The Hellenizing Muse

Trends in Classics –
Pathways of Reception

General Editors
Franco Montanari and Antonios Rengakos

Editorial Board
Lorna Hardwick, Craig Kallendorf, Fiona Macintosh,
Miltos Pechlivanos

Associate Editors
Anastasia Bakogianni and Rosanna Lauriola

Volume 6

The Hellenizing Muse

A European Anthology of Poetry in Ancient Greek
from the Renaissance to the Present

Edited by
Filippomaria Pontani and Stefan Weise

DE GRUYTER

ISBN 978-3-11-125596-5
e-ISBN (PDF) 978-3-11-065275-8
e-ISBN (EPUB) 978-3-11-065287-1
ISSN 2629-2556

Library of Congress Control Number: 2021942022

Bibliographic information published by the Deutsche Nationalbibliothek
The Deutsche Nationalbibliothek lists this publication in the Deutsche Nationalbibliografie; detailed bibliographic data are available on the Internet at http://dnb.dnb.de.

© 2023 Walter de Gruyter GmbH, Berlin/Boston
This volume is text- and page-identical with the hardback published in 2022.
Cover image: Paul Klee, Hauptweg und Nebenwege
Printing and binding: CPI books GmbH, Leck

www.degruyter.com

Contents

List of Figures —— VII

Filippomaria Pontani and Stefan Weise
General Introduction —— 1

Timeline —— 25

Gerasimos Zoras, Kostas Yiavis, and Filippomaria Pontani
Greece —— 30

Filippomaria Pontani
Italy —— 82

Stefan Weise
Germany —— 146

Han Lamers and Raf Van Rooy
The Low Countries —— 216

Marcela Slavíková
The Bohemian Lands —— 280

Janika Päll and Martin Steinrück
Switzerland —— 306

Luigi-Alberto Sanchi, Jean-Marie Flamand, and Romain Menini
France —— 358

Vlado Rezar
Balkans —— 403

Farkas Gábor Kiss and András Németh
Hungary —— 451

Stefan Weise
Great Britain —— 482

Filippomaria Pontani
Iberia —— 558

Tomas Veteikis (in collaboration with Gościwit Malinowski and Bartosz Awianowicz)
Poland and Lithuania —— 604

Elena Ermolaeva
Russia —— 648

William M. Barton, Martin M. Bauer, and Martin Korenjak
Austria —— 688

Johanna Akujärvi, Tua Korhonen, Janika Päll, and Erkki Sironen
Nordic Countries —— 722

List of Contributors —— 803
Index Librorum Manuscriptorum —— 809
Index Selectivus Personarum —— 811
Index Selectivus Rerum Memorabilium —— 823
Index Graecitatis (neologismi, hapax legomena, verba rara) —— 829

List of Figures

Fig. 1: Mesolonghi (Aetolia-Acarnania), Garden of Heroes: statue of Lord Byron with the Greek verse inscription by Demetrios Semitelos. (Photo: Filippomaria Pontani). —— 30

Fig. 2a: Bagno Vignoni (Siena, Tuscany): Greek inscription by Lattanzio Tolomei on the porch of the bath. (Fondazione A. Tagliolini – Centro per lo studio del paesaggio e del giardino – San Quirico d'Orcia). —— 82

Fig. 2b: Bagno Vignoni (Siena, Tuscany): Loggiato di Santa Caterina, where the inscription by Tolomei is installed. (Photo: Silvia Rizzo). —— 82

Fig. 3: Heidelberg, Bergfriedhof: Funerary monument for Hermann Köchly with the Greek inscription composed by himself. Phaeton1, CC BY-SA 3.0, https://creativecommons.org/licenses/by-sa/3.0>, via Wikimedia Commons (https://de.wikipedia.org/wiki/Hermann_Köchly#/media/Datei:Koechly.JPG [accessed: January 2021]). —— 146

Fig. 4: Anthonis Mor van Dashorst (Antonio Moro), Self-portrait (1558) with a Greek epigram by Dominicus Lampsonius. (Florence, Galleria degli Uffizi, inv. 1637). —— 216

Fig. 5: Last page of the Greek manuscript text (fol. 210v) of Jan Křesadlo's *Astronautilia* (see below) illustrating the 'universal translator' Franta while writing the text and fixing the dates of composition: 28 December 1993–20 January 1994. [Václav Z.J. Pinkava. The original manuscript is now preserved at Literární archiv Památníku národního písemnictví (The Museum of Czech Literature Literary Archive), Prague/Litoměřice (no. 2110; www.badatelna.cz/fond/3417)]. —— 280

Fig. 6: *Musarum Limagidum vicinarumque applausus votivi...summis...honoribus... D. Andreae Meieri*, Tiguri: typis Henrici Bodmeri, 1696, 89 (M IIr): acrostichic poem by Johann Heinrich Herder. (Zentralbibliothek Zürich, 18.228: 20, https://doi.org/10.3931/e-rara-11991 / Public Domain Mark). —— 306

Fig. 7: *Les Amours de P. de Ronsard Vandomoys...*, Paris 1552, 2: portrait of Pierre Ronsard with the Greek inscription ὡς ἴδον ὡς ἐμάνην (Theoc. *Id*. 2.82) and the epigram by J.-A. de Baïf. (gallica.bnf.fr / Paris, Bibliothèque nationale de France, RES P-YE-1482). —— 358

Fig. 8: Budapest, National Széchényi Library, ms Fol. Lat. 3606.II, f. 31v: autograph of Georg Wyrffel's poem *In victoriam quam reverendissimus episcopus Zagrabiensis habuit de Turcis apud Glynam fluvium*. (Budapest, National Széchényi Library). —— 410

Fig. 9: *Emblemata cum aliquot nummis antiqui operis, Ioannis Sambuci Tirnaviensis Pannonii*, Antverpiae: ex officina Christophori Plantini, 1564, 228: Greek epigram by Sambucus. (München, Bayerische Staatsbibliothek, L.impr.c.n.mss. 200, p. 228, urn:nbn:de:bvb:12-bsb00035710-6). —— 456

Fig. 10: Oxford, The Queen's College (on the wall of the Senior Common Room): War memorial with a Greek inscription by Edgar Lobel at its bottom. (Michael Riordan by permission of the Provost and Fellows of The Queen's College, Oxford). —— 482

Fig. 11: *Enchiridion mythyco-physico-ethicum complectens expositionem in Hesiodi Theogoniam... Accedit Hymnus in B. Virginem Mariam Graecè, idemque Latinè pro opere finito authore D. Antonio Martinez de Quesada...*, Universidad Complutense de Madrid, Biblioteca, BH MSS 191, f. 227r: first page of Antonio Martínez de Quesada's Greek hymn to the Virgin Mary. (Madrid, Biblioteca de la Universidad Complutense, BH MSS 191, f. 227r, https://patrimoniodigital.ucm.es/r/item/5320288456, CC BY 2.0 ES). —— 558

Fig. 12: *Thesauri Polonolatinograeci Gregorii Cnapii e Societate Iesu tomus secundus* [...], Cracoviae: Sumptu & Typis Francisci Caesarii, 1626, 941: alphabetic hymn on Ignatius of Loyola by Gregorius Cnapius. (München, Bayerische Staatsbibliothek, 4 Polygl. 14, p. 941, urn:nbn:de:bvb:12-bsb10691010-0). —— **604**

Fig. 13: St Petersburg, Russian National Library, ms. F. 608, I, 4802, f. 5v: autograph of Σιγη Ερωτος by Christian Friedrich Graefe (one may note that Graefe does not use accents in his autograph). —— **648**

Fig. 14: First page of Kollár's poem *Charites* from Franz Christoph Scheyb (ed.) (1756), *Musae Francisco et Mariae Theresiae augustis congratulantur ob scientias, bonasque artes eorum iussu et munificentia Vindobonae restitutas*, Vindobonae, p. 130. (Photo: GoogleBooks. Wien, Österreichische Nationalbibliothek, 48.E.10 ALT PRUNK, p. 130, http://data.onb.ac.at/rec/AC10146752). —— **688**

Fig. 15: *Carmina Graeca JOSEPHI THUNII Autographa*: manuscript page providing a Greek poem by Josef Thun to his fellow poet Laurentius Norrmannus. Linköping Diocesan Library, W 40, p. S5 (http://urn.kb.se/resolve?urn=urn:nbn:se:alvin:portal:record-265976). —— **722**

ΔΙΑΛΟΓΟΣ

Ἀνθολόγῳ Στέφανον πλέξαντ' ὦ τόνδε, Φιλίππῳ
  ἕσπεσθον νεαρῶν δρεψαμένῳ κάλυκας; –
Ναί, φίλε· πάντα γὰρ ἴσθ' ἡμᾶς ἅτε παῖδας ἄθυρμα
  Ἑλλήνων τέρπει καινὰ παλαιά θ' ὁμῶς.

Filippomaria Pontani and Stefan Weise
General Introduction

1 Goals and Limitations

In combination with the renewal in the domain of Latin style and the new paradigmatic value attributed to classical antiquity in the realm of visual arts, the learning of Greek was probably one of the key elements of the humanistic movement which started in Italy in the second half of the 14th century and spread all over Europe in the subsequent two hundred years. As is well known, the early times of this phenomenon were all but easy: despite the efforts of Petrarch and Boccaccio, no curricular teaching was established before the very last years of the 14th century, and even then few Italians could reach an adequate *niveau* of familiarity with the language. No wonder, then, that – while poetry was frequently practised by the Byzantine emigres working as scribes, scholars, and teachers on Italian soil – the first Westerner to embark on the writing of elegies and Sapphic stanzas in Greek was an intellectual who had spent a long time in Constantinople: Francesco Filelfo. And it was only in the later years of the 15th century that a proper European tradition of Greek versification was inaugurated: a key role was played in this respect by Angelo Poliziano, whose *Liber epigrammatum Graecorum* (1498) represented not only a masterly achievement in terms of the imitation of ancient poetic forms, but also the first sylloge of this kind to appear in print.

This new tradition soon left the shores of the Mediterranean and reached its heyday and most impressive peaks between the 16th and the early 17th century in Germany, the Low Countries and partly in France: despite a certain decline since the mid-17th century, and its rather elitarian (if conspicuous) reviviscence in the 19th-century academic circles, it never petered out down to our own day. This anthology aims to give an overview and shed some light on the history of this hitherto mostly neglected phenomenon of versification in ancient Greek, by offering selections from all parts of Europe, from the Renaissance to the present.[1] The volume is the result of the collaboration of several scholars from various European countries, and as such it has the modest ambition to contribute to the investigation of a forgotten aspect of the cultural identity of the continent.

The selection is arranged in regional sections, which by and large follow the political segmentation of present-day Europe. Each section has been prepared by

---

[1] Cf. also with a somewhat different focus the volume of Oliveira/Ramón 2019.

https://doi.org/10.1515/9783110652758-001

one or more editors, and is organised in strict chronological order (the only exception being the chapter on the Nordic Countries, where a geographical criterion also applies) (see also 3, below). Although we did keep an eye on the relevance and bulk of the respective outputs, it was neither possible nor reasonable to represent all modern European countries with the same breadth and intensity: hence some evident differences between chapters in terms of length and scope.

As deep research is only at the beginning, we are well aware of the limitations of our endeavour. First of all, an obvious difficulty lies in the decision to consider only poetry. From the very beginning, prose composition in Greek was also widespread: it may suffice to recall the Greek letters penned by scholars from Filelfo up to Wilamowitz and Gilbert Murray, as well as the academic speeches, the dissertations and conversational guides which were especially popular in Central and Northern Europe between the 16th and the 17th centuries. However, poetry represents in general a more learned, elaborated and characteristic phenomenon, easier to analyse in its re-use of classical models, and granting a more distinct opportunity to compare intra- and interregional developments and trends.

Another limitation concerns our geographical scope. Although there is no doubt that most Greek poetry was written in Europe, it was certainly not confined to it. The deep influence of European education systems through colonisation or mission spread the teaching of Greek all over the world: hence, Greek composition is certainly attested since the 18th century in scholarly *milieux* of Mexico, the Philippines, Australia, and above all in North America. Yet for these areas – and for other territories even more remote from the Western learned tradition, such as Asia or Africa – the data is still too fragmentary to allow the outline of a coherent picture.

On a similar note, we are well aware that even in Europe much still has to be discovered and unearthed from libraries: research on manuscripts is stronger and more advanced in some regions than in others, and it is very possible that by our decision to mine primarily printed material (and even then, in a selective manner) we may have missed many representative pieces, or even single authors or scholarly circles that would have been relevant to our inquiry.

However, even if some of our choices or general conclusions are bound to be regarded as temporary or to undergo revision and re-assessment in the near future, we still hope to have given, thanks to the generous efforts of a wonderful team of colleagues from all over the continent, a flavour of an intellectual production that probably deserves more interest both as an aspect of the classical tradition and as a cultural phenomenon *per se*, and which certainly awaits further research in the decades to come.

2 General Survey

As opposed to writing in Latin, literary composition in Greek has not been a continuous activity in Europe from classical antiquity through the modern age: with the exception of Greece proper and of some small territories once linked to the Eastern Roman Empire (sporadic Greek-speaking communities still alive in the Balkan region or Southern Italy), by 1400 the very knowledge of Greek had been almost entirely lost in the West. Therefore, when Byzantine émigrés, starting with Manuel Chrysoloras, started to throw on Italian soil the seeds of a new blossoming of Greek studies, autonomous composition in that language became a much bolder, more arbitrary and eccentric idea than any attempt to revive Latin poetry and prose by adopting ancient models and thereby departing from medieval standards – an idea that only a restricted elite of learned figures could reasonably conceive.

'We can never hope to get the whole fling of a sentence in Greek as we do in English', once wrote Virgina Woolf (*On Not Knowing Greek*, 1925). Because the knowledge of Greek (and especially the high degree of proficiency required to write poetry in that language) was such a tremendous challenge in the first place and the advantage (or the illusion) of a limited number of intellectuals, most of the authors presented in this anthology are scholars, teachers, professors, philologists, and only by way of exception free-standing intellectuals or poets *stricto sensu*; some of the most notable exceptions to this rule come from England, where Greek has been (and partly still is) an integral part of the education of the cultivated elite, and was perceived at least since the 18th century as (again V. Woolf speaking) 'the language that has us most in bondage; the desire for that which perpetually lures us back'.

When most authors of this anthology decided to write Greek verse, they did so mostly either for their own pleasure and *divertissement*, or for a small audience of virtuosos and *savants*; they did so in order to impress their colleagues or to acquire reputation for their esoteric learning, sometimes even to use it as an encrypted medium for mockery (e.g., Milton); they did so not only in large political or academic capitals of European countries, but also in smaller centres whose Hellenic pedigree this volume attempts to unravel at least partly (from Coimbra, Valencia, and Dubrovnik to Ilfeld, Cracow, and Vilnius); and when they wrote odes and epigrams outside of the narrow domain of academic communication, they could not seriously believe in the linguistic skills of their patrons or entertain the illusion of a real communication with their addressees. This is no doubt one of the reasons why Greek poetry of the modern age, down to the present day, has been so often neglected or looked upon by readers and historians alike as a paradigmatic instance of a pedantic exercise, practised by erudites in their *tour d'ivoire;* it may appear to exhibit in an extreme form the negative aspects – frigidity, derivativeness, lack of inspiration – that have long marred the consideration and the reception of Neo-Latin poetry after the romantic revolution.

Indeed, this charge cannot be deemed wholly unfounded. On the one hand, some of these pieces – especially, though not exclusively, in the early stages of the appropriation of Greek – live to an insufficient poetic and linguistic standard, rather resembling exercises of enthusiastic neophytes wishing to display their proficiency and skill in a difficult tongue than full-fledged poetic attempts seeking to exploit the potential of an ancestral literary idiom. On the other hand, in a number of cases, even when the linguistic competence rises to a more acceptable *niveau,* the imitation of ancient prototypes remains often at a very superficial level, without an adequate aesthetic appropriation. This is why some of the pieces gathered in this anthology (chiefly, shorter epigrams of various kinds) may appear *prima facie* rather unattractive to the modern reader.

And yet, even apparently jejune and occasional epigrams fulfil a very important cultural role as documents both of the state of classical learning in a given time and place, and of the development, enthusiasm, and ambition of some literary personalities. **François Rabelais'** epigram on a book by André Tiraqueau (1524), **Martin Crusius'** scoptic epigram against the Catholics ('Antichrists', 1550), **Algernon Charles Swinburne'**s epitaph for the death of Théophile Gautier (1872) or **Demetrios Semitelos'** funerary inscription on Byron's tomb at Mesolonghi (1881) are texts that, independently of their aesthetic value, carry an immense cultural value, and earn their deeper sense from being written in Greek rather than in Latin or in any modern language.

Even more importantly, from Poliziano to Wilamowitz, there are many cases in which 'the internalization of models grows to the point of total fluency of recall and recombination':[2] the ability to recombine very different (and sometimes rather remote) sources, the originality of some neologisms or *hapax legomena,* the genuine inspiration of poems describing new realities or ideas, made for small masterpieces that can stand all sort of literary criticism: from the heartfelt appeal of **Markos Mousouros** for the liberation of Greece in his *Ode to Plato* (1513) to **Laurentius Rhodoman'**s hexametrical poem *Arion* (c. 1567/1588), from **Samuel Taylor Coleridge'**s Sapphic ode against slavery in America (1792) to **Johan Andreas dèr Mouw'**s philosophical elegy called *Pim* (c. 1912).

---

[2] See Hardie, Philip (1992), "Vida's *De arte poetica* and the Transformation of Models", in: *Apodosis. Essays presented to Dr W.W. Cruickshank,* London, 47–53: 48.

Because of the lack of a centuries-old pre-existing tradition, and because of the highly personal and highly demanding challenge posed by versification in Greek, the variety of the results in terms of quality, genre, and poetical status of the pieces collected in this anthology is truly manifold. Predictably, the lion's share goes to more 'obvious' genres such as epigram and poetic paraphrases, but hexametrical epic and various kinds of lyric odes are all but absent, and other so-called 'minor' genres live a life of their own throughout the ages of the Republic of Letters. Most of these typologies made their first significant appearance in Italy – the region where, *inter alia*, the Greek text of most ancient models was first rediscovered and made available to scholars as an object of study and autonomous imitation (from Homer to the *Greek Anthology*, from Gregory of Nazianzus to Nonnus of Panopolis – though for instance the *Anacreontea* were first published in Paris by Henri Estienne).

It is therefore easy to understand that, e.g., several functions of the epigram (above all the *Buchepigramme*, the epitaphs, the encomiastic or epideictic pieces) were premiered by texts published in Aldine editions, conceived for Italian patrons, penned on manuscripts in Rome or inscribed on the walls of Tuscan spas. This obviously exerted a strong influence on the numerous scholars who received a linguistic training either in Italy or through 'Italian' teachers, such as (just to mention some of the authors of this anthology, which leaves out outstanding figures like Thomas Linacre or Guillaume Budé) the Germans **Celtis**, **Pirckheimer** and **Reuchlin**, the Croatian **Benessa**, the French **de Brie**, the Hungarian **Istvánffy**, or even the later Russian citizen **Maxim the Greek**. Collaterally, many Greek scribes and scholars of the 15th, 16th and 17th centuries were obviously deeply marked by their participation in the intellectual climate of the Italian Renaissance, either through their contacts with courts and universities, or through their links with institutions such as the Collegio Romano and the Vatican Curia (the case of the Chiot **Leone Allacci** being perhaps the most representative). Furthermore, the very fact that the first published sylloge of Greek epigrams was **Poliziano**'s *Liber* (1498) influenced deeply the evolution of this editorial genre, from **Ianos Laskaris**' own *Epigrammata* in 1527 down to the numerous German, Dutch, and later also British collections of this kind. That Poliziano's Greek epigrams should be closely imitated by Johannes Reuchlin in his epigram for Constantia Peutinger, by **Miguel de Ledesma**'s cento on the Passion of Christ, and by **Johan Paulinus** in Finland, shows how important the Italian incunable continued to be considered throughout the 16th and the 17th centuries.

And yet, whereas on a European level Neo-Latin elegy, love lyric, pastoral, and epic were literally and durably shaped by the prototypes of Petrarch, Pontano, Poliziano, Battista Spagnoli, and Sannazaro, in the domain of Greek versification the prominence of Italy was far less lasting and definitive: authors from other areas of Europe soon flanked their Ausonian predecessors, surpassing them in terms of variety, breadth, and scope of literary output. This development is partly due to the steady decline of classical (and particularly Greek) learning in Italy and in other Catholic regions since the late 16th century, in connection with the 'appropriation' of Greek by the Lutheran Reform (one need just think of the impact of Erasmus' New Testament or of the activity of **Melanchthon** and **Camerarius**, both engaged in Greek versification), with the cultural tenets of the post-Tridentine reform, and with the establishment of the new, most influential Jesuit curriculum (the *Ratio studiorum*), where preeminence was given to Latin, and Greek remained the heritage of a relatively small elite. Good examples of the difficulties Catholic scholars had to face in the proper acquisition of the language can be seen, e.g., in the poetic attempts penned by **Arnoldus Engel** (→ **Bohemian lands**), **José Rodríguez de Castro** (→ **Iberia**), or by members of the Accademia dell'Arcadia in 17th-century Rome or of the Jesuit college of Villagarcía de Campos in the 1740s; a nice example is the rudimentary Greek spoken by the personification of this language in the Latin play written in the Hungarian gymnasium of Eperjes (Prešov) in 1661. However, we should not understate the persistence of a good *niveau* of Greek learning in single centres and cities all through the 17th century, from Valencia (the home to, *inter alios*, Ledesma, Esteve, Palmireno, and then to the amazing translator and prolific versifier **Vicente Mariner**) to Rome (a pope such as Urbanus VIII, born **Maffeo Barberini**, not only gathered in the Vatican a gallery of Greek scholars and poets, but was even able to fashion himself an almost 'sensual' Greek epigram on the martyrdom of St Sebastian).

Indeed, the religious factor became paramount in a number of ways, above all because the regions where Protestantism took the lead, starting with Germany, Switzerland, and the Low Countries, soon allotted Greek a conspicuous place in the average educated culture and in the school curriculum – the case of France, with the precocious establishment of a chair of Greek at Francis I's newly founded Collège Royal in Paris, and the rise of the 'Greek-speaking' constellation of poets known as *Pléiade*, is analogous though partly different due to the more complex and long-standing confessional struggle between Catholics and Protestants in that country. This state of affairs, in which **Erasmus of Rotterdam** played a key role of transition (witness – amongst other things – the proliferation of Greek epigrams on his passing away, from the Portuguese **Diogo Pires** to the Hungarian **Nicolaus Oláh**), explains why some of the most outstanding classical scholars of the 16th century were trained and worked in Central or Northern Europe: Dorat, Budé, Camerarius, Rhodoman, Crusius, H. Stephanus, J.J. Scaliger, D. Heinsius, and many others.

New centres of Greek learning and composition arose between the 16th and the 17th century: on one side Leuven, Antwerp, Bruges, then Amsterdam and Leiden, and on the other side particularly Basel, Geneva, Wittenberg, and the school of Ilfeld, where Michael Neander trained two generations of pupils who numbered among the most brilliant Greek poets of their times (namely Rhodoman, **Gothus**, and **Mylius**). In these contexts, between the mid-16th and the mid-17th century, Greek verse grew into something more serious than a pure exercise or a *divertissement*, and vindicated the status of a full-fledged literary medium. This resulted in the production of a vast number of poetic attempts: while Greek versification seems to have occupied French scholars chiefly in terms of a learned communication between erudites (from literary polemics to funerary encomia, from **Bérault** to **Chrestien** to Montaigne – cf. in later times the witty epigrams of **Ménage**, **Huet**, **La Monnoye**), it is particularly German, Flemish, and Dutch scholars who engaged in bold experiments opening to Greek the path of entirely new literary genres.

One need just think of the historical epics in hexameters (**Wassenaer**'s *Harlemias*; later, in the Nordic context, Paulinus' *laus patriae* known as *Finlandia*), of mythological epyllia (Rhodoman's *Arion* or *Troica* and **Foreest**'s *Idyllia sive Heroes*; but see also the sapiential *Heracles* by the Dane **Petrus Borrichius**), of bucolic or encomiastic idyllia (**Herrichen**, **Dawes**; but also the French **J.-A. de Baïf** wrote a *Medanis*), of long elegiac encomia (**Scaliger**'s and **Heinsius**' *De mirandis Bataviae*), of versified letters (Reusner, Clajus), etc. It is interesting that in this frame lyric odes did not earn pride of place: Sapphic odes certainly enjoyed some popularity since the times of Filelfo (and were later practiced, again in a Christian vein, by **Jean Dorat**, **Jakub Strabo**, **Martín Miguel Navarro**, and others), and occasional attempts at writing phalaecians, epodic verses, and Alcaic stanzas are registered across Europe between Poland (Mylius' paraphrase of the *Pater Noster*), Switzerland (**Gessner**) and France (La Monnoye's translation of Catullus' *carmen 3*; interestingly, an epodic Greek encomium opens the works of Louise Labé, the 'modern Sappho'). But on the whole these experiments suffered from the undeniable lack of a solid ancient Greek background (only lyric texts known through indirect tradition were available until the late 19th century), and leaned to a remarkable extent – both in terms of metrical structure and of contents – on their Latin counterparts, from Catullus to Horace. The only significant exception was of course the Pindaric ode, which came in fashion since the 16th century, with a religious thrust (e.g., **Reusner**, **Philaras**) or, more commonly, an encomiastic purpose (e.g. Dorat, **Amalteo, Niegoszewski, Grotius,** all the way down to the Swedish academic *gratulationes*, the modern Olympic odes, and **Danielewicz'** *natalicium*).

On the German-Flemish axis, the ingenious and sometimes aesthetically remarkable struggle with ancient prototypes brought excellent results in a number of domains: for instance, many Greek poems with a strictly Christian content were written, such as **Posselius'** paraphrase of the gospel lectures, Rhodoman's *Palaestina*, Gothus' *Historia vitae et doctrinae Iesu Christi*, the unpublished work of **Bonaventura Vulcanius**, etc.; in neighbouring areas, one ought to recall **Polanus'** and Spiegel's versified renderings of the *Psalms*; **Cnapius'** alphabetical hymn to St Ignatius of Loyola; later, **Thun**'s hymns to the Son of God. And there is little doubt that this popularity of religious odes in the German milieu indirectly fostered similar attempts in 'Latin' countries, from **Tito Prospero Martinengo**'s outstanding *Poëmata* to **Denis Pétau**'s hymn to St Geneviève.

In terms of broader cultural influence, the neighbouring areas of Central Europe, which in an earlier stage had been dependent on the trends of Italian humanism, now largely revolved around the German achievements – this is for example the case for the Bohemian lands (especially before their turn to Catholicism, from **Aerichalcus** to **Crinesius**), Austria (**Charopus**), Hungary (from **Szikszai** to **Guttovieni**: the link with the university of Wittenberg was particularly strong in the mid-16th century, and it held for the Lutheran part of the country), Croatia (**Garbitius Illyricus** and others: here the pivotal role of the city of Ragusa should be stressed), Poland and Lithuania (Mylius, **Retell**), and later the Nordic countries (Gregor Krüger, Olaus Martini, Jonas Kylander, **Georg Dunte**, Aeschillus Petraeus; see esp. the Uppsala school of the 17th century, with its large production of *encomia* and *epithalamia*). A special case is Switzerland, where many French printers and scholars (e.g. the Stephani/Estiennes, Crespin, Beza) took refuge in the reformed city of Geneva, or hosted foreign intellectuals and poets such as the Spaniard **Núñez Vela** in Lausanne, while the German-speaking area trained a number of printers, editors, and scholars (Oporinus, **Ceporinus**, Gessner, etc.).

And yet, after this peak, in most of Central and Northern Europe the later part of the 17th and then the 18th century represented a moment of pause in the story of Greek poetic composition. Several factors may have contributed to the decreasing popularity of this practice: the sense that an acme had been reached in earlier generations; the gradual loss of the centrality of classical learning in the broader frame of European civilisation (the 17th and 18th centuries witness the rise of polyglot compositions, showing rather the exotic character of Greek among other oriental languages); the gradual decline in Jesuit instruction. To be sure, pieces in rococo taste were in fact produced, from **Francius'** and Herrichen's Anacreontic odes on tea to **Boivin**'s equally Anacreontic epitaph for the death of Anne Dacier, from **Manuel Martí**'s sympotic elegies to **Kollár**'s elegant bucolic idyll. And in later years, some peculiar poetical experiments marked the transition to a new romantic spirit (**Chénier**'s erotic epigrams; **Tóth**'s sentimental idyllia; **Leopardi**'s ode to the moon).

More interestingly, however, the 18th century witnessed some significant cross-fertilisations throughout Europe: Greek scholars and communities of the diaspora started to produce and print books in several hotspots throughout the continent – from Rome (and the Vatican) to Vienna (the cradle of the Greek Enlightenment, but also of Makraios' *Orthodox Hymnody*), from single 'eccentric' experiments such as in the Albanian city of Moschopole (the home-town to the well-travelled mathematician and poet Konstantinos Tzechanes) to the vast and culturally ambitious principalities of Wallachia and the Danubian area, where printing houses flourished from Bucharest to Iași, and dozens of book epigrams or encomiastic pieces were published (**Ioannes Molyvdos Comnenos, Georgios Chrysogonos**, etc.; **Polyzoes Kondos**, a fan of Napoleon, wrote Greek epigrams between Pest and Bucharest). Spanish and Portuguese Jesuits, after the ban on their congregation issued in Iberia, took refuge in Italy: the city of Bologna proved in this context a particularly attractive centre, where locals (**Clotilde Tambroni**) and foreigners (**Manuel Lassala, Manuel Aponte**, etc.) shared the same environment, and the same enthusiasm for original Greek verse. After Maxim the Greek, Russia could not boast a significant indigenous tradition of Greek composition: from the end of the 18th through the early 19th century, however, the court of St Petersburg witnessed a remarkable development of Greek poetry, at the crossroads between the enthusiasm aroused by the cultural and political reforms of Catherine II (**Boulgaris, Palladoklis**, and others; encomiastic odes in Greek were addressed to the empress also by foreign authors such as **Pasquale Baffi** or Lord North) and the establishment of the teaching of Greek in academia (the German input – **Graefe**, Nauck et al. – was pivotal in this respect, also as concerns the practice of translating Russian lyric into Greek).

Yet this overall panorama, while it takes into account the continent proper, not only overlooks the peculiar case of Sweden, where hexametrical orations continued to be written and published from the 1620s through the 1820s (this uninterrupted fancy led, in later decades, to remarkable results such as the delicate and melancholic poems by **Erik E. Östling** and the philosophical elegies of **Johan Bergman**), but above all does not tally to the special case of Great Britain. In England, a relatively late start was followed, particularly after the establishment of Protestantism in the 1560s, by a remarkable *essor* of Greek studies, and then of

Greek composition under various forms: this phenomenon went well beyond the more usual flow of epigrams, or the encomiastic and epideictic vein for kings and queens: hexameters were used by **Richard Dawes** for a splendid bucolic idyllion, by **Edward Wells** for a didascalic poem on contemporary geography. **John Christopherson** in the 1540s produced with the tragedy called *Iephthaë* one of the earliest and most convincing iambic dramas in our overview, only to be matched 300 years later by **Julius Richter**'s Aristophanic comedies or Albert Johansson's Greek tragedy *Nupta fluvii*/Νύμφη ἡ τοῦ ποταμοῦ, and then partly by Graefe's translations from Schiller, by dèr Mouw's Shakespearian *rheseis* or by occasional 20th-century academic parodies such as **Knox**'s *Telephoniazusae*, or **Vitelli**'s and **Rissa**'s comic dialogues (the iambic trimeter was otherwise often used in epigrams, but also in such a masterpiece as **Allacci**'s *Hellas*, perhaps the acme of a long tradition of mourning songs on the fall of Greece and Byzantium to the Turks).

More 'rare' metres encountered an unexpected success between Oxford and Cambridge, partly in the frame of the long-standing tradition of the Greek poetry competition between pupils of the various colleges, a tradition that lasts to the present day and that has located in England, since the times of Joshua Barnes and Richard Bentley, the most impressive continuity of this practice in the Western world. We thus find epitaphs in anacreontics (**Herbert**) or asclepiads (Swinburne), epinicians in anacreontics (**Barnes**), Pindaric (**Robertson**) or Alcaic stanzas (**D'Angour**), gnomic texts in a mixture of lyric metres (**Geddes**), and Sapphic stanzas used for encomiastic celebrations (**Moore**) or love poems (**Headlam**).

The obvious fate of Greek poetry over the last two hundred years was academia: with some exceptions involving diplomats, ecclesiasticals, or independent intellectuals, most authors of Greek verse have been (and still are, down to the present day) college or university professors of classics, and most of them have been writing chiefly for their colleagues. The products of this self-referential quest for an ever more refined and 'ancient-looking' poetic expression, were often epigrams directed to mock, mourn, or celebrate other professors, or to share thoughts about contingent or eternal truths. Germany, where the curriculum of 'Klassische Philologie' was first consolidated, and where theories of a special cognation between Greeks and Germans gained ground, played once again a leading role: the skill and fame of its academic elite (headed by Wilamowitz, with his indefatigable and eclectic poetic output) not only spread to larger areas of intellectuals (**Friedrich Engels**, the co-author of the Communist manifesto, was a refined author of Greek verse), but also exerted a significant echo in Austria (**Ludwig Mayr**'s panegyric epyllion on the city of Graz is a notable achievement), Italy (Vitelli), Russia (**Borovsky**), and Poland (Danielewicz); the phenomenon was on the other hand less conspicuous in French and Dutch academia. England, as mentioned above, followed a parallel development, producing between Oxford, Cambridge, and London a tradition of unexpected vitality down to this day, mirrored in several pieces wittily relating to contemporary reality (from Napoleon to slavery), and in a number of anthologies of competition pieces stemming from the various colleges or universities (*Musae Etonenses, Musae Cantabrigienses, Anthologia Oxoniensis*, etc.). It can well be argued that in this domain the English influence helped shape the German tradition as well. Within this narrow frame Greek became even a spoken language (one may recall that from the 15th century onwards a lot of poems or Greek orations were actually performed before being printed) and sometimes an encrypted code used to veil intimate or delicate information. Yet, even if someone will disqualify as frigid **Korsch**'s lines to Rudolf Westphal, **Niedermühlbichler**'s pious prayers, or **Rebelo Gonçalves**' epigrams to his wife, there is no reason to forget that even in recent times several authors, through a skilful handling of Greek words, have achieved a remarkable poetic and philosophical force. Amongst other achievements, some well-thought parodies of the academic or scholastic world have been written in Greek over the last decades (**Runeberg**'s ludicrous *Academic Examination*; **Fehér**'s elegiac satire of psychoanalysis; Rissa's macaronic 'comedies'), while other poets, following the footsteps of **Georgios Koressios**' hexametrical poem on Florentine football (1611!), have admirably succeeded in describing contemporary reality in ancient Greek garb, from **Philippos Ioannou**'s epigrams on the aerostatic balloon and telegraph to **Jan Křesadlo**'s *Ode to Stalin*. Křesadlo's extensive 1995 poem *Astronautilia* can be considered – despite some linguistic and metrical shortcomings – as an interesting mixture of ancient epic, contemporary science-fiction, and satire: together with Alvaro Rissa's experiments, it may hint at a way in which poetry in ancient Greek could avoid the fate of a pure exercise, and turn fresh, thoughtful, and provocative through elegance and linguistic wit. After all, the very opportunity of so handling ancient words and of thereby fashioning new verse is a privilege that most authors have been and no doubt will always be deeply aware of: in the words of the contemporary Cypriot poet Kostas Mondis ("Ἕλληνες ποιητές – 'Greek Poets'), 'Few people read us, / Very few know our language, / we remain without recognition and applause / in this remote corner: / in return, however, we write in Greek.'[3]

---

3 Ἐλάχιστοι μᾶς διαβάζουν, / ἐλάχιστοι ξέρουν τὴ γλώσσα μας, / μένουμε ἀδικαίωτοι κι ἀχειροκρότητοι / σ' αὐτὴ τὴ μακρυνὴ γωνιά, / ὅμως ἀντισταθμίζει ποὺ γράφουμε Ἑλληνικά (from: Ποιήματα γιὰ μικρὰ καὶ μεγάλα παιδιά, 1976).

3 Metre, Dialects, Editorial Practice, Presentation, History of Scholarship

This section gathers some general observations and remarks about technical issues such as metre, dialects, orthography, and our editorial practice. Detailed information on these topics is added after each poem under the rubrics 'metre' and 'notes'.

3.1 Metre

As can be expected in such a diverse picture, the treatment of prosody and metre varies greatly from one author to another and from one region to another. A whole range of authors, particularly in the early centuries, do not hesitate to neglect elementary rules and produce wholly unmetrical pieces, whereas others, like Matthaeus Gothus (→ **Germany**), are keen on following the strictest rules down to the number of hexameter patterns in Nonnus of Panopolis!

Between these two poles, some general tendencies can be highlighted. First of all, prosodical problems or *abusiones* represent a very common phenomenon, especially in cases of the so-called *dichrona* (vowels α, ι, and υ), whose quantity is not self-evident: a recurrent case is that of the verb ἄδω 'to sing' (often written without *iota subscriptum*, see below) taken with short α. Consonant combinations such as ψ, ζ, σπ, στ, or even στρ are often treated as one consonant, causing no length by position – a trend for which we can find some Homeric or later parallels, but that is certainly also influenced by the Latin practice (cf. Rhein 1987, 47–50). Lengthening by final -ς, -ν, or -ρ, according to Homeric practice, is quite frequent as well. Hiatus is another delicate issue: most authors are not very careful with hiatuses both within the verse and at *caesurae* (e.g., the pentameter's middle caesura). In terms of verse construction, amongst hexameters we find a number of *versus bipartiti* (with diaeresis after the third foot), perhaps the heritage of a Byzantine practice or simply the fruit of carelessness. Of course, modern 'laws' such as Hermann's Bridge and Porson's Law were unknown before their discovery in the 19th century (for Hermann's Bridge in particular, however, see Rhein 1987, 45), and are therefore largely ignored before that time, although particularly refined poets respect them simply by imitating closely good examples. Among lyric metres, Pindaric odes often reproduce the strophic pattern of one specific epinician of the Theban poet; more 'eccentric' metres such as phalaecian hendecasyllables, epodic verses, asclepiads, Sapphic and Alcaic stanzas tend to lean on Latin prototypes such as Catullus and Horace. Other forms and combinations are newly invented (Herrichen, Klopstock → **Germany**) or taken from vernacular compositions (e.g., rhyme and sonnet structure, see Crusius → **Germany**, anonymous Odarion → **Poland and Lithuania**, Fehér → **Hungary**).

3.2 Dialects

Most poems in this anthology tend to make use of Homeric diction (a mixture of different forms with a strong Ionic flavour), without any regard to genre or metre. At times, from Filelfo to D'Angour, we find a preference for the more obvious forms of Attic Greek.

Predictably, Doric forms appear with varying degrees of consistency in the context of bucolic poetry (e.g., Herrichen, Kollár, Dawes) and of Pindaric odes (e.g., Amalteo, Reusner, Robertson, Baffi, Jebb, Danielewicz): much as in ancient models, however, this most often amounts to little more than an overall patina. A peculiar mixture of epic and bucolic is the Doric epyllion *Arion* by Rhodoman (→ **Germany**). Inspired by the Doric touch of some pieces of the *Greek Anthology*, some humanists (from Aldus to Benessa) also resort to sporadic Doric forms in their epigrams.

Aeolic poems, on the other hand, are exceedingly rare before the 19th century, when the scientific study of the Lesbian dialect and lyric was revolutionised by papyrological discoveries. Although we find a considerable number of poems written in Sapphic stanzas, most of them either stick to Ionic or – as in the English odes of the Browne Medal – import Doric features taken from Pindar. In more recent times, however, we do find single gems written in the Aeolic dialect: Korsch's little Alcaic poem Πρὸς Οὐεστφάλιον (→ **Russia**), and Headlam's *To Mary* (→ **Great Britain**). A peculiar mixture of Homeric language and Aeolic accentuation can be found in Křesadlo's Ἀστροναυτιλία (→ **Bohemian Lands**).

3.3 Orthography and Editorial Practice

Greek orthography, with all its breathings, accents, and diacritical signs, has always been a major problem in the West, both for the uneven and sometimes inconsistent linguistic knowledge of authors, and for the technical inadequacy of a large number of printers, particularly in the early times of humanism and the Renaissance. Let us list only some critical points that emerge from the inspection and collation of both original manuscripts and early prints of the 15th–17th centuries (we shall neglect here the use of 'Byzantine' abbreviations and tachygraphic signs) (cf. e.g., Weise 2016, 124):

- *Iota subscriptum* is often (though not consistently) omitted
- Final σ is occasionally used instead of (or along with) final ς
- Initials of proper names are often not capitalised
- Capital or initial letters dispense with diacritical signs altogether
- Enclitics (esp. τε) may be grouped together with the preceding word
- Accents (and breathings) are either wrong or different from modern practice (e.g., *gravis* before punctuation marks, τὶς instead of τίς, diacritics on the first element of diphthongs, not to mention the extreme variability in accentuation with enclitics, partly linked to the peculiarities of Byzantine rules)
- Punctuation differs considerably from modern practice

As time went by, western, 'Porsonian' printing rules became increasingly popular both in schools (and thus in the poets' autograph writing) and in typographies. Single exceptions may reflect a special historical intention: we might recall here the use of capital letters for real or fictional inscriptions, or the conscious omission of all diacritical signs (see Klopstock, Menchaca, Macías; a forerunner was Poliziano's edition of Callimachus' fifth hymn in the *Miscellanea*), whether or not the latter feature was influenced by contemporary theories suggesting that accentuation was absent from ancient Greek and proposing Latin stress rules for Greek (prominent supporters were Isaac Vossius and Henricus Christianus Henninius, cf. Minaoglou 2018, 122f.).

Several of the peculiarities in the above list correspond to writing habits of the authors, whether inherited from Byzantine scribal practice or not: insofar as this can be ascertained through the painstaking study of both the authors' autographs (where extant) and the contemporary usage prevailing in their *milieux*, these details may well deserve a thorough study in view of the adoption of a strictly conservative, historical orthography in editing the texts (cf. Gastgeber 2018).

But this will be a task for future generations of researchers, when manuscripts and prints are systematically investigated, and single national traditions properly outlined: this study will be important in order to distinguish more clearly between what can be ascribed to the authors' own will and what should rather be regarded as the fruit of the printers' inaccuracy or idiosyncrasy. The primary goal of the present anthology, however, is to make the texts available and readable for a larger public who is chiefly familiar with classical Greek in the orthographic form which has been dominant over the past two centuries. Hence, while we do lay some importance on orthographic peculiarities and we do attempt to preserve 'eccentric' features of the originals as long as we gauge that they mirror the authors' last will, we are sometimes ready to adapt the texts to modern practice for the sake of clarity (punctuation, in particular, consistently follows modern rules): one could call this model a 'critical *Lesefassung*'.

Furthermore, a certain degree of autonomy in this respect has been given to the editors of single sections: some of them have investigated the matter more deeply than others (see, e.g., the careful analysis of capitalisation in Johan Paulinus' *Finlandia*), some of them have been more generous and systematic than others in registering orthographic peculiarities in the *apparatus criticus*.

3.4 Presentation

Texts are arranged by sections roughly corresponding to modern countries or geographical areas; in the case where this is particularly problematic (e.g., Balkans, Poland and Lithuania) the introductions explain the historical evolution of the respective cultural and political space; the Nordic Countries are grouped in one chapter, which however deals separately with every single country of that area.

Sections are ordered chronologically according to the date of their first text. We are well aware that it has not always been possible to identify with certainty or to reproduce in our selections the earliest example of Greek poetry from every single country or region, and we admit that several texts are hard to date and that the difference of one or two years may be deemed irrelevant: we are nonetheless confident that this criterion, for all its roughness, helps to give a realistic picture of the gradual spreading of the phenomenon of Greek versification throughout Europe.

Each section has a similar structure: a short introduction summarises the development of Greek studies and writing in the relevant country or area, and ends with a **General Bibliography**. Titles included in the general bibliography will be quoted by short title within the whole section. After the introduction, texts are ordered chronologically, with the only limitation that texts by the same author are presented consecutively (preceded by Roman numerals: I, II, etc.). For every piece the following elements appear:
– author (when known) with dates of birth and death
– title (when known or extant: when lacking a Latin title is given in angular brackets < >) followed by the date of writing in square brackets [ ] (when known: in most cases, the date of the *editio princeps* is given, or else the more or less exact date of the manuscript source)
– the critical edition of the Greek text

- the sources (manuscripts or prints) on which the edition is based (**Textus**)
- the critical apparatus (**Crit.**): lemmata from different lines are separated by ‖, lemmata within the same line are separated by |
- the *apparatus fontium et comparandorum* (**Sim.**), gathering *loci similes*, possible literary sources, parallel or peculiar forms; classical authors are here quoted according to the *Oxford Classical Dictionary* (OCD)
- an English translation, mostly in prose or in non-poetic lines
- a short paragraph on **Metre** and a usually longer section of **Notes** referring to some features of the poem, though by no means aiming at a full commentary
- a short **Biography** of the author, mostly compiled from published dictionaries or historical essays
- a **Bibliography** gathering the most easily available sources on the author and – where available – on his poetic output in Greek.

A point of debate might sometimes be the assignment of authors to certain regional sections. In most cases the essential criteria were either the place of birth (e.g., Casaubon in → **Switzerland**, Erasmus in → **Low Countries**, Bessarion, Laskaris, Moschos, Mousouros, Allacci in → **Greece**) or the centre of activity (e.g., Graefe in → **Russia**, Mylius in → **Poland and Lithuania**, Reusner in → **Germany**).

4 History of Scholarship

The exploration of Humanist Greek or *Neualtgriechisch* is a very young field of studies,[4] which 'overlaps with many different established disciplines' (Päll/Volt 2018, 9): Classical (Greek) Philology, Byzantine Studies, Modern Greek Studies, Neo-Latin Studies, Renaissance Studies, Classical Reception Studies, Codicology, (Greek) Palaeography. The very denomination of the subject is controversial: 'Humanist Greek' or 'Renaissance Greek' (stressing the peak in the Renaissance), *Neualtgriechisch* (stressing persistence from the Renaissance to the present in

---

4 Cf. the title of the 2018 conference at Helsinki University: 'Humanist Greek (HUG) – Perspectives for a New Field of Studies'.

parallel to Neo-Latin), 'Neo-Greek' (R. Hunter), 'Neo-Hellenic' (Ermolaeva), *Hellenistik* (R. Glei).⁵

As a matter of fact, the first attempts to collect this kind of texts and biographic information on their authors go back to the late 17th and 18th century. Whereas Lorenzo Crasso in his 1678 volume *Istoria de' poeti greci e di que' che'n Greca lingua han poetato* put ancient and 'modern' poets in the same box, Georgius Lizelius in his 1730 *Historia poetarum Graecorum Germaniae* was the first to focus exclusively on 'modern' poets, and moreover on poets from one specific region; in later decades Erik Michael Fant and Matthias Floderus will do the same for Sweden (cf. Akujärvi 2020, 63f.). These attempts to single out the literary and cultural phenomenon, however, did not generate a new branch of research *suo iure*, but were often silently collapsed in the great national biographical dictionaries of the 19th and 20th centuries.

The history of anthologies has an equally slow start: collections of texts, mostly contemporary ones in combination with Neo-Latin poems, appear since the 18th century (e.g. Freyer's 1715 *Fasciculus poematum Graecorum*, Olivet's 1743 *Recentiores poetae Latini et Graeci selecti quinque*, Floderus' 1785–1789 *De poetis in Svio-Gothia Graecis*, and Mitscherlich's 1793 *Eclogae recentiorum carminum Latinorum*) and particularly in the 19th century (of special interest is an attempt of a larger collection by the Braunschweig physician Karl Friedrich Arend Scheller, cf. Päll 2020b; then we often find collections of Greek translations). However, the scientific vogue of 19th-century German gymnasia brought about the first critical editions of some Renaissance Greek poets. A culmination and a milestone for studies in Humanist Greek, Émile Legrand started his gigantic *Bibliographie hellénique* in 1885.

A true surge in the study of 'Humanist Greek' (an expression first attested in a book title with Roberto Weiss's posthumous collected papers, published in 1977) took place in post-WWII Italian philology, when new critical editions of Italian and Greek poets were produced (Filelfo, Gaurico, Poliziano, Laskaris, Moschos, Allacci, Pascoli) – this trend continues to the present day. After important contributions by Dieter Harlfinger (1989) and Walther Ludwig (1998), the last decades of the 20th century witnessed an increasing number of critical editions in other European countries as well: special attention has been devoted to Humanist Greek over the last 20 years in Scandinavia, the Baltic area and Eastern Europe; the abundant German poetic output has equally been made the object of

---

5 For discussions cf., e.g., Päll/Volt 2018, 9–11; Weise 2011, 401; Weise 2019, 7 fn. 5; Korhonen in Kajava/Korhonen/Vesterinen 2020, ii. See also Glei, Reinhold (2018), Rev. „HELLENISTI!", in: *Neulateinisches Jahrbuch* 20, 544–549; Hunter in Beron/Weise 2020, 198.

deep study (from Rhein's 1987 dissertation onwards). In recent years, the perspective has been broadened in a number of ways: regional surveys, studies in the field of intellectual history, and large scientific conferences on Humanist Greek (Tartu 2014, Wuppertal 2015, Helsinki 2018).[6]

Much remains to be done, above all in terms of proper critical editions of poetic texts in ancient Greek: the investigation of single genres and of transnational erudite networks, the historical contextualisation of this cultural phenomenon, the detection of reception clusters (e.g., Nonnus of Panopolis, Gregory of Nazianzus, the gnomic poets, the Greek epigrammatists, the Hellenistic poets). We conceive this anthology chiefly as a first tool that may help other scholars to take into consideration areas and personalities they are not familiar with, and to follow the threads of interregional developments and connections in various moments of Europe's intellectual history.

Schöningen/Venice, December 2020
τοῦ νοσήματος ἐπιδημοῦντος

---

[6] For conference volumes, see Päll/Volt 2018 (Tartu conference); Weise 2017 (Wuppertal conference); Kajava/Korhonen/Vesterinen 2020 (Helsinki conference). Preliminary versions of some chapters in the present volume were discussed during a workshop in Venice in 2018.

Selective Bibliography

Collected Papers

Kajava, Mika/Korhonen, Tua/Vesterinen, Jamie (eds.) (2020), *MEILICHA DÔRA. Poems and Prose in Greek from Renaissance and Early Modern Europe*, Helsinki.
Lamers, Han/Constantinidou, Natasha (eds.) (2020), *Receptions of Hellenism in Early Modern Europe 15th–17th Centuries*, Leiden.
Päll, Janika/Volt, Ivo (eds.) (2018), *Hellenostephanos. Humanist Greek in Early Modern Europe. Learned Communities between Antiquity and Contemporary Culture*, Tartu.
Weise, Stefan (ed.) (2017), *HELLENISTI! Altgriechisch als Literatursprache im neuzeitlichen Europa*, Stuttgart.

Some Single Editions and Collections

Andrist, Patrick/Lukinovich, Alessandra (2005), "POESIS ET MORES: Florent Chrestien, Joseph-Juste Scaliger, et les *Psaumes* en vers du *Bernensis* A 69", in: Antje Kolde/Alessandra Lukinovich/André-Louis Rey (eds.), κορυφαίῳ ἀνδρί. *Mélanges offerts à André Hurst*, Genève, 673–715.
Aydin, Elisabeth (ed.) (forthcoming), *Daniel Heinsius. Peplus*, Paris.
Baldwin, Barry (1995), *The Latin & Greek Poems of Samuel Johnson. Text, Translation and Commentary*, London.
Buchwald, Wolfgang (ed.) (1938), *Ulrich von Wilamowitz-Moellendorff. Elegeia*, Berlin.
Citti, Vittorio (1998), "Bessomachos: un inedito greco pascoliano", in: *Lexis* 1, 87–104.
Cortassa, Guido/Maltese, Enrico V. (1997), *Francesco Filelfo. De Psychagogia*, Alessandria.
Czerniatowicz, Janina (ed.) (1991), *Corpusculum poesis Polono-Graecae saeculorum XVI–XVII (1531–1648)*, Wrocław.
de Vries, Meta (2007), *Het dichtwerk van Jan van Foreest (1585–1651)*, PhD dissertation, Radboud Universiteit Nijmegen.
Flach, Johannes (ed.) (1876), *ΕΤΕΟΣΤΕΨΙΑΣ ΒΙΒΛΙΟΝ ΤΡΙΤΟΝ. Carminis ab Alberto Kunio compositi librum tertium e codice Tubingensi*, Tubingae.
Fobes, Francis Howard (ed.)/Sypherd, Wilbur Owen (1928), *Jephthah by John Christopherson. The Greek text edited and translated into English*, Newark, Delaware.
Gallo, Italo (1998), *Pomponio Gaurico. Inno greco a Fabrizio Brancia*, Napoli.
Gärtner, Thomas (2020a), "Die diversen Reflexe des *Epitaphios Bionos* bei Lorenz Rhodoman", in: Anne-Elisabeth Beron/Stefan Weise (eds.), *Hyblaea avena. Theokrit in römischer Kaiserzeit und Früher Neuzeit*, Stuttgart, 115–154: 130–149 (edition and translation of Rhodoman's *Totenklage um Luther*).
Gärtner, Thomas (2020b), "Tierische Kampfansage. Die Paränesen der Mäusekämpfer in der *Anthropomyomachie* des Eduard Eyth (1840) vor dem Hintergrund der späthellenistischen *Batrachomyomachie*", in: Hedwig Schmalzgruber (ed.), *Speaking Animals in Ancient Literature*, Heidelberg, 553–595: 566–595 (edition and translation of Eyth's *Anthropomyomachia*).

Giannachi, Francesco G. (2017), "Lettere ed epigrammi di Francesco Arcudi (1590–1641)", in: *Studi sull'Oriente Cristiano* 21, 77–151.
Gürsching, Mauritius (ed.) (1894), "Alberti Kuni Leonbergensis ΕΤΕΟΣΤΕΨΙΑΣ libros I, II, IV e codice Tubingensi", in: *K. B. Humanistisches Gymnasium in Bayreuth. Programm am Schlusse des Jahres 1893/94*, Bayreuth, 1–52.
Hillgruber, Michael (2017), "Archäologie als Opferdienst. Das Hyperboreer-Gedicht Eduard Gerhards", in: Stefan Weise (ed.), *HELLENISTI! Altgriechisch als Literatursprache im neuzeitlichen Europa*, Stuttgart, 221–251: 238–248 (edition and commentary).
Korhonen, Tua/Oksala, Teivas/Sironen, Erkki (eds.) (2000), *Johan Paulinus (Lillienstedt), Magnus Principatus Finlandia*, Helsinki.
Lamata Meana, Silvia (1998), "Un texto en griego inédito del humanismo español del siglo XVIII", in: *Epos* 14, 563–580.
Legrand, Émile (1885–1906), *Bibliographie Hellénique ou description raisonnée des ouvrages publiés par des grecs aux XVe et XVIe siècles*, vol. I–IV, Paris.
Legrand, Émile (1892), *Cent-dix lettres grecques de François Filelfe*, Paris.
Legrand, Émile (1894–1903), *Bibliographie Hellénique ou description des ouvrages publiés par des grecs au XVIIe siècle*, vol. I–IV, Paris.
Meschini, Anna (1976a), *Demetrio Mosco. La storia di Elena e Alessandro*, Padova.
Meschini, Anna (1976b), *Giano Laskaris. Epigrammi Greci*, Padova.
Morrison, Anthea (1983), "Samuel Taylor Coleridge's Greek Prize Ode on the Slave Trade", in: John Richard Watson (ed.), *An Infinite Complexity: Essays in Romanticism*, Edinburgh, 145–160.
Musae Cantabrigienses; seu carmina quaedam numismate aureo Cantabrigiae ornata et Procancellarii permissu edita, Londini 1810.
Neuendorf, Paul A. (2017), "Griechische Versepisteln im 16. Jahrhundert. Johannes Clajus d. Ä. (1535–1592) an die Gelehrten seiner Zeit", in: Stefan Weise (ed.), *HELLENISTI! Altgriechisch als Literatursprache im neuzeitlichen Europa*, Stuttgart, 63–108.
Opelt, Ilona (1968), "Zwei griechische pindarische Oden aus dem frühen 17. Jahrhundert", in: *Mnemosyne* 21/4, 374–385.
Pontani, Filippomaria (ed.) (2002), *Angeli Politiani Liber epigrammatum Graecorum*, Roma.
Pontani, Filippomaria (2002–3), "Musurus' Creed", in: *Greek, Roman, and Byzantine Studies* 43, 175–213.
Pontani, Filippomaria (2014), "Preghiere, parafrasi e grammatiche: Il *Credo* e l'*Ave Maria* di Marco Musuro", in: *Bibliothèque d'Humanisme et Renaissance* 76/2, 325–340.
Pontani, Filippomaria (2015), "Sognando la crociata. Un'ode saffica di Giano Làskaris su Carlo VIII", in: *Italia Medioevale e Umanistica* 56, 251–294.
Rhein, Stefan (1987), *Philologie und Dichtung. Melanchthons griechische Gedichte (Edition, Übersetzung und Kommentar)*, Diss. Heidelberg.
Richtsteig, Eberhard (1927), *Deutsche Dichtungen in griechischem Gewande*, Breslau.
Rotolo, Vincenzo (1966), *Il Carme «HELLAS» di Leone Allacci*, Palermo.
Schmitz, Thomas (1991), "Les odes grecques de Frédéric Jamot († ca. 1609)", in: *Bibliothèque d'Humanisme et Renaissance* 53/2, 281–303.
Tosi, Renzo (2011), *I carmi greci di Clotilde Tambroni*, Bologna.
van den Berg, R.M./Buijs, M./Gieben, C.J.S./van den Hoorn, R.-J./Nijland, J.M./Pfeijffer, I.L./Roskam, H.N. (eds.) (1993), *Bataafs Athene. Een bloemlezing van Klassiek Griekse poëzie van de hand van Leidse humanisten van de zestiende tot en met de twintigste eeuw. Kritische teksteditie met inleidingen, vertaling en noten*, Leiden.

van Walsem, Gerard Christiaan (ed.) (1930), *Harlemias. Het beleg der stad Haarlem in een Grieksch gedicht verhaald...*, Leiden.
Volckmar, Karl (1854), "Laurentius Rhodomann's Lobgedicht auf Ilfeld", in: *Programm des Königlichen Pädagogiums zu Ilfeld Ostern 1854*, Nordhausen, 1–54 (edition and translation).
Weise, Stefan (2017), "Dichten und Teetrinken. Zum anakreontischen griechischen Teegedicht *De Thea herba* von Johann Gottfried Herrichen (1629–1705)", in: Id. (ed.), *HELLENISTI! Altgriechisch als Literatursprache im neuzeitlichen Europa*, Stuttgart, 149–201: 180–196 (edition and translation).
Weise, Stefan (2019), *Der Arion des Lorenz Rhodoman. Ein altgriechisches Epyllion der Renaissance. Einleitung, Text, Übersetzung, Wortindex*, Stuttgart.
Wilson, Nigel G. (2016), *Aldus Manutius. The Greek Classics*, Cambridge Mass.
Zoras, Gerasimos (1994), *Ἑλληνόγλωσσα στιχουργήματα Ἰταλῶν λογίων (ΙΖ΄ – ΙΘ΄ αἰῶνες)*, Athina.

Catalogues

Chamay, Jacques/Cottier, Jean-Pierre (eds.) (2000), *Homère chez Calvin*, Genève.
Harlfinger, Dieter (ed.) (1989), *Graecogermania. Griechischstudien deutscher Humanisten. Die Editionstätigkeit der Griechen in der italienischen Renaissance (1469 – 1523)*, Weinheim/ New York.
Hieronymus, Frank (ed.) (1992), *En Basileia polei tes Germanias. Griechischer Geist aus Basler Pressen*, Basel.
Korhonen, Tua/Sironen, Erkki (2018), *The Exhibition «Humanist Greek from Finland" 22 August – 5 October 2018,* Helsinki.
Päll, Janika/Valper, Eve (eds.) (2014), *Βάρβαρος οὐ πέλομαι*, Tartu.

Regional and General Surveys

Akujärvi, Johanna (2020), "Greek occasional poetry from the Swedish Empire. The case of Josephus Thun", in: Arne Jönsson *et al.* (eds.), *Att dikta för livet, döden och evigheten. Tillfällesdiktning 1500–1800*. Göteborg/Stockholm, 61–86.
Bauer, Martin M./Rainer, Rupert (2019), "Austria (Autriche)", in: Francisco Oliveira/Ramón Martínez (eds.), *Europatrida*, Coimbra, 13–25.
Bērziņa, Gita (2018), "16th–17th-century Greek texts at the Academic Library of the University of Latvia", in: Janika Päll/Ivo Volt (eds.), *Hellenostephanos. Humanist Greek in Early Modern Europe. Learned Communities between Antiquity and Contemporary Culture,* Tartu, 40–56.
Crasso, Lorenzo (1678), *Istoria de' poeti greci e di que' che'n Greca lingua han poetato,* Napoli.
Czerniatowicz, Janina (2013), "Greek Poetry Composed by Polish Authors in the 16th and 17th Centuries", in: *Eos* C 2013/fasciculus extra ordinem editus electronicus (ISSN 0012-7825), 403–423 (= ptf.edu.pl/eos/wp-content/uploads/2016/07/407_EOS-2013-CD.pdf).
de Andrés, Enriqueta (1988), *Helenistas españoles del siglo XVII*, Madrid.
Ermolaeva, Elena (2019), "Neo-Hellenic poetry in Russia: Antonios Palladoklis (1747–1801) and Georgios Baldani (about 1760–1789)", in: *Hyperboreus* 25/2, 375–386.
Fant, Erik Michael (1775–1786), *Historiola litteraturae Graecae in Svecia. Diss. Specimen I–XII*, Uppsala.

Floderus, Matthias (1785–1789), *De poetis in Svio-Gothia Graecis. Diss. Specimen I–IV.*
Gastgeber, Christian (2018), "Transalpine Greek Humanism (Pannonian Area). A Methodological Approach", in: Janika Päll/Ivo Volt (eds.) (2018), *Hellenostephanos. Humanist Greek in Early Modern Europe. Learned Communities between Antiquity and Contemporary Culture*, Tartu, 19–39.
Gottschalck, Rasmus (2019), "Denmark (Danemark)", in: Francisco Oliveira/Ramón Martínez (eds.), *Europatrida*, Coimbra, 59–70.
Hernando, Concepción (1975), *Helenismo e Ilustración (el griego en el siglo XVIII español)*, Madrid.
Korhonen, Tua (2004), Ateena Auran rannoilla: Humanistikreikkaa Kuninkaallisesta Turun akatemiasta, http://urn.fi/URN:ISBN:952-10-1812-7, Diss. Helsinki.
Král, Josef (1898), "Řecké básnictví humanistické v Čechách až do konce samostatné university Karlovy", in: *Rozpravy filologické věnované Janu Gebauerovi*, Praha, 86–105.
Lizelius, Georgius (1730), *Historia poetarum Graecorum Germaniae a renatis litteris ad nostra usque tempora…*, Francofurti et Lipsiae.
López Rueda, José (1973), *Helenistas españoles del siglo XVI*, Madrid.
Ludwig, Walther (1998), *Hellas in Deutschland. Darstellungen der Gräzistik im deutschsprachigen Raum aus dem 16. und 17. Jahrhundert*, Hamburg.
Maillard, Jean-François/Kecskeméti, Judit/Magnien, Catherine/Portalier, Monique (1999), *La France des Humanistes: Hellénistes I*, Turnhout.
Maillard, Jean-François/Flamand, Jean-Marie/Kecskeméti, Judit (2010), *La France des Humanistes: Hellénistes II*, Turnhout.
Nordgren, Lars (2019), "Sweden (Suède)", in: Francisco Oliveira/Ramón Martínez (eds.), *Europatrida*, Coimbra, 265–276.
Päll, Janika (2010), "Humanistengriechisch im alten Estland und Nord-Livland", in: Janika Päll/Ivo Volt/Martin Steinrück (eds.), *Classical Tradition from the 16th Century to Nietzsche*, Tartu, 114–147.
Päll, Janika (2018), "Humanist Greek in Early Modern Estonia and Livonia", in: Janika Päll/Ivo Volt (eds.), *Hellenostephanos. Humanist Greek in Early Modern Europe. Learned Communities between Antiquity and Contemporary Culture*, Tartu, 57–112.
Päll, Janika (2020a), "Hyperborean flowers: Humanist Greek around the Baltic Sea", in: Natasha Constantinidou/Han Lamers (eds.), *Receptions of Hellenism in Early Modern Europe*, Leiden/Boston, 410–438.
Päll, Janika (2020b), "German Neo-Humanism *versus* Rising Professionalism. *Carmina Hellenica Teutonum* by the Braunschweig Physician and Philhellene Karl Friedrich Arend Scheller (1773–1842)", in: Mika Kajava/Tua Korhonen/Jamie Vesterinen (eds.), *MEILICHA DÔRA. Poems and Prose in Greek from Renaissance and Early Modern Europe*, Helsinki, 299–332.
Pontani, Filippomaria (2017), "*Graeca per Italiae fines*. Greek poetry in Italy from Poliziano to the present", in: Stefan Weise (ed.), *HELLENISTI! Altgriechisch als Literatursprache im neuzeitlichen Europa*, Stuttgart, 311–347.
Slavíková, Marcela (2020), "Γενεὴν Βοίημος. Humanist Greek Poetry in the Bohemian Lands", in: Mika Kajava/Tua Korhonen/Jamie Vesterinen (eds.), *MEILICHA DÔRA. Poems and Prose in Greek from Renaissance and Early Modern Europe*, Helsinki, 247–267.
Veteikis, Tomas (2004), *Graikų kalbos studijos ir graikiškoji kūryba Lietuvoje XVI–XVII amžiuje*, Daktaro disertacija. Humanitariniai mokslai, filologija, 04H. Vilnius.
Weise, Stefan (2011), "Μοῦσα Ἀλληνική. Griechische Gedichte hallescher Gelehrter", in: *Archiv für Papyrusforschung und verwandte Gebiete* 57/2, 399–429.

Weise, Stefan (2016), "Ἑλληνίδ' αἶαν εἰσιδεῖν ἱμείρομαι – Neualtgriechische Literatur in Deutschland (Versuch eines Überblicks)", in: *Antike und Abendland* 62, 114–181.
Weise, Stefan (2020), *"Graecia transvolavit Alpes:* Humanist Greek Writing in Germany (15th–17th Centuries) Through the Eyes of Georg Lizel (1694-1761)", in: Han Lamers/Natasha Constantinidou (eds.), *Receptions of Hellenism in Early Modern Europe 15th–17th Centuries*, Leiden, 379–409.

Single Genres and Themes

Beron, Anne-Elisabeth/Weise, Stefan (eds.) (2020), *Hyblaea avena. Theokrit in römischer Kaiserzeit und Früher Neuzeit*, Stuttgart.
Gärtner, Thomas (2020), "Jonische Hexameter als Träger der norddeutschen Reformation", in: Mika Kajava/Tua Korhonen/Jamie Vesterinen (eds.), *MEILICHA DÔRA. Poems and Prose in Greek from the Renaissance and Early Modern Europe*, Helsinki, 217–243.
Harrison, Thomas (2020), "Herodotus's Travels in Britain and Beyond. Prose Composition and Pseudo-Ethnography", in: Thomas Harrison/Joseph Skinner (eds.), *Herodotus in the Long Nineteenth Century*, Cambridge et al., 244–273.
Ludwig, Walther (2017), *"Scitis, quanto semper amore Graecarum rerum flagrem.* Motive für den Höhepunkt des humanistischen griechischen Dichtens um 1600", in: Stefan Weise (ed.), *HELLENISTI! Altgriechisch als Literatursprache im neuzeitlichen Europa*, Stuttgart.
Päll, Janika (2017), "The Transfer of Greek Pindaric Ode from Italy to the Northern Shores: From Robortello to Vogelmann and further", in: Stefan Weise (ed.), *HELLENISTI! Altgriechisch als Literatursprache im neuzeitlichen Europa*, Stuttgart, 349–368.
Päll, Janika (forthcoming), "Greek Pindaric ode in the United Kingdom", in: Ivo Volt/Janika Päll/Neeme Näripä (eds.), *Hortus Floridus*, Tartu.
Pontani, Filippomaria (2018), "Hellenic Verse and Christian Humanism: From Nonnus to Musurus", in: *International Journal of Classical Tradition* 25, 216–240.

Multilingualism, 'Greekness', and History of Greek Studies

Ben-Tov, Asaph (2009), *Lutheran Humanists and Greek Antiquity: Melanchthonian Scholarship Between Universal History and Pedagogy*, Leiden et al.
Botley, Paul (2010), *Learning Greek in Western Europe 1396–1529*, Philadelphia.
Bursian, Conrad (1883), *Geschichte der classischen Philologie in Deutschland von den Anfängen bis zur Gegenwart*, München/Leipzig.
Geanakoplos, Deno J. (1962), *Greek Scholars in Venice*, Cambridge Mass.
Haynes, Kenneth (2003), *English Literature and Ancient Languages*, Oxford.
Lamers, Han (2015), *Greece Reinvented*, Leiden/Boston.
Hutton, James (1935), *The Greek Anthology in Italy to the Year 1800*, Ithaca/New York.
Saladin, Jean-Christophe (2000), *La bataille du grec à la Renaissance*, Paris.
Sandys, John Edwin (1908), *A History of Classical Scholarship*, vol. ii–iii, Cambridge.
Stray, Christopher (1998), *Classics Transformed. Schools, Universities, and Society in England, 1830–1960*, Oxford.

Weiss, Roberto (1977), *Medieval and Humanist Greek. Collected Essays*, Padova.
Wilson, Nigel G. (1992), *From Byzantium to Italy*, London.

Orthography, Language, and Metrics (see also Single Editions)

Kallergis, H. E. (1998), "Μετρικὲς παρατηρήσεις σὲ ἀρχαιόγλωσσα ἐπιγράμματα Ἑλλήνων λογίων του 16ου καὶ του 17ου αἰώνα", in: *Θησαυρίσματα* 28, 223–237.
Minaoglou, Charalampos (2018), "Anastasius Michael Macedo and His Speech on Hellenism", in: Päll/Volt 2018, 115–129.
Päll, Janika (2005), "Far Away from Byzantium: Pronunciation and Orthography of Greek in the 17th Century Estonia", in: Ivo Volt/Janika Päll (eds.), *Byzantino-Nordica. Acta Societatis Morgensternianae* 2, Tartu, 86–119.
Sironen, Erkki (2000), "Notes on the Language of Johan Paulinus' *Finlandia*. A Baroque Eulogy in Greek Verse", in: *Arctos* 24, 129–147.
Sironen, Erkki (2018), "'Dialectal' Variation in Humanist Greek Prose orations from the Great Sweden", in: Päll/Volt 2018, 130–143.

Online Resources

https://www.dbbe.ugent.be (database of Byzantine book epigrams)
http://hellenic-institute.uk/research/Etheridge/ (digital edition of Etheridge's Greek encomium)
http://humgraeca.utlib.ut.ee (Helleno-Nordica project database)
https://www.pantoia.de (valuable database of translations into Greek and Latin)

Timeline

Year	Humanist Greek/'Neualtgriechisch'	General history/History of Greek scholarship	
1397		Manuel Chrysoloras becomes the first professor of Greek at the Studio in Florence	14th c.
1453		Conquest of Constantinople by the Turks	
1488		Editio princeps of Homer	
1494		Editio princeps of the *Anthologia Graeca* (Planudea)	15th c.
1494–1495		Aldo Manuzio founds his press in Venice	
1498	Angelo Poliziano (†1494), *Liber epigrammatum Graecorum*		
1501	Demetrios Moschos, Τὸ καθ' Ἑλένην καὶ Ἀλέξανδρον		
1502		Foundation of Wittenberg University	
1513	Markos Mousouros, *Ode to Plato*	Editio princeps of Pindar; Demetrios Doukas appointed at the Chair of Greek at the Universidad Complutense, Madrid	
1516		Publication of Erasmus' New Testament in Greek and Latin (*Novum Instrumentum omne*); Maxim the Greek (Michael Trivolis) arrives in Moscow	16th c.
1517		Foundation of the *Collegium Trilingue* in Leuven; beginning of the Lutheran Reformation	
1518		Philipp Melanchthon becomes professor of Greek at Wittenberg	
1527	Ianos Laskaris, *Epigrammata* (first edition)		
1530		Foundation of the Collège royal in Paris, Pierre Danès becomes its first professor of Greek	
ca. 1535		Johannes Oporinus starts his press in Basel	

Year	Humanist Greek/'Neualtgriechisch'	General history/History of Greek scholarship
1538	Joachim Camerarius/Jakob Micyllus, *Epigrammata veterum poetarum*	
1540		John Cheke becomes the first Regius Professor of Greek at Cambridge; the Jesuit order is acknowledged by the pope
1541		Matouš Collinus becomes the first professor of Greek at the University of Prague
1544	Ianos Laskaris, *Epigrammata* (second edition) John Christopherson, Τραγῳδία Ἰεφθάε (between 1544 and 1547)	
1545	Sebastian Castellio (Châtillon), *Vita Ioannis Baptistae*	
1547		Jean Dorat starts lecturing at the Collège de Coqueret in Paris
1548	Francesco Robortello, Βιοχρησμῳδία (first known Pindarising ode in Humanist Greek)	
1550		Michael Neander becomes headmaster at Ilfeld
1551		Robert Estienne prints the Greek New Testament in Geneva, where Jean Calvin will found the Academy in 1559
1554		Editio princeps of the *Carmina Anacreontea*
1555	Pietro Cortona, *Varia Carmina Graeca*	Peace of Augsburg: Lutheran Protestantism is officially acknowledged within the Holy Roman Empire
1555–1557		Establishment of the Jesuits in the Colleges of Coimbra and Évora
1559		Diogo Pires (Didacus Pyrrhus) settles in Ragusa
1569		Editio princeps of Nonnus' *Dionysiaca*
1571	Michael Retellius, *Poematum Graecorum libri duo*	

Year	Humanist Greek/'Neualtgriechisch'	General history/History of Greek scholarship
1573	Matthaeus Gothus, *Historiae vitae et doctrinae Jesu Christi...libri duo*	
1576		Foundation of the Collegio Greco di Sant'Atanasio in Rome
1582	Tito Prospero Martinengo, *Poëmata diversa*	
1585	Martin Crusius, *Germanograeciae libri sex*	
1588	[Laurentius Rhodoman], *Argonautica. Thebaica. Troica. Ilias parva* (+ *Arion*)	
1589	Laurentius Rhodoman, *Palaestina*	
1595	Hugo Grotius, *Ode ad illustrissimum comitem Henricum-Fredericum Nassavium*; Petrus Ivarus Borrichius, Ξενοφῶντος Ἡρακλῆς	
1599		Publication of the definitive version of the Jesuit *Ratio studiorum*
1605	Johannes Foreestius, *Idyllia sive Heroes*; Nicolaes Jansz. van Wassenaer, *Harlemias*	
1613	Daniel Heinsius, *Peplus Graecorum epigrammatum*	
1622		The University of Prague is closed
1632		Foundation of Tartu University (*Academia Gustaviana*), the first university in Estonia
1640	Maffeo Barberini (Urban VIII), *Poemata* (1st ed. 1629, some Greek pieces)	Foundation of Turku University (Royal Academy of Turku/Åbo), the first university in Finland
1641	Denis Pétau, *Graeca varii generis carmina*	
1642	Leone Allacci, *Hellas*	
1648		Peace of Westphalia
1678	Johan Paulinus, *Magnus Principatus Finlandia*	
1682	Josef Thun, *Amores sacri*	

17th c.

Year	Humanist Greek/'Neualtgriechisch'	General history/History of Greek scholarship	
1717	Johann Gottfried Herrichen (†1705), *Poemata Graeca et Latina*		
1730	Georgius Lizelius, *Historia poetarum Graecorum Germaniae*		
1744		Foundation of the New Academy in Moschopole	
1756	Adam František Kollár, *Χάριτες, εἰδύλλιον*		
1762		Catherine II becomes Empress of Russia	
1771		The *Plan de Estudios* of Antonio Campomanes is introduced in Spain	
1772	Pasquale Baffi, *Ode for Catherine*		18th c.
1773		Suppression of the Jesuit order (1759 Portugal, 1764 France, 1767 Spain, 1782 Austria)	
1775		Establishment of the Browne Medal at the University of Cambridge	
ca. 1780		Vienna becomes a centre of the Greek Enlightenment	
1791	Eugenius Boulgaris, *Aeneidis P. Virgilii Maronis libri XII Graeco carmine heroico expressi*		
1792	Samuel Taylor Coleridge, *Sors misera Servorum in insulis Indiae occidentalis* (Browne Medal)		
1795		Friedrich August Wolf, *Prolegomena ad Homerum*	
1797	Polyzoes Kondos, *Carmen heroicum*		
1818	László Ungvárnémeti Tóth, *Görög versei magyar tolmácsolattal*		
1819		Department of Classics at St Petersburg (professor: Chr. F. Graefe)	19th c.
1821		Start of the Greek Revolution	
1826	Johan Ludvig Runeberg, *Ἡ Ἀνάκρισις ἀκαδημαϊκή. Ἔπος γελοῖον*		

Year	Humanist Greek/'Neualtgriechisch'	General history/History of Greek scholarship	
1830		Foundation of the Kingdom of Greece, Otto of Wittelsbach becomes its first king	
1831	Eduard Eyth, *Hilarolypos* (first edition; second edition in 1840)		
1837	Friedrich Engels, *Duel of Eteocles and Polynices*		
1871	Julius Richter, *Ipes*		
1874	Philippos Ioannou, *Philologika parerga*		
1886	Theodorus Korsch, *ΣΤΕΦΑΝΟΣ*		
1896	George Stuart Robertson, *Athenais* (Pindaric ode for the Olympic Games)	'Games of the I Olympiad' in Athens	
1897	Ludwig Mayr, *Chariton polis* (first edition)		
ca. 1912	Johan Andreas dèr Mouw, *Pim*		
1918	Ronald A. Knox, *Telephoniazusae*		
1938	Ulrich von Wilamowitz-Moellendorff (†1931), *Elegeia*		
1990	Jerzy Kazimierz Danielewicz, *Professori Georgio Łanowski septuagenario* (Pindaric ode)		20th c.
1995	Jan Křesadlo (= Václav Pinkava, †1995), *Astronautilia*		
2012	Armand D'Angour, Alcaic Greek Ode for the London Olympics		
2014		First conference on Humanist Greek held at Tartu University	21th c.
2015	Alvaro Rissa (= Walter Lapini), *Il culo non esiste solo per andare di corpo*		

Fig. 1: Mesolonghi (Aetolia-Acarnania), Garden of Heroes: statue of Lord Byron with the Greek verse inscription by Demetrios Semitelos (see below, p. 77f.). Photo: Filippomaria Pontani.

Gerasimos Zoras, Kostas Yiavis, and Filippomaria Pontani
Greece

The Eastern Roman Empire was the only place in Europe where the tradition of poetry in ancient Greek language and metre was not entirely disrupted during the Middle Ages. Due to the loss of many texts in the manuscript tradition, to the selections of the Byzantine school curricula, and to the rapid decline in metrical competence, this continuity affected above all iambic and dactylic verse: after Romanos the Melodist (6th century), no author could present himself as a legitimate heir of Pindar (the only lyric author to be consistently, if partially, transmitted and read throughout the Middle Ages), and the very knowledge of lyric metre was confined to a restricted number of scholars, from Isaac Tzetzes in the 12th century to Demetrios Triklinios in the 14th. On the other hand, the 'easier' dactylic rhythms (chiefly the hexameter and, to a lesser extent, the elegiac couplet) continued to be practised, if occasionally, by poets and scholar-poets from John Geometres (10th century) to Theodore Prodromos and John Tzetzes (12th century) down to Maximos Planoudes (late 13th century). Irregularities and mistakes of various kinds affect the prosody and, above all, the metrical structure of these lines, but a number of epigrams, odes, and even idylls or short epics show that some awareness of hexametrical poetry was constantly kept alive in Byzantium, even in times when liturgical poetry and versification in the 'vulgar' language followed entirely different paths. An even deeper transformation affected the old iambic trimeter, which changed into a similar line based on different (and stricter) metrical and prosodic principles, the Byzantine dodecasyllable: this verse was not used in dramatic poetry (theatre had almost no place in Byzantium), but it soon earned pride of place as the most popular rhythm for *poésies d'occasion*, inscriptions, and short epigrams of all kinds. It should be recalled that in the transmission of Greek classical verse into a new Christian context, a key role was played by the heritage of late antique poetry, from Synesios' Anacreontic hymns to Nonnos of Panopolis' evangelic paraphrase; in particular, the immense output in hexameters and trimeters by Gregory of Nazianzus (4th century) represented a major source of inspiration for Byzantine poets throughout the centuries.

Our thanks to Theokritos Kouremenos (Univ. of Thessaloniki) and to Evgenia Makrigianni (Univ. of Athens) for help, improvements, and wise suggestions.

Against this background, the fall of Constantinople to the Ottomans in 1453, the ensuing decline of cultural centres such as Thessalonica, Mystras, and Trebizond, and the massive emigration of Byzantine scholars to Italy, led to a radical change: the contact and cross-fertilisation with Italian humanism produced not only the first instances of Greek poetry on European soil since antiquity (the cases of Filelfo, Poliziano, and others: → **Italy**), but also a major shift in the process of poetic emulation on the part of the Byzantines themselves, who were esteemed and recruited in the West chiefly on the basis of their familiarity with classical literature.

A good case in point is Cardinal **Bessarion** (1403–1472), both a churchman and a humanist: the owner of a vast library of Greek classics, he practised versification in dodecasyllables, but also resorted to elegiac couplets in ancient garb when devising epitaphs for himself or for his colleagues and friends. The tribute paid by Bessarion to his master Georgios Gemistos Pletho – a Platonic philosopher who was later condemned for heresy by the Eastern Church, and whose teachings indirectly influenced the Platonic and Neoplatonic revival in 15th-century Italy – embodies a departure from the purely Byzantine tradition through the adoption of new, mostly pagan models and conventions. It is not by chance that one of the longest book-epigrams of this age was composed precisely in praise of Bessarion's treatise in defence of Plato: its author, **Andronikos Kallistos** (†1475/1484), is a typical case of an intellectual who was active in various Italian cities as a teacher of Greek, as a prolific scribe (*inter alios* for Bessarion himself), and as a philosopher and a poet.

In his capacity as a teacher in Florence, Kallistos might be held responsible for introducing Angelo Poliziano to the riches of the *Greek Anthology*, a text that had remained rather marginal to Byzantine education but enjoyed great success in the Western Renaissance. Because Greek verse (with the notable exception of **Demetrios Moschos'** epyllion on *Helen and Alexander*) remained almost entirely confined to epigrammatic poetry, the pieces of the *Greek Anthology* (then known in its Planudean *facies*) provided inspiration for a number of encomia, *Buchepigramme* or the like, from Theodore Gazes, Konstantinos Laskaris and Demetrios Chalkondyles, down to John Argyropoulos and the Cretan **Demetrios Doukas** (ca. 1480–1527). In this frame, we can well appreciate the significance of the *editio princeps* of the *Greek Anthology* prepared in Florence in 1494 by **Ianos Laskaris** (1445–1535), an outstanding philologist, book-hunter and diplomat, and perhaps the most talented (certainly the most difficult) Greek poet of his time. Laskaris' witty and allusive epigrams, first published in an autonomous sylloge in 1527, were sometimes so erudite and 'Alexandrian' as to become obscure: while often conceived for scholarly topics or books, they sometimes addressed the celebrities the author had met in his incredibly active and adventurous public life, from his rival Poliziano to the painter Michelangelo, from Spanish dukes to the king of France (Laskaris' 1494 Sapphic ode for Charles VIII, not included in the sylloge, was a *tour de force* with a heavy political message).

The only poet who could rise to the level of Laskaris in this field (apart from Poliziano, his competitor in erudition but also in the bid for the heart of Alessandra Scala), was his Cretan pupil and protégé **Markos Mousouros** (1470–1517), the smartest connoisseur of Greek poetic diction and the most precious collaborator of Aldo Manuzio in the correction and edition of classical texts (→ **Italy**). Mousouros' versification spans from epigrams directed to his Venetian pupils down to hexametrical paraphrases of Christian prayers (the *Creed* and the *Ave Maria*), from a series of conventional book-epigrams to the long and ambitious *Ode to Plato* (1513), his masterpiece and the most overt plea to Pope Leo X and to the Western leaders for a Crusade against the Turks.

Thanks to their *studia*, to their printing houses, and to the large number of noblemen who were interested in learning Greek, Florence and Venice played a decisive role in the early phase of Greco-Italian humanism. So did Rome at a slightly later stage: the Ginnasio Greco created by pope Leo X on the Quirinale hill in 1514–1515 was entrusted to Laskaris, who hired Mousouros as a professor in 1516; after Mousouros' death, one of the collaborators was the Cretan **Arsenios Apostolis** (ca. 1465–1535), a prolific scribe but also a judicious scholar and editor of classical texts, and the author of witty epigrams and elegies addressed to his readers or to his patrons, such as Pope Paul III. Even if the Ginnasio Greco, with its innovative press, had a very short life, it sowed a seed that was fundamental for at least two reasons: it propagated the image of Rome as a sort of 'new Athens', a cultural and religious spearhead in an imaginary anti-Ottoman front of all Christian nations; and it inaugurated the idea that in the age of the Greek diaspora it was Catholic Rome that could equip a number of young intellectuals coming from Greece or Asia Minor with the necessary degree of education (among the pupils of Leo's first Gymnasium were good epigrammatists such as Matthaios Devaris, who worked for a long time at the Vatican library, and Christophoros Kondoleon).

Until the mid-16th century the political plight of the Greek nation, and the need for a new Crusade that might free both Greece and Constantinople from the Turkish yoke, represented a fixed idea for the most ambitious émigrés in Italy: the lament of the Corfiot **Antonios Eparchos** (1491–1571) stands precisely in this tradition, and was designed – much like Kallistos' monody or Mousouros' ode in previous decades – to stir the sympathy and the interest of an European *intellighentsija* that had long begun to view Greece through the lens of Homer, Pericles and the Acropolis.

However, the situation in Italy after the Counter-reformation, and the steady decline of the interest of Italian elites in Greek language and culture, changed this state of affairs profoundly. On the one hand, some cities continued to attract young Greeks in search of instruction: this was the case of Padua and Venice, the former through its university, where generations of Greeks were trained in medicine, philosophy and law, and through the famous Colleges of J. Paleocappa and then of Ioannes Kottounios; in Venice, many Greek printing houses remained active for centuries, and so did the Greek community of St George (most relevant is the foundation of the Greek School of Gabriel Severos in 1593, and then of the Flanginian College in 1665). This cultural environment fostered *inter alia* the production of several good Hellenic epigrams: leaving aside the Ionian islands (which were the home to many intellectuals and poets in the 16th century, from Alexandros and Leonardos Phortios to Ioannes Demisiani), we find Cretans such as the priest and teacher **Zacharias Skordylis** (†after 1572), the Calvinist philologist and commentator Phrangiskos Portos (Francesco Porto), and the theologian **Maximos Margounios** (1549–1602). Crete and the Ionian islands were under Venetian rule, whereas Chios (the home to other important scholars such as Hermodoros Lestarchos and Ioannes Mindonios) belonged to the Genoese: the Chiots Michael Sophianos and later **Georgios Koressios** (ca. 1570–1660) were both active as Greek poets, the former within the Paduan circle of Gian Vincenzo Pinelli, the latter moving from Padua to Tuscany, where he penned a remarkable (if formally poor) elegiac poem on football.

Aside from isolated cases of migration to Italy such as that of the 'Neapolitan' painter **Belisario Corenzio** (1558–after 1646), after the new opening of the Collegio Greco di S. Atanasio in 1576 it was again Catholic Rome that became the first port of refuge of the Greek elite, both for Italians of Greek descent such as Francesco Arcudi or Gregorio Porzio (→ **Italy**), and for Greeks by birth such as (to mention but a couple of those who practised the Hellenizing Muse) the Macedonian Ioannes Kottounios, the Cretan **Ioannes Matthaios Karyophylles** (ca. 1566–1633), the Chiot **Leone Allacci** (1588–1669), the Naxian Phrangiskos Kokkos, the Cypriot Ioannes Kigalas, and the Athenians Theophilos Korydalleus (later a philosopher and a controversial theologian in Constantinople) and **Leonardos Philaras** (ca. 1595–1673). The Collegio Greco, taken over by the Jesuits in 1591, became the institution where so many bishops, deacons, and intellectuals were educated during their youth, some of them indeed remaining to teach and study in house for a longer time. The quality of the Greek verse produced by the pupils of this institution attests to a special appreciation of verse in classical garb even beyond the conventional status of *poésies d'occasion* or book-epigrams, and to a conversation with Greek models that went well beyond curricular instruction and might also have benefited from the revival of Greek poetry under the papacy of Urbanus VIII (→ **Italy**).

This is true especially for three outstanding poets: Leone Allacci, an extremely prolific writer and perhaps the most remarkable researcher of the Vatican library in the 17th century, wrote with his iambic *Hellas* a memorable encomium of old Greek greatness, designed to impress the international élite, especially the French crown. Ioannes Kottounios, who taught rhetoric and philosophy in Bologna and Padua, dedicated an entire essay to Louis XIV on the art of epigram, which he himself practised in two rare books of Ἑλληνικὰ ἐπιγράμματα published in Padua in 1653. Finally, Philaras, who lived for a long time as a diplomat in Paris and London, promoting in all quarters the cause of the liberation of Greece, tested his poetic vein in a long Pindaric ode for the Virgin Mary, thus reviving a metrical form that had long been neglected in Greek quarters.

The present overview, by considering Italy as a sort of 'second home' to the Greek nation, does not take into account some later developments of the diaspora of Greek intellectuals between the late 17th and the early 19th century: we leave the sections on the **Balkans** and **Russia**, in particular, to document the importance of the Greek émigrés (especially, though not exclusively, belonging to the hierarchy of the Orthodox church) in the transmission and defence of Greek wisdom (including the study of classical language and literature) in the Danubian Principates, at the court of the Tsars, and even in such remote areas as Albania. Limiting our scope to the Greco-Italian context, we can state that since the late 17th century, as the dynamism of the Collegio Greco diminished and Venice (as the pole of attraction for intellectuals from the Ionian islands) remained the most important centre in Europe for the printing of Greek, the amount and the quality of published Greek verse diminished steadily: epigrams were indeed sometimes prefixed to liturgical, theological, or erudite works (one can recall *exempli gratia* the names of the Cretans Antonios Strategos, Liberios Kolettis and Alexios Spanos, of the Athenian **Georgios Patousas** (1687–1761), of Nikolaos Bouboulios, and others), but they were mostly unsatisfying from the point of view of classical metre, language, and artistic value.

This development went hand in hand with the progressive affirmation of 'vulgar' Greek (however defined) as the new language of the nation, and thus as the right vehicle for a new, proud literary and poetic expression – an ideological and cultural evolution that especially involved intellectuals from the Ionian islands since the second half of the 18th century. At the end of this story, once Greece recovered its independence (1827–1832) and modern Greek literature started a radically new parcours, epigrams in the ancient Greek fashion became erudite rarities and virtuoso pieces of purely archaeological interest. Some items of this output proved witty (the clever epigrams of **Philippos Ioannou** on modern inventions), others particularly touching (the epigram for the monument to Lord Byron at Mesolonghi written by the philologist **Demetrios Semitelos**); yet others, especially in the learned circles of 20th-century professors, remained within the conventions of academic communication (see here the examples of **Antonios Keramopoulos** and **Stylianos Alexiou**).

General Bibliography

BH XV/XVI = Legrand, Émile (1885–1906), *Bibliographie hellénique ou Description raisonnée des ouvrages publiés en grec par des Grecs aux XVe et XVIe siècles*, I–IV, Paris.
BH XVII = Legrand, Émile (1894–1903), *Bibliographie hellénique ou Description raisonnée des ouvrages publiés en grec par des Grecs au XVIIe siècle*, I–V, Paris.
Bianca, Concetta/Ferreri, Luigi/Delle Donne, Saulo (eds.) (2017), *Le prime edizioni greche a Roma*, Turnhout.
DBI = *Dizionario biografico degli Italiani*, Roma 1960–.
Fiaccadori, Gianfranco (ed.) (1994), *Bessarione e l'Umanesimo*, Napoli.
Geanakoplos, Deno J. (1962), *Greek Scholars in Venice*, Cambridge Mass.
Hutton, James (1935), *The Greek Anthology in Italy to the year 1800*, Ithaca/New York.
Lauxtermann, Marc (2003–2019), *Byzantine Poetry from Pisides to Geometres*, I–II, Oxford.
Petrakos, Vassilis (2016), "Τα αρχαία Ελληνικά στη ζωή των Ελλήνων", in: *O Mentor* 29/118, 123–211.
Podskalsky, Gerhard (1988), *Griechische Theologie in der Zeit der Türkenherrschaft (1453–1821)*, München.
RGK = Gamillscheg, Ernst/Harlfinger, Dieter/Eleuteri, Paolo (eds.) (1981–1997), *Repertorium der griechischen Kopisten*, I–III, Wien.
Tsirpanlis, Zacharias (1980), *Το Ελληνικό Κολλέγιο της Ρώμης και οι μαθητές του (1576–1700)*, Athens.

Basilios Bessarion (1403–1472)

I. Ἐπίγραμμα εἰς τὸν σοφὸν Γεώργιον τὸν Γεμιστόν [1452]

Πολλοὺς μὲν φῦσεν θεοειδέας ἀνέρας Ἑλλὰς
προὔχοντας σοφίῃ, τῇ τε ὅλῃ ἀρετῇ.
ἀλλὰ Γεμιστός, ὅσον Φαέθων ἄστρων ὑπερίσχει,
τόσον τῶν ἄλλων ἀμφότερον κρατέει.

Textus: Venezia, Biblioteca Nazionale Marciana, ms. Marc. gr. 333, f. 8r, manu ipsius auctoris (unde Mohler, Ludwig (1942), *Kardinal Bessarion* III, Paderborn, 469)

Crit.: tit. proprie ad prius epigramma (f. 7v) spectat, ad hoc τοῦ αὐτοῦ εἰς τὸν αὐτὸν ἕτερον ἐπίγραμμα adscr. auctor || **4** τόσσον debuit

Sim.: 1 θεοειδέας ἀνέρας] cf. *Anth. Pal.* 8.1.1 || **2** σοφίῃ...ἀρετῇ] de iunctura cf. e.g. Thgn. 1.1074 al. | ὅλῃ ἀρετῇ] cf. Aristot. *Eth. Eud.* 1219ab etc. || **2–4** de hyperbola et excessu sapientiae cf. *Anth. Pal.* 7.125

Epigram on the wise Georgios Gemistos

Greece gave birth to many godlike men
excellent in wisdom and in general virtue.
But as much as Phaethon is superior to the stars, Gemistos
wins over the others in both fields.

II. <*Sui ipsius epitaphium*> [1466]

Τοῦτ' ἔτι Βησσαρίων ζῶν ἄνυσα σώματι σῆμα·
πνεῦμα δὲ φευξεῖται πρὸς Θεὸν ἀθάνατον.

Textus: Romae in monumento sepulchrali cardinalis Bessarionis litteris maiusculis inscriptum in ecclesia Sanctorum XII Apostolorum, sub verbis *Bessario episcopus Thusculanus Sanctae Romanae Ecclesiae Cardinalis Patriarcha Constantinopolitanus nobili Graecia ortus oriundusque sibi vivens posuit anno salutis MCCCCLXVI* (hinc Mohler, Ludwig (1923), *Kardinal Bessarion* I, Paderborn, 323; lapidis imaginem praebet Fiaccadori 1994, 235)

Sim.: 1 σώματι σῆμα] cf. Plat. *Gorg.* 493a3 al. || **2** cf. *Anth. Pal.* 10.88.3–4

⟨Epitaph for himself⟩

> I, Bessarion made this grave for my body while I was still alive:
> my spirit will fly to the immortal God.

Metre: Elegiac couplets (note the harsh hiatus in l.2 and the prosodic mistake in l.4).

Notes: Bessarion was a prolific writer of theological and philosophical works, but he did not produce many poems (beside the epitaphs for Gemistos Pletho, one can recall the long encomium in dodecasyllables for Empress Theodora, for whose death he also penned some shorter epigrams). The hommage paid to his master Pletho (not an uncontroversial intellectual in his own time) takes the shape of a hyperbolic praise along the lines of an ancient epigram in praise of Epicharmus: it was added, along with other short texts, in the blank space of ff. 7–8 of ms. Marc. gr. 333, probably in the very days after Pletho's passing. The more sober funerary inscription devised by Bessarion for his own grave in the Church of Santi Apostoli in Rome (where it was later replaced by a different monument, and moved to the cloister where it is still to be seen today) insists on an obvious Platonic reminiscence (the pun σῶμα – σῆμα), coupled with the allusion to an epigram by Palladas, also insisting on the Platonic idea of the liberation of the soul from corporal bonds.

Biography: A protégé of Archbishop Dositheos of Trebizond, Basilios Bessarion (Trebizond 1403 – Ravenna 1472) was educated as a lay pupil in a monastery at Constantinople. At the age of twenty, he took monastic orders, and studied under the humanist Francesco Filelfo (→ **Italy**), then in Byzantium, and possibly under Markos Eugenikos. A pivotal experience for him was his stay at Mystras in the Peloponnese, where he joined the school of the renowned Neo-platonist Georgios Gemistos Pletho: there he also became acquainted with the imperial family of the Palaiologoi, recommending them social reforms and a closer dialogue with the Western Church. His advice was not acted on, but it was appreciated, and he was created bishop of Nicaea and became one of the main negotiators of the Byzantine delegation at the Council of Ferrara-Florence (1428–1449). Although Bessarion's main concern was to secure military support for the struggling Empire, he was able to seek compromise on the finer points of theological debates: this earned him popularity in the humanistic circles of Florence, a cardinalship from the catholic Pope, and, in due course, fierce disapproval in Byzantium. After a short time spent in a monastery (where he delved into patristic and ancient sources in order to provide arguments for the Ferrara bid for unity), he again found refuge in Italy, where he became the abbot of the Basilian monastery of Grottaferrata near Rome. He then followed the Pope to Rome, where he established his residence: his house became a centre for humanists, and he championed many Greek scholars; he had a huge library (which he later donated to the Republic of Venice), he commissioned translations and copies of many books, and generously financed the studies of Greek pupils. Ten years after the Fall of Constantinople, Bessarion became the Latin Patriarch of the City: in this capacity, he tried for several years to persuade the European rulers to organise a crusade in order to regain Constantinople, though in vain.

Bibliography: Lamers, Han (2015), *Greece Reinvented*, Leiden/Boston (esp. 115 for epigram II); Bianca, Concetta (1999), *Da Bisanzio a Roma*, Roma; Fiaccadori 1994, esp. 239 (E. Mioni) and 409f. (P. Eleuteri); Labowsky, Lotte (1979), *Bessarion's Library and the Biblioteca Marciana*, Roma; Pontani, Filippo Maria (1968) "Epicedi inediti del Bessarione", in: *Rivista di studi bizantini e neoellenici* 5, 105–121; Mohler, Ludwig (1923–1942), *Kardinal Bessarion als Theologe, Humanist, und Staatsmann*, I–III, Paderborn.

Andronikos Kallistos († 1475/1484)

Ἀνδρονίκου Βυζαντίου ἐπίγραμμα ἐν ἑξαμέτρῳ εἰς τὸ Βησσαρίωνος καρδινάλεως καὶ πατριάρχου Κωνσταντινουπόλεως ὑπὲρ Πλάτωνος βυβλίον [1458/59]

(excerptum, vv. 35–48)

35 Ἀλλὰ σὺ χαῖρε, Πλάτων, πρόμον αὐχῶν Βησσαρίωνα
    δῖον· ὃ δή τοι αἰὲν ἀεικέα λοιγὸν ἀμύνει,
    ὅς καὶ τήνδε τέτευχε καλὴν δέλτον, μέγα ἔργον
    ἠδὲ τεῆς σοφίης μνημήϊον ἐσσομένοισιν.
    Ἀλλ', ὦ Βησσαρίων μάκαρ, οὐλέ τε καὶ μέγα χαῖρε,
40 σεῖο δ' ἀεὶ φάτις ἄμβροτος οὐρανὸν εὐρὺν ἱκάνοι,
    οὕνεκά σ' ὑψιμέδων Θεὸς ἄφθιτος αἰθέρι ναίων
    ὄλβιον οἷς δώροισι μετ' ἀνθρώποισιν ἔθηκε,
    παντοίην ἀρετὴν ἠδὲ κλέος ἐσθλὸν ὀπάσσας·
    αὐτὰρ ἐγὼ σέο καὶ μετέπειτα μνήσομαι αἰὲν
45 σὴν σοφίην θαμὰ κλείων πᾶσι μετ' ἀνθρώποισιν
    σήν τ' ἀγανοφροσύνην, σὴν μειλιχίην τε,
    λισσόμενος κρατερὸν Θεόν, ἄμβροτον ἄρχον Ὀλύμπου,
    ὄφρα τοι ἐς πολέας λυκάβαντας γῆρας ὀπάζῃ
    ὄλβιον, ἄκρον ἀωτεῦντι σοφίης ἁγνὸν ἄνθος.

Textus: Venezia, Biblioteca Nazionale Marciana, ms. Marc. gr. 198, ff. 1v–2r (manu ipsius auctoris); Firenze, Biblioteca Medicea Laurenziana, mss. Laur. 31.24, ff. 145r–146r (manu Georgii Hermonymi) et Laur. 31.21, ff. 129r–30r (manu Alexii Celadeni); e Laurentianis ed. Legrand, Émile (1892), *Cent-dix lettres grecques de François Filelfe*, Paris, 220–221

Crit.: 36 ὁ Laur. 31.21 || **46** μειλιχείην Laur. 31.24 || **47** θυμόν a.c. Laur. 31.24

Sim.: 36 ἀεικέα λοιγὸν ἀμύνει] cf. *Il.* 1.341, 398, 456 al. || **38** μνημήϊον ἐσσομένοισιν] cf. *Anth. Pal.* 9.197.6 || **39** οὖλέ τε καὶ μέγα χαῖρε] cf. *Od.* 24.402 || **40** οὐρανὸν εὐρὺν ἱκάνοι] cf. *Od.* 8.74; 19.108 || **41** ὑψιμέδων Θεός] cf. *Anth. Pal.* 8.5.1 | Θεὸς ἄφθιτος αἰθέρι ναίων] cf. *Orac. Sib.* 5.298 al. || **42** ὄλβιον...μετ' ἀνθρώποισιν] cf. e.g. *Od.* 17.419–420 || **43** παντοίην ἀρετήν] cf. *Il.* 15.642; 22.268; *Od.* 13.45–46 | κλέος ἐσθλὸν ὀπάσσας] cf. Orph. *Arg.* 3 || **44** αὐτὰρ – μνήσομαι] sim. *Hymn. Hom. Cer.* 495, *Ap.* 546 etc. || **46** σήν τ' ἀγανοφροσύνην] cf. *Il.* 24.772; *Od.* 11.203 || **47** ἀρχὸν Ὀλύμπου] cf. Nonn. *Dion.* 7.119 || **48** γῆρας ὀπάζῃ] cf. *Il.* 4.321; 8.103 || **49** cf. Pind. *Isthm.* 7.18 (σοφίας ἄκρον ἄωτον)

Epigram in hexameters by Andronikos Kallistos on the book *In defence of Plato* written by Cardinal Bessarion, patriarch of Constantinople

(excerpt, ll. 35–48)

> [35] Hail, o Plato, you who can boast as your first defender the divine
> Bessarion. He averts from you shameful ruin,
> he who has produced this nice book, a big work
> and a memento of your wisdom for future generations.
> O merry Bessarion, health and joy be with thee,
> [40] and may your eternal glory reach the broad sky,
> because the immortal God, ruling on high and dwelling in the sky
> through his gifts made you fortunate amongst men,
> providing you with every virtue and good fame:
> and I shall remember you even in the future,
> [45] celebrating frequently amongst all men your wisdom,
> your gentleness and your kindness,
> when invoking the powerful God, immortal head of the Olymp,
> that he may yield you a happy old age for many years,
> while you cull the choicest, purest flower of wisdom.

Metre: Hexameters; the prosody is good (irrational lengthening of the last syllable of ἀωτεῦντι in l. 48; note also the *correptio Attica* in ἀγνόν, not operating in other lines), the metre is at times problematic (ll. 39, 40, 45, and 47 are bipartite, and l. 46 is conspicuously defective of one dactylic foot).

Notes: These are the last lines of a long epigram, concluded in the Laurentian manuscripts by an invocation Εὐτύχει μουσηγέτα ('Fare well, leader of the Muses'): it is preserved at the beginning of Kallistos' own manuscript of Bessarion's *In calumniatorem Platonis* (Marc. gr. 198), and by the hand of other scribes in manuscripts of Hesiod and Euripides. It contains a rather conventional praise of Bessarion's wisdom and his passion for Plato, particularly of his work *In calumniatorem Platonis* (started in Greek in 1458–59, first printed in Latin in 1469): this treatise was a defence of Christian Platonism (in its Neoplatonic form, as well as in its possible harmony with Aristotelian teachings) against the doctrines of George of Trebizond (the alleged *calumniator*, in his *Comparatio philosophorum Platonis et Aristotelis* of 1458), which favoured Aristotelian orthodoxy while describing the dangers of Plato and his alleged 'followers' (from Epicurus to Muhammad to Pletho himself). In 1462 Kallistos himself intervened in the polemic with a defence of Theodore Gaza against Michael Apostolis (the father of Arsenios, see below). Kallistos' re-use of hemistichs and poetic terms shows his deep familiarity with hexametric (particularly cletic hymns) and epigrammatic poetry – this is in keeping with his activity as a copyist, and with his role as a teacher of Angelo Poliziano (→ **Italy**), who borrowed precisely from this ode some *iuncturae* of his early Greek epigrams.

Biography: Andronikos Kallistos (Constantinople, early 15th c. – London, 1475/1484) is a Byzantine scholar first attested in Italy in 1441. He lived and taught in Padua, Bologna, Rome, and Florence. He was in touch with many humanists such as Bessarion, Demetrios Chalkondyles, and others; in 1475 for unknown reasons he left for London, where he died in poverty before 1484. His teaching in Florence was particularly original and productive, as it involved authors hitherto almost unknown to Italian Hellenists, such as Pindar and Apollonius Rhodius. His unceasing activity as a copyist (and one capable of making many conjectures *inter scribendum*) earns him pride of place in the transmission to the West of the achievements of the Byzantine scholarship, particularly on scenic texts. Kallistos was not a prolific poet: he translated a Latin epigram of Poliziano, and wrote one epigram for Homer and one for the death of Bessarion.

Bibliography: Cammelli, Giuseppe (1942), *I dotti bizantini e le origini dell'umanesimo: Andronico Callisto*, Firenze; Perosa, Alessandro (1953), "Inediti di Andronico Callisto", in: *Rinascimento* 4, 3–15 (Id., *Studi di filologia umanistica* III, Roma 2000, 89–102); Bigi, Emilio (1961), "Callisto, Andronico", in: *DBI* 3, 163; Fiaccadori 1994, 462; Speranzi, David (2011), "Il ritratto dell'anonimo", in: Nunzio Bianchi (ed.), *La tradizione dei testi greci in Italia meridionale*, Bari, 113–124: 116; Orlandi, Luigi (2014), "Andronico Callisto e l'epigramma per la tomba di Mida", in: *Medioevo greco* 14, 163–175; del Soldato, Eva (ed.) (2014), *Basilio Bessarione. Contro il calunniatore di Platone*,

Roma; Chinellato, Martha (2018), "L'Odissea secondo Andronico Callisto", in: *Medioevo greco* 18, 82–109.

Demetrios Moschos (ca. 1450–post 1519?)

Τὸ καθ' Ἑλένην καὶ Ἀλέξανδρον [ante 1493]

(excerptum, vv. 357–374)

    Τὴν δ' Ἑλένη μετέειπεν ἀγαζομένη βασίλειαν·
    "δῖ' Ἑκάβη, Πριάμου κλεινὴ δάμαρ, ὅν τε θεὸν ὣς
    δῆμος ἅπας τίουσι κρατιστεύοντα θέμιστας,
360 ὑμῖν μὲν παρέχοιεν Ὀλύμπιοι ὄλβια πάντα
    ὅσσοι ναιετάοιτε θεόδμητον πόλιν ἀμφίς·
    ὡς δέ σε θυμὸς ἄνωγεν ἐμὸν γένος ἐξερεείνειν,
    αὐτίκα νῦν τάδε πάντα δαήσεαι ὡς ἐπέοικε.
    Θέστιος, ὃς Λακόνεσσιν ἀπόπροθι ἐμβασίλευε,
365 γείνατο ἐκ Δαναοῖο θυγατρὸς κάλλεϊ πρώτας
    Λήδαν καὶ Κλυτίην τε Μελίππην θ' ἱμερόεσσαν,
    ὃν Δαναὸν πρόγονον πατρὸς σέθεν ἴσμεν ἐόντα·
    τοῦ γὰρ Ἀγήνωρ ἦεν ἀδελφεός, ὃς σέο πατρὸς
    ἔσκε πατήρ· ἀπάνευθε δὲ εἴσεαι τῶν πέρι αὐτή.
370 Λήδαν Τυνδάρεος περικαλλέα θῆκεν ἄκοιτιν·
    Λήδη δ' αὖτέ μ' ἔτικτε πάτρης ἐπὶ τηλόθ' ἐούσης·
    ὡς ἐγὼ ἐκ γένεος σέθεν οὐκ ἀλλότριός εἰμι
    οὐδ' αὐτοῦ Πριάμοιο, ἐπεὶ καὶ Δάρδανος ἦεν
    ἔκγονος ἐκ Δαναοῖο θυγατρῶν αἷμα λελογχώς."

Textus: Roma, Biblioteca Angelica, ms. C.4.13, ff. 53–62 et 71–74 (manu ipsius auctoris); Δημητρίου Μόσχου τοῦ Λάκωνος *Τὸ καθ' Ἑλένην καὶ Ἀλέξανδρον*/ *Demetri Moschi Laconis hoc ad Helenam et Alexandrum* Pontico Virunio interprete, Rhegii Lingobardiae: presbyter Dionysius impressit, s.d. [sed 1501]; ed. crit. confecit Meschini, Anna (1976), *Demetrio Mosco. La storia di Elena e Alessandro*, Padova.

Sim.: 357 ἀγαζομένη] de verbo cf. *Od.* 10.249; Pind. *Isthm.* 11.6 || **358** Πριάμου...δάμαρ] cf. Eur. *Hec.* 493 | θεὸν ὣς...τίουσι] sim. *Il.* 9.155 et spec. 302–303 || **360** sim. *Od.* 8.413 (θεοὶ δέ τοι ὄλβια δοῖεν) || **361** ὅσσοι ναιετάοιτε] sim. Musae. *Hero et L.* 45 | θεόδμητον πόλιν] Eur. *Andr.* 1263 || **362** γένος ἐξερεείνειν] cf. *Od.* 19.116 || **363** δαήσεαι] cf. *Od.* 3.187 | ὡς ἐπέοικε] cf. *Od.* 24.481 || **364** ἐμβασίλευε] cf. *Od.* 15.413 || **364–366** de historia cf. Malal. 4.12; Jo. Antioch. fr. 37 Rob.; Cedr. 1.212.4; vide Dict. *bell. Troi.* 1.9 || **367–368** et **373–374** de historia cf. Malal. 5.4; Jo. Antioch. fr. 40.43–48 Rob.; Cedr. 1.218.7 || **369** εἴσεαι...αὐτή] cf. *Od.* 24.506 || **370** θῆκεν ἄκοιτιν] cf. Quint. Smyrn. 3.568 al. || **371** cf. *Il.* 1.30 al. (τηλόθι πάτρης) || **374** αἷμα λελογχώς] cf. Orph. *Arg.* 81; Luc. *Alex.* 11.10

The story of Helen and Alexander

(excerpt, ll. 357–374)

> And Helen replied to the queen, with the utmost respect:
> 'O divine Hecuba, illustrious wife of Priam, whom all the people
> venerate like a god, mightiest in justice,
> [360] may the Olympian gods yield every prosperity to all of you
> who dwell in and nearby the god-built city:
> since your spirit induces you to ask me about my family,
> you will know all this immediately, as it is appropriate.
> Thestios, who reigned far away on the Laconians,
> [365] generated from a daughter of Danaos three very beautiful girls,
> Leda, Klytia and lovely Melippe;
> we know that this Danaos is the ancestor of your father,
> for his brother was Agenor, who was the father
> of your father: I'm sure you know about all this yourself.
> [370] Tyndareos married the beautiful Leda:
> and Leda generated me in my so distant fatherland:
> thus I am not foreign to your stock
> nor to that of Priamos himself, for even Dardanos
> descended from Danaos' daughters by kin of blood.'

Metre: Hexameters; wrong prosody in l. 364 Λακόνεσσιν (the right declension would require an ω); a harsh lengthening of the first syllable of πατρός in ll. 367–368; ugly hiatuses in ll. 364, 365, 369.

Notes: This is an excerpt of a long epyllion in 462 lines devoted to the birth, the youth, and the marriage of Helen in Sparta, and above all to her abduction by Paris: after their arrival at Troy, Helen is much admired by everyone and she tries to show her new mother-in-law that she can boast some genealogical affinity with the Trojans; at the same time, Menelaos is back in Sparta and with the help of Odysseus he starts conceiving the Achaean expedition to Troy. A copy of this poem, which was the only creative output of Moschos to reach the press during his lifetime, was requested by Pietro Bembo from Moschos himself in 1493 (incidentally, the *terminus ante quem* for the composition of the piece). The *Story of Helen and Alexander* stands out as the only instance of frankly epic poetry among the Greek scholars of the Renaissance diaspora: it borrows many lexical and expressive features of the Homeric epic, and it shows some knowledge of the fragmentary archaic epic and the Euripidean tragedies dealing with *antehomerica* and *posthomerica*. But Moschos also displays a *penchant* for mythography that culminates in the massive re-use of the material from Dictys and John of Antioch found in Malalas and Cedrenus. One may compare Moschos' epyllion with the later mythological epyllia by Rhodoman (→ **Germany**) and Foreestius (→ **Low Countries**).

Biography: Demetrios Moschos (Sparta ca. 1450 – *post* 1519) was a prolific scribe and scholar of the Italian Renaissance, whose creative production is limited to some epigrams and elegies, to the *Story of Helen and Alexander* and to a prose comedy called *Neaira*. Little is known of Moschos' biography: he might have been in Italy as early as 1470, and was certainly teaching in Venice in 1492–93; he then taught in Ferrara and Mantua (where he became acquainted with Mario Equicola and Isabella d'Este), and we lose trace of him after 1519.

Bibliography: *RGK* I.97, II.131, III.165; Zorzi, Niccolò (1997), "Demetrio Mosco e Mario Equicola", in: *Giornale storico della letteratura italiana* 174, 522–572; Eleuteri, Paolo/Canart, Paul (1991), *Scrittura greca nell'Umanesimo italiano*, Milano, 86–89; Pontani, Anna (1987), "Su una commedia umanistica greca", in: *Museum Patavinum* 4, 267–288; Ead. (1986), "La «Neera» di Demetrio Mosco", in: *Orpheus* n.s. 7, 365–392; Homeyer, Helene (1982–87), "Bemerkungen zu einem Epos des Demetrios Moschos über die Entführung der Helena durch Paris", in: *Helikon* 22–27, 467–476.

Ianos Laskaris (1445–1535)

I. Εἰς Μιχαλάγγελον τὸν ζωογράφον [post 1512]

Ἡ Μιχαλαγγέλεω· πῶς δ' ὕπτιος ἔγραφ' ἀερθεὶς
κοῖλα τέγους; λέχρις πῶς ἐπέτεινε χέρα;
βλέμματι δ' ἐν κύκλῳ πῶς ἔσχατον ἐς περιωπὴν
ἥπτετο, συμμετρίαις ὀπτικὸς ἑσπόμενος;
5 εἰκόσι δ' ὡς πλείσταις, οὐκ εἰν ὀλίγαισιν, Ἀπελλῆς
ὡς πάρος ἢ Ζεῦξις κλῄζεται ἠὲ Μύκων.

Textus: Ἰανοῦ Λασκάρεως τοῦ Ῥυνδακηνοῦ Ἐπιγράμματα / Iani Lascaris Rhyndaceni *Epigrammata*, Parisiis: apud Iacobum Bogardum 1544 (unde Meschini, Anna (1976), *Giano Laskaris. Epigrammi Greci*, Padova, 79: no. 62)

Sim.: 1 ἀερθείς] in clausula cf. *Od.* 8.375; 12.432 || 2 λέχρις] cf. Ap. Rhod. *Argon.* 1.1235 al. || 3 ἐς περιωπήν] cf. *Il.* 14.8; *Anth. Pal.* 6.167.1 al. || 6 Μύκων] scil. Micon pictor Atheniensis (Paus. 1.17.1; Ael. *Nat. Anim.* 4.50 al.; forma Μύκων hic illic in codd. occurrit)

On Michelangelo the painter

Lo and behold Michelangelo! But how did he paint the roof
up there on his back? How did he twist and stretch his arm out?
How did he take in every detail, gazing everywhere all around
and following the analogies of perspective?
[5] He is renowned for many paintings, not just a handful,
as in the case of Zeuxis, Apelles and Micon in the past.

II. Εἰς Φράγκισκον τὸν Κελτῶν βασιλέα βαρέως φέροντα τὴν τῆς βασιλίσσης τελευτήν [1524]

Μηκέτ' ἄναξ ἀλόχου κατοδύρεο μοῖραν ἄτεγκτον
κουριδίης· θρήνων ἄξιον οὔ μ' ἀπάγει.
Σοί με Ζεὺς κατέπεμψε Προμηθέος ἐννεσίῃσι
ψυχῶν φαιδροτάτης πίδακος ἐκ λογικῶν·
5 καὶ βασιλεῖς Κέλταις ξυνὸν γένος ἔμπεδον αἰὲν
κεῖς ἔτε' ἐξ ἐτέων στήσαμεν ἡμετέροις.
Νῦν δὲ Διὸς βουλαῖσι τεὸν γόνον ἀλλοδαπή σοι
νύμφη ἀλλοδαπῶν κράντορας ἐκφανέει.
Τῷ τοι κἂν βιοτῇ καὶ οἰχομένη τριπόθητον
10 ἄλκαρ ἔφυν πολέμων Κλαυδίη Ἑσπερίοις.

Textus: Iani Lascaris Rhyndaceni *Epigrammata*, Parisiis, in Chalcographeio Iodoci Badii Ascensii, 1527, c. a8v–b1r (hinc Meschini, *Giano Laskaris. Epigrammi Greci*, 55: no. 29)

Crit.: 9 κἂν debuit

Sim.: 1 cf. *Anth. Pal.* 9.87.1 (μηκέτι νῦν μινύριζε) et sim. | ἀλόχου...κουριδίης] cf. *Il.* 1.114 al. | μοῖραν ἄτεγκτον] cf. Ar. *Thesm.* 1047 || 2 de forma sim. *Anth. Pal.* 7.260.2 (οὐδὲν ἔχω θρήνων ἄξιον οὐδὲ θανών), 667.2 || 3 κατέπεμψε] de verbo cf. Hes. *Theog.* 515 || 5 ἔμπεδον αἰέν] cf. Thgn. 1.317; Ap. Rhod. *Argon.* 1.1076 etc. || 6 κεῖς ἔτε'ἐξ ἐτέων] cf. Theoc. *Id.* 18.15 || 7 Διὸς βουλαῖσι] cf. *Il.* 13.524 et saep. || 8 κράντορας] de subst. cf. Eur. *Andr.* 507; *Anth. Pal.* 6.108.2 al. || 10 ἄλκαρ...πολέμων] cf. Quint. Smyrn. 1.160 et 2.11

For Francis the king of the Gauls, in despair for the death of the Queen

O Lord, stop crying over the implacable fate of your spouse:
I am worthy of mourning if it carries me away.
Zeus sent me to you by the advice of Prometheus,
from the brightest source of rational souls:
[5] we gave kings to our dear Gauls, one year after another

remaining always a common and stable stock.
But now by Zeus' will a foreign wife will give birth
to your offspring, who will rule over foreign folks.
For this reason I, Claude, both alive and dead, am for you a necessary
[10] defence from the wars to the Western peoples.

Metre: Elegiac couplets (flawless).

Notes: The first edition of Laskaris' epigrams (60 in Greek + 60 in Latin) was published in Paris in 1527; a radically new one came out in 1544, with the addition of 12 Greek pieces; several epigrams are preserved in (partly autograph) manuscripts such as Vat. gr. 12 and Par. gr. 2879. In his characteristically learned, obscure and allusive style, Laskaris tackled several genres (epitaphs, encomia, love poems, dedicatory pieces, book epigrams, gnomic epigrams, epideictic epigrams, invectives against Poliziano); all are in elegiac metre, with the exception of no. 22 in iambics. In very recent times a long and refined Sapphic ode on Charles VIII's descent to Italy and prospective Crusade (1494) has been attributed to Laskaris' pen. Epigr. 62 (which presents a morphologically implausible genitive in -εω in l. 1) celebrates against the background of Hellenic predecessors the great enterprise of Michelangelo's frescoes on the vault of the Sixtine Chapel: this suggests a dating shortly after their completion in 1512. Epigr. 29 was written for the untimely death of Queen Claude (1524), since 1514 the wife of Francis of Valois, then King Francis I: in those days, Laskaris was long active as a diplomat and minister for the king of France. The 'source of rational souls' (l. 4) might be a Platonic reminiscence, while ll. 7–8 might represent an allusion to the project of a marriage between Francis I and Mary of England.

Biography: The offspring of an illustrious Byzantine family, Ianos Laskaris (Constantinople 1445 – Rome 1534) moved to Italy (perhaps to Venice and Padua, perhaps to Rome) at an unknown date, and eventually landed in Florence at the court of the Medici. He performed diplomatic missions to continental Greece, Crete, and Constantinople in the years 1490–1492, during which he purchased a number of manuscripts, and brought several young pupils to Italy (amongst them Markos Mousouros and Arsenios Apostolis). In 1492 he obtained the professorship of Greek at the Florentine Studio, and started editing texts for Lorenzo d'Alopa, most notably Apollonius Rhodius, Lucian, and the *Greek Anthology*. In 1495 he followed King Charles VIII to France, and worked for the following decades as a diplomat for the French crown (from 1504 until 1509 in Venice, then in Milan). In close contact with Manuzio, Guillaume Budé, and the papacy, in 1515 he was charged by Pope Leo X with the creation and organisation of the short-lived Ginnasio Greco on the Quirinale hill in Rome – for the printing-house of this institution he will edit some difficult texts. Now at the service of the pope, he travelled often to France, to Spain, and elsewhere, while simultaneously working on translations and other works, and adding to his impressive collection of manuscripts (mostly acquired by Cardinal Niccolò Ridolfi).

Bibliography: Ceresa, Mario (2004), "Làskaris, Giano", in: *DBI* 63, 785–791; Pagliaroli, Stefano (2004), "Giano Lascari e il Ginnasio greco", in: *Studi medievali e umanistici* 2, 215–293; Flamand, Jean-Marie (2017), "Giano Lascari", in: Bianca/ Ferreri/Delle Donne 2017, 207–211. On his Greek poems: Meschini 1976 (see above Textus); Pontani, Filippomaria (2015), "Sognando la Crociata", in: *Italia Medioevale e Umanistica* 56, 251–294.

Markos Mousouros (1470–1517)

Ὠιδὴ εἰς Πλάτωνα [1513]

(excerptum, vv. 1–20, 153–174)

    Θεῖε Πλάτων, ξυνοπαδὲ θεοῖς καὶ δαίμοσιν ἥρως
      πασσυδίῃ μεγάλῳ Ζηνὶ παρεσπομένοις,
    ἅρμα κατ' οὐρανὸν εὐρὺν ἀελλοπόδων ὅτε πώλων
      κεῖνος ἐλᾷ πτηνῷ δίφρῳ ἐφεζόμενος,
5   εἰ δ' ἄγε νῦν κατάβηθι λιπὼν χορὸν οὐρανιώνων
      ἐς γᾶν ψυχοφυῶν εἰρεσίῃ πτερύγων,
    καὶ λάζευ τόδε τεῦχος, ὃ Σωκρατικὴν ὀαριστὺν
      ἀμφὶς ἔχει καὶ σῆς κεδνὰ γένεθλα φρενός·
    ᾧ ἔνι κοσμοτέχνης ὀκτὼ πτύχας Οὐλύμποιο
10   ἐξ ἰδίων ἕλκων ἀρχέτυπον πραπίδων
    δείματο καρπαλίμως, ὑπάτην σελάεσσιν ἀπείροις
      δαιδάλλων τήν περ κλείομεν ἀπλανέα.
    Τὰς δ' ἄρ ὑφεξείης μονοφεγγέας ἐξετόρευσεν
      αὐτόθεν ἀκροτάτης ἀντία κινυμένας·
15 ἣ σφέας ἁρπάζουσα παλιμπλάγκτοιο κελεύθου
      σύρει ἀναγκαίῃ· ταὶ δὲ βιηζόμεναι
    οὐκ ἀέκουσαι ἕπονται, ὅμως ἑὸν οἶμον ἑκάστη
      ἔμπαλιν ἐξανύει βάρδιον ἢ τάχιον·
    ᾧ ἔνι κυδρὸς ἔρως ἀπὸ γαίης ὑψόσ' ἀείρων
20   ἱμέρῳ ἄμμε φλέγει κάλλεος οὐρανίου.
[...]
    Καὶ τὰ μὲν εἴθε γένοιτο· μαθήμασι νῦν δὲ παλαιῶν
      Ἑλλήνων, ὦναξ, ἄρκεσον οἰχομένοις·
155 Θάρσυνον δ' Ἑκάτοιο φιλαγρύπνους ὑποφήτας
      δώροις μειλίσσων καὶ γεράεσσι θεῶν.

Παντοδαπούς τε, πάτερ, ξυναγείρας ἡμὲν Ἀχαιῶν
    ἠδὲ πολυσπορέων υἱέας Ἑσπερίων
πρωθήβας καὶ μήτε φρενῶν ἐπιδευέας ἐσθλῶν
160 μήτε φυῆς μήτ' οὖν αἵματος εὐγενέος,
    ἐν Ῥώμῃ κατάνασσον ἐπιστήσας σφίσιν ἄνδρας,
    οἳ σώζουσι λόγων ζώπυρον ὠγυγίων.
Ναίοιεν δ' ἀπάνευθε πολυσκάρθμοιο κυδοιμοῦ
    Νηϊάδων προχοαῖς γειτονέοντα δόμον,
165 τῷ δ' Ἑκαδημείης ὄνομ' εἴη κυδιανείρης
    ζήλῳ τῷ προτέρης, ἥν ποτ' ἐγὼ νεμόμην,
κούροις εὐφυέεσσιν ἐπισταμένως ὀαρίζων,
    τούς γ' ἀναμιμνήσκων, ὧν πάρος αὐτοὶ ἴσαν.
Ἀλλ' ἡ μὲν δὴ ὄλωλε· σὺ δ' ἦν καινὴν ἀναφήνῃς
170 ἔνθεν ἄρ' εὐμαθίης πυρσὸς ἀναπτόμενος
βαιοῦ ἀπὸ σπινθῆρος ἀναπλήσει μάλα πολλῶν
    ψυχὰς ἠϊθέων φωτὸς ἀκηρασίου,
ἐν Ῥώμῃ δέ κεν αὖθις ἀνηβήσειαν Ἀθῆναι
    ἀντί τοι Ἰλισσοῦ Θύμβριν ἀμειψάμεναι.

Textus: Ἅπαντα τὰ τοῦ Πλάτωνος / *Omnia Platonis opera*, Venetiis: in aedibus Aldi et Andreae soceri, mense Septembri 1513, cc. I 3r–4v (vide novissime Ferreri, Luigi (2014), *L'Italia degli umanisti. I. Marco Musuro*, Turnhout, 140–146 et Wilson, Nigel G. (2016), *Aldus Manutius. The Greek Classics*, Cambridge Mass.)

Crit.: 17 ὁμῶς Wilson || **167** ἐπισταμένων Ald. || **169** ἀναφήνης Ald.

Sim.: 1 ξυνοπαδὲ θεοῖς] cf. Plat. *Phaedr*. 248c3 (de anima) || **3–4** de re cf. Plat. *Phaedr*. 246e || **3** οὐρανὸν εὐρύν] saep. apud Hom. || **4** δίφρῳ ἐφεζόμενος] cf. *Od.* 4.717 || **5** εἰ δ' ἄγε νῦν κατάβηθι] cf. *Od.* 23.20 || **6** ψυχοφυῶν hapax | εἰρεσίῃ πτερύγων] cf. Ang. Polit. *epigr. gr.* 57.2 || **7** λάζευ] cf. Theocr. *Id.* 15.21 || **8** sim. Aesch. *Sept.* 593–594 (apud Plat. *resp.* 362a8) || **9–18** de re cf. Plat. *Tim.* 92c et praes. *resp.* 616d–617b || **9** κοσμοτέχνης] cf. Synes. *Hymn.* 1.425 et 5.30 | πτύχας Οὐλύμποιο] cf. *Il.* 11.77 || **10** cf. *Anth. Pal.* 16.204.2 (ἐξ ἰδίης ἕλκων ἀρχέτυπον κραδίης, de Praxitele) || **13** ὑφεξείης hapax | μονοφεγγέας] verbum recentius, cf. lex. Vind. α 141 G. || **15** παλιμπλάγκτοιο] de adi. cf. Aesch. *Prom.* 838; Greg. Naz. *carm.*, PG 37.1005.5 || **19** ἀπὸ γαίης ὑψόσ' ἀείρων] cf. *Il.* 20.325 || **20** κάλλεος οὐρανίου] cf. Greg. Naz. *carm.*, PG 37.1470.6 al.
153 εἴθε γένοιτο] cf. Thgn. 1.731 || **158** πολυσπερέων debuit (adi. cum πολύσπορος contaminatum) || **159** πρωθήβας] cf. *Il.* 8.518; *Od.* 8.263 | φρενῶν...ἐσθλῶν] cf. *Od.* 2.117 al. || **160** αἵματος εὐγενέος] cf. *Anth. Pal.* 8.159.1 || **163** ἀπάνευθε πολυσκάρθμοιο κυδοιμοῦ] cf. Nonn. *Dion.* 22.93 (de adi. *Il.* 2.814) || **164** Νηϊάδων προχοαῖς] cf. *Anth. Pal.* 9.663.4 || **165** Ἑκαδημείης] cf. Diog. Laert. 3.8.1 || **167–168** de methodo docendi per anamnesin cf. e.g. Plat. *Phaed*. 72e, 92d || **170** εὐμαθίης πυρσὸς ἀναπτόμενος] cf. *Anth. Pal.* 16.201.7–8 || **172** ψυχὰς ἠϊθέων] cf. *Anth. Pal.* 11.36.2 | φωτὸς ἀκηρασίου] cf. *Anth. Pal.* 8.1.4 || **174** Θύμβριν ἀμειψάμεναι] cf. *Anth. Pal.* 9.219.4

Ode to Plato

(excerpt, ll. 1–20, 153–174)

    Divine Plato, hero accompanying gods and demons
        who at high speed follow the great Zeus
    when he drives through the wide sky a wagon of swift-footed horses,
        sitting on a winged chariot,
    [5] descend now to the earth from the company of celestial gods,
        flapping the wings that grow out of your soul,
    and accept this book that combines Socratic
        dialogue with the noble products of your mind.
    In it the creator of the world swiftly built the eight layers of Olympus
    [10] drawing the wise design out of his own mind
    and decorating with countless stars the outermost
        level, which we call the unmoved one.
    He placed the lower ravines each carrying one individual light,
        all moving in the opposite direction of the outermost level:
    [15] this layer grabs the others and drags them forcibly
        along the reverse path, and despite being forced,
    they follow it willingly, though each alike completes
        its own backward journey later or sooner:
    in this work, glorious love, raising us above the earth,
    [20] sets us on fire with desire of celestial beauty.
    [...]
    'And may all this happen; but now, my lord, give support to the study
        of the ancient Greeks, which has disappeared.
    [155] And encourage the wakeful interpreters of the far-shooting god,
        soothing him with presents and divine gifts.
    Gathering, o father, the variegated sons of the Achaeans
        and of the populous nations of the West,
    in their early youth and provided with intelligence,
    [160] good character and noble blood,
    settle them in Rome, placing them under the rule of men
        who preserve the spark of the ancient culture.
    May they live far from loud confusion,
        in a house close to the fountain of the Naiads.
    [165] May its name be that of the renowned Academy,
        in emulation of the previous one, which I once directed,
    discussing knowledgeably with noble youths,
        reminding them of what they formerly knew.
    But that school has perished; if you establish a new one,
    [170] from it a beacon of learning
    will rise from a small spark, and fill the souls
        of a great number of young men with pure light.
    Athens would then rise again in Rome,
        taking the Tiber in exchange for the Ilissus.

Metre: Elegiac couplets.

Notes: Mousouros penned a number of Greek epigrams celebrating manuscripts, ancient authors, contemporary scholars or friends; he also produced smart hexametrical paraphrases of the Christian *Creed* and of the *Ave Maria*. The *Ode to Plato* is his poetical masterpiece, for it joins the praise of an ancient author with the pressing demand to Leo X for political and military help for the liberation of Greece. The beginning of the poem, in pure pagan fashion, describes Plato as a hero and a divine being, echoing Plato's *Phaedrus* (Zeus' chariot in ll. 3–4), *Timaeus* and *Republic* (ll. 9–18 with the layers of the stars and planets) and *Symposium* (love in ll. 19–20). In what follows, Plato is invited to come to Rome and to address Pope Leo X with a long invocation requesting help against the Turks and an intervention for the freedom and cultural growth of the Greek people. In the final part of his speech (ll. 153–186) Plato specifically asks Pope Leo to grant the foundation of a new Greek academy: what is implied here is the creation of the Ginnasio greco on the Quirinale, directed by Laskaris and joined by Mousouros in 1516.

Biography: A pupil of Arsenios-Aristoboulos Apostolis in Crete (see below), Markos Mousouros (Marcus Musurus, Candia, ca. 1475 – Rome, 1517) was already versed in classical Greek and Latin when he was brought to Florence by Ianos Laskaris (see above) in 1492. In Florence he worked as a scribe, copying several important manuscripts of classical authors. In 1494–95 and then in 1497 he is attested in Venice, where he cooperated with Aldo Manuzio (→ **Italy**) in the editions of Musaeus, Aristophanes, the Greek epistolographers, and of Poliziano's *Opera*. In 1499 he participated in the grand edition of the *Etymologicum Magnum* for the other Cretan printers Zacharias Kalliergis and Nicholas Vlastos (his epigram celebrating this enterprise is full of national pride). After a couple of years at Ferrara and Carpi as a tutor to Prince Alberto Pio, in 1503 he was summoned to Padua as a professor of Greek (he lectured on Homer, Theocritus, and particularly the *Greek Anthology*): amongst his pupils were the German Johannes Cuno, the Italians Lazaro Bonamico (→ **Italy**) and Gerolamo Aleandro; from 1509 to 1516 he lived and taught in Venice, only to move to Rome in 1516 as the professor of the newly founded Ginnasio Greco of Pope Leo X. There he suddenly died in 1517. Mousouros was a prolific scribe, an active poet, and the most important collaborator of the Aldine press for the Greek classics (from Sophocles to Plato, from Plutarch to Hesychius), constantly displaying his skill as the most ingenious and learned Greek philologist of his time.

Bibliography: Ferreri, Luigi (2014), *L'Europa degli umanisti. I. Marco Musuro*, Turnhout; Speranzi, David (2013), *La scrittura di Marco Musuro*, Roma; Pontani, Anna (2002), "L'umanesimo greco a Venezia: Marco Musuro, Girolamo Aleandro e l'*Antologia greca*", in: *I Greci a Venezia*, Venezia, 381–466. On his Greek verse: Dijkstra, Roald/Hermans, Erik (2015), "Musurus' Homeric Ode to Plato and his Requests to Pope Leo X", in: *Akroterion* 60, 33–63; Pontani, Filippomaria (2014), "Preghiere, parafrasi e grammatiche", in: *Bibliothèque d'Humanisme et Renaissance* 76, 325–340; Pontani, Filippomaria (2003), "Musurus' Creed", in: *Greek, Roman and Byzantine Studies* 43 175–213; Sifakis, Gregorios M. (1954), "Μάρκου Μουσούρου τοῦ Κρητὸς Ποίημα εἰς τὸν Πλάτωνα", in: *Κρητικὰ Χρονικὰ* 3, 366–388.

Demetrios Doukas (ca. 1480–1527)

Δημητρίου Δούκα τοῦ Κρητός [1514]

Καὶ μέγα μικρὸν καὶ σμικρὸν μέγα, καὶ τόδε ὡς δεῖ
πρᾶξαι, ὑμνοπόλοις Φοῖβος ἔδωκε μόνοις.
Παρθένος Ἡρὼ Λείανδρός τε, βροτοί περ ἐόντες,
εἰσὶ δὲ ἀθάνατοι τερψινόοις ἔπεσιν.
5   Εἰ δὴ Μουσαῖός τις ἐμ' ὑμνήσαιτο θανόντα,
αὐτίκα τεθναίην, ὄφρα βίοιο τύχω.

Textus: Μουσαίου ποιημάτιον τὰ κατ' Ἡρὼ καὶ Λέανδρον / Musaei opusculum *de Erone et Leandro*, <Alcalà de Henares>: in Academia Complutensi, s.d. [sed 1514], c. Iv (Legrand, *Bibl. XV/XVI*, I, Paris 1885, 121)

Crit.: 5 ἔμ' debuit

Sim.: 3 Λείανδρος] forma saepius in Musaei epyllio invenitur || 4 τερψινόοις] de adi. cf. *Anth. Pal.* 9.505.3 et saep. apud Nonnum || 6 αὐτίκα τεθναίην] cf. *Il.* 18.98 et praes. Musae. *Hero et L.* 79

By the Cretan Demetrios Doukas

The ability to turn big into small, and small into big, and do this
   as it should be done, Phoebus bequeathed only to poets.
(H)Ero the virgin and Leander, albeit mortal,
   are immortal in the verse that delights the mind.
[5] If a Musaeus were to praise me after my death,
   may I die immediately, so as to obtain life.

Metre: Elegiac couplets, with ugly hiatuses (ll. 1, 4).

Notes: This book-epigram belongs to the front matter of the Complutensian edition of Musaeus, largely indebted to the 1494 Aldine edition curated by Markos Mousouros (who had also penned in it a much more refined epigram on Musaeus' poem). While the wit about immortality is elegant, Doukas' poetic diction is rather hesitant (see e.g. l. 2 πρᾶξαι for ποιῆσαι, l. 4 misplaced δέ).

Biography: Demetrios Doukas (Candia, ca. 1480 – Rome, ca. 1527) arrived in Venice around 1505. He cooperated with Aldo's printing house for the *Rhetores Graeci* and for Plutarch's *Moralia* (1508 and 1509), and then in 1513 he was invited by Cardinal Jiménez to the newly founded chair of Greek at the Collegium Trilingue of Alcalà (→ **Iberia**). There he worked at the Greek section of the New Testament in the famous Polyglot Bible, and he curated the edition of some poetical and grammatical texts. After the cardinal's death in 1517 he came back to Rome, where he was still teaching Greek in 1523. In Rome he published patristic writings and Juan Sepúlveda's Latin translation of Alexander of Aphrodisias' commentary on Aristotle's *Metaphysics*. He may have died during the sack of Rome in 1527.

Bibliography: Geanakoplos 1962, 223–255; Martínez Manzano, Teresa (2009), "Hacia la identificación de la biblioteca y la mano de Demetrio Ducas", in: *Byzantinische Zeitschrift* 102, 717–730.

Aristoboulos (Arsenios) Apostolis (ca. 1465–1535)

Διάλογος

Τὰ τοῦ διαλόγου πρόσωπα· Φιλομαθής, βιβλιοπώλης καὶ βίβλος.
Προλογίζει ὁ Φιλομαθής. [1519]

– Ἦ ῥά τι καινόν γ' ἐκτετύπωκας, βιβλιοπῶλα;
– Ναί, φίλ', ἔναγχος, ναί· κεῖνο τὸ βιβλάριον.
– Βωκαίης ἔπη, ἢ Ἀσκραίης ἔνδον ἐέργεις
Μώσης, ὦ βίβλε; Εἰπέ μοι εἰρομένῳ.
5   – Ῥήτορας ἠδὲ σοφοὺς δήπουθεν ἐγὼ κατελέγχω,
καὐτὸν Μαιονίδην, λωποδύτας προτέρων.
Ἀλλὰ δραχμὴν κάτθου, πρίν μ' ἀνὰ χεῖρας ἀείρῃς,
καί κεν ἴδοις παρ' ἐμοὶ πολλά γε τῶν σπανίων.
Ὡς βραχύς ἐσθ' ὁ βίος, κακοδαιμονίης τ' ἀνάμεστος,
10 γνώσεαι, ὡς δεῖ σοι, πάρ τε Σιμωνίδεω,
πάρ τε Φιλήμονος ἠδὲ Μενάνδρου· ἀλλὰ καὶ αὐτοῦ
ἔκφρασιν εἰδείης τοῦ ἀθλίου βιότου.
Αὖθις Ψελλοῦ ἰάμβους εἰς ἀρετὰς κακίας τε,
καὶ ἀναγωγὰς τρεῖς ἱστορίης μυθικῆς

15 Ταντάλου ἠδὲ Σφιγγὸς Κίρκης φαρμακίδος τε,
      αἵ γ' ἑρμηνείης ἔμμορον οὐρανίης.
    Ταῦτ' ἀναλεξάμενος, σπάνιον χρῆμα σπουδαίοις,
      τῆς Μουνεμβασίης προὔθετο Ἀρσένιος.
    – Τὴν δραχμὴν λαβέ, Βιβλιοπῶλ', ἰδού. – Ἀλλὰ καὶ αὐτὸς
20 τὴν βίβλον σχών, ἀσπασίως ἄπιθι.
    Καὶ μετὰ μικρὸν λήψῃ πάντως, ἤν γ' ἐπανέλθῃς,
      τἀποφθέγματα δὴ τῶν Σοφίης τροφίμων.

Textus: Γέρας εἴ μ' ὀνομάσειας σπάνιον τῶν σπουδαίων οὐκ ἂν ἁμάρτοις δηλαδή, τῆς ἀληθείας φίλε, <Romae: apud Collegium Graecum, ca. 1519>, c. a2r–v (unde nuper Ferreri, in: Bianca/Ferreri/Delle Donne 2017, 242)

Crit.: 20 prius hemistichium pentametri syllaba caret, fort. τὴν βίβλον <νῦν> σχών vel. sim.

Sim.: 3 βωκαίης] resp. nomen pastoris apud Theoc. Id. 10 (vide *schol. Theoc.* 10.1–3 et Hsch. β 895 βουκαῖος) | ἔνδον ἐέργεις: cf. *Il.* 2.617 al. (ἐντὸς ἐέργει) || **4** εἰπέ μοι εἰρομένῳ] cf. *Od.* 15.263, 24.114 al.; *Anth. Pal.* 11.274.1 et 14.1.2 || **6** λωποδύτας] cf. *Anth. Pal.* 11.130.2 || **7** ἀνὰ χεῖρας ἀείρης] cf. *Il.* 7.130 || **10** Σιμωνίδεω] de forma cf. *Anth. Pal.* 4.1.8; 9.184.5 et 571.2 || **17** ἀναλεξάμενος] cf. *Anth. Pal.* 7.471.4; 9.428.4 || **22** Σοφίης τροφίμων] cf. Eust. *in Il.* 1.42 al.

Dialogue

Characters of the dialogue: a reader, a bookseller, and a book.
The reader begins.

  – Have you published perchance anything new, o bookseller?
  – Yes, my friend, this little book just now.
  – O book, do you contain verses of the bucolic Muse
    or of the Ascran one? Answer my question.
  [5] – I scrutinise orators and wise men in every detail,
    and even the Maeonides himself, plagiarists of their predecessors.
  But pay your money before you pick me up,
    and you will see in me many rarities.
  You will learn (you need to) from Simonides, from Philemon,
  [10] and from Menander that life is short
  and full of adversities; but moreover
    you will see a description of wretched life.
  Then Psellos' iambi on virtue and vice,
    three anagogical interpretations of myths
  [15] (those of Tantalus, of Sphinx and of Circe the witch),
    whose stories obtain a celestial meaning.
  Having collected all this, Arsenios of Monemvasia
    offered this rare object to the scholars.
  – Take my money, bookseller, here it is.

[20] – And you take the book and depart happy.
And soon you will also get, if you return,
   the apophthegms of Wisdom's pupils.

Metre: Elegiac couplets, with bipartite hexameters (ll. 7, 13, 15, 21) and an untenable pentameter (l. 20, see app. crit.); there are some problems of prosody (l. 14 the υ in μυθικῆς should be long; in l. 8 the lengthening of Μουν- is analogic) and hiatus (l. 4 has a problematic caesura; l. 17).

Notes: This uncommon instance of lively dialogue in elegiac verse is in fact a strategy for the self-presentation of the book with all its manifold contents. The allusions to literary authors are relatively easy to disentangle: l. 3 the Ascraean Muse refers to Hesiod; l. 6 the Maeonides is Homer; l. 11 Philemo and Menander are the 'gnomic' poets of the so-called 'New Comedy' of the 4th/3rd c. BC, whereas the description of wretched life might be a reference to Theodore Prodromos' *In vitam sub imagine allegorica*; ll. 13–16 allude to the iambi on *Virtues and Vices* falsely attributed to the 11th-century scholar Michael Psellos (in ms. Par. gr. 3068: see Westerink, Leenert G. (1992), *M. Pselli Poemata*, Stuttgart/Leipzig 1992, xxxv), and to his writings of Homeric allegory (*opusc.* 43–44 Duffy, though there is nothing on Circe). These periphrases are essential to situate the *Γέρας σπάνιον* within the tradition where it belongs, namely in the genre of Byzantine florilegia (materials derive from Porphyry, Clement of Alexandria, Stobaeus, Ps.-Psellus, Tzetzes, and other authors). The final couplet announces the publication of the *Apophthegmata*, the book Apostolis will edit a few months later in the same year 1519.

Biography: The son of the eminent scholar and scribe Michael Apostolis (ca. 1422–1480), Aristoboulos Apostolis (Candia, after 1465 – Venice, 1535) was brought to Florence by Ianos Laskaris in 1492 together with other promising scholars (Markos Mousouros, Kaisar Strategos, etc.). He soon moved to Venice, where he edited Theodore Prodromos' *Galeomyomachia* for Aldo Manuzio (1495). In those days he was already working on the edition of his father's *Violarium* (Ἰωνιά), a collection of proverbs, *gnomai*, apophthegms, and anecdotes. Perhaps in 1514 Aristoboulos was named by Pope Leo X as Archbishop of Monemvasia: he thus changed his name into Arsenios. In 1518 he succeeded Ianos Laskaris in the direction of the Ginnasio greco on the Quirinale hill, for whose press he published the aforementioned apophthegms and the short collection of philosophical and moral texts known as *Γέρας σπάνιον* ('Rare gift'). An indefatigable copyist of Greek manuscripts, with a special interest for philosophical and exegetical works, he published in 1534 the scholia to seven tragedies of Euripides.

Bibliography: *RGK* I.27, II.38, III.46; Pratesi, Alessandro (1961), "Apostolis, Aristobulo", in: *DBI* 3, 611–613; Geanakoplos 1962, 167–200; Flamand, Jean-Marie, in: Bianca/Ferreri/Delle Donne 2017, 211–213. On his Greek poems: Cavarzeran, Jacopo (2018), "La lettera e il carme di Arsenio Apostolis per Paolo III", in: *Medioevo greco* 18, 53–79; Bianca/Ferreri/Delle Donne 2017, 241–267.

Antonios Eparchos (1491–1571)

Θρῆνος εἰς τὴν Ἑλλάδος καταστροφὴν
Ἀντωνίου τοῦ Ἐπάρχου [1544]

(excerptum, vv. 1–22)

  Νῦν ὀλοφυδνῆς, Πιερίδες, νῦν ἄρχετ' ἀοιδῆς,
   δάκρυα νῦν, Ἑλικών, λεῖβ' ἄμοτον γοάων.
  Νῦν, Χάριτες τρισσαί, Ζηνὸς περικαλλέα τέκνα,
   Ἑλλάδος οὐλομένην συντυχίην κλάετε.
5 Ἄγχει θὴρ ὀλοὸς γναμπτοῖς ὀνύχεσσι κιχήσας
   πρόρριζον Δαναῶν ἱμερόεντα δόμον.
  Δεινὸν ἐπιβρωμᾶται δ' ἄλλοις αἰὲν ὁρούων,
   οὐδέποτ' ἀφρικτὶ δέρκεται ὅν κεν ἴδοι.
  Ἄθρει, Ζεῦ, περίσημον, ἄθρει, γένος οἷον ὀλεῖται·
10 μύρεο σήν, Ἑλλάς, μύρεο δυσμορίην.
  Ἀλκείδην κικλήσκω· ποῦ νῦν παῖς ἀγέρωχος
   Ἀλκμήνης; ἢ γὰρ τοῦδ' ἄποθεν προσιδὼν
  οὐκ ἂν μεῖνεν ἐπισκύνιον καὶ χεῖρα βαρεῖαν,
   θὴρ ὁ τόδ' ὑβρίζων ἔθνος ὑπερφιάλως.
15 Ἀλλ' ἀστοῖσι φάνηθι ἀνήμερα φῦλ' ἀπελαύνων,
   Ἀμφιτρυωνιάδη, σοῖσιν ἀπ' οὐρανόθεν.
  Καδμηῒς γὰρ Θήβη κεδνὴ σεῖο τιθήνη,
   ῥίγιον ἔνδον ἔχει Γηρυόνοιο κύνα.
  Τίρυνθος περιβώτου δέδμηται μέγα δ' ἄστυ,
20 δούλειόν τ' ἦμαρ δίψιον Ἄργος ἴδεν.
  Οἱ δὲ Μυκήνας καὶ Πέλοπος χθόνα πᾶσαν ἐπεῖχον
   αἴ, αἴ, βαρβαρικὰ νῦν ζυγόδεσμ' ἔλαβον.

Textus: Città del Vaticano, Biblioteca Apostolica Vaticana, ms. Vat. gr. 1462, ff. 3r–8v (manu ipsius auctoris); Ἀντωνίου Ἐπάρχου τοῦ Κερκυραίου Εἰς τὴν Ἑλλάδος καταστροφὴν θρῆνος. τοῦ αὐτοῦ ἐπιστολαί.../ *Antonii Eparchi In eversionem Graeciae Deploratio. Eiusdem epistolae...*, Venetiis 1544 (versionem impressam dedimus, sicut iam Legrand, Émile (1870), Ἀντωνίου τοῦ Ἐπάρχου τοῦ Κερκυραίου εἰς τὴν Ἑλλάδος καταστροφὴν θρῆνος, Paris).

Crit.: 2 δάκρυ δὲ λεῖβ' Ἑλικὼν νῦν ἄμοτον γοάων Vat. | ἄμοτων ed. || 3 νῦν: καὶ Vat. || 4 Ἑλλάδος οὐλομένας δεῦτε τύχας κλάετε Vat. || 9 περίσημον: περίβωτον Vat. || 15 φῦλλ', correxi || 21 οἵ debuit

Sim.: 1 ὀλοφυδνῆς] de adi. cf. *Il.* 5.683; 23.102; *Od.* 19.362 || ἄρχετ' ἀοιδῆς] cf. Theoc. *Id.* 1.64 etc., necnon Mosch. *epit. Bion.* 1 || **3** Χάριτες τρισσαί] cf. *Anth. Pal.* 5.140.4, 195.1 al. | Ζηνὸς περικαλλέα τέκνα: cf. *Hymn. Hom. Herm.* 323, 397, 504 || **5** θὴρ ὀλοός] cf. Opp. *H.* 4.267; 5.228 | γναμπτοῖς ὀνύχεσσι] cf. Hes. *Op.* 205 || **7** ἐπιβρωμᾶται] de verbo cf. Nic. Chon. 590.24 v.D. || **8** οὐδέποτ' ἀφρικτί] cf. Call. *Hymn.* 3.65 || **10** μύρεο] cf. Bion. *epit. Adon.* 68; *Orac. Sib.* 5.214 || **13** χεῖρα βαρεῖαν] cf. *Il.* 1.219; 5.81 || **14** ὑβρίζων ὑπερφιάλως] cf. *Od.* 1.227 || **16** Ἀμφιτρυωνιάδη] cf. *Anth. Pal.* 6.114.2 al. || **17** Καδμηΐς Θήβη] cf. *Vit. metr. Pindari* 1, vide Hes. *Op.* 162 || **19** περιβώτου] de adi. cf. *Anth. Pal.* 8.140.3, 204.1, 9.62.1 || **20** δούλειόν τ' ἦμαρ: cf. Eur. *Andr.* 99, *Hec.* 56 || δίψιον Ἄργος] cf. Eur. *Alc.* 560; Nonn. *Dion.* 4.257

Lament on the destruction of Greece by Antonios Eparchos

(excerpt, ll. 1–22)

> Begin now the sad ode, o Muses of Pieria,
>   shed unceasing tears of lament, o Helicon.
> Now, threefold Graces, beautiful children of Zeus,
>   weep for the disastrous event that fell on Greece.
> [5] With his crooked talons the deadly beast is suffocating
>   from the foundations the beautiful palace of the Greeks.
> It growls frightfully constantly attacking others
>   and never looks at anyone without causing fear.
> Behold, Zeus, behold what a brilliant stock will disappear:
> [10] Wail, Greece, wail your evil fate.
> I am calling on Hercules — where is the proud child
>   of Alcmene? If he had seen all this from far,
> the beast that insults our nation with insolence
>   would not have withheld his eyebrows and his strong arm.
> [15] Do appear from the sky to your fellow citizens,
>   driving away the wild tribes, o son of Amphitryon.
> The famous Cadmean Thebes, your nurse,
>   bears inside a more frightful dog than Geryones.
> The great city of Tiryns has been enslaved,
> [20] and dry Argos has seen the day of captivity.
> And those who occupied Mycenae and the entire land of Pelops,
>   alas, alas, are now tied under barbaric yokes.

Metre: Elegiac couplets, with bipartite hexameters (ll. 7, 11, 17, 19) and prosodical flaws in l. 4 (κλάετε should have long α); lengthening at pentameter's caesura in l. 22.

Notes: The *Lament on the destruction of Greece*, addressed to Pope Paul III, is Eparchos' most important work: it consists of 103 elegiac couplets written as an appeal to European rulers to find reconcilement among themselves and fight together against the Turks. The work stands in the grand tradition of laments on the sad fate of Greece (from Andronikos Kallistos' prose monody to Mousouros' *Ode to Plato*), and it insists on the past grandeur of the country, evoking not only the powerful city-states of ancient myth and history (ll. 17–22), but also figures such as Leonidas, Themistocles, and Pericles. It displays a somewhat problematic poetic diction (e.g. l. 18 the genitive Γηρυόνοιο is morphologically untenable, l. 19 the δέ is misplaced to avoid the hiatus, etc.). Nonetheless, it obtained a merciful judgement from Philipp Melanchthon in a letter of 1545 to Joachim Camerarius (Legrand, *BH XV/XVI*, I.262).

Biography: The offspring of an illustrious Byzantine family of scholars, Antonios Eparchos (Corfu 1491–1571) was appointed by his relative Ianos Laskaris (see above) at the short-lived school created by the French Francis I in Milan in 1520. Back to Kerkyra in 1522, he fled the island after the sack perpetrated by the Turks in 1537. In Venice he taught classical Greek, he worked as a scribe, and after selling his large library to King Francis I he established himself as one of the leading book dealers of his generation: through various, sometimes indeed very indirect and tortuous channels (he was on particularly good terms with ambassadors and book collectors such as Diego Hurtado de Mendoza and Guillaume Pellicier), his Greek manuscripts (sometimes obtained in special missions to the East) ended up in the libraries at Fontainebleau, Rome, Florence, Augsburg, Vienna, El Escorial. Throughout his life he maintained a strong relationship with several cardinals (particularly with the powerful Roman bibliophile Marcello Cervini), and he proved a strong believer in the dialogue between the Eastern and the Western Churches, in the perspective of European solidarity in a common fight against the Ottomans: he corresponded on this topic with such prominent figures as Philipp Melanchthon and Cardinal Gasparo Contarini, and he wrote a *Presentation of the Ottoman tyranny* (1538–39) which offered not only military advice but also useful remarks on the ethos and the habits of the Turks. In 1552 he came back to Corfu, where he spent the rest of his life.

Bibliography: *RGK* I.23, II.32, III.36; Yotopoulou-Sisilianou, Elly (1978), Αντώνιος ο Έπαρχος, Athina; Ceresa, Massimo (1993), "Eparco, Antonio", in: *DBI* 43, 13–17; Mondrain, Brigitte (2000), "Les Éparque, une famille de médecins collectionneurs de manuscrits aux XVe–XVIe siècles", in: *The Greek Script in the 15th and 16th c.*, Athens, 145–163; Benz, Ernst ([2]1971), *Wittenberg und Byzanz. Zur Begegnung und Auseinandersetzung der Reformation und der östlich - orthodoxen Kirche*, München; Weise, Stefan (2020), "Gespräche auf Augenhöhe. Deutsch-griechischer Dialog im Humanismus und heute", in: Stefan Freund/Nina Mindt (eds.), *Antike Konzepte für ein modernes Europa. Die Klassische Philologie und die Zukunft eines Jahrhundertprojekts*, Wuppertal, 115–129.

Zacharias Skordylis († post 1572)

Ζαχαρίου ἱερέως Σκορδυλίου Κρητός [1563]

Ἤΰτε καρποφόρον δένδρον κατὰ δάσκιον ὕλην
    λανθάνει, πυκινῶν κρυπτὸν ὑπ' ἀκρεμόνων,
καί μιν θηρητὴρ ἐφράσσατο, αἶψα δ' ὀπώρης
    πλήσατο, καὶ δ' ἄλλοις δεῖξεν ἐπιστάμενος,
5   ὡς ἄρα τήνδε βίβλον μυχάτοις ὑπὸ βένθεσι λήθης
    Φραγκίσκος πολλοῖς ἤμασι κευθομένην
πολλὰ καμὼν ἐσάωσε καὶ ἐς φάος ἤγαγεν αὖθις
    καὶ προῖκα ξυνὴν προὔθετ' ὄνησιν ἔχειν.
Δεῦρ' ἴτε δὴ μετ' ἐδητὺν ὅσοι Χριστοῦ βασιλῆος
10 λάτριες, οἵ θ' ἱεραῖς μεμβλόμενοι σελίσι·
δὴ γὰρ ὑπ' ἐννεσίῃσι θεοπρεπέων ἱερήων
    ζωοφόροις καρπὸν δήετ' ἀκηράσιον.

Textus: Νικήτα Φιλοσόφου τοῦ καὶ Δαβὶδ *ἑρμηνεία εἰς τὰ τετράστιχα τοῦ μεγάλου πατρὸς Γρηγορίου τοῦ Ναζιανζηνοῦ*, Venetiis: apud Franciscum Zanetum, 1563, c. 18r (unde Legrand, *BH XV/XVI*, I, 318)

Crit.: 5 ὣς debuit

Sim.: nota multas clausulas pentametri (2 ἀκρεμόνων, 4 ἐπιστάμενος, 6 κευθομένην) in epigrammatis obvias ‖ **1** κατὰ δάσκιον ὕλην] cf. *Od.* 5.470; *Opp. C.* 2.530 al. ‖ **5** πολλὰ καμών] cf. *Anth. Pal.* 5.75.5; 9.472.1 al. | ἐς φάος ἤγαγεν αὖθις] cf. *Anth. Pal.* 16.42.3 ‖ **9** Χριστοῦ βασιλῆος] cf. Greg. Naz. *carm.*, PG 37.620.7 al. ‖ **10** λάτριες] cf. e.g. Greg. Naz. *carm.*, PG 37.1373.12 | ἱεραῖς...σελίσι] cf. *Anth. Pal.* 9.496.2

By the Cretan priest Zacharias Skordylis

Just as the fruit-bearing tree in a dense forest
    is latent, hidden by thick branches,
but it is detected by a predator, who quickly snatches
    the fruit and shows it to the others, since he knows it,
[5] so now Francisco has saved this book, hidden for a long time
    in the remotest depths of forgetfulness:
he worked hard and brought it back to life,
    and offered it as a common gift to all, for general utility.
Come here after your meal, all ye lovers of Christ the King,
[10] ye who take care of the sacred pages:
thanks to the life-giving advice of divinely illustrious priests
    you will find an unpolluted fruit.

Metre: Elegiac couplets. Incorrect prosody in the second α of l. 2 λανθάνει.

Notes: This book-epigram introduces the edition of the exegesis of the Byzantine scholar Nicetas David (9th/10th c.) on Gregory of Nazianzus' gnomic tetrastichs, a book which Skordylis co-funded with its printer, the famous Francesco Zanetti, later active in Rome. The hero of this poem, Φραγκίσκος (l. 6), is the Jesuit Hellenist Francisco Torres (1509–1584), who searched libraries for works by the Greek Church Fathers. In his *Διαταγαὶ τῶν ἁγίων ἀποστόλων / Constitutiones sanctorum apostolorum* (Venice 1563, c. 17v), Torres extolled Skordylis as ἀνὴρ πεπαιδευμένος καὶ λόγου ἔμπειρος, and Skordylis reciprocated the compliment with the present piece. The lines reveal at times a somewhat uncertain diction (in l. 4 πλήσατο is a problematic form, and the δ' is clearly misplaced; in l. 10 the construction of μέμβλεσθαι is wrong).

Biography: Little is known of the early life of the Cretan scholar Zacharias Skordylis (Kydonia ca. 1530 – post 1572), except for his studies in Padua, his early ordination as a priest in 1559 in Naxos, and his work as a scribe for the French ambassador Jean Hurault de Boistaillé in Venice between 1562 and 1564; he was later named *epitropos* (overseer) of the patriarch of Constantinople Ioasaph (in office 1551–1565), a position in which he took pride long after his term had ended. While in Venice he preached at San Giorgio dei Greci, and even tried to be selected for one of the two priest positions there. In 1566 we find him again in Crete, where he took exception to the fact that the Venetian government forced the Orthodox Cretans to participate in common liturgies with the Catholics. His editorial activity concerned mainly liturgical works, such as a *Horologion* (with ecclesiastical rules to boot), various treatises on fasting, and an essay on kinship (1564); he also represented the Orthodox point of view in the 12 questions on dogma posed by Charles de Guise, Cardinal of Lorraine (later printed in Lami's *Deliciae eruditorum*).

Bibliography: *RGK* II.157; Layton, Evro (1994), *The Sixteenth-Century Greek Book in Italy. Printers and Publishers for the Greek World*, Venice, 455–459. Lucà, Santo (2017), "Traduzioni patristiche autografe dal greco al latino del gesuita Francisco Torres (†1584)", in: Francesca P. Barone et al. (eds.), *Philologie, herméneutique et histoire des textes*, Turnhout, 71–117.

Maximos Margounios (1549–1602)

Ὕμνος ἔννατος ἱκετήριος εἰς τὴν Ἁγίαν Τριάδα, ἔχων ἀκροστιχίδα τήνδε· Μάξιμος τάδ'ἔγραψεν [1601]

    Μέμνησό μου, ἀνάρχου
    ἄρρητε βλαστὲ ῥίζης,
    ξένον τ' ἆημα ἀμφοῖν
    ἴσον γόνῳ καὶ ἀρχῇ,
5 μορφὴ τρισήλιός μοι·
    ὅταν κρίνῃς μ' ἀλιτρὸν
    σῶσον πυρός με λάτριν
    τὸν σόν, ζάλης τε πάσης
    ἄλαλκε, σῶτερ, αἰνῆς·
10 δεσμόν τε λῦσον αἶψα
    ἑσμοῦ λυγρῶν κακῶν μου·
    γράψον δὲ σῇ με βίβλῳ
    ῥόον φυγόντα τόνδε
    ἄτρωτον ἠδὲ σῶον·
15 ψάλλειν τε καὶ γεραίρειν
    ἐν ἀπλέτοις χρόνοισι
    νεῦσον τεὸν κράτος με.

Textus: Μαξίμου τοῦ Μαργουνίου ἐπισκόπου Κυθήρων Ὕμνοι ἀνακρεόντειοι / Maximi Margunii episcopi Cytherorum *Hymni Anacreontici*, Augustae 1601, cc. G8v–H1r

Crit.: λύσον, correxi

Sim.: 1–2 cf. Synes. *Hymn.* 3.10–11; de ἄναρχος ῥίζα cf. Greg. Naz. *carm.*, PG 37.412.11 || **5** τρισήλιος] de Trinitate apud scriptores theologiae sim. || **10** cf. Eur. fr. 128.2 Kn. al. || **16** sim. Plat. *leg.* 683a6 || **17** νεῦσον] cf. Synes. *Hymn.* 3.37

Ninth hymn of supplication to the Holy Trinity, with this acrostic: 'Maximos wrote this'

    Remember me, ineffable
    blossom of an eternal root,
    and you foreign spirit of both,
    similar to the Son and the Father,
    [5] form of threefold sun for me:
    when you judge me, poor sinner,
    save me, your servant, from the flames,
    and keep me, o saviour, far from

every terrible storm:
[10] loosen immediately the chain
of the mass of my awful evils:
write my name in your book
while I escape from that stream
unwounded and safe:
[15] let me sing and venerate
your power
in the endless times.

Metre: Anacreontic hymn in iambic catalectic dimeters (in the fashion of the III hymn of Synesius of Cyrene).

Notes: Margounios' output in verse is vast, and consists above all of epigrams in elegiac couplets, written for books or for encomiastic purposes. His book of Anacreontic hymns, all of religious content and mostly of a rather conventional nature, follow in the footsteps of a century-old Byzantine tradition stretching its roots back to the works of Synesios (4th c. CE), Sophronios of Jerusalem (7th c.), and the circle of Leo the Philosopher (9th c.): characteristically, the book is dedicated to the German Konrad Rittershausen, and published in Augsburg.

Biography: The Cretan Maximos Margounios (Candia 1549 – Venice 1602) studied in Padua and later taught for a long time in Venice: he became archbishop of Kythera, but never reached his see. The owner of a very rich library (most of which ended up in the Iviron Monastery on Mt. Athos and later partly in Moscow), a prolific translator from Greek into Latin and vice versa, in the domain of theology he stood out as a supporter of the union between the Eastern and the Catholic Churches (he wrote for this purpose a treatise in three books on the procession of the Holy Spirit, which earned him disagreement even from his former fellow pupils Meletios Pigas and Gabriel Severos).

Bibliography: *RGK* I.259, II.356, III.427; Geanakoplos, Deno J. (1966), *Byzantine East and Latin West*, Oxford, 165–193; Fedalto, Giorgio (1967), *Massimo Margunio*, Brescia; Podskalsky 1988, 135–151; Karamanolis, Yorgos E. (1998), "Ανέκδοτα επιγράμματα του Μάξιμου Μαργούνιου σε χειρόγραφα και έντυπα της Μαρκιανής βιβλιοθήκης", in: *Thesaurismata* 28, 197–207; Ciccolella, Federica (2020), "Maximos Margounios (*c.* 1549–1602), his Anacreontic Hymns, and the Byzantine Revival in Early Modern Germany", in: Natasha Constantinidou/Han Lamers (eds.), *Receptions of Hellenism in Early Modern Europe 15th–17th Centuries*, Leiden/Boston, 215–229.

Georgios Koressios (ca. 1570–1660)

Διήγησις τοῦ κλεινοῦ ἀγῶνος τῶν Φλωρεντινῶν διὰ στίχων, ὅστις παρ' ἐκείνοις μὲν Κάλτζιον, παρὰ δὲ τοῖς ἀρχαίοις ἀποκαλεῖται Ἄρπαστόν [1611]

(excerptum, vv. 241–256)

    Πῶς δρόμοι ἠδὲ πλοκαί, πυγμαὶ καὶ πτώσιες ἀνδρῶν,
       σήμαντρα κρατεροῦ δὴ γίνεται πολέμου.
    Πῶς ῥα λεοντηδὸν σταδιεὺς ὠστίζεται ἄλλον,
       ἀμφότερος πτήνοις ἶσος ἔει δὲ δρόμον.
245 Καὶ ὁ μὲν ἐν κονίαις πρηνὴς πέσε, τῇδε καὶ ἄλλος,
       ἦ που εἷς δ' ἑτέρου κάππεσεν ἔστιν ὅτε.
    Τόσσοι Πουλυδάμαντες δ' ἀλκὰν ἠδὲ Μίλωνες
       φαίνονται πυγμῇ χρώμενοι οἱ σταδιεῖς.
    Ἕν τέλος ἀντιπάλων φρεσὶ δ' ἔπλετο· μή ῥά γ' ἀνύσειν
250   τὴν σφαίρην δι' ὅρου μεσσατίου ἰέναι.
    Ἀστέρι δ' οὐρανίῳ τάχος εἴκελος ἔπλετο πάντως
       σφαίρη, τὴν δὲ βίην τηλεβόλου βολίδι.
    Εἰσέτι τῶν προτέρων τάξις δύναταί περ ἰοῦσα
       κάρτεϊ καὶ τέχνῃ τοῖς σφετέροις ἀμύνειν.
255 Τῆμος ἐπεὶ σφαίρη δ' ἐκινήθη, χρὴ ἰσαρίθμους
       τοὺς μέροπας λευκοὺς καὶ ἐρυθροὺς διιέναι.

Textus: *Διήγησις τοῦ κλεινοῦ ἀγῶνος τῶν Φλωρεντίνων διὰ στίχων, ὅστις παρ' ἐκείνοις μὲν Κάλτζιον, παρὰ δὲ τοῖς ἀρχαίοις καλεῖται Ἄρπαστόν, ποιηθεῖσα παρὰ Γεωργίου Κορεσσίου τοῦ Χίου...* / Venetiis: apud Antonium Pinelli, 1611 (transl. Latina: *Narratio inclyti certaminis Florentinorum Graecis versibus, quos apud illos Calcio, apud antiquos vero Arpastum appellatur, facta a D. Georgio Coresio Chiensi,* Venetiis: ex Typographia Antonii Pinelli, 1611).

Crit.: 242 δέ, correxi

Sim.: Tit. ἁρπαστός] cf. Athen. 1.14f || **241** sim. catalogus ludorum, cf. e.g. Hld. *Aeth.* 4.1.1; Nonn. *Dion.* 19.229 etc. || **243** λεοντηδόν] cf. LXX *Mach* 2.11.11 et Hsch. λ 654 | σταδιεύς] cf. *Anth. Pal.* 9.557.1, 11.163.2; Greg. Naz. *carm.*, PG 37.1206.9 | ὠστίζεται] cf. Ar. *Ach.* 42 || **244** ἔει] de forma cf. *Etym. Magn.* 431.11 || **245** ἐν κονίαις πρηνής] cf. *Il.* 2.418; 4.554; 6.43 || **247** Πουλυδάμαντες...Μίλωνες] cf. Philostr. *gymn.* 2.2.16 || **251** ἀστέρι δ' οὐρανίῳ] cf. Pind. *Pyth.* 3.75; *Hymn. Orph.* 7.3

Versified account of the famous game of the Florentines, called by them 'calcio', by the ancients *harpastos*

(excerpt, ll. 241–256)

> Look how the running and battling, the beating and the falling of men
>   become symbols of a great war!
> Look how each combatant, like a lion, pushes the other away,
>   and both resemble a swift bird!
> [245] One lands on his face in dust here, another one in that other corner,
>   and at times they fall one on top of the other.
> Like so many Polydamases and Milos, with all their strength,
>   it seems as if the players were wrestling.
> One thing only is on the minds of the antagonists: not to let
> [250] the ball get across the central line.
> The ball is swift like a star from heaven,
>   violent like a shuttle from a far-reaching cannon.
> The line of the forward players can come
>   and help their side with their skill and strength.
> [255] As soon as the ball has moved, an equal number
>   of Whites and Reds must cross the pitch.

Metre: Elegiac couplets. Bipartite hexameter in l. 247; l. 256 (with διέναι) does not scan; wrong prosody of ι in l. 242 γίνεται and l. 255 ἐκινήθη, and of υ in l. 254 ἀμύνειν.

Notes: Koressios' *Diegesis*, a delightful description of the ancestor of modern football, runs to 216 elegiac couplets. The poem, which traces the origins of the game back to Greece and Rome albeit giving the Florentines a decisive role in its development, is dedicated to the Grand Duke of Florence, Cosimo II de' Medici (1590–1621), who is referred to at the beginning (Κόσμῳ, ἡγεμόνι κρατερῷ, τόδε ἆθλον ἀείδω) and at the end of the poem (Δέχνυσο ἀσπασίως ἄρα, Κόσμε ἀρήϊε, δῶρον). Despite its hesitant Greek form, the poem also saw a Latin version (printed in the same year) and an Italian version (1688, transl. by Anton Maria Salvini).

Biography: A doctor, a philosopher and a theologian, Georgios Koressios (Chios ca. 1570–1660) probably studied philosophy and medicine in Padua and Pisa, and taught Greek language at the University of Pisa from 1609 to 1615. A personal friend of the Medici family (the Duke Cosimo II and his younger brother Francesco), he also worked as a doctor in Pisa, Livorno, and Marseille and, before 1618, he finally returned to Chios, where he worked as a doctor and a teacher until his death. His impressive literary and scholarly production ranges from medicine to physics (he wrote against Galilei's theory), but his main concern was the theological dispute against the Latins (polemical writings against Bellarmino and Karyophylles) and against the Protestant doctrine.

Bibliography: Podskalsky 1988, 183–190; Stoupakis, Nikos M. (2000), *Γεώργιος Κορέσσιος (1570 ci. – 1659/60)*, Chios; Zoras, Gerasimos G. (2002–2005), "Ἡ ἀναβίωσις τοῦ Ἅρπαστοῦ εἰς τὴν Φλωρεντίαν καὶ ἡ *Διήγησις τοῦ Γεωργίου Κορεσσίου*", in: *Ἀθηνᾶ* 83, 483–500.

Ioannes Matthaios Karyophylles (ca. 1566–1633)

Εἰς τὸν αὐτὸν ἀναγραμματισμὸς Ἰσάακος Κασαύβωνος [1612]

> Εἰ ποθέεις ἀνάγραμμα σαφές, ξένε, τῇ τὸ δὲ <δὴ> πῶς·
> ΑΙΣΑ ΒΟΩΣΑ λέγει· ΝΟΥΣ ΚΑΚΟΣ ἀνδρὶ πέλει.

Textus: R.P. Andreae Eudaemon-Ioannis Cydonii e societate Iesu *Responsio ad Epistolam Isaaci Casauboni*, Coloniae Agrippinae: apud Ioannem Kinckium, 1612, c. <I> (unde Legrand, *BH XVII*, I.83)

Crit.: 1 δὴ addidi

Sim.: 1 εἰ...ποθέεις] cf. Greg. Naz. *carm.*, PG 37.560.10 | ἀνάγραμμα] verbum Latine expressum, Graece potius ἀναγραμματισμός vel sim. || 2 νοῦς κακός] cf. Soph. *OT* 600

Anagrammatic verse on the same: Isaac Casaubon

> O stranger, if you want a clear anagram, here it is, somehow:
> 'Fate cries' and it says this man has 'an evil mind'.

Metre: Elegiac couplet.

Notes: Karyophylles enjoyed puns, and re-named himself 'Kairophilos'. The present distich introduces the reply by the Jesuit father Andreas Eudaimon-Ioannes, the then rector of Rome's Collegio Greco, against the criticism of the Protestant scholar Isaac Casaubon (1559–1614); → **Switzerland**); the complicated theological quarrel, inaugurated by Casaubon's letter to the French Jesuit Fronton du Duc, was later continued by the English Regius Professor of Divinity John

Prideaux. The first three pages of Eudaimon-Ioannes' book carry epigrams by Ioannes Matthaios Karyophylles εἰς Κασαούβωνον τὸν αἱρετικόν.

Biography: In 1583 Ioannes Matthaios Karyophylles (Chania 1566 – Rome 1633) entered the Collegio Greco of St Athanasius in Rome, where he graduated in theology and philosophy in 1595, and taught Greek since 1592. In 1596 he was sent back to Crete as *vicarius* of the diocese of Kissamos, where he proved such a stern defender of the Catholic faith that the Venetian authorities favoured his return to Rome. In 1603 Clement VIII awarded him a post in the *familia* of Cardinal Silvestro Aldobrandini; in 1622 he received the titularity of the archbishopric of Iconium. Acquainted with important cardinals such as Luigi Ludovisi and Francesco Barberini, Karyophylles wrote erudite works on Greek pronounciation and on the syntax of Theodore Gaza, a number of theological treatises (he particularly enjoyed polemic and controversy), and several letters.

Bibliography: Tsirpanlis 1980, 289–292; Podskalsky 1988, 181–183.

Belisario Corenzio (1558–after 1646)

Εἰς Βελισσάριον οἱ μοναχοί [1615]

Ἀρκαδίη μὲν ἔφυσε Κορένσιον, ἔσχε δὲ γαῖα
Παρθενόπη γραφέων Πρωτογένην ἕτερον.

Textus: Neapoli in lapide marmoreo inscriptum, qui nunc in pavimento ecclesiae Sanctorum Severini et Sossii servatur

Sim.: 1–2 cf. epitaphium Vergilii "Mantua me genuit...tenet nunc / Parthenope"

The monks for Belisario

Arcadia gave birth to Corenzio, the land of Parthenope
has kept him, a second Protogenes among the painters.

Metre: Elegiac couplet.

Notes: This epitaph, allegedly written by the Benedictine monks of Ss. Severino e Sossio to commemorate Corenzio (whose frescoes are still visible in the church and the sacristy), was inscribed on a stone for the funerary monument that the painter had in fact designed for himself and his family as early as 1615. The stone is now to be seen in the floor of the same church. The epigram clearly echoes the famous epitaph for Virgil, and evokes antonomastically the famous Carian painter Protogenes (4th century BC).

Biography: Born to a family of Greek agents at the service of Spain, Belisario Corenzio (Kyparissia, Peloponnesos, 1558 – Naples, *post* 1646) moved to Italy after the battle of Lepanto and settled down in Naples, while spending some time in Rome during his youth. Since 1589 he became one of the most successful and popular painters of early Neapolitan Baroque, and frescoed a number of churches in town, from San Paolo Maggiore to the Gesù Nuovo, not to mention the dome of the abbey church at Monte Cassino; many of his works were destroyed during World War II. Albeit an Orthodox and a member of the Hellenic Fraternity of Naples, he followed the Catholic rite in his two marriages and the baptism of his children. The legend that he died falling off from a scaffolding in Ss. Severino e Sossio at 85 years of age should not be trusted.

Bibliography: Ioannou, Panayotis K. (2011), *Belisario Corenzio. Η ζωή και το έργο του*, Iraklio/Venice (with earlier bibliography); Lampros, Spyridon (1871), "Περὶ Βελισσαρίου Κορενσίου", in: *Pandora* 22, 367–374, 385–390.

Leone Allacci (1588–1669)

Ἑλλάς [1642]

(excerptum, vv. 715–754)

715 Τοσαῦτ' ἔφη ΕΛΛΑΣ, ἀμφὶ δ' ὠλέναις
αὖθις περισφίγξασα νήδυμον τόκον,
φίλημ' ἔθηκ' ὅσσοισι δεύτερον φίλοις.
Παῖς δ' ἱστορούσης πημοναῖς σύννους γεγώς,
ὕβρει τ' ἀνάσσης κάρτ' ἐποχθίσας τόσῃ
720 οἰκτρὸν στέναξεν ἄλγος ἐκθύμῳ φρενί.
Γοργοῖς ἔπειτ' ὄμμασιν ἀντωπὸν βλέπος
τοκεῖ προσίσχων, σύν τε θεὶς γλυκὺν γέλων,
βάζειν ἔοικε ταῦτα φραδμόνως πατρί.
"Θυμῷ πίεσσον μῆνιν, ἢν ἐλᾷς, πάτερ.
725 Μέθες δαφοινὸν ἔγχος, Εὐρώπης τ' ἄπο
πρὸς Ἀντολὰς ὅρμισσον, ἔνθ' ἀνδρηλάτης,
ἄτην τ' ἄθεσμος λαὸς ὁπλίζει βροτοῖς
αὐτὸς σὺ παιδὸς ἐμπνέοντος δηΐοις

φόνον, πάθας τ' εἰ καὶ νεογνὰ νηπίῳ
730 ἄψῃ χόλον δύσοργον εἰκαίως πεδᾷ,
ὁρμῇ προηγοῦ εὐθρασέστερος φανείς,
φίλην τ' ἄνασσαν ἀμφιβὰς λυτήριος
ὄνησον, ἠδ' ἔκλυσσον, ὧν ἔχει κακῶν,
μέσφ' αὐτὸς ἐς γυιαρκὲς αὐξηθεὶς μέτρον
735 ἥβης, μένει τε κεχλαδὼς εὐανθέμῳ
αὐτὸς τύχης ῥύσαιμι μορσίμου φίλην,
πρός τ' ὄλβον, ὃν κέκτητο πορθμεύσας ξένως,
καλοῖς πρέπουσαν, καὶ περίβλεπτον κράτῃ,
βίου τ' ἐν ἅλμῃ μειδιῶσαν εὐδίῳ,
740 εὐδαιμονούσης πολλὰ κομπάσω γάμους,
τούς μοι δίδωσιν ἐκ γένους κλῆρος λαχών.
'Ἐμὴ γάρ ἐστι, κ' οὐκ ἀπαρνοῦμαι τὸ μή.
Ἔνθεν μόναρχον αἷμα βλαστήσει πέδῳ,
αἰὲν προσαρκοῦν, οὔ τι γηράσκον χρόνοις."
745 Παιδὸς πρόθυμον ἦτορ ἐξειδὼς πατήρ,
ἄνασσαν ἦγε, δεξιούμενος γόνῳ,
πίστιν λαβών τ' ἔδωκε, δεξιάς θ' ὁμοῦ
ὅρκοις συνῆψαν. "Καὶ δὴ εἰργάσθω τόδε
τοὖργον, προσεῖπε, τεῦ μακρὰν τείνω μάτην;
750 Ἐμοῖς ὅπλοισιν, οὐδ' ἄτερ βουλῆς θεοῦ,
ἐλευθερούσθω γαῖα, τεχνέων τροφός,
δεινῆς ἀνάγκης, καὶ γενέσθω σύννομος
τέκνῳ νεογνῷ, τῆσδε κοιράνῳ χθονός,
πλέον γ' ἢ τὸ πρόσθεν ΕΛΛΑΣ εὐτυχεστέρα."

Textus: Leonis Allatii *Hellas*, Romae: excudebat Mascardus, 1642, vv. 715–754 (unde Rotolo, Vincenzo (1966), *Il Carme «HELLAS» di Leone Allacci*, Palermo)

Crit.: 715 ἡ Ἑλλὰς vel sim. debuit || 717 ὅσσοισιν ed., correxi || 719 ἐποχθήσας ed., corr. Rotolo || 731 εὐθρασέστερος pro εὐθαρσ- metri gratia || 733 ὤνησον ed., corr. Rotolo | ἔκλυσον debuit

Sim.: 716 περισφίγξασα] cf. Nonn. *Dion.* 4.67 al. || 719 ἐποχθίσας] de verbo cf. Opp. *H.* 5.170 || 720 cf. Aesch. *PV* 435 (στένουσιν ἄλγος οἰκτρόν) || 721 γοργοῖς ὄμμασι] sim. Aesch. *PV* 356 | βλέπος] cf. Ar. *Nub.* 1176 || 722 γλυκὺν γέλων] cf. Pind. *Pyth.* 8.85 || 723 adv. φραδμόνως hapax ut vid. || 724 sim. Pind. *Ol.* 6.37 (ἐν θυμῷ πιέσαις χόλον) || 726 ἀνδρηλάτης] cf. Aesch. *Sept.* 637 || 730 δύσοργον] cf. Soph. *Trach.* 1118; *Ai.* 1017; *Phil.* 377 || 732 λυτήριος] cf. Aesch. *Eum.* 298 || 733 ὧν ἔχει κακῶν] cf. Eur. *Hec.* 1268 || 734 γυιαρκές] cf. Pind. *Pyth.* 3.6 || 735 κεχλαδώς] cf. Pind. *Ol.* 9.2 et *Pyth.* 4.179 | εὐανθέμῳ] cf. Pind. *Ol.* 1.67 et *Anth. Pal.* 7.602.3 || 736 τύχης μορσίμου] cf. Heracl. Lemb. fr. 5 Müller (ex Alexarchi epistula, vide Athen. 3.98f) || 740 κομπάσω γάμους] cf. Aesch. *PV* 947 || 742 cf. Soph. *Ant.* 443; *Ai.* 96 || 744 προσαρκοῦν] verbum tragicum, cf. Soph. *OT* 141 al. | de clausula sim. Aesch. *PV* 981 || 745 ἐξειδώς] cf. Soph. *OT* 37, *Trach.* 399; Eur. *Phoen.* 95 || 749 μακρὰν τείνω] cf. Soph. *Ai.* 1040 || 750 ἄτερ...θεοῦ] cf. *Od.* 2.372 || 752 δεινῆς ἀνάγκης] cf. Eur. *Hel.* 514 || 753 τῆσδε κοιράνῳ χθονός] cf. Eur. *Alc.* 507, *Med.* 71, *HF* 139, *IT* 1080

Hellas

(excerpt, ll. 715–754)

[715] Thus spoke HELLAS, and, holding
the sweet little child in her arms,
kissed his eyes one more time.
And the child, learning her pains from her words
and sighing deeply for the grave injustice done to the Queen,
[720] uttered from his angered soul a wailing cry.
Then, turning swiftly his gaze and his swift eyes
towards his father, and smiling sweetly,
he thoughtfully said the following words:
'Suppress in your heart the rage you feel, O Father.
[725] Set aside your blood-stained sword, and from Europe
proceed East-bound where a ruler who drives people away
and a lawless kin provide a catastrophe to the mortals;
and you, while your son urges you to slaughter
the enemy (even if my baby limbs naturally
[730] impede my passions and my sharp rage),
show yourself braver and run before me,
protecting the Queen as a saviour;
help her and free her from the evils that harass her,
until I, reaching the bloom of my youth
[735] in my limbs, and relying on flourishing strength,
manage to help her come round her gloomy fate.
And miraculously restoring her to her previous wealth,
glowing with beauty and illustrious with power,
smiling quietly in the calm sea of life,
[740] I shall be proud to marry her happy as ever,
a task assigned to me by the fate of my kin.
For she is mine, there can be no objection about this.
From this marriage a royal race will spring in the world,
always in blossom and never ageing as time goes by.'
[745] The father, seeing the zest in the heart of his child,
led the Queen, hand in hand, to his son,
they exchanged vows, shook hands and made
their pledges: 'So let this plan be realised –
he said – why should we tarry for no reason?
[750] With my weapons, and not without the will of God,
let the land that bore all arts be freed
from her terrible slavery, and let her unite
with my son, the ruler of this country:
may HELLAS be happier than ever before.'

Metre: Iambic trimeters; Allacci's trimeter does not share features with the Byzantine dodecasyllable, and follows the ancient pattern; if the text is sound (the print looks in many points rather careless), there are occasional mistakes (one syllable is missing in l. 715; the α in l. 721 ὄμμασιν should be short).

Notes: Allacci had a *faible* for versification in Greek (hexameters and trimeters), especially for *épigrammes d'occasion*, for erudite compositions (the Ὁμήρου γοναί printed at the end of his erudite study *De patria Homeri*) and for encomiastic pieces such as the *Eridanus* (1635) and the *Barberinocomis* (1640), written for the Barberini family. The *Hellas*, in 754 iambic trimeters, is a more ambitious poem, dedicated to the then four-year-old Dolphin of France, Louis XIV (who became king in 1654): the fiction has it that Greece, a beautiful noblewoman, comes to Louis' cradle and begs him to take the initiative of freeing her from the cruel Turkish yoke. The passage presented here contains Louis XIV's exhortation to his father Louis XIII, and the *dextrarum iunctio* that binds together the fates of France and Greece. The use of iambic verse enables Allacci to allude to the tragedy of his nation by interweaving in his poem quotations from Attic drama.

Biography: Leone Allacci (Greek name Leon Alatzes, Chios 1588 – Rome 1669) was brought to Italy as a child and enrolled in the Collegio greco, where he graduated in philosophy and Divinity in 1610. After a short stay in Anglona (where he was the vicar of Bishop Bernardo Giustiniani) and in his homeland Chios, he came back to Rome where he graduated in medicine in 1616, and later taught Greek at the Collegio greco (he had to resign after a quarrel with I.M. Karyophylles). Highly praised by Gregory XV, who hired him as *scriptor Graecus* at the Vatican Library in 1618, and in 1622 entrusted to him the delicate mission of bringing to Rome the Heidelberg manuscripts donated by Maximilian I, he was less appreciated by Urbanus VIII, and it was only with Alexander VII that he received due honours (in 1661 he succeeded Lucas Holste as *primo custode* of the Library). His scholarly output is immense and stretches from theology (see in particular his *De Ecclesiae occidentalis atque orientalis perpetua consensione*, 1648) to Byzantine literature and history, not to mention his erudite interest in epigraphy and etruscology, and his editions and translations of Greek classical works (from Socrates' letters to Saloustios to Philo of Alexandria). His immense epistolary (preserved in manuscripts kept at the Biblioteca Vallicelliana in Rome) still awaits closer scrutiny.

Bibliography: Musti, Domenico (1960), "Allacci, Leone", in: *DBI* 2, 467–471; Jacono, Carmela (1962), *Bibliografia di Leone Allacci (1588–1669)*, Palermo; Rotolo 1966 (see above Textus); Tsirpanlis 1980, 377–383; Podskalsky 1988, 213–219; Papadopoulos, Thomàs I. (1989), "Ο Λέων Αλλάτιος και η Χίος", in: *Χιακὰ Χρονικά* 20, 3–144.

Leonardos Philaras (ca. 1595–1673)

Τῇ Θεοτόκῳ καὶ ἀειπαρθένῳ Μαρίᾳ ἁγνῶς καὶ ἀμώμως συλληφθείσῃ [1644]

(excerptum, vv. 16–45)

      ἀντιστροφή. κώλων ιε′
Ὁ τρισσοφαὴς ἁνίκα μέδων
ἐξ οὐδενὸς πρόπασαν ἕλκε γένναν,
λιάσας ὑδάτων γᾶν καὶ σκότου φάος,
τὸν ἁμὸν ἀρχιγονέταν
20 τεκτήνατ' ἰδίαις παλάμαις
ἀπήμον', ἐτήτυμον, ᾧ τε
εἴκελον εἴδει λαμπρῷ,
ὅλων μὶν πρύτανιν θᾶκεν, ὑπάκοον
δέ οἱ πάντα· θεσπέσια χάρματα
25 χεῦεν ἄναξ, ἕδος χαρίτων
ἔρυσθαι δῶκ', ἀγαναῖς
ἐν χαρίτεσσι τερπνὸν
ὃς δὲ βίοτον ἑλὼν
ἀκάκης, νόσφι μόχθου,
30 θυμὸν ἰαίνων νέμε.

      ἐπῳδὸς α′. κώλων ιε′
Πάντ' ἐκ θεοῖο ἕσπεται βροτοῖσιν
ἐσλὰ τέλεια. Οὐδὲν ἔρδειν ἀκράαντον
δύναται δωτὴρ ἑάων·
ἀλλ' ὑπερκωμάσδων οὐχ ὑπέμεινε δαρὸν
35 εὐτυχίας ἄωτον. Χρόνον ἐς μακρὸν
οὐκ ἔρχεται θνατοῖσιν ὄλβος·
οἷα δὲ σκιᾶς ἠὲ ὀνείρων
οἴχεται φάσματα.
Ὦ πρωτόγονον κάρα,
40 γλυκὺ ψεῦδος μαιμάσσων
ἄιδρις, ὀλέθριον
ἕλκος ἔπαξας βροτῶν
γένει. Δεινά τις ἐρινννὺς τάδε

πήματα μήσατο, ἀνίκ' ἄπαφεν
45 σοῖο ἄνακτος λάθεν ἐφετμέων.

Textus: *Ὠιδὴ εἰς τὴν ἀναμάρτητον σύλληψιν τῆς Θεοτόκου...τοῦ χρησιμωτάτου κυρίου Λεονάρδου τοῦ Φιλαρᾶ τοῦ Ἀθηναίου.../ Ode in immaculatam Conceptionem Deiparae...*authore viro praestantissimo D. Leonardo Philara Atheniensi, ἐν Παρισίοις αχμδ' (Parisiis 1644) (unde *Recueil de pièces lues dans les séances publiques de l'Académie établie à Rouen*, Rouen 1784, et novissime Legrand, *BH XVII* I.470-473)

Crit.: 19 ἁμόν ed., correxi || 34 οὐκ ed., correxi

Sim.: 16 τρισσοφαής] cf. Greg. Naz. *carm.*, PG 37.421.1 al. || 18 λιάσας] de verbo cf. Hsch. λ 929 || 19 ἀρχιγονέταν hapax || 20 ἰδίαις παλάμαις] cf. *Orac. sib.* 11.269 || 25 ἕδος χαρίτων] cf. *Anth. Pal.* 9.246.2 || 26 ἀγαναῖς...χαρίτεσσι] cf. Pind. *Isthm.* 3/4.8 || 29 ἀκάκης] cf. Aesch. *Pers.* 855 || 32 ἐσλὰ τέλεια] cf. Pind. *Pyth.* 9.89 || 33 δωτὴρ ἑάων] cf. *Od.* 8.325 || 35-36 cf. Pind. *Pyth.* 3.105 (ὄλβος οὐκ ἐς μακρὸν ἀνδρῶν ἔρχεται) || 37-38 cf. Pind. *Pyth.* 8.95 (σκιᾶς ὄναρ) || 40-41 cf. Pind. *Pyth.* 2.37 (ψεῦδος γλυκὺ μεθέπων ἄιδρις) || 44 πήματα μήσατο] cf. Eur. *Phoen.* 799

To the Virgin Mary, the Mother of God, the fruit of a pure and immaculate conception

(excerpt, ll. 16-45)

    antistrophe (15 cola)
When the Threefold Ruler
created from no one our entire stock,
having separated land from waters and light from darkness,
He fashioned with His own hands
[20] our forefather,
far from sorrow and lie, similar
to His own blazing aspect,
he made him the governor of all things, constantly
obedient to Him: the Lord poured
[25] divine gifts, and He gave him
a graceful land to inhabit: and choosing
a pleasant life among
gentle graces,
he lived warming his own spirit
[30] far from evil and toil.

    epode 1 (15 cola)
All good and perfect things come to mortals
from God. The giver of goods cannot
do anything idle:
however, overwhelmed by goods, he did not stand long

[35] the flower of happiness. Wealth does not come to mortals
for a long time:
like ghosts of a shadow
or of a dream it disappears.
O first-created head,
[40] you preferred a sweet lie
out of ignorance, you delivered
a mortal wound to the human species.
A terrible Erinys made these
sorrowful thoughts, when she deceived you
[45] into forgetting the orders of your Lord.

Metre: Pindaric strophes. As opposed to similar Italian attempts (e.g., Robortello and Amalteo), and as opposed to the 18th-century author Sergios Makraios, whose Ὀρθόδοξος Ὑμνῳδός followed directly the various metrical systems of Pindar's odes, Philaras improvises here a metrical pattern of his own, however implausible and full of hiatuses and infelicities.

Notes: The ode starts from the creation of man and the original sin: Adam is the protagonist of the first triad. Beside the aforementioned metrical hardships, one should note a probably wrong infinitive (l. 45 λάθεν) and a lack of aspiration in l. 34 (perhaps to be ascribed to the author). The passage here selected displays the adoption of Pindaric diction less in terms of dialect or vocabulary, than in terms of ideology – see esp. the ethical *gnomai* in the epode.

Biography: Born to a distinguished Athenian family, Leonardos Philaras (Athens ca. 1595 – Paris 1673) was trained at the Collegio Greco until 1617, and later worked as the ambassador of the Duke of Parma to the French court, and as an advisor to Cardinal Richelieu. From Paris he travelled to England (1652–54), where he became acquainted with John Milton (→ **Great Britain**). After a period in Venice (1657–61) he came back to Paris where he died in 1673. His devotion to the Catholic cause is confirmed by his translation of Bellarmino's *Catechism*; more importantly, he made a crucial contribution to the support of the Greek cause throughout Europe and the European rulers.

Bibliography: Legrand, *BH XVII*, III.407–409; Knös, Börje (1953), "Ὁ Λεονάρδος ὁ Φιλαράς", in: *Προσφορά εις Στίλπωνα Κυριακίδην*, Thessaloniki, 345–357; Tsirpanlis 1980, 424–426; Pontani, Filippomaria (2012), "Pindar's liberal songs", in: *Bulletin of the Institute of Classical Studies* 55, 193–210.

Georgios Patousas (1687–1761)

Εἰς τὴν Φιλολογικὴν Ἐγκυκλοπαιδείαν ἐπίγραμμα [1710]

    Τίπτε μάτην φιλόμουσε πονεῖς, τὴν δ' αὖ Ἑλικῶνος
        ἀμβαίνεις ἀτραπὸν Πιερίδας πορίσων;
    Βούλει ῥᾷστα κ' ἄμοχθος πασῶν τῶν δ' ἐπιτεῦξαι;
        Σπουδῇ ἐνδελεχεῖ εἴλυε τάσδε βίβλους·
5   ὧδ' ἐν θειοφρόνων λατρίων Χριστοῖο λόγοισι
        ἥ τε Πολυμνίη, Οὐρανίη τε πέλει·
    πὰρ ῥητῆρσι Θάλεια, τραγῳδοῖς Τερψιχόρη τε
        θάλλει· πὰρ λυρικοῖς Μελπομένη ἀΐδει.
    Εὐτέρπης, Κλειοῦς τ' ἐράεις, ἐρατῆς Ἐρατοῦς τε;
10 Διαλόγους, γνώμας, ἠδ' ἐπιγράμματ' ἔχε.
    Ἡ παρ' ἑκάστῳ στίλβει ἑκάστη θάμβεῖ πάντων,
        πᾶσι δὲ τῶν ἄλλων ἔξοχα Καλλιόπη.
    Θαῦμα δὲ οὐδὲν ναιετάειν Μουσῶν χορὸν ὧδε·
        καὶ γάρ κ' ἂν δέλτοις ᾤκεον Ἡροδότου.

                        Ὁ ἐν ἱερεῦσιν ἐλάχιστος Γεώργιος Πατούσας Ἀθηναῖος

Textus: *Ἐγκυκλοπαιδεία Φιλολογική*,…παρὰ τοῦ ἐν ἱερεῦσιν αἰδεσιμωτάτου καὶ λογιωτάτου Ἰωάννου Πατούσα τοῦ ἐξ Ἀθηνῶν…, Ἑνετίησιν: παρὰ Νικολάῳ τῷ Σάρῳ, αψι' (Venetiis 1710), cc. 8–9 (unde Legrand, Émile (1918), *Bibliographie Hellénique…XVIIIe siècle*, I, Paris)

Sim.: 1 Τίπτε μάτην…πονεῖς] cf. *Anth. Pal.* 10.77.1 | Ἑλικῶνος…ἀμβαίνεις] cf. *Anth. Pal.* 9.230.1 ‖ 4 σπουδῇ ἐνδελεχεῖ] cf. e.g. Dio Cass. 53.27.4 ‖ 5 λατρίων Χριστοῖο] cf. *Anth. Pal.* 8.2.2 ‖ 7 de Musis cf. *Anth. Pal.* 9.504 | πὰρ ῥητῆρσι] cf. *Anth. Pal.* 8.122.1 ‖ 12 ἔξοχα Καλλιόπη] cf. *Anth. Pal.* 7.8.6

Epigram on the *Philological Encyclopaedia*

    Why are you toiling in vain, curious reader, and why are you once again
        ascending the path of the Helicon in order to find the Muses?
    Do you want to reach all of them easily and without effort?
        Flip through these books with continuous study:
[5] Here in the words of the divinely inspired servants of Christ
        there are both Polymnia and Urania.
    And Thalia blossoms for the orators, Terpsichore for the tragedians;
        Melpomene sings to the lyrical poets.
    Do you desire Euterpe, Clio and desirable Erato?
[10] Take these dialogues, sentences, and epigrams.
    To be sure, in every piece each Muse shines amazing everyone,
        but above all others Calliope.

No wonder that the chorus of the Muses dwells here:
they would also dwell in the books of Herodotus.

The least of priests, Georgios Patousas from Athens

Metre: Elegiac couplets, with one bipartite hexameter (l. 3), an objectionable use of hiatuses (see esp. the unelided δέ in l. 13) and some prosodical mistakes (l. 3 the crasis κ' ἄμοχθος is counted as short; there are vagaries in the iotas, see ll. 6 and especially διαλόγους in 10).

Notes: This epigram celebrates the bulky *Philological Encyclopaedia* in four volumes (1675 pages) produced in 1710 by Ioannes Patousas, the distinguished brother of Georgios. This encyclopaedia, dedicated to the doctor and philosopher Spyridon Petroulios, remained an essential tool for the instruction of pupils until well into the 19th century. The epigram by Georgios anthologised here is part of the introductory material.

Biography: After an early training in Athens, Georgios Patousas (Athens 1687 – Venice 1761) continued his studies in Italy, and became a deacon at the church of San Giorgio dei Greci in Venice, as well as a teacher at the nearby Flanginian College.

Bibliography: Abdale, Athanasia K. (1984), *Η Εγκυκλοπαιδεία Φιλολογική του Ιωάννη Πατούσα*, Athens.

Philippos Ioannou (1796–1880)

I. Εἰς τὴν ἀεροστατικὴν σφαῖραν [1865]

Πολλάκι μῦθον ἄκουσα τὸν Ἰκάρου, ὃν πτερύγεσσι
   τυκτῇσι πτάσθαι φασὶ διηέριον.
Ἀλλὰ τόδ' ὠϊόμην κενεὴν φάτιν ἔμμεν ἀοιδῶν,
   ποικίλ' ἐνὶ φρεσσὶ ψεύδεα πλασσομένων.
5 Νῦν δ' ἄρα πῶς κε τέρας φαίη τις ἄπιστον ἐκεῖνο,
   κοῦφον τόνδ' ὁρόων ἠερόπλαγκτον ὄχον,
ἠέρος ἔμπλειον, διά τ' ἠέρος οὐχ ἕνα μοῦνον,
   ἀλλ' ἄμυδις πολλοὺς ὕψι φέροντ' ἀνέρας;
Ἠνίδ' ὑπὲρ νεφέων θρασυμήχανος ἤρθη ὅμιλος,
10   καὶ τάχ' ἑλιξοπόροις τείρεσι προσπελάσει.

Textus: Ioannou, Philippos (1874, 1865¹), *Φιλολογικὰ πάρεργα*, Athens, 586.

Crit.: **5** τις κε τέρας φήσειεν ἄπιστον 1865

Sim.: 1 cf. *Il.* 1.386 (Πολλάκι...ἄκουσα) ǁ **2** τυκτῇσι] cf. *Il.* 12.105 ǁ **3** κενεὴν φάτιν] cf. Opp. *C.* 3.357 ǁ **4** ποικίλ'...ψεύδεα] cf. Pind. *Ol.* 1.29 ǁ **5** τέρας...ἄπιστον] cf. Aesch. *PV* 832 ǁ **6** ἠερόπλαγκτον] cf. *Hymn. Orph.* 7.8 ǁ **9** θρασυμήχανος] cf. Pind. *Ol.* 6.67 ǁ **10** ἑλιξοπόροις] cf. Maneth. *Apotel.* 4.437 | τείρεσι] cf. Maxim. 6.220; 9.450

On the aerostatic balloon

> I have time and again heard the myth of Icarus: they say
>   he flew with artificial wings.
> But I thought it was just empty words of poets,
>   who create manifold lies in their minds.
> [5] And yet, how could anyone say now that it was unbelievable,
>   seeing this light mobile vehicle wandering in the sky,
> full of air and transporting high through the air
>   not one man, but many at the same time?
> Look, the bold group of people has lifted over the clouds,
> [10] and it will soon approach the celestial bodies which move in spires.

II. Εἰς τὸν ἠλεκτρικὸν Τηλέγραφον [1865]

> Οὔνομ' ἀπ' ἠλέκτρου τις ἔχουσα, τεράστιος ὁρμήν,
>   ἐνδέδυκεν πᾶσαν τήνδε φύσιν δύναμις,
> δαίμων δή τις ἄοπτος, ὁρατὰ δὲ πᾶσι τελεῦσα
>   ἔργα, σοφοῖς ἀσόφοις τ' ἀνδράσι θαῦμα μέγα.
> 5 Ἥδ' ὅπλον αἰθαλόεν τεύχει Διός, ἥδε χάλαζαν
>   πρηστήρων τε μένος τίκτει ἀμαιμακέτων,
> ἥδε καὶ ἀνθρώποις νῦν γίγνεται εὑρεσιτέχνοις
>   Ἴριδος Ἑρμείω τ' ἄγγελος ὠκυτέρη.
> Ἠνὶ σιδηρείῃ ἐπὶ μέρμιθ' ὀξὺ θέουσα
> 10   ὥστε νόημα, φέρει πανταχοῦ ἀγγελίας.

Textus: Ioannou, Philippos (1874, 1865¹), *Φιλολογικὰ πάρεργα*, Athens, 588

Crit: 3 τελεοῦσα 1865 ǁ **4** τ' ἀσόφοις ἀνδράσι 1865 ǁ **8** Ἴριδος ἠδ' Ἑρμοῦ ἄγγελος 1865 ǁ **9** σιδηρείης διὰ μέρμιθος 1865

Sim.: 3 ἄοπτος] cf. Antiph. fr. 87B4 D.-K. ǁ **4** σοφοῖς ἀσόφοις τ'] cf. *Anth. Pal.* 15.14.6 ǁ **6** πρηστήρων...ἀμαιμακέτων] cf. *Hymn. Orph.* 19.11 ǁ **7** εὑρεσιτέχνοις] cf. *Hymn. Orph.* 32.17 ǁ **8** Ἑρμείῳ] de forma cf. *Il.* 15.214 ǁ **9** μέρμιθ'] cf. *Od.* 10.23 ǁ **10** ὥστε νόημα] cf. Thgn. 1.985; Opp. *H.* 5.660

On the electric telegraph

A power deriving its name from electron, amazing for its force,
  has penetrated this entire world,
an invisible divine might performing works visible to all,
  an object of great admiration for the wise and the lay people.
[5] This power creates Zeus' flaming weapon; this power gives rise
  to hail and generates the violence of irresistible typhoons;
this power becomes a messenger swifter than Iris and Hermes,
  for men, who are inventors of the arts.
Look: running on an iron string as swiftly
[10] as thought, it delivers messages everywhere.

Metre: Elegiac couplets (the υ in II.2 ἐνδέδυκεν should be long).

Notes: Ioannou's *Philologika parerga* (Athens 1859, 1874[2]) embrace an assortment of pieces in ancient Greek, from metrical translations (Catullus, Ovid, Virgil, Schiller, even modern Greek folk songs) to prose works (Tacitus' *Germania*). His original output includes various encomiastic and celebrative pieces, such as an epico-lyrical poem on the death of Lord Byron, a Sapphic Doric ode on Otto's 25th jubilee (1858), a Pindaric one on the anniversary of Otto and Amalia's wedding (1861), various anacreontics, elegies on the death of his own brother and of King Otto, as well as scoptic, epideictic, and funerary epigrams. The poems presented here belong to series of three (I) and two (II) pieces on the same subject, and attempt to cloth in ancient Greek terms (see esp. II.1 on *elektron*, but also the mythological allusions to Icarus, Zeus, Hermes etc.) the most recent achievements of science.

Biography: In his youth Philippos Ioannou (Zagora 1796 – Athens 1880) visited Constantinople and was initiated to the ideas and principles of the Philike Hetaireia, the secret society which helped prepare the Greek Revolution in 1821. He later moved to Munich where he studied classics and natural sciences, received his doctorate in 1836, and taught Greek to Prince Otto, later to become the first king of Modern Greece. In 1837 he returned to Greece and worked for the Foreign Office, only to be appointed in 1839 to the chair of philosophy at the university, where he earned several distinctions in his later years (he was also the president of the prestigious Archaeological Society from 1850 until 1879).

Bibliography: Patriarcheas, Panayotis N. (1936), *Φίλιππος Ιωάννου. Ο από καθέδρας Έλλην φιλόσοφος του 19ου αιώνος*, Athens; Michalopoulos, Andreas N. (2015), "Translating and interpreting Ovid's *Heroides* in 19th century Greece", in: Kostas A. Dimadis (ed.), *Continuities, Discontinuities, Ruptures in the Greek World (1204–2014)*, II, Athens, 287–297.

Demetrios Semitelos (1830–1898)

<In monumentum Georgii G. Byron> [1881]

Βρεττανίης ὁμότιμον ἄθρει στάς, ξεῖνε, Βύρωνα
ὃν περὶ κῆρι φίλευν Μνημοσύνης θύγατρες·
τῶν δ' εὐεργεσιῶν μνῆστιν σῴζοντες ἀγήρω
Ἕλληνες στῆσαν λάϊνον ἐξ ἐράνου.
5   Εὖτε γὰρ Ἑλλὰς ἐτείρετ' ἐλευθερίης ἐν ἀέθλῳ
ἤλυθε θαλπωρὴ χάρμα τε μαρναμένοις.

Textus: litteris maiusculis inscriptum in lapide marmoreo sub statua Georgii G. Byronis in horto Heroum apud urbem Mesolongium dicata (vid. fig. 1).

Sim.: 2 περὶ κῆρι φίλευν] e.g. *Il.* 13.430 al. || 3 sim. e.g. *Anth. Pal.* 7.250.6 (ἀντ' εὐεργεσίης μνῆμ') || 6 θαλπωρή] cf. *Il.* 6.412; 10.223 al.

<On the monument of Lord Byron>

O stranger, stand and look at Byron, peer of Britain,
   whom the daughters of Mnemosyne loved from heart.
Keeping an imperishable memory of his benefacts,
   the Greeks set up a marble sculpture, each contributing his share.
[5] For when Greece was suffering in the war for its freedom,
   he came bringing hope and joy to the fighters.

Metre: Elegiac couplets (but the α in l. 2 θύγατρες is otherwise generally counted as long).

Notes: The epigram was inscribed on the statue of Lord George Gordon Byron (1788–1824) at Mesolonghi, where the English philhellene died fighting for the liberation of Greece. The statue was unveiled on 25 October 1881, and in this circumstance the poet Achilleas Paraschos declaimed a long poem. Semitelos' epigram, which blends epic reminiscences with the celebration of Byron's bravery and art, was chosen among 21 participants of a nation-wide competition.

Biography: The philologist Demetrios Semitelos (Monodendrion, Epirus 1830 – Athens 1898) studied in Athens and in Germany. He taught from 1856 at the Gymnasium of Patras and then at Athens; in 1868 he was appointed to the chair of Greek Philology at the University of Athens, a position he held until his death. Amongst his greatest achievements one should recall the edition of the Patmian scholia on Pindar, and an important historical essay on Epirus. He is recalled in the memories of several major intellectuals who were his students at the university at the time, from Alexandros Papadiamantis to Georgios Souris and Ioannis Gryparis.

Bibliography: Mavromichali, Efthimia (2007), "Εθνική ιδεολογία και νεοελληνική γλυπτική", in: Elizabeth Close et al. (eds.), *Greek Resarch in Australia*, Adelaide, 549–564.

Antonios Keramopoulos (1870–1960)

Τὸ ἀρχαιολογικὸν συμβούλιον τοῦ Ὑπουργείου Θρησκευμάτων κ. Ἐθν. Παιδείας πρὸς τὴν Γαλλικὴν Ἀρχαιολογικὴν Σχολὴν Ἀθηνῶν ἐπὶ τῇ ἑκατονταετηρίδι αὐτῆς [1947]

    Γαλλίαν αἰνέομεν, ἣ θῆκε κατ' ἄστυ Ἀθήνης
      οἶκον ἀρίγνωτον, μέρμερα δ' ἐστέγασεν
    ἀρχαίης σοφίης μελετήματ', ἰδ' ἐκπροέηκεν
      ἄνδρας ἀριπρεπέας ἐν καμάτοις ἱεροῖς.
5   Δρηστοσύνην δὲ λέγοι κε Νότος, Βορέης Ζέφυρός τε
      Ἑλλάδος ἠδ' Εὖρος, πάντες ἐπιστάμενοι·
    Θεσπιὰ καὶ Δῆλος ἱερὴ Θάσσος θ' ἁλίπλαγκτος
      Παρνάσιοι Δελφοί, Μαντινέη, Τεγέη,
    Πτώιον ἠδὲ Φίλιπποι ἰδὲ Στράτος Εἰλατίη τε,
10 Κρήτη, πόλλ' ἕτερα ἔργ' ἀγλαὰ πραπίδων,
      πάνθ' ἑκατονταετῆ Γάλλων πόνον ἄσπετον ᾄδει.
    Χαίρετε τοὶ ζῶντες, οἱ φθίμενοι μάκαρες.

                                       Ἄντων. Δ. Κεραμόπουλος ἐποίησε

Textus: *Bulletin de correspondance hellénique* 70, 1946, Supplément (Le Centenaire de l'École Française d'Athènes, Paris 1948), 222

Crit.: 7 Θάσος debuit, metri causa produxit || 9 Πτώιον ed., correxi

Sim.: 3 ἀρχαίης σοφίης] cf. *Anth. Pal.* 6.293.4 | ἐκπροέηκεν] de forma cf. Greg. Naz. *carm.*, PG 37.1503.1 || 4 ἄνδρας ἀριπρεπέας] cf. *Il.* 9.441 || 5 δρηστοσύνην] cf. *Od.* 15.321 | Νότος...Εὖρος] cf. *Od.* 5.295–296 al. || 7 Δῆλος ἱερή] cf. Ar. *Thesm.* 316 || 8 Μαντινέη Τεγέη] cf. *Il.* 2.607

The Archaeological Council of the Ministry of National Education and Cults to the French Archaeological School at Athens on its 100th anniversary

> We praise France, who established in the city of Athens
>   a famous house, accommodated there the difficult
> research in ancient wisdom, and produced
>   brilliant men thriving in hallowed toil.
> [5] Notos, Boreas, Zephyrus, and the Greek Euros might tell
>   about this activity, for they all know.
> Thespies, holy Delos, and Thasos wandering in the sea,
>   the Parnassian Delphi, Mantinea, Tegea,
> Ptōon, Philippi, Stratos, Elateia
> [10] Crete, and many more glorious works of the intellect,
> all sing the hundred-year-old hard work of the French.
>   Hail, then, to the living, let the deceased be blessed.

By Antonios D. Keramopoulos

Metre: Elegiac couplets (l. 1 Γαλλίαν might be taken as bisyllabic by synizesis; l. 10 the hiatus is harsh).

Notes: The epigram was composed by Keramopoulos on behalf of the Archaeological Council of the Ministry of Education and Cults in order to celebrate the centenary of the French Archaeological School in Athens, founded in 1846. The sites mentioned in the poem correspond to the major excavations of the French School.

Biography: The archaeologist Antonios Keramopoulos (Vlasti, Kozani 1870 – Athens 1960) studied at Athens and did post-graduate work in Germany, Italy, and Austria. He taught history of art and archaeology at Athens, and since 1904 he was head of the department of the national Archaeological Service specialising in ancient coins. He participated in many excavations, for instance in the Athenian Agora, in Mycenae, Florina, Kastoria, and Zakros. A member of the Academy of Athens, he was elected its president in 1938; he was a supporter of Metaxas' regime, and endorsed nationalistic and irredentist views, fostering the creation of a stable Greek identity through the study of the past.

Bibliography: Stephanides, Ioannis D. (2007), *Stirring the Greek Nation*, Burlington; Karamanolakis, Vassilis (2008), "University of Athens and archaeological studies", in: Dimitris Damaskos/Dimitris Plantzos (eds.), *A Singular Antiquity*, Athens, 185–195.

Stylianos Alexiou (1921–2013)

<Ad Henricum van Effenterre> [1982]

Ἐφφεντέρρε φίλε, κλεινῆς Κρήτης ξένε πιστὲ
χαίροις σὺν Μισελὶν κουριδίῃ ἀλόχῳ·
ἀλκὴν σὴν πολέμῳ Λίλλης πεδίον μὲν ἂν εἴποι,
σῆς σοφίης δὲ βυθοὺς ἔργα τὰ Μαλλιακά.

Textus: Petrakos 2016, 208–209.

Sim.: 2 κουριδίῃ ἀλόχῳ] cf. *Il.* 1.114 etc. || **3** cf. Aesch. test. 162.3 Radt = *FGE* 478 Page (ἀλκὴν δ' εὐδόκιμον Μαραθώνιον ἄλσος ἂν εἴποι)

<To Henri van Effenterre>

Dear van Effenterre, faithful guest of famous Crete,
  may you be happy with your wife Micheline:
The fields of Lille might tell about your military prowess,
  your work at Mallia about the depths of your learning.

Metre: Elegiac couplets.

Notes: This epigram, the fruit of private communication, was written for the French archaeologist and epigraphist Henri van Effenterre (1912–2007), who taught for many years at the University of Caen (where he also held the post of Directeur d'Archéologie et Beaux-Arts de Normandie), and later at the Sorbonne. A hero of the French Resistance (he was badly injured in Lille during the German occupation), after the war he wrote a large number of essays on ancient Greece, some of which he co-authored with his wife Micheline; his work on the Minoan palace of Mallia remains fundamental to this day.

Biography: The philologist Stylianos Alexiou (Heraklion 1921–2013) was trained in Athens, where he received his doctoral degree in 1959. He became supervisor of antiquities in Rhodes, then moved to the Museum of Heraklion, which he directed from 1962 until 1977 when he took up teaching at the University of Crete (first archaeology, later medieval and modern Greek Literature). In 1981 he was made a supernumerary member of the Academy of Athens. He published an impressive amount of editions, essays, and publications concerning Cretan art and archaeology, the Cretan literature of the Renaissance, and Greek literature from Digenis Akritas to Dionysios Solomos.

Bibliography: Panagiotakis, Nikolaos (2001), "Για το έργο του Στ. Αλεξίου", in: *Nea Estia* 150, 639–644.

Fig. 2a: Bagno Vignoni (Siena, Tuscany): Greek inscription by Lattanzio Tolomei on the porch of the bath (see below, p. 105–107).

Fig. 2b: Bagno Vignoni: Loggiato di Santa Caterina, where the inscription by Tolomei is installed.

Filippomaria Pontani
Italy

The surge of Italian humanism in the early 15th century[1] was made possible by the cross-fertilisation of two momentous inputs, namely a genuine, renewed interest for antiquity and the classical world (embodied by Francesco Petrarca, who notoriously deplored his inability to read Plato and Homer), and the contribution of the Byzantine émigrés summoned to teach ancient Greek in various Italian cities and universities, starting with Manuel Chrysoloras' appointment in Florence in 1397.[2] This extraordinary cultural phenomenon, to which we owe much of the extant heritage of ancient Greek literature, resulted in the rise or growth of several public and private libraries, and in a massive wave of translations from ancient works,[3] but it proved less successful in providing the pupils with sufficient skills for autonomous composition in that language. This is after all understandable if we take into account that, despite all the efforts devoted to grammatical teaching and the production of handbooks and lexica,[4] thorough linguistic competence was hard to achieve, and that even in the Byzantine tradition versification in ancient Greek style and metre (hexameter, elegiac couplet, not to mention lyric metres) represented the exception rather than the rule (→ **Greece**).

Of course we do possess a number of epigrams and poems written by Byzantine scholars in Italy (from Theodore Gaza to Andronikos Kallistos, from John Argyropoulos to Demetrios Chalkondylas), but seldom did the impulse to emulation find its way to their Italian pupils. If we neglect some uncertain *terzine* jotted down *ex tempore* by the great epigraphist and antiquarian Ciriaco of Ancona (1391–1452),[5] the earliest attempts in this field stem from one of the few intellectuals who moved

---

[1] This introduction largely summarises Pontani 2017. No complete study of Greek poetry in Italy has been produced after the (largely unreliable) Crasso, Lorenzo (1678), *Istoria de' poeti greci e di que' che'n Greca lingua han poetato*, Napoli.
[2] There are many accounts of this process: perhaps the most obvious reference works are Wilson 1992 and Cortesi, Mariarosa (1995), "Umanesimo Greco", in: *Lo spazio letterario del Medio Evo* III, Roma, 457–508.
[3] See e.g. the inventory of Cortesi, Mariarosa/Fiaschi, Silvia (eds.) (2008), *Repertorio delle traduzioni umanistiche a stampa (secoli XV–XVI)*, Firenze, and some special case-studies (Fryde, Edmund B. (1996), *Greek Manuscripts in the Private Library of the Medici*, Aberystwyth; Fiaccadori, Gianfranco (ed.) (1994), *Bessarione e l'Umanesimo*, Venezia), as well as Staikos, Konstantinos Sp. (1998), *Charta of Greek Printing*, I, Cologne 1998.
[4] Botley, Paul (2010), *Learning Greek in Western Europe 1396–1529*, Philadelphia.
[5] Pontani, Anna (1994), "I *Graeca* di Ciriaco d'Ancona", in: *Thesaurismata* 24, 37–148: 70–71 and 75–76.

to Constantinople for some years (1420–1427), namely **Francesco Filelfo** (1398–1481): his sylloge by the title of *De psychagogia* (three books of elegies and Sapphic odes), albeit largely unknown and unpublished until as late as 1997, stands out today as a real *première* in Western culture. Indeed, Filelfo declaredly wished to introduce Greek versification in the Latin world, a practice for which he could find no real parallel in either ancient or modern times (the few epigrams by Germanicus, Hadrian, or Julia Balbilla representing marginal exceptions).[6] His ambition was thus to ground in Western culture a new kind of 'poetic bilingualism';[7] while we may remain sceptical about the outcome of this challenge (most of Filelfo's encomiastic pieces sound empty and partly awkward to our ears), it certainly commands respect in an age when Greek literature was still a largely uncharted territory.

The scholar who managed to surpass Filelfo's achievement by far was the greatest connoisseur of Greek in the entire Quattrocento, and one of the key figures of Florentine humanism, namely **Angelo Poliziano** (1454–1494): his *Liber epigrammatum Graecorum* (in the posthumous *Opera* of 1498: but the first epigrams belong to Poliziano's teens), the fruit of a refined meditation on various ancient Greek prototypes (from Homer to Theocritus, from Nonnus to the *Greek Anthology*), is not only the first book of original Greek poetry to be printed in the West, but also a masterpiece in terms of poetic skill: it witnesses to that long-standing interchange between three languages (Italian, Latin, and Greek) which characterised the author's poetic and philological activity. Poliziano's Greek verse, embracing love poems, sceptic and encomiastic pieces, and plausible imitations from the *Greek Anthology*, proceeded not only from the ambition to startle the audience through the novelty of such a feat of learning, but also from the conviction that no decent Greek poetry had been produced over the last six centuries (not even in Byzantium), and that versification was conducive to a better acquaintance with the workings of Greek language and style.[8] Incidentally, the latter idea was shared by Poliziano's great rival Ianos Laskaris (→ **Greece**), an

---

6 See Hutchinson, Gregory O. (2013), *Greek to Latin*, Oxford, 135–146; Adams, James N./Janse, Mark/Swain, Simon (eds.) (2003), *Bilingualism in Ancient Society*, Oxford.
7 I use the term in the sense of Traina, Alfonso/Paradisi, Patrizia (2006³), *Il latino del Pascoli: saggio sul bilinguismo poetico*, Bologna.
8 *Epist.* 5.7 to Antonio Codro Urceo: *Non enim poema reperitur ullum citra sexcentos annos a Graecis conditum, quod patienter legas...Prius tamen illud testabor, me non ideo certasse cum tam praeclaris ingeniis, quae diu comprobavit antiquitas, praesertim in arena ipsorum, quod inde mihi victoriam vel sperarem, vel quaererem: sed quod hoc magis videbar illa cogniturus, quo minus in experiundo consequerer.* See Pontani 2002, xxiv–xxvi. On the problematic negotiation between Classical and Byzantine Greekness during the Italian Renaissance see now Lamers, Han (2015), *Greece Reinvented. Transformations of Byzantine Hellenism in Renaissance Italy*, Leiden/Boston.

outstanding philologist and diplomat who, throughout his long life, practised an even more ambitious, allusive, and partly obscure poetic style (his book of epigrams was published in 1527).[9]

This historical moment proved essential for European humanism for a number of reasons, and above all because it marked the rediscovery of the *Greek Anthology*, which was edited by Laskaris in Florence in 1494.[10] On the one hand, Poliziano's example was followed by some of his pupils and by other Tuscan intellectuals at the turn of the century, from **Scipione Forteguerri Carteromaco** (1466–1515) to **Lattanzio Tolomei** (1487–1543) and Andrea Dazzi,[11] who all displayed their Greek vein in well-thought occasional encomiastic or epideictic epigrams, or even (this is particularly Forteguerri's case) in the peculiar genre of book-epigrams; indeed, the Venetian publishing house of **Aldo Manuzio** (himself a Greek poet as well as the host of the so-called *Neakademia*, a private society imposing on its members the exclusive oral and written use of Greek),[12] and particularly the prefatory materials to its memorable editions of Greek and Latin classics, represented the ideal venue for this kind of *lusus*.[13]

Yet other intellectuals of the late 15th and early 16th century derived their familiarity with Greek epigram from Laskaris: these are humanists from the North-Eastern regions of Italy (chiefly Veneto and Friuli) such as Girolamo Aleandro[14] and **Lazaro Bonamico** (1477–1552). This specific local tradition – for which the Venetian Pietro Bembo, a good writer of Greek prose but a terrible Greek poet, was no

---

9 See his words on the study of Greek in Meschini, Anna (1983), "Una prolusione fiorentina di Giano Làskaris", in: *Umanesimo e Rinascimento a Firenze e Venezia. Miscellanea V. Branca*, III, Firenze, 69–113; more recently on this kind of texts Gastgeber, Christian (2014), "Griechischstudium im italienischen Humanismus", in: *Jahrbuch der Österreichischen Byzantinistik* 64, 67–104.
10 See e.g. Lauxtermann, Marc (2009), "Janus Lascaris and the Greek Anthology", in: Susanna de Beer et al. (eds.), *The Neo-Latin Epigram*, Leuven, 39–63.
11 On Dazzi's epigrams see now Pontani, Filippomaria (2019), "Knocking on Charon's Door", in: *Humanistica Lovaniensia* 68, 297–315.
12 On this institution, and on its *Nomos* written by Forteguerri, see Dionisotti, in Orlandi/Dionisotti 1975, xliii; Lowry, Martin (1979), *The World of Aldus Manutius*, London, 195–199; Wilson 1992, 129–131.
13 See the beautiful collection of prefaces by Orlandi/Dionisotti 1975, and now Wilson 2016.
14 See Venier, Matteo (2009), "Aleandro, Girolamo", in: *Nuovo Liruti* II/1, Udine, 165–171, and particularly Pontani, Anna (2002), "L'umanesimo greco a Venezia: Marco Musuro, Girolamo Aleandro e l'Antologia planudea", in: Maria Francesca Tiepolo/Eurigio Tonetti (eds.), *I Greci a Venezia*, Venezia, 381–466.

initiator[15] – may have influenced the only South Italian writer of Greek verse, **Pomponio Gaurico** (long active in Padua),[16] and it survived in later times under the pen of such intellectuals as Francesco Robortello, **Giovan Battista Amalteo** (1525–1573) and **Pietro Cortona** († ca. 1598). These three authors, all active between the second and the seventh decade of the 16th century, wrote Greek poetry for different reasons: Robortello, a specialist of Greek poetic and literary genres, developed a full-fledged theory of the epigram, and practiced above all the Pindaric ode;[17] Amalteo, who also tried his hand at the Pindaric ode, inscribed his few Greek pieces in the broader frame of a sizeable encomiastic output in Latin and Italian; the little-known Cortona, who spent most of his life as a court physician in Munich, certainly resented the growing popularity of Greek verse in German-speaking countries – hence probably the idea of publishing in 1555, for the first time after Poliziano, an entire book of *Varia carmina Graeca* embracing pieces devoted to both Italian and Bavarian friends, from Venetian noblemen and Dogi, to Joachim Camerarius (→ **Germany**) and the Fugger family.

However, by the mid-16th century the merry times of Italian humanism, when pagan and even licentious poetry could stand side-by-side with more serious and even religious pieces, had long expired, and Italy had lost its leading role in Classical studies to the advantage of other competitors, chiefly France, the Low Countries, and Germany. The European spread of Greek language and literature benefited from the more stable institutional support of e.g. the Collège Royal in Paris and the *Collegium Trilingue* in Leuven – nothing of that size and scale could have been conceived in any of the small Italian states, particularly since the country had become a battlefield for the territorial ambitions of other European nations.[18] More importantly, however, the very knowledge of Greek fell the victim to

---

15 Pagliaroli, Stefano (2013), "Per gli studi greci di Pietro Bembo", in: Howard Burns et al. (ed.), *Pietro Bembo e le arti*, Venezia, 89–118, esp. 93–96. Wilson, Nigel G. (ed.) (2003), *Pietro Bembo. Oratio pro litteris Graecis*, Messina. Pontani 2017, 318–319.
16 Gallo, Italo (1990), "Pomponio Gaurico e la poesia umanistica meridionale in lingua greca", in: *Res publica litterarum* 13, 93–100.
17 On Robortello see Carlini, Antonio (1967), *L'attività filologica di Francesco Robortello*, Udine, and Hutton 1935, 60–62; on his Βιοχρησμῳδία see Päll, Janika (2017), "The Transfer of Greek Pindaric Ode from Italy to the Northen Shores", in: Stefan Weise (ed.), *HELLENISTI! [...]*, Stuttgart, 349–368.
18 See, most generally, Saladin, Jean-Christophe (2000), *La bataille du grec à la Renaissance*, Paris; Momigliano, Arnaldo (1960), "L'eredità della filologia antica e il metodo storico", in: Id., *Secondo contributo alla storia degli studi classici*, Roma, 463–480; Id. (1988), "Introduzione", in: Karl Christ/Arnaldo Momigliano (eds.), *L'antichità nell'Ottocento in Italia e Germania*, Bologna/Berlin, 10.

the stern confrontation between the danger of the Lutheran Reform and the Counter-Reformation. The increasing mistrust towards a direct, personal approach to the Holy Writ (and to the New Testament in particular), along with the growing centrality of the Jesuit curriculum (the *Ratio studiorum*, while emphasising a strong mastery of Latin, left a relatively small space for the teaching of Greek, and an even smaller one for autonomous exercise in that language),[19] entailed a rapid decay of Greek studies on Italian soil. While the story of this decline has never been told in depth (the most recent overview dates back to 1941),[20] and while we should beware of apportioning blame only to the Counter-Reformation for the decline of Italian humanism,[21] it is doubtless that the wealth and variety of Greek poetic output petered out relentlessly decade after decade, in the same years when they blossomed elsewhere in the continent.

Two exceptions should be singled out: one is the Benedictine monk **Tito Prospero Martinengo** (†1594), the only Italian who wrote an entire book of lengthy Greek odes praising Christ, the Virgin Mary, the Saints, the Holy Spirit, etc. (1582); it may be no chance that this remarkable feat of erudite poetry, carried out with a very special literary taste, and refined through an unprecedented familiarity with Hellenistic and imperial hexametric poetry, stems from a monk whom the Inquisition put on trial for heresy and for his alleged sympathy for the reformed faith – incidentally, Martinengo was a contemporary of the Ferrarese 'Calvinist amazon' Olympia Morata (→ **Germany**). Another exception to the decline of Greek versification comes from the heart of the Roman curia, and is represented by the *milieu* of **Maffeo Barberini** (from 1623 Pope Urban VIII): both Barberini himself and some intellectuals of his court produced short *virtuoso* compositions in various metres, of encomiastic, ekphrastic or paraphrastic content. Amongst the authors of this circle number both Greeks such as Leone Allacci (→ **Greece**), and Italians of Greek descent (e.g., **Francesco Arcudi** and **Gregorio Porzio**), often trained at the Collegio Greco of Rome:[22] it is to be regretted that, despite the active presence of learned scholars from the Ionian islands, from Crete and continental Greece in various Italian cities (not only Rome, but also Florence, Padua, and Venice; → **Greece**), so little cross-fertilisation took place.

---

19 Benedetto, Giovanni (2013), "Rifar da capo: l'istruzione classica dopo l'Unità", in: Carlo G. Lacaita/Mariachiara Fugazza (eds.), *L'istruzione secondaria nell'Italia unita*, Milano, 65–87: 72–73. Pontani 2017, 321–324.
20 Curione 1941.
21 See e.g. Monfasani, John (2015), "The Rise and Fall of Renaissance Italy", in: *Aevum* 89, 465–481; Ricci, Saverio (1997), "La crisi dell'Umanesimo italiano", in: Enrico Malato (ed.), *Storia della letteratura italiana*, V, Roma, 57–109.
22 Tsirpanlis 1980.

Since the second half of the 17th century, academies played an essential role for the preservation and the production of culture in several Italian centres: however, the scholars who could boast some active familiarity with Greek verse were very few, e.g. the Pisan professor Benedetto Averani (from the Accademia degli Apatisti in Florence), who wrote a series of 86 dissertations on the epigrams of the *Greek Anthology*, and the Benedictine monk from Naples Giovan Battista de Miro.[23] The latter, whose 1695 ode to Cardinal Gaspare Carpegna is a fine Pindaric cento, was a member of the glorious Accademia dell'Arcadia in Rome: many of his fellow academics also tried their hand at writing Greek verse, with embarrassing results marred by all sorts of prosodical, metrical and grammatical flaws.[24]

The antiquarian revival in several cities of 18th-century Italy (Scipione Maffei in Verona, Angelo Maria Bandini in Florence, Jacopo Morelli in Venice, Giovan Battista Mingarelli in Bologna, the Tipografia del Seminario in Padova) did not entail a real erudite interest in Greek versification:[25] the latter had to wait for external reagents, which appeared at the end of the century. The Bolognese professor **Clotilde Tambroni** (1758–1817), celebrated by her contemporaries as *Sappho rediviva*, probably inherited the impulse to write a number of (conventional and encomiastic) Greek odes from her teacher, the Spaniard Jesuit Manuel Aponte (→ **Iberia**).[26] The Neapolitan Hellenist and papyrologist **Pasquale Baffi** (one of the intellectuals killed in the bloody repression of the 1799 revolution against the Bourbons) was probably inspired to write a Greek Pindaric ode for Catherine II of Russia by his contacts with the lively local Greek community and by his contacts with many European colleagues (from Zoega to Villoison) with whom he debated *per epistulas* on the treasuries revealed by the newly discovered Herculaneum papyri: in an age when Naples was the most important centre of Greek studies in Italy, the Greek form given to this political manifesto of support to Catherine's ideal of enlightened rule is a remarkable fact.[27]

---

23 See Pontani 2017, 327–330. Hutton 1935, 52–53 and 377–381.
24 See the annotated edition by Zoras, Gerasimos (1994), *Ἑλληνόγλωσσα στιχουργήματα Ἰταλῶν λογίων (ΙΖ' – ΙΘ' αἰῶνες)*, Athina.
25 See Curione 1941, 71–85 and Mancini, Augusto (1939), "Spirito e caratteri dello studio del greco in Italia", in: *Italia e Grecia*, Firenze, 409–424: 417–421.
26 See Tosi, Renzo (2002), "Appunti sulla storia dell'insegnamento delle lingue classiche in Italia", in: *Quaderni del CIRSIL (Bologna)* 2, 1–6. Degani, Enzo (1989), *Da Gaetano Pelliccioni a Vittorio Puntoni*, Bologna.
27 See La Torraca, Umberto (2012), *Lo studio del greco a Napoli nel Settecento*, Napoli. See d'Oria, Filippo (1989), "Arcadia e fillelenismo a Napoli nel Settecento: Tommaso Stanislao Velasti", in: *Italoellenika* 2, 253–266; d'Oria, Filippo (1999), "Greco classico e greco volgare nella tradizione

However unsystematic, the strength of this erudite tradition should not be underrated: in few other European countries did no less than three outstanding 19th-century poets try their hand at writing Greek verse. The first published poem of a 19-year-old **Giacomo Leopardi** (1798–1837), the greatest Italian Romantic poet and an accomplished Classical scholar since his childhood at Recanati, was an Anacreontic *Hymn to the Moon* (allegedly found in a lost Greek manuscript), which in 1817 anticipated some features of his later Italian verse on the same topic.[28] Around the same years a very young Niccolò Tommaseo, later to become the greatest collector of Greek popular ballads after Claude Fauriel, sent a Greek epigram on the Lake Garda to a priest from Brescia.[29] Several decades later, after Italy had become a unified nation and after the national legislation – amidst all sorts of criticisms and hardships – had established the study of Greek as an integral part of the humanistic curriculum,[30] a young **Giovanni Pascoli** (1855–1912) – later to become one of the best Latin poets in Europe, and a milestone of contemporary Italian literature – toyed with the idea of writing a Greek epic on Giuseppe Garibaldi's heroic deeds, of which only a few lines are extant.

Pascoli was also a professor at Bologna University: as elsewhere in Europe over the past two centuries, the practice of writing Greek epigrams became the heritage almost exclusively of university professors. While many of them – from Diego Vitrioli to Ignazio Cazzaniga, from **Luigi Illuminati** (1881–1962) to Saverio Siciliano[31] – attained uncertain results, the ability to combine a deep linguistic

---

umanistica partenopea", in: *Vichiana* s. IV, I/2, 135–154; Venturi, Franco (1979), *Settecento Riformatore*, III, Torino, 109–127.

28 On the context of Leopardi's Classical philology see Timpanaro, Sebastiano (1977), *La filologia di Giacomo Leopardi*, Firenze, and Degani, Enzo (1999), "Filologia e storia", in: *Eikasmos* 10, 279–314.

29 See Tommaseo, Niccolò/Capponi, Gino (1911), *Carteggio inedito*, ed. Isidoro del Lungo/Paolo Prunas, I, Bologna, 43. On Tommaseo's Hellenism, see most recently Maiolini, Elena (2018), *Niccolò Tommaseo. Canti greci*, Milano.

30 See Bonetta, Gaetano (1995), "L'istruzione classica nell'Italia liberale", in: G. Bonetta/Gigliola Fioravanti (eds.), *L'istruzione classica (1860–1910)*, Roma, 17–97, esp. 23 and 70–75. Cerasuolo, Salvatore et al. (eds.) (2014), *La tradizione classica e l'unità d'Italia*, I–II, Napoli.

31 See Megna, Paola (2006), "Gli epigrammi greci di Diego Vitrioli", in: Vincenzo Fera/Daniela Gionta/Elena Morabito (eds.), *La poesia latina nell'area dello Stretto fra Ottocento e Novecento*, Messina, 157–181; Renna, Enrico (2014), "Le «Meleagridi» di Ignazio Cazzaniga", in: *Atene e Roma* 8, 50–62 (but Cazzaniga's poem dates back to 1972); Gardini, Nicola (1998), *Atlas*, Milano, 11–14; Siciliano, Saverio (1998), *Ritorno al classico. Poesie in greco antico e in volgare*, Napoli, and Id. (2006), "Ἔρως καὶ ὄναρ", *Rivista di cultura classica e medioevale* 1, 207–208. The Greek verses of Filippo Maria Pontani (e.g. Id. (1982–83) "Ludicra", in: *Atti e Memorie dell'Accademia Patavina di scienze, lettere ed arti* 95, 149–157) ought to be mentioned. The free verse in ancient

and philological knowledge with a witty and refined literary skill unites two otherwise very different, indeed almost antithetic, authors. **Girolamo Vitelli**'s *Subsiciva* (1927) is a remarkable collection of Greek (and Latin) poems, stretching from mere *épigrammes d'occasion* to longer, and generally humorous, *tranches de vie*: Vitelli's philological and linguistic training – which made him an outstanding papyrologist and an experienced textual critic – was influenced by the German rather than by the Italian scholarly tradition, and this probably also explains his peculiar enthusiasm for Greek versification. In much more recent years, **Alvaro Rissa** (a pseudonym for a professor of Greek literature at the University of Genoa) has opened a new path of Greek poetry by concocting learned *pastiches* of different genres and applying terms, images, and scenes of ancient Greek epic, lyric, and tragedy to the humble reality of our present world, with a high degree of lexical creativity (sometimes bordering on 'macaronic') and with hilarious effects of paradox and parody.

General Bibliography

Curione, Alessandro (1941), *Sullo studio del greco in Italia nei secoli XVII e XVIII*, Roma.
DBI = Dizionario biografico degli Italiani, I–, Roma 1960–.
Hutton, James (1935), *The Greek Anthology in Italy to the Year 1800*, Ithaca/New York.
Orlandi, Giovanni/Dionisotti, Carlo (1975), *Aldo Manuzio editore*, Milano.
Pontani, Filippomaria (ed.) (2002), *Angeli Politiani Liber epigrammatum Graecorum*, Roma.
Pontani, Filippomaria (2017), "*Graeca per Italiae fines*. Greek poetry in Italy from Poliziano to the present", in: Stefan Weise (ed.), *HELLENISTI! Altgriechisch als Literatursprache im neuzeitlichen Europa*, Stuttgart, 311–347.
Tsirpanlis, Zacharias (1980), *Τὸ Ἑλληνικό Κολλέγιο τῆς Ρώμης καὶ οἱ μαθητές του (1576–1700)*, Thessaloniki.
Wilson, Nigel G. (1992), *From Byzantium to Italy*, London.
Wilson, Nigel G. (ed.) (2016), *Aldus Manutius. The Greek Classics*, Cambridge/London.

Greek by the eccentric Milanese artist Emilio Villa (e.g. Τὰ Θήβησι τείχη/*Le mure di Tebe*, Brescia 1981), albeit inspired, is marred by a number of gross mistakes.

Francesco Filelfo (1398–1481)

Τὸν θεὸν ἐν καιρῷ ἀποδοῦναι τοῖς ἀνθρώποις μισθὸν κατὰ τὰ αὐτῶν ἔργα [1457–1465]

  Ἐλπὶς ἀνθρώπους ἀπατᾷ ματαίη,
  ἡγεμὼν οὔσπερ λόγος οὐδὲ θεῖον
  ὄμμα φωτίζει, πάθος ἀλλὰ μοῦνον
4 πάντοθεν εἴργει.
  Εἰ καὶ ὦν γαίης βασιλεὺς ἀπάσης
  ἠδὲ τοῦ πόντου, ἀνέμων καὶ ἄστρων,
  εἷς θεὸς πολλοῖς δύναμιν τυράννοις
8 πολλάκ' ἐχώρει,
  ἀλλ' ὅμως οὐδὲν τελέως ἀφῆκεν
  τούτου ἐν κόσμου πελάγει περάσσαι
  χωρὶς ἀμοιβῆς· πέλεται βροτοῖσιν
12 ἶσος ἑκάστοις.
  Οὗτος ἐν πᾶσιν φοβερὸς πολίταις
  ἔσχε τὴν γαίην ὑπὸ χειρὶ δοῦλον
  πᾶσαν ὠμώδης πάτριον, θεοῖο
16 οὐκ ἀλεγίζων.
  Ἀλλ' ὅδ' ἀνθρώπων ὑπερίσχε πάντων
  ἀξίας ὕψει, ἔτι καὶ μεγίστῳ
  χρημάτων πλήθει, βλαβεροῖς ἐν ὅπλοις
20 αἰὲν ὑπάρχων.
  Ἔστιν ἡ θείης κρίσεως βραδεῖα
  ὥρα· αὐλεῖ γὰρ κύριος δικαίου
  καιρὸν ὁ κρίνων ἀποδοὺς κατ' ἔργον
24 μισθὸν ἑκάστοις·
  ὡς πέλει θνητοῖς θάνατος μονάρχης
  ἐσθλός, ὃς μοῦνος πολέμους, ἀγῶνας
  κᾆριν ἀνθρώπων λύει ἀσεβούντων,
28 πάντα πιέζων.

Textus: Firenze, Biblioteca Medicea Laurenziana, ms. Plut. 58.15, ff. 74v–75v (manu ipsius auctoris); primum ed. Cortassa, Guido/Maltese, Enrico V. (1997), *Francesco Filelfo. De Psychagogia*, Alessandria, 135f. (III.12)

Crit.: 2 ουδέ ms. || 5 γαίης in mg. add. || 9 ὅμος vel sim. a.c. || 10 πέλαγει ms. || 25 ὥς debuit

Sim.: tit. (cf. 21–24)] cf. NT, *Apoc.* 22.12 || **2** ἡγεμών...λόγος] cf. Arist. *Magn. Mor.* 2.6.36; Men. *sent.* 68–69 J. || **2–3** θεῖον ὄμμα] scil. animae, cf. Arist. *de mund.* 391a15; Porph. *vita Plot.* 10.29; Greg. Nyss. *contra Eunom.* 2.1.626 || **4** πάντοθεν εἴργει] cf. Xen. *Anab.* 3.1.12 || **5–6** scil. de Deo omnipotente, cf. e.g. Polit. *epigr.* IX || **8** ἐχώρει] scil. παρεχώρει || **11** χωρὶς ἀμοιβῆς] de re cf. e.g. Io. Chrys. *ad pop. Antioch.*, PG 49.23d–24a || **13–20** de re cf. e.g. NT, *Apoc.* 18.16–19 || **15** ὠμώδης] hapax legomenon, cf. ὠμός || **15–16** θεοῖο οὐκ ἀλεγίζων] cf. Quint. Smyrn. 3.45 || **18** ἀξίας ὕψει] cf. Basil. *serm*. 60.29 etc. || **21–22** κρίσεως...ὥρα] cf. NT, *Apoc*. 14.7 al. || **22** αὐλεῖ] scil. prob. tuba angelorum (cf. NT, *Apoc*. 8.6) sive Dei, qui est κύριος δικαίου (cf. e.g. *Apoc*. 16.5 al.)

In due course, God gives men a reward according to their deeds

Vain hope deceives mankind
who is not enlightened by sovereign reason
nor by the divine eye, but is oppressed from all sides
[4] by suffering alone.
Even if, being the king of the entire earth,
of the sea, the winds, and the stars
the one God has often yielded power
[8] to several tyrants,
still He has never let anything pass
through the sea of this world
without due reward: He is fair
[12] to each and every man.
This man, feared by all his fellow-citizens,
has cruelly ruled over his entire
native land, enslaving it, without
[16] any respect for God.
That other man has outdone all others
through his high honours and his huge
wealth, being always busy
[20] in noxious arms.
The time of divine judgement comes
slowly: for the ruling Lord trumpets
the time of justice, giving everyone
[24] the reward for his deeds:
death is a good monarch for mortals,
for death alone solves wars, fights,
and the strife of impious men,
[28] repressing all these things.

Metre: Sapphic stanzas, with occasional prosodical mistakes (long α in l. 11 ἀμοιβῆς, l. 28 ἀσεβούντων) and objectionable phenomena (hiatus in l. 22; crasis in l. 27 κἄριν).

Notes: In a letter to Gerolamo Castelli of April 1458, Filelfo – who beside his poems wrote more than a hundred private letters in good Attic Greek – observed that virtually no Latin had been writing Greek verse in either ancient or modern times: hence his decision to attempt this new undertaking, despite his insufficient familiarity with the secrets of Greek poetic diction. His *De psychagogia*, a collection of 44 Greek poems in three books written between 1457 and 1465, remained buried and unpublished for centuries in ms. Laur. 58.15: the author's request not to circulate these texts (the note on f. 80r reads: *hi tres libri neque aediti sunt a me Francisco Philelfo nec emendati. quare cum multa mutanda sient, ne quis ex hisce quicquam exscribat rogo*, 'these three books have not been edited nor corrected by me, Francesco Filelfo: therefore, since much has to be changed, I beg no one copy anything from here') was respected until the *editio princeps* in 1997. Alternatively elegiac couplets and Sapphic stanzas (in an age when Aeolic poetry was virtually unknown, this metre could only be emulated from Latin prototypes), Filelfo's poems are *poésies d'occasion*, and above all encomiastic pieces for his patrons, for rulers and cardinals: while it is unlikely that they could really be understood and appreciated by the addressees, they were also designed to impress Filelfo's fellow-humanists. The present ode is the only one with a purely philosophical/theological content, and it clearly takes its cue from the idea of distributive justice in a passage of John's *Apocalypse* (22.12); we can hardly detect any clear poetic reminiscence, and several prosaic expressions are drawn directly from philosophical and patristic texts; a poetic flavour is given by dialectal features such as l. 1 ματαίη, l. 15 θεοῖο, ll. 3 and 26 μοῦνος or lexical items such as l. 25 πέλει.

Biography: One of the protagonists of the first generation of Italian humanists, Francesco Filelfo (Tolentino 1398 – Florence 1481) studied in Padua and held his first teaching posts in Venice and Vicenza; he then spent seven years (1420–1427) in Constantinople as the secretary to the Venetian *bailo*, and later to the emperor John VIII Palaiologos, for whom he also served in diplomatic missions. In the East he was trained at the school of Ioannes Chrysoloras, and he collected many manuscripts which he sent back to Venice in 1427 (he numbers as one of the greatest book collectors of his age). Due to his linguistic skills, he was able to start a career as a translator (above all of prose authors such as Hippocrates, Lysias, Xenophon, Dio Chrysostom, Plutarch, Basil of Caesarea) and as a teacher of Greek in various Italian cities (Venice, Bologna, Florence, Siena, Milan, Naples, and Rome). During his Italian peregrinations, Filelfo became acquainted (sometimes in hostile terms) with many of the brightest minds and rulers of the Italian Quattrocento, from Poggio Bracciolini to Federico da Montefeltro, from Lorenzo de' Medici to Francesco Sforza: his huge epistolary is an excellent witness to the breadth of his acquaintances. One of the first Italian exegetes of Dante and Petrarch, he also wrote Latin orations, odes, and satires, an epic poem for Francesco Sforza, some philosophical and political treatises, and commentaries on Juvenal and Quintilian.

Bibliography: Viti, Paolo (1997), "Filelfo, Francesco", in: *DBI* 47, 613–626; Wilson 1992, 48–53; de Keyser, Jeroen (2015), *Francesco Filelfo and Francesco Sforza*, Hildesheim; Id. (ed.) (2015), *F. Filelfo. Collected Letters*, I–IV, Alessandria; Robin, Diana (1991), *Filelfo in Milan*, Princeton; Eleuteri, Paolo (1991), "Francesco Filelfo copista e possessore di codici greci", in: Dieter Harlfinger/Giancarlo Prato (eds.), *Paleografia e codicologia greca*, Alessandria, 163–179; Cortesi, Mariarosa (1986), "Aspetti linguistici della cultura greca di Francesco Filelfo", in: *Francesco Filelfo nel quinto centenario della morte*, Padova, 163–206. On his Greek poems: Cortassa, Guido/Maltese, Enrico V. (1997), *Francesco Filelfo. De Psychagogia*, Alessandria, 9–26; Pontani 2017, 313–315; Thomas, Oliver (2016), "Homeric and/or Hymns: Some Fifteenth-Century Approaches", in: Andrew Faulkner/Athanassios Vergados/Andreas Schwab (eds.), *The Reception of the Homeric Hymns*, Oxford 2016, 277–299; Pontani, Filippomaria (2018), "Hellenic Verse and Christian Humanism", in: *International Journal of the Classical Tradition* 25, 216–240.

Angelo Poliziano (1454–1494)

I. *18. aetatis anno*. Προσευχὴ πρὸς τὸν Θεόν [1472]

Ὦ πάτερ ἡμέτερε χρυσόθρονε, αἰθέρι ναίων,
ὦ πάντων βασιλεῦ, Θεὸς ἄφθιτε, αἰθέριε Πάν,
πάντα ἰδὼν καὶ πάντα κινῶν καὶ πάντα κατασχών,
πρεσβύτερός τε χρόνου, πάντων ἀρχή τε τέλος τε·
5   παμμακάρων δάπεδον καὶ οὐρανίων σέλας ἄστρων,
σύ, πάτερ, ἠέλιόν τε μέγαν λαμπράν τε σελήνην,
πηγὰς καὶ ποταμοὺς καὶ γῆν καὶ πόντον ἔτευξας,
πάντα ζωογονῶν, σῷ πάντα πνεύματι πληρῶν·
οὐράνιοι χθόνιοί τε καὶ οἱ ὑπένερθε καμόντες
10   πάντες ὑποχθόνιοι σὴν ἐκτελέουσιν ἐφετμήν.
νῦν δὴ κικλήσκω σὲ τεῇ κτίσις ἔνθα χαμευνάς,
ἄθλιος ὠκύμορος, Θεέ, γήϊνος ἀνθρωπίσκος,
ἀλγῶν ὧν ἥμαρτόν σοι καὶ δάκρυα χεύων.
εἰ δ' ἄγε μοι, λίτομαι, πάτερ ἄφθιτε, ἵλαος ἴσθι,
15   κἀξ ἐμέθεν δὴ κόσμου θελξινόοιο ἔρωτα
δαίμονος ἠδ' ἀπάτας καὶ ἀτάσθαλον ὕβριν ἔλαυνε·
δεῦε δ' ἐμὴν κραδίην σέο πνεύματος ἀσπέτῳ ὄμβρῳ
ὥστε ἀεί σε μόνον στέργειν, ὕπατε κρειόντων.

Textus: Angeli Politiani *Opera*, Venetiis: in aedibus Aldi, 1498, c. κκ3r (unde Pontani 2002, 38: epigr. 9)

Crit.: 2 Πάν: Ζάν Lavagnini ǁ 3 κατασχών (vel κατίσχων) Ardizzoni: κατέσχων Ald. ǁ 4–5 ipse distinxi

Sim.: 1 ὦ πάτερ ἡμέτερε] cf. *Il.* 8.31; *Od.* 1.45 | αἰθέρι ναίων] cf. *Il.* 2.412 etc. ǁ 2 ὦ πάντων βασιλεῦ] cf. Greg. Naz. *carm.* 1.1.34.1 | Θεὸς ἄφθιτε] cf. *Hymn. Orph.* 15.1 | αἰθέριε] cf. *Anth. Pal.* 9.453.1 ǁ

3 πάντα...πάντα...πάντα] cf. *Il.* 3.277 etc. || **4** πρεσβύτερός τε χρόνου] cf. e.g. Eus. *Demonstr. evang.* 4.1.3.7 | πάντων ἀρχή τε τέλος τε] cf. NT, *Apoc.* 21.6 et *Hymn. Orph.* 15.7 || **5** παμμακάρων δάπεδον] cf. *Hymn. Orph.* 19.3 | οὐρανίων σέλας ἄστρων] cf. *Hymn. Orph.* 7.1 || **6** ἥλιον...σελήνην] cf. Hes. *Theog.* 19 (371) || **7–8** πηγάς...πληρῶν] cf. Greg. Naz. *carm.* 1.1.31.5–6 || **9–10** cf. NT, *Matth.* 6.10 | οὐράνιοι χθόνιοί τε] cf. *Hymn. Orph.* 1.2 etc., necnon Greg. Naz. *carm.* 1.1.3.6 et 4.41 | οἱ ὑπένερθε καμόντες] cf. *Il.* 3.278–279 || **11** χαμευνάς] cf. *Il.* 16.235 al. || **12** ὠκύμορος] cf. *Il.* 1.417 || **13** δάκρυα χεύων] cf. Greg. Naz. *carm.* 1.1.34.17 || **14** εἰ δ' ἄγε μοι] cf. *Il.* 6.376 et *Od.* 4.382 | λίτομαι...ἴσθι] cf. Greg. Naz. *carm.* 1.1.34.14 et 19 || **15–16** cf. NT, *Matth.* 6.13 | θελξινόοιο] cf. fort. Musae. 147 | ἀτάσθαλον ὕβριν] cf. *Od.* 16.86 et 24.352 || **17** ἀσπέτῳ ὄμβρῳ] cf. *Il.* 13.139 et 3.4 || **18** ὕπατε κρειόντων] cf. *Il.* 8.31; *Od.* 1.45

Written at the age of 18. Prayer to God

O, our Father living in the aether on a golden throne,
king of all, immortal God, ethereal Pan,
You who see, move, and master everything,
older than time, beginning and end of all things:
[5] You, Father, made the floor of the blessed
and the splendour of the heavenly stars, the great sun and the bright moon,
the springs and the rivers, the earth and the sea,
giving life to everything, filling everything with Your spirit;
those living in heaven and on earth, and the dead below,
[10] under the earth, all execute Your order.
Now I invoke You, here, Your creature lying on the ground,
a small, wretched, quickly-dying man made of earth, my God,
suffering and shedding tears for my sins against You.
Please, o imperishable Father, be gracious towards me,
[15] and drive away from me the love of the mind-beguiling world,
the deceptions of the devil and the wicked insolence:
cleanse my heart through the unceasing rain of Your spirit
so that I may love You alone, o highest of masters.

II. *MVIID.* Εἰς Ἀλεξάνδραν τὴν ποιήτριαν [1493]

Ἠλέκτρην ὑπέκριν' ὁπότ' ἄζυξ ἄζυγα κούρην
  κούρη Ἀλεξάνδρη τήν γε Σοφοκλεΐην,
θαμβέομεν πάντες πῶς εὐμαρὲς Ἀτθίδα γλῶτταν
  ἤπυεν ἀπταίστως, Αὐσονὶς οὖσα γένος,
5   πῶς δέ γε μιμηλὴν προΐει καὶ ἐτήτυμον αὐδήν,
  τἀκριβὲς ἐντέχνου τήρεε πῶς θυμέλης,
πῶς ἦθος δ' ἐφύλαττεν ἀκήρατον· ὄμματα γαίῃ
  πήξασ' οὐδ' ὁρμῆς ἤμβροτεν, οὐ βάσεως·
οὐδ' ἀσχημόνεεν φωνὴν βαρύδακρυν ἰεῖσα,
10   βλέμματι μυδαλέῳ σὺν δ' ἔχεεν θεατάς.

πάντες ἄρ' ἐξεπλάγημεν· ἐμὲ ζῆλος δ' ὑπένυξεν
ὡς τὸν ὅμαιμον ἑῆς εἶδον ἐν ἀγκαλίσιν.

Textus: Angeli Politiani *Opera*, Venetiis, in aedibus Aldi 1498, c. κκ5v (unde Pontani 2002, 129: epigr. 28)

Crit.: 12 ἐῆς Ald., corr. Del Lungo

Sim.: 1 ἄζυγα κούρην] cf. Nonn. *Dion.* 1.345 etc. (Theoc. *Id.* 27.7) || **3** Ἀτθίδα γλῶτταν] cf. Nonn. *Dion.* 37.319 et 19.99 || **4** Αὐσονίς] cf. *Anth. Pal.* 2.305 || **7** ἦθος...ἀκήρατον] cf fort. Plat. *Leg.* 5.735c || **7–8** ὄμματα...πήξασ'] cf. e.g. *Il.* 3.217; Ap. Rhod. *Argon.* 3.22, 422 || **9** ἀσχημόνεεν] cf. fort. Long. *subl.* 3.5 | βαρύδακρυν] cf. *Anth. Pal.* 2.221; 9.262.5; Nonn. *Dion.* 35.16 || **10** βλέμματι μυδαλέῳ] cf. Soph. *El.* 166 || **11** ὑπένυξεν] cf. Theoc. *Id.* 19.3 || **12** ἐν ἀγκαλίσιν] cf. *Anth. Pal.* 9.517.6

1493. On Alexandra the poetess

When the young maid Alexandra played on stage
  the young maid Electra of Sophocles,
we were all amazed at how naturally and correctly
  she spoke Attic, being Ausonian by birth,
[5] at how imitative and genuine a voice she uttered,
  how she followed the good rules of stagecraft,
how she kept an undefiled character: fixing her eyes
  to the ground, she never missed a gesture or a step;
nor did she misbehave when giving out a tearful utterance,
[10] and by her wet gaze she troubled the spectators.
We were all surprised: and I felt some jealousy
  as I saw her brother in her arms.

III. 1493. Εἰς τοὺς κώνωπας

Τοὺς κώνωπας ἐρᾶν μᾶλλον πρέπει ἠέπερ ἄνδρας,
  φύντας τῶν γονίμων ὡς Κύπρις ἐξ ὑδάτων,
καὶ μιμησαμένους ἀερσιπότητον Ἔρωτα
  εἰρεσίῃ πτερύγων τῷ τ' ἔμεν αἱμοπότας,
5 τὸν κῶμον τ' ᾄδοντας ἐγερσιγύναικα πλανήτην,
  αἰνῶς ὑπναπατῶν ἱεμένους ὀάρων,
ἐς λέχος ἐμπταίοντας, ἐπ' αὐτοὺς πολλάκι μαστούς,
  κἀμφαφόωντας ὅλης ἅψεα θηλυτέρης,
ψαύοντας χειλῶν τε καὶ ἐκμυζῶντας ὀπωπῆς
10 μαρμαρυγάς, γλώσσης τ' ἠρέμα γευομένους,
  ἀγρύπνους, ἰταμούς, σκοτοδερκέας· ἆρά τις ἀνδρῶν
  ὅσσα γε κώνωπες δείγματ' ἔρωτος ἔχει;

Textus: Angeli Politiani *Opera*, Venetiis: in aedibus Aldi, 1498, c. κκ8v in Libro Epigrammatum Graecorum (Ald.) et cc. q3r–4v in Libro Epistularum XII.8 (Epist.) (vide Pontani 2002, 129: epigr. 57)

Crit.: Tit. om. Epist. || **4** εἰρεσίῃ Epist.: εἰρεσίους Ald. | ἔμεν' Ald.: ἔμεν Epist. || **5** κῶμόν τ' recte Del Lungo || **7** ἐπ' Ald.: ἐς Epist. | μασθους Epist. || **8** κάμφαφόοντας Epist. | ἄψεα Epist. || **9–10** om. Ald. || **9** ἐκμυξῶντας Epist., corr. Del Lungo || **11** ἆρα τίς Epist.

Sim.: 2 γονίμων…ὑδάτων] cf. Plut. *qu. conv.* 664d et fort. *Anth. Pal.* 9.277.6 || **3** ἀερσιπότητον] cf. Hes. *Op.* 777 et e.g. Nonn. *Dion.* 33.86 || **4** εἰρεσίῃ πτερύγων] cf. Luc. *musc. enc.* 2 | αἱμοπότας] cf. *Orac. Sib.* 8.94; Vett. Val. 2.17.87; Suid. αι 207 || **5** κῶμον τ' ᾄδοντας] cf. fort. Suid. κ 2252 | ἐγερσιγύναικα] cf. *PMG* 1003 Page || **6** ὑπναπατῶν] cf. *Anth. Pal.* 5.197.2 || **7** ἐμπταίοντας] cf. Lycophr. 105 || **8** ἄψεα θηλυτέρης] cf. *Anth. Pal.* 5.218.6 || **9–10** ὀπωπῆς μαρμαρυγάς] cf. e.g. Nonn. *Dion.* 30.255; *Anth. Pal.* 2.281–282; Opp. *C.* 3.349–350 || **11** ἰταμούς] cf. *Anth. Pal.* 9.440.12 | σκοτοδερκέας] cf. Suid. ζ 106 || **12** δείγματ' ἔρωτος] cf. Luc. *dial. mer.* 8.1.4 et Jo. Chrys. *epist. ad Olymp.* 10.6.45–46

1493. On mosquitos

> Mosquitos must certainly love more than men do:
>   they are generated, like Venus, from fertile waters,
> they imitate high-soaring Eros by the rowing
>   of their wings and by drinking blood,
> [5] they sing the wandering revel-song that wakes up women,
>   they are badly fond of sleep-deceiving encounters,
> they fall in beds, often on the very breasts,
>   and touch all around the limbs of the female body,
> they skim lips, suck the sparkles of the gaze,
> [10] they slowly savour the tongue,
> being sleepless and reckless, and seeing in the dark: can any man
>   show as many signs of love as mosquitos?

Metre: Hexameters (I) and elegiac couplets (II and III): while the latter two epigrams are flawless (the only exception is the wrong quantity of the α in II.10 θεατάς and in III.3 ἀερσιπότητον), the earlier piece, whose poetic texture is less fluid, displays some prosodical mistakes (the clausula of l. 2 that creates a στίχος μείουρος; l. 3 κινῶν; l. 6 σύ) and some ugly hiatuses (ll. 1, 2, 9, 15 etc.; note in l. 5 the absence of *correptio epica*).

Notes: Poliziano's *Liber epigrammatum Graecorum* – the second book of this kind after Filelfo's *De psychagogia*, and the first one to reach the press in 1498 – contains 57 pieces (+ the answer of Alessandra Scala to epigram 30, most probably written or at least inspired by Alessandra's other teacher and admirer Ianos Laskaris, rather than by her future husband Michael Marullus). With one exception (epigr. 27 sculpted on a stone in the house of Giovanni Ciampolini in 1490), these texts date back to two distinct periods of the author's life: the youthful epigrams written in 1471–81, and a later output of 1493–94. Although the edition of the *Liber* was curated by Zanobi Acciaiuoli in 1495 after the author's premature death (and then collected in the 1498 Aldine edition of the *Opera*), we know from Poliziano's letters (especially *epist.* 5.7 to Antonio Codro Urceo, of June 1494) that the book had been prepared by the author himself; we also possess some autographs of single poems jotted down in the author's later years. While the texts of these epigrams show that Poliziano improved his poetic skill over the years, passing from a period of Homeric and partly bucolic inspiration to a deeper familiarity with the style of the Greek epigrammatists and of Nonnus of Panopolis, the variety of the texts gathered in the *Liber* is quite impressive in terms of both genre (encomiastic, erotic, epideictic, scoptic) and metre (hexameters, elegiac couplets, iambics, phalaecian hendecasyllables).

The tradition of paraphrasing Christian prayers in (ancient) Greek verse is a long and prolific one, from Nonnus of Panopolis through Markos Mousouros. Epigram 9 of the *Liber* (our no. I) takes its cue from the *Pater Noster* (NT, *Matth.* 6.9–10), and clothes the most important prayer of the Christian faith in epic garments (see above all ll. 1 and 18, each featuring a hemistich of the same Homeric formula); however, the intermingling of pagan and Christian sources emerges in borrowings from the *Orphic Hymns* (ll. 4–5, 9) side by side with quotations from poems of Gregory of Nazianzus (ll. 2, 7–8, 14) – more precisely, from the same poems that Marsilio Ficino had copied in the last folia of ms. Vat. Borg. gr. 22. And it was probably the Orphic tradition of Pan as the god of 'All' that induced Poliziano to apply this very theonym to the Christian God (l. 2). This shows that, albeit not engaging in any deep philosophical speculation, the 18-year-old Poliziano must have nonetheless felt the influence of the Platonic circles of Medicean Florence; his epigram 9 does not represent a document of his (otherwise unlikely) commitment to Catholic faith, but rather a rhetorical paraphrase that displays both his linguistic skill and the underlying tension between the expressive modes of Hellenism and Christianism.

Our epigram II is the starting point of a cycle of epigrams (nos. 28, 30–33, 48, 50) dedicated to the beautiful and unfortunate Alessandra Scala (1475–1506), a pupil of the Studio where she attended the classes of Poliziano himself, of Demetrios Chalkondyles and of Ianos Laskaris (who also fell in love with her and wrote six Greek epigrams in honour of her beauty and talents). The episode here described is a historical one: Alessandra's performance of *Electra* in a recitation of

Sophocles' play in the Scala mansion in Florence in 1493, before an audience packed with learned men and *familiares*. In a long Latin letter to the Venetian noblewoman Cassandra Fedele, Poliziano recalled this event with even more emphatic overtones: *Erat in verbis lepos ille Atticus prorsus genuinus et nativus, gestus ubique ita promptus et efficax...Verecunde omnia et pudenter, non modo ad terram demissis sed pene in terram semper defixis oculis....* The literary reminiscences of the epigram range from Homer to Theocritus to Nonnus, and are augmented by exact references to the play (beside the verbal echo of l. 10, l. 12 refers to the scene where Electra and Orestes meet, see Soph. *El.* 1226).

Alessandra's father, Bartolomeo Scala, chancellor of the Republic of Florence, was the recipient of our epigram III, which was appended by Poliziano to a letter dealing with the grammatical gender of the term *culex* / κώνωψ (this philological debate later grew into a much broader and harsher polemic between Scala and Poliziano). As opposed to other epigrams that draw directly on prototypes from the *Greek Anthology* (e.g., 42 of the Panhellenic games, 51 on the organ, or 54–55 on Aphrodite Anadyomene and on the armed Aphrodite), this piece is the fruit of Poliziano's own invention (although the Latin text to which it responds was probably inspired by Meleager's *Anth. Pal.* 5.151), and it represents a perfect achievement in terms of stylistic elegance, of judicious inspiration from ancient sources (besides the epigrams of the *Anthology*, especially Nonnus), and of interesting neologisms *à l'ancienne* (l. 5 ἐγερσιγύναιξ, l. 11 σκοτοδερκής).

Biography: Angelo Poliziano (Montepulciano 1454 – Florence 1494) is probably the most outstanding classical scholar of Italian humanism, and the best Italian poet of the Quattrocento. Born in what is called in Latin *Mons Politianus* (hence his humanistic name), after the death of his father he moved to Florence, where he immediately displayed an extraordinary ability (his translations from the *Iliad* earned him the nickname of *Homericus adulescens*), and he got acquainted with Marsilio Ficino, John Argyropoulos, Demetrios Chalkondyles, and other Greek and Italian scholars. Under the protection of Lorenzo il Magnifico from 1473, he obtained an ecclesiastical privilege and wrote for Lorenzo's brother Giuliano the epic poem *Stanze per la giostra* (1475–78). After a short quarrel with Lorenzo (during which time he wrote the *Fabula di Orfeo* at the court of Mantova), he was summoned to Florence in 1480 as a teacher at the Studio, and started to lecture there on several Greek and Latin authors – we still possess the texts of most of his courses, as well as the invaluable *zibaldoni* in which he gathered his reading notes from ancient authors. A Latin poet (epigrams, elegies, the learned *Sylvae*), an amateur of philosophy (he followed Platonism until his 'conversion' to Aristotelianism in 1490), a prolific translator (Herodian's historical work, Epictetus'

Manual, etc.), a connoisseur of manuscripts at the Medicean Library, and a firstrate philologist (his *Miscellanea*, based on the model of Gellius' *Noctes Atticae*, tackle textual issues in a totally new manner, and break new ground in the domain of philological method), Poliziano was no easy character, and his epigrams and epistles testify to his many quarrels with colleagues and friends. The quality of his innumerable literary and scholarly achievements (in such a short life) affords him a central place in the history of Italian humanism.

Bibliography: Branca, Vittore (1983), *Poliziano e l'Umanesimo della parola*, Torino; Bausi, Francesco (2006), *Angelo Poliziano. Poesie*, Torino; Orvieto, Paolo (2009), *Poliziano e l'ambiente mediceo*, Roma; Megna, Paola (2009), *Le note del Poliziano alla traduzione dell'Iliade*, Messina; Silvano, Luigi (2010), *Angelo Poliziano. Appunti per un corso sull'Odissea*, Alessandria; Viti, Paolo (ed.) (2016), *Cultura e filologia di Angelo Poliziano*, Firenze. On his Greek poems: Pontani 2002; Pontani, Filippomaria (2018), "Hellenic Verse and Christian Humanism", in: *International Journal of the Classical Tradition* 25, 216–240; Steinrück, Martin (2018), "Metric 'mistakes' in the Greek Epigrams of Angelo Poliziano", in: Janika Päll/Ivo Volt (eds.), *Hellenostephanos*, Tartu, 318–335.

Scipione Forteguerri (1466–1515) and Aldo Manuzio (1449–1515)

I. Σκιπίωνος Καρτερομάχου [1496]

Βίβλον ὁ γραμματικῆς ἐργώδεα τήνδε πονήσας,
  Ἕλλησιν φρονέων ἶσα, Βαρῖνος ἔην,
ὅς τέχνης τε λύων γρίφους ἅμα καὶ λαβυρίνθους
  ἡγητὴς χαλεπῆς γίγνεθ' ἅπασιν ὁδοῦ.
5 Θαρραλέως βᾶτε δὴ ταύτην νέοι ἠδὲ γέροντες·
  Ἑλλάδ' ἐς αὐτὴν ἤδ' Ἰταλίηθεν ἄγει.
Μηδένα δ' ἐντεῦθεν μηδέν ποτε λήσεται ἡμῶν,
  τοῖς δ' αὖ ταῦτα σοφοῖς πᾶς τις ὅμοιος ἔσῃ·
ὅσσα μαθεῖν δ' ἄρα τις ζητήσει, τόσσα καὶ ἕξει,
10   καὶ τοῦ ἔχειν ἔσται πᾶσι μέτρον τὸ θέλειν.

II. Ἄλδου

Λῇς γνῶν' Ἡσίοδον καὶ Σιμιχίδαν καὶ Ὅμηρον
  ποιητάς τ' ἄλλως; τὰν λαβὲ πραξομέναν.
Κεὶς γὰρ Λατοΐδα γλυκερὸν δῶ κεῖς τε πορευσεῖ
  μεστά ῥ' ἀηδονέων ἄλσεα Πιερίδων.

Textus: *Thesaurus Cornucopiae et Horti Adonidis*, Venetiis: in aedibus Aldi, 1496, c. *iv r; leguntur Scipionis versus (quos ex Aldina ed. Chiti, Alfredo (1902), *Scipione Forteguerri il Carteromaco*, Firenze, 67–68) etiam in ms. Firenze, Biblioteca Medicea Laurenziana, Plut. 55.18, f. 3v (Laur.); Aldi epigramma (quod denuo ed. Orlandi/Dionisotti 1975, 13 et Wilson 2016, 36) in Aldina tantum invenitur

Crit.: I. Tit. Σκιπίωνος Πιστοριησίου Laur. || **1** ὁ om. Laur. || **2** καὶ καλὰ συντάξας οὗτος ὁ Γωαρινὸς Laur. || **6** Ἰταλίηθεν: ἀκριβέως γὰρ Laur. || **8** ἔσσῃ Laur.

Sim.: I.1 πονήσας] de verbo cf. *Anth. Pal.* 9.93.2 || **5** νέοι ἠδὲ γέροντες] cf. *Il.* 2.789 al. || **6** Ἰταλίηθεν non apud auctores (nondum innotuerat *Fragm. Epic. Hist.* 1v.2 Heitsch) || **10** cf. fort. e.g. Greg. Nyss. *apol. in hexaëm.* 69.2 μέτρον τῆς δυνάμεως τοῦ Θεοῦ τὸ θέλημα γίνεται
II.1 Λῇς] saep. apud Theoc., e.g. *Id.* 1.12 | Σιμιχίδαν] cf. Theoc. *Id.* 7.21 || **4** ἀηδονέων] de philomelis saepe, cf. e.g. Call. *Anth. Pal.* 7.80.2 (epigr. 5.2 Pf.)

By Scipio Carteromachus

> The man who realised this laborious grammar book,
>   thinking like a native Greek, was Varinus:
> solving the riddles and labyrinths of the art
>   he became for everyone a guide in this difficult journey.
> [5] Take this road confidently, o young and old,
>   for it leads from Italy straight to Greece.
> None of you will ever forget any of these doctrines,
>   and you, whoever you are, will rival the experts in these matters.
> The more one seeks to learn, the more one will have,
> [10] and for everyone the limit of learning will be his wish.

By Aldus

> Do you wish to know Hesiod, Simichidas [*scil.* Theocritus] and Homer
>   and other poets? Take this book and study it.
> You will go to the sweet house of Apollo, and to the groves
>   of the Pierides, full of nightingales.

Metre: Elegiac couplets. Both pieces are very correct (I.4: incorrect quantity in the first syllable of ἅπασιν).

Notes: Both epigrams appeared in the *editio princeps* of a book Aldus had been cherishing since the beginnings of his publishing house, the *Thesaurus Cornucopiae* (1496), a bulky sylloge of Greek lexicographical and grammatical works assembled in 1494 (this is the date of ms. Laur. 55.18, the dedication copy to Pietro de' Medici) by Poliziano's pupil (and future tutor of Giovanni de' Medici) Guarino Favorino from Camerino (†1537) with the help of the Florentine nobleman Carlo Antinori (†1503). Two more epigrams appeared on the same page of the Aldine, one by Poliziano, evoking the debt of the West towards Greece 'now lost in its labyrinths' (no. XLVII Pontani), and one by the Cretan scholar Aristoboulos Apostolis (→ **Greece**). Three of these four texts (all except Apostolis') were then republished on the first page of Favorino's later lexicographical masterpiece (the Λεξικὸν Μέγα καὶ πάνυ ὠφέλιμον / *Magnum ac perutile Dictionarium*, published by Zacharias Kalliergis in Rome in 1523); all four were engraved in stone in the funeral monument of Guarino Favorino in the cathedral of Nocera Umbra, the city of which he became a bishop in his later years (the monument was destroyed in the early 19th century, but we still possess drawings and transcriptions).

As for the *Thesaurus Cornucopiae*, largely based on ms. San Marco 303 and other grammatical manuscripts of the Medicean library, it was not only an alphabetical monolingual lexicon, but also embraced a number of minor grammatical treatises, which had been chosen and collected with a clear pedagogical goal. The Aldine edition of the *Thesaurus* is opened by a section of introductory texts, including Aldus' preface (which claims a decisive role of editing for himself and for Urbano Bolzanio from Belluno), Poliziano's Latin letter to Favorino, a Greek letter by Forteguerri, and finally the dedicatory epistle in Greek by Favorino himself to Piero de' Medici. The four Greek epigrams follow Poliziano's Latin letter: Forteguerri's text develops the commonplace of grammatical teaching as a complex journey to be undertaken with the help of a guide (i.e. the *Thesaurus* itself): the Greek diction is rather prosaic, and sometimes harsh (see the change of subject in l. 8; note the curious Doric future ἐξεῖ in l. 9). Aldus, on the other hand, who had written only one other Greek book-epigram (on Aristotle's *Organon* in 1495) and would never return to Greek verse in the rest of his life (although he did write Greek prose prefaces, e.g. to the 1503 Xenophon, the 1505 *Horae* and the 1514 Suda), insists here on the importance of the *Thesaurus Cornucopiae* for the study of ancient Greek poetry, and adorns his lines with a very prominent, if not entirely consistent Doric patina (see the reference to Theocritus in l. 1; particularly disturbing is the untenable genitive ἀηδονέων in l. 4; πραξομέναν in l. 2 must refer to an implicit βίβλον, and be intended in a passive sense, 'to be studied').

Biographies: Scipione Forteguerri (Pistoia 1466–1515), known since 1495 by his humanist name of Carteromaco, was trained in Rome and then particularly in Florence, where he became one of the dearest pupils of Angelo Poliziano. After studying philosophy in Padova, he moved to Venice where he cooperated with

Aldo Manuzio, both in the philological care of his editions and in the management of the so-called 'New Academy' (*Neakademia*, 1502–1505), a peculiar institution which imposed spoken ancient Greek on its members, and whose statutes he also famously wrote in Greek; during this period Forteguerri printed a short oration in support of Greek studies in the West. In his later years he was active as a teacher and a translator (Aelius Aristides, Ptolemy's *Geography*), and he travelled a lot in various Italian cities; most of his Greek and Latin books entered the Vatican Library shortly after his death.

While originally a grammarian (he printed a Latin grammar in 1493 and he left behind an unpublished Greek grammar), Aldo Manuzio (Bassiano Romano 1449 – Venice 1515), after his studies in Rome and Ferrara, moved to Venice in the early 1490s and implanted there the greatest printing house for the publication of classical authors (1495–1515). He was able to recruit for his enterprise a number of the most brilliant Greek and Italian philologists, from Markos Mousouros to the Gregoropoulos brothers, from Francesco Negri to Forteguerri himself; through the 'New Academy', established at his house in Sant'Agostin, he became acquainted with such important personalities as Erasmus of Rotterdam (→ **Low Countries**), Pietro Bembo, and Thomas Linacre, who all cooperated in various ways with his press. The sheer number, quality, and ambition of Aldo's editions of classical authors (both in the more expensive format of his early years, and in the smaller format since 1501), as well as his innovations in terms of printing technique, punctuation, italic characters etc., make the Aldine press a revolutionary enterprise in European culture, and a landmark in the history and spread of Greek cultural heritage: the *editiones principes* of Aristotle and Plato, the tragedians, Aristophanes (with scholia), Herodotus, Thucydides, the Greek orators, Athenaeus, Hesychius, and many others, will remain essential points of reference for all later editions and scholarly works.

Bibliography: Piovan, Francesco (1997), "Forteguerri, Scipione", in: *DBI* 49, 163–167; Chiti, Alfredo (1902), *Scipione Forteguerri (il Carteromaco)*, Firenze; Lowry, Martin (2000²), *Il mondo di Aldo Manuzio*, Roma; Orlandi/Dionisotti 1975, esp. 13 and 201–203. Barker, Nicholas (1985), *Aldus Manutius and the Development of the Greek Script and Type in the Fifteenth Century*, Sandy Hook; Bigliazzi, Lucia et al. (eds.) (1994), *Aldo Manuzio tipografo*, Firenze; Zeidberg, David S. (ed.) (1998), *Aldus Manutius and Renaissance Culture*, Firenze; Sicherl, Martin (1997), *Griechische Erstausgaben des Aldus Manutius*, Paderborn/München; Wilson 2016, 26–37; Pontani 2002, 198–199; Villani, Eva (2013), "Il *Magnum ac penutile Dictionarium* di Varino Favorino Camerte", in: *Aevum* 87, 579–598; Ucciardello, Giuseppe (2017), "Guarini Favorini Magnum Dictionarium graecum", in: Concetta Bianca et al. (eds.), *Le prime edizioni greche a Roma (1510–1526)*, Turnhout, 171–204.

Lazaro Bonamico (1477–1552)

<*In mortem Herculis Cantelmi*> [1509–1510]

    Οὔνομα καὶ στιβαρὰν πανομοίϊος ἄρρενα χεῖρα
      κῆρ τε λεοντοπάλᾳ τῷ Διός, Ἡρακλέης,
    χῆττον ὃς οὐδὲν ἔλαμπεν ἐν ἀμφιπόλοισι θυγατρῶν,
      ἤπιος ἀλλοίας συστολίσας χάριτας,
5   Ἄρεΐ καὶ Φοίβῳ κλέος ἀμφιμάχητον ἀείρας
      κάππεσε, δουλοσύνας ῥυόμενος πατρίδα.

Textus: Milano, Biblioteca Ambrosiana, ms. D 450 inf., f. 68v (manu ipsius auctoris: hinc Pontani, Filippomaria (2015), "Sognando la Crociata", in: *Italia Medioevale e Umanistica* 56, 251–295: 256 adn. 17)

Crit.: 6 aliter in mg. versum excogitavit ipse auctor, scil. κάππεσεν ἠρεμέων ἐνθάδε κηδόμενος et mox κάππεσεν ἐν πολλοῖς μόνος

Sim.: 1 στιβαρὰν...χεῖρα] cf. *Od.* 5.454 | πανομοίϊος] cf. Nonn. *Dion.* 2.344 al.; vide *Anth. Pal.* 7.599.3 (etiam de incipit οὔνομα...) || 2 λεοντοπάλᾳ hapax leg. (cf. μουνοπάλης) || 4 συστολίσας Χάριτας] cf. *Anth. Pal.* 7.419.4 || 5 ἀμφιμάχητον] cf. Soph. *Tr.* 527 cum schol. || 6 κάππεσε] in hac sede versus cf. *Il.* 23.278 et 881, al. | δουλοσύνας ῥυόμενος πατρίδα] cf. *Anth. Pal.* 7.255.2 et 7.72.2

<On the death of Ercole Cantelmo>

    Hercules, most similar to Zeus' lion-fighting son for his name,
      his strong virile hand and his courage,
    he who shone no less brightly among the servants of Zeus' daughters,
      gently uniting them with other Graces,
    [5] having acquired a fame fought for by Ares and Apollo,
      has fallen, saving his fatherland from slavery.

Metre: Elegiac couplets (flawless).

Notes: Bonamico's Greek epigrams – mostly elegiac, but in at least one case iambic – were partly published as book-epigrams, partly unearthed in modern times from manuscripts preserved in Milan's Biblioteca Ambrosiana. The present poem features along with other Latin and Greek autograph writings in ms. Ambr. D 450 inf.: on the lower half of f. 68v, otherwise occupied by the rough draft of a Latin letter and by a chaotic jumble of unruly *scriptiunculae*, our text is surrounded by a series of hemistichs or poetic formulae (all Greek, except Propertius 2.7.19). These fragments (e.g., σὺ δέ γ' ἄτεγκτε πολύστονε βάρβαρε, χρήσων τοσσούτων πληθόμενον χαρίτων, αὐτὰρ ἄνοπλον ὅτι κτείνας, σοὶ μόρος ἀμπλακίης οἷος ἐπικρέμαται, εἰ γάρ γ᾽ ἃ δείλαιε Θεῶ νόμος ἔμπεδον εἴη, οὐ γὰρ ἀρηϊφίλων γένος ἄφθιτον οὐ γὰρ ἀοιδῶν: the latter may indeed have been intended as a continuation of our epigram) were probably jotted down by the author to indulge his poetic vein. The epigram is dedicated to Ercole Cantelmo, the offspring of a wealthy family from Mantova, who died during the victorious battle of Polesella (1509) between the troops of Ferrara and Venice. Cantelmo was celebrated by no less than Ludovico Ariosto as 'il più ardito garzon che di sua etade / fosse da un polo a l'altro' (*Orlando Furioso* 36.9.3); a few months later, Bonamico was hired as the preceptor to his brother Francesco. The epitaph is structured around the comparison with Heracles, the ancient hero, and it insists on the *topos* of the simultaneous excellence of the deceased in both warfare and the arts; the neologism (λεοντοπάλης) is an easy if smart reconstruction on ancient prototypes.

Biography: Lazaro Bonamico (Bassano del Grappa 1477 – Padua 1552) studied in Padua under the guide of Giovanni Calfurnio, Raffaele Regio, Niccolò Leoniceno and later of Markos Mousouros (→ **Greece**). We find him in Mantua from 1510 as the preceptor of Galeazzo Gonzaga, he was then summoned to Rome by the pope in 1521, and after the sack of Rome he went back to Venice and again Padua, where he became a lecturer in Greek and Latin at the Studio in 1530. An Aristotelian philosopher (he followed Pomponazzi) and a member of the Accademia degli Infiammati, he left a considerable poetic production in Latin (later to be read in the collective volume: Lazari Bonamici Bassanensis *Carminum liber*, Venetiis 1572); his output embraced a number of epigrams and poems dedicated to some of the leading personalities of his time, from Ranuccio Farnese to Paolo Giovio, from Marco Loredan to Reginald Pole.

Bibliography: Avesani, Rino (1969), "Bonamico, Lazzaro", in: *DBI* 11, 533–540; Piovan, Francesco (1988), *Per la biografia di Lazzaro Bonamico*, Trieste; Villani, Eva (2015), "*Notulae* e lemmi greco-latini/volgari di Lazzaro Bonamico", in: *Aevum* 89, 409–426. On his Greek poems: Meschini, Anna (1979), "Inediti greci di Lazaro Bonamico", in: *Medioevo e Rinascimento Veneto*, Padova, 51–68

Lattanzio Tolomei (1487–1543)

‹De balneo› [ca. 1510–1530]

Νηιάδες ναίουσαι ἔσω φλογιθαλπέος οἴκου,
πῦρ συνεχῶς σμίγδην ὕδασι χευόμεναι,

νάμασιν ὑμετέροισιν ἀεὶ πλείστους βαρυνούσων
ἀνθρώπων στυγεροῦ ῥυσάμεναι θανάτου,
5   χαίρετε καὶ μερόπων ἄλκαρ πτύετ' ἄφθονον ὕδωρ·
βλύζετε, ὦ καλαὶ πίδακες, ὦ ἀγαθαί,
χεύετέ τ' ἀρρώστοισιν ὑγείαν, τοῖς δὲ λοετρὸν
εὐρώστοις, ἀμφοῖν πολλὰ χαριζόμεναι.

Λακταντίου Πτολεμαίου τοῦ Σεναίου

Textus: epigramma litteris maiusculis inscriptum in porticu balnei legitur, quod nunc Bagno Vignoni in Etruria prope Senas cognominatur (cf. fig. 2ab); primum edidit Meschini, Anna (1982), "Lattanzio Tolomei e l'Antologia Greca", in: *Bollettino dei Classici* s. III, 3, 23–62: 29 adn. 19.

Sim.: 1 φλογιθαλπέος] hapax legomenon, sim. πυριθαλπής (Ap. Rhod. 4.926; *Anth. Pal.* 9.632.4; Nonn. *Dion.* 1.236 etc.) || **2** cf. Paul. Sil. *in Therm. Pyth.* 158 (ὕδωρ τε καὶ πῦρ μίγδην); nota σμίγδην hapax leg. (cf. verbum σμίγω = μίγνυμι) || **3** νάμασιν] de veriloquio Naiadum cf. *schol*. D in *Il*. 6.21; Hsch. ν 19; synag. ν 3 Cunn.; Suid. ν 14 | βαρυνούσων] adi. apud Nonn. *Par. Jo.* 6.5 tantum || **4** στυγεροῦ] cf. *Od.* 12.341, 24.14 etc. | ῥυσάμεναι θανάτου] cf. *Anth. Pal.* 9.40.6 || **8** πολλὰ χαριζόμεναι] cf. *Anth. Pal.* 10.56.8; 12.250.4

<Inscription on a bath>

O Naiads, you who dwell in a house heated by flames,
   you who unceasingly pour out fire mixed with water,
you who by your streams keep protecting
   most seriously ill men from dreadful death,
[5] hail to you! Spill out abundant water, a remedy for mortals:
   gush forth, o beautiful and propitious springs,
and pour out health for the sick and baths for the strong,
   a great benefit for the ones and for the others.

By Lattanzio Tolomei from Siena

Metre: Elegiac couplets; the quantity of the υ in πτύετε (l. 5) is wrong.

Notes: This 'pagan' invocation to the Nymphs is particularly appropriate in the context of Bagno Vignoni (a small *borgo* near San Quirico d'Orcia, in the heart of the Terra di Siena), one of the most reputed thermal sites in Tuscany down to the present day: the epigram, inscribed on the fourth pillar of the loggiato in the Piazza delle Sorgenti, is still visible and legible. The literary fiction is smart, and it probably takes its cue from a similar invocation to the Naiads in *Anth. Pal.* 9.814, as well as from a Latin inscription (*CIL* XI.2595, now lost) then preserved nearby.

The text is enriched by several echos of hexametric poetry (including the late antique one), by the paronomastic and etymological play on the Nymphs' name (ll. 1 ναίω and 3 νᾶμα), by some rare or utterly new compound adjectives (ll. 1, 3), and by the repeated oxymoric interplay between water, fire, and medicine.

Biography: The offspring of one of the wealthiest and most illustrious families of Siena, Lattanzio Tolomei (Siena 1487 – Rome 1543) was a dedicated catholic (he immediately adhered to the doctrine of Ignatius of Loyola), and an acquaintance of such important humanists and poets as Ludovico Ariosto, Reginald Pole, and Pierio Valeriano. He served as a secretary to Siena's Accademia degli Intronati, and according to some of his biographers he could boast a written and spoken knowledge of various ancient languages, including Greek, Hebrew, and Syriac. He owned a large library of Greek and Latin books, divided today, above all, between the Biblioteca Vaticana and the Bibliothèque Nationale de France. Despite his fame of learning and his conspicuous scholarly activity, his only known writings are three Greek epigrams (the present one, one in honour of the Portuguese ambassador Miguel da Silva, and one for the printer Zacharias Kalliergis, featuring in the edition of Thomas Magister's Ἀτθίδος διαλέκτου ἐκλογαί, Kalliergis, Rome 1517): his special interest for the *Greek Anthology* is documented by the abundant notes he collected in ms. Vat. Gr. 1169.

Bibliography: Mercati, Giuseppe (1926), *Scritti d'Isidoro il Cardinale Ruteno*, Roma, 138–150; Deswarte, Sylvie (1989), *Il «perfetto cortegiano» D. Miguel da Silva*, Roma, 39–51. On his Greek poems: Meschini, Anna (1982), "Lattanzio Tolomei e l'Antologia Greca", in: *Bollettino dei Classici* s. III, 3, 23–62; Gaspari, Anna (2017), "Thomae Magistri Attici Eloquii Elegantiae", in: Concetta Bianca et al. (eds.), *Le prime edizioni greche a Roma (1510–1526)*, Turnhout, 147–156: 150–154.

Pomponio Gaurico (1481/82–1528/30)

Πομπωνίου τοῦ Γαυρικοῦ ὕμνος εἰς Φαβρίκιον Βράγκειον [ca. 1512–1521]

(excerptum, vv. 34–46)

"Τέκνον ἐμόν, τί κλαίεις; τί κλαίεις, φίλε κοῦρε;
35 παῖ καλέ, τίς γε κακὸς κακὰ μήσατο σοὶ τάδε ἔργα;
φαῦλος Ἔρως, φθονέων σῷ κάλλεϊ, τοιάδε ῥέξε.
μὴ κλαίειν, φίλε κοῦρε, βίος μοῦ, μηκέτι κλαίειν·
τοῦτο μὲν ἀργαλέον νῦν νῦν καταπαύσομεν ἄλγος,
ἀλλ᾽ αὕτη πυρόεντος ἀπ᾽ ἄνθρακος ἔσσεται οὐλή.

40 Ἔσσεται ἀργαλέου φθονερὸν σημεῖον Ἔρωτος,
    καὶ δὴ τοῦθ' ἕλκος πολλῶν ἔσετ' αἴτιος ἑλκῶν,
    κουριδίαις τε κόραις καὶ ὁμηλικέεσσι νέοισι,
    οἵτινες ἱμερόεν τόδε σῆμα φιλοῦσι φιλῆσαι.
    Μὴ κλαίειν, φίλε κοῦρε, βίος μοῦ, μηκέτι κλαίειν.
45 πολλοὺς μὲν κλαῦσαι ποιήσεις εἵνεκα σεῖο,
    εἵνεκα σοῖο πόθου πολλοὶ κλαύσουσιν ἐρασταί."

Textus: ms. Napoli, Biblioteca Nazionale, XIII.AA.63, cc. 46r–49v (unde Gallo, Italo (1998), *Pomponio Gaurico. Inno greco a Fabrizio Brancia*, Napoli, 20–30)

Crit.: accentus libri ms. neglego (e.g. 35 σόι, 37 κλάιειν, 38 ἀργαλεον etc.)

Sim.: 34 cf. *Il.* 1.362 et 18.73 (τέκνον τί κλαίεις) | φίλε κοῦρε] cf. Theoc. *Id.* 12.1, Call. *Aet.* fr. 27 et praes. *Anth. Pal.* 16.344.1 (τίς τελέθεις φίλε κοῦρε) ‖ **35** κακὰ — ἔργα] cf. *Od.* 24.199 et 444 ‖ **36** τοιάδε ῥέξε] cf. *Il.* 5.373 et 21.509 ‖ **37** μὴ κλαίειν] cf. *Anth. Pal.* 5.43.5–6 ‖ **38** ἀργαλέον...ἄλγος] est figura etymologica, cf. *Etym. Magn.* 135.19–20 | καταπαύσομεν] cf. fort. Theogn. 1.1133 ‖ **40** ἀργαλέου...Ἔρωτος] cf. Theoc. *Id.* 1.98 ‖ **45** εἵνεκα σεῖο] cf. *Il.* 6.525, *Od.* 6.156

Pomponio Gaurico's hymn for Fabrizio Brancia

(excerpt, ll. 34–46)

> 'Oh my son, why are you crying? Why are you crying, dear boy?
> [35] Dear child, what evil man devised for you these evils?
> Bad Eros, envious for your beauty, did this.
> Don't cry, dear boy, my life, don't cry any longer:
> this dreadful pain we shall appease in short,
> though this scar made by fiery coal will remain.
> [40] It will remain as a sign of the envy of dreadful Eros,
> and this wound will be the cause of many other wounds,
> for married girls and for youngsters of your age,
> who will wish to kiss this charming sign.
> Don't cry, dear boy, my life, don't cry any longer.
> [45] You will make many people cry because of you,
> many lovers will cry because of the longing for you.'

Metre: Hexameters, with some prosodical mistakes (none in the present passage) and some metrical flaws (above all the bipartite hexameters such as here l. 34).

Notes: Probably the only South Italian humanist capable of writing Greek verse, Gaurico composed the 182 hexameters in praise of his noble pupil Fabrizio Brancia in Naples during the second decade of the 16th century. Full of conventional *topoi*, and largely occupied by Apollo's instructions to Fabrizio, Gaurico's poem (which remained unpublished until the 19th century) explains the scar on the dedicatee's face as the wound inflicted on him by Eros, envious of his beauty (the Charites and the Muses then rush to console him: our passage is the Charites' speech to baby Fabrizio). The hymn further celebrates the wealth of the Brancia family, which derived from a special privilege on the commerce of fish (later dismissed in 1522, which thus also becomes a *terminus ante quem*): in this section, Apollo enumerates all the harbours of the Naples area where the privilege is in vigour, from Amalfi to Capri and Pozzuoli (the hexameters embrace here an impressive series of Italian toponyms clad in Greek garb). Built on the imitation of epic and especially Homeric vocabulary, with some linguistic infelicities (the infinitive as imperative, l. 37 etc., is attested in classical Greek, but l. 42 ὁμηλικής is not) and some transparent Latinisms (l. 37 βίος μοῦ looks like a vocative *vita mea*, l. 38 the anaphora is modelled on *nunc nunc*), Gaurico's text presents many instances of word- and verse-repetition, with some virtuoso puns such as l. 43 φιλοῦσι φιλῆσαι. The general rhythm and style appear to be reminiscent of the contemporary Latin poetry of Sannazaro and Pontano (see especially the latter's *Naeniae*, to be compared with Herrichen → **Germany**).

Biography: Pomponio Gaurico (Gauro, Salerno 1481/82–ca. 1528/30), the brother of the famous astrologist Luca (1475–1558), was a precocious admirer of Greek language and learning. He may have travelled to Constantinople during his youth, but we know for sure that after spending his early years in Campania he studied in Padua, where in the early years of the 16th century he practised Greek language and literature together with some outstanding humanists, from Leonico Tomeo to Markos Mousouros (→ **Greece**). In his capacity as a classical scholar, between 1502 and 1504 he edited the elegies of the Latin poet Maximianus, and he published a translation of Ammonius' commentary to Porphyry's *Isagoge* (his version of Aristophanes' *Plutus* is lost). A versatile and creative talent, he also worked as a sculptor (his 1504 treatise *De sculptura* remains a landmark in Renaissance artistic literature) and as a first-rate Latin poet: he wrote eclogues and epigrams on the model of Virgil and the *Greek Anthology*, but also elegies, Sapphic odes, *sylvae* etc., later collected in the posthumous edition: Pomponii Gaurici Neapolitani *Elegiae XXIX* etc., Venice 1526. The importance of Greek models in his literary output emerges not only from some titles, e.g. the *sylvae* δυστυχία and ζωγραφία or the eclogues ἐρωτικὴ διαλλήλως and ἐρωτικὴ ἁπλῶς, not only from the very conventional Greek distich that rounds off the epigram for G.B. Ramusio (ἐνθάδε νυμφάων χορός, / ἐνθάδε Φοῖβος Ἀπόλλων, ἐνθάδε Πιερίδες, ἐνθάδε καὶ Χάριτες, *Elegiae*, c. FIv), but above all from the literary references already partly detected (with special reference to tragic poets) by Catosso Trotta in his *Annotationes* published in Naples in 1524. In his Roman years (1509–1512) he wrote an important commentary to Horace's *Ars poetica*; upon his return to Naples he held, until 1519, the chair of Greek and Latin, writing *inter alia* an apparently lost 'Greco-Latin grammar', and entering the circle of literati around Jacopo Sannazaro.

Bibliography: Bacchelli, Franco (1999), "Gaurico, Pomponio", in: *DBI* 52, 705–707; Percopo, Erasmo (1891–93), "Pomponio Gaurico umanista napoletano", in: *Atti della R. Accademia di archeologia, lettere e belle arti* 16, 145–261; Chastel, André/Klein, Robert (eds.) (1969), *Pomponius Gauricus. De sculptura*, Genève; Granese, Alberto/Martelli, Sebastiano/Spinelli, Enrico (eds.) (1992), *I Gaurico e il Rinascimento meridionale*, Salerno; Gallo, Italo (ed.) (1998), *Pomponio Gaurico. Inno greco a Fabrizio Brancia*, Napoli.

Pietro Cortona (†ca. 1598)

Εἰς ἰατρῶν ἀγέλην [1555]

Ψαῦε χερὸς καύσῳ πυρετῷ κάμνοντος ἰατρός,
    οὐδέ τι μὶν νοσέειν ὄμνυεν ἀθανάτους·
ἄλλος ἐς ἡμιθανῆ καὶ τηξιμελεῖ ἐπὶ νούσῳ
    ἦλθε μαραινόμενον φάρμακα πολλὰ φέρων,
5 καὶ τάδε πάντα κινῶν δυνατώτερα ἠὲ φορῆναι
    ἄμμιγα τῇ νούσῳ πνεῦμα συνεξέβαλεν.
Ἱπποκράτους ἄλλος προφερέστερος ἠδὲ Γαληνοῦ
    εὔχετ' ἄνουν ἀπατῶν καὶ ταχυπειθῆ ὄχλον.
ἄλλος φυσιόων κενεῇ ἐπὶ δόξῃ ἀγείρει
10   πλοῦτον ἀκηδείας τῶν θεραπευομένων.
ἄλλος ἐς ἐμπορίην σπεύδων καὶ κέρδος ἐλαφρόν
    θῆκεν ἰητήρων δόξαν ἀφαυροτέρην.
ἐστὶ δὲ καὶ φρενοπλὴξ ἄλλος μέγαν οὐρανὸν εἴσω
    κλίμακι τῆς βροτέης χειρὸς ἐελπόμενος.
15 Ὦ παιηοσύνης, πῶς ἐνθάδε κεῖται ἄτιμος
    χερσὶν ἐν οὐτιδανῶν ἠδὲ κακῶν μερόπων.
Δείδια, μὴ τὸ πάλιν, νὴ τὸν Δία, κόσμος ὀλισθῇ
    οὐ πυρός, οὐχ ὑδάτων, ἀλλ' ἰατρῶν δυνάμει.

Textus: Petri Cortonaei Utinensis *Varia Carmina Graeca*, Venetiis, Ioan. Gryphius excudebat, 1555, p. 18

Crit.: 2 οὐδέ τί μιν debuit

Sim.: 3 τηξιμελεῖ...νούσῳ] ex *Anth. Pal.* 7.234.3 | νούσῳ...μαραινόμενον] cf. *Anth. Pal.* 7.508.3 || **4** φάρμακα πολλά] cf. *Anth. Pal.* 9.212.1 || **5** φορῆναι] cf. *Il.* 2.107 al. || **7** προφερέστερος] cf. *Anth.*

Pal. 9.211.2 || **8** ταχυπειθῇ] cf. Theoc. *Id.* 2.138 et 7.38, necnon Nonn. *Par. Jo.* 4.182 (de populo) al. || **9** φυσιόων] cf. e.g. Opp. *hal.* 2.325 al.; vide Greg. Naz. *carm.* 1.2.1.369 (de κενεὴ δόξα *carm.* 2.1.2.159) || **10** τῶν θεραπευομένων] cf. *Anth. Pal.* 11.188.2 || **11** κέρδος ἐλαφρόν] cf. Greg. Naz. *carm.* 1.2.1.576 || **13** φρενοπλήξ] cf. *Anth. Pal.* 9.141.1; Greg. Naz. *carm.* 1.1.6.99 | μέγαν οὐρανὸν εἴσω] cf. *Il.* 8.549 et 1.497 || **15** παιηοσύνης] de verbo cf. Hsch. π 86 || **16** οὐτιδανῶν...μερόπων] cf. *Anth. Pal.* 9.482.1 || **18** κόσμος ὀλισθῇ] cf. *Anth. Pal.* 11.238.6

On the herd of physicians

> One doctor touched the hand of a man ill with bilious fever,
>   and swore by the gods that he was in full health.
> Another one visited a half-dead man, wasted away by a pernicious
>   illness, bringing all sorts of medicines,
> [5] and attempting all these remedies, too strong for the patient's resistance,
>   he cast out his soul along with his illness.
> Another one boasted to be better than Hippocrates and Galen,
>   taking in the stupid and credulous crowd.
> Yet another one, inflated with vain glory, grows rich
> [10] on the carelessness of his patients.
> Another one, speeding towards commerce and easy gain
>   makes weaker the reputation of physicians.
> There is also another frenzied one who hopes to get
>   to the great sky through the ladder of human hand.
> [15] O art of healing, how dishonoured you lie hereabouts,
>   in the hands of worthless and evil men.
> I fear, by Zeus, that the world may collapse again,
>   not by the force of waters or fire, but of doctors.

Metre: Elegiac couplets, with occasional prosodical mistakes (the ι in l. 5 κινῶν and l. 12 ἰητήρων, the α in l. 18 ἰατρῶν).

Notes: A smart *epigramma longum* in the long-standing tradition of the *Contra medicos* (particularly dear to the author, who was a physician himself): see e.g. *Anth. Pal.* 11.112–126; Mart. 1.47, 5.9, 8.74. The text shows Cortona's familiarity with Galen's vocabulary (e.g., l. 1 καῦσος πυρετός), but above all with the language of the *Greek Anthology* and of Gregory of Nazianzus.

Biography: Very little is known about Pietro Cortona from Udine (perhaps a relative of the painter and cartographer Giovanni Antonio Cortona, †1560; no relation of the famous Tuscan painter Pietro da Cortona): an expert in Galen and an acquaintance of some important Italian intellectuals such as Lazaro Bonamico and Vettore Trincavelli, he became the physician of the duke of Bavaria Albrecht V, and published in 1555 a book of *Varia carmina Graeca* that remains the first one of its kind after Filelfo's *De Psychagogia* and Poliziano's *Liber epigrammatum Graecorum*. Clearly influenced by his German environment, Cortona produced mostly *épigrammes d'occasion*, and amongst his addressees we find Venetian noblemen and bishops, Melanchthon and Camerarius (→ **Germany**), members of the Fugger family, Samuel Quiccheberg, and Olympia Morata.

Bibliography: Liruti, Gian Giuseppe (1830), *Notizie delle vite ed opere scritte da' letterati del Friuli*, IV, Venezia, 381; Meadow, Mark A./Robertson, Bruce (eds.) (2013), *Samuel Quiccheberg. The First Treatise on Museums*, Los Angeles, 35 and 115.

Giovan Battista Amalteo (1525–1573)

Ἰωάννῃ τῷ Αὐστρίῳ [1571]

       Στροφή
Κυδίμων Εὔκλεια καλὸν φάος ἄθλων
σὰν ἐς αὐγὰν ἐκ πολέμου δέχεο
Καίσαρος παῖδ' ἀντιθέου,
ὃν δὴ ἀγλαοῖς ἐν ἀγκώνεσσιν ἐνήνοχε νίκα,
5 Θραξὶ δεινῶς ναυμαχήσανθ' ὑπὲρ
κόλπους Ἐχινάδων ἐπὶ Τρινακρίας

       Ἀντιστροφή
πιστὸν ὅρμον, πῖνε δὲ νέκταρος εὐώ-
δεις γλυκείας ἐκ κύλικος λιβάδας
ἄρτι κιρνωσᾶν χαρίτων.
10 ἀγλαΐζεται δ' ἀεὶ κῦδος μετὰ κύκλον ἀέθλων
ἡλιειδὲς καὶ χρόνον μυρίον
ἀνθεῖ· πόνοι γὰρ εὔχεος ἐντὶ τροφοί.

       Ἐπῳδός
ᾤχετο δ' Ἰονίας περάων θαλάσσας
κύματα, καὶ πολὺν ἴθυνε στόλον
15 ἱερόν, οἷος ἔπλεεν Αἰσονίδας
Κολχίδος χρυσαυγέ' ἐς πόλιν μολών,
ἔνθ' ἀριστεύων θεοστυγεῖ ταχὺν
ἔμβαλε στρατῷ μόρον,
γηγενέων δὲ θανόντων, ὡς δράκονθ' ὕπνος δάμε,
20 χρύσεον εἶθαρ κῶας εἷλε,
καὐτοῦ εὔπλοος φαεινοῖς
ἐν ἄστροις λάμπει Ἀργώ.

Textus: Trium fratrum Amaltheorum Hieronymi, Io. Baptistae, Cornelii *Carmina*, Venetiis: ex typographia Andreae Muschii, 1627, pp. 149–150 (mox Amstelaedami: apud H. Wetstenium, 1689², pp. 103–104); Milano, Biblioteca Ambrosiana, ms. R 110 sup., f. 185v (manu ipsius auctoris)

Crit.: tit. Ἰωάννῃ Αὐστρίῳ Ἀμαλθείου εἶδος Ambr. ‖ **4** ἀγκώνεσιν Ambr. ‖ **5** δεινῶς Ambr. ‖ **6** Θρινακίας Ambr. ‖ **8** γλυκείας: χρυσείας Ambr. ‖ **11** ἡλιοειδές ed. ‖ **14** καὶ πολὺν ἴθυνε στόλον ἱερόν omiserat, in mg. add. Ambr. ‖ **15** Αἰσωνίδας a.c. ut vid. Ambr. ‖ **16** μολῶν ed. | versum toto caelo mutatum (τᾶς Ἰωλκοῦ κλεινὸν ἐς πτολίεθρον) praebet Ambr.

Sim.: 1 κυδίμων...ἄθλων] cf. Pind. *Ol.* 14.24 ‖ **4** ἐν ἀγκώνεσσιν...νίκα] cf. Pind. *Nem.* 5.42 ‖ **5–6** δεινῶς...κόλπους] cf. fort. *Od.* 5.52 ‖ **10** ἀγλαΐζεται] cf. Pind. *Ol.* 1.14 | μετὰ κύκλον ἀέθλων] cf. *Anth. Pal.* 9.468.3 ‖ **11** χρόνον μυρίον] Pind. *Isthm.* 5.28 ‖ **13** Ἰονίας...θαλάσσας] cf. Pind. *Pyth.* 3.68 ‖ **14** στόλον ἱερόν] cf. fort. *Anth. Pal.* 9.236.3 ‖ **15** ἔπλεεν Αἰσονίδας] cf. Theoc. *Id.* 13.17 ‖ **17** ταχὺν μόρον] cf. Mosch. *epit. Bion.* 26 ‖ **20** χρύσεον κῶας] cf. Pind. *Ol.* 4.231; Theoc. *Id.* 13.16 ‖ **21–22** εὔπλοος Ἀργώ] cf. Greg. Naz. *carm.* 2.1.34.71 | de Argus catasterismo cf. e.g. Arat. *Phaen.* 348–352 al.

To John of Austria

            Strophe
O Fame, shining light of glorious deeds,
embrace in your splendour the son
of the godlike Emperor who comes back from war:
Victory has carried him in her blazing arms
[5] when he fought ardently the Thracians over the straits
of the Echinades, towards the safe harbour

            Antistrophe
of Trinacria; and he drank the fragrant liquid of nectar
just poured by the Graces
from a sweet cup.
[10] Sun-like glory always rejoices after a number
of deeds, and it blossoms for a long time,
for toils are the rearers of fame.

            Epode
He travelled passing over the waves of the Ionian
sea, and he directed the large, holy
[15] naval army, just as Aeson's son [Jason] travelled
to the gold-gleaming city of Colchis,
where through his deeds he inflicted a quick death
to the army hated by the gods,
and killing the earth-born giants, as sleep befell the Dragon,
[20] he immediately took the golden fleece.

And his Argo, after its safe journey, shines
among the bright stars.

Metre: The metrical pattern (described by C. De Stefani *apud* Venier 2016, 342) is calqued on the 11th *Olympian* of Pindar, also made of one triad only (an exception is l. 14, which is much longer in Amalteo's ode): the responsion between strophe and antistrophe is perfect, but then in l. 11 the ms.'s ἠλιειδές is indispensable, and in l. 8 γλυκείας must be preferred to the ms.'s χρυσείας (which has a long υ: hence perhaps the insertion of the 'gold' element in l. 14).

Notes: The ode celebrates the battle of Lepanto/Naupaktos (7th October 1571), during which an alliance of Catholic troops defeated the Ottoman Turks: Amalteo devoted to the same battle a Latin ode in hexameters (to the commander of the Venetian troops, Sebastiano Venier) and an Italian *canzone* (to the general of the papal army, Marco Antonio Colonna). This ode is dedicated to John of Austria (1546–1578), the son of Emperor Charles V and the chief of the Spanish troops at Lepanto. First published in the sylloge of the Amalteos' poetry curated by Girolamo Aleandro the Younger in 1627, this ode also appears on a loose folium of ms. Ambr. R 110 sup., a miscellaneous codex carrying various poems and writings of 16th-century scholars and erudites. Given the variants (note especially l. 14), it is likely that the manuscript should be regarded as an earlier attempt vis-à-vis the posthumous print. The Echinades (l. 6) are the Curzolari islands, west of the gulf of Patras, where the battle actually took place; the 'safe harbour' of Sicily (ll. 6–7) is Messina, where the Christian army gathered before the battle. The parallelism with Jason's expedition of the Argonauts (also featuring in Amalteo's other poems on Lepanto) is of course reminiscent of Pindar's fourth *Olympian* and of the epic of Apollonius of Rhodes, although the catasterism of the ship (ll. 21–22) is mentioned in other classical sources, from Aratus 342–352 down to Manil. 1.412–415 etc.

Biography: Giovanni Battista Amalteo (Oderzo 1525 – Rome 1573) belongs to a family of humanists (his father Francesco and his brothers Girolamo and Cornelio). He studied arts and rhetoric in Padua, where he got acquainted with Pietro Aretino, Sperone Speroni, Paolo Manuzio, and others; he then graduated in law in 1552. He visited Northen Europe and England as an envoy, he spent four years as a secretary in Dubrovnik, and in 1562 he settled in Rome as a secretary to Cardinal Carlo Borromeo: he stood out as one of the most active members of the *Accademia delle Notti Vaticane*. He followed Borromeo to Milan, only to come back in 1568 to the papal court, where he worked as a private secretary. Amalteo's Latin poetry (eclogues, idylls, epistles, odes, etc.) displays some familiarity with Greek epigrams and Anacreontics, whereas his Italian output follows the Petrarchist trend.

Bibliography: Venier, Matteo (ed.) (2016), *Amaltheae favilla domus*, Pordenone, esp. 36 note 49, 39, and 342–343 (epigr. V.a.17). Buiatti, Anna (1960), "Amalteo, Giovan Battista", in: *DBI* 2, 629–631; Päll, Janika/Valper, Eve (eds.) (2014), *Βάρβαρος οὐ πέλομαι*, Tartu, 16 no. 27.

Tito Prospero Martinengo (†1594)

Εἰς τὴν ὑπεραγίαν δέσποιναν ἡμῶν Μαρίαν παρθένον τὴν θεοτόκον [1550–1580]

(excerptum, vv. 1–34)

  Πάντα χρεωστεῦσι μὲν σοί, θεόνυμφε πάναγνε,
  παρθένε κυδίστη, Μαριὰμ μακάρων βασίλεια,
  ἀνθρώπων κλυτὰ φῦλα κατὰ χθόνα βωτιάνειραν.
  ὅσσα γὰρ ἠρινὰ φῦλλα καὶ ἄνθεα γίγνεται ὥρῃ,
5 ὅσσά τε τείρεα λαμπρὰ κατ' αἰθέρα βουκολέονται,
  ψάμμος ὅσος πεφόρηται ἐπὶ ῥηγμῖνι θαλάσσης,
  ὁππότε πόντιον οἶδμα κακαὶ κλονέουσι θύελλαι,
  χάρματα τόσσα τιθεῖς πρόφρων, μεγαλώνυμε κούρη,
  ἀνδράσιν ἠδὲ γυναιξὶ χαριζομένη χατέουσιν.
10 ἀλλὰ τὸ τέλθος ἐμὸν περιώσιον. ἦ γὰρ ἀπ' ἀρχῆς
  κυδιάνειρα κόρη, μῆτηρ ἅτε φίλτατον υἷα
  φίλαο κηδομένη με καὶ ἐν πρώτοισιν ἔτισας,
  καὶ κρυερῆς κακότητος ὑπεξείρυσσας ἁπάσης
  λοίσθια τειρόμενον, χαροπὴν τ' ἀπέκρυψας ὀπωπὴν
15 πολλάκις ἀχνυμένῳ, καὶ ὀφέλσιμα πάντα παρέσχες
  ῥεῖα φιλοστόργῳ με περιστέλλουσα μενοινῇ.
  ἦ ῥ' ἐτεόν σε θεοῦ ἱεροὶ κλείουσιν ἀοιδοὶ
  μητέρα μειλιχίης τ' ἀγανῆς χάριτός τ' ἐρατεινῆς
  μητέρα θ' ἱμερτῆς ἀγάπης ἠδ' ἐλπίδος ἁγνῆς.
20 ἴστε, φίλοι, τόπερ ἥδε τορῶς πάντεσσι γεγωνεῖ
  ᾆσμα καλὸν λαοῖς καὶ φύλοις γαῖαν ἔχουσιν·
  "αὐτὴ ἐγὼ μήτηρ τελέθω ἀγαπήσιος ἰρῆς,
  μήτηρ τ' ἠνορέης σθεναρῆς ἀλκῆς τε τέτυγμαι,
  ἐλπωρῆς θ' ὁσίης μεγαλοπρεπίης τ' ἐριτίμου.
25 δωτίναισι βρύω τιμαλφέσι παντοδαπῇσιν.
  οἷς κε θέλω ζωῆς πορσαίνω τέρμ' ἀπέραντον,
  ὄλβον ἅπαντα φέρω, κειμήλιά τ' ἄφθονα πάντα,
  καὶ τιμῆς στεφάνωμα, τὸ μὴ χρόνος οἶδε μαραίνειν
  καὶ πλοῦτον καρποῦσθαι ἀκήρατον ὀλβιόμοιρον,

30 ἠδ' εὐδαιμοσύνης εὐανθέα τέρψιν ἀτειρῆ.
    τοῖσιν ἔμ' ἀμφαγαπῶσι καὶ ἐκζητεῦσιν ἐρασταῖς
    καρπὸς ἐμὸς χρυσοῖο καὶ ἀργύρου ἔπλετ' ἀρείων,
    καὶ πολυτιμήτους βλαστήματα λᾶας ἐμεῖο
    νικᾷ ἀπειρεσίῳ τιμῇ καὶ μάργαρα λευκά."

Textus: Πρὸς Γρηγόριον τρισκαιδέκατον ὕπατον ἀρχιερέα Τίτου Προσπέρου Μαρτινεγγίου μονα- χοῦ Βριξιανοῦ *Ποιήματα διάφορα ἑλληνικὰ καὶ λατινικά* / T. Prosperi Martinenegii Brixiani Monachi *Poëmata diversa cum Graeca tum Latina*, Romae: Fr. Zannettus, 1582, pp. 34–35.

Crit.: 21 ἄσμα ed., correxi

Sim.: 1 θεόνυμφε πάναγνε] saep. in precibus ecclesiae Graecae orthodoxae || **2** παρθένε κυδίστη] sim. e.g. Greg. Naz. *carm.* 1.2.2.3 || **3** ἀνθρώπων κλυτὰ φῦλ'] cf. *Il.* 14.361, *Hymn. Hom. Apoll.* 273 | κατὰ χθόνα βωτιάνειραν] cf. *Od.* 19.408, *Hymn. Hom. Apoll.* 363 || **4** cf. *Il.* 2.468, *Od.* 9.51 || **5** cf. Call. *hymn. Del.* 176 || **6** ἐπὶ ῥηγμῖνι θαλάσσης] cf. *Il.* 1.437 etc. || **7** πόντιον οἶδμα] cf. Eur. *Hel.* 400, Ar. *av.* 250 etc. | κλονέουσιν θύελλαι] Quint. Smyrn. 13.396–397 || **8** μεγαλώνυμε κούρη] cf. fort. *Hymn. Orph.* 36.1–2 (de Artemide) || **9** ἀνδράσιν ἠδὲ γυναιξίν] cf. *Od.* 19.408 | χαριζομένη χατέου- σιν] cf. *Od.* 1.140 al. χαριζομένη παρεόντων || **10** τέλθος] ex Call. *lav. Pall.* 106 et *hymn. Cer.* 77 || **11** κυδιάνειρα] raro de hominibus (e.g. *Il.* 1.490 de pugna), fort. sensu "glorificans" || **12** φίλαο] Call. *hymn. Dian.* 185; de κηδομένη cf. iuncturam φιλέουσά τε κηδομένη τε (*Il.* 1.196 al.) || **13** ὑπε- ξείρυσσας] de verbo cf. fort. Ap. Rhod. *Argon.* 2.1181 || **14** λοίσθια] adv. cf. *Anth. Pal.* 7.646.1, vide iam Ap. Rhod. *Argon.* 4.471 | χαροπὴν...ὀπωπήν] cf. Opp. *C.* 1.421 || **15** πολλάκις ἀχνυμένῳ] ex Nonn. *Dion.* 33.104 | ὀφέλσιμα] Call. *hymn. Apoll.* 94 || **16** φιλοστόργῳ...μενοινῇ] iunctura Nonni- ana, cf. *Dion.* 4.15 al. || **17** κλείουσιν ἀοιδοί] cf. *Od.* 1.338, Call. *hymn. Ap.* 18 || **20** ἴστε φίλοι] cf. Nonn. *Dion.* 36.430 || **27** ὄλβον ἅπαντα] cf. Greg. Naz. *carm.* 2.1.51.15 | ἄφθονα πάντα] cf. *Hymn. Hom. Ap.* 536 || **28** στεφάνωμα] cf. e.g. Pind. *Pyth.* 1.50 | μὴ χρόνος οἶδε μαραίνειν] cf. Nonn. *Dion.* 24.205, 34.109 || **29** ὀλβιόμοιρον] cf. *Hymn. Orph.* 34.12

To Our Blessed Lady the Virgin Mary, the Mother of Christ

(excerpt, ll. 1–34)

> All-hallowed spouse of God, glorious virgin Mary,
> queen of the Blest, all famous generations of humans
> on man-feeding earth are indebted to you.
> For as many flowers and leaves blossom in the spring,
> [5] as many blazing stars range through the sky,
> as many grains of sand whirl on the seashore
> when harsh storms perturb the waves of the sea,
> that many joys you graciously provide, o highly named girl,
> donating them to the men and women in need.
> [10] But my debt is very large: for from the beginning,
> o glorified maid, like a mother with her dearest child
> you loved and cherished and honoured me greatly,

and you drew away from me every cold evil, when I was succumbing
to the outmost distress, and you hid your graceful face
[15] often when I was grieving, and you offered me all useful things,
swiftly wrapping me up in a tenderly love.
The holy poets of God rightly celebrate you as
the mother of gentle kindness, of beautiful grace,
the mother of lovely desire and of pure hope.
[20] O friends, recall the marvellous song that she shouted
to all the peoples and the generations that live on earth.
'I am the mother of holy love,
I am the mother of powerful manhood and strength,
of pious hope and of precious magnificence:
[25] I swell with all sorts of costly gifts,
and to those I want I concede a boundless limit of life,
I bring every prosperity, and abundant treasures,
and the wreath of honour, that time cannot waste away,
I give undefiled, blessed wealth to be cropped,
[30] and the indestructible, flowery pleasure of merriness.
For the lovers who cherish and seek out for me
my fruit is better than gold and silver,
and my offshoots overcome the precious stones
and the white pearls by means of their endless value.'

Metre: Hexameters (flawless).

Notes: This cletic hymn to the Virgin Mary belongs to the large number of religious poems in Martinengo's sylloge. By combining lexical items and entire expressions taken from Homeric, Hellenistic and even late antique hexametrical poetry, the author uses pagan vocabulary and form for a Christian content (the same applies conspicuously to the long Pindaric ode to the Virgin Mary in 24 stanzas). This peculiar expressive thrust, together with the declared ambition to produce a genre of poetry that was neglected in Italy and typical of Northern Europe (see particularly his contemporary Laurentius Rhodoman, → **Germany**), endow this sylloge with a special cultural relevance.

Biography: A member of one of the most distinguished families of Brescia, some time in the 1540s Tito Prospero Martinengo († Brescia 1594) became a Benedictine monk at the abbey of Sant'Eufemia, where he spent the rest of his life except for some years at the abbey of Santa Giustina in Padua. In 1566 he was put under trial and five years later he was sentenced for heresy by the Roman inquisition, as an adept of the sect of Giorgio Siculo. After his rehabilitation, as a *protégé* of Cardinal Antonio Carafa, he cooperated to the Roman edition of Jerome's *Epistles* and to the 1587 Roman Septuagint; he also published with the Vatican printer Francesco

Zanetti a *Theotocodia* (1583) and a conspicuous volume of Greek verse, the *Poëmata diversa* (1582, 1590²), embracing hexameters, elegiac couplets, iambic trimeters, Sapphic and Alcaic stanzas, glyconeans, Anacreontics, Pindaric odes, etc.

Bibliography: Zaggia, Massimo (2003), *Tra Mantova e la Sicilia nel Cinquecento*, Firenze, II, 681–685 and III, 896–897; Prosperi, Adriano (2000), *L'eresia del Libro Grande*, Milano, 292f.; Bossi da Modena, Arcangelo (1983), *Matricula Monachorum congregationis Casinensis ordinis S. Benedicti*, ed. Leandro Novelli/Giovanni Spinelli, I, Cesena, 362f. On his Greek poems: Pontani 2017, 324–326; Weise, Stefan (2019), *Der Arion des Lorenz Rhodoman. Einleitung, Text, Übersetzung, Wortindex*, Stuttgart, 105f.

Gregorio Porzio (ca. 1584–1646)

Πτερύγιον
Τῷ λαμπροτάτῳ καὶ Γενναιοτάτῳ Ἀνδρὶ
Μαφφαίῳ τῷ Βαρβερίνῳ
Γρηγόριος ὁ Πόρκιος [1620–1623?]

Οὔνομα Μαφφείοιο καὶ ἔργματα καὶ κλέος ᾄδω

Εὔπτερον Ἀτλαντίδος υἱὸν σκοπιάζων ἰδὲ πέτροιο Ῥέας δάμαρτος
Παιδοφόνου, ὅς κε γενέθλαν κτάνε πουλυσθενέων Γιγάντων
Βροντᾷ ἀσιγάτῳ ἀκοντισσάμενος δι' αἴθρας,
Μὴ μέγα θάμβει, ἕδος ἀκμόνειον
5 Τῆλε λιπόντ', ἐς αἶαν
Ἐρεμνὰν
Ἱκάνειν.
Κάλλει θέλγομαι γὰρ
Ἄνθεος Ἄνθευς πολυποικίλοιο,
10 Τὸ ζαθέα γαῖα κλυτῶν Αἰνεαδῶν ἐς ἕδραν
Αἰὲν ἀρίζηλον ἀερτάσσει, ἅπασιν τὸ θοῶς πιφαύσκω·
Καὶ γὰρ ἐγὼν ἀγγελιώτας Διὸς εἴμ' ὀτραλέως ἦρα φέρων βροτοῖσι.

Textus: Città del Vaticano, Biblioteca Apostolica Vaticana, ms. Barb. Gr. 279, f. 281r (manu ipsius auctoris): verba in imagine alarum inclusa.

Sim.: 1 εὔπτερον] de Mercurio cf. *carm. astrol.* 4 Heitsch (= Sphaera 4 Maass) || **2** πουλυσθενέων] de Titanibus cf. Quint. Smyrn. 2.205 al. || **3** δι' αἴθρας] cf. *Anth. Pal.* 15.24.6 (Simiae alae) || **4** μὴ...θάμβει] cf. *Anth. Pal.* 7.425.1; 9.295.3; vide etiam μέγα θάμβος, e.g. Ap. Rhod. *Argon.* 1.220; Nonn. *Dion.* 12.173 al. || **5–6** αἶαν ἐρεμνάν] cf. *Od.* 24.106; Ap. Rhod. *Argon.* 3.864 || **9** πολυποικίλοιο] cf. *Orac. Sib.* 1.291 || **11** ἀρίζηλον] cf. fort. Colluth. *rapt. Hel.* 248 || **13** ἀγγελιώτας] cf. e.g.

Hymn. Hom. Herm. 296; Call. *hymn.* 1.68 al. | ἦρα φέρων βροτοῖσι] de Heracle cf. Pyth. fr. 443 P.-W. (Aelian. *VH* 2.32.8; Diod. Sic. 4.10.1 etc.).

Wing
for the excellent and most honourable
Maffeo Barberini
by Gregorio Porzio

I sing Maffeo's name, deeds and glory

When you watch the winged son of Atlas' daughter and of the stone of Rhea, the wife
of the child-killer (he annihilated the generation of the strong Giants
hitting them with a noisy thunder through the air),
do not be really amazed that he left behind
[5] his celestial seat, and arrived at this
obscure
land.
For I am charmed by the beauty
of the variegated Flower's Flower,
[10] which the divine land of the illustrious Aeneads will extol
to the ever conspicuous seat. This I hasten to proclaim to everyone:
for, me too, I am a messenger of Zeus, and I diligently bring help to men.

Metre: After the lone hexameter introducing the poem, the wing proper consists of choriambic lines made of a varying number of choriambs (from 5 to 0) followed by one bacchaeus. The metre is taken from Simias' *Wings* (*Anth. Pal.* 15.24), which is clearly the model of this piece.

Notes: This *carmen figuratum* features in ms. Barb. gr. 279, a dazzling codex containing Greek poems dedicated to the Barberini family by a number of erudites linked to the Collegio Greco or to the Academia Basiliana (Leone Allacci, Giuseppe Carpano, Giovanni Matteo Cariofilli [→ **Greece**], Fabio Olivadisio, Francesco Arcudi, Henri Dormal, Denis Pétau [→ **France**], and others). It owes its form to the model of the Hellenistic poet Simias of Rhodes. While it does not display a special elegance in terms of Greek poetic diction, it does imply good familiarity with Greek mythology (a topic also popular in e.g. the *Syrinx*): Hermes is called the son of Maia (Atlas' daughter) and Zeus (the son of Rhea and Kronos: Rhea famously substituted a stone so as to save him from Kronos' gnaws: see e.g. Paus. 9.2.7); the 'akmonean seat' (l. 5) is the sky, for Akmon was the father of Ouranos. The dedicatee is of course Maffeo Barberini, the future Pope Urbanus

VIII, but it looks as if at the time of this epigram he was still on the verge of ascending to the papal throne (see l. 11 ἀερτάσσει, and the lack of any reference to Maffeo's dignity in the title).

Biography: Not much is known about Gregorio Porzio (Ancona 1581 – Rome 1646), who was born in Italy to a Cretan father, and a pupil of the Collegio Greco in Rome between 1594 and 1603. He worked as a *scriptor Graecus* of the Vatican library from 1614 until his death, and later as a secretary *ab epistulis* to Pope Paul V and to Cardinal Scipione Borghese. The author of many encomiastic and ecphrastic pieces (including a lost piece on the game of chess, an *epithalamium* for Marco Antonio Borghese of 1619, a *Panegyris* to Urbanus VIII printed in 1632, and an unpublished description of the *Horti* of the Borghese family on the hill of Quirinale), Porzio was a member of the Accademia degli Umoristi, his satirical vein emerging in the *Cynopithecomachia* (*The War of dogs and apes*, Rome 1638).

Bibliography: Tsirpanlis 1980, 341f.; Faedo, Lucia (2005), "Girolamo Tezi e il suo edificio di parole", in: Girolamo Tezi, *Aedes Barberinae ad Quirinalem descriptae*, ed. Lucia Faedo/Thomas Frangenberg, Pisa, 3–115 (with further bibliography); von Flemming, Victoria (1996), *Arma amoris*, Mainz, 194; Papadopoulos, Thomas (1983), "Libri degli studenti greci del Collegio greco di Sant'Atanasio di Roma", in: Andonios Fyrigos (ed.), *Il Collegio greco di Roma*, Roma, 303–328: 324; Legrand, Émile (1895), *Bibliographie Hellénique du XVIIème siècle*, III, Paris, 302–308; Nicius Erythraeus, Ianus (1729), *Pinacotheca Imaginum Illustrium Doctrinae vel Ingenii*, Guelferbyti, 676–684.

Francesco Arcudi (1590–1641)

I. *Urbano Octavo P.O.M.*
εἰς τὴν περὶ ἁγνείας βίβλον Μεθοδίου τοῦ μάρτυρος [1639]

Ἡ Κύπρις τὸν Ἄδωνιν ἰχνηλατέουσ', ὑπ' ἀκάνθης
τὸν πόδα ἐτρώθη· αἷμα δ' ἔβαψε ῥόδα.
Μειθόδιος δὲ θανὼν περὶ πίστιος, αἵματι βάψεν
4   ἄνθεα παρθενίης, ἄφθιτα, λευκὰ πάλαι.

II. *Idem emendatum et correctum ab auctore sui, ex censura URBANI Octavi P.O.M. doctissimi et sapientissimi Poësis Principis*

    Ψευδὲς μουσοπόλων φῦλον μυθεύσατο, ὅττι
       τρωθείσης Παφίης αἷμα ἔβαψε ῥόδα.   vel λύθρος
    κάλλος ὅμως γε ῥόδοιο ἀπόλλυται· ὤλετο Κύπρις,
       ὡς σκιά, ὡς ὄναρ, ὡς μῦθος ἀοιδοπόλων.
5 Μειθόδιος δὲ θανὼν περὶ πίστιος, αἵματι βάψεν
       ἄνθεα ἁγνείης, κ' ἄφθιτος ἔστιν ἔτι.
    κ' ἄφθιτα ἁγνείης ἔπλε κάλλεα, πορφύροντα
       λύθρῳ Μειθοδίου. ταῦτ' ἔχει ἥδε βίβλος.

Textus: Città del Vaticano, Biblioteca Apostolica Vaticana, ms. Barb. Gr. 279, f. 61r, manu ipsius auctoris (hinc ed. Giannachi, Francesco G. (2017), "Lettere ed epigrammi di Francesco Arcudi (1590–1641)", in: *Studi sull'Oriente Cristiano* 21, 77–151: 116)

Crit.: II 2 v.l. "vel λύθρος" (scil. ad αἷμα) in mg. add. ipse auctor

Sim.: I.1–2 τὸν Ἄδωνιν...ἔβαψε ῥόδα] de re cf. Bion. *epit. Adon.* (praes. 64–67); de forma cf. Mosch. *Amor fugit.* 1 (ἁ Κύπρις τὸν Ἔρωτα) || **II.2** τρωθείσης] cf. Anacr. 3; vide etiam I.1–2 || **3** ὤλετο] fort. ad Bion. *epit. Adon.* 2 (ὤλετο καλὸς Ἄδωνις) alludit || **4** ὡς σκιά, ὡς ὄναρ] cf. Pind. *Pyth.* 8.95 | ἀοιδοπόλων] in sim. contextu vide Greg. Naz. *carm.* 2.2.7.239 (*Anth. Pal.* 7.595.1; 9.343.5) || **6** ἄνθεα ἁγνείης] cf. Ps.-Jo. Chrys. *PG* 62.727.39; Theod. Stud. *PG* 96.684.24 || **7** ἔπλε] cf. *Il.* 12.11; Ap. Rhod. 1.1012

For Pope Urbanus VIII
On the book *On Purity* by the martyr Methodius

    Cypris, while chasing Adonis, was wounded
       by a thorn in her foot: the blood stained the roses.
    Methodius, having died for his faith, stained in blood
       the immortal flowers of virginity, formerly white.

The same, emended and corrected by the author, following the criticism of Pope Urbanus VIII, most learned and wise Prince of Poetry

    The false kin of the poets wrote that
       the blood of wounded Paphia stained the roses.
    But the beauty of a rose dies out. And Cypris has died,

like a shade, like a dream, like the tale of singers.
[5] Methodius, on the other hand, having died for his faith, stained with his blood
the flowers of purity, and he is still immortal.
And immortal are the beauties of purity, reddish
for Methodius' blood, which are in this book.

Metre: Elegiac couplets; legitimate metrical lengthening in Methodius' name (ll. I.2, II.5 and 8); disturbing hiatuses in I.2 and in II.1 and 7.

Notes: Arcudi's massive verse production embraces above all dedicatory epigrams for the manuscripts he copied, and encomiastic pieces dedicated to members of the Barberini family. Many of these compositions, including beautiful *carmina figurata* and celebrative pieces for the Museum of Antiquities set up by Francesco Barberini on Monte Mario, are preserved in autograph form in ms. Barb. Gr. 279. The present epigram, conceived for a manuscript of Methodius of Olympus' *Symposium* (Barb. Gr. 463, written by Arcudi himself soon after becoming a bishop in 1639) had a turbulent history: a first version (I), consisting of just 2 couplets, was criticised by Pope Urbanus VIII, who urged the author to produce a less 'pagan' poem (now II); and yet, as Giannachi points out, on f. 104r of the same ms. we find a longer *Fassung* of version I (4 couplets).

Biography: The offspring of a family of Corfiot provenance (his father, the *protopapas* Antonio Arcudi, compiled in 1598 the Νέον Ἀνθολόγιον, a Byzantine *breviarium* designed for priests and monks), Francesco Arcudi (Soleto 1590 – Nusco 1641) belonged to the Salentine Greek-speaking community that subsists down to our own day, and that gave rise, from the late Middle Ages, to a flourishing production of Greek manuscripts and to a solid scholastic tradition, which at times also included some sort of poetic activity. From 1600, Francesco Arcudi was trained at the Collegio Greco in Rome, where he got acquainted with Leone Allacci (→ **Greece**) and other scholars; he then went back to Soleto, and inherited in 1613 from his father the role of Latin archpriest of the local Collegiata. His letters and epigrams attest to his unceasing search for Greek manuscripts and his passion for the local history of ancient Salento (he believed e.g. that Salentine Greek went back to the Greek of the ancient Southern Italian colonies rather than to the Byzantine times), as well as to his longing for a new position in Rome, which he eventually obtained through his acquaintance with Cardinal Francesco Barberini and with his uncle Maffeo (later Urbanus VIII): in 1637 he moved to Rome (where he became a member of the Academia Basiliana), only to be named two years later Bishop of Nusco, near Avellino. It is no chance that most of Arcudi's manuscripts – both those written and those owned by him – are preserved today in the Vatican Library among the *Barberiniani Graeci*.

Bibliography: Giannachi, Francesco G. (2017), "Lettere ed epigrammi di Francesco Arcudi (1590–1641)", in: *Studi sull'Oriente Cristiano* 21, 77–151; Impellizzeri, Salvatore (1961), "Arcudi, Francesco", in: *DBI* 2, Rome, 15; Tsirpanlis 1980, 376f. See also Manni, Luigi (2005), "Tracce testamentarie e biografiche di Nicola Viva e Antonio Arcudi", in: *Bollettino storico di Terra d'Otranto* 14, 51–68. On our epigram and Methodius' text, see Lucà, Santo (2000), "Il Vat. gr. 2020 e Metodio d'Olimpo", in: *Bollettino della Badia greca di Grottaferrata* 54, 155–191, esp. 168–170.

Maffeo Barberini (1568–1644)

Εἰς τὴν τοῦ ἁγίου Σεβαστιανοῦ εἰκόνα [1630–1640]

Δεσμευθέντα βέλη πρόμαχον Χριστοῦ διαπείρει,
ὃν μὴ ζῶντα γραφεύς, μήτε θανόντα γράφεν.
Ζῆν μὲν ἔτ' ἀθρέομεν, νεκρὸν δὲ φοβούμεθα πίπτειν,
καὶ μέγα δείν' ἡμῖν τραύματ' ἐνῶρσε πάθος.
5   Ἔμπαγε τραυματίου ἐπιλεύσσετον ἀστέρας ὄσσε,
καὶ στόμα μὲν χαῖνον λισσομένου δοκέει.
Οὐκ ἔξεστι τέχνη φωνὴν ἀπὸ χρώματι δεῖξαι,
νοῦς δὲ γραφέντα βλέπει χείλεα τοῦτο λέγειν·
"Ἄμμα λύειν, ψυχὴ γὰρ ἐμὴ μεμαυῖα φέρεσθαι,
10   ὡς ἔλαφος διψῶν πίδακα, πρός σε, Θεός."

Textus: Maphaei Barberini (nunc Urbani Papae VIII) *Poëmata*, Romae: ex typogr. Cam. Apost. 1640, p. 155

Crit.: 4 δείν' correxi] δειν' ed.

Sim.: 1 cf. e.g. Gr. Nyss. *in Basil.* 2.3 (τὸν Χριστοῦ στρατιώτην...καὶ πρόμαχον τῆς ὑπὲρ Χριστοῦ παρρησίας etc.), sed vide etiam Paul. *hymn.* 3.59; Sym. Thessal. *mirac. s. Dem.* 3.1.12 de πρόμαχος Χριστοῦ Ι διαπείρει verbum pedestre || **2** ζῶντα...θανόντα] de oxymoro cf. e.g. *Anth. Pal.* 7.394.6 et saepius || **4** ἐνῶρσε] cf. *Il.* 6.499; 15.366; Eur. *suppl.* 713 || **5** ἔμπαγε] Greg. Naz. *carm.* 1.2.2.570 et 2.1.15.13 (cum μήν) Ι ἐπιλεύσσετον] verbum apud *Il.* 3.12 tantum; de ὄσσε cum forma dualis cf. e.g. *Il.* 23.464, 477 || **7** φωνήν...χρώματι] cf. *Anth. Pal.* 11.433.2; de re cf. e.g. Plut. *de glor. Ath.* 346f; *Rhet. Her.* 4.28 || **9** ἄμμα λύειν] cf. Eur. *Hipp.* 781 Ι μεμαυῖα] cum inf. cf. *Od.* 16.171 || **10** ὡς ἔλαφος κτλ.] cf. *Psalm.* 41.2

On the picture of St Sebastian

> Arrows transfix the enchained soldier of Christ,
>   whom the painter has represented neither dead nor alive.
> We see he is still alive, but we fear he might fall dead,
>   and his horrible wounds arouse our great sorrow.
> [5] Even so, the victim's eyes watch the stars,
>   and his open mouth seems that of a praying man.
> Art cannot show the voice through colours,
>   but the mind can see that the depicted lips are saying:
> 'Loosen the knot, for my soul wants to rush to You,
> [10] God, like a thirsty deer to a spring.'

Metre: Elegiac couplets (flawless).

Notes: Barberini's *Poëmata* also included some Greek items, mostly *poésies d'occasion* (e.g. an eulogy of Pope Leo III, and a short praise of the Greek language), but also a poetic paraphrase of *Psalm 75*. This *ekphrasis* of a painting of St Sebastian – equipped with a rather free and equally metrical Latin translation – might refer to one of the several canvasses of this kind that were once kept in the Palazzo Barberini alle Quattro Fontane in Rome (the inventories do not record the famous painting by Pietro Perugino, now at the Louvre, before 1648; the explicit reference to a painting rules out Bernini's 1617 sculpture commissioned by Cardinal Maffeo Barberini, now kept at the Thyssen-Bornemisza National Museum, Madrid). While adopting the obvious *topos* of *ut pictura poësis* and of the 'speaking' images (see in particular the oxymora in ll. 2–3 and 7–8), and displaying a certain familiarity with epic and scriptural diction (ll. 4, 5, 9, 10), Barberini's text does belong to the vast domain of Baroque lyric.

Biography: The offspring of a wealthy Florentine family of merchants, Maffeo Barberini (Florence 1568 – Rome 1644) entered the ecclesiastical career early: a cardinal from 1606, he was elected to the Holy See in 1623, becoming one of the most influential popes of his century. Beside his activity as a reformer of the Church and as a distinguished diplomat and politician on the European scene, Barberini had a rich cultural agenda, which included the propagation of the Christian faith, more power to the Inquisition (e.g., the famous court case against Galileo Galilei; one should also recall the anathema against the 'pagan' Baroque style of Marino's *Adone*), and an important activity of artistic patronage (Bernini, Caravaggio, Pietro da Cortona, and others). Barberini's education, first in the Jesuit College of Florence, later at the Collegio Romano and the University of Pisa, made him a proficient Latin writer. Due to the personality of their author rather than to their intrinsic literary value, Barberini's Latin epigrams and odes – mostly of religious and hagiographical content (though bucolic eclogues and Biblical paraphrases are also included), and sometimes in relatively unusual metres – were gathered in various collections of *Poëmata*, the first one published in 1595, the final, comprehensive one in 1644. Illustrated by Rubens and Bernini, set to music by J.H. Kapsberger, commented by Tommaso Campanella, they were widely read throughout Europe.

Bibliography: Lutz, Georg (2000), "Urbano VIII", in: *Enciclopedia dei Papi*, III, Roma, 298–321; see also Rietbergen, Peter (2006), *Power and Religion in Baroque Rome*, Leiden/Boston. On his *Poëmata*: Fumaroli, Marc (1980), *L'âge de l'éloquence*, Genève, 202–226; Formichetti, Gianfranco (1983), *Campanella critico letterario. I "Commentaria" ai "Poemata" di Urbano VIII*, Roma; Spini, Giorgio (1996), *Galileo, Campanella e il "divinus poeta"*, Bologna, 41–57. On his Greek poems: Pontani 2017, 327.

Pasquale Baffi (1749–1799)

Αἰκατερίνῃ βασιλίσσῃ καὶ αὐτοκρατορίσσῃ πάσης Ῥωσίας Εἶδος [1772]

(excerptum, vv. 1–46)

       στροφ. α' κώλ. θ'
Καινὸν Ὑπερβορέων φάος πτυχαῖς,
ὦ Μοῖσαι ἰοπλόκαμοι,
ποίαις κελαδήσομεν ὕμνων κεδνοτά-
ταν Αἰκατερίναν; ἀοιδᾶν
5 δὴ ὁδοὶ παντᾶ μυρίαι· φλέγεται
δ' ἁ ἐσλοῖς ἀπείροις
καὶ πέραν γᾶς τερμάτων μιν
ἁ φάτις ἀρτιεπὴς κάρυξε, καὶ
θῆκε ζηλωτὰν ποτὶ ξείνων τε κ' ἀστῶν.
       ἀντιστροφ. κώλ. θ'
10 Ἀλλὰ τίν' ἀγλαΐαν, ἀμάχανε
τᾶν Πιερίδων ἀρότα,
πρώταν φάμεν εὐλογίαις, θύμ', ἔλδεαι;
Ἦ ῥ' ἀρχεδικᾶν προγόνων εὖτ'
ἴχνεσιν ἀρχὰν ἐφέποισα, δίκας
15 ἀστοῖς κατ' αἶσαν
κ' ὀρθοβούλοισιν διαιτᾷ
μήδεσιν; Ἦ θεμιπλέκτοις ἁνίκα
στεμμάτεσσιν καδμένα χαίτας σεβαστὰς

ἐπῳδ. κώλ. θ'
εὐνόμοις ὤρθωσε τεθμοῖς,
20 κ' ἔμπεδον ὄλβον ἄγεν;
"Η κλυτᾶν τόλμας μεγαλανοριᾶν;
"Η ῥ' ἀνίκ' ἐν Μοισᾶν μυχοῖς
τᾶν ἀρετᾶν κορυφὰς πᾶν
τέρμα προβᾶσα λέλογχεν, ταῖς ὄπα
25 καὶ δέμας εἰδομένα μορφὰν θαητά;
Ἀλλὰ μακραγορίαν
ἄσχολος γάρ εἰμι πᾶσαν θεῖμεν αὐλῷ.
στροφ. β' κώλ. θ'
εὐπραγίαν δὲ νέαν λέγειν χρεὼν
νικαφορίαισι στρατὸν
30 ἁ προσέμιξε βιατάν. Δωριεῖ
κῶμον πεδίλῳ κελαδῶμεν,
οὐκ ἀέθλων τῶν πάρος, Ἑλλαδικὸς
τὰ θαύμαινε δᾶμος,
ἀμφὶ νικατᾶν ἀγαστῶν·
35 Θησέος οὐδὲ πόνους χ' Ἡρακλέους
ψευδέσιν δαιδαλμένους μύθοις κλύωμεν·
ἀντιστρ. κώλ. θ'
οὐ θοᾶς Ἄργους μαχατὰς
καὶ ποικιλόνωτον ὄφιν
χρυσοῦ τε νάκους βαθυμάλλου ἁρπαγάν·
40 κεύθοι πανδαμάτωρ τάδε λάθα.
Τεῦ γὰρ εἴκει τὰ λήμασιν ἀθλοφόροις
Αἰκατερίνα
τὰ ῥοαῖς Μοισᾶν ὀπάζει
ποικιλογάρυας ὕμνους; Πινδαρι-
45 κᾷ ἐφαπτοίμαν ἀοιδᾷ τὴν ἀγάλλεν
ἐπῳδ. κώλ. θ'
μαχανᾷ. [...]

Textus: Firenze, Biblioteca Marucelliana, ms. B.I.12, ff. 285r–287v (manu ipsius auctoris; f. 287v, post finem odae, scripsit idem: Ἀνθεστηριῶνος δεκάτῃ φθίνοντος ἐν τῷ ἀπὸ τῆς θεογονίας ἔτει αψοβ' Πασχάλιος ὁ Βάφιος ἐποίει).

Crit.: 8 κάρηξε ms., correxi || 9 ζαλωτάν debuit || 15 καθ' αἶσαν ms., correxi || 18 στεμάτεσσιν ms., correxi || 37 Ἀργοῦς debuit || 40 πανδαμάτειρα debuit

Sim.: 1 Ὑπερβορέων] cf. Pind. *Ol.* 3.16 | πτυχαῖς...ὕμνων (3)] cf. Pind. *Ol.* 1.105 || 2 Μοῖσαι ἰοπλό-καμοι] cf. Pind. *Pyth.* 1.1–2 || 3 κελαδήσομεν] cf. Pind. *Ol.* 2.2 || 4 ἀοιδᾶν...ὁδοί] cf. Pind. *Ol.* 1.110–111 (ὁδὸν λόγων), sed iam *Hymn. Hom. Herm.* 451 (οἶμον ἀοιδῆς) || 5 παντᾶ μυρίαι] cf. Pind. *Isthm.* 3/4.19 | φλέγεται] cf. Pind. *Nem.* 10.2 || 8 ἀρτιεπής] cf. Pind. *Ol.* 6.60 | κάρυξε] cf. Pind. *Isthm.* 3/4.12 || 9 θῆκε ζηλωτάν] cf. Pind. *Ol.* 7.6 | ποτὶ ξείνων τε κ' ἀστῶν] cf. Pind. *Ol.* 7.90 || 11 Πιερίδων ἀρότα] cf. Pind. *Nem.* 6.32 || 12 ἔλδεαι] cf. Pind. *Ol.* 1.4 || 13 ἀρχεδικᾶν] cf. Pind. *Pyth.* 4.110 || 16 ὀρθοβούλοισιν] cf. Pind. *Pyth.* 4.262 | διαιτᾷ] de verbo cf. Pind. *Ol.* 9.66 || 17 θεμιπλέκτοις] cf. Pind.

Nem. 9.52 || **18** καδμένα] scil. κεκαδμένα, cf. Pind. *Ol.* 1.27 || **21** μεγαλανοριᾶν] cf. Pind. *Nem.* 11.44 || **22** ἐν Μοισᾶν μυχοῖς] cf. Pind. *Pyth.* 6.49 || **23** ἀρετᾶν κορυφάς] cf. Pind. *Ol.* 1.13 || **24** τέρμα προβᾶσα] cf. Pind. *Nem.* 7.71 || **25** δέμας εἰδομένα] cf. Hom. *Od.* 2.268 al. || **26–27** cf. Pind. *Pyth.* 8.29–31 || **28** εὐπραγίαν...νέαν] cf. Pind. *Pyth.* 7.18 || **29** νικαφορίαισι] cf. Pind. *Nem.* 10.41 al. || **30** προσέμιξε] de verbo cf. Pind. *Ol.* 1.10 | βιατάν] de Marte cf. Pind. *Pyth.* 1.22 | Δωριεῖ...πεδίλῳ] cf. Pind. *Ol.* 3.5 || **36** ψευδ. δαιδ. μύθοις] cf. Pind. *Ol.* 1.29 || **37** θοᾶς Ἄργους] cf. Pind. *Pyth.* 4.25 || **38** cf. Pind. *Pyth.* 4.249 || **39** χρυσοῦ νάκους] cf. Pind. *Pyth.* 4.68 | βαθυμάλλου] cf. Pind. *Pyth.* 4.161 || **41** λήμασιν ἀθλοφόροις] cf. Pind. *Nem.* 3.83 || **43** ῥοαῖς Μοισᾶν] cf. Pind. *Nem.* 7.12 || **44** ποικιλογάρυας] cf. Pind. *Ol.* 3.8 || **46** μαχανᾷ] cf. fort. Pind. *Pyth.* 3.109

Ode
For Catherine, the queen and empress of all Russia

(excerpt, ll. 1–46)

strophe 1 (nine cola)
O Muses with dark locks, through which
sinuous hymns shall we celebrate
the new light of the Hyperboreans, the
noblest Catherine? The ways of songs
[5] are certainly innumerable: and she
becomes illustrious through her endless goods,
and beyond the boundaries of the earth
a solid fame has proclaimed her, and has made her
envied by both strangers and citizens.

antistrophe (nine cola)
[10] But which triumph do you wish
to tell first in eulogy,
o my spirit, helpless plougher of the Pierides?
Perchance when, practising her rule
in the footsteps of her prime ancestors, she administers
[15] justice to the citizens in a balanced way,
wisely and correctly?
Or when, with justly wrought crowns
adorning her venerable hair,

epode (nine cola)
she raised up with lawful decrees
[20] and brought stable prosperity?
Or her illustrious brave deeds of manliness?
Or when in the farthest nooks of the Muses
she overcame every boundary
attaining the peaks of virtue, admirable in her aspect
[25] for the resemblance with them in voice and body?

But I have no time to sing on my flute
a tedious story.

                              strophe 2 (nine cola)

I must tell of the new success
that bound a powerful army
[30] to victories. Let us sing in a revel
with Dorian sandals
not about the celebrated winners
of the games of old, which the Greek
people admired;
[35] nor shall we hear the toils of Theseus and Heracles
chiselled with false tales,

                              antistrophe (nine cola)

nor the soldiers of swift Argo
and the snake with back of various hues
and the rape of the thick golden fleece:
[40] may all-taming oblivion hide all this.
For what is similar to what with victorious determination
Catherine
gives to the streams of the Muses,
the many-toned hymns? May I apply myself
[45] to the Pindaric song so as to praise her

                              epode (nine cola)

with my art. [...]

Metre: The metre follows closely that of Pindar's *Olympian* 3: immediately below the title, Baffi added the note: ἡ μελοποιΐα συνίσταται πρὸς τὸ τῶν Πινδάρου Ὀλυμπίων εἶδος γ' Τυνδαρίδαις τε κ.τ.λ.; the same pattern had been used in 1695 by the member of the Accademia dell'Arcadia Giovan Battista de Miro in his ode to Gaspare Carpegna (see Pontani 2017, 329). The prosody is sometimes erroneous (beside the synaeresis between ἁ and ἐσλ- on l. 6, see esp. l. 9 short ε in θῆκε despite following ζ, l. 14 irrationally long ι in the ending of l. 14 ἴχνεσιν; l. 29 short ι in νικαφορίαισι despite following στρ-; l. 30 short ι in πεδίλῳ; long τὰ in l. 43), and the metre presents some superfluous syllables (at the beginning of ll. 33 and 40; see also the τὰ in l. 41), and at least one missing syllable (at the beginning of l. 30); furthermore, l. 37 is metrically untenable (clearly the metre of the first line of the epode has been wrongly applied to the antistrophe).

Notes: Most of Baffi's works never reached the press, but his ode for Catherine II of Russia – preserved in the autograph quire he gave to the Florentine erudite

Angelo Maria Bandini during their meeting in Naples in March 1781 – is remarkable under at least two aspects: first, as a unique example of 18th century Pindaric versification, virtually a 'cento' of Pindaric terms and expressions, following the Theban's patterns of praise both in the introductory part (here reproduced) and in the more plainly encomiastic section, where the family and deeds of the Empress are duly celebrated; secondly, this ode attests to the poet's veneration for Catherine II, the tsarina who had inflamed the political sympathies of the most progressive circles of the Neapolitan *intelligentsija*, both for her apparent *penchant* for the Enlightenment and for her struggle against the Turks (which they hoped would lead to the liberation of Greece). This veneration was shared by others in Europe, e.g. by the Englishman Lord Frederick North who also wrote a Pindaric ode for Catherine II (see → **Russia**).

Biography: Pasquale Baffi (Santa Sofia d'Epiro, Cosenza 1749 – Napoli 1799) belonged to the Albanian community of Calabria, and was trained in Greek language and rite since his childhood. He became the head of Naples' Royal Library, one of the first scholars to study properly the newly discovered Herculaneum papyri, and an expert on Greek grammar and manuscripts, in epistolary contact with the brightest European scholars of his time, from Zoega to Villoison to Harles. A fervent partisan of the short-lived 1799 Revolution against the oppression of the Spanish regime – the most significant political feat of the Italian Enlightenment –, after the return of the Bourbons he was executed together with a large number of Neapolitan intellectuals.

Bibliography: d'Oria, Filippo (1987), "Pasquale Baffi", in: Marcello Gigante (ed.) (1987), *La cultura classica a Napoli nell'Ottocento*, Napoli, 93–121; d'Oria, Filippo (1980), "Pasquale Baffi e i papiri d'Ercolano", in: *Contributi alla storia della Officina dei papiri ercolanesi*, Napoli, 103–158; Venturi, Franco (1979), *Settecento riformatore*, III, Torino, 109–127; Pontani 2017, 333–335.

Clotilde Tambroni (1758–1817)

Εἰς Ἰωάννην Βαπτιστὴν τὸν Βοδώνιον Ἐλεγεῖα [1795]

(excerptum, ll. 1–10)

Εὖτε ποδήνεμος Ὄσσα κατήλυθεν ἀγγελιῶτις
εἰς ἔδαφος μακάρων σοὺς ἐρέουσα πόνους,
καὶ σπεύδουσα κόμιζε, Βοδώνιε, ἀγκαλίδεσσι

τεῦχος, ὅπερ κέκαμες τοῦτο πανυστάτιον,
5   λαμπράς τ' ἀμφιλαφεῖς σελίδας, κλέος εὐρὺ λαχοίσας,
    θαῦμα μέγα θνητοῖς, χάρμα τ' ἐπουρανίοις.
    Αἶψα μάλ' ἐξ ἑδέων ἀνστῆσαν πάντες ἀοιδοὶ
    Ἑλλάδος εὐρυχόρου Αὐσονίης τε καλῆς,
    ὥς μιν ἑώρουν πλησίον ἤδη· καὶ τόθ' ἕκαστος
10 εἰδέμεν ὅττι φέρει βούλετ' ἐπαντιάσας
    [...]

Textus: *Elegia greca* di Clotilde Tambroni in onore del celebre tipografo Giambattista Bodoni con la versione italiana del Padre Maestro Giuseppe Maria Pagnini, dalla Reale Tipografia Parmense 1795, pp. 7–11 (unde Tosi, Renzo (2011), *I carmi greci di Clotilde Tambroni*, Bologna, pp. 89–99).

Crit.: 9 ἑώρων debuit

Sim.: 1 ποδήνεμος] de Iride dictum apud Hom. *Il.* 2.786 etc. | ἀγγελιῶτις] Call. *hymn. Del.* 216 || 3 ἀγκαλίδεσσι] cf. *Il.* 18.555, Call. *hymn. Dian.* 73 || 4 πανυστάτιον] Call. *Lav. Pall.* 54 || 5 ἀμφιλαφεῖς] cf. e.g. Call. *hymn. Dian.* 3, *Cer.* 26 al. | κλέος εὐρύ] cf. *Od.* 1.344 etc. | λαχοίσας] de forma Dorica cf. Pind. *Ol.* 14.2 || 6 sim. e.g. *hymn. Hom. Cer.* 403, vide Hes. *Theog.* 588 etc. || **7** de re cf. *Il.* 1.533–534; ἀνστῆσαν cf. *Il.* 18.358 ἀνστήσασα || **8** εὐρυχόρου] de Graecia cf. *Il.* 9.474 al. || **10** ἐπαντιάσας] cf. *hymn. Hom. Ap.* 152

Elegy for Giovan Battista Bodoni

(excerpt, ll. 1–10)

> When wind-swift Fame came down to the dwelling of the gods
>   in order to announce and celebrate your achievements,
> o Bodoni, and she hurried carrying
>   this most recent book of yours,
> [5] with its wide and brilliant pages, full of glory,
>   a miracle for men and a joy for the heavenly ones,
> immediately all the singers of large Greece
>   and beautiful Ausonia rose from their stalls,
> as soon as they saw her approaching: and then everyone
> [10] wanted to know what she was carrying with her
> [...]

Metre: Elegiac couplets, with a bipartite hexameter in l. 9, and an ugly hiatus in l. 3 and 8.

Notes: The ode, consisting of 74 lines, is a celebration of Giambattista Bodoni (1740–1813), the most prolific and refined printer of his times, and the founder of an extremely ambitious printing house in Parma, where his working tools and his creations (books in an amazing variety of different alphabets) are still to be admired in the Museo Bodoniano. Indeed, the book here extolled by Fame might be the catalogue of the *Edizioni bodoniane eseguite in Parma*, printed by Bodoni in 1794. Tambroni's couplets show a number of poetic reminiscences, and it is quite possible that the presence of Callimachean expressions could be ascribed to the fact that Bodoni had printed a *Callimaco greco-italiano* (hymns and epigrams) in 1792. The perfect κέκαμα, from the verb κάμνω (see l. 3), is a grammatical recreation on the basis of an incorrect subdivision of the Homeric formula κε κάμω (see e.g. Choerob. *in Th. Alex. can.* 104.11; *Etym. Magn.* 488.29, etc.); the imperfect ἑώρουν (l. 9) is wrong for ἑώρων; the infinite εἰδέμεν (l. 10) is extremely rare, probably recreated *ad hoc* from εἴδω.

Biography: Despite her humble origins (she was the daughter of a cook), the *Sappho rediviva* of the Bolognese Studio, Clotilde Tambroni (Bologna 1758–1817), became during her life not only a member of various academies (including the Arcadia from 1792), but above all the first woman to hold a chair of Greek (1793), and a bright star of international Hellenism (she corresponded with Mme de Staël, Richard Porson, F.-A. Wolf, and Villoison). In 1798 she refused to swear fidelity to the Cisalpine Republic, and left for Spain together with her former teacher Manuel Aponte (→ **Iberia**), who introduced her to the Real Academia de España; the next year, however, she was allowed by Napoleon to return to Bologna, where she continued to teach until early retirement in 1808. Despite her lack of originality, which betrays the fact that she was not a genuine scholar herself, her numerous Greek compositions display good familiarity with archaic and Hellenistic poetic diction.

Bibliography: Tosi, Renzo (1988), "Clotilde Tambroni e il classicismo tra Parma e Bologna alla fine del XVIII secolo", in: *Alma mater studiorum. La presenza femminile dal XVIII al XX secolo*, Bologna, 119–134; Tosi, Renzo (2011), *I carmi greci di Clotilde Tambroni*, Bologna.

Giacomo Leopardi (1798–1837)

Εἰς Σελήνην [1816]

Βούλομ' ὑμνεῖν (β) Σελήνην.
Σ' ἀναμέλψομεν, Σελήνη,
Μετέωρον, ἀργυρῶπιν.
Σὺ γὰρ οὐρανοῦ κρατοῦσα,
5   Ἡσύχου τε νυκτὸς ἀρχὴν

Μελάνων τ' ἔχεις ὀνείρων.
Σὲ δὲ κ' ἀστέρες σέβονται
Οὐρανὸν καταυγάζουσαν.
Σὺ δὲ λευκὸν ἅρμ' ἐλαύνεις
10 Λιπαροχρόους τε πώλους
Ἀναβάντας ἐκ θαλάσσης·
Χ' ὅτε πανταχοῦ καμόντες (γ)
Μέροπες σιωπάουσι,
Μέσον οὐρανὸν σιωπῇ
15 Ἔννυχος μόνη θ' ὁδεύεις,
Ἐπ' ὄρη τε, κἀπὶ δένδρων
Κορυφάς, δόμους τ' ἐπ' ἄκρους
Ἐφ' ὁδούς τε (δ), κἀπὶ λίμνας
Πόλυ ὂν (ε) βαλοῦσα φέγγος.
20 Τρομέουσι μέν σε κλέπται,
Πάντα κόσμον εἰσορῶσαν·
Ὑμνέουσιν ἀδόνες δέ,
Πάννυχον θέρους ἐν ὥρῃ
Μινυρίσματ' ἠχέουσαι
25 Πυκινοῖσιν ἐν κλάδοισιν.
Σὺ δὲ προσφιλὴς ὁδίταις,
Ὑδάτων ποτ' ἐξιοῦσα.
Σὲ δὲ καὶ θεοὶ φιλοῦνται,
Σὲ δὲ τιμῶσιν (ζ) ἄνδρες,
30 Μετέωρον, ἀργυρῶπιν
Ποτνίαν, καλήν, φεραυγῇ.

(β) Legendum, quo constet metri ratio: ὑμνέειν.
(γ) MS. Codex habet: κομῶντες.
(δ) Ἐφόδους τε habet Codex.
(ε) Lego: Πολιὸν.
(ζ) Legitimo sono gaudebit versus, si legeris: τιμάουσιν.

Textus: *Lo Spettatore Italiano* 8 (quad. 75, 1.5.1817), pp. 142–163; *Inno a Nettuno d'incerto autore nuovamente scoperto*. Traduzione dal greco del conte Giacomo Leopardi da Recanati, Milano: presso Antonio Fortunato Stella 1817; exemplar huius editionis ab ipso auctore correctum (Napoli, Biblioteca Nazionale Centrale, C.L. XXIV.11.b): vide ed. crit. a Claudia Catalano et al., apud Gavazzeni, Franco (ed.) (2009), *Giacomo Leopardi. Canti e poesie disperse*, III, Firenze, pp. 263–284 confectam.

Crit.: 5 Ἡσυχοῦ ed., corr. Pistelli || **30–31** μετέωρε κ' ἀργυρῶπι / Πότνα παγκάλη φεραυγές habent edd., in exemplari Neapolitano corr. ipse auctor

Sim.: 2 ἀναμέλψομεν] cf. Anacreont. 38.2 et 27 W. || **3** ἀργυρῶπιν hapax, cf. βοῶπις, γλαυκῶπις || **4** (de Iove) cf. Archil. fr. 174.1 W. || **6** μελάνων...ὀνείρων] de nocte cf. Eur. *Hec.* 71 || **7–8** de luna plena cf. *Il.* 8.555–856; Sapph. fr. 34.1–3 V. || **9–11** cf. *Hymn. Hom.* 32.7–9 | λιπαροχρόους] de adi. cf. Theoc. *Id.* 2.165 et Anacreont. 20.7 W. || **12–13** sim. Verg. *Aen.* 2.250–255 || **14** μέσον οὐρανόν] sim. Theoc. *Id.* 21.19, sed de itinere Solis *Il.* 8.68 etc. || **16-19** sim. *Il.* 8.555-859 || **20-21** sim. [Mosch.] 8.4-8 || **22-25** cf. [Mosch.] 3.9 (ἀδόνες); *Od.* 19.518-522 || **23** θέρους ἐν ὥρῃ] cf. Hes. *Op.* 582-584 || **24** cf. [Theoc.] *Epigr.* 4.9-11 || **28-29** sim. Hes. *Theog.* 415-418; Anacreont. 34.10-13 W. || **30-31** cf. *Hymn. Hom.* 32.17-18; Anacreont. 34.16-17 W.; πότνα de Luna saep. apud Theoc. *Id.* 2 (69, 75 etc.)

To Selene

I want to celebrate Selene. / We shall praise thee, Selene, / you high above, you silver-faced. / You dominate the sky / [5] and rule over the calm night / and over the black dreams. / The stars honour you / when you light up the sky. / You drive the white cart / [10] and the gleaming horses / emerging from the sea: / and when everywhere men / are silent and tired, / alone in the silence of the night / [15] you travel through the sky, / sending off a grey light / over the mountains and the tree-tops / and above the roofs, / over roads and lakes. / [20] Thieves are afraid of you / for you see the whole world: / nightingales invoke you, / singing warblings all night long / in the summer season / [25] from the dense boughs. / You are dear to the wanderers / when you finally emerge from the water. / Gods love you, / men honour you, / [30] you high above, silver-faced, / beautiful Lady who bring the light.

Metre: Anacreontics (Ionic anaclastic dimeters): Leopardi wrongly believed that the first syllable of each line could be alternatively long or short, and this error (affecting ll. 1, 5, 8, 15, 21-23, 31) was pointed out to him by the German scholar Theobald Fix in 1831, when a new edition of his *Odae adespotae* was planned, though never realised.

Notes: This is one of two *Odae adespotae* published by the 18-year-old Leopardi in the important Italian periodical *Lo Spettatore Italiano*, together with a Latin translation: while the present one is clearly anacreontic, the other (and shorter) one, Εἰς Ἔρωτα, is written in pherecrateans. Both odes were fictitiously presented as drawn from a lost 14th-century manuscript owned by an unnamed friend, who was responsible for their transcription and Latin version; the same ms. allegedly contained a long hexametric hymn to Poseidon, of which Leopardi printed his own Italian translation, while quoting only the first and last line (incidentally, far from metrically satisfying: Ἐννοσιγαῖον κυανοχαίτην ἄρχομ' ἀείδειν and Ἀμφ' ἄρ' ἀοιδὸς βαῖν', ὕμνων γὰρ τοῖσι μέμηλε). It should be stressed that these are Leopardi's earliest original poems in any language to appear in print.

While the *Inno a Nettuno* is equipped with a series of mythological or exegetical notes, the shorter odes (but especially the one to Selene) are equipped with critical notes purportedly devoted to correct the manuscript's mistakes. While perpetuating an academic tradition of alleged 'Greek' compositions published in their Italian translation (from Vincenzo Imperiali's 1780 *Faoniade* to Cesare

Arici's 1815 *Inni di Bacchilide*), these odes and the hymn appeared in the same years when Angelo Mai – later the dedicatee of a famous *canzone* by Leopardi – was really unearthing new texts in the Ambrosian and Vatican libraries: this may well be the reason why they were taken as genuinely ancient by some Italian scholars upon their publication. However, Leopardi's goal was not only to mock erudite pedantry, but also to tackle *in re* the delicate issue of poetic translation from Greek epic and lyric poetry, Homer and Anacreon representing the two major poles of his attention. While devoid of any proper poetic value ('senza dubbio io ho fatto tutt'altro che poesia', he writes in a letter of 1817), these texts are exceptional documents of his precocious familiarity with Greek poetic language (epic, bucolic, and lyric: he had just produced translations from the *Odyssey* and Moschus), but also valuable experiments in the laboratory of his brand-new Italian poetic vein. This explains why some lines or *iuncturae* of the *Ode to Selene* will find their way into the great Italian idylls of his maturity.

Bibliography: Bazzocchi, Marco (2008), *Leopardi*, Bologna; Gigante, Marcello (2002), *Leopardi e l'antico*, Bologna; Dotti, Ugo (1999), *Lo sguardo sul mondo*, Roma/Bari; Timpanaro, Sebastiano (1997³), *La filologia di Giacomo Leopardi*, Roma. On his Greek poems: Catalano, Claudia et al., *Odae adespotae [1816–1817]*, in: Gavazzeni, Franco (ed.), *Giacomo Leopardi*, III, Firenze, 263–284; Centenari, Margherita (ed.) (2016), *G. Leopardi. Inno a Nettuno, Odae adespotae (1816–1817)*, Venezia.

Giovanni Pascoli (1855–1912)

Βησσόμαχος [1884]
Ῥαψῳδία αʹ

Ὣς ὅγε κοιρανέων δηίους πολέμοιό τ' ἔπαυσεν
καὶ ξύμπαντας ἔτισεν ὑπερβασίης ἀλεγεινῆς·
παυσάμενοι δ' ἄρα λαοὶ ὀιζυροῦ πολέμοιο
πάντες μὲν φιλότητα καὶ ὅρκια τάμνον ἑκόντες·
5 ὃς δ' ἐπεὶ ἄσβεστον κλέος ᾗ περὶ πατρίδι θῆκεν,
ἀσφαλέως δ' ὤρθωσε Πανιταλίδας μεγαθύμους,
οἱ μὲν ἔχον πάσην ἐρατεινὴν πατρίδα γαίην
ἐξ Ἄλπεων νιφοεσσάων ἐς ἀπείρονα πόντον,
γυμνασίων τε νέοις ἔμελεν βουλῆς τε γέρουσιν,
10 μοῦσα δὲ καὶ θῆλεν καὶ δίκα εὐρυάγεια.
Δράγμασι γὰρ τέμενοι σταφυλῇσί τ' ἔβριθον ἀλωαί,
εὐσσέλμοις τ' ἔγεμεν πολιὴ νήεσσι θάλαττα.
Ταῦτα γὰρ εἰρήνη τέκεν ὄλβια, λαοὶ δ' ἀμφὶς
ὄλβιοι ἦσαν ἰδ' ἐσθλοί, ὁ δ' ἀπῆλθεν ἄφαντος.

15 Τόν γέ φασιν ληφθῆναι ἐν ἀθανάτοισι θεοῖσι,
    τέρπεται οὗ ῥα μεθ' ἡρώων πατρίων τε θεῶν τε...
    πορφυρέη δὲ χιτών, χαίτη δ' ἀΐσσεται ὤμοις
    ξανθὴ χρυσείη, γλαυκὼ δ' ὡς οὐρανὸς ὄσσε
    ἠὲ θάλαττα φάανθεν· θάμβησεν δ' ἄρα ποιμὴν
20 ἀλλοδαπὸς καί μιν τρόμος ἔσχ', εἴπεσκε δὲ παισὶν...

Textus: Castelvecchio, Archivio Pascoli, cart. LXII, busta 4, ff. 37–39, ubi tres versiones servantur manu ipsius auctoris (hinc Citti, Vittorio (1998), "Bessomachos: un inedito greco pascoliano", in: *Lexis* 1, 87–104 et Traina, Alfonso/Paradisi, Patrizia (2008²), *Appendix Pascoliana*, Bologna, 43–50)

Crit.: (Trainam secutus versionem C, quae novissima videtur, dedi, praeter vv. 17–20) **7** οἱ μὲν ἔχον πάσην...γαίην versio C: οἱ μὲν πᾶσαν ἔχον...γαῖαν (fort. rectius) versio B || **9** βουλῆς: ἀγορῆς in mg. versio B || **10** καὶ εὐρυάγει' εἰρήνη in mg. ut vid. addidit auctor; εὐρυάγυια debuit || **11** τεμένη debuit || **13** ταῦτα: πάντα versio B || **15–16** om. versio B || **17–20** versio B tantum servat || **17** πορφύρεος debuit | χαίτη: κόμη a.c. || **18** ξαντῆ, correxi || **19** θάμβησε δ' ἰδὼν φρένα ποιμήν (quod deinde varie correxit) a.c. || **20** ἔσχ': ἔλλαβεν a.c.

Sim.: 1 ὥς...κοιρανέων] cf. *Il.* 2.207, 4.250 | πολέμοιό τ' ἔπαυσεν] sim. *Il.* 18.125 || **2** ἔτισεν – ἀλεγεινῆς] cf. *Od.* 3.206 || **3** cf. *Il.* 3.112 et (de παυσάμενοι) 15.58 al. || **4** cf. *Il.* 3.73, 256 || **5** ἄσβ. κλέος] cf. *Od.* 4.584, 7.333 || **6** ἀσφ. ὤρθωσε] cf. Soph. *Ant.* 162–163 | Πανιταλίδας] hapax legomenon, ex Πανέλληνες sim. creatum | μεγαθύμους] cf. *Il.* 2.631 || **7** πατρίδα γαίην] saep. apud Hom. (*Il.* 2.140 etc.) || **8** ἐς ἀπείρονα πόντον] cf. *Il.* 1.350 || **9** γυμν. – ἔμελεν] cf. Bacch. *pae.* 4.67 | βουλῆς τε γέρουσιν] cf. Pind. fr. 199 M. (Plut. *Lyc.* 21.6) || **10** cf. Terpandr. fr. 5 Gostoli (Plut. *Lyc.* 21.4–5) || **11** cf. *Il.* 18.561 et (de δράγματα) 552 || **12** εὐσσέλμοις] de navibus epitheton, cf. *Il.* 2.170 et saep. | πολιή] de mari cf. *Il.* 4.248 al. || **13** εἰρήνη τέκεν] cf. Bacch. *pae.* 4.61 | λαοί...ὄλβιοι] cf. e.g. *Od.* 11.136–137 (ἀμφὶ δὲ λαοὶ / ὄλβιοι ἔσσονται) || **14** sim. fort. Eur. *Or.* 1557 (ἄφαντος οἴχεται) || **15** ἐν ἀθ. θεοῖσι] cf. *Il.* 1.520 al. || **17** cf. *Od.* 19.241–242 (δίπλακα / πορφυρέην καὶ τερμιόεντα χιτῶνα); etiam Bacch. *dith.* 18.52 | χαίτη... ὤμοις] cf. *Il.* 6.509–510 || **18** ξανθὴ χρυσείη] sim. *Il.* 14.351, *Od.* 1.137 al. || **18–19** cf. *Il.* 1.200 (δεινὼ δέ οἱ ὄσσε φάανθεν) || **19** θάλαττα] est γλαυκή apud *Il.* 16.34 | θάμβησεν δ'ἄρα] cf. Quint. Smyrn. 4.443 al. || **20** cf. *Il.* 6.137 al. ἔχε τρόμος

Bessomachos – Book I

Thus, being the commander in chief, he stopped the enemies from fighting
and he repaid them all for their harmful outrage:
and all the people, giving up woeful war
happily swore fidelity and friendship.
[5] Once he had given imperishable glory to his fatherland,
and steadily restored to wealth the great-hearted Italians,
they dwelled throughout the entire beautiful fatherland
from the snowy Alps to the boundless sea,
and the young cared for sport, and the old for the government,
[10] and the Muse and the public justice flourished.

The fields swelled with corn, and the vineyards with grapes,
and the grey sea was full of well-benched ships.
These were the blessings brought by peace, and the people all around
were happy and honest, while he had become invisible.
[15] They say that he was subsumed among the immortal gods
where he rejoices with the national heroes and the gods...

He had a red mantle, and blond, golden hair
fell on his shoulders, and his eyes glazed as blue
as the sky or the sea: the foreign shepherd was scared
[20] and terror seized him, and he said to his children...

Metre: Hexameters, with bipartite lines (ll. 5, 13, 19, 20) and one metrically mistaken verse (l. 14). The α of φασιν in l. 15 should be counted as long.

Notes: From eyewitnesses we know that on the second anniversary of the death of the national hero Giuseppe Garibaldi (1807–1882), Pascoli – then a teacher at the Liceo Classico of Matera – wanted to 'translate' in Homeric hexameters a section of the official funeral speech delivered by the famous poet and scholar Giosuè Carducci, former professor of Pascoli himself at Bologna (*Per la morte di Giuseppe Garibaldi*: 'Liberato e restituito negli antichi diritti il popolo suo, conciliati i popoli intorno, fermata la pace la libertà la felicità, l'eroe scomparve: dicono fosse assunto ai concilii degli dèi della patria. Ma ogni giorno il sole...disegna tra gli abeti e i larici una grande ombra, che ha rossa la veste e bionda la cappelliera errante su i venti e sereno lo sguardo siccome il cielo. Il pastore straniero guarda ammirato, e dice ai figliuoli: – È l'eroe dell'Italia che veglia su le Alpi della sua patria'). Carducci's words explain Pascoli's lines, but not the title, which might refer to someone fighting 'against the Bessoi', i.e. the barbarians (the Βησσοί were a Thracian population renowned for their cruelty). The outcome of Pascoli's effort, an unfinished battlefield autograph of various words and hemistichs, can be categorised in three different attempts, with the last version leaving out some of the lines previously conceived (here ll. 17–20). On the whole, this looks like a Homeric cento, with uncertain dialectal character (see e.g. the hyper-Ionic πάσην...γαίην in l. 7; the Doric δίκα in l. 10; the Attic θάλαττα in l. 12), problematic syntax, and some gross grammatical mistakes (the non-existent aorist θῆλεν in l. 10; the genre of τέμενος in l. 11 and of χιτών in l. 17; the orthography of ξανθή in l. 18; I believe l. 10 εὐρυάγεια (instead of εὐρυάγυια) is simply a mistake rather than a neologism coined on the root of the verb ἄγειν).

Biography: Giovanni Pascoli (San Mauro di Romagna 1855 – Bologna 1912), one of the greatest poets of Italian literature, was trained at the University of Bologna, and in 1882 he started teaching in secondary school at the 'Licei' of Matera and then Massa. He finally landed in Bologna as a university professor, but he still spent most of his time first in his country house at San Mauro, and then, from 1895, in a mansion near Castelvecchio di Barga (in northern Tuscany), where he fled together with his sister Maria. A Latinist and a renowned expert of Dante, Pascoli stands out not only for a number of poetic syllogae that revolutionised the entire panorama of Italian literature (*Myricae, Canti di Castelvecchio, Poemi conviviali*, etc.), but also for his unparalleled skill in Latin versification, which earned him international admiration, and a series of gold medals from the prestigious *certamen Hoeufftianum* held every year in Amsterdam: due to their vividness and poetic inspiration, as well as to Pascoli's formidable familiarity with the secrets of Latin verse (chiefly the hexameter, but also many other metres), his *Carmina* are regarded by many critics as his masterpiece, and as the finest embodiment of a 'poetic bilingualism' that few other poets could realise during the last two centuries. Pascoli's Greek verse, however, cannot be compared with the Latin verse, and amounts to a few short *épigrammes d'occasion* (interestingly, one composed for a restaurant in Livorno).

Bibliography: Garboli, Cesare et al. (eds.) (2002), *Giovanni Pascoli. Poesie e prose scelte*, Milano; Pianezzola, Emilio (ed.) (2009), *Il latino del Pascoli e il bilinguismo poetico*, Venezia; Traina, Alfonso/Paradisi, Patrizia (2006³), *Il latino del Pascoli: saggio sul bilinguismo poetico*, Bologna; Pazzaglia, Mario (2003), *Pascoli*, Roma. On his Greek poems: Citti, Vittorio (1998), "Bessomachos: un inedito greco pascoliano", in: *Lexis* 1, 87–104; Traina, Alfonso/Paradisi, Patrizia (2008²), *Appendix Pascoliana*, Bologna; Pontani 2017, 337f.

Girolamo Vitelli (1849–1935)

Per la laurea di Raffaello Bianchi
Ἀπόσπασμα ἐπικολυρικοδραματικὸν πολύμετρον [1915]

(excerptum, vv. 49–78: loquuntur Medea, Mathilda, Leucius)

<u>Μήδεια</u>. ὀρθῶς ἔλεξας. νῦν δὲ Λεῦκον ἱστορῶ.
50 τίμιε σὲ Λεῦκε γλυκέσι προσφωνῶ λόγοις·
    εἰδότι δὲ λέξω θαρσαλέως τάδε· "θέινον"
    ξανθὸν βορείων Ἀγγλοσαξόνων ποτὸν
    ἡμῖν ὑπέσχου δῶρον –
    <u>Μαθίλδα</u>.   ἐσφάλης, φίλη·
    ἡμῖν γὰρ οὔτι ποτὸν ἁπλῶς ὑπέσχετο,
55 ἀλλ' ἅμα πλακοῦντας κἀπικυκλίους – "ὅσους
    ἐὰν θέληθ'" – ἑκὼν δ' ἔλεξεν, οὐ βίᾳ.

ταύταις τοιαύταις συλλαβαῖσι χρώμενος –
γλυκίνας τε συχνούς, κᾆτι διπυριτῶν δύο
λίτρας ἑκατέρᾳ τοὐλάχιστον, ἔτι δὲ καὶ... –
60 Μήδεια. ἅλις, Μαθίλδα· μηδέν, ὡς λέγουσ', ἄγαν.
τούτων δὲ Λεῦκος ἐμμελῶς μεμνημένος,
εὐθὺς χρέος φίλαισιν ἀποδοῦναι θέλει·
γενναιόφρων γάρ· χἠ χάρις προσκείσεται.
Λεύκιος. (ᾔδειν γυναῖκας τρυγόνων λαλιστέρας,   σ ͫ τοὺς πέντε στίχους
65 πρὸς δ', ὡς ἔοικεν, αἵδε – τἆλλά γ' εὐλαβεῖς –   λεπτοφώνως φθέγγε-
ἀδηφάγοι πέλουσι καὶ ποτίσταται,   ται ὁ Λεῦκος, ἵνα μὴ
ὡς ἐν παλαιαῖς Ἀττικαῖς κωμῳδίαις.   συνιῶσιν αἱ κόραι.
πόθεν, τάλας, ἐγώ σφε χορτάζειν ἔχω;)
ὦ λῆμ' ἄριστον, ἔρνος Ἰστρικῆς χθονός,
70 γλυκερὸν δὲ σὺ φάος ἀρτοποιϊκῆς πόλεως
– οὗ δὴ συχνὰς εὕροις ἂν ἀρτοπώλιδας –,
χάριν πρόσοιδα κἀς ἀεὶ προσείσομαι
ὑμῖν τε μεγάλην, ὅτι καλῶς ὑπόσχεσιν
ἐμὴν ἐγείρεθ', ἧς κακῶς ἐπελαθόμην·
75 τὸν δ' ἔρανον, ὥσπερ εἰκός, οὐκ ἀγνωμόνως
τελεσφορήσω – κατά γε τὸ δυνατόν, φίλαι.
ὄκνον δὲ παρέχει τοῦδέ μου βαλλαντίου
ἀράχνι', αἰεὶ πολλά, νῦν δὲ... πλείονα. ⸔

⸔ (ἡ διπλῆ)... ψευδέλληνα εἶναι τὸν ψευδοποιητὴν τοῦτον καὶ ἐκ τούτου ὑπολάβοι ἄν τις, ὅτι φαίνεται χρώμενος βαρβάρων ποιητῶν εἰκόνι· plenus sacculus est aranearum, arcula tua plena est aranearum κτλ. ὅμ.

Textus: Girolamo Vitelli, *Subsiciva*, ed. Ermenegildo Pistelli, Firenze: L'arte della stampa, 1927, no. IX

Sim.: 49 ὀρθῶς ἔλεξας] cf. Soph. *Phil.* 341, Eur. *Or.* 100 etc. || 55 κἀπικυκλίους] Epich. fr. 23 K.-A. || 58 γλυκίνας] cf. Athen. 14.645d | διπυριτῶν] cf. Phryn. fr. 40 K.-A. (Poll. 7.23) || 60 μηδὲν ἄγαν] cf. *Sept. Sap. dicta*, Chil. 22 Tz.-Papag. || 63 γενναιόφρων] vox serioris Graecitatis, e.g. Rom. Mel. dub. 69.7.3 etc. | χἠ χάρις προσκείσεται] cf. Soph. *OT* 232 || 64 τρυγόνων λαλιστέρας] Men. fr. 346 Koerte; Diogen. 8.34.1 etc. || 66 ποτίσταται] cf. Aristoph. *Thesm.* 735 || 69 ὦ λῆμ' ἄριστον] cf. Eur. *IT* 609; *IA* 1421 || 70 γλυκερὸν...φάος] cf. *Od.* 16.23 | ἀρτοποιϊκῆς] de adi. cf. Athen. 3.113a || 71 ἀρτοπώλιδας] de subst. feminino cf. Ar. *Ran.* 858; *Vesp.* 238 || 72 χάριν...προσείσομαι] cf. Ar. *Vesp.* 1420

For the graduation of Raffaello Bianchi
epic-lyric-dramatic fragment in many metres

(excerpt, ll. 49–78)

<blockquote>

Medea: Well said. Now let me ask Bianchi.
[50] O venerable Bianchi, I'll address you with sweet words:
since you know the issue, I dare speak: you promised us
as a gift the blond beverage of the Northern Anglosaxons,
the 'tea' –
Mathilda: You are wrong, my dear:
he did not only promise us some drinks,
[55] but also cakes and donuts – 'as many
as you wish' – this he said spontaneously, not by force,
using precisely these words –
and many wine cakes, and then at least two pounds
of biscuits for each of us, and then...
[60] Medea: Enough, Mathilda: 'nothing too much', as they say.
Bianchi, having aptly remembered all these things,
wants to pay immediately the debt to his friends,
for he is a generous man; and he will have gratitude in exchange.
Bianchi: (I knew that women are more garrulous than turtledoves,
[65] but these ones, it seems, albeit otherwise wise,
are also gluttonous and exceedingly thirsty,
like in the old Attic comedies.
How shall I manage to feed them, poor me?)*
O excellent spirit, offspring of the Istrian land,
[70] sweet light of the bread-making city
– where you can find a great many female bakers –,
I am and will always be very grateful to you
for having reminded me of a promise
which I had lamentably forgotten;
[75] as appropriate, I shall not ignore my debt, and contribute
my share of the food – as best I can, my dears.
My only hesitation is due to the cobwebs
in this purse – they are many, but now... even more**.

</blockquote>

* note that these 5 lines are pronounced by Lucius in a whisper, so that the ladies may not hear.
** (the diple)... One could argue that the pseudo-poet is a pseudo-Greek from the fact that he seems to use an image taken from barbarian poets: *plenus sacculus est aranearum, arcula tua plena est aranearum* and the like

Metre: (comic) iambic trimeters (flawless).

Notes: Vitelli's *poèmes d'occasion* in Greek and Latin – above all short epigrams for his colleagues and pupils, but sometimes longer encomiastic or scoptic compositions – were gathered by his pupil Ermenegildo Pistelli (with the aid of Medea Norsa and Goffredo Coppola) in a sylloge entitled *Subsiciva*: they stand out for their high linguistic and literary quality, and clearly follow in the footsteps of the glorious German academic tradition (more epigrams of this kind are to be found in Vitelli's later correspondence with Rudolf Pfeiffer). The 'epic-lyric-dramatic' fragment under consideration is a tribute to the young student Raffaello Bianchi (Hellenised as *Leukos*), who after his graduation had promised some tea and some *Delikatessen* to Matilde Sansoni and Medea Norsa, both young collaborators of Vitelli (the former was born in Pistoia, Latin 'Pistoria', cp. *pistor* = 'baker', ll. 70f.; the latter was born in Trieste, see l. 69). Humorously presented as the *editio princeps* of a new papyrological find (hence the critical signs and the marginal annotations, fully in the style of ancient rolls: the Latin passages evoked in the note marked with the *keraunion* are Catull. 13.8 and Afranius fr. 410), *Per la laurea di Raffaello Bianchi* is composed by a hexametrical presentation of the three main characters, a dialogue between them (including a lyric stanza celebrating the party), and a final scene where Pistelli reproaches the youths for their partying while the country is at war, and Vitelli himself (*Moschos*) intervenes to appease the atmosphere and bring the meeting to a peaceful end.

Biography: One of the greatest Classical scholars of contemporary Italy, Girolamo Vitelli (Santa Croce del Sannio 1849 – Spotorno 1935) was trained at the Scuola Normale Superiore di Pisa; from his youth (also thanks to the teachings provided by his mentors Alessandro d'Ancona and Domenico Comparetti) he had a special *penchant* for the methods and approaches of German classical philology, as opposed to the wave of cultural chauvinism and autarchy that dominated Italy at the turn of the century. From 1886 until his retirement, he taught Greek literature at the University of Florence, and became an expert in Greek palaeography and, later, papyrology – he founded the Società Italiana per la ricerca dei papiri greci e latini in Egitto (then transformed into the Papyrological Institute that still carries his name); together with his pupil Medea Norsa he edited many new texts of classical literature recovered from the sands of Egypt. In 1920 he was nominated a Senator of the Italian Kingdom, but in 1934 he refused to swear fidelity to the Fascist regime.

Bibliography: Treves, Piero (1962), "Girolamo Vitelli", in: *Lo studio dell'antichità classica nell'Ottocento*, V, Milano/Napoli, 1113–1126; Gigante, Marcello (1986), *Girolamo Vitelli e la nuova filologia*, Santa Croce del Sannio; Canfora, Luciano (2005), *Il papiro di Dongo*, Milano; Debernardi, Davide (2014), "Ritratto bibliografico di Girolamo Vitelli", in: *Analecta Papyrologica 26*,

441–490. On his Greek poems: Pontani 2017, 338f.; Bossina, Luigi/Bergamo, Max/Cannavale, Serena (2013), "Il carteggio tra Girolamo Vitelli e Rudolf Pfeiffer", in: *Atene e Roma* n.s. II/7, 391–463: 407 and 420.

Luigi Illuminati (1881–1962)

Εἰς τὴν μακαρτάτην Παρθένον
Χριστοῦ Μητέρα καὶ Εἰρήνης ἄνασσαν
Ἀτριανοὶ πολῖται
εὐσεβείας μνημόσυνον
ἐποίησαν [1942]

    Ἤτορος εἰρήνην μερόπεσσι, κόρη χαρίεσσα,
        δὸς χατέουσιν ἀεὶ καὶ φάος οὐρανόθεν.

                      καὶ τόδε Ἀ. Ἰλλουμινάτι

Textus: inscriptio in muro viae Picenae invenitur (sub arcu qui ad forum ducit, quod nunc Piazza Duchi d'Acquaviva cognominatur) in urbe Atri (in provincia urbis Teramo).

Sim.: 1 κόρη χαρίεσσα] cf. *Anth. Pal.* 1.44.1 (de Deipara; vide iam Theoc. *Id.* 11.30) || **2** χατέουσιν absolute cf. *Il.* 9.518; *Od.* 2.249 etc. | φάος οὐρανόθεν] cf. fort. Nonn. *Par. Jo.* 12.181–182

To the Blessed Virgin Mother of Christ, Lady of Peace, the citizens of Atri dedicated this memorial of piety

    Give people the peace of the soul, o gracious Lady,
        for they are always in need, and send them light from above.
                      This too is by L. Illuminati

Metre: Elegiac couplet (flawless).

Notes: The inscription, conceived for a *sacellum* of the Virgin Mary established in 1942, appears on a marble plaque immediately below a Latin invocation graffitoed in earlier times (*Pacis mater opem cunctis da cordibus alma / atque fidem firma, virgo fidelis, ave*): our distich might be considered a loose translation of this prayer. Illuminati's signature is reminiscent of Phocylides' *sphragis* καὶ τόδε Φωκυλίδεω.

Biography: A priest of Atri's Cathedral, then a professor of Latin Literature at the University of Messina, and later of Greek and Latin Grammar at the University of Genoa, Luigi Illuminati (Atri 1881 – 1962) was a follower of Croce's idealism and investigated Latin poetry from an aesthetical point of view (he wrote books on Caesar, on Cicero, on Latin elegy and satire). A laborious scholar, interested in various fields of knowledge and profoundly devoted to his hometown, Illuminati wrote several Latin epigrams and poems, including a *Carmen in Benitum Mussolini Ducem* (1930).

Bibliography: Cupaiuolo, Giovanni (1993), "Luigi Illuminati a Messina", in: *Messana* n.s. 17, 127–160; Verna, Giovanni (ed.) (1994), *Omaggio a Luigi Illuminati*, Atri; Traina, Alfonso (2003), *La lyra e la libra*, Bologna, 287f. (= *Studi e problemi di critica testuale* 62, 2001, 199f.).

Alvaro Rissa (1962–)

Πρόεδροι [2015]

(excerptum, vv. 131–160, 203–210: Pappus et Maccus loquuntur)

    ΠΑ. Ἐγὼ μαθητὰς ποικίλως ποιῶ χλιδᾶν
    ἁβρῶς τε μυρίοις διαιτᾶσθαι τρόποις·
    ὁσημέραι γὰρ αὐτοβοῦς αὐτοὺς ἄγει,
    ἐμοῦ κυβερνητοῦντος, εἰς Δάντου στάσιν,
135 καὶ ῥᾴδι' ἔνδον καὶ στερεοὺς ἱδρύσαμεν.
    ΜΑ. Κἄν τῷδε νικῶ σ'· ἀλλὰ καὶ φρουροῖς ἐῶ
    χρῆσθαι μαθητὰς χαρτοπώλαις ἐμφανῶς.
    ΠΑ. Ἀλλ' οὐκ ἐῶσιν οἱ νόμοι τοιαῦτα δρᾶν.
    ΜΑ. Ἡμεῖς ἑαυτοῖς τοὺς νόμους πορίζομεν.
140 Ὅπως δ' ἀρέσκω, κἂν προφυλακτίκ' ἐν σχολῇ
    πωλεῖν ἐῴην, τοῖς μαθηταῖς ὢν φίλος.
    ΠΑ. Ἔμοιγ' ἀσελγεῖς κἄνομοι φρουροὶ πάρα.
    ΜΑ. Ἐμοὶ δὲ μᾶλλον, οἷσπερ οὐ κόσμος ποτέ,
    οὐ νοῦς ἀραρώς, οὐ φρενῶν πειθαρχία.
145 Εἰ λευκὸν εἶπας, ἐξακούουσιν μέλαν·
    εἰ μέν τις ἦλθεν ὢν φύλαξ αὐλῆς ἔσω,
    εἰσῆλθ' ἄκλητος οὐδὲ τὴν θύραν ψοφεῖ·
    δέον δ' ἀπελθεῖν ἐν χρόνοις τεταγμένοις,
    ὅταν θέλῃ τις παρὰ χρόνους ἀπηλλάγη·
150 ἅπερ δ' ἐν αὐλαῖς εὗρε, λαμβάνων ἔχει,
    κοὐ ταῦτα κρύβδην, ἀλλ' ὑπ' ὀφθαλμοῖς ἐμοῖς.
    Αὐτοὺς κολάζειν; τίς με δρᾷ δρᾶσαι τόδε;
    μωρὸς γὰρ εἴην τοῦσδε τιμωρούμενος·
    οὕτως μὲν αἰεὶ συμμάχους δεινοὺς ἔχω,

155 ἄλλως δ' ἔχοιμ' ἂν πάντας ὡς ἐναντίους·
πᾶσιν γὰρ εἶναι συμφέρει προέδρῳ φίλῳ.
Πονηρὰ δ' ἔστω τἄνδον, ἢν μηδεὶς ὁρᾷ·
οἴκοι πινώδεις κρεῖσσον ἐκπλύνειν στολάς.
Τοιγὰρ σιωπῶ κοὐκ ἀκούω κοὐχ ὁρῶ·
160 ἐμοῦ κρατοῦντος ἥδε Γαλιλαίου θέμις.
[...]
ΧΟΡΟΣ ΔΙΔΑΣΚΑΛΩΝ
Ποῖ ποῖ πρόεδροι γάνος ἡμέτερον,
ἐνθένδ' ἦλθον ταχυτῆτι ποδῶν;
205 πράγματα δείδω μὴ πολὺ μείζω
πάσχωσι χρόνου περιτελλομένου.
Ὁρμῇ δὲ βραβεὺς Δάντου τυφλῇ
καὶ Γαλιλαίου περίεργος ἄναξ,
ἔποχοι ζήλῳ,
210 πολέμους ἀσχήμονας ἦρον.

Textus: Alvaro Rissa, *Il culo non esiste solo per andare di corpo*, Genova: il melangolo, 2015, pp. 54–56, 60.

Sim.: 132 ἁβρῶς...διαιτᾶσθαι] cf. adi. ἁβροδίαιτος || 133 αὐτοβοῦς] scil. Ital. "autobus" || 134 verbum κυβερνητέω inauditum || 135 scil. ex Ital. "radio" et "stereo" (machinis ad musicam audiendam) || 137 χαρτοπώλαις verbum novae fere Graecitatis || 140 προφυλακτίκ'] scil. Ital. "profilattici" | σχολῇ] scil. schola || 144 cf. Aesch. *Pers.* 374 (πειθάρχῳ φρενί) || 146 αὐλῆς] scil. Ital. "aula" || 147 τὴν θύραν ψοφεῖ] cf. Men. *Dys.* 586, *Pk.* 316 etc. || 148 ἐν χρόνοις τεταγμένοις] cf. Aesch. *Eum.* 945 || 158 πινώδεις] cf. Eur. *Or.* 225, ceterum proverbium Ital. resp. "lavare in casa i panni sporchi" || 203 ποῖ ποῖ] cf. e.g. Eur. *Or.* 278, *IT* 1435 al., et in anap. ποῖ πᾷ Eur. *Hec.* 1075 || 204 ταχυτῆτι ποδῶν] cf. Pind. *Isthm.* 5.10 || 205 πράγματα μείζω] cf. Ar. *Lys.* 617 || 206 χρ. περιτ.] cf. *Orac. Sib.* 3.158 al., sed sim. vide *Il.* 2.551 al.

The school heads

(excerpt, ll. 131–160, 203–210)

> Pappus: I let pupils have a good time in manifold ways
> and live smoothly and at their ease with every comfort:
> every day a bus brings them
> to the 'Dante' stop: I am the driver,
> [135] and we have installed inside both radio and stereos.
> Maccus: In this too I defeat you: I let the pupils buy openly
> stationery from the janitors.
> Pappus: But the laws prohibit this.
> Maccus: We establish the laws for ourselves.
> [140] For the sake of popularity, I would even authorise the trade
> of condoms in the school, because I am a friend of the pupils.

> Pappus: I have insolent and lawless janitors.
> Maccus: Mine are even worse, they have no manners at all,
> no stable common sense, no countenance or obedience.
> [145] If you say white, they understand black:
> if a janitor enters the classroom,
> he gets in uninvited and without knocking on the door:
> while one should leave at fixed hours,
> he goes away whenever he likes, against the timetable;
> [150] whatever he finds in the classroom, he takes away,
> and not secretly, but under my very eyes.
> Punish them? Why on earth should I do that?
> I would be a fool to punish these people:
> this way I have them as skilful allies,
> [155] otherwise I would have all of them against me:
> it is better for the school head to be a friend of everybody.
> Let things go badly inside, if no one sees it:
> it's better to wash the dirty laundry at home.
> So I shut up, I do not hear, I do not see:
> [160] under my direction this is the rule at the Galilei.
> [...]
> CHORUS OF THE TEACHERS:
> Where, where did the school heads, our pride, go
> leaving with swift foot this place?
> [205] I fear they might suffer much greater evils
> with the change of the year.
> The chief of the Dante and the clumsy
> leader of the Galilei, with blind impulse,
> mounting upon their envy,
> [210] raised obscene wars.

Metre: Iambic trimeters (ll. 131–160), flawless and with very few solutions (e.g., ll. 135, 156, 160); anapaests (ll. 203–210), flawless. The model is that of Greek dramatic poetry (esp. comedy and paratragedy).

Notes: The collection *Il culo non esiste solo per andare di corpo*, despite its obscene title, embraces a number of parodic, grotesque, satirical, and erotic Greek and Latin poems in various metres. The passage considered here is an excerpt from a dialogue between the headmasters of two important secondary schools (*Licei Classici*) in Florence, both named after the characters of archaic and Plautine Roman comedy: Pappus is the head of the 'Dante' (l. 134), Maccus of the 'Galilei' (l. 160). Besides the many Italianisms in both neologisms and ancient words endowed with new meanings (see the app. sim.), the syntax is also often adapted to that of Italian colloquial language (see e.g. the causative 'fare' in ll. 131 and 152, and 'lasciare' in ll. 136, 138, 141; the proverbs in ll. 145, 158).

Biography: Alvaro Rissa is a witty pseudonym for the Italian classicist Walter Lapini (Florence 1962), professor of Greek literature at the University of Genoa: an expert in the philological reconstruction of philosophical texts (particularly Epicurus and the Epicurean corpus; he has also published on Ps.-Xenophon and Heraclides Ponticus), Lapini has devoted serious philological studies to Greek epigrammatists, such as Strato and Posidippus of Pella. Alongside his academic activity, Lapini has written a number of poems in Greek and Latin, using the parodic and evocative potential of the ancient languages in order to produce allusive texts linking in a humorous and clever manner ancient and modern situations and themes (amongst them a Greek translation of a contemporary Italian pop song, *Tutto molto interessante*, and a Latin ode to the football player Francesco Totti, *Cochlear Dei*).

Bibliography: Pontani 2017, 340–342.

Fig. 3: Heidelberg, Bergfriedhof: Funerary monument for Hermann Köchly with the Greek inscription composed by himself (see below, p. 203f.).

Stefan Weise
Germany

As in the other sections, a strict definition of the 'German' area with regard to its changing shapes and borders throughout history is difficult. Nevertheless, for practical reasons the present selection of authors and texts will concentrate on the area of modern Germany. The difficulty becomes eminent, however, in cases like those of Johannes Mylius and Nicolaus Reusner. Although Mylius was born in the area of present-day Germany, he was later active in present-day Poland. He is, therefore, located in the Polish-Lithuanian section. Reusner, on the other hand, was born in present-day Poland (Silesia) but was later active mainly in present-day Germany and is, therefore, placed in the German section. Cases like these show the interconnectedness between areas in the history of Europe, which invites us not only to consider their differences but, more importantly, their overlaps and links with one another.

One may wonder why Greek studies and literature have played such an eminent role in the 'German' area that its works gained a leading position among the European nations. A potential reason to explain the prominence of Greek language and literature is its early connection with the Protestant movement where Greek became a distinguishing mark against Roman Catholicism. Of course, Greek never superseded the importance of Latin in the German educational system (even Melanchthon stated *Latina discenda, Graeca tentanda*)[1] but it was often seen as a symbol of a specifically Protestant humanism in Germany (especially by scholars in the second half of the sixteenth century, such as Crusius and Rhodoman).

The pure mass of texts and authors makes it impossible to give a thorough evaluation of the phenomenon as a whole,[2] but as a preliminary impression one can distinguish two major periods. The first begins in the Renaissance of the 16th

---

I owe my special thanks to Thomas Gärtner (Cologne) who gave me very valuable guidance on various parts of this section (esp. Rhodoman, Gothus, and Eyth).

---

1 Short version of a quotation from Melanchthon's inaugural speech *De corrigendis adolescentiae studiis*, delivered on 29 August 1518. See Bretschneider, Carolus Gottlieb (1843), *Philippi Melanthonis Opera quae supersunt omnia*, vol. XI, Halis Saxonum, 16. The full version is: *docebo quibus auspiciis Latina discenda sint, et Graeca tentanda*. On this speech, see also Rhein 2020, 113–115.
2 General surveys are given by Ludwig 1998 and Weise 2016, for larger collections of singular studies see esp. Harlfinger et al. 1989 and Weise 2017. See also Päll 2020.

century and continues until the first half of the 18th century. A possible turning-point was perhaps in 1730, when Georgius Lizelius (1694–1761) published his *Historia Poetarum Graecorum Germaniae*, summing up the preceding tradition of Greek versification from Johannes Reuchlin through to his own time.[3] A new period then starts at the beginning of the 19th century and ends with the Second World War. We could use the label 'Neo-humanism' to summarise this renewed flourishing of Greek writing. Greek versification can also be found between these periods and after, but in a much smaller quantity.[4]

This introduction will now consider these two periods in greater detail. The introduction of Greek literature and letters in Germany can be fixed quite precisely around the year 1500.[5] From 1500 to the 1530s, we find only some isolated short epigrams, mostly paratexts, accompanying editions of other texts. An early enthusiast of Greek was **Nicolaus Marschalk** (1460s–1525), who composed a simple but elegant Greek epigram for one of his humanistic books. Other famous humanists tried their hands at such epigrams as well, although not yet all with the necessary competence, such as **Conrad Celtis** (1459–1508), **Willibald Pirckheimer** (1470–1530), and **Johannes Reuchlin** (1455–1522).[6] They had all spent some time in Italy and we can, therefore, assume that there was an Italian influence on this habit. They were mainly inspired by the famous editions of Aldo Manuzio (→ **Italy**) bearing Greek poems such as those by Angelo Poliziano (→ **Italy**), Markos Mousouros (→ **Greece**), and Ianos Laskaris (→ **Greece**).[7] The importance of Poliziano as a rôle model becomes clear when we look at the Greek epigram which Reuchlin wrote about Constantia Peutinger, perhaps one of the most interesting examples from this early period (see below). The poem is almost completely a cento of verses by Poliziano and should perhaps present an obvious parallel to Poliziano's epigrams about his beloved, Alessandra Scala. Reuchlin never published these verses, however. Instead, he later published various Greek (and Hebrew) letters written to him by Byzantine teachers from Italy in his letter collection *Clarorum virorum epistolae*, showing himself as a true *vir trilinguis* of European renown.

---

3 Cf. Weise 2020.
4 For this periodisation model cf. Weise 2016.
5 For a general picture of the situation of Greek studies in "Germany" around 1500, see Holzberg 1981, 83–86.
6 Cf. esp. Bauch 1896.
7 The great desire for Aldus' elegant editions of Greek authors can be seen in the letter collections of early German humanists. For the influence of Aldus, see also Bauch 1896, 193.

The next important step towards a Greek literature of German descent was the implementation of Greek professorships at the universities – a process which took some time.[8] The first professor of Greek at Leipzig University was a foreigner, Richard Croke, who officially started teaching there in 1515,[9] but he appears not to have written Greek epigrams himself.

The first humanists to spread Greek writing on a larger scale were Reuchlin's protégé, **Philipp Melanchthon** (1497–1560), and his student and close friend, **Joachim Camerarius** (1500–1574). They not only published their Greek verses and letters but encouraged others to do so as well. Camerarius added a first larger collection of Greek verses by Jacob Micyllus and himself to his *Epigrammata veterum poetarum* in 1538.[10] Their efforts to inspire others to emulate them were obviously successful as an increasing number of Greek poetic texts appeared since the 1540s. They also attracted and inspired many foreign students to write Greek verses. The most prominent 'German' poets who were students of Melanchthon were Paul Dolscius,[11] **Johannes Caselius** (1533–1613), **Johannes Posselius** (1528–1591), and Michael Neander (1525–1595).[12] Neander, in particular, being headmaster of Ilfeld, a former monastery at the bottom of the Harz mountains, became a key figure for the following generation. He not only initiated special phrasebooks,[13] as did Johannes Posselius, but also inspired many of his pupils to compose larger Greek paraphrases and epic pieces.[14] By far the most famous product of the Neander school and perhaps one of the best Greek poets of the Renaissance period, besides Poliziano and Mousouros, was **Laurentius Rhodoman** (1545/6–1606). A Greek philologist as well as a poet, he was highly esteemed and even praised as *Homerus alter* or *biblicus* by his contemporaries. His voluminous epic poems are of interest as he not only covers Christian and Protestant themes (following the Melanchthonian aim of *docta pietas*) but also includes Greek mythology. His Doric epyllion *Arion*, culminating in a description of Zeus seducing beautiful Leda, is certainly a masterpiece in this regard and an exception.[15]

---

8 Cf. esp. Rhein 2020.
9 For Croke, see Bauch 1896, 177–183.
10 For this collection, see Schultheiß 2020.
11 See esp. Flogaus 2015a.
12 Cf. esp. Rhein 2017.
13 *De re poetica Graecorum* (Leipzig 1582, 1592, 1613) for poetry, *Elegantiae Graecae linguae* (Leipzig 1583 and 1589) for prose.
14 As there is a larger group of Greek poems and poets with connections to Neander, one may indeed summarize them as a sort of 'Ilfelder Dichterschule'. Cf. Weise 2019, 20–26 and Gärtner 2020.
15 See Weise 2019, but cf. also Moschos (→ **Greece**).

Finally, Greek writing peaked around 1600 culminating in the *triga* of Laurentius Rhodoman, **Nikolaus Reusner** (1545–1602), and **Martin Crusius** (1526–1607), the latter being a pupil of Johannes Sturm in Strasbourg.[16] Whereas Rhodoman concentrated mainly on epic poetry, the latter two used a great variety of forms. As an example, a rhymed piece by Crusius and a Pindaric ode by Reusner are included here. Other poets who deserve mention are **Nicodemus Frischlin** (1547–1590), particularly excelling in Greek epigrams, and **Matthaeus Gothus** (1548–1619), a pupil of Neander like Rhodoman, who refined his style and metre to Nonnian rules. Another interesting figure is the Italian poetess Olympia Fulvia Morata (1526–1555) (see → **Italy**) who went to Germany because of her reformatory convictions. Her Greek, Latin, and Italian writings were published by Celio Secondo Curione in 1558, shortly after her death.[17] Thus, during the sixteenth century, particularly in the second half of the century when Protestantism gained an official status within the Holy Roman Empire through the Peace of Augsburg treaty of 1555, Greek versification became an important sign of Protestant humanism. Poems by Catholic poets are extant but in a far smaller number. That we find within this period not only separate epigrams but also larger collections and even voluminous epics can further be regarded from a stylistic perspective to be a phenomenon of contemporary mannerism. Factors which might have fostered the intensive study of Greek could have been contacts with the Orthodox church in Constantinople as well as the constant danger from the Turks during the century.[18]

Greek versification, therefore, entered schools and universities and became a cultural practice which continued into the seventeenth and the beginning of the eighteenth centuries despite the devastating results of the Thirty Years' War. Throughout the course of the seventeenth and eighteenth centuries, the forms became more playful and showed the influence of the new baroque taste. We find, for example, polyglot pieces and figurative poems, etc. Greek was no longer a discipline of its own but rather a part of studies in connection with other Oriental languages – a sign of its decreasing importance in the context of polyhistorism.

---

16 Cf. Ludwig 2017.
17 For her Greek writings, see esp. Holzberg, Niklas (2017), "Livius und die *Vulgata* mit der Gräzität beschenkt. Olympia Moratas *Laus Q. Mucii Scaevolae* und ihre Paraphrase des 46. Psalms", in: Weise 2017, 47–62.
18 For Protestant contacts with Greek emigrants and the Orthodox patriarch, see Benz 1971 and Wendebourg 1986. For the "Turkish danger" as an important factor in developing a new European identity, cf. Kaufmann 2017, 19–22.

Nevertheless, there are still some remarkable authors from this period. An outstanding poet of the baroque era is **Johann Gottfried Herrichen** (1629–1705), who was a very creative writer of Theocritean and Anacreontic verse. The posthumous collection of his poems, published in 1717, is also significant in portraying the changing tastes of the time. Whereas in Germany the collection was still praised, in France, it was already rejected as pedantic and old-fashioned, an attitude, which was later adopted, under French influence, in Germany as well. Thus, we can observe a decline in Greek writing after the 1730s.

An important exception to this general decline is the famous Saxon *Fürstenschulen*, especially Schulpforta, where Greek verse composition continued. A Greek translation by **Friedrich Gottlieb Klopstock** (1724–1803) of one of his own German poems is included below. Klopstock was no outstanding Greek poet. In fact, there are only two known Greek translations of his own odes. He was, however, a very famous and influential forerunner of German classicism as he introduced classical metres into German poetry and imitated Homeric wording. He was also a pupil at Schulpforta and, therefore, serves as a witness to the continuing tradition there.

At the beginning of the nineteenth century, Greek literature saw a sort of relaunch, which was perhaps inspired also by the English practice of writing Greek (→ **Great Britain**) and of course by the philhellenic movement around the time of the liberation of Greece. Early collections of Greek poems from this period were published by Friedrich Thiersch, a classical scholar who was also involved in the reorganisation of the German education system to a Neo-humanistic form.[19] As in Melanchthon's time, there appear to have been distinct circles of Greek poets which could be traced back to influential masters, such as Gottfried Hermann and August Boeckh.[20] Concerning the forms, however, we see a major tendency towards translating classical German poems into Greek instead of making free compositions. The aim of these translations was of course linguistic training but they also had a competitive element, which should reveal the mental cognation between Greeks and Germans, a theory which was cultivated by various scholars of this age (esp. Wilhelm von Humboldt and Franz Passow).[21] The trend of translating pieces of classical vernacular poets was, perhaps, also influenced by contemporary trends in Great Britain. There are, however, still original pieces to be found as well. Until the middle of the nineteenth century, pupils used to produce Greek

---

19 An important collection of earlier Greek poems from Germany was made by the Braunschweig physician Karl Friedrich Arend Scheller (1773–1842). See Päll 2020.
20 Cf. Richtsteig 1927.
21 Cf. Landfester 1988, 86–88.

verse compositions on themes of ancient or German history and perform them at the end of the school year. Of these compositions, we know of those by classicists such as Friedrich Wilhelm Ritschl, but also those by the later communist leader **Friedrich Engels** (1820–1895), a portion of whose epic description of the duel between Eteocles and Polynices has been chosen for this selection. Also included are parts of a parodistic epic by **Eduard Eyth** (1809–1884), who wrote elegant Anacreontic verses as well, and an excerpt from one of the three comedies in Aristophanic manner by **Julius Richter** (1816–1877). Richter, who wrote his comedies after the foundation of the *Deutsches Kaiserreich* in 1871, shows a strong satirical and conservative attitude. This could, perhaps, be compared to similar tendencies in contemporary Neo-Latin literature. Being a student of August Boeckh, Richter also denounced the strict fixation on textual criticism by German scholars like Lachmann, Haupt, and Bekker.

A final influential scholar, writing Greek, was **Ulrich von Wilamowitz-Moellendorff** (1848–1931), the famous German philologist. After his death, his Greek and Latin poems were collected and his students continued to write small Greek pieces. It is interesting to note that he was a pupil at Schulpforta, and thus, we can again observe the continuation of the old humanistic tradition from this school. As he was particularly concerned with different styles and genres, a Hellenistic congratulatory poem and two translations of Goethe in epigrammatic and Sapphic style have been included here. The selection culminates in an epigram of Wilamowitz' student **Paul Friedländer** (1882–1968), a classical scholar of Jewish descent. In this epigram, Friedländer says goodbye to his former homeland, Germany, from his position as an exile in America.

Greek versification has continued from the end of World War II until today, but a school or greater community of poets is no longer discernible.[22] An exception to this general development was the short period, from 1954 to 1967, when the journal *Alindethra* (Bad Dürkheim), containing older and also some new texts in ancient Greek, was published.

---

[22] Some contemporary classicists who have written Greek epigrams on different occasions are, e.g., Uwe Dubielzig (*1955) and Michael Gronewald (*1944) (*ZPE* 86, 1991, 1; *ZPE* 97, 1993, 1).

General Bibliography

Bauch, Gustav (1896): "Die Anfänge des Studiums der griechischen Sprache und Litteratur in Norddeutschland", in: *Mitteilungen der Gesellschaft für Deutsche Erziehungs- und Schulgeschichte* 6, 47–74, 75–98, 163–193.

Benz, Ernst (^{2}1971), *Wittenberg und Byzanz. Zur Begegnung und Auseinandersetzung der Reformation und der östlich - orthodoxen Kirche*, München.

Flogaus, Reinhard (2015a), "Eine orthodoxe Interpretation der lutherischen Lehre? Neue Erkenntnisse zur Entstehung der Confessio Augustana Graeca und ihrer Sendung an Patriarch Joasaph II.", in: Reinhard Flogaus/Jennifer Wasmuth (eds.), *Orthodoxie im Dialog. Historische und aktuelle Perspektiven. Festschrift für Heinz Ohme*, Berlin/New York, 3–42.

Flogaus, Reinhard (2015b), "Die griechischen Übersetzungen des Heidelberger Katechismus. Entstehung, historischer Kontext, Wirkungsgeschichte", in: Christoph Strohm/Jan Stievermann (ed.), *Profil und Wirkung des Heidelberger Katechismus*, Gütersloh, 242–268.

Gärtner, Thomas (2020), "Jonische Hexameter als Träger der norddeutschen Reformation", in: Mika Kajava/Tua Korhonen/Jamie Vesterinen (eds.), *MEILICHA DÔRA. Poems and Prose in Greek from Renaissance and Early Modern Europe*, Helsinki, 217–243.

Harlfinger, Dieter et al. (eds.) (1989), *Graecogermania = Graecogermania. Griechischstudien deutscher Humanisten. Die Editionstätigkeit der Griechen in der italienischen Renaissance (1469 - 1523)*, Weinheim/New York.

Holzberg, Niklas (1981), *Willibald Pirckheimer. Griechischer Humanismus in Deutschland*, München.

Horawitz, Adalbert (1884), *Griechische Studien. Beiträge zur Geschichte des Griechischen in Deutschland*, 411–450.

Kaufmann, Thomas (^{2}2017), *Erlöste und Verdammte. Eine Geschichte der Reformation*, München.

Landfester, Manfred (1988), *Humanismus und Gesellschaft im 19. Jahrhundert. Untersuchungen zur politischen und gesellschaftlichen Bedeutung der humanistischen Bildung in Deutschland*, Darmstadt.

Lizelius, Georgius (1730), *Historia poetarum Graecorum Germaniae a renatis literis ad nostra usque tempora…*, Francofurti et Lipsiae.

Ludwig, Walther (1998), *Hellas in Deutschland. Darstellungen der Gräzistik im deutschsprachigen Raum aus dem 16. und 17. Jahrhundert*, Hamburg.

Ludwig, Walther (2017), "*Scitis, quanto semper amore Graecarum rerum flagrem*. Motive für den Höhepunkt des humanistischen griechischen Dichtens um 1600", in: Weise 2017, 125–145.

Päll, Janika (2020), "German Neo-Humanism versus Rising Professionalism. *Carmina Hellenica Teutonum* by the Braunschweig Physician and Philhellene Karl Friedrich Arend Scheller (1773–1842)", in: Mika Kajava/Tua Korhonen/Jamie Vesterinen (eds.), *MEILICHA DÔRA. Poems and Prose in Greek from Renaissance and Early Modern Europe*, Helsinki, 299–332.

Rhein, Stefan (2017), "Philipp Melanchthon und seine griechischen Dichterschüler", in: Weise 2017, 15–46.

Rhein, Stefan (2020), "Die Griechischstudien in Deutschland und ihre universitäre Institutionalisierung im 16. Jahrhundert. Ein Überblick", in: Mika Kajava/Tua Korhonen/Jamie Vesterinen (eds.), *MEILICHA DÔRA. Poems and Prose in Greek from Renaissance and Early Modern Europe*, Helsinki, 107–147.

Richtsteig, Eberhard (1927), *Deutsche Dichtungen in griechischem Gewande*, Breslau.

Schultheiß, Jochen (2020), "Profilbildung eines Dichterphilologen – Joachim Camerarius d.Ä. als Verfasser, Übersetzer und Herausgeber griechischer Epigramme", in: Mika Kajava/ Tua Korhonen/Jamie Vesterinen (eds.), *MEILICHA DÔRA. Poems and Prose in Greek from Renaissance and Early Modern Europe*, Helsinki, 149–184.

Weise, Stefan (2011), "Μοῦσα Ἀλληνική. Griechische Gedichte hallescher Gelehrter", in: Michael Hillgruber/Rainer Lenk/Stefan Weise (eds.), *HYPOTHESEIS. Festschrift für Wolfgang Luppe zum 80. Geburtstag = Archiv für Papyrusforschung und verwandte Gebiete* 57/2, 399–429.

Weise, Stefan (2016), "'Ἑλληνίδ' αἶαν εἰσιδεῖν ἱμείρομαι – Neualtgriechische Literatur in Deutschland (Versuch eines Überblicks)", in: *Antike und Abendland* 62, 2016, 114–181.

Weise, Stefan (ed.) (2017), *HELLENISTI! Altgriechisch als Literatursprache im neuzeitlichen Europa*, Stuttgart.

Weise, Stefan (2019), *Der Arion des Lorenz Rhodoman. Ein altgriechisches Epyllion der Renaissance. Einleitung, Text, Übersetzung, Wortindex*, Stuttgart.

Weise, Stefan (2020), "Graecia transvolavit Alpes: Humanist Greek Writing in Germany (15th–17th Centuries) Through the Eyes of Georg Lizel (1694–1761)", in: Natasha Constantinidou/Han Lamers (eds.), *Receptions of Hellenism in Early Modern Europe. 15th–17th Centuries*, Leiden/Boston, 379–409.

Wendebourg, Dorothea (1986), *Reformation und Orthodoxie. Der ökumenische Briefwechsel zwischen der Leitung der Württembergischen Kirche und Patriarch Jeremias II. von Konstantinopel in den Jahren 1573–1581*, Göttingen.

Abbreviated Titles

ADB = Historische Commission bei der Königlichen Akademie der Wissenschaften (ed.) (1875–1912), *Allgemeine deutsche Biographie*, vol. 1–56, Leipzig.

NDB = Historische Kommission bei der Bayerischen Akademie der Wissenschaften (ed.) (1953–), *Neue deutsche Biographie*, Bd. 1–, Berlin.

VLHum = Worstbrock, Franz Josef (2008–2015), *Verfasser-Lexikon – Deutscher Humanismus 1480–1520*, vol. 1–3, Berlin.

VL16 = Kühlmann, Wilhelm et al. (ed.) (2011–2019), *Frühe Neuzeit in Deutschland 1520–1620. Literaturwissenschaftliches Verfasserlexikon*, vol. 1–7, Berlin u.a.

Flood = Flood, John L. (2006), *Poets laureate in the Holy Roman Empire: a bio-bibliographical handbook*, vol. 1–4, Berlin.

Early Experiments by Celtis, Pirckheimer and Marschalk

Conrad Celtis (1459–1508)

I. Gręcum. [ante 1500]

> Ἐξ αἵματοσ κήλτης γερμάνου τάχα ποιητὴς
> Ἑλληνικὴν γλῶσσην εἴσφερει τὴν πατρίδα.[23]

II. δίστιχον ἐλεγιακον [ante 1500]

> Ἄρξεται πρώτην κόνραδοσ κήλτησ εἰσ ὥραν
> Στίχιον ἑλληνικῶν ἐνδόματὸς ἰδίου.[24]

Textus: a) Mss.: K = Kassel, Universitätsbibliothek Kassel, Landesbibliothek und Murhardsche Bibliothek der Stadt Kassel, Sign. 2° Ms. poet. et roman. 7, f. 55r (IV 61, 63); N = Nürnberg, Stadtbibliothek Nürnberg, Sign. Cent. V App. 3, f. 102v (IV 48f.), b) ed.: Hartfelder, Karl (ed.) (1881), *Fünf Bücher Epigramme von Konrad Celtes*, Berlin, 85 (IV 48f.).[25]

Crit.: Accentus et spiritus in K postea additi, in N prorsus desunt ‖ **I.2** ελλινικην γλόσσην N | τὴν N in marg. | εἴσφερει τὴν] metro repugnat, an voluerit εἴσφερεν ἐς? ‖ **II.1** προτην K ante correcturam

Greek (epigram)

> Celtis, the poet from German blood, happens
>   to have brought the Greek language to his homeland.

Elegiac couplet

> Conrad Celtis will start (to teach)
>   the Greek alphabet in his own house at one o'clock.

---

[23] **Author's Latin version:** *Germano Celtis de sanguine forte poeta / Gręcorum linguam protulit in patriam.*
[24] **Author's Latin version:** *Incipiet primam Conradus Celtis ad horam / Alphabeton graion ędibus in propriis.*
[25] In order to illustrate the development of Greek studies in Germany the texts of Celtis, Pirckheimer, and Marschalk are not normalised as in the rest of the section.

Metre: Elegiac couplets. The prosody is very problematic: I.1 αἵματοσ (short diphthong αι), τάχα ποιητής (lengthening of α in τάχα and internal correption in ποιητής), I.2 εἴσφερει τὴν *contra metrum*, II.1 ἄρξεται ... κήλτης εἰς (-ται, -της and εἰς are obviously considered short by Celtis), II.2 στίχιον = στοιχείων (?)

Notes: In book IV of his epigrams, which were first published in print by Hartfelder in 1881, the famous German humanist Conrad Celtis (1459–1508) inserted two short Greek distichs with their Latin poetic translations. In the first one, Celtis proudly claims to have introduced Greek to Germany. The second seems to be an announcement for personal training in Greek in his own house. Perhaps both texts (together with their Latin translations) were used as advertisements for private courses in Greek.

Biography: Conrad Celtis was an important figure in early German humanism. He was a poet and networker, hence his title in older literature as 'Erzhumanist'. In 1487, he became the first German humanist to be made poet laureate by Emperor Frederick III in Nürnberg; thereafter, he went to Italy, where he met *inter alios* Marsilio Ficino, Pomponio Leto, and Filippo Beroaldo Sr. Later, he became a professor in Ingolstadt (1494) and Vienna (1497). His Latin work consists of influential didactic texts (*Ars versificandi et carminum* 1486), poetical collections (*Amores* 1502; *Odae* published posthumously in 1513), and even editions of earlier medieval authors (*Opera Hrotsvithae* 1501; *Ligurinus* 1507). He skilfully combined his poetic ambitions with art (Albrecht Dürer) and self-presentation (this is seen in the artificial Romanisation of his name: Conradus Protucius Celtis, whose last two elements are renderings of his German surname *Bickel/Pickel* in Greek [πρό + τύκος] and Latin [*celtis*]). Although he presented himself as a *vir trilinguis*, his knowledge of Greek was rather superficial. Aldo Manuzio, therefore, refused to print the Greek grammar penned by Celtis.

Bibliography: Harlfinger et al. 1989, 303; Robert, Jörg (2008), "Celtis (Bickel, Pickel), Konrad (Conradus Celtis Protucius)", in: *VLHum* 1, 375–427; Wuttke, Dieter (1970), "Zur griechischen Grammatik des Konrad Celtis", in: Michael von Albrecht (ed.), *Silvae. Festschrift für Ernst Zinn zum 60. Geburtstag*, Tübingen, 289–303.

Willibald Pirckheimer (1470–1530)

⟨*Epigramma de Hrotsvitha poetria*⟩ [1501]

Εἰ σαπφὼ δεκάτη μουσάων ἐστὶν ἀδόντων
'Ρόσβίθ ἔνδεκατη μοῦσα καταγράφεται.[26]

Textus: Celtis, Conrad (1501), *Opera Hrosvite illustris virginis et monialis Germane gente Saxonica orte...*, Norunbergae, a IIIv

Crit.: 1 ἀδόντων] pro ᾀδόντων contra metrum (sed apud poetas humanisticos saepius α in verbo ᾄδειν corripitur) ‖ **2** P'όσβίθ ed., ft. pro 'Ρόσβιθ' | ἐνδεκάτη debuit

Sim.: 1–2 imitatur noster *Anth. Pal.* 9.571.7–8 (ἀνδρῶν δ' οὐκ ἐνάτη Σαπφὼ πέλεν, ἀλλ' ἐρατειναῖς / ἐν Μούσαις δεκάτη Μοῦσα καταγράφεται)

⟨Epigram on the poetess Hrotsvitha⟩

If Sappho is the tenth of the singing Muses,
then Rosvith is recorded as the eleventh Muse.

Metre: Elegiac couplet. The prosody is flawless except for ἀδόντων with short α, but this seems to be a fairly common scansion in early humanist Greek.

Notes: This early epigram by Pirckheimer (the only one in Greek we know of) is printed in Celtis' edition of Hrotsvith of Gandersheim, a medieval poetess, together with other Latin paratexts. It shows Pirckheimer's knowledge of the *Greek Anthology* and underscores the humanistic idea of *aemulatio veterum* by equating 'German' Hrotsvith with Sappho and the Muses.

Biography: Like Celtis, Willibald Pirckheimer (1470–1530) was an important figure in early German humanism. He studied in Italy at the universities of Padua (1489–92) and Pavia (1492–95). Thereafter, he became a member of Nuremberg's city council (1496–1502, 1505–1523) and was on friendly terms with many contemporary humanists, amongst them Albrecht Dürer, the famous painter, and Conrad Celtis (see above). Since 1502, Pirckheimer translated many Greek writings into Latin, and some into German as well (notably Plutarch, Lucian, Horapollo,

---

26 **Author's Latin version:** *Si sapho decima est musarum dulce canentum / Hrosuitha scribenda est undecima aonidum.*

Gregory of Nazianzus, and Ptolemy). His most important original works are the satire *Eckius dedolatus* (1520) and the *Apologia seu podagrae laus* (1522).

Bibliography: Holzberg 1981; Holzberg, Niklas (2013), "Pirckheimer (Birck-, Pirk-, -eymer, -heymer, -her), Willibald (Bilibaldus)", in: *VLHum* 2, 465–487.

Nicolaus Marschalk (c. 1470–1525)

Epigramma graecum de laude litterarum graecarum [1502]

> ελληνων αιγλη του δεινου λειψανα καδμου
> ρωμαιοισ πηγη δωρα τα κλεια θεων[27]

Textus: Marschalk, Nicolaus (1502), *Introductio ad litteras hebraicas utilissima*, [Erfurt], pag. ult.

Crit.: noster omisit accentus et spiritus. Quos si addere velis, possis scribere: Ἑλλήνων αἴγλη, τοῦ δεινοῦ λείψανα Κάδμου / Ῥωμαίοις πηγή, δῶρα τὰ κλει‹ν›ὰ θεῶν ‖ **2** κλεια ed., ft. voluit κλεινά

Greek epigram on the praise of the Greek alphabet

> Glory of the Greeks, heritage of powerful Cadmus,
>   source for the Romans, illustrious gifts of the Gods.

Metre: Elegiac couplet. The prosody is flawless.

Notes: This distich by Marschalk is printed at the end of an introductory manual for Hebrew (a reprint of Aldo's *Introductio perbrevis ad Hebraicam linguam*). The manifest intention was to present the author as a *vir trilinguis* who knows Latin, Hebrew, and Greek alike. Although the language is very simple and consists only of a list of praising nouns, the metre is flawless and the simple distich seems to be constructed very carefully, with Ἑλλήνων and Ῥωμαίοις at the beginning of the two lines, Κάδμου and θεῶν at their end. The mention of Cadmus is an allusion to his invention of the Greek alphabet. This distich is indeed a fine humanistic advertisement for learning Greek, hinting at its usefulness for the study of

---

27 *Author's Latin version:* Graecorum splendor: Romanae gloria linguae: / Cadmea proles: munera clara deum.

Latin (Ῥωμαίοις πηγή) and its divine origin (δῶρα…θεῶν). Marschalk also makes careful use of prosody by contrasting the heavy spondees of the first halves of the lines with the (necessary) dactyls at their end.

Biography: Nicolaus Marschalk was one of the first scholars to teach Greek at German universities, notably in Erfurt, and to use Greek types for his prints. He studied perhaps in Leuven and Erfurt, where he acquired the degrees of *baccalaureus* (1492) and *magister* (1496). In Erfurt, he also opened his own printing house with Greek types from Wolfgang Schenck, and mostly printed his own humanistic books for training in Latin, Greek, and Hebrew (*Orthographia* 1500, *Introductio ad litteras hebraicas* 1502, *Introductorium in idioma Graecanicum* 1502, *Enchiridion poetarum clarorum* 1502). He appears to have assembled a group of humanistic students around himself, some of whom went with him to Wittenberg in 1502. Later, he was active at the University of Rostock, where he died in 1525. The selected Greek epigram seems to be his only Greek composition. As he clearly used Aldine prints for the redaction of his training books in Greek and Hebrew and even integrated two Greek epigrams by Poliziano (→ **Italy**) into his *Enchiridion poetarum clarorum* (P IIIv–Vr), it can be assumed that these were his sources of inspiration for trying his hand at a Greek epigram himself.

Bibliography: Bauch 1896, 49–74; Haye, Thomas (1994), "Notizen zu Nikolaus Marschalk", in: *Daphnis* 23, 205–236; Huber-Rebenich, Gerlinde (2013), "Marschalk, Nikolaus ([de Gronenberg]; Nicolaus Marescalcus/Marscalcus Thurius [= aus Thüringen])", in: *VLHum* 2, 161–203.

Johannes Reuchlin (Capnio) (1455–1522)

‹*Epigramma ad Constantiam Peutingeri filiam*› [ante 1514]

Τοξευθεὶς Πευτιγγερίδος φλεχθείς θ' ὑπ' Ἐρώτων
Κωνσταντίης, Κρονίδης παρθένου ὡς Δανάης,
Ἄσομαι οὕτως· "Χαῖρε, κόρη Πευτιγγερί, χαῖρε
Ἀντιδιδοῦσ' εἰ‹ς› σὰς ζῶντά με πυρκαϊάς.
5   Καὶ πυρὶ φλέξε τὸ πῦρ ἠδ' ὄμμασι δᾷδας ἄναπτε·
Νῶν μετὰ σεῖο φλογὸς καινὸς †ἀνεστιντ† ἔρως.
Δός μοι παρθενικήν, κούρη, μετὰ σὸν στόμα γλῶσσαν,
Καπνίων ἔσομαι ὄλβιος ὧ τρὶς ἐγώ.
Φωναῖς ἐν πλείσταις τὸ ἐμὸν κλέος, ἀλλὰ σὺ φθέγξη
10   Ἑλλάδι, τευτονικῇ, ῥωμαϊκ', ἑβραϊκῇ."

Textus: Staatsbibliothek Berlin, Ms. lat. Fol. 239, f. 25r (unde Rhein 1989, 74).

Crit.: 3 Ἄισομαι debuit ‖ 4 εἰς σὰς scripsi coll. Politian. *ep. gr.* 29,4: εἰ σὰς ms.: ἐς ἴσας deliberat Gärtner ǀ ζῶντα με ms. ǀ πυρκαϊᾶς ms. ‖ 5 φλέξε: an pro φλέξον? ǀ δᾷδας debuit ‖ 6 νῷν debuit ǀ ἄνεστιν ms.: mihi suspectum, ft. ἄνεισιν vel ἔνεστιν ‖ 9 φθέγξῃ debuit ‖ 10 ῥωμαϊκ': ῥωμαϊχ' debuit: ῥωμαϊκῇ, 'βραϊκῇ Pontani ǀ ἐβραϊκῇ: -ῇ ms.

Sim.: 1 Τοξευθεὶς...φλεχθεὶς θ' ὑπ' Ἐρώτων] ~ Politian. *ep. gr.* 53.1 (de Pico Mirandulensi): τοξευθεὶς φλεχθεὶς θ' ὑπὸ Πίκος Ἐρώτων ‖ 4 cf. Politian. *ep. gr.* 29.4 (de Alexandria poetria): ὦ ἐμὲ δοὺς ἐς ὅλας ζῶντ' ἔτι πυρκαϊάς ‖ 5 καὶ πυρὶ φλέξε τὸ πῦρ] = Politian. *ep. gr.* 53.7 ǀ ὄμμασι δᾷδας ἀνάπτε] ~ Politian. *ep. gr.* 29.3 (ἐν ὄμμασι δᾷδας ἀνάπτει) ‖ 8 ὄλβιος ὦ τρὶς ἐγώ] = Politian. *ep. gr.* 26,5 ‖ 9–10 ~ Politian. *ep. gr.* 30b.9–10 (φωναῖς δ' ἐν πλείσταις σόν τοι κλέος ἠέρ' ἐλαστρεῖ, / Ἑλλάδι, Ῥωμαϊκῇ, Ἑβραϊκῇ, ἰδίῃ)

⟨Epigram to Constantia Peutinger⟩

> Shot and inflamed by the Cupids of the Peutinger-girl Constantia like the son of Kronos [= Zeus] by the ones of maiden Danae, I will sing like this: 'Be happy, Peutinger-girl, be happy since you put me alive onto your pyre: [5] And the fire burnt with fire and lit up the torches in my eyes. Together with your flame, a new love is in both of us. Give me your virginal tongue, girl, after your mouth: and I will be a thrice happy Capnion [Reuchlin ~ 'little smoke']! My glory is in most languages, but you will say it in [10] Greek, German, Latin, and Hebrew.'

Metre: Elegiac couplets; in general, the metre is treated quite well, in comparison with pieces by other German humanists of the time, but there are also some peculiarities. Note, especially, consonantic ι in l. 2 (Κωνσταντίης), the lengthening of ι in l. 8 (Καπνίων) and the short υ before φθέγξῃ in l. 9. One may also note the hiatus at the caesura of the pentameter in l. 8.

Notes: Bernardino Trebazio (1480–1548) who, in a letter to Stephanus Rosinus from 1514, transmitted this Greek epigram together with a Greek letter by Reuchlin, gives us some information about the circumstances of its composition, saying: *Libuit et versiculos quosdam subtexere, quos ille cum certatim Constantiam lectissimam virginem, Peutingeri filiam laudaremus, non minus apte quam facile dictavit; eos ego cum memoria tenerem epistolae subnectendos putavi* (Friedlaender 1837, 106) – 'I also added some verses, which he dictated as adequately as easily when we had a competition in praising the excellent girl Constantia, Peutinger's daughter. As I still kept them in mind, I thought that I should add them at the end of the letter.' Thus, the epigram was a result of a poetic contest between Reuchlin and Trebazio about Conrad Peutinger's (1465–1547) daughter Constantia (1503–?). Constantia was famous as she later made the laurel wreath for the poet Ulrich von Hutten (1488–1523), who praised her as the most beautiful and virtuous of all maidens in Augsburg. The epigram is not only remarkable because of its erotic character but also because it is almost a cento of phrases borrowed from the Italian humanist Angelo Poliziano (→ **Italy**). The sources are epigrams 26, 29, 30b and 53 from Poliziano's *Liber epigrammatum Graecorum*, which addressed a boy named Chrysocomus (26), an unknown boy (29), Giovanni Pico della Mirandola (53), and Poliziano himself (30b; the response of Alessandra Scala, probably written or inspired by Ianos Laskaris). Therefore, it seems reasonable to assume that Reuchlin did not directly know the ancient sources for Poliziano's phrasing, but used Poliziano instead. One may also assume that the epigram was later polished by Trebazio himself. Most notable is an additional remark by Trebazio about its supposed erotic nature: *Et ne quis posset dubitare, de quali amore locutus esset, subjunxit epigrammati*: καὶ ἔστι δὲ θεῖος ἔρως, ἀγαθὸς ἀγαθοῦ διὰ τὸ ἀγαθόν (*Dionysius de divinis nominibus capite IIII.*). – 'And in order that nobody could have doubts about the nature of the love he had talked about, he added beneath the epigram: 'and there is a divine love, good of good because of the good' (Dionysius [Areopagita], *De divinis nominibus*, chapter IV).'

Biography: Johannes Reuchlin (1455–1522) was one of the most influential German humanists in the period before the reformation. He studied at the universities of Freiburg im Breisgau and Basel and became *Doctor iuris utriusque* at the University of Tübingen in 1484. During his three visits to Italy, he became familiar with several Italian humanists including Angelo Poliziano, Cristoforo Landino, and Giovanni Pico della Mirandola. His quarrel with Johannes Pfefferkorn and the Theological Faculty in Cologne about the destruction of all Hebrew books in Germany made him famous beyond the boundaries of Germany, as it was considered by his defenders to be a fight between the old scholastic tradition and the new humanistic movement. His opponents were depicted as stupid and ignorant in the anonymously published *Epistolae obscurorum virorum* (1515/17). In 1520, he became professor of Greek and Hebrew at the University of Ingolstadt, and in 1521, he returned to Stuttgart, where he died in 1522. His most important works are the two dialogues, *De verbo mirifico* (1494) and *De arte cabalistica* (1517). These are religious works seeking to unify Jewish, Ancient, and Christian thinking. He fostered Hebrew and Greek studies in particular, claiming to be the first person to introduce them to Germany. He was, therefore, celebrated as a *vir trilinguis* by his contemporaries. Among his philological works are a guide to Hebrew grammar (*Rudimenta Hebraica*, 1506) and several translations from Greek into Latin and Latin into German. His Latin and Greek poems are very few but he wrote two Latin comedies (*Sergius, Scaenica Progymnasmata*) around 1498.

Bibliography: Geiger, Ludwig (1889), "Reuchlin, Johannes", in: *ADB* 28, 785–799; Roloff, Hans-Gert (2003), "Reuchlin, Johannes", in: *NDB* 21, 451–453; Dörner, Gerald (2013), "Reuchlin (Rochlin, Roechlin; Capnion), Johannes", in: *VLHum* 2, 579–633; on his Greek poems: Friedlaender, Gottlieb (1837), *Beiträge zur Reformationsgeschichte. Sammlung ungedruckter Briefe des Reuchlin, Beza und Bullinger nebst einem Anhange zur Geschichte der Jesuiten*, Berlin; Rhein, Stefan (1989), "Johannes Reuchlin als Dichter. Vorläufige Anmerkungen zu unbekannten Texten", in: Hans-Peter Becht (ed.), *Pforzheim in der frühen Neuzeit*, Sigmaringen, 51–80.

Philipp Melanchthon (1497–1560)

Τῇ παιδείᾳ [1525]

Οὔπω ἐγὼ πρόλιπον θνητοὺς θεὰ οὐδ', ὅτ' ἀραίας
ἀθάνατ' ἐκ γαίας σὺν ἅμα πάντες ἔβαν.
οὐδέ με ἱππομάχων ἀραβημιγῆ ἔθνεα Θρηϊκῶν,
οὐκ ἀπέλαυνε Γοθῶν βαρβαρόφωνος ἄρης·
5   αἰεὶ γάρ τ' ἐχόμην ἐνί που μέρει Ἑλλάδος ἠδὲ
Ἰταλίας, δηΐους ἔνθα μένουσ' ἔλαθον.
νῦν δ' ὅτε νικηθέντες ἐς ἔσχατα γῆς φύγον ἐχθροί,
ἥκω Γερμανῶν λαὸν ἐς ὀψιμαθῶν.
οἱ δέ με γηθήσαντες ἐὴν βασίλειαν ἔθηκαν,
10 οὐδὲν ἐγὼ Θρᾳκῶν οὐδὲ Γοθῶν ἀλέγω.
δεῦτ' οὖν, Γερμανῶν παῖδες, κάμῆς ἀπὸ πατρῶν
ἀντ' εὐεργεσίης δῶρα λάβοιτε χερὸς
ὠκυγράφον κάλαμον, τόν μοι πόρε μείλιχος Ἑρμῆς·
ὅπλα γάρ ἐστι δέον ταῦτα μάλ' ὔμμε φορεῖν,
15 παιδείας φίλα δῶρ', ὑμέας δ' εἰς ἀνέρας ἄξω,
ἔσται ἐφ' ὧν χρυσέη δεύτερον αὖ γενεή.

Textus: Melanchthon, Philipp (1525), *Institutio puerilis literarum Graecarum*, Hagenau, ee iii rv; Rhein 1987, 144 (Nr. XIV).

Crit.: 4 ἀπέλαυνε scripsi: ἀπέλαυε ed. || 6 δηΐους scripsi: δηϊοὺς ed.

Sim.: 3 ἀραβημιγῆ] neologismus || 4 βαρβαρόφωνος ἄρης] cf. Nonn. *Dion.* 23.122 (β. Ἑώσιος ὤκλασεν ἄρης); Marc. Musur. *Od. in Plat.* 190 (eadem sede) || 12 ἀντ' εὐεργεσίης] cf. Theoc. *Id.* 17.116 (eadem sede) || 13 ὠκυγράφον] neologismus || 14 μείλιχος Ἑρμῆς] clausula Nonniana, cf. *Dion.* 36.108; 38.103

To *Paideia* [personified 'Education']

I, the goddess, have not yet left the mortals, not even when all immortals together had left the accursed earth. Neither the mixed Arabic tribes of the Thracians fighting on horsebacks nor the war of the Goths, speaking a foreign tongue, expelled me. [5] For always I stayed somewhere in one part of Greece and Italy, where my enemies did not notice my abode. But now, as the beaten enemies have taken flight to the end of the world, I have come to the people of the Germans, who are late in learning. But they rejoiced and made me their queen, [10] and I am not afraid of the Thracians or the Goths. Come ye, children of the Germans, and take from my hand gifts in exchange for your fathers' kindness: the fast writing reed which pleasant Mercury gave to me. For it is much needed that you carry these arms, [15] the dear gifts of *Paideia*; and I will bring you to men, under whose guidance there will be a new Golden Age.

Metre: Elegiac couplets. Note elision of -οι and lengthening of σύν in l. 2, hiatus in l. 3, synizesis in ll. 3 (Θρηϊκῶν), 6 (δηΐους), 16 (χρυσέη).

Notes: This poem was first printed at the end of Melanchthon's *Institutio puerilis literarum Graecarum* (1525), a short collection of Greek texts for school education. In addition to various ancient texts ranging from Homer to the New Testament, the collection also contained some Greek hexameters entitled *Capita sacrosanctae fidei*, which were obviously written by Melanchthon's friend Joachim Camerarius. Camerarius later separately edited an extended version in a book called *Capita pietatis et religionis christianae versibus Graecis comprehensa ad institutionem puerilem* (Leipzig 1545) (see Walter 2017). Melanchthon's epigram is significant in various ways. At first, Melanchthon is evoking the idea of *translatio studiorum*. After being hidden from the attacks of Goths and Thracians (probably Turks), *Paideia* finally comes to Germany where she is warmly welcomed. In the second part, Melanchthon then combines this with the idea of *aemulatio*, as *Paideia* now – in return for her admission – wants to give a reed to the children which will bring them to a new Golden Age. Melanchthon uses the form of *prosopopoeia* in his epigram, as *Paideia* ('Education') is herself speaking. The gift of a reed at the end of the poem recalls, perhaps, a famous Latin epigram by Erasmus: Erasmus handed the reed he had received from Johannes Reuchlin over to Wilhelm Nesen (ca. 1494–1524). Melanchthon did the same in 1523. The Greek epigram, therefore, shows a kind of humanistic *Dichterweihe* and invites the readers to take the gift and write in Greek themselves (cf. Rhein 1987 & 2017). Melanchthon, who had a major influence on the propagation of Greek learning and writing, supports this intention in the Latin text which precedes the epigram. In it, he asks the teachers to combine reading of Greek texts with writing, that is, passive and active knowledge of the language: *Nam haec, id est lectionem & scriptionem,* *si coniunxeris, plane alterius alterum habebit alleviationem, & perfectius ac foelicius efficiet.* – It is interesting to note that Melanchthon uses two Nonnian hexameter-endings, only attested in the *Dionysiaca*, which were first printed in 1569. It is reasonable to assume that he did not take them directly from Nonnus (cf. Weise 2019, 18, fn. 55) but used other sources (e.g., Mousouros → **Greece**).

Biography: Philipp Melanchthon was one of the key figures in the introduction and establishment of Greek studies and writing in Protestant Germany. Born in Bretten in 1497, he attended the Latin school in Pforzheim, supported and promoted by Johannes Reuchlin (see above). Reuchlin also gave him his humanist name, rendering the original German 'Schwarzerdt' ('black earth') into the Greek Μελάγχθων. From 1509, Melanchthon studied first in Heidelberg and later in Tübingen, where he acquired a master's degree in 1514. Alongside his teaching at the university, he worked as a corrector in the publishing office of Thomas Anshelm. It is there that he performed his first work as a poet on a short epigram for an edition of Theodore Gaza's *De rudimentis literarum Graecarum* in 1515 (cf. Rhein 2017, 20–21). In 1518, upon a recommendation by Reuchlin, he became professor of Greek at the newly-founded Wittenberg University, the second officially salaried professorship of Greek in Germany after that attained by Richard Croke at Leipzig University in 1515. In Wittenberg, Melanchthon quickly became a close friend and collaborator of Martin Luther, although he kept his professorship of Greek at the Faculty of Arts until his death in 1560. It is not necessary to list his achievements as a Protestant reformer, but only to highlight his influence as a propagator of Greek. His tastes and predilections had a lasting influence on his students. He made Latin translations of Euripides, Pindar, Theognis, Demosthenes, and other Greek authors (including Hellenistic and later poets), and he authored an important Greek grammar and a collection of Greek texts for beginners (see above). Although he wrote only a dozen Greek epigrams and letters himself, he encouraged his students to do so with great success. In an important article, Stefan Rhein lists the following among his students who proved capable of writing in Greek: David Chytraeus, Paul Dolscius, Matthias Garbitius (→ **Balkans**), Michael Neander (see below Rhodoman and Gothus), and Johannes Caselius (see below).

Bibliography: Scheible, Heinz (2016), *Melanchthon. Vermittler der Reformation. Eine Biographie*, München. On his Greek poetry and Greek contacts: Benz 1971; Rhein, Stefan (1987), *Philologie und Dichtung. Melanchthons griechische Gedichte (Edition, Übersetzung und Kommentar)*, Diss. Heidelberg; Rhein, Stefan (2017), "Philipp Melanchthon und seine griechischen Dichterschüler", in: Weise 2017, 15–46; Walter, Jochen (2017), "Die Capita pietatis et religionis Christianae versibus Graecis comprehensa ad institutionem puerilem des Joachim Camerarius (1545) und ihre kürzere

Erstfassung in Melanchthons Institutio puerilis literarum Graecarum (1525)", in: Thomas Baier (ed.), *Camerarius Polyhistor. Wissensvermittlung im deutschen Humanismus*, Tübingen, 23-57.

Joachim Camerarius (1500-1574)

I. <*Epigramma de Camerario poeta*> [ante 1538]

    Οὐδ' ἐγὼ αὐτὸς ποιητὴν ἐμέ φημι γενέσθαι
      οὐδέ τε Παρνασσοῦ βῆν' ἐπ' ὄρους κορυφήν,
    οὐδ' ἔμ' ἐν ἱππογένους ἐποτίσθη χείλεα κρήνης,
      οὐδέ με Πιερίδων ὅσσα προσῆλθε θεῶν.
5   Καὶ δέ θ' ὅμως αἰεί τι γράφων στιχόεντ' ἐν ἀριθμῷ
      καὶ πεδίων Κλειοῦς ἄνθος ἀποδρέπομαι.
    ἡ δ' ἔμ' ἐᾷ βελτίστη ὅπως τινὰ παῖδ' ἀλιταίνειν
      ἡδύ τ' ἐπὶ σπουδῆς τῆσδε κενῆς γελάᾳ.
    οὐκ ἀλέγω· τέρψις μὲν ἔμ' εὑρέθη ἥδε βίοιο
10   παυσωλή τ' ἀγαθὴ φροντίδος ἀργαλέης.
    Μοῦσα, μόνον μ' εἴασσον ἀνώνυμόν τ' ἀκλεῆ τε
      ἀφραδέειν σφετέρης ἂν δρίον Ἀονίης.

Textus: Camerarius, Joachim/Micyllus, Jacobus (1538), *Epigrammata veterum poetarum*, Basileae, 119.

Crit.: 3 ἔμ' (= ἐμά) scripsi: ἐμ' ed. | ἱππογενοῦς debuit || 5 αἰεί scripsi: ἀεί ed. | στιχόεντ' temptavi: στίχοεν τ' ed. || 7 ἔμ' (= ἐμέ) scripsi (melius δέ μ'): ἐμ' ed. || 7-8 ἐᾷ...γελάᾳ scripsi: ἐᾶ...γελάα ed. || 8 τῆσδε: τῆς δε ed. || 9 ἔμ' (= ἐμοί) scripsi suadente Pontani: ἐμ' ed. | ἥδε: ἡδὲ ed.

Sim.: 1-3 cf. Pers. *prol.* 1-3 || 3 ἱππογένους] neologismus || 10 παυσωλή...φροντίδος ἀργαλέης] cf. *Anth. Pal.* 11.54.6 (παύω φροντίδας ἀργαλέας)

<Epigram on Camerarius as a poet>

I do not say that I have become a poet nor that I have gone to the top of mount Parnassus. Neither were my lips irrigated by the fountain which originated from the horse nor did the voice of the Pierides [Muses] come to me. [5] Nevertheless, always writing something in verses and metre, I pluck off the flower of Klio's plains. And she, the dearest one, lets me sin like some child and laughs gently at this vain effort. I do not care. I have found this as a joy of life [10] and a good rest from painful thought. Muse, just let me anonymously and without glory play on the thicket of your Aonia.

II. Τῇ μητρὶ Ἰωαχεῖμος υἱὸς ἐποίει [1522?]

Μαῖα φίλη, τὶς μοῖρα τεὴν ζωὴν ἀπόλεσσε,
 ὤμοι τὶς πότμος σεῖο δάμασσε βίον;
ὡς σοῦ μὲν τεθνευίας ἡμέτερος δόμος ἔρρει
 σοί θ' ἅμα παντόλεθρος συντάκη οἰχομένη
5 καὶ σύ που αἰθερίαις ἐνὶ πτυξὶν νυνὶ κάθησαι
 ἀθανάτοις ἡμᾶς ὄμμασι δερκομένη,
νῶ δ' αὖ σήματα ταῦτα τεῇ μνήμῃ προθέμεσθα,
 ὄφρα καὶ ὀψιγόνων ἡμέας εὖ τις ἐρῇ.

Textus: Camerarius/Micyllus 1538, 133–134.

Crit.: 1–2 τὶς (cf. etiam infra Herrichen)] debuit τίς ‖ 4 σοί Gärtner: σῇ ed. | συντάκη οἰχομένη Gärtner: συντάκετ' οἰχομένη ed. ‖ 8 an ἐρεῖ?

Sim.: 1 μαῖα φίλη] iunctura Homerica, cf. *Od.* 20,129; 23,11.59.81 ‖ 4 παντόλεθρος] apud veteres tantum παντολέτειρα (*Hymn. Orph.* 26.2) vel πανόλεθρος legitur ‖ 6 ὄμμασι δερκομένη] cf. eadem sede Greg. Naz. *carm.* PG 37.1377.8 (ὄμμασι δερκόμενος) ‖ 8 cf. Hom. *Il.* 3.353 (ὄφρα τις ἐρρίγησι καὶ ὀψιγόνων ἀνθρώπων)

The son Joachim wrote this for his mother

My dear good mother, which Moira took your life away, o, which fate overcame your life? Hence, since you are dead, our house disappears, and together with your passing, it has melted away. [5] And you sit now somewhere in the folds of heaven and look upon us with immortal eyes. But we have set this monument for your memory so that someone of the after-born will praise us as well.

Metre: Elegiac couplets; almost flawless, but in the first epigram note the elision of -οι in ἐμοί (l. 9) and the wrong scansion of ἀνώνυμον (l. 11: υ should be short), and in the second epigram there is a *versus bipartitus* in l. 3, πτ does not cause position in l. 5, and νυνί (l. 5) has a short ι.

Notes: The two epigrams selected here belong to an epigram collection from 1538 (*Epigrammata veterum poetarum*) containing Camerarius' own Greek poems together with those of Jacob Micyllus as an appendix to a collection of ancient epigrams. The poems in this collection cover many different forms (funerary epigrams, hymns, astronomical poems, riddles) and metres (even epodic forms; cf. → **France**) and are, therefore, of high interest (cf. Schultheiß 2020). The first epigram presented here gives an interesting self-assessment of Camerarius as a poet. He judges himself – certainly with humanistic and Protestant understatement –

not as a born poet but as an amateur poet playing just for fun. It is also noteworthy that Camerarius alludes to the Latin poet Persius in lines 1–3 (Camerarius even uses a more Latin-like *accusativus cum infinitivo* in the first line instead of the *nominativus cum infinitivo* one would expect in Greek). The second poem is a funerary epigram for his dead mother, showing again a personal touch. It should be mentioned that Camerarius also included some pieces by Poliziano (→ **Italy**) and Laskaris (→ **Greece**) in the collection before his own pieces. In the Greek foreword, he explains the addition of his own epigrams as follows: Τὰ δὲ [Τά δε ed.] μεταγενέστερα ταυτὶ ἐν ᾧπερ [ὧπερ ed.] αὐτοὶ ἐθέλοιτε λόγῳ τε καὶ ἀριθμῷ θήσετε, οὐδὲν δ' οὖν οἷον δεῖγμά [δειγμά ed.] τι παρασκευάσασθαι τῆς τῶν νεωτέρων σπουδῆς καὶ ὥσπερ κατ' ἴχνη τῶν προτέρων ὁδοιπορίας [...]. (a 5r) – 'And you will judge these later (poems) as you like, but nothing else than just to give an example of the zeal of the recent people and as an example of their following the traces of the Ancients.'

Biography: Born in 1500, Camerarius studied at the University of Leipzig where he attended the Greek lectures of Richard Croke (1516) and Petrus Mosellanus (1517). After a short period in Erfurt, he moved to Wittenberg in 1521 and became a close friend of Philipp Melanchthon. Melanchthon recommended him to become headmaster and teacher of Greek at the Protestant model-school in Nürnberg (1526–35). From 1535 to 1541, he held a professorship of Greek at the University of Tübingen and finally, returned to Leipzig to be professor of Greek and Latin at the university there. He died in Leipzig in 1574. Camerarius was an important philologist and edited many Greek and Latin authors. He was a keen writer of Greek. He not only exchanged Greek letters and poems with his friend Melanchthon but also composed a remarkable Greek prose history of the Schmalkaldic War (the text remained a fragment – perhaps in imitation of Thucydides – and was later supplemented with a short Greek closure by Simon Stenius) (cf. Voigt 1874, 115–121). His numerous Greek poems range from epigrams to longer pieces (Walter 2017), idylls (Orth 2020), and even supplements for defective Greek literature (Weise 2018). A complete overview of his printed writings with descriptions and bibliography is now accessible at: http://www.camerarius.de/ [accessed: August 2020].

Bibliography: Hamm, Joachim (2011), "Camerarius (Kammermeister), Joachim d. Ä.", in: *VL16*, vol. 1, 425–438. On his Greek writings: Schultheiß 2020; Orth, Christian (2020), "Die Rezeption der griechischen Bukoliker in Camerarius' *Ekloge* über den Tod des Johannes Stigelius (*ecl.* 17)", in: Anne-Elisabeth Beron/Stefan Weise (eds.), *Hyblaea avena. Theokrit in römischer Kaiserzeit und Früher Neuzeit*, Stuttgart, 99–114; Weise, Stefan (2020), "Gespräche auf Augenhöhe. Deutsch-griechischer Dialog im Humanismus und heute", in: Stefan Freund/Nina Mindt (eds.),

Antike Konzepte für ein modernes Europa. Die Klassische Philologie und die Zukunft eines Jahrhundertprojekts, Wuppertal, 115–129: 117–125; Id. (2018), *"Alter Theocritus?* Joachim Camerarius'griechische Supplemente zu Theokrits *Herakliskos* und dem sogenannten *Herakles leontophonos*", in: *Humanistica Lovaniensia* 67, 257–299; Walter, Jochen (2017), "Die *Capita pietatis et religionis Christianae versibus Graecis comprehensa ad institutionem puerilem* des Joachim Camerarius (1545) und ihre kürzere Erstfassung in Melanchthons *Institutio puerilis literarum Graecarum* (1525)", in: Thomas Baier (ed.), *Camerarius Polyhistor. Wissensvermittlung im deutschen Humanismus*, Tübingen, 23–57; Weng, Gerhard (2003), "Camerarius' griechische Gestaltung des 133. Psalms – nur eine Paraphrase?", in: Rainer Kößling/Günther Wartenberg (eds.), *Joachim Camerarius*, Tübingen, 175–205; Voigt, Georg (1874), *Die Geschichtschreibung über den Schmalkaldischen Krieg*, Leipzig.

Martin Crusius (1526–1607)

I. <*Versus rhythmici paraphrasi poeticae Ieremiae prophetae praepositi*> [1571]

Ὡς Ἱρμίας ὠδύρατο
Ἱρουσαλὴμ τὸ πτῶμα
καὶ φρικτὸν ὠλοφύρατο
Λαοῦ Θεοῖο χῶμα·
5 Οὕτως ὅπλοις πορθουμένων
Χριστωνύμων σκοτεινοῖς
Ἡμῶν λίην κακουμένων
Κακοῖσιν οὐ ποθεινοῖς
Τί δεῖ ποιεῖν; τί χρὴ λέγειν;
10 Οὐ σφάλματ' ἀμὰ κεύθειν,
Ἀλλ' ὡς μάλιστ' αὐτὰ ψέγειν,
Οὐκ ἐν δύῃ καθεύδειν·
Πιστῇ προσευχῇ τὸν Θεὸν
Συγγνώμον' αὖθι θεῖναι,
15 Πάντας βίον τρέπειν ἐὸν
Καλοῖς τρόποις συνεῖναι
Λήγοντες ἤθους νηπίου
καὶ βέλτιον φρονεῦντες
Πατρὸς τύχοιμεν ἠπίου
20 Ἐν πᾶσιν εὐτυχεῦντες.
Ταῦθ' ὁ Προφήτης ἐμπαθῶς
Θρήνοις δίδαξ' ἑοῖσι,
Τοὺς Φιγκελθοῦσος εὐμαθῶς
Φράζει μέτροις καλοῖσι·
25 Φράζει νέος Νορθούσιος,
Ὡς οὐκ ἂν ἔφρασ' ἄλλος·

Γεραίτερος Ῥαμνούσιος
Οὐκ ἂν λάβοι τὸ κάλλος.

Textus: Finckelthaus, Wolfang (1571), *Hieremię Prophetae ΘΡΗΝΟΙ. Graeco Heroico Carmine expositi*, Tubingae, c. [A4r]; Crusius, Martin (1585), *Germanograeciae libri sex...*, Basileae, 143 (una cum versione Latina).

Crit.: post v. 28 apposuit Ετει ᾳ φ ο α

<Rhymed verses accompanying a Greek paraphrasis of Jeremiah>

As Jeremiah mourned the fall of Jerusalem and lamented the awful ruin of God's people, [5] so when we Christians are destroyed by dark weapons and maltreated by undesirable evils, what should we do, what should we say? [10] We should not hide our mistakes but expose them as strongly as we can, and we should not sleep in anguish! We should make God indulgent again through pious prayer, [15] everybody should change their life and should adopt good manners; we should end our childish customs und think better: then, we may get a gentle father [20] and succeed in everything. This was what the prophet passionately taught through his *Lamentations*. Finckelthaus, [25] the young man from Nordhausen, skilfully explains them in beautiful verses like no other elder Rhamnusian [Attic] could have explained them nor could have captured their beauty.[28]

Metre: Distichs of alternating acatalectic and catalectic iambic dimeters (with cross rhyme).

II. ΑΝΤΙΧΡΙΣΤΟΙ [12 November 1550]

Εἱματολευκοφόροι, φαινοσκυθρωποπρόσωποι,
  Ζητοδ<ι>εργόβιοι, χρηματομισσοπρᾶται,
Χριστοκαθηματιοσταυροί, εἰδωλοσεβασταί,

---

28 Author's Latin translation: *Vt flevit Hirmias trucem / Hirusalae ruinam: / Populi Dei plorans crucem, / manum plicando binam: / [5] Sic arma gentem cùm premunt / cruenta Christianam: / hostesque dira cùm fremunt, / non iam habendo vanam: / Quid facere licet [correxit Pontani: dicet ed.]: aut dicere? / [10] peccata non tacere: / Sed maximè reprehendere: / ac propter ipsa flere, / Deum, benignum reddere / fida precatione: / [15] vitae bonae convertere / nos institutione. / Pravam relinquunt, qui viam: / fidam geruntque mentem: / emergere queunt per piam / [20] vitam Deo placentem. / Hoc omne Vatis tormina / huius docent disertè: / dant Finckelthusi carmina, / spectanda, docta certè. / [25] Iuvenis dat en Germanicus, / quale haud daret Poema / maior aliquis natu Atticus, / doctaque mente schema.*

Λεκτροδικαιόφυγοι, πορνολαθραιοτρόφοι,
5   Ἐξαπατησιάδαι, κοσμουπαντηπεροπευταί,
Καλλιτριχιπποβάται, κερματοθηρασίδαι,
Φαιναγιόφθαλμοι, ὀλοοφρενιλαθραφυτευταί,
Αἱματοδιψαλέοι, κερδαλεοφρόνιμοι,
Βομβαρδοξιφεσισχοινεγχεσιπυρδιαλέκται,
10   Βιβλοθεουφυγάδες, κοσμοματαιόσοφοι,
Διαβολοσπερέες, παχυοσκοτοεργοδιῶκται,
Ὀρθοφρενιπλανέες, ταρταρεριννύμοροι.

Textus: Crusius, Martin (1567), *Poematum Graecorum libri duo*..., Basileae, lib. II, p. 62.

Crit.: 2 ζητοδιεργόβιοι scripsi: ζητοδεργόβιοι ed. metro repugnante ‖ **4** λεκτροδικαιοφύγοι Pontani

Sim.: imitatur noster poema ex Hegesandro sumptum et in Athenaei *Deipnosophistis* 4.162ab traditum

Antichrists

You white-clothes-wearers, you severe-face-simulators,
    You life-through-works-seekers, you masses-with-money-buyers,
You daily Christ-crucifiers, you idol-worshippers,
    You righteous-marriage-escapers, you secret prostitute-pimps,
You frauds, you through-the-whole-world-travellers,
    You beautiful-haired-horses-riders, you money hunters,
You holy-eyes-simulators, you secret evil-mind-planters,
    You thirsty for blood, you greedy of gain,
You cannon-sword-rope-spear-fire-speakers,
    You holy-Bible-escapers, you wordly sophists,
You devil's seed, you works-in-thick-darkness-seekers,
    You deprived of right mind, you underworld's Erinys-seekers.[29]

Metre: Elegiac couplets (note hiatus in l. 7).

---

29 Author's Latin translation: *Candidauestigeri, faciesimulanteseueri, / Pulchroperotumidi, missapecunifices. / QuottidieChristocrucifigi, idolicolentes. / Connubisanctifugae, clammeretricitegae. / [5] Versidolopelles, totorbiperambulitechnae, / Alticaballequites, fraudepecunilegi. / Fictoculosancti, mentexitiosiferentes, / Sanguinicrudibibae, pectorecelidoli. / Bombardagladiofunhastaflammiloquentes, / [10] Bibliasacrifugae, desipidiscioli. / Nigrideonati, crassaetenebrisstudiosi, / Mentebonapriui, tartarerinnypetae.*

Notes: The two selected poems show both Crusius' (unclassical) predilection for formal experiments and the deeply Protestant nature of his poetry. The first poem, accompanying a Greek paraphrase of *Jeremiah* by Wolfgang Finckelthaus (a pupil of Michael Neander and a friend of Laurentius Rhodoman), is remarkable in the use of rhymed endings, a feature taken, perhaps, from popular German songs and poetry, combined here with ancient metre. The second poem is a list of negative epithets characterising the Antichrists (the Catholics in Crusius' eyes). There is also a counterpart praising the (Protestant) Christians. For the characterisation, Crusius uses only longer composite neologisms (*verba plaustralia*). This feature, together with its satirical intention, is obviously inspired by Hegesander (Ath. 4.162ab) and Aristophanes who used similar artificial composites (see also Gilles Ménage → **France**). Regarding this poem, Lizel notes in his *Historia*: *Poëta noster verbis plaustralibus, phaleretis & sesquipedalibus, id est, rei convenientibus, naturam eorum, qui contra Christi membra pugnant, depingit. [...] Ejusmodi carminis genus, si modo, ut CRVSIVS fecit, parcius & naturae rei conveniens usurpetur, non plane spernendum esse puto, quod instar aromatum sit, quibus cibi saporati fiunt. Talia verba plaustralia, quae justum plaustri onus videri possunt, reperiuntur quoque apud veteres* (Lizelius 1730, 110–111).

Biography: Although his own Greek poems are not particularly sublime and show no exquisite taste for the Greek poetic language, Martin Crusius was an enthusiastic and influential philhellenist. His career progression was quick and straightforward. Born in 1526, he attended the famous gymnasium of Johannes Sturm in Strasbourg. Thereafter, he was school rector in Memmingen (1554) and from 1559, professor of Greek and Latin at the University of Tübingen until his death in 1607. He was a successful academic teacher and was part of a wide network of important Hellenists, notably Michael Neander and Laurentius Rhodoman (see below). He even built up a correspondence with the Greek patriarch of Constantinople and his administration (cf. Wendebourg 1986). Although his theological dialogue was unsuccessful, Crusius was one of the first Westerners to gather specific knowledge not only about ancient but also about modern Greek. His main works are the two programmatic books *Turcograecia* (1584) and *Germanograecia* (1585), the former being a presentation of contemporary Greece under Turkish rule (also containing his letter exchange with Patriarch Jeremiah II), the latter being a presentation of Greek literature and poetry in Germany (containing, e.g., three poetic letters by Laurentius Rhodoman, most notably his autobiographical Greek poem, *Bioporikon*). His restless activity is also shown by his handwritten *Diarium* in which he meticulously noted his readings, contacts, and activities – a valuable source for sixteenth-century scientific life (cf. Mährle 2019).

In order to improve his competence in writing Greek, he simultaneously translated into Greek church sermons which are still preserved together with other handwritten volumes by him in the library of the University of Tübingen. His first major poetic work in Greek was a poetic paraphrase of the Susanna-Story form the Old Testament (1555) (see Weise 2020). The first collection of his Greek poems and orations entitled *Martini Crusii Poematum Graecorum libri duo…Orationum liber unus* was published by the important humanist printer, Johannes Oporinus, in 1567. A bilingual (Latin/Greek) prose narration on the sufferings of his parents during the Schmalkaldic War, published as an appendix to a Latin *epitome* of Heliodorus' novel *Aethiopica* in 1584, is of some interest too.

Bibliography: Wildmann, Hans (1957), "Crusius, Martin", in: *NDB* 3, 433–434; Wendebourg 1986; Ludwig 1998; Ludwig, Walther (1998a), "Martin Crusius und das Studium des Griechischen im 16. Jahrhundert", in: *Humanistische Bildung* 20, 1–13; Id. (1998b), "Martin Crusius und das Studium des Griechischen in Nordeuropa", in: *Arctos* 32, 133–148; Id. 2017, 125–131; Mährle, Wolfgang (2019), "Der Tag des Gelehrten. Das ‚Diarium' des Martin Crusius als frühneuzeitliches Selbstzeugnis", in: Id. (ed.), *Spätrenaissance in Schwaben: Wissen – Literatur – Kunst*, Stuttgart, 229–247; Weise, Stefan (2020), "Χελκιάδος μέλλων θυμοῦ περὶ σώφρονος εἰπεῖν. Griechische Paraphrasen der Susanna-Geschichte aus der Renaissance (Martin Crusius und Georg Koch)", in: Eberhard Bons/Michaela Geiger/Frank Ueberschaer/Marcus Sigismund/Martin Meiser (eds.), *Die Septuaginta – Themen, Manuskripte, Wirkungen*, Tübingen, 868–885.

Johannes Posselius (1528–1591)

ΙΩΑΝΝΗΣ ΠΟΣΣΕΛΙΟΣ ΤΟΙΣ ΝΕΑΝΙΣΚΟΙΣ, ΤΟΙΣ περὶ τὴν Ἑλληνικὴν σοφίαν σπουδάζουσι, χαίρειν [1585]

Ἔστιν ἀνὴρ φρόνιμος, βίοτον καματώδεος ὥρῃ
  Ἀμητοῦ ὅστις συλλέγει ἁρμόδιον.
Οὗτος γὰρ πλούτῳ κεκορημένος ἄφθονα πάντα
  Αἰὲν ἔχει, ζωὴν τερπνοτάτην διάγων.
5 Ὅς δὲ ἀεργὸς ἐὼν ἐνὶ εἴαρος ἤματι εὕδει,
  Οὗτος τῇ πενίῃ τείρεται ἐξοπίσω.
Ἀμβολιεργὸς ἀνὴρ βιότου ἐπιδεύεται αἰσχρῶς,
  Χρήμασ' ἐπ' ἀλλοτρίοις χεῖρας ἰάλλει ἑάς.
Τῷδε Θεὸς νεμεσᾷ πανυπέρτατος, ὅστις ἀεργὸς
10 Σπάρτην οὐ κοσμεῖ, ἣν λάχεν, ἐμμελέως.
Ταῦτ' οὖν φραζόμενος σὺ μετὰ φρεσὶ καιροῦ ἀόκνως
  Ἅπτου ἰδ' ἐργάζευ πᾶς ὅτις ἐσσὶ νέος.
Μάνθανε εὖ φρονέειν προσέχων ἀρετῇσιν ἀγαυῇς
  Καὶ σοφίῃ, καιρὸς μέχρι πάρεστι καλός.

15 Γράμματα ὀτραλέως Ἑλληνικὰ γνῶθι, ἀληθῶς
    Εἰ μέμαας σώφρων καὶ πολύϊδρις ἔμεν.
    Ἑλλήνεσσιν ἄγαν κομψῶς φρονίμως τε ἅπαντα
    Ἀνδράσιν ἡδυεπὴς Μοῦσα ἔδωκε λαλεῖν.
    Οὐκ αἰέν, νέοι ὦ ἀγαπητοί, καιρὸς ἐσεῖται
20 Τοῦ μαθέειν· νυνὶ χρήσιμα μανθάνετε.
    Ἀμητοῦ νῦν ἐστὶ χρόνος, συλλέξατε καρπούς·
    Καιρὸς καὶ νεότης οὐ παρέασιν ἀεί.

Textus: Posselius, Johannes (1585), *Calligraphia oratoria linguae Graecae* [...], Frankfurt, *2.

Sim.: 1 καματώδεος ὥρῃ] = Hes. *Op.* 584 (θέρεος κ. ὤ.) || **7** ἀμβολιεργὸς ἀνήρ] iunctura Hesiodica, vid. *Op.* 413 || **10** σπάρτην–λάχεν] paroemia, cf. Plut. *De tranq. anim.* 472d (σπάρταν ἔλαχες, ταύταν κόσμει), Apostol. 8,59 (ἣν ἔλαχες σπάρταν, ταύτην κόσμει) et al. || **17–18** de re cf. Hor. *AP* 323-324 (*Grais ingenium, Grais dedit ore rotundo / Musa loqui*) || **18** ἡδυεπὴς μοῦσα] cf. *Hymn. Hom.* 32,1-2 (Μοῦσαι / ἡδυεπεῖς); Hes. *Theog.* 965-966, 1021-1022

Johannes Posselius greets the youths who are eager to study Greek wisdom

A wise man is the one who gathers enough substance for life at the time of wearisome harvest. For this one has everything in plenty, satisfied with wealth, and has a life full of enjoyment. [5] But whoever is not working and sleeps at the day of spring, that one is later oppressed by poverty. A man who dilates work is shamefully in need for life-substance and puts forth his hands on possessions belonging to others. God, the highest of all, has wrath with every not working man who [10] does not rule the part which he obtained rightly. Therefore, consider this in your mind and take the opportunity without hesitation. Work, when you are young. Learn to be prudent by turning your mind on the noble virtues and wisdom, as long as the good opportunity is there. [15] Learn Greek letters readily, if you want to be truly prudent and have much knowledge. The sweet-speaking Muse gave to the Greeks the gift to say everything very pleasantly and prudently. The opportunity for learning, O beloved children, will not be forever: [20] Learn useful things now! The time of harvest is now, gather the fruits: For opportunity and youth are not always at hand.

Metre: Elegiac couplets; Posselius' metric is flawless but he frequently admits hiatus (l. 2, 5, 7, 10, 13, 15, 17, 19).

Notes: This paratext accompanying Posselius' *Calligraphia oratoria linguae Graecae*, a Greek prose phraseology, is a recommendation to study Greek at a young age as a worthy investment for later life. The argument of usefulness is an important part of humanistic propaganda for Greek and the *humaniora* altogether.

Biography: Johannes Posselius, born in 1528 in Parchim, was a teacher and professor of Greek at the University of Rostock, where he had also studied from 1542 to 1545. After smaller posts elsewhere, he returned to Rostock in 1550, became *magister* in 1552, and taught at the university college from 1553. He was made rector of the university twice and was closely connected with David Chytraeus (1531–1600), whom he also accompanied on diplomatic missions. His working tools for writing and speaking Greek were very influential and successful. For this reason, he composed a *Syntaxis Graeca* (1565; more than ten reprints in the 16th and eight in the 17th century) and an Οἰκείων διαλόγων βιβλίον, a Greek translation of Erasmus' *Familiarium colloquiorum formulae* (at least four prints in the 16th and eight in the 17th century). This was one of the very few examples of Greek *Gesprächsbüchlein*. In addition to these successful didactic instruments for prose composition and conversation, Posselius also published poetic works. The most important were a Greek-Latin paraphrase of the gospel lectures (1565 and later: Εὐαγγέλια τῶν κυριακῶν καὶ ἑορταστικῶν ἡμερῶν στίχοις ἡρωικοῖς περιειλημμένα/*Evangelia Dominicorum et festorum dierum versibus Heroicis reddita*), a collection of Greek funerary poems for citizens who died during the plague (1565: *Epitaphia clarorum et piorum aliquot hominum*), and a collection of gnomic verses (1588: *Regulae vitae*).

Bibliography: Krause (1888), "Posselius, Johannes", in: *ADB* 26, 460–461; Johnson, Diane L. (2006), "Musa Posseliana: Johannes Posselius the Elder (1528–91) and the Lutheran Greek Program", in: *Reformation & Renaissance Review* 8, 186–209.

Johannes Caselius (1533–1613)

Εἰς πολυπράγμονα [ante 1613]

Πᾶς πουλυπράγμων δυστυχὴς πέφυκ' ἀνήρ.
Πῶς εὐτυχὲς γὰρ ἢ 'γαθοῦ τὸ αἴτιον
Τἄλλων ἐρευνᾶν, πάντα δ' αὐτοῦ ἀγνοεῖν;
Τὰ μὲν γὰρ ἄλλων πάντα γνοὺς σαυτὸν λαθών,
5 Κενὴν μέριμναν νηπίᾳ τρέφων φρενὶ
Φόβους παραυτίκ', εἰς τέλος δὲ πολλάκις
Ὄλεθρον αὐτόν, ὦ τάλαν, σοὶ κερδανεῖς.
Ὥς, εἰ φρονεῖς, ἀπὸ τῆλε τἄλλο πᾶν βαλών
Τὸ πρὸς σεαυτὸν ἐν βίῳ μόνον σκόπει,
10 Ζήτει θ' ἕκαστά σοι κατ' ἴχνος, ἐννοῶν
Ὧν ἐνδεὴς ἤτοι φρενῶν ἢ χρημάτων
Ἤπου φίλων ἢ καὶ τύχης. τῶν δ' οὐδενὸς

Γένοιτ' ἄμοιρος, ᾧ μέλει, ἃ μέλειν χρεών·
Ἰδιοπραγῶν δέ τις γένοιτο καὶ μάκαρ.

Textus: Caselius, Johannes (1624), *Carmina gnomica Graeca, et Latina* [...], Hamburg, 15–16.

Sim.: 1 πέφυκ' ἀνήρ] clausula Euripidea, vid. *Med.* 294; *Heracl.* 2 etc.

On a restless man

Unfortunate is the man who is ever restless and distracted. How could it be fortunate or the reason of good to inquire into others' business, but to know nothing about oneself? Hence, knowing everything about others, but being hidden from yourself, [5] you will nourish a vain sorrow in your childish mind and will gain fears and in the end, often death itself. So, if you are prudent, throw any other thing away and concentrate only on your own business in life. [10] Search everything for yourself along its trace, considering what you need, be it understanding or money or friends or also luck. The one who cares what he should take care of, will not be without any of this things. Whoever pursues his own business, may also be happy.

Metre: Iambic trimeters.

Notes: A gnomic piece on a typical Greek subject, the πολυπραγμοσύνη. The subject is consistent with Caselius' pedagogical intentions and his longing for peace and cultivated exchange.

Biography: Johannes Caselius (born in 1533) was an influential humanist and professor at the universities of Rostock (from 1563) and Helmstedt (from 1576). Among his teachers were Michael Neander in Nordhausen (later rector of the important monastery school in Ilfeld, see Rhodoman), Philipp Melanchthon in Wittenberg, and Joachim Camerarius in Leipzig. To complete his humanistic learning he twice visited Italy where, on his second visit in 1566, he acquired a doctorate in law at the University of Pisa and became friends with other important humanists such as Muret, Robortello, and Manutius Jr. Caselius died while a professor at Helmstedt in 1613. Some of his Greek poems are collected in *Carminum Graecorum et Latinorum centuria prima* (Göttingen 1608). An earlier collection is *Triumphus Domini et redemptoris nostri Iesu Christi...Quaedam alia eiusdem autoris Graeca poëmata* (Wittenberg 1552). His friend, Laurentius Rhodoman (see below), composed a lengthier hexametric congratulatory poem for Caselius' seventieth birthday in 1602 (Γενέθλια ἤτοι ἑβδομηκονταετηρὶς Κασηλίου). At request of Caselius, Rhodoman also wrote one of his last poems, a commemorative piece for the influential Polish nobleman and politician Jan Zamojski (*Epos manibus magni*

Zamoscii, published posthumously by Caselius in 1606) (see also Niegoszewski → **Poland and Lithuania**).

Bibliography: Kämmel, Heinrich (1876), "Caselius, Johannes", in: *ADB* 4, 40–43; Newald, Richard (1957), "Caselius, Johannes", in: *NDB* 3, 164; Sdzuj, Reimund B. (2011), "Caselius (Κασήλιος, Kesselius, Chesselius), Johannes ('Ιωάννης)", in: *VL16*, vol. 1, 478–497; Ludwig, Walther (2003), "Paideia bei Johannes Caselius und die Rezeption des Isokrates", in: *Würzburger Jahrbücher für die Altertumswissenschaft* 27, 195–216 = Id., *Miscella Neolatina*, vol. 1, Hildesheim/Zürich/New York 2004, 333–355.

Nicolaus Reusner (1545–1602)

In natalem diem filii Dei [1593]

   ὀγδοὰς α'

Θεὸν δεῦτε νέοι νέον
κωμάζετε παῖδα, καὶ κροτεῖτε
φωνᾷ ἀδυμελεῖ. χαρὰ δὴ
ἀμετέρα, εὔ-
5 χαρι βρεφύλλιον ἐν καπαῖς νῦν
κνώσσει μαλακῶς ἄδοξον·
καὶ μητρὸς ἐν ἁγνᾶς
κόλλοπι λάμπει, ἥλιος ὡς κλει-

   ὀγδοὰς β'

νός, ἀρχὰ ἄμα καὶ τέλος.
10 Ὦ τυτθὲ σαῶτερ, ἀμφὶ τίν μοι
ἦτορ δαίεται αἰθερῶδες,
τὺ δ' ἀπὸ βηλοῦ.
Τὺ κέαρ ἀχνύμενόν μοι ἀμπαύ-
σῃς ἄν σέο χρηστότητι.
15 ὦ παῖ πανάριστε,
ἄφθιτ' ἄναξ δόξας καὶ ἀγητέ,

   ὀγδοὰς γ'

ἐμὲ πρὸς σὲ τάχ' ἕλκυε.
ὦ πρᾳότατον νόον γονῆος,
ὦ υἱοῦ ἀγάπαν μεγίστην.
20 Πάντες ἀπωλό-
μεθα βροτοὶ διὰ δυσσέβειαν.

ἀλλ' οὐρανίας χαρᾶς αὖ
ἀμῖν μετέδωκεν:
εἴθε κέν, εἴθ' εἴημεν ἐκεῖθι.

ὀγδοὰς δ'

25 χαρὰ δὲ ποῖ μακάρων πέλει
τόσση; πλέον οὔποτ' ἢ ἐν οὐρα-
νοῖς: ἔνθα γλυκεροῖς ἐν ὕμνοις
ἄγγελοι ἁγνοὶ
κελαδέοντι θεὸν καὶ ἔνθα
30 αὐλὰ ἰάχει ἄνακτος
οἴμαις λιγυφθόγγοις:
εἴθε κέν, εἴθ' εἴημεν ἐκεῖθι.

Textus: Reusner, Nicolaus (1593), *Operum Nicolai Reusneri Leorini Silesii iurisconsulti et consiliarii Saxonici pars secunda* [...], Jena, 212–213.

Sim.: 3 φωνᾷ ἀδυμελεῖ] iunctura Pindarica, cf. *Nem.* 2.25 || 5 βρεφύλλιον] forma diminutiva pedestris, quae saepius apud Lucianum (cf. *Fug.* 19) legitur, in poesi inde a Michaele Psello || 8 κόλλοπι] fort. ex Hom. *Od.* 21.407, sed partim alio sensu || 10–11 cf. Hom. *Od.* 1.48 (ἀμφ' Ὀδυσῆι...δαίεται ἦτορ) || 12 ἀπὸ βηλοῦ] ex Hom. *Il.* 1.591 cum *schol.* (ἀπὸ τοῦ οὐρανοῦ) || 31 οἴμαις λιγυφθόγγοις] iunctura apud veteres inaudita, sed verba iam Homerica

On the birthday of God's son

First octet

Come on, young children, honour God, the young child, and yield with your sweet-singing voice: Our joy, [5] a charming small baby is now sleeping softly in a manger without glory and he shines at the neck of his pure mother like the fam-

Second octet

ous sun, beginning and end in one. [10] O small saviour, my heavenly heart is divided about you, but you are from the sky. You will stop my heart from grieving with your goodness. [15] O best child of all, eternal and admirable Lord of glory,

Third octet

draw me quickly towards Thee, O most gentle sense of the father, O greatest love of the son. [20] All we mortals perished because of our impiety. But he shared the heavenly joy with us. If only, if we could be there.

Fourth octet

[25] Where is such a joy of the Gods? Never more than in heaven: There pure angels celebrate God and there [30] the court of the Lord shouts with clearvoiced songs. If only, if we could be there.

Metre: Monostrophic ode in imitation of Pind. *Nem.* 2.

Notes: A fine Pindaric ode celebrating Christmas joy. The poem exploits the paradox of the baby child saving the world. The third and fourth stanzas end with the same line as a sort of refrain. This is one of eleven Pindaric odes within Reusner's two books of Greek epodes, all of them with a purely Christian subject. In this ode Reusner uses a repeated monostrophic form modelled after Pind. *Nem.* 2. A hint is given in l. 3, where Reusner reuses the combination φωνᾷ ἀδυμελεῖ from the end of Pindar's ode (*Nem.* 2.25). The short cola, however, reflect the Byzantine colometry of Pindar, representing the pre-Boeckhian practice. Reusner also uses features of Pindar's Doric dialect, notably Doric ᾱ (ll. 3ff.), the pronoun τύ (ll. 12–13), and -οντι for Attic -ουσι (l. 29).

Biography: The polyhistor Nicolaus Reusner (ennobled as *comes Palatinus* by Emperor Rudolf II in 1594) was a *doctor iuris* (from 1583 in Basel) and a professor of law at the universities of Basel and Jena. His native home (1545), however, was Löwenberg (today Lwówek Śląski in Poland). He attended the gymnasia in Goldberg/Złotoryja (under Valentin Friedland called Trozendorf, a very important Protestant pedagogue) and Breslau/Wrocław, where he gained a profound, humanistic education. Thereafter, he studied in Wittenberg and Leipzig. In addition to the humanistic disciplines, he also focused first on medicine and later, on law. After his studies, he became a teacher in Augsburg under Hieronymus Wolf and in Lauingen (1566, rector from 1572). He died while a professor at Jena in 1602. – His writings comprise a wide range of subjects: juridical, biographic, historic, rhetoric, philosophical, and poetic. He gained great success with his *Icones*, a collection of *Gelehrtenporträts* with praising verses from different authors. His own poetic works were published in an *opera*-collection in 1593–94. This collection also contains several books in Greek: one book of Greek elegies, one book of Greek *Heroides* (a translation of the first two Latin *Heroides* by the German Neo-Latin poet Eobanus Hessus), two books of Greek epodes, and one book of Greek epigrams. The Greek poems are of high quality with a great variety of subjects, metres, and genres. He especially excelled as a lyric poet with Christian themes.

Bibliography: Eisenhart, August Ritter von (1889), "Reusner, Nikolaus von", in: *ADB* 28, 299–303; Schilling, Michael (2016), "Reusner, Nikolaus", in: Wilhelm Kühlmann et al. (eds.), *Frühe Neuzeit in Deutschland 1520-1620. Literaturwissenschaftliches Verfasserlexikon*, Band 5, Berlin/Boston, 259–266; Ludwig 2017, 137–141; Päll, Janika (2017), "The Transfer of Greek Pindaric Ode from Italy to the Northern Shores: From Robortello to Vogelmann and further", in: Weise 2017, 349–368: 361–354.

Laurentius Rhodoman (1545/46–1606)

I. *Arion* [1567?/1588]

(excerptum, vv. 936–959: Leda visa Iuppiter cygnus fit)

αὐτὰρ ἐπεὶ τὰ καὶ ἄλλα διήλυθε μητιόωσα,
ἴθμα παραστρέψασα τανύσφυρον ὦρτο βαδίσδεν
εἰς κροκάλαν ποταμοῖο κατώφορον. ἤθελε γάρ που
ἄσυχα παφλάζοντος ἐπισχεδὸν ἄχον ἀκοῦσαι.
940 φράσσατο δ' οὔτ' ἀμέλασε θεῶν γενετήρ τε καὶ ἀνδρῶν
ἀργυφέας νεφέλας ὑπερήμενος εὐρύοπα Ζεύς.
ὡς δ' ἴδεν, ὥς σφε τάχ' οἶστρος ἀθέσφατος ἦτορ ἀνᾶψεν
ἐκ Παφίης, πυρόεις δὲ πάϊς φρένας ἆσε τόξῳ.
ἀλλ' οὔ μιν τόκα πρῶτα νόσος λάβε· δὴν γὰρ ὄνασθαι
945 ἵμειρεν φιλότατος ἐϋζώνοιο γυναικός,
ἐξότε οἱ ταπρῶτ' ἐπενήνοθεν εὔδροσος ἄβα.
αἶψα δέ οἱ πυκιναῖσι μεληδόσι πλήσσετο θυμός.
Ἥρας γὰρ μάλα μῆνιν ὀπίζετο, μή οἱ ἐνικλᾷ
ζαλοσύναισιν ἄεθλον, ὅν οἱ παρεθήκατο Κύπρις.
950 ὡς δ' ἄλοχον λελάθοι νεμεσάμονα, κλέψεν ἑαυτόν,
σκᾶπτρα μὲν ἐκ χερὸς ἦκε, θεῷ δ' ἀπεδύσατο μορφάν,
ἕσσατο δ' ὄρνιχος μαλακὰ πτίλα. πάντα δὲ κύκνῳ
εἴσατο χιονόμορφον ἔχων δέμας. αἶψα δ' ἄνοιξεν
οὐράνιον πυλεῶνα λάθρῃ. διὰ δ' αὐτὸς ὄρουσεν
955 αὔρας ἢ καπνοῖο θοώτερος. οὐδέ τις ἔγνω
ἀθανάτων, οὐδ' αὐτὸς ὁ πάνσκοπος ὄρχαμος αἴγλας,
ὅς τοπρὶν ἐνόησε καὶ Ἡφαίστῳ κρύφ' ἔλεξεν
Ἄρεα κουριδίοισι μιγαζόμενον λεχέεσσι
Κύπριδος, ἄσβεστον δὲ γέλων μακάρεσσιν ἐνῶρσεν.

Textus: Neander, Michael (ed.) (1588), *Argonautica. Thebaica. Troica. Ilias parva. Poematia Graeca auctoris anonymi, sed pereruditi* [...], Lipsiae, P 5rv; Weise 2019, 218.

Crit.: 938 ποταμοῖο corr.: ποτάμοιο ed. || **945** ἐϋζώνοιο corr.: ἐϋζώνοι ed. || **946** ἐπενήνοθεν corr.: -νυθεν ed. || **948** μή οἱ scripsi: μὴ οἱ ed. || **949** ζαλοσύναισιν corr.: Ζαλυ- ed. || **951** σκᾶπτρα corr.:

σκάπτρα ed. || **955** καπνοῖο corr.: κάπνοιο ed. | οὐδέ scripsi: οὐ δέ ed. || **956** οὐδ' Gärtner: οὔτ' ed. | πάνσκοπος corr.: πανσκόπος ed., contra normam defendit Pontani (fort. recte)

Sim.: 939 ἄσυχα παφλάζοντος] cf. Dionys. Per. 838 || **940** θεῶν γενετήρ τε καὶ ἀνδρῶν] imitatur clausulam Hom. πατὴρ ἀνδρῶν τε θεῶν τε, vide *Il.* 1.544 et al. || **941** εὐρύοπα Ζεύς] clausula Hom., cf. *Il.* 5.265 et al. || **942** ὡς δ' ἴδεν, ὥς...] cf. Theoc. 3.42 (ὡς ἴδεν, ὡς ἐμάνη) || **943** πυρόεις δὲ πάϊς] iunctura Nonniana, vid. *Dion.* 24.8 (de Baccho) | φρένας ἄασε] cf. Hom. *Od.* 21.297 (φ. ἄασεν οἴνῳ); Quint. Smyrn. 13.429 (φ. ἄ. Κύπρις) || **945** ~ Hes. *Sc.* 31 || **946** εὔδροσος] cf. Eur. *IA* 1517; Ar. *Av.* 245 || **947** πυκιναῖσι μεληδόσι] cf. *Anth. Pal.* 2.16 (στείνετο γὰρ πυκινῇσι μεληδόσι) || **948** Ἥρας...μῆνιν ὀπίζετο] cf. Hom. *Od.* 14.283 (Διὸς δ' ὠπίζετο μῆνιν); Hes. *Sc.* 21 (τῶν ὅ γ' ὀπίζετο μῆνιν) || **949** ζαλοσύναισιν] cf. *Hymn. Hom. Ap.* 100 (de iracundia Iunonis) || **952** ὄρνιχος] de forma cf. Pi. *Isthm.* 6.53; Theoc. 7.47 || **953** χιονόμορφον] neologismus || **954** οὐράνιον πυλεῶνα] cf. Greg. Naz. *Carm.*, PG 37.1346.8 (eadem sede); Nonn. *Dion.* 38.330 || **955** αὔρας...θοώτερος] cf. Nonn. *Dion.* 37.279; 42.160 (θοώτερα...αὔρης) | οὐδέ τις ἔγνω] clausula epica, cf. Hom. *Il.* 24.691; Ap. Rhod. *Argon.* 4.48; Nonn. *Par. Jo.* 13.117 || **956** πάνσκοπος] cf. Jul.Aegypt. *Anth. Pal.* 7.580.2 (πάνσκοπον ὄμμα Δίκης) | ὄρχαμος αἴγλας] cf. *Anth. Pal.* 9.634.1 (κοίρανον αἴγλης) || **957–958** de re cf. Hom. *Od.* 8.271 (Ἥλιος, ὅ σφ' ἐνόησε μιγαζομένους φιλότητι) || **959** ἄσβεστον—ἐνῶρσεν] cf. Hom. *Od.* 8.326 (ἄσβεστος δ' ἄρ ἐνῶρτο γέλως μακάρεσσι θεοῖσι)

Arion

(excerpt, ll. 936–959: Seeing Leda alone, Zeus becomes a swan)

> But when she [sc. Leda] had considered this and other thoughts in her mind, she turned her tender feet and started to go to the deeper shore of the river [Eurotas]. For she wanted to hear the nearby echo of the silently flowing water. [940] But the father of Gods and men, far-looking Zeus, noticed and did not neglect her, while sitting on a silvery cloud. As soon as he saw her, an unutterable passion, coming from the Paphian goddess [Aphrodite], quickly inflamed his heart, and the fiery boy [Eros] wounded his mind with his bow. But this was not the first time that this sickness had occupied him: For he [945] had already been desiring to enjoy the love of the well-girdled woman for a long time, since dewy youth was on her. But immediately his mind filled with numerous sorrows. For he was fearing Hera's wrath that she would ruin with her jealousy the prize Cypris [Aphrodite] had set before him. [950] Therefore, in order to escape his angry wife, he disguised himself, took the sceptre away, stripped off his divine form and put on the soft wings of a bird. In every detail, he made himself like a swan with a snow-like dress. Immediately, he secretly opened the door of heaven. And he himself moved through it [955] more quickly than air or smoke. Nobody of the immortals noticed him nor even the all-seeing lord of light [Helios], who had noticed before and secretly told Hephaestus that Ares was having intercourse with Cypris in their nuptial bed and therefore caused inextinguishable laughter to the gods.

Metre: Hexameters; hiatuses in ll. 946, 947, 948, lengthening by final ν in 957.

Notes: The selected lines describing Zeus' metamorphosis from a god into a swan are taken from the epyllion *Arion*. Although in the present form only known as an appendix to the collection *Argonautica. Thebaica. Troica. Ilias parva* (see below) from 1588, there must have been an earlier print from about 1567, realised by the famous humanist printer Johannes Oporinus (1507–1568) in Basel. This highly refined poem consisting of about 1250 Doric hexameters retells the story of the singer Arion known from Herodotus' *Histories* (1.23–24). Rhodoman weaves into the plot two longer insertions: The first is a lengthy consolatory song (ἐπικάδιον ᾆσμα) by Arion before he jumps into the sea (ll. 430–688). The second is a hymn (*hymnus genethliacus*) by the same after his salvation, retelling Zeus' seduction of the beautiful Leda. This almost Hellenistic or neoteric interweaving of stories with erotic elements secures Rhodoman's poem a special place among humanist Greek literature (but cf. also Moschos → **Greece**, and Foreestius → **Low Countries**). He wanted to present himself and his art to a learned public while honouring the printer Oporinus, who used Arion sitting on the dolphin as his signet.

II. *Troica* [1588/²1604]

(excerptum, vv. 1–22: prooemium)

Μνημοσύνη λιγυράς ποτ' ἐγείνατο πότνια Μούσας,
δῶκε δὲ Παρνησοῦ ζάθεον κλέτας ἀμφιπολεύειν.
νῦν δὲ πατὴρ μετένασσεν Ὀλύμπιος ἐς χθόνα σεμνῶν
Γερμανῶν καὶ ἄνωγε παλαιά τε καινά τ' ἀείδειν,
5   ὅσσα θεῷ τ' ἐπίηρα βροτῶν τ' εἰς χρῆσιν ἱκάνει·
καὶ ταῖς νῦν θαλερῇσιν ὀρώρεται ἐν φρεσὶν ὁρμὴ
εἰπεῖν ἐξ ἀρχῆς Τρώων φάτιν ἄχρι τελευτῆς
Ἀργείων θ' ἱδρῶτα κακόν τ' εἰς πατρίδα νόστον
καὶ δέμας εἰς ἓν ἄγειν, σποράδην ὅσα χεῦαν ἀοιδοὶ
10 πλειοτέροις ἐπέεσσιν· ἐγὼ δ' ὀλίγοισιν ἐνίψω.
οὐ μέλπω πινυτοῖσι καὶ ἀνδράσιν, οἷς ἅλις ἐστὶν
ἰδμοσύνης, ποθέω δὲ νέοις παίδεσσιν ὑφαίνειν
χρήσιμ', ὅσοι φιλέουσιν Ἀχαιΐδος ἤθεα μούσης.
οὐ κρύπτειν γὰρ ἔοικε θεοῦ πολυκυδέα δῶρα,
15 ἀλλὰ βροτοῖς πολέεσσιν, ὅσον σθένος, ἔνθεν ἀρήγειν
χείρεσιν ἐσθλοπόνοισι καὶ εὐβούλοις πραπίδεσσι.
τοὔνεκεν εἰ ζητεῖ τὶς ἐς Ἑλλάδα ῥᾴδιον οἶμον,
ἡγεσίης ἀπόναιτο καὶ ἀγχινόοισι πεδίλοις
τῇδε μολὼν δρέψαιτο παλαιῶν καρπὸν ἀοιδῶν,
20 καρπὸν ἐπιστήμης τε καὶ ἤθεος ἠδὲ καὶ αὐδῆς.
νῦν δ' ἄρ' ἐγὼν ἄρχοιμι, φίλον δέ μοι ἔργον ἀρωγῆς
θεσπεσίης, ᾧ πείθομ', ἐλαφρίσσειεν ἀήτης.

Textus: Neander, Michael (ed.) (1588), *Argonautica. Thebaica. Troica. Ilias parva. Poematia Graeca auctoris anonymi, sed perernditi* [...], Lipsiae, Z1v–Z2r; Rhodoman, Laurentius (1604), *Ἰλιὰς Κοίντου Σμυρναίου; seu Quinti Calabri Paraleipomena, Id est, Derelicta ab Homero, XIV. libris comprehensa...*, Hanoviae (nitor editione posteriori).

Crit.: 1–5 aliter editio prior (1588): Δεῦτε θεαὶ λιγυροῖσιν ἀγαλλόμεναι μελέεσσιν, / ἃς Διΐ Μνημοσύνη ποτ' ἐγείνατο, δῶκε δὲ ναίειν / Παρνησοῦ κορυφὰς καὶ ἐΰφρονος ἄντρ' Ἑλικῶνος / κρήνης θ' ἱππογενοῦς ζάθεον ῥόον ἀμφιπολεύειν. / Δεῦτε θεαὶ πρὸς ἐμὸν νεοειδέος ἔργον ἀοιδῆς. || **17** τὶς] more temporis pro τις scripsit noster || **22** ᾧ πείθομ' ed. 1604: εὔκαιρος ed. 1588

Sim.: 2 Παρνησοῦ...κλέτας] cf. Lycoph. *Alex.* 703 (Ληθαιῶνος ὑψηλὸν κλέτας); κλέτας etiam apud Nonnum saepius legitur, cf. *Dion.* 5.59 al. || **7** ὀρώρεται] ex Hom. *Od.* 19.377 et 524 || **13** Ἀχαιΐδος ἤθεα μούσης] cf. *Anth. Pal.* 2.390 (Πλατωνίδος ἤθεϊ Μούσης) || **14** πολυκυδέα] cf. *Anth. Pal.* 1.8.4 (πολυκυδέα τιμήν) || **16** ἐσθλοπόνοισι] neologismus

Story of Troy

(excerpt, ll. 1–22: proem)

> Revered Mnemosyne once gave birth to the clear-sounding Muses and allowed them to live in the sacred hillside of the Parnassos. But now the Olympian father transferred them to the land of the noble Germans and told them to sing of things, old and new alike, [5] which please to God and are useful for the mortals. And from these now-blooming Muses an impulse has risen up in my mind to tell from beginning to end the rumour about the Trojans and the sweat and bad return to home of the Greeks, and to bring together in one frame what the singers have diffused [10] with more words: I will tell it with few words. I do not sing for the learned men and those who have enough knowledge, but I want to weave useful things for young boys who love the character of the Achaean [Greek] Muse, as it is not appropriate to hide God's glorious givings, [15] but to help many people according to one's power with hands doing good and a prudent mind. Therefore, if someone is seeking an easy way to Greece, may he have the use of (my) command and may he cull, once he has come here with shrewd shoes, the fruit of the old singers, [20] the fruit of science, ethics, and rhetoric alike. Thus, now, I would like to start and may a blast of divine help, whom I obey, make my work lighter.[30]

---

30 Author's Latin (verse) translation: *Mnemosyne doctas peperit veneranda Camoenas, / Parnassique dedit sacras habitare latebras: / Nunc pater aetherius claros in Teutonis agros / Transtulit has: nova ut inveniant antiquaque condant, / [5] Quae sint grata Deo; Quae sint accommoda vitae, / Quas nunc afflatas caelo sacer impetus urget, / Historiam Troiae facili deducere versu, / Praeliaque Argivûm, reditumque per omnia tristem. / Quae sparsim cantant vates, ceu corpore in uno, / [10] nunc damus: & sic multa iuvat comprendere paucis. / Nec doctis canimus, quorum sapientia mentem / Imbuit ante satis: docili sed commoda turbae / Teximus, arridet Graiae cui Gratia*

Metre: Hexameters.

Notes: The lines presented here belong to the proem of the second edition of Rhodoman's *Troica* from 1604. The poem on the Trojan war was first published anonymously together with four other mythological poems (*Argonautica, Thebaica, Ilias parva, Arion*) by Rhodoman's teacher, Michael Neander, in 1588. The proem of the *Troica* is the lengthiest one and the most explicit concerning the intentions of this peculiar collection of hexametrical poems on the most important stories of Greek mythology: It can be assumed that they were written as short poetic introductions for pupils studying Greek mythology and epic diction. For this reason, Rhodoman presents the myths comprehensively from the beginning to the end (l. 7 ἐξ ἀρχῆς…ἄχρι τελευτῆς) – in the case of the *Troica*, from the foundation of Troy by Dardanus until the murder of Helen in Rhodes. The first lines of the poem are indicative of Rhodoman's consciousness as a German-Greek poet: Rhodoman describes the transfer of the Muses from their Greek homeland to Germany, where they should now continue to sing 'pious and useful songs' (l. 5) – a sort of poetic program many times repeated in Rhodoman's poems. Although Rhodoman's presentation of the Trojan myth is, on the whole, very short and concentrated (the poem consists of about 1700 lines), it appears that he tries to surpass Homer and Quintus, whom he mentions in a second proem in the middle of the poem, by giving a more comprehensive and chronological account of events. Notable is the contrast with the interwoven stories in Rhodoman's *Arion*, primarily not written for pupils but for learned people. It is, perhaps, also due to this fact that in the second version, Rhodoman even adds a damnation of the pagan gods, especially of Zeus and of his many love affairs.

Biography: Laurentius (Lorenz) Rhodoman was not only one of the most famous German poets in Greek in the Renaissance period, but also a remarkable philologist whose achievements in the edition of Quintus of Smyrna and Diodorus Siculus are still valuable today. His special affection for Greek originated at Ilfeld, where he became familiar with Greek literature and verse composition under the guidance of Michael Neander, a pupil of Melanchthon. Thereafter, he served as headmaster of various schools in Northern and Central Germany (1571 Schwerin,

---

linguae. / *Non decet acceptas è caelo abscondere dotes:* / [15] *Sed potius consulto animo, manibusque benignis,* / *Inservire aliis, quantum sinit usque facultas.* / *Quisquis ad Argolicos igitur compendia vates* / *Expetit, huc veniat, duce me non segniter aptum* / *Ingrediatur iter: Veterum ut se flore coronet,* / [20] *Artis & eloquii & morum qui spiret odorem.* / *Ergo opus aggredior. Superi sed gratia flatus* / *Allevet auxilio: hos quo fretus tracto labores.*

1572 Lüneburg, 1584 Walkenried and 1598 Stralsund). In 1592, he obtained a professorship at the University of Jena and from 1601 until his death in 1606, he served as a professor at Wittenberg. His major Greek poems were published between 1572 and 1591, while he was headmaster in Lüneburg and Walkenried. Most of them have a strong Protestant and pedagogical tendency and are written in hexameters, for example, the *Lutherus* (1579), a biography of the Protestant leader, and the *Palaestina* (1589), a history of the Holy Land from the Biblical fathers up until Rhodoman's own time. Of special interest are his Greek autobiography, *Bioporikon* (1585), and a series of mythological poems, *Argonautica, Thebaica, Troica, Ilias parva* (1588), which present the major Greek mythical stories in a comprehensive manner. Over time, Rhodoman developed a special consciousness as a Greek poet, regarding himself as a continuation of antiquity as well as a promoter of Protestantism. This combination is highlighted by his motto σὺν θεῷ καὶ μούσαις ('with God and the Muses').

Bibliography: Gärtner, Thomas (2016), "Rhodoman(nus), Lorenz (Laurentius)", in: *VL16*, vol. 5, 300–310 (with comprehensive bibliography); *Id.* (2017a), "Der Troja-Mythos in den eigenen Dichtungen Lorenz Rhodomans", in: Weise 2017, 109–123; *Id.* (2017b), "Lorenz Rhodoman – ein homerisierender Dichter im Dienste der lutherischen Reformation", in: *Neulateinisches Jahrbuch* 19, 175–197; *Id.* 2020 (see General Bibliography); *Id.* (2020), "Die diversen Reflexe des *Epitaphios Bionos* bei Lorenz Rhodoman", in: Anne-Elisabeth Beron/Stefan Weise (eds.), *Hyblaea avena. Theokrit in römischer Kaiserzeit und Früher Neuzeit*, Stuttgart, 115–154; Ludwig, Walther (2014), "Der Humanist Laurentius Rhodomanus als griechischer Dichter Laurentios Rhodoman und seine Autobiographie von 1582", in: *Neulateinisches Jahrbuch* 16, 137–171; Ludwig 2017, 131–137; *Id.* (2018), "Der deutsche Dichter Laurentios Rodoman", in: Janika Päll/Ivo Volt (eds.), *Hellenostephanos. Humanist Greek in Early Modern Europe. Learned Communities between Antiquity and Contemporary Culture*, Tartu, 249–259; Weise 2016, 133–136; Weise 2019; *Id.* (2020), "Griechische Mythologie im Dienste reformatorischer Pädagogik: Zur Epensammlung Argonautica. Thebaica. Troica. Ilias parva von Lorenz Rhodoman (1588)", in: Mika Kajava/Tua Korhonen/Jamie Vesterinen (eds.), *MEILICHA DÔRA. Poems and Prose in Greek from Renaissance and Early Modern Europe*, Helsinki, 185–215.

Nicodemus Frischlin (1547–1590)

Εἰς τύμβον ἱερέος [ante 1589]

Ἤριον οἰνηροῦ κεύθει τόδε σῶμ' ἱερῆος,
γλυπτὴν ἐκ πέτρης αὐτὸς ὁρᾷς κύλικα·
ζωὸς μὲν γὰρ ἐὼν οὐ τέκνα φίλ', οὐ γάμον ἐσθλὸν
στέρξ', ἀλλὰ Βρομίου δῶρ' ἐρατεινὰ θεοῦ.
5   Οὓς δὲ λέλοιπε νόθους μετὰ συγκοίτου Σαλαβάκχης,

τῶν ὑπὲρ ἀκτεάνων οὐ στένει οὐδὲ τόσον.
Ἓν δὲ τόδ' αἰάζει καὶ ὑπὸ χθονὶ διψαλέος φώς·
ὅττι τάφῳ ξηρῷ ξηρὸς ἔπεστι κύλιξ.

Textus: Frischlin, Nicodemus (ed.) (1589), *Callimachi Cyrenaei Hymni et Epigrammata*, [...], Basileae, 395.

Sim.: poeta imitatur Antip. Sid. *Anth. Pal.* 7.353 = HE XXVII (de Maronide) || **3** γάμον ἐσθλόν] clausula eadem sede legitur in Greg. Naz. *carm.* PG 37.1462.6 || **4** Βρομίου δῶρ'] cf. Nonn. *Dion.* 47.71 (δῶρα...Βρομίοιο)

On a tomb of a priest

This tomb covers the body of a priest who loved wine: you see for yourself the cup carved of stone. When he was alive, he did not love his children nor the good marriage, but the lovely gifts of god Bromios [Dionysus]. [5] And he does not mourn so much for the bastard children he has left with his bedfellow, Salabakche, without any possession. But there is only one thing which this thirsty man laments under the earth too: that a dry cup is on his dry tomb.

Metre: Elegiac couplets (flawless).

Notes: This epigram imitates a funerary epigram by Antipater of Sidon (*Anth. Pal.* 7.353) about an alcoholic woman named Maronis, who left her children and her husband in poverty and longed only that the cup on her grave should be filled with wine. Frischlin uses an alcoholic priest instead of the woman, thus giving the epigram an anti-clerical leaning. In order to sharpen his criticism, he makes him not only the father of legitimate children with one woman but also of illegitimate children with another bedfellow. Frischlin also tries to sharpen this point on the linguistic level. He combines the first and the last couplet by using a form of κύλιξ in each case as the last word (Antipater has τάφῳ in the last couplet). Furthermore, whereas Antipater starts the ὅττι-sentence already in the hexameter (ἓν δὲ τόδ' αἰάζει καὶ ὑπ' ἠρίον, ὅττι τὸ Βάκχου / ἄρμενον οὐ Βάκχου πλῆρες ἔπεστι τάφῳ), Frischlin compresses it to the pentameter and puts τάφῳ ξηρῷ and ξηρὸς κύλιξ (Frischlin wrongly regards κύλιξ as a masculine noun!) side by side.

Biography: The humanist poet and scholar Nicodemus Frischlin is known as a playwright and author of Latin comedies (e.g., the famous *Iulius redivivus*). His biography is tragically eventful, although it started quite successfully. Born in 1547, he studied at the University of Tübingen, where he became *baccalaureus* in 1564, *magister* in 1565 and finally, *professor poetices* in 1568. His career took a dramatic turn, however, when he got involved in a bitter dispute with his former teacher and influential colleague Martin Crusius (see above). The quarrel forced him to leave Tübingen and be in constant search of new positions in various places (Ljubljana, Prague, Wittenberg, Braunschweig, Kassel, Marburg, Frankfurt, Mainz), until he was arrested in Hohenurach, where he died while trying to escape in 1590. A collection of his Greek poems (*Epitaphia et quaedam alia scripta amicis*) was appended to his edition, with Latin translation and notes, of the *Hymns* of Callimachus (Basel 1589). Many of his epigrams were inspired by poems of the *Greek Anthology*. The metres used include elegiac couplets, phalaecians, iambic dimeters (Anacreontics), a Pindaric ode, and hexameters for a hymn on Jesus Christ.

Bibliography: Bebermeyer, Gustav (1961), "Frischlin, Nicodemus", in: *NDB* 5, 620–621; Seidel, Robert (2012), "Frischlin, Nicodemus", in: *VL16*, vol. 2, 460–477; Weise 2016, 144; *Id.* (forthcoming), "Alexandria und Wittenberg – Zur Rezeption alexandrinischer Dichter im protestantischen Philhellenismus des 16. Jahrhunderts in Deutschland", in: Joachim Hamm/Marion Gindhart (eds.), *Camerarius im Kontext*.

Matthaeus Gothus (1548–1619)

Historiae vitae et doctrinae Iesu Christi, Apostolorum, & discipulorum eorundem libri duo [1573]

(excerptum, lib. I, vv. 108–118: Gabriel Mariam salutat)

  Χαῖρε, πέπον Μαρίη φιλοπάρθενε δῖα γυναικῶν,
  ὀλβίη ἐν πάσαισι θυγατράσι θηλυτεράων,
110 χαῖρε· σὺ δ' ἐνδομύχοισιν ὑπὸ σπλάγχνοισι κύημα
  αὐξήσεις, καὶ ἔπειτα πεπαινομένου τοκετοῖο
  μουνοτόκοις ὠδῖσι φέροις θεόπαιδα φόωσδε.
  τῷ δὲ λοχευομένῳ κλυτὸν οὔνομα, πότνια, θήσεις
  Ἰησοῦν καλέσασα βιοσσόον ἴδμονι φωνῇ.
115 ῥεῖα γὰρ ὑψιμέδων τελέει, φρεσὶν ὅ,ττι μενοινᾷ,
  ἐμμαπέως δ' ὅ,τι κεῖνος ὑπὸ πραπίδεσσιν ἑλίσσει,
  ἔργον ἔφυ, καὶ μηδὲν ἀνήνυτον ἕρκος ὀδόντων
  ἐξέπτη βασιλῆος ἔπος, δύναται γὰρ ἅπαντα.

Textus: Gothus, Matthaeus (1573), ΠΕΡΙ ΧΡΙΣΤΟΥ ΚΑΙ ΤΩΝ ΑΠΟΣΤΟΛΩΝ ΚΑΙ ΑΛΛΩΝ τινῶν ἁγίων μαθητῶν χριστοῦ τε καὶ τῶν ἀποστόλων αὐτοῦ, βιβλίω δύω. Id est: Historiae vitae et doctrinae Iesu Christi, Apostolorum, & discipulorum erundem, libri duo…, Basileae, 15.

Crit.: 110 σὺ δ' corr.: σύδ' ed.

Sim.: 108 δῖα γυναικῶν] clausula Homerica, vid. *Il.* 2.714; 3.171 etc. || **111** πεπαινομένου τοκετοῖο] clausula Nonniana, vid. *Dion.* 8.197; 24.210 etc. || **113** κλυτὸν οὔνομα] iunctura Homerica, vid. *Od.* 9.364; 19.153 (ὄνομα κλυτόν) || **114** ἴδμονι φωνῇ] clausula Nonniana, vid. *Par. Jo.* 3.57; 4.34; 21.114 || **115** ὅ,ττι μενοινᾷ] cf. *Hymn. Hom. Merc.* 474, 489 (ὅττι μενοινᾷς) || **117** ἕρκος ὀδόντων] clausula Homerica, vid. *Il.* 4.350; 9.409 etc. || **118** δύναται γὰρ ἅπαντα] clausula Homerica, vid. *Od.* 4.237

History of the life and doctrine of Jesus Christ, the apostles and their disciples in two books

(excerpt, ll. 108–118: Gabriel addressing Mary)

Hail to you, dear Mary, divine amongst women, loving virginity! You are blessed among all daughters of women. [110] Hail to you! You will nourish a baby in your inner organs and then when the time is ripe, you may bring God's child in a single birth to the light. You, my lady, will give the newborn child a famous name by calling him life-saving Jesus with your knowing voice. [115] For high-ruling God easily accomplishes whatever he is planning in his mind, and what he is revolving in his head, becomes quickly true, and there is no word of the King which passes the fence of his teeth without fulfillment, for he can everything.

Metre: Hexameters (flawless with Nonnian metrics: no line in this section has more than one spondaic foot, elision is very rare, no other scheme besides the nine Nonnian hexameter schemes: DDDDD, SDDDD, DSDDD, DDDSD).

Notes: Gothus' *Historia vitae et doctrinae Iesu Christi, Apostolorum, & discipulorum eorundem* is a two-book epic retelling of the evangelical history from Jesus' birth to the appearance of the Holy Spirit in the first book, and the deeds of the Apostles (especially Paul) and evangelists until the destruction of Jerusalem by Emperor Titus in the second book. Gothus is clearly emulating Nonnus' style in two senses: firstly, he uses Nonnian phrases and metrics (with admirable talent), and secondly, he tries to surpass Nonnus by integrating not only the Johannine story but also the other Gospels, the Acts, and further material into the piece as well as coining new phrases and neologisms. Together with Rhodoman, he certainly is one of the finest Greek poets of the time in this technical regard.

Biography: Like Laurentius Rhodoman (see above), Matthaeus Gothus, originating from Ellrich, gained his exquisite training in Greek poetry at the monastery school in Ilfeld under the guidance of Michael Neander. Not much is known about his biography. He was headmaster of the school in Stolberg from 1574, and later, archdeacon (from 1579) and a court as well as city preacher at the same place from 1608 until his death in 1619. His son, bearing the same name, became poet laureate (before 1603). Three major hexametrical poems in Greek were written and published by Gothus: The first one, Περὶ Χριστοῦ καὶ τῶν ἀποστόλων καὶ ἄλλων τινῶν ἁγίων μαθητῶν Χριστοῦ τε καὶ ἀποστόλων αὐτοῦ βιβλίω δύω, was printed by Johannes Oporinus in 1573, the second one Κατηχητικὰ συν ἀντιθέσει τῶν ἐναντιουμένων and the third one, Θεολογίας σύνοψις, were both printed in Frankfurt/Main in 1574. The front page of the first poem states that it was composed in Ilfeld. The two other poems were reissued in Leipzig in 1621 by Gothus' sons, Matthaeus and Nicolaus, together with a pair of Greek letter-poems by Gothus Sr and Rhodoman. Here, Rhodoman acknowledges and praises the Nonnian character of Gothus' poetry: The Nonnian 'graces bring your verses to perfection. The magniloquent Muse of the dead man has transmigrated into your mind and distributes all to the praise of Christ.' (Νόννου, τοῦ χάριτές σοι τελέουσιν ἔπη: / μοῦσα δ' ἀποφθιμένου μεγαλήγορος εἰς φρένα σεῖο / νάσσατο, καὶ χριστοῦ κύδεϊ πάντα [πάνδα ed.] νέμει).[31] It is noteworthy that Gothus' Greek poetry was imitated by Theodosius Fabricius, another pupil of Neander, in his Greek *Paean de Jesu Christo vero deo et homine, redemptore generis humani* (Wittenberg 1579).

Bibliography: Lizelius 1730, 128–129; Flood 2, 697–700; Ludwig, Walther (2016), "Das protestantische Bild der Universalgeschichte im 16./17. Jahrhundert. Epigramme von Melanchthon und Stigel, die Daniel-Paraphrase des Matthaeus Gothus, Friedrich von Nostitz' Lehrdichtung über die vier Monarchien und das Theatrum historicum des Christian Matthiae", in: *Neulateinisches Jahrbuch* 18, 237–281 (= *Florilegium Neolatinum*, Hildesheim 2019, 243–285); Gärtner 2020, 227–232; Gärtner, Thomas (forthcoming), "Nonnos von Panopolis im protestantischen Philhellenismus des 16./17. Jahrhunderts. Zur Nonnos-Rezeption bei Lorenz Rhodoman und Matthaeus Gothus", in: Berenice Verhelst (ed.), *Nonnus of Panopolis in Context IV: Poetry at the Crossroads.*

---

[31] Gothus, Matthaeus (1621), *ΚΑΤΗΧΗΤΙΚΑ, ΣΥΝ ΑΝΤΙΘΕΣΕΙ…*, Leipzig,)†(7r. Cf. esp. Gärtner (forthcoming).

Johann Gottfried Herrichen (1629–1705)

I. <*Idyllium*> *primum, quo Androthei natales Orontas, Sosthenes, et Mariallis sermone amoebaeo celebrant* [1668]

(excerptum, vv. 139–172)

Orontas (Ὀρ.), Sosthenes (Σω.), Mariallis (Μα.)

       Ὀρ.   Νῦν τιν' ἐπειρωτῶμες ἄφαρ, πᾶ Χριστὸς ἐτέχθη.
140 **Σω.**   Οὔ τις ἐναντίβιον φοιτῇ. θάνον ἐνθάδε θνατοί.
       Ὀρ.   Ἔνδοθι δωματίων ἀστοὺς τάχα ῥῖγος ἐέργει.
       Σω.   Τάνδε θύραν, τὶς ἔσω, βλέψων κορύναφι πατάξω,
            Ὄλλα! **Μα.** τίς ἀγροίκως, ἄτε δάμιος, ἔκτοθι κρούει;
       Ὀρ.   Χαῖρε γύναι! τεχθέντα βροτῶν Σωτῆρα ματεύω.
145 **Μα.**   Τίς, πόθεν εἶς; <**Ὀρ.**> οἴων ἄμφω πελόμεσθα βοτῆρες.
       Σω.   Χαῖρε γύναι! σύγγωθι θύραν κρούσαντι βιαίως·
            Ἤνθομες ἐκ πεδίω, ποίμναν ὅθι βόσκομες ἄμφω.
       Μα.   Σφῶϊ τὶς ἡγεμονεὺς πρὸς ἐμὴν γόνεν αὔλιδα δεῦρο;
       Σω.   Δεῦρό με μαλοβότης φιλοποίμνιον ἦγεν Ὀρόντας.
150 **Ὀρ.**   Ἄγγελος ὧδε μολεῖν ταύτας ἐμὲ κέκλετο νυκτός.
       Μα.   Οὐκ ἀθεεὶ κλισίηθεν ἐμὸν ποτὶ βώτορε σταθμὸν
            Νεισσομένω, λίην κεκμῶτε θαάσσετον ἄμφω
            Ἐνθάδε παυσομένω. Καθαρῖνα, θὲς ἀνδράσι θώκους.
       Ὀρ.   Οὔ τέο τι χρειώ, πασᾶν περὶ νύμφα κοράων
155   Καλλίστα, χρήσδουσιν ἄφαρ ποτὶ ποίμνιον ἐλθεῖν.
              Ἔννεπε, παρθενικά, μῶν ἤλφομες υἱέα θεῖον;
       Μα.   Εὕρετε κοῦρον ἐμόν, τριφιλέστατον υἷα Θεοῖο,
            Ἰσαΐδαο γένος, κλυμένου θάλος εὐθὺ Δαβίδω.
       Ὀρ.   Παῖδα σὸν ἁμετέρῃσι γονυκλισίῃσι σεβίσδειν
160   Δός, Τάλι, καὶ γενύδεσσιν ἕοι γένυν ἁδὺ φιλᾶσαι.
       Σω.   Προπροκυλινδομένοιϊν ἔα σὸν νῶϊ γεραίρειν,
            Παρθένε, παῖδα φίλον καὶ χείλεσι χείλεα θλίβειν.
       Μα.   Ἑζομένω σιγᾶτον· ἐμοὶ διεγείρετον υἷα.
       Σω.   Σὸν τέκος ὀρσολόπευε χεροῖν, καὶ σαύσιον ᾆδε.

              ΜΑΡΙΑΛΛΙΔΟΣ ΚΑΤΑΒΑΥΚΑΛΙΣΜΟΣ

165   Σαῦσε, φίλη κεφαλή, θεῖον βρέφος, ἡδέα τέρψις,
                 Σαῦσε, γλυκὺ γλυκερὴν παῦσιν ἴαυε τέκος.
              Σαῦσε, νιφοβλήτοιο κρύος χειμῶνος ἀνάσσει,
                 Σμερδαλέου ζαῆς ἲς ἀνέμοιο βρέμει.
              Σαῦσε, βορειαίῃσι νέφη χιόνεσσι δονεῖται,

170   Νωΐτερον κρούει πάγχυ χάλαζα στέγος.
        Σαῦσε, πενιχραλέης πεφιλημένε κοῦρε τιθήνης,
        Πατέρος ἀφνειοῦ σαῦσε πενιχρὲ πάϊς.

Textus: Herrichen, August (ed.) (1717), I.G. CYRILLI sive HERRICHEN *Poemata Graeca et Latina*, Hamburgi, 102–104.

Crit.: 142/148 τὶς: exspectaveris τίς || **169** δονεῖται scripsi: δονοῦται ed. || **171** τιθήνης scripsi (coll. versione Latina *nutricis*): τιτήνης ed.

Sim.: 144 χαῖρε γύναι] cf. *Hymn. Hom. Cer.* 213 || **145** Τίς, πόθεν εἶς] iunctura Homerica, cf. *Il.* 21.150; *Od.* 1.170 et al. || **148** γόνεν] forma irregularis pro γέγονεν || **149** φιλοποίμνιον] cf. Theoc. *Id.* 5.106 || **151** οὐκ ἀθεεί] cf. Hom. *Od.* 18.353 || **160** Τάλι] apud veteres α semper longum, cf. Soph. *Ant.* 629; Callim. *Aet.* fr. 75.3 Pf. || ἀδὺ φιλᾶσαι] cf. [Theoc.] *Id.* 20.1 || **161** προπροκυλινδομένοιϋν] cf. eadem sede Hom. *Il.* 22.221; *Od.* 17.525 || **162** χείλεα θλίβειν] cf. [Theoc.] *Id.* 20.4 || **164** ὀρσολόπευε] cf. *Hymn. Hom. Merc.* 308; Aesch. *Pers.* 10 (sed utroque loco alio sensu) | σαύσιον] neologismus || **165** σαῦσε] alibi non legitur | φίλη κεφαλή] salutatio Homerica, cf. (eadem sede) Hom. *Il.* 12.281 (de Teucro) | ἡδέα τέρψις] cf. Theoc. *Id.* 3.20; 27.4 || **168** ἲς ἀνέμοιο βρέμει] cf. Hom. *Il.* 17.739 (ἐπιβρέμει ἲς ἀνέμοιο) || **169** νέφη χιόνεσσι δονεῖται] cf. Hom. *Il.* 12.156–157 (νιφάδες…/ ἅς τ' ἄνεμος ζαὴς νέφεα σκιόεντα δονήσας) || **171** πενιχραλέης] de forma cf. *Anth. Pal.* 6.190.6

First <Idyll> in which Orontas, Sosthenes and Mariallis celebrate the birth of Christ in dialogue

(excerpt, ll. 139–172)

Or. Now, let us ask someone quickly, where Christ is born. [140] **So.** Nobody comes face to face. Men have died here. **Or.** Perhaps the cold keeps the citizens in their houses. **So.** I will knock at this door with my staff in order to see if someone is in. Hello! **Ma.** Who is knocking so rudely like a public executioner from the outside? **Or.** Greetings, woman! I am looking for the born Saviour of the mortals. [145] **Ma.** Who are you and where are you from? **Or.** We both are shepherds. **So.** Greetings, woman! Please excuse me for having knocked at the door so violently. We came from the field, where both of us are tending a flock. **Ma.** Who led you both to my resting place here? **So.** It was Orontas the shepherd who led me here, being a shepherd myself. [150] **Or.** An angel ordered me to go here tonight. **Ma.** It was not without the aid of God that you shepherds have come here from your tent to my barn. So, sit down, as you must be very tired, in order to relax here. Catherine, put out chairs for the men. **Or.** We don't need anything, most beautiful bride of all girls, [155] as we want to return immediately to our flock. Just tell us, girl, whether we have found the divine son? **Ma.** You have found my child, the thrice-beloved son of God, the offspring of Jesse, the direct scion of famous David. **Or.** Concede, maiden, that we honour your child with our genuflections [160] and that we kiss his sweet jaw with our jaws. **So.** Let us, maiden, honour your beloved child by rolling at his feet and let us press lips with lips. **Ma.** Sit down and be quiet. You wake up my son. **So.** Rock your child with your hands and sing a lullaby.

MARIALLIS' LULLABY: [165] *Sause*, my dear head, divine baby, sweet joy, *sause*, sleep sweetly, my sweet child. *Sause*, the icy cold of snowy winter dominates, the stormy force of the terrible wind roars. *Sause*, the clouds are shaken by the northern snow, hail severely knocks at our roof. *Sause*, beloved child of your poor nurse, *sause*, poor child of your wealthy father.[32]

Metre: Hexameters and elegiac couplets (l. 165ff.); note πᾰτέρος in l. 172, and στ- causing no position in l. 170.

Notes: This text is an excerpt from one of three Greek idylls Herrichen composed for recitation at the Nicolaischule in Leipzig in the 1660s. The three idylls are arranged according to the three ecclesiastic festivals, Christmas (*Id.* 1), Easter (*Id.* 2), and St Michael's Day (*Id.* 3). The 'Christmas idyll' (321 verses) seems to be the most recent, composed and performed by Herrichen's pupils in 1668. The three speakers (all played by boys) are the two shepherds, Orontas and Sosthenes, and Mariallis (a bucolised version of Mary, fashioned after the bucolic Amaryllis). The idyll, following Luke's account, begins after the vision of the angels in the fields: Excited Orontas wakes up his sleeping companion, Sosthenes, who is in the midst of a pleasant dream. After quarrelling about the interpretation of their dreams (a reference to [Theoc.] *id.* 21), they go together to wintry Bethlehem where they knock on Mariallis' door. At the centre of the idyll is a lullaby song by Mariallis for sleeping Jesus (ll. 165–200). In the end, the child wakes up, the shepherds can

---

32 Author's Latin prose translation: OR. *Nunc aliquem percontabimur, ubi Christus natus sit.* / [140] SO. *Nemo obviam procedit. Mortui sunt hic homines.* / OR. *Intra domicilia cives fortassis frigus continet.* / SO. *Hanc januam, visurus quis intus sit, pedo feriam,* / Holla! MAR. *Quis rusticè, ut apparitor, foris pulsat?* / OR. *Salve Mulier! Natum hominum Servatorem quaero.* / [145] MAR. *Quis, & unde es?* OR. *Ovium ambo sumus pastores.* / SO. *Salve, Mulier! Ignosce fores vehementer pulsanti;* / *Venimus è campo, ubi gregem ambo pascimus.* / MAR. *Vobis quinam dux fuit huc ad meum stabulum?* / SO. *Huc me pastorem Pastor deduxit Orontas.* / [150] OR. *Angelus huc concedere hâc mihi imperavit nocte.* / MAR. *Non sine numine à tuguriis pastores ad meam casam* / *Venientes, valdè fessi, capite sessum ambo* / *hîc requieturi. Catharina, appone viris sellas.* / OR. *Non equidem opus est, omnium Nympha Virginum* / [155] *Pulcherrima, volentibus statim ad gregem redire,* / *Dic saltem, Virgo, an invenerimus filium divinum?* / MAR. *Re<p>peristis filium meum, dilectissimum Filium Dei,* / *Isaidae stirpem, celebrati germen rectum Davidae.* / OR. *Filium tuum nostris geniculationibus venerari* / [160] *Concede, Puella, & genis ei genas suaviter osculari.* / SO. *Provolutis ad pedes sine tuum nobis honorare* / *Virgo, filium dilectum, labraque labris libare.* / MA. *Sedete, & tacete. Mihi excitatis filium meum.* / SO. *Natum tuum jactato manibus, & sausion cane.*

MARIALLIDIS LALLUS: [165] *Sause, carum caput, divine infans, jucunda voluptas,* / *Sause, dulcis dulcem quietem dormi, mi Fili.* / *Sause, nivosae frigus hyemis dominatur,* / *Horrendi vehemens vis venti murmurat.* / *Sause, borealibus nubes nivibus agitantur,* / [170] *Nostrumque pulsat undique grando tectum.* / *Sause, pauperis dilecte Puer nutricis,* / *Patris divitis Sause pauper Soboles.*

kiss him, and Mariallis sends them to tell the news to everybody. – Herrichen cleverly uses references to and reminiscences of Theocritus' bucolics and his other songs. The lullaby song has an equivalent in Theocritus' *Herakliskos* (*id.* 24.7–9), where Alcmene sings a similar song, although much shorter and in hexameters, for the babies Hercules and Iphicles. The change from hexameters to elegiac couplets is certainly inspired by idyll 8 from the *Corpus Theocriteum*, but perhaps is also reminiscent of the Latin lullaby songs (*Naeniae*) by the Neapolitan poet Giovanni Pontano. The lullaby character is further underscored by the elsewhere unattested onomatopoetic form σαῦσε, repeated in every couplet (note especially the sound effect with αυ and υ in l. 166: σαῦσε, γλυκὺ γλυκερὴν παῦσιν ἴαυε).[33] Finally, the detail that Mariallis calls an otherwise unmentioned female servant, *Katharina*, to prepare seats for the two shepherds (l. 153) may allude to the beginning of the Theocritean *Adoniazusae* (*id.* 15.1–3).

II. *DE THEA HERBA ad Nobilissimum Virum FRIDER. BENED. CARPZOVIUM, Melydrion* [c. 1685/86]

(excerptum, vv. 1–24, 37–40, 173–180)

    Σὺ μὲν Εὔϊου πεπωκώς
    Ἑκατοντάκις δέπαστρον,
        Ἀνάκρεον, καθεύδεις
        Χάλκεον ὕπνον.
5   Τί δὲ σὰ λύρη λιγεῖα,
    Λαλιεστάτα τί φόρμιγξ
        Μεταξύ; μῶν καρώθη
        Σοὶ σὺν ἀοιδῷ;
    Ἄνα! σῶν ἀπ' ὀμμάτων σμᾶ
10 Βαθὺ νῶκαρ. οὐ καθῆκον
        Ἐσαιὲν ὡς Σελάνας
        Ἀνέρα κνώσσειν.
    Βλεφάρων δὲ καμμυόντων
    Ἐὰν οὐ δύνῃ δίεσθαι
15   τὸ κῶμ', ἐμοὶ χαρίζευ
        Σεῖο χελώναν.
    Ἐθέλω γὰρ οὐ παλαιοῖς
    Βοτάναν βροτοῖσι γνωστάν,
        Ὕδωρ τε τοὶ βδελυκτόν

---

[33] The form may be inspired by the Hesychian lemma (σ 285) σαυσαρόν· ψίθυρον ('whispering/whisperer'), meaning perhaps just 'hist/shush'.

20 Γάρυϊ φράσδειν.
    Σοφὸς εὑρετὰς ποάων
    Ἰδὲ φαρμάκων ὁ Φοῖβος
    Συναινέοι μενοινὰν
    Τάνδε μελῳδός.
    [...]
    Ἔνιοι καλεῦντι Θῖαν,
    Ἔνιοι Τζίαν καλεῦντι,
    Καλεῦντι Θῇ δὲ θεῖον
40 Θαμνίον ἄλλοι.
    [...]
    Λάλον οὖν ῥοφῶμεν ὕδωρ,
    Ἵνα νύχθ' ὅλαν, ἑταῖροι,
175 Ἀπ' ὀμμάτων σοβῶμεν
    Νήδυμον ὕπνον.
    Ὁ πιῶν γάρ ἐστι ζωῷ
    Ἐναλίγκιος, καθεύδων
    θανόντι. Τίς πρὸ ζωᾶς
180 Μοῖραν ἕλοιτο;

Textus: Herrichen 1717 (vide supra), 263–269; Weise 2017, 180–191.

Sim.: 1–8 de re cf. *Anth. Pal.* 7.29.1–2 (εὕδεις ἐν φθιμένοισιν, Ἀνάκρεον, ἐσθλὰ πονήσας, / εὕδει δ' ἡ γλυκερὴ νυκτιλάλος κιθάρη); 7.33.1 (πολλὰ πιὼν τέθνηκας, Ἀνάκρεον) || **4** χάλκεον ὕπνον] clausula Homerica, vid. *Il.* 11.241 || **10** νώκαρ] cf. Nic. *Ther.* 189 || **173** λάλον οὖν ῥοφῶμεν ὕδωρ] cf. Anacreont. 12.7 (λάλον πιόντες ὕδωρ) || **176** νήδυμον ὕπνον] clausula Homerica, vid. *Il.* 16.454

On the tea-plant to the most noble man Friedrich Benedikt Carpzov, a ditty

(excerpt, ll. 1–24, 37–40, 173–180)

> Having drunk Euios' [Dionysus] beaker a hundred times, Anacreon, you are now sleeping a brazen sleep. [5] What does your sweet lyre do, what your loquacious phorminx in the meantime? Was it plunged into deep sleep together with you, the singer? Come on! Wipe the [10] deep coma from your eyes, as it is not convenient to slumber forever like Selene's man [sc. Endymion]. If you cannot put to flight [15] the coma from your dozing eyes, give me your lyre! For it is a plant not known to the Ancients and the water being disgusting for you, [20] which I want to show with my voice. Phoebus, the wise discoverer of herbs and medicine, he, the singer, may agree with my wish. [...]
> Some call it *Thia*, some call it *Tzia*, others, however, call the divine [40] bush *The*. [...]
> Well, let us sip the loquacious water so that we can clear away, my friends, [175] the sweet sleep from our eyes the whole night long. For, who has drunk it, resembles a living person, but who is sleeping, a dead man. Who would choose [180] death instead of life?

Metre: New anacreontic stanza consisting of two anaclastic ionic dimeters (uu – u – u – x), one catalectic iambic dimeter (x – u – u – x) and an adonian (– uu – x). Zeta in derivative forms of ζῆν is used as a simple consonant, causing no position (ll. 177, 179).³⁴

Notes: This Anacreontic ode to tea is an interesting mingling of Anacreontic tradition and didactic poetry. The inspiration for this poem was likely a Latin didactic poem by the French poet Pierre Petit (1617–1687), and two Greek Anacreontic odes by Petrus Francius (→ **Low Countries**). Herrichen creates something new by combining Doric dialect and a new Anacreontic stanza to praise an unanacreontic subject: tea. The tea is consciously called just 'water' by Herrichen in order to evoke the ancient antithesis of wine and water drinkers. His poem, relying on contemporary scientific writings, wishes to prove the superiority of 'Apollonic' tea over 'Dionysiac' wine. One can, therefore, see here a reflection of early enlightenment, polyhistorism, and self-conscious emancipation from the Ancients.

Biography: Johann Gottfried Herrichen (born in 1629) can be considered one of the most productive and gifted German poets in Greek of the late 17th century. He was vice-rector and thereafter rector at the Nicolai School in Leipzig. Among his pupils were the polyhistorian Johann Albert Fabricius (1668–1736), compiler of the famous *Bibliotheca Graeca*, and the Leipzig senator Friedrich Benedikt Carpzov (1649–99), who later promoted Herrichen as a Greek poet by publishing several of his poems. Herrichen's primarily Greek and fewer Latin poems were collected and published again after his death in 1717. They consist mainly of Christian lyric odes and occasional poetry. Herrichen covers a wide range of forms and metres: Sapphic stanzas, tetrameters, hexameters, Pindaric odes, Theocritean idylls, and Anacreontic poetry (with newly-created stanzas). While still praised in Germany, the contemporary *Journal des Sçavans* (1720) notes about the collection: 'Ceux qui ne cherchent dans la Poësie qu'une verité exprimée d'une maniere fort commune, & la mesure des vers, pourront ne pas desaprouver le Recuëil; mais ceux qui ont du gout pour ce qui fait la veritable Poësie, seront surpris qu'on se soit donné la peine de recuëillir ces Pieces' (cited after Weise 2020, 160).

Bibliography: Weise, Stefan (2017), "Dichten und Teetrinken. Zum anakreontischen griechischen Teegedicht *De Thea herba* von Johann Gottfried Herrichen (1629–1705)", in: Weise 2017, 149–201; *Id.* (2020), "'Der berühmte Leipziger Theocritus' – Zu Theokritrezeption und Performanz

---

34 Cf. West 1982, 17; Rhein 1987, 47.

in den *Idyllia Graeca solennia* von Johann Gottfried Herrichen", in: Anne-Elisabeth Beron/Stefan Weise (eds.), *Hyblaea avena. Theokrit in römischer Kaiserzeit und Früher Neuzeit*, Stuttgart, 157–175.

Johann Heinrich Schulze (1687–1744)

Ἰωάννου Ἑρρίκου Σχουλζίου μελέτημα περὶ φθόνου εὐκαταφρονήτου

Τίπτ' αἰὲν στοναχῶν, νήπι', ἀδημονεῖς
χεύεις θ' ὡς ποταμοὺς δάκρυ ἀένναον·
ὅς τ' εἴωθε καλοῖς πάντοθ' ὁμαρτέειν
φαύλων αἰσθόμενος δυσκέλαδον φθόνον;
5   Κεδνὸς πὰρ παλαιοῖς ἀνδράσιν ἐμπρέπει,
ὑψηλῶν ἀρετῶν τὰς κορυφὰς δραπών,
κώνειον δὲ πιὼν κάππεσε Σωκράτης
ζήλῳ δυσσεβέων οὐλεθρίῳ δαμείς.
τίς νίκης στεφάνων τ' ἐνθάδ' ἐτύγχανεν;
10 οὐ μέν τοι Μελίτου, οὐδ' Ἀνύτου βίη,
οὐδ' οὖν τηκόμενος βασκανίῃ Λύκων·
μούνη παντοδαπῶν ἀτρεκίη δόλων
καὶ τήνης θεράπων πανδαμάτωρ πέλει.

Textus: Freyer, Hieronymus (ed.) (1715), *Fasciculus poematum Graecorum ex antiquis ac recentioribus poetis collectus et ad innoxium scholasticae iuventutis usum accommodatus*, Halae Magdeburgicae, 129–130.

Crit.: 10 Μελήτου debuit

Sim.: 3-4 ὁμαρτέειν / ... δυσκέλαδον φθόνον] cf. Hes. *Op.* 195–196 (ζῆλος δ' ἀνθρώποισιν ... / δύσκελαδος ... ὁμαρτήσει) || **6** ὑψηλῶν ἀρετῶν τὰς κορυφὰς δραπών] ~ Pind. *Ol.* 1.13 (δρέπων μὲν κορυφὰς ἀρετᾶν ἄπο πασᾶν)

Exercise by Johann Heinrich Schulze about the contemptible envy

Why are you constantly in anguish and groaning, you stupid one,
and shedding ever-flowing tears like rivers,
whenever you see bad men's shrieking envy,
which usually accompanies good men everywhere?
[5] One noble man is famous among ancient men,
as he gained the top of high virtues:

He, Socrates, drank the hemlock-juice and died,
overcome by the destructive zeal of impious men.
Who gained the crown of victory here?
[10] Not the violence of Melitos nor the one of Anytos
nor Lycon, consumed by jealousy.
Only truth and its servant are capable
of overcoming every sort of cunning.[35]

Metre: Stichic asclepiads. Hiatuses in l. 2 and 10.

Notes: As a teacher at August Hermann Francke's *Paedagogium* in Halle, Schulze composed two short Greek poems for a school collection of Greek poetic texts, *Fasciculus poematum Graecorum*, issued by Hieronymus Freyer in 1715. This collection is structured according to metres and is interesting as it included not only texts by ancient poets but also those by humanist or contemporary poets. In addition to Greek texts by Freyer and Schulze, it contains further texts by Olympia Morata, Johannes Mylius (→ **Poland and Lithuania**), Henri Estienne (→ **France**), Johannes Posselius (see above), Florent Chrestien (→ **France**), Aemilius Portus (→ **Switzerland**), Nicolaus Reusner (see above), Martin Crusius (see above), Erasmus Schmidius, Georg Leuschner, James Duport (→ **Great Britain**), Johann Gottfried Herrichen (see above), Samuel Knauth, and Georg Friedrich Thryllitsch. As such, Freyer's volume was an important source for Lizelius' *Historia Poetarum Graecorum Germaniae* (see introduction). The integration of humanist and contemporary texts was due to three main factors: Freyer wanted 1) texts appropriate for pupils, 2) a mixture of old and new, and 3) texts for all metres. Schulze's two poems filled the lack of stichic asclepiads and stichic glyconics. The metric treatment is geared towards Horatian practice. Schulze chose an ethical theme: envy of the good. Socrates serves as an example.

Biography: The baroque polyhistorian Johann Heinrich Schulze (born in 1687) was a professor at the universities of Altdorf (from 1720) and Halle (from 1732), where he had attended as a child and later as a teacher the famous pietistic *Paedagogium*, founded by August Hermann Francke. He also studied at the then

---

35 **Accompanying Latin prose translation:** *Cur semper gemens, stulte, inquietus es et fundis, ceu flumina, lacrimam perennem: quae consueuit bonos ubique comitari, inertium quoties sentis infamem invidiam? Venerabilis inter priscos homines excellit, qui excelsarum virtutum summitates decerpsit, cicuta autem hausta prostratus est, Socrates invidia impiorum perniciosa subactus. Quis victoria coronisque hic potiebatur? Non sane Meliti neque Anyti violentia; neque vero tabescens invidentia Lycon: sola omnigenarum veritas fraudum et huius minister domitor est.*

newly-founded university there. He studied both theology (with a special interest in Greek and oriental languages) and medicine. Therefore, his professorship in Halle was in eloquence and antiquities as well as medicine. To foster the study of antiquity, he founded a Latin society. In science history, he is famous for his experiments with silver nitrate as an important step towards the discovery of photography; he is also remembered for the decipherment of the Cufic letters on the Coronation Mantle of the Roman emperors, as a medical historian, and as a numismatic. He died in Halle in 1744. Alongside the two known short Greek epigrams, he contributed to an influential Greek grammar.

Bibliography: Weise 2011.

Friedrich Gottlieb Klopstock (1724–1803)

<*Versio Graeca odae c.t.* "Die frühen Gräber">

    Χαιρ', Ἄρτεμι ἀργυρεα,
    καλα νυκτος ἑταιρεα,
    Πεφυγας· φευγε μη, της φρενος φιλη·
    Ἡ κε μενει, ἀπεβη δε νεφελα.

Textus: Gronemeyer, Horst/Hurlebusch, Karl (eds.) (2010), *Friedrich Gottlieb Klopstock. Oden*, vol. 1: Text, Berlin/New York, 610.

Sim.: 2 νυκτος ἑταιρεα] cf. Triph. 503 νυκτὸς ἑταίρη (de quiete) || **5** δε νεφέλα] cf. Hom. *Il.* 14.350 (δέ etiam producitur)

<Greek translation of his ode *Die frühen Gräber*>

    Hail, silvery Artemis,
    night's beautiful companion!
    You have escaped: Do not go, friend of my mind.
    Perhaps she will stay, but the cloud has gone.[36]

Metre: Newly built lyric stanza according to the German original.

---

[36] German original: "Willkommen, o silberner Mond, / Schöner, stiller Gefährt der Nacht! / Du entfliehst? Eile nicht, bleib, Gedankenfreund! / Sehet, er bleibt, das Gewölk wallte nur hin."

Notes: We know of partial Greek translations by Klopstock of only two of his own German odes. One translates stanzas 1–6 of his ode *An Fanny*, and the other translates only the first stanza of his ode *Die frühen Gräber*. These originated in different periods. The first translation was done in 1749 while Klopstock lived in Langensalza, and the second was written for a visit by the scholar Karl August Böttiger, in Hamburg in 1795. Their purpose was not only to show Klopstock's command of the language to renowned scholars (the first translation was sent to Johann Jakob Bodmer, the second performed with music before Böttiger) but also, according to Klopstock himself, to demonstrate the superiority of German over Greek. In both cases, Klopstock uses formulae and phrases from Greek poets, al-though his Greek has serious shortcomings, especially in the selected second translation: ἑταιρεα instead of ἑταίρα, πέφυγας instead of πέφευγας, Ἡ κε μένει instead of ἥ κε μένῃ (prospective subjunctive) or ἥ κε μένοι (*potentialis*). The complete absence of accents may be due to contemporary theories on Greek accentuation (see also **General Introduction**).[37]

Biography: Friedrich Gottlieb Klopstock (born in Quedlinburg in 1724) was a famous German poet and forerunner of German classicism. Important stages of his life took place in Copenhagen and also in Hamburg, where he died in 1803. With his German epic titled *Der Messias* (first edition of songs I–V in 1751) and his odes, he influenced the poets and the poetic language of his time. He adapted the German language for the rhythmical reproduction of ancient metres. His humanistic training is rooted in his education at Schulpforta from 1739 to 1745, where he is said to have composed not only Latin and German but also Greek verses. Nothing has survived from this period, however, besides his Latin valediction which announced his epic project, *Der Messias*.

Bibliography: Füssli, Hans Heinrich (1810), *Eine Reliquie von Klopstock*, Zürich; Böttiger, Karl August (1814), "Klopstock, im Sommer 1795. Ein Bruchstück aus meinem Tagebuche", in: *Minerva Taschenbuch* 6, 313–352; Hurlebusch, Klaus (2003), *Friedrich Gottlieb Klopstock*, Hamburg; Weise 2016, 159, 161.

---

[37] Cf. Minaoglou, Charalampos (2018), "Anastasius Michael Macedo and His Speech on Hellenism", in: Janika Päll/Ivo Volt (eds.), *Hellenostephanos. Humanist Greek in Early Modern Europe. Learned Communities between Antiquity and Contemporary Culture*, Tartu, 115–129 (120–121).

Eduard Eyth (1809–1884)

Ἀνθρωπομυομαχία [1840]

(excerptum, vv. 1–31, 89–106).

    Ἄνθρωπός περ ἐὼν μύας ᾄσομαι ἀργιόδοντας,
    Ὠκύποδας, τοῖς αὐτὸς Ἄρης ποτ' ἀμύμονα θυμὸν
    Ἔνσταξεν, τρόμον οὔτιν' ἐνὶ σμικροῖσι πόδεσσιν,
    Οὔτε δέος χλωρόν ποτ' ἔχειν, ἀλλ' ἀντιβίοισι
5 Δεινὸν ὀδοῦσι μάχεσθαι ἐπ' ἄνδρας χαλκοκορυστάς.
    Τῶν ἀμόθεν γε φίλον μοι ἐπείγεται ἦτορ ἀείδειν.
    Τοὔνομα Μυονίη χώρη τις ἀπόπροθέν ἐστι,
    Τῆς μέρος ἐν ξηρᾷ κεῖται Ῥήνοιο παρ' ὄχθαις
    Καλλιρρόου ποταμοῦ, ἕτερον μέρος ἀμφικέκλυσται.
10 Κεῖθι μύες δ' ὑπὸ γῇ ἐὰ δώματα ναιετάασκον,
    Αὐτὰρ ὕπερθε φέρεσκον ἀγροὶ μάλα πίονα καρπόν,
    Ἄνθεα καλά, πόην, κρῖ λευκὸν ἰδ' ἄλφιτα πυκνά.
    Ἀνθρώπων δ' οὐδεὶς κώμας καὶ ἄστεα οἶδε
    Καλὰ μυῶν, τέχνῃ τάπερ αὐτοὶ ᾠκοδόμησαν.
15 Πάντα γάρ ἐσθ' ὑπόγεια, ζόφῳ κεκαλυμμένα νυκτός.
    Εἷς δ' ἐκεῖ οἶκον ἕκαστος ἔχει καλόν τε μικρόν τε
    Σύν τε γυναικὶ φίλῃ καὶ σὺν τέκνοισι φίλοισι.
    Πὰρ δὲ μυχοί, ἐνὶ τοῖσι πάτρη 'γαθὰ βρωτὰ φυλάττει
    Παντοῖ', ὄφρα φαγεῖν ὥρῃ χειμῶνος ἔχωσιν.
20 Τὴν δὲ πόσιν φρεάτων βαθέων ἐξ αὐτὸς ἀφύσσει
    Οὐδείς, ἀλλὰ θεοῦ ὑετὸν πίνουσιν ἅπαντες.
    Οὐδ' ἄρα τοῦτο φιλοῦσι, μυῶν βιόειν ἑκὰς ἄλλων·
    Ὤρυξαν γὰρ ὁδοὺς πρὸς πλησίον ὄντας ἕκαστος,
    Τῶν διὰ ὦκα φέροντ', εὖ εἰδότες, ᾗπερ ἄγουσιν.
25 Οὔθ' οἱ δεύονται ἀρχόντων ἡγεμόνων τε,
    Οὔτε μυὸς βασιλῆος, ὅου κράτος ἐστὶ μέγιστον.
    Μυοκρέων δ' ἄρ' ἄναξ κατ' ἐπωνυμίην κέκληται,
    Ἀργεννῇ δ' ἐσθῆτι πυκασμένος ἐστὶν ἁπάντων
    Οἶος· ἐπ' αὖ κεφαλῇ κόσμηται στέμματι χρυσοῦ.
30 Χρυσὸν γὰρ Ῥήνοιο φέρουσιν κύματα πολλόν·
    Ἀλλ' ἄγε, Μοῦσ', ἀρχὴν ᾆδε κρυεροῦ πολέμοιο.
    [...]
    Ἄρτι γὰρ ἀνθρώπων εἰσήλυθον ἄστεα μοῦνος
90 Αὐτὸς σκεψάμενος ῥ', ὅσσοι ποτ' ἔασι καὶ οἷοι·
    Κώμας δ' αὖ πόλεάς τε διέδραμον, οὐδέ τις εἶδεν,
    Καὶ ἀγοράς, ναοὺς τε θεῶν καὶ βιβλιοθήκας,
    Καὶ ταμιεῖ', ἐνὶ τοῖσι γυνὴ 'γαθὰ βρωτὰ φυλάττει.
    Αὐτὰρ ἅπαξ ἔμ' ἴδον· κουρῶν τε γὰρ ἠδὲ γυναικῶν
95 Πουλὺς ὅμιλος ἔην· μία τὰς δ' ἄλλας ἐκάλεσσεν

Ὥρᾳ ἑσπερινῇ, δόμου ἐν μυχῷ· αἱ δ' ἄρ' ἔπινον
Ἡδὺ ποτὸν χλωρόν τι, καὶ εἰς γάλα λευκὸν ἔχευον,
Πολλὰ δὲ βαττολόγουν καὶ λοιδορέεσκον ἀπούσας.
Σῖγα δ' ἔγωγ' ἤμην πεπτηώς, πάντα δ' ἄκουον.
100 Αὐτὰρ ἐπεὶ ἐβόασκον ἅπασαι, ἄλλαι ἐπ' ἄλλαις,
Δὴ τότ' ἔγωγ' ἔθελον ψωμὸν καὶ αὐτὸς ἑλέσθαι·
Ἁλλόμενος δὲ προῆλθον, ἐμοῖσι πόδεσσι πεποιθώς·
Καὶ μία γνῶ, καὶ ἴδεν, καὶ ἔκραγε· "μῦς!" αἱ δ' ἄλλαι
Μηδὲν ἰδοῦσαι, ἀκούσασαι μυὸς οὔνομα μοῦνον
105 Ἔτρεμον αὐτίκ', ἔφευγον ἰδ' ἐκθορέοντο θύραζε.
Ὥς αἱ μὲν μάλα δειλαὶ ἐφαίνοντ' ἔμμεν ἅπασαι·

Textus: Eyth, Eduard (1840²), *Hilarolypos*, Basel, 31–32, 34–35 (unde Gärtner 2020, 566–567, 570).

Crit.: 6 ἦτορ: ητορ ed. || **15** ἐστ' ed., correxit Gärtner || **18** πάτρη Gärtner: πατὴρ ed. || **28** πυκασμένος] πεπυκασμένος debuit, sed metro repugnat || **29** κεκόσμηται debuit (sed vide v. 28) || **89** εἰσήλυθον] ed. pro εἰσήλυθον (cf. Kühner-Blass [1890], *Ausf. Gr. d. Gr. Sprache*, I.1 § 2, p. 41)

Sim.: 1 ἀργιόδοντας] epitheton Homericum, cf. Hom. *Il.* 10.264 (de apro); 11.292 (de canibus) || **2** ἀμύμονα θυμόν] iunctura Homerica, cf. *Il.* 16.119 etc. || **4** δέος χλωρόν] iunctura Homerica, cf. *Il.* 8.77; 12.243 || **5** ἄνδρας χαλκοκορυστάς] cf. eadem sede *Orac. Sib.* 12.197 || **6** τῶν ἀμόθεν γε] = Hom. *Od.* 1.10 || **7** χώρη τις ἀπόπροθέν ἐστι] cf. Hom. *Od.* 7.244 (Ὠγυγίη τις νῆσος ἀπόπροθεν εἰν ἁλὶ κεῖται) || **8** Ῥήνοιο παρ' ὄχθαις] cf. Hom. *Il.* 4.475 (Σιμόεντος παρ' ὄχθῃσι), 487 (ποταμοῖο παρ' ὄχθας) et sim. || **9** Καλλίρρου ποταμοῦ] cf. Hes. *Op.* 737 (ποταμῶν καλλίρροον ὕδωρ) || **10–19** de re cf. Verg. *georg.* 1.181–182 (*saepe exiguus mus / sub terris posuitque domos atque horrea fecit*) || **12** κρῖ λευκόν] cf. Hom. *Il.* 4.604 || **13** Ἀνθρώπων...ἄστεα οἶδε] cf. Hom. *Od.* 1.3 (ἀνθρώπων ἴδεν ἄστεα) || **15** ζόφῳ...νυκτός] cf. Hes. *Sc.* 227 || **26** ὅου κράτος ἐστὶ μέγιστον] = Hom. *Od.* 1.70 (de Polyphemo) || **98** βαττολόγουν] verbum pedestre || **102** πόδεσσι πεποιθώς] cf. Hom. *Il.* 6.505; 22.138 (ποσὶ κραιπνοῖσι πεποιθώς) || **105** ἐκθορέοντο θύραζε] cf. Hom. *Il.* 8.29–30 (ἐκ δὲ θύραζε / ἔδραμον)

The war between men and mice

(excerpt, ll. 1–31, 89–106)

Though being human, I will sing of the mice with white teeth and fast feet in whom Ares himself once instilled excellent courage, so that they never have any tremble in their small feet nor any green fear, but [5] they fight terribly with hostile teeth against bronze-armed men. Starting from some place, my dear heart urges to sing about this. – There is a place far away, named Myonia. Part of it lies on the dry land near the shores of the Rhine, the beautiful-flowing river. Another part is covered by water. [10] There, the mice had their dwellings beneath earth. But the fields above bore very rich fruit, beautiful flowers, grass, white barley, and dense groat. No human knows the villages and beautiful cities of the mice which they have skilfully built, [15] for everything is subterraneous, hidden by the darkness of night. Everyone there has a beautiful and small house together with his wife and his children. There are store-chambers, where the clan keeps all kind of edible goods, in order to have something to eat in the winter season. [20] Nobody draws water from deep wells by himself but all alike they drink God's rain. So, they don't like to live separated from the other mice. Hence, everyone has dug tunnels to his neighbours. Through these tunnels they quickly hurry, as they know well where they are heading for. [25] They don't lack rulers and leaders nor a mouse king whose power is greatest. Thus, Myocreon is called their ruler by name. He alone of all is clothed with a white dress. On his head, he is adorned with a wreath of gold, [30] for the waves of the Rhine carry a lot of gold: But now, Muse, sing the beginning of the cruel war. [...]

[Myocreon speaking:] 'Just now, I entered alone the cities of men [90] and saw for myself, how many they are and of which kind: Without being noted, I passed through villages and cities, through market places, temples of gods, libraries, and storehouses, where the wife keeps good food. But once they saw me, for there was [95] a huge assembly of girls and women. One of them invited the others in the inner part of her house in the evening. Hence, they were drinking some hot green drink and poured white milk into it. All the time, they were chatting a lot and were making fun of those who were absent. I was sitting silently on the floor and could hear everything. [100] But when they all began to shout, the one to the other, then I wanted to get a morsel of bread for myself too: With a jump I attacked trusting in my feet. Then, one acknowledged and saw and shouted: 'A mouse!' The others, although they had not seen anything, hearing just the word 'mouse', [105] were quivering immediately, taking flight, and running out. So, they all seemed to be very cowardly.'

Metre: Hexameters. Elegant verses, but very liberal with hiatuses (see ll. 9, 10, 13, 14, 18, 21, 24, 25, 96, 100, 103); in l. 15, ζ does not cause position; l. 103 is a *versus spondiacus* with dramatic effect.

Notes: Eyth added the epic fragment Ἀνθρωπομυομαχία (*'The War between Men and Mice'*) to the second edition of his otherwise lyric collection from 1840, *Hilarolypos* (*'Happy and Sad'*). The text consists of 321 hexameters and is inspired by the pseudo-Homeric *Batrachomyomachia* but with clear differences (e.g., no divine apparatus, no Homeric weaponry, location on the shores of the Rhine). In his text, Eyth describes the preparation for a war between mankind and mice over the supply of food. The text ends with the mice killing the human spy with their teeth. Perhaps the text is partly inspired by E.T.A. Hoffmann's famous story *The Nutcracker and the Mouse King* (*'Nussknacker und Mäusekönig'*, first published in 1816). According to Thomas Gärtner, who published a thorough study with edition and translation, in his text Eyth contrasts an idealised, unified mouse society with the corruptible and discordant human society in order to criticise, through allegory, the contemporary state of Germany's fragmentation into many different territories. The open end may allude to Virgil's *Aeneid* or Plato's *Critias* and should, perhaps, suggest that if human society changes and Germany is unified, there might still be a possibility for victory, even though the mice are strong through their joint strength. Eyth cleverly integrates references to other ancient and modern literature, for example, he alludes to Horace's famous line *parturient montes, nascetur ridiculus mus* (*Ars* 139) with a witty *oppositio in imitando* in letting the mice sing: τοῦτ' ἠδύνατο μῦς – 'this the mouse could do' (l. 164) (cf. Gärtner 2020, 558). The wit of this clausula becomes even more evident if one does not assume that the *monosyllabum* μῦς lengthens the preceding syllable but that it is to be thought of as short on purpose in order to create a line with a short, penultimate syllable, traditionally called μύ- or μείουρος – 'mouse-tailed'.[38]

Biography: Eduard Eyth was a German classical scholar, teacher, and poet. Born in 1809, he obtained his philological and theological education in Maulbronn (1823–27) and Tübingen (1827–31). During his studies, he was mainly influenced by the German poet Ludwig Uhland (1787–1862), to whom he dedicated several of his works including the mentioned collection of Greek poems. In 1841, he became a professor at the Seminar of Schönthal, where he taught Greek, Latin, and History, and in 1868, he was promoted to headmaster of the Seminar in Blaubeuren. He retired in 1877 and died in 1884. While he later concentrated mainly on translations (*Odyssey* 1834/5; *Iliad* 1–8, 1851; Sophocles 1854; Hesiod; Plutarch; Plato), pedagogical questions, and German poetry (with a strong Christian focus), his first publication was a volume of Greek poetry titled *Hilarolypos*. The first edition from 1831 consisted of 37 epigrams in elegiac couplets, 18 Anacreontics, and a series of 5 small poems on the flea, called Ψυλλιάς. In the second edition from 1840, he reworked some poems, enlarged the sections with new poems, and added a section of Γνῶμαι as well as the fragmentary epic Ἀνθρωπομυομαχία. His Greek poetry originated from his time as a student and the years before he became a professor at Maulbronn. It is marked by a special lightness and humour in tone. The Ἀνθρωπομυομαχία is of special interest as an example of a mock-epic (cf. also Duport → **Great Britain**).

Bibliography: Gärtner, Thomas (2020), "Tierische Kampfansage. Die Paränesen der Mäusekämpfer in der Anthropomyomachie des Eduard Eyth (1840) vor dem Hintergrund der späthellenistischen Batrachomyomachie", in: Hedwig Schmalzgruber (ed.), *Speaking Animals in Ancient Literature*, Heidelberg, 553–596 (with complete edition and German translation of the Ἀνθρωπομυομαχία); Krauß, Rudolf (1904), "Eyth, Eduard", in: *ADB* 48, 464–465; Kraut, K. (1884), "Eduard Eyth", in: *Biographisches Jahrbuch für Alterthumskunde* 7, 107–108; Weise 2016, 139, 146–147.

---

[38] Cf. West, Martin L. (1982), *Greek Metre*, Oxford, 173–174.

Hermann Köchly (1815–1876)

‹Inscriptio Graeca sepulchri Koechliani› [1876]

ΑΡΜΙΝΙΟΣΚ
ΟΙΧΛΥΣΟΤΑ
ΕΙΓΕΠΟΘΗΣ
ΕΝΑΘΗΝΑΣ
ΟΨΕΤΥΧΩΝ
ΙΔΕΕΙΝΜΟΙΡ
ΑΝΙΔΕΝΘΑ
ΝΑΤΟΥ

Minuscule version with diacritics:

Ἀρμίνιος Κοιχλύς, ὅ τ' ἀεί γ' ἐπόθησεν, Ἀθήνας
ὀψὲ τυχὼν ἰδέειν μοῖραν ἴδεν θανάτου.

Textus: Heidelberg, Bergfriedhof (see fig. 3, above).

Sim.: 2 μοῖραν…θανάτου] cf. eadem sede Theogn. 1.340, 820; Mimn. fr. 6.2 West; Solon fr. 20.4 West. Vide etiam Hom. *Od.* 17.326.

‹Greek inscription on Köchly's gravestone›

When *Arminios Koichlys* [Hermann Köchly] finally managed to see, what he had always longed for: Athens, he saw the lot of death.

Metre: Elegiac couplet (slight violation of Hermann's bridge in l. 1 depending on whether one reads γε πόθησεν or γ' ἐπόθησεν).

Notes: Köchly died in Trieste on 3 December 1876, while returning from a trip to Greece. He is said to have composed his own gravestone inscription and to have noted it in his diary before his death. Köchly made wise use of the form, framing the first line with his own name and Athens, doubling ἰδέειν and ἴδεν in the second line, and ending with θανάτου. The inscription is realised in Greek capitals without respecting word separation and metre, thereby imitating ancient inscriptional practice.

Biography: Hermann Köchly (1815–1876) was a classicist and professor at the universities of Zurich (from 1851) and Heidelberg (from 1864). He received his humanistic education at the Saxonian *Fürstenschule* in Grimma, where he delivered a Greek hexametrical composition on Brasidas (274 lines!) upon leaving the school to study in Leipzig under Gottfried Hermann. As an important text critic with a focus on later Greek epic, he made influential editions of Quintus Smyrnaeus (1850), Manetho's *Apotelesmata* (1858), and Nonnus' *Dionysiaca* (1858).

Bibliography: Hug, Arnold (1882), "Köchly, Hermann", in: *ADB* 16, 410–411; Weise 2016, 164–165.

Julius Richter (1816–1877)

Ἶπες [1871]

(excerptum, vv. 257–291: Καρ. = Καρδαμοῦχος, Ῥει. = Ῥεισκία, Δακ. = Δακηρία, Χορ. = Χορός)

	Καρ.	ποτέον φίλοι νῦν, νῦν ἐλευθέρῳ ποδί.
	Ῥει.	Ὁράτιός γ' ἄμεινον εἶπε ταυταγί.
	Καρ.	ἀλλ' οὖν ποσὶν κραιπνοῖσι κορδακιστέον.
260	Δακ.	εὖ Καρδαμοῦχε καὶ σοφῶς, πέραινε δή.
	Καρ.	κόρδαξ ἰατρός ἐστιν αἵματος σαπροῦ.
	Δακ.	κόρδαξ γὰρ ἐμμελείας, ὦ θεοί, κρατεῖ.
	Χορ.	ἀτεχνῶς, ἐπεὶ τὰ χερείονα νικᾷ πανταχοῦ.
	Καρ.	ὦ εἶα δὴ νῦν ᾄδετε στροφὴν νέαν.
265	Χορ.	οὐκ ἴσμεν, οὐκ ἦν παρὰ διδασκάλου λαβεῖν.
	Ῥει.	λέγοις ἂν αὐτός, ὢν σοφὸς καὶ φιλόλογος.
	Καρ.	πειράσομαι δῆτ' ὦν ἄμουσος θαῦμ' ὅσον.
		Τύριον οἶδμα λιποῦσ' ἔβαν
	Χορ.	ὀψομένα πατροκτόνον
270		καὶ μιαρὰν Ἰοκάσταν.
		αἰβοῖ, φόνων τε καὶ γάμων ἀγάμων γέμει.
	Καρ.	Ἀκτὶς ἀελίου τὸ κάλ-
	Δακ.	λιστον ἑπταπέπλῳ φάος
		κούρῃ πρὸς γάμου ὥραν, –
275		ἰδοὺ μάλ' αὖθις ἑπτάπεπλον γάμον λέγεις.
	Καρ.	πῶς ἑπτάπεπλον;
	Δακ.	σαφῶς τόδ', ὥς γε τήμερον
		κόραι μὲν εἰσὶν ἑπτάπεπλοι καὶ μονόπυλοι.
	Καρ.	Ἔρως ἀνίκατε μάχαν,
		Ἔρως ὃς ἐν κτήμασι πίπτεις –
280	Χορ.	νὴ Δία γελοῖόν ἐστι τᾆσμα καὶ παχύ

περὶ γραοσόβων καὶ πλουσίων γεροντίων.
ὁ τραγικὸς οὐδὲν εἶπε κωμικώτερον.
Καρ.   δέδυκε μὲν ἁ σελάνα –
Χορ.   ἆ δειλὲ μόνος καθεύδεις;
285   κακή 'στιν αὕτη τῶν μοναχῶν μονῳδία·
σὺ δ' ἔκλεψας αὐτὸ τᾆσμα παρὰ Σαπφοῦς σαφῶς.
Καρ.   τί δὲ δεῖ χορεύειν, εἴ γε φαῦλος ὁ Σοφοκλῆς;
Χορ.   ἔα τὸν ἄνδρα τὸν πολυτίμητον κάτω.
ἀλλ' ἐκ σεαυτοῦ νῦν πρόφαιν' ᾠδήν τινα.
290 Καρ.   φιλόλογος ᾠδῆς οὐ τοκεὺς ἀλλὰ φθορεύς.
Χορ.   φεῦ φεῦ, μέγαν τιν' εἶπας ἐν βραχεῖ λόγον.

Textus: Richter, Julius (1871), *Das Ungeziefer. Eine griechische Komödie*, Jena, 15–17.

Crit.: 281 an γραοσοβῶν?

Sim.: 257 cf. Hor. *carm.* 1.37.1 *(nunc est bibendum, nunc pede libero)* || **259** ποσὶν κραιπνοῖσι] iunctura epica, cf. e.g. Hom. *Il.* 6.505; 17.909 || **263** ἐπεὶ τὰ χερείονα νικᾷ] cf. Hom. *Il.* 1.576; *Od.* 18.404 || **268** = Eur. *Phoen.* 202 || **271** γάμων ἀγάμων] iunctura tragica, cf. Soph. *OT* 1214; Eur. *Hel.* 690 || **272** = Soph. *Ant.* 100 || **278–279** = Soph. *Ant.* 781–782 || **281** γραοσόβων] cf. Ar. *Plut.* 812 || **283–284** ~ Sapph. fr. 168 B,1.4 Voigt

Ipes ['The Bugs']

(excerpt, ll. 257–291)

Kar. Now, we have to drink, my friends, now with free foot – **Rei.** Horace has said this much better! **Kar.** So, we have to dance the *kordax* with fast feet. [260] **Dac.** Well, Kardamuchos, fine! Continue! **Kar.** The *kordax* heals rotten blood. **Dac.** Yes, the *kordax*, O gods, is superior to tragic dance. **Cho.** Absolutely, as the worse always wins. **Kar.** Come on then, sing a new stanza! [265] **Cho.** We don't know any. It was not possible to get one from our trainer. **Rei.** Say one yourself, as you are wise and a philologist. **Kar.** I will try it then, despite being completely unmusical. *When I left the Tyrian sea, I went...* **Cho.** to see the murder of his father [270] and polluted Iocasta. – Faugh! That is full of murders and illegitimate weddings! **Kar.** *Beam of the sun, the most...* **Dac.** beautiful day for the maiden wearing seven mantles for the nuptial hour – [275] Behold, again you are telling of a wedding with seven mantles. **Kar.** What do you mean by 'seven mantles'? **Dac.** Most certainly, that today the girls are wearing seven mantles and still have just one gate. **Kar.** *Eros, unconquered in battle, Eros, who attacks our possessions* – [280] **Cho.** By Zeus, this song is ridiculous and disgusting about lovers of old women and rich old men. The tragic poet didn't write anything more ridiculous. **Kar.** *The moon has sunk* – **Cho.** and you, miserable man, sleep alone? [285] This is the bad song of the monks: You have obviously stolen the song from Sappho! **Kar.** What are we to dance to, if Sophocles is bad? **Cho.** Let the highly-honoured man beneath. Show us now a song by yourself! [290] **Kar.** A philologist does not generate poetry, but destroys it. **Cho.** Alas, alas! There, you have spoken a great sentence in few words.

Metre: Iambic trimeters and inserted lyric lines.

Notes: Julius Richter, who called himself κριτής in Greek, wrote three comedies in Aristophanic manner. This is an excerpt from the first one titled Ἶπες, i.e., 'wood-worms' or simply 'bugs' (a Homeric *hapax*: fittingly chosen for a comedy on philologists!). This comedy is about contemporary philology and its exclusive focus on textual criticism. The main characters are Κέφαλος and Καρδαμοῦχος, the first one being a caricature of the contemporary classicist Moriz Haupt (1807–1874), and the second one perhaps representative of the famous editor Immanuel Bekker (1785–1871) (the Greek name apparently should evoke the classical phrase κάρδαμα βλέπειν: 'to look sharp and stinging'). Within the piece, the dead female philologists Δακηρία and Ῥεισκία, i.e. Anne Dacier (1647–1720) and Ernestine Christine Reiske (1735–1798), visit earth to see the current status of classical philology. The present scene displays some interesting details of Richter's technique. Here, he is imitating *paratragodia*, a typical element of the Old Comedy of Aristophanes, where scenes from tragedy are parodied. Furthermore, Richter integrates quotations from Latin (Horace in l. 257; especially funny, since Horace himself is imitating Alcaeus fr. 332 V. in this *carmen*), and German classics (l. 291 reminds the reader of a famous line from Goethe's *Iphigenie auf Tauris*: 'Du sprichst ein großes Wort gelassen aus'; the Thracian king, Thoas, says this after learning that Iphigenia is a descendant of Tantalus). The reference to Goethe here comments on a central phrase of the piece that a philologist cannot create poetry himself, but rather destroys it (l. 290). Kardamuchos is not able to invent a comical dancing song for the choir, consisting of bugs (the *kordax* was a frivolous dance in Old Comedy). A last remarkable feature is the 'dirty joke' in l. 277, a very common element in Attic comedy but not common in ancient Greek poetry of modern times until the 20th century.

Biography: Julius Hermann Richter (1816–1877) was a German classical scholar and teacher. He received his philological training at the universities of Bonn and Berlin, where he specialised in Greek drama with a thesis titled *De Aeschyli, Sophoclis, Euripidis interpretibus Graecis* (1839). He later became a teacher at the Friedrich Werdersches Gymnasium in Berlin. He maintained this position until his retirement in 1872. His major philological achievements consist of annotated editions of Aristophanes' *Wasps* (1858) and *Peace* (1869). Among his Greek poems are a parabase for the anniversary of the University of Bonn (1868), three comedies (Ἶπες, 1871; Χελιδόνες, 1873; Κόκκυγες, 1874), and some lyric pieces and translations from German into Greek, assembled in two minor collections

(*Griechische Lieder*, 1870; *Griechische und lateinische Lieder*, 1871). A strong patriotic touch is significant in all of his Greek poetry.

Bibliography: Süss, Wilhelm (1911), *Aristophanes und die Nachwelt*, Leipzig, 164–174; Kloft, Hans (1995), "(Un-) Demokratisches Gelächter. Überlegungen und Materialien zur Rezeption des Aristophanes im 19. Jahrhundert", in: Inge Marßolek/Till Schelz-Brandenburg (eds.), *Soziale Demokratie und sozialistische Theorie. Festschrift für Hans-Josef Steinberg zum 60. Geburtstag*, Bremen, 351–361; Weise 2016, 140–142, 152–153; Holtermann, Martin (2017), "Von der Philologenzunft und anderem Ungeziefer. Zu den altgriechischen Komödien von Julius Richter (1816–1877)", in: Weise 2017, 285–307.

Friedrich Engels (1820–1895)

Ἐτεοκλοῦς καὶ Πολυνείκους μονομαχία [1837]

(excerptum, vv. 67–80: finis carminis)

Ἔγχος ἄρα προΐει δολιχόσκιον νῦν Ἐτεοκλῆς
καὶ τὸ μὲν ἄντα ἰδὼν ἠλεύατο Κῆρα μέλαιναν
δῖος Ἀγηνορίδης, τὸ δ' ὑπέρπτατο χάλκεον ἔγχος.
70 Αὐτὰρ ὅγ' αὖ μὲν ἐρυσσάμενος ξίφος ἀργυρόηλον
ἦλθε δρόμῳ ἐπὶ τόνδε τάχ', ἀντίθεος Πολυνείκης –
ἀντίπαλος δὲ κατὰ ζώνην θώρηκος ἔνερθεν
νύξ'· ἐπὶ δ' αὐτὸς ἔρεισε, βαρείῃ χειρὶ πιθήσας,
αὐτίκα δ' ἔρρεεν αἷμα κελαινεφὲς ἐξ ὠτειλῆς.
75 ἤτοι ἄρα ξίφος ὀξὺ κατ' ὀμφαλὸν αὖτ' Ἐτεοκλοῦς
θώρηκος δί' ἐλήλατ' ἄναξ ἀνδρῶν Πολυνείκης.
Καί ῥ' ἔπεσον πρὸς γῆν, τοὺς δὲ σκότος ὄσσε κάλυψεν
καὶ Πολυνείκη καί τ' ἄρ' ἄνακτ' ἀνδρῶν Ἐτεοκλῆ·
ἤτοι ἀδελφὸς ἀδελφὸν ἔπεφνέ τε δουρὶ σιδηρῷ,
80 καί ῥα σεσίγηταί τε κενὸς δόμος Οἰδιπόδαο.

Textus: Engels, Friedrich (1976), "Der Zweikampf des Eteokles und Polyneikes. Griechisches Gedicht", in: *Karl Marx Friedrich Engels Gesamtausgabe (MEGA), Vierte Abteilung: Exzerpte, Notizen, Marginalien, Band 1: Karl Marx Friedrich Engels Exzerpte und Notizen bis 1842, Text*, Berlin, 533–535: 534–535.

Crit.: tit. Ἐτεοκλοῦς] Ἐτεοκλέους exspectaveris ‖ 67 δολιχόσκιον νῦν] lapsu auctoris claudicat versus, nisi -κιον pro una syllaba longa duxeris ‖ 75 ὄμφαλον] ὀμφαλὸν debuit

Sim.: 67–69 noster imitatur Hom. *Il.* 22.273–275 (...προΐει δολιχόσκιον ἔγχος· / καὶ τὸ μὲν ἄντα ἰδὼν ἠλεύατο.../ ...τὸ δ' ὑπέρπτατο χάλκεον ἔγχος) ‖ 68 ἠλεύατο Κῆρα μέλαιναν] clausula Homerica, vid. *Il.* 3.360; 7.254 et al. (sed ibi semper ἀλεύατο) ‖ **70** ἐρυσσάμενος ξίφος ἀργυρόηλον clausula Homerica, vid. *Il.* 3.361; 13.610 || **74** = Hom. *Il.* 4.140 || **75** ξίφος ὀξύ] iunctura Homerica, vid. *Il.* 4.530; 12.190 etc. || **76** θώρηκος δί' ἐλήλατ'] cf. Tyrt. fr. 12.26 (διὰ θώρηκος...ἐληλάμενος) || **77** τοὺς δὲ σκότος ὄσσε κάλυψεν] hemistichium Homericum, vid. *Il.* 4.503,526 etc. (sed ibi semper τὸν δὲ κτλ.) || **80** σεσίγηταί...δόμος Οἰδιπόδαο] cf. Eur. *Alc.* 78 (τί σεσίγηται δόμος Ἀδμήτου;)

The duel of Eteocles and Polynices

(excerpt, ll. 67–80: final part)

> Thus now Eteocles threw his long spear, but the divine offspring of Agenor [Polynices], seeing it in front of him, avoided the dark goddess of death and the brazen spear flew over him. [70] But god-like Polynices drew his silver-studded sword and, running quickly, attacked his brother. The enemy however pierced him at the belt beneath the corslet. He drove himself against him trusting his strong hand. Immediately black blood flowed out of the wound. [75] Yes, Polynices, the lord of men, had driven his sharp sword at Eteocles' navel through his corslet. And so they fell on earth, and darkness covered the eyes of Polynices as well as Eteocles, the lord of men. So, brother killed brother with the brazen spear [80] and the empty house of Oedipus became silent.

Metre: Hexameters (l. 74 *spondiacus*). Almost flawless, but with a problem in l. 67 and hiatus in l. 71.

Notes: Engels' presentation of the duel of Oedipus' children, Eteocles and Polynices, consists of 80 hexameters. It was delivered by him along with other contributions by pupils in German and Latin, at the valediction ceremony of the gymnasium in Elberfeld on 15 September 1837. The composition demonstrates that Engels had a very good command of Homeric language and formulae.[39] From the *Schulprogramm*, we know the titles of other such compositions delivered at the so-called *Rede-Actus* at the end of the school year. Amongst others, the later famous philosopher Friedrich Ueberweg (1826–1871), like Engels a pupil of Elberfeld Gymnasium, delivered a composition Ἡ ἐν Μαραθῶνι μάχη in 1845. Another pupil, Heinrich Christoph Gottlieb Stier (1825–1896), who composed a funny epic description of the current teachers at Elberfeld Gymnasium at the time, wrote an artistic Pindaric ode on the rebirth of Greece in 1844.[40] An important stimulus for

---

[39] Among his released papers there are also detailed notes on Homer's *Iliad* from his time at the gymnasium in Elberfeld.

[40] Both compositions and other poems in Greek and Latin are published in Stier, Theoph(ilus) (1884), *Seria mixta jocis. Carmina XXXVII Graeca Latina Theotisca*, Servestae, 1–5 (*De Graecia resurgente*, Pindaric ode), 5–12 (*Gymnasio vale dicitur*, epic narration). They are both inspired by other Greek compositions from Schulpforta. See Gärtner (forthcoming).

writing these verses seems to have been a strong philhellenic spirit, fervent in Elberfeld and other German gymnasia of the time because of the 'German' regency of Otto I in Greece after its liberation (1832–1862). At Elberfeld, however, Greek composition ceased after the departure of Dr. Karl Eichhoff (1805–1882) in 1845, a former student at the universities of Bonn and Berlin, whereas Latin compositions continued.

Biography: It is not necessary to give an account of the life of the later famous communist leader Friedrich Engels, but it may suffice to explain his extraordinary knowledge of Greek. Engels was born in Barmen (part of present-day Wuppertal) in 1820. From 1834 to 1837, he attended the then-famous gymnasium of neighbouring Elberfeld (now part of Wuppertal as well).[41] There he acquired his training in Greek, Latin, and Hebrew before leaving his home for Bremen where he published his first papers, especially his *Briefe aus dem Wuppertal* (1839).

Bibliography: Gärtner, Thomas (2021), "Die griechischen Freiheitskriege in den altgriechischen Dichtungen des Gottlieb Stier", in: Pontani, Filippomaria (ed.), *Dalle sacre ossa degli Elleni – La Rivoluzione greca due secoli dopo = Costellazioni – Rivista di lingue e letterature* 14, 97–130; Wittmütz, Volkmar (2020), "Friedrich Engels in der Schule", in: *Geschichte im Wuppertal* 29, 12–37.

Ulrich von Wilamowitz-Moellendorff (1848–1931)

I. An Georg Kaibels Kinder zur Geburt einer Schwester [1.4.1886]

>Ἦλθ' ἦλθε πελαργός,
>ὁ Πρωσσικὸς ὄρνις,
>γενέθλιος ἦρος
>ῥίγευς τε τῆς τ' ἐπ' ἱστίηι λυτήριος
>5   βροτοῖσι φωλείης λυγρῆς.
>ἦλθεν δὲ τῆιδ' ἐν ἡμέρηι πάλαι ποτέ
>(εἰσ' ἐννέα ὀκτάδες σχεδόν)
>σιδήρεόν τ' ἤνεικεν ἔρσεν ἐς χθόνα
>πελαργόχρωτα παιδίον.
>10 Τοῦ δ' ἡρακλειόθυμος ἐξέβλαστ' ἀνήρ,
>ὃς κἀνεσώσατ' ἀργύρου
>ἐπώνυμον τῆς Κελτοδουλείης πόλιν

---

41 See esp. Wittmütz 2020.

Μούσηισιν ἀρχαίην ἕδρην.
ὅκοι πελαργὸς ωὑτὸς ἦλθε σήμερον
15 τύννον φέρων κοράσιον
φίλον φίλοισι καὶ γονεῦσι καὶ γονέων
    φίλοισιν· ἀλλ' οὔπω φίλον
ἀδελφεοῖσιν· ὡς ἔπληξε μητέρα
πελαργὸς ὁ σκαιὸς σκέλος.
20 ὦ παῖδες, ἀλλὰ νηπίωι τε χαίρετε
– τὸ θῆλυ δεξιώτερον –
τῶι Πρωσσικῶι τ' ἐν Ἀργυρῖτι σήμερον
μὴ λοιδορήσητ' ὀρνέωι·
τὸ μαμμίον γὰρ ἐξαναστήσει τάχα
25 ἥδιον' ἤπερ ἦν πρὸ τοῦ.
ὑμῖν δὲ τοῖς τρίζυξι νῦν πέμπει τάδε,
ὅπως ἀείδητ' ἄσμενοι·
        ἦλθ' ἦλθε πελαργός,
        ὁ Πρωσσικὸς ὄρνις·
30   ἤνεικε τὸ τυτθόν
        μάμμηι τε πάπαι τε,
        ἡμῖν δὲ γλύκιστα
        μελίπηκτα μυριστά
        τραγημάτια

Textus: Wilamowitz-Moellendorf, Ulrich von (1938), Ἐλεγεῖα, Berlin, 9–10.

Crit.: 15 τυννὸν debuit || **25** an ἥδιον ἤπερ?

Sim.: 1 (28) ἦλθ' ἦλθε πελαργός] imitatur *Carm.Pop.* 2.1 (ἦλθ' ἦλθε χελιδών) || **9** πελαργόχρωτα] cf. Lycoph. *Alex.* 24 || **10** ἡρακλειόθυμος] neologismus || **12** Κελτοδουλείης] neologismus

To the children of Georg Kaibel on the occasion of the birth of a sister

He has come, he has come: the stork, the Prussian bird, parent of spring and deliverer from frost and [5] from the sad hibernation mortals are passing at the hearth. On the same day, he came once (it is about nine octades now) and carried a small child made of iron into the stork-coloured land. [10] A man with Herculean bravery [Bismarck] grew out of this, a man, who also saved from the French slavery the city named after silver [Argentoratum/Argentina, i.e. Strasbourg], the old seat of the Muses. The same stork has come there today [15] carrying a small girl, dear to the dear parents and the friends of the parents, but not yet dear to her brothers, as the stupid stork has struck the mother at her leg. [20] Boys, be happy about the baby – the female is better – and don't abuse the Prussian bird in Strasbourg today: For he will quickly raise up your mummy [25] better than she was before. But for you three, he sends this so that you can sing happily: 'He has come, he has come: the stork, the

Prussian bird. [30] He brought the little baby to mummy and daddy, but for us, he brought sweetest honey-cakes and small fragrant fruits.'

Metre: ll. 1–3 and 28–32 ^pher ('Reizianus'), 4–27 alternating iambic trimeters and dimeters, 33–34 pher^{2d} (pherecratean with double dactylic expansion).

Notes: This congratulatory piece for Georg Kaibel (1849–1901), who wrote Greek epi-grams himself (a selection is printed in *Biographisches Jahrbuch für Alter-tums-kunde* 27, 1904, 63–65), is carefully structured. The poem has a frame of verses imitating the popular spring song ἦλθ' ἦλθε χελιδών (*Carm. Pop.* 2). Instead of the swallow, Wilamowitz puts the stork bringing a baby. The choice has strong political implications. Wilamowitz calls him the 'Prussian bird'. This is not without reason – the date of birth coincides with that of the famous Prussian chancellor, Otto von Bismarck, who was born on 1 April 1815. Another connection to Bismarck is made through the place. Strasbourg became part of the 'Deutsches Reich' again in 1871, after having been French-controlled since 1681. Wilamowitz calls the French period Κελτοδουλεία ('Celtic slavery').

II. <*Duae versiones Graecae carminis Goethiani c.t.* "Wandrers Nachtlied"> [1891]

IIa. <*Versio epigrammatica*>

Πρῳόνες εὕδουσιν, καὶ ἐνὶ δρυσὶ νήνεμος αἰθήρ,
πτηνῶν δ' ἐν λόχμῃ πᾶν κατέδαρθε γένος·
τέτλαθι δή, φίλε θυμέ· μετ' οὐ πολὺ καὶ σὲ μέτεισιν
ἠρέμα κοιμήσων ὕπνος ὁ παυσανίας.

Textus: Wilamowitz-Moellendorff, Ulrich von (1891), *Euripides. Hippolytos. Griechisch und Deutsch*, Berlin, 16–17.

Sim.: 1–2 cf. Alcm. PMG 89.1–2 (εὕδουσι... / πρῳόνες τε) || 1 νήνεμος αἰθήρ] clausula Homerica, vid. *Il.* 8.556 || 2 de re cf. Alcm. PMG 89.6 (εὕδουσι δ' οἰωνῶν φῦλα τανυπτερύγων) || 3 τέτλαθι δή, φίλε θυμέ] cf. Hom. *Od.* 20.18 τέτλαθι δή, κραδίη || 4 παυσανίας] cf. Soph. fr. 887,2 (νόστον)

‹Two Greek translations of Goethe's poem *Wandrers Nachtlied*›

‹Translation in epigrammatic style›

> The mountains are sleeping and so is the calm air in the oaks;
>   the whole race of birds has fallen asleep in the thicket.
> Be patient, my soul: not after long, it will be you
>   whom Sleep, the allayer of sorrow, will come over in order to gently calm you down.

Metre: Elegiac couplets.

IIb. ‹*Versio Sapphica*›

> κορύφαις μὲν ἀπαίσαις
>   κάτεσχε σίγα·
> ἐπὶ δ' ἀκρεμόνεσσι
>   σίγαισ' ἄηται·
> 5 ὀρνέων δὲ θρόος κατ' ὕ-
>   λαν εὕδει· σὺ δὲ βαῖον ὄμ-
>   μεννον, ὄδωτα, καὶ σὺ κοιμάσῃ.

Textus: Wilamowitz 1891, 17.

‹Translation in Sappho's style›

> Silence has taken every
> top of the hills,
> on the branches,
> the winds are silent.
> [5] The noise of the birds is sleeping in the forest. But you, traveller, wait
> a bit: you also will fall asleep.

Metre: Aeolic (ll. 1–4: 2x pher ia –, ll. 5–6: 2x gl, l. 7: cho ia sp).

Notes: The translation of German classics into Greek was a popular exercise throughout the ninteenth century and later. Gottfried Hermann (1772–1848) translated parts of Schiller's dramas (→ **Russia**), Theodor Kock (1820–1901) translated the whole of Goethe's *Iphigenie auf Tauris*,⁴² and August Dühr (1806–1896) translated Goethe's epic *Hermann und Dorothea*,⁴³ to name a few.⁴⁴ The two different translations of Goethe's *Wanderers Nachtlied* ('*Traveller's Night Song*') are taken from Wilamowitz' own translation of Euripides' *Hippolytos*. In the preface under the heading *was ist übersetzen?* (Wilamowitz 1891, 1–22), he explains the principles of his translation, which does not simply use German rhythmical equivalents of ancient metres but tries to find a style from the German tradition equivalent to the Greek. In referring to Gottfried Hermann, Wilamowitz postulates that a translator should be able to translate in either direction: from Greek to German and vice versa. In order to illustrate this idea, Wilamowitz gives some examples himself including an archaising Greek hexameter version of parts from the medieval *Nibelungenlied*⁴⁵ and the two versions of Goethe's poem. According to Wilamowitz, there are two equivalent choices of form for Goethe's composition: On the one hand, one may use the epigrammatic style of the third century BC (Wilamowitz perhaps had Anyte and other epigrammatists in mind), on the other hand, one might use the Aeolic style of Sappho. To give his translations a Greek flavour, Wilamowitz also integrates formulae from Greek literature (νήνεμος αἰθήρ, τέτλαθι δή, φίλε θυμέ).

Biography: Ulrich von Wilamowitz-Moellendorff was one of the most famous German classicists and Hellenists. He held professorships at the universities of Greifswald (1876), Göttingen (1883), and finally Berlin (1897). He made important contributions to almost all fields of Greek philology, especially to lyric, bucolics, Hellenistic poetry, Greek tragedy, Plato, and Homer. He learned Greek versification at Schulpforta and continued to write Greek verses throughout his career. This attitude influenced his pupils who wrote and published Greek verses themselves. One may, therefore, postulate a sort of *schola Wilamowitziana*. Amongst his pupils and friends writing small Greek addresses and congratulatory poems were Georg Kaibel (1849–1901), Wolfgang Schadewaldt (1900–1974), and Paul Friedländer (see below). His Greek and Latin poems were collected after his death in 1931 and published under the title *ΕΛΕΓΕΙΑ*.

---

42 Kock, Theodor (1861), *Goethii Iphigenia Graece*, Berlin.
43 Dühr, August (1888), Γοιθίου εἰδύλλιον Ἀρμίνιος καὶ Δωροθέα, Gotha.
44 Cf. Weise 2016, 161–164.
45 Wilamowitz 1891, 12–15. Cf. Weise 2016, 162–163.

Bibliography: Calder III, William Musgrave (2012), "Wilamowitz-Moellendorff, Ulrich von", in: Peter Kuhlmann/Helmut Schneider (eds.), *Geschichte der Altertumswissenschaften. Biographisches Lexikon*, Stuttgart/Weimar (= Der Neue Pauly Supplemente; 6), 1312–1317. On his Greek poetry: Körte, Alfred (1939), "Rez. Wilamowitz-Moellendorff, Elegeia (1938)", in: *Gnomon* 15, 1939, 46–53; Weise 2016, 123, 148–150, 162–163.

Paul Friedländer (1882–1968)

<*Epigramma*> [1948]

Ἥ μέ ποτ' ἔθρεψας καὶ ἐγείναο σαῖς ἐν ἀρούραις
ἠδ' ἱερῶν πολίων σῶν ἐνὶ χαρμοσύναις·
ἥ με τεὴν φωνὴν ἐδιδάξαο καὶ σέο Μούσας
καὶ ἤθεα τῶν προτέρων· ἧς κεν ὑπερθανέειν
5 Μοίραις εἰ τὸ ἄδοι πέλεν εὔχαρι· νῦν χεόμεσθα
δάκρυα καὶ λοιβὴν πατρίδι τῆι τὸ πάλαι.

Textus: Friedländer, Paul/Hoffleit, Herbert Benno (1948), *Epigrammata. Greek Inscriptions in Verse from the Beginnings to the Persian Wars*, Berkeley/Los Angeles; Friedländer, Paul (1969), *Studien zur antiken Literatur und Kunst*, Berlin, 682.

Sim.: 1 Ἥ—ἐγείναο] cf. Hom. *Od.* 2.131 (Telemachus de Penelopa matre): ἥ μ' ἔτεχ', ἥ μ' ἔθρεψε (hic tamen *hysteron proteron*, cf. etiam Hom. *Il.* 1.251 τράφεν ἠδ' ἐγένοντο); de ἐγείναο in hac versus sede cf. *Il.* 5.330 et Callim. *Hymn.* 5.105; de ἐν ἀρούραις cf. fort. Hom. *Od.* 1.407 al. πατρὶς ἄρουρα || **2** χαρμοσύναις] verbum magis pedestre quam poeticum, sed cf. *Hymn. Orph.* 60.4 || **3** ἥ με τεὴν φωνήν: sim. incipit *Anth. Gr.* 16.268.1 || **4** ἧς...ὑπερθανέειν] cf. Eur. *Phoen.* 998 (τῆσδ' ὑπερθανεῖν χθονός) || **5–6** χεόμεσθα / δάκρυα] iunctura Hom., cf. e.g. *Il.* 7.426 (δάκρυα θερμὰ χέοντες) || **6** δάκρυα καὶ λοιβήν] cf. Orph. *A.* 547–548 (λοιβὰς / δοῦναι ὑποχθονίοισι καὶ δάκρυα λειβέμεν ὄσσων).

<Epigram>

For Thee who once have brought me up and have given me birth on your fields
and in the happiness of your holy cities,
for Thee who have taught me your language and your Muses
and the customs of the ancestors, for Thee for whom it would have been merry to die,
[5] had this pleased the Moirai: for Thee, we now shed
tears and libations, O Fatherland of old.

Metre: Elegiac couplets (note the synizesis in l. 4 καὶ ἤθεα).

Notes: The epigram was first published on the front page of a collection of ancient Greek verse inscriptions in 1948, nine years after Friedländer's emigration from Germany. It is very thoughtfully structured with the classical scheme of *Erwartung* ('expectation') and *Aufschluss* ('solution'), as Lessing calls it. The author addresses Germany in three relative clauses, without naming it. Reference is made in ll. 4–5 to Friedländer's service in WWI, and the sad *pointe* of this dedicational epigram is spared until the very last words: πατρίδι τῆι τὸ πάλαι ('Fatherland of old').

Biography: Paul Friedländer was a German classicist of Jewish descent. Born in Berlin in 1882, he studied classics at the universities of Berlin and Bonn and was awarded a doctorate under the supervision of Ulrich von Wilamowitz-Moellendorff in 1905. He volunteered in WWI and was honoured with the so-called Iron Cross ('Eisernes Kreuz'). He then became a *professor ordinarius* at Marburg University in 1920 and at Halle University in 1932, but in 1935, he was relieved of his duty for being 'Nicht-Arier'. In 1938, he was even interned for some weeks in the concentration camp of Sachsenhausen. He managed, however, to flee to the United States in 1939, where he taught at the universities of Baltimore and then California in Los Angeles. He died in Los Angeles in 1968. Friedländer's studies on Plato and on late antique literature are still important today. The Greek epigram presented here is collected together with others dedicated to his wife, Charlotte, and to Wilamowitz, in Friedländer's *Studien zur antiken Literatur und Kunst* (pp. 681f.). It was Wilamowitz who inspired him to write Greek poetry.

Bibliography: Bühler, Winfried (1969), "Paul Friedländer", in: *Gnomon* 41, 619–623; Calder III, William Musgrave (1994), "Friedländer, Paul", in: Ward W. Briggs Jr. (ed.), *Biographical Dictionary of North American Classists*, Westport, Connecticut/London 1994, 200–202; Mensching, Eckart (2003), "Professor Paul Friedländer (1882–1968): Von Halle über Berlin nach Los Angeles", in: Id., *Nugae zur Philologie-Geschichte*, XII, Berlin, 82–92; Berner, Hans-Ulrich/Pait, Mayya (2012), "Friedländer, Paul", in: Peter Kuhlmann/Helmuth Schneider (edd.), *Geschichte der Altertumswissenschaften. Biographisches Lexikon*, Stuttgart/Weimar (= Der Neue Pauly Supplemente; 6), 427f. On his Greek poetry: Weise 2011, 424f.; Hillgruber, Michael (2013), "Paul Friedländer", in: Friedemann Stengel (ed.), *Ausgeschlossen. Zum Gedenken an die 1933–1945 entlassenen Hochschullehrer der Martin-Luther-Universität Halle-Wittenberg*, Halle an der Saale, 101–109 (105); Weise 2016, 148, 151; Ludwig 2017, 137.

Fig. 4: Anthonis Mor van Dashorst (Antonio Moro), Self-portrait (1558) with a Greek epigram (see below, p. 228–231) by Dominicus Lampsonius (Florence, Galleria degli Uffizi, inv. 1637).

Han Lamers and Raf Van Rooy
The Low Countries

It is too early to tell the story of Greek poetry composition in the Low Countries, which begins with **Erasmus'** first attempts in the early 1500s and continues to the present day.[1] Hardly any systematic research has been done, apart from some isolated case studies and one small anthology concentrating on Leiden University.[2] The present selection results from an initial survey of the field, addressing the Low Countries in their entirety. The selection of Greek poems we offer here covers the main genres and subject areas we have found so far. Our selection also reflects some of the imbalances in the corpus, including a strong emphasis on the sixteenth and seventeenth centuries, a relative lack of evidence from some southern centres of Greek studies (mainly Leuven), and a notable lacuna in the eighteenth century.[3]

The historical Low Countries today largely coincide with the Netherlands and Belgium (especially Dutch-speaking Flanders), but the area has had a complex history. Politically speaking, the northern and southern Low Countries have been in shifting regional constellations. Before borders hardened in 1830 with the separation of the kingdom of Belgium from that of the Netherlands, cultural boundaries between the regions were fluid, especially in the sixteenth and seventeenth centuries, and despite confessional differences. Moreover, members of the cultural elite travelled extensively among different political and cultural centres throughout Europe. These combined factors sometimes make it difficult to decide who belonged to the Low Countries and who did not. We have been rather inclusive in this regard, including men like **Frédéric Jamot** (*fl.* 1552–1611) and **Joseph Justus Scaliger** (1540–1609), whose biographies are closely connected with the Low Countries.

---

1 The early humanist Rodolphus Agricola (1443/44–1485), sometimes considered the founder of Greek studies in the Low Countries, could write Greek, but so far no Greek verses by his hand have surfaced. On his Greek knowledge, see IJsewijn (1988). A letter from Agricola to Johannes Reuchlin, written from Heidelberg, is partly composed in Greek: see *Clarorum virorum epistolae* 1514, fol. gv^v–gvi^r.
2 The Pindaric odes of Frédéric Jamot and those of Petrus Bovillius (Pierre Bouille), for instance, have been the topics of scholarly articles. See, respectively, Schmitz 1991 and Opelt 1968. For the anthology, see van den Berg *et al.* 1993. See also the references concerning individual poets in the anthology below.
3 The apparent lack of Greek verse from the circle of Hellenists around Tiberius Hemsterhuis (1685–1766) is particularly striking in this regard. For Leuven, evidence is relatively limited, but see Feys/Van Rooy 2020 for a collection of epitaphs for Rutger Rescius, for the greater part written in defective Greek.

https://doi.org/10.1515/9783110652758-006

Greek verse composition in this part of Europe generally followed trends in Greek studies. Interest in Greek started to intensify in the Low Countries from about 1515 in Leuven. Students from all over Europe flocked towards the city's Collegium Trilingue, founded in 1517. Leuven remained, together with Antwerp, Ghent, and Liège, a principal centre of Greek studies until about 1580, when the wars of religion stimulated a northward 'brain drain'.[4] The centre of gravity then shifted to Leiden and, to a lesser extent, cities such as Franeker and Amsterdam. During this phase of transition, the southern cities of Bruges and Douai were notably animated – albeit largely forgotten – centres of Greek learning.[5] In compliance with these general trends, Greek poetry composition moved from south to north after 1580 and had its Golden Age in the century or so between c. 1550 and c. 1650, peaking between 1580 and 1610,[6] when writers north and south celebrated the Greek Muse. Greek composition rapidly declined afterwards. This has to do, among other factors, with the fact that, unlike England, the Low Countries did not maintain a strong tradition of composition in Greek teaching.[7] Greek poems by modern authors are, therefore, rare and isolated phenomena; the small oeuvre of **Bernard Abraham van Groningen** (1894–1987) – professor of Greek at Leiden University between 1929 and 1964 – is the most substantial printed collection we know of from the modern period. In terms of quality, the few scattered Greek poems of **Johan Andreas dèr Mouw** (1863–1919) are the most spectacular. Both van Groningen and dèr Mouw are represented in the present anthology.

Most poems we have found so far were produced in circles connected to universities or prestigious printing houses, principally in Antwerp, Bruges, Amsterdam, and Leiden. A notable exception is **Willem van de Ven** (b. 1548), who worked in relative isolation in the small town of Sint-Oedenrode, where he wrote a Theognis-inspired prayer to St Oda of Scotland (represented in this anthology). The poets are mostly students and scholars, professors and teachers, and clerics and Jesuits. And they are invariably *men*. The polyglot Anna Maria van Schurman (1607–1678), who corresponded in Greek, reportedly also wrote Greek poems, but none of them has so far resurfaced.[8] Most writers were involved in philological studies or teach-

---

4 On Leuven as a centre of Greek studies in the early modern period, see Van Rooy/Van Hal 2018. Greek studies in sixteenth-century Antwerp, Ghent, and Liège deserve a closer study.
5 On Bruges, see Lamers/Van Rooy fc.
6 Cf. also the German section.
7 See, e.g., Sicking in van den Berg et al. 1993, xi.
8 The theologian Gisbertus Voetius (1589–1676) addressed an extant Greek poem to her (Voetius 1655, ***3ʳ, with a Latin translation). In personal correspondence, both Pieta van Beek and Anne Larsen have confirmed that they have so far not found any Greek poems by van Schurman. The

ing, but learned men of other disciplines – including medicine and botany – occasionally tried their hands at Greek verse.⁹ Only a few of these writers can be regarded as Greek poets in the sense that they produced a sizeable oeuvre over an extended period of time. In terms of quantity, the *poetae maiores* of the Low Countries include **Bonaventura Vulcanius** (1538–1614; for the most part unpublished), Frédéric Jamot, **Nicolaes van Wassenaer** (c. 1572–1629), **Daniel Heinsius** (1580–1655), **Johannes Foreestius** (1586–1651), **Petrus Francius** (1645–1704), and – to a lesser extent – van Groningen, all included in this anthology.

The readership of Greek compositions was obviously limited. We have, however, found incidental evidence showing that some of the compositions were actually read and appreciated. The dialogue between a scholar and a bookseller, authored by Erasmus and Simon Grynaeus (1493–1541), for instance, was translated into Latin in humanist hand in a copy of Grynaeus' Aristotle edition, the title page of which features the poem.¹⁰ Exceptionally, Greek poems enjoyed wider popularity, mainly in Latin or Dutch translations, as did Scaliger's poem on Holland, which was reprinted many times and was even parodied by his brilliant student Daniel Heinsius (included in our anthology).

The corpus is metrically diverse and features dactylic hexameters, elegiac couplets, iambic metre (e.g., anaclasts and Anacreontics), as well as Pindaric strophes. Hexameters and elegiac couplets prevail, even though Pindaric odes also enjoyed some popularity in the Renaissance. Dramatic and didactic poetry, on the other hand, is conspicuous by its absence, even if there is one fairly late poem in Aeschylean style (see dèr Mouw). The range of poetic genres is quite diverse as well. Most poems were composed for specific occasions, and these were many: birth, death, and almost everything in between. We have included various examples of this genre, from varied periods and contexts: Erasmus' epitaph to Jacob Batt (1502), an anonymous wedding poem to Balthasar II Moretus (1645), and van Groningen's farewell poem to the famous German Classicist Bruno Snell (1869–1986). Among the occasional poems, *carmina liminaria* are particularly numerous. Poems on national, regional, or even local topics were also en vogue. This is, for example, reflected in Nicolaes van Wassenaer's 1605 Ἁρλεμιάς (*Harlemias*), a Homer-style epic

---

suggestion that van Schurman wrote Greek poems is in van Beek 2010, 35f. For van Schurman's Greek letters, see van Beek 2018.

9 For example, the physician and botanist Adolphus Vorstius (1597–1663) from Delft. A Greek poem by his hand, a book dedication, is in the British Library, Sloane MS 2764, fol. 57ʳ (with Latin translation, signed "A. V.").

10 This refers to a copy of the 1539 edition in the Bayerische Staatsbibliothek in Munich: Handschriftenabteilung, 4° L.impr.c.n.mss. 114, also available online via the Münchener DigitalisierungsZentrum and its Digitale Bibliothek.

dealing with the Spanish siege of Haarlem (1571/72) (a selection of which is printed below).

A greater diversity of subjects appears in the work of some of the *poetae maiores* – especially Heinsius and Francius – as well as in dèr Mouw's eccentric collection. In Heinsius' oeuvre, for example, we find a cycle of love poems for Demophile, poems about ancient Greek authors in his *Peplus*, as well as more humorous poems (all represented in our anthology). Francius' collection is perhaps even more heterogeneous, featuring among its disparate topics poems on Chinese herbal tea in the form of Anacreontic drinking songs (see below). As can be expected, poets creatively adapted ancient genres, themes, and *topoi*. Many poems moreover show a tension between ancient Greek (pagan) and contemporary (Christian) references, most obviously in van Wassenaer's epic account of the siege of Haarlem, mentioned above, in which both the Hellenic pantheon and the Christian God are involved.

In terms of style and language, the poems differ greatly. They show some quite unidiomatic expressions and unattested forms, as well as features that suggest the influence of the poet's mother tongue or Latin. Most poets are also fond of neologisms, rare words, and *hapax legomena* (found in lexica and commentaries as well as the ancient poets themselves). At least some poets try their hands at writing in the correct literary dialects. This sometimes leads to excess, as in a poem written by the 11- or 12-year-old **Hugo Grotius** (1583–1645), who Doricizes beyond the standards of Pindar himself (represented below).

In order to understand the peculiarities of the style and language of these poems, the poets' own views on grammatical correctness and style are particularly important. To give just one example: we can appreciate Erasmus' choice to use a nominative instead of a vocative only when we realise that, by premodern standards, this counted as a feature of Atticism (see his epitaph for Jérôme de Busleyden in Vredeveld 1993, 152). In this context, it may be worthwhile to look at the ways in which the poets reflected on their own poetic language. Their correspondence is a particularly informative source in this regard. To stay with the example of Erasmus: in one of his letters, he observed that it was not so much idiomatic accuracy as the efficacy of the expression that counted. Such explicit statements can cast light on the ways in which Greek poets conceptualised their own poetic language, how their literary views related to their writing praxis, and how these views may have changed over time.[11]

---

[11] Editorial note: in our editions of the Greek texts, we have normalised spelling and accentuation in compliance with the anthology's editorial principles. In the critical notes, we have recorded all

General Bibliography

van Beek, Pieta (2010), *The First Female University Student. Anna Maria van Schurman (1636)*, Utrecht.
van Beek, Pieta (2018), "῟Ως ῥόδον ἐν ἀκάνθαις – As a Rose among the Thorns. Anna Maria van Schurman and Her Correspondences in Greek", in: Janika Päll/Ivo Volt (eds.), *Hellenostephanos. Humanist Greek in Early Modern Europe. Learned Communities between Antiquity and Contemporary Culture*, Tartu, 414–437.
van den Berg, R.M./Buijs, M./Gieben, C.J.S./van den Hoorn, R.-J./Nijland, J.M./Pfeijffer, I.L./Roskam, H.N. (eds.) (1993), *Bataafs Athene. Een bloemlezing van Klassiek Griekse poëzie van de hand van Leidse humanisten van de zestiende tot en met de twintigste eeuw. Kritische teksteditie met inleidingen, vertaling en noten*, Leiden.
Clarorum virorum epistolae (1514), *Clarorum virorum epistolae Latinae Graecae et Hebraicae variis temporibus missae ad Joannem Reuchlin Phorcensem ll. doctorem* (1514), Tubingae.
Feys, Xander/Van Rooy, Raf (2020), "Louvain Lyrical about Greek: A Funerary Collection for Rutger Rescius (†1545) Retrieved", in: *Lias* 47/1, 17–66.
IJsewijn, Jozef (1988), "Agricola as a Greek Scholar", in: Fokke Akkerman/Arie Johan Vanderjagt (eds.), *Rodolphus Agricola Phrisius, 1444–1485. Proceedings of the International Conference at the University of Groningen, 28–30 October 1985*, Leiden, 21–37.
Lamers, Han/Van Rooy, Raf (forthcoming), "*Athenae Belgicae*: Greek Studies in Renaissance Bruges", in: Federica Ciccolella (ed.), *Graecia transvolavit Alpes. The Study of Greek in Early Modern Europe*, Leiden/Boston.
Lauxtermann, Marc D. (2019), "Appendix Metrica", in: Id., *Byzantine Poetry from Pisides to Geometres*, vol. 2, Vienna, 265–383.
Opelt, Ilona (1968), "Zwei griechische pindarische Oden aus dem frühen 17. Jahrhundert", in: *Mnemosyne* 21/4, 374–385.
Schmitz, Thomas (1991), "Les odes grecques de Frédéric Jamot († ca. 1609)", in: *Bibliothèque d'Humanisme et Renaissance* 53/2, 281–303.
Van Rooy, Raf/Van Hal, Toon (2018), "Studying Ancient Greek at the Old University of Leuven: An outline in a European context", in: Jan Papy (ed.), *The Leuven Collegium Trilingue 1517–1797. Erasmus, humanist educational practice and the new language institute Latin – Greek – Hebrew*, Leuven/Paris/Bristol, CT, 129–153.
Voetius, Gisbertus (1655), *Selectarum disputationum theologicarum pars secunda*, Ultrajecti.
Vredeveld, Harry (ed.) (1993), *Erasmus. Poems*, Translated by Clarence H. Miller, Collected Works of Erasmus 85–86, Toronto/Buffalo/London.

---

significant variations, including matters of punctuation and accentuation, except where they represent established practice in early modern editions, e.g. *gravis* instead of *acutus* before a comma, full stop, or enclitic and accentuation of diphthongs on the first rather than the second vowel.

Desiderius Erasmus of Rotterdam (1466/67/69–1536)

I. *Iacobo Batto, Graeco dimetro iambico* [paulo post 02.VII.1502]

Ἰάκωβε Βάττε, θάρσεο·
καλῶς θανὼν παλιμφύει.

Textus: Edd. a: *Varia epigrammata*, [Parisiis], in aedibus Nicolai depratis, 1507, fol. Biii^r (sine accentibus, spiritibus spatiisque). b: *Auctarium selectarum aliquot epistolarum Erasmi Roterodami ad eruditos, et horum ad illum*, Apud inclytam Basileam: apud Io. Frobenium, 1518, 312. c: *Omnia opera…, quaecunque ipse autor pro suis agnovit, novem tomis distincta…*, Basileae: ex officina Frobeniana, 1540, vol. 1, 1025. d: *Opera omnia emendatiora et auctiora…*, Lugduni Batavorum: Cura & impensis Petri vander Aa, 1703, vol. 3/1, 1219. Editiones recentiores: Reedijk 1956, 262; Vredeveld 1993, 60.[12]

Crit.: 2 καλῳς a

Sim.: 1 Βάττε, θάρσεο] cf. Theoc. *Id.* 4.41 (θαρσεῖν χρή, φίλε Βάττε)

To Jacob Batt, in Greek iambic dimeter

Jacob Batt, have courage:
he who dies well is born again.[13]

Metre: Iambic dimeter.

Notes: This poem by Erasmus may be the first Greek verse by a Hellenist from the Low Countries, as it was written between the death of Jacob Batt, which occurred prior to 2 July 1502, and January 1507, when the first edition of Erasmus' *Varia epigrammata* appeared. Jacob Batt (c. 1466–1502) originated from the village of Bat(h) near Bergen op Zoom, studied in Paris, and was a close friend of Erasmus. Erasmus is inspired by Theocritus' *Idyllia*, in which Corydon comforts the pastor

---

[12] Identical reissues have been omitted for reasons of space: see Reedijk 1956, where they are listed both for this and the following poems.

[13] English translations of Erasmus' Greek poems are our own, inspired by the translations of Clarence H. Miller in Vredeveld 1993. Erasmus translated the poem himself into Latin: *Iacobe Batte, ne time, / bene moriens renascitur*. See Citti 2007, 430.

Battus.¹⁴ Both Erasmus and Theocritus contrast life and death, but Erasmus does so in a Christian framework, as he alludes to the Last Judgement and the resurrection of the dead. Erasmus probably also took inspiration from a Greek inscription. Citti 2007, 430 cites a Greek epitaph in Rome, which bears striking similarity to this poem: Θαρσον [sic] ἄδελφε, καλῶς θνήσκων πάλιν φυέται. Perhaps Erasmus read the inscription in a travel account or in a letter from one of his many contacts (Citti 2007, 430f.). The poem contains two peculiar words. The imperative form θάρσεο has no parallels in other Greek texts. One would expect θάρσει, frequent in epitaphs and the New Testament (Vredeveld 1993, 472), but a trisyllabic form is necessary *metri causa*; one might propose the uncontracted variant θάρσεε as an alternative reading. This form might suggest an incomplete mastery of Greek (an argument in favour of an early dating of the poem). Vredeveld 1993, 472 attributes it to 'metrical reasons', claiming that Erasmus wanted 'to avoid rhyme'. The form παλιμφύει is also rare. Pseudo-Lucian has the adjective παλιμφυής, 'growing again' (*Am.* 2), but note that the Roman epitaph cited earlier also has πάλιν φυέται.

II. *Illustrissimo principi Philippo reduci Homerocenton* [c. IX.1503]

Χαῖρε Φίλιππε, πάτρας γλυκερὸν φάος, ὄρχαμε λαῶν.
Ὦ φίλ', ἐπεὶ νόστησας ἐελδομένοισι μάλ' ἡμῖν
σῶός τ' ἠΰς τε μέγας τε, θεοὶ δέ σε ἤγαγον αὐτοί,
οὐλέ τε καὶ μάλα χαῖρε, θεοὶ δέ τοι ὄλβια δοῖεν
5   καὶ παισὶν παίδων καὶ τοὶ μετόπισθε γένωνται.
Ἄλκιμος ἔσσ' αἰεί, καὶ σοῦ κλέος οὐκ ἀπολεῖται.

                                                                        Τέλος.

Textus: Edd. a: *Ad illustrissimum principem Philippum, archiducem Austriae, ducem Burgundiae etcetera. de triumphali profectione Hispaniensi, deque felici eiusdem in patriam reditu gratulatorius panegyricus...*, Antwerpiae: [Theodoricus Martens], 1504, in pagina tituli (sine spiritibus spatiisque et accentus rari sunt). b: *Ad illustrissimum principem Philippum Austriae ducem, Maximiliani Caesaris filium, de triumphali profectione Hispaniensi, deque felici in patriam reditu Panegyricus...*, [Parisiis]: Vaenundatur apud Ascensium, 1516, in pagina tituli. c: *Quae toto volumine continentur. Pacis querela. De regno administrando. Institutio principis Christiani. Panegyricus ad Philippum et carmen. Item ex Plutarcho. De discrimine adulatoris et amici...*, Venetiis: in aedibus Aldi, et Andreae Soceri, 1518, fol. 165ʳ. d: *Quae toto volumine continentur. Pacis querela. De regno administrando. Institutio principis Christiani. Panegyricus ad Philippum et carmen. Item*

---

14 Theoc. *Id.* 4.41–42: θαρσεῖν χρή, φίλε Βάττε· τάχ' αὔριον ἔσσετ' ἄμεινον. / ἐλπίδες ἐν ζωοῖσιν, ἀνέλπιστοι δὲ θανόντες.

ex Plutarcho. De discrimine adulatoris et amici..., Impressum Florentiae, per haeredes Philippi Iuntae, 1519, fol. 155ᵛ. Editiones recentiores: Reedijk 1956, 277; Vredeveld 1993, 138.

Crit.: tit. Εἰς φίλιππον ὁμηρόκεντρον cd || **1** πάτρης c: πάτρις d || **2** ἐελδομένουσι d | ἡμεῖν ab || **3** σῶος τ' abcd: σῶός τε Reedijk: σῶς τε Vredeveld | ἥης b || **5** καὶ τοι ab || **6** καί σου cd || **8** Τέλος omittunt cd

Sim.:[15] **1** Χαῖρε] cf. e.g. Hom. *Il.* 10.277; *Od.* 1.123; 13.229 || πάτρας] cf. Hom. *Il.* 1.30; *Od.* 24.310 (πάτρης, solum in fine versuum) || γλυκερὸν φάος] cf. Hom. *Od.* 16.23; 17.41 (ἦλθες, Τηλέμαχε, γλυκερὸν φάος) || ὄρχαμε λαῶν] clausula Hom., vid. *Il.* 14.102; 17.12 etc. || **2** Ὦ–ἡμῖν] = Hom. *Od.* 24.400 || **3** σῶς] cf. eadem sede Hom. *Il.* 22.332 | ἠύς τε μέγας τε] iunctura Hom., vid. *Il.* 2.653; 3.167 etc.; *Od.* 9.508 (sed semper in fine versuum) || **3–4** θεοὶ–δοῖεν] = Hom. *Od.* 24.401–402 (sed μέγα pro μάλα in editionibus recentioribus) || **5** καὶ–γένωνται] cf. Hom. *Il.* 20.308 (καὶ παίδων παῖδες, τοί κεν μετόπισθε γένωνται); Verg. *Aen.* 3.98 (*et nati natorum, et qui nascentur ab illis*) || **6** Ἄλκιμος ἔσσ'] = Hom. *Od.* 1.302; 3.200 || κλέος–ἀπολεῖται] cf. Hom. *Il.* 2.325 (ὅου κλέος οὔ ποτ' ὀλεῖται); *Od.* 24.196 (τῷ οἱ κλέος οὔ ποτ' ὀλεῖται)

A Homeric cento to the most illustrious Prince Philip, upon his return

> Welcome Philip, sweet light of the fatherland, leader of nations.
> Dear prince, now that you have returned to us, who desired it so much,
> safe and sound, and brave, and great, and the gods have guided you themselves,
> health and great joy be with you, and may the gods grant prosperity to you
> [5] and to your children's children and to those who will be born afterwards.
> Always be brave, and your fame will not perish.
>
> The end.

Metre: Hexameters (σῶος in l. 3: unusual synizesis?).

Notes: This is the first Greek poem attributed to Erasmus that appeared in print; even though the attribution is uncertain, most humanists took his authorship for granted (Reedijk 1956, 276). The cento accompanied Erasmus' *Panegyricus* for Philip the Handsome (1478–1506) of Habsburg, who returned from Spain in 1503. Erasmus recited part of his panegyric in Brussels on 6 January 1504 before it was printed in February 1504 by Thierry Martens in Antwerp (Reedijk 1956, 272; Vredeveld 1993, 533). The poem is patched together out of verse fragments and typical phrases from Homer's epics (abounding in *epitheta ornantia* for kings).

---

[15] Cf. already Reedijk 1956, 277; Vredeveld 1993, 534.

Erasmus also inserted a lengthy passage based on *Od.* 24.400–402. Perhaps Erasmus was influenced by Eudocia's *Homerocentones*, the *editio princeps* of which appeared as part of the *Poetae Christiani veteres* at the Aldine press in 1502. Erasmus expressed a dim view of cento poetry in his later work (MacPhail 2014, 77). Despite its cento form, the poem's language and style are not entirely Homeric. Erasmus writes the Attic πάτρας instead of Ionic πάτρης (Vredeveld 1993, 534) and σῶος instead of Homeric σῶς. σῶος does not fit the metre; perhaps it should be understood as a peculiar synizesis (cf. Lauxtermann 2019, 293 for similar examples from Byzantine poetry). The poem's Latin title has been replaced by a Greek one in Italian editions: Εἰς Φίλιππον Ὁμηρόκεντρον ('Patchwork of Homeric tags for Philip'), a title also reminding readers of the *Anthologia Palatina*.[16]

III. *Per Desiderium Erasmum Roterodamum* φιλολόγου καὶ βιβλιοπώλου διάλογος [1530–1531]

    Φιλ. Τί νέον κομίζεις; Βίβλον; Βιβ. Οὐδαμῶς. Φιλ. Τί δή;
    Βιβ. Χρυσοῦ ῥέεθρα. Φιλ. Ναὶ σὺ πλουσίως λέγεις.
    Παχύτερον εἰπέ. Βιβ. Τὸν Σταγειρίτην λέγω,
    ὃν ἔλαθεν οὐδὲν τῶν μαθημάτων μέρος,
5   οὗτός γ' ἀνέζησ' ὡς πρὸ τοῦ πολὺ καλλίων.
    Φιλ. Λέγεις ἀληθῶς τῆς Ἀμαλθείας κέρας.
    Βιβ. Οὐ μέν γ' ὀπώρας μεστόν, ἀλλ' ἀμεινόνων.
    Φιλ Καὶ τίς τοσοῦτον πλοῦτον ἡμῖν ἐμφέρει;
    Βιβ. Τοῦτόν γε παρέχει φιλόπονος Βεβέλλιος.
10 Φιλ. Χρυσέμπορος γοῦν ἐστιν, οὐ λογέμπορος;
    Βιβ. Ναί. Κεῖ τι χρυσοῦ καὶ λίθων προφερέστερον,
    θείας δὲ σοφίας οὐδέν ἐστ' ἀντάξιον.

Textus: Edd. a: *Ἀριστοτέλους ἅπαντα...*, Basileae: apud Io. Beb., 1531, in pagina tituli. b: *Ἀριστοτέλους ἅπαντα...*, Basileae: per Io. Beb. et Mich. Ising., 1539, in pagina tituli. c: *Ἀριστοτέλους ἅπαντα...*, Basileae: per Io. Beb. et Mich. Ising., 1550, in pagina tituli. Editiones recentiores: Reedijk 1956, 349f.; Vredeveld 1993, 166.

Crit.: 7 ὀπώρας a || 11 Κεῖτι abc

Sim.:[17] 1 Τί νέον] cf. e.g. Aesch. *Ag.* 85 (τί νέον;); Eur. *Alc.* 932 (τί νέον τόδε) || 2 Χρυσοῦ ῥέεθρα] cf. Cic. *ac.* 2.38.119 (*flumen orationis aureum fundens Aristoteles*; cf. Vredeveld 1993, 556), sed cf. etiam *Anthologiae Graecae app.*, *Epigrammata demonstrativa* 356.2 de Iesu Christo (τὰ χρυσᾶ

---

16 See e.g. *Anth. Pal.* 1.119, entitled Ὑπόθεσις τῶν Ὁμηροκέντρων. The term also appears in the Suda and in the work of Eustathius of Thessalonica.
17 Cf. already Vredeveld 1993, 556.

ῥεῖθρα, Χριστέ, σῶν λόγων) || **3** παχύτερον εἰπέ] cf. Origen. *comm. in ev. Joh.* 1.19.116 (Οὐ χαλεπὸν μὲν οὖν παχύτερον εἰπεῖν) || **5** τοῦ πολὺ καλλίων] cf. Isae. 2.15 (καίτοι πολὺ κάλλιον; vide epistolam Grynaei ad Erasmum in Allen/Garrod 1938, 141) || **6–7** τῆς Ἀμαλθείας κέρας...ὀπώρας μεστόν, ἀλλ' ἀμεινόνων] cf. Plut. *De fort. Rom.* 318a (τὸ δ' ὑμνούμενον ἐκεῖνο τοῦ πλούτου κέρας ἔχει διὰ χειρός, οὐκ ὀπώρας ἀεὶ θαλλούσης μεστόν, ἀλλ' ὅσα φέρει πᾶσα γῆ); cf. etiam Erasm. *Adag.* 1.6.2 || **10** λογέμπορος] verbum rarum, cf. fort. iambos G. Acropolitae in laudem epistularum Theodori Lascaris || **11** ex Orig. *hom. in Job,* PG 11.89D (de lapidibus cf. ibidem et Job ipsum)

Dialogue between a philologist and a bookseller by Desiderius Erasmus of Rotterdam

> Phil[ologist]: 'What is the new thing you are bringing? A book?' Books[eller]: 'By no means.' Phil.: 'What then?' Books.: 'Streams of gold.' Phil.: 'You are certainly using rich language; elaborate a bit.' Books.: 'I am talking about the Stagirite,[18] whose notice no branch of learning escaped, [5] he indeed came back to life much more beautiful than before.' Phil.: 'You are truly talking about the horn of plenty.' Books.: 'It is at any rate not full of fruit, but of better things.' Phil.: 'And who is bringing in such great riches for us?' Books.: 'Well, these are provided by the industrious Bebel.'[19] [10] Phil.: 'Is he then a dealer in gold, not a dealer in words?' Books.: 'Yes! And whatever else is more excellent than gold and precious stones, but nothing is worth as much as divine wisdom.'

Metre: Iambic trimeters.

Notes: Even though the three sixteenth-century editions only mention Erasmus as the author, his correspondence shows that he co-authored it with the Swabian Hellenist Simon Grynaeus (c. 1494–1541). Grynaeus (professor of Greek in Basel since 1529) was the editor of the Aristotle volume in which the poem first appeared and for which Erasmus also wrote the preface. Formally, the poem might have been influenced by a similar dialogue poem by Arsenios Apostolis (see → **Greece**). Grynaeus discussed the poem in a letter to Erasmus, showing dissatisfaction with the result. He complained that the printers had forced them to compose the verses hastily, referring to the dialogue as 'our limping iambs' (*scazontes nostri*). He also suggested changing χρυσῶν ῥέεθρα to χρυσοῦ or χρύσεια ῥέεθρα. Erasmus answered, expressing his preference for the former suggestion and claiming that this collocation does not require justification (*patrocinium*) (Reedijk 1956, 349; Vredeveld 1993, 556). The authors were rather free in their word choice. They coined the phrase λέγω πλουσίως as well as the noun χρυσέμπορος, formed

---

[18] Aristotle, who originated from the ancient city of Stagira, in Chalcidice, northern Greece.
[19] Johann Bebel (documented 1517–39), printer in Basel (see Bietenholz 1995). His relationship with Erasmus was turbulent, as he printed some treatises directed against him in the 1520s.

after analogy with the rare λογέμπορος (which they perhaps knew from Eustathius' commentary on Homer) or perhaps inspired by the thirteenth-century Byzantine author George Akropolites (see source apparatus).

The poem refers to the horn of Amalthea, the goat who secretly nursed Zeus in a Cretan cave. When they were playing one day, Zeus accidentally broke off Amalthea's horn. The young god felt bad and graced the horn with magic powers; it would always be filled with whatever its owner wanted. Erasmus knew this myth very well and referred to it in his *Adagia* (1.6.2 on the *copiae cornu*).

Biography: Born in 1466, 1467, or 1469 as the illegitimate son of a Dutch priest and a physician's daughter, Erasmus received his first education in Deventer. There, he was taught by the German humanist Alexander Hegius, who may have initiated him in Greek grammar. After staying at the monastery of Steyn (near Gouda), Erasmus became the secretary of Henry of Bergen, the bishop of Cambrai. Disappointed by the scholastic approach of the theologians at the University of Paris, he devoted his life to classical studies. He was constantly looking for funding throughout Europe. Soon he must have realised that Greek was indispensable for classical studies and that to truly explore theology, one must have a thorough mastery of the language of the New Testament. Around 1500, he began studying Greek as an autodidact and started composing short poems almost immediately. He perfected his knowledge of Greek in Leuven by reading, among others, the Early Christian author Origen and works by St Paul. His main aim in studying Greek was to produce a more adequate Latin translation of the New Testament. This he achieved in 1516 with his *Novum instrumentum*, which he kept on revising throughout his life. Erasmus also translated numerous pagan Greek works into Latin and was the guiding spirit of the Leuven *Collegium Trilingue* in 1517, which materialised thanks to Jérôme de Busleyden's financial support. Seven Greek poems, dating to the period from c. 1502 to 1531, are known today, but Erasmus' authorship is not always uncontested. He most certainly was, however, the author of a Greek poem in iambic trimeters (1518), commemorating the death of Jérôme de Busleyden and accompanying a now-lost portrait of this humanist. This piece did not make our final selection, but Lampsonius' poem on Antonio Moro's self-portrait, treated next, exemplifies portrait poetry.

Bibliography: The bibliography on Erasmus is vast. We therefore limit ourselves to literature relevant to his Greek poetry, cited above. For the latest complete edition of Erasmus' Greek poems with an English translation and a very useful commentary, see Vredeveld, Harry (ed.) (1993), *Erasmus. Poems*, Translated by Clarence H. Miller, Collected Works of Erasmus 85–86, Toronto/Buffalo/London, 85f. See also Reedijk, Cornelis (ed.) (1956), *The Poems of Desiderius Erasmus*, PhD dissertation, University of Leiden, in many respects much more thorough than

Vredeveld's edition. For the Battus poem, see Citti, Francesco (2007), "Gli epigrammi dell'*Anthologia Graeca* negli *Adagia* di Erasmo", in: *Lexis* 25, 401–432: 430f. For the Busleyden epitaph, see especially De Vocht, Henry (1950), *Jerome de Busleyden. Founder of the Louvain Collegium Trilingue. His Life and Writings Edited for the First Time in their Entirety from the Original Manuscript*, Turnhout, 99–103. Other literature: Allen, Percy S./Garrod, Heathcote W. (eds.) (1938), *Opus epistolarum Des. Erasmi Roterodami*, Tom. IX: 1530–1532, Oxonii; Bietenholz, Peter G. (1995), "Johann Bebel", in: Peter G. Bietenholz/Thomas Brian Deutscher (eds.), *Contemporaries of Erasmus. A Biographical Register of the Renaissance and Reformation*, Toronto/Buffalo/London, vol. 1, 112–113; van Leijenhorst, C.G. (1995), "Jacob Batt", in: Peter G. Bietenholz/Thomas Brian Deutscher (eds.), *Contemporaries of Erasmus. A Biographical Register of the Renaissance and Reformation*, Toronto/Buffalo/London, vol. 1, 100–101; MacPhail, Eric M. (2014), *Dancing around the Well. The Circulation of Commonplaces in Renaissance Humanism*, Leiden/Boston.

Dominicus Lampsonius (1532–1599)

<*De Antonii Mori pictura sui ipsius*> [1558]

    Βαβαί. Τίνος γὰρ εἰκών;
    τοῦ ζωγράφων ἀρίστου,
    τοῦ Ἀπελλέ' ἠδὲ Ζεῦξιν
    ἑτέρους τε τῶν παλαιῶν
5   νεωτέρους θ' ἅπαντας
    τέχνῃ ὑπερβαλόντος.
    Αὑτοῦ μὲν αὐτὸς εἶδος
    ἐῇ ἔγραψε χειρί
    χαλυβδινῷ σκοπήσας
10 ἑαυτὸν ἐν κατόπτρῳ
    ὦ ἐξόχου τεχνίτου.
    Ὁ ψευδόμωρος οὗτος
    τάχα, Μῶρε, καὶ λαλήσει.

    Λαμψον.

Textus: A: epigramma tabulae dilutis coloribus oleo depictae et in Museo Officiorum Florentiae conservatae (num. inv. 1637) manu ipsius pictoris anno 1558 additum. Editiones recentiores: Baldinucci 1769, 148 (transcriptio cum versione Latina et Italica Antonii Mariae Salvinii, 1653–1729); Obreen 1888–1890, 288 (transcriptio cum versione Nederlandica Augusti Ioannis Flament, 1856–1925); Pontani 1996, 242 (cum versione Italica et imagine photographica); Puraye 1949, 176 (transcriptio cum versione Gallica Julii Labarbe, 1920–1997).

Crit.: 1 τινός A || 2 τῶν Baldinucci | ὑψίστου Obreen || 3 Ἀπελλέ', ἠδὲ Baldinucci Obreen: Ἀπελλέην δὲ Puraye || 6 τεχνῃ A Baldinucci || 7 αυτῶν γὰρ Baldinucci | εἶδος Baldinucci || 8 χειρεὶ Baldinucci || 9 χαλιβδίνῳ Baldinucci: χαλυβδικῷ Puraye || 10 *om.* Obreen | εαυτῶν Baldinucci ||

12 ὄψει δ' ὁ Μῶρος Obreen || **13** τάχω Baldinucci | Μῶρος Obreen || **Subscr.** omisit Baldinucci: Λάμψων Puraye: Λαμψόνίου [sic] Obreen: Λαμψονίου fortasse

Sim.: 1 *Anacreon*. 3.1 et 16.1 (ζωγράφων ἄριστε) || **13** *Anacreon*. 16.34 (τάχα κηρὲ καὶ λαλήσεις)

<On Antonio Moro's self-portrait>

> Oh my! Whose portrait is this? Of the very best of painters, who in his craft outweighs Apelles and Zeuxis and all others of the ancients as well as all moderns. He painted his own image with his own hand, looking at himself in a mirror of steel. Oh, what a superb artist! This counterfeit Moro here will perhaps even talk, o Moro!

Metre: Catalectic iambic dimeters (hemiambs) with anaclastic ionic dimeters (anacreontics) in ll. 4 and 13 (there is no need, therefore, to read κ'λαλήσει in the final verse, *contra* Flement in Obreen 1888–1890, 288n1).

Notes: Lampsonius wrote this poem about the self-portrait of the Dutch portrait painter Anthonis Mor van Dashorst (Antonio Moro, Utrecht, c. 1518–Antwerp, c. 1577), greatly influenced by Titian's style. Mor travelled extensively across Europe in order to paint portraits of some of the leading aristocrats of his day, including Cardinal Granvelle, the Duke of Alba, Maximilian of Austria, Philip II, Catherine of Austria, Queen Mary I of England, William of Orange, and Anna of Austria. Such high-profile commissions made him widely known in the highest echelons of European aristocracy, and he was especially popular among the Habsburgs. He painted his self-portrait during his brief stay in Utrecht in 1558; he depicted Lampsonius' poem on a paper note fixed, with a thin pin, to an empty canvas. The Greek letters are well-shaped and overall clearly readable. As the *Anacreontea* were first published in print in 1554, Lampsonius' poem counts as an early example of humanist Greek verse in Anacreontic style, and his language and metre are indebted to the poems associated with Anacreon. Lamsponius' usage of the form χαλυβδινῷ is notable: the usual form in classical Greek would be χαλυβδικῷ, while his spelling reflects later Greek (cf. modern Greek χαλύβδινος; cf. also χαλύβινος in Schol. *Soph. Tr.* 1259). ψευδόμωρος is a witty invention of the author. Due to its prominent position in Moro's painting, Lampsonius' poem is among the better-known Greek verses composed in the Low Countries and has been translated several times. Apart from the Latin, French, and Italian translations facing the editions mentioned in the *apparatus*, there are different English, Dutch, and French versions in resp. Woodall 2007, 10; Frerichs 1947, 45n1; and Hymans 1910, 101. Lampsonius also wrote an Anacreontic poem to Moro's son, the humanist Philips Mor van Dashorst (d. 1578), which remains, to the best of our current knowledge, unpublished (Paris, Bibliothèque Nationale de France, Ms. Dupuy 951, fol. 38v).

Biography: Dominicus Lampsonius (1532–1599) was born in Bruges and studied classical languages in Leuven (from 1549). In 1554, he entered the service of the English cardinal and humanist Reginald Pole (1500–1558). After Pole's death, he left England and settled in Liège, where he served as the secretary of three successive Prince-Bishops until his death in 1599. Interested in literature, history, and art, Lampsonius maintained an extensive correspondence with humanists and artists. He was vividly interested in painting in particular. He wrote a laudatory biography of the Bruges painter Lambertus Lombardus (1506–1566), printed by Hubertus Goltzius (1526–1583) in 1565. The book opens with an engraved version of Lombardus' self-portrait, followed by a Greek distich, probably by the Bruges Hellenist Adolphus Mekerchus (1528–1591): Αὐτὸς ἑαυτοῦ σῶμα γράφεν Λόμβαρδος ἄριστος· / ἤθεα καὶ ψυχὴν Λαμψονίοιο γραφίς ('Lombardus himself depicted his own body best: / Lampsonius' stylus described his character and spirit'; see Leroy 1948, 75). Lombardus had trained Lampsonius in the arts of drawing and painting and also brought him in contact with Giorgio Vasari and other famous Italian artists (Lampsonius corresponded with, among others, Titian and Giulio Clovio). In 1572, Volcxken Diericx, the widow of the Antwerp printer Hieronymus Cock, published a set of 23 engraved portraits of Netherlandish painters, including Jan van Eyck, Hieronymus Bosch, and Rogier van der Weyden. For each portrait, Lampsonius wrote a brief Latin poem in praise of the depicted painter. The work marks an important step in the formation of a canon of painters from the Low Countries. The only surviving painting by Lampsonius himself, depicting the Crucifixion (1576), is in St Quentin Cathedral in Hasselt. While some of his Dutch and Latin poems were published, the extent of his corpus of Greek verses remains thus far unknown.

Bibliography: On Lampsonius' life and work, see Becker, Jochen (1973), "Zur niederländischen Kunstliteratur des 16. Jahrhunderts: Domenicus Lampsonius", in: *Nederlands Kunsthistorisch Jaarboek* 24, 45–61; De Baets, Peter (2008), "Familiale achtergrond van drie Brugse humanisten: Lampsonius, Fruterius en Colvius", in: *Brugs Ommeland* 3, 154–172; De Landtsheer, Jeanine (2005), "Lampsonius, Dominicus", in: *Nationaal Biografisch Woordenboek*, vol. 17, Brussels, 417–421. On his relationship with Moro in particular, see Puraye, Jean (1949), "Antonio Moro et Dominique Lampson", in: *Oud Holland* 64 (5/6), 175–183. On Hellenism in Renaissance Bruges, see Lamers/Van Rooy (forthcoming). Further literature: Baldinucci, Filippo (1769), *Notizie de' professori del disegno da Cimabue in qua. Della parte 2 del secolo IV dal 1550 al 1560...*, Florence; Frerichs, Lieneke C.J. (1947), *Antonio Moro*, Amsterdam; Hymans, Henri (1910), *Antonio Moro, son oeuvre et son temps*, Brussels; Leroy, Antoon (1948), *Adolphus Mekerchus (Adolf Van Meetkerke) 1528–1591. Leven en werken*, MA thesis, University of Ghent; Obreen, Frederik D.O.

(1888–1890), "Iets over Antonis Moor (Antonio Moro)", in: *Archief voor Nederlandsche kunstgeschiedenis* 7, 286–288; Pontani, Anna (1996), "Iscrizioni greche nell'arte occidentale: Specimen di un catalogo", in: *Scrittura e civiltà* 20, 205–279; Woodall, Joanna (2007), *Anthonis Mor: Art and Authority*, Zwolle.

Willem van de Ven (b. 1548)

Προσευχὴ τοῦ ποιητοῦ [16.XII.1570]

> Πότνια τῶν Σκωτῶν τε θεὰ θύγατέρ τε κρατίστου
> τοῦ βασιλῆος, ἐμοῦ κλῦθι, καὶ ἐσθλὰ δίδου·
> εὐχομένῳ σὺ δὲ κλῦθι, κακὰς δ' ἀπὸ κῆρας ἄλαλκε,
> ὡς πολλῇ μάκαρος ζήσοιμ' ἐν ἡσυχίῃ·
> 5 ἀθάνατον θεόν, ᾧ κράτος ἐστὶ μέγ', εὔχεο, Κούρη,
> ὃν τιμῶσιν ἀνὴρ ἐσθλὸς ὁμῶς τε κακός·
> χεῖρα πεσόντι δοίη, μὲ κ' ἐπεί ποτε γαῖα καλύψει
> πρὸς θρόνον οὐράνιον τῷδε θανόντα φέρῃ.

Textus: Ms. A: Brussels, Royal Library, Ms. 8471–75, fol. 13r. Editio recentior: Verweij 2016, 197 (sine accentibus).

Crit.: 1 Πότνεα A | θύγατερτε A: θυγατερ τε Verweij || 3 δὲ] δέ A || 4 φησοιμ' Verweij | ἡσιχίῃ A || 6 ὀν A || 7 καλύψ<...> A: καλυψ(ει) Verweij

Sim.: 1 θεὰ θύγατερ] cf. Hom. *Il.* 5.815 (de Minerva); 14.194, 14.243 (de Hera); *Od.* 1.10 (de Musa), 20.61 (de Diana) || 2 cf. Thgn. 1.4 (ad Apollinem: μοι κλῦθι καὶ ἐσθλὰ δίδου) || 3 cf. Thgn. 1.13 (ad Dianam: εὐχομένῳ μοι κλῦθι, κακὰς δ' ἀπὸ κῆρας ἄλαλκε) || 4 πολλῇ ἡσυχίῃ] cf. Thgn. 369.486 || 7 cf. Ps.-Phoc. 26; *Orac. Sib.* 2.86 (χείρα πεσόντι δίδου) | γαῖα καλύψει] = Triph. 407; *Orac.Sib.* 4.185, etc. || 8 θρόνον οὐράνιον] cf. *Orac. Sib.* 2.240 (eadem sede).

The poet's prayer

> Queen of the Scots, goddess, daughter of the mightiest king, please hear me and grant success; do lend your ear to me praying, and ward off pernicious fates so that I can live a happy life in perfect peace. [5] Address your prayers, Daughter, to the immortal god, whose powers are vast, and who is equally worshipped by the good and the bad. May He offer His hand to me when fallen, and let Him, when at some point earth will cover me, bring me to his heavenly throne at my death.

Metre: Elegiac couplets (l. 4: ζήσοιμ' does not fit the pentameter).

Notes: Van de Ven composed his prayer on 16 December 1570, at the age of 22. He added it to an epic poem in Latin about the life of St Oda of Scotland (c. 680–c. 726). Oda was venerated in Sint-Oedenrode, a village in the Duchy of Brabant (now in the Dutch province of North-Brabant), where she was believed to have lived as a hermit after having fled her native Scotland. The saint's relics remain in the local St Martin's church. Van de Ven's prayer, and his work more generally, reflect a renewed interest in the veneration of saints, resulting from the Counter-reformation. Van de Ven addresses Oda in a manner reminiscent of prayers to the gods in Homer and Theognis in particular; Κούρη is a common way to address the daughter of Demeter, Persephone. The poet intended to publish his poem but never did so. The verb form ζήσοιμ' (l. 4) in the manuscript seems to be a mistake for ζήσομ' for ζήσομαι. The subjunctive φέρῃ (l. 8) is unexpected, since an optative (φέροι) is required to convey the connotation of a wish implied here. Perhaps the poet had an optative in mind, but was misled by iotacist pronunciation.

Biography: Nothing is known about the life of Willem van de Ven (Vennius, b. 1548) apart from the fact that, in 1570–1572, he taught at the chapter school of Sint-Oedenrode. Even though he probably did not attend university, he clearly enjoyed a decent humanist education. Other works by van de Ven, including a Latin poem on the Holy Blood Miracle of Boxtel (which took place in 1380), also survive in manuscript.

Bibliography: Verweij, Michiel (2016), "Vergilius aan de Dommel. Het Odagedicht van Willem van de Ven (1570). Inleiding, editie en vertaling", in: Arnoud-Jan Bijsterveld/Veronique Roelvink (eds.), *Rondom Sint-Oedenrode. Macht, religie en cultuur in de Meierij*, Woudrichem, 167–201.

Frédéric Jamot (*fl.* 1552–1611)

Εἰς Ἔρωτος ἀνδριάντα διαλογισμός [1593]

Λέγε ζωγράφων ἄριστε,
ὅδε παῖς τίνος καλεῖται;
Ὅδε παῖς ὁ τῆς Κυθήρης.
Τί δ' ἄγει βέλη φαρέτρης;
5 Ὅτι καρδίας δαΐζειν
μερόπων ἕτοιμός ἐστιν.
Τί δὲ ψιλός ἐστι σῶμα;
Ὅτι νήπιοι χιτώνων
λόγον οὐκ ἔχουσι παῖδες.
10 Τί δὲ παῖς ἄνηβός ἐστιν;

Ὅτι νήπιοι δοκοῦσιν
ἅμα παιδίοις ἐρασταί.
Πτερὰ πῶς φέρει κατ' ὤμων;
Ὅτι πολλὰ πεπλάνηται
15 ἐπὶ καρδίαισιν ἀνδρῶν.
Τί γὰρ οὐκ ἔχει μέτωπον;
Τί δ' ἔρωτι καὶ μετώπῳ;
Φιλοπάρθενον γὰρ αἰδῶ
ἰδίων ἀπεῖρξε θώκων.
20 Ἆρα τίς μιν ἐστέρησε
πολυφεγγέων ὀπωπῶν;
Παφίης ἄπληστος ὀρμή.
Τίνα δ' ἡγέτην λέλογχεν;
Ἀνάπαυσιν, οἶνον, ὕπνον.
25 Τίνα σύγγονον λέλογχε;
Κακὸν ἔχθος, ἄλγος, Ἄρην.
Τί πελιδνός ἐστιν ὄψιν;
Ὅτι πάντοθεν δονοῦνται
στοναχαί τε καὶ μέριμναι.
30 Ὁ δὲ πῶς θεοῖς ἐμίχθη;
Ἀσεβεῖ βροτῶν μενοινῇ.
Ἀθέμιστον ἔθνος ἀνδρῶν
κακίην ὅταν φιλήσῃ,
κακίην δόλῳ σκεπάζει.

Textus: *Varia poemata Graeca et Latina: Hymni, idyllia, funera, odae, epigrammata, anagrammata*, Antverpiae: ex officina Plantiniana, 1593, 102–105.

Crit.: 2 καλεῖται ed.

Sim.: 1 cf. *Anacreont.* 3.1; 16.1 (Ἄγε, ζωγράφων ἄριστε) || **3** cf. *Anacreont.* 16.21 (Κυθήρης); 44.9 (παῖς ὁ Κυθήρης); Georg. *Carmina anacreontea* 1.165 (Ὁ Ἔρως ὁ τῆς Κυθήρης) || **4** cf. Pind. *Ol.* 2.83–84 (ὠκέα βέλη / ἔνδον ἐντὶ φαρέτρας) || **5–6** cf. *Anth. Pal.* 1.32.2 (κραδίην...μερόπων); 9.627.4 (κραδίης μερόπων) || **18** cf. Nonn. *Dion.* 48.335; 48.930 (σέβας φιλοπάρθενον αἰδοῦς) || **22** cf. Dion. Cass. 12.50.3 (ὁρμῇ ἀπλήστῳ); 40.39.3 (ὁρμαῖς ἀπλήστοις) || **28–29** cf. Jo.Chrys. *Ad populum Antiochenum*, PG 49.119 (ταραττόμενοι καὶ δονούμενοι πάντοθεν); Nonn. *Dion.* 10.242 (φθονερῇ δεδόνητο μερίμνῃ) || **30** cf. Hom. *Hymn. Dem.* 354–355 (θεοῖσι / μίσγεται) || **32** cf. Pind. *Ol.* 1.66 (ἀνέρων ἔθνος)

Discussion about a statue of Love

'Do tell, most excellent of painters, this child here, whose is it?' – 'This child is Aphrodite's.'[20] – 'And why does he carry arrows in a quiver?' – [5] 'Because he is ready to pierce through the hearts of men.' – 'And why does he have a naked body?' – 'Because little children do not care for clothes.' – [10] 'And why is he a young child?' – 'Because lovers seem silly together with little boys.' – 'Why does he bear wings on his shoulders?' – 'Because he often roams [15] over the hearts of men.' – 'Yet why does he not have a brow?'[21] – 'What use does Love have for a brow? For he has barred virginal decency from its proper seats.' – [20] 'Who has deprived him of bright-shining eyes?' – 'An insatiate desire for the Paphian [Aphrodite].' – 'But whom does he have as a guide?' – 'Repose, wine, sleep.' – [25] 'Whom does he have as a cognate?' – 'Terrible hate, pain, Ares.' – 'Why does he look flushed?' – 'Because from all sides sighs and cares are buzzing.' – [30] 'But how did he join the gods?' – 'By the impious desire of mortals. The unlawful nation of men, when it entertains vice, it covers vice with cunning.'

Metre: Anaclast, an Ionic dimeter in which the fourth and fifth elements are reversed (⏑⏑ – ⏑ – ⏑ – x), frequently used by Sappho and especially Anacreon (Halporn/Ostwald/Rosenmeyer 1980, 24). Like Lampsonius, Jamot is inspired by the *Anacreontea* (discovered and first printed by Stephanus in 1554).

Notes: Jamot's poem constitutes a dialogue about a statue of Eros between a beholder and a painter. The opening line quotes from *Anacreontea* 16, which is about a painter and his (future) painting. It is not entirely clear why Jamot would introduce a painter (ζωγράφος) instead of a sculptor. Even though the word he uses for 'statue' in the poem's title (ἀνδριάς) may also mean 'image', Jamot's own Latin rendering – printed with the Greek – shows that he actually took it to denote a 'statue' (*In Amoris statuam dialogismus*). Perhaps he wanted ζωγράφος to refer to someone who paints statues (cf. Pl. *Resp.* 420c, with apparent reference to an ἀνδριάς being coloured with pigments). While Jamot explicitly refers to his ancient models in some of his poems, he does not do so in this case. Apart from the *Anacrontea*, Jamot also imitates Pindar's language (e.g., the verb form λέλογχε(ν) in l. 23, l. 25). Notwithstanding his ancient models, his Greek is occasionally idiosyncratic (e.g., νήπιοι ἐρασταί in ll. 11–12 and ἀσεβὴς μενοινή in l. 31). Jamot's usage of the word μέτωπον, 'brow, forehead' (ll. 16–17), is perhaps most striking. Apparently, he wanted to evoke the image of a blindfolded Eros, which was a

---

20 Aphrodite is referred to here by means of the unusual word Κυθήρη, as in the Anacreontic poem Jamot is imitating (*Anacreont.* 16.21). The goddess was closely connected to the Greek island of Cythera (τὰ Κύθηρα).
21 For Jamot's idiosyncratic use of μέτωπον, see the Notes below.

common iconographical motif, symbolising blind, i.e. irrational and indiscriminate, lust, in contrast to the seeing Cupid of rational love (cf. also ll. 20–34, where other negative traits of blind love are identified). In his Latin version of the Greek poem, Jamot used the Latin word *frons*, which likewise means 'brow, forehead', while it also denotes 'shame' in medieval Latin. Perhaps the double meaning of the Latin is applied to the Greek here as well. Sometimes the poet combines existing collocations (e.g., φέρω κατ' ὤμων) idiosyncratically with other words, in this case πτερόν (l. 13). This is unusual, since the phrase φέρω κατ' ὤμων is normally employed in combination with things carried on one's shoulders – either literally or figuratively – and not with things *attached* to them.

Biography: Hardly anything is known about the life of Frédéric Jamot (Federicus Jamotius, *fl.* 1552–1611). Born in Béthune, now in France, but then in Flanders, Jamot likely had French as his mother tongue. In Paris, he studied Greek with Johannes Straselius (Jan van Strazeele, d. 1558) and Jean Dorat (Auratus, 1508–1588) at the Collège Royal. His friends included the two Bruges-born Hellenists Bonaventura Vulcanius (see below) and Andreas Hoius (1551–1635).[22] In later life, he seems to have moved to Antwerp and Douai (then also in Flanders). Jamot worked as a physician, while also publishing Latin and Greek poems as well as several philological works, including a Theocritus commentary (1552). Combining his two fields of interest, he translated a fifteenth-century Byzantine treatise on gout into French. Jamot's Greek poems are mostly occasional in nature, but he also translated one of Ausonius' poems into Greek, which enjoyed some success in France (Schmitz 1991, 284). A variety of genres is represented in his poetry, ranging from Pindaric odes – for instance, in honour of the Scottish poet George Buchanan (1506–1582) – over elegiac couplets to various kinds of dimeters, Sapphic stanzas, and anagrammatic poems.

Bibliography: Sacré, Dirk (1994), "Andreas Hoius' sterfjaar (met een noot over zijn familie)", in: *Biekorf. Westvlaams archief voor geschiedenis, archeologie, taal- en volkskunde* 94, 387–392; Schmitz, Thomas (1991), "Les odes grecques de Frédéric Jamot († ca. 1609)", in: *Bibliothèque d'Humanisme et Renaissance* 53/2, 281–303.

---

22 Sacré 1994, 388.

Hugo Grotius (1583–1645)

Hugeiani Grotii ode ad illustrissimum comitem Henricum-Fredericum Nassavium Guilielmi filium / Ὑγειάνου τοῦ Γροτίου εἶδος [1595]

(excerptum, vv. 141–175)

Στρ. ε. κώ. ιβ.

    Ἒν μερόπων ἔθνος, ἒν δὲ θεῶν ἔθνος,
    μάτηρ δ' ἐστι μία δυοῖν·
    πολλὰ δ' ἦ διείργει
    αἰὲν ἀμφότερ' ὡς τὸ μὲν γὰρ οὐδὲν
145 ἐστὶν ἠδ' ἐπάμερον·
    ἀσφαλὲς αἰὲν ἔδος δὲ ὁ χάλκεος
    μένει οὐρανὸς ὑψικάρηνος.
    Ἀλλὰ μέν τι μέροπες ἄνδρες
    φέρομες ποτὶ ὀλβίοις θεοῖσι,
150 τὰν φρένα μὰν ἄτερ ἆσ-
    γε τὸ δὲ γρὺ πελόμεσθα μόγις,
    ἄνθρωπος δ' ὄναρ ἐστι σκιᾶς.

Ἀντ. κώ. ιβ.

    Ἀλλ' ὄκα Μουσόδοτος βροτέοις ἔλθῃ
    αἴγλα, λαμπρὸν ἔπεστι φῶς,
155 μείλιχός τε αἰών.
    Τὰ δὲ νῦν ὅ γε ταλικοῦτον ὄλβον,
    ἠδὲ θησαυρὸν μάει,
    οὔ ποτε χειμέριος τὸν ἐριβρόμου
    νεφέλας στρατὸς ὄμβρος ἐπακτός,
160 οὐ σίδηρος, οὔποτ' ἀλκὴ
    ἀνεμόδρομος ἂν δύνητ' ἀπόλλειν,
    οὐ πότμος, οὐδ' ἄποτμος,
    ἀνάριθμος ἀριθμὸς δ' ἐτέων
    τοῦτον μηδὲν ἔχει βλαβέειν.

Ἐπ. κώ. ια.

165 Φέρτερον δὲ Νασσάβιος νέος
    νοῦν ἀλικίας φέρει, ἐκ
    δὲ σμικροῦ φρυγάνοιο
    γίγνεται ἶφι δένδρον,
    ναὶ δίκην κάσεως, ἀρωγῇ

170 ξυνῶν τ' ἀνδρῶν πραπίδεσσι.
Τήνῳ δὲ ποτνίᾳ τε ματέρι
ὑψόθι τὸν χρόνον εἴη
νῦν ὀπίσω τ' ἀεὶ πατέειν·
καλοῖς μοι δὲ θεοὶ διδοῖτε πανδοτῆρες
175 καλῶς ὁμιλέειν.

Textus: Ed. a: *Ode ad illustriss. comitem Henricum-Fredericum Nassavium Guilielmi f.*, Lugduni Batavorum: Apud Franciscum Raphelengium, 1595, 10–11. Editiones recentiores: Tiele/Cohen/ter Meulen 1941–1942, 34–36; Meulenbroek 1972, 43–47 (facsimile); van den Berg *et al.* 1993, 82–84.

Crit.: 143 ἦ a || **146** ἄσφαλες a || **147** οὔρανος a || **148** ἀνδρὲς a || **150** ἀτὲρ a || **151** γρὺ a et edd. recc. pro γρῦ || **159** νεφελᾶς a | ἔπακτος a || **170** ἀνδρῶν a

Sim.:[23] **141–150** cf. Pind. *Nem.* 6.1–7 (Ἓν ἀνδρῶν, ἓν θεῶν γένος· ἐκ μιᾶς δὲ πνέομεν / ματρὸς ἀμφότεροι· διείργει δὲ πᾶσα κεκριμένα / δύναμις, ὡς τὸ μὲν οὐδέν, ὁ δὲ / χάλκεος ἀσφαλὲς αἰὲν ἕδος / μένει οὐρανός. ἀλλά τι προσφέρομεν ἔμπαν ἢ μέγαν / νόον ἤτοι φύσιν ἀθανάτοις / καίπερ ἐφαμερίαν οὐκ εἰδότες οὐδὲ μετὰ νύκτας ἄμμε πότμος / ἄντιν' ἔγραψε δραμεῖν ποτὶ στάθμαν) || **151** τὸ δὲ γρὺ [sic]] γρῦ in comoedia saepius legitur, sed semper cum negatione coniunctum, cf. e.g. Ar. *Plut.* 17 (οὐδὲ γρῦ) || **151–155** cf. Pind. *Pyth.* 8.95–97 (ἐπάμεροι· τί δέ τις; τί δ' οὔ τις; σκιᾶς ὄναρ / ἄνθρωπος. ἀλλ' ὅταν αἴγλα διόσδοτος ἔλθῃ, / λαμπρὸν φέγγος ἔπεστιν ἀνδρῶν καὶ μείλιχος αἰών) || **157–161** cf. Pind. *Pyth.* 6.7–14 (ἑτοῖμος ὕμνων θησαυρὸς ἐν πολυχρύσῳ / Ἀπολλωνίᾳ τετείχισται νάπᾳ· / τὸν οὔτε χειμέριος ὄμβρος, ἐπακτὸς ἐλθών / ἐριβρόμου νεφέλας / στρατὸς ἀμείλιχος, οὔτ' ἄνεμος ἐς μυχοὺς ἁλὸς ἄξοισι παμφόρῳ χεράδει / τυπτόμενον) || **160–164** cf. Hor. *Carm.* 3.30.3–5 (*quod non imber edax, non Aquilo impotens / possit diruere aut innumerabilis / annorum series et fuga temporum*) || **161** ἀνεμόδρομος] cf. Luc. *Ver. hist.* 1.13 || **162** cf. Eur. *Hipp.* 1143–1144 (διοίσω / πότμον ἄποτμον); *Phoen.* 1306–1307 (πότμος ἄποτμος ὁ φόνος ἕνεκ' Ἐρινύων) || **165–166** cf. Pind. *Pyth.* 5.109–111 (κρέσσονα μὲν ἁλικίας / νόον φέρβεται / γλῶσσάν τε) || **169–170** cf. Pind. *Ol.* 11.10 (ἐκ θεοῦ δ' ἀνὴρ σοφαῖς ἀνθεῖ πραπίδεσσιν ὁμοίως) || **172–175** cf. Pind. *Ol.* 1.115–116 (εἴη σέ τε τοῦτον ὑψοῦ χρόνον πατεῖν, / ἐμέ τε τοσσάδε νικαφόροις / ὁμιλεῖν πρόφαντον σοφίᾳ καθ' Ἕλλανας ἐόντα παντᾷ) || **174–175** cf. etiam Pind. *Pyth.* 2.96 (ἁδόντα δ' εἴη με τοῖς ἀγαθοῖς ὁμιλεῖν)

---

[23] See also the highly detailed analysis by Meulenbroek 1973, 30–32. Cf. van den Berg *et al.* 1993, 82–84.

Ode by Hugo-Jan de Groot to the most illustrious count Hendrik Frederik of Nassau, Willem's son

(excerpt, ll. 141–175)

Strophe 5, 12 verses

There's one nation of men and one of gods, and both have one mother; but there is, yes, a lot separating them forever, since the one is indeed [145] nothing and ephemeral, while the bronze, high-topped heaven stands forever as a steadfast abode. Yet there is some way in which we, reasonable men, bear resemblance to the blessed gods: [150] our mind, without which we are barely anything, and man is but a shadow's dream.

Antistrophe 5, 12 verses

Yet when the splendour given by the Muses comes to the mortals, a radiant light is set over them, [155] and their life is joyful. And now is he [Frederik Hendrik of Nassau] pursuing such a great bliss, and a treasure, which neither an invading army of stormy rain from a loud-roaring cloud, [160] nor iron, nor a force swift as the wind, could ever destroy. Neither can destiny, not even an ill-starred one, nor an innumerable number of years in any way harm it.

Epode 5, 11 verses

[165] And the young Nassau has an intellect ahead of his age, and from the tiny branch a tree is growing forcefully, very much like his brother, with the help [170] and wits of statesmen. And may it be possible for him and his revered mother to tread aloft for a long time, now and always hereafter; and may the all-giving gods allow me to nobly [175] consort with the noble.

Metre: The poem follows the triadic structure of Pindaric odes (cf. West 1982, 60–76) and does not seem to adopt the pattern of one specific ode, reflecting different compositions by Pindar.

Notes: Following the emerging fashion of Pindar-style poetry, Hugo Grotius composed this ode in 1595, when he was only 11 or 12 years old. The poem, one of his very first publications, is addressed to the young Frederik Hendrik of Nassau (1584–1647), then 11 years of age; he was like Grotius born in Delft, and they must have spent considerable time together studying in Leiden (Tiele/Cohen/ter Meulen 1941–42, esp. 11–14). Frederik Hendrik was the son of William the Silent (1533–1584) and his fourth wife Louise de Coligny (1555–1620), who also plays a prominent role in the ode. He was the half-brother of Maurice of Orange (1567–1625), whom he succeeded as Prince of Orange and stadtholder. Grotius alludes to Maurice's credo *Tandem fit surculus arbor* ('In the end the sprig becomes a tree') in ll. 166–168. The ode was printed only once in the early modern period and does not seem to have achieved a wide distribution. One copy (now in Leiden) is accompanied by a handwritten Latin poem by Grotius, dedicating the booklet to Janus Dousa the Elder (1545–1604), curator of Leiden University; in it, the poet apologises for imitating Pindar without emulating him.[24] Grotius' mastery of Greek was already remarkable at this point. The text shows quite a few accentual mistakes. Some of these might have been introduced in the typesetting process, yet Grotius is responsible for at least one of them: in l. 151, he writes γρύ (with a short vowel) instead of γρῦ (with a long vowel), apparently for metrical reasons (compare van den Berg *et al.* 1993, 82 with Meulenbroek 1973, 30). He also tends to hyperdoricize his Greek and writes, for instance, φέρομες ποτί (l. 149) and ἀλλ' ὅκα (l. 153), perhaps in imitation of Theocritus, where Pindar wrote, respectively, προσφέρομεν and ἀλλ' ὅταν (Meulenbroek 1973, 20). Following contemporary grammar, he also adopts the allegedly Doric practice of dropping the *jota subscriptum* in certain cases (Meulenbroek 1973, 31; l. 153: ἔλθη instead of ἔλθῃ). Sometimes he prefers Attic forms, writing contracted νοῦν instead of Pindaric νόον (l. 166). His Greek is not always idiomatic; idiosyncratic are, for instance, οὐρανὸς ὑψικάρηνος (l. 147, varying on the clausula of *Il.* 12.132), μέροπες ἄνδρες (l. 148), ὄλβιοι θεοί (l. 149), and γρὺ πελόμεσθα μόγις (l. 151). Grotius shows some creativity by coining neologisms, including Μουσόδοτος (l. 153), formed by analogy with Διόσδοτος, and πανδοτήρ (l. 174), a masculine backformation of πανδώτειρα. Sometimes he follows the language of Homer and other poets rather than that of Pindar (e.g., by using μόγις instead of μόλις; Meulenbroek 1973, 30), and he also relies on early modern grammars and lexica for certain Greek forms (e.g., μάει in l. 157 and βλαβέειν in l. 164; Meulenbroek 1973, 31). Moreover, Grotius' Greek is influenced by Latin syntax and phraseology, as he uses, for instance, a subjunctive (l. 161) where one would expect an optative (Meulenbroek 1973, 31).

Biography: Born in Delft, Hugo Grotius (de Groot, 1583–1645) studied with Joseph Justus Scaliger in Leiden from age 11. One of his fellow students was the poet Daniel Heinsius, who became a close friend of Grotius' (see below). From 1599, he was active as a lawyer. Two years later, Grotius was appointed historiographer of the States of Holland. In 1607, he became public prosecutor. He later went on

---

24 Van den Berg *et al.* 1993, 84. The poem is quoted in Tiele/Cohen/ter Meulen 1941–42, 17f. and Meulenbroek 1972, 26–29, with Dutch translation.

a diplomatic mission to England in order to settle a number of conflicts over Indian trade. During the religious disputes of the Twelve Years' Truce (1609–1621), Grotius was imprisoned for life, as he had argued in favour of freedom of worship. He succeeded in spectacularly escaping from Loevestein Castle in 1621 by hiding inside a book chest and managed to flee to Paris. His friend Heinsius wrote a Greek poem on the chest in which Grotius escaped (see below). Admired by the Swedish king Gustav II Adolf, Grotius became Swedish ambassador to France in 1634. Ten years later, he was briefly called back to Sweden; on his return trip to France, he was shipwrecked, which eventually led to his death in August 1645. We have only included Grotius' earliest Greek poem, but he composed Greek poetry during his later life as well. Most notably, he wrote an interesting gratulatory poem upon receiving a Chinese book, most likely in 1601 (text in van den Berg *et al.* 1993, 86–87).

Bibliography: For a biographical account, see Nellen, Henk (2015), *Hugo Grotius: A Lifelong Struggle for Peace in Church and State, 1583 – 1645*, translated by J.C. Grayson, Leiden/Boston. For his Greek poetry, including the complete ode with a Dutch translation, see Tiele, H.J./Cohen, M. C./ter Meulen, J. (1941–1942), "Grotius' eerste publicatie: De aan Frederik Hendrik opgedragen ode. Griekse tekst met Nederlandsche vertaling door Dr. H.J. Tiele", in: *Grotiana* 9, 11–37; van den Berg *et al.* 1993, 71–87. See also the edition and commentary in Meulenbroek, Bernard L. (1972), *De dichtwerken van Hugo Grotius* (I. Oorspronkelijke dichtwerken. Tweede deel, pars 1. A. Tekst en vertaling), Assen; Id. (1973), *De dichtwerken van Hugo Grotius* (I. Oorspronkelijke dichtwerken. Tweede deel, pars 1. B. Toelichting), Assen. On the reception of Pindar in the Low Countries in general, see Veenman, René (1992), "De Thebaensche Swaen: De receptie van Pindarus in de Nederlanden", in: *Voortgang. Jaarboek voor de Neerlandistiek* 13, 65–90. Further literature: West, Martin L. (1982), *Greek Metre*, Oxford.

Bonaventura Vulcanius (1538–1614)

I. <*In Ioannem Arcerium Theodoretum*> [c. 1598]

Πυθαγόρῃ φρούδῳ σωτήρ ποτ' Ἰάμβλιχος ἦεν,
Ἀρκέριος δ' ὀλέθρου πρόξενος ἀμφοτέρῳ.

Textus: Mss. A: Leiden, Universiteitsbibliotheek, VUL 103 II, autographus, *Carmina*, fol. 71r (secundum num. fol. a C.L. Heesakkers anno 1974 insertos). B: London, British Library, Burney MS 371, autographus, fol. 104r.

Crit.: 1 σωτὴρ AB

Sim.: 2 ὀλέθρου πρόξενος] iunctura Cyrilli Alexandrini

<Against Johannes Arcerius Theodoretus>

Whereas Iamblichus once saved Pythagoras from further ruin,
Arcerius inflicts ruin on both men.

Metre: Elegiac couplet.

Notes: The poem constitutes a brief invective against Johannes Arcerius Theodoretus (1568–1604), professor of Greek at Franeker University and editor/ translator of Iamblichus' biography of Pythagoras (Franeker, 1598). The word φροῦδος is rarely used in any case except the nom. sg. and pl. Vulcanius signed this poem in Greek in both A and B: Ἡφαιστίωνος (elsewhere, in VUL 97, fol. 48r, also: Ἡφαιστίωνος τοῦ Βρουγιέως). Two poems by Arcerius on Vulcanius' *editio princeps* of Agathias (Leiden, 1594) survive in VUL 103, s.v. *Arcerius*, fol. 67 (both Latin and Greek).

II. *In clarissimi viri Ioannis Meursii Glossarium* [c. 1610]

Ἤθεα καὶ λέξεις, αἷς χρήσατο πρίν ποτε πᾶσα
συζῶσ' αὐτονόμῳ Ἑλλὰς ἐλευθερίῃ,
Ἡσύχιος τάδε πάντα καὶ ἄλλοι λεξικοράπται
γράψαν ἑνὶ γλαφυραῖς Μνημοσύνης σελίσιν.
5 αὐτὰρ ὑπ' ἀλλογενῶν ὁπότε ζυγὸν ἤλυθεν Ἑλλὰς
ἔγχεσι βαρβαρικοῖς κάρτα δαμαζομένη,
ἤθεσιν ὀθνείοις καὶ λέξεσι βαρβαροφώνοις,
χώρα τε καὶ γλώσσῃ φύρετο πασσυδίῃ.
δρεψάμενος δ' ἐκ συγγραφέων πινυτὸς τάδε πολλῶν
10 Μευρσιάδης βιβλίῳ ἐγκατέερξεν ἑνί,
οὗ ἄτερ ἱστορικῶν νεαρῶν νόος οὐ καταληπτός,
οὐδ' ἄτερ Ἡσυχίου τῶν παλαιῶν πέλεται.

Textus: Ms. A: Leiden, Universiteitsbibliotheek, VUL 103, autographus, duae poematis versiones, scil. A1: VUL 103 I B, *B. Vulcanius ad Jo. Meursium*, s. fol., et A2: VUL 103 II, *Carmina*, fol. 14ᵛ (secundum num. fol. a C.L. Heesakkers anno 1974 insertos). Edd. b: Johannes Meursius, *Glossarium Graecobarbarum...*, Lugduni Batavorum: Ex Officina Thomae Basson, 1610, fol.)0(iv. c: Johannes Meursius, *Glossarium Graeco-barbarum...Editio altera...*, Lugduni Batavorum: Apud Ludovicum Elzevirium, 1614, fol. *iiij*ʳ. Editio recentior: van den Berg *et al.* 1993, 12.

Crit.: 2 συζῶσα A2 || **4** γράψαν A1 ante rasuram A2 bc : θῆκαν A1 post rasuram || **5** ἤλυθεν A1 ante rasuram A2 bc : ἐρείπον/ἔριπον[?] A1 in margine || **6** κάρτα A1 bc : πάντα A2 || **8** φύρετο μισγομένη A1 ante rasuram : μίσγετο κεκροπίδων A1 super rasuram et πασσυδίως in margine : λείπετο φυρομένη A2 : φύρεται d || **11** ἄτερ οὐκ ἱστορικῶν A2 ante rasuram || **12** οὐδ' A2 bc : ὡς A1 | ἔσκεν ὁ τῶν παλαιῶν A1 infra rasuram || οὗ ἄτερ οὐ νεαρὰς Ἑλλήνων λέξεις νοῆσαι / ἱστορικῶν νεαρούς οὐκ ἐννοῆσαι A2 infra finem et οὗ ἄτερ ἱστορικῶν παλαιῶν νοῦς δυσκατάληπτός / ὡς ἄτερ Ἡσυχίου ἔσκεν ὁ τῶν παλαιῶν in margine.

Sim.: 2 cf. Paus. 9.15.6.8 || **9** δρεψάμενος] cf. *Anth. Pal.* 9.197.1–2 || **7** βαρβαροφώνοις] cf. Hom. *Il.* 2.867 (de Caribus in Anatolia vel Turcia antiqua)

On the *Glossarium* of the eminent man Johannes Meursius

> The customs and words that all Hellas used in the past,
>   when it still lived in autonomous freedom –
> Hesychius and other word-stitchers
> noted them all down on Mnemosyne's polished pages.
> [5] But when Hellas came under the yoke of foreigners,
>   entirely subdued by barbarian armies,
> both country and language rapidly mingled
>   with foreign customs and barbaric-sounding words.
> The clever Meursius picked them from many writers
> [10] and collected them in one single book.
> Without him, the meaning of younger historians would not be understandable,
>   no less than without Hesychius, that of the ancients is incomprehensible.

Metre: Elegiac couplets (with some metrical anomalies such as e.g. χώρα with short α in l. 8; cf. Lauxtermann 2019, 275).

Notes: The text appears in the *Glossarium Graecobarbarum* (Leiden, 1610) by the Dutch scholar Johannes Meursius (1579–1639), together with epigrams of, among others, Hugo Grotius and Daniel Heinsius. As the first full dictionary specifically dedicated to later Greek, the *Glossarium* is a hallmark of early Greek studies in the Low Countries, and Vulcanius places it on a level with the lexicon of Hesychius of Alexandria (5th/6th cent.). λεξικοράπτης is a neologism. Vulcanius might have reworked this poem after publication, since the two manuscript versions exhibit variants and corrections not reflected in the printed versions (see app. crit.). The relationship between the manuscript versions remains unclear, but they are, in any case, both drafts, containing numerous corrections. Perhaps Vulcanius reworked them for a separate publication of his poetry, which never materialised. Daniel Heinsius and Gulielmus Coddaeus also composed poems on Meursius' lexicon (see van den Berg *et al.* 1993, 38, 63). Vulcanius used a very similar phrasing as in l. 4 in a poem for Paul Merula's edition of Ennius' *Annales*, published in Leiden in 1595 (fol. 4r) (also in VUL 103 I A, *Anonymi*, s. fol. and VUL 103 I B, *Vulcanius*, items 2 and 4). His choice for the rare adjective βαρβαρόφωνος (l. 7) is probably no coincidence. In the *Iliad*, it refers to the Carians, a non-Greek

Anatolian people, and Vulcanius applies it to the current inhabitants of the area, the Turks, who were usually thought to have corrupted the Greek language. The adjective is also used in this context in Mousouros' *Ode to Plato* and in an epigram by Melanchthon (→ **Greece, Germany**).

Biography: Bonaventura Vulcanius (De Smet) was born on 30 June 1538 in Bruges. Between 1559 and 1570, he was librarian to Francisco de Mendoza and his brother Ferdinand, archdeacon of Toledo. In 1573, he moved to Cologne, where he was offered a professorship in Greek in 1574. After a brief stay in Switzerland with the printers Estienne (Geneva) and Froben (Basel), he moved to Antwerp, where he acted as secretary to Marnix van Sint Aldegonde. In 1580, he moved to Leiden, where he taught Greek for 30 years, counting Daniel Heinsius and Hugo Grotius among his students. His Leiden period witnessed the publication of numerous editions, including the poems of Callimachus, Moschus, and Bion (1584), Constantine VII's *De thematibus* (1588), Agathias (1594), and Apuleius (1594). Vulcanius kept his university post until blindness forced him to resign in 1610. He died four years later, on 9 October 1614. He was a prolific writer of Greek and Latin verse, which he produced from a young age. Among his more interesting pieces is a eulogy on the city of Dordrecht and an epitaph for Christophe Plantin, extant in different versions. He also wrote a collection of religious odes, in both Latin and Greek, and dedicated to Johan van Oldebarneveldt (1609). For his Greek poetry, which still awaits a modern critical edition, the most important manuscripts are VUL 97 and VUL 103 (Leiden University Library).

Bibliography: On his life and work, see the essays in Cazes, Hélène (2010) (ed.), *Bonaventura Vulcanius, Works and Networks: Bruges 1538-Leiden 1614*, Leiden/Boston. On his Greek poetry in particular, see van den Berg *et al.* 1993, 11–15 and van Dam, Harm-Jan (2010), "'The Honour of Letters': Bonaventura Vulcanius, Scholar and Poet", in: Hélène Cazes (ed.), *Bonaventura Vulcanius, Works and Networks: Bruges 1538 – Leiden 1614*, Leiden/Boston, 47–68. For an edition of a youthful piece by Vulcanius, an epitaph on Johannes Straselius, Greek professor at the Collège Royal in Paris, see Feys/Van Rooy (2020).

Joseph Justus Scaliger (1540–1609)

Carmen de mirandis Bataviae [c. 1600–1602]

Ὑμετέρης ἐρέω νηπευθέα θαύματα γαίης,
Δουσιάδη, δύσπιστ' ἀλλοδαποῖς ἀΐειν.
ἐνταῦθ' οὐκ ἀρκοῦσ' ἐρίοις ἱστῶνες Ἀθήνης·
πῶϋ δὲ φροῦδον ἅπαν εἰροπόκων ὀΐων.

5 ἄστεα χειροβίους οὐ χωρεῖ τέκτονας ἄνδρας·
ἐργασίμης δ' ὕλης ἔστ' ἀχόρηγον ἕδος.
σιτοδόκους πυροῦ σωροὶ ῥηγνῦσι καλιάς·
βούβοτος ἡ γαίη δ', οὐ φιλόπυρος ἔφυ.
ἄπλετοι ὧδ' οἴνοιο νενασμέναι εἰσὶ πιθάκναι·
10 οὐδενὸς οἰνοπέδου δ' ἐστὶ φυτηκομίη.
οὐδαμὸς ἢ σπάνιος τῇδε σπόρος ἐστὶ λίνοιο·
ποῦ ποτὲ δ' εἰσὶ λίνου πλείονες ἐργασίαι;
οἰκίαι εἰσὶ μέσοισιν ἐν ὕδασιν. τίς κε πίθοιτο;
ὑδροποτεῖ δ' οὐδεὶς ἐνθάδε, Δουσιάδη.

Textus: Ms. A: Leiden, Universiteitsbibliotheek, SCAL 25, fol. 140r, autographus. Edd. b: Daniel Heinsius, *Auriacus, sive Libertas saucia...*, Lugduni Batavorum: Apud Andream Cloucquium, 1602, 87 (= Bloemendal, Jan (ed.) (1997), *Daniel Heinsius: Auriacus, sive Libertas saucia (1602)*, Voorthuizen, II, 270). c: Daniel Heinsius, *Poematum nova editio...*, Lugduni Batavorum: Apud Iohannem Maire, 1606, 190–191 (prima series). d: *Opuscula varia antehac non edita*, Parisiis, Apud Hadrianum Beys / Apud Hieronymum Drouart, 1610, 294–295. e: *Opuscula varia antehac non edita: Nunc vero multis partibus aucta*, Francofurti: Apud Iacobum Fischerum, 1612, 358. f: *Poemata omnia, ex museo Petri Scriverii*, [Lugduni Batavorum]: Ex Officina Plantiniana Raphelengii, 1615, 43–44 (= *Poemata omnia, ex museo Petri Scriverii*, Berolini: Verlag von A. Bath, 1864, 46). Editio recentior: van den Berg et al. 1993, 2.

Crit.: **1–2** super rasuram A | θαύματα πᾶσιν ἄπιστα ὀθνείοισιν [ἐθ- van den Berg et al.] ἀκοῦσαι, / Δουσιάδη, φράσω, πατρίδος ὑμετέρης ante rasuram A || **6** ἐργασίμου A || **7** ῥηγνῦσι δὲ δοχὰς Δημήτερος ὄμπνια δῶρα ante rasuram A | σιτοδόκους β πυροῦ σωροὶ πιμπλᾶσι καλιάς in margine A | ῥηγνῦσι bcdefg: πιμπλᾶσι A || **9** ἐνδόμυχοι τ' οἴνοιο νενασμέναι εἰσὶ πιθάχναι ante rasuram A | ἄπλετοι ~~εἰσὶ~~ ὧδ' οἴνοιο νενασμέναι εἰσὶ πιθάχναι infra rasuram A | πιθάχναι Abcde || **12** ποτε possis || **13** ὕδασι f

Sim.: **1** νηπευθέα] cf. *Orac. ap. Macr. Sat.* 1.18.20 (hapax leg.) | θαύματα γαίης] cf. *Anth. Pal.* 9.656.10 || **4** εἰροπόκων ὀίων] cf. Hom. *Od.* 9.443; Hes. *Theog.* 446 al. || **5** χειροβίους] de subst. cf. Suid. χ 248 | cf. Hom. *Il.* 6.315; 13.390; 16.483 (τέκτονες ἄνδρες) || **6** ἀχόρηγον] cf. *schol. vet.* Pind. *Ol.* 2.96b (hapax leg.) || **8** βούβοτος] cf. Hom. *Od.* 13.246 || **10** cf. Opp. *C.* 4.331; Nonn. *Dion.* 47.72

Poem on Batavia's wonders

I will speak about your country's unheard-of wonders,
  Dousa, which foreigners can hardly believe.
Here, Athena's waving-mills are not sufficient for the wool;
  but there is no flock of woolly sheep to be seen anywhere.
[5] The cities cannot contain the carpenters who live by their handiwork;
  yet the place is barren of workable wood.
Heaps of wheat have the granaries bursting apart;
  yet, although grazed by cattle, the land is not particularly welcoming to wheat.
Huge numbers of jars, full of wine, are lined up;

[10] but there is no viniculture to be found anywhere.
Here, too, little or no flax is grown to make linen;
   yet where in the world would you find more linen-workshops than here?
Houses stand in the midst of water – who would believe this?
   And yet, nobody here drinks water, Dousa!

Metre: Elegiac couplets.

Notes: The poem is addressed to the Dutch humanist and politician Janus Dousa (1545–1604), who had invited Scaliger to come to Leiden as successor to Justus Lipsius (1547–1606). Scaliger as usual delights in rare, learned words (e.g. νηπευθέα, ἀχόρηγον). Note that ἀχόρηγος is not a neologism but is attested in the scholia on Pindar, which the poet knew well (*pace* van den Berg *et al*. 1993, 2, n. 4). Scaliger's poem has a rich reception history. Daniel Heinsius, one of his students, parodied it in Greek (see below). Later in the seventeenth century, the Greek poem enjoyed particular popularity in patriotic circles. It circulated, anonymously, in the 1630 edition of Grotius' *Liber de antiquitate Reipublicae Batavicae* (reproducing the text of *b*, with many errors; Grotius 1630, 13). It was also translated into German (Opitz 1645, 331f.) and Dutch (Pars 1701, 410f.), from the Latin version.[25] The Latin rendering was attached to the 1616 Dutch translation of Tacitus' *Historiae* by Johannes Fenacolius (1577–1645). Bernhard von Mallinckrodt (1591–1664) wrote a critical response in Latin, adding some Dutch wonders which Scaliger, according to him, had deliberately left unmentioned (*Epigramma de miraculis Hollandiae, a Scaligero dissimulatis aut neglectis,* in Mallinckrodt 1640).

Biography: Born and raised in France, Joseph Justus Scaliger's later life is closely connected with the Low Countries, where he stayed from 1593 until his death in 1609. Scaliger was born in Agen (southern France) on 5 August 1540. He received his early education in Latin from his father, Julius Caesar Scaliger (1484–1558). After his father's death, he studied in Paris, where he became fluent in ancient Greek under Adrien Turnèbe (1512–1565). During his travels through Europe, starting in 1563, he became a Protestant and, after the St Bartholomew's Day massacre (24 August 1572), he was forced to leave his home country. He settled in Geneva and remained there until 1574, when he returned to France. In the following decade, he composed some of his most important philological works, including editions of the *Catalecta* (1575), Festus (1574–1575), Ausonius (1575), Catullus,

---

25 The final lines were also rendered in Dutch in *Bagchus op zijn' troon* 1715, 110: "Ons land schijnt midden in het water als verzonken / En nochtans wordt hier 't minste die laffe vocht gedronken."

Tibullus and Propertius (1577), Manilius (1579), and his study on ancient chronology (1583). In 1590, he was offered a position at Leiden University, which he accepted after some hesitation in 1591, arriving in 1593. In Leiden, he continued his work on ancient chronology, culminating, in 1606, with the publication of the *Thesaurus temporum*. He died there on 21 January 1609. Scaliger was not only a scholar of wide-ranging topics but also a prolific poet, mainly in Greek and Latin. He also translated others' poems into Greek, including the mimes of Publilius Syrus, the *Disticha Catonis*, a good part of Martial, and poems by Catullus and Petrarch. Collections of his poetry were published in 1610 and 1615, while some of it remained in manuscript. He was also a friend of, among others, the German Hellenist Laurentius Rhodoman (→ **Germany**) who composed a gratulatory piece for him in Greek.

Bibliography: Biographical accounts: Bernays, Jacob (1855), *Joseph Justus Scaliger*, Berlin; Robinson, George W. (ed.) (1927), *Autobiography of Joseph Scaliger with Autobiographical Selections from His Letters, His Testament and the Funeral Orations by Daniel Heinsius and Dominicus Baudius*, Cambridge; Grafton, Anthony T. (1983–93), *Joseph Scaliger: A Study in the History of Classical Scholarship*, 2 vols, Oxford. On his Greek poetry: Grafton 1983, 103f.; van den Berg et al. 1993, 1–9. Some previously unpublished poems are in De Jonge, Henk Jan (ed.) (1980), *Josephi J. Scaligeri Poemata Anecdota*, Leiden. Further literature: *Bagchus op zijn' troon* (1715), *Bagchus op zyn' troon, of De nuttigheid des wyns in zyn' aart en Eigenschap. Uyt de Aaloude en Nieuwe Grieksche, Latynsche en Fransche Historiën opgeheldert. En met aartige poëtische gedachten verreikt*, Te Leiden en in 's Gr. Hage; Grotius, Hugo (1630), *De antiquitate Reipublicae Batavicae liber singularis*, ed. Petrus Scriverius, Lugduni Batavorum; von Mallinkrodt, Bernhard (1640), *De ortu ac progressu artis typographicae dissertatio historica...*, Coloniae Agrippinae; Opitz, Martin (1645), *Weltliche Poëmata, letzte Truck auffs fleissigst ubersehen und verbessert*, vol. 2, Amsterdam; Pars, Adriaan (1701), *Index Batavicus, of naamrol van de Batavise en Hollandse schrijvers: Van Julius Cesar af, tot dese tijden toe...*, Tot Leiden.

Daniel Heinsius (1580–1655)

I. *De mirandis Bataviae* [1602 vel paulo ante]

Ἴλαθι Δουσιάδη, τὰ τεῶν μεμάθηκα Βαταυῶν,
παῦρα, λίην δὲ φέρω θαύμασιν εἰδόμενα.
Εὔρεα μὲν πάσας σφίσιν ἐπλήρωσε πόληας·
εἰροπόκους δ' οὐδεὶς ὧδ' ὄϊας κομέει.
5 Ξυλοκόποι πέλον ἄνδρες ἀπειρέσιοι ξύλα θ' ὧδε·
ἄξυλος αὐτὰρ ὅλη γῆ πέλει ἡμετέρη.
Πάντῃ δῶρα πέλει Δημήτερος· οὐδέ μιν ὑμέων
ἔτρεφε γῆ, βουσὶν πλεῖστα χαριζομένη.
Πᾶς δὲ πίθος, Διόνυσε, σέθεν γέμε· πολλοὶ ἔασιν

10 ἀμπελινοὶ καρποί, ἄμπελος οὐδεμίη.
    Οὐδὲ λίνοις ἁπαλοῖσι καταβρίθουσιν ἄρουραι·
    τὰς δὲ λίνα πλήθει χειροβίων παλάμας.
    Τανταλικὸν γένος ἐσμέν, ἐπεὶ ποταμοῖς στεφόμεσθα·
    τίς δὲ τόσων γεύει, Δουσιάδη, ποταμῶν;[26]

Textus: Edd. a: Daniel Heinsius, *Auriacus, sive Libertas saucia...*, Lugduni Batavorum: Apud Andream Cloucquium, 1602, 88 (= Bloemendal, Jan (ed.) (1997), *Daniel Heinsius: Auriacus, sive Libertas saucia (1602)*, Voorthuizen, II, 272). b: *Poematum nova editio auctior emendatiorque*, Lugduni Batavorum: Apud Iohannem Maire, 1606, 191-192 (prima series). c: *Poematum editio tertia...*, Lugd. Batavorum: Apud Ioannem Maire, 1610, 201-202. d: *Poemata emendata locis infinitis et aucta, editio quarta*, Lugd. Batavorum: Apud Joh. Orlers et Iohan. Maire, 1613, 412. e: *Poemata emendata nunc postremo et aucta*, Lugd. Batavorum: Apud Iohannem Maire, 1617, 429. f: *Poematum editio nova*, Lugduni Batavorum: Sumptibus Elzeviriorum, et Iohannis Mairii, 1621, 358. g: *Poemata auctiora ed. Nicolao Heinsio, Dan. filio*, Lugduni Batavorum: Apud Francis. Hegerum, 1640, 102-103. h: *Poematum editio nova, longe auctior, editore Nicolao Heinsio, Danielis filio...*, Amstelodami: Apud Joannem Janssonium, 1649, 586. Editio recentior: van den Berg *et al.* 1993, 58.

Crit.: 1 Ἴλαθι d ‖ 4 εἰροπόκους δ' ὑμῶν τίς κομέει ὄϊας; abcd ‖ 5 ξύλαθ' ὧδε abcdefgh ‖ 6 ἄξυλον αὐτὰρ ὅλον σφιν γέγονεν πέδιον abc | ὑμετέρη f ‖ 7 οὐδαμόθι πλεῖον Δημήτερος. οὐδέ μιν ὑμῶν abc

On the wonders of Holland

Be gracious, Dousa! What I know about your Batavians,
   is not much, but let me report the things that seem exceptionally wondrous.
Wool fills all their cities,
   but nobody actually keeps woolly sheep here.
[5] Carpenters are numerous, as is wood;
   our entire country is devoid of trees, though.
The offers of Demeter are to be found everywhere, but your
   country does not foster her, generous as it is, above all, to cattle.
Every jar is full of you, Dionysus; the vine's
[10] fruits are numerous, but there is not a single vineyard.
And the fields are not weighed down by tender flax plants,
   yet linen overwhelms the handcrafters' palms.
We belong to Tantalus' stock, as we are surrounded by rivers,
   but who can taste of so many rivers, Dousa?

Metre: Elegiac couplets.

---

26 Our edition of Heinsius' Greek poems is the result of a first collation. His poetry has a complex textual history, making it impossible to establish a definitive edition at this stage.

Notes: Heinsius emulates Scaliger's poem on the same subject, which was included in the many editions of Heinsius' poetry, and gives it a new ending. Heinsius' version is less rigidly organised than Scaliger's and stylistically more supple (e.g. in its usage of particles). In terms of reception, however, the laurel goes to Scaliger, whose poem enjoyed particular popularity. Van den Berg *et al.* 1993, 59 offers a brief stylistic comparison of Heinsius' and Scaliger's pieces.

II. Ἐν τῷ παραπλέειν τὴν τῆς ἐρωμένης πατρίδα [?c. 1610–1613]

Χαῖρε πόλι τριπόθητε, μακάρτατον ἄστυ Βαταύων·
τὴν γὰρ ἐμὴν κατέχεις, πότνια, Δημοφίλην.
Χαῖρε πόλι· πνοιαί με παραρπάζουσι γὰρ ἄλλῃ·
καὶ τάχα καλλείψω σοι λόγον ἡμιτελῆ.
5 Ἀλλὰ σύ μοι τόδε λέξον ἐν οὔασιν ἓν τόδε κείνης
ῥημάτιον, δοκέω ναί, φίλον ἐσσόμενον·
ὡς μέσσοις κατακείμεθ᾽ ἐν ὕδασιν· ἀλλὰ καὶ ἔμπης
ὡς πάρος, ἀρχαίῳ νῦν πυρὶ καιόμεθα.

Textus: Edd. a: *Peplus Graecorum epigrammatum...*, Lugduni Batavorum: Ex officina Ioannis Patii; Prostant apud Ludovicum Elzevirium, 1613, 30. b: *Poemata emendata locis infinitis et aucta, editio quarta*, Lugd. Batavorum: Apud Joh. Orlers et Iohan. Maire, 1613, 387. c: *Poemata emendata nunc postremo et aucta*, Lugd. Batavorum: Apud Iohannem Maire, 1617, 395. d: *Poematum editio nova*, Lugduni Batavorum: Sumptibus Elzeviriorum, et Iohannis Mairii, 1621, 314. e: *Poemata auctiora ed. Nicolao Heinsio, Dan. filio*, Lugduni Batavorum: Apud Francis. Hegerum, 1640, 59. f: *Poematum editio nova, longe auctior, editore Nicolao Heinsio, Danielis filio...*, Amstelodami: Apud Joannem Janssonium, 1649, 551. Editio recentior: van den Berg *et al.* 1993, 51.

Crit.: tit. Cum amicae patriam praeternavigaret bcdefg || **3** παραπάζουσι a || **7** ἔμπης c || **8** ἀρχαίῳ τῷ πυρὶ abg

Sim.: 3 παραρπάζουσι] cf. *Anth. Pal.* 11.153.3 || **4** cf. Hipp. *De sem.* 27.37; Xen. *Cyr.* 8.1.3; Sozom. *Hist. eccl.* 8.18.8.7 || **6** cf. *Anth. Pal.* 5.163.5; 7.421.7; 7.422.6 (ναὶ δοκέω) || **7** cf. Hom. *Il.* 2.297; 19.422; *Anth. Pal.* 1.101.5; 2.1.232; 8.147.3 (...ἀλλὰ καὶ ἔμπης)

On when he sailed by his girlfriend's home city

Hail, city of my intense desire, most blessed town of the Batavians;
for you, revered city, hold my Demophile.
Hail, city, for the winds already snatch me away to somewhere else,
and I will perhaps leave you a half-finished phrase.
[5] But whisper for me at least this one small sentence here in her ear,
which, I firmly believe, will be endearing:

'We lie in the middle of the water, but even now
we are burning, just like we used to, with the fire of old.'

Metre: Elegiac couplets.

Notes: This poem is part of a cycle of six poems to and about Demophile (van den Berg *et al.* 1993, 48–53). This poem can be read as responding to Catullus 11.15–16. Like many of Heinsius' poems, it is not indebted to specific authors in particular. It contains some rare words (e.g., late antique παραρπάζουσι in l. 3) and expressions (e.g., τὸν λόγον ἡμιτελῆ καταλείπειν in l. 4). In some turns of phrase, the poem is clearly reminiscent of the *Greek Anthology* (e.g., δοκέω ναί and ἀλλὰ καὶ ἔμπης in this position in the verse).

III. Ὡς ἀπὸ Διογένους τοῦ κυνός [c. 1613]

Ἁ μερόπων μάστιξ, ὁ Διὸς μεγάλοιο προφάτας,
    πάντολμος γυμνᾶς μάρτυς ἀλαθείας,
μηδένα μὲν σαίνων, πάντας δ' ὑλάων κατ' ἀγυιάς,
    ἐμμὶ κύων. Θεῖον δ' ὤνομα Διογένας.
5 Μώναν τὰν ἀρετὰν γυμνάσδομαι· ἁ δ' ἄλοχός μευ·
    οὐ γὰρ τὰν ἀρχὰν ἐμμι γυναικοφίλας.
Ἀφράτωρ δ', ἄπολις, πίθον οἰκέω, οἶκον ἄοικον,
    τῶ μέτα μευ κτᾶσις πᾶσα περιστρέφεται.
Μώνα δ' ἁ πήρα μοι ἀεὶ καὶ βάκτρον ὀπαδεῖ,
10   πιστὸν ἀκιβδάλω σκᾶπτρον ἐλευθερίας.
Θέρμοι δεῖπνον ἔασι· τὸ δ' αὐτόχυτον καλὸν ὕδωρ
    διψῶμες· κοτύλα δ' ἐντί μοι ἁ παλάμα.
Ὕμμες πολλὰ πέπασθε, πολὺ πλῆω ποθέοντες·
    αὐτὸς δ' οὐδὲν ἔχων, οὐδενὸς ἐνδέομαι.

Textus & crit.: *vide* Aydin, Elisabeth (ed.), *Daniel Heinsius. Peplus*, Paris, *paratur*. Editio princeps : *Peplus Graecorum epigrammatum*..., Lugduni Batavorum: Ex officina Ioannis Patii; Prostant apud Ludovicum Elzevirium, 1613, 14–15.

Sim. : 1 ὁ Διὸς μεγάλοιο προφάτας] cf. Pind. *Nem.* 1.60 (Διὸς ὑψίστου προφάταν ἔξοχον) ‖ 2 μηδένα μὲν σαίνων] cf. NT, *1 Ep.Thess.* 3.3 (τὸ μηδένα σαίνεσθαι) ‖ 6 γυναικοφίλας] cf. Theoc. *Id.* 8.60 ‖ 7 Ἀφράτωρ δ', ἄπολις] cf. *schol.* Hom. *Il.* 9.63a (ἀφρήτωρ : ἄπολις καὶ συγγένειαν οὐκ ἔχων) | πίθον οἰκέω] cf. e.g. Orig. *Cels.* 2.41; Greg. Naz. *Fun. or. Basil.* 60.5; Ps.-Nonn. *schol. mythol.* 4.26; *Anth. Pal.* 7.64.3 | οἶκον ἄοικον] cf. Nonn. *Dion.* 17.42 | ἄπολις... ἄοικον] cf. fragmentum tragicum anonymum in D.L. 6.38 (ἄπολις, ἄοικος, πατρίδος ἐστερημένος, / πτωχός, πλανήτης, βίον ἔχων τοὐφ' ἡμέραν) ‖ **9** cf. Diog. Sin. *epist.* 26.1 (σὺ δὲ τὸν τρίβωνα λεοντῆν νόει, τὸ δὲ βάκτρον ῥόπαλον, τὴν δὲ πήραν γῆν καὶ θάλατταν, ἀφ' ἧς τρέφῃ); Honest. in *Anth. Pal.* 7.66.1–2 (Βάκτρον καὶ πήρη καὶ διπλόον εἷμα σοφοῖο / Διογένευς βιότου φόρτος ὁ κουφότατος) ‖ **11** cf. Nonn. *Dion.* 42.97 (νέκταρος αὐτοχύτοιο πιὼν γλυκερώτερον ὕδωρ) ‖ **13** πολλὰ πέπασθε] cf. Thgn. 1.663 (πολλὰ πέπαται)

As if written by Diogenes the Cynic

>Whip of mortals, prophet of the great Zeus,
>   fearless witness of the naked truth,
>wagging the tail to no one, but barking at everyone in the streets,
>   I am a dog, and I have the divine name of Diogenes.
>[5] I only practise virtue; it is my spouse.
>   Indeed, I am not a lover of women.
>Rather, without any family or country, I live in a barrel, a home that is no home,
>   and my entire fortune lies in that barrel.
>Only a leather bag goes along with me, and a stick,
>[10] infallible support of genuine freedom.
>Lupines are my meals. The fine flowing water is enough
>   to quench my thirst, and I use my hand as a small cup.
>You, you possess many things, but you ask for even more;
>   and I who have nothing, I do not lack anything.
>[transl. Elisabeth Aydin]

Metre: Elegiac couplets.

Notes: The poem is part of Heinsius' *pièce de resistance* of Greek composition: the *Peplus Graecorum epigrammatum*, published for the first time in Leiden in 1613, and dedicated to his friend and fellow poet Hugo Grotius. It was revised and reprinted at least five times (1613, 1617, 1621, 1640, and 1649). The original collection contained 63 poems: 56 poems discussing ancient Greek philosophers, and 7 love poems (including poem II, edited above). After the first edition, the love poems were removed from the *Peplus* to be integrated into the *Poemata*. The collection is inspired by the pseudo-Aristotelian *Peplus* (containing epitaphs on Greek epic heroes) and Diogenes Laertius' *Vitae Philosophorum*. In 1618, the Tübingen humanist and poet Friedrich Hermann Flayder (1596–1644) published a Latin translation. On the *Peplus* and its sources, see mainly Aydin (2018). The poem printed here is written in the *persona* of Diogenes the Cynic (412/404 BC–323 BC), humorously advertising his Cynic philosophy. Heinsius imitates Doric, the dialect of Corinth, where Diogenes – originally from the Ionian colony of Sinope – lived for a long time. As Heinsius explained to Grotius in his letter of dedication, the dialect befitted the Cynic and Stoic philosophers in particular because of qualities such as its 'masculinity' and 'robustness' (Heinsius 1613,):(5r). The poem thus also reflects the poet's interest in the Greek dialects and evidences his ability to use them creatively. Notwithstanding the poem's subject matter, the language equally betrays some features of Christian Greek, e.g., the collocation γυμνὴ ἀλήθεια. Like Scaliger, Heinsius delights in using rare words; cf., e.g., the word γυναικοφίλης, which Heinsius probably took from Theocritus (*Id.* 8.60) or the *Greek Anthology* (6.78.2).

IV. *In pulices et culices a se interfectos, cum ab iis totam noctem Swindrechti exagitatus esset* [?c. 1613–1617]

> Ἐνθάδε κωνώπεσσιν ὅλην τὴν νύκτα παλαίων
> ψύλλαις τ' ἀγχιμάχοις εὗδέ ποθ' Εἰνσιάδης·
> αὐτὰρ ἀνιστάμενος στυγερῆς ἐξ ὄρθριος εὐνῆς,
> πολλοὺς εὗρεν ἑῇ χειρὶ κατακταμένους.
> 5 Περσεφόνη, σὺ δὲ δέξαι ἀνάρσια φῦλα καμόντων,
> νυκτιλάλους, ὕπνων ἡμετέρων φθορέας.

Textus: Edd. a: *Poemata emendata nunc postremo et aucta*, Lugd. Batavorum: Apud Iohannem Maire, 1617, 406. b: *Poematum editio nova*, Lugduni Batavorum: Sumptibus Elzeviriorum, et Iohannis Mairii, 1621, 337. c: *Poemata auctiora ed. Nicolao Heinsio, Dan. filio*, Lugduni Batavorum: Apud Francis. Hegerum, 1640, 80–81. d: *Poematum editio nova, longe auctior, editore Nicolao Heinsio, Danielis filio...*, Amstelodami: Apud Joannem Janssonium, 1649, 568–569. Editio recentior: van den Berg *et al.* 1993, 54.

Crit.: 3 ὄρθιος van den Berg *et al.*

Sim.: 5 ἀνάρσια φῦλα] cf. Quint. Smyrn. 2.57 vel potius Nonn. *Dion.* 28.277 || 6 νυκτιλάλους] cf. *Anth. Pal.* 7.29.2

On the mosquitoes and fleas he killed, when he was plagued by them all night in Zwijndrecht

> Heinsius once slept here and wrestled all night with mosquitoes
> and fleas, hand-to-hand.
> After rising from his hated bed at daybreak,
> he found many of them slain by his own hand.
> [5] Persephone, please receive the hostile races of the dead,
> those night-revellers, destroyers of our sleep.

Metre: Elegiac couplets.

Notes: It is unclear whether Heinsius here refers to the city of Zwijndrecht near Antwerp or the city of the same name not too far from Rotterdam. The verb δέχεσθαι might just mean 'receive' but also, with reference to hostile troops, 'await the attack'. Mosquitoes are a popular subject in Humanist Greek poetry (cf. Poliziano → **Italy**; Duport → **Great Britain**)

V. *In arcam libris onustam, qua servatus est Grotius* [paulo post 22.III.1621]

> Μουσῶν κτῆμα κιβωτέ, καλεῖ σε μὲν ἐς χορὸν ἄστρων
>   Ζεὺς μέγας, ἢ Ζηνὸς τέκνον Ἐλευθερίη·
> θεῖον ἐπεὶ μετὰ πότμον ἐς ἠελίου τέκες αὐγήν,
>   καὶ πάλιν ἐκ θανάτου ῥύσαο Γρωτιάδην.
> 5 Δευτερόποτμέ μοι οὖλε, βιοῦν δέ μοι ἔμπαλιν ἄρχου,
>   σῶς μετὰ τοὺς δεσμούς, ζῶν μετὰ τὸν θάνατον.

Textus : Mss. A: Paris, BNF, Département des Manuscrits, Dupuy 837, n° 83. B: *Ibid.*, n° 112. Edd. c: *Poemata auctiora ed. Nicolao Heinsio, Dan. filio*, Lugduni Batavorum: Apud Francis. Hegerum, 1640, 110. d: *Poematum editio nova, longe auctior, editore Nicolao Heinsio, Danielis filio...*, Amstelodami: Apud Joannem Janssonium, 1649, 592.

Crit.: tit. In cistam qua evasit Grotius AB || **1** Μοῦσῶν B || **3** ζωὸν AB | τεκες A || **4** καὶ cd : ἢ AB || **5** Δευτερόποτμε, σὺ δ' οὖλε· AB | δέ μεν B || **6** σῶς cd

Sim.: 1 χορὸν ἄστρων] cf. e.g. Dion. Per. 909; Nonn. *Dion.* 2.228; 9.238; 35.337 || **3** μετὰ πότμον] cf. e.g. Nonn. *Dion.* 47.725 || **4** ἐκ θανάτου ῥύσαο] cf. Aristid. *Or.* 49.4 || **5** Δευτερόποτμε] cf. Hsch. δ 746

On the chest heavy with books, by means of which Grotius was saved

> Property of the Muses, chest, you are called to the choir of stars
>   by great Zeus, or Zeus' child Freedom:
> for you have brought divine Grotius back to the sunlight after his death
>   and you have delivered him from death.
> [5] Man with a second fate, may you be healthy, and please do start living again,
>   safe and sound after the chains, alive after death.

Metre: Elegiac couplets.

Notes: The poem refers to a famous episode in Netherlandish history: the escape of the polymath Hugo Grotius from Loevestein Castle (Gelderland). Grotius had been serving a life sentence in the castle since, in the religious struggles, he had sided with the Remonstrants. Books were brought to him on a regular basis, carried to his prison in a large chest. After two years in custody, Grotius managed to escape by hiding in the book chest with the help of his wife, who also stayed in the castle, and a maidservant. After his escape, he dressed as a bricklayer to avoid being recognised and made his way to Paris, where he soon became a diplomat for Sweden. Two Dutch museums claim possession of the chest in question: the Rijksmuseum in Amsterdam and Het Prinsenhof in Delft. As with many other poems by Heinsius, there is no model which he follows closely. Certain phrases do suggest, however, that he had Nonnus' *Dionysiaca* in mind. More than a decade earlier, he had composed a dissertation on Nonnus' epic (1610). Heinsius wrote learned poetry, using rare words taken from lexica, such as δευτερόποτμος. The last half verse contains the collocation ζάω μετὰ (τὸν) θάνατον – frequent in Christian Greek texts – but Heinsius cleverly applies it to Grotius' escape, suggesting that life imprisonment is basically as bad as death. Heinsius also composed a Latin poem on this event, which bears some resemblance to its Greek counterpart (Heinsius 1640, 291f.). The poems on Grotius' escape were published only in 1640, by Heinsius' son Nicolaas, as Heinsius did not dare to publish them earlier because of the religious climate.[27]

Biography: Daniel Heinsius (Heins) was born in Ghent on 9 June 1580. The Spanish war forced his parents to move to England. They eventually returned to the Low Countries, where, in 1596, Heinsius started studying law at the then University of Franeker. Two years later, in 1598, he moved to Leiden, where he studied under J.J. Scaliger. In 1603, Heinsius was offered a professorship in poetics and in 1605 one in Greek, and in 1607 he was made librarian of the university's collections. In 1612, he was appointed *professor politices*. Heinsius remained in Leiden until his death on 25 February 1655. As a classical scholar, he edited many texts, including Hesiod (1603), Theocritus, Bion, and Moschus (1603), Aristotle's *Ars poetica* (1610), and Terentius (1618). He also edited the correspondence of Scaliger (1627). Heinsius was a gifted poet and wrote a treatise on how to write a tragedy (1611, 1643). Drawing inspiration from Greek models in particular, he not only wrote Latin and Dutch poems – under the pseudonym 'Theocritus from Ghent' – but frequently tried his hand at Greek, starting in 1602 at the latest, when his Neo-Latin tragedy *Auriacus* was published. This book contains a lengthy Greek letter to J.J. Scaliger as well as the witty poem *In Hispanum et Batavum*, consisting of 14

---

[27] See the letter Willem de Groot wrote to his brother Hugo on 8 October 1640, edited by Meulenbroek/Witkam 1981, 556.

elegiac couplets in Greek (Bloemendal 1997, I, 202–207), followed by Greek poems by Vulcanius and Gulielmus Coddaeus (Willem van der Codde; 1575–after 1625). Heinsius' first standalone collection of poetry (1603) has no Greek poems apart from an opening address to Aphrodite in alexandrines (Heinsius 1603: *6v), but he published many Greek poems afterwards. His main contribution to humanist Hellenism was his *Peplus* (1613), a collection of poems about ancient Greek writers, mainly philosophers. It was well received and widely praised in the Republic of Letters. Moreover, Heinsius published Greek verses in his *Poemata* (from the second edition of 1606 on), which went through many editions even after his death. Some of his Greek verses are scattered in publications and editions, while others remain in manuscript. Some believe that an epigram traditionally attributed to Philodemus is actually by Heinsius (*Ep.* 38 ed. Sider, for which see Sider 1997, 201). In his preface to the *Peplus*, Heinsius shows keen awareness of the tradition of humanist Greek poetry written before him, citing Mousouros' *Ode to Plato*, Laskaris' epigrams (which he had long sought), the liminary verses by Aldo and Carteromaco, and Poliziano's epigrams (Heinsius 1613,):(3ᵛ) (→ **Greece, Italy**).

Bibliography: Biographical accounts: ter Horst, Dirk J.H. (1935), *Daniel Heinsius (1580–1655)*, Utrecht; Sellin, Paul R. (1968), *Daniel Heinsius and Stuart England. With a Short-Title Checklist of the Works of Daniel Heinsius*, Leiden/London; Becker-Cantarino, Barbara (1978), *Daniel Heinsius*, Boston. On various aspects of his poetical and scholarly work, see the essays in Lefèvre, Eckard/Schäfer, Eckart (eds.) (2008), *Daniel Heinsius klassischer Philologe und Poet*, Tübingen. More in particular about his literary theories, see Meter, Jan Hendrik (1975), *De literaire theorieën van Daniël Heinsius*, Amsterdam. On Heinsius' Greek poems: Golla, Korbinian (2008), "Daniel Heinsius' Epigramme auf Hesiod", in: Eckard Lefèvre/ Eckart Schäfer (eds.), *Daniel Heinsius. Klassischer Philologe und Poet*, Tübingen, 31–55; Hintzen, Beate (2014), "Daniel Heinsius, Martin Opitz und Paul Fleming. Übersetzung und Transfer vom Griechischen ins Deutsche und vom Deutschen ins Lateinische", in: Tom Deneire (ed.), *Dynamics of Neo-Latin and the Vernacular*, Leiden, 177–201: 191–200; Aydin, Elisabeth (2018), "Le Peplus Graecorum Epigrammatum de Daniel Heinsius, une adaptation de Diogène Laërce à la Renaissance", in: *Neulateinisches Jahrbuch* 20, 29–55. Further literature: Aydin, Elisabeth (ed./transl.) (forthcoming), *Daniel Heinsius. Peplus*, Paris; van den Berg et al. 1993; Bloemendal, Jan (1997), *Daniel Heinsius. Auriacus, sive Libertas saucia (1602)*, 2 vols., Voorthuizen; Heinsius, Daniel (1603), *Elegiarum lib. III. Monobiblos, sylvae, in quibus varia*, Lugduni Batavorum; Heinsius, Daniel (1613), *Peplus Graecorum epigrammatum. In quo omnes celebriores Graeciae philosophi, encomia eorum, vita et opiniones recensentur aut exponuntur*, Lugduni Batavorum; Heinsius, Daniel (1640), *Poemata auctiora*, ed. Nicolaus Heinsius, Lugduni Batavorum; Meulenbroek, Bernard Lambert/Witkam, Paula P. (eds.) (1981), *Briefwisseling van Hugo Grotius*, vol. 11, 's-Gravenhage; Sider, David (1997), *The Epigrams of Philodemos. Introduction, Text, and Commentary*, Oxford/New York.

Nicolaes Jansz. van Wassenaer (c. 1572–1629)

Ἁρλεμιὰς ἢ Ἐξήγησις τῆς πολιορκίας τῆς πόλεως Ἁρλεμίης, γενομένης τῷ ἔτει ͵αφοβ΄ [1605]

(excerptum, vv. 425–452: Hispanorum copiae Harlemum deveniunt et urbis incolae ad obsidionem parantur)

425 Πάντες ἐπασσύτεροι καὶ λαοῦ ἡγεμονῆες,
 λαοί τ' ἐρρώοντο μάχην ἐπὶ κυδιάνειραν,
 ὡς παρὰ κασσιτέρου λεκάναις μάλα λαμπομένῃσι,
 καὶ λοπάσιν σμήκταις πυροδαίσια[28] καλὰ πολιτῶν,
 κ' ἀργεννοὶ τοῖχοι διὰ ἱδρῶτ' ἀνδραποδώδη
430 στίλβουσι καθαρῶν παμπόλλων Ἁρλεμιώνων
 ὣς καὶ χαλκεοθωρήκων τότε τεύχεα καλά,
 ἔγχεα τεῖχόσδ' ἐρχομένων σελάωσι πολιτῶν.
 Αὐτίκα θηλύτεραι καὶ ἀολλέες ἀμφαγέροντο
 οὐκ ἄοπλ', ἀλλὰ ἐϋπλέκτους μετὰ χερσὶν ἔχουσαι
435 ἐχθροφόνοισι, λύγους πιττωτούς, Ἀΐδος ἕρκος.
 Πολλῇσι θρασὺς ἀμφιπόλοισι, καὶ ἀντιανείραις
 θυμὸς χεῖρας ὁπλίζει, τεῖχόσδ' ἐσσεύοντο
 σὺν μακροῖς ὀβελοῖσιν· καὶ ἐν πλεκτοῖς ταλάροισιν,
 λάϊνα κοῦρ' ἁπαλοῖσι φέρον νώτοισι βέλεμνα·
440 ὣς οἱ μὲν μάλα πάντες ὅσοι πτολίεθρον ἔχουσι,
 ἄνδρες γηραλέοι πολλοί τε καὶ οἷς γόνυ χλωρόν,
 ἀνδράσι δυσμενέεσσι μαχησόμεν' ἐσσεύοντο.
 Ὅσσον ἐλευθερίη φάεος γλυκερώτερός ἐστι,
 τόσσον ἔρως πόλεως καὶ ἐνέστακτο φρεσὶ πάντων.
445 Ζεὺς δὲ μὲν ἀργινόεντα, καὶ ὄρθιον ὑψικολωνὸν
 δέρκεσθαι ἐπίβαινεν ἐνυαλίων πόνον ἀνδρῶν
 Μαυρῶν ἱπποδάμων τε, καὶ ἀστῶν χαλκοχιτώνων.
 Μιχθεῖσ' ἀστοῖσιν δὲ παρίστατο Τριτογένεια,
 χρυσείην τρυφάλην τε, καὶ ἔγχος χείρεσ' ἔχουσα.
450 Οὐλομένη τε τέως στρατιὴ στυγεραί τε φάλαγγες
 Ἰσπάνων ἑτέρωθεν ἐκαρτύναντο, καὶ ὅπλα
 αἴγλην παμφανόωσαν ἀποστράπτουσι δαφοινά.

Textus: Ed. a: Ἁρλεμιὰς ἢ Ἐξήγησις τῆς πολιορκίας τῆς πόλεως Ἁρλεμίης, γενομένης τῷ ἔτει, αφοβ. *Harlemias sive Enarratio obsidionis urbis Harlemi, quae accidit anno 1572*, Lugduni Batavorum: Ex Officina Ioannis Patii, 1605, fol. C4v & D1v. Editio recentior: van Walsem, Gerard

---

28 This peculiar spelling of the word is attested in the *editio princeps* of Hesychius' lexicon, printed by Aldo in Venice in 1514 (Hsch. s.v. πυροδανεῖον vol. 3, p. 218 ed. Hansen with *app. crit.*).

Christiaan (ed.) (1930), *Harlemias. Het beleg der stad Haarlem in een Grieksch gedicht verhaald...*, Leiden, 26 & 28.

Crit.: 428 σπήκταις van Walsem ‖ 429 άργυρυνοὶ van Walsem ǀ ἱδρῶτ' a van Walsem ‖ 430 καθάρων a ‖ 432 τεῖχοσδ' a van Walsem ‖ 433 θηλύτεραι a ǀ ἀμφιγέροντο a van Walsem: ἀμφαγέροντο corr. ‖ 434 εὐπλέκτους corr. (cf. Hom. *Il.* 23.115): ἐϋπλήκτους a van Walsem ‖ 436 ἀμφιπόλοισι a ‖ 437 τεῖχοσδ' a van Walsem ‖ 438 ταλάροισιν corr.: ταλέροισιν a van Walsem ‖ 439 ἀπαλοῖσι debuit ‖ 443 φάεθος van Walsem ‖ 444 πολεως a ‖ 450 στρατιή van Walsem ‖ 452 αἴχλην van Walsem ǀ ἀπαστράπτουσι debuit

Sim.: 425 Nonn. *Dion.* 14.105, 14.186, 14.330, etc. (...ἡγεμονῆες) ‖ 426 cf. Hom. *Il.* 4.225 (σπεύδοντα μάχην ἐς κυδιάνειραν) ‖ 431 τεύχεα καλά] cf. Hom. *Il.* 3.328; 5.621; 7.103, etc. ‖ 433 ἀμφαγέροντο] Hom. *Il.* 18.37; Ap. Rhod. *Argon.* 4.1527 ‖ 434 μετὰ χέρσιν ἔχουσαι] Hom. *Il.* 24.647; 4.300; 7.339; 22.497 ‖ 435 ἄϊδος ἕρκος] Opp. *H.* 4.97 ‖ 436 ἀντιανείραις] cf. Hom. *Il.* 3.189; 6.186 (*de Amazonibus*) (cf. Ap. Soph. 33.19) ‖ 437 θυμὸς χεῖρας ὁπλίζει] cf. Basil. *leg. lib. gent.* 7.17 (ἁπλῶς...ἐπ' ἐχθροὺς θυμὸς ὁπλίζει χέρα) ‖ 438–439 cf. Hom. *Il.* 18.568 (πλεκτοῖς ἐν ταλάροισι φέρον...) ‖ 441 γόνυ χλωρόν] Theoc. *Id.* 14.70 (cf. Eust. *Il.* 1001.19–20) ‖ 442 cf. Hom. *Il.* 19.232 (ἀνδράσι δυσμενέεσσι μαχώμεθα...) ‖ 443–444 cf. Antip. Sid. *Anth. Pal.* 9.23.7–8 (ὅσσον μητρυιᾶς γλυκερωτέρη ἔπλετο μήτηρ, / τόσσον...) ‖ 445 cf. Opp. *C.* 4.87 (...ὄρθιον, ὑψικόλωνον) (cf. Hsch. υ 935, *s.v.* ὑψικόλωνον vol. 4, p. 136 ed. Hansen) ‖ 446 cf. Opp. *H.* 5.245 (...ἐνυάλιον πόνον ἀνδρῶν) ‖ 447 cf. Hom. *Il.* 3.127; 3.131; 3.251; 8.71 (Τρώων θ' ἱπποδάμων καὶ Ἀχαιῶν χαλκοχιτώνων) ‖ 449 cf. Nonn. *Dion.* 38.292 (χρυσείην τρυφάλειαν...); Hsch. τ 1572, *s.v.* τρυφάλη ‖ 450 Οὐλομένη] cf. Hom. *Il.* 1.2 (οὐλομένην) ǀ στυγεραί τε φάλαγγες] cf. Opp. *C.* 2.257 (...στυγεραί τε φάλαγγες) ‖ 451 cf. Hom. *Il.* 11.215; 12.415 (Ἀργεῖοι δ' ἑτέρωθεν ἐκαρτύναντο φάλαγγας) (cf. Hes. *Theog.* 676) ‖ 452 cf. Opp. *C.* 3.479 (αἴγλην παμφανόωσαν ἀπαστράπτουσιν...)

Harlemias, or Account of the siege of the city of Haarlem, which took place in the year 1572

(excerpt, ll. 425–452)

> [425] All the people's leaders, one after another, and the people [of Haarlem] rushed into the battle that brings glory to men; just as, thanks to the brightly shining tin pots and the polished plates, the kitchens of the citizens are beautiful, and just as the white walls of so many of Haarlem's clean inhabitants [430] shine due to the hard work of their servants, so beautiful were the harnesses of men armoured with bronze breastplates, so shone the spears of the citizens who came to the walls. Soon women were also gathered in throngs; they came not unarmed but their enemy-killing hands held [435] well-twisted twigs, dipped in tar: a wall of death.[29] A spirit of audacity equipped the numerous handmaids, truly

---

29 Reference to the burning tar wreaths that the women of Haarlem, according to some sources, threw around the necks of the enemy.

matches for men, with arms; they rushed to the wall with long lances. And in plaited baskets, lads carried, on their young backs, stones to throw with. [440] Thus, all who lived in the citadel, both a large number of elderly men and boys whose knees were still nimble, hastened to fight the enemy men. As much as freedom was dearer to them than life, so much love for their city was in all of their hearts. [445] Zeus, in turn, arrived at a shining and high hill to inspect the toil of warlike men, the horse-taming Moors and the bronze-clad citizens. And the Trito-born [Pallas Athena] stood amidst the citizens, wearing her golden helmet and holding a spear in her hand. [450] In the meantime, the accursed army, the hated ranks of the Spaniards, strengthened themselves on the other side, and the blood-reeking weapons flashed forth a radiant gleam.

Metre: Hexameters (with some bipartite lines and elision of diphthongs, as in ll. 434, 439 and 442).

Notes: This passage is part of an epic poem of 1460 verses about an episode from the Eighty Years' War in 1572–73, when the troops of Philip II of Spain besieged the Dutch city of Haarlem. Although Haarlem had held a moderate position in the religious wars, the political atmosphere turned against Philip II in the summer of 1572. The king responded by massacring the inhabitants of two cities near Haarlem. When Haarlem reaffirmed its anti-Spanish position, replacing its officials with supporters of the Prince of Orange, Spanish troops, commanded by Don Fadrique of Toledo, began a siege of the city in December 1572. Half a year later, in July 1573, Haarlem eventually surrendered and saw its garrison massacred. The poem, printed in 1605, was dedicated to the Mayor of Haarlem; the city also paid for its publication. The poet recounts the main stages of the siege of Haarlem, rounding off with a eulogy for the city and its most famous inhabitants. The protagonists are treated like heroes from the *Iliad*, while Zeus and Athena constantly attempt to influence the course of events. The poem is accompanied by a Latin prose translation 'for beginners', and it might have been intended for school use. The book opens with several shorter poems by colleagues and friends, including two Greek ones: two elegiac couplets by a certain 'T. [Γ.?] Κοδδαῖος' (Gulielmus Coddaeus [1574–after 1625]?), praising the poet as Haarlem's Homer, and 13 couplets by the English theologian Hugh Broughton (1549–1612). The Greek text of the *Harlemias* was imperfectly reprinted by G.C. van Walsem in 1930 with a Dutch translation. The poem abounds in Homeric idiom, as reflected in words such as ἀολλέες, ἀμφίπολοι, and χαλκεοθώρηκες and in phrasings such as ἀμφαγέροντο. Wassenaer also tries to homericize his modern battle scenes by introducing Homeric similes and reusing Homeric epithets, as in the passage cited above. The epithet Homer usually applied to the Amazons is, for instance, applied here to the female servants coming to the city's defence (l. 436). The Spaniards take the usual epithet of the Trojans, while the inhabitants of Haarlem are described with the adjective the ancient poet applied to the Achaeans (l. 447). The poem's language is not merely indebted to Homer all the same. In its phraseology, the influence of both Oppian (*Halieutica*) and pseudo-Oppian (*Cynegetica*) stands out. The most distinctive borrowing from pseudo-Oppian is the word ὑψικόλωνον, which is only attested in the *Cynegetica* and, via that work, Hesychius. Unusual forms employed by Wassenaer include πυροδαίσια in l. 428 (probably derived from the Aldine *editio princeps* of Hesychius' lexicon) and ἐχθροφόνοισι in l. 435 (apparently a word of the poet's own invention).

Biography: Nicolaes Jansz. van Wassenaer (c. 1572–1629) was born in Heusden or, more probably, in Enkhuizen, although contemporaries believed he was born in Amsterdam. He briefly studied theology in Leiden (1592–1594) but fled from college due to a student revolt. He returned to Amsterdam, where, in 1599, he was living with his mother. In 1601, however, he moved to Weesp, where he opened a private school. When he published his *Harlemias* in 1605, he had recently been appointed at the Great Latin School of Haarlem, where he worked as a teacher (*lector*) and 'writing-master' (*schrijfmeester*). In 1607, he returned to Amsterdam to become vice principal of the Great School there. He remained at this institute until c. 1612, when he started a new career as a physician. In the following years, he published, in Dutch, several treatises about medicine as well as Ottoman and European history (the seventeen issues of his *Historisch Verhael* were particularly popular). Apart from his *Harlemias*, Wassenaer wrote a new year's poem for the Haarlem city council in Greek, also in 1605. He died on 24 or 25 September 1629.

Bibliography: Biographical accounts: Kannegieter, J.Z. (1964), "Dr. Nicolaes Jansz. van Wassenaer (1571/2–1629)", in: *Jaarboek van het Genootschap Amstelodamum* 56, 71–99; Kannegieter, J.Z. (1967), "Dr. Nicolaes Jansz. van Wassenaer (1571/2–1629)", in: *Amstelodamum: Maandblad voor de Kennis van Amsterdam* 54, 150–151; more recently, van de Venne, Hans (2000), "A Greek Xenion in Latin Dress: Nicolaus a Wassenaer and Theodorus Schrevelius", in: Dirk Sacré/Gilbert Tournoy (eds.), *Myricae: Essays on Neo-Latin Literature in Memory of Jozef Ijsewijn*, Leuven, 415–442: 417–421. On his Greek poems: Kannegieter 1964, 75f.; van de Venne, Hans (1997), "Een Grieks lofdicht op Haarlem (1605) in Latijnse vertaling: Nicolaes van Wassenaer en Theodorus Schrevelius", in: *Haerlem Jaarboek*, 9–35 and van de Venne 2000; Veenman, René (2009), *De klassieke traditie in de Lage Landen*, Nijmegen, 125–128, 131–133; van Walsem, Gerard Christiaan (ed.) (1930), *Harlemias. Het beleg der stad Haarlem in een Grieksch gedicht verhaald...*, Leiden.

Johannes Foreestius (1586–1651)

Βερόη [1605]

(excerptum, vv. 48–62)

48 Τὴν πρότερος προσέειπεν ἐϋστέφανος Διόνυσος·
 "Παρθένε, τί πτώκας μεθέπεις; Οὐκ ἄξιος ἄγρη·
50 μητέρος ἥτε θεῶν πέλε θηρήτειρα καὶ ἀνδρῶν.
 Καὶ σὺ θεοὺς θήρευε, κακαῖς λίπε θηρία κούραις.
 Μηδ' ἐρέοις 'ἑτέρων πέλομαι ἀδίδακτος ἀέθλων',
 παρθενικὴ οὕτως ἑτέρων ἀδίδακτος ἀέθλων
 βέβληκας Διόνυσον ἄτερ τόξων καὶ ὀϊστῶν.
55 Τῷ κεν ἐγὼ κόσμοιο μέρος τρίτον ἄστεά θ' εἷλον
 μυρία, παρθενικῇ ἀταλῇ ἵνα κύρμα γένωμαι;
 Ἀλλά με κουρίδιον μοῦνον τελέσειας ἀκοίτην,
 ὅσσον ἐγὼν ἵδρωσα πόνον τοι προῖκα παρέξω,
 Βάκχον δ' Ἰνδοφόνον, σὺ δὲ Βακχοφόνος καλέσαιο.
60 Ἄρτιός ἐστι γάμος, σὺ γὰρ ἔσσεαι Ἀφρογένεια,
 αὐτὰρ ἐγὼν ἑὸς υἱός· ἐπεὶ σταφυλῇσιν ὀπώρης
 ἡμετέρης δύναμαι τόδ' Ἔρως μαλεροῖσιν ὀϊστοῖς."

Textus: Ed. a: *Εἰδύλλια ἢ Ἥρωες, καὶ ἄλλα ποιημάτιά τινα. Idyllia siue Heroes, et alia poematia quædam*, [Lugduni Batavorum]: Ex Officina Plantiniana Raphelengii, 1605, 55. Editio recentior: de Vries 2007, 112–113 (transcriptio cum versione Nederlandica editoris).

Crit.: 55 κὲν a

Sim.: 48 Τὴν πρότερος προσέειπεν] clausula Homerica; vide e.g. Hom. *Il.* 5.275; 7.22; etc. Cf. etiam Theoc. *Id.* 22.52 | προσέειπεν ἐϋστέφανος] Hom. *Il.* 21.511; *Hom. Hymn. Cer.* 224 | ἐϋστέφανος Διόνυσος] cf. *Hymn. Orph.* 74.2 (ἐϋστεφάνου Διονύσου) || 49 cf. eadem sede Nonn. *Dion.* 9.171 (μεθέπων κεμαδοσσόον ἄγρην); 10.224 (μεθέπων ἐλαφηβόλον ἄγρην); 32.134 (μεθέπων ὀρεσίδρομον ἄγρην) || 50 θηρήτειρα] hapax legomenon: Call. *Del.* 230 || 52–53 cf. eadem sede Nonn. *Dion.* 29.335–336 (ἀδίδακτος Ἀθήνη, / παρθενικῇ) || 55 cf. eadem sede Hom. *Il.* 17.563–564 (τώ κεν ἔγωγ' ἐθέλοιμι παρεστάμεναι καὶ ἀμύνειν / Πατρόκλῳ); secundum Eustathium Thessalonicensem: τῷ κεν ἔγωγ' ἐθέλοιμι παρεστάμεναι καὶ ἀμύνειν || 55–56 cf. fortasse *Anth. Pal.* 11.58.1 (ἄστεα μυρία); vide etiam Ap. Rhod. *Argon.* 4.274 (μυρία δ' ἄστη) || 56 cf. Hom. *Od.* 11.38 (παρθενικαί τ' ἀταλαί) | cf. e.g. eadem sede Hom. *Il.* 5.488 (κύρμα γένησθε); 17.272 (κύρμα γενέσθαι); *Od.* 5.473 (κύρμα γένωμαι); etc. || 57 cf. Ap. Rhod. *Argon.* 4.1071–1072 (ἀκοίτην / κουρίδιον); Nonn. *Dion.* 4.113 (μοῦνον ἐμοὶ πόρε τοῦτον ἀκοίτην); 32.35 (κουριδίης φιλότητος ἵνα μνήσειεν ἀκοίτην) || 58 cf. e.g. Demosth. 30.36 (παρεχόμενος τὴν προῖχ' ὡς ἀπέδωκεν) || 59 cf. Nonn. *Dion.* 25.84 (Βάκχου δ' Ἰνδοφόνου) || 60 epithetum Veneris in e.g. Mosch. *Europa* 71; Bion fr. 11.1; Nonn. *Dion.* 6.353; 31.269; etc. || 61 ἑὸς υἱός] clausula Homerica; vide e.g. Hom. *Il.* 12.292; *Od.* 11.142 | cf. fortasse Nonn. *Dion.* 12.345–346 (ἔστρωσεν ὀπώρην ὀγκώσας σταφυλῇσι) || 62 cf. Nonn. *Dion.* 48.472 (ἡδυβόλῳ Διόνυσον Ἔρως οἴστρησεν οἰστῷ)

Beroe

(excerpt, ll. 48–62)

> The beautifully crowned Dionysus addressed her [Beroe] first: 'Maiden, why do you pursue hares? It is not a worthy prey: [50] not for a mother [Aphrodite] who was a huntress of gods and men. You, too, should hunt gods, leave the wild animals to base girls. May you not say 'I'm not trained for other contests', you maiden, so lacking training for other contests, have hit Dionysus without bows and arrows. [55] For this I would have taken one third of the world and countless cities, to become the booty of a tender maiden? But may you make me alone your lawful husband, I will offer you as dowry everything I have toiled for, and may you call Bacchus 'killer of Indians', but yourself 'killer of Bacchus'. [60] It is a suitable marriage, for you will be the foam-born [Aphrodite], but I am her son, since with the grapes of our harvest I can do this, an Eros with destructive arrows.'

Metre: Hexameters.

Notes: This passage, in which Dionysus is fruitlessly wooing Beroe in competition with Poseidon, is part of a youthful epyllion by Foreestius, addressed to Daniel Heinsius, with whom he lived together as a student. The poem itself is one of a series on mythological women. The extract above is representative of Foreestius' Greek poetry as a whole. His collection is largely bucolic in nature, focusing on the cruelty of Eros and with a prominent place for the figure of Dionysus, popularised through Nonnus' *Dionysiaca*, of which Heinsius published a new edition in 1605, in the same year that Foreestius' Greek poetry appeared. Foreestius also tended to feature large sections of direct speech in his compositions. In addition to Nonnus, the poet clearly had Homer in mind. There are occasional echoes of other poets, especially bucolic ones such as Moschus and Bion and the scholar-poet Callimachus, author of learned hymns. The passage shows some linguistic peculiarities and even errors. There are various mistakes, especially on the syntactic level, such as the lack of congruence between ἄξιος and ἄγρη (l. 49) – did the poet erroneously conceptualise ἄξιος as a kind of composed adjective (ἄ-ξιος)? The use of an unattested future optative in a main clause is likewise awkward (l. 52: ἐρέοις), whereas the meaning of the particle κεν, accentuated in the original edition and joined with an aorist indicative, is obscure (l. 55). In the final verse, a conjunction seems to be lacking, making it unclear how the second part of the verse should be fitted into the sentence. In general, the clarity and correctness of the syntactic flow seems to have been sacrificed in favour of the metre. Foreestius moreover seems to have had a dislike of the Greek article, which features only very rarely in his poetry, and if it does, it is often pronominally used (ll. 48 and 55); this might be due to interference from Latin, a language in which he was more accustomed to composing poetry. The composition Βακχοφόνος seems to be an invention of Foreestius, coined *ad locum* after the example of Ἰνδοφόνος, an epithet of Dionysus/Bacchus only appearing in Nonnus' *Dionysiaca*. The middle optative aorist second person singular καλέσαιο (< καλέω) is correctly formed, but attested nowhere in the extant corpus of ancient and Byzantine Greek texts.

Biography: Born in Alkmaar as Jan van Foreest on 9 October 1586, Johannes Foreestius was a member of an old noble family and related to the renowned doctor Pieter van Foreest (1521–1597). Foreestius studied at the Latin school of Hoorn and, from 1600, at the University of Leiden, coming into contact with the leading humanists of the day, including Josephus Justus Scaliger, Bonaventura Vulcanius, and especially Daniel Heinsius, one of his main sources of inspiration for writing Greek poetry. After his arts and law studies, Foreestius followed the usual path of his ancestors, taking on various political duties, in particular that of mayor of Hoorn. Despite his busy life, he made the time to write poetry, first during his studies, when he composed in Greek and Latin, and later in his professional life, when he only composed in Latin, mainly on patriotic themes, including some Orangist propaganda. He produced a quite extensive oeuvre, which has thus far attracted only limited attention. Foreestius had a large network across Europe, corresponding with, among others, René Descartes and Christina of Sweden. He died in Hoorn on 27 October 1651.

Bibliography: de Vries, Meta (2007), *Het dichtwerk van Jan van Foreest (1585–1651)*, PhD dissertation, Radboud Universiteit Nijmegen.

Anonymus (?Martin Binnart, d. 1653/1654)

Τὸ πιεστήριον Ἑλληνικὸν τῷ Βαλθάσαρι Μωρήτῳ τῶν Μουσῶν ἀρχηγῷ νυμφαγωγοῦντι συγχαίρει· ἅμα καὶ πατριάζοντας εὔχεται υἱούς, κἂν ἀληθινῇ σοφίᾳ καὶ ἐπιστήμῃ ἐξαιρετούς [23.VII.1645]

    Ἀργολική, ἂν θεσπεσίων σοι κῆδος Ἀχαιῶν,
    ἔννεπε Μοῦσα γάμον πολλῶν ἀντάξιον ἄλλων
    ἀρχηγοῖο χοροῦ, Μωρήτῳ χάρματα παῦρα
    νυμφεύοντι ἄειδε, θεά, μελιγήρυας ὕμνους.
5   Ἔργα μέγιστα μέλοντα νόον νύκτας τε καὶ ἦμαρ
    τοξοφόρος θάμβησεν Ἔρως, ἀδάμαντά σε δέρκων

ἐν μόχθοισι μένοντα, ὅταν καλὰ ἔργα τοσαῦτα
χαλκογράφοισι τύποις εὐκλήων Ἑλλάδος ἀνδρῶν,
Ῥωμαϊκοῦ τε μέλους διακούης ἔμμεν' ἀμύντωρ,
10   ὄργανα Μουσάων τὰ σοφώτατα βιβλία πωλῶν,
ὥστε καταστίλβειν σέλας ὕψοθεν ἐς βιότητα,
καὶ τῶν ἀρχαϊκῶν πολὺ φέρτερον ἔμμεν' ἀοιδῶν.
Αὐτὰρ ὁμῶς χαλέπαινε γαμοστόλος ὄρνις ἐρώτων
ἡρώων ἡττᾶσθαι νόον φρενοθελγέϊ κέντρῳ,
15   ἔνθα δέ σου μισόνυμφον Ἀθηνᾶν τὴν φλόγα σβέννειν·
κυρτὸν ὀπισθοτόνοιο κέρας κυκλώσατο τόξου,
ἄτρομον οὐτάζων τὸν σὸν πολυφρόντιδα θυμόν.
Νῦν ἔγνως τὸν Ἔρωτα βαρὺν σφόδρ' ὅστις ἑαυτοῦ
κήδεσί σου δυνατὸς μελέτας ἔστ' ἐκπολεμίζειν.
20   Ἀλλὰ δέχου νόμιμον τὸν Ἔρωτα, ποθῶν τὸ καθῆκον,
ὄφρα ἔπειτα πονήσῃς ἔμπαλιν, ὅττεό σε χρή.
Ἐκ δὲ γάμων παλίνορσον γὰρ μάλα πολλὰ δοκοῦσιν
ἔργα σοφῶν. Γλυκερός σε μὲν αἱρεῖ μηρὸς Ἔρωτος,
βέλτιον ἀλλὰ μέρος ταῖς Μούσαις σεῖο φύλαττε.
25   Οὕτω πατρώζοντά τε σοι τέξει παράκοιτις
τέκνα, Ὀλυμπιάδων Μουσάων ἔκγονα Φοίβου.
Τοῦτο δέ μοι χαρίεν, μητρός τε καὶ Ἑλλάδος εὐχὴ
ἑπτὰ Σοφῶν, σοι τοῦτο ἐπεύχει Παλλὰς Ἀθηνᾶ.

Textus: *Officina Plantiniana, Acroamata nuptialia typographo regio Balthasari Moreto et lectissimae virgini Annae Goos, dominis suis, felici auspicio matrimonium ineuntibus, Officina Plantiniana debiti obsequii ergo gratulabunda pangebat Antverpiae X. Kal. Aug. M. DC. XLV.*, Antverpiae: Officina Plantiniana, 1645, 8–11 (cum versione Latina).

Crit.: 1 Ἀχαίων ed. || 8 Ἕλλαδος ed. || 12 πολυφέρτερον ed. || 13 γαμόστολος ed. || 16 ὀπιστόνοιο ed. || 17 πολυφροντίδα ed. || 27 Ἕλλαδος ed.

Sim.: 1–2 cf. e.g. Hom. *Od.* 1.1 (Ἄνδρα μοι ἔννεπε, Μοῦσα) || 2 πολλῶν ἀντάξιον ἄλλων] cf. Hom. *Il.* 11.514 || 4 cf. e.g. Pind. *Isthm.* 2.3 (μελιγάρυας ὕμνους) || 5 cf. Hom. *Il.* 5.490 (σοὶ δὲ χρὴ τάδε πάντα μέλειν νύκτας τε καὶ ἦμαρ) || 6 cf. Nonn. *Dion.* 47.312 (αὐτὸς Ἔρως θάμβησεν); *Epigrammatum Anthologiae appendix*, ed. Cougny, vol. 3, p. 406 (61.1: τοξοφόρον...Ἔρωτα) || 10 cf. *Anth. Pal.* 9.171.1 (Pall.: Ὄργανα Μουσάων, τὰ πολύστονα βιβλία πωλῶ) || 11 cf. *Hymn. Hom. Mart.* 10 (πρηῢ καταστίλβων σέλας ὑψόθεν ἐς βιότητα) || 13 cf. e.g. Nonn. *Dion.* 33.121 (γαμοκλόπον ὄρνιν Ἐρώτων) || 14 φρενοθελγέϊ κέντρῳ] cf. Nonn. *Dion.* 7.278 || 15 μισόνυμφον] cf. Lycoph. *Alex.* 356 (hap. leg.) || 16 = Nonn. *Dion.* 15.366 || 17 cf. Hom. *Il.* 16.162–163 (ἐν δέ τε θυμὸς / στήθεσιν ἄτρομός ἐστι) | cf. Hom. *Il.* 20.458–459 (τὸν μὲν ἔπειτα / οὐτάζων ξιφεῖ μεγάλῳ ἐξαίνυτο θυμόν) || 18 cf. Theoc. *Id.* 3.15 (νῦν ἔγνων τὸν Ἔρωτα· βαρὺς θεός) || 21 ὅττεό σε χρή] cf. Hom. *Od.* 1.124 || 22 cf. Gr. Naz. *Carm.* PG 37.503.4–5; 37.609.11–12 (ambo ἐκ δὲ γάμων παλίνορσος ἄναξ ἐμὸς εὖτ' ἂν ἐπέλθῃ, / Ἐξαπίνης δοκέουσι) || 26 cf. e.g. Hom. *Il.* 2.491 (Ὀλυμπιάδες Μοῦσαι); Hes. *Theog.* 25, 52, 966, 1022 (Μοῦσαι Ὀλυμπιάδες)

The Greek press congratulates Balthasar Moretus, patron of the Muses, who is taking home a bride; at the same time it also wishes him sons who might take after their father, excelling both in true wisdom and in knowledge

Argolic Muse, if you care about the divine-sounding Achaeans, tell me of the marriage of the patron of dance that is worth many others; please sing for marrying Moretus of small delights, goddess, sing sweet-voiced hymns. [5] Your mind, busied with great works night and day, astonished bow-bearing Eros, who saw that you remained unbreakable amidst hard work, as you print so many excellent works of famous men of Greece with your copper writing plates, and you are renowned for being the defender of Roman poetry; [10] selling the wisest of books, instruments of the Muses, you thus shed a ray from high above down to life and greatly excel the ancient bards. But even so, the wedding-preparing love-bird was angry that while your mind was overwhelmed by the heart-charming sting of the heroes, [15] and that marriage-hating Athena then quenched the flame in you; he rounded the curved horn of the back-bent bow, hitting your mind, which is fearless and full of thought. Now you have come to know exceedingly powerful Eros, who is capable of making your concerns conflict with his own priorities. [20] But accept legitimate Love, while longing for your duty, so that you will work hard again on whatever befits you. And very many works of wise men indeed expect you to return from your marriage affairs. The sweet thigh of Eros seizes you, but preserve your better half for the Muses. [25] Thus your wife will give birth for you to children who take after their father, grandchildren of Phoebus' Olympian Muses. And this pleases me, this is the wish of Greece, mother of the seven Sages; this is what Pallas Athena wishes for you.

Metre: Hexameters.

Notes: The poem is part of a collection printed on the occasion of the marriage of Balthasar II Moretus (1615–1674) with Anna Goos (1627–1691) on 23 July 1645. Balthasar II led the Plantin Press (*Officina Plantiniana*) in Antwerp from 1641 until his death. Under his guidance, the printing house increasingly set itself to producing liturgical texts, even though in his early years Balthasar still also printed works of ancient history and literature, as this poem reflects. The collection in which it appears, entitled *Acroamata nuptialia*, was probably edited by the Antwerp Jesuit Jacob de Cater (Caterus, 1593–1657) (Sacré 1998). The poems are in the principal languages of the Plantin Press, i.e. the three 'sacred' languages as well as Spanish, Italian, French, and Dutch. In the collection, each press addresses its newly-wed owner in its 'own' language. The poems were likely performed during the wedding celebration, perhaps to the accompaniment of the moving presses (Sacré 1998, 155). Although the poems are anonymous, the Greek piece might have been composed by Martin Binnart (d. 1653/54), who first worked as corrector in the Plantin Press before becoming a bookseller (from 1634) and printer (1644–

1649) in Antwerp. He also authored a popular Dutch–Latin dictionary (on his life, see Claes 1972). A long Greek poem by Binnart's hand, lamenting Balthasar I's death, exists in manuscript in the archives of the Plantin-Moretus Museum in Antwerp.[30] Both poems exhibit similar stylistic and linguistic infelicities, especially in terms of morphology. The poem presented here has e.g. ἐπεύχει (l. 28), which is an unattested active usage of the verb ἐπεύχομαι, as well as the equally unattested thematic infinitive σβέννειν from σβέννυμι (l. 15). A number of verbs are moreover used with unusual meanings, e.g. διακούω (l. 9). The manuscript poem equally abounds in incorrect or unattested forms, including over-Ionicized φθοῦνος for φθόνος (l. 7) and the verb ὑφαῖρον (l. 15), an incorrect form of ὑφαιρέω. The address by Plantin's Greek press is, partly, a kind of cento from authors such as Homer and Nonnus but also alludes to many others, including the Christian author Gregory of Nazianzus. A free Latin rendering, also in hexameters, was printed facing the Greek text.

Bibliography: De Schepper, Marcus (1996), "*Acroamata nuptialia* (1645). Een typografisch epithalamium voor Balthasar II Moretus en Anna Goos", in: *De Gulden Passer* 74, 377–402 (offers a facsimile of the *epithalamia* collection). On the editorship, see esp. Sacré, Dirk (1998), "*Acroamata Nuptialia* (1645) voor Balthasar II Moretus en Anna Goos. Jacobus Caterus s.j. in plaats van Casperius Gevartius?", in: *De Gulden Passer* 76–77, 155–174. Further literature: Claes, Frans (1972), "Het woordenboek van Martin Binnart", in: *Tijdschrift voor Nederlandse Taal- en Letterkunde* 88, 256–272.

Petrus Francius (1645–1704)

I. Εἰς Θέαν βοτάνην [1685/1697]

Ὅταν πίνω μὲν ὕδωρ
τὴν Σηρικήν τε ποίην,
Θέαν ἣν καλῶς καλοῦσιν,
ὕδωρ μὲν οὐχὶ πίνω,
5 πίνω μὲν οὐχὶ ποίην·
πίνω δ' ἄριστον οἶνον,
μέλι μὲν πίνω φέριστον·
πίνω δὲ νέκταρ αὐτό·
ὃ θεοὶ πίνουσι πίνω.

---

30 The title of this poem is Θρῆνος ἐπὶ τοῦ θανάτου τοῦ παγκλυτοῦ ἀνδρὸς Βαλθασάρου Μωρήτου τυπογράφων πάλαι φοίνικος. See Antwerp, Plantin-Moretus Museum, Arch. 1150 a. misc., item 83.

10 Ὅταν πίνω μὲν ὕδωρ
τὴν Σηρικήν τε ποίην,
οὔ μοι μέλει ποτοῖο,
ὑποληνίου δρόσοιο,
μέλιτός τε νέκταρός τε.
15 Ὅταν πίνω μὲν ὕδωρ
τὴν Σηρικήν τε ποίην
ἀνθρώπινόν τε νέκταρ,
λείπω τὸ νέκταρ ὑμῖν,
νέκταρ πίνοντες ἡδύ.
20 Ὅταν πίνω μὲν ὕδωρ
τὴν Σηρικήν τε ποίην,
ἀποδράουσι πᾶσαι
λύπαι τε καὶ μέριμναι.
Ὅταν πίνω μὲν ὕδωρ
25 τὴν Σηρικήν τε ποίην,
στήθεσσιν ἐν φίλοισι
πολλὴν ἔχω γαλήνην.
Ὅταν πίνω μὲν ὕδωρ
τὴν Σηρικήν τε ποίην,
30 θέλω θέλω τ' ἀείδειν,
θέλω θέλω χορεύειν,
θέλω θέλω μανῆναι.
Ὅταν πίνω μὲν ὕδωρ,
τὴν Σηρικήν τε ποίην,
35 σοφῶν ἔγωγε κουρῶν,
αὐτοῦ ἔγωγε Φοίβου
λάλον πίνω τόθ' ὕδωρ.
Πίωμεν οὖν ἑταῖροι,
πίωμεν οὖν ἀοιδοί,
40 πίωμεν οὖν, πίωμεν.
Πίνοι τὸν οἶνον ἄλλος.
Ἐμοὶ σαόφρον ὕδωρ,
ἐμοὶ τὸ νᾶμα τοῦτο,
φίλον τὸ νᾶμα, φίλοι,
45 τὴν Σηρικήν τε ταύτην
ἐρασμίην, ποθεινήν,
θέαν, ποτῶν φερίστην,
δότε μοι πίνοντι ποίην.

Textus: Edd. a: Petri Petiti *Epos de vi et praestantia thiae sinensis, quae vulgo Thé dicitur...*, [Parisiis, 1685,] p. 20–21. b: *In laudem Thiae Sinensis Anacreontica duo*, Amstelodami [Lipsiae?, s.n.], 1685. c: *Poëmata: Editio altera...*, Amstelaedami: Apud Henr. Wetstenium, 1697, 468–470. Editiones recentiores: Pescheck 1821, 454–455 (sec. editionem b); Weise 2017, 193–194 (editio critica cum versione Germanica).

Crit.: tit. Εἰς Θέαν βοτάνην c: Ὠδάριον 1. a | ΩΔΑΡΙΟΝ A. b || **2 (et 5, 11, 16, 21, 29, 34,** non etiam 48) ποίην c || **3** ἦν a || **5** οὐχὶ a || **6** ἐρυθρὸν ab || **7** μὲν a || **8** αὐτὸ, ab || **9** Θεοὶ b || **10** ὕδωρ a || **12** Οὔ a || **16** Σηρικήν a || **17** ἀνθρώπινον a || **19** πίνουσιν ab || **22** ἀποφεύγουσίν με ab || **23** κόπαι a: κοπαί b || **26** φίλοισιν b: -οιον a || **28** Ὅταν a || **28** Σηρικήν a || **30** τ' ἀείδειν ab || **31** χερεύεν a || **34** Σηρικήν a || **36** Αὐτοῦ ἔγωγε c: Ἀπόλλωνὸς τε a : Ἀπόλλωνός τε b || **37** τόθ' c: μὲν ab || **38** ἑταίροι c || **41** Οἶνον πίνοι μὲν ab || **45** τῆν Σηρικῆν, τε τάντην a || **48** μοῖ a

Sim.: **1 (et 10, 15, 20, 24, 28, 33)** cf. *Anacreont.* 45.1 (Ὅταν πίνω τὸν οἶνον) || **6** *Anacreont.* 9.8 (πιὼν δ' ἐρυθρὸν οἶνον) || **20–23** cf. *Anacreont.* 45.1–2; 50.6 || **26** cf. e.g. Hom. *Il.* 4.313; *Od.* 23.215 (ἐνὶ στήθεσσι φίλοισιν) || **30** cf. e.g. *Anacreont.* 48.4 (θέλω καλῶς ἀείδειν) || **31** cf. *Anacreont.* 38.21 (μεθύων θέλω χορεύειν); 49.10 (πάλιν θέλω χορεύειν) || **32** cf. e.g. *Anacreont.* 9.3 (θέλω, θέλω μανῆναι) || **37** cf. *Anacreont.* 12.7 (λάλον πιόντες ὕδωρ) || **44** cf. *Epigrammatum Anthologiae Appendix*, ed. Cougny, vol. 3, p. 33 (217.2: νᾶμα φίλον)

On herbal tea

When I'm drinking water with Chinese herbs, called 'thea' ['tea'] with good reason,[31] it's not water I'm drinking, [5] I'm not drinking herbs; but I'm drinking excellent wine, I'm drinking marvellous honey, I'm drinking nectar pure and simple: what the gods drink, that's what I'm drinking! [10] When I'm drinking water with Chinese herbs, I don't care about drinking the dew from under the winepress, honey, and nectar. [15] When I'm drinking water with Chinese herbs, human nectar, I leave the nectar to you – you, nectar-drinkers! [20] When I'm drinking water with Chinese herbs, troubles and cares all flee. When I'm drinking water [25] with Chinese herbs, I experience a great calm in my chest. When I'm drinking water with Chinese herbs, [30] I so desire to sing, I so desire to dance, I so desire to be a madman. When I'm drinking water with Chinese herbs, [35] I'm drinking the babbling water of the wise maidens [i.e. Muses] and Apollo himself. So let's drink, fellows, so let's drink, singers, [40] so let's drink, let's drink. May someone else drink the wine. Give to me sound water, to me this stream, this beloved stream, my friends, [45] with Chinese herbs, lovely, desirable, tea, most excellent among drinks, give me herbs, when I am drinking.

Metre: Catalectic iambic dimeters (hemiambs) with anaclastic ionic dimeters (anacreontics) in ll. 3, 7, 9, 13, 14, 22 (only in editions ab), 48 (brief discussion in Weise 2017, 174 fn. 107; cf. Lampsonius' usage).

Notes: This poem is one of two 'drinking poems' Francius devoted to the subject of tea. Exotic and luxurious products such as tea, coffee, and tobacco were more often the topic of Latin poetry, usually didactic in nature. Poems on the subject in Greek are, however, less common. In his poems, Francius parodies anacreontic

---

[31] Francius plays with the word for 'tea', *thee* in Dutch, θέα in Greek, suggesting it has a divine nature (cf. θεά).

wine poems by applying the excited enthusiasm of drinking wine to tea. In doing so, he departs from the more common didactic approach to exotic subjects. Francius' two poems were first published in 1685 together with the Latin tea poem of Pierre Petit (1617–1687), dedicated to Pierre-Daniel Huet (1630–1721), bishop of Avranches (→ **France**). Francius also addressed three Greek elegiac distichs to his fellow tea fanatics, Petit and Huet, in which he alludes to Pindar's dictum ἄριστον μὲν ὕδωρ (*Ol.* 1.1).[32] After the fairly sloppy *editio princeps* of the poems (a), Francius' verses were reprinted in a self-standing publication (with a better text) in the same year (b). In 1697, the poet published a second edition of his Latin work, to which he appended Greek poems, including slightly revised versions of his anacreontic drinking songs (c) (the first edition of Francius' poems, published in 1686, included Latin translations of epigrams from the *Greek Anthology* – with the original texts – but did not contain Greek verses from his own hand). The text presented here follows Francius' second redaction (Weise followed the 1685 edition). The odd form ἀποδράουσι in l. 22, which replaces the ἀποφεύγουσίν με present in the previous editions, is not attested in the ancient sources. The poet seems to take it as an equivalent to ἀποδιδράσκουσι, oddly omitting the reduplication (δι-) and σκ-suffix. Francius' tea poems were soon imitated by the German poet Johann Gottfried Herrichen, who wrote a Doric song on the same subject (→ **Germany**).

II. Περὶ τοῦ Σλάδου, ὃς μὴ καθεύδειν δυνάμενος ποιητὴς ἐγένετο [c. 1689–97]

Οὐ μία πρὸς Μούσας ἐστ' ἀτραπός· οὐ μία Σλάδῳ
ἔστι γὰρ ἰατρῷ ποιμένι θ' Ἡσιόδῳ.
Τὰς Μούσας ἐῷ Ἡσίοδος πάλαι εἶδεν ἐν ὕπνῳ·
τὰς νῦν μὲν Μούσας Σλᾶδος ἄϋπνος ἴδεν.
5 Αἴθε μοι ἀγραυλεῖν οὕτως οὕτως τε καθεύδειν
ἢ Σλάδου Μοῦσαι δοῖεν ἢ Ἡσιόδου.

Textus: Ed. a: *Poëmata: Editio altera...*, Amstelaedami: Apud Henr. Wetstenium, 1697, 483.

Crit.: 5 ἀγραυλεῖν : ἀγρυπνεῖν fortasse potius legendum

Sim.: 1 cf. Plut. *Mor.* 418c9

---

[32] Huet zestily recounts his addiction to tea in his memoirs, which include a long Latin poem in elegiac couplets by his own hand praising the potion (Huet 1718, 303–307). See also the English translation in Huet 1810, 180f., where the Latin poem is, however, left untranslated.

On Slade, who became a poet when he could not sleep

> There is not one sole path to the Muses; for there is not one sole
>   path for doctor Slade and for shepherd Hesiod.
> Hesiod saw the Muses long ago in his sleep;
>   just now Slade saw the Muses when he was sleepless.
> [5] May either Slade's or Hesiod's Muses grant me to live in the open [pass sleepless nights?]
>   like that or to sleep like that.

Metre: Elegiac couplets.

Notes: In this brief metapoetic piece, Francius expresses the hope that the Muses would inspire him both while asleep, as they did with the ancient poet Hesiod, and while awake, as they did with his recently deceased friend and fellow Greek poet Matthew Slade (1628–1689). Francius is probably alluding to the beginning of Hesiod's *Theogony* (ll. 9–10), where the poet invokes the Muses who travel by night. The image of a sleeping Hesiod became popular in early modern times, especially in emblem books. Pierre Cousteau's *Pegme* (Lyon, 1560), for instance, features an emblem showing Hesiod sleeping at the Castalian Spring. The accompanying poems begins as follows : 'Dy moy de grace, o toy Poëte Ascrée / si en dormant aux mons de Thessalie, / tu as receu de la Muse sacrée, / le gentil don de noble Poësie ?' (p. 346). The poem displays one lexical oddity: in l. 5 Francius apparently mistook ἀγραυλεῖν ('to live in the open') for ἀγρυπνεῖν ('to pass sleepless nights'), which makes more sense in this context. Matthew Slade was a doctor from Amsterdam with English roots who had studied in Leiden and Helmstedt. He published on different medical topics, including asthma and embryology, often under pseudonyms, and was active in the field of philology too. He worked on commentaries of, among others, Hesychius. Slade is the topic of several poems by Francius, in one of which he is even granted the title of 'king of the Greek epigram'.[33] Slade's Greek poetical oeuvre still awaits further study. It seems, however, that he composed Greek poems for several decades. A 1658 book on natural and medical aspects of both Indies, authored by Willem Piso (1611–1678) and printed in Amsterdam, contains a Greek poem in 11 elegiac couplets by Slade (see Piso 1658, ** 6ᵛ). A year later he addressed a laudatory poem to the book collector Paul(us) Terhaar(ius), a friend of Marcus Zuerius Boxhorn and acquaintance of Claude de Saumaise (Rhodes 1976). To a collection of Latin poems on the victories of the Christian Europeans over the Muslim Turks written by Francius and published in 1687, a cycle of four Greek poems by Slade is appended (Francius 1687,

---

33 See Francius 1697, 492: Ἑλλαδικοῦ βασιλεῦ ἐπιγράμματος.

117f.). In a copy of the 1554 *editio princeps* of the ancient doctor Aretaeus now preserved at the Gennadius Library in Athens, a handwritten poem by Slade can be found (Mavroudis 1993). Further study will likely bring to light more Greek compositions by this interesting figure.

Biography: Born in Amsterdam on 19 August 1645, Petrus Francius (Pieter de Frans) spent almost his entire life in his home city. He attended a Latin school, where his attention was drawn to Latin poetry and Ovid in particular. From age 17, he studied in Leiden under Johann Friedrich Gronovius (1611–1671) and others. His first Latin poem dates to this time. In 1669–1671, Francius undertook a *peregrinatio academica* to England, France, Switzerland, and Italy, meeting among others the star poet René Rapin (1621–1687) in Paris. He moreover obtained a doctoral degree in both laws from the university of Angers. During his *peregrinatio*, he also visited Virgil's alleged tomb in Naples. In early 1674, aged 28, Francius was appointed professor of eloquence at the Amsterdam *Athenaeum Illustre*. He consolidated his career as a Latin poet and orator, reciting his work for large and enthusiastic audiences. He also translated Greek poems from the *Anthologia Palatina* into Latin verses. After he had published his first collection of Latin poems (1682), he started composing poetry in Greek, and obtained the chair of Greek in 1686. He ended his inaugural lecture with an outburst of Greek verses. He published his Greek poems, appended to his Latin collection, in 1697. He stimulated Greek composition among his students, having them translate part of Ovid's *Metamorphoses* (1691) and two of Cicero's orations (*Pro Archia* and *Pro Marcello*; 1693) into Greek. The students had to perform their Greek work, and Francius himself introduced these events with short Greek orations (Francius 1705, 279–281, 344–346). Francius was part of a circle of poets which included Matthew Slade, who might have been one of his examples. He was also involved in a heated dispute about Greek poetry. When Jacob Perizonius (1651–1715) was inaugurated as professor of eloquence at Leiden University – a chair previously offered to Francius – one of his students, Johannes Jensius, recited a Greek poem of his own composition. Francius, unimpressed, published a scathing criticism of the poem, which resulted in a years-long, bitter controversy. He died on 19 August 1704.

Bibliography: On Francius' life: see Heesakkers, Chris L. (1997), "De hoogleraar in de welsprekendheid Petrus Francius (1645–1704)", in: Eco O. G. Haitsma Mulier (ed.), *Athenaeum Illustre. Elf studies over de Doorluchtige School 1632–1877*, Amsterdam, 91–134: 94–106. On his tea poems, see Weise, Stefan (2017), "Dichten und Teetrinken. Zum anakreontischen griechischen Teegedicht De Thea herba von Johann Gottfried Herrichen (1629–1705)", in: Id. (ed.), *HELLENISTI! Altgriechisch als Literatursprache im neuzeitlichen Europa*, Stuttgart, 149–201. Further literature:

Francius, Petrus (1682), *Poëmata*, Amsterdam; Francius, Petrus (1687), *Laurus Europaea, seu Celebres christianorum de Turcis victoriae*, Amsterdam; Francius, Petrus (1697), *Poëmata*, 2nd ed., Amsterdam; Francius, Petrus (1705), *Orationes*, 2nd ed., Amsterdam; Huet, Pierre-Daniel (1718), *Commentarius de rebus ad eum pertinentibus*, Amsterdam; Huet, Pierre-Daniel, (1810), *Memoirs of the Life of Peter Daniel Huet, Bishop of Avranches*, vol. 2, London; Mavroudis (Μαυρουδής), Aimilios (1993), "Το επίγραμμα Εις Αρεταίον του «Μ. Σλάδου, ιατρού Αμστελοδαμαίου»", in: *Ελληνικά* 43, 209–213; Pescheck, Christian Adolph (1821), "Griechische Theegedichte", in: *Kritische Bibliothek für das Schul- und Unterrichtswesen*, 3/1, 453–455; Piso, Willem (1658), *De Indiae utriusque re naturali et medica libri quatuordecim*, Amsterdam; Rhodes, Dennis E. (1976), "A Dutch Seventeenth-Century Book-Collector: Paulus Terhaarius", in: *Quaerendo* 6/4, 347–351.

Johan Andreas dèr Mouw (1863–1919)

I. Ἀντώνιος τοῦ Καίσαρος πεφονευμένου δημηγορεῖ τῇ Αἰσχύλου λέξει χρώμενος [?1888–1902/?1904]

(excerptum, vv. 53–79)

οὕτω γὰρ αὐδᾶν μοι δοκεῖ, χρανθεὶς ἄγει,
λόγοισι μαστίκτορσι Φοῖβος ἔγκοτος·
55 "Ἦ κάρτ' ἀναιδεῖς ἐστε, φοίνιον γένος,
τὸν Καίσαρα φθείραντες οἵτινες βλέπειν
πρὸς ἁγνὸν εὔτολμοι πέλεσθ' ἐμὸν φάος,
πᾶσιν στύγος θεοῖσι καὐτοῖσιν βλάβῃ!
τέθνηκεν ἥρως πάντ' ἀλίγκιος θεῷ,
60 οἱ δ' αὐτοένται ζῶσι, χλίοντες φόνῳ!
Τί δ' ἀνθέμοισι δένδρον ἢ βρίθει χλόῃ,
ὅτου γ' ἀφέλκει δίψιος λειχὴν βίον;
καὶ πῶς πολιτεύσεσθε θάλλοντες κράτει,
ἐὰν τοὺς λεωργούς, μὴ 'κταμόντες πρεμνόθεν,
65 ἐᾶθ' ὑπεκπίνοντας αὐαίνειν πόλιν;"
Τοιαῦτα Φοίβου τρανὲς ἀστράπτει σέλας.
Ἡ δ' αὖτε νυκτίσεμνος ἐνστάζει φρεσὶν
ἄστρων σιωπὴ τηλεπόμποις φθέγμασιν,
ὡς χρή με τιμαλφεῖν τε τὸν προύχοντ' ἀεί,
70 πάντας τ' ἀνοιστρεῖν φερτάτων[34] τιμαόρους.
Ἐγρέσθ', ἐγρέσθε, σοῦσθε καὶ πιστοὶ χόλῳ
φέρεσθ', ἅπερ κεραυνὸς αἰχμάζων φόβον. –
Στεροπαῖσι παμφθάρτοισι δαιμόνων βραβεὺς

---

[34] Νερτέρ<ων> as an alternative reading in ms. N. Fresco hesitantly opts for the current reading on grounds of content (Fresco 1972, IIb, 528).

βρύοντ' ἄϊστοῖ φοιτάδος τόλμης βροτόν·
75 πρὶν οὖν διαρραισθεῖσαν ὄλλυσθαι πόλιν
θείαις θυέλλαις, ὦ ταλαίπωροι φίλοι,
αὐτοὶ γενέσθε σκηπτός, ᾧ πεδάρσιον
θυμὸν καθίζων, ὑψίπυργον ὡς θρόνον,
Δίκης ἄναγνα φεψαλῷ μισήματα.

Textus & crit.: *vide* Fresco, Marcel F. (1972), *De dichter dèr Mouw en de klassieke oudheid*, Amsterdam, IIa, 325–327.

Sim.: 54 ἔγκοτος] cf. e.g. Aesch. *Cho.* 392 || 55 ἦ κάρτ(α)] cf. e.g. Aesch. *Cho.* 929 || **55–56** βλέπειν...φάος] cf. e.g. Aesch. *Ag.* 1646; *Pers.* 299; *Eum.* 746 || **56** ἁγνὸν...φάος] cf. e.g. Eur. *El.* 86 || **58** στύγος] cf. e.g. Aesch. *Cho.* 392 (ἔγκοτον στύγος); *Sept.* 653 (ὦ θεομανές τε καὶ θεῶν μέγα στύγος) || **59** cf. Pind. *Pyth.* 1.53 (ἥρωας ἀντιθέους) et *Nem.* 3.22 (ἥρως θεός) || **60** αὐτοέντα] cf. Soph. *OT* 107; *El.* 272 | χλίοντες] cf. Aesch. *Cho.* 137; *Supp.* 236 || **61** δένδρον...βρίθει] cf. Hom. *Od.* 19.112 || **62** δίψιος] cf. Aesch. *Ag.* 495 | λειχήν] cf. Aesch. *Eum.* 785 = 815; *Cho.* 281 || **64** λεωργούς] cf. Aesch. *PV* 5 | πρεμνόθεν] cf. Aesch. *Sept.* 71, 1056 (vid. αὐτόπρεμνον in *Eum.* 401) || **65** ὑπεκπίνοντας] hap. leg. (cf. ἐκπίνειν: Aesch. *Ag.* 1398) || **66** cf. Aesch. *PV* 356 (ἤστραπτε γοργωπὸν σέλας) || **67** νυκτίσεμνος] cf. Aesch. *Eum.* 108 (hap. leg.) | cf. Bacchyl. 13.196 (ἐνέσταξ[εν φρασίν]); Opp. *C.* 2.314 (ἐνέστακται φρεσί) || **68** τηλεπόμποις] cf. Aesch. *Ag.* 300 (hap. leg.) || **69** cf. Aesch. *Ag.* 922 (θεούς τοι τοῖσδε τιμαλφεῖν χρεών) || **70** ἀνοιστρεῖν] Eur. *Bacch.* 979 || **72** cf. Nonn. *Dion.* 1.392 (αἰχμάζοντα κεραυνῷ) || **73** παμφθάρτοισι] cf. Aesch. *Cho.* 296 (hap. leg.) || **75** διαρραισθεῖσαν...πόλιν] cf. Aesch. *PV* 238 & Nonn. *Dion.* 25.367 || **77** πεδάρσιον] cf. e.g. Aesch. *PV* 271 & *Cho.* 846 || **78** ὑψίπυργον] cf. e.g. Aesch. *Supp.* 97 || **79** φεψαλῷ] cf. Aesch. *PV* 362 (ἐφεψαλώθη < φεψαλόομαι; quasi hap. leg.) & Nicet. Eugen., *De Drosillae et Chariclis amoribus* 5.245–246 (Τοιούσδε πικροὺς εἰσδεδεγμένην λόγους / πρηστὴρ κεραυνὸς φεψαλοῖ τὴν παρθένον).

Antony speaks to the assembly after Caesar's murder, using Aeschylus' style

(excerpt, ll. 53–79)

For, defiled by guilt, he seems to me to be speaking as follows, with scourging words, spiteful Phoebus: [55] 'Very shameless is indeed what you are, blood-stained clan, who after killing Caesar have the courage to look at my pure light,[35] you abomination before all gods and your own mischief! Dead is the hero, in all respects resembling a god, [60] but his assassins live, revelling in murder. But what tree is heavy with flowers or verdure, out of which a thirsty moss sucks the life? And how will you be a community, thriving with strength, if you let the villains, instead of cutting them out [65] from the stem, suck out and

---

35 Fresco 1972, IIb, 518 observes that dèr Mouw plays with the double meaning of the phrase βλέπειν...φάος: 'looking at the light' and 'live' (for the latter meaning, see Aesch. *Ag.* 1646, *Pers.* 299, and *Eum.* 746).

wither the city?' Such things Phoebus' bright light flashes. And on the other hand the silence of the stars, solemnised by the night, drops into my mind with far-journeyed words, that I have to honour him who always excelled [70] and incite madly all avengers of the bravest. Wake up, wake up, hurry up, and move with trust in your wrath, like lightning spearing fear. – With all-consuming lightning flashes the leader of the gods destroys the mortal, full of mad boldness; [75] so before the city is dashed to pieces and annihilated by divine storms, my miserable friends, become a thunderbolt yourself, with which I, residing on my rage high in the air as if on a high-towered throne, burn the unholy objects of Justice's hate to ashes.

Metre: Iambic trimeters (analysis in Fresco 1972, IIb, 456f.).

Notes: The poem, consisting of 98 verses, offers a poetic interpretation of Marc Antony's speech at the death of Caesar (dèr Mouw's alternative title was Ἀντώνιος λέγει τὸν Καίσαρος ἐπιτάφιον; Fresco 1972, IIa, 320); Antony exhorts the Romans to take revenge on Caesar's murderers. The poem can be regarded as a poetic reflection on Δίκη, with Zeus as the restorer of order. It has sometimes been interpreted in the light of dèr Mouw's dismissal from the gymnasium in Doetinchem in 1904, but this seems for various reasons unlikely (compare the views of Fresco 1972, IIb, 422–425, 473–475 and Meijer 1980 on this subject). The passage reproduced here concerns Apollo's speech to the Romans, reported by Antony as part of his exhortation. In a previous version, dèr Mouw might have envisioned a speech by Zeus rather than Apollo (Fresco 1972, IIb, 516f.). A thorough discussion of the poem's style and content is in Fresco 1972, IIb, 407–478, with very detailed commentary and *apparatus fontium* on pp. 479–556. For the date of the poem in particular, see Fresco 1972, IIb, 473–475. Both the poem's central theme and style recall Aeschylus, referenced in one of the titles Mouw gave to this poem, which we have adopted here. This makes the poem a unique specimen for the Low Countries, as tragedy-style Greek poetry was barely produced in that area.[36] The motif of the slain leader resonates with the central subject of Aeschylus' *Choephoroi*, while Zeus as protector of Δίκη is central to Aeschylus' work in general (analysis in Fresco 1972, IIb, 442–446). Dèr Mouw's language and style also echo Aeschylus'. This appears, among other things, from the many expressions the poet borrowed from Aeschylus, including multiple *hapax legomena* (3, and perhaps 4, in this passage alone). One particularly interesting Aeschylean borrowing in the passage under discussion is the verb τιμαλφεῖν: according to the *Scholia vetera*, at Aesch. *Eum.* 626, the ancient playwright was even mocked for his predilection

---

36 Greek translations in the style of Attic tragedy were very common in Britain at this time (e.g., among the poetic submissions to the Gaisford Prize → **Great Britain**).

for the word by the comic poet Epicharmus. On the other hand, some features are not particularly tragic at all (e.g. πέλεσθαι in l. 57 instead of πέλειν), or even prosaic (e.g., πολιτεύεσθαι in l. 63). More generally, the poem abounds in rare and learned words (e.g., ἄγος, εὔτολμος, ἄνθεμον, δίψιος, λεωργός, ἀνοιστρεῖν). On dèr Mouw's vocabulary, see Fresco 1972, IIb, 447–457, with word list on pp. 457–471. Apart from the violations of Porson's Law (ll. 64 & 68), the passage offered here shows some peculiarities of language: an unusual synizesis in l. 64 (ἐάν instead of ἤν); a neologism in l. 65 (ὑπεκπίνειν); unusual accentuation of the imperative in l. 71 and 77 (γενέσθε); and uncommon usage of the article (ἡ in l. 67), perhaps to be understood as a demonstrative in Homeric fashion (in apposition with σιωπή in l. 68). The work also contains some daring phrasings, most notably πεδάρσιον θυμὸν καθίζων in l. 78 (Fresco 1972, IIb, 534–535). In 1902, Koster (1902, 53) observed that dèr Mouw had translated Antony's speech from Shakespeare's *Julius Caesar* into Greek iambic trimeters. This cannot refer to the poem here (Custers 2018, 86), as dèr Mouw's *Antonios* is by no means a translation of *Julius Caesar*, even though it does respond to it (compare e.g. l. 71 with *Julius Caesar* 2.1, with the discussion of Fresco 1972, IIb, 426–435).

II. Πίμ [c. 1912]

Πομπόν, Πίμ, πέμπω πάμπαν σοι καιρίου εὐχῆς
　　χάρτην, σῆς ῥώμης, φίλτατε, κηδόμενος.
Μὴ γάρ σοι, μελετῶντι τρέχειν δικυκλεῖν τε Πλάτωνα
　　μέμφεσθαι νομίσῃς, ἐκκατιδόντα τόπου,
5　ἔνθα θανόντι θανὼν ἰδέας δείκνυσιν ἑταίρῳ,
　　ἃς ζωὸς ζωὸν πόλλ' ἐδίδασκε λόγοις,
καὶ μάκαρες σιγῶσι, τὰ δ' ὄντως ὄντα θεῶνται,
　　δίνη δ' ἐκστατικοὺς ἠρέμα κυκλοφορεῖ.
Ἔνθ' εἰ καί του ἔρις ζῶντος διέλυσεν ἔρωτα,
10　ὥστε δοκεῖν φροῦδον πάντ' ἀφανιζόμενον,
ἀλλὰ τὸν αὐτὸν ἔρωτ' ἀναλήψεται, ὅνπερ ἔκλαυσεν,
　　ἀσπάσεται δ' εὔφρων, ὡς πρὶν ἐρῶντος ἐρῶν.
Ὅς γὰρ ἔρως κατέδυ ψυχῆς κευθμῶν' ἐς ἄβυσσον,
　　ἀνθεῖ ἀκίνδυνος Βράχμανι σῳζόμενος,
15　οἶαι ποντιάδες μαλακαὶ θάλλουσ' ἀνεμῶναι
　　οὐδέποτ' οὐδεμιᾷ λαίλαπι σειόμεναι.
Βούλῃ μὲν γνῶναι ῥιζώματ' ἀγήρατα κόσμου,
　　ῥώννυσθαι δ', ὡς χρή, νήπιος οὐκ ἐθέλεις.
Εἴρηται· "Τίς ἀνὴρ θεὸν ὄψεται οὐδὲ θανεῖται;"
20　Δεῖ δ' ὑπὲρ ἄνθρωπον καρτερὰ νεῦρά σ' ἔχειν,
ὅστις ἐπιστήμης γένεσιν, φιλόκαντε, θεωρεῖς
　　καί, Ἀρτμαννιάδη, θεσμὰ σοφῆς φύσεως.

Ὥστε διπλῆν ῥώμην, φίλε Πίμ, σε πρέπει παρέχεσθαι
νεῦρά τε θεῖα, διπλοῦν τὸν θεὸν ὀψόμενον.
25 Εὑρήσεις γὰρ ἴσως, νέος ὤν, ἃ γέρων οὐχ ηὗρον,
σκεψάμενος πολλῶν δόγματα πολλὰ σοφῶν.
Πρῶτον μὲν τὸ κενόν, πότερον ψυχαῖς μόνον ἐστὶν
ἔμφυτον ἡμετέραις, ἢ φύσεως ἰδέα·
δεύτερον αὖ πότερον τὸ τέλος μόνον ἐστι νόησις
30 ἀνδρῶν, ἢ τάττει κόσμον ἅπαντα καλῶς.
Οὐκοῦν ἢν ἐθέλῃς ἐμέ τ' εὐφραίνειν καὶ Ἀθήνην
(ἡδέα δ' ἄν, ποιῶν ὧδε, γενέθλι' ἄγοις!),
χρή σ' εὖ γιγνώσκειν ὁδόν, ὦ φίλε Πίμ, μίαν εἶναι·
Πρὸς τἀληθὲς νεῖ, καὶ τρέχε καὶ δικύκλει.

Textus & crit.: *vide* Fresco, Marcel F. (1972, IIa), *De dichter dèr Mouw en de klassieke oudheid*, Amsterdam, 336–339.

Sim.:[37] **1** Πομπὸν...πέμπω] cf. Hom. *Il.* 16.671 & 16.681 (πέμπε δέ μιν πομποῖσιν ἅμα κραιπνοῖσι φέρεσθαι) || καιρίου εὐχῆς] cf. Thgn. 1.341 (καίριον εὐχήν) || **4** ἐκκατιδόντα] cf. Hom. *Il.* 4.508 & 7.21 (Περγάμου ἐκκατιδών [*de Apolline*]) || **19** "Τίς ἀνὴρ θεὸν ὄψεται οὐδὲ θανεῖται;"] cf. LXX *Ex.* 33.20

Pim

I'm sending you, Pim, a card carrying a very timely wish, concerned as I am, my dearest, over your strength. For you should not believe that, if you train yourself in running and biking, Plato blames you, when he looks down from the place, [5] where, one dead man to the other, he is showing to a friend the ideas, which in their lifetime he had often tried to teach to him with words, and they are blissfully silent, while they admire the truly existing beings, and a whirlwind is gently carrying them around in ecstasy. And there, even if a quarrel destroyed someone's love during lifetime, [10] so that it seems to be gone, forever vanished, he will still retrieve the same love he had lamented, and he will salute it cheerfully, as if he is in love with a former lover. For love that has sunk into the bottomless hole of the soul flourishes far from danger, saved through Brahman, [15] like delicate sea anemones thrive, never disturbed by any hurricane. You want to get to know the cosmos' ageless elements, but you refuse to gather the necessary strength, in your silliness. The saying goes: 'What man will see God and won't die?' [20] And you have to possess superhumanly strong muscles, you who study the birth of knowledge, Kant-lover and Hartmann enthusiast, the laws of wise nature. So, my dear Pim, you have to exhibit double strength and divine muscles, if you want to see God doubly. [25] For perhaps you will find, young as you are, what an old man like me has not found, even though I have considered many doctrines of many wise men. Firstly, whether the void of space is only planted into our souls or is a form of

---

[37] Cf. Fresco 1972, 571–579 and van den Berg *et al.* 1993, 98.

nature; secondly, in turn, whether the final cause is merely a concept [30] of men, or it righteously rules the entire cosmos. Surely, if you want to cheer me and Athena (and you could spend a pleasant birthday by doing so!), you have to be well aware, my dear Pim, that there is one road only: swim, run, and bike to the truth.

Metre: Elegiac couplets (*spondiacus* in l. 25, emphasising the poet's advanced age: γέρων οὐχ ηὗρον).

Notes: The poem is addressed to the young Guillaume 'Pim' Nijhoff on the occasion of his birthday and sends a clear philosophical message, i.e. to find the truth one needs to have the strength of a youngster (Fresco 1972, IIb, 571). The year of composition is unknown. Pim was born in 1895 and lived in The Hague, where dèr Mouw was his teacher from 1910 onwards. Assuming that Pim was probably able to understand dèr Mouw's poem, Fresco 1972, IIb, 571 suggests that it was written around 1912. The first verse contains an impressive play on the sounds of the nicknames of the brothers Guillaume (1895–1932) and Martinus (1894–1953) Nijhoff, known as Pim and Pom. The latter became a successful author and found fame as a Dutch poet – one of his most famous poems, *De Moeder de Vrouw* (1934), was translated into Greek verse by Bernard van Groningen 1972, 22. Dèr Mouw expresses the classical ideal of a healthy mind in a healthy body, which reaches a witty climax in the final verse. The topic of this poem is more philosophical than those of his other Greek compositions, which might also explain why the language is less poetical. Dèr Mouw shows himself to be very creative with the Greek language, composing neologisms to refer to the philosophers Immanuel Kant (l. 21: φιλόκαντε) and Eduard von Hartmann (l. 22: Ἀρτμαννιάδη), whose ideas Pim cherished. The Greek expressions dèr Mouw uses moreover demonstrate that he was thoroughly acquainted with Greek philosophical concepts such as τὸ κενόν, τὸ τέλος, and τὰ ὄντως ὄντα, the last being a typically Platonic phrase to refer to what really exists. He moreover alludes to Plato's theory of ideas. Other aspects of his work suggest a thorough acquaintance with ancient Greek classics as well. The double usage of the participle θανών, for instance, might be inspired by the oeuvre of Euripides, in which this occurs frequently (e.g., *Alc.* 541). Dèr Mouw also plays with *homoioptota* and sounds in general, e.g. the emphatic alliteration in the poem's very first line: Πομπόν, Πίμ, πέμπω πάμπαν.

Biography: Born in Westervoort on 24 July 1863 and raised in Zwolle and Deventer, Johan Andreas dèr Mouw studied Classics, Sanskrit, and philosophy at Leiden University. In 1890, he successfully defended his dissertation *Quomodo* *antiqui naturam mirati sunt?*, written under the supervision of Johannes van Leeuwen. From 1888 until 1904, he taught at the gymnasium in Doetinchem. Dèr Mouw enjoyed close friendships with some of his students and felt strong affection for at least two of them, including the son of the gymnasium's director, the later Classicist and translator Maximiliaan August (Max) Schwartz (1884–1973), whom he considered 'one of the greatest loves of [his] life' (Custers 2018, 142–145). In 1904, he was fired, mainly because of his anti-Christian ideas. This was a difficult period for dèr Mouw, who tried to commit suicide twice. Afterwards he worked as a private tutor in Rijswijk, publishing at the same time two books on philosophical themes. In 1907, he moved with his wife and his daughter-by-adoption to The Hague, where he continued to teach in private. In his later years he also composed Brahmanic poetry. The bulk of his poetry is in Dutch, but there is also a small collection of Latin and Greek poems, usually on themes from classical antiquity. He exchanged Latin, Greek, and Dutch poems with his colleague and friend Edward Bernard Koster (1861–1937). According to Koster (1902, 53), dèr Mouw's Greek and Latin poems were not just meant to be funny but were serious stylistic exercises as well. All of his poetry was published only after his death on 8 July 1919; his personal archive is now kept in The Hague at the Literatuurmuseum. Apart from *Antonios* and *Pim*, he also composed a love poem in Sapphic strophes entitled *Anna* (?1889), written in Attic rather than Aeolic, and three very short epigrams.

Bibliography: Biographical accounts: most recently, Custers, Lucien (2018), *Alleen in wervelende wereld. Het leven van Johan Andreas dèr Mouw (1863-1919)*, Nijmegen. See also Meijer, Jaap (1976), *Het ivoren aapje. J.A. dèr Mouw en Victor van Vriesland*, Heemstede; Id. (1979), *Over het nut van biografische gegevens bij het lezen van gedichten van J.A. dèr Mouw*, Heemstede; Id. (1980), *Ook gij, Brutus. J.A. dèr Mouw en de biografische methode*, Heemstede. For dèr Mouw's poetry: Fresco, Marcel F. (ed.) (1986), *Johan Andreas dèr Mouw. Volledig dichtwerk*, Amsterdam (latest edition); see also the extensive commentary and notes in Fresco, Marcel F. (1971–1972), *De dichter dèr Mouw en de klassieke oudheid*, 2 vols, Amsterdam. On his Greek poetry: Koster, Edward B. (1902), "Een oude schuld II", in: *De Nederlandsche Spectator* 7, 52–55. For some historical context regarding Pim: van Rij, Lennard (2011), "Platoonse liefde in tijden van decadentisme: J.A. dèr Mouw, Victor van Vriesland en Martinus Nijhoff", in: *De Parelduiker* 16, 38–56: 49f.

Bernard van Groningen (1894–1987)

Viro clarissimo Br. Snell fundationem Hardt linquenti [post 1950]

> Ὄμματα δακρύοφιν πλήσθη, πάντες δ' ἐγόησαν
> ξανθὸν ἐπείτε Ταχὺν οἴκαδ' ἰόντ' ἔπιδον,
> ζηλωτὴν τραγικῆς ποιήσιος, ἀλλὰ γέλωτος
> αἴτιον ὡσαύτως τοῖς ἑτάροισιν ἀεί.
> 5 Εὐχὴ δ' Οὐλυμπόνδε πολυφθόγγος ἐπαέρθη·
> τοιοῦτοι πολλοί τ' ἄμμι γένοιντο φίλοι.

Textus: van Groningen, Bernard A. (1972), *Carmina et epigrammata Graece*, Leiden, 8.

Crit.: 2 Ταχύν ed. ‖ 5 Οὐλυμπόνδε ed. | fortasse πολυφθόγγως

Sim.: 1 cf. Hom. *Od.* 4.704f., 19.472f. ‖ 2 ξανθόν] Hom. passim (de Menelao), e.g. *Il.* 3.284; *Od.* 4.30 | ἐπείτε] forma Herodotea | οἴκαδ' ἰόντ'] cf. Hom. *Od.* 7.188; 13.121, 305; 14.181, etc. ‖ 6 cf. *Comicorum Graecorum fragmenta in papyris reperta*, fr. 257.88 Austin (εἰ γὰρ τοιοῦτοι τρεῖς γένοιντό σοι φίλοι)

To the most illustrious Bruno Snell leaving the Hardt Foundation

> Eyes filled with tears, all wept after they had seen
>   the fair-haired Swift (Ταχύς)[38] was going home;
> he is a great admirer of tragedy but always
>   makes his comrades laugh too.
> [5] A prayer with many voices was borne up to the Olympus:
>   that we may have many friends like him.

Metre: Elegiac couplets (note the lengthening of Ταχύν in l. 2 and πολυφθόγγος[39] in l. 5).

---

[38] The Greek Ταχύς is a pun on the name *Snell*, evoking the German and Dutch words for 'swift' (*schnell* and *snel*, respectively).

[39] Perhaps van Groningen intended the otherwise unattested adverb πολυφθόγγως here, which would solve both the accentual and the metrical issues with the form πολυφθόγγος (normally πολύφθογγος) in this context. πολυφθόγγως does feature sporadically in later *katharevousa* Greek.

Notes: Bruno Snell (1898–1986) was a German classical scholar who, from 1931 to 1959, held the chair of classical philology at the University of Hamburg. In 1944, he established the research centre of the *Thesaurus Linguae Graecae*. The epigram, echoing the *Greek Anthology*, refers to one of Snell's visits to the Hardt Foundation, a research centre for Classics in Vandœuvres, not too far from Geneva (Switzerland), established in 1950. Van Groningen emphasises Snell's work on Greek tragedy, which included his *Habilitation* on Aeschylus (1925), an edition of Euripidean and anonymous fragments (1964) appended to Nauck's *Tragicorum Graecorum Fragmenta* (1856), and the first two volumes of the revised *TrGF* (1971, 1981). Van Groningen constructs an opposition between Snell's interest in tragedy and his humorous character. In the final verse, he adopts a phrasing from an anonymous piece of New Comedy, thus also alluding to Snell's interest in dramatic *adespota* (l. 6, with *app. fontium*). The language of the poem is fairly free but betrays the influence of Homeric idiom, most notably in the epithet applied to Snell (ξανθός), which Homer usually applied to Menelaos and Achilles. Van Groningen additionally uses some rare forms, including ἐγόησαν in l. 1 and ἐπαέρθη in l. 5 (the more usual form in this position is ἀέρθη as, e.g., in Hom. *Od.* 19.540). The expression εὐχὴ πολυφθόγγος in l. 5 is also unusual: the uncommon adjective πολύφθογγος, first attested in Plutarch (*Mor.* 827a, 973c), is particularly frequent in Christian Greek texts. Here, it may suggest that the prayer or wish was expressed in many languages, given the international company of scholars at the Hardt Foundation.

Biography: Bernard Abraham van Groningen (Twello, 1894 – Leiderdorp, 1987) spent his early youth in Brussels, where he studied Classics at the Université Libre de Bruxelles before relocating to Groningen. After obtaining his PhD degree there in 1921, he taught Greek and Latin at high schools for some time and worked at the Papyrological Institute of Groningen University. In 1928 he accepted the chair of Greek at Leiden University, which he held from 1929 until his retirement in 1964. Van Groningen specialised in Greek papyrology and was co-founder of the Leids Papyrologisch Instituut (1935) and the *Papyrologica Lugduno-Batava* (first issue in 1941). Another area of interest was Greek lyricism (e.g., *La composition littéraire archaïque grecque: procédés et réalisations*, Amsterdam 1958). Van Groningen also published the *skolia* of Pindar (*Pindare au banquet*, Leiden 1960). On 30 May 1942, during the German occupation, he resigned at his own request and was put into custody and exiled to Steenwijk. After the war, he resumed his duties in Leiden and, from 1949 to 1950, served as the university's *rector magnificus*. Van Groningen also contributed to the Dutch literary periodical *De Gids* (and from 1950 to 1952, acted as a member of the editorial board). Snell and van Groningen were close contemporaries with shared interests; they seem to have been on friendly terms (in any case, they exchanged letters).[40] Van Groningen published a small collection of Greek verse in 1972, mainly occasional poems and some translations from Dutch. Some of these poems were included, with Dutch translation, in van den Berg et al. 1993, 104–109.

Bibliography: van Groningen, Bernard (1972), *Carmina et epigrammata Graece*, Leiden. Biographical accounts: Sijpesteijn, P.J. (1988), "Levensbericht B. A. van Groningen", in: *Jaarboek der Koninklijke Nederlandse Akademie van Wetenschappen*, 19–24. On van Groningen's Greek poems: van den Berg et al. 1993, 103–109.

---

40 See Munich, Bayerische Staatsbibliothek, Nachlass Bruno Snell, Sign. Ana 490.B.II. Groningen, Bernard Abraham van (Hamburg, 08.11.1955).

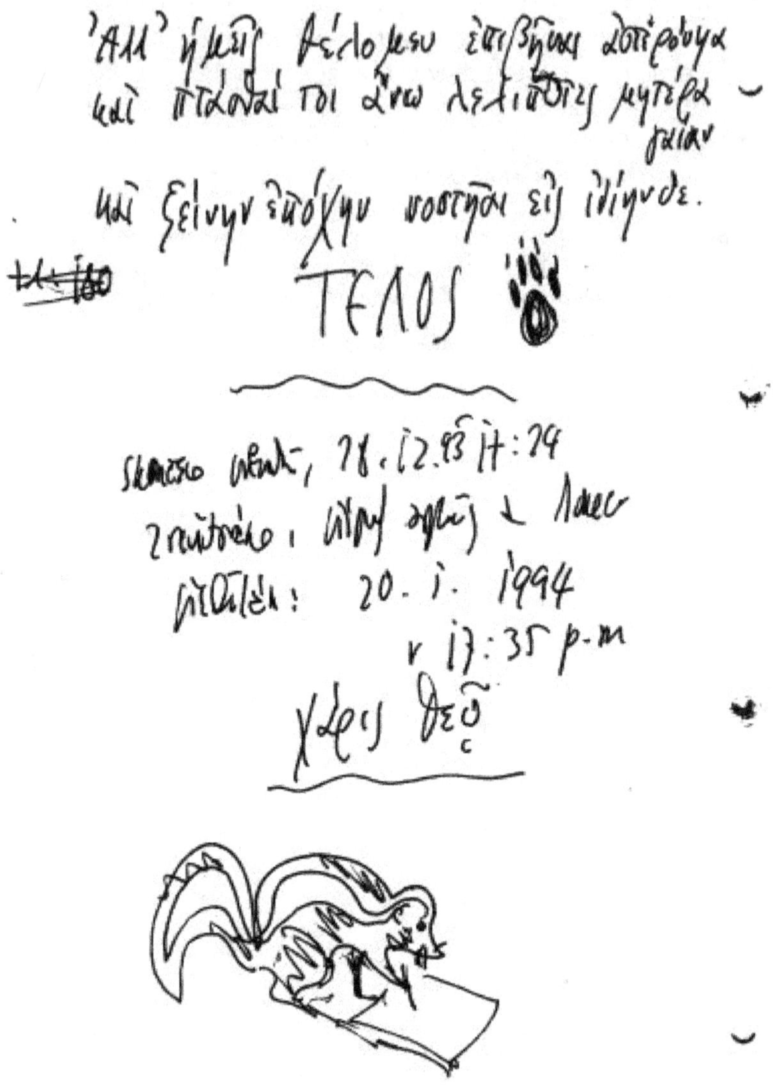

Ἀλλ' ἡμῖν μέλομεν ἐπιβῆναι ἀστέρουχα
καὶ πλόναι τοι ἄνω λετιοῦσης μητέρα
     γαίαν
καὶ ξείνην ἐνοχήν νοστῆσαι εἰς ἰδίην δε.

ΤΕΛΟΣ

Fig. 5: Last page of the Greek manuscript text (fol. 210v) of Jan Křesadlo's *Astronautilia* (see below, p. 301–305) illustrating the 'universal translator' Franta while writing the text and fixing the dates of composition: 28 December 1993–20 January 1994.

Marcela Slavíková
The Bohemian Lands

The University of Prague was founded in 1348 by Charles IV, whose reign was a time of prosperity for the Bohemian lands. However, the early reformation led by Jan Hus, who was the rector of the University of Prague in 1409–1410, and the Hussite wars (1419–1434) that followed his execution slowed the beginnings of Renaissance Humanism in the Bohemian lands to a considerable extent.[1] The majority of the Bohemian population was Hussite by that time and the University of Prague was Hussite too, which led to severe restrictions: from 1419 there was only the Faculty of Arts (also called the *Academia Pragensis*), which retained its Reformed disposition[2] until 1622 when it was closed to be united with the Jesuit college.[3] Renaissance Humanism, therefore, started rather late in the Bohemian lands (in the last third of the 15th century) and it also came to an early end as it was mostly associated with Reformed intellectuals who either had to convert to Catholicism or emigrate after the disastrous defeat of the Protestant Bohemian Estates in 1620.[4] The sudden loss of the intellectual elite resulted in a drastic decline in literary production.

Humanist Greek poetry had an even shorter life given that the department of Greek studies was only founded in 1537 at the University of Prague. Before that date, several people learned Greek abroad, the most famous being **Bohuslav Hasištejnský z Lobkovic** (ca. 1461–1510). Others studied in Wittenberg, such as **Matouš Collinus** (1516–1566),[5] who, as the first professor of Greek at the University of Prague, gave classes on Greek grammar and lectures on Homer's *Iliad*. The few poems he composed in Greek are short and are usually provided with a word-to-word Latin translation, evidently because he did not expect that many people

---

With assistance by Stefan Weise (SW) in the chapters on Engel and Křesadlo.

---

1 For the Hussite wars, see Kaminsky 2004.
2 For the most part of the Bohemian Renaissance Humanism, the University of Prague was in fact Utraquist. Utraquists were a faction of the Hussite movement, but their views of the Catholic Church were usually moderate. For further information on the Utraquist church, see Haberkern 2016, 3–4.
3 For the history of Prague University, see Čornejová/Svatoš/Svobodný 2001.
4 For the Battle of White Mountain and its repercussions, see Thomas 2010, 251–294.
5 For another Bohemian graduate of Wittenberg University, see below Šebestián (Sebastianus) Aerichalcus.

https://doi.org/10.1515/9783110652758-007

would understand Greek at the time. However, with Collinus's and his colleagues' efforts, knowledge of Greek increased considerably, although it remained very exclusive. It was not unusual, even in the first decade of the 17th century, for some authors to provide their Greek poems with Latin translations. Nevertheless, most Greek poems, and the best ones, appear in the first twenty years of the 17th century. There are approximately twenty authors who can be considered major, given that they wrote more than one Greek poem and were clearly skilled in Greek composition.[6] They were mainly connected to the University of Prague, but it was customary to study abroad too, usually in Wittenberg or Leipzig. Some of them, after having completed their studies, accepted offers to teach at local Latin schools (e.g., in Žatec,[7] Čáslav, Kutná Hora, Jihlava, etc.).[8] It is possible that they also occasionally taught Greek there, although there is little evidence to prove it.

The genres of Humanist Greek poetry copy the patterns of Latin composition, which usually served a particular purpose. On the one hand, it was a means of learned communication among friends and colleagues (congratulations and condolences, etc.). On the other hand, the ability to write quality occasional poetry was invaluable for those who needed an influential patron. Last but not least, some genres were specifically linked to university events, such as graduations. The most frequent example of artificial poetry that is to be found in the Bohemian lands of the time is certainly the epigram, while epic and elegy, usually concerning the Christian faith, are in a minority.[9]

After the University of Prague was closed in 1622, this practice began to wane. Some authors still published abroad, but in the end, the ability to compose Greek poetry died with them. The university education was in the hands of Jesuits whose objectives for learning and teaching Greek were so very different from those of the Humanists who wrote poetry mostly as a means of communication. There are Greek grammar books, multilingual dictionaries and studies on Greek pronunciation published by the Jesuit order in the 17th and 18th centuries. It is therefore clear that ancient Greek was still taught, but the main reasons were probably similar to modern ones, that is, to understand and translate the works of Greek authors rather than actively write poetry in ancient Greek. There is a rare

---

6 Some accomplished authors could not fit within the frame of this anthology, e.g. Pavel (Paulus) Saphirides (died in 1599), Martin Faberius (died in 1599), Jan Prosdokonymus (before 1572–1625), et al. For Prosdokonymus, see Slavíková 2020, 240 and 250–252.
7 See below Jakub (Jacobus) Strabo, below.
8 For the local Latin schools, see Storchová 2011, 231–255.
9 For the genres of Latin occasional poetry, see Martínek 2014, 200–212. For further detail on Humanist Greek poetry in the Bohemian Lands, see Slavíková 2020, 233–253.

epic work by the Jesuit priest **Arnoldus Engel** (1620–1690), which is unlike anything the Humanist authors wrote, regardless of whether its genre or its extent are taken into account. However, Engel provided his Greek text with a Latin translation, which means that, once again, he did not expect a very wide readership. Then, in the last third of the 18th century the Czech national revival movement began[10] and consequently most Czech intellectual efforts were directed towards the production of Czech literature rather than that of Latin, let alone Greek. Finally, at the end of the 19th century and in the 20th century, only a classical philologist or a professor of ancient Greek would probably compose poetry in ancient Greek. Paradoxically, the 20th century is somewhat richer in Greek poetry than the 19th century, which is mostly due to **Jan Křesadlo** (1926–1995),[11] whose extensive epic poem titled *Astronautilia* surpasses any Greek work that has been written in the Czech lands since the Renaissance.

General Bibliography

Čornejová, Ivana/Svatoš, Michal/Svobodný, Petr (eds.) (2001), *A History of Charles University. Volume I (1348–1802)*, Prague.
Haberkern Phillip, N. (2016), *Patron Saint and Prophet in the Bohemian and German Reformations*, New York.
Hejnic, Josef/Martínek, Jan (2011), *Rukověť humanistického básnictví v Čechách a na Moravě/ Enchiridion renatae poesis in Bohemia et Moravia cultae*, Dodatky A-Ž, Praha.
Jakubcová, Alena/Pernerstorfer, Matthias J. (2013), *Theater in Böhmen, Mähren und Schlesien von den Anfängen bis zum Ausgang des 18. Jahrhunderts: ein Lexikon*, Wien.
Kaminsky, Howard (2004), *A History of the Hussite Revolution*, Eugene.
Král, Josef (1898), "Řecké básnictví humanistické v Čechách až do konce samostatné university Karlovy", in: *Rozpravy filologické věnované Janu Gebauerovi*, Praha, 86–105.
Macura, Vladimír (1998), "Problems and paradoxes of the national revival", in: Mikuláš Teich (ed.), *Bohemia in History*, Cambridge, 182–197.

---

10 For the Czech national revival, see Macura 1998, 182–197.
11 Recently, four Greek poems by the Czech composer and musicologist Jarmil Burghauser (1921–1997) were discovered in the course of the Charles University student project titled *Skauting za 2. světové války: Jarmil Burghauser a jeho deníky ve starořečtině* (*Scouting Activities during the 2nd World War: Jarmil Burghauser and His Diaries in Ancient Greek*, 2017). The poems which are a part of Burghauser's diary nr. 3 (dated between the 24th of June and the 28th of August, 1940) and nr. 6 (dated between the 16th of September, 1941 and the 31st of July, 1942) are an odd mixture of epic vocabulary and Sapphic inspiration combined with bucolic motifs, and appear to have been a result of his school efforts.

Martínek, Jan (2014), "Lateinische Gelegenheitspoesie in den Böhmischen Ländern und in Deutschland im 16. und 17. Jahrhundert", in: *Martiniana, Studie o latinském humanismu v českých zemích*, Praha.

Slavíková, Marcela (2020), "Γενεὴν Βοίημος. Humanist Greek Poetry in the Bohemian Lands", in: Mika Kajava/Tua Korhonen/Jamie Vesterinen (eds.), *MEILICHA DÔRA. Poems and Prose in Greek from Renaissance and Early Modern Europe*, Helsinki, 247–267.

Storchová, Lucie (2011), *Paupertate styloque connecti, Utváření humanistické učenecké komunity v českých zemích*, Praha.

Storchová, Lucie (ed.) (2020), *Companion to Central and Eastern European Humanism*, vol. 2: Czech Lands: Part 1 (A–L).

Storchová, Lucie (ed.) (forthcoming), *Companion to Central and Eastern European Humanism*, vol. 2: Czech Lands: Part 2 (M–Z).

Thomas, Andrew L. (2010), *A House Divided, Wittelsbach Confessional Court Cultures in the Holy Roman Empire, C. 1550–1650*, Leiden/Boston.

Truhlář, Antonín/Hrdina, Karel/Hejnic, Josef/Martínek, Jan (1966–1982), *Rukověť humanistického básnictví v Čechách a na Moravě od konce 15. století do začátku 17. století/Enchiridion renatae poesis in Bohemia et Moravia cultae*, Praha: vol. 1 (A–C) 1966; vol. 3 (K–M) 1969; vol. 4 (N–Ř) 1973; vol. 5 (S–Ž) 1982.

Bohuslav Hasištejnský z Lobkovic (ca. 1461–1510)/ Bohuslaus of Lobkowicz and Hassenstein

Ad Psarum [inter 1501/02 et 1510]

> Τεύχεσιν οἱ λαοὶ χαίρουσιν, Ψαρέ, τί ποιῶ
> τῶν ἐν τοῖς πολέμοις Πιερίδων ἱερεύς;

Textus: Bohuslaus Hasisteynius a Lobkowitz, *Farrago poematum in ordinem digestorum ac editorum*, Pragae 1570, 193; Vaculínová, Marta (ed.) (2012), *Bohuslaw Lobkowitz von Hassenstein, Opera poetica*, Leipzig, 204 (Graeca ed. Barbora Krylová).

Crit.: 1 τί Krylová: τι ed.

Sim.: 1 Τεύχεσιν οἱ λαοὶ χαίρουσιν] cf. Thgn., ubi similia dicuntur; e.g. 1.53 (Κύρνε, πόλις μὲν ἔθ' ἥδε πόλις, λαοὶ δὲ δὴ ἄλλοι); Thgn. 1.886 (κακοῦ δ' οὐκ ἔραμαι πολέμου) ‖ **2** Πιερίδων ἱερεύς] cf. *Anth. Pal.* 7.35.2 (Πιερίδων πρόπολος); cf. Plu. *Sept.* 150a1 (ἱερεὺς τῶν Ἀρδαλείων Μουσῶν).

To Psarus

> People are pleased to wear armour again. Psarus, what am I to do in war, being a priest of the Muses?

Metre: Elegiac couplet.

Notes: Hasištenjský was a prolific poet who composed in various genres. He also wrote several treatises on moral philosophy, but he was never keen on publishing his works himself. His poems were edited by Tomáš Mitis, a member of Jan Hodějovský's circle (see below, Matouš Collinus), and published in a book of collected poems *(Illustris ac generosi D. Bohuslai Hasisteynii a Lobkowitz...farrago poematum)* in 1562 and 1570, but only the latter edition survives. Two books of epigrams are included which abound in witty sarcasm and are clearly indicative of the author's talent and erudition. There are several Latin translations from Greek in the books as well as numerous allusions to Greek texts and the literary tradition (Homer, Hesiod, Sappho, Theognis, et al.). However, only two short epigrams are Greek, while one is composed in Latin combined with Greek. All Greek epigrams are addressed to Jan Sturnus *(Psarus)*, who was Hasištejnský's colleague at Hasištejn School from 1501 or 1502. The epigram evokes the dichotomy of warrior and poet, notably combined in Archilochus fr. 1 W.

Biography: Bohuslav Hasištejnský z Lobkovic (Bohuslaw Lobkowitz von Hassenstein, etc.) was a Bohemian nobleman of considerable erudition and influence. Born ca. 1461, he studied in Italy from 1475 (Bologna, Ferrara), where he obtained the degree of Doctor in canon law (1482). Despite his Utraquist family background, he converted to Catholicism. During his life he visited most of the countries in the Mediterranean including Syria, Palestine, Egypt, and Tunisia. He was in close contact with influential people throughout all of Europe, either in person or through correspondence. He aspired to the office of bishop (both in Olomouc and in Prague) and held several state offices. From 1503 he led a private school for his noble young relatives in Hasištejn Castle, where he died in 1510.

Bibliography: Ford, Philip/Bloemendal, Jan/Fantazzi, Charles E. (eds.) (2014), *Brill's Encyclopedia of the Neo-latin World*, Leiden/Boston, 416f.; "Lobkowicz und Hassenstein, Bohuslaus von", in: Walther Killy (ed.) (1990), *Literaturlexikon. Autoren und Werke deutscher Sprache*, vol. 7, Gütersloh/München, 315f.; Kyzourová, Ivana (ed.) (2007), *Básník a král. Bohuslav Hasištejnský z Lobkovic v zrcadle jagellonské doby*, Praha; Slavíková 2020, 235f.; Vaculínová, Marta (2009), "Humanistische Dichter aus den böhmischen Ländern und ihre Präsenz in den gedruckten nicht bohemikalen Anthologien des 16.–17. Jahrhunderts", in: *Listy filologické/ Folia philologica* 132, no. 1/2, 9–23; Vaculínová, Marta/Slavíková, Marcela (2020), "Lobkowicz and Hassenstein, Bohuslaus of", in: Storchová 2020, 688–701; "z Lobkovic, Bohuslav Hasištejnský", in: Truhlář/Hrdina/Hejnic/Martínek (3) 1969, 170–203.

Šebestián (Sebastianus) Aerichalcus (ca. 1515–1555)

S. AE. P. Lectori [post 1546]

    Ἔλδεαι, ὑψίβατον πτερύγεσσιν ἐς ἠέρα βαίνων,
        ὀπτεύειν μεγάλου μέρμερα ἔργα θεοῦ·
    οὐ σοὶ ταῦθ', ἃ ποθεῖς, πορέει φύσις, οὐδ' ἄρ' ἀνάγκη
        Ἰκαρίην σε λαχεῖν Δαιδαλέην τε φύσιν.
5   Ὄμματ' ἐνὶ κραδίῃ σαυτοῦ παμφεγγέα πῆξον,
        τεύξεαι ἠγαθέῃ σύμφορα πολλὰ φρενί.
    Γνώσεαι ἀμφαδίην σεμναῖς πραπίδεσσιν, ἔδωκε
        πολλὰ φύσις κραδίῃ ὡς χαρίεντα τεῇ.
    Ταῦτα σὺ μὴ κρατερῶν ὕβριζ' ὡς φῦλα γιγάντων,
10   ἀλλ' ὥσπερ μεγάλου θαῦμα σέβαζε θεοῦ.

Textus: Aerichalcus, Sebastianus (ca. 1546), *Descriptiones affectuum, quae extant in libello de Anima*, Pragae?, in fronte operis; Král 1898, 88 (vv. 1–6).

Crit.: 3 οὐ σοὶ ταῦθ' corr.: ὂυ σὸι ταυθ' ed. | ἃ Král: ἄ ed. || 5 πῆξον Král: πήξον ed. || 6 ἠγαθέῃ Král: ἠ- ed. || 8 κραδίῃ: -η ed. | τεῇ: -ῇ ed. || 9 Ταῦτα σὺ: ταῦτὰ συ ed. | ὕβριζ' ὡς: ὕβριζ, ὣς ed.

Sim.: 1 Ἔλδεαι] cf. Hom. *Od.* 23.6; cf. Pind. *Ol.* 1.4 | ἐς ἠέρα] cf. *Anth. Pal.* 7.699.1 (Ἰκάρου ὦ νεόφοιτον ἐς ἠέρα πωτηθέντος) || 2 ὀπτεύειν] cf. Ar. *Av.* 1061 (Πᾶσαν μὲν γὰρ γᾶν ὀπτεύω) | μέρμερα ἔργα] cf. Hom. *Il.* 8.453; 10.524; cf. etiam Hes. *Theog.* 603 || 5 Ὄμματ'– πῆξον] cf. Hom. *Il.* 3.217 (ὄμματα πήξας); Ap. Rhod. *Argon.* 3.422 | παμφεγγέα] cf. Soph. *El.* 105–106 (παμφεγγεῖς ἄστρων ῥιπάς) || 6 τεύξεαι] cf. Hes. *Op.* 401 || 9 φῦλα γιγάντων] cf. Hom. *Od.* 7.206; Hom. *Batr.* 283; Nonn. *Dion.* 1.18.

S(ebastianus) Ae(richalcus) from Přeštice to the reader

You wish to fly high up the air and see the miraculous deeds of the great God. But your nature does not allow you to do what you long for, and there is also no need to become Icarus or Daedalus. [5] You just have to keep looking into your own heart with bright eyes and you will create many useful things in your sacred soul. You will openly realise in your holy mind that nature has bestowed many graces upon your heart. Do not be arrogant about it as the tribe of fierce giants used to be, [10] but revere it as a miracle of the great God.

Metre: Elegiac couplets.

Notes: The five Greek elegiac couplets by Šebestián Aerichalcus were printed on the title page of his philosophical poem *Descriptiones affectuum*, in which he faithfully followed Melanchthon's *Commentarius de anima*. There is no date of publication on the title page. However, one of the additional poems included in the book addresses the solar eclipse of 9 June 1546. There are no further Greek poems preserved under Aerichalcus's name, but it is evident that he had a solid knowledge of Greek grammar and phraseology and was clearly well-versed in Greek literature, particularly the Homeric epic, Hesiod, and the *Greek (Planudean) Anthology*.

Biography: Šebestián Aerichalcus (Sebastianus Aerichalcus Praesticenus; abbrev. S. AE. P.) was born ca 1515. From 1540 he studied in Wittenberg, where he got his Master's degree in 1544. For the rest of his life he was a professor of Classics at the University of Prague, where he also held several major offices, including those of dean and rector. He died of the plague in 1555. He specialised in the comedy of Terence and introduced Greek classes into Latin schools.

Bibliography: Jakubcová/Pernerstorfer 2013, 1 (s.v. "Sebastianus Aerichalcus"); Storchová, Lucie (2020), "Aerichalcus, Sebastianus", in: Storchová 2020, 84–88; Truhlář/Hrdina/Hejnic/ Martínek (1) 1966, 49–52 (s.v. "Aerichalcus, Šebestián"); on his Greek poems: Král 1898, 88.

Matouš (Matthaeus) Collinus (1516–1566)

Epitaphium M. Martini Hannonis, vita functi 22. Novembris. Anno 1550. Autore Mattheo Collino [1551]

Ἄννων Μαρτῖνος γενεὴν Βοίημος ἐν αἴῃ
  τῇδε θανὼν μέμορεν κηρὸς ἀερσίποδος.
Εἴκοσι γὰρ βιότοιο μόγις καὶ τέσσαρ' ἔφηβος
  πλῆσεν ἔτη, ὅτε μιν ὄσσε κάλυψε μόρος.
5 Ἐσθλὸς ἀοιδὸς ἔην, ἐσθλὸς δέ τε μάντις, ὃς αὐδᾶν
  ἐσσόμεν' ἐκ διδαχῆς οἶδε μαθηματικῆς.
Ἀλλ' ὅτι ζηλώσας Φοῖβον καὶ ἰατρικὰ στέρξεν,
  τῷ μιν ἀπεχθήρας ἐξεμάρηνε θεός.

Textus: *Epicedia scripta honestis et eruditis viris M. Martino Hannoni...*, Wittenbergae 1551, c. A IIIv; Král 1898, 88–89.

Crit.: 1 Βοιημός Král ǁ 2 κηρὸς Král: -ος ed. ǁ 3 βιότοιο Král: βιοτοῖο ed. ǁ 5 ἐσθλὸς δέ: ἐσθλος δέ ed. | ὃς Král: ὅς ed. | αὐδᾶν: αυ- ed. ǁ 6 ἐσσόμεν': ἐσσομεν' ed. ǁ 8 ἀπεχθήρας correxi: ἐπεχθήρας ed.

Sim.: 2 μέμορεν] sc. ἔμμορεν; cf. Hrd. Περὶ παθῶν 383.3 (μείρω μέμαρκα μέμορε ἔμμορε) | ἀερσίποδος] cf. Hom. *Il.* 3.327 (ἵπποι ἀερσίποδες); cf. etiam Hom. *Il.* 23.475; Nonn. *Dion.* 2.22 (ἀερσιπόδης δὲ Τυφωεύς) ǁ 4 πλῆσεν ἔτη] cf. *Anth. Gr. App.* 100.2 (παντὸς μοῖραν ἔπλησε βίου) | ὄσσε κάλυψε μόρος] cf. Hom. *Il.* 4.461 (τὸν δὲ σκότος ὄσσε κάλυψεν); cf. etiam Hom. *Il.* 4.503; 4.526; 6.11 et al. ǁ 6 ἐσσόμεν'] cf. Hom. *Il.* 1.70 (ὅς ᾔδη τά τ' ἐόντα τά τ' ἐσσόμενα πρό τ' ἐόντα); cf. etiam Hes. *Theog.* 38 ǁ 8 ἀπεχθήρας] cf. Hom. *Il.* 3.415 (τὼς δέ σ' ἀπεχθήρω ὡς νῦν ἔκπαγλ' ἐφίλησα) | ἐξεμάρηνε] cf. *Anth. Pal.* 12.234.4 (ταῦτα δ' ὁμῇ φθονέων ἐξεμάρανε χρόνος).

Epitaph on Master Martin Hanno, died on 22 November 1550, by Matthaeus Collinus

Martin Hanno, Bohemian by birth, has died in this land; he had been allotted a rapid death. He was a youth who had hardly completed four and twenty years, when fate closed his eyes. [5] He was a great poet, he was a great prophet too, who could predict the future through his knowledge of mathematics. But because he emulated Apollo and was also fond of medicine, the god became jealous and let him fade away.[12]

---

[12] **Author's Latin translation:** *Hanno Martinus, patria Boiemus, in ora / Mortuus hac, celerem lapsus in interitum est. / Nam vix viginti iuvenis compleverat annos / Bisque duos, ipsum dum rapit*

Metre: Elegiac couplets.

Notes: The poem is an epicedium for Martin Hanno, Collinus's student and a cherished member of Hodějovský's circle. He enrolled at Wittenberg University to complete his academic education, but died shortly after his matriculation, in 1550, after an outbreak of plague in Wittenberg. Collinus's Greek epicedium for Hanno is one of the eight Greek poems that have been preserved under his name. The poem, which Collinus provided with a parallel Latin version, is clearly indicative of the author's sound knowledge of Homeric epic and the *Greek Anthology*. Despite a certain rigidity in expression, the poem is extremely valuable, since it is one of the earliest poems in Greek that was written in the Bohemian lands.

Biography: Matouš Collinus (Matthaeus Collinus a Choterina) was one of the most influential Humanist scholars in Bohemia. Born in 1516, he studied in Prague and from 1534 in Wittenberg, where he attended Philipp Melanchthon's classes, although his teacher of Greek was Veit Winsheim. After having received his Master's degree in 1540, he returned to Prague and was appointed to be the first professor of Greek at the University. He gave lectures on Homer's *Iliad*, Greek grammar, as well as on numerous Latin authors. Apart from Melanchthon, he maintained correspondence with scholars around Europe. His educational and literary efforts gained him support among the Bohemian nobility, most importantly from Jan the Elder Hodějovský. With his help, Collinus built a wide circle of poets who represented the first generation of Humanist poetry in the Bohemian lands. However, only very few of the poems were composed in Greek.

Bibliography: Hejnic, Josef (1964), "Filip Melanchton, Matouš Collinus a počátky měšťanského humanismu v Čechách", in: *Listy filologické/Folia philologica* 87, no. 2, 1964, 361–379; Říčan, Rudolf (1963), "Melanchthon und die böhmischen Länder", in: *Philipp Melanchthon, Humanist, Reformator, Praeceptor Germaniae*, Berlin, 237–260; Slavíková 2020, 236–238; Storchová, Lucie (ed.) (2014), "Biographical Sketches of Humanist Editors Active in the Literary Field of Prague University: Matthaeus Collinus (1516–1566)", in: *Europa Humanistica 16, Bohemia and Moravia*, vol. II, *Bohemian School Humanism and its Editorial Practices (ca. 1550–1610)*, Turnhout, 73–76; Storchová, Lucie (2020), "Collinus, Matthaeus", in: Storchová 2020, 298–316; "Collinus, Matouš", in: Truhlář/Hrdina/Hejnic/Martínek (1) 1966, 416–451; on his Greek poems: Král 1898, 88–89; Slavíková 2020, 248.

---

atra dies. / Cantor erat praestans et noverat ille futura / Dicere per geneses arte Mathematica. / Sed quia zelatus Phoebum coluisse parabat, / Artem etiam medicam Paeoniumque decus, / Hinc illum Phoebus corpus siccante marasmo, / Percussit nigra percitus invidia.

Jakub (Jacobus) Strabo (ca. 1553-1582)

Πρὸς Χριστὸν δέησις περὶ λύσεως τοῦ βίου [1575]

(excerptum, vv. 1-16)

>Ἔστιν ὡς κύμβη βιότου πορεία,
>συμφορῶν κόσμῳ ἐν ἄκρῳ τυχοῦσα
>κύμασι φλοίσβοις τε κακῶν φορεῖται
>ἔνθα καὶ ἔνθα.
>5 Ἥκει ἐκ βαθμῶν στυγεροῖο ᾅδου
>καὶ ἑῷ θυμῷ κακότητα τεύχει,
>τὴν κολυμβούσην ἀπολεῖν μεμηλὼς
>ἀχλύος ἄρχων.
>Σὰρξ παθῶν οἶδμ᾽ ἀργαλέων βαρείας
>10 χεῖρας εἰς πράξεις ἀδίκων ἄγουσα,
>καὶ νόον φθαρτὸν φρονέειν ἐγείρει
>αἰσχρὰ ὀλοιά.
>Φαῦλοι ἄνθρωποι δόμον οὐρανοῖο
>θεῖον ἐχθαίροντες, ἑοῖς ἀτάκτοις
>15 δείγμασ᾽ εἰς τάφρον θανάτοιο αὐτὴν
>ἐμφορέουσιν.

Textus: *Symbolum viri pietate, doctrina, prudentia...praestantis D. Ioannis Balbini*, ex coetu scholae Zatecensis 1575; Král 1898, 93 (vv. 1-8 tantum).

Crit.: tit. λύσεως Král: λούσεως ed. || **1** ὡς Král: ὣς ed. || **5** Ἥκει Král: Ἡ- ed. || **7** κολυμβούσην ed.: κολυμβῶσαν malim || **9** βαρείας temptavi: βαρεῖ ἥν ed. || **10** ἀδίκων corr.: ἀδικῶν ed. || **12** ὀλοιά Weise: ὀλειά ed. || **14** ἐχθαίροντες corr.: αἰθχαίροντες ed. || **16** ἐμφορέουσιν corr.: Εμφορεούσιν ed.

Sim.: 3 κύμασι φλοίσβοις] cf. Hom. *Il.* 13.798 (κύματα παφλάζοντα πολυφλοίσβοιο θαλάσσης) || **4** ἔνθα καὶ ἔνθα] cf. Hom. *Il.* 2.476; 2.799; 2.812 et al. || **5** Ἥκει ἐκ βαθμῶν στυγεροῖο ᾅδου] cf. Ap. Rhod. *Argon.* 3.810 (στυγεροῖο κατὰ φρένας ἦλθ᾽ Ἀίδαο) || **9** βαρείας χεῖρας] cf. Hom. *Il.* 1.89; 21.548; Ap. Rhod. *Argon.* 2.69-70 || **13** Φαῦλοι ἄνθρωποι] cf. Pl. *Euthyd.* 305a7

A Prayer to Christ for the End of Life

(excerpt, ll. 1-16)

>The journey of life is like a boat which by a series of misfortunes on the surface of the world is snatched up by roaring waves of evils and is carried to and fro. [5] The ruler of mist is coming from the depths of dreadful hell and is devising evil in his mind, as he wants to destroy the boat that is already sinking. The body is a sea of violent passions; [10] it makes

the strong hands do unjust things and rouses the mortal mind to conceive ignoble and deadly thoughts. Ordinary people hate the divine house of heaven and by their [15] evident lawlessness, they carry the boat to the grave of death.

Metre: Sapphic stanzas.

Notes: Strabo's poem titled Πρὸς Χριστὸν δέησις περὶ λύσεως τοῦ βίου (1575) is one of the two Greek poems that have been preserved under Strabo's name and was, apparently, the earliest Greek piece that a Bohemian author composed in a metre different from the elegiac couplet, which had been prevalent until then. The extent of the poem, consisting of nine Sapphic stanzas, is rather ambitious and the choice of the Sapphic metre suggests that the author was adept in Greek prosody, although there are some grammatical mistakes that might not be solely ascribed to the typographer's incompetence. Despite the Sapphic metre, the vocabulary is mostly epic.

Biography: Jakub Strabo was born in the South Bohemian town of Klatovy. The date of his birth is uncertain, however, he matriculated at Wittenberg University in 1571. He continued his studies at the University of Prague, from which he graduated with a Master's degree in 1576. From 1573 to 1577 he was the director of a Latin school in Žatec, but he then preferred an administrative position at the town hall. He died of the plague in 1582, praised by his contemporaries for his knowledge of Hebrew and Greek.

Bibliography: Storchová (forthcoming); Storchová 2011, 245–249; Truhlář/Hrdina/Hejnic/Martínek (5) 1982, 207–208; on his Greek poems: Král 1898, 92–93.

Henricus Polanus (active around 1599)

Psalmus CVI. [1599]

(excerptum, vv. 1–12)

    Ὅς ῥα θεοῦ σκιεραῖσιν ὑπὸ πτερύγεσσι κάθηται,
    ὅστε πανυψίστοιο κραταιῇ χειρὶ πέποιθε,
    τοιάδ' ἀτάρβητόν τε καὶ ἄτρομον ἦτορ ἀέξων,
    ὃν θεόν, ὃν γενετῆρα τεθαρσηκὼς προσέειπε·
5   Ἐλπὶς ἐμή, θεός, ἔσσι, σύ μοι σάκος, ᾧ ῥα κατ' ἐχθρῶν
    ὥπλισμαι στιβαρῶς, καὶ χαλκεόπτυκτος ἐτύχθης
    πυργὸς ἐμοὶ καὶ ἔρυμμα, θοῶν θοὸν ἔχμα βελέμνων.
    Καίπερ ἐμοὶ παγίδας καὶ ἐμοὶ κακὰ μυρία τεύχοι

ἐχθρὸς ὁ θηρητὴρ καὶ δίκτυα μυρία τείνοι,
10 οὔθ᾽ ἓν ἔγωγε κακὸν δειδίσσομαι οὔτε φοβοῦμαι
δίκτυ᾽, ἐπεὶ μέν, ἄναξ, πρόσθ᾽ ἵστασαι ἠδὲ φυλάσσεις
σῶον ἄτερθε κακῶν καὶ ἐμοὶ ἀπὸ λοιγὸν ἀμύνεις.

Textus: *Psalmus XCI. Graecolatino heroico carmine expressus: addita elegia succincta De sanctis angelis*, Gorlicii 1599 (versus omnes 74).

Crit.: 1 Ὅς ῥα corr.: Ὸς ῥά ed. || **3** ἀτάρβητόν τε corr.: ἀτάρβητόντε ed. || **5** Ἐλπὶς corr.: Ελπίς ed. | θεός, ἐσσι corr.: θεός ἐσσί ed. | σύ μοι corr.: σύ μοὶ ed. | ᾧ ῥα corr.: ὣ ῥά ed. || **6** ὥπλισμαι corr.: ὤπλισμαι ed. | χαλκεόπτυκτος temptavi: χαλκώπυκτος ed. (incert.) || **7** ἔρυμμα] ἔρυμα malim || **10** οὔθ᾽ ἓν corr.: οὐθ᾽ ἕν ed. | κακὸν corr.: κακόν ed. || **11** ἐπεὶ μὲν corr.: ἐπεί μεν ed. || **12** ἐμοὶ ἀπὸ corr.: ἐμοί ἀπό ed.

Sim.: 1 σκιεραῖσιν ὑπὸ πτερύγεσσι] cf. Nonn. *Dion.* 48.635 (σκιεραῖς πτερύγεσσι) || **2** κραταιῇ χειρί] cf. Eur. *HF* 964 (κραταιᾶς χειρός) || **4** προσέειπε] cf. Hom. *Il.* 1.105 et al. || **7** θοὸν ἔχμα βελέμνων] cf. Ap. Rhod. *Argon.* 4.201 (θοὸν ἔχμα βολάων) || **8** κακὰ μυρία] cf. Plu. *Agis* 37.4.4; Pl. *Leg.* 789a1 (μυρία κακά) || **12** ἀπὸ λοιγὸν ἀμύνεις] cf. Hom. *Il.* 1.67 (ἀπὸ λοιγὸν ἀμῦναι); cf. etiam Hom. *Il.* 16.75

Psalm 106

(excerpt, ll. 1–12)

> Whoever sits protected by the shadowy wings of God and trusts the powerful hand of the Highest, they cherish it in their fearless, intrepid heart and address their God, their Creator, with confidence: [5] 'God, you are my hope, you are my strong armour which I wear against my foes, and you are my defensive tower panelled with bronze, my wall, my quick defence against quick darts. So even if my enemy, the hunter, lays thousands of traps and causes thousands of troubles, if he spreads out thousands of nets, [10] I will not fear even one of those troubles; I am not afraid of nets, when you, my Lord, stand close and protect me so as to be safe from evil, and when you defend me from harm.'[13]

Metre: Hexameters.

---

13 Author's Latin translation: *Quem Deus alarum sub opaca contegit umbra, / Quem virtus summique levat manus alma Tonantis, / Ille Deum, ille suum scit compellare parentem / Intrepido tales depromens pectore voces: / Spes mihi firma Deus, scutum, quo fortiter hostes / Contra eo. Tu mihi, quae iaculatur perfidus hostis, / Telorum tutela ingens atque aenea turris. / In te tuta mihi spes et fiducia fixa est. / Et mihi mille licet laqueos et retia mille, / Mille astus nectat, fallacibus undique technis / Infestans miserorum hominum genus, haud tamen ipse / Mille dolos metuam, non mille pericla pavescam. / Incolumem me namque Dei custodia servat.*

Notes: The poem, inspired by Psalm 91, was published in 1599. It is dedicated to Charles the Younger of Žerotín, whose family helped Polanus to find an occupation as a preceptor a year later. The author provided the poem with a parallel Latin version which is close enough to the Greek original to convey the same meaning but has individual artistic qualities in part due to the author's knowledge of correct Latin phraseology. The same applies to the Greek version which, although being lexically and syntactically rather simple, is very impressive in its religiosity.

Biography: Henricus Polanus Iunior a Polansdorf was born in Opava where his father, of the same name, held an administrative position at the town hall. The date of Polanus's birth is uncertain. However, he matriculated at Basel University in 1599. Through his uncle Amandus Polanus, who had made influential contacts among the Moravian nobility, he became a preceptor in 1600 and visited Strasbourg. After he left the service without notice, no further information about him is attested.

Bibliography: Hrubý, František (1970), *Étudiants Tchèques aux écoles protestantes de l'Europe occidentale à la fin du 16ᵉ et au début du 17ᵉ siècle*, Brno, 89; Truhlář/Hrdina/Hejnic/Martínek (4) 1973, 219 (s.v. "Polanus a Polansdorf, Henricus").

Leonhartus Albertus (before 1583–after 1607)

Per leviora ad graviora [1603]

>   Οὐ τυχὸν ἀνθρώπῳ συμβήσεται, ὅττι μενοινᾷ.
>   Ἔργοις, ὡς εἰκός, χρηστέον ἐστὶ μέσοις.
>   Οὕτω σπευδομένῳ ἐρατῆς ἀρετῆς ποτὶ ἄκρα
>   πρὸς χαλέπ᾽ οἶμος ἀεί ἐστι δι᾽ εὐχερέων.

Textus: Leonhartus Albertus, *Epigrammatum liber I.*, Pragae 1603, A8.

Crit.: 1 Οὐ corr.: Ου ed. | μενοινᾷ corr.: -ᾶ ed. || 2 Ἔργοις corr.: Ε- ed. | ὡς εἰκός corr.: ὡς ἐικὸς ed. || 3 Οὕτω corr.: Ὕυτω ed.

Sim.: 3 ἀρετῆς ποτὶ ἄκρα] cf. Hes. *Op.* 289–292, ubi similia dicuntur; cf. etiam Stob. *Anth.* 3.1.205b22.

Through easier to heavier business

Whatever people desire, they cannot have it by mere chance, but they evidently must make an effort in the meanwhile. Therefore, whoever strives to reach the peak of lovely prowess, they must always take the path which is easy in the beginning, but leads towards the difficult.[14]

Metre: Elegiac couplets.

Notes: There are five Greek pieces in Albertus's *Epigrammaton liber I.* (1603), all composed in the elegiac couplet. The poem titled *Per leviora ad graviora* is provided with two parallel Latin versions. It was clearly inspired by Hesiod's *Opera et dies* 289–292, although the original idea is somewhat modified.

Biography: Leonhartus Albertus (Schlacovaldensis) was born before 1583 near Schlaggenwald in West Bohemia (hence the epithet). He studied in Prague where he then lived from 1601 to 1607, giving private classes of Latin and Greek. Some of his students were from noble families, which provided him with influential patrons and other contacts. His contemporaries appreciated his poetry on biblical and other religious matters. In 1603, he published his *Epigrammatum liber I.*, which, apart from occasional poems, contains Latin and Greek epigrams of good artistic quality. After 1607, there is no further information about him attested.

Bibliography: Hejnic/Martínek 2011, 35 (s.v. "Albertus, Leonhartus"); El Kholi, Susann (2013), "Ein poetisches Zeugnis für Buchausleihe im frühen 17. Jahrhundert: das Briefgedicht des Leonhartus Albertus an Jan Theodor von Ottersdorf", in: *Wolfenbütteler Notizen zur Buchgeschichte* 38/1–2, 49–55; El Kholi, Susann/Lněničková, Jitka/Vaculínová, Marta, "Leonhartus Albertus und sein Gedicht über die Glasherstellung", in: *Listy filologické/Folia Philologica* 135, no. 3/4, 2012, 367–402; Truhlář/Hrdina/Hejnic/Martínek (1) 1966, 67–69 (s.v. "Albertus, Leonhartus"); Vaculínová, Marta/Slavíková, Marcela (2020), "Albertus Schlacovaldensis, Leonhartus", in: Storchová 2020, 97–101.

---

14 Author's Latin translations: 1) *Haud casu obtingunt homini, quae pectore versat, / Utendum mediis convenienter erit. / Culmina sic quisquis virtutis ad ardua tendit, / Ad graviora feret per leviora gradum.* 2) *Per leviora prius qui discit figere gressum, / Huic aditus posthac ad graviora patet.*

Jan (Johannes) Campanus (1572–1622)

Allusio ad autoris cognomen [1616]

  Μέλισσε τῆς Ἀθήνης,
  σεμνῶν Μέλισσε Μουσῶν,
  τίς μάντις ᾗ ἄριστος,
  ζητεῖς λόγοισι τοῖσι;
5 Οἰωνὸς εἷς ἄριστος
  ἐμοὶ θεῷ ἕπεσθαι,
  πατρίδ' ἐῇ ἀρήγειν.
  Μάντις δέ μοι φέριστος
  σοφὸς γέρων ὀπίσσω
10 πρόσσω τε πάντα λεύσσων,
  ἄριστα ὡς γένηται.
  Μάντις δέ μοι καὶ ἄστρων
  εἰδὼς φύσιν βλέπων τε
  μέλλοντα ὡς ἐόντα.
15 Οὕτως ἐμοὶ σὺ ἴσθι
  τὴν εἴαρος καθ' ὥραν
  πάντων φέρων ἀπ' ἀνθῶν
  καρποὺς τρόπον μελίσσης.
  Μέλισσε τῆς Ἀθήνης,
20 σεμνῶν Μέλισσε Μουσῶν.

Textus: *Oratio de praesagiis astrologorum ex horoscopo...*, per Jacobum Wczelinum Lstiborenum, Pragae 1616, C2b; Král 1898, 97 (vv. 1–7).

Crit.: 3 τίς μάντις corr. Král: Τις μαντις ed. || 4 σοῖσι deliberat Weise || 5 Οἰωνὸς corr. Král: Ὀιωνός ed. | εἷς corr. Král: εῖς ed. || 6 ἐμοὶ corr.: Εμοι ed.: ἐμοί Král | ἕπεσθαι corr. Král: ἔπεσσαι ed. || 7 πατρίδ' ἐῇ corr.: Πάτρι δ' εῇ ed.: πάτρη δ' ἐῇ Král || 8 δέ μοι corr.: δὲ μοι ed. || 10 λεύσσων corr.: λευσσων ed. || 12 δέ μοι corr.: δὲ μοι ed. || 13 εἰδὼς corr.: Ἐιδὼς ed. | βλέπων τε corr.: βλέπωντε ed. || 15 Οὕτως ἐμοὶ σὺ corr.: Ὀυτως ἔμοὶ συ ed.

Sim.: 3 μάντις ᾗ ἄριστος] cf. Soph. *El.* 1481 (καὶ μάντις ὢν ἄριστος); Eur. fr. 973.1 (μάντις δ' ἄριστος ὅστις εἰκάζει καλῶς) || 5 Οἰωνὸς εἷς ἄριστος] cf. Hom. *Il.* 12.243 (εἷς οἰωνὸς ἄριστος ἀμύνεσθαι περὶ πάτρης) || 9 σοφὸς γέρων] cf. Eur. *Ba.* 185–186 (ἐξηγοῦ σύ μοι γέρων γέροντι, Τειρεσία· σὺ γὰρ σοφός) || 9–10 ὀπίσσω / πρόσσω] cf. Hom. *Il.* 1.343 (ἅμα πρόσσω καὶ ὀπίσσω); 3.109; 18.250; *Od.* 24.452 || 10 πάντα λεύσσων] cf. Soph. *OC* 869 (ὁ πάντα λεύσσων Ἥλιος) || 14 μέλλοντα ὡς ἐόντα] cf. Hom. *Il.* 1.70 (ὃς ᾔδη τά τ' ἐόντα τά τ' ἐσσόμενα πρό τ' ἐόντα) || 16 τὴν εἴαρος καθ' ὥραν] cf. *Anth. Pal.* 11.407.1 (εἴαρος ὥρῃ).

Allusion to the author's name

Beehive of Athena, Beehive of the holy Muses, are you asking in this book who is the most excellent prophet? [5] For me, the most excellent omen is to follow God and help one's country. The best prophet, in my opinion, is a wise old man who can see best past [10] and future, so that everything will be fine. I think that a prophet knows the nature of stars and sees the future as if it were present. [15] Be like this for me, and when the spring comes, collect honey from all the flowers just like a bee. Beehive of Athena, [20] Beehive of the holy Muses.

Metre: Catalectic iambic dimeter.

Notes: This playful iambic piece is an accompanying poem to an astrological treatise by Jakub Včelín (lit. Beehive), whose name Campanus translated into Greek as Μέλισσος. This gives him the welcome opportunity to conclude the poem with lyrical motifs, when he compares the addressee to a bee (μέλισσα) which collects the fruits of assiduous work. The first two verses recur at the end of the poem, providing the perfect closure to the piece. The vocabulary employed indicates Campanus's knowledge of Homeric epic and the Greek dramatists. The repetitions and the simple tune allude to Anacreontic songs where the bee is also a common motif.

Biography: Jan Campanus (Vodňanský) was a Humanist scholar with unparalleled skill in Greek composition. Born in the South Bohemian town of Vodňany (hence his epithet) in 1572, he attended several Latin schools in the region, where he perfected his Latin, even before he enrolled at the University of Prague in 1590. During his university years he had already started publishing poetry, while mastering Greek at the same time. Soon after graduation he became a professor of Greek and Latin literature at the University of Prague. Later he also gave lectures on the history of the Czech lands. Campanus stayed at the University all his life, until it was handed over to the Jesuit Order. He died shortly after, on 13 December 1622. His poetry, composed in both classical languages with equal skill and art, is the creation of a witty and gifted poet, even though his poems are mostly occasional.

Bibliography: Hemelík, Martin (2012), *Jan Campanus Vodňanský: portrét renesančního básníka*, Jihlava; Jakubcová/Pernerstorfer 2013, 104–107 (s.v. "Johannes Campanus Vodňanský"); Martínek, Jan (1990), "De Magistro Campano regni Hungarici laudatore", in: *Listy filologické/Folia Philologica* 113/1, 52–56; Odložilík, Otakar (1938), *Mistr Jan Campanus*, Praha; Slavíková 2020, 240; Vaculínová, Marta/Slavíková, Marcela/Jacková, Magdaléna (2020), "Campanus Vodnianus, Ioannes", in: Storchová 2020, 219–236; Storchová 2011, 192–197; Truhlář/Hrdina/Hejnic/Martínek (1) 1966, 254–299 (s.v. "Campanus [Kumpán], Jan"); on his Greek poems: Král 1898, 96–99; Slavíková 2020, 248–249.

Christophorus Crinesius (1583–1629)

Γαμήλιον *Graeco-Syrum* [1612]

    Σὺ καὶ βουλῇ νόῳ τε
    ἐπιστήμων ἄκοιτιν
    ὡς λαὸς ποιέεις νῦν.
    Γυνὴ ναὶ ἐμπόδισμα;
5   Οὐ δῆτα· ἀνδρὶ μᾶλλον
    ἀλεξιφάρμακον καὶ
    παρήγορος τυχήσει
    πένθους, ἢν τἆλλα κεδνή.
    Ἄξον τοίνυν, ἑταῖρε,
10 πρὸς δῶμά σου γυναῖκα,
    νύμφαν μάλ᾽ αἰγλήεσσαν,
    καὶ ζῶε πουλύτεκνος.

Textus: *Nuptiis Clarissimi Excellentissimique Viri Dn. M. Tobiae Tilemanni... Celebrandis Gratulantur Collegae et Amici*, Wittenberg 1612, A3.

Crit.: 1 νόῳτε ed. || 4 ἐμποδισμα ed. || 5 δεῖτα ed.

Sim.: 1 βουλῇ νόῳ τε ἐπιστήμων] cf. Hom. *Od.* 16.374 (αὐτὸς μὲν γὰρ ἐπιστήμων βουλῇ τε νόῳ τε) || 2–3 ἄκοιτιν...ποιέεις] cf. Hom. *Il.* 9.397 (ποιήσομ᾽ ἄκοιτιν) || 6 ἀλεξιφάρμακον] cf. Men. fr. 313.1–2 (Ἐφέσια τοῖς γαμοῦσιν οὗτος περιπατεῖ λέγων ἀλεξιφάρμακα) || 7–8 παρήγορος...πένθους] cf. Greg. Naz. *De vita* 1324 (τῶν κακῶν παρήγορος) || 11 νύμφαν μάλ᾽ αἰγλήεσσαν] cf. Greg. Naz. *Carm. mor.*, PG 37.907.7–8 (Παρθένος αἰγλήεσσα, περίφρων, ἀγλαόμητις, / Νυμφίον ἧς κραδίης ἁγνὸν ἔχουσα Λόγον) || 12 πουλύτεκνος] cf. Aesch. *PV* 137; Nonn. *Dion.* 25.261 (sed sine productione litterae o: πολύτεκνος)

Greek-Syrian wedding song

You are taking a wife now, as common people do, you, who are wise both in decisions and in mind. Is a wife really an impediment? [5] Oh no! She rather will be an antidote and a comforter in grief if she is good in general. Therefore lead your wife, that very beautiful girl, [10] to your home, my friend, and live blessed with many children.

Metre: Catalectic iambic dimeter.

Notes: This short poem, which the author provided with a parallel Syriac version, is an epithalamion for Tobias Tilemann, who was a professor of mathematics at Wittenberg University. It is a playful dialogue between the author and the bridegroom and, despite its brevity, it is clearly indicative of Crinesius's knowledge of ancient Greek vocabulary and phraseology. Considering that he probably only learned Greek to complete his knowledge of biblical languages, the level of his Greek is all the more extraordinary.

Biography: Christophorus Crinesius (Schlaccowaldo-Bohemus) was born in the West Bohemian town of Schlaggenwald (hence the epithet) in 1583. He studied at the Latin school in his home town and then he proceeded to Leipzig, Jena, and Wittenberg Universities. Apart from Latin and Greek, he acquired a mastery of oriental languages, which he taught at Wittenberg University for several years after his graduation in 1607. However, he also showed an active interest in theology and religious matters and was ordained as a minister of the Lutheran Church. From 1624 until his death in 1629 he was a professor of theology at the University of Altdorf. He composed poetry both in classical and oriental languages, such as Hebrew, Arabic, Syriac, and Aramaic. Most of his poems have several language variations; it was not unusual for him to provide a poem with two, or even three, parallel versions.

Bibliography: "Crinesius, Christophorus", in: Hejnic/Martínek 2011, 88–89; Huber, Karl (1944–45), "Magister Christoph Crinesius", in: *Jahrbuch der Gesellschaft für Geschichte des Protestantismus in Österreich* 65–66, 54–61; Slavíková 2020, 241; Vaculínová, Marta/Slavíková, Marcela/Veselá, Lenka (2020), "Crinesius, Christophorus", in: Storchová 2020, 316–322; "Crinesius (Grünes), Christophorus", in: Truhlář/Hrdina/Hejnic/Martínek (1) 1966, 471–472; on his Greek poems: Slavíková 2020, 252–253.

Arnoldus Engel/Angelus (1620–1690)

Ἐγώ εἰμι τὸ Α.
Ἰησοῦ τοῦ Ἀρχιστρατηγοῦ τεραστία γένεσις ἤγουν Ἀρχὴ Θεανθρώπου.
ΠΟΙΗΜΑ I. [1666]

(excerptum, vv. 1–16)

  Ἐκ Διὸς ἄρχεσθαι, μετὰ πίδακος ἔρρετε, Μοῦσαι·
  ἐκ Διὸς ἄρχεσθαι, οὐ μὴν ὃν ἐγείνατο πατρὸς
  ἀντίον ἡ Κυβέλη, ὃν μὴ Δικταῖα φόρεισκεν
  ἄντρ' ἀμαθοῦς Κρήτης, ὃν μὴ θῆσ' εἷο Μελίσσῃ
5 Ἀδράστεια λέγῃ· ὃν μὴ στενάχοντα πεφάσσων
  χαλκὸς ὑπ' Ἰδαίῳ Κορυβάντων θρέψε κυδοιμῷ,
  ἀλλ' ὃν δὴ γεγαῶτα πατρὶ προ-ἀμήτορα πάντων

Ἡελίου πρὸ φάους καιροῦ πόρρωθεν ἅπαντος
πρόσθε πόλου καὶ γῆς καὶ πόντου δεύτερον ἡ παῖς
10 γείνατο ἀνδρὸς ἄνευ, πόλις ὃν κ' ἀπέδειξεν Ἰέσσης
οἶκον ὑπ' ὀρφναῖον, ΜΑΡΙΑΣ ὃν καὶ γάλα θῆσθαι
ἄστρ' ὑμνοῖ βηλοῖς, ὃν Ἐρήνη, ὃν οὐρανόδοξ', ὃν
Ἀγγελικοὶ φανερῶς γεγαῶτ' ἤκασσι χορηγοί.
Παρθένος ᾧ τόσσου γενετείρα πρόδρομος Ὄρθρου
15 Ἠὼς εὐπράττειν, πελάταις καὶ ὕμνον ἀείδειν,
φῶς δόμεν ἆρ' ἔξεστιν ἀρείονος Ἡελίοιο.

Textus: Prague, Královská kanonie premonstrátů na Strahově, DF V 20, fol. 16r (ms.); Arnoldus Angelus, *Virtutis & honoris aedes In Heroibus et Poëmatis XXV. Graeco-Latinis Ordine Litterarum deductis Adaperta.* Micro-Pragae 1666, 2 (ed.).

Crit.: 3 φόρεισκεν ed., ms.: an φόρεσκεν? || **4** εἶο ed.: ἦγε ms. || **5** Ἀδράστεια λέγῃ ed.: Ἀδράστει' ἐνέπῃ ms. in marg. | πεφάσσων] φρενοπλήξ ms. p.c. in marg., *Ab ἐκπεφάσσω vel pone φρενοπλήξ* ed. in marg. || **8** καίροιο πρὸ παντὸς ἀριθμῶν ms. || **12** Ἐρήνη] *Ἐρήνη & Ἰρήνη abjecta subjunctivâ vel prępositivâ Poëticè adnotat* ed. in marg. | οὐρανόδοξα ms. || **14** γενέτειρα debuit || **16** φῶς ms. in marg.

Sim.: 1 Ἐκ Διὸς ἄρχεσθαι] cf. Theocr. 17.1 (ἐκ Διὸς ἀρχώμεσθα) | ἔρρετε, Μοῦσαι] cf. Greg. Naz. *Carm.*, PG 37.1495.7; *Anth. Gr. App.* 255.1 || **4** θῆσ'] cf. Hsch. θ 542 (θῆσαι· θρέψαι, θηλάσαι) || **4–5** de Adrastea et Melissa filiis regis Melissei, quae Iovem infantem nutriverunt, cf. Apollod. *Bibl.* 1.5 (Adrastea et Ida); Callim. *Hymn.* 1.47–49 (Adrastea); Lactant. *Div. inst.* 1.22 (Melissa) || **6** Κορυβάντων θρέψε κυδοιμῷ] cf. Nonn. *Dion.* 28.276; 29.216 (Δικταῖοι Κορύβαντες ἐπεστρατόωντο κυδοιμῷ) || **11** γάλα θῆσθαι] cf. Hom. *Od.* 4.89

I am the Alpha.
The prodigious birth of Jesus, the commander-in-chief, or the beginning of the God-man.
First Poem

(excerpt, ll. 1–16)

Start with Zeus! Away, Muses, with your fountain! Start with Zeus! But not the one to whom Cybele gave birth as an enemy of his father; nor the one whom the Dictean groves of ignorant Crete sustained; nor the one whom [5] Adrastea says to have suckled for (with?) her Melissa; nor the one whom the furious metal brought up under the noise of the Idean Corybants: But the one who was born for his father without a mother before everything, before the light of the sun away from all time, before heaven, earth and sea, the one to whom for the second time a maiden [10] gave birth without a man; and the one whom the city of Iesse revealed in a dark house; the one who suckled the milk of Mary as the stars sing to the Sacred; whom Peace, the glory of heaven and the angelic chorus-leaders sung as clearly born. O maiden, O mother, O [15] dawn preceding such a light, hail to you. Sing a song for your clients whether it is possible to give the light of a better sun.[15]

Metre: Hexameters.

Notes: Engel's book *Virtutis et honoris aedes* (1666) contains 25 short epic poems describing actions of mythical, ancient, and early modern heroes. The poems are composed both in Greek and Latin and their titles are in alphabetical order. Although the Greek versions precede the Latin ones, the original was most probably Latin (cf. Weise 2016, 137), considering that the entire accompanying text is in Latin and that Engel was clearly far more skilled in Latin than in Greek, where he often struggles both grammatically (ll. 3ff. μή with indicative, l. 7 προ-ἀμήτορα πάντων) and lexically (l. 3 φόρεισκεν, l. 5 πεφάσσων, l. 12 Ἐρήνη), sometimes to the point of obscurity. That the Latin version preceded the Greek is also clear from a comparison between the Greek text and the Latin version of our passage. The Latin version illustrates the title of the poem *Ego sum A* by starting each line with an A whereas the Greek version misses this special effect. The prefaces to the poems, which serve the role of a rhetorical exercise, and the Latin annotations in the margins that explain idioms and difficult passages, suggest that the book was probably intended for scholastic purposes. In the context of Engel's times, the extent of his Greek text is remarkable.

Biography: Arnoldus Engel (Angelus), born in Utrecht in 1620, studied in Prague, where he joined the Jesuit order in 1640. He then worked as a priest and a missionary and throughout his life he taught in several colleges and schools throughout Bohemia and Moravia. He died in the North Bohemian town of Chomutov in 1690. Apart from his Greek-Latin epic poems, there are several Jesuit plays preserved under his name.[16]

---

15 Author's Latin version: *A Jove Principium! Cum fonte facessite, Musae, / A Jove Principium; Non quem Berecynthia Patri / Adversum genuit; non quem Dictaea tulerunt / Antra rudis Cretae; non quem lactâsse Melissae / [5] Adrastea ferat; non quem furiosa gementem / Aera sub Idaeo Corybantum aluêre tumultu, / Ast quem jam genitum sinè matre ante omnia Patri, / Ante jubar Solis, procul omni temporis aevô, / Ante Polum & Terram, & refugum mare, Virgo secundùm / [10] Absque viro genuit: quémque Urbs Jessaea retexit / Aede sub obscura: quem Lac suxisse MARIAE / Astra canunt Superis, quem Pax, quem gloria Coeli, / Angelicíque palàm Natum cecinêre Choragi. / Alma Parens Virgo tantae praenuncia Lucis / [15] Aurora, ô! Faveas, pandásque Clientibus hymnum, / Anne dari Solis possit melioris origo.*

16 The critical edition of Engel's text, the English translation, and the central part of the notes were prepared by Stefan Weise. The rest of the notes and the biography was provided by Marcela Slavíková.

Bibliography: Jacková, Magdaléna (2016), "The End of School Year on the Stage of Jesuit Schools in the Bohemian Province", in: *Acta Universitatis Carolinae Philologica 2/Graecolatina Pragensia*, 125–135; "Arnoldus Angelus", in: Jakubcová/Pernerstorfer 2013, 6–8; Weise, Stefan (2016), "Ἑλληνίδ' αἶαν εἰσιδεῖν ἱμείρομαι – Neualtgriechische Literatur in Deutschland (Versuch eines Überblicks)", in: *Antike und Abendland* 62, 114–181 (136–137).

Jan Křesadlo (1926–1995)

I. Óda na Stalina [1984/1990]

Στᾶλιν ἄναξ, ἄγαμαί σε. Σὺ λευκολίθῳ ἐνὶ Κρέμλῳ
ἑζόμενος κρατέεις πάντων Ῥώσσων Τατάρων τε
καὶ πολλῶν ἐθνῶν ξείνων ἀμενηνῶν κράτων.
Ἐν κονίῃ ἕρποντες θεὸν ὥς εἰσορόωσιν.
5   Σοὶ δὲ μέγας στρατός ἐστι βροτοκτόνος, ὅς δ' ἐνὶ χώραις
ἀλλοδαπῶν φορέει ὀϊζύν καὶ κῆρα μέλαιναν·
Ἄνδρας συλεύουσι βιάζουσίν τε γυναῖκας,
ὡρολόγους γὰρ κλέπτουσιν, τοὺς ἄνδρες ἀγαυοί
ἐν καρποῖς φορέουσι· τὸ γὰρ μέγα θαῦμα ἰδέσθαι.
10   Ἄλλοι γάρ ῥ' ἐκάμοντο ἰδυίῃσι πραπίδεσσιν,
σὺ δ' ἐλθὼν αἱρεῖς, ὅτι τοι κράτος ἐστὶ μέγιστον.
Χεῖρας βεβριθὼς παμπόλλοις ὡρολόγοισιν
ἑζόμενος ὁράας χρονοδείγματα κύδεϊ γαίων.
Πάντες δειδιότες κυνέουσι πόδας τε πυγήν τε.
15   Αὐτὸς γὰρ κρατέεις, ἢν δή τινας οὐκ ἐφίλησας
πέμψας Σειβερίην εἰς λάγερα, ᾗ ψύχωνται
δεσμοῖσι στυγεροῖσι δεδεμένοι ἠὲ θάνωσι.
Ῥωσιακῆς γαίης πάντες ῥ' ἄνδρες τε γυναῖκες
εὐχόμενοι στυγέουσιν, ἐπεὶ θεός ἐσσι μέγιστος.
20   Ἥλιον δ' αὐτόν φασιν σόν τ' ἔμμεναι ὄμμα
καὶ Στάλινος πορδήν φασι ψολόεντα κεραυνόν.

Textus: A = Křesadlo, Jan (1984), *Mrchopěvci*, Toronto (editio princeps); B = Křesadlo, Jan (1990), *Mrchopěvci*, in: *Bestseller 4*, Praha (editio, quae ultima ab auctore ipso redacta est); Weise = Weise, Stefan (2010), "Graeca recentiora – Jan Křesadlos homerische Ode an Stalin", in: Thomas Brüggemann/Burkhard Meissner/Christian Mileta/Angela Pabst/Oliver Schmitt (eds.), *Studia Hellenistica et Historiographica. Festschrift für Andreas Mehl*, Gutenberg, 437–451 (editio critica: 440–441).

Crit.: 1 σε. Σὺ B: σε· σὺ A || 2 κράτεεις A | πάντας Ῥώσσας Τατάρους τε A || 3 ἔθνων A | ξείνων ἀναρίθμα κάρηνα A || 4 θεόν ὡς A || 5 Σοὶ δὲ Weise: Σοί δε AB | βροτόκτονος A | ὅς δ' AB] pro ὅς τ' | ἐνὶ A || 6 κηρὰ A || 7 Ἄνδρὰς σιλήσουσί δε τε καὶ βιάζουσι γυναικάς A || 8 ὡρολόγους δε τε κλέπτουσιν A | τοὺς ἀνδρές ἀγαυνοί A || 9 τό γαρ A | ἴδεσθαι A || 10 Ἄλλοί γαρ κεκάμηκαν ἰδιεσὶ πραπιδεέσσιν A || 11 σὺ δ' ἐλθων αἴρεις, ὅτι τοι A | κράτος ἐστί Weise: κρατός ἐστι A: κράτος ἐστὶ B ||

12 βεβριθὼς παμπόλλοις Β: καλλύμμενος πολλοῖσιν Α ǁ 13 ὁράας ΑΒ: ὁράᾳς debuit ǁ 14 κινέουσι Α ǁ 15 Αὐτός γαρ Α ǀ κράτεεις Α ǀ ἦν δή τινας οὐκ ἐφίλησας Β: καὶ ὁντινὰ οὐκ ἐφίλησας Α ǁ 16 Σειβερίην εἰς λάγερα, Β: Σειβερίης χώρης εἰς λάγερα· Α ǀ ᾗ ψύχωνται corr.: ῇ ψύχωνται Β: ἥδε κρύουσι Α ǁ 17 δεδημενοὶ ᾖε θάνωσιν Α ǀ ἠὲ] pro ἠδὲ ǁ 18 Ῥωσιακῆς: P- Β: Ῥωσσιῆς Α ǁ ῥ': ῥ' Β, deest in Α ǀ ἀνδρές τε γυναικές Α ǁ 19 ἐπεί θεός ἔσσι Β ǀ μεγίστος Α ǁ 20 δ' deest in Α ǀ αὐτὸν φησίν Α ǀ σόν τ' Β: σου Α ǁ 21 καὶ Α ǀ πορδήν φασι Weise: πορδήν φασὶ Β: πόρδην φησὶν Α ǀ ψολοέντα Α

Sim.: 1 ἄγαμαί σε] cf. Pl. *Prt.* 361e3 ǀ λευκολίθῳ] cf. Strab. *Geogr.* 5.3.8.45; 9.5.16.30; 12.5.3.8 ǁ 2 κρατέεις πάντων] cf. *Hymn. Orph.* 16.7 (πάντων γὰρ κρατέεις μούνη πάντεσσί τ' ἀνάσσεις) et al. ǁ 4 θεὸν ὣς εἰσορόωσιν] cf. Hom. *Od.* 8.173; cf. etiam Hom. *Il.* 12.312 (θεοὺς ὣς εἰσορόωσι) ǁ 5 βροτοκτόνος] cf. *Hymn. Orph.* 65.2; Eur. *IT.* 384 ǁ 6 ὀϊζύν] cf. Hom. *Il.* 15.365; *Od.* 7.211; et al. ǀ κῆρα μέλαιναν] clausula Hom., vid. *Il.* 2.859; 3.360 et al. ǁ 8 ἄνδρες ἀγαυοί] cf. Hom. *Il.* 3.268 (κήρυκες ἀγαυοί); cf. etiam *Il.* 10.563 (Τρῶες ἀ.); *Od.* 4.681 (μνηστῆρες ἀ.) et al. ǁ 9 θαῦμα ἰδέσθαι] clausula Hom., vid. *Il.* 5.725; 10.439; 18.83 et al. ǁ 10 ἰδυίῃσι πραπίδεσσιν] clausula Hom., vid. *Il* 1.608 etc.; *Od.* 7.92 ǁ 11 κράτος ἐστὶ μέγιστον] clausula Hom., vid. *Il.* 2.118; 9.25,39 et al. ǁ 13 κύδεΐ γαίων] clausula Hom., vid. *Il.* 1.405; 5.906; 8.51 et al. (semper καθέζετο antecedit) ǁ 14 πυγήν] cf. Ar. *Ran.* 1095 ǁ 17 δεσμοῖσι στυγεροῖσι] cf. Hom. *Od.* 11.81,465 (ἐπέεσσιν ἀμειβομένω στυγεροῖσιν) ǁ 21 ψολόεντα κεραυνόν] clausula Hom., vid. *Od.* 24.539 ; cf. etiam *Od.* 23.330 (ἔβαλε ψολόεντι κεραυνῷ) ; Hes. *Theog.* 515.

Ode to Stalin

Ruler Stalin, I honour you. Sitting in the white-walled Kremlin, you rule powerfully over the Russians and the Tartars and countless heads of many nations. Crawling in the dust they look up to you as to a god. [5] You have a great army, killing mortals, which brings destruction and Black Death to the lands of foreigners. They kill men and rape women, they also steal watches worn by honoured men on their wrists, which is a wondrous sight. [10] Other men forged them with knowledge, and you, having come, then take them, for you are all-powerful. Having covered your arms with many watches, you sit beholding your indicators of time, proud of your glory. They all kiss your feet and arse in terror. [15] For you yourself rule and, those who displease you, you send to the land of Siberia to a camp where they freeze, bound in strong chains, and die. All the men and women of the land of Russia pray to you in terror, for you are the supreme god. [20] It is said the sun himself is your eye and the smouldering thunderbolt is Stalin's fart.

(Transl. from the Czech, Václav Z.J. Pinkava 1999)[17]

Metre: Hexameters; note the two *spondiaci* (l. 3 and 16). There are many *hiatus* in the text, ll. 1 (λευκολίθῳ ἑ-), 3 (κονίῃ ἐ-), 6 (φορέει ὁ-), 10 (ἐκάμοντο ἰ-), 16 (λάγερα,

---

17 Křesadlo, Jan (1999), *Mrchopěvci/GraveLarks*, Praha, 38 (Czech-English edition).

ᾗ). In l. 16, the poet uses *metri causa* the unattested form δεδημένοι for δεδεμένοι. πυγήν in l. 14 must be scanned short here although it is long (πῡγή).

Notes: This Homeric 'ode' to Stalin is an integral part of Křesadlo's novel titled *Mrchopěvci*, which was first published by Josef Škvorecký in Toronto in 1984. The second edition of the novel followed in 1990. It included a revised version of the hymn whose first edition had contained some metrical and grammatical errors. Two versions were published by Křesadlo's heirs after the author's death (1999, 2015). The poem is an excellent example of Křesadlo's wit and poetic inspiration that later culminated in his *Astronautilia*. Křesadlo's Greek has some strange peculiarities obviously resulting from the fact that he did not use an edition of Homer, but recited from memory. For example, ἠέ in l. 17 actually means 'and' not 'or' (Křesadlo confused probably ἠδέ and ἠέ). Furthermore, Křesadlo often uses δέ like the epic τε (cf. l. 5). Finally, we should note that he moves forward the accent of participles and infinitives of strong aorist stems, perhaps influenced by Aeolic barytonesis as he also knew and imitated Sappho and Alcaeus.[18]

II. ΑΣΤΡΟΝΑΥΤΙΛΙΑ, προοίμιον [1995]

(excerptum, α 1–9)[19]

> Ἀρχόμενος πρῶτον Μουσῶν χορῷ εἰξ Ἑλικῶνος
> εὔχομαι ἐκπάγλως καὶ Ἀπόλλωνι ἄνακτι
> Μουσάων ἄρχοντι καλῷ ἰδὲ δαίμον' ἀοιδῶν
> ὄφρ' εἴποιεν ἐμὴν κόσμου γλαφυροῖο πόρευσιν
> 5 θαύματα πλανήτων καὶ ἀνδρῶν ὄμβριμα ἔργα
> οἷα τε δειξάμενοι πλέομεν δνόφερον διὰ χάσμα
> πλοίαρχος μὲν ἐγὼ καὶ ἐμοὶ ἐρίηρες ἑταῖροι
> Μανδὺν ζητοῦντες καὶ μῆλον κοσμοθεωροῦν.
> Ἔσπετε νῦν ἡμῖν τάδε, ὦ θεός, ἠὲ θέαιναι.

Textus: Křesadlo, Jan (1995), *Ποιήτου* [sic] *ἀδήλου Ἀστροναυτιλία ἢ ἡ Μικροοδυσσεία* [sic] *ἡ κοσμική*, Praha, 2; exemplaria manu auctoris scripta nunc asservantur in archivo musei literarum Bohemicarum Pragensi (The Museum of Czech Literature, Literary Archive, Prague/Litoměřice; collection Jan Křesadlo, no. 2110; Astronautilia: 127–129).

---

18 Linguistic hints by SW.
19 This section is by SW.

Crit.: 6 οἷά τε debuit | δνόφερον debuit, sed fortasse colorem quendam Aeolicum affectat noster || 9 ἠὲ: ἠδὲ exspectaveris (cf. versionem Bohemicam auctoris: "ty, bože, vy bohyně také"), sed ἠέ lapsu memoriae pro ἠδέ saepius adhibet noster, cf. supra *Odam in Stal.*, v. 17

Sim.: 1 cf. Batr. 1 (ἀρχόμενος πρῶτον Μουσῶν χορὸν ἐξ Ἑλικῶνος) || 2 Ἀπόλλωνι ἄνακτι] cf. Hom. *Il.* 1.36; Hes. *Theog.* 347 (eadem sede) || 4 κόσμου γλαφυροῖο] nova iunctura | πόρευσιν] verbum pedestre || 7 πλοίαρχος] nomen neograecum | καὶ ἐμοὶ ἐρίηρες ἑταῖροι] clausula Homerica, cf. *Od.* 9.555 (vide etiam *Il.* 23.6; *Od.* 9.172; 12.199,397; 14.249) || 8 κοσμοθεωροῦν] neologismus ad theoriam quantalem respiciens || 9 ἔσπετε νῦν ἡμῖν] cf. Hom. *Il.* 2.484; 11.218; 14.508; 16.112 (ἔσπετε νῦν μοι, Μοῦσαι Ὀλύμπια δώματ' ἔχουσαι)

Astronautilia ['Star-voyage'], Proem

(excerpt: book 1, ll. 1–9)

> In the beginning I strongly beg the choir of the Muses from mount Helicon and lord Apollo, the beautiful ruler of the Muses and the god of the singers, that they tell my journey through the hollow space, [5] the miracles of the planets, and the great deeds of men we showed during our journey through dark space, I, the captain, and my dear comrades, while searching for Mandys and the space-regarding sheep. Tell us now these things, O god and goddesses!

Metre: Hexameters; note hiatuses in ll. 2, 3, 5, 7 and 9.

Notes: Křesadlo starts his Greek science-fiction epic with a traditional proem invoking the Muses and Apollo to tell the journey of his main character Nemo or Οὐδείς in Greek (the obvious difference from the Homeric Οὖτις from the *Odyssey* seems deliberate). The author uses some peculiar forms like εἰς and ὄμβριμα to evoke hyper-archaic language. The first line imitates the Homeric *Batrachomyomachia*, indicating that Křesadlo intends a witty play with Homeric references (Křesadlo also completed a Czech translation of the *Batrachomyomachia*). Like the *Ode to Stalin*, the *Astronautilia* is therefore full of Homeric reminiscences and phrases (l. 2 Ἀπόλλωνι ἄνακτι, 7 ἐμοὶ ἐρίηρες ἑταῖροι, 9 ἔσπετε νῦν), but Křesadlo also uses newly invented junctures and verbs like κόσμου γλαφυροῖο (l. 4), δνόφερον διὰ χάσμα (l. 6), μῆλον κοσμοθεωροῦν (l. 8). The line Μανδὺν ζητοῦντες καὶ μῆλον κοσμοθεωροῦν (8) is repeated throughout the whole poem. It states the goal of Nemo's space quest: the engineer Mandys and a sheep on whose existence the whole cosmos depends according to quantum mechanics (hence κοσμο**θεωροῦν**). The character of the sheep is inspired by the famous *Lunovis* poem of the German poet Christian Morgenstern (1871–1914). In the Czech and Latin preface to the *Astronautilia* the reader learns that the Greek version was a *lapsus* of the universal translator Franta (a character inspired by a short story of Stanislaw Lem, *Invasion from Aldebaran*), who mistook modern times for the Renaissance (see fig. 5, above). Beside these fictional characters from other literatures (Greek as well as vernacular), Křesadlo also integrates real people (Pavel Mandys was a literary critic, the robot Ivo is reminiscent of Křesadlo's Czech publisher Ivo Železný) and film characters (RoboCop; the seer Onufrius alludes to the Homeric Tiresias from the *Nekyia* as to the frozen Commander Powell from the movie *Dark Star*) in his *opus magnum*. The first-person narrative of Nemo clearly imitates the *apologoi* from the *Odyssey*, a main pretext for the whole poem and its episodic nature. The posthumous *editio princeps* from 1995 has a handwritten (!) copy of the Greek text with facing Czech verse translation, a Czech preface with a Latin summary and an English glossary. The edition is preceded by a letter of the Canadian philologist Wallace McLeod, who was involved in the revision of the earlier *Ode to Stalin*. [SW]

Biography: Jan Křesadlo, born as Václav Jaroslav Karel Pinkava in 1926, in Prague, was a Czech author and a poet who had an exceptional talent for foreign languages. After having learned ancient Greek at grammar school, he enrolled at the university to study English language and literature, but was expelled for political reasons. Later, however, he returned and graduated in psychology and finally received a Doctor's degree in 1968. In August 1968, he emigrated to the United Kingdom, where he then worked as a clinical psychologist. He died in Colchester in 1995. Apart from the *Ode to Stalin* and a few short pieces published in a book of poems titled *Sedmihlásek* (1988), his works composed in ancient Greek include an ingenious epic poem titled Ἀστροναυτιλία ἢ ἡ Μικροοδυσσεία [sic] ἡ κοσμική (published in Prague shortly after the author's death in 1995), which is an extensive Homeric inspiration of more than 6500 hexameters. Křesadlo's command of the Homeric language and expression is remarkable and the extent of his Greek work is entirely unprecedented in the Czech lands. [MS]

Bibliography: Czaplińska, Joanna (2003), "Alegorie – groteska – postmoderna. Postmodernistický ráz Mrchopěvců Jana Křesadla", in: Libor Pavera (ed.), *Posmodernismus v české a slovenské próze*, Opava, 191–196; "Křesadlo, Jan: Mrchopěvci", in: Zbyněk Fišer (1994), *Slovník české prózy*, Ostrava, 199–201; Hanuška, Petr (1996), "Vzájemná korespondence Jana Křesadla a Josefa Škvoreckého", in: *Česká literatura* 44/6, 625–642; on his Greek poems: Δανιήλ, Γιώργος (1989), "'Ἕνας «Ὁμηρικός» Ὕμνος στὸν Στάλιν", in: *Τὸ τράμ* 3/9–10, 65f.; Weise, Stefan (2010), "Graeca recentiora – Jan Křesadlos homerische Ode an Stalin", in: Thomas Brüggemann/Burkhard Meissner/Christian Mileta/Angela Pabst/Oliver Schmitt (eds.), *Studia Hellenistica et Historiographica. Festschrift für Andreas Mehl*, Gutenberg 2010, 437–451; Balthussen, Han (2015), "A 'Homeric' hymn to Stalin: performing safe criticism in ancient Greek?", in: *Classical Receptions Journal* 7/2, 223–241.

XLIX.
I.

Ἀρχὸς	Ἁγνὸς	Ἀμ'	Ἀρτεπὴς	Ἀμάρυσσε	Ἀμύμων;
Νημερτὴς	νοέη,	νεμεσῶν	νέα	νείκεα	νικῶν;
Δωτὴρ	Δημάσιος	δώρων	δὺς	δήνεα	δαίφρων;
Ῥηξήνωρ	ῥητὸς,	ῥέζων	ῥέα	ῥήματα	ῥήτωρ;
Ἐρέας	εὔσκεν	ἐρρώσατο	εὔφρων;	εὔκηλος	ἔσκε;
Αὐγάζων	ἄρα	ἄφθονος;	αὐτὰρ	αὐγαρὸν	ἁλύσκει;
Στείχων	συνεχέως	σοβαρὸς;	σώζων	σῶμα	σφοδρῶς;
Μιν	Μάλα	Μὲν	Μελιηδέα	Μοίρα	Μητιόεντες
Ἐκλεκτόνκεν	ἐπῆρεν	ἐς	ἔδρεν	ἐκόντες,	ἔπωντες;
Ἴσχτε,	Ἰθυδίκης	ἴθι	ἰδμων,	ἴφθιμος	ἴσθι,
Ἡσυχος	ἧς	Ἥρως	ἢ	ἠπιος	ἡγεμονεύῃ;
Ῥιγηλῶν	ῥήξων	ῥαδιέργημα	ῥίμφα	ῥα	ῥαβδίῳ;
Ὀλβιος	Οὔνεκ	Ὄλυμπον	ὁμῶς	ὅσιον τ'	ὀπηδεύῃ;
Σώματι	σφοδρῶς	σὺν	σήθεσσι	Σεβάσματα	σπένδων.

Μετάφρασις.

A cceptus, Castus, vitæ integer ipse coruscat;
N arrans Vera, simul succensens litibus ortis;
D onorum largúsque dator; Consultor amandus;
R ector Mavortis clarus, Rhetorque disertus;
E lectósque colens coetûs; rutilat quóque mitis;
A spectu blandus; Vitans fugiensque superbos;
S emper robustus gradiens os suave fovebat;
M ellitum hunc equidem Magnates sorte Canóra
E lectum in solium tolluntque sequentia fantur;
I ncedas fortis; judex sis scitus & æquus,
E gregiúsque Héros, Dux sis moderamine suavis;
R umpens horrendûm citius malefacta bacillo;
U t sancto tandem felix coelóque fruaris
S emper carne simul quoque pectore sacra sacrando;

Fig. 6: *Musarum Limagidum vicinarumque applausus votivi...summis...honoribus...D. Andreae Meieri*, Tiguri: typis Henrici Bodmeri, 1696, 89 (M IIr): acrostichic poem by Johann Heinrich Herder (see below, p. 353–355).

Janika Päll and Martin Steinrück
Switzerland

The Helvetia of the humanists – more or less loosely connected towns, republics, and cantons in the region, which roughly corresponds to modern Switzerland (*Confoederatio Helvetica*)[1] – had a glorious past and a flourishing literary life.[2] Its activities included the editing of ancient authors and of scholarly works about Greek in two printing towns of Europe-wide significance: Basel and Geneva.

Initially, many printers from nearby regions came to Basel for business. Johannes Froben (ca. 1460 Hammelburg, Bavaria – 1527 Basel), Andreas Cratander (ca. 1490 Strasbourg – 1540 Basel), Johannes Herwagen (ca. 1497 Wadendinger near Bodensee – 1558 Basel), Valentin Curio (ca. 1500 Alsace – 1532/1533 Basel), to name but a few examples, were followed by Basel-born humanists Johannes Oporinus (Herbst, 1505–1568), Sebastian Henricpetri (1546–1627), Eusebius Episcopius (1540–1590), and others.[3] In the Republic of Geneva, French Protestants, such as Robert I Estienne (1503 Paris – 1559 Geneva), Henri II Estienne (1531 Paris – 1598 Lyon), Jean Crespin (1520 Arras – 1572 Geneva), Eustache Vignon (1530 Arras – 1588 Frankfurt am Main) and others found safety from religious prosecution, a place in the local humanist network and sometimes very intricate ways of working for the French and European book market.[4] In Zürich, Christoph Froschauer (ca. 1490 in Bavaria – 1564 Zürich) brought new skills from Augsburg; in the 17th century Greek printing was in the hands of the Wolff and Bodmer families.[5]

---

1 The name of Helvetians and outline of their territories goes back to Caesar's *Gallic War*. Today's German part of Switzerland (meanwhile inhabited by Alemanni) gained *de facto* independance from the Holy Roman Empire after the Swabian war in 1499, resulting in Basel City joining the Old Confederation (already expanded by Zürich and Bern), which grew gradually by wars (Bern and Fribourg conquering Vaud), bilateral agreements (with the Republic of Geneva, the County of Neuchâtel), or looser ties (with the Prince-Bishopric of Basel). Each region had close connections to its neighbours: Swabia (Baden-Württemberg and Bavaria in today's Germany), Alsace (Upper and Lower Rhine), Franche-Comté and Rhône-Alpes (Savoy, Auvergne, Dauphiné, Ardèche) in today's France.
2 For the notion of literary life, comprising literature written or published in a certain region (by or for the people living in that region) and works published elsewhere, but connected to that same region, see Klöker 2005, 47f. and the Nordic part of this anthology.
3 Hieronymus 1992; *ITB*.
4 Reverdin 2000, 50–90; Kecskeméti/Boudou/Cazès 2003; Boudou/Kecskeméti 2009; Bremme 1969; GLN15-16; Gilmont 1981.
5 Benzing 1982; Meyer, Helmut (2018), "Froschauer, Christoph", in: *Historisches Lexikon der Schweiz (HLS)*, https://hls-dhs-dss.ch/de/articles/010612/2018-01-11/ [accessed: November 2020].

Besides offering the technical means with their Greek types (sometimes superb ones, like the *grec du Roi,* used by the Estiennes), the printers in Basel and Geneva became enablers in a much larger sense, creating the demand for Hellenizing poetry and prose. Some Greek poems featured in collections of Latin *carmina*, but initially Hellenizing Greek texts appeared mostly as paratexts in Greek lexica, grammars, and editions of ancient and Christian Greek authors, including dedicatory poems and letters or addresses to the readers which functioned in the same way as blurbs on modern book covers.[6] Many authors of such liminary texts – Erasmus, Melanchthon, Wolf (Lykios), Frischlin, Rhodoman, Crusius, Micyllus, Neander, Dolscius, Olympia Fulvia Morata, Camerarius, Canter, Bonaventura Vulcanius, Julius Caesar and Joseph Justus Scaliger, and numerous others – did not live in Switzerland, but had good relations with Swiss printers and publishers, often because of their common background (homeland, instruction, or friendship).

As elsewhere in Europe, several other factors shaped the fate of Humanist Greek in Helvetia: the Reformation and the emergence of important centres of scholarship which drew students and mature scholars from near and from far.[7] The independence of the regions, the republican nature of the governments, the absence of great courts, and (relatively) peaceful times promoted economy and nurtured literary life.

The mapping of Humanist Greek poetry from Switzerland is still in progress: hence, only some general features of this corpus of several hundreds of Greek poems are presented in what follows.[8] The first examples from its Golden Age (ca. 1545–1599) represent the initial phase of passionate immersion into Greek by Protestant humanists, which brought along many book paratexts, but also lengthy and sublime poems which often expressed deeply personal religious feelings (see the end of this introduction). From the initial close-knit circles of colleagues and humanist families, the practice of Greek poetry expanded almost explosively at the end of the 16th and in the first half of the 17th century, bringing along less prominent peaks, but more poems (and personal poetry quires) and greater variety in forms and genres, displaying the love for the Hellenizing fashion among numerous Swiss scholars and students. In the first part of the 18th

---

6 For the notion, see van Dam 2015 (p. 64 for analogous invitations in the Low Countries).
7 For the role of the Reformation, see Saladin 2013; Ludwig 1998, 102 (and Ludwig elswhere).
8 Thanks to the e-rara project, most of Swiss humanist prints are also digitised. E-rara has also furnished the biographical data (birth- and lifetimes), with external links to biographical databases.

century, Greek poetry became rare, only to be revived by isolated Hellenists in the following centuries.[9]

The Swiss readers of this anthology might be quite astonished that there is not more to find in the field of Humanist Greek poetry from Helvetia. Yet we must consider that during the peak of Humanist Greek poetry in the 16th century,[10] the majority of authors in the humanist editions were either visiting scholars and correspondents from abroad (see above) or immigrants. This anthology's criterion of including, in general, only native authors allows us to present just a small, sometimes less attractive part of Hellenizing Helvetia. Whereas some poems have been reclaimed by the authors' countries of birth and are thus presented in other sections of the anthology, some poets will be nonetheless mentioned in the present introduction.

The Reformation, the New School System, and Greek Poetry

As a result of the Reformation, the school system in Swiss towns was reorganised according to the example of Leiden's *Collegium trilingue* and Melanchthon's ideas of the sacred languages in the service of the Reform.[11] The change affected every stage and field of education from theology and philosophy, to medicine, the natural sciences, and even law.

The literary circles in the Basel humanist movement moved around the university and the printers, in close connection to the town council and the church. The University of Basel (founded in 1460)[12] was reorganised in 1532, but its first professor of Greek, Simon Grynaeus (1493–1541) had been invited from Heidelberg already in 1529 by the reformer Johannes Oecolampadius (1482–1531). Grynaeus' successor was Basel's own printer, Johannes Oporinus. Many following professors of Greek were active Hellenizers. Sebastian Castellion (Châtillon, 1515–1563 Dauphiné, France) arrived from Geneva where he had disagreements

---

9 From the 19th century, Emanuel Linder, from the 20th Yves Gerhard, from the 21st Martin Steinrück can be named.
10 The Golden Age of Greek between 1530–1560 (according to Saladin 2013, 305–361) is slightly early, the end of the 16th century (according to Ludwig 2014) slightly late for Switzerland.
11 Ludwig 2014, 138; Saladin 2013, 355–361. For schools, see Crousaz 2012, 45–68 (general) and below.
12 See Herzog 1778 and Staehelin 1957 (for the whole paragraph).

with Calvin; Oporinus printed his Bible-inspired poetry and provided him with a livelihood as the editor and translator of religious works until he received the professorship.[13] Greek scholarship often flourished within learned families: the doctors of medicine, the physician Theodor Zwinger the Elder (1564–1671), Oporinus' nephew, and his son Jacob Zwinger (1595–1610) taught Greek and wrote Greek poems.[14] The Wettstein family produced five professors of Greek and Hellenizing poets in the 17th century, of whom the most important were **Johann Rudolf Wettstein the Father and the Son**. Greek poetry was also written by numerous other Basel professors and students, both from Switzerland and from nearby or farther Europe (as far as Silesia). Among them the talented Johann Jakob Battier should not remain unmentioned. In the 18th century Greek poetry became rare in Basel,[15] and the 19th century is represented only by Emanuel Linder (1768–1843) who, differently from earlier times, preferred a professorship of Greek and Hebrew at the university to the position of a pastor.[16]

In Zürich, the reformers took care of teaching the sacred languages:[17] Ulrich Zwingli (1484–1531) founded the *Schola Tigurina* (1525) which was reorganised by Heinrich Bullinger (1504–1575) into a higher school (later named *Collegium humanitatis* and *Collegium Carolinum*). Zwingli invited the talented **Jacobus Ceporinus** (1499/1500–1525) as the Professor of Greek, but he died early, leaving his Greek grammar for future generations. In the mid-16th century the most active Hellenizer was the polymath physician **Konrad Gessner** (1516–1565). The collection of epicedia for the death of Bullinger (in 1575) is characteristic of Zürich's Greek poetry at the end of the century: amongst authors there are evangelical pastors and/or persons connected to higher schools, such as Rudolf Gwalther (Gualtherus, 1519–1586) and Sadrach Tomann (†1598).[18] The 17th century is represented here by **Johann Rudolf Stucki** (1596–1660) and **Johannes Lavater** (1624–1695), but the choice might

---

13 See Buisson 1892 and the end of this introduction.
14 Steinke, Hubert (2014), "Zwinger, Jakob", in: *Historisches Lexikon der Schweiz (HLS)*, https://hls-dhs-dss.ch/de/articles/025309/2014-03-03/ [accessed: September 2020].
15 For example by J.B. Merian (1723–1807), see Wichers, Hermann (2008), "Merian, Johann Bernhard", in: *Historisches Lexikon der Schweiz*, https://hls-dhs-dss.ch/de/articles/042205/ 2008-10-30/ [accessed: September 2020] and Merian, Matthäus (1740), *Mathusalems Gesegneter Ehestand... Todt. Herrns Hans Bernhard Burckhardts*. Basel, Mechel, sen.
16 See https://personenlexikon.bl.ch/Emanuel_Linder and manuscripts at Basel University Library, NL 204.
17 For the whole paragraph, see Bächtold 2000; Ernst 1879; Goeing 2016.
18 Simmler, Josias (1575), *Narratio de ortu, vita ed obitu...Bullingeri*, Zürich. The collection also includes Greek *epicedia* by Johann(?) Jacob Ulrich and Johann Jacob Haller; a generation later

also include Greek poems by the Evangelical theologian Johann (Hans) Kaspar Schweizer (Suicerus, 1619–1688), Professor of Greek in Zürich's Collegium.[19]

In the Republic of Geneva, Greek scholarship flourished among the refugees fleeing from religious persecution. Its starting point is in 1551, when Robert I Estienne printed the Greek New Testament and published his son Henri II Estienne's Greek translation of Calvin's catechism. Henri II was an excellent Hellenizer and published his most important editions in Geneva, including *Thesaurus Graecae Linguae,* Plato, Plutarch, and several Greek poets. His competitor Jean Crespin took great interest in Greek, editing ancient authors and investing a great deal in publishing Greek-Latin lexica (the first as early as 1554), as well as inviting scholars to write Greek liminary poems.[20]

The role of Genevan printers as promotors of Hellenizing literature is inseparable from the Academy under its two leaders. When Jean Calvin (1509 Nyon – 1564 Geneva) was invited to Geneva in 1541, he reorganised the Old College and soon founded the Academy (1559).[21] Franciscus Portus (1511 Candia – 1581 Geneva) was its first professor of Greek (1561–1581), sticking to the Byzantine manner of pronunciation (and creating some confusion, as Theodore de Bèze was at the same time promoting the Erasmian pronunciation) and publishing numerous liminary poems in Greek. His son Aemilius Portus (1550 Ferrara – 1614 Stadthagen) published Greek poetry (including biblical paraphrases) and taught Greek in Geneva and Lausanne before leaving for Germany.[22] **Isaac Casaubon** (1559–1614), from the second generation of immigrants, became the next Professor of Greek (1581–1596), published Greek authors and wrote Greek poetry. Many youngsters who came from France or the Low Countries to study at Geneva's Academy joined in the exchange of Greek poems: these include Lambert Daneau (1530–1590), Franciscus Junius (de Jon; 1545–1602 Leiden), or Antoine de la Faye (Fayus; 1540 Châteaudon – 1614 Geneva), who arrived in Geneva in 1561 and taught both in Geneva and in Lausanne, later becoming the Rector of the Lausanne Academy.[23]

Greek poems were written by Johann Wilhelm Stucki (1542–1607), Hans Konrad Ochsner (1556–1611), and Heinrich Erni (1565–1639). For Bullinger, see Campi/Opitz 2007.

19 Ryssel, Viktor (1894), "Suicerus, Johann Caspar", in: *Allgemeine Deutsche Biographie* 37, 141–143.
20 See Furno 2009; Gilmont 1981; Reverdin 2000, 36–48.
21 See Reverdin 2000 loc.cit.; Borgeaud 1900; Maag 1995 (for the whole paragraph).
22 For the Portuses, see Geanakoplos 1966, 158–160; Weber, Karl Friedrich (1854), *Vita Aemilii Porti*, Marburg.
23 See Maag 1995.

The last flowering of Greek poetry in Geneva is connected to the time and activity of Theodore de Bèze (1519 Vézelay – 1605 Geneva) who in his youth had been friends with the French poets Dorat, Ronsard and du Bellay (→ **France**), and fought for his faith on the battleground; after teaching Greek in Lausanne, he succeeded Calvin as the head of the Genevan Academy, but preferred preaching to the work of a professor, and continued to love and write Greek poetry.[24]

The Academy of Lausanne opened in 1537, after Vaud had been conquered by Bern. Its first professor of Greek (1537–1540), Konrad Gessner, was invited from Zürich, but later there were closer ties to Geneva. All Lausanne professors were excellent Hellenists and many of them wrote Greek poetry:[25] Theodore de Bèze was Professor of Greek in 1549–1558, Pedro Nuñez de Vela (ca. 1502 Avila – 1580 Lausanne) in 1567–1580 (for Vela's Greek poems, published in 1570 in Basel, see → **Iberia**);[26] the Savoyard Johannes Scapula (Jean Espaulaz, 1540–1600), the author of a very popular Greek-Latin lexicon, also studied and taught at Lausanne;[27] Jean de Serres (Serranus, 1540 Villeneuve-de-Berg – 1598) from Ardèche studied in Lausanne and Geneva and dedicated himself to the study of Plato while he was the rector of the Lausanne Academy (1572–1578) before becoming the historian of Henri IV; he also translated Buchanan's paraphrases into Greek.[28] In 1598 Stephanus a Castrobello became Professor of Greek, in 1617–1628 Franciscus Blondetus: both were probably local and published short Greek epigrams.[29]

The Higher School in Bern (opened in 1528) was reorganised in 1549 under the head of its church, Johannes Haller (1523–1575).[30] The Alsatian reformer Wolfgang Musculus (see below on Gessner) and Bern's own Benedictus Marti (Aretius, 1522–1574) promoted Greek studies, but only a few Greek poems were written here, e.g. the epigram by Valentin Rebmann (Ampelander; 1520–1587) for the death of his father-in-law Musculus, or a psalm by Abraham Champ-Renaud in 1706.[31]

---

24 See Haag, Eugène and Émile (1879), *La France Protestante*. Vol. 2, Paris, 503–541; Maag 1995.
25 Crousaz 2012 (incl., 240 for Greek); Graf 1888–1889.
26 See Gilmont 1981, 137, 195; Boehmer 1883, 145–162.
27 For more exact biographical information, see Hieronymus 1992, 103.
28 See Boehmer 1883, 151–152 (for Scapula); Gilmont 1981, 154; Dardier 1883 (for Serres).
29 See Meillerus, below.
30 van Wijnkoop Lüthi, Marc (2006), "Haller, Johannes", in: *Historisches Lexikon der Schweiz (HLS)*, https://hls-dhs-dss.ch/de/articles/010458/2006-02-17/ [accessed: November 2020]; Immenhauser 2008; Haag 1903; Graf 1888–1889.
31 See Mathys, Hans-Peter (2001), "Aretius, Benedikt", in: *Historisches Lexikon der Schweiz (HLS)*, https://hls-dhs-dss.ch/de/articles/010508/2001-08-29/ [accessed: November 2020], and the end of the introduction, below.

The Genres and Forms of Humanist Greek in Switzerland

As often in Humanist Greek poetry, the most frequent genre in the Swiss tradition is occasional poetry, from liminary poems in books to poems for weddings, funerals, studies, graduations, etc. The variety of forms extends from two-line epigrams to verse orations, epyllia, dialogues, idyllia, Circles of Muses[32] and polyglot poems; the poetic devices include anagrams, acrostics, and pangrammatic poems. Although the most popular metres are hexameter and elegiac couplets, like in the early years, gradually other metres were added, down to the most complex ones, such as Pindaric strophes, or metres inspired by Roman poetry and the psalm paraphrase books (much like the church songbooks in Lutheran regions). Other genres of Humanist Greek in Switzerland concern prose and include the earliest Greek disputation presently known,[33] as well as frequent letters that appeared in prints and manuscript collections.

The development and popularity of two genres of Humanist Greek poetry is especially connected to the preferences of Basel and Genevan printers: biblical poetry,[34] particularly paraphrastic, and the Pindarising Ode.

In Basel, Oporinus started to promote Bible-inspired literature in Greek: in 1545 he printed Sebastian Châtillon's Greek epyllion *Life of St John the Baptist* as an appendix to the latter's Latin paraphrase of the Book of Jonas; in 1555 he printed the Greek *Psalms of David* by Halle Rector and City Physician Paul Dolscius (1526–1589), who later also published other Christian epyllia in Germany; finally in 1573, the *Life of Jesus* by Matthaeus Gothus (Götze, 1548–1619) from Ellrich in Nordhausen (→ **Germany**).[35] In 1581, the Greek paraphrases of the Psalms by Aemilius Portus were printed in Basel, with an introductory letter by

---

32 See Ludwig 2001, esp. 31–34.
33 See Päll 2020, 730–731.
34 See Czapla 2013 (for the notion of biblical epic and a great number of examples).
35 Châtillon, Sebastian (1545), *Jonas Propheta...vita Ioannis Baptistae*, Basel; Dolcius, Paul (1555), *Psalterium prophetae et regis Davidis versibus elegiacis*, Basel. Cf. Eckstein, Friedrich August (1877), "Dolscius, Paul" in: *Allgemeine Deutsche Biographie* 5, 321f. For the importance and promotion of biblical paraphrases by Oporinus, see also Weise, Stefan (2020), "Griechische Mythologie im Dienste reformatorischer Pädagogik: Zur Epensammlung *Argonautica. Thebaica. Troica. Ilias parva* von Lorenz Rhodoman (1588)", in: Mika Kajava/Tua Korhonen/Jamie Vesterinen (eds.), *MEILICHA DÔRA. Poems and Prose in Greek from Renaissance and Early Modern Europe*, Helsinki, 185–215: 189–190.

his already very ill father, Franciscus Portus.³⁶ In Geneva, Henri II Estienne's edition of Buchanan's paraphrases (1566) stood out among remaining paraphrase literature because of its extension with Greek paraphrases in different verse forms.³⁷ Estienne also published his own translations of the Psalms of David into anacreontic and Sapphic metres in 1568³⁸ and printed, in 1575, the Greek translation of Buchanan's Latin paraphrases by Jean de Serres with some of the latter's own paraphrases, as well as Greek gratulations by colleagues.³⁹ Matthieu Berjon printed **Meillerus'** paraphrases of the Book of Solomon in 1599 in Geneva. In 1658, Johann Kaspar Schweizer published the paraphrase of the Book of Jonas and of some Greek psalms by the English classicist John Aylmer (†1672). Apart from the big editions, students also wrote paraphrases of single psalms: as late as 1706 Abraham Champ-Renaud from Bienne published his Greek-Latin paraphrase of Psalm 101 in Sapphic stanzas in Bern.⁴⁰

The development of the Pindarising Ode in Greek had started in Italy, but its further flourishing is due in part to the activity of Henri II Estienne, who published his editions of Pindar (with other lyric poets) in Geneva in 1560 and 1566;⁴¹ it appears that he invited two French students to add paraphrases in Greek Pindaric verses to his edition of Buchanan's Psalm paraphrases in 1566.⁴² These were Frédéric Jamot (1552 Béthune – after 1600 in Netherlands; → **Low Countries**)⁴³ and Florent Chrestien (1540–1590 in Orléans; → **France**), who had enrolled as a student in Geneva in 1559;⁴⁴ both left Geneva after their youth. Apart from the re-editions of Estienne's Buchanan, some of their Genevan odes have been reprinted many times: Chrestien's Pindaric ode commemorating Jean Calvin's death (probably from 1564) was reprinted in 1569, 1597, 1598, 1713 and 1879, and Jamot's congratulation for Buchanan in 1566, 1568; 1572, 1575, and 1593. Also, at least two

---

36 See *Omnes Dauidis Psalmi...ab Aemylio Francisci Porti f(ilio)*, Basel, by printer Leonhard Ostenius, with the dotation by Strasbourg printer Bernhard Jobin.
37 See *Psalmorum Dauidis Paraphrasis poetica...auctore Georgio Buchanano*, Geneva 1566. Its popularity was rapid, numerous reprints (and pirate editions) appeared and it became a recommended Greek schoolbook as late and far as in Tartu in the 1650s.
38 *Psalmi Davidis aliquot metro anacreontio et sapphico. Autore Henr. Stephano*, Geneva 1568.
39 See n. 29 above and *Psalmorum Dauidis aliquot*, Geneva 1575.
40 Schweizer, Johann Caspar (1658), in: Ἐμπύρευμα εὐσεβείας, Tiguri, 115–128; Champ-Renaud, A. (1706), *Sacrae eclogae seu idyllae*, Bern.
41 See *Pindari Olympia, Pythia, Nemea, Isthmia*, Geneva 1560; Geneva 1566.
42 See Lukinovich 2018; Päll 2017.
43 Gilmont 1981, 229 qualifies him as a friend of Crespin. For his odes, see Schmitz 1991.
44 See Jacobsen 1973.

Basel citizens have written Pindaric odes: the student of theology Andreas Hey and the Hellenist Martin Steinrück.[45]

Greek poetry in Switzerland emerged initially in connection to the book production through paratexts in humanist editions and versified expressions of religious piety. It was written in the 16th century by French (or other) Protestant immigrants in Geneva and Lausanne, but also by local and foreign humanists in Zürich and Basel (considerably less so in smaller towns). From the 17th century onwards it was mainly connected to the universities of Basel and Zürich, composed by numerous academics of Swiss origin, but also by foreign students, and it included a great variety of occasional poetry.

[JP/MS]

General Bibliography

Bächtold, Hans Ulrich (2000), *Schola Tigurina: die Zürcher Hohe Schule und ihre Gelehrten um 1550; Katalog zur Ausstellung*, Zürich/Freiburg im Breisgau.
Benzing, Josef (1982), *Die Buchdrucker des 16. und 17. Jahrhunderts im deutschen Sprachgebiet*, Wiesbaden.
Boehmer, Edward (1883), *Spanish reformers*. Vol. 2, Strasbourg/London.
Borgeaud, Charles (1900), *Histoire de l'Université de Genève. L'Academie de Calvin. 1559–1798*, Geneva.
Bremme, Hans Joachim (1969), *Buchdrucker und Buchhändler zur Zeit der Glaubenskämpfe. Studien zur Genfer Druckgeschichte 1565–1580*, Geneva.
Campi, Emidio/Opitz, Peter (eds.) (2007), *Heinrich Bullinger: Life – Thought – Influence*, I–II, Zürich.
Cazès, Hélène (2003), "Étude introductive: La passion et les épreuves d'Henri II Estienne, imprimeur humaniste", in: Judit Kecskeméti/Bénédicte Boudou/Hélène Cazès (eds.), *La France des Humanistes. Henri II Estienne, Éditeur et Écrivain*, Turnhout, XI–XLVIII.
Crousaz, Karine (2012), *L'Académie de Lausanne entre Humanisme et Réforme (ca. 1637–1560)*, Leiden/Boston.
Czapla, Ralf Georg (2013), *Das Bibelepos in der frühen Neuzeit. Zur deutschen Geschichte einer europäischen Gattung*, Berlin/Boston.
Dardier, Charles (1883), "Jean de Serres, historiographe du Roi; sa vie et ses écrits", in: *Revue Historique* 22, 291–328; 23, 28–76.
Ernst, Ulrich (1879), *Geschichte des Zürcherischen Schulwesens bis gegen das Ende des sechzehnten Jahrhunderts*, Winterthur.

---

45 See *Benedicto Mitzio...laureae*, Basel: Betsche 1579; he also published some other Greek poems. Steinrück's *propemptikon* to Claude Calame is unpublished.

Furno, Martine (2009), "Robert I Estienne", in: Bénédicte Boudou/Judit Kecskeméti (eds.), *La France des Humanistes: Robert et Charles Estienne. Des imprimeurs pédagogues*, Turnhout, 21–26.

Gilmont, Jean-François (1981), *Jean Crespin. Un éditeur réformé du XVIe siècle*, Genève.

GLN 15-16 = Gilmont, Jean-François & Ville de Genève, *Bibliographie de la production imprimée des 15ᵉ et 16ᵉ siècles des villes de Genève*, Lausanne et Neuchâtel (et Morges), http://www.ville-ge.ch/musinfo/bd/bge/gln/index.php.

Goeing, Anja-Silvia (2016), *Storing, Archivising, Originizing. The Changing Dynamics of Scholarly Information management in Post-Reformation Zurich*, Leiden/Boston.

Graf, Johann Heinrich (1888–1889), *Geschichte der Mathematik und der Naturwissenschaften in Bernischen Landen. Heft I.-Heft III*, Bern.

Haag, Friedrich (2003), *Die hohen Schulen zu Bern in ihrer geschichtlichen Entwicklung von 1528 bis 1834*, Bern.

Herzog, Johann Werner (1778), *Athenae Rauricae, sive catalogus professorum Academiae Basiliensis ab a. MCCCCLX ad a. MDCCLXXVII*, Basel.

Hieronymus, Frank (ed.) (1992), Ἐν Βασιλείᾳ πόλει τῆς Γερμανίας. *Griechischer Geist aus Basler Pressen*, Basel: Universitätsbibliothek. See also https://ub.unibas.ch/cmsdata/spezialkataloge/gg/

Immenhauser, Beat (2008), "Hohe Schule oder Universität? Zur Pfarrerausbildung in Bern im 16. Jahrhundert", in: *Berner Zeitschrift für Geschichte und Heimatkunde* 70, 1–36.

ITB = Index typographorum editorumque Basiliensium, https://ub2.unibas.ch/itb.

Jacobsen, Brigitte (1973), *Florent Chrestien. Ein Protestant und Humanist in Frankreich zur Zeit der Religionskriege*, München.

Klöker, Martin (2005), *Literarisches Leben in Reval in der ersten Hälfte des 17ten Jahrhunderts (1600–1657). Institutionen der Gelehrsamkeit und Dichten bei Gelegenheit. Teil I. Darstellung*, Tübingen.

Ludwig, Walther (1998), *Hellas in Deutschland. Darstellung der Gräzistik im deutschsprachigen Raum aus dem 16. und 17. Jahrhundert*, Hamburg.

Ludwig, Walther (2014), "Der Humanist Laurentius Rhodomanus als griechischer Dichter Laurentios Rhodoman und seine Autobiographie von 1582", in: *Neulateinisches Jahrbuch* 16, 137–171.

Ludwig, Walther (2001), "Musenkult und Gottesdienst", in: Walther Ludwig (ed.), *Die Musen im Reformationszeitalter*, Leipzig, 9–51.

Lukinovich, Alessandra (2018), "Florent Chrestien pindarise sous la houlette d'Henri Estienne. Un psaume des montées en vers grecs (Ps. 127 hébreu) dans la version publiée en 1566 et dans un autographe", in: Janika Päll/Ivo Volt (eds.), *Hellenostephanos. Humanist Greek in Early Modern Europe*, Tartu, 260–298.

Maag, Karin (1995), *Seminary or University? The Genevan Academy and Reformed Higher Education*, Aldershot.

Päll, Janika (2017), "The Transfer of Greek Pindaric Ode from Italy to the Northern Shores: From Robortello to Vogelmann and further", in: Stefan Weise (ed.), *HELLENISTI! Altgriechisch als Literatursprache im neuzeitlichen Europa*, Stuttgart, 349–368.

Päll, Janika (2020), "Greek Disputations in German and Swedish Universities and Academic Gymnasia in the 17th and Early 18th Century", in: Meelis Friedenthal/Hanspeter Marti/Robert Seidel (eds.), *Early Modern Disputations and Dissertations in an Interdisciplinary and European context*. Leiden/Boston, 728–778.

Reverdin, Olivier (2000), "Figures de l'Héllenisme à Genève", in: *Homère chez Calvin. Figures de l'hellénisme à Genève. Mélanges Olivier Reverdin*, Geneva, 27–101.
Staehelin, Andreas (1957), *Geschichte der Universität Basel*, Basel.
Schmitz, Thomas (1991), "Les odes grecques de Frédéric Jamot", in: *Bibliothèque d'Humanisme et Renaissance* 53, 281–330.
Van Dam, Harm-Jan (2015), "Poems on the Threshold: Neo-Latin carmina liminaria", in: Astrid Steiner-Weber et al. (eds.), *Acta Conventus Neo-Latini Monasteriensis*, Leiden, 50–81.

Jakob Wiesendanger/Jacobus Ceporinus (1499/1500–1525)

Εἰς εὐζωΐαν καὶ ἀποθέωσιν Καίσαρος τοῦ Μαξιμιλιανοῦ [1519]

Ὁππότε ζωὸς ἔην, πολλῶν ἐμὲ ποιμένα λαῶν
ἀθάνατοι ποίησαν, ἐνὶ φρεσὶ μήδεα θέντες.
Καὶ τότε πειθόμενον λαὸν μαλακοῖσιν ἔπεσσι
παρφάμενος, πάντων γε πατὴρ μάλα ἤπιος ἦρχον.
5 Οὔποτε δημοβόρος γενόμην, καὶ οὐ μάλα πολλὰ
ὁπλοτέρων ἀνδρῶν κρατερῇ ὑσμίνῃ ἐμίχθην.
Ἀλλ' ἐνὶ ἡμετέροις μεγάροις αἰδώς τε δίκη τε,
παρθένῳ ἀλφοδότᾳ, πολλῇ πραότητι φίληθεν
μηδοφόρους τε πάνυ πολυΐδριας ἄνδρας ἔφερβον.
10 Καὶ μᾶλλόν μοι ἄρεσκον ἀεὶ λιγύφωνοι ἀοιδοί,
οἷς μέλει αὐδῇσι καὶ εὐφροσύνῃ αἰδοίῃ
τερπέμεν ἡρώων ἀγαθὰς φρένας, οὐδ' ἂν ἔτ' ἄλλοι
αὐτῶν κλειόντων δυσπενθέα θυμὸν ἔχοιεν.
Τῶν ἀναμὶξ ἔζων, πάντ' ἤματα ἐν θαλίῃσι
15 ἥσυχος ἐξετέλουν, θυμὸν ἀκαχημένος οὔπω.
Αὐτὰρ ὅτ' αἶσα ἐμοὶ ἀμετάτροπος ἱστὸν ὕφηνε
νείατον, ἥτε βροτοῖς ἀλίαστα νεήματ' ἀριθμεῖ,
ἀθανάτων μεθ' ὅμιλον ἔβην, θεοὶ ᾗχιπερ ἄλλοι
εὔκηλοι ζώουσι κακῶν ἔκτοσθε μεριμνῶν.

Textus: Philipp Gundelius, *In divum imp(eratorem) Maximilianum... Epicoedion...Epitaphia item quaedam Graeca atque Latina eidem Principi.... posita*, Vienna 1520, Eij v.

Crit.: 4 ἤπιος correxi: ἥ- ed. || 6 ὁπλοτέρων ed., correxi || 7 μεγαροῖς ed., correxi | αἰδώς correxi: αἰδός ed. || 8 ἀλφοδότα] hapax ex ἀλφή cf. ὀλβοδότειραι | πραότητι α brevi | φίληθεν correxi: φίλιθεν ed. || 9 Μηδοφόρους] hapax ex μῆδος cf. βουληφόρος | πολυΐδριας correxi: πολυϋΐδριας ed. || 10 λιγύφωνοι correxi: λιγύφωνι ed. || 11 αἰδοίῃ debuit || 14 ἔζων] act. pro med. || 15 θυμὸν] brevis in caesura | ἐξετέλουν cum ictu ed. || 16 αἶσσα pro αἶσα | ἱστόν correxi: ὑστὸν ed. ||17 νεήματ' pro νήματα

Sim.: 1 ποιμένα λαῶν] cf. Hom. *Il.* 2.242 et al. || **2** ἀθάνατοι ποίησαν] cf. Hes. *Op.* 110 | ἐνὶ φρεσί] formula Homerica, cf. *Il.* 17.325 (φρεσὶ μήδεα εἰδώς) et *Od.* 11.445 || **3–4** μαλακοῖσιν ἔπεσσι / Παρφάμενος] Hes. *Theog.* 90 (ῥηιδίως, μαλακοῖσι παραιφάμενοι ἐπέεσσιν) || **4** Παρφάμενος] cf. Hom. *Il.* 12.249; *Od.* 2.189 | πάντων γε πατὴρ...ἤπιος] passim de Deo; cf. Pind. *Ol.* 2.17 (de tempore); NT *Ep. Pauli ad Eph.* 4.6.2 (εἷς θεὸς καὶ πατὴρ πάντων); Hom. *Od.* 2.47, 15.152 (πατὴρ δ᾽ ὣς ἤπιος ἦεν) || **5** δημοβόρος] cf. Hom. *Il.* 1.231 (δημοβόρος βασιλεύς) | μάλα πολλά] cf. Hom. *Od.* 1.1 et al. || **6** Ὁπλοτέρων ἀνδρῶν] cf. Hom. *Il.* 3.108 (αἰεὶ δ᾽ ὁπλοτέρων ἀνδρῶν) | κρατερῇ ὑσμίνη ἐμίχθην] cf. formulas Homericas κρατερῇ ὑσμίνη et προμάχοισιν ἐμίχθη || **7** ἐνὶ ἡμετέροις μεγάροις] cf. Hom. *Od.* 3.186 (ἐνὶ μεγάροισι καθήμενος ἡμετέροισι | αἰδώς) τε δίκη τε] cf. Tyrt. 12. 38 (οὔτ᾽ αἰδοῦς οὔτε δίκης) et Plat. *Prot.* 322c || **8** φίληθεν] cf. Hesych. ε 7492 (ἐφιλήθησαν) et *Il.* 2.668 || **9** cf. Hom. *Il.* 9.86 (τὸν δ᾽ εὗρον φρένα τερπόμενον φόρμιγγι λιγείῃ) | ἔφερβον] cf. Arat. *Phaen.* 114 (ὄφρ᾽ ἔτι γαῖα γένος χρύσειον ἔφερβεν) || **10** λιγύφωνοι ἀοιδοί] cf. Orph. *Arg.* 5 (λιγύφωνον ἀοιδήν) || **13** cf. Hom. *Od.* 1.338 (ἔργ᾽ ἀνδρῶν τε θεῶν τε, τά τε κλείουσιν ἀοιδοί); 5.222 (ταλαπενθέα θυμόν); 11.39 (νεοπενθέα θυμὸν ἔχουσαι); *Od.* 23.15 (πολυπενθέα θυμὸν ἔχουσαν) || **14** πάντ᾽ ἤματα] cf. *Hymn. Hom. Ven.* 28 (παρθένος ἔσσεσθαι πάντ᾽ ἤματα) pro formula ἤματα πάντα | ἐν θαλίῃσι] Hes. *Op.* 115 (τέρποντ᾽ ἐν θαλίῃσι) || **15** ἀκαχήμενος] cf. Hom. *Od.* 10.313 (ἀκαχήμενος ἦτορ) et al. || **16** ἀμετάτροπος] cf. *Anth. Gr. App.*, *Orac.* 146.19; Ars. *Par. Cent.* 185.7c.19 (τέτλατε Μοιράων ἀμετάτροπα δήνεα) | ἱστὸν ὕφηνε] cf. Hom. *Il.* 3.125 (ἣ δὲ μέγαν ἱστὸν ὕφαινε) et al. || **18** ἧχιπερ] cf. Hom. *Od.* 19.553 (ᾗχι πάρος περ) || **19** ζώουσι κακῶν ἔκτοσθε] cf. Thgn. 1.1121 (ὄφρα δίκῃ ζώοιμι κακῶν ἔκτοσθεν ἁπάντων)

On the Good Life and Apotheosis of Emperor Maximilian

When I was still alive, the shepherd of so many people
I was made by Immortals who gave me intelligent reason;
since I persuaded them all with sweet and softened speeches,
I could rule them all as gentle in mood as a father.
[5] Never devouring fat of the people I was, and not mingled
so many times in the gruesome and violent quarrel with youngsters.
In my palace I cherished respect of the other and justice,
growth-bringing maiden the two, with the use of caring and goodness;
men with ideas did I nourish, the really replenished of knowledge.
[10] Or let me say: I did always enjoy the clear-pitched singers
whose is a beautiful voice and a taste for festivity-music,
able to entertain high spirits of heroes, so no one
anymore could, when they sing, have a single pain in their feelings.
So among them I was sitting and spending my time in the banquets
[15] peacefully every day, never harmed in my soul by the darkness.
When unavoidable fate however was spinning my life's thread's
end, she who counts the unabating pensum of life for the humans,
then I joined the Immortals, and went to the place of the other
carefree gods who are all living outside of unhappy sorrows.

Metre: Hexameters.

Notes: Ceporinus' poem reveals traces of Byzantine pronunciation and adherence to Reuchlin's school of pronunciation: ι = η = i in φίλιθεν (l. 8), ι = οι = i in λιγύφωνι (l. 10), and υ = ι = i in ὑστὸν (l. 16). However, it is not clear whether these misspellings are Ceporinus' or the printer's fault. Ceporinus admits occasional hiatus and *brevis in caesura*, adhering to the principles of metrics, which he discussed in the 2nd edition of his grammar.[46] He introduces several *hapax legomena*, based on the analogy with epic forms: the epithet ἀλφοδότα (l. 7, from ἀλφή) might also be a reminiscence of Horace's banker Alfius, Mr. Growth, and could be understood in the economic sense: peace is good for business; μηδοφόρους (from μήδεα, l. 9) is probably a *metri causa* invention for βουληφόρος; he also uses the epic infinitive τερπέμεν and epic prolongations.

This poem, commemorating the death of the Holy Roman Emperor Maximilian I (1459–1519) was probably written in 1519, while Ceporinus was a student in Vienna.[47] The collection begins with a verse oration by Philipp Gundelius in Latin hexameters, followed by several Latin *epicedia* by different authors. In Ceporinus' poem Maximilian seems to be speaking from his grave (actually in Vienna), here imagined as coming from his cenotaph in Innsbruck, where he had surrounded himself by more than 100 statues of 'heroes and heroines of the past'. Ceporinus could have thanked the Emperor for signing the Treaty of Basel (and thus *de facto* Swiss independence from the Holy Roman Empire) in 1499, but of course, after the defeat in the battle of Dornach in 1499 the Emperor had no other choice. Maximilian's message in the beginning is clearly referring to this controversy, stressing: 'I'm no Agamemnon (cf. l. 6), I'm not a fat- or people-devouring king'.[48]

The poem is constructed in a Byzantine, *oikos*-like ABBA-pattern, framed by the motives *alive-immortal – immortal-living*, where the theme of Agamemnon announces the theme of heroes as an audience. The centre of the poem leaves place for praising Maximilian I as a benefactor of arts. The word δίκη (l. 7) was in Hesiod's times the equivalent of our 'Realpolitik', but Ceporinus used it probably in the foggy sense of justice. The reference to the abolishment of Maximilian's pain

---

46 Ceporinus 1522b, 148–156.
47 According to the date of Gundel's address to the reader which dates from 1 December 1519.
48 The double-entendre between δημός 'fat', reserved in feasts to kings, and δῆμος, 'people' or 'district', i.e. the taxes, is used here as in the *Iliad* against Agamemnon by the youngster Achilles, but there are allusions to Ulysses as well, see Steinrück, Martin (2001), *La pierre et la graisse: Lecture dans l'intertexte grec antique*, Amsterdam.

(in the end) could be linked by historians (and Ceporinus) to the biographeme according to which the Emperor once fell from his horse, was in pain for the rest of his life, and inclined to depression.

Biography: Jakob Wiesendanger or Ceporin(us) (Ἰάκωβος ὁ Κηπωρός) was born in 1499 or 1500 in Dinghard near Winterthur, Switzerland; he studied at Winterthur Gymnasium, the Universities of Cologne and Vienna (1518–1520), as well as with Johannes Reuchlin (→ **Germany**) in Ingolstadt (1520); in 1520 he was praised for his good knowledge of Greek as someone who makes Vienna speak Greek (*greçissare*).[49] Ceporin was a protégé of Zwingli, worked initially as a corrector for the Basel printer Andreas Cratander (Hartmann, c. 1490–1540) and received his first teaching post of Greek and Latin from Zwingli in 1522 (whereas Zwingli himself studied Hebrew with him); in 1525, shortly before his premature death, he became professor of Greek and Hebrew in Zwingli's school of Theology in Zürich; Ceporin however continued to work with Basel printers, participating in the editions of Dionysius Periegetes' *Descriptio*, Aratus' *Phaenomena*, and Proclus' *Sphaera* in 1523 and of the New Testament in 1524, both in Johannes Bebel's printing house.[50] He also wrote the address to the readers for Zwingli's work on the principles of teaching (*Quo pacto ingenui adolescentes formandi sint*), published by Bebel in 1523.[51]

Ceporin is mostly famous for two works: firstly, his Greek grammar, which was printed in 1522 in Basel at Valentin Crato's printing house in two different editions and stayed in use in numerous reprints and new editions till the 18th century; and secondly, his edition of Pindar which appeared after his death with a preface by Zwingli (1526).[52] Presently, no other Greek poems by Ceporin are known. His addressee, Emperor Maximilian I (1459–1519), was proclaimed Holy Roman Emperor in 1508, but he had already been crowned as king in 1486. Maximilian had hugely broadened the reign of the Habsburg house, both peacefully and in war, whereas Switzerland was one of the countries which retained their independence as a result of the battle of Dornach in 1499 and the ensuing peace treaty of Basel. Maximilian I is known as a protector of the arts and of humanist scholars, thus it is no wonder that his death was commemorated with numerous poems, speeches, and poetry collections.[53]

---

[49] Bächtold 2003, for more details, Riedweg 2000, 204f., Suter-Meyer 2017, 27f.
[50] Riedweg 2000, 206f., 213–215.
[51] See VD16 Z 88.
[52] For more details, see Riedweg 2000.
[53] Friedhuber 2003; Mühlberger 2007.

Bibliography: Bächtold, Hans Ulrich (2003), "Ceporin, Jakob", in: *Historisches Lexikon der Schweiz (HLS)*, Version vom 01.09.2003. Online: https://hls-dhs-dss.ch/de/articles/010566/ 2003-09-01/ [accessed: September 2020]; Schnabel, C. (2000), "Ceporinus/Wiesendanger", https://www.zhref.ch/themen/reformationsjubilaeum/allgemeine-informationen/huldrych-zwingli/zwingli-lexikon-von-a-bis-z-1/lexikon-c/ceporinus-wiesendanger [accessed: September 2020]; Riedweg, Christoph (2000), "Ein Philologe an Zwinglis Seite. Zum 500. Geburtstag des Zürcher Humanisten Jacob Wiesendanger, gen. Ceporinus (1500–1525)", in: *Museum Helveticum* 57, 201–219; Egli, Emil (1901), "Ceporins Leben und Schreiben", in: *Analecta reformatoria*, Bd. 2, Zürich, 145–160; Katharina Suter-Meyer (2017), "Der Rhein: Fluss der Germanen oder der Helvetier? Patriotismus und Apologie in Vadian's Kommentar zu Pomponius Mela (1522)", in: Carmen Cardelle de Hartmann/Ulrich Eigler (eds.), *Latein am Rhein. Zur Kulturtopographie und Literaturgeographie eines Europäischen Stromes*, Berlin, 22–52; Friedhuber, Ingrid (2003), "Emperor Maximilian I.", in: Peter G. Bietenholz/Thomas B. Deutscher, *Contemporaries of Erasmus*, Volume II, Toronto et al., 410–414; Mühlberger, Kurt (2007), "Poetenkolleg und Dichterkrönung in Wien", in: Rainer A. Müller et al. (eds.), *Bilder-Daten-Promotionen. Studien zum Promotionswesen an deutschen Universitäten der frühen Neuzeit*, Stuttgart, 84–119. Some of Ceporinus' editions: *Compendium Grammaticae Graecae iam recens editum*, Basel: Curio, 1522; *Compendium Grammaticae Graecae: iam de integro ab ipso authore & castigatum & locupletatum*, Basel: Curio, 1522; *Pindari Olympia, Pythia, Nemea, Isthmia*, Basel: Cratander, 1526.

[JP/MS]

Konrad Gessner (1516–1565)

I. *Conradi Gesneri Tigurini ad studiosos pueros Hendecasyllabum hendecastichum* [1542]

Νίγρου ἑνδεκασύλλαβον ποίημα
Χερσὶν ἀμφοτέρῃσι δεῦτε παῖδες
Δέξασθ'. Ἐνθάδε γὰρ μαθεῖν ἔνεστι
Τρέψεις θαυμασίας τε ποικίλας τε
5   Φύσιος προτέρης ἐς εἶδος ἄλλο.
Οὐκ εἰκῆ δὲ παλαιοὶ ἄνδρες αὕτως
Πλάττοντες τάδε, φημίσαντο μύθους,
Ἀλλὰ σεμνοτέρας τινὰς μαθήσεις,
Ὥσπερ ἐν λέπεϊ πυρῆνα, κρύψαν.
10 Λάβετ' οὖν τόδε παῖδες εὐπρόσωποι
Νίγρου ἑνδεκασύλλαβον ποίημα.

Textus: *Ovidianae Metamorphoseos epitome* per Franciscum Nigrum Bassianatem collecta, Tiguri [1542] (VD16 O 1668), [C7 = p. 23r]. Iterum ed. Bartholomaei Bolognini Bononiensis *Epitome elegiaca in Publ. Ovidij Nasonis Libros XV. Metamorphoseon*. Francisci Nigri Bassianatis *Epitome in Metamorphosin Ovidianam*, carmine Sapphico, Basileae 1544 (VD16 ZV 2237), d2v.

Sim.: 2 Χερσὶν ἀμφοτέρῃσι] cf. formulam epicam ἀμφοτέρῃσι(ν) (δὲ) χερσί(ν) apud Hom. *Il.* 18.23, 123 et al.

Eleven hendecasyllabic verses for boy students by Konrad Gessner from Zurich

This hendecasyllabic poem by Negri
come and take it in both your hands, my pupils,
for in here you can learn a lot on changings,
marvelous and also as manifolded,
[5] from old nature to different appearance:
Not just so did in older times the people
create and tell us just for fun those stories
but they hid therein some higher learnings
just like stone in the husk (or in the fruitflesh).
[10] This is why you should take, you fairfaced pupils,
this hendecasyllabic poem by Negri.

Metre: Phalaecian hendecasyllables (called Sapphic).

Notes: The poem is addressed to the readers of the Latin verse epitome of Ovid's *Metamorphoses* by Francesco Negri (Niger, 1500 Bassano – 1563 Pinczow), a Franciscan monk and scholar who turned to Protestantism. Gessner uses the same metre as Negri and frames the poem with allusions to his name (*niger* 'black'). Gessner also refers to the subject of Negri's epitome, the *metamorphoses* ('changings') and the possibility of allegorical interpretations ('hidden meanings') of these. The circular structure and references to the metre may be influenced by Negri's Latin poem in this book (see below). Gessner combines Attic and epic forms as usual for Humanist Greek poetry, but avoids hiatus (as he should in a lyric poem). By the time of the edition of this poem Negri had found refuge in the Three Leagues territory of Switzerland (corresponding roughly to modern Graubünden) and was in contact with Gessner, as well as with several other Italian scholars who had been corresponding with Heinrich Bullinger (1504–1574) and turned to Protestantism; later Negri also attended Gessner's classes in Zürich school.[54] Negri had worked on Roman literature, translated from Italian to Latin and published polemical works on theological and philosophical questions, but

---

54 Bernhard 2019, 341–344.

he also published Latin paraphrases of the psalms. His *Epitome* of Ovid's *Metamorphoses* in hendecasyllables appeared for the first time in 1542 in Zürich and was designed for schoolboys. In its beginning, there is an unsigned Latin poem in 'Catullan hendecasyllables' (inspired by Catullus' *carmen* 42), most probably by Negri himself. Negri had in the 1540s a close relationship also with some Basel printers, so the poem was included in Bassi's new edition of Ovid's paraphrases in other metres in 1544.

II. *In tumulum* / ἄλλο εἰς αὐτόν [1563?]

Ἰχθὺς ἐνὶ πελάγει μῦς κήτεσίν ἐστιν ὁδηγός·
   καὶ ΜΥΣ ἀνὴρ ἄριστος,
μύστης Χριστοσεβής, ΛΥΚΟΒΑΤΗΣ δ' οὔνομα πρώτου
   ἐκ μυστικοῦ βαπτίσματος,
5   ἀνδράσιν ἡγητὴρ διδαχῇ τε βίῳ τε βροτοῖσιν,
   ἕως ἂν ἔζη, γέγονε.
Νῦν δ' ἱερῷ λυκάβαντι λογιζομένῳ ἐνὶ δυσσὶν
   αὐτοῦ ὀνόμασιν ἧλε,
ῥιφθέντος, μετὰ τόνδε βίον πρὸς κρεῖττον' ἀπῆλθεν
10   αἰωνίως ζησόμενος.

Textus: Simmler, Josiah (1566), *Vita clarissimi philosophi et medici excellentissimi Conradi Gessneri Tigurini*, Zürich, L3v (= 43v). Editio postrema in: *Synopsis festalium concionum*, Basileae 1595, 91 (In Tumulum excellentis doctrina et pietate viri Wolfgangi Musculi); cf. exemplar manu scriptum in Wolfenbüttel HAB, Cod. Guelf. 872 Novi, scil. Karl Scheller, *Carmina Hellenica Teutonum III*, p. 164, sub titulo: "In Wolfg. Musculum, Dusae Lotharing. oppid. Alsat. finitimo, nat.1497, †1563. 3 Kal. Sept."

Crit.: 3 ΛΥΚΟΒΆΤΗΣ Vita 1566: ΛΥΚοβάτης Synopsis || 8 ἧλε Vita, Scheller: ηλο linea suprascripta Synopsis; ab ἀλάω (de peregrinatione vel haeresi) || 9 ἀπῆλθεν] ἀπῆλθε Synopsis

Sim.: 1 de re cf. Plin. *NH* 9.186 (*amicitiae exempla sunt...ballaena et musculus*); vid. etiam Plut. *De soll. an.* 980f–981a; Ael. *NA* 2.13 || 7 λυκάβαντι] cf. *Od.* 19.306

On the grave / Another poem on the same

The Mouse-fish is in the open sea for the whales their own pilot,
   and Mouse-man, he excels here.
Mice-ter-believer of Christ, his lycambic first name is Wolf-step [Lykobates]
   so Mystical his baptism.
[5] Leader of mortal men, in his wisdom and life an example,
   he always was in lifetime,

> Now in the holy year/wolf-step [*lykabas*], counted with both of his names,
>   he has been thrown out and wanders
>   and he has gone after this one now to a much better lifetime,
> [10] bound for eternal living.⁵⁵

Metre: Epodic; hexameter with an iambic dimeter sometimes catalectic (l. 6 γέγονε, l. 9 ζησόμενος with accentuated short vowels for longum, as in Greg. Naz.).

Notes: The poem's addressee is the Alsacian reformator Wolfgang Musculus/ Müslin (1497 Dieuse – 1563 Bern), known also as Εὐτύχιος (a translation of another version of his surname, Meusel/ Mosel). He studied in different schools in Dieuze, Ribeauville, Colmar, and Sélestat, but so briefly, that he has been called an autodidact.⁵⁶ He became a novice in the Benedictine monastery in Bixville and was ordained as a priest in Metz, but soon turned to Protestantism and married. As a vicar in Strasbourg, he studied Hebrew with Capito and Bucerus, and Greek on his own. He had a major role in the Augsburg reformation, but as a result of the Schmalkaldic war and the Augsburg interim he had to flee and spent his last years from 1549 until his death as a professor of theology (and Hebrew) in Bern. He was brilliant in exegesis (he published several commentaries on the Old and New Testaments), wrote liturgical (protestant) songs in German, but was condemned because of his theological views by Rome. Although he had an opportunity to return to Augsburg, he chose to remain in Bern, where he had become deeply rooted: his sons became priests and teachers in Switzerland, his daughter Esther was married to his colleague, the Professor of Greek at Bern Gymnasium, Valentin Rebmann/Ampelander, founding one of the eminent Bern families for centuries to come. After his death, the description of his life was published together with a selection of his occasional Latin poems and a collection of *epicedia* by his friends and colleagues.⁵⁷ The latter included the above-presented poem by Gessner, but also Greek poems by Musculus' friend, the reformed pastor and theologian Johannes Haller (1523 Amsoldingen – 1575

---

55 Latin version of the poem in *Vita* and in *Synopsis*: *Musculus vt vastis immensa per aequora cetis / Praenando piscis dux solet esse viae: / Ne breuia, aut syrtes, scopuliue, pericula vitae, / Insidiaeue vllae, dira creare queant. / MVSCVLE sic BΩLGANGE viam mortalibus aegris / Foelicem ad caelum, nomen vt insinuat, / Monstrabas viuendo pie, sancteque docendo: / Nunc terra hac corpus, sydera habent animam.*
56 Bodenmann 2000.
57 The *Vita* and the collection have both been published at least twice, see above, but although the manuscript of the *Vita* has been found, the poems, which had once been attached to it, are now lost (Bodenmann 2000, 27).

Bern),[58] who had even been on his deathbed, by his son-in-law, Valentin Ampelander, and by Franciscus Portus, as well as Latin poetry by other friends and colleagues.[59]

This poem represents a precious sign of vitality of the iambic tradition in epodes, although neither Archilochus nor any other Greek iambographer used exactly this metre: combining hexameter with a (freely) catalectic iambic dimeter (which Servius and Perotti called *Anacreontium*), as in Horace's epodes 14 and 15, close to Müslin's own choral's second verses (*O Herre Gott begnade mich,/ Der Vater in sein Throne*). As was usual in occasional poetry, the name of the addressee is the main source of the word-play,[60] but in the case of Wolfgang Müslin, an additional role might have been played by Gessner's interest in zoology. However, there is also a link to Greek iambographers (Semonides, Archilochos): In the *Odyssey*, Lykabas is the rite for Apollon (around Christmas), which could explain the strange adjective *hieros* (sacred/strong). Gessner may have seen, not unlike modern scholars, in Lykabas/Wolfstep, the name of Archilochus' enemy Lykambes. Gessner attacks in a typically ethic, deflected manner, the pope for not condemning a wolf, but a mouse.

Biography: Konrad (Conrad) Gessner (1516 Zürich – 1565 Zürich) is a universal historian, philologist, medical doctor, and botanist who does not need a presentation.[61] He belonged to the circles of Zwingli, studied at the Universities of Bourges and Paris, and after starting to teach in Zürich, he was soon (1537) invited to the Lausanne Academy as a Professor of Greek.[62] After his promotion in Basel in medicine in 1541 he returned to Zürich, where he worked as a physician and a natural historian. Gessner's interest in philology is expressed in his *Mithridates* (1555), but already in 1537 he had published a lexicon of Greek (in Basel, by Walder). Gessner wrote numerous Greek poems, including fourteen poems commemorating the death of Zwingli and numerous book epigrams, as well as some Greek letters, partly still unedited. He had a wide circle of

---

58 See van Wijnkoop Lüthi, Marc (2006), "Haller, Johannes", in: *Historisches Lexikon der Schweiz (HLS)*, Version vom 17.02.2006. Online: https://hls-dhs-dss.ch/de/articles/010458/2006-02-17/ [accessed: November 2020].
59 See Simmer 1566, including 2 Greek and 3 Latin epigrams (by Haller, p. 93), two Greek poems (Ampelander/Rebmann, p. 104, 105) and one Greek poem by Franciscus Portus (p. 105).
60 In the same collection, Johannes Haller presents two Greek epigrams which also rely on the word-play with mouse (see Synopsis 1595, 93).
61 For biographical data, see Simmler 1566; Leu 2020 (newest general discussion); Leu/Opitz 2019.
62 See Crousaz 2012, 72.

correspondents, to whom he also dedicated poetry, and received several poems from others, including some Greek poems (by Franciscus Portus, Adolph Occo III, Henri Estienne) in the collection commemorating his death.⁶³

Bibliography: Leu, Urs (2020), "Gessner, Konrad", in: *Historisches Lexikon der Schweiz (HLS)*, Version vom 08.05.2020. Online: https://hls-dhs-dss.ch/de/articles/014376/2020-05-08/ [accessed: September 2020]; Crousaz, Karine (2012), *L'Académie de Lausanne entre Humanisme et Réforme (ca.1537–1560)*, Leiden/Boston; Vogel, Katja (2019), "Thrinodiae Herois Huldrychi Zwinglii – Conrad Gessners dichterischer Nachruf auf Huldrych Zwingli", in: Urs Leu/Peter Opitz (eds.), *Conrad Gessner (1516–1565): die Renaissance der Wissenschaften*, Berlin, 465–484. For Negri: Biasiori, Lucio (2013), "Francesco Negri", in: *Dizionario Biografico degli Italiani* 78, 120–123. For Musculus: Bodenmann, Reinhard (2000), *Wolfgang Musculus (1497–1563)*, Genève; Dellsperger, Rudolf/Freudenberger, Rudolf/Weber, Wolfgang (eds.) (1997), *Wolfgang Musculus (1497–1563) und die Oberdeutsche Reformation*, Berlin 1997.

[JP/MS]

Gédéon Perrot (active in 1592–1622)

Aliud [1594]

  Ἑρμ. Ἥκω νῦν κήρυξ, Διὸς αἰθερίοιο κελεύσει.
     Ἴλδιον ὅττι θέλει ἆθλον ἔχειν ἀρετᾶς.
  Ἀπόλλ. Εὖγε, διακτορίην τίν' ἀπαγγέλλοντα ἀκούω·
     Ποῦ θέμις αἰδοίη Πάλλας ὅπη τε πέλει;
5 Παλλ. Ἴλδιος ἀθανάτου ἀρετῆς ἆθλον στέφος ἕξει,
     εἵνεκε τοῖο βροτοὶ πολλὰ φέρουσι κακά.

     Haec amicitiae symbolum extare voluit Gedeon Perrotus Neocomensis.

Textus: *Carmina gratulatoria In honorem...Dn. Ioannis Hildii Mulheimensis Marchici...Cum...supremam in philosophia lauream consequeretur*, Basel: Foiletus 1593, A2v.

Crit.: 4 Παλλὰς debuit ‖ 6 εἵνεκε] pro εἵνεκεν metri causa

---

63 Cf. Vogel 2019 (including an edition of the longest among these, a Homeric cento) and Leu/Opitz 2019 passim. Some of these Greek poems have been printed after the speech by Simmler 1566, E2v–E3r (by Gessner to Occa), L3rv (*in tumulum Musculi*); H3v–H4r (*epicedia* by others for Gessner).

Sim.: 1 Διὸς αἰθερίοιο] cf. Nonn. *Dion.* 7.267 || **2, 4** ἀρετᾶς] dorice || **3** διακτορίην] cf. Nonn. *Par. Jo.* 12.8; Mus. *Hero et Leander* 6 (λύχνον ἀπαγγέλλοντα διακτορίην Ἀφροδίτης)

Another one (on the same topic)

> Hermes: Now I arrive as a herald with heavenly Zeus's commandment,
> his wish is: virtue's prize Hildius has to receive.
> Apollo: Good! What a message I'm listening here to be told me by the herald?
> Where is Themis revered, where is Pallas the wise?
> [5] Pallas: Hildius will receive the prize-garland of virtue immortal,
> for which the mortals have so many troubles to bear.
>
> *Gedeon Perrot from Neuchâtel has wished to leave these lines, as token of friendship*

Metre: Elegiac couplets (with hiatus in l. 5).

Notes: The addressee Johannes Hildius from Mühlheim in Baden was enrolled at the University of Basel in 1588 and received his degree in philosophy there in 1593.[64] This poem follows another, much longer poem by Perrot, which tells in Latin hexameters that in the midst of the storms of life, the practice of virtue and arts (acknowledged by Apollo and Pallas) will bring consolation, joy, and honour. The Greek poem accomplishes the prediction of honour in a short dialogue between the messenger-god Hermes and the guardians of the arts, Apollo and Pallas Athena, who will crown the new Master.

Biography: The author Gédéon Perrot from St. Imier entered the University of Basel in 1592, was still studying there in 1594 and worked as a pastor in St. Imier in 1617–1622, displaying his religious zeal in Horace-style inscriptions in the local church.[65] This is his only known Greek poem.

---

64 Also Mvlheimensis, Milhensis, Myllensis Marchicus, considered to be identical with Johann Jacob Hildius, pastor in Fischingen in Thurgau, Switzerland (1608) and in Buggingen in Baden-Württemberg (1636–1639), see Wackernagel 1956, 359.
65 Gedeon Perrotus Neocomensis (of Neuchâtel) is probably the same person as Gedeon Perrotus Sanctimeriensis (Sanctimerinensis Rauracus) from St. Imier in Jura (not far from Neuchâtel), see Wackernagel 1959, 399; Gerber 1928, 50; cf. *Dictionnaire du Jura*, https://www.diju.ch/f/notices/detail/1642 [accessed: November 2020].

Bibliography: Wackernagel, Hans Georg (1956), *Die Matrikel der Universität Basel. II. Band. 1532/33–1600/01*, Basel; Gerber, Robert (1928), "Le Folklore du Haut-Erguel", in: *Actes de la Société jurassienne d'émulation* 33, 47–60.

[JP]

Isaac Casaubon (1559–1614)

Auctoris de hac editione δεκάστιχον. ὡς ἀπὸ τῆς βίβλου [1596]

Ὁπλοτέρου τόδε γράμμ', ἄγονος γονή, ἥνπερ ἔφυσεν
 στοργῆς γλυκείας τεκνικῆς νῆϊς τοκεύς.
Ὃς πάρος ἠλιτόμηνον ἔμ', εἰν ἀβάτοισι βάτοισιν
 Ἀτημέλητον εἴα, οὐ φήσας τεκεῖν.
5 Ἄρτι με κεῖνος ἀνεῖλεν, ἐῷ πήχυνέ τ' ἀγοστῷ,
 Ἄλλων παραιφασίῃσι, τῶν ἐμοὶ φίλων
Οὕτω δὴ κομιδῆς ἔτυχόν τινος· ἀμφὶ δὲ γυῖα
 πατὴρ ἔμ' ἀμφέβαλλε λιτὰ γοῦν τάδε.
Τῷ Σκαλάνῳ καὶ Κομμελίνῳ χάρις· οὕνεκεν ὑμέων
10 ἔχει γόνος γονῆα καὶ γονεὺς γόνον.

Textus: *Isaaci Casauboni Theocriticarum lectionum libellus. Editio altera*, [Genève]: Commelin 1596, A1v; (in editione priori anno 1584 deest carmen graecum).

Crit.: 3, 8 ἔμ' ed., correxi

Sim.: 1 ἄγονος] cf. *Anth. Pal.* 14.111.1 (Ἄγονος ἐξ ἀγόνων); Eubul. *Sph. fr.* 1.11 (αἰχμητής, παίδων ἀγόνων γόνον ἐξαφανίζων) || 2 τεκνικῆς] hapax; de re cf. Philem. 200 (ἡδύ γε πατὴρ τέκνοισιν, εἰ στοργὴν ἔχοι) || 3 ἀβάτοισι βάτοισιν] cf. Hermesian. (FGrHist 691T2) apud Agatharch. *de mari Erythr.* 21.89 || 5 πήχυνέ τ' ἀγοστῷ] cf. Nonn. *Dion.* 8.187; 12.378 al. (πήχυνεν ἀγοστῷ) || 7 γυῖα] de brachiis cf. Theocr. *Id.* 22.81 || 9 Σκαλάνῳ] cf. J.C. Scaliger, *Poemata*, Heidelberg 1600, Tit. verso, v. 3 (Ἦν δὲ Σκαλανῶν θείων γένος)

A decastich on this edition, by its author. As if spoken by the book

This writing of a younger man is a childless offspring, begotten
 by a father unaware of sweet parental care;
who me in tender age, in inaccessible brambles,
 had left to the fates, denying that he brought me forth.
[5] Just now, freshly he took me again in his arms and embraced me,

encouraged by the others was he, by my friends,
thus I received some attention and then around me my father
did put his hands, around these limbs, unadorned.
Grateful I am to you, Skalanos [Scaliger] and Commelinus, by your doing
[10] the child has now a father, and the father his child.

Metre: Epodic (hexameter, iambic trimeter).

Notes: The poem uses an old device of Greek epigrams, making the book speak for itself. Word-plays on the begetting, father and offspring occur as frame of the poem (l. 1 ἄγονος γονή, l. 10 γόνος γονῆα...γονεὺς γόνον), others in the middle (ll. 2 and 4 τεκνικῆς...τοκεύς...τεκεῖν and l. 3 ἀβάτοισι βάτοισιν). The possibly intendedly ambiguous τεκνικῆς (instead of τεχνικῆς) in line 2 might allude either to the fact that Casaubon's daughter from his first marriage had not yet been born (she died probably soon after birth in 1585) or that the author was not yet familiar with editing techniques.

Biography: Isaac Casaubon (Hortibonus, 'Goodgarden') was born in 1559 in Geneva in a French refugee family. His father was the Huguenot activist Arnaut Casaubon.[66] Soon the family returned to France and settled down in Crest (Dauphiné) where Isaac was taught by his father. In 1578 Isaac returned to Geneva and became the student of Franciscus Portus (1511–1581), the famous Cretan who had been the Professor of Greek at the Academy of Geneva since 1562. Portus appreciated Casaubon's zeal and talent and recommended him as his follower. His son Aemilius Portus wrote about Casaubon the following words: Κήπων ἐξ ἀγαθῶν καρπὸς πέλε φέρτατος... ('From good gardens the best fruit comes...') on the occastion of Casaubon's first scholarly work, the *Critical notes to the Lives of the Philosophers by Diogenes Laertius* (1583). After the death of Portus, Casaubon became the Professor of Greek (1582) in the Academy. In 1583 he married Marie Perlyot, who soon died (1585), followed a few months later by Casaubon's father. In 1586 Casaubon married Florence, the daughter of the printer Henri II Estienne (1531–1598; → **France**), with whom he had a long and affectionate marriage, and begot 18 children. The life in Geneva was difficult at the time. The fight against the dukes of Savoy brought the city under a siege, the plague killed many of its inhabitants and the economy was faltering. The only industry left, printing, did not bring much income either. Casaubon had hoped to get access to Estienne's book and manuscript collection through his wife, but this

---

66 See Barrelet 2005; Pattison 1892; Reverdin 1961 and 2000 (here and below).

did not happen.⁶⁷ Actually, the relationship with his father-in-law was clouded by Casaubon's interference in the conflicts between Genevan printers in 1584. In 1566, Estienne published his edition of Theocritus and the bucolic poets, to which Crespin responded with a pocket volume of *Bucolici* and *Gnomici* (1569), after which Estienne published the *Idyllic* poets (1579). Crespin's successor, Eustache Vignon, published a new edition in 1584, to which he attached critical notes on Theocritus and a salutatory letter to Estienne by Casaubon. Although the words of address were flattering, the story must have not pleased Estienne.⁶⁸ Casaubon continued to teach Greek, to edit and translate the ancient authors, trying to provide for his increasing family and to acquire the books he needed for his scholarly work. He had many friends and supporters: the aging Théodore de Bèze kept humanist ardour and love for Greek alive at Geneva and looked at him as a son; his friendly relationship with the printer Jérôme Commelin (Commelinus, ca. 1550–1597) was beneficial for both; the initial mutual admiration with Joseph Justus Scaliger (1540–1609) grew into a friendship in letters.⁶⁹ When Commelin published a new edition of Theocritus and its Greek scholia with Scaliger's critical notes in 1596 in Heidelberg, he invited Casaubon to re-publish his notes on Theocritus, which he did, with some revisions and omitting the plea for advice from his letter to Estienne. On the verso of the title page of this part of the edition (printed separately in Geneva) he also added the above poem, alluding to the previous edition of his notes and thanking Commelinus and Scaliger (Σκάλανος).⁷⁰ Still under economic pressure, Causaubon left Geneva and became a professor at the University of Montpellier in France (1596), after which he moved to Lyon (1598) and to Paris (1600). In Lyon he received the news of the death of his father-in-law, but the hope of finally obtaining his wife's dowry was not fulfilled, although he became involved in the printing house, which now

---

67 Pattison 1875, 22ff.
68 The story is told by Pattison 1875, 29–31. See Οἱ τῆς ἡρωικῆς ποιήσεως πρωτεύοντες ποιηταί...*Poetae graeci principes heroici carminis et alii*, [Geneva]: Henri II Estienne, 1566; Τὰ σωζόμενα τῶν παλαιοτάτων ποιητῶν γεωργικά...*Vetustissimorum authorum Georgica*..., Geneva: Jean Crespin, 1569; *Theocriti aliorumque poetarum Idyllia. Ejusdem epigrammata*, [Geneva]: Henri II Estienne, 1579; Casaubon's critical notes are printed in Τὰ σωζόμενα τῶν παλαιοτάτων ποιητῶν γεωργικά...*Vetustissimorum authorum Georgica*...*Accessit huic editioni Isaaci Hortiboni libellus*, [Geneva]: Eustache Vignon, 1584 (Casaubon's notes on pp. 361–413).
69 Pattison 1875, 63–64, 69sqq.
70 He had adopted this name probably from Julius Caesar, see critical notes above. J.J. Scaliger has signed his poems as Ἰώσηππος Σκάλανος Ἰουλιάδης, in: *Agathiae Epigrammata Graeca*, Leiden 1594, 4v. On this publication, see Casaubon's letter to Scaliger from March 1596: Casaubon 1638, 494.

belonged to Paul Estienne. Casaubon found a new protector, King Henry IV, but after Henry's death he was no longer secure in France and left for England, where he spent the last years of his life (1610–1614). Casaubon published many important editions of classical authors: Strabo, Polyaenus, Aristotle, Pliny, Theophrastus, Diogenes Laertius, Suetonius, Athenaeus, Persius, but also the New Testament, Dio Chrysostomus, Gregory of Nyssa, and Joseph Justus Scaliger, as well as critical comments on the ancient authors. His surviving immense correspondence is invaluable as a source for intellectual (and not only) history. He also left many Latin and Greek occasional poems.

Bibliography: Barrelet, Jacques (2005), "Casaubon, Isaac", in: *Historisches Lexikon der Schweiz (HLS)*, https://hls-dhs-dss.ch/de/articles/035175/2005-07-06/ [accessed: November 2020]; Pattison, Mark (1875), *Isaac Casaubon 1559-1614*, Oxford (with a list of Casaubon's published books); *Homère chez Calvin. Mélanges O. Reverdin*, Genève 2000, 37–40; Parenty, Hélène (2009), *Isaac Casaubon helléniste*, Genève. Among Casaubon's works: *Isaaci Casauboni Epistolae*, Hague: Maire, 1638; Casaubon's Greek poems from the Geneva period: Jacquemot, Jean (1591), *Lamentationes prophetae Jermiae*, Geneva, **2rv; Lect, Jaques (1595), *Iac. Lectii poematum liber unus*, Geneva, *iiij v; Jacquemot, Jean (1591), *Joannis Jacomoti Barrensis Lyrica*, Geneva, A4rv.

[JP]

Jacob Meiler (*fl.* 1599)

Παροιμίαι Σολομῶντος. Κεφ. α΄ [1599]

(excerptum, vv. 1–14)

    Αἱ γνῶμαι Σολομῶντος τοῦ Δαβὶδ βασιλῆος
    Ἰσραήλ, γνῶναι τὴν ἀγαθὴν σοφίην,
    Θέσπιν ἐπιστήμην νοέμεν καὶ νουθετέεσθαι,
    Καὶ λαβέμεν τὸν νοῦν τήν τε δικαιοσύνην.
5   Ὡς θεῖναι μερόπων εὐήθεσι μὲν φρένας ἐσθλάς,
    Τοῖς δὲ νέοις γνῶσιν τήν τε διδασκαλίαν.
    Οὓς πινυτὸς παρέχων, ἄλλων πινυτώτερος ἔσται
    Λαθριδίας γνώμας τῶν συνετῶν μαθέμεν.
    Ἰδμοσύνης ἐρατῆς ἀρχὴ φόβος ἐστὶ θεοῖο.
10 Ἀλλ' ὀλιγωροῦσι γνώσεος ἀφραδέες.
    Σοῖο πατρός, τέκνον, τὰ μαθήματα φίλτατ' ἄκουσον,
    Καὶ δέξαι μητρὸς σεῖο δίδαγμα καλόν.
    Ταῦτα γάρ, ὦ τέκνον, κεφαλῇ σέθεν ὡς χάρις ἔσται,
    ὥς θ' ὅρμος δειρῇ χρύσεός ἐστι τεῇ.

Textus: *Proverbiorum Salomonis metaphrasis graeca metrica Jacobi Meilerii. Cui versio latina ad verbum reddita e regione respondet*, Genevae: M. Berjon, 1599, 11

Sim.: 2 τὴν ἀγαθὴν σοφίην] cf. Xenoph. fr. 2.14 West (ἀγαθῆς σοφίης) || **5** φρένας ἐσθλάς] cf. Hom. *Il.* 17.470; *Od.* 2.117; 7.111 || **14** ὅρμος δειρῇ χρύσεος] cf. Hom. *Od.* 15.460 (χρύσεον ὅρμον ἔχων)

The Proverbs of Salomon, Chapter 1

(excerpt, ll. 1–14)

> The proverbs of Solomon, the son of David, the king of
>   Israel tell how to know blessing of wisdom so good;
> to perceive divine knowledge, to get some recommendations,
>   and to obtain prudent minds and the righteousness;
> [5] and to give understanding minds to the simple among mortals,
>   and to the younger men wisdom and lessons as well.
> The man whose ears are sagacious, will be more sagacious than others;
>   and he will understand the hidden sayings of the wise.
> Fear of God is the beginning of knowledge, which is beloved
> [10] but of this wisdom of yours fools have little esteem.
> Pay attention, my child, to the dearest instructions of your father,
>   from your mother accept all her teachings so fair.
> All this, my child, will be as a lovely grace upon your head,
>   just like a golden chain which is surrounding your neck.[71]

Biography: Little, if anything at all is known of Jacob(us) Meiler(us) (Meiller, Meilerius, Giacomo Meillerio). His inclusion among the Swiss Greek poets is based on the uncertain information that he taught at the Academy of Lausanne.[72] However, as many of the academy's Hellenizing professors were foreign refugees,

---

[71] The translation has been in some places inspired by the King James version of the Bible. The Greek text paraphrased is the following: LXX *Prov.* 1.1–9 Παροιμίαι Σαλωμῶντος υἱοῦ Δαυιδ, ὃς ἐβασίλευσεν ἐν Ισραηλ, γνῶναι σοφίαν καὶ παιδείαν νοῆσαί τε λόγους φρονήσεως δέξασθαί τε στροφὰς λόγων νοῆσαί τε δικαιοσύνην ἀληθῆ καὶ κρίμα κατευθύνειν, ἵνα δῷ ἀκάκοις πανουργίαν, παιδὶ δὲ νέῳ αἴσθησίν τε καὶ ἔννοιαν· τῶνδε γὰρ ἀκούσας σοφὸς σοφώτερος ἔσται, ὁ δὲ νοήμων κυβέρνησιν κτήσεται νοήσει τε παραβολὴν καὶ σκοτεινὸν λόγον ῥήσεις τε σοφῶν καὶ αἰνίγματα. Ἀρχὴ σοφίας φόβος θεοῦ, σύνεσις δὲ ἀγαθὴ πᾶσι τοῖς ποιοῦσιν αὐτήν· εὐσέβεια δὲ εἰς θεὸν ἀρχὴ αἰσθήσεως, σοφίαν δὲ καὶ παιδείαν ἀσεβεῖς ἐξουθενήσουσιν. ἄκουε, υἱέ, παιδείαν πατρός σου καὶ μὴ ἀπώσῃ θεσμοὺς μητρός σου· στέφανον γὰρ χαρίτων δέξῃ σῇ κορυφῇ καὶ κλοιὸν χρύσεον περὶ σῷ τραχήλῳ.

[72] One Petrus Meillerus congratulates a professor of Lausanne Academy some years later with poems in Greek and Latin, see Molery, Elie (1606–1607), *Astronomicus τῆς ψηφοφορίας*, Genève, qq1v–qq2.

this might – very typically for the French part of Switzerland – also be the case with Meiler. This verse paraphrase of the *Book of Salomon* is his only known work, printed in 1599 in Geneva by Matthieu Berjon, who had in 1597 published the French verse paraphrases of the *Psalms* by Théodore de Bèze and a Latin poetry book by Jean Jacquemot which included several paraphrases of the *Proverbs of Salomon*.[73] The choice of the dedicatees (Johannes Steiger, the Baron of Rolle and his brother Georg, Baron of Mont-le-Grand, both in the vicinity of Lausanne) and the gratulation in Greek to the author by Stephanus a Castrobello (Étienne de Beauchasteau, the Professor of Greek and Ethics in Lausanne Academy), indicate that Meiler had connections to Lausanne, if not the roots there.[74]

Metre: Elegiac couplets.

Notes: Following the Latin versions, Biblical paraphrases in Greek verse appeared from the middle of the 16th century onwards. The influence of Basel and Genevan prints of paraphrases (see above) might have been the inspiration for this book. Biblical paraphrases were considered good both for moral instruction and for learning the language, as the dedication by the author tells us, but with the additional promise of pleasure.[75] Indeed, Meilerus' distichs have a true Greek flavour with his avoidance of hiatus, central caesurae and Homeric forms, at the same time remaining quite true to the text of the Proverbs, and translating it all, not only some chosen pieces. No wonder that Lizelius would have liked to welcome him in Germany![76]

Bibliography: Jöcher, Christian Gottlieb (1751), *Allgemeines Gelehrten-Lexikon. Dritter Theil. M–R*, Leipzig, 1234; Lizelius, Georg (1730), *Historia poetarum graecorum Germaniae*, Frankfurt, 211–212; Crasso, Lorenzo (1678), *Istoria de' poeti greci*, Napoli, 254; Draudius, Georgius (1611), *Bibliotheca classica*, Frankfurt, 1123.

[JP]

---

73 See Bèze, Théodore (1597), *Les saincts cantiques...mis de nouveau en rime*, Genève; Jacquemot, Johannes (1597), *Musae Neocomenses*, Geneva, 199ff.
74 See Graf 1888, 69. In 1612 Castrobello was the pastor in the Church of Lutry (diocese of Lausanne) and participated in the Greek-Latin edition of Pseudo-Longinus, where he referred to the academy and the city of Lausanne as *nostra*; the same edition includes a Greek epigram by Franciscus Blondetus from Grand-Vaux (near Lausanne), see Διονυσίου Λογγίνου ῥήτορος περὶ ὕψους βιβλίων, A Gab. de Petra, Geneva 1612, 13, 19.
75 See Meilerus 1599, 7–8.
76 See Lizelius 1730, 212.

Heinrich Jeckelmann (1565–1633)

ΕΛΕΕΙΝΟΛΟΓΙΑ ΕΠΙ ΤΗ ΠΑΝΩΛΙΑ ΤΗΣ ΒΑΣΙΛΕΙΩΝ ΠΟΛΕΩΣ [1611]

(excerptum, vv. 1–8)

> Αἴθ' ὄφελον τυχέμεν κρατὸς οὗ κρῆναι μελάνυδρες
> δακρυχέωσιν ἀπ' ὄσσοιν πικροῖν νωλεμὲς ὕδωρ·
> θρηνέμεν ᾗ θέμις ἐστίν, τὴν ὀλεσίπτολιν ἄτην
> καί τε μιαιφόνον, ἠδὲ ἀεικέα λοιγόν, ἐπῶρσε
> 5 τὸν θεὸς ὑψιμέδων ἀνὰ δῆμον Βασσιλεείων,
> ὀργισθεὶς στυγερῇσι ἀλιτροσύνῃσιν ἁπάντων,
> ὅττι ἐπειγόμενοι θεραπόντων κήρυκι φωνῇ
> οὐκ ἠκούσαμεν ἥ ῥα ἐφετμάων ἀπλανείων.

Textus: *Deploratio cladis Basileensis, postremis quinque mensibus superioris Anni, Dei voluntate grassante Peste, illatae*, Basel: J.J. Genath, 1611,):(2r.

Crit.: 1 κρῆναι ed., correxi || 2 πικροῖν] πικρῶς malim | νωλεμές] sensu adverbiali || 3 ᾗ: ἦ vel ἢ malim | θέμις ἐστίν corr.: θέμίς ἐστιν ed. || 4 ἠδὲ scripsi: ἢ δὲ ed. || λοιγὸν corr.: λοίγον cum ictu ed. || 6 στυγερῇσιν possis || 7 κήρυκι] dactylus, cf. *Anth. Pal.* 11.124.6 κηρύκιον γὰρ.

Sim.: 1 αἴθ' ὄφελον] Hom. *Od.* 13.204 (αἴθ' ὄφελον μεῖναι) || 1–2 κρατὸς...ὕδωρ] cf. e.g. Hom. *Il.* 9.14 (ἵστατο δάκρυ χέων ὥς τε κρήνη μελάνυδρος); LXX *Jer.* 8.23 (τίς δώσει κεφαλῇ μου ὕδωρ καὶ ὀφθαλμοῖς μου πηγὴν δακρύων) || 3 ᾗ θέμις ἐστίν] Hom. *Il.* 2.73 (ἣ θέμις), *Il.* 9.33 (ἦ θέμις) | ὀλεσίπτολιν ἄτην] Tryph. 683 || 4 μιαιφόνον] cf. *Il.* 5.31, 5.455 (Ἄρες Ἄρες βροτολοιγὲ μιαιφόνε) | ἀεικέα λοιγόν] cf. Hom. *Il.* 1.97 (οὐδ' ὅ γε πρὶν Δαναοῖσιν ἀεικέα λοιγὸν ἀπώσει) et *Anth. Pal.* 9.460.4 (Τρωσὶν ἀεικέα λοιγὸν ἐγείρει) || 6 στυγερῇσι] Hom. *Od.* 20.78 (στυγερῇσιν Ἐρινύσιν) | ἀλιτροσύνῃσιν] cf. Tryph. 491 (ἀλιτροσύναι σε φέρουσι) || 7 θεραπόντων κήρυκι] cf. Hom. *Il.* 1.321 (τώ οἱ ἔσαν κήρυκε καὶ ὀτρηρὼ θεράποντε) || 8 ἐφετμάων] cf. Hom. *Il.* 5.818 (μέμνημαι ἐφετμέων); Ap. Rhod. *Argon.* 2.1152 (πατρὸς ἐφετμάων ἀλέγοντες)

Commiseration on the catastrophe in the city of Basel

(excerpt, ll. 1–8)

> I wish I could get hold of the head whence the springs of black water
> shed their tears from the two bitter eyes, the hard, cruel water,
> so I could weep with right the mischief crushing the city,
> mean and murderous, and this undeserved plague that
> [5] God in high heaven has sent all over the Canton of Basel,
> out of wrath for the wicked sins, the community's doings
> since although we were urged we had no ear for the warnings
> of his servants' voice that is for the righteous advices.

Metre: Hexameters, with occasional liberties (e.g., l. 7 κήρυκι = – ⏑⏑, unclassical use of caesurae), and several bipartite lines.

Notes: The author's moralising tone, his Greek expression (for example l. 2 ὄσσοιν πικροῖν νωλεμὲς ὕδωρ) and his bad metrics which ignores classical norms allows to appreciate the other authors. And yet, when Jeckelmann wrote his 163 lines on the Basel Plague and its victims in 1611, the university was pleased and made him the *Ordinarius* of Greek.[77] Nowadays, the text with its marginal comments is perhaps a valuable source for historians. Jeckelmann's epyllion (like his occasional poems) is equipped with explanatory marginal notes in Latin. It begins with a reference to Jeremiah 9.1: 'Oh that my head were waters and mine eyes a fountain of tears, That I might weep day and night for the slain of the daughter of my people,'[78] but his choice of words does not coincide with the Septuagint, relying on Homeric diction instead, and merging pagan and Christian imagery. The proemium (ll. 1–16) states that the plague was God's punishment for disobeying his will, but that it hit everyone without discrimination, including women and innocent children. Jeckelmann continues with a lament about the dead whose fame will last forever and praises some eminent citizens who are loved by the Muses, including the Professor of Theology Amandus Polanus, the Professor of Logic Heinrich Justus, the Professor of Medicine and Ethics Thomas Coccius, the Professor of Greek Jakob Zwinger, and the Professor of Physics and Mathematics Johann Georg Leo. Other victims are not mentioned by name (ll. 17–49). The following part begins with a simile which compares the plague with a storm, brought about by Zeus (ll. 50–63), and continues with a list of different professions and social classes who all suffered despite their profession, time, or place (ll. 64–75). As a conclusion, Jeckelmann exhorts the readers to think about their mortality, to remember that Zeus has his own ways (ll. 76–88) and to pray for his forgiveness (ll. 89–95). The address to God praises his might and beseeches health and safety for the magistrates and the academics, so that they may glorify him with hymns (ll. 96–120). In the end, he turns once more to Zeus the Father (standing for the Christian God), reflecting on his might and the instability of the

---

[77] The story of his brilliant mastering of Greek is based on the funeral eulogy by Theodor Zwinger (Zwinger 1633). Historians have explained that the chair of Greek was the lowest level and usually served as a ladder to the theology chair or a post in the community. Twenty years later Jeckelmann was still there.

[78] This is the marginal note: *Ieremiae 9.1. Ut olim Propheta deflevit populi Jud. calamitatem, sic et nos nostram miseriam pub. deplorare convenit quam nobis immisit DEUS peccatis nostris offensus. Quod non oboedivimus ipsius S.S. Verbo.*

human condition (ll. 121–150) and concluding the poem with a new, more general prayer (ll. 151–163).

Biography: Heinrich Jeckelmann was born in 1565 in Basel, where his father Franciscus was a surgeon and a physician.[79] He entered the University of Basel in 1581, received the degree of Magister Artium in 1587 and continued to study theology, but soon left his hometown for 14 years of travels abroad, first to Germany, then through France to England, where he spent nine years in the service of the governor of Dover (1592–1601). After his return to Basel, in 1611 he became the Professor of Greek and remained in this position till his death in 1633. Jeckelmann has been praised for his ability to speak Greek and Latin fluently, as well as for his knowledge of oriental and modern languages. Apart from some theological works from the period of his studies, the remaining works of his maturity consist in Greek poetry: in 1610, two *epicedia* in elegiac couplets for the victims of the Basel Plague (the Professor of Theology Amandus Polanus and the Professor of Greek Jacob Zwinger), accompanied by a verse paraphrase of Psalm 91 in hexameters; in 1611, a verse oration commemorating the same plague.[80] In 1629 he published two congratulatory poems in Greek for Felix Platter on the occasion of his doctorate in medicine.

Bibliography: Zwinger, Theodor (1633), *Christliche Leich-Predigt von der seligmachenden Erkantnuss Jesu Christi...Bestattung des...Henrici Jeckelmann*, Basel; Herzog, Johann Werner (1778), *Athenae Rauricae, sive catalogus professorum Academiae Basiliensis ab a. MCCCLX ad a. MDCCLXXVII*, Basel; Marti-Weissenbach, Karin (2005), "Jeckelmann, Heinrich", in: *Historisches Lexikon der Schweiz (HLS)*, https://hls-dhs-dss.ch/de/articles/026015/2005-06-30/ [accessed: November 2020]; Lötscher, Valentin (ed.) (1987), *Felix Platter, Beschreibung der Stadt Basel 1610 und Pestbericht 1610/1611*, Basel; Jeckelmann's other Greek poems can be read in his *Inferiae Sacratae, memoriae...D. Amandi Polani...D. Iacobi Zvingeri...*, Basel 1610, and in his Συγχάρματα *in honorem...M. Felicis Plateri...Cum in arte Apollinea supremo axiomate doctoris cohonestaretur*, Basel 1629.

[JP/MS]

---

[79] Cf. Marti-Weissenbach 2005; Herzog 1778, 365–366. Jeckelmanns were related to the family of Platter, see Jeckelmann 1629, A3v. For the Plague, see Felix Platter's account, edited in Lötscher 1987.
[80] These poems may have helped him gain the vacant post of the Professor of Greek: the poem to Jacob Zwinger was dedicated to the influential Basel merchant and Zwinger's half-brother Johann Lucas Iselin, and presented a eulogy of his family.

Johann Rudolf Stucki (1596–1660)

ΓΑΜΗΛΙΟΝ *Ad ornatissimum Dn. Sponsum* [1620]

Ἰωάννη, γλυκερὸν φάος, ὦ κεχαρισμένα εἰδώς,
Οὐασῆρ' ὦ φίλ' ἑταῖρε πολύτροπε καὶ πολύιδρις,
ἐσθλέ, ἐμοὶ οὐ μέν τι κασιγνήτοιο χερείων,
σοὶ σχεδόν ἐστι γάμος, μέγα πάντων χάρμα ἑταίρων.
5 Ὅττι Θεὸς κύδιστος, ὀλύμπιος, αἰθέρι ναίων,
μοῦνος ἐπιχθονίοις ὄλβον καὶ κῦδος ὀπάζων,
αὐτὸς σοὶ ἄλοχον περικαλλέα καὶ ἐχέθυμον,
ἐκπρεπὲς εἶδος ἔχουσαν ἔδωκε ὁ δῶτορ ἐάων.
Ἥν τε κασιγνήτη δέδαεν μάλα πότνια πατρὸς
10 τέχνην παντοίην, χαρίεντα δὲ ἔργα τελείει.
Συγχαίρουσι φίλοι πάντες, μάλα πού σφισι θυμὸς
αἰὲν ἐυφροσύνῃσιν ἰαίνεται εἵνεκα σεῖο,
λευσσόντων τοιόνδε θάλος σοι εἶναι ἄκοιτιν.
Οὖλέ τε καὶ μέγα χαῖρε, Θεὸς δέ τοι ὄλβια δοίη,
15 ὄλβια πάντα πατρὸς δοίη, φωτὸς πολυμήτου.
Τέκνα τε εἰρήνης τε μένειν ἐν ἀπήμοσι θεσμοῖς.
Αἴ μοι τοῦτο ἔπος τελέσειε πατὴρ θεὸς ἡμῶν!
Καὶ σὺ μὲν οὕτω χαῖρε, πατρὸς σέο ἀγλαὲ υἱέ,
αὐτὰρ ἐγὼ φιλότητα τεὴν μετόπισθε φυλάξω.

Textus: *Prosphonesis amica ad nuptias...Joannis Waseri...cum...Domina Susanna...Heinrici Tomanni...filia*, Tiguri: I.R. Wolphius [1620].

Crit.: 2 πολύιδρις ed. cum ictu, correxi || **7** περικάλλεα ed. cum ictu, correxi || **8** δῶτορ] pro nominativo metri causa || **11** πού σφίσι ed., correxi || **13** τοοιὸν δὲ ed., correxi || **15** πολυμήτου] pro πολυμήτιος metri causa || **17** αἴ μοὶ ed., correxi || **19** αὖταρ ed., correxi

Sim.: 1 γλυκερὸν φάος] cf. Hom. *Od.* 16.23 al. || **1–3** κεχαρισμένα...χερείων] cf. Hom. *Od.* 8.584–585 (ἤ τίς που καὶ ἑταῖρος ἀνὴρ κεχαρισμένα εἰδώς, / ἐσθλός; ἐπεὶ οὐ μέν τι κασιγνήτοιο χερείων) || **2** πολύτροπε] cf. Hom. *Od.* 1.1 | πολύιδρις] cf. Hom. *Od.* 15.459 || **4** Σοὶ σχεδόν ἐστι γάμος] cf. Hom. *Od.* 6.27 (σοὶ δὲ γάμος σχεδόν ἐστιν) | μέγα πάντων χάρμα] cf. Hom. *Il.* 24.706 (μέγα χάρμα πόλει) || **5** Ὅττι Θεὸς κύδιστος...ναίων] cf. Hom. *Il.* 2.412 (Ζεῦ κύδιστε μέγιστε κελαινεφὲς αἰθέρι ναίων) || **6** ὄλβον...ὀπάζων] cf. Hom. *Od.* 19.161 (Ζεὺς ὄλβον ὀπάζει) || **8** ἐκπρεπὲς εἶδος ἔχουσαν] cf. *Hymn. Hom. Lun.* 16 | δῶτορ ἐάων] *Hymn. Hom. Merc.* 12, *Vest.* 8 || **9–10** δέδαεν...τελείει] cf. Hom. *Od.* 6.233, 23.160 (ἴδρις, ὃν Ἥφαιστος δέδαεν καὶ Παλλὰς Ἀθήνη / τέχνην παντοίην, χαρίεντα δὲ ἔργα τελείει) || **11–13** μάλα...θάλος] = Hom. *Od.* 6.155–157 || **14** Οὖλέ τε...δοίη] cf. Hom. *Od.* 24.402 (οὖλέ τε...θεοὶ δέ τοι ὄλβια δοῖεν) || **16** Τέκνα τε εἰρήνης...θεσμοῖς] cf. *Hymn. Hom. Mart.* 16 (δὸς μάκαρ, εἰρήνης τε...θεσμοῖς) || **17** Αἴ μοι...τελέσειε] cf. Hom. *Od.* 20.236 (αἲ γὰρ τοῦτο, ξεῖνε, ἔπος τελέσειε Κρονίων) || **18** Καὶ σὺ...υἱέ] cf. *Hymn. Hom. Apoll.* 545 (Καὶ σὺ...Διὸς καὶ Λητοῦς υἱέ); *Hymn. Hom. Merc.* 10, 579 (Καὶ σὺ...Διὸς καὶ Μαιάδος υἱέ) || **19** Αὐτὰρ...φυλάξω] cf. Hom. *Il.* 24.111 (αἰδῶ καὶ φιλότητα τεὴν μετόπισθε φυλάσσων)

Wedding-song for the most illustrious master Groom

> John, sweet light, who has always been a friend to me, Waser,
> dearest companion who knows many ways, of manifold knowledge,
> noble man who counts no less to me than my own brother,
> wedding is near to you, really for all your friends a great pleasure.
> [5] Since most glorious God, the Olympian, living in heaven
> solely is granting to mortal men the riches and glory,
> gave you himself a wife, of good standing and of behaviour
> and standing out for her good looks – he is the giver of riches!
> And as your father's revered sister has taught her to master
> [10] so many trades, she produces things rather charming and graceful.
> All your friends are together with you in joy and their heart is
> always warm to you when they see you, observing with pleasure
> that the woman you marry, your wife, is such a nice flower.
> So be blessed and happy, may God too give you his riches,
> [15] all the riches he gave to your father, a man rich in thinking.
> And may your children remain in Peace's foundations and safety:
> may God the Father fulfilment grant to these verses and prayer!
> Greetings to you thus, my friend, the splendid son of your father;
> I, however will cherish the friendship for you in the future!

Metre: Hexameters.

Notes: This poem is the first in a trilingual set of *epithalamia*, followed by Latin anagram poems which attack the monks who avoid love and marriage, and by two other poems which allude to the names of the newlyweds in Latin and in English. The addressees are from important Zürich families: the groom Johann Waser was the eldest son of Stucki's colleague Kaspar Waser (1565–1625), an evangelical theologian and orientalist, first a Professor of Greek and then of Theology at the Collegium Carolinum; Johann's maternal grandfather was the influential pastor Josias Simmler. The bride, Susanna, was the daughter of Heinrich Thomann, a member of Zürich's Small Council, who was related to Sadrach Thomann, another Hellenizing poet from Zürich.[81] Here, Stucki sometimes follows the German ictus in Greek accents (forced long before Opitz on Greek rhythm), but it is evident that he knows his Homer well: the poem is almost cento-like, combining words, phrases and occasionally full verses from Homer and the Homeric hymns. The poem follows a composition pattern suggested by the *Odyssey*, where Ulysses' ironic flattery returns to him like a boomerang in the strong

---

81 See Lassner 2012.

ring composition of the 6th book and he presents himself as the victim of Nausicaa's wedding wishes. Almost three verses are quoted from this epic *makarismos* of the beauty of the bride (ll. 11–13), followed in l. 14 by another whole-verse quote from the *Odyssey* (24.402), where the Greek gods stand for the Christian God; by this quotation Stucki takes the position of Dolios, the closest servant of Penelope and Laertes, speaking to Ulysses almost as a friend. The groom Waser is identified with the trickster-hero Ulysses already in the second line (πολύτροπε). The rhythm and the syntax of the 19 hexameters reveal some traces of exhaustion: the phrases consist of 4–4–2–3–2–1–1–1–1 verses. The number of lines might hint at the age of the bridegroom, but his exact date of birth is a mystery.

Biography: Johann Rudolf Stucki was born in Zürich in 1596. He belonged to a family of evangelical pastors. His father, Johann Wilhelm Stucki (1521–1608), had studied with Konrad Gessner and Rudolf Pellikan and worked first as professor of sacred languages and then of theology in Zürich; when he died, he was honoured with Greek *epicedia* by the Basel physician and professor of Greek Jacob Zwinger and by the Zürich Professor of Greek Konrad Ochsner.[82] Johann Rudolf studied theology at Saumur Protestant Academy until 1619. Back in Zürich, he held different positions in the churches of the region, worked as a professor of Hebrew and Logic in the Collegium Humanitatis and eventually became the Professor of Logic at the Collegium Carolinum in 1639, where he advanced to the positions of the Professor of Theology and Rector. He died in 1660. Stucki's works include numerous theological disputations, he also re-edited Ceporin's Greek compendium with a Latin verse address to the schoolboys, exhorting them to study Greek and praising previous Zürich professors of Greek. He wrote many Latin and some Greek occasional poems, including at least one other trilingual set (Hebrew-Greek-Latin), followed by a Greek poem on the death of his fellow professor Kaspar Waser.[83]

Bibliography: Waser, Konrad (1608), *De vita et obitu...Dn. Ioh. Guilielmi Stuckii*. Zürich; Koldewey, Friedrich (1893), "Stucki, Johann Wilhelm", in: *Allgemeine Deutsche Biographie* 36, 717–720; Moser, Christian (2012), "Stucki, Johann Rudolf", in: *Historisches Lexikon der Schweiz (HLS)*, https://hls-dhs-dss.ch/de/articles/010866/2012-07-02/ [accessed: November 2020]. On his works: Kvosen, Jodocus (1626), *De Vita et Obitu...Domini Caspari Waseri*, Basel; Lassner, Martin (2012), "Thomann, Heinrich", in: *Historisches Lexikon der Schweiz (HLS)*, https://hls-dhs-dss.ch/de/articles/018200/2012-03-06/ [accessed: November 2020]; Bigler-Marschall, Ingrid

---

82 See Waser 1608; Koldewey 1893.
83 See Kvosen 1626, 50–51.

(2014), "Waser, Caspar", in: *Historisches Lexikon der Schweiz (HLS)*, https://hls-dhs-dss.ch/de/articles/010902/ 2014-12-27/ [accessed: November 2020].

[JP/MS]

Johannes Lavater (1624–1695)

Εὐχωλὴ *Carmine Archilochio* μελῳδίᾳ *Psalmi CXXXIV accinenda* [1643]

Α.
Ὦ παμμέδων ἐμεῦ Θεός,
οἷς νυμφίοις ὀπάζεο
τὸ σεῖο παμφαὲς φάος
ᾗ εἰνὶ αἴῃ ἀσκελές!

Β.
5 Ὦ μεῦ Θεὸς ζείδωρος ὤν,
τὺ οἶσιν ὄλβον ὃν πόρε,
καὶ ὧν πολυζήλων πτερῶν
αἰὲν πυκάζοις οὓς κνέφᾳ!

Γ.
Ὦ ἄμβροτος Θεὸς βροτῶν,
10 ἄγκλευε οἶσιν νυμφίοις
σαόφρονον λέκτρον λίην,
εὐπαιδίῃφι καὶ φανόν!

Δ.
Ὦ, ὦ ἀόσσητερ Θεός,
πόρσυνε κείνοισιν δ' ἐπάψ
15 ζωὴν λυγρήν τ' ἐπώδυνον,
ἥν τ' ἀμβροσείην, πάντροφον!

Textus: *Epithalamion in nuptias secundissimas...Dn. Joh. Huldrichi Grebelii...necnon...Susannae Werdmullerae...a Johanne Lavatero*, Tiguri 1643,)(3r

Crit.: 3 τὸ σεῖο correxi: ὁ σεῖο ed. || 10 ἄγκλευε] pro ἐκέλευε, vel ex ἀγκαλίζομαι vel ἀγκλάω metri causa || 13 ἀόσσητερ correxi: ἀοσσήτερ ed. || 14 ἐπάψ] cum acc. cf. *EM* 354.25 et Hom. *Il.* 21.537 cum scholiis.

A prayer. To be sung in Archilochean rhythm to the melody of Psalm 134

1
I pray, my God, almighty God
to give to your own newlyweds
your light, your own, so fully bright
in their own country undisturbed!

2
My God, who gives the zea to us,
now give your people too your wealth,
and cover them with the shade of
your always much-admired wings!

3
Immortal God of mortal men,
prevent the newlyweds of yours
of a too chaste bed of love:
let there as well the children shine!

4
Our ally, oh our helping God
provide them now anew with life
which after sorrow, sadness will
be then immortal, nourishing!

Metre: Iambic dimeters. What we call iambic dimeter was for Servius in his *Centimetrum* (as it was for Perotti and their followers) an Archilochean metre, from the epodes of Horace (*amore percussum gravi*) and Archilochus. For modern scholars, the name of Archilochus also implies an allusion to the iambic tradition, obsessed with heterosexuality and marriage, which seems to be in accordance with the fertility-wish of the 3rd stanza (usual, if not obligatory, in *epithalamia*).

Notes: This is the third part of Lavater's set of *epithalamia* for Grebel and Werdmüller. The groom and the bride are not well known: Johann Ulrich Grebel was the son of Johann Heinrich Grebel, from an old and influential Zürich family, and Susanna Werdmüller was a daughter of the Zürich citizen Balthasar Werdmüller. The first two poems of the book are in Greek hexameters: 17 lines address the bridegroom and 16 lines the bride. The third poem (above) is a prayer in 16 lines which asks for God's protection; its German version follows as the fourth poem,[84] and the fifth and the sixth poems (also in German) are presented as sung correspondingly by the men and women at the wedding party. Like Gessner's poem ('eleven hendecasyllabi', see above), Lavater's wedding-song plays with numbers: four stanzas of four lines of four feet. These are to be sung according to the melody of Psalm 134, either from the Genevan Psalter (its present German text, *Herr Gott, dich loben alle wir* is, however, later in date) or from Ambrosius Lobwasser's Psalter from 1573, which was used in the evangelical churches of Basel and Zürich in many different prints.[85]

Biography: Johannes Lavater (1624–1695 in Zürich), belonged to another branch of the same influential Zürich family as the physiognomist Johann Kaspar Lavater 100 years later.[86] He studied theology at the Collegium Carolinum in Zürich, continued his studies in Groningen and started to work as a pastor in Uitikon in 1649. He worked later at the Collegium Carolinum, first as a Professor of Rhetoric, then of Philosophy; he finally became also the school headmaster of the Großmünsterstift. Lavater was involved in theological controversies and numerous theological and philosophical disputations were published under his guidance, but today he is mainly known as a researcher on deaf-muteness, because of three disputations he supervised, known as *Schola mutorum ac surdorum*. He published several occasional poems in Greek, Latin, and German, including an *epicedium* in Latin for his friend, the eminent evangelical theologian and Hebraist Johann Heinrich Hottinger,[87] and at least ten *epithalamia* in Greek.

---

84 See: IV. Μεταβολὴ in vernaculam, Εὐχωλῆς carmine Archilochio conceptae, ad idem μέλος decantanda. 'I. O könig, o du höchster Gott, / Lass den Ehleüthen dein Gebott / Klar leüchten, als ein Lichte schon, / Auff diser Erd gib freüwd und wohn! 2. O treüwer Gott, o unser Herz, / Erhalte sy bey Gut und Ehr, / Und, under deinen flüglein gut, / in diser zeit gib schirm und hut! 3. O Gott, der du unsterblich bist, / Vermehre sy zu aller frist: / Sy auch begaab mit Leibes frucht, / Erhalte sy in Ehr und Zucht! 4. O heyland, o Erlöser mein, / Auch dise zwey Ehmenschen dein, / Nach diser so betrübten zeit, / Mit freüwden in den himmel gleit!'
85 For the history of the Genevan Psalter, see Cordier, L. (1929), *Der deutsche Evangelische Liederpsalter*, Berlin; Bernoulli, Peter E./Fuller, Frieder (ed.) (2001), *Der Genfer Psalter*, Zürich. Numerous prints of Lobwasser's 1576 edition were available in Lavater's time, see for example Ps. 134: *O Gott der Du ein Heerfür bist* in Lobwasser, Ambrosius [1633], *Psalmen Davids*, Zürich, 352. Lavater similarly uses the melodies of Christian hymns in one of his five Greek *epithalamia* for Johann Ludwig Keller and Ursula Lavatera in the same year (1643) and one of his German *epithalamia* (*Was lebet, was schwebet* from *Nürnbergisches Gesangbuch*, 1677, 419).
86 See Bächtold 2007.
87 Heidegger, Johann Heinrich (1671), *Oratio funebris reverendi atque clarissimi viri, dn. Ioh. Henrici Hottingeri*, Zürich, [I4r].

Bibliography: Bächtold, Hans Ulrich (2007), "Lavater, Johannes", in: *Historisches Lexikon der Schweiz (HLS)*, https://hls-dhs-dss.ch/de/articles/010727/ 2007-03-19/ [accessed: November 2020]. Works by Lavater: J.L./Ott, Johann Heinrich (1664), *Disquisitio physica De Mutorum Ac Surdorum Ab Ortu Sermone, Auditu, Cognitione atque Institutione prior*, Zürich; J.L./Muraltus, Johannes (1664), *Schola Mutorum ac surdorum…Disquisitio secunda: quae est de eorundem cognitione ac institutione.* Zürich; J.L./Wiser, Johann Balthasar (1665), *Schola Mutorum Ac Surdorum, Seu Disquisitio exoterica tertia: Quae est De eorundem Institutione*, Zürich.

[JP/MS]

Johann Rudolf Wettstein I (1614–1684)

Ὠιδή [1666]

(excerptum, vv. 69–90)

    ΚΑΛΛΙΟΠΗ.
 ἘΓΛΙΓΓΗΡ στεφάνη ἀριδεικέτα ἰητήρων,
70 ἐλλογίμως ζωήν, παμμάκαρ εἶ, διάγων!
    ΚΛΕΙΩ.
 Ἔρως μαθημάτων τεῖν κόμην δέει
 φύλλῳ δάφνης· καρποὺς φέρον θάλλοι ἀεί!
    ἘΡΑΤΩ.
 Γλεύκους εἰνὶ βροτοῖς ἢ ἐρατώτερον
 ἔνδοξόν τε τεοῦ πότνιον οὔνομα!
    ΘΑΛΕΙΑ
75 Λητοΐδης φιλότητα ἀμῶν ὡς κοσμεῖ Ἀπόλλων,
 Αὖ μετὰ ταῦτα σέβου, πλείονα τῶν πορίσει!
    ΜΕΛΠΟΜΕΝΗ.
 Ἴσος ἀγλαοῖς νικηταῖς, ἐξ ἐναντίοις ἄγεις
 νῦν θρίαμβον, εὖχος, εὔχομαι, ἀμέτρως αὐξάμεν·
    ΤΕΡΨΙΧΟΡΗ.
 Γαίη ἡλίου ἐφ᾽ ὅσσον αὐγὴ
80 μαρμαίρει, μέχρις οὐρανοῦ ἰκάνοις·
    ΕΥΤΕΡΠΗ.
 Γαίεις νῦν δάφνῃ, ἀρετῇσι κεκασμένε, πολλά·
 Νούσῳ θηκομένοις ἥδυμος ἴσθι ὁμῶς·
    ΠΟΛΥΜΝΙΑ
 Ἤματι δοίη παντὶ βίοιο τοί γ᾽ ἀγακλειτέ
 Τερπικέραυνος ὄλβια φαιδρῷ!
    ΟΥΡΑΝΙΗ.
85 Ῥαυρακέων δηθὰ φάνοις ἄστρον
 ἄκρον, ἕως τ᾽ οὐλύμπι᾽ ἔποιντο!

Ταῦτα Μουσῶν χρυσᾶ ἔπη ἀκούσας
λανθανόντως, γηθόσυνος μάλιστα
ἐν παρεζεύγνυν τὸ ἔγωγε ῥῆμα·
90   ΠΆΝΤΑ ΓΈΝΟΙΤΟ.

Textus: *Votivi applausus...Nicolao Eglingero Basiliensi, cum a...Joh. Casparo Bauhino...in florentiss. Basiliens. Universit. ...medicinae doctor proclamaretur, fusi ab amicis*, Basileae: J.J. Decker, 1666, A3v–A4r (cf. Steinrück 2018, 316–317).

Crit.: tit. Ἀρετῇ τε καὶ παιδείᾳ παντοδαπῇ διαφέροντι Κυρίῳ Νικολάῳ τῷ Ἐγλιγγήρῳ Βασιλειώτῃ δάφνην Ἀσκληπιάδα τῇ δεκάτῃ ἱσταμένου μηνὸς μεταγειτνιῶνος ἔτει ἀπὸ τῆς Θεογονίας ͵α χ ξ ϛ ʹ κατ' ἀξίαν μάλιστα λάβοντι, φίλης ἐκ κραδίης ᾠδῇ τῇδε συγχαίρει Ἰωάννης Ῥάθυλφος ὁ Οὐεττιστένιος. || **69** ἀριδεικέτα] forma fem. Dorica (vel pro vocativo ἀρειδείκετε) || **77** ἐξ ἐναντίοις] ft. pro ἐξ ἐναντίας vel ἐξ ἐναντίων aut ἐξ cum ἄγεις coniungendum et ἐναντίοις dativus (in)commodi || **78** αὐξάμεν] ft. pro αὐξέμεν, αὐξάμην possis || **82** ἤδυμος correxi: ἤδιμος ed.

Sim.: 74 πότνιον οὔνομα] forma neoclassica, cf. Calvin, Στοιχείωσις 1531, 126, Ἡ Κυριακὴ προσευχή, v. 2 || **77** νικητής] cf. Eust. In Il. 157.1 || **81** Γαίεις] cf. Hom. *Il.* 1.405; 5.906 al. (κύδεϊ γαίων; cf. Hsch. γ 45) | κεκασμένε] cf. Hom. *Il.* 4.339 (δόλοισι κεκασμένε) || **84** τερπικέραυνος] cf. Hom. *Il.* 24.529 (δώῃ Ζεὺς τερπικέραυνος)

Song

(excerpt, ll. 69–90)

       CALLIOPE
Eglinger, you are the crown, the most visible of the doctors
[70] and in a high repute, blessed you are, leading your life!
       CLIO
E ros of studies puts a band around your head
  of laurel leaves! May it blossom and bear fruits!
       ERATO
G rapewine, sweet among men, can't be desired more
  and have greater renown than the good name of yours!
       THALIA
[75] **L** ike does Apollo, the offspring of Leto, help our friendship:
  worship him afterwards too and he will bring you more goods!
       MELPOMENE
I n the shining light of winners over your feinds you celebrate
  now the triumph! May, I pray, this fame without measure be increased!
       TERPSICHORE
G lowing light of the sun as long as will shine
[80] on earth, may you reach up to heaven!
       EUTERPE
G lorify yourself with laurels, oh so excelling in virtue,

to the sickly depressed, be to them nice all the same.
    POLYHYMNIA
E very day of your lifetime may give to you, O my famous,
he who throws thunders blessings to your brightness.
    URANIA
[85] **R** aurachians long time may see your star
high, as long as heaven may follow.

> Reading of the Muses these golden verses
> secretly, I joined to them for my pleasure,
> as a further one word, myself, I added:
>   MAY IT ALL HAPPEN!

Metre: Mixed (after the first 17 Sapphic stanzas, the lines of our excerpts are: ll. 69–70 elegiac couplet / ll. 71–72: 2 iambic trimeters / ll. 73–74: 2 minor asclepiads / ll. 75–76: elegiac couplet / ll. 77–78: 2 catalectic trochaic tetrameters / ll. 79–80: 2 phalaecian hendecasyllables / ll. 81–82: elegiac couplet / ll. 83–84: 3+2 adonians / ll. 85–86: choriambus + sapphicus and choriambus + reizianus / ll. 87–90: Sapphic stanza).

Notes: The addressee of this poem, Nicolaus Eglinger (1645–1711),[88] was the son of Hans Heinrich Eglinger (a salt-accountant) and Anna Herzog. As a young talent, Eglinger received his Master's degree in philosophy in 1661 and continued with his studies of medicine, receiving his doctorate in 1666 with a dissertation on the plague. He held different professorships in Physics, Botany, Anatomy, and Medicine at the University of Basel from 1675 onwards. He married twice: in 1676 with Rosina Mangold and in 1684 with Judith Burckhardt, both daughters of illustrious fathers. His son Christopher became Professor of Logic and Rhetoric at the University of Basel. According to *Anthologia Palatina* 9.751.7–8, Sappho should be inserted into the catalogue of the nine Muses: Wettstein does so 'to his own pleasure' (l. 88) by starting and ending the chorus of the Muses in Sapphic stanzas. If the theologian and Greek professor tried to steer free from the somewhat monotone humanist metrics, he did not follow the Greek models,[89] nor Perotti or Celtis, but Seneca's *metra libera*, seemingly derived from Caesius Bassus' transformation of Horatian odes (but with a Sapphic undertone). However, instead of giving each Muse her own metre, as is often the case in such circles of Muses, Wettstein divides the poem into three parts, starting every triplet of Muses

---

[88] Gernler 1711, 49–52; Herzog 1778, 194–196, 221.
[89] Such as Hephaestio's Περὶ ποιημάτων (Scaliger did, already in 1561).

with the eternal elegiac couplet (for Euterpe, Calliope, and Thalia). The Muses who stand in the second position in each triplet receive metres based on repeated feet (iambics, trochaics, and adoneans for Clio, Melpomene, and Polyhymnia), whereas each triplet ends with a more complex verse type (for Erato, Terpsichore, and Urania), and the crown is the *Votum* in Sapphics. The halfmoon-acrostic starts with the introduction of the addressee's name.[90] Although Wettstein uses epic vocabulary, he does not work with patch-work methods and often creates his own forms by analogy or takes peculiar forms from other humanist authors, such as πότνιον (l. 78), which we find in the Lord's prayer in Greek verses printed by Robert I Estienne at the end of Calvin's *Greek Cathechism*, as translated by his son Henri II (Στοιχείωσις 1531, Geneva, 126).

Biography: Johann Rudolf Wettstein I (1614–1684, also known as the Father), one of the many carrying this name in the family, was born in Basel in 1614.[91] His father was the famous Mayor Johann Rudolf Wettstein (1594–1666, also called the Grandfather), a participant in the negotiations of the Peace of Westphalia, who had obtained Switzerland's *de jure* independence from the Holy Roman Empire. The author of our poem, Johann Rudolf, was a brilliant young man: he entered the University of Basel in 1628, received his master's degree in arts in 1631 and subsequently studied theology (with a licentiate in 1634). He soon became Professor of Greek (1634) and later Professor of Philosophy (Organon) in 1643. In the same year he married Margarethe Zäslin, with whom he had 12 sons and 5 daughters, including Johann Rudolph Wettstein II (see below). In 1649, Wettstein I received the degree of Theology, in 1654 he became a Professor of Theology (in Dogmatics), and in 1656 Professor of the New Testament. He wrote many theological works and much occasional poetry (mostly in Latin). At present we know four Greek poems by him: to Nicolaus Eglinger, to Emmanuel König, and jointly to Hieronymus Zenoin and Peter Falkeisen for their doctorates in medicine, and to Sebastian Faesch (see below) for his doctorate in Law.

Bibliography: Salis, Arnold von (1897), "Wettstein, Johann Rudolf", in: *Allgemeine Deutsche Biographie* 42, 248–250; Egger, Franz (2015), "Wettstein, Johann Rudolf", in: *Historisches Lexikon der Schweiz (HLS)*, https://hls-dhs-dss.ch/de/articles/019086/2015-01-11/ [accessed: November 2020]; Gernler, Johann Heinrich (1711), Ἀλεξιφάρμακον, *Oder Der Sünde Gegen-Gifft...als...bestattet ward Der...Herr Nicolaus Eglinger*. Basel. His other Greek poems: Ἔπος προσφθεγκτήριον...τὸν Ζηνώινον...τὸν Φαλκίσιον, Basel: Decker, 1641; *Clarissimo viro Sebastiano*

---

90 For the function of acrostics, cf. Steinrück 2018, 299–302, 315–316.
91 See Egger 2015.

Feschio, philosopho...sub doctorali corona...triumfanti, Basel: Bertsche, 1681; *Nobilissimo, clarissimo...Emmanueli König...*, Basel: typis Regiis, 1682. On this poem: Steinrück, Martin (2018), "Springlesen: eine akrostichische Form bei Propertius und Filelfo", in: Janika Päll/Ivo Volt (eds.), *Hellenostephanos*, Tartu, 299–317.

[MS/JP]

Sebastian Faesch (1647–1712)

XIII. [1674]

 Ὦ ψάμεθ᾽ Ἐγλιγγῆρον ἐς οὐρανὸν ἀστερόεντα
  χρυσέοις ἐν φήμης ἅρμασιν ὀρνύμενον,
 Ἄ μμι δὲ εἰσορόωσιν ἑνὶ φρεσὶ θυμὸς ἰάνθη,
  εἶπέ θ᾽, ὅδ᾽ αὐξήσει πατρίδος εὐρὺ κλέος.
5 Ὦ πόποι! αὐτὰρ ἕως τά τε τείρεα λαμπετόωντα,
  ἄστρα θ᾽, ἅ τ᾽ Οὔλυμπος ἐστεφάνωτ᾽, ἐφορᾷ,
 Α ἶψ᾽ ὑπὲρ Ὠρίωνα καὶ ὀψὲ δύοντα Βοώτην
  ἠέρθη, γνώμης ἔμπαλιν ἡμετέρης.
 Ὥ ς κρυεροῦ θανάτου νέφεα σκιόεντα καλύπτει
10   φέγγος, ὃ μὲν πάτρῃ λάμπε μινυνθάδιον.
 Ἀ λλ᾽ ὅγε παμφαίνων μακάρων μεθ᾽ ὁμήγυριν ἀνδρῶν,
  ἀστὴρ ὡς αὐγὴν ἔννυται ἀϊδίην.

     ὀλίγα ταῦτα ὡς νομιζόμενα τῷ μακαρίτῃ ποιεῖν ἔμελλε
     ΣΕΒΑΣΤΙΑΝῸΣ Ὁ ΦΈΣΧΙΟΣ

Textus: Rüdin, Jakob (1674), *Samuel Eglingerus Phil. & Med. D. Mathematum in Acad. Basiliensi Profess. ...oratione parentali...illustratus*, Basileae: J. Werenfels, 43 (= F2r).

Sim.: 1 ἐς οὐρανὸν ἀστερόεντα] Hom. *Il.* 15.371; *Od.* 9.527; 12.380 (εἰς) || **2** χρυσέοις ἐν φήμης ἅρμασιν] cf. *Hymn. Hom. Cer.* 431 (ἐν ἅρμασι χρυσείοισι) || **3** εἰσορόωσι] cf. Hom. *Od.* 8.327 | ἐνὶ φρεσὶ θυμὸς ἰάνθη] cf. Hom. *Il.* 24.321; *Od.* 15.165 || **4** πατρίδος εὐρὺ κλέος] cf. Hom. *Od.* 3.82 (πατρὸς ἐμοῦ κλέος εὐρύ) || **5** τείρεα λαμπετόωντα] cf. Ap. Rhod. *Argon.* 3.1362, vide Hes. *Theog.* 110, 382 (ἄστρά τε λαμπετόωντα) || **5–6** τείρεα...ἐστεφάνωτ᾽] cf. Hom. *Il.* 18.485 (ἐν δὲ τὰ τείρεα πάντα, τά τ᾽ οὐρανὸς ἐστεφάνωται) || **6** ἠέρθη] ex analogia metri causa cf. Simon. PMG 516 || **7** καὶ ὀψὲ δύοντα Βοώτην] cf. Hom. *Od.* 5.272 || **8** γνώμης ἔμπαλιν] cf. Pind. *Pyth.* 12.32 (ἔμπαλιν γνώμας) || **9** κρυεροῦ θανάτου] cf. Eus. *Praep.* 5.6.1.12; *Anth. App. Orac.* 129.8 (κρυεροῦ θανάτοιο) | νέφεα σκιόεντα] cf. Hom. *Il.* 5.522 al. || **11** μεθ᾽ ὁμήγυριν] cf. Hom. *Il.* 20.142; *Hom. Hymn.* 2.484; 3.187 (θεῶν μεθ᾽ ὁμήγυριν ἄλλων)

<Epitaph for S. Eglinger>

> **O**ur friend Eglinger we have seen into star-sparkling heaven
>   mounting on his fame, with golden chariot there,
> **A**nd we looked with joy in our souls at how he ascended
>   and the heart said: he will give fame to his land far and wide.
> [5] **O,** alas! While he was looking at all those glittering wonders
>   and those stars, which were made into Olympian crown,
> **A**y! he rapidly lifted above Orion and Bootes,
>   late-setting star, against all what were hoping in thoughts
> **O**rcus' clouds now, frisky and shadowy, cover his lustre
> [10] that had been giving to his city so shortly its light.
> **A**ll bright, shining he is among blessed men, in their assembly,
>   like a star puts on the cloak's brilliance, eternally bright.

Sebastian Faesch composed these few verses for
the deceased according to the custom

Metre: Elegiac couplets.

Notes: The addressee of the poem is Samuel Eglinger (Basel 1638–1673), the son of the Basel pharmacist and/or court assessor Samuel Eglinger and of Monica Melville.[92] He acquired the doctorates in philosophy (1655) and medicine (1661) at the University of Basel, and became there Professor of Mathematics (1655). In 1673 he made a trip to his brother in Frankfurt, and died on his way home in Heidelberg. His printed works include above all medical disputations. The gratulations for his academic achievements and the *epicedia* for him reveal that he lived in the same circles as the Wettsteins and Faesch. Omega and Alpha of the acrostic mark the high hopes for and the short life of Samuel Eglinger. Faesch combines words and phrases from classical authors (mainly Homer), but without favouring one author or work. The ring composition, the ascendance of a star and its disappearance among the illustrious deceased in 6 elegiac couplets, might be typical motives for his times and the genre of the *epicedium*, but for us it might also be a school reminiscence of the beginning of *Oresteia*, Aeschylus' most juridical text, where the shadowy politics of Argos are compared to the assembly of the stars (but Pindar's *Pythian* 12 is closer both in form and theme).

Biography: Sebastian Faesch was born in 1647 in Basel. His father was Christopher Faesch, a Professor of Law and History at the University of Basel, and his

---

[92] See Herzog 1778, 415f.; Rüdin 1674, 3–5, 16–20.

mother Catharina Güntzer.⁹³ He excelled in language studies (Greek, Hebrew, and Latin) and oratory, and received the degree of master in 1664 with a Greek verse oration *De literarum graecarum ad studium juris necessitate* (not found). Thereafter he studied law and spent time in France and Britain together with his friend Johann Rudolph Wettstein II (see below), returning home through Belgium and France. In 1678 he left again, in order to study antiquities in Italy, where he wrote a Greek and Latin poem in honour of Venice (*Rei publicae Venetae laudes,* not found) and started studying Roman coins. In 1681 he received his doctorate and started to work as the Professor of Law at the University of Basel; afterwards he moved to the position of the City Secretary and the Deputy for Church and Schools. In 1685 he married Anna Maria Winckelblech with whom he had 6 children. He died in Basel in 1712. Faesch published several juridical disputations, occasional speeches and poems in Latin, and at least five Greek poems. Most of his work on numismatics, many speeches and numerous letters to and by him are unpublished. One of his Greek poems is a good illustration of the circles of friendship and relations among Hellenists: the doctorate of Johann Wettstein was celebrated with Greek poems by his cousins, brothers Johann Rudolf Wettstein II and Samuel Wettstein, as well as by Sebastian Faesch.⁹⁴

Bibliography: Bühler, Theodor (2014), "Faesch, Sebastian", in: *Historisches Lexikon der Schweiz (HLS)*, https://hls-dhs-dss.ch/it/articles/015832/2004-12-01/ [accessed: November 2020]; Huber, Johann Jacob (1712), *Der Ruhm Eines Guten Gewissens/....Leich-Predigt Uber...Herr Sebastian Fäsch...*, Basel; Herzog, Johann Werner (1778), *Athenae Rauricae, sive catalogus professorum Academiae Basiliensis ab a.* MCCCLX *ad a.* MDCCLXXVII, Basel.

[MS/JP]

---

93 See Huber 1712, 50–57; Herzog, 1778, 145f.
94 See *Viro...Iohanne Wetstenio...laurum doctoralem a Sebast. Faeschio...collatam...gratulantur fautores et amici*, Basileae: J. Bertsch, 1685. His Greek poems are for Johannes Tonjola and Paul Tsernatorni (1665), Thomas Siegfried Ring from Silesia (1683), and Leonhard Laurenz Högger from Sankt Gall (1683).

Johann Rudolf Wettstein II (1647–1711)

שיר חתנה [1670]
Τὸ αὐτὸ ἑλληνιστί.

Δῶρον πανταγαθοῦ ἄλοχος πέλε κέδν' εἰδυῖα,
  Ἀνδρὶ ἑῷ, καὶ Ζεὺς ἀμφοτέροισι πάρα.
Χαῖρ' οὖν ἐκ κραδίης, πολυφέρτατε Νύμφιε, Νύμφην
  Εὐκλέα καὶ πάντως οὐρανόδεικτον ἔχεις,
5 Σύγγαμον ἐσσομένην μογεροῦ μέγα χάρμα βίοιο,
  Ἄμπελον, ἣ καρπόν Σοι γλυκὺν ἐκφορέει.
Ἄμβροτος οὐρανόθεν τελέσειε ἃ ἤρξατο καλά,
  Ἀρκετὸν ὧδε, ἄνω, δοὺς γάνος ἀΐδιον.

Textus: Joh. Rodolfus Wetstenius, *Felicissimo neogamorum pari...Ioh. Iacobo Buxtorfio et...Cleophae Brandmylleriae...pia vota*, Basileae: Decker, 1670, 1v.

Crit.: 1 πανταγάθου debuit || 3 νυμφίε debuit

Sim.: 1 cf. LXX, *Prov.* 19.14; πανταγαθοῦ] cf. *Anth. Pal.* 11.340.4 | κέδν' εἰδυῖα] cf. *Hymn. Hom. Ap.* 313 et *Ven.* 43–44 (Ζεὺς...ἄλοχον ποιήσατο κέδν' εἰδυῖαν) || 4 οὐρανόδεικτον cf. *Hymn. Hom. Lun.* 3 || 5 μογεροῦ...βίοιο] cf. Greg. Naz. *carm.*, PG 37.1240; *Anth. Pal.* 9.500.4 || 6 ἄμπελον] cf. NT *Ioh.* 15.1 (Ἐγώ εἰμι ἡ ἄμπελος ἡ ἀληθινή)

Wedding song
The same in Greek

A prudent wife is for her husband a gift of the Almighty and Zeus is together with both of them. Therefore rejoice from your heart, most valiant bridegroom, as you have received a bride of good fame and in every sense created from heaven. She will be your spouse, a great joy in the distressful life, a vine which will bring you sweet fruits. And let the Immortal from heaven bring to fulfillment what has nicely started, thus giving you sufficiently everlasting happiness in the future.[95]

Metre: Hexameters (with liberties, such as the hiatus in l. 7).

---

[95] This is the English version contained in the book (heading 'The same in English'): 'Blessed is wel the MAN, who had a wife, I say / From GOD a godly WIFE, the LORD is in this way: / Therfore be in your heart SIR! Rejoyce with your BRIDE, / Which to your great honour is joyned to your side, / Which shall give to your house prosperitie and peace, / And lik'th fruitfull vines render you good increase: / To you the living LORD wil multiply his grace, / That blessing after you shall follow on your race!'

Notes: In most collections of his time, the most prolific of the Wettsteins to write in Greek, Johann Rudolf the Son, appears with a poem in Greek, the finest available, always using twists the other contributors to the anthology were not able to produce. Instead of his usual bilingual poem pairs, this time he surpassed himself in using nine languages, starting with Hebrew and adding Greek, Latin, Italian, French, Spanish, English, Dutch, and German translations, quite in accordance with the *poikilia* of wedding poetry.[96] A couple of years earlier, he had written a Hebrew poem with translations into Greek, Latin, and German for the Mangold brothers (who were his friends and the relatives of his wife Ursula), accompanied by a pangrammatic poem (on the letter M) in both Greek and Latin.

As in his usual bilingual Greek-Latin poem pairs, Wettstein's translation is quite free, because he relies on the poetic formulae which are specific to the language in question. His wedding poem is based on the well-known passages from the Bible and from classical authors such as Hesiod (*Op.* 702–703: οὐ μὲν γάρ τι γυναικὸς ἀνὴρ ληΐζετ' ἄμεινον τῆς ἀγαθῆς) or Theognis (1225: Οὐδέν, Κύρν', ἀγαθῆς γλυκερώτερόν ἐστι γυναικός). Wettstein proceeds according to the simplest pattern from the statement, first premise of the rhetorical syllogism (a good wife is a gift of God) to the conclusion (therefore Buxtorf has to be congratulated) and the *Votum*. Both addressees come from old Basel humanist families: Johann Jakob Buxtorf (1605–1704), the son of the professor of Hebrew and theologian Johann Buxtorf (1599–1664), became the Professor of Hebrew at Basel University after his father's death in 1664, and, as an exception, made his grand tour (which included the studies of Arabic in England) after receiving this position. His bride Cleophe Brandmüller (1655–1733), who was to bear him six children, was the daughter of Jacob Brandmüller, the Professor of Law at Basel University, and of Salome König, descendant of the family of printers and book merchants.[97]

Biography: The grandson of the famous Mayor of Basel, Johann Rudolf Wettstein II (1647–1711, also known as the Son) was born in Basel.[98] His father was the Professor of Theology Johann Rudolf Wettstein I (see above), his mother Margaretha Zäslin. His father, an excellent Hellenist himself, sent his son to study with the

---

96 See Wettstein, J.R. (1667), *Pari fratrum indolis...Ioh. Georgio Mathiae Mangoldiis...quum summam philosophiae lauream...obtinerent*, Basel. For polyglottism as a special feature of wedding poetry (especially in the absence of courts), see Päll 2020a.
97 See Werner 1778, 449–452 and "Emanuel König I", in: *Index typographorum editorumque Basileensium* https://ub2.unibas.ch/itb/druckerverleger/emanuel-koenig-i/ [accessed: November 2020].
98 Werner 1778, 55–56, 79, 323, 373, cf. Marti-Weissbach 2012; von Salis 1897.

best teachers in 1660: as a young boy of 13 years Johann Rudolf II learned Greek in Zürich under Johann Caspar Schweizer/Suicerus (1620–1688), the Professor of Greek at the Zürich Collegium and another of Switzerland's Hellenizing poets. Back in Basel, Johann Rudolf II graduated in philosophy (1663) and started his studies of theology. Wettstein the Son was famous for his mastery of Greek and Latin, being called *Latii Graeciaeque non hospes sed civis*. In 1667 he revealed his excellence in Greek in a rather scandalous way: he presented a disputation for the vacancy of the chair of Greek, and in order to show his rank to his cunning opponent, he insisted on disputing in Greek and even answered to the opponent's Latin questions in Greek.[99] He received his degree in theology in 1668, left for his Grand Tour together with his friend Sebastian Faesch (see above) and after his return he started to teach at the University of Basel; in 1673 he became Professor of Eloquence, in 1684 Professor of Greek. He received his Doctorate in Theology in 1685, and then advanced from the position of Professor of Loci (1685) to that of Professor of the Old (1686) and the New Testament (1703 or 1704). He was married to Ursula Mangold, with whom he had 7 children. Johann Rudolf II has written and presided over numerous theological and philosophical-(philological) disputations. Today he is mostly known for his Greco-Latin commented editions of Origen's *Dialogus contra Marcionitas* (1673–1674) and *Exhortatio ad Martyrium* (1673), as well as for his treatises about the Greek language: nine disputations about the pronunciation of Greek (1676–1678), and disputations about the Greek accentuation and the fate of the poetry of Homer.[100] He wrote numerous occasional poems and speeches in Latin, a long elegy praising the thermal waters of Pfeffers (*Thermae Favarienses*) and at least thirty Greek poems, most of which are equipped with his own Latin translations. As often happens, the longest and most elaborate poems stem from the author's youth: in 1668 he dedicated a Greek-Latin poem pair in elegiac couplets to Theobald Schönauer for his laureate in Philosophy, presenting a beautiful description of the dwelling place of Apollo and the Muses.[101]

Bibliography: Herzog 1778; Salis, Arnold von (1897), "Wettstein, Johann Rudolf", in: *Allgemeine Deutsche Biographie* 42), 250–251 [Online-Version]; Marti-Weissenbach, K. (2012), "Wettstein, Jo-

---

[99] See Werner 1778; Wettstein 1667. For disputations in Greek, see Päll 2020b (in the Nordic section).
[100] For *Pro Graeca & genuina linguae Graecae pronuntiatione* (ed. prima 1680), *De accentuum Gr. antiquitate et usu* (1685); *De fato scriptorum Homeri* (1684), see Wettstein 1686 in the bibliography.
[101] Wettstein, J.R. (1668), *Vernam vernantemque coronam qua dexter Apollo*, Basel: Decker.

hann Rudolf", in: *Historisches Lexikon der Schweiz (HLS)*, https://hls-dhs-dss.ch/de/articles/026283/2012-11-16/ [accessed: November 2020]. Other works by Wettstein: *Pro Graeca et genuina linguae Graecae pronunciatione...orationes apologeticae...adiectae sunt orationes quaedam miscellae*, Basel 1686; *Thermae Favarienses*, Basel: Bertsche 1706 (written in 1672); *Philosophorum ordinis specimen hoc philologicum Graeca p.t. vacante*, Basel 1676.

[JP]

Johann Heinrich Herder (1661–1716)

XLIX. [1696]

	Ἄρχιος	Ἁγνὸς	Ἄμ'	Ἀρτιεπὴς	Ἀμάρυσσεν	Ἀμύμων
	Νημερτὴς	νοέῃ,	νεμεσῶν	νέα	νείκεα	νικῶν,
	Δωτὴρ	δημόσιος	δώρων	δοὺς	δήνεα	δαίφρων,
	Ῥηξήνωρ	ῥητός,	ῥέζων	ῥέα	ῥήματα	ῥήτωρ,
5	Ἐρέας	εὖς κεν	ἐράσσατο	εὔφρων,	εὔκηλος	ἔσκε,
	Αὐγάζων	ἄρα	ἄφθονος;	αὐτὰρ	αὐγαρὸν	ἀλύσκει;
	Στείχων	συνεχέως	στιβαρὸς;	σώζων	στόμα	σφοδρῶς,
	Μιν	Μάλα	Μὲν	Μελιηδέα	Μοίρα	Μητιόεντες
	Ἐκλεκτόν	κεν ἐπῆραν	ἐς	ἕδραν	ἑκόντες,	ἕποντες,
10	ἼΣΧΥΕ	Ἰθυδίκης	ἴθι	ἴδμων	ἴφθιμος	ἴσθι,
	Ἥσυχος	ἧς	Ἥρως	ἢ	ἤπιος	ἡγεμονεύῃ,
	Ῥιγηλῶν	ῥήξων	ῥαδιούργημα	ῥίμφα	ῥα	ῥάβδῳ,
	Ὄλβιος	οὕνεκ'	Ὄλυμπον	ὁμῶς	ὁσιόν τ'	ὀπιπεύῃ,
	Σώματι	σφοδρῶς	σὺν	στήθεσσι	σεβάσματα	σπένδων.

Textus: *Musarum Limagidum vicinarumque applausus votivi...summis...honoribus...D. Andreae Meieri*, Tiguri: H. Bodmer 1696, M IIr (cf. fig. 6)

Crit.: 2 νεμεσῶν scripsi: νεμεσῶν ed. || 3 δαίφρων scripsi: δαΐφρων ed. || 6 αὐγαρὸν pro αὐγηρόν || 9 Ἐκλεκτόν κεν] ed. Ἐκλεκτόνκεν, || 13 ὅσιόντ ὀπιπτεύῃ ed., correxi

Sim.: 10–14 (acrostichis ΙΗΡΟΣ), cf. *Anth. Pal.* 7.3; A. Politianus, epigr. gr. 10.17 (Ὦ χαῖρ' ἱηρὴ κεφαλή)

<Acrostic for Andreas Meyer>

A lways best and pure, without blame, bright, readily talking,
N either mistaken in thoughts nor seeking for victory-quarrels,
D onor of public donations with all his thoughtful advises,
R ealizer by the law, an easily speaking orator,

[5] **E** ager for children, the good-thinking, mild man, he doesn't worry!
A ye, he is brilliant for sure, but then he avoids too much brilliance,
S turdily setting his steps, one by one, with words very careful,
M uch for this sweet man the wise were hoping by fate the promotion,
E lected man to be for the chair, and then readily told him:
[10] '**I** n your judgement, be STRONG, go and be knowledgeable, with power,
E asy and gentle, as hero or mild wherever you lead us,
R ise your sceptre against the scary men, breaking them swiftly,
O lympus' heights and religion respecting, you shall be happy,
S oul and body, you give them both in your veneration.'

Metre: Hexameters (with liberties: l. 5 εὔκηλος and 7 ἴφθιμος dactylic, 5 acephalous, 6 αὐγαρὸν (αὐγηρὸν) counted as ᴗ – ᴗ, 7 συνεχέως choriambic, 12 ῥᾳδιούργημα counted as ᴗᴗ – ᴗᴗ)

Notes: The addressee of the poem, Andreas Meyer (Meier, 1635–1711), is well-known.[102] From an old Zürich family of merchants, he was a member of the *Zunft zur Waag* (Balance) and the master of this guild from 1668 until 1696, when he became Mayor of Zürich. He had also served in the military and during his service he completed the reorganisation of the Zürich army. In the translation the sixfold pangrammatic ἀκροστιχίς (cf Cicero, *De divinatione* 2.111) *Andreas Meieros* is reduced to a single acrostic like in the Latin translation by the author.[103] But this is not enough: Herder hid a second acrostic in Greek within the first: *hieros*, 'sacred' marked by the beginning of a word in capitals ΙΣΧΥΕ, 'be STRONG'[104] (a half-moon-shaped form inherited from Aratus' ΛΕΠΤΗ-acrostic), which introduces the direct speech. The acrostic's etymologic quality (Meyer = mayor) hints at the fact that in 1673 Meyer had been a major in the army. His first name Andreas ('the manly') adds to the military ring and is reminiscent of Meyer's work in the Tigurine army. The initial description (less respectful in Greek than in the Latin 'translation') sketches the Mayor as a man of few words, advancing step by step, an

---

102 See Lassner 2009.
103 Ibidem: Μετάφρασις. *A cceptus, Castus, vitae integer ipse coruscat; N arrans Vera, simul succensens litibus ortis; D onorum largusque dator; Consultor amandus; R ector Mavortis clarus, Rhetorque disertus; E lectosque colens coetus; rutilat quoque mitis; A spectu blandus; Vitans fugiensque superbos; S emper robustus gradiens os suave fovebat; M ellitum hunc equidem Magnates sorte Canora; E lectum in solium tolluntque sequentia fantur; I ncedas fortis; judex sis scitus & aequus; E gregiusque Heros, Dux sis moderamine suavis; R umpens horrendûm citius malefacta bacillo; U t sancto tandem felix coeloque fruaris S emper carne simul quoque pectore sacra sacrando.*
104 He probably thought, like many classical scholars today, that the word actually means 'STRONG'.

allusion perhaps to his actual position as a powerful society-headmaster of the guild of the *Shieldbearers to the Balance*. The seven hexameters of the description part (6 words in each) are detached from the following by the majuscules which run through the eighth line, and the following 2 verses of the speech-introduction – all of it in the third person. Only then does the text slip into the second person of direct speech. After this poem, Herder added a Latin numerical anagrammatic poem, which indicated the year when Meier became Mayor, and a chronogrammatic poem, also based on the anagram of Meyer's name (also in Latin), as well as an elegiac couplet in Greek.

Biography: The author is probably Hans (Johannes) Heinrich Herder (1661–1716), a pastor in Wildenberg (near Zürich), who had been a student of the Zürich Collegium and participated in philosophical and theological disputations there in 1683.[105] A Latin letter by him to the Zürich physician Johann Jakob Scheutzer (who studied thermal waters) is preserved in manuscript form.

Bibliography: Lassner, Martin (2009), "Meyer, Andreas", in: *Historisches Lexikon der Schweiz (HLS)*, https://hls-dhs-dss.ch/de/articles/018093/2009-11-05/ [accessed: November 2020].

[MS]

Yves Gerhard (1948–)

ΕΓΚΩΜΙΟΝ [1989]

Ἄνδρα σοφόν θ᾽ ὑμνῶ πολυτέχνεά θ᾽, ὃς μάλ᾽ ἀκριβῆ
τοῖσι φιλέλλησιν διδαχὴν πόρεν. Ἄστυ μὲν οἰκεῖ
Λωζάννης τριλόφου, ἐδίδαξέν ἑ δ᾽ ἐν Βασιλείᾳ
αὖτε Μυλωνιάδης, ἀριδείκετος ἡγητήρων.
5   Αὐτὰρ ἐπεὶ μὲν ἔγραψε τὸ βιβλίον εἰς τὸν Ἔρωτα,
ἔνθα πρὸς Ἀρχιλόχου μέλεα σπούδαζε καὶ οὕτως
τοῦ τὰ ἐρείπι᾽ ἄγειρε τά τ᾽ ἀστρολόγου πάλιν αὐτοῦ
χώρης τῆς Κνιδίης Εὐδόξοο, ἔνθα δ᾽ ἔπειτα
ἔκδωκεν Στράβωνα Γεωγραφικῶν τὸν ὑφάντην
10 καὶ ταῦτ᾽ εἰς γλῶσσαν μετεφράσσατο τῶν Γαλατάων.
Νῦν δ᾽ οὐ ῥήσιος ἔστιν ἀκούειν τοῖς γε μαθηταῖς
λεπτῆς οὐδ᾽ ἀγαθῶν ἐπέων κομψῶν τ᾽ ἀπολαύειν

---

105 See Weber-Steiner, Regula (2006), *Glückwünschende Ruhm- und Ehrengedichte*, Bern, 409.

καί ῥ' ἂν ὁ τῶν Μουσῶν θεράπων παύσαιτο τοῦ ἔργου·
οὐ μὴν ἀλλ' ὑπόμνημα νέον φέρει ἐμμενὲς αἰεὶ
15 τῆς δεκάτης Μούσης ἕνεκεν καὶ λεξικὰ ῥάπτει,
τῆς δ' Ἀκαδημείης ἀτρεκῶς μνήμην ἐφύλαξεν
καὶ τὰ Πλατωνείων συγγράμματα ἄμμι παρέσχεν.
Αὐτὰρ ἐπεὶ πάντως δεκετηρίδας ἤνυσεν ἑπτά,
μικρὰ τάδ' αὖτε γραφέντα προείλετο εἰς ἓν ἀγείρας,
20 ὡς ἄρα ἀστάχυες ταναοί, οἳ ἐν ἐλλεδανοῖσιν
ἀρχομένου θέρεός γε δέδενται. Νῦν δ', ἀναγνῶστα,
χαῖρέ νυ πολλάκι μηδὲ λαθοῦ τόπερ εἶπεν ἀοιδὸς
ὑμνῶν τὴν Δήμητρα· "μέγ' ὄλβιος, ὄντινα Μοῦσαι
προφρονέως φίλωνται ἐπιχθονίων ἀνθρώπων."

Textus: scheda impressa, quae die 20 Iunii a. 1989 Losanae (Lausanne) in festo ad honorem Francisci Lasserre celebrato publici iuris facta est

Sim. 1 ἄνδρα σοφόν] in hac sede cf. *Anth. Pal.* 7.618.1 | πολυτέχνεα] cf. Solon. fr. 13.49 W. || **3** τριλόφου] cf. Nonn. *Dion.* 6.124 al. || **4** ἀριδείκετος] cum gen. part. (ἀνδρῶν) cf. Hom. *Il.* 11.248; 14.320 || **12** ἀγαθῶν ἐπέων] cf. e.g. Greg. Naz. *Carm.*, PG 37.1537.7 || **13** Μουσάων θεράπων] cf. Hes. *Op.* 100 al. || **14** ἐμμενὲς αἰεί] cf. Hom. *Il.* 10.361, 364 etc. || **15** δεκάτης Μούσης] saep. de Sapphone, cf. *Anth. Pal.* 9.66.2 et 571.8 || **19** εἰς ἓν ἀγείρας] de clausula cf. *Anth. Pal.* 5.300.1; 8.17.3; 16.138.5 al. || **20–21** ἀστάχυες...δέδενται] cf. *Hymn. Hom. Dem.* 454–456 || **22** χαῖρέ νυ πολλάκι] cf. Theoc. *Id.* 1.144 || **23–24** *Hymn. Hom. Dem.* 486–487

Encomium

I praise the wise and skilful man, who provided the lovers of Greek
with a very precise teaching. He lives in the three-hilled
town of Lausanne, but in Basel he was the pupil
of the remarkable among professors, Von der Mühll.
[5] After writing a book devoted to Eros,
he studied here the poems of Archilochus, thus gathering
his fragments, as well as those of the Cnidian
astronomer, Eudoxus; later here he edited
Strabo, the weaver of the *Geography*,
[10] which he translated in the language of the Gauls.
But now students can no longer listen to his fine discourse
nor profit from his excellent and ingenious words:
the servant of the Muses could thus stop working;
and yet, indefatigably, he produces a new commentary
[15] about the tenth Muse, he has woven lexica,
he has cherished the memory of the Academy
and he has given us the writings of Plato's school.
Now, since he has completed seven times ten years
he has chosen and gathered these short articles in a volume

[20] like long spikes, that at the beginning of the summer
have been bound together with ropes. Now, reader,
rejoice often and do not forget the words of the poet
who sang to Demeter: 'Merry he whom the Muses
love with benevolence, among the men on the earth.'

Metre: Hexameters (note hiatuses in ll. 7, 17).

Notes: This epigram was conceived for the *Kleine Schriften* of the great Swiss philologist François Lasserre (1919–1989): *Nouveaux chapitres de littérature grecque (1947–1986)*, Genève 1989. It was publicly recited on the event of the book's presentation to Lasserre himself on 20 June 1989, organised by the curator Claude Calame, Lasserre's successor on the Lausanne chair. Gerhard's piece was partly inspired by Rudolf Führer's long encomiastic epigram for the Hellenist Eva-Maria Voigt, the famous editor of Sappho and Alcaeus (Θησαυρὸς σπουδαιογέλοιος *für EMV*, Hamburg 1983). Reference is made in the poem to some of Lasserre's most important books: the texts of Archilochus (*Les épodes d'Archiloque*, Paris 1950; *Fragments*, Paris 1958), Eudoxus (*Die Fragmente des Eudoxos von Knidos*, Berlin 1966), and Strabo (ed. of books 1, 3–6, and 10–12 of the *Geography*, Paris 1966–1967, 1969, 1971, 1975, 1981), the essay on Sappho (*Sappho: une autre lecture*, Padua 1989), the edition of letters α–β of the *Etymologicum Genuinum, Magnum* and *Symeonis* (with Nikolaos Livadaras: I, Athens 1976; II, Rome 1992), and finally the studies on Plato and Platonism (*La naissance des mathématiques à l'époque de Platon*, Paris 1990).

Biography: A pupil of François Lasserre and André Rivier at Lausanne, Yves Gerhard worked mainly as a teacher of Greek, Latin, and French in secondary school. In 1972–1974 he cooperated with the *Lexikon des frühgriechischen Epos* in Hamburg, and in more recent times he was active as a biographer (*André Bonnard et l'hellénisme à Lausanne au XXe siècle*, Vevey 2011) and as a translator of epic and lyric poetry (see esp. Hésiode, *La Théogonie*, Vevey 2005).

Bibliography: Marcotte, Didier (2018), "François Lasserre face à Strabon: le texte et les muses", in: *FuturoClassico* 4, 227–260; Calame, Claude (1990), "François Lasserre (1919–1989)", in: *Quaderni Urbinati di Cultura Classica* 34, 165–168.

[FP]

Fig. 7: *Les Amours de P. de Ronsard Vandomoys…*, Paris 1552, 2: portrait of Pierre Ronsard with the Greek inscription ὡς ἴδον ὡς ἐμάνην (Theoc. *Id.* 2.82) and the epigram by J.-A. de Baïf (see below, p. 370–372).

Luigi-Alberto Sanchi, Jean-Marie Flamand, and Romain Menini
France

To understand the dynamics of French poetry production in Greek, a well-known comedy written in 1672 by Molière, *Les Femmes savantes* ('*The Learned Ladies*'), is worth quoting. Molière ridicules the attitude of a couple of parasites, Trissotin and Vadius, who claim to write poems in the ancient style and make a display of their Greco-Roman knowledge. In Act iii, scene v, Vadius quarrels with Trissotin addressing him with these words (l. 1043): 'Je te défie en vers, prose, grec, et latin' ('I defy you in verse, prose, Greek and Latin'), thus declaring his ability to write even Greek verse. The character of Vadius was inspired by one of the poets in our selection, the remarkable philologist **Gilles Ménage** (1613–1692), author of *Historia mulierum philosopharum* ('*History of Women Philosophers*') and *Observationes et emendationes in Diogenem Laertium* ('*Remarks and Emendations on Diogenes Laertius*'), as well as several Greek and Latin poems. Among his circle of scholars, we find Anne Dacier, the daughter of the professor of Greek literature, Tanguy Lefèvre, and the dedicatee of a Greek poem written by **Jean Boivin** (1663–1726), another friend of Ménage, as well as **Bernard de La Monnoye** (1641–1728). If Ménage did not show disappointment when watching Molière's comedy, the fact that the erudite poets were parodied indicates in itself the end of a golden era for the '*neualtgriechisch*' verse production in France.[1] It is well known that being seen as ridiculous was a French citizen's worst nightmare. This may help explain why, with the exception of the 1743 edition *Recentiores poetae Latini et Graeci selecti*, this kind of literary *divertissement* is almost impossible to find after the Renaissance, even in academic circles. The present selection nevertheless includes a few meaningful pieces, written by **André Chénier** (1762–1794), **Léon Vernier** (1855–1926) and **Fernand Chapouthier** (1899–1953).

In his 1672 play, Molière wanted to ensure the elimination of a practice which was almost dead. He perhaps ignored, however, the extent to which it had been eagerly pursued, and its relatively widespread nature, during a century running from approximately 1520 to 1620, or rather, from the Reformation to the end of

---

1 Cf. also the interesting statement by François de Callières in his *Histoire poétique de la guerre nouvellement déclarée entre les Anciens et les Modernes* (Paris 1688, 287) on Greek verse production, which banishes such efforts to Germany and the Nordic nations: '[...] il [sc. Apollo] met au plus bas étage du Parnasse tous ceux qui au lieu de cultiver leur langue maternelle s'amusent à écrire en Vers Grecs ou Latins, declare tous ces ouvrages de contre-bande, ainsi que toutes *Anagrammes, Acrostiches*, & autres amusemens de Pedans, les bannit de la societé des Nations polies, & les relegue à perpetuité dans les Coleges & chez les Allemans & autres nations du Nord.'

the Civil Wars. Excellent Greek professors, scholars and eminent literary authors tried to pursue the Hellenic Muse, starting with **François Rabelais** (c. 1500?–1553), who is also the first modern author in the history of French literature. Making a selection for this period is thus as difficult as being spoilt for choice: an anthology dedicated to Greek production in Renaissance France (prose and verse) would require a large volume. One pivotal institution, whose existence provides an explanation for the wealth of poems produced during the 16th century, was the French King's College, *Collège royal*, formed by its professors (*lecteurs du roi*) and later enriched by the King's printers, of whom Robert Estienne (Robertus Stephanus) was one. Among the first representatives of this College was Jacques Toussain, or Iacobus Tusanus (†1547), the dedicatee of **François Bérauld**'s (c. 1517–1574) poem in the present selection. Toussain had been trained by Guillaume Budé (1468–1540), who is associated with the appointment of the first King's lecturers in 1530. However, despite their sincere interest in ancient Greek epigrams, as far as we know neither Toussain nor Budé wrote Greek poetry.[2]

During the years following the establishment of these lecturers and printers, in spite of the tense situation leading to the Wars of Religion (1562–1598), France enjoyed an extraordinary intellectual development led by humanists and scholars.[3] The flowering of poetic output was then paralleled in French as well as in humanistic Latin and Greek. The famous *lecteur du roi* **Jean Dorat** (1508–1588) was both a generous author of fine Greek poems, producing some sixty pieces, and the professor of the generation of poets which, in 1554, was baptised *La Pléiade*, including **Jean-Antoine de Baïf** (1532–1589) and **Rémy Belleau** (1528–1577); a few Greek poems were dedicated to the leader of the *Pléiade*, Pierre de Ronsard. The founder of this group, Joachim Du Bellay, must also be mentioned, as, in 1549, he published the manifesto of the new French literature, *La Deffence*

---

2 Ianos Laskaris (→ **Greece**), the author of the *editio princeps* of the *Planudean Anthology* in 1494, became an ambassador for the kings of France from 1495 and contributed to the development of Greek studies in Paris, especially for Toussain's preceptor, Budé. No evidence of his influence concerning the epigrams is acknowledged until 1527, when Laskaris published his *Epigrammata* in Paris with Josse Bade's press, or 1531, when Bade published his own edition of the *Planudea*, based on the second Aldine edition of 1521.
3 The conflicts between the first Hellenists and the Parisian Faculty of Theology occupied the years from c. 1520 to c. 1540, mostly prior to the beginnings of the *Collège des lecteurs du roi*. The battleground was mainly represented by biblical studies, particularly as concerns the value placed on the Latin Vulgate. But this apparently did not impact the enthusiasm for Greek literature and poetry in the scholarly *élite*. By the end of the 16th century, however, the teaching of Greek was the stronghold of the Jesuits and spread all over the kingdom.

et illustration de la langue francoyse ('*The Defence and Illustration of the French language*'), inspired by Sperone Speroni's Italian *Dialogo delle lingue* ('*Dialogue of the languages*', 1542). Du Bellay successfully spoke in favour of a reform of the French language and its literature through the large-scale, humanistic imitation of words, subject-matters and genres imported from Greek and Latin Antiquity. On the erudite side, Greek poems were composed by **Henri II Estienne** (Henricus Stephanus; 1528?–1598) and his pupil **Florent Chrestien** (1541–1596), whose praise of typography is worth mentioning. It should be recalled that the theory that the French language was derived directly from ancient Greek was quite popular throughout the humanist age: it was hinted at by Guillaume Budé and other authors of his generation, like Geoffroy Tory (c. 1530), and then clearly stated by Henricus Stephanus in his *Traité de la conformité du langage français avec le grec* ('*Essay on the Conformity of the French language with the Greek tongue*', 1569). Thus, for several decades, practising Greek became a political issue, and this may explain part of the enthusiasm shown by our poets in the 16th century. The case of Michel de Montaigne's cenotaph in Bordeaux is both unique and symbolic: each side of the monument bears an epigraph, one in Greek and one in Latin. There are also examples of Greek religious poems, such as **Denis Pétau**'s (1583–1652) hymn to the Parisian saint, Sainte Geneviève.

General Bibliography

Barbier-Mueller, Jean-Paul (1973–2005), *Ma Bibliothèque poétique*, Pt. I–IV, Genève.
Barbier-Mueller, Jean-Paul (2015–), *Dictionnaire des poètes français de la seconde moitié du XVIe siècle (1549–1615)*, vol. I–, Genève.
Maillard, Jean-François/Kecskeméti, Judit/Magnien, Catherine/Portalier, Monique (1999), *La France des Humanistes: Hellénistes* I, Turnhout.
Maillard, Jean-François/Flamand, Jean-Marie et al. (2010), *La France des humanistes. Hellénistes* II, Turnhout.

François Rabelais (c. 1500?–1553)

Φραγκίσκου τοῦ Ῥαβελαίσου [1524]

    Βίβλον ἐν οἴκοισιν τήνδ' Ἠλυσίοισιν ἰδόντες
    Ἄμμιγα τὴν ἄνδρες θηλυτέραι τέ φάσαν·
    "Οἷσι νόμοις ὅδ' ἑοὺς Ἀνδρέας τήν γε διδάσκει
    Συζυγίην Γαλάτας ἠδὲ γάμοιο κλέος,
5 Τοὺς ἐδίδαξε Πλάτων ἄν γ' ἡμέας· εἰν ἀνθρώποις
    Κεδνότερος τίς κ' ἄν τοῦ γε Πλάτωνος ἔῃ;"

Textus: Andreae Tiraquelli...*Ex commentariis in Pictonum consuetudines Sectio de legibus connubialibus et iure maritali*, Parisiis: G. a Prato (G. du Pré), 1524, [a i]v (unde Rabelais, François [1994], *Œuvres complètes*, Paris, 1021).

Crit.: tit. Φραγκήσκου ed. || **2** θηλύτεραί τε debuit || **3** ἑοὺς ed. || **6** ἔῃ ed., possis et ἔην vel ἔοι

By François Rabelais

    As they saw this book in the Elysian dwellings,
      Men and women together said about it:
    'The laws by which this man, André, explains to the French,
      his fellow-citizens, the marriage and the glory of matrimony,
    Plato could have taught them to us. And among humans
      who could be better than Plato?'

Metre: Elegiac couplets (l. 3 Ἀνδρέας must be read with lengthened ε). Note the *spondiacus* in l. 5.

Notes: These six lines must be considered a particularly early fruit in France, where Greek was not yet a commonly practised language, with the notable exception of a few Parisian scholars. When he composed this poem in 1524, for the revised edition of *De legibus connubialibus* by his friend André Tiraqueau, a scholar of law, Rabelais was perhaps still the *adulescens* he had claimed to be three years earlier in a letter to Guillaume Budé. The Greek piece is set at the beginning of the volume, and immediately followed by a Latin quatrain written by the humanist Pierre Lamy in honour of Rabelais, presented as his own trustful Pylades in the Franciscan convent at Fontenay-le-Comte (*P. Amici ad F. Rabelaesum*). Tiraqueau also tells us in his dissertation that Rabelais, when still a friar, had translated Herodotus' Book I into Latin and thereby completed Lorenzo Valla's version, which had been carried out on a mutilated manuscript. This achievement is, however, now lost. There is also further evidence that Rabelais, as a young Hellenist, translated some of Lucian of Samosata's writings during these years. This Greek poem shows a few Ionising forms, which prove Rabelais' precocious interest in Ionic Greek, to be developed later in his 1532 edition of Hippocrates. The mention of Plato and his *Laws*, as the term of comparison evoked for Tiraqueau's book, is not surprising: Rabelais had a lifelong familiarity with the Platonic corpus, as his fictional works attest. No doubt he also consulted one of the first printed editions of Planudes' *Greek Anthology*, since Tiraqueau quotes a few poems from it during the same period in which he wrote his *De legibus connubialibus*. We must consider that Rabelais' taste for Greek poetry never abandoned him: in his last work, *Le Quart Livre* ('*The Fourth Book*', 1552), he shows a careful study of Jean Brodeau's erudite commentaries on the *Epigrammata graeca* (Basel, 1549).

Biography: Rabelais' birthdate is still unknown (†1553). An author of successful novels, he also realised the edition of Hippocrates' *Aphorisms* (1532) and *Prognosticon* (1537). Celebrated for his vernacular masterpieces, Rabelais was in fact one of the best French scholars of Greek in his day. In 1521, the future author of *Pantagruel* claimed to be still *adulescens* in a letter to Guillaume Budé, which meant that he was less than 30 years old. At that time, Rabelais was a friar in the Puy-Saint-Martin convent at Fontenay-le-Comte, in Poitou, where he studied Greek together with Pierre Lamy. This period's threefold correspondence between Rabelais, Lamy, and Budé tells us a lot about the difficulties encountered by the former two scholars in peacefully studying Greek literature: in 1523, their convent's Fathers Superiors confiscated their Greek books, suspecting them of proximity to Lutheranism. The volumes were returned only upon Budé's intervention. Two Greek books with friar François' *ex libris* still survive from that period, by Plutarch and Pseudo-Dionysius the Areopagite, respectively. Thanks to an indult that he and his friend Lamy solicited from Pope Clement VII, Rabelais left the Franciscan order and joined the Benedictines of Maillezais, under the protection of Geoffroy d'Estissac, a rich sponsor of humanists.

Bibliography: Plattard, Jean (1923), *L'Adolescence de Rabelais en Poitou*, Paris; Huchon, Mireille (2011), *Rabelais*, Paris; Menini, Romain/Pédeflous, Olivier (2010), "Les marginales de l'amitié. Pierre Lamy et Nicolas Bérauld lecteurs de Lucien de Samosate (BnF Rés. Z. 247)", in: *Bibliothèque d'Humanisme et Renaissance* 74, 35–70. On his Greek poems: Menini, Romain (2009), *Rabelais et l'intertexte platonicien*, Geneva, 67–69; Id. (2013), "Rabelais helléniste", in: *Bulletin de l'Association Guillaume Budé* 1, 216–240; Id. (2014), *Rabelais altérateur. "Græciser en François"*, Paris; Cappellen, Raphaël (2015), "Rabelais lecteur des *Epigrammatum graecorum libri VII* commentés par Jean Brodeau (1549)", in: Rosanna Gorris Camos/Alexandre Vanautgaerden (eds.), *Les Labyrinthes de l'esprit. Collections et bibliothèques à la Renaissance*, Geneva, 105–127.

Germain de Brie (c. 1490–1538)

Ad idem argumentum [scil. de Venere marmorea Francisco regi ab Renzo equite donata] Eiusdem [scil. Germani Brixii] [1531]

Οὐρανόθεν ποτ' ἐς Ἀμβασίην, Φραγκίσκε, μολοῦσα
τὴν σεῦ τὴν Κύπριν Κύπρις ἰδοῦσ', ἔλεγεν·
"καὶ σὲ πρέπεν, βασιλεῦ κρείσσων Ἀρεῖος ἐμοῖο,
κἀμεῦ θειοτέραν τὴν Παφίην κατέχειν."

Textus: Germani Brixii...*Gratulatoriae quatuor ad totidem viros clarissimos;* eiusdem *epistolae quatuor ad totidem viros doctissimos;* eiusdem *Versus aliquot ad Franciscum Galliarum regem*, Paris: Chr. Wechel 1531, k3r.

Crit.: 1 Φράγκισκε ed. || 3 Ἀρεῖος ed: Ἄρηος debuit || 4 κἀμεῦ debuit

Sim.: 2 cf. *Anth. Pal.* 16.162.1 (Ἁ Κύπρις τὰν Κύπριν...ἰδοῦσα)

On the same subject [scil. on the statue of Venus offered by Knight Renzo to King Francis in 1530] by the same author [scil. Germain de Brie]

One day, coming down to Amboise from the sky, o Francis,
   Cypris declared, after she saw your own Cypris:
'O King, since you're stronger than my dear Ares, you definitely had
   to possess a more divine Paphian than I am!'

Metre: Elegiac couplets (the long α in the clumsy genitive Ἀρεῖος follows *Il.* 5.31 etc.).

Notes: In 1531, with the composition of nine epigrams, Germain de Brie welcomed a majestic gift that had been offered to Francis I in the autumn of 1530, in Amboise: an ancient, Parian marble statue of Venus holding an apple, brought from Italy. It was a present from the *condottiere* Renzo da Ceri degli Orsini, serving the King of France in Naples. Germain de Brie, then Grand Almoner of France, was sejourning at the royal castle in Amboise. The admiration inspired by this gift was the starting point for several poems, in Greek (Germain de Brie), Latin (Guillaume Du Bellay, Théodore de Bèze, Théocrène, Gilbert Ducher) and French (Clément Marot and the King himself), and Germain de Brie took the opportunity to praise the King's political ambitions, as the apple in Venus' hand represented the global empire now promised to Francis I.

Biography: The son of a wealthy family, Germain de Brie was born in c. 1490 near Auxerre, possibly in Saint-Bris-le-Vineux. After studying law in Orléans, he spent two years in Italy (1508–1510), where he met Ianos Laskaris – who hosted him in Venice and became his friend –, Erasmus, Girolamo Aleandro, and Pietro Bembo, and eventually attended Aldo Manuzio's academy. In Padua, de Brie studied under Markos Mousouros and became a remarkable Hellenist (for these scholars see → **Greece, Italy, Low Countries**); in Rome, he met his sponsor, Louis d'Amboise, who appointed him canon in Albi. Back in France, he came under the protection of chancellor Jean de Ganay, until the latter's death in 1512, and subsequently under Queen Ann of Brittany, to whom de Brie dedicated a Latin poem, *Chordigerae navis conflagratio* (1513), celebrating a contemporary naval battle against the English and thus creating a quarrel with Thomas More, who wrote his ironical *Epigrammata* (1518) against him and was then countered by de Brie's *Antimorus* in 1519. Only Erasmus could eventually appease the feud. Appointed canon of Notre Dame in Paris, de Brie dedicated the rest of his life (†1538) to studying the classics and entertained a friendly correspondence with the best scholars of his day: Guillaume Budé, Jacques Toussain, Pierre Danès, and Girolamo Fondulo from Cremona. In particular, de Brie focused on St John Chrysostom and translated several of his writings into Latin. He was also celebrated for his Latin poems and his rich Greek and Latin correspondence.

Bibliography: Maillard/Kecskeméti/Magnien/Portalier 1999, 11–40; Provini, Sandra (ed.) (2004), Humbert de Montmoret/Germain de Brie/Pierre Choque, *L'incendie de la Cordelière*, La Rochelle, 99–119; La Garanderie, Marie Madeleine de (1995), "Germain de Brie", in: *Christianisme et lettres profanes*, Paris, 133–160; La Garanderie, Marie-Madeleine de (1986), "Germain de Brie", in: Peter Gerard Bietenholz/Thomas Brian Deutscher (eds.), *Contemporaries of Erasmus. A Biographical Register of the Renaissance and Reformation*, Toronto/Buffalo/London, 200–202. On his Greek poems and on this one in particular: Picot, Émile (1902), "Sur une statue de Vénus envoyée par Renzo da Ceri au roi François Ier", in: *Revue archéologique*, 3e série, 41, 223–231; Murarasu, Dumitru (1928), *La poésie néo-latine et la Renaissance des lettres antiques en France*, Paris, 55–63; Galand-Hallyn, Perrine (1999), "Autour de la Vénus d'Amboise (1530): une refloraison du genre de l'*ekphrasis*", in: *Bibliothèque d'Humanisme et Renaissance* 61, 345–374; La Garanderie, Marie Madeleine de (2010), *Guillaume Budé, philosophe de la culture*, Paris, 70–83 (and *passim*); Cooper, Richard (2013), *Roman Antiquities in Renaissance France, 1515–65*, London, 131f.

Jean Dorat (1508–1588)

I. <De Terpandro> [1552]

Τέρπανδρος πρὶν ἔτερπ' ἄνδρας μόνον, ἀλλὰ γυναῖκας
νῦν τέρπει· νῦν ἂρ Τερπογυνὴς ἔσεται.

Αὑρατοῦ

Textus: *Les Amours de P. de Ronsard Vandomoys*, Paris, veuve La Porte, 1552, in fronte operis.

Crit.: 2 Τερπογύνης debuit || Αὑρατοῦ] de nominis accentu, cf. *infra* II. tit. Αὑράτου

<On Terpander>

Terpander used to cheer only men, but now
he cheers women: from now on, he will be Terpogynes.

By Dorat

Metre: Elegiac couplet.

Notes: This short epigram is a pun on the Greek anagram of Ronsard's name (Τέρπανδρος ὁ σῶς ['Terpander the Saved'] = Πέτρος Ῥώνσαρδος). The new generation of French poets owed a debt to Dorat for their discovery of the Hellenistic poet Lycophron, whose *Alexandra* was the model acknowledged by Ronsard for his own *Cassandre*. We still have the Greek copy of the 1546 Oporinus edition of Lycophron (now in Pierpont Morgan Library, Heineman 243) that both Dorat and Ronsard annotated, as professor and student, in order to decipher the *obscurum poema*, of which Dorat produced his own edition the year after (Paris: J. Bogard, 1547). Lycophron also inspired Dorat when it came to the revival of anagrams in French literature. He was thus able to turn his most brilliant student, Ronsard, into the new 'Terpander', since the front page of Ronsard's *Quatre premiers livres des Odes* (Paris: G. Cavellat, 1550), where this couplet appears, reads: Σῶς ὁ Τέρπανδρος. | Πέτρος ὁ Ῥώνσαρδος μοι ἐναίσιμον οὔνομα κεῖται, / Σῶς γὰρ ὁ Τέρπανδρος, τερψίβροτός τε χέλυς. | Ιω. Αὑρατοῦ ('Terpander resurrected. | My name is Pierre de Ronsard for a good reason: / Terpander [the 'men-cheering'] is resurrected, and his lyre cheers the mortals. | By Jean Dorat'). The anagram on Terpander, a legendary citharede and poet, continues with our distich, which opens Ronsard's *Amours* in 1552–1553: the pun on Τερπογύνης ('woman-cheering', a *hapax legomenon* re-constructed on the basis of Τέρπανδρος) is a transparent allusion to the dedicatees of Ronsard's love poems, but also a prediction of the success of these poems among a public composed of ladies.

II. Εἰς Ὕμνους Ῥωνσάρδου σαπφικά Ἰωάννου Αὐράτου, πρὸς Ὄδητον Καστιλιονέα [1555]

(excerptum, vv. 1–8, 21–28, 36–56)

    Εἰς νέους ὕμνους, νέον ὕμνον ᾄδω,
    "χείρ γε τὴν χεῖρ'", ὡς φθονερῶν ἐρεῖ τις
    ἀνέρων ἴσως "πόδα πούς τε νίπτων" –
        ἀλλ' ὅ, τι θυμῷ
5 οἱ φίλον φάσθω κατ' ἐμοῦ φθόνος, καὶ
    φὰς ἔπειθ' ὡς ἄξιος ἐκραγείη.
    Σοὶ δ' ἔγωγ' ἔμπης, σὺ δ' ἐμοὶ φιλοῦντι
        φίλτατος εἴης.
    […]
    Ὦ φίλη Μοῦσ', ἀλλὰ σὺ νῦν ἔλεγξον
    ψεῦδος Ἀσκραῖον. Δὸς ἐμοὶ δὲ καλὰ
    αἰὲν αὐτὸν μέν γε ποεῖν, ποοὐντων δ'
        ἄμφι κάλ' εἰπεῖν.
25 Οἷον ὁ Ῥώνσαρδος ὁ Θρᾷξ ἅτ' Ὀρφεὺς
    τὰς πέτρας ἕλκων ποτε καὶ τὰ δένδρα
    ὧν μελῶν κηληδόσι, καὐτὸς ἕλκει
        οὔατα Κελτῶν.
    […]
    Νῦν δὲ καὐτὴν τὴν φύσιν οἷα μέλπειν
    ἄρχεται, τά τ' ἐκ φύσεως ἅπαντα,
    τοὺς θεούς, τοὺς δαίμονας, οὐρανόν, γῆν,
40 καὶ τὰ μετ' ἀμφοῖν,
    καὶ βίον καὶ τὸν θάνατον, Δίκην τε
    τοῦ Διὸς τὴν πρεσβυτάτην θύγατρα,
    χρυσὸν αὐτόν, μυρία θ' ὅσσα τἆλλα
        λυγρὰ καὶ ἐσθλά·
45 Σὺν γὰρ ἀεὶ κίρναται ἐσθλὰ λυγροῖς
    Ζεὺς παρ' ἀνθρώποις, ὁ σοφὸς δὲ καὶ τὰ
    καὶ τὰ γινώσκει, διὰ δ' ἐσθλὰ κρίνας
        θάτερα φεύγει.
    Ὧν χάρις πολλὴ μὲν ὀφείλεθ' ὕμνων
50 τῷ γε ποιητῇ, μεγάλη δ' ὌΔΗΤΕ
    μουσάναξ, καὶ σοί· σὺ γὰρ εἶ πατὴρ ὣς
        ἐσθλὸς ἀοιδοῖς,
    Ἀξίοις δῶρ' ἄξια δούς τε τιμὴν

αὐτός, οὐ μὴν ἀλλὰ καὶ ἄλλα πλείω
55 προτρέπων δοῦναι βασιλῆ' ἄριστον
 ἦμαρ ἐπ' ἦμαρ.
[...]

Textus: *Hymne de Bacus par Pierre de Ronsard, avec la version latine de Jean Dorat*, Paris: André Wechel, 1555, 30–32.

Crit.: 26 ποτὲ debuit || **36** οἶα (neutrum) fort. pro femin. οἴα metri causa adhibuit

Sim.: 2 χείρ—χεῖρ' (*scil.* νίπτει)] cf. Epicharm. fr. 30 D.-K.; Men. *sent.* 830 Jäkel, vide Erasm. *Adag.* 33 || **23** ψεῦδος Ἀσκραῖον] ad Hes. *Op.* 25–26 alludit || **27** κηληδόσι] cf. Pind. fr. 52i, 71 M. || **42** πρεσβυτάτην θύγατρα] cf. Hom. *Il.* 11.740 (de Agamede) || **44–46** λυγρὰ καὶ ἐσθλά—ἐσθλὰ λυγροῖς] cf. Hom. *Il.* 24.529–531 || **51** μουσάναξ] hapax leg. ut vid. | πατὴρ ὥς] cf. *Od.* 2.46–47 || **56** ἦμαρ ἐπ' ἦμαρ] cf. Theoc. *Id.* 11.69 (ἆμαρ ἐπ' ἆμαρ)

Sapphic stanzas for Ronsard's *Hymns* by Jean Dorat, to Odet de Châtillon

(excerpt, ll. 1–8, 21–28, 36–56)

To honour new hymns, I sing a new hymn;
'one hand washes...' – or as a jealous man
might say, 'one foot washes the other' –
 but let jealousy
[5] say against me what it wants, and then,
having said that, explode as it deserves.
But may I nonetheless be dearest to you, and you
 to me, your best friend.
[...]
O beloved Muse, please confute now
the Ascraean lie! And always concede me
to do him good, to say the best about those
 who do good.
[25] So Ronsard – like Orpheus the Thracian
who once drew the rocks and the trees
thanks to his charming melodies – draws in the same way
 the ears of the French.
[...]
Now he also starts celebrating how Nature itself is,
and how is all which comes from Nature,
The gods, the daemons, the sky, the earth,
[40] and what is in between,
and life and death, and Justice,
the oldest of Zeus' daughters,

gold itself and several other things,
>   the bad and the good ones.
[45] For the latter are always mixed with the former
by Zeus in people's lives, and the wise man can
sort out each side: distinguishing the good things,
>   he flees the others.
The poet must be warmly thanked
[50] for these hymns, and you too, great Odet,
lord of the Muses, for you are good like a father
>   for the poets,
yourself giving worthy presents and honour to those
who deserve it, as well as persuading
[55] the excellent King to give many more
>   day after day.
[...]

Metre: Sapphic stanzas (with some dubious prosodies, e.g. long alphas in l. 3 ἀνέρων and l. 45 ἀεί, the α alternatively long and short in l. 22 and 24 καλά).

Notes: This long poem, a celebration of Ronsard's skill and of Dorat's friendship (as opposed to the Hesiodic 'envy' between poets evoked in the first part of the ode), is dedicated to Odet de Châtillon (or de Coligny) and his literary patronage. At the time the poem was composed, Odet was a Catholic cardinal, a member of the royal court, one of Ronsard's most important protectors and a generous sponsor of poets and artists. He eventually became a Huguenot after 1562; he was excommunicated and ended his life in England.

Biography: A remarkable Hellenist and a trilingual poet (Greek, Latin, and French), Jean Dorat was called 'the French Homer' or 'the Gallic Pindar'. Coming to Paris from Limoges, he was introduced to King Francis I around 1540. In 1544, Lazare de Baïf appointed him as a preceptor for his son Jean-Antoine, aged 12, as well as for Ronsard, who was then 20 years old. In 1547, after Lazare de Baïf's death, Dorat started lecturing at the *Collège de Coqueret.* His students, both the elder ones, such as Jean-Antoine de Baïf and Ronsard, and the younger ones, such as Joachim Du Bellay, greatly admired this brilliant professor and fuelled his celebrity. Sharing his enthusiasm, Dorat let them discover Antiquity as well as the rules of poetic art through the study of Pindar, Aeschylus, Lycophron and, above all, Homer. While lecturing, Dorat worked as a proof corrector for the King's printer Robert Estienne. Appointed *lecteur royal* of Greek in 1556, he held this tenure until 1567. Officially appointed 'King's poet', he eventually became a soothsayer-poet. In fact, fascinated by divinatory arts and prophecy, he dared to couple poetic and prophetic inspiration. Under King Charles IX, he had the title of *interpres regius*, meaning not only 'interpreter of texts', but also of all sorts of signs: indeed, he almost played the role of an official soothsayer. He suffered a serious illness during the winter of 1570–1571, but survived, and his religious attitude profoundly changed as he moved from a vaguely deistic position to orthodox Catholicism, and even to anti-Protestant fanaticism.

Bibliography: Demerson, Geneviève (1983), *Dorat en son temps: culture classique et présence au monde*, Clermont-Ferrand; de Buzon, Christine/Girot, Jean-Eudes (eds.) (2007), *Jean Dorat, poète humaniste de la Renaissance*, Geneva (see particularly the inventory of his sparse writings by Catherine Magnien-Simonin, pp. 439–452); Ford, Philip (ed.) (2000), *Mythologicum, ou interprétation allégorique de l'Odyssée X–XII et de l'Hymne à Aphrodite*, Geneva [critical edition of Ms. Milan, Bibl. Ambros. A 184[suss], a notebook including the class notes taken between 1569 and 1571 by an anonymous student of Dorat on the *Odyssey*]. On his Greek poems: Robiquet, Paul (1887), *De Ioannis Aurati poetae regii uita et Latine scriptis poematibus*, Paris.

Jean-Antoine de Baïf (1532–1589)

I. Εἰς τὴν εἰκόνα τοῦ Ῥωνσάρδου μύρτῳ ἐστεφανωμένου [1552]

Κύπριδος ἔργ' ᾄδοντα τὸ Κύπριδος ἔστεφε δένδρον·
Κύπριδος ὑμνοπόλῳ στέμμα πρέπει Κύπριδος.

Βαϊφίου

II. Ὡς ἀπὸ Ῥωνσάρδου εἰς τὴν Κάσσανδραν [1552]

Φοιβάδα τὴν Κάσσανδραν, ἔρως τὸν ἔτειρεν ἐκείνης,
Φοιβομανῆ τεῦξεν Φοῖβος ἐρωμανέων.
Ἡ δ' ἄλλη Κάσσανδρ' ἡ 'κ Κελτίδος, οὐκέτι φοιβάς,
Νῦν ἔμ' ἐρωμανέα ῥέξ' ἰδὲ φοιβομανῆ.

Ἰα. Ἀντω. Βαϊφίου

Textus: *Les Amours de P. de Ronsard Vandomoys*, Paris, veuve M. de la Porte, 1552, 2–3.

Crit.: II.1, 3 Κάσσανδραν, Κάσσανδρ': Κασσάνδρᾶν, Κασσάνδρᾶ debuit || 4 ἔμ' debuit

Sim.: I.1 Κύπριδος ἔργ'] cf. *Anth. Pal.* 7.221.1 et 9.437.4, necnon Musae. 141
II. 1 φοιβάδα] cf. Eur. *Hec.* 827 (ἡ φοιβάς, ἣν καλοῦσι Κασάνδραν Φρύγες) | ἔρως...ἔτειρεν] cf. Plut. *Thes.* 20.1 || 2 φοιβομανῆ] hapax leg. ut vid. | ἐρωμανέων] verbum ἐρωμανέω saepius apud Nonn. (vide iam Opp. *C.* 3.368; *Anth. Pal.* 5.267.10 etc.); idem de adi. ἐρωμανής (v. 4; cf. etiam Musae. 11 al.)

On Ronsard's portrait crowned with myrtle

The singer of Cypris' deeds was wreathed with Cypris' tree.
Cypris' wreath suits him who celebrates Cypris with hymns.

By Baïf

As if written by Ronsard to Cassandra

Being crazily in love, Phoebus made Phoebus' priestess Cassandra
(love for whom consumed him) crazy for Phoebus.
The other Cassandra, the one from France, is no longer a priestess of Phoebus,
but she made me crazily in love and crazy for Phoebus as well.

By J.Ant. de Baïf

Metre: Elegiac couplets.

Notes: The few, witty verses introduced here accompanied the portraits of Ronsard (see fig. 7, above) and Cassandra respectively, which face one another at the beginning of the 1552 edition of Ronsard's *Amours*. Aged 27, the poet is represented as turned to the right, with a myrtle wreath on his head, in an oval medallion that carries as its inscription a line from Theocritus in capitals (*id*. 2.82): ΏΣ ΊΔΟΝ ΏΣ ’ΕΜΆΝΗΝ ('as soon as I saw her, I went crazy'). The lady, aged 20, keeps her eyes to the left in a similar medallion, surrounded by Ovid's words (*Met*. 2.781): *CARPITQUE, ET CARPITUR UNA* ('She consumes and at the same time is consumed', clearly detached from the reference to *Invidia* in the Latin source).

Biography: The natural son of Lazare de Baïf (†1547), a scholar who translated Sophocles and Euripides into French, Jean-Antoine de Baïf became a pupil of Jean Dorat at the age of 11 and followed him to the *Collège de Coqueret* where he met Ronsard, whom Lazare de Baïf had previously hosted at the royal court under his protection. After intense study of Greek literature, Ronsard and Jean-Antoine de Baïf both published a French collection of *Amours* ('*Love poems*') in 1552. Dedicated to Cassandra, Ronsard's *canzoniere* was especially inspired by the *Alexandra* (i.e. Cassandra), the difficult poem by the Hellenistic poet Lycophron on which Dorat lectured for the two young men. Besides his vernacular poems, Jean-Antoine de Baïf was one of the most prolific authors of Greek verse in 16th-century France, after Dorat himself. Published in 1577, Baïf's *Medanis* is a long Greek and Latin epideictic idyll of no less than 172 lines, written in 1552–1553 to celebrate Jean Brinon, lord of Médan and Villennes, thus creating a parallel with Dorat's Latin poem *Villanis*.

Bibliography: Jurgens, Madeleine (1985), "II. Lazare et Jean-Antoine de Baïf", in: *Ronsard et ses amis. Documents du Minutier Central des Notaires de Paris*, Paris, 23–43, 124–201; Vignes, Jean (1999), *Bibliographie des écrivains français: Jean-Antoine de Baïf*, Paris; Barbier-Mueller, Jean-Paul (1994), *Ma Bibliothèque poétique*, vol. III, Genève, 291–361; Id. (2015), *Dictionnaire des poètes français de la seconde moitié du XVIᵉ siècle (1549–1615)*, vol. I, Genève, 267–296. On his Greek poems: Rigolot, François (1988), "Ronsard et Muret: Les pièces liminaires aux *Amours* de 1553", in: *Revue d'histoire littéraire de la France* 1, 3–16; de Buzon, Christine/Martin, Pierre (eds.) (1999), Ronsard, Muret, *Les Amours, leurs commentaires (1553)*, Paris, 4.

François Bérauld (*ca.* 1517–1574)

Francisci Beraldi Nicolai filii Parisiensis In Jacobum Tusanum praeceptorem suum, carmen [1552]

    Ἑλλάδα Τοῦρκος Ἄρης ἐξήλασε πατρίδος αἴης
        Αἰσχρὸν δουλοσύνης ζεῦγος ἀνηναμένην.
    Ἡ δὲ μετοικήσασα πρὸς ἔθνεα γείτονα, πάντη
        Σκίδνατο, καὶ πολλοὺς ἄστεγος εὗρε δόμους.
5   Οὐ μέντοι γυμνή, πλοῦτον δ' ἀναφαίρετον ἦγεν
        Τῷ πολέμῳ, χρυσοῦ χρῆμα βεβαιότερον.
    Οἱ πρῶτοι δ' Ἐνετοὶ πολύπλαγκτον ἀλήτιδα παῦσαν
        Τῆς τε πλάνης κ' ἀστοῖς ἴσα δίκαι' ἔπορον.
    Τοὺς μιμησάμενοι λοιποὶ πάλιν Αὐσονιῆες
10 Τῶν Κελτῶν ἰκέλην εἰς φρένας ὦρσαν ἔριν.
    Αὐτὴν γοῦν βασιλεῖς Κελτῶν κληθεῖσαν ἐπάθλοις
        Πλείοσιν, ἐν σταθερῷ εὔθρονον εἶσαν ἔδει.
    Ἀλλ' ὅτε δὴ κρυερὰς Ἄλπεις διαβᾶσα νεηλὺς
        Ἥγγισεν, ὁ πρῶτος Τουσανὸς ἐξένισε
15 Ὧι πάρ', ἕως ἔζη καταλύτης τοῖος, ἔμεινε
        Τὴν ἀγανοφροσύνην τ' ἀνδρὸς ἀγασσαμένη.
    Τοῦ δὲ μεταλλάξαντος, ἄτ' αὖθις ἀνάστατος οὖσα
        Ἡ τλήμων δολιχῆς ἤρχετ' ὁδοιπορίας,
    Εἰ μὴ τοῖς αὐτοῖς Φεδερῖκος ἀνεῖλκε Μόρελλος
20 Εἴδασι, τοῖς αὐτὴν Τουσανὸς εἱστίασε.
    Εἶτα δ' ἀείμνηστον κείνου κλέος, εὐκλεὲς αὐτῇ
        Κῦδος ἄγει, λήθην καὶ προτέρων ὀδυνῶν.

Textus: *Lexicon Graecolatinum...Jacobi Tusani...studio et industria locupletatum...*, Parisiis: apud Carolam Guillard, 1552, c. a iiii v.

Crit.: 8 κἀστοῖς debuit || 13 νέηλυς debuit || 16 τἀνδρός debuit || 18 ἤρχεθ' debuit

Sim.: 1 πατρίδος αἴης] clausula Homerica, cf. Hom. *Il.* 2.162 et saep. || 2 δουλοσύνης ζεῦγος] cf. Nonn. *Dion.* 33.253 al. || 5 πλοῦτον ἀναφαίρετον] saepe apud Christianos, cf. e.g. Clem. *paedag.*

3.6.36; Jo. Chrys. *PG* 53.175.33 etc. || **7** ἀλήτιδα] verbum rarum, e.g. Greg. Nyss. *PG* 46.117c al.; *Lexicon* ipsum, c. Iii v || **9** Αὐσονιῆες] cf. Dion. Per. 78 || **10** ὧρσαν ἔριν] cf. Hom. *Od.* 3.161 || **12** εὔθρονον] de Aurora apud Homerum (*Il.* 8.565 et saep.), alibi de aliis (de Horis Pind. *Pyth.* 9.60 etc.) || **15** καταλύτης] "hospes" ex LXX, *Sapient.* 5.14 (cum καταλυτής significet "destructor", cf. *Lexicon* ipsum, c. Mm iiii r) || **16** ἀγανοφροσύνην] cf. Hom. *Il.* 24.772; *Od.* 11.202 || **21** ἀείμνηστον— κλέος] cf. Eur. *IT* 1531; Xen. *Cyn.* 1.6.

By François Bérauld from Paris, son of Nicolas, Poem for his preceptor Jacques Toussain

> The Turkish Ares forced Greece out of her fatherland,
> once she refused the shameful yoke of slavery.
> But, emigrating to neighbouring peoples, Greece spread
> everywhere, and albeit homeless, it found several homes.
> [5] Yet she was not naked, but carried a treasure
> that war could not steal, a wealth firmer than gold.
> The Venetians were the first who stopped the journey of this never stopping
> wanderer, and gave her citizens equal rights.
> Then the other Italians imitated them,
> [10] and sparked a similar emulation in the heart of the French.
> So the kings of France attracted her with even more prizes
> and settled her on an honourable, stable seat.
> As the newcomer crossed the icy Alps to join us,
> Toussain was the first to give her hospitality.
> [15] Greece stayed in his house as long as such a host lived,
> charmed by the benignity of this man.
> When he died, the poor lady, as she was homeless again,
> would have resumed her long wandering,
> if Frédéric Morel had not brought her back, thanks to the same
> [20] dishes Toussain had served to her in his day.
> Unforgettable is now his glory: he brings her a glorious
> fame, and the oblivion of her previous tribulations!

Metre: Elegiac couplets (flawless).

Notes: The lament over the sad fate of Greece, after the fall of Constantinople to the Turks in May 1453, was a frequent poetic theme (→ **Italy**, **Greece**, **Germany**). Here, it is coupled with the *topos* of the *translatio studii* in the countries that welcomed the Greek *émigrés* as well as their prestigious culture, beginning with Venice (l. 7), the first city to host Greek immigrants in the 15th century. The kings of France (βασιλεῖς Κελτῶν, l. 11), and especially Francis I, also played a major role in the protection of Greek culture. On Jacques Toussain, see below. Fédéric II Morel (1523–1583), celebrated in l. 19, was a *lecteur royal* for Greek and an important Parisian printer.

Biography: Son of the humanist Nicolas Bérauld, François learned Greek as a young man and became a student of Jacques Tusan (called Toussain), the first *lecteur royal* in Greek. Bérauld was eventually sent by his father to Orléans, to study civil law. Having quickly sided with the Reformation, he was forced to leave Paris, probably in 1554, and thereupon went to Lausanne to teach Greek (1555–1558), then to Geneva, where he arrived in 1559. He finally settled down in La Rochelle, a centre of Protestant culture. Henri Estienne entrusted to him the translation of the two books of Appian on the Roman wars against Hannibal and Spain; this Latin translation was included in the 1592 bilingual edition printed in Geneva (*Appiani Alexandrini Rom. Historiarum*, pp. 255–349). François Bérauld, who was a distinguished scholar of Hebrew as well, also translated into Latin one of John Chrysostom's homilies, on being moderate in drinking wine. When he died, in about 1575, François Bérauld was head of the *Collège* at La Rochelle.

Bibliography: Doinel, Jules (1878–1882), "Notes sur les deux Bérauld et quelques-uns de leurs contemporains", in: *Bulletin de la Société historique et archéologique de l'Orléanais* 7, 242–247; Béraut, Armand (1909), "François Béraud avant son professorat", in: *Bulletin de la Soc. hist. et archéol. de l'Orléanais* 15 (n° 195), 326–357; Haag, Eugène and Émile, *La France protestante*, t. II, Paris, 1847, 189–190; Maillard, Jean-François/Flamand, Jean-Marie et al. (2010), *La France des humanistes. Hellénistes II*, Turnhout, 521–522. On Fr. Bérauld's teaching: Béraut, Armand (1910), "Les Béraud au collège de La Rochelle (1571–1619)", in: *Revue de Saintonge et d'Aunis* 30, 164–182, 245–260 [booklet, La Rochelle: 1910]; Bourchenin, Pierre Daniel (1882), *Études sur les Académies protestantes au XVIe et au XVIIe siècle*, Paris (repr. Geneva: 1969).

Anonymous

Εἰς ᾠδὰς Λοΐσης Λαβαίας [1556]

Τὰς Σαπφοῦς ᾠδὰς γλυκυφώνου ἃς ἀπόλεσσεν
  Ἡ παμφάγου χρόνου βίη,
Μειλιχίῳ Παφίης καὶ ἐρώτων νῦν γὲ Λαβαίη
  Κόλπῳ τραφεῖσ' ἀνήγαγε.
5 Εἰ δέ τις ὡς καινὸν θαυμάζει, καὶ "πόθεν ἐστί",
  Φησίν, "νέη ποιήτρια;",
Γνοίη ὡς γοργὸν καὶ ἄκαμπτον δυστυχέουσα
  Ἔχει Φάων' ἐρώμενον·
Τοῦ πληχθεῖσα φυγῇ, λιγυρὸν μέλος ἦρξε τάλαινα

10   Χορδαῖς ἐναρμόζειν λύρης.
     Σφοδρὰ δὲ πρὸς ταύτας ποιήσεις οἴστρ' ἐνίησι
     Παιδῶν ἐρᾶν ὑπερηφάνων.

Textus: *Euvres de Louïze Labé Lionnoize*, Lyon: J. de Tournes, 1556, 125 ("Escriz de divers Poëtes, à la louenge de Louïze Labé Lionnoize"), unde nuperrime Labé, Louise (2004), *Œuvres complètes*, Paris, 142–143.

Crit.: 12 Παίδων ἐρᾶν debuit

Sim.: 1 Σαπφοῦς...γλυκυφώνου] cf. *Anth. Pal.* 9.66.1–2 (μελιφώνου / Σαπφοῦς) || **9** λιγυρὸν μέλος] Anacreont. 60.6

For the odes of Louise Labé

> The odes of sweet-speaking Sappho, destroyed by the
>   assault of all-devouring Time,
> are now ours again, thanks to Labé, nourished in the gentle
>   bosom of the Paphian and the Erotes.
> [5] If, surprised by the novelty, someone asks 'Where does
>   this new poetess come from?',
> he should know that – o ill-fated Lady! –, she loved Phaon,
>   a savage and irremovable man.
> Saddened by his refusal, the poor Lady started to adapt
> [10] a pleasant melody on the strings of her lyre.
> She sends strong stimuli with these poems to
>   love scornful young men.

Metre: Dactylic hexameters and iambic dimeters (cf. Hor. *Epod.* XIV and XV).

Notes: Not much is known with certainty about the life of the poetess Louise Labé, to the point that Mireille Huchon has doubted her very existence, dubbing her 'a paper creature', a forgery created by her supposed fellow poets, such as Maurice Scève and Claude de Taillemont, both poets from Lyons, or Clément Marot. She was apparently born in c. 1524 in Lyons, died in 1566 and was celebrated as *La Belle Cordière* ('the beautiful Ropemaker') in the *milieu* of Lyons literary circles. Though she was married, the object of her love was the poet Olivier de Magny, whom she sang about in passionate lyrics, in which she introduced herself as *Sappho rediviva*. Who is the author of this piece? These twelve Greek verses open the collection of poetry *Escriz de divers Poëtes, à la louenge de Louïze Labé Lionnoize* ('Writings of different poets in praise of Lyons-born Louise Labé'), following the first edition of the poetess' *Works*. This poem shows the will to define Labé as the new Sappho. None of the attributions proposed to date, such as Henri Estienne, Marc-Antoine Muret and others, have managed to persuade the critics: it looks as if the author of these somehow clumsy verses were rather an *amateur* Hellenist who first conceived his poetry in Latin, on Horatian models. The rediscovery of Sappho coincided with this poem's publication; the *Ode to the loved one* (Sapph. fr. 31 V.) and the *Ode to Aphrodite* (Sapph. fr. 1 V.) had been published in 1554. When our author states (ll. 1–2) that all Sappho's poems are lost, he surely refers to the loss of most of them. The optative γνοίη (l. 7) is used instead of an imperative form. The elision οἶστρ' ἐνίησι (l. 11) must be explained: Is it a Latinism derived from *oestrum inicit* or should we suppose an unattested plural form οἶστρα? This problem led T. Vigliano to suggest the attribution be to an *amateur* Hellenist acquainted with Latin poetry. Be that as it may, one should be aware that the Horatian combination of hexameter with iambic dimeter had already been used by Joachim Camerarius (Camerarius the Elder → **Germany**) in his collection of *Epigrammata* published in 1538 by Herwagen-Froben (Παράπτωμα τοῦ Ἀδάμου, pp. 128–129).

Bibliography: Rigolot, François (1983), "Louise Labé et la redécouverte de Sappho", in: *Nouvelle revue du seizième siècle* 1, 19–31; Id. (1997), *Louise Labé Lyonnaise ou la Renaissance au féminin*, Paris; Huchon, Mireille (2006), *Louise Labé, une créature de papier*, Geneva; Martin, Daniel (2006), "Louise Labé est-elle une créature de papier?", in: *Réforme Humanisme et Renaissance*, 63, 7–37. On this Greek poem: Vigliano, Tristan (2012), "Note sur l'ode grecque à Louise Labé", in: *Réforme, Humanisme, Renaissance* 75, 191–197; Cazes, Hélène/Dupèbe, Jean (forthcoming), "Louise Labé et Sappho", in: *Mélanges Mireille Huchon*.

Rémy Belleau (1528–1577)

Remigii Bellei Nogentaei Epigramma [1558]

Τήνδ' ἐθέων τε νόμων τε γραφὴν ἀνέθηκε Νόγεντον
σοί, μεγάλου σεμνὴ παῖ Κρονίδαο Δίκη.
Χθὲς γὰρ ἔτ' ἀμφήριστα πόλιν συνέχευε θεμιστέων
τάγματα, λοξοδίκαις ἀνδράσι πειθομένην·
5 νῦν δ' ἐπεὶ ἐξ ἀγράφων γραπτοὺς ἐχαρίσσαο πρόφρων
ἄμμι νόμους, στυγερὰς τηλόσ' ἀλιτροσύνας
ἐξέβαλες πόλεως, ἐξ οὗ τεὸν ὄμμα φαεινὸν
τρέψας, ἐμῆς γλυκερᾶς κηδομένη πατρίδος.
Οὐδὲ δικορράπταισι τόδ' ἦν φίλον, ἀλλὰ γένοιο
10 δυσμενέουσα κακοῖς, τοῖς δ' ἀγαθοῖσι φίλη.

Textus: [Faye, Barthélémy/Thou, Christophe de/Viole, Jacques], *Coustumes des pays, comte et bailliage du Grand Perche*, Paris: J. Dallier, 1558, c. e2v.

Crit.: 1 γραφὴν scripsi: γράφην ed.

Sim.: 3 θεμιστέων] forma peculiaris (θεμίστων enim debuit) apud Hes. *Theog.* 235 reperitur || 4 λοξοδίκαις hapax ut vid. || ἀνδράσι πειθομένην] cf. Thgn. 948 || 6 ἀλιτροσύνας] cf. Ap. Rhod. *Argon.* 4.699; *Anth. Pal.* 5.302.8 etc. || 7 ὄμμα φαεινόν] cf. Opp. *C.* 3.69; *Anth. Pal.* 8.5.3 || 8 γλυκερᾶς... πατρίδος] cf. Hom. *Od.* 22.323; Pind. *Pyth.* 4.32 || 9 δικορράπταισι] verbum apud Phryn. *praep. soph.* 62.15

Epigram of Rémy Belleau from Nogent

> Nogent dedicated this text on customs and rules
>   to you, Justice, revered daughter of the great son of Cronus.
> For, until yesterday, disputed rules of righteousness troubled our town,
>   that was obeying a few ambiguous lawyers;
> [5] but now, after you prudently gratified us with written laws,
>   replacing the unwritten ones, you threw all loathed mischiefs
> far away from our town, since the time when you turned your bright
>   eyes with care on my sweet fatherland.
> Nor such an action was meant to favour the pettifoggers, but please,
> [10] be hostile to the mean and friendly to the good men.

Metre: Elegiac couplets (flawless).

Notes: Belleau's poem, written in his capacity as a citizen of Nogent like all other liminary pieces of the 1558 volume, celebrates the edition of the customary laws that ruled the region of Perche, and that he collected upon the King's order. As the law of Northern France was customary, the process of writing and editing local practices and customs, started at the end of the 15th century, became a major issue during the Renaissance, and was favoured by humanists.

Biography: Born in 1528 in Nogent-le-Rotrou, the *Pléiade* poet Rémy Belleau was Ronsard's disciple and friend. Not much is known of his early years. In 1550, Belleau eventually met the abbot of *Les Mureaux* Chrestophle de Choiseul, a friend of Ronsard and an epicurean, who sponsored him for some ten years, giving him the opportunity to study in Paris at the *Collège de Boncourt*, under Marc-Antoine Muret and George Buchanan. Belleau also followed the lectures of Jean Dorat and Ramus. Fond of erudite Hellenistic poetry (Callimachus, Nicander, Aratus), he translated Anacreon into French verse, a work published in 1556 by Henri Estienne, during the same period in which he published his first poems. His main poetical work was *Bergerie* (1565), imitating Sannazaro's *Arcadia*. As a humanist, he was in contact with Denys Lambin, Adrien Turnèbe, and Léger du Chesne; in 1567, he was part of the jury in charge of evaluating Nicolas Goulu's application for the chair of Greek literature at the *Collège royal*. An excellent Hellenist, his scholarly masterpiece was an erudite collection of hymns about precious stones (*Amours et Nouveaux Eschanges des pierres precieuses*, 1576), dedicated to King Henry III.

Bibliography: Eckhardt, Alexandre (1917), *Rémy Belleau, sa vie, sa Bergerie. Étude historique et critique*, Budapest/Paris; Connat, Madeleine (1945), "Mort et testament de Rémy Belleau", in: *Bibliothèque d'Humanisme et Renaissance* 6, 328–356 (on Belleau's library, approx. 200 titles of which 16 in Greek); Barbier, Jean Paul (1994), *Ma Bibliothèque poétique*, vol. III: *Ceux de la Pléiade*, Genève, 413–444; Barbier-Mueller, Jean Paul (2015), *Dictionnaire des poètes français de la seconde moitié du XVIe siècle (1549–1615)*, vol. I, Genève, 398–407; Belleau, Rémy (1995–2003), *Œuvres poétiques* (G. Demerson ed.), 6 vols., Paris; Chayes, Evelien/Smith, Paul J. (2004), "Structures changeantes des *Pierres précieuses* (1576) de Rémy Belleau", in: *Revue d'Histoire littéraire de la France* 104, 25–44; Braybrook, Jean (2013), *Rémy Belleau et l'art de guérir*, London.

Florent Chrestien (1541–1596)

Εἰς χαλκοτυπίαν ὕμνος Φλωρ. Χριστιανοῦ [c. 1556]

Ἀμφὶ Τυπογραφίην ἐριούνιον, εὑρεσιτέχνου
  Ἀμφιγυήεντος ἀγλαόπαιδα κόραν,
Πάντας ἀοιδοπόλους νῦν ἄξιον ἐστὶν ἀείδειν·
  Σοῦσθε νῦν ὦ μοῦσαι, σοῦσθε δ' ἀοιδοπόλοι.
5 Ἠνὶ θεᾶς φιλαοίδου ἐτήσιος ἦλθεν ἑορτή·
  Πασσυδίῃ μοῦσαι σπεύδετε χ' ὑμνοπόλοι.
Ἔξιτε δ', οὐ κισσῷ ἀλλὰ στεφάνοισιν ἐλαίας
  Καλλικόμου λαμπρὸν κρᾶτα πυκασδόμενοι.
Οὐδὲν γὰρ τῆνα ξυνὸν ποτὲ καὶ Διονύσῳ
10 Ἔπλετ' Ἀθηναίης οὐδὲν ἀφαυροτέρα,
Ἔργα δὲ τεχνήεντα (νῦν οὐ θέμις) οὐ μελέτωσαν
  Χαλκοτύποις μύσταις ἀνδράσιν ἐργατίναις.
Οὐδὲ θέμις ἀΐειν ληνοῦ πολυδινέα φθόγγον,
  Οὐ πλατάγημα καλὸν γραμμοτόκων σελίδων.
15 Τούς τε χαρακτῆρας καὶ τυμπανοδέγμονα χαλκὸν
  Καλλίπετ', εὖτε τέλος ἔργμασι νὺξ ὀπάσῃ.
Ἀλλὰ πολυρροθίοις μεγάλην θεὸν εἴπατε μολπαῖς
  Ἑσπόμενοι πάντες μοὶ τάδε μελπομένῳ·
"Χαῖρε θεὰ φιλαοιδέ, μέγ' ἀνθρώποισιν ὄνειαρ,
20 Ἡ Διὸς ἐννεσίῃ Πιερίδας ἔτεκες,
Ἀχλὺν ἀποσκεδάσασ' ὀλεσίμβροτον, ᾗ φίλοι ἄνδρες

Ἴδριες, ᾗ μουσέων νήϊδες ἐχθόμενοι.
Ἡ μούνη φεύγουσα μίτον κρατερῶν μοιράων
Πευκεδανόν, φεύγουσ' ἠδὲ Κρόνου δρεπάνην
25 Ἀμβλεῖαν· μούνη σὺ Διὸς ψολόεντα κεραυνὸν
Οὐδέποτε τρομέεις, χαλκομέτωπε θεά.
Χαῖρε θεὰ Χαλκογραφίη, σὲ δ' ἐτήσιον αὖθις,
Ὦ πολύολβε θεά, ἄμμες ἀεισόμεθα."

Textus: F. Chrestien, *In typographiam* [Paris, R. Estienne, ca. 1556], sive unicum huius operis exemplar: Paris, BnF Rés. g-Y-3.

Crit.: 4 et 11 νύν haud encliticum sed accentu praeditum (sicut saepe in mss.): l. 11 νῦν exstabat, deinde accentum calamo mutavit scriba || 14 οὖ possis ("ubi rumor...") || 18 μοι debuit || 23 κηράων a.c. ed. (κη deleto μοι- in mg. adposuit scriba quidam)

Sim.: 1 εὑρεσιτέχνου] *Hymn. Orph.* 31.14 || 2 Ἀμφιγυήεντος] epitheton Hephaesti apud Homerum (*Il.* 1.607 et saep.) | ἀγλαόπαιδα] Opp. *H.* 2.41 et saep. apud Nonn. (*Dion.* 9.321 al.) || 4 σοῦσθε] cf. Aesch. *suppl.* 842 et praes. Callim. *Hymn.* 6.4 || 5 φιλαοιδοῦ] Theoc. *Id.* 28.23; *Anth. Pal.* 9.372.4 || 8 πυκασδόμενοι] de forma Dorica cf. Theoc. 3.14 || 10 οὐδὲν ἀφαυροτέρᾳ] cf. *Anth. Pal.* 9.764.6 et 5.270.6 || 11 ἔργα δὲ τεχνήεντα] cf. *Anth. Pal.* 9.363.13 || 12 ἀνδράσιν ἐργατίναις] cf. Theoc. *Id.* 21.3 || 13 πολυδινέα] cf. Opp. *H.* 4.585; *Anth. Pal.* 6.39.3 || 14 πλατάγημα] cf. Theoc. *Id.* 3.29 | γραμμοτόκων] cf. *Anth. Pal.* 6.63.1 || 15 τυμπανοδέγμονα] hapax leg. ut vid. || 16 τέλος ἔργμασι] cf. Thgn. 164; Pind. *Isthm.* 1.27 || 17 πολυρροθίοις] cf. Quint. Smyrn. 7.395; Arat. 412; Aesch. *Sept.* 7 (πολυρρόθοις) || 19 μέγ' ἀνθρώποισιν ὄνειαρ] cf. Arat. *Phaen.* 15 || 20 Διὸς ἐννεσίῃ] cf. *Anth. Pal.* 9.485.3 || 21 ἀχλὺν ἀποσκ. ὄλεσ.] ex Procl. *hymn.* 1.41 || 22 μουσέων νήϊδες] cf. Callim. *Aet.* 1.2 || 25 ἀμβλεῖαν] cf. *Anth. Pal.* 6.36.4 | ψολόεντα κεραυνόν] clausula epica, cf. e.g. Hom. *Od.* 23.330; 24.539; *Batr.* 287; Hes. *Theog.* 515 || 26 χαλκομέτωπε] hapax leg. ut vid. || 28 ἀεισόμεθα] cf. *Anth. Pal.* 7.518.4 (et 16.49.2)

A Hymn to Typography, by Florent Chrestien

It is a duty for all poets to sing now
    of beneficent Typography, daughter
of the lame inventor of arts [Hephaestus] and mother to beautiful children.
    Jig now, Muses, jig, you poets:
[5] Here has come the annual celebration of the poetry-loving goddess.
    Hurry up, Muses and you, authors of hymns.
And come out, wreathing your radiant head not with ivy, but with crowns
    of the olive tree, beautiful as hair.
For there has never been anything in common between her and Dionysus
[10] and she is no less mighty than Athena.
Artistic works should not be carried out (it is not allowed)
    by hard-working typographers initiated to the mysteries.
Nor is it allowed to hear the much-whirling sound of a wine-vat
    nor the nice noise of letter-mothering pages.

[15] And leave the fonts and the bronze receiving the panels,
    when the night puts an end to your work!
Please celebrate the great Goddess with loud songs,
    following, you all, the song I start:
'Hail, poetry-loving Goddess, grand benefit for humans,
[20] you who gave birth to the Pierides on Zeus' advice,
as you dispelled the mists fatal to mankind, you who cherish educated men,
    and hate those who ignore the Muses.
Only you escape the bitter thread of the deadly Moirai,
    and escape Kronos' unsharp
[25] Scythe: only you are never frightened by Zeus'
    smoking lightning, o bronze-faced Goddess!
Hail, Goddess Chalcography! Every year again,
    O happy and wealthy Goddess, we shall sing for you.'

Metre: Elegiac couplets. Note lengthening and hiatus at the caesura of the pentameter: ll. 2, 16, 28. -ς causes lengthening in l. 13, double consonant does not in l. 13.

Notes: A full-page poster printed perhaps by Robert Estienne (1556?) to celebrate Typography (we know of other Greek poems with *laudes typographiae*, e.g. by Utenhovius) included this hymn written by Florent Chrestien, a Latin elegy of twelve distichs by Camille de Morel (presented as the translation of a Greek hymn by Dorat on the same subject, not included), and a French ode, set on three columns, written by Jacques Grévin in honour of Robert Estienne; finally, there is a single line in Hebrew (*Proverbs* XV, 14: 'The discerning heart seeks knowledge, but the mouth of a fool feeds on folly'). In the poem, which includes some Doric elements (e.g. l. 8 πυκασδόμενοι), we find an obvious allusion (l. 9 στεφάνοισιν ἐλαίας) to the Estienne family brand, the famous *Oliva Stephani* which figured together with St Paul's motto *Noli altum sapere*. Starting from the olive tree, which Athena is associated with, ll. 9–12 extend the metaphor of this symbol, here opposed to Dionysus' ivy, and underline the powers of the new goddess, similar to those of Athena. Dionysus stands for wine and drunkenness, the great enemies of a typographer, along with night's obscurity (ll. 13–14), for all these elements jeopardise the accuracy of printing.

Biography: Born in Orléans, Florent Chrestien (1541–1596), poet and preceptor of the future King Henry IV, was the son of a doctor appointed at the court of Francis I and Henry II. Having declared himself quite early in favour of the Reformation, Chrestien left France for Geneva, where he followed the teaching of Henri Estienne. An excellent Latinist and Hellenist, he was both a poet (he had a quarrel with Ronsard), and an important translator of such authors as Aristophanes, Oppian, Aeschylus, Sophocles, and Euripides.

Bibliography: Pinvert, Lucien (1898), *Jacques Grévin (1538–1570). Étude biographique et littéraire*, Paris (esp. 247–250); Jacobsen, Brigitte (1973), *Florent Chrestien. Ein Protestant und Humanist in Frankreich zur Zeit der Religionskriege*, München; Barbier, Jean-Paul (1998), *Ma bibliothèque poétique*, IV, Genève, 408–421; Cazes, Hélène (2006), "Florent Chrestien", in: Nativel, Colette ([et al.] eds.), *Centuriae Latinae II*, Genève, 211–220. On his Greek poems: Lukinovich, Alexandra (2018), "Florent Chrestien pindarise sous la houlette d'Henri Estienne. Un psaume des montées en vers grecs (Ps. 127 hébreu) dans la version publiée en 1566 et dans un autographe", in: Päll, Janika/Volt, Ivo (eds.), *Hellenostephanos. Humanist Greek in Early Modern Europe*, Tartu, 260–298.

Henri II Estienne (1528?–1598)

Ἄλδου Μανουτίου ἐπιτάφιον [1569]

Ἄλδος ὅδ', ὃς τέχνης φάος ἦν μέγα βιβλοδοτείρας,
  Ἄλδος, ἔρεισμα τέχνης καὶ μέγ' ὄνειαρ ἐών.
Παιδείης γὰρ ἑῆς καμάτων τε καὶ ὄλβου ἀφειδῶν,
  Ἠΰτε τηλυγέτην τήνδ' ἀτίταλλε πάϊν.
5 Βίβλων οὖν τέχνη πολέων τελέθεσκε δότειρα,
  Ἄλδος δ' αὖ τέχνῃ ἦν βιόδωρος ἐῇ.

Textus: H. Stephanus, "Epitaphia Graeca & Latina doctorum quorundam typographorum (Ἐπιτάφια τυπογράφων τινῶν εὐπαιδεύτων)", in: Id., *Artis typographicae querimonia*, [Genevae]: H. Stephanus, 1569, a1r–v [= 17–18].

Sim.: 1 βιβλοδοτείρας] hapax leg. ut vid. || **2** cf. *Anth. Pal.* 7.81.4 (ἔρεισμα Δίκας) | μέγ' ὄνειαρ] cf. e.g. *Od.* 4.444; Hes. *Op.* 41 et 346 etc. || **4** ἀτίταλλε πάϊν] cf. e.g. *Od.* 18.323 || **5** τελέθεσκε] verbum rarum, vide *Hymn. Hom. Cer.* 241; Call. *Iav. Pall.* 67; *Anth. Pal.* 9.597.1 || **6** βιόδωρος] Aesch. fr. 168.17 R.; Soph. *Ph.* 1162

Epitaph for Aldus Manutius

This is Aldus, who was a bright light of the art of providing books,
  Aldus, a pillar of the art and a huge resource.
For he generously gave out his knowledge, work and bliss,
  in bringing this art up as a cherished child.
[5] Thus did the art of books become a giver of many goods:
  and Aldus was the lifegiver for his own art.

Metre: Elegiac couplets (note the hiatus in l. 6).

Notes: This is the first of a number of Greek and Latin epigrams written by Henri Estienne for the most illustrious of his colleagues, from Aldus to Josse Bade and Oporinus, from Morel to his father Robert Estienne (the book closes *honoris causa* with two epitaphs by Erasmus of Rotterdam for Froben). This collection is appended to the *Artis typographicae querimonia*, a short and satirical pamphlet in Latin hexameters against the careless printers who stain the reputation of the printing press by their inadequacy.

Biography: Probably born in 1528, son of the famous royal printer Robert, Henri II was a prince among Hellenists and the key printer of his time. His only Parisian edition was the *editio princeps* of the *Anacreontea* (1554). After a journey to Italy in 1555, he joined his father in Geneva and settled there, even though he qualified himself as a *typographus Parisiensis*. His beautiful and accurate editions of ancient authors were so influential that in several cases (e.g. Plato) they are still used today for the subdivision of the text. His scholarly activity was remarkable: he published, among other books, an *Apology on behalf of Herodotus* (1566) and the celebrated *Thesaurus linguae Graecae* (1572), an investment that led him to bankruptcy. He had fourteen children from three wives; his daughter Florence married Isaac Casaubon (→ **Switzerland**).

Bibliography: Boudou, Bénédicte/Cazes, Hélène/Kecskeméti, Judit (2006), *La France des Humanistes. Henri II Estienne, imprimeur et écrivain*, Turnhout; Cazes, Hélène (2002), "Les mille et une pages d'Henri Estienne: le recueil infini", in: *Études françaises* [Montréal, Canada] 38/3, 71–80; Boudou, Bénédicte (2005), "Proverbes et formules gnomiques chez Henri Estienne: de l'histoire à la poésie", in: *Seizième siècle* 1, 161–174 (online); Demaizière, Colette (2006), "Henri Estienne", in: *Centuriae Latinae* II, 313–318; Boudou, Bénédicte (2015), "Henri Estienne", in: Méniel, Bruno (ed.) *Écrivains juristes et juristes écrivains, du Moyen Âge au Siècle des Lumières*, Paris, 424–432.

Anonymous (prob. Jean de Saint-Martin, † *post* 1617)

<*Epitaphium Michaëlis Montani*> [c. 1593]

Ἠρίον ὅστις ἰδὼν ἠδ' οὔνομα τοὐμὸν ἐρωτᾷς
"μῶν θάνε Μώντανος;" παύεο θαμβοπαθεῖν.
Οὐκ ἐμὰ ταῦτα· δέμας, γένος εὐγενές, ὄλβος ἄνολβος,
προστασίαι, δυνάμεις, παίγνια θνητὰ τύχης.
5 Οὐρανόθεν κατέβην θεῖον φυτὸν εἰς χθόνα Κελτῶν,
οὐ σοφὸς Ἑλλήνων ὄγδοος οὔτε τρίτος

Αὐσονίων, ἀλλ' εἷς πάντων ἀντάξιος ἄλλων
    τῆς τε βάθει σοφίης ἄνθεσί τ' εὐεπίης,
ὅς καὶ χριστοσεβεῖ ξύνωσα διδάγματι σκέψιν
10   τὴν πυρρωνείην. Ἑλλάδα δ' εἷλε φθόνος,
εἷλε καὶ Αὐσονίην· φθονερὴν δ' ἔριν αὐτὸς ἐπισχὼν
    τάξιν ἐπ' οὐρανίδων πατρίδα μευ ἀνέβην.

Textus: inscriptio in monumento sepulchrali Michaelis de Montaigne nunc Burdigalae in Museo Aquitaniae asservato; inde transcripsit Legros, Alain (2008), "Deux épitaphes pour un tombeau", in: *Nouveau Bulletin de la Société Internationale des Amis de Montaigne* 4, 391–400.[4]

Crit.: spiritus accentusque fere semper tamquam in lapide servavimus || **12** οὐρανιδῶν debuit

Sim.: 2 θαμβοπαθεῖν] hapax leg. ut vid. || **3** οὐκ ἐμὰ ταῦτα] cf. *Anth. Pal.* 9.322.1 | γένος εὐγενές] cf. Phoc. *sent.* 3.1 | ὄλβος ἄνολβος] primum dictum ut vid., sed cf. e.g. Aesch. *Ag.* 1545 (ἄχαριν χάριν); Soph. *Aj.* 665 (ἄδωρα δῶρα) etc. || **4** παίγνια...τύχης] cf. *Anth. Pal.* 9.768.1 (et 10.80.1) || **5** cf. Hom. *Il.* 11.184 al. (οὐρανόθεν καταβάς) || **6** ὄγδοος] cf. Call. fr. 587 Pf. || **7** cf. Hom. *Il.* 11.514 (πολλῶν ἀντάξιος ἄλλων) || **8** βάθει σοφίης] cf. Paul. *ep. Rom.* 11.33 | ἄνθεσί τ' εὐεπίης] cf. fort. *Anth. Pal.* 2.1.381 et Dioscor. fr. 20.6 (sed utrumque locum ignorabat noster) || **9** χριστοσεβεῖ] hapax leg., ut vid. (sed saepius apud poetas recentiores, cf. e.g. L. Rhodoman, *Palaestina* 9.347) || **10** εἷλε φθόνος] cf. Eur. *Or.* 974

<Greek epitaph on Montaigne's monument>

If having seen this tomb and my name, you ask:
    'Is Montaigne dead?' – give up your worried amazement:
All this is not me: my body, my noble family, my unhappy happiness,
    my honours, my powers: they are the mortal preys of fortune.
[5] A divine breed, I came down from heaven to the land of the Celts,
    not the eighth of the Wise men of Greece, nor the third
among the Ausonians, but worth to myself all the others
    by the depth of my wisdom and my flowery language;
I, who allied the Pyrrhonian Doubt to the Christian
[10] doctrine. Envy seized Greece,
and seized even Ausonia [*scil.* Italy], but, taming the envious strife,
    I ascended back to the rank of the angels, my homeland.

---

4 See also the website of the CESR Tours: http://www.bvh.univ-tours.fr/MONLOE/INSCRIPTIONS_Tombeau.pdf. We warmly thank Prof. Alain Legros for his help with the edition and commentary of this epigraph. The poem is transcribed here in lower-case letters.

Metre: Elegiac couplets (in l. 9 the short vowel before σκ- has parallels in bucolic and epic poetry, in l. 10 the short vowel before φθ- is somewhat harsher)

Notes: The original text is engraved in gilded capitals on a black marble plaque inserted on the right flank of the funerary monument of Michel de Montaigne (1533–1592), installed on 1 May 1614 above his tomb in a chapel of the Feuillants church in Bordeaux. The monument is preserved today in the Musée d'Aquitaine. A remarkable feat of linguistic skill (see the paronomasia at the beginning, of l. 2, the neologisms in ll. 2 and 9), and a blend of reminiscences from epic, epigrammatic, and tragic diction, this poem also deals with philosophy (the verb ἐπέχω, here l. 11, is the Pyrrhonians' refrain and Montaigne's own motto). Αὐσονίων in l. 7 seems to be referring to 'inhabitants of Ausonia' (see l. 11 Αὐσονίην = Italy), but could as well be applied to the town of Bordeaux, fatherland of the Latin poet Ausonius.

Biography: This epitaph has been attributed by Reinhold Dezeimeris, with high likelihood, to the poet Jean de Saint-Martin, *alias* Johannes Sammartinus, who gave it to a friend, Geoffroy de Malvyn. Dezeimeris found only that Saint-Martin, born in Dax, was a lawyer at the Parlement de Bordeaux and that he wrote other poems, including a couple in Greek, for Professor Élie Vinet in a posthumous literary tribute published in 1590, two years before Montaigne's death. Saint-Martin was still alive in 1617.

Bibliography: Montaigne, Michel de (1745), *Essais*, Pierre Coste (ed.), London [first transcription of the epigram]; Lapaume, Jean (1859), *Le Tombeau de Michel Montaigne*, Rennes; Dezeimeris, Reinhold (1861), *Recherches sur l'auteur des épitaphes de Montaigne*, Bordeaux; Marin, Louis (1981), "Tombeau de Montaigne", in: *La Voix excommuniée*, Paris, 133–156; Millet, Olivier (1995), *La première réception des Essais de Montaigne (1580–1640)*, Paris; Legros, Alain (1999), "La dédicace de l'*Adversus Mathematicos* au cardinal de Lorraine, ou du bon usage de Sextus Empiricus selon Gentian Hervet et Montaigne", in: *Bulletin de la Société des Amis de Montaigne* 8, 41–72; Millet, Olivier (2008), "Le tombeau de Montaigne", in: *Nouveau Bulletin de la Société Internationale des Amis de Montaigne* 4, 377–390; Legros, Alain (2008), "Deux épitaphes pour un tombeau", in: *Nouveau Bulletin de la Société Internationale des Amis de Montaigne* 4, 391–400.

Denis Pétau (1583–1652)

Εἰς τὴν Ἁγίαν Γενοβήφαν, Πανηγυρικὸς α΄ [1620]

(excerptum, vv. 1–24)

    Οὐκ ἀρετῆς μέγα χρῆμα θοῇ κεχρημένον ὁρμῇ
    Ἀθρόον ἐξανόρουσε, καὶ ἐν πραπίδεσσι φαάνθη,
    Ἀλλὰ μάλ' ἐκ πολλοῖο καὶ ἡλικίης ἀπὸ πρώτης
    Ἀνδρῶν ἐν στήθεσσιν ἀέξεται· ἧχι διαπρὸ
5 Εἰς ψυχὴν καταδῦσα βαθείην αὔλακα τέμνει.
    Ἥ τ' ἔνδον σελάουσα σαφῆ τεκμήρι' ὀπάζει.
    Οἷον ἅπαι γενετῆς καὶ ἔτ' ἐν λίκνοισι τέθηπεν
    Μητρυιὴ κοτέουσα Διὸς γόνον Ἡρακλῆα,
    Ἧμος δεινὰ πέλωρα, δαφοινοὺς ἧκε δράκοντας,
10 Ἀρτιγενοῦς μεμαυῖα πρὶν ἥβης ἄνθος ἱκέσθαι
    Ἰῷ δηλητῆρι μελῶν ἄπο θυμὸν ἀποῦραι.
    Ἀλλ' ὅγε δραξάμενός τε καὶ ἀμφοτέρῃσι μεμαρπὼς
    Σφίγξατο καὶ κατέπεφνε περὶ σπείρῃσι πλακέντας.
    Τοίη παρθένος, ἣν σεμνοῖς ἐπέεσσι γεραίρειν
15 Ἀρχαῖον κατὰ χρεῖος ἔμ' αὐτίκα θυμὸς ἄνωγεν,
    Ἀντίθεος Γενοβήφα, ἀρηϊφίλων μέγα Κελτῶν
    Κῦδος ὁμοῦ τε καὶ ἄλκαρ, ἐϋκτίστου δὲ πόληος
    Ἔξοχα, ἣ Φράγκων ἕδος ἔλλαχεν ἔμμεν' ἀνάκτων.
    Αὕτη γοῦν νεογιλὸν ἔτι βρέφος οὖσα καὶ ἄρτι
20 Μητρὸς ἐν ἀγκοίνῃσιν ἀειρομένη, ἐκέκαστο
    Παντοίης ἀρετῇσι, καὶ εὐσεβὴς κατέφαινε
    Δείγματα πόλλ' ἀρίδηλα, τά περ προϊοῦσα κράτυνεν
    Ἐκπάγλως περί τ' οὖσ' ἀνδρῶν περί τ' οὖσα γυναικῶν
    Τῶν πλείστων, γαίης ὅσον οὐρανός ἐστιν ὕπερθεν.

Textus: Διονυσίου τοῦ Πεταβίου Αὐρηλιανέως... *Ἑλληνικὰ ἔπη παντοδαπά* / Dionysii Petavii Aurelianensis... *Graeca varii generis carmina*, Paris: Sébastien Cramoisy, 1641², 86–89.

Sim.: 4 cf. Hom. *Il.* 18.110 (ἀνδρῶν ἐν στήθεσσιν ἀέξεται) || **5** αὔλακα τέμνει] cf. e.g. *Anth. Pal.* 9.274.1 al. || **6** σαφῆ...ὀπάζει] cf. Eur. *Med.* 517 || **7** τέθηπεν potius intransitive, cf. Hom. *Od.* 23.105 || **8** Διὸς γόνον Ἡρακλῆα] cf. Dion. Per. 454; Opp. *C.* 2.109 | δεινὰ...δράκοντας] cf. Hom. *Il.* 2.308 et 321 || **9** δράκοντας] de historia cf. e.g. Pind. *Nem.* 1.33–72; Theoc. *Id.* 24 || **10** ἥβης ἄνθος] cf. Hom. *Il.* 13.484, sed cf. Hom. *Od.* 4.668 (πρὶν ἥβης μέτρον ἱκέσθαι) || **11** θυμὸν ἀποῦραι] cf. Hom. *Il.* 21.296; *Od.* 13.270 || **19** νεογιλὸν...βρέφος] cf. Theoc. *Id.* 17.58 || **20** μητρὸς ἐν ἀγκοίνῃσιν] cf. Opp. *H.* 3.34 || **21** cf. Hom. *Od.* 4.725 (παντοίησ' ἀρετῇσι κεκασμένον) etc. || **24** sim. Hom. *Il.* 15.36 al. (γαῖα καὶ οὐρανὸς εὐρὺς ὕπερθε)

Panegyric I to Saint Geneviève

(excerpt, ll. 1–24)

> It is not that the huge bulk of virtue, with a rapid impulse,
> springs up suddenly and appears in the heart;
> but it is since a long time, and since early childhood,
> that virtue grows in the breast of men, where,
> [5] entering well down into the soul, it digs a deep furrow.
> Shining from inside, it gives clear signs of herself.
> Like when the stepmother hating Heracles, the son of Zeus,
> from his birth and still in the cradle,
> sent him prodigious monsters, bloodthirsty dragons,
> [10] in her ardent desire to remove, by a fatal poison, the life from his limbs,
> before he could reach the flower of new-born youth.
> But he grabbed them and grasped them with both his hands:
> He strangled them and killed them, as they hugged him with their knots.
> Such is the virgin whom, according to an old vow,
> [15] my heart orders me to honour now, in holy verses:
> The divine Geneviève, both great glory and support
> of the warlike Celts, and especially of the well-built City
> which has had the fate of being the see of the kings of France.
> So she, being still a new-born child, and being just lifted up
> [20] in the arms of her mother, shone
> with all virtues, and displayed bright evidence of her piety,
> which she strengthened as she grew up,
> showing herself to be superior to most men, to most women,
> as much as heaven is superior to the earth. [5]

Metre: Hexameters (almost flawless: some hiatuses e.g. ll. 16, 18, and a possible bipartite verse in l. 18).

---

5 Author's Latin translation: *Numquam virtus excellens subita erumpens vi | Tota simul emicuit, et in praecordiis extitit: | Sed longe ante, et aetate a prima | Hominum in pectoribus gliscit ; ubi penitus | [5] In animam ingrediens, profundum sulcum ducit. | Tum intus refulgens clara indicia exhibet. | Qualem ab ortu, et incunabulis admirata est | Noverca infensa Iovis filium Herculem: | Quando gravia monstra, sanguineos immisit dracones, | [10] Recens nati cupiens, priusquam ad pubertatis florem pervenisset | Veneno nocenti a membris animam auferre. | Ille vero amplexus, et ambabus comprehendens | Strinxit, et occidit circum spiris implicatos. | Talis virgo, quam honestis versibus decorare, | [15] Antiquum iuxta debitum, me iam animus admonet, | Divina Genovefa, bellicosorum magnum Celtarum | Decus iuxta, et propugnaculum: belle conditae civitatis | Praesertim, cui Francorum sedi contigit esse regum. | Illa igitur recens nata adhuc infans, atque adeo | [20] Matris in ulnis sublata, praedita erat | Omnibus virtutibus; pietatis autem praebuit | Argumenta multa perspicua, quae progrediens confirmabat | Vehementer, superans viros et feminas | Plurimas, terram quantum coelum est supra.*

Notes: Patron saint of the city of Paris, Geneviève (c. 420–c. 502 or 512) avoided the storming of the city by Attila in 451 and ensured the wheat supply during the siege of 465. In 1617, suffering from a serious illness, Denis Pétau made a vow to this saint (l. 15: ἀρχαῖον χρέος). Having recovered his health, he wrote from 1619 several long and grateful poems in her honour, especially the *Panegyric* and the *Soteria ad s. Genovefam*. The comparison with the myth of Hercules' birth in ll. 7–13, inspired by Theocritus 24 (Ἡρακλίσκος) is worth noting.

Biography: Denis Pétau (1583–1652), the son of an educated trader, studied in Orléans and Paris. Still very young, he learned Greek, Latin, and Hebrew, and did particularly well in Greek. He came into contact with the great scholar Isaac Casaubon (they exchanged several Greek letters; → **Switzerland**) and started research into Greek manuscripts, while preparing a complete edition of Synesius (*Synesii...Opera quae extant omnia*, Paris 1612). He entered the Jesuit order in 1605 and lectured on rhetoric and moral theology in various Jesuit colleges: first La Flèche (1613–1615), then Clermont, in Paris, where he became librarian after Fronton du Duc (†1623). A remarkable scholar and a prolific author of Greek and Latin poems, Pétau gained fame for his philological works, such as his editions of Themistius, Julian, Nicephorus, and Epiphanius, as well as for his studies on chronology (*Opus de doctrina temporum*, 1627), which continued J.J. Scaliger's research *De emendatione temporum*. Pétau's publications dealing with the history of dogma and moral theology (*Dogmata theologica*, 1644 and 1650) were authoritative – if debated – for more than two centuries. He wrote poetry until the very final days of his life.

Bibliography: Stanonik, Franz (1876), *Dionysius Petavius. Ein Beitrag zur Gelehrten-Geschichte des XVII. Jahrhunderts*, Graz; Vital Chatellain, Jules-Charles (1884), *Le Père Denys Petau d'Orléans, jésuite: sa vie et ses œuvres*, Paris; Martin, Jules (1910), *Denis Petau (1583–1652)*, Paris; Hofmann, Michael (1976), *Theologie, Dogma und Dogmenentwicklung im theologischen Werk Denis Petau's*, Frankfurt am Main/München; Thill, Andrée/Banderier, Gilles (ed.) (1999), *La Lyre jésuite, anthologie de poèmes latins 1620–1730*, Genève, 11–19.

Gilles Ménage (1613–1692)

Εἰς Γαργίλιον [1652]

Ἀλλοπροσαλλοκόλαξ, ἱπποτρεχεδειπνοσοφιστής,
Ἀκρατοχανδοπότης, κρειοφαγαινοβόρος,
Δοξοπαλαιομαθής, ἀναγραμματοτεχνοποιητής,
Γραμματοληρολόγος, μωρεπιμωρότατος.

Textus: Aegidii Menagii *Miscellanea*, Paris, A. Courbé 1652, 79 (mox in: *Poemata. Secunda editio auctior et emendatior*, Paris 1656, 53)

Sim.: 1 cf. verba composita sicut δημοκόλαξ, μαλακοκόλαξ etc. | ἱπποτρεχεδειπνοσοφιστής] cf. Athen. 1.4a (ὁ τρεχέδειπνος, φησὶ σοφιστής); Plut. *Mor.* 726a || **2** ἀκρατοχανδοπότης] cf. *Anth. Pal.* 11.59.1 (χανδοπόται, sed etiam ἀκρατοπότης) | κρειοφαγαινοβόρος] cf. Nic. *Ther.* 50 (dub.: κρειοφάγος); αἰνοβόρος prob. ex αἱμοβόρος parodice creatum || **3** cf. δοξοματαιοσοφοί apud Athen. 4.162a || **4** cf. ληρολόγος et composita a γραμματο- incohantia

To Gargilius

> One-after-another Toady, Horse-running Professor of Parasitism,
>   Pure-wine Toper, Beef-eater-like-a-sick-man,
> Fake Antiquarian, Poor-anagram Writer,
>   Grammar Babbler, Hyper-stupid More-than-stupid.[6]

Metre: Elegiac couplets.

Notes: These two distichs are formed of only eight portmanteau words, *sesquipedalia verba* or *plaustralia* (*cf.* Erasmus *Adagia* 3.2.69); they may be compared to a couple of similar pieces found among Martin Crusius' *Poemata graeca* (→ **Germany**). The use of portmanteau barbarisms is typical of all Greco-Latin production on the 'Montmaur affair': see also *Monmori Parasitosycophantosophistae* ἀποχυτραποθέωσις ('The Saucepandeification of Montmaur the Parasite, Sycophant and Sophist'). A model for this kind of compounds can be found in Aristophanes, e.g. *Pax* 810–811, where a bad poet and a bad singer are mocked, but a more direct inspiration is a poem (*FGE* anon. 155 Page) transmitted by Athenaeus, 4.162ab,[7] and remarkably 'translated' into Latin by Joseph Justus Scaliger (*Coniectanea in M. Terentium Varronem*, Paris 1565, 2).[8]

---

[6] Another possible translation: 'Kisser of any and all asses, gold medalist in racing to learned banquets, / Bottomless sack of wine who wolfs down his meat raw, / Classicist in his own mind, repeated anagram offender, / Grammatician of gobbledegook, moron to beat all morons.'

[7] A quotation from Book 6 of Hegesander of Delphi's *Commentaries*: Ὀφρυανασπασίδαι, ῥινεγκαταπηξιγένειοι, / σακκογενειοτρόφοι καὶ λοπαδαρπαγίδαι, / εἱματανωπερίβαλλοι, ἀνηλιποκαιβλεπέλαιοι, / νυκτιλαθραιοφάγοι, νυκτιπαταιπλάγιοι, / μειρακιεξαπάται ⟨καὶ⟩ συλλαβοπευσιλαληταί, / δοξοματαιόσοφοι, ζηταρετησιάδαι.

[8] See Porter, David A. (2019), "The Early Modern lyric: a literary wilderness of world literature", in: *University of Toronto Quarterly* 88/2, 195–209: 205.

Biography: This classical scholar, who was also a gallant abbot, wrote poems in Latin, Greek, French, and Italian. According to Pierre Bayle, Gilles Ménage (1613–1692) was 'the Varro of his day' – which suffices to illustrate how powerful this scholar's fame was. Ménage left his career as a lawyer to devote himself entirely to literature and scholarship. Two years after the publication of his famous *Origines de la langue française* ('*Origins of the French language*', 1650), Ménage produced a book of *Miscellanea*, including some Greek, Latin, and French poems. Among the Greek ones, a short, satirical cycle embraces a few caustic epigrams (called διασυρτικά) against 'Gargilius', introduced by the author as a 'babbling orator' (ῥήτωρ ἀδόλεσχος). Before beginning his famous controversy with Vaugelas and Bouhours about the French language, Ménage taunted Pierre de Montmaur (1576–1648), a bibliophile and a poet who had been the royal professor of Greek literature for over twenty-five years at *Collège royal*, for being a parasite among literary circles. Ménage went so far as to write a parodic *Biography* and *Will* of this man, whom he and others called 'Gargilius Mamurra' (*Vita M. Gargilii Mamurrae parasitopaedagogi*, 1643), by harking back to the name of the ridiculous man once mocked by Catullus.

Bibliography: Samfiresco, Elvire (1902), *Ménage. Polémiste, philologue, poète*, Paris (repr. Geneva 1971); Leroy-Turcan, Isabelle/Russon Wooldrigde, Terence (eds.) (1995), *Gilles Ménage (1613–1692) grammairien et lexicographe*, Lyons; Trivisani-Moreau, Isabelle (ed.) (2015), *Gilles Ménage: un homme de langue dans la République des Lettres* (monographic volume of *Littératures classiques* 88). On this epigram: Bannister, Mark (1979), "The Montmaur Affair: poetry versus pedantry in the seventeenth century", in: *French Studies* 33, 397–410; Turcan, Isabelle (1994), "Gilles Ménage (1613–1692), philologue d'avant-garde, conseiller des poètes", in: *Œuvres et Critiques* 19/1, 79–87; De Smet, Ingrid A.R. (1996), *Menippean Satire and the Republic of Letters, 1581–1655*, Geneva; Barbafieri, Carine/Civardi, Jean-Marc (eds.) (forthcoming), *L'Affaire Pierre de Montmaur*.

Pierre-Daniel Huet (1630–1721)

Εἰς τρεχέδειπνον παράσιτον [1694]

Εὔχομαί σοι, Γένετορ πάντων, ὃς Ὀλύμπια ναίεις
Δώματα, εἴ ποτε βῇ, θάνατον μετά, εἰς Ἄϊδος δῶ
Νυκτιλαθραιοφάγος τε καὶ ὠμοβόρος τρεχέδειπνος,
Εὐμεγέθους στόματος μέγ' ἀφαιρεῖν ἕρκος ὀδόντων,
5 Καὶ παρὰ τοῖς φλοιοῖς ἐσσάμεν' ἀμύγδαλα θεῖναι·
Αἰτίας μιαροῦ παρασίτου τῇδε κολάξεις.

Textus: Petri Danielis Huetii *Poemata Latina et Graeca*, Utrecht: W. Broedelet, 1694, 46.

Crit.: 2 μέτα debuit

Sim.: 1 γένετορ πάντων] cf. *Hymn. Orph.* 11.10 || **1–2** Ὀλύμπια.../ δώματα] cf. Hom. *Il.* 1.8 et saep. || **2** Ἄιδος δῶ] cf. Hom. *Il.* 23.74; *Od.* 11.571 || **3** Νυκτιλαθραιοφάγος] Athen. 4.162a (*FGE* 155) | τρεχέδειπνος] vide supra, cf. Alciphr. 3.1; Athen. 1.4a; Plut. *Mor.* 726a || **4** ἕρκος ὀδόντων] Hom. *Il.* 4.370; 9.409 al.

To a banquet-running parasite

> I beg you, All-Creator, who dwell in the houses of Olymp
> if ever, after his death, come to the House of Hades
> a night-clandestine eater and raw-flesh-devouring parasite,
> please remove from his big mouth his teeth's huge fence
> [5] and set next to him almonds coated with their bark:
> Thus you'll punish him for having been a dirty parasite!

Metre: Dactylic hexameters (serious prosodical flaws in l. 1 εὔχομαι and in l. 5 ἐσσάμεν').

Notes: Huet's *Poëmata* is a collection of very diverse Latin pieces of encomiastic, didascalic, or personal content. The section including our epigram shows a special attention to *sesquipedalia verba* and scoptic tones. The only other Greek poem of the book is a touching elegy for the death of a young boy.

Biography: Pierre-Daniel Huet (1630–1721) received a thorough training in Latin and Greek from the Jesuits in Caen, where he was born, before being appointed to the nearby abbey of Aulnay. He was chosen to become *sous-précepteur* of the *Grand Dauphin* under Bossuet and edited, with Anne Dacier, a number of Latin authors for the famous series *Ad usum Delphini*. After taking up the position of Bishop of Avranches between 1692 and 1699, he decided to leave this role and retire to the peace of the abbey of Fontenay (Calvados). A man of vast erudition, especially in theology, history, and literature, he published at the beginning of his career the results of his research on the Bible and on the origins of the novel, as well as translations of ancient authors. Interested in natural sciences and astronomy, he was also willing to learn such literary tongues as Hebrew, Syriac, and Arabic, and to study oriental religions, in particular those of India, and he pursued comparative studies in a variety of works, written either in Latin or French. A smart polemist against the followers of Jansenius, he acquired his renown thanks to his critical remarks on Descartes' philosophy, which he had previously admired. He was elected to the *Académie française* in 1674. Being an outstanding scholar in Greek philology, both pagan and Christian, he translated

Origen as well as the novel of *Daphnis and Chloe*. He loved poetry and composed several poems such as odes, eclogues, and short pieces, mostly in Latin, but also a few in Greek, like his poems on tea (cf. Francius → **Low Countries**, Herrichen → **Germany**).

Bibliography: Huet, Daniel (1853), *Mémoires de Daniel Huet, évêque d'Avranches, traduits pour la première fois du latin en français par Charles Nisard*, Paris (see 24–35 for Huet's Greek studies and 189f. for his praise of tea); Dupront, Alphonse (1930), *Pierre Daniel Huet et l'exégèse comparatiste au XVIIe siècle*, Paris; Guellouz, Suzanne (ed.) (1994), *Pierre-Daniel Huet (1630–1721). Actes du Colloque de Caen (12–13 novembre 1993)*, Paris/Seattle/Tübingen; Rapetti, Elena (1999), *Pierre-Daniel Huet: erudizione, filosofia, apologetica*, Milan; Ducœur, Guillaume (2013), "Les religions indiennes comme *argumentatio* dans les *Alnetanae quaestiones* de Pierre-Daniel Huet", in: *Dix-septième siècle* 259, 281–299.

Jean Boivin (1663–1726)

Ἄννης τῆς Δακερίας τελευτησάσης Ἀνακρέων κλαίων [1720]

Ἀνάκρεον, τί κλαίεις,
Τὰ πρὶν γελῶν καὶ ἁβρὰ
Γελῶσι συγχορεύων
Ἔρωτι καὶ Λυαίῳ;
5   – Αἶ αἶ, ὄλωλεν Ἄννη,
Ὄλωλεν ἡ φίλυμνος
Ἐμῶν μελῶν ἀοιδός·
Ὄλωλεν ἡ λυθέντα
Τῆς βαρβίτου τὰ νεῦρα
10 Ὅλην τε βάρβιτόν μοι
Ἐς βέλτιον μαθοῦσα
Μόνη μεθαρμόσασθαι.
Αἶ αἶ, ὄλωλεν Ἄννη·
Ἄννη, σοφῶν τὸ θαῦμα·
15 Ἄννη, μέλημα Μουσῶν·
Ἄννη, κλέος γυναικῶν.
Ὄλωλε· σὺν δ᾽ ἅπαντα
Ἀπώλεθ᾽ οἷς γέγηθα·
Λοιπὸν δ᾽ ἐμοὶ τὸ πενθεῖν,
20 Στένειν τε καὶ βοῆσαι,
Αἶ αἶ, ὄλωλεν Ἄννη.

Textus: *Recentiores poetae latini et graeci selecti quinque, curis Josephi Oliveti collecti ac editi. Editio auctior et correctior*, Lugduni Batavorum, Francofurti ad Moenum et Hagae-Comitum: sumptibus Societatis, 1743, 266.

Sim.: 2–3 γελῶν καὶ ἁβρά / γελῶσι] *Anacreont.* 43,3 (ἁβρὰ γελῶντες, = 44,5) ‖ **3** γελῶσι συγχορεύων] *Anacreont.* 44,11 (Χαρίτεσσι συγχορεύων) ‖ **6** φίλυμνος] *Anacreont.* 34,16 (φίλυμνε, corr. Stephanus: φίλυπνε cod.) ‖ **9–10** βαρβίτου... βάρβιτον] *Anacreont.* passim ‖ **15** μέλημα Μουσῶν] *Anacreont.* 55.9–10 (τόδε καὶ μέλημα μύθοις / χαρίεν φυτόν τε Μουσῶν)

Anacreon mourns the death of Anne Dacier

Anacreon, why are you mourning?
You were formerly laughing and dancing
with your smiling gentle fellows,
Eros and Sorrow-lifting Bacchus?
[5] – Alas! Anne is dead!
Dead, the melodious
poet, singer of my songs!
Dead, she the only one
who taught me how to adjust
[10] at their best the loosened
strings of my lyre
and the whole lyre!
Alas, Anne is dead!
Anne, the scholars' wonder!
[15] Anne, darling of the Muses!
Anne, women's glory!
She is dead; and with her
I lost all my joy.
Now I cannot but languish,
[20] mourn, and cry these words:
Alas, Anne is dead!

Metre: Catalectic iambic dimeter ('Anacreontic').

Notes: In the manner of Anacreon, whose style, words, and metre Boivin closely imitates, the poem mourns the loss of Anne Dacier (1645–1720), a scholar who is best known for her annotated translations of Homer into French (1711, 1716), but who began her career by translating into the vernacular Anacreon and Sappho's poems (1681). During the famous *Querelle d'Homère*, a literary dispute (part of the grander 'Battle of the Books') opposing, from 1714 on, Anne Dacier against Antoine Houdar de la Motte, Jean Boivin had sided with the learned translator, notably in the introduction to his *Apologie d'Homère* (1715).

Biography: Jean Boivin, also known by the pseudonym 'Œnopion', Οἰνοπίων (1663–1726), was the son of Louis Boivin, a lawyer, and of Marie Vattier, sister of

Pierre Vattier, the King's lecturer in Arabic. He was appointed to the King's Library in 1686, and five years later he joined the King's Guard as *commis en second*. Based on royal manuscripts, he published the writings of the major mathematicians of Antiquity (*Veterum mathematicorum Athenaei, Apollodori, Philonis, Bitonis, Heronis et aliorum opera graece et latine*, 1693) as well as an important edition of Nicephorus Gregoras' *Roman History* (1702). He was eventually appointed as the King's lecturer in Greek at the *Collège royal*, where he taught from 1706 to 1726. He was first associated member (1705), then pensionary (1724) of the *Académie des inscriptions et médailles*. He also served as the director of the manuscript department at the King's Library (1720–1726) and entered the *Académie française* in 1721. He left several translations from Greek into French: Sophocles, Aristophanes, and the *Batrachomyomachia*. One of the best Hellenists of his day, he wrote a few Greek poems (*Poësies Anacréontiques Grecques de M. Boivin* (ΟΙΝΟΠΙΩΝΟΣ ΜΕΛΗ) *au nombre d'onze Pièces*, Paris 1722; see also *Poëtarum ex Academiâ Gallicâ, qui latinè aut graecè scripserunt, Carmina*, Paris 1738), and in particular some odes referring to the family of Chancellor Henri François d'Aguessau. Boivin combined a vast erudition with a deep knowledge of poetry: his passion for the Homeric poems explains why he chose Homer as a subject for his lectures at the *Collège royal*.

Bibliography: Fossier, François (2019*), Jean Boivin et l'histoire de la Bibliothèque du Roi*, Paris. On the Querelle: Rigault, Hippolyte (1856), *Histoire de la Querelle des Anciens et des Modernes*, Paris; Lecoq, Anne-Marie (ed.) (2001), *La Querelle des Anciens et des Modernes, 17ᵉ–18ᵉ siècles*, Paris.

Bernard de La Monnoye (1641–1728)

Θρῆνος ἐπὶ τῷ Λεσβίας στρουθῷ [1743]

Ἰοὺ κλαίετε, Κύπρι καὶ Ἔρωτες
Ὅσσοι θ' ἱμερόεντες ἄνδρες εἰσίν.
Ἰοὺ στρουθὸς <ἐμῆς> ὄλωλε Κούρης,
Ὃν αὐτοῖς ἴσον ὄμμασιν φίλησεν.
5   Ἦν γὰρ μειλίχιος, φίλην τε κείνην
Ἔγνω δεσπότιν, ὡς τεκοῦσαν ἡ παῖς.
Οὐδ' αὐτῆς ποθ' ἑκὼν λέλοιπε κόλπους,
Ἀλλ' ἔνθα πτάμενος καὶ ἔνθα, μούνην
Πιππίζων ἐς ἄνασσαν ἷκεν αἰεί·
10 Ὃς νῦν βῆ διὰ νύκτα πρὸς τὸν οἶκον,
Ὅθεν νόστιμός ἐστι, φασίν, οὔτις.
Σὲ δ' ὁ Ζεὺς ὀλέσειε, νὺξ κακίστη,

Εἰς ἧς δώματα πᾶν καλὸν καταρρεῖ,
Ἥ μοι στρουθὸν ἔλες ποθεινὸν οὕτω.
15 Φεῦ τὸ σχέτλιον ἔργον, αἴ σὺ δειλέ,
Αἴ στρουθὲ τριπόθητέ, σου χάριν νῦν
Κούρης ὄμματα τῆς ἐμῆς ὑποιδεῖ
Τῶν πικρῶν ἀπὸ δακρύων ἐρυθρά.

Textus: *Recentiores poetae latini et graeci selecti quinque, curis Josephi Oliveti collecti ac editi. Editio auctior et correctior*, Lugduni Batavorum, Francofurti ad Mœnum et Hagae-Comitum: sumptibus Societatis, 1743, 323.

Crit.: 3 ἐμῆς addidi ‖ 12 ὀλέσειε scripsi: ὀλέσει ed. ‖ 16 σοῦ debuit ‖ 18 ἐρυθρά scripsi: ἐρυτρά ed.

Sim.: poeta carmen Catulli (3) in sermonem Graecum vertit ‖ 1 cf. Mosch. *epit. Bion.* 67 (κλαίουσιν Ἔρωτες) etc. ‖ 4 de re cf. Mosch. *Meg.* 9 ‖ 9 Πιππίζων] Ar. *Av.* 307 ‖ 16 τριπόθητε] Bion *Id.* 1.58; Mosch. *Id.* 3.51

Lament on Lesbia's sparrow

Ah! Mourn, Aphrodite and Cupids,
and all you charming men!
Ah! My girlfriend's sparrow is dead,
whom she loved no less than her eyes.
[5] He was sweet as honey and knew her as his
loving mistress as a girl knows her mother.
He never quit her lap on purpose,
but, hopping about here and there,
he just chirped to his lady, alone.
[10] Now he went through the night to the home
no one ever returns from, as they say.
May Zeus kill you, o horrible night,
to whose houses every beauty flows:
You have stolen the charming sparrow from me.
[15] Oh miserable deed! Oh you, poor little one!
Oh much-wanted sparrow, now because of you
my girl's eyes are swollen
red with weeping bitter tears!

Metre: Phalaecian hendecasyllable.

Notes: This is a faithful translation of Catullus's famous poem 3, on the death of Lesbia's sparrow. La Monnoye excelled in imitations and translations from short poems of Antiquity, chiefly epigrams.

Biography: Bernard de La Monnoye was an erudite poet and scholar born in Dijon in 1641; he died in Paris in 1728. Educated by the Jesuits, he studied law in Orléans and became a lawyer in his hometown, eventually abandoning this career in order to become a scholar. La Monnoye's first and brilliant success came through writing a poem on the abolition of duels, which obtained first prize from the *Académie française*. He learned Greek only at the age of forty but mastered it so well that he was able to write Greek compositions and to translate into Greek hexameters the famous sixth Satire of Boileau, *The Embarrassment of Paris*. Kind and jovial in character, he practised poetry in French, Latin, and Greek, preferring rather light and playful trends rather than a noble and solemn tone. He earned celebrity thanks to his 1700 edition, which included a collection of *Noëls* or popular verses usually sung for Christmas, written in Burgundian dialect. A learned polygraph, modest and scrupulous, he carefully studied many ancient authors and corresponded with scholars from all over Europe, such as Pierre Bayle, Étienne Baluze, and Bernard de Montfaucon. He settled in Paris in 1707 and was elected to the *Académie française* in 1713.

Bibliography: Peignot, Gabriel (1832), *Nouvelles recherches chronologiques, littéraires et philologiques sur la vie et les ouvrages de Bernard de la Monnoye*, Dijon; Michaud, Louis-Gabriel (1854), *Biographie universelle*, Paris, vol. 20, 640–644; Lex, Léonce (1905), "Lettre de La Monnoye à Bernard de Montfaucon", in: *Bibliothèque de l'École des chartes* 66, 628–631; Jacquin, Lucie (2016), *Les Noëls bourguignons de Bernard de La Monnoye*, Lyon.

André Chénier (1762–1794)

‹De Aglaia puella› [1788–1790]

> Τρὶς μάκαρ Ἀνδρεία· τὴν Ἀγλαΐην ῥοδόμαζον
> γυμνὴν λαμποπύγην ὡς ἴδες, ὡς ἐμάνης·
> ὡς δέ τε πολλὰ μιγεὶς ἐν σεισοπύγῃ φιλότητι
> μείλιχα στήθεσσιν, χείλεσι, χέρσ' ἔπαθες!
> 5 ὡς νῦν κ' ἔγραψας ἡδὺ πνείουσαν ἑταίραν,
> ὄμμασι βακχευθεὶς τὰς φρένας ἠδὲ πόθῳ!

Textus: Paris, Bibliothèque Nationale de France, ms. *N.A.F.* 6851, n° 23 (manu scriptum litteris minusculis sine accentibus spiritibusve, praeter diaeresin ï in αγλαϊην)⁹: hinc Chénier, André (1950), *Œuvres complètes*, ed. Gérald Walter, Paris, 619.

---

9 See the image of this page on Gallica: https://gallica.bnf.fr/ark:/12148/btv1b10090499q/f25.item.zoom.

Sim.: 1 Τρὶς μάκαρ] Hes. fr. 211.7 M.-W.; *Anth. Pal.* 15.22; Callim. fr. 114 Pf. et saep. | Ἀγλαΐην ῥοδόμαζον] cf. Mosch. 2.70 (Ἀγλαΐην πυρσοῖο ῥόδου χείρεσσι λέγουσα); ῥοδόμαζος hapax leg. ut vid. || **2** λαμποπύγην] hapax leg., ut vid., cf. λευκόπυγος, καλλίπυγος etc. | ὡς—ἐμάνης] cf. Theoc. *Id.* 2.82 || **3** μιγεὶς—φιλότητι] cf. Hom. *Il.* 6.25 (μίγη φιλότητι καὶ εὐνῇ); 2.32 (ἵνα μίσγεαι ἐν φιλότητι) etc. | σεισοπύγῃ] cf. Suid. ι 760 ("Ἴϋγξ τὸ ὄρνεον, τὸ λεγόμενον σεισοπυγής); *Etym. Magn.* 479.55; *schol. Theoc.* 2.17 ("Ἴϋγξ, ἡ λεγομένη σεισοπυγίς) || **5** ἡδὺ πνείουσαν] cf. Hom. *Od.* 4.446 (ἀμβροσίην...ἡδὺ μάλα πνείουσαν) || **6** βακχευθεὶς τὰς φρένας] cf. Eur. *HF* 1122

‹On Aglaia›

> Thrice blessed are you, André, for when you saw rosy-bosomed Aglaia
>   nude, her buttocks shining with a healthy glow, how you were driven wild:
> how you often had intercourse with her in buttocks-moving love,
>   you experienced sweetness with chest, hands and lips.
> [5] How much you'd have drawn right now the beautiful lady, who sighs gently,
>   and, watching her, your spirits would have been excited by desire!

Metre: Elegiac couplets (l. 2 λαμποπύγην with short υ, l. 4 inusual correptio before στ-, though attested in ancient verse; l. 5 -ας lengthened *in arsi*).

Notes: During his journey to England (1788–1790), André Chénier composed six poems in Greek, ranging from one to ten lines. Each of these celebrated, with an erotic tension the poet never showed in his French poetry, the 'young British nymphs' (παρθενικαὶ νύμφαι τε Βριτανίδες) whom Chénier met on the banks of the 'divine Thames', as 'Rhodope's cantor' (Ἀνδρείας ὁ Ῥοδόπειος). These short poetic exercises offer an image of the poet as a lover and as a draftsman of the female body, keen to evoke in the most suggestive language the meanderings of physical love. The bashfulness of the 1958 editor of these pieces for the prestigious *Bibliothèque de la Pléiade* series deserves to be quoted here: 'I hesitate to offer the reader a French version of these Greek and Latin verses of Ch[énier]. There are certain things that can only be said in the language of the Ancients, who had a conception of decency very different from ours.' The name of the youngest Grace, here Ἀγλαΐη (Hes. *Theog.* 909; 945), also considered Aphrodite's messenger (Nonn. *Dion.* 33.57), is the pseudonym of a presumably real English girl, the protagonist of this erotic poem inspired by the long epigrammatic tradition on the theme, cf. e.g. *Anth. Pal.* 5.35; the name Byblis is used in another Greek piece of Chénier's. As a name, Aglaia/Aglaie tells the 'brightness' of beauty and should be likened to the following epithet λαμποπύγη (2), related to beauty shining under the belt. Another of Chénier's Greek distichs introduces the poet proclaiming himself a 'Thracian' and repeatedly kissing this same part of his lover's body (πολλὰ κύσας τὴν πυγήν). Chénier uses the word σεισοπύγη (3) as an adjective and seems to go back to its etymological meaning to evoke the act of love making with vibrant vivacity. If ancient lexica sometimes consider σεισοπυγής/σεισοπυγίς as a noun and a synonym of ἔρως, Chénier made it an epithet of φιλότης (a word taken here in its epic meaning of the physical act of love), and combined it with the participle μιγείς, often found in Homer.

Biography: André Chénier was born in 1762 in Galata, Constantinople, to a Greek mother and a French merchant father. As early as 1765, the family moved to France, where André could conduct his studies at the *Collège de Navarre*, a liberal and open-minded Parisian school. The poet insisted in his verse on his French-Byzantine origin, which in his opinion implied an 'Orphic' destiny: 'Hail, Thrace: mother to me and mother to Orpheus! / Hail, Galata that my eyes long have desired! / For a Greek young lady there, a beauty in her / Spring, in the bed of a French-born husband / Gave birth to me, a Frenchman in Byzantium's breast.'[10] This personal, legendary heritage helped Chénier become one of the leading poetic authors who tried to revive French poetry by drawing on the springs of Greek literature. His work remained unfinished: Chénier was a victim of the French Revolution and died on the scaffold on 25 July 1794. While being led to the guillotine, it is said that he turned down the corner of a page of the Sophocles text he was reading and put it in his pocket, as if he planned to read it again. Apocryphal or not, this anecdote shows Chénier's attachment to the Hellenic models he demonstrated throughout his life. In fact, his French work draws tirelessly on Greek sources (epic, tragedy, lyric), whether in personal elegies, philosophical poems, or political productions connected with the revolutionary context. An inspirer of French Romanticism, he was one of the three tutelary figures in Alfred de Musset's *Stello* (1832), and his poetic production acquired, little by little, the posthumous fame it deserved.

Bibliography: Dimoff, Paul (1936), *La Vie et l'œuvre d'André Chénier jusqu'à la Révolution française*, Paris (repr. Geneva 1970); Id. (1947), "Winckelmann et André Chénier", in: *Revue de littérature comparée* 83, 321–333; Egger, Émile (1869), *L'Hellénisme en France: Leçons sur l'influence des études grecques dans le développement de la langue et de la littérature françaises*, Paris, 331–94; Quillen, Elisabeth (1982), *L'Angleterre et l'Amérique dans la vie et la poésie d'André Chénier*, Bern/Frankfurt; Chénier, André (2005; 2010), *Œuvres poétiques*, eds. Georges Buisson/Édouard

---

10 Chénier, André (1889), *Œuvres poétiques*, vol. 1, ed. Louis Moland, Paris, 308–9: '[...] Salut, Thrace ma mère et la mère d'Orphée, / Galata, que mes yeux désiraient dès longtemps; / Car c'est là qu'une Grecque, en son jeune printemps, / Belle, au lit d'un époux nourrisson de la France, / Me fit naître Français dans les murs de Byzance. [...]'.

Guitton, Orléans. On the Greek poem: Becq de Fouquières, Louis (1879), *Œuvres poétiques de André Chénier, précédées d'une étude sur André Chénier par Sainte-Beuve*, Paris, vol. 2, 354.

Léon Vernier (1855–1926)

Εἰς Ἐρρῖκον Οὐείλλιον [1898]

(excerptum, vv. 23-38, 75-78, 91-98)

  Καί σε θεὸς δέδαέν ποτε βάρβαρος, ἡνίκ' ἔλαμψας
   δαιδαλέην λέξεων σύνθεσιν ἐξετάσας,
25 ῥωμαϊκῆς δ' αὐδῆς διελὼν φώνημα, λατίνων
   οὐνομάτων ψυχὰς ἤλασας ἐξ Ἀίδεω.
  Τοὔνεκά μ' οἶστρος ἄγεν, πάντες δέ τε πειθόμεθ' οἴστρῳ,
   ἐκ σέθεν, ὀτρύνων Ἑλλάδος ἐξιέναι.
  Καί σοι ἀπαιτηθεὶς τίνειν ἐπιεικέ' ἄποινα,
30 τεύχεσί μ' ἐκτοπίοις ἦλθον ὁπλισσάμενος·
   ῥωμαϊκὰς κνημῖδας ἔχων καὶ γαλλικὸν ἔγχος
   χερσὶν ἑλών, τιμὴν βαρβαρικὴν ἔφερον·
  δαίμων δ' αὖ μ' ἐκέλευσε, τὸ δὴ πρέπον, ἔνδοθι νεύσας
   ἐκστάνθ' Ἑσπερίης Ἑλλάδα γαῖαν ἔχειν.
35 Τίς δὲ τραφεὶς ὑπὸ σεῖο, λέγοι ποτ' ἂν Ἑλλάδι χαίρειν
   οὐκ ἀσεβῶν; Πολλοὶ ῥήματά γ' ἀμβρόσια
  ἠδὲ θεοπλάστων ἐπέων ἄσβεστον ἀοιδὴν
   οὔασι δεξάμενοι κἀγκατέθεντο φρεσίν.
  [...]
75 Μνήσασθαι δ' ἡμῶν κέλομαί σε μάλ', οἵπερ ἔχοντες
   Σηκοανῶν γαῖαν, μητρόπολίν τε μικρήν,
  ὡς σὺ πάλαι, φιλοχωρέομεν, μὴ δῆτα γένηται
   μικροτέρη· καί σοι πολλὰ χαριζόμεθα,
  [...]
91 Ἀνδρὶ γὰρ εὐμούσῳ τόγε δὴ λῷστον καὶ ἄριστον,
   θνητοῖς τ' οὐ παύροις τ' Ἀθανάτοισι φίλῳ,
  πυκνὰ πολυστέφανον καταβήμεναι ἐς Πρυτανεῖον
   ἀστείου ποταμοῦ κείμενον ἀμφὶ ῥοάς,
95 ἔνθα περ εὔπυργόν τε πάλαι θεὸς ἔκτισε νηόν,
   καὶ τέγος ἵδρυσεν στρογγύλον ὑψιφαές,
  χἠ Σοφίη πολύμορφος ἄγει χορὸν ἀττικὸν ἀνδρῶν
   πᾶσί τ' ἀριστότοκον κἀκχέει ἠνορέην.

Textus: Mélanges Henri Weil. *Recueil de mémoires concernant l'histoire et la littérature grecques, dédié à Henri Weil...à l'occasion de son 80ᵉ anniversaire...*, Paris: A. Fontemoing, 1898, 445-448.

Sim.: 38 κἀγκατέθεντο φρεσίν] cf. Theoc. 17.14; Hom. *Od.* 11.614 (θυμῷ); Hes. *Op.* 27 (στέρνοις) || **77–78** cf. Plut. *Dem.* 2 || **78** cf. e.g. *Anth. Pal.* 12.280.4 πολλὰ χαριζόμενος || **96** ὑψιφαές] de adiectivo cf. *Anth. Pal.* 7.701.4

For Henri Weil

(excerpt, ll. 23–38, 75–78, 91–98)

> And one day a barbaric god taught you, when you brilliantly
>   investigated the cunning word-composition,
> [25] and by distinguishing the sound of Roman speech
>   you brought out of Hades the souls of Latin names.
> This is why a passion drove me (and we all obey passions)
>   urging me to leave you, to go out of Greece.
> And, at your request to pay a suitable ransom,
> [30] I came, armed with foreign books:
> wearing Roman greaves and with a Gallic spear
>   in my hand, I brought a barbaric ransom;
> but then a god, nodding inside, invited me to a fair duty:
>   to leave Hesperia and get back to the Greek soil.
> [35] Of your alumni, who could ever say goodbye to Greece
>   without impiety? So many people heard immortal words
> and the inextinguishable song of God-made expressions
>   and stored them in their hearts!
> [...]
> [75] Please, please, do not forget us, who inhabit
>   the land of the *Sequani* and a small mother-town.
> Like you once we love this place, so that it may not
>   get smaller: we are very thankful to you
> [...]
> This is the best thing for a man skilled in the most excellent arts,
>   dear to mortals as well as to several Immortals:
> to enter often the Prytaneum [= *scil.* Académie française] charged with many wreaths
>   lying by the flows of our city's river,
> [95] where long ago a god founded a well-towered temple,
>   and built a round dome seen from afar,
> and where the multiform Wisdom leads an Attic choir of men
>   pouring out to all your manhood that produces the best offspring.

Metre: Elegiac couplets.

Notes: The poem's dedicatee is Heinrich Weil (born in 1818 in Frankfurt am Main, died in Paris on 9 November 1909). Following his brilliant achievements studying classics at Heidelberg University, then in Berlin, under the direction of August

Boeckh, Weil became a French citizen in 1848 and lectured at the Faculty of Literature at Strasbourg University and, one year later, at the University of Besançon, finishing his career as a professor in Paris (*École Pratique des Hautes Études, École normale supérieure*), from 1876 until 1891. Most appreciated for his erudition, but also for his righteousness, kindness, and courtesy, this scholar was among the founders, in Paris, of the *Association pour l'encouragement des études grecques*. An outstanding expert in the Greek language and its literature, especially poetry and Greek history, he gave his students a strong impetus for these studies. His remarkable editions of Demosthenes, Aeschylus, and Euripides (*Sept tragédies*) show the quality of his scholarship as well as the pertinence of his annotations. Vernier's praise includes a short description of the *Académie française* (ll. 92–96), founded by 'a god' (Cardinal Mazarin), whose members are called 'Immortals' (l. 92): its building lies by the Seine in central Paris (l. 94), it can be considered a 'temple' (l. 95) and has a vaulted dome (l. 96 τέγος…στρογγύλον); there, Wisdom helps men to become *humaniores* (l. 98 ἠνορέην). The expression καί σοι πολλὰ χαριζόμεθα (l. 78) is possibly a misinterpretation of χαρίζομαι, which in the context is apparently meant as 'be thankful', whereas its usual meaning is 'gratify', 'be pleasant to' someone.

Biography: Léon Vernier was a classical scholar, trained at *École normale supérieure*, and a disciple of the important Hellenist Heinrich Weil, to whom he sent his season's greetings in ancient Greek every year. He lectured in classics at the University of Besançon. Not much is known about the life of this professor, described as 'one of the last ancient poets' (Dalmeyda 1927). Besides his PhD thesis, a treatise on Voltaire's French grammar (*Études sur Voltaire grammairien et sur la grammaire au XVIIIe siècle*, 1888), Vernier published commentaries on the *Odyssey* and a few studies on ancient metre and verse, his main scientific interest: *De Senariis Italicis* (1888), *Étude sur la versification populaire des Romains à l'époque classique* (1888, 1891), *Les Inscriptions métriques de l'Afrique romaine* (1891), and *Petit Traité de métrique grecque et latine* (1894), which was considered an original contribution, inspired by Vernier's rhythmic and musical sense of Greek poetry.

Bibliography: Dalmeyda, Georges (1927), "Allocution prononcée le 19 mai 1927", in: *Revue des études grecques* 40, LII–LXII [on Vernier, LVIII–LIX].

Fernand Chapouthier (1899–1953)

Ἡ ἐν Λουκοτοκίᾳ τῇ ἐν Ἀθήναις Ἀκαδημίᾳ χαίρειν [1946]

Σκάπτε καὶ σκέπτου

Χαῖρε, φίλη κάσι, χαῖρε· σὲ κἀμέ τε γείνατο μήτηρ
αὐτή, τοὺς αὐτοὺς δὲ καὶ υἷας ἐθρεψάμεθ' ἄμφω·
ἀλλ' ἐμὲ πρεσβυτέρην γε νεώτερα τέκνα πέλασσαν,
σοὶ δὲ νεωτέρῃ ἀμφὶ γεραίτεροι εἴαται υἷες
5 καὶ σοφοί · οἱ γὰρ ἐμοῦ νέοι οὔπω χερσὶ πίθοντο,
ἀλλ' ἔτ' ἐν ὄμμασιν οἷσι τὸν οὐρανὸν εὐρὺν ἔχουσι,
νήπιοι, οἳ μεμάασι πόλιν κτίσαι ἐν νεφέλαισιν·
σοὶ δὲ μελάγχειρες παῖδες καὶ καμπύλοι ὤμους,
χρυσὸν θηρῶντες καὶ ὁπόσσα κε γαῖα κεκεύθῃ,
10 σκάπτουσιν τὰ βάθη διά τ' ἄγκεα καὶ διὰ βήσσας,
σκεπτόμενοι δὲ πόλεις κτίσσαν νηούς τε δόμους τε.
Χαῖρε, κασιγνήτη χρυσοστέφαν', ἥ με διδάσκεις,
ὡς ὕπατος μακάρων, οὐκ Οὐρανός, ἀλλά τοι Αἶα.

Textus: *Bulletin de correspondance hellénique* 70, 1946, Supplément (Le Centenaire de l'École Française d'Athènes, Paris 1948), 211.

Crit.: 7 οἳ: οἵ ed. || **10** διά τ': διὰ τ' ed.

Sim.: tit. Λουκοτοκίᾳ] cf. Strab. 4.3.5.20 de Lutetia || **1** κάσι] cf. Soph. *OC* 1440 || **6** cf. Hom. *Il.* 20.299 al. (τοὶ οὐρανὸν εὐρὺν ἔχουσι) || **7** νήπιοι] cf. Hom. *Il.* 8.177; *Od.* 1.8 al. || **8** μελάγχειρες] hapax leg. ut vid. || **9** γαῖα κεκεύθῃ] cf. Hes. *Theog.* 505; Quint. Smyrn. 1.2 || **10** διά...βήσσας] cf. Hom. *Il.* 22.190

The Paris Academy greets the Academy of Athens

'Dig and study!'

Hail, dear sister, hail! One and the same mother gave birth to you and me,
and we also both raised the same offspring:
But, being the elder one, I was approached by younger children,
while you, the younger one, are surrounded by elder sons,
[5] and wise ones; for my own children, being too young, could not yet rely on their hands,
but they still have at sight in their eyes the wide sky,
silly boys, who strive to build a city on the clouds!
Your sons, with browned arms and bent shoulders
look for gold and all that the earth might hide:
[10] they dig at deep levels by hollows and by glens,

and, by their study, they have rebuilt cities, temples, and houses.
Hail, o gold-crowned sister: you teach me
that the Earth, not the Sky, is leader of the Blest.

Metre: Hexameters.

Notes: This poem celebrates the anniversary of the prestigious *École française d'Athènes*, founded in 1846 and subsequently the leader of some of the most important archaeological excavations in Greece, from Delos and Delphi to Argos. The *Witz* consists of a dialogue between the University of Paris (more devoted to speculation and theoretical studies) and the archaeological school at Athens, whose members are more devoted to working in the field.

Biography: A well-known Hellenist from Bordeaux, educated at the *École normale supérieure*, Fernand Chapouthier was a member of the *École française d'Athènes* and a professor at the Sorbonne. Working in both the archaeological and textual domains, he published an edition of a number of plays by Euripides, as well as essays on several subjects, including studies on ancient Greek religion and more popular, illustrated books about Greece. He also participated in excavations at Delos and particularly Mallia, on the island of Crete.

Bibliography: de Romilly, Jacqueline (1954), "Fernand Chapouthier", in: *Bulletin de l'Association Guillaume Budé* 3, 10–11; Demargne, Pierre (1956), "Fernand Chapouthier", in: *Revue Archéologique* s. 6, 47, 204–211; *L'École française d'Athènes*, special issue of the *Bulletin de Correspondance Hellénique* 120, 1996.

Vlado Rezar
Balkans

The rule of the Ottoman Sultan Mehmed II began with the conquest of Constantinople (1453), symbolically marking the end of the Eastern Roman Empire, which had lasted for more than a thousand years. The fall of Constantinople gave impetus to a new phase of Ottoman expansion into southeastern Europe: Mehmed himself subdued most of the area known as the Balkans today, while his grandson, Suleiman the Magnificent, completed the territorial extension of the Empire, terrifying the Christian West by advancing all the way to Vienna (1529). This major political turn also had profound cultural repercussions, including the exodus of the Greek intellectual elite from the mid-15th century onwards, just as Renaissance humanism was gathering momentum in Italy. This migration, together with the invention of the printing press, was instrumental in making the Muse of ancient Greek poetry sing again: first in Italy, and from the 16th century onwards in western and northern Europe as well. On the other hand, the Balkans, a peculiar meeting point of the Catholic ('Latin') West and the Orthodox ('Greek') East and now the site of Islamic political and cultural domination, remained for the most part out of touch with the intellectual trends of the European humanist *Res publica litterarum*. Humanist influence extended only as far as its westernmost, mostly Catholic, fringe areas that had not fallen under Ottoman rule. Even there, however, instances of poetry in classical Greek were few and far between. In the eastern, mostly Orthodox, parts of the Balkans, classical Greek scholarship, and poetry in particular, was to take root only at the end of the 17th century as a prelude to the Greek Enlightenment (for the Greek part of the Balkans, see → **Greece**).

The Catholic West

As a result of their political and cultural connection with the Italian peninsula, Adriatic city communes such as Istrian Koper (Justinopolis), Dalmatian Zadar (Zara), Šibenik (Sibenicum), Trogir (Tragurium), Split (Spalatum), Dubrovnik (Ragusa), and Kotor (Catharum) – all of them important strongholds lying along the trade route to the Levant and, except for Dubrovnik, for centuries under the rule of the Republic of Venice (*Stato da Mar*) – embraced the spirit of Renaissance humanism early on. Predominantly Italian humanists, who were often well versed in Greek (Palladio Fosco Negri of Padua, to name but one, was in charge of schools in Šibenik, Trogir, Zadar, and Koper), were active in these areas from the 15th century onwards, and their talented students went on to become not only accomplished Latin poets but also internationally recognised translators from Greek (e.g., Andreas Divus of Justinopolis, who published the complete works of Homer, Aristophanes, and Theocritus in Latin translation). Nevertheless, active Greek literacy on the eastern Adriatic coast took roots effectively only in Ragusa (Dubrovnik). The latter was a wealthy and independent trading city which in its collective memory still fondly remembered Byzantine rule from the early centuries of its existence. Good relations with Constantinople were continually confirmed by the prerogatives awarded to Ragusa until as late as 1451. Soon after, a large number of Greek refugees sought asylum in Ragusa on their way to Italy (including Ianos Laskaris, Demetrios Chalkokondyles, and Michael Tarchaniota Marullus). Given the fact that Senofonte Filelfo, the son of the prominent humanist and ancient Greek poet Francesco Filelfo, worked as chancellor of Ragusa for 10 years (1460–1470), and that the city administration preferred hiring teachers of both Latin and Greek (in 1490, for example, the city fathers were about to hire the famous Demetrios Chalkokondyles, though he eventually opted to teach in Milan instead), it is small wonder that as early as the late 15th century the Ragusan nobleman Ioannes Gozze was praised by his contemporaries for composing poetry in both ancient Greek and Latin. Gozze's poetry, which was commended by Angelo Poliziano as well, has unfortunately been lost. Hence the only preserved Ragusan humanist poetry in ancient Greek remains a small epigrammatic cycle by **Damianus Benessa** (1476–1539). Yet, his poetic endeavour had no significant influence on the Ragusan cultural milieu as these Greek verses, dispersed in the large corpus of Latin poetry, have until recently remained in manuscript form only. Unlike his fellow citizens – including Michael Coelius Gradi (a poet and translator of Xenophon's *Anabasis* and Demosthenes' orations), who was taught Greek by Chalkokondyles in Milan, and Nicolaus Petreus Corcyraeus (a Ragusan teacher, poet, and author of widely commended translations of Greek philosophical and medical texts), who acquired a command of Greek under the guidance of the Greek scholar Sergio Stiso in southern Italy – Benessa mastered the art of writing ancient Greek verse without attending any of the centres of European humanism. He was probably helped by the fact that, despite Ragusa's remoteness, newly printed Greek titles were reaching the city more easily than expected, as the Ragusan teacher Daniele Clario of Parma (to whom Aldo Manuzio dedicated his *Aristophanes* in 1498 and his *Demosthenes* in 1504) was at the same time Aldo's book-selling 'concessionaire' for Greece. By the mid-16th century ancient Greek had officially become part of the school curriculum, and in the second half of the 16th century Greek scholarship in Ragusa received a great boost by the Italian Benedictine and Ragusan archbishop Chrysostomus Calvini (1494–1575), a translator of Greek theological authors; by the Italian humanist poet Giovanni Battista Amalteo (1525–1573; see → **Italy**), a notary public in Ragusa (1557–1561); and by **Didacus Pyrrhus** (1517–1599). The latter was a persecuted Portuguese Jew who found refuge in Ragusa in the last few decades of his life and privately taught a large number of Ragusan citizens who would themselves go on to try their hand at translating classical Greek texts. Along with the above-mentioned humanists active in Ragusa, he laid a solid foundation for Greek literacy in Ragusa, to the point that this became an essential component of the cultural heritage of the city. This tradition would culminate two centuries later in the works of the internationally renowned names of Greek philology: the Ragusan Jesuit Raimondo Cunich (1719–1794), a Latin translator of the *Iliad* and the *Greek Anthology*; his student Bernardo Zamagna (1735–1820), a Latin translator of the *Odyssey* and the Greek bucolic poets; and **Nicolaus Androvich** (1798–1857), an occasional poet who in the first half of the 19th century tried his hand at ancient Greek poetry with great success and is remembered now as the last Hellenist of Ragusa.

When it comes to Greek humanism and especially poetry in ancient Greek in traditionally Catholic parts of the Balkans (often called the *Antemurale Christianitatis* in the West), the Ragusan 'Greek Muse' seems to stand out even more considering the fact that on the eastern Adriatic coast it has no equal. On the humanist foundations laid throughout the 15th century, and in spite of constant threat of war just outside the city walls, cultural life in the Adriatic city communes under Venetian rule continued, though Latin poetry predominated and hardly gave ancient Greek a chance. Beyond this narrow coastline stretch, inland areas turned into a de facto military border for centuries to come and had no opportunity to develop any learned literature until the Turkish threat was over. Many abandoned these areas in order to save themselves, including **Matthias Garbitius Illyricus** (1503–1559), who as a young man was forced to flee war-ravaged Istria at the beginning of the 16th century. Like his famous compatriot Matthias Flacius Illyricus, Garbitius was soon recognised of as a talented philologist by Protestant German scholars; under Luther's and Melanchthon's tutelage he became one of the best-known Hellenists and occasional Greek poets of his time. Instances of the reverse process – a foreigner versed in ancient Greek coming *ex officio* to Croatian lands and leaving his mark as a Greek poet there – were rare, the most interesting case being **Georgius Wyrffel** (1535–1585), a canon of Zagreb.

The keepers and providers of classical education on what was left of the free territory of Croatia (the so-called *reliquiae reliquiarum*) remained some local Franciscan and particularly Jesuit monasteries. However, although the Jesuit *ratio studiorum* encompassed instruction in both classical languages, Latin was to remain the exclusive language of learned literature in these areas over the next few centuries. All the more exotic, then, was the isolated epigrammatic poetry in ancient Greek by the Croat Franciscan **Raphael Levakovich** (1597–1650). Even this 'excursion into the unknown', however, is understandable given his philological involvement in attempts by the Roman Church to extend its influence in the Orthodox East in the 17th century.

To conclude, the survey of early modern poetry in ancient Greek in the western Balkans necessarily points to the rather anomalous nature of the phenomenon. It cannot be argued that the western parts of the Balkans were not familiar with ancient Greek scholarship during the rise and heyday of humanism. Owing to specific political circumstances in the first half of the 16th century, however, no tradition of Greek literary production, and particularly poetry in ancient Greek, ever emerged in the 'Latin' Balkans, with the single exception of Ragusa.

The Orthodox East

In the eastern part of the Balkans Greek literacy was best preserved in the Danubian principalities of Moldavia and Wallachia (then known as Hungaro-Wallachia). Although they were conquered by the Ottomans as early as the 15th century, these areas succeeded in gaining a certain level of autonomy – cultural as well as political – through their vassalage. In the second half of the 16th century, the Moldavian voivode Jacobus Heraclides, a Greek soldier and a humanist of Protestant faith, tried with little success to recreate the cultural atmosphere of Renaissance humanism by opening an academy in Cotnari (*Schola Latina*, 1562–1563), where ancient Greek was taught in addition to Latin. However, the flowering of classical Greek, in both prose and verse, only began with the so-called Wallachian Renaissance (during the rule of the native boyar Constantine Brâncoveanu) at the end of the 17th century, when the Princely Academy of Bucharest was founded. Almost simultaneously the Porte started to appoint members of the Phanariot families as rulers of the principalities, and they introduced Greek as an official language of the courts. Whether a symbolic proof of ascendancy and prestige for the emerging Phanariot elite, who tried to dissociate themselves, as some scholars have put it, from the local society, or merely a cultural consequence of the wider European intellectual movement of the time, this literary phenomenon was to last throughout the 18th century. Its beginnings (the era of the enlightened rule by the Mavrokordatos family until 1830), however, were also its apogee in terms of quality.

Intellectual activities in the Danubian principalities were also facilitated by the establishment of several Greek printing offices from 1690 onwards (Iasi in Moldavia, and Bucharest, Snagov and Târgovişte in Wallachia being the most important), led by the learned monk Anthim the Iberian, later bishop of Wallachia. In that time Greek printing offices did not exist anywhere else in the Ottoman Empire. With the rare exception of Plutarch's *Parallel Lives*, these printers published mostly doctrinal and liturgical texts in response to Catholic proselytising, for the most part in modern Greek. Still, forewords to these editions became a perfect stage for the most prominent intellectuals, predominantly of Greek origin, who had gathered around the Wallachian court, to present their learned occasional poetry, most of which merely praised the achievements of their royal patrons. In the first half of the 18th century, among the verses of eminent professors and editors such as Sebastos Kyminetes, Metrophanes Gregoras of Dodone and Ioannes Postelnikos, the poetry of **Ioannes Molyvdos Comnenos** (1657–1719), one of the most learned men in the Greek world at the time, stands out because of its large number of classically styled verses. The iambic poetry of **Georgios Chrysogonos of Trebizond** (†1739) is also worthy of mention. **Demetrios Georgoulis Notaras**, a doctor and classical philologist, managed to publish only two epigrams in ancient Greek, but their elegance reflects the intellectual atmosphere at the court of the Mavrokordatos family. This literary practice continued until the end of the 18th century, but it never measured up to the aesthetic achievements of ancient Greek poetry from the earlier period, which can be gauged from the iambic poetry of Parthenios Metaxopoulos and Nikolaos Belaras. In 1777, the latter, a professor at the Princely Academy, published a collection of as many as 45 commendatory poems in ancient Greek by various authors in honour of the Wallachian ruler and patron of literature, Alexander Ypsilanti, who had provided the Academy with its own printing office. According to Legrand, however, this collection, as a whole, is of little aesthetic value.

One of the authors represented in Belaras' collection is **Konstantinos Tzechanes** (1741–1800), a mathematician and professor of Greek at Leiden University. He was one of the most prolific 18th-century ancient Greek poets in the Balkans, and, unlike his compatriots, he published most of his poetry in various cities in western Europe. Tzechanes was a native of Moschopole, an Aromanian commercial metropolis with a Greek-speaking population. Today Moschopole is just a small village in Albania, but in the early 18th century it emerged as a leading centre of Greek intellectual activity in the Balkans. In 1744, the local Greek *frontistirion* was upgraded and renamed 'New Academy'; it was headed by Tzechanes' teacher, Theodoros Kavalliotes, an all-round scholar who promoted the philological disciplines in particular, including poetry. The short-lasting cultural and educational flourishing of the city was mainly due to the presence of the only working Greek printing office in a Balkan region under direct Ottoman rule. It was established around 1730 by Gregorios Konstantinos Moschopolites, an occasional classical Greek poet himself who was closely connected with the Academy and the metropolitan church of Ohrid. By the year 1769, when the city was destroyed by Albanian Muslims, the local press had issued at least 22 editions of mostly liturgical works. Some of the books were edited and supplied with ancient Greek epigrams by another notable professor at the Academy, **Michael Goras Hypischiotes** (c. 1700–1790).

Serbian territories were mostly rural and under strict Ottoman rule and thus lacked a sizable Greek intellectual elite, so Greek cultural influence was not felt there as in other parts of the eastern Balkans. However, in the first half of the 18th century Greek schools began open on Serbian soil as well: the first Greek *frontistirion* was founded in Belgrade in 1718, when the city became part of the Habsburg Empire after centuries of Ottoman rule. But when the city fell into Ottoman hands again in 1738, Greek literacy continued to be nurtured in schools across the Danube river in the Austrian-ruled region of Vojvodina, particularly in the cities of Novi Sad and Zemun. The latter, because of its strategic position, was accorded special privileges by the Austrian emperors, which aroused the interest of the Greek inhabitants of the Turkish-occupied areas, who consequently migrated to the town and created one of the most flourishing Greek colonies in the northwestern Balkans. **Jovan Mladenovich** (1721–1753) and **Demetrios Darvaris** (1757–1823), a native Serbian and a Greek of Aromanian descent, respectively, were the best-known alumni and promoters of Greek literacy in these areas, and they composed some occasional poetry in ancient Greek. Their verses were published in Vienna, another important printing centre of Greek literacy from the second half of the 18th century until the end of the *Tourkokratia* (→ **Austria**).

General Bibliography

Bouchard, Jacques (2016), "Refined Attic Greek: Hallmark of the Emerging Phanariot Nobility", in: *American Romanian Academy 40th Conference Proceedings*, 11–17.

Camariano-Cioran, Ariadna (1974), *Les Académies Princières de Bucarest et de Jassy et Leurs Professeurs*, Thessaloniki.

Crijević, Serafin Marija (1975–1980), *Dubrovačka biblioteka / Bibliotheca Ragusina*, ed. Stjepan Krasić, 3 vol., Zagreb.

Dobrescu, Caius/Matei, Sorin Adam (2011), "Latent Crusaders: Narrative Strategies of Survival in Early Modern Danubian Principalities, 1550–1750", in: *Journal of Global Initiatives: Policy, Pedagogy, Perspective* 6/2, 31–48.

Legrand, Émile (1885–1906), *Bibliographie hellénique ou Description raisonnée des ouvrages publiés en grec par des Grecs aux XVe et XVIe siècles*, I–IV, Paris.

Legrand, Émile (1894–1903), *Bibliographie hellénique ou Description raisonnée des ouvrages publiés en grec par des Grecs au XVIIe siècle*, I–V, Paris.

Legrand, Émile (1918–1928), *Bibliographie hellénique ou Description raisonnée des ouvrages publiés en grec par des Grecs au XVIIIe siècle*, I–II, Paris.

Papachristou, Panayotis Alexandrou (1992), *The Three Faces of the Phanariots: An Inquiry into the Role and Motivations of the Greek Nobility under Ottoman Rule (1683–1821)*, Vancouver.

Peyfuss, Max Demeter (1989), *Die Druckerei von Moschopolis, 1731 – 1769: Buchdruck und Heiligenverehrung im Erzbistum Achrida*, Wien/Köln.

Staikos, Konstantinos/Sklavenitis, Triantaphyllos E. (2001), *The Publishing Centres of the Greeks from the Renaissance to the Neohellenic Enlightenment*, Athens.

Supičić, Ivan (2008), *Croatia and Europe: Croatia in the Late Middle Ages and the Renaissance (A Cultural Survey)*, London/Zagreb.

Zaviras, Georgios I. (1872), *Νέα Ἑλλὰς ἢ Ἑλληνικὸν Θέατρον*, Ἀθῆναι.

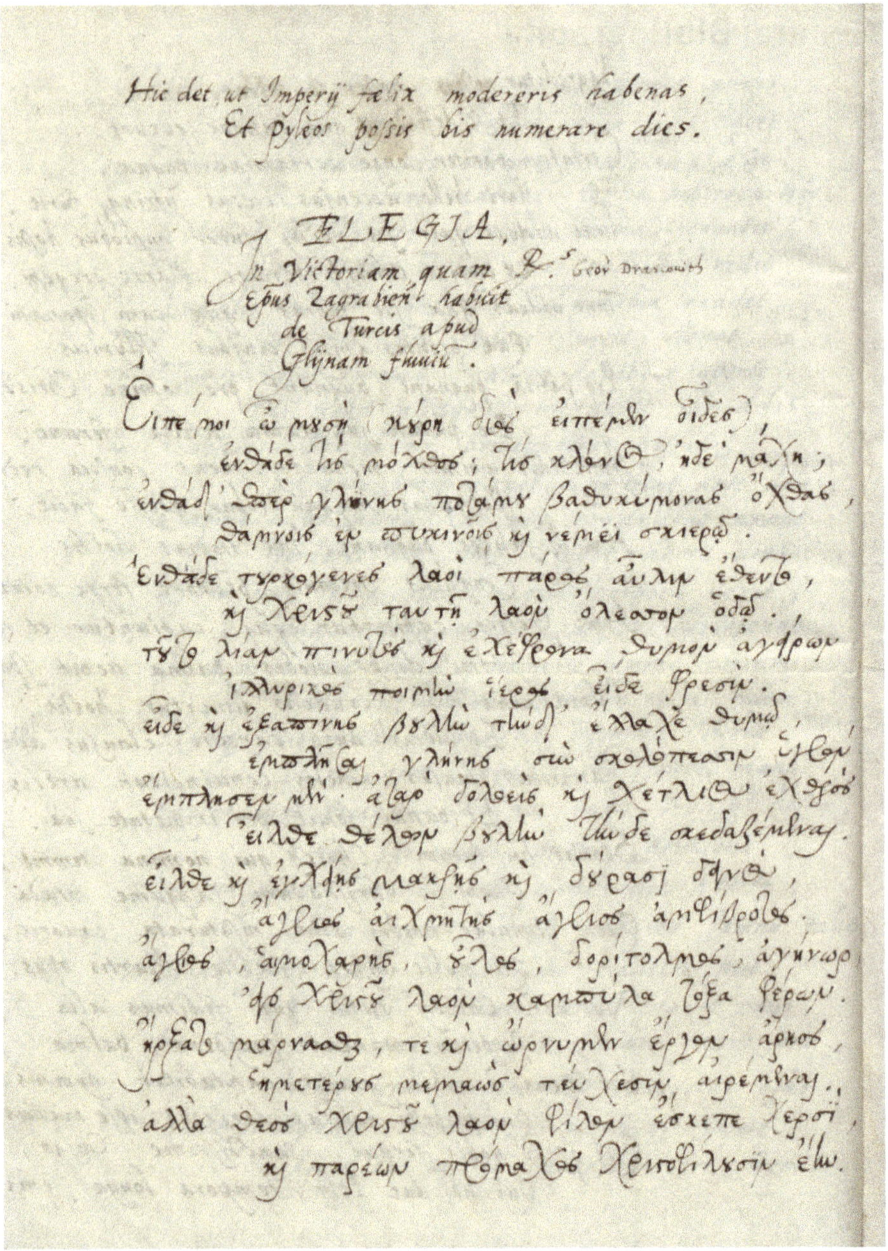
Hic det, ut Imperii felix modereris habenas,
Et Pyleos possis bis numerare dies.

ELEGIA.
In Victoriam quam R.^s Geor. Draschowitz
Epus Zagrabien. habuit
de Turcis apud
Glynam fluuiu.

Fig. 8: Budapest, National Széchényi Library, ms Fol. Lat. 3606.II, f. 31v: autograph of Georg Wyrffel's poem *In victoriam quam reverendissimus episcopus Zagrabiensis habuit de Turcis apud Glynam fluvium* (see below, p. 421–424).

Damianus Benessa (1476–1539)

I. <*De Terra et Caelo*> [c. 1530]

  Οὐρανοῦ ἀστερόεντος ἐγὼ γὰρ ἰσόχρονος εἰμί,
  Καίπερ τοῦδ' ἄλλως πολλὰ στεριζόμενος –
  Τοῦδε γὰρ ἦν ἀεὶ αὐγάζοντος ἀείδιον εἶδος,
  Πασσυδίῃ πολλοῖς ἄστρεσι λαμπόμενον,
5 Ἀλλὰ κάτω ζοφερὸς καὶ τοῦδ' ὑποκείμενος αὐτὴ
  Οὐρανόθεν πολλοῖς ὄμμασι βλεψάμενος –
  Ἀρσενικὴ δύναμις κεῖνος, τὸ δὲ θηλυκὸν αὐτή,
  Τίκτω καὶ μήτηρ ὥσπερ ἅπαντα τρέφω.

II. Περὶ Εἰράνας

  Ἔγγονος ἡ Διὸς Εἰράνα πόλιν ἣν δὲ κατεῖχε,
  Αὐτίκα μὲν πλοῦτος τῇδε πάρεστι μέγας.
  Καὶ γὰρ ἑαυτῆς οὐκ ἄλλην δοξάζετο σπουδῆς
  Ἠμή, ποῦ τέμενος δυσὶν ἔνεστι θεαῖς,
5 Εὐνομίη τε καλῇ καί σοι δ' ἅμα, πότνια Δίκα –
  Ἄμφω γὰρ μεγάλων ὄντε κλέος πτολίων –
  Ὑμῖν γοῦν, ἀγαθῶν ὅσσοι γλίχεσθε διδόντος,
  Μέλλοι τοῦ τεμένους κείμενα καλλὸν ἔχειν.

III. Κονσταντίνῳ

  Ἄλγεα καὶ νοῦσοι, πάντως κακὰ μύρια δ' ἄλλα,
  Οἷς ἡμῶν ἔνοχος ἄθλιός ἐστι βίος·
  Πᾶν μὲν τῆς ἀρετῆς ἀγαθὸν λυμαίνεται αἰέν,
  Ἠδ' ἀλαὸς κρατέει οὐλόμενός τε τύχῃ.
5 Τούτων οὖν μετέχοντα ἰδὼν νῦν ἄχνυμαι αὔτως,
  Πένθος γὰρ τόδε τοι, πένθεος οὐδὲν ἄκος,
  Δειλὸς καὶ δοκέω μοι οὐτιδανός τε γενέσθαι,
  Αὐτίκα μὴ παρέχειν οὐ δυνατὸς μάκαρα.

Textus: Dubrovnik, Archivum Monasterii Ragusini Fratrum Minorum, ms. 78, fol. 41v.

Crit.: plurimos spiritus et accentus, in autographo passim male positos, hic juxta normam orthographicam hodiernam vocibus apposui
I.2 στεριζόμενος] ita, forsan forma secundaria verbi στερέω (pro στερούμενος) || **4** ἄστρεσι] ita
II.4 Ἠμή] ita, forsan metri causa pro Ἐμή, aut pro Ἡμή (videlicet Ἡ ἐμή) || **8** Μέλλοι] ita, metri causa pro μέλοι | καλλὸν] ita, forsitan pro καλῶς

III. Tit. Κονσταντίνῳ] ita || **8 μὴ**] ita, metri causa pro με

Sim.: I.1–8 cf. Hes. *Theog.* 104–127 || **6** cf. *Anth. Pal.* 7.669.2
II.1–8 cf. Pind. *Ol.* 13.6–7
III.1–8 cf. Greg. Naz. *Carm.*, PG 37.1016.5–9 et 37.755.7–8 || **1** κακὰ...ἄλλα] cf. Hes. *Op.* 100

<On Heaven and Earth>

The starry Heaven and I, Earth, are peers in age,
  although I am made different in many ways:
with unchanging face, lo, the Heaven ever shines,
  while myriad stars strive to give it their brightest light;
[5] I, however, lie down in the darkness, exposed to the Heaven,
  being watched by its myriad eyes.
While Heaven reveals his masculine nature, mine is feminine:
  I give birth and like a mother nurture all.

On *Eirene* [Peace]

Whatever city Eirene, Zeus' daughter, bestows her patronage upon,
  it immediately becomes a place of prosperity.
This very goddess is esteemed to be worthy of worship
  by my city, where two more goddesses have their temples:
[5] fair *Eunomia* [Good order] and you, honourable *Dike* [Justice],
  for both of you are a source of pride for large cities.
Therefore, all of you seeking a benefactor,
  take good care of her temple!

To Constantine

Misery and disease, and a thousand other misfortunes
  there are which enthral our miserable life:
All good virtue is always ruined
  while the world is governed by blind and baneful Chance.
[5] My heart aches to see that my fate is no different,
  being miserable, and with no means of alleviation:
I deem myself a worthless weakling
  being unable to instantly procure merriness.

Metre: Elegiac couplets, with a number of orthographic and morphological adaptations due to the prosodic requirements of the metre, resulting in lesser comprehensibility of the text, a number of prosodic problems (I.3 ἀεί should have long α, etc.) and weak metre.

Notes: Apart from his voluminous Christian epic *De morte Christi*, Benessa wrote smaller-scale poetry as well (more than 8,000 Latin verses in epigrams, eclogues, lyric poetry, and satires). His humanistic proclivity is emphasised by his Latin renditions of seven Greek epigrams from the *Planudean Anthology* and especially by nine epigrams of his own – a total of 30 elegiac couplets – composed in ancient Greek. It seems that Benessa's Greek cycle was to some extent a reaction to Laskaris' edition of the *Anthologia Graeca* (1494) and Poliziano's *Liber epigrammatum Graecorum* (1498). Benessa's first Greek epigram was certainly composed before 1515 and represents the poet's farewell to love poetry. In the remainder of the cycle one can find epitaphs, religious poems, and echoes of motifs taken from classical and postclassical Greek authors. The first of the three epigrams featured here explains the relationship between Earth and Heaven, reinterpreting the verses from Hesiod's *Theogony*; the second is an interpretation of Pindar *Ol.* 13.6–7 and discusses the importance of peace for the welfare of the people; and the last, echoing verses of Gregory of Nazianzus, pessimistically laments the poet's whimsical fate. Although the notable 19th-century Vatican librarian Girolamo Amati considered Benessa's Greek epigrams mostly incomprehensible and of no value in terms of content, aesthetics, and grammar, they have remained an *unicum* among the surviving works of Dalmatian humanist poets and are therefore of particular cultural value.

Biography: Damianus Benessa (Republic of Ragusa/Dubrovnik, c. 1476–1539) was a nobleman and humanist. His only formal instruction in Latin and Greek was provided by the notable Italian teacher Daniele Clario at Ragusa's Gymnasium. Benessa was not a professional humanist but a *dilettante*, yet he is remarkable in that he surpassed his more acclaimed Dalmatian contemporaries (Aelius Cervinus, Jacobus Bonus, and Marcus Marulus) in the variety of his humanistic commitment. The only work published during his lifetime was his *octavo* edition of the longest Roman epic, *Opus de secundo bello Punico* by Silius Italicus (Lyon 1514). All of his own literary oeuvre, in spite of his intention to publish it, remained buried in two autograph manuscripts until recently.

Bibliography: Rezar, Vlado (ed.) (2017), *Damianus Benessa, Poemata*, Split, 7–38; Rezar, Vlado (2018), "The Greek Verses of Damianus Benessa", in: Janika Päll/Ivo Volt (eds.), *Hellenostephanos. Humanist Greek in Early Modern Europe: Learned Communities Between Antiquity and Contemporary Culture*, Tartu, 391–413.

Didacus Pyrrhus (1517–1599)

I. *Didaci Pyrrhi in Erasmum* [1537]

Ἀθάνατος σοφίαν, ζωὴν δὲ θνητὸς Ἔρασμος
Ὧδ' ἐν τοῖς κόλποις κρύπτεται Ἑλβετίας.
Γαῖα μὲν οἰμώζει, μακρὸς συγχαίρει Ὄλυμπος,
Αὐτὴ ὅτι στέρεται, αὐτὸς ὅτι μετέχει.

II. *Aliud eiusdem*

Ἐνθάδε κεῖται ἀνὴρ θεῖος τρισέραστος Ἔρασμος,
Ψυχὰ δὲ τῶν μακάρων οἶκον Ὄλυμπον ἔχει.

III. *Aliud eiusdem*

Quod bonus atque pius fueris, quod doctus, Erasme,
    Τοῦτό γε τοῖς ἀγαθοῖς πᾶσι διὰ στόματος.
Quod non ipse tuos mores culpaverit unquam
    Ζώϊλος, οὐκ αὐτὸς Μῶμος, Ἔρασμε, neget.
5 Quod divorum auges numerum novus incola coeli,
    Δείκνυται ἡ ἀρετὴ τοῦτο τεός τε βίος.
Quod proferre parem valeant tibi secula nostra,
    Μὴ νέμεσις ῥητοῖς, τοῦτο μὲν ἀδύνατον.

Textus: *D. Erasmi Roterodami epitaphia, per eruditissimos aliquot viros Academiae Lovaniensis aedita*, Lovanii: ex officina Rutgeri Rescii, 1537, ff. 3–4.

Crit.: I.4 στέρεται Petrač: στἄρται ed. 1537 || III.4 Ζωΐλος debuit

Sim.: II.2 cf. *Anth. Pal.* 7.60.2
III.2 πᾶσι διὰ στόματος] cf. Theoc. *Id.* 12.21; *Anth. Pal.* 8.126.2

Didacus Pyrrhus on Erasmus

Immortal for his wisdom, though mortal in his life, Erasmus
  lies hidden here in the bosom of Helvetian earth.
Earth is mourning, whereas high Olympus rejoices:
  the one for losing him, the other for having received him.

Another one by the same author

Here rests a divine man, triply loved Erasmus:
  His soul resides on Olympus, the home of the blessed.

Another one by the same author

That you were kind and pious, and a learned man, Erasmus,
  this is what fair people never cease to talk about.
That your habits have never been criticised by Zoilus,
  this is, Erasmus, what Momus [the critic God] himself would confirm.
[5] That as a new inhabitant of Heaven you increase the number of gods,
  this is demonstrated by your virtue and your life.
That our age might yield your equal –
  may what I say not appear unjust – this is impossible.

Metre: Elegiac couplets, with some glaring prosodical mistakes, such as ψυχά with a short α in II.2.

Notes: Pyrrhus wrote the poems featured here as a teenager, during his stay in Leuven (for the Leuven context, see the **Low Countries** section), on the occasion of the death of Erasmus (at Basel in 1536). Although his literary endeavours in ancient Greek resulted in these three short epigrams only, Pyrrhus must have contributed significantly to the spread of Greek scholarship in Ragusa/Dubrovnik, as some of his pupils and colleagues (Dominicus Zlatarich, Matthaeus Benessa, Michael Monaldi, Nicolaus Gozze, and Antonius Medus) later distinguished themselves as translators of classical Greek authors and commentators of Aristotle of international renown.

Biography: Didacus Pyrrhus Lusitanus (Jacobus Flavius Eborensis; Évora, Portugal 1517 – Ragusa/Dubrovnik 1599) was born as Isaia Coen into a Jewish family. At the University of Salamanca he was taught Latin and Greek by the famous Hernán Núñez, *el Comendador Griego* (for the Iberian context, see → **Iberia**), and in

1536 he graduated at the University of Leuven. Afterwards he went to Italy and lived in Ferrara and Rome, having become acquainted with many prominent Italian humanists of the time, such as Lilio Giraldi and Paolo Giovio. In 1555 he moved to Constantinople and in 1558, after twenty years of wandering, settled in the Republic of Ragusa, where he remained for the rest of his life (†1599). It has been generally thought that Didacus was active as a professor at Dubrovnik Public School, because ancient Greek had officially become part of the school curriculum by the time of his arrival; however, no archival evidence supports this assumption. Nevertheless, his Latin poems, especially his major work *Cato Minor sive Disticha moralia* (Venice 1592), dedicated to the schoolteachers from Lisbon, suggest that he shared his profound classical knowledge with the community as a private tutor to the most important Ragusan intellectual figures of the time.

Bibliography: Tucker, George Hugo (2003), *Homo Viator: Itineraries of Exile, Displacement and Writings in Renaissance Europe*, Geneve, 195–238; Petrač, Petra (2014), "Didacus Pyrrhus and Erasmus", in: *Classical heritage from the epigraphic to the digital: Academia Ragusina 2009 and 2011*, Zagreb, 209–219.

Matthias Garbitius Illyricus (1503–1559)

I. Πρὸς τοὺς ἐντυχόντας τῶν νέων τούτῳ τῷ βιβλίῳ Ματθίου Ἰλλυριοῦ [1538]

Δεῦρο, νεογνὲ πάϊς, τόδε δὴ πολυειδὲς ἄθυρμα
    Ἀμφιέπων χρηστῶς νοῦν ἐπίθελγε σέθεν.
Ἔνθα ἀριφραδέως δήεις πεπυκασμένα πάντα
    Ἐσθλοῖς ἠδὲ καλοῖς σύν τε καὶ εὐμαρέσι·
5   Ἔνθα φρονεῖν σε καλῶς τε καὶ ἤθεα κεδνὰ διδάξει
    Ῥάβδου ἄτερ τ' ἐνιπῆς, πλάσμα μάλ' αἱμύλιον.
Τοὔνεκ' ἄρ' εὖ εἰδὼς τά γε μὲν κεχαρηότι θυμῷ
    Παίγνια σῇσι λίην ἄρμενα φρεσσὶν ἔλε.

Textus: Camerarius, Joachimus (1538), *Aesopi Phrygis fabularum celeberrimi autoris vita...*, Tübingen: apud U. Morhard, f. 1v.

Crit.: 8 φρεσσὶν] ita, metri causa

Sim.: 4 Ἐσθλοῖς ἠδὲ καλοῖς] cf. Hom. *Od.* 6.189 || 5 ἤθεα κεδνὰ διδάξει] cf. Hes. *Op.* 699 || 7 κεχαρηότι θυμῷ] cf. Orph. *Hymn.* 1.10; 31.7; 51.17

To the younger readers of this book by Matthias Illyricus

Young lad, don't be afraid to take this motley toy
  into your hands; let it be a useful balm for your soul.
You will find there all clearly said, with a plethora of examples,
  decent, fair, and simple to boot:
[5] You will be taught how to reason and be chaste,
  without a cane or rebuke, by these very wise stories.
Therefore, study them closely and happily
  embrace these playful thoughts, particularly well-suited to your mind.

II. Ὑμέναιος αὐτοσχεδιασθεὶς παρὰ Ματθίου Ἰλλυρικοῦ τοῦ Γαρβικίου πρὸς τὴν τῆς Τυβίγγης Ἀκαδημίαν περὶ γάμου ἄρχοντος ἡμῶν λαμπροτάτου τοῦ Χριστοφόρου ἐν τῇ Βιρτεβέργῃ [1544]

(excerptum, vv. 1–28)

Χαίρετε, Νικαρίδες Μοῦσαι, κεχάροιο, Τύβιγγα,
  Νῦν πρέπον ἀγλαΐαν πᾶσαν ἀειρόμεναι.
Ἠνίδε ἡμέτερος, δηρὸν πεποθημένος, ἄρχων
  Ἄμμιν ἵκει νύμφην οὗ ἐρίηρον ἄγων.
5 Φεῦ τῆς εὐτυχίης, ὅσσον γ' ἀριδείκετοι ἄμφω
  Πᾶσιν ὁμοῦ θεόθεν τοῖσι καλοῖσι βίου·
Ἓν γένος, ἐν δὲ φυή, ἐν καὶ θεοείκελον εἶδος,
  Σύν τε κράτει ὄλβον ἄφθονά τ' ἄλλα πάρα,
Πρὸς δ' ἔτι θαυμασίως τῶν δ' ἐκπρέπει ἀγλαὸν ἦθος
10   Ἔκ τε σαοφροσύνη πευκαλίμοιο νόου.
Τίς δ' ἄρα σφωὲ βροτῶν μάλα περ πεφραδμένος ἀμῶν
  Εὖ κατὰ κόσμον ἄδοι ἀξιάγαστον ἅλις;
Κυδάλιμόν κε ἔοι τόδε θείου ἔργον Ὁμήρου
  Ἠέ γε Θηβαίῳ ἄρμενον ὑψαγόρᾳ.
15 Αὐτὰρ ἰαινομένως αὐτοῖς εὐδαίμονα παστὸν
  Εὔξασθαι χ' ἡμᾶς εὐφρονέοντας ἔνι,
Ἠδὲ βίον χρόνιον καὶ ὁμοφροσύνην ἐρατεινήν,
  Σύν τ' ἄλλοις ἀγαθοῖς παῖδας ἀγηνορίδας·
Τοῦτο καλὸν καὶ ἐνὸν τὸ δὲ καὶ μάλα ἔσσετ' ἀγαστὸν
20   Δέξασθαι φιλικῶς πὰρ φρονέουσι φίλα.
Οὐδέ κεν ἐκ πολλῶν εἴ τις κατὰ μοῖραν ἐπέλθοι
  Παυρά τιν' εὖ κλείων, τοῦτ' ἀνέραστον ἔσῃ·
Τῷ δ' ἄρα, Νικαρίδες Μοῦσαι, ἀρίδηλον ἱεῖσαι
  Κὰδ δύναμιν φωνήν, καλὸν ἀείδετ' ἔπος
25 Καί ῥ' ὑμέναιον ὁμοῦ συναγαλλόμεναι πραπίδεσσι,
  Ἂμ πόλιν ἐμμαπέως παντόθι γηρύετε,

Ὦδε μάλ' ἐνδυκέως σύμπαντα μὲν εὐχετόωσαι,
Ὡς ἐπέοικε, καλοῖς ἡγεμόνεσσιν, ἔα.

Textus: *De nuptiis illustrissimi principis ac domini, domini Christophori Wirtembergensis et Deccensis ducis, comitis Montis Peligardi etc*, Tübingen 1544, ff. B7–B9.

Crit.: 7 δὲ: δ' ed. || 11 ἀμῶν: ἀμῶν ed. || 22 ἔσῃ ed., ultima vocis pars quasi prorsus atramento deformata: ἔοι exspectaveris || 24 Κὰδ: Καδ' ed. || 26 Ἄμ: Ἄν ed.

Sim.: 11 Τίς...βροτῶν] cf. Hom. *Il.* 1.8 || 17 ὁμοφροσύνην ἐρατεινήν] cf. Greg. Naz. *Carm. mor.*, PG 37.553.4 || 24 Κὰδ δύναμιν] cf. Hes. *Op.* 336 || 27 Ὦδε...ἐνδυκέως] cf. Hes. [*Sc.*] 427

An *hymenaeus* celebrating the wedding of our illustrious Duke Christopher of Württemberg, written *ex tempore* by Matthias Garbitius Illyricus to the University of Tübingen

(excerpt, ll. 1–28)

Make merry, Muses of Neckar; be joyful, Tübingen,
   for time is ripe for celebrations.
Lo, our champion, for whom we've longed so much,
   is coming with his lovely wife-to-be.
[5] Ah, what bliss! How excellent they both are,
   in all God-given things for life:
A noble birth, beauty, and godlike appearance,
   add to that, among other things, authority and immense fortune,
a wondrously impeccable character of theirs to boot,
[10]   alongside prudence of their brilliant mind.
Who of us mortals would, even if brave enough,
   be capable of singing their praises to the world in an adequate and admirable manner?
It would have to be the illustrious work of divine Homer
   or a poem composed by the Theban [Pindar] who employed an elevated style.
[15] However, to heartily wish them a blessed marital bed,
   we too, being good-willed to them, are free to do,
as well as to wish them a long life and harmony in love,
   and, among other benefits, a heroic progeny:
And it will be nice and decorous, admirable indeed,
[20]   if they receive this as a gift from friends, in a friendly manner.
So if by chance someone out of the multitude appeared
   who would fain say a few words of praise, that wouldn't be amiss:
Join him, Muses of Neckar, with a clear voice
   at the top of your lungs sing a beautiful song,
[25] and, celebrating together in your hearts this wedding song,
   spread it quickly around the city,

and pray devoutly that every kind of wellness,
as it is only fit, befall them, the good rulers, oho!

III. M. Garbitius Illyricus in obitum D. Martini Lutheri [1546]

Ὃν δέμας ἐξαπόλεσσε, ψυχὴν πάμπαν γ' ἀδυνά<μει>
Καὶ μάλα περ στυγερὸς παντοδάμας τε μόρ<ος>,
Οὔτε θεοπνεύστως διδαχὴν κραδίηθε χυθεῖσαν
Πάντοθι χριστοφίλοις αἶσα δύναιτο σβέσαι·
5   Αὐτὰρ ἐς οὐράνιόν γε ψυχὴ κενεῶνα μολοῦσα
Αὐτόθι σὺν Χριστῷ ζήσεται ἀθανάτως,
Ἠδὲ πολυσπερέας διδαχὴ διαβᾶσα πρὸς ἄνδρα<ς>
Ὧδε μάλ' ἄσβεστος πιστιδότειρα μενεῖ.
Τῇδ' ἄρα διπλασίως ζώεις, Μαρτῖνε θεουδής,
10   Ἄμβροτος ὡς ἐτεῶς ἔνθα καὶ ἔνθα βίῳ.
Ζήσεται ἀσκελέως καὶ ἐξηγήματα ταῦτα
Μάντιος ἀρχηγοῦ πάντη ἀριφραδέα·
Τόφρα γε χριστοπόλος σπουδάσσεται οὗτος ἀοιδ<ός>
Καὶ τάδ' ἀεὶ ἔσται ἀξιάγαστά σεο.

Textus: *In Esaiam scholia ex d. Martini Lutheri praelectionibus collecta*, Tübingen: apud U. Morhard, 1546, 2.

Crit.: 1 ἀδυνά<μει>] lacunam supplevi || 2 Ἠδὲ: Ἡδὲ ed. | μόρ<ος>] lacunam supplevi || 7 ἄνδρα<ς>] lacunam supplevi || 13 ἀοιδ<ός>] lacunam supplevi

Sim.: 2 στυγερὸς...μόρος] cf. Greg. Naz. *Carm.*, PG 37.1015.4 | παντοδάμας] hapax legomenon || 3 κραδίηθε] hapax legomenon || 5 οὐράνιον κενεῶνα] cf. *Anth. Pal.* 9.207.2; Nonn. *Dion.* 1.232 || 7 πολυσπερέας...ἄνδρας] cf. *Orac. Sib.* 11.1; Nonn. *Par. Jo.* 8.75 || 8 πιστιδότειρα] hapax legomenon || 13 χριστοπόλος] hapax legomenon

Matthias Garbitius Illyricus on the death of Martin Luther

Death took his body, yet could not take his soul,
    even though it fells everything when it's on the march:
God-inspired teachings that flowed from his heart
    to all who love Christ could not be destroyed by Death.
[5] His soul has repaired to the vast heaven
    to live there forever in the company of Christ,
while his teachings, having passed to dispersed peoples,
    are here to stay as the indestructible apostles of faith.
Thus, divine Martin, you live twofold,
[10] as it is only fit, verily immortal here and there.
Forever will also live these interpretations

> of the first of the prophets, clearly outlined in every sense:
> As long as this prophet, the herald of Christ, is studied,
> so long will these interpretations give glory to you.

Metre: Elegiac couplets, with several prosodic mistakes, like the short ι in ἵκει (II, 4) and the long α in ἀδυνά<μει> (III, 1).

Notes: Apart from lecturing on Greek and Latin authors, Garbitius edited and profusely commented translations of Aeschylus' *Prometheus* and Hesiod's *Erga* (Basel 1559), Aristeas' letter *De legis Divinae ex Hebraica lingua in Graecam translatione* (Basel 1561) and Dionysius of Halicarnassus' *De Thucydidis historia* (Basel 1579). He also composed and published poetry in both Greek and Latin. Of the ca. 500 Greek verses he composed, 82 elegiac couplets belong to an *epithalamium* celebrating the wedding of Melanchthon's daughter Anna to Georg Sabinus in 1536, and additional 60 couplets to the wedding poem for Duke Christoph of Württemberg in 1544, presented here partially (no. II). The remainder of the verses belong to shorter dedicatory epigrams and several *epitaphia*. All the extant Greek poems were published during his lifetime.

Biography: Matthias Garbitius Illyricus (Ματθίας Γαρβύκιος/Γαρβύτιος Ἰλλυρικός/Ἰλλυριός; Istria ca. 1505 – Tübingen 1559) was a classical scholar, teacher, and poet. Nothing is known about his childhood in his native land, nor did he ever speak of his roots, but he never gave up using his ethnonym along with his name. He came to Germany in 1520 and enrolled as a *pauper* in the St Egidien Monastery School in Nuremberg. In 1526 he continued his studies at the newly founded Gymnasium in the same city under the direction of Joachim Camerarius (→ **Germany**). In 1533 Garbitius went to Heidelberg, where he studied under the notable Hellenist Jacobus Micyllus. In 1534 he moved to Wittenberg and was enrolled at the University, where he met Martin Luther and became a student of the *Praeceptor Germaniae*, Philipp Melanchthon. The latter helped him to obtain a position as teacher of Greek literature at Wittenberg University. In 1537 he moved to Tübingen, where he took up a post of professor. In 1541 he inherited the chair of Greek from his former teacher, Camerarius, and kept it until the end of his life in 1559. In 1540 Garbitius hosted and helped his compatriot, the famous Protestant theologian and philosopher Matthias Flacius Illyricus (Labin, Istria 1520 – Frankfurt am Main 1575), to become Melanchthon's student as well. Garbitius himself never became a fervent Lutheran like Flacius.

Bibliography: Körbler, Đuro (1901), "Humanista Matija Grbić (Mathias Garbitius Illyricus)", in: *Rad JAZU* 145, 30–104; Ilić, Luka (2011), "Praeceptor humanissimus et duo Illyrii", in: Irene

Dingel/Armin Kohnle (eds.), *Philipp Melanchthon. Lehrer Deutschlands, Reformator Europas*, Leipzig, 65–79.

Georgius Wyrffel (1535–1585)

Elegia in victoriam quam reverendissimus episcopus Zagrabiensis habuit de Turcis apud Glynam fluvium [1573]

    Εἰπέ μοι, ὦ Μούση – κούρη Διός, εἰπέμεν οἶδες –
       Ἐνθάδε τίς μόχθος, τίς κλόνος ἠδὲ μάχη;
    Ἐνθάδ' ὑπὲρ Γλήνης ποταμοῦ βαθυκύμονας ὄχθας
       Θάμνοις ἐν πυκινοῖς καὶ νέμεϊ σκιερῷ,
5   Ἐνθάδε Τουρκόγενες λαοὶ πάρος αὖλιν ἔθεντο,
       Καὶ Χριστοῦ ταύτῃ λαὸν ὄλεσσον ὁδῷ.
    Τοῦτο λίαν πινυτὸς καὶ ἐχέφρονα θυμὸν ἀγείρων
       Ἰλλυρικὸς ποιμὴν ἱερὸς εἶδε φρεσίν,
    Εἶδε καὶ ἐξαπίνης βουλὴν τήνδ' ἔλλαχε θυμῷ
10   Ἐμπλῆσαι Γλήνης σὺν σκολόπεσσιν ὑγρόν.
    Ἔμπλησεν μέν· ἀτὰρ δολόεις καὶ σχέτλιος ἐχθρὸς
       Εἶλθε θέλων βουλὴν τήνδε σκεδαζέμεναι,
    Εἶλθε καὶ ἐγχείης μακρῆς καὶ δούρασι δεινός,
       Ἄγριος αἰχμητής, ἄγριος ἀμφίβροτος,
15 Ἄγριος, αἱμοχαρής, οὖλος, δορίτολμος, ἀγήνωρ,
       Εἰς Χριστοῦ λαὸν καμπύλα τόξα φέρων.
    Ἤρξατο μάρνασθαί τε καὶ ὠρνύμεν ἔργον Ἄρηος,
       Ἡμετέρους μεμαὼς τεύχεσιν αἱρέμεναι,
    Ἀλλὰ Θεὸς Χριστοῦ λαὸν φίλον ἔσκεπε χερσί,
20   Καὶ παρεὼν πρόμαχος Χριστοφιλοῦσιν ἔην.
    Λαὲ φίλου Χριστοῖο, σέθεν μοι ἀγάλλεο θυμῷ·
       Τουρκογενὴς λαὸς πότμον ἔψεψεν ἑόν,
    Τουρκογενὴς λαὸς στυγερὴν δόμον Ἄιδος εἶσε,
       Μηκέτι σε βλάπτειν ὡς τὸ πάροιθεν ἔχει.
25 Τέρπεαι, ὦ φίλε λαὲ Θεοῦ τε καὶ ᾄσματα μέλπε,
       Ἄισματα μέλπε Θεῷ πάντοθι γηθόσυνος,
    Ὡς καὶ ἐγὼ σὺν σοι γεγανωμένος ἀσκελὲς αἰέν
       Ἤνδε βοὴν μέλψω παμμεδέοντι Θεῷ.
    Κῦδος ἔοι καὶ δόξα Θεῷ, καὶ ἀγήραον εὖχος,
30   Ὃς νικᾶν ἡμᾶς τῇδε δίδασκε μάχῃ.

Textus: Budapest, National Széchényi Library, ms Fol. Lat. 3606.II, ff. 31v–32r.

Crit.: spiritus et accentus aliquot in manuscripto autographo male positos necnon litteras subscriptas iuxta normam orthographicam hodiernam vocibus apposui || **1** Μούσῃ] ita, sc. metri causa pro Μοῦσα | οἶδες] ita || **5** Τουρκόγενες] ita, sc. pro Τουρκογενεῖς || **13 (14)** Εἶλθε] ita, sc. pro ἦλθε || **17** ὠρνύμεν] ita, sc. pro ὀρνύμεν || **22** ἔφεψεν] ita, sc. pro ἐπέσπεν (ἐφέπω)

Sim.: 3 βαθυκύμονας ὄχθας] cf. Musae. 189 || **4** Θάμνοις ἐν πυκινοῖς] cf. Hom. *Od.* 5.471 | νέμεϊ σκιερῷ] cf. Hom. *Il.* 11.480 || **5** αὖλιν ἔθεντο] cf. Hom. *Il.* 9.232 || **7** Τοῦτο...ἀγείρων] cf. Quint. Smyrn. 10.9 || **13** ἐγχείης μακρῆς] cf. Hom. *Il.* 3.37, 254 || **14** ἄγριος αἰχμητής] cf. Hom *Il.* 6.97 et 278 || **16** καμπύλα τόξα] cf. Hom. *Il.* 3.17 et saepius || **17** ἔργον Ἄρηος] cf. Hom. *Il.* 11.734 || **20** Χριστοφιλοῦσιν] hapax legomenon || **22** πότμον ἔψεψεν] cf. Hom. *Od.* 24.471 || **23** δόμον Ἄιδος εἶσε] cf. Hom. *Il.* 3.322 et saepius || **24** ὡς τὸ πάροιθεν] cf. Hom. *Od.* 2.312; Ap. Rhod. *Argon.* 1.816 et saep. || **27** ἀσκελὲς αἰέν] cf. Hom. *Od.* 1.68 || **28** παμμεδέοντι] adiect. Nonnianum (cf. *Dion.* 1.368 et saepius)

An elegy on the victory of the reverend bishop of Zagreb over the Turks at the river Glina

Tell me, Muse – daughter of Zeus, thou knowest to tell –
what adversity, commotion, and fray does this happen to be?
Here, above the shores of the deep and rolling Glina river
in the boscage and shady grove,
[5] here have the Turkish troops recently made camp,
where they started to destroy Christianity.
Very wise and full of prudence
a holy Illyrian shepherd noticed it,
he noticed it and in his heart decided
[10] with spiked pales to fence the course of Glina.
Thus he did. But the cunning and cruel enemy
came to foil that decision,
arriving dauntingly with his long wooden spears –
a wild spearbearer in full armour,
[15] cruel, bloodthirsty, death-dealing, a daring and defiant warrior –
and directing crooked arrows at Christ's followers.
He started warring and plying Ares' trade,
willing with weapons to take the lives of our warriors,
but God with his hands protected his beloved Christian people,
[20] and stood in the first fighting lines of those who love Christ.
O people of our dear Christ, rejoice in your hearts,
for the Turkish army have met their doom.
The Turkish army depart to Hades' sad abode,
and can harm you no longer as before.
[25] Rejoice, oh dear people of Christ, and sing songs,
sing songs to God and rejoice everywhere,
as I will, with you constantly rejoicing,
this celebratory cry at Almighty God direct:
God be honoured and praised, and eternal glory be his,
[30] for instructing us on how to win this battle.

Metre: Elegiac couplets.

Notes: Among a large number of poetic treatments of Christian-Muslim battles written by humanists in Latin, this poem is a unique Croatian example of a 'Turcomachia' written in ancient Greek. It refers to a little-known battle between Turkish and Croatian troops on the river Glina in the vicinity of Zagreb in August 1573, in which Count Juraj Drašković, a humanist and Wyrffel's patron, led the Croatian troops to victory. In spite of a number of orthographical and morphological errors, the poem contains a plethora of Homeric and epic stylistic reminiscences, suggesting that the author had a thorough classical education and that he was an accomplished writer of Greek verse. His only printed Greek epigram (1569) suggests that he received his education in ancient Greek from the famous Hellenist Hieronymus Wolf. Since humanism had not gained as much momentum in northern Croatia as in Dalmatia at the time, and ancient Greek was not yet an official part of the local school curriculum, we cannot but wonder about the poem's intended audience. It is possible that, in addition to a Latin poem on the same subject (*Elegia ad Caesarem*) which can be found in the manuscript together with the Greek one, this elegy accompanied the official report that Drašković sent to Emperor Maximilian II, that is, it was written for the German imperial court. However, considering the fact that a distinguished late-humanist circle gathered around the Chapter of Zagreb School during Wyrffel's 10-year spell in Croatia, it is not far-fetched to imagine that this Greek elegy written in what was then an exotic linguistic medium had contemporary readers even in Zagreb. At any rate, ancient Greek education in these lands would be established systematically only a few decades later, upon the arrival of the Jesuits and their *ratio studiorum* in 1607.

Biography: Georgius Wyrffel (also Vurffel, Wyrffelius, Vurffelius, Virffelius; Ulm, c. 1535 – Eisenstadt, c. 1585) was a doctor of theology and a humanist. The existing biographical entries on him are incomplete; they wrongly point to two different persons of the same name who were simultaneously active in both Germany and Croatia. The first mention of Wyrffel's name can be found in the register of Ingolstadt University from 1552; after that, at the beginning of the 1560s, his name appears as a copyist of Greek manuscripts kept in the Fugger family collection in Augsburg (e.g., the *Dionysiaca* of Nonnus copied in 1561, Vindob. *phil. gr.* 52). Although he came from a Protestant background, he began his ecclesiastical career as a Catholic priest in Croatia. Bishop Juraj Drašković brought him from the Tridentine Council to Zagreb, where he served from 1563 until 1573 as canon and head of the newly established school by the Chapter of Zagreb, and as personal secretary to the bishop. He was named Latin poet laureate in Vienna in 1568 and studied in Rome at the Collegium Germanicum, collaborating closely with Cardinal Sirleto, a renowned Hellenist. He then returned to Germany, and from 1574 he was a counsellor to the Bavarian Duke Albert V and the librarian in charge of the Greek manuscripts in his court library in Munich. He spent the last few years of his life as a parish priest in Eisenstadt, Austria. A small part of his literary work – a few hundred verses, mostly in Latin but also in Greek, dedicated to German, Italian, and Croatian patrons – was published during his life, while the rest is preserved in manuscripts.

Bibliography: Flood, John (2001), *Poets Laureate in the Holy Roman Empire. A Bio-bibliographical Handbook*, vol. IV, Berlin/New York, 2271–2272; Hartig, Otto (1917), "Die Gründung der Münchener Hofbibliothek durch Albrecht V. und Johann Jakob Fugger", in: *Abhandlungen der Königlich Bayerischen Akademie der Wissenschaften, Philosophisch-philologische Klasse* XXVIII, 3. Abhandlung, 69–70; Kerschbaum, Roland Peter (1998), "Die Verhandlungen zur Gründung eines Salzburger Priesterseminars und seine Entstehung", in: *Mitteilungen der Gesellschaft für Salzburger Landeskunde* 138, 46–49; Rittsteuer, Josef (1950), "Pfarrer Hoffmann von Eisenstadt (1586–1595): Ein Beitrag zur Geschichte der Landeshauptstadt", in: *Burgenländische Heimatblätter* 12, 66–76; Rezar, Vlado (forthcoming), "The Canon of Zagreb and a Humanist: Georg Wyrffel", in: *Colloquia Maruliana* 30.

Raphael Levakovich (1597–1650)

Ῥαφαὴλ ἱερομονάχου φραγκισκάνου τοῦ Κροβάτου εἰς τὴν βίβλον Νεοφύτου τοῦ Ῥοδινοῦ [1636]

    Οὐ πάϊς Οἰάγρου Θρηΐκιος, ἀλλὰ καὶ αὐτὸς
    Μαιονίδης ὕμνους γράψαν ἀπειρεσίους
    Ἀνδρῶν ἠδὲ θεῶν, πολλούς τε ἔρωτας ἀνάγνων,
    Λήρους, οὐχ ὕμνους, ἔργματ' ἀτασθαλίης.
5   Ἠνίδε παρθενικῆς Μαρίης ὕμνος, ὅν ποτε Λουκᾶς
    Ἐν σελίσι στίξε Πνεύματι κρουόμενος·
    Τοῦτον πολλὰ καμὼν Ῥοδινὸς δυοκαίδεκ' ἀρίστοις
    Χριστολάτραισι σαφῶς δῆλον ἔθηκε λόγοις.

Textus: Νεοφύτου Ῥοδινοῦ *Ἐξήγησις εἰς τὴν ᾠδὴν τῆς Θεοτόκου etc*, Romae 1636 (hoc transcriptum iuxta ed. Legrand, Émile [1894], *Bibliographie hellénique XVII*, 1, Paris, 340).

Sim.: 1 πάϊς Οἰάγρου Θρηΐκιος] cf. Ap. Rhod. *Argon*. 4.905 | ἀλλὰ καὶ αὐτός] cf. Hom. *Il*. 11.650 et saep. || **3** Ἀνδρῶν...θεῶν] cf. Hom *Il*. 13.632 || **6** Πνεύματι κρουόμενος] cf. Greg. Naz. *carm*., PG

37.1364.10 || **7** πολλὰ καμών] cf. Nonn. *Dion.* 25.197; *Anth. Pal.* 5.75.5 et saep. | δυοκαίδεκ' ἀρίστοις] cf. Hom. *Il.* 9.195

The Franciscan friar Raphael the Croat praises the book by Neophytos Rhodinos

Not only the Thracian, Oeagrus' son [Orpheus], but
   the Maeonides [Homer] himself wrote countless hymns
on men and gods, many sinful love stories they put into verse:
   Yet those are not hymns, but rattle resulting from folly.
[5] Behold the hymn to the Virgin Mary, which once Luke
   wrote on leaves, touched by the Holy Spirit:
After devoting a great deal of effort to it, in twelve most excellent
   sermons Rhodinos made the hymn clear to the worshippers of Christ.

Metre: Elegiac couplets with some prosodical flaws (cf. the long ι in Θρηΐκιος).

Notes: Levakovich was not only a scholar (most of his historiographic works in Latin are still in manuscript form), but also a poet. His poetry is of an occasional nature, mostly in Croatian; the epigram featured here is his only known composition in ancient Greek. Nevertheless, this text testifies to the thorough classical education Levakovich received in Franciscan houses in Croatia. The epigram accompanied a vernacular Greek edition of the sermons on the Canticle of the Virgin Mary, written by Neophytos Rhodinos of Cyprus, a Greek proselyte monk and scholar, and printed by the Congregation in Rome in 1636 (see below).

Biography: Raphael Levakovich (Rafael Levaković, fra Rafaele Croato, Ῥαφαὴλ Ἱερομόναχος Φραγκισκάνος ὁ Κροβάτος; Jastrebarsko, Croatia 1597 – Zadar, Croatia 1650) joined the Order of the Minor Friars at an early age and was ordained a priest. Having become an excellent philologist in his homeland, in 1626 Levakovich was invited to Rome by the Sacred Congregation for the Propagation of the Faith to help with the re-editing and printing of Old Church Slavonic liturgical books for the purpose of spreading Catholicism in non-Catholic southern and eastern Slavic countries. He was sent by the Pope on several missions to the Orthodox East (Romania, Bulgaria, Ukraine), and was consecrated as Archbishop of Achrida (Ohrid, Macedonia) in 1647, but died while travelling to his archiepiscopal see.

Bibliography: Kukuljević Sakcinski, Ivan (1868), "Književnici u Hrvatah s ove strane Velebita, živivši u prvoj polovini XVII. Vieka", in: *Arkiv za povjestnicu jugoslavensku* 9, 278–312; Giammanco, Amanda Danielle (2015), *(Self) Fashioning of an Ottoman Christian Prince: Jachia Ibm Mehmed in Confessional Diplomacy of the Early Seventeenth-Century*, Budapest, 51–54.

Ioannes Comnenos Molyvdos (1657–1719)

Εἰς τὸν ἀοίδιμον συγγραφέα καὶ τοὺς εὐγενεστάτους υἱοὺς αὐτοῦ, καὶ τὴν πανάριστον ταύτην βίβλον ἐπίγραμμα τοῦ πανιερωτάτου μητροπολίτου Δρύστρας κυρίου Ἱεροθέου [1716]

(excerptum, vv. 1–38)

  Ηὔχετο γῆ Μακεδὼν ἐπ' Ἀλεξάνδρῳ βασιλῆϊ,
   Ἦρξε γὰρ Εὐρώπης ἠδ' Ἀσίης πολέμοις.
  Νῦν δέ γε Βυζαντὶς πλέον εὔχεται ἤπερ ἐκείνη,
   Ἄλλον Ἀλέξανδρον κρείσσονα γειναμένη·
5 Ἀντολίη τε Δύσις τε καὶ Εὐρώπη γὰρ ἀείδει,
   Ἥ τε ὑπὲρ βορέην ἔξοχα τοῦδε κλέα.
  Κεῖνος ἐν ὅπλοις, οὗτος ἐν ἰδμοσύνῃ μέγ' ἄριστος,
   Γαίης ὠφελέων πείρατα πάντα λόγοις·
  Κεῖνος Ἀριστοτέλους συγγράμμασιν αἰὲν ἐχρῆτο,
10 Τῶν τούτου χατέει χ' ᾧ κλέος ἐν σοφίῃ.
  Κεῖνος ἐνὶ πτολέμοις μερόπων χέεν αἵματα, οὗτος
   Στήσατο πρεσβεύσας αἱματόεντα ῥόον,
  Ἔς γε μάχας κεῖνος ὀξύς ποτε ᾔδετο εἶναι,
   Πεῖσεν ὅδ' εἰρήνην πάντας ἄνακτας ἄγειν.
15 Κεῖνος μὲν πολέας κτείνων Ἄϊδι προΐαπτεν,
   Οὗτος ἀκεστορίῃ σώετο ἐκ θανάτου.
  Οὐ τέκε κεῖνος ὁμοῖον ἑαυτῷ φίλτατον υἷα,
   Οὗτός οἱ ἐμφερέας καὶ φρενὶ καὶ σοφίῃ·
  Ὧν ὁ μὲν ἐνδυκέως γῆς Μολδαβίης ποτὲ ἄρξας,
20 Νῦν Οὐγγροβλαχίης σκῆπτρον ἔχει ζαθέης,
  Νικόλεως κλῆσιν, μάλα δ' ἔξοχος ἡγεμονήων,
   Κλειτὸς ἐπ' εὐσεβίῃ ἔν τε δικασπολίαις,
  Ἥρως, ἄκρα φέρων σοφίης κορυφάς τ' ἀρετάων,
   Λάμπων παντοίαις ἀγλαΐαις χαρίτων,
25 Δαψιλέως πενίην ἐλεαίρων, κ' ἴδμονας ἄνδρας
   Τιμαῖς ἀμφιέπων, κηδόμενος σοφίης,
  Ὅς καὶ τήνδ' ἱερὴν δαπάνησιν ἑῇσι τύπωσεν,
   Αἴσια πατρὶ νέμων, βίβλον ἐπωφελέα.
  Ἄτερος υἱήων δ' Ἰωάννης μέγας ἤδη
30 Ἑρμηνεὺς σεκρέτων κραντορίης Ὀθμάνων,

Τῆς τ' ἐκκλησιέων μεγάλης οἰκουμενικοῦ τε
Πατράρχου τελέθει Λογοθέτης ὁ Μέγας.
Εὐσεβέων πρόμος, ἠδὲ φίλος Μουσῶν τε σοφῶν τε,
Εὖ τε δράων προφρόνως δαμναμένους πενίῃ.
35 Τοῖος Ἀλέξανδρος Βυζάντιος, ὃς μετὰ πλείστας
Σύγγραφε καὶ ταύτην φροντίδι λεπτοτάτῃ,
Ἥτις ἰουδαϊκῶν θειογραφικὴν περιίσχει
Ἱστορίαν πᾶσαν [...]

Textus: *Ἱστορία ἱερά, ἤτοι τὰ Ἰουδαϊκὰ παρὰ τοῦ εὐσεβεστάτου κυρίου Ἀλεξάνδρου Μαυροκορδάτου*, Bucharest 1716, 3v-4v (hoc transcriptum iuxta ed. Legrand, Émile [1918], *Bibliographie hellénique XVIII*, 1, Paris, 135-136).

Crit.: 27 ἐῇσι scripsi: ἐῇσι ed.

Sim.: 12 αἱματόεντα ῥόον] cf. Greg. Naz. *carm. mor.*, PG 37.618.1 || **15** Ἄϊδι προΐαπτεν] cf. Hom. *Il.* 1.3 || **21-22** ἡγεμονήων...δικασπολίαις] cf. *Anth. Pal.* 7.334.9-10 || **23** κορυφᾶς τ' ἀρετάων] cf. Pind. *Ol.* 1.13 || **24** ἀγλαΐαις χαρίτων] cf. *Anth. Pal.* 10.71.6 || **30** κραντορίης] hapax legomenon || **34** δαμναμένους πενίῃ] cf. Thgn. 1.173

Epigram by the most holy Metropolitan of Dristra, Sir Hierotheos [John Molyvdos Comnenos], commending the famous writer and his noblest sons, as well as this excellent book

(excerpt, ll. 1-38)

The land of Macedonia was proud of Alexander the Great,
   for he ruled by war Europe and Asia.
Even prouder than Macedonia is Byzantium now,
   for it gave birth to another Alexander, a greater one:
[5] Both the East and the West, as well as Europe, praise him,
   even the northernmost lands extol his famous deeds.
Alexander the Great was the best by far in combat, whereas this one excelled in knowledge:
   All the parts of the world have derived benefit from his words.
That one was constantly taking advantage of Aristotle's writings,
[10] and the writings of this one are wanted even by those famous for their wisdom.
That one shed the blood of mortals in war,
   while this one prevented through negotiation the rivers of blood from flowing.
That one was known for starting battles quickly,
   while this one for swaying rulers towards peace.
[15] That one killed many men and sent them to Hades,
   while this one was saving them from death through the art of medicine.
That one did not give birth to a son resembling him,

while this one has produced his peers in heart and mind.
One of them ruled the state of Moldavia fondly,
[20] and now holds the sceptre of holy Wallachia.
Nicholas is his name, the greatest of rulers,
  famed for his piety and judicial decisions,
a hero, reaching the outermost limits of wisdom and virtue,
  radiating gracefully and charmingly,
[25] generously aiding the poor, and bestowing the wise
  with honours: for he is fond of wisdom.
So this holy and useful book he prints at his own expense,
  honouring his father deservingly.
The second of his sons, John, already
[30] a great Dragoman of the Ottoman Porte,
is now the great logothete of the ecumenical
  Patriarch of the Great Church.
The first in piety and a friend of the Muses and wisdom,
  he is a prudent benefactor to those struck by poverty.
[35] That kind of a man was Alexander the Byzantine, who, apart from many other books,
  with the utmost care compiled this book,
which contains the whole history of the divine books
  of the Jews. [...]

Metre: Elegiac couplets, with some minor prosodical flaws (e.g., λογοθέτης with the first omikron taken for a long in l. 32, though this is obligatory for that noun, *metri causa*).

Notes: Molyvdos was one of the most remarkable intellectuals of his time under Ottoman rule. Besides writing works in history, theology, and even astronomy, and translations from ancient Greek and Latin into vernacular Greek, he greatly helped the development of Greek printing in Wallachia. He also wrote occasional poetry in ancient Greek, starting as early as 1683, his last poem dating from 1719. Of 22 mostly laudatory epigrams (c. 300 verses in all), the majority were published in various editions during his lifetime. The selected poem, presented here only partially (38 out of 60 lines), praises Alexander Mavrocordatos (1641–1709), an already deceased Phanariot nobleman and a notable writer of medical, philosophical, historical, and philological treatises, as well as his sons Nicholas (1670–1730) and John Nicholas (1684–1719), the rulers of Wallachia and Moldavia since 1709. The latter, a scholar himself, edited his father's work and printed it posthumously in 1716.

Biography: John Comnenos Molyvdos (Ἰωάννης Κομνηνὸς Μόλυβδος, Perinthus 1657 – Bucharest 1719) was a Greek physician and scholar. After completing his elementary education in his home town of Molyvdos, he attended the Patriarchal

Academy in Constantinople (1676–1680) and studied theology, philosophy, grammar, and medicine. In 1686 he continued his studies at the University of Padua, received his diploma as 'doctor-philosopher' (ἰατροφιλόσοφος) and left Italy. He became the head physician at the court of the Russian Tsar and in 1697 moved to Bucharest and became a court physician (ἀρχιατρός) to Constantin Brâncoveanu, Prince of Wallachia. This period was intellectually the most productive time in Molyvdos' career, as he was not only closely associated with the Princely Academy of Bucharest, but also intensively engaged in literary and translation activities. In 1698 he made a pilgrimage to Mount Athos, which became the topic of what is perhaps his most famous work, the *Pilgrim's Guidebook to the Holy Mount Athos* (Προσκυνητάριον τοῦ Ἁγίου Ὄρους τοῦ Ἄθωνος), published in 1701 at Snagov Monastery. In 1702, Molyvdos resigned as court physician, in order to enter the clergy. In 1703 he is already recorded as a monk, assuming the monastic name Ἱερόθεος, and a year later he became titular bishop of Side (in modern-day Turkey). In 1711 he was made metropolitan bishop of Dristra (modern-day Silistra, Bulgaria) and held that position until his death.

Bibliography: Pantos, Demetrios Charalampos (2007), *Ἰωάννης-Ἱερόθεος Κομνηνός μητροπολίτης Δρύστρας (1657–1719): βίος – ἐκκλησιαστική δράση – συγγραφικό ἔργο*, Athens.

Demetrios Notaras (ca. 1685–1741)

Εἰς τὴν παροῦσαν περὶ τῶν καθηκόντων βίβλον [1719]

    Εὗδον παννύχιος μαλακῷ δεδμημένος ὕπνῳ·
    Τερψίνοον τότ' ὄναρ πέμψε μοι Αἰγίοχος.
    Δόρκα θεοπνεύστου σοφίης πὰρ θεῷ Ἑλικῶνος
    Παῖδας ἀγειρομένους, νιφοβόλῳ ἐν ὄρει,
5   Οἷς ἐνὶ πᾶσιν Φοῖβος Ἀπόλλων μῦθον ἔειπε
    Τοῖον, ἀνιστάμενος, καρτερὸν ἠδὲ μέγαν·
    "Ὦ πόποι, οἷον ὄνειδος ἱκάνει δέλτου ἄμοιρον
    Τῆς γε καθηκόντων Ἑλλάδα ἡμετέρην.
    Ὑμμέων οὔ τις ἔτευχεν ἐόντων φιλοσοφούντων
10   Ταύτην τὴν δέλτον, μηδὲ θέλει ἀλέγειν."
    Ὣς φάτο. Αὐτὰρ Ἀριστοτέλης ἠμείβετο Φοῖβον
    Μύθοις μειλιχίοις ὀργῇ ἐλαυνόμενον·
    "Ὦ ἄνα Λητοΐδη, μὴ σκύζεο, λάμβανε δέλτον
    (Ἴσχεν ὑπαί γε μάλης) πρόσφατον ἠδὲ σοφήν."
15   Γηθόσυνος λάβε τὴν δέλτον τότε, ἠδὲ ἀνέγνω,
    Κἀγάμενος· "Δάφνης ἄξιος ἡμετέρης."
    Ἔπλακον οὖν Μοῦσαι δάφνης στέφος, ἀγλαὰ δῶρα,

Καὶ ἐπέθηκε κάρᾳ κοιράνου Οὐγγροβλάχων.
Ἦσαν δ' ἠδ' ἐκρότησαν Μοῦσαι ἴστορες ᾠδῆς,
20   Ὕπνος δ' ἀμβρόσιος μεῖο ἀφῆκε ῥέθη.

Εἰς δουλικῆς εὐλαβείας τεκμήριον Δημήτριος Γεωργούλης Νοταρᾶς, ἀκέστωρ

Textus: *Περὶ τῶν καθηκόντων βίβλος* κυρίου Ἰωάννου Νικολάου Ἀλεξάνδρου Μαυροκορδάτου βοίβοδα, Bucharest 1719, 4v–5r (hoc transcriptum iuxta ed. Legrand, Émile [1918], *Bibliographie Hellénique XVIII*, 1, Paris, 157–158).

Crit.: 3 Δόρκα] hapax legomenon, scilicet pro δέδορκα || 13 Λητοΐδη: Λητοΐδης ed. || 17 Ἔπλακον: Ἔπλαγον ed.

Sim.: 1 Εὗδον παννύχιος] cf. Hom. *Od.* 7.288 | μαλακῷ...ὕπνῳ] cf. Hom. *Od.* 15.6 || 2 τερψίνοον] cf. Nonn. *Dion.* 1.418 et saep. || 3 θεοπνεύστου σοφίης] cf. Ps.Phocyl. *Sent.* 129 || 4 νιφοβόλῳ ἐν ὄρει] cf. Eur. *Phoen.* 234 al. || 5 μῦθον ἔειπε] cf. Hom. *Il.* 3.303 et saep. || 6 καρτερὸν ἠδὲ μέγαν] cf. Ar. *Ran.* 1398 || 7 Ὦ...ἱκάνει] cf. Hom. *Od.* 9.507 || 11 cf. Hom. *Il.* 24.424 || 13 Ὦ...σκύζεο] cf. Quint. Smyrn. 5.428–429 || 17 ἀγλαὰ δῶρα] cf. Hom. *Il.* 1.213 et saep. || 19 Μοῦσαι...ᾠδῆς] cf. *Hymn. Hom. in Lunam* 1–2 || 20 cf. Hom. *Il.* 16.856 al.

On the present book *On Duties*

The whole night I was sleeping possessed by tender rest
   when the Aegis-bearer sent a dream that delights the soul.
Around the Heliconian deity of God-given wisdom I saw
   children gathered on the snowy mountain,
[5] and among them all Phoebus Apollo uttered standing up,
   a speech of this kind, ferocious and loud:
'Woe is me! What an embarrassment comes on our Greece,
   that has no book which speaks of duties.
Of you, who are philosophers, nobody wrote
[10] a book like that, nor wants to take care of this task.'
Thus he said. Aristotle however answered Phoebus
   with suavity, for the latter was driven by rage:
'Don't be mad, lord, son of Leto: take this book'–
   He carried it under his arm – 'new and wise.'
[15] Happily Phoebus then took the book and read it,
   and then in amazement he said: 'It is worthy of our laurel.'
Accordingly, the Muses made a laurel wreath, a great gift,
   and he put it on the head of the lord of Wallachia.
The Muses, adept at singing, started the song and clapped their hands,
[20] and the divine dream departed from my limbs.

As a proof of my humble reverence,
Demetrios Georgoulis Notaras, the healer

Metre: Elegiac couplets, with some minor prosodical and metrical problems (cf. bipartite hexameter in l. 19).

Notes: During his studies in Italy, Notaras mastered Latin, which enabled him to translate several philosophical and natural-scientific works from Latin into vulgar Greek during the first two decades of the 18th century. As for his poetry, only two epigrams written in ancient Greek have been preserved. The one presented here praises the literary accomplishments of the Wallachian duke John Nicholas Mavrocordatos, son of Alexander (see Molyvdos' epigram above), especially his *Book on Duties*, which was well received and translated into Latin (Leipzig 1722). Although credited with only a small number of verses, Notaras' elegant style has an Homeric flair and attests to his thorough classical education and the refinement of the intellectual environment at the Wallachian court in the early decades of the Phanariots' rule.

Biography: Demetrios Georgoulis Notaras (Δημήτριος Γεωργούλης Νοταράς; Trikala, ca. 1685 – Bucharest, 1741) was a physician (ἰατροφιλόσοφος). He was the nephew of the famous Patriarch of Jerusalem and scholar Chrysanthes Notaras (1660–1731). Existing biographical data suggest that he studied liberal arts, medicine, and theology at Rome and Padua; he later held the post of court physician (ἀρχιατρός) to the dukes of Wallachia in Bucharest.

Bibliography: Sathas, Konstantinos (1872), *Μεσαιωνική Βιβλιοθήκη*, Γ΄, Βενετία, 200, 500; Αποστολόπουλος, Δημήτρης Γ. (1999), "Το πρωτότυπο του Περί της των συμβουλιών ματαιότητος", in: *The Gleaner* 22, 251–252; Camariano-Cioran 1974, 221f.; Glykophrydi-Leontsini, Athanasia (2006), "Δημήτριος Νοταράς και Emanuele Tesauro: μία ανέκδοτη μετάφραση αριστοτελικής ηθικής και ο ρόλος των διανοουμένων της Διασποράς στη διακίνηση των ιδεών", in: *Ο ελληνικός κόσμος ανάμεσα στην εποχή του διαφωτισμού και στον εικοστό αιώνα: πρακτικά του Γ΄ Ευρωπαϊκού Συνεδρίου Νεοελληνικών Σπουδών (ΕΕΝΣ)*, 1, 379–392.

Georgios Chrysogonos of Trebizond (†1739)

Πρὸς τὸν αὐτὸν (θεοφρουρητὸν καὶ σοφώτατον ἡγεμόνα) ἕτερον ἡρωελεγεῖον [1719]

Μοῦσαι Πιερίδες, μέγ' ἀείσατε πάνσοφον ἄνδρα,
    Πρίν ποτε Μολδαβίης, νῦν δ' ἀγὸν Οὐγγροβλάχων,
Ἀστέρα παμφανόωντα, ἐν ἔργμασιν ἔξοχον ὄντα,
    Φαίδιμον ἐκ προγόνων ἡγεμόνων τὸ κλέος,
5 Πράξεσιν αἰθερίῃσιν εὖ ἔρδοντ' ὀρθοφρονοῦντας,

Οἷα πατὴρ πάντων κηδόμενον προφρόνως·
Ὃς καὶ τήνδε βίβλον πραπίδεσσιν ἔτευξεν ἐοῖσι,
Λαμπρότατον Μουσῶν φέγγος ἀνασχόμενος,
Ἤθεα καὶ μερόπων καλλώπισεν ἔξοχα βίον,
10   Εὐσεβέσιν δῶκε πρὸς πόλον ὡς κλίμακα.
Τῆς ἱερῆς σοφίης ἐρικυδέα πυρσὸν ἀνάψας,
Δεινὴν τῆς κακίης ἀχλὺν ἀπεσκέδασε,
Φύτλης θ' ἡμετέρης χαλεπὴν σκοτόμαιναν ἔλυσε,
Λαμπρὸν ἐς εὐμαθίης φέγγος ἀμειψάμενος.
15   Ἣν θυμῷ μεμαῶτι κρατῶν Βλαχίης ἐτύπωσε,
Τεύξας Οὑγγαρίῃ κλίμακα χριστολάτραις·
Τῷ τοι καὶ ἐὸν οὔνομ' ἀκήρατον ἔσσεται αἰεί,
Ἀθανάτῳ μνήμῃ συμπαρατεινόμενον.

Τῆς ὑμετέρας ἐκλαμπροσοφωτάτης μεγαλειότητος ἐλάχιστος τῶν οἰκετῶν ὁ προρρηθεὶς Γεώργιος Τραπεζούντιος, δεύτερος διδάσκαλος τῆς ἐν Βουκουρεστίῳ αὐθεντικῆς σχολῆς

Textus: *Περὶ τῶν καθηκόντων βίβλος* κυρίου Ἰωάννου Νικολάου Ἀλεξάνδρου Μαυροκορδάτου βοΐβοδα, Bucharest 1719 (hoc transcriptum iuxta ed. Legrand, Émile [1918], *Bibliographie Hellénique XVIII*, 1, Paris, 160–161).

Crit.: 7 ἐοῖσι: debuit ἑαῖσι || **17** Τῷ: Τώ ed.

Sim.: 1 Μοῦσαι...ἀείσατε] cf. Theoc. *Id.* 10.24 | πάνσοφον ἄνδρα] cf. *Certamen Hom. et Hes.* 40 || **3** ἀστέρα παμφανόωντα] cf. Quint. Smyrn. 7.346; Orph. *Arg.* 781 || **7** πραπίδεσσιν...ἐοῖσι] cf. Greg. Naz. *Carm.*, PG 37.1264.11 || **8** cf. *Anth. Pal.* 9.24.4 || **11** πυρσὸν ἀνάψας] cf. *Anth. Pal.* 2.1.25 al. || **12–13** cf. Const. Man. *Chron.* 6306 || **15** θυμῷ μεμαῶτι] cf. Hom. *Il.* 3.9

Elegiac couplets to the same wise ruler protected by God

Pierian Muses, sing loudly of the very learned man,
   once the ruler of Moldavia, now of Wallachia,
a bright star standing out for its heroic exploits,
   invested by the glory of his preceding rulers,
[5] a benefactor of the faithful with celestial deeds,
   like a father earnestly concerned for everyone.
His mind conceived this book,
   emitting the splendid light of the Muses,
and exceedingly embellishing the customs and the life of mortals:
[10] Thus he offered it to the devout as a ladder leading to heaven.
He lit the glorious torch of holy wisdom
   and dispersed the fearful fog of mischief,
our people he saved from perilous darkness,
   replacing it with the intense light of learning.
[15] With the greatest of wills he printed this book as the ruler of Wallachia,

a part of Hungary, providing a ladder to heaven to the worshippers of Christ.
For ever will his name therefore remain untainted,
resounding through history as an enduring memory.

The aforementioned Georgios Trapezuntios, the least of courtiers to Your Illustrious and Wisest Highness, second teacher at the court school in Bucharest

Metre: Elegiac couplets, with some metrical and prosodical flaws (e.g., βίον with a long ι in l. 9, κλίμακα with a short ι in l. 10, but with a long ι in l. 16).

Notes: Chrysogonos translated the *Nomokanon* into modern Greek (1730) and composed two books of divine services (Bucharest 1726, Venice 1748). Apart from some 20 epistles in ancient Greek (published recently), he wrote occasional poetry, including three laudatory epigrams (130 verses both in iambics and elegiac couplets, published in 1719 in the *Book on Duties*, of which he was chief editor as well) and an elaborate acrostic iambic poem (Κανών ἰαμβικὸς ἐγκωμιαστικός, 130 verses) in praise of the Wallachian duke Georgios Ghikas (around 1735), published only recently from the manuscript (British Library, Add MS 8236).

Biography: Georgios Chrysogonos of Trebizond (Γεώργιος Χρυσόγονος Τραπεζούντιος; Trebizond ? – Bucharest 1739) was a teacher, translator, religious writer, and poet. His biographical data are a matter of dispute, especially because in the past his name was not distinguished clearly from another Georgios of Trebizond (ἰατροφιλόσοφος), called Hypomenas (1689–1745), who was active as a teacher in the same Academy at roughly the same time. Chrysogonos' father, Theodoros Symeonos, a director of the School (Φροντιστήριον) of Trebizond, was invited in 1692 to take a post at the Princely Academy of Bucharest, so he took his son along with him to Wallachia. It is very likely that Chrysogonos studied there as well and received a thorough classical education. He was appointed as a teacher at the Academy in 1715, eventually serving as its director from 1724 to 1736. He taught ancient Greek grammar, classical and ecclesiastical literature, and Platonic philosophy.

Bibliography: Angelomati-Tsougkaraki, Eleni (2011), "Γεώργιος Χρυσόγονος Τραπεζούντιος: νέα στοιχεία για τον βίο και το έργο του", in: *Ιόνιος Λόγος*, τ. 3, 11–68.

Michael Goras Hypischiotes (c. 1700–1790)

I. Τοῦ αὐτοῦ Μιχαὴλ ἐπίγραμμα εἰς τὴν πεῖναν [1740]

Τῷ χιλιοστῷ εἰν ἔτεϊ ἠδ' ἑπτακοσιοστῷ
Τεσσαρακοστ' ταῖ ποτ'† θεογουνιέης
Λευγαλέῳ λιμῷ φύτλης βεβολήατο ἦτορ
Αἰνομόρων μερόπων τῆς Μακεδονιέης.
5   Πείνη δ' οὐλομένη μορφὰς μεταθεῖσα βροτείας
Ψυχὰς εἰν Ἀΐδῃ, φεῦ, προΐαψ' ἀτυχῶς.

Textus: *Σύντομος ἱστορία τῆς κατὰ τὸ 1740 ἔτος Μεγάλης γενομένης πείνας συντεθεῖσα παρὰ τοῦ κυρίου Μιχαὴλ Γκόρας*, Moschopolis 1740 (hoc transcriptum iuxta ed. Politis, N. G. [1883], "Περὶ τοῦ ἐν Μακεδονίᾳ λιμοῦ ἐν ἔτει 1740", in: *Δελτίον τῆς ἱστορικῆς καὶ ἐθνολογικῆς ἑταιρίας τῆς Ἑλλάδος*, t. 1, Athens, 273).

Crit.: 2 Τεσσαρρακοστ' αἶ ποτ' ed., sed male intellegitur: Τεσσαρακοσταί ποτ' Politis

Sim.: 3 Λευγαλέῳ λιμῷ] cf. Hom. *Od.* 5.312; 15.359 || 4 Αἰνομόρων μερόπων] cf. *Orac. Sib.* 5.455 || 5–6 cf. Hom. *Il.* 1.2–3

Epigram by Michael <Goras> on the famine

In the year seventeen hundred, alas,
   and forty since the birth of our Lord
the direst famine crushed the heart
   of the unfortunate mortals of Macedonia.
[5] Fatal hunger distorted the mortal bodies
   and with ill fate their souls, alas, cast into Hades.

II. Ἐπίγραμμα Μιχαὴλ Ὑπισχιώτου εἰς τὸν μακαριώτατον Ἀχρειδῶν Ἰωάσαφ [1742]

Οὐκ ἔτι ὀρνιέων πτερύγεσσιν ἐπαγγελίη νῦν
   Φάμαν θειάζειν Ἄμμονος ἀνάτροπον·
Δικραέος ἀετοῖο Ἰωάσαφ ὠκυπτέροισι
   Χύδην θρυλλῆσαι δαιμονίην ἀρετάν.
5   Τὰν φάνεν οὐχὶ μύθοις τρίποδι χρυσηλατέῳ γε,
   Τρισσοφαεῖ δὲ ἕδρῃ Ἀχρίδος ἀτρεκίῃ.

III. Ἐπίγραμμα Μιχαὴλ εἰς τὴν Ἀχρίδα [1742]

"Τοῦ, πόλε, γηθόσυνος;" "Χριστοῖο πέλω ὅτι θρᾶνος,
  Μυστῶν ἠδ' ἕδρας δωδεκάτων γε φέρω."
"Καὶ τύ, ἔρει μοι, Ἀχρὶς πρῶτ' Ἰουστιννιανή τε;"
  "Τοῦ πατριάρχου ὅττ' εἰμὶ ἕδρ' ἀρχιθύτου,
5 Δὶς στηλιτευτοῦ ἀμύμωνος Ἰωάσαφ ἦ μοι,
  Ἀρχιθυτῶν τε φέρω ἰσαρίθμως τὰ ἕδη."
"Ἢν δὶς ἥβησεν δ', ἔθ' ἅπαξ, Ἠοῦς ὁ Τιθωνός,
  Πόρσιον οὔποτ' ἴδης ἠνιαρὴν ἀνίην."

Textus: Ἀκολουθία...ἀφιερωθεῖσα τῷ μακαριωτάτῳ ἀρχιεπισκόπῳ τῆς Πρώτης Ἰουστιννιανῆς Ἀχρειδῶν κυρίῳ Ἰωάσαφ, Moschopolis 1742 (iuxta ed. É. Legrand, *Bibliographie hellénique XVIII*, 1, Paris, 1918, p. 289).

Crit.: III, 4 ὅττ'] ita, metri causa | ἕδρ': ἔρδ' ed. || 5 ἀμύμωνος] ita, metri causa || 7 δὶς ἥβησεν conieci: δισσήβησεν Legrand || 8 ἠνιαρὴν] ita, metri causa

Sim.: II.1 ὀρνιέων πτερύγεσσιν] cf. Nonn. *Dion.* 6.388 || 3 δικραέος] cf. Ael. Dion. δ 25; Phot. δ 609 al. || 4 δαιμονίαν ἀρετάν] cf. Pind. *Nem.* 1.9 || 5 τρίποδι χρυσηλατέῳ] cf. Ar. *Plut.* 9
III.1 θρᾶνος] verbum rarum, cf. Suid. θ 456 al. || 8 πόρσιον] cf. Pind. *Ol.* 1.114

Epigram by Michael Hypischiotes in praise of the most blessed Archbishop of Ochrid, Joasaph

No longer is it now a task for bird wings
  to extol the worthless prophecies of Ammon:
Let the fast wings of the double-headed eagle
  announce Joasaph's divine virtue to the world at large.
[5] He didn't exhibit it prophesying on the golden tripod,
  but preaching the truth in the seat of the triune God in Ochrid.

Michael's epigram in praise of Ochrid

'Heaven, why are you so happy?' 'Because I am the throne of Christ,
  and I'm the seat of the twelve disciples of his.'
'And why are you happy, tell me, Ochrid, that is, Justiniana Prima?'
  'Because I am the seat of the great father Archbishop,
[5] of the truly honourable Joasaph, whose name has been twice in marble engraved,
  as I contain two archiepiscopal sees.'
'If Eos' Tithonus had become young once more, that is, had he obtained his youth twice,
  great sorrows and pain of his later years wouldn't have been seen.'

Metre: Elegiac couplets, with a number of impossible prosodical and metrical solutions.

Notes: In the 1740s Hypischiotes collaborated closely with the Moschopole press: in 1740 he published a poem (115 verses in vulgar Greek) on the great famine that ravaged Macedonia that year, containing three epigrams on the same subject in ancient Greek (I). In 1742 he supervised the printing of a book of divine services and contributed five laudatory epigrams (two of which are collected here, II–III), along with a dedicatory epistle in ancient Greek, to Joasaph, the archbishop of Ochrid (1719–1745), who was a patron of Moschopole's cultural renaissance. Two additional epigrams were published in 1746, accompanying another religious book printed under his supervision. Epigram II recalls the myth of a bird that flew from Egypt to Dodona to announce that a sanctuary to Zeus Ammon should be built there. The bird became the symbol of this oracular deity, as seen on coins from the Hellenistic period. In the poet's time the bird is still a symbol in the Greek world, but is has morphed into a double-headed eagle symbolising the dual power of Byzantium and the Orthodox Church. This bird's task is to spread a far more valuable message than Ammon's bird, i.e. Joasaph's words of Christian truth. Epigram III reminds the reader that the Archbishopric of Ochrid was a heir to the Archbishopric of Justiniana Prima from the 6th century; in that sense, Joasaph was an archbishop with double archiepiscopal honours. Consequently, the archiepiscopal see of Ochrid would have been considered twice-blessed, as Tithonus would have been, had he been given his youth again.

Biography: Michael Goras Hypischiotes (Μιχαὴλ τοῦ Γκόρας Ὑπισχιώτης; Schipiska, c. 1700 – Moschopole, 1790) was a scholar of Aromanian descent. As son of the bishop of Gora, Hypischiotes received a thorough education at the Greek School of Moschopole (today Voskopoja, Albania). He was a layman, highly esteemed in his time for his education; his intellectual acme coincided with the foundation of the famous New Academy in 1744, and some sources even number him among its teachers. After the sack of Moschopole in 1769 he retreated to a nearby monastery.

Bibliography: Zaviras 1872, 456; Kourilas, Eulogios (1935), Γρηγόριος ὁ Ἀργυροκαστρίτης: ὁ μεταφραστὴς τῆς Καινῆς Διαθήκης εἰς τὸ Ἀλβανικόν: ἤτοι αἱ βάσεις τῆς Ἀλβανικῆς φιλολογίας καὶ γλώσσης ἢ Ἀκαδημία τῆς Μοσχοπόλεως, Ἀθῆναι, 131–133; Martinianos, Ioakeim (1939), "Η Ιερά Μονή του Τιμίου Προδρόμου κατά τον εν αυτή κώδικα 1630 – 1875", in: Id., Συμβολαί εις την Ιστορίαν της Μοσχοπόλεως – Α', Athens, 18–31.

Jovan Mladenovich (1721–1753)

Ἰαμβικοὶ στίχοι εἰς τὸν πανοσιώτατον ἀρχιμανδρίτην τοῦ παναγίου καὶ ζωοδόχου τάφου, κύριον Συμεὼν τὸν φροντιστὴν τῆς νέας τυπώσεως ταύτης [1749]

    Οἴκου ὁ ζῆλος θεῖος βεβρώκει ὥς σε,
    Βαβαὶ ὃν θαυμάζειν γε κάρτα σοῦ πόνου·
    Χώροις ἄγεις οἷς στῆσαν τοῦ Θεοῦ πόδες,
    Τούτους ἐναργεῖς πᾶσι ποιῶν τοῖς τύποις.
5 Ὄντως κἄγαμαι, καί σε αἰνέω σφόδρα,
    Ἀμείψοι ἵνα θεῖον αἰτέω δέ σοι,
    Ὡς τημελοῦς τῆς γ' εἴνεκα σπουδῆς πόνων
    Ὀρεκτὰ χωρηγοῖ τὰ τῆς ἄμφω χρόνοις.

                                    Ἰωάννης Μλαδενίδης, οἰκονόμος Νεοφύτου

Textus: Mladenovich, Jovan (1749), "Ἰαμβικοὶ στίχοι ...", in: *Προσκυνητάριον τῆς ἁγίας πόλεως Ἰερουσαλὴμ καὶ πάσης Παλαιστίνης*...παρὰ τοῦ πανοσιωτάτου ἀρχιμανδρίτου τοῦ παναγίου καὶ ζωοδόχου τάφου, κυρίου Συμεὼν τυπωθέν, παρὰ τῷ ἱεροδιακόνῳ Χριστοφόρῳ Ζέφαρ καὶ τῶν Ἰλλυρικο-σερβῶν κοινῷ ζωγράφῳ, Vienna, 2.

Crit.: 8 χωρηγοῖ] ita, metri causa

Iambic verses in praise of the most blessed archimandrite of the Church of the Holy and Life-receiving Grave, Master Simeon, the curator of this new edition

    Since you are devoured by a divine love for home,
    behold now a great admiration for your effort:
    You guide others where Christ's feet have trodden,
    and with this edition you reveal these places to everybody.
    [5] I truly admire you and highly praise you,
    and I want God to return you the favour,
    that on account of your devoted and considerable effort
    both of your books be blessed with keen readers for a long time.

                                    Jovan Mladenovich, a state official of Novi Sad

Metre: Iambic trimeters, or rather a kind of dodecasyllabic line replete with all sorts of prosodical mistakes and grammatical flaws.

Notes: Beside several translations of Greek books of religious character into Serbian and Russian, Mladenovich composed, as far as is known today, only two laudatory epigrams in ancient Greek. They accompanied a vernacular Greek edition of a pilgrimage book (Προσκυνητάριον) printed at Vienna in 1749, with extraordinary etchings by the painter Hristofor Zefarovich, who was at that time a Novi Sad (Νεόφυτον) resident as well. The featured epigram, however, praises the Serbian archimandrite of the Holy Grave in Jerusalem, Simeon Simeonovich, who carried out the editing of the book and financed it. It is not clear whether Simeonovich also wrote the text (the epigram insists on his immense efforts and merits), nor whether the last verse of the epigram commemorates the fact that there was another edition of the same book, a Serbian one in Cyrillic characters. Such a book was indeed prepared in 1748, but, as Legrand inferred, it was not printed until four years later in Vienna.

Biography: Jovan Mladenovich (Ἰωάννης Μλαδενίδης; Novi Sad, 1721 – Moscow, 1781) was a teacher of Greek and a translator. He was educated in the Greek School of Belgrade and continued his studies at the Orthodox Spiritual College in Novi Sad. In 1741 he is mentioned as a teacher of Greek at the Petrovaradin School. Since 1757 Mladenovich led a monastic life under the name Sophronios; in 1759 he left for Ukraine and Russia, where he ended his life.

Bibliography: Ramazanova, Dzhamilia N. (2018), "Historicodogmatic Treatise by Elias Meniates and its 18th-century Serbian Translators from Greek", in: *Slověne* 7/2, 134–178.

Konstantinos Tzechanes (1741–1800)

I. *Belisarius habet iam oculos, quibus lynceis uti, prout par est, misero non licet: date ergo ei obolum!* [1776]

Ἧκε Βελισσάριος διζήμενος Ἑλλάδος ἄνδρα
   Κλεινὸν ἐς Ὀξόνιον Πιερίδων τὸ ὄρος.
Εὗρε δ' ὁδηγηθεὶς Λόνδρῃ ἐνὶ εὐρυαγυίῃ
   Τοῦ πάρα οὐκ ὀβολὸν δέξατο ἀλλ' ὀβολούς,
5   Ὄμμασιν ἀτρεκέως μὴ δοῦναι σχόντας ἀρωγήν,
   Μᾶλλον ἀτὰρ φθεῖραι, δεῖξε τὸ ὡς ὁ χρόνος.
Ζηνὸς δ' εὐδοκίῃ νηπενθές, πλαζόμενος δήν,
   Εὗρε Βελισσάριος, ὄμματα δεξάμενος.
Λυγκεὺς δὴ γεγαὼς μακάρων νῆσον τριπόθητον
10 Βρεττανίην ναίειν ἦλθε Βελισσάριος·
Αὐτίκα δ' εἰσελθὼν ὡς Λυγκεὺς σήματα δόρκε,

Αἰόλα ὡς πάντως τερπνά τε κ' ἀντίβια.
Ἀστείων Γάλλων διὸ σπεύδων ᾤχετο γαῖαν
    Ἕλληνος βουλῇ ὁπλοφόρου πίσυνος,
15 Τοῦ μᾶλλον δοκέειν ἢ ἔμμεναι οἷον ἔδει δὴν
    Βουλομένου σπορέων ζιζανίων φιλίης.
Ἐλπίδος οὖν ψευσθεὶς καὶ γνοὺς ἐπανῆλθε τὰ αὐτὰ
    Πρὸς Διὸς ἠδ' αὐτῶν Μνημοσύνης τεκέων
Ἄγγλων νῦν δίων δεῖσθαι, Βελγῶν τ' ὀνομαστῶν,
20 Τῶν τε φιλανθρώπων, φιλοθέων τε λίην,
Ἔξοχα Πιερίδων θεραπόντων ἀξιαγάστων,
    Καὶ τούτων ὀπαδῶν τῶν ἐρατεινοτάτων
Μὴ παρορᾶν αἰτοῦντ' ἔλεος σμικρόν γ' ἀλεωρὴν
    Λοίσθι' ἀπειλούσης ἀργαλέης πενίης.

II. Ἐπίγραμμα ἡρωελεγεῖον [1776]

Δέξατο φιλόσοφος γέρας ἄμβροτον οὔνομα Νεύτων
    Μισθόν γ' ἰδμοσύνης ἄξιον ἀμφιλαφοῦς.
Γήθεο γοῦν μακάρων νῆσος τοίου λελαχυῖα
    Φωτός, Βρεττανίη ἀμφιβόητος ἀεί·
5 Τοῦ γὰρ λαμπηδὼν σοφίης φαεσίμβροτος αἰεὶ
    Αὐγάζει σφαίρην τὴν περίγειον ὅλην,
Ἔκλυσιν ἀρχαίων σκοτομαίνης πᾶσι διδοῦσα,
    Τοῖσι φίλον τ' ἀγαθὸν ἀτρεκίη τε μόνη,
Ἧς μέτοχος γεγαὼς ναὶ πᾶς τις ἐλεύθερος ἔσται
10 Τῆς τ' ἀδαημονίης δεισιθέου τε πλάνης.

Textus: Tzechani, Constantinus (1776), *Carmen heroico-elegiacum quod temporis praesentis circumstantiarum effectum breviter expositis exponendis humillime offert Anglis Belgisque, philomusis generosissimis ac studiosis nobilissimis*, Cambridge, 3–4.

Crit.: I.11 δόρκε] ita, sed cf. supra Demetrium Notaram || **12** κ' ἀντίβια ed. || **19** Ἄγγλων debuit

Sim.: I.4 νηπενθές] cf. Hom. *Od.* 4.221 || **24** ἀργαλέης πενίης] cf. Alc. fr. 364 V || **II.10** ἀδαημονίης] cf. Hom. *Od.* 24.244 | δεισιθέου] cf. Hsch. δ 1966, vox rarissima

Belisarius now has eyes like Lynceus, but he is unable to use them well, so give him an obol!

Belisarius, following the path of the Greek man, came
    to famous Oxford, the mountain of the Pierian Muses:
But when he was taken to the wide streets of London by the man
    from whom he had received not one but many obols,

[5] he found out that the rich, in truth, do not succour one-eyed beggars,
   but rather crush them, as it has been proven over time.
After a long wandering and by the good will of Zeus
   Belisarius then was relieved of sorrow, having recovered his sight:
This time being sharp-eyed, Belisarius, another Lynceus,
[10] came to Britain, the island of the blessed, ready to settle there.
But as soon as he arrived, Lynceus spotted the signs,
   varying, as ever, from friendly to hostile.
Therefore, he quickly moved to the land of the witty French,
   relying on advice given by a Greek of noble descent:
[15] But the man was more into pretending than being honest,
   and this friendship turned out to be darnel for his crops.
Deceived in his hopes and having experienced the same again,
   under the protection of the children of Zeus and Mnemosyne,
he returned to beg the divine and famous Angles and Belgae –
[20] and they are benevolent to men and highly reverent of God,
   esteemed above others as admirers of the Pierian Muses,
      as well as their most fervent attendants –
asking them not to oversee his cry for mercy, a bit of shelter
   from grievous poverty that threathens to be his end.

Epigram in elegiac couplets

Newton the philosopher received, as a gift of honour, an immortal name,
   a decent pay for his abundant knowledge.
Rejoice, therefore, Island of the blessed, that Fate gave you
   such a hero, and that you, Britain, will be far-famed forever:
[5] Because the brightness of his fame bringing light to mortals
   shines forever over the whole Earth globe,
giving redemption from the darkness of the past
   to those who hold dear the good and the truth alone.
Verily, everyone who becomes its sharer will set himself free
[10] from ignorance and religious erring.

III. Ἔπος ἡρωελεγεῖον εἰς τὴν φιλόσοφον τῶν ἀηττήτων Ῥωσσῶν αὐτοκράτορα Αἰκατερίναν τὴν Δευτέραν [1776]

(excerptum, vv. 9–32)

  Τίς δέ με δὴ νομιεῖ τολμῶντα ψεκτέον ἄνδρα
10 Νῦν Αὐτοκράτορ' ὡς θυμὸς ἀνώγει ὕδειν;
  Τοίην εὑραμένην θεόθεν χάριν Αἰκατερίνην,
  Οἵην νοῦς νοέειν γλῶττά τ' ἐρεῖν ἀπορεῖ;

Τοίην, ἧς πλεῖστοι αὐτοκρατόρων ἐράοντες
　　　Τῶν ὀνομαστοτάτων ἤμβροτον, ὧν ὁ Πέτρος
15　Πρῶτος ὁ ὑψιπέτης ἀετὸς Ῥωσσῶν μεγαθύμων
　　　Μουνάρχης Καῖσαρ, τοῦ κλέος εὑρύτατον.
　　　Γήθετε οὖν, Ῥῶσσοι πιστοὶ θεράποντες Ἄρηος
　　　Νῦν αὐτοκράτορος Παλλάδος ἐμμορότες,
　　　Αἰγιόχοιο Διὸς κούρης τῆς τριτογενείης
20　Οὔσης ἀσφαλέος κ' ἀτρόμου αἰγίδ' ὕπο,
　　　Ἄσπετον ὤπασ' ὅθεν Ζεὺς ναὶ κλέος ἠδ' ἔτι δώσει
　　　Πάμμεγα κῦδος ἀεὶ τῇ πινυτόφρονι τῇ,
　　　Κρείττονα δυσμενέων ἐχθίστων τήνδ' ἀποφαίνων
　　　Ἥπερ ἡ ἀτρεκίη καὶ ἀγαθὸν τὰ φίλα.
25　Τοίην οὖν γε θεάν, Ῥωσσῶν ἰφθιμοτάτων τε
　　　Ἠδὲ ἀρειμανέων εὖχος ἀπειρέσιον,
　　　Ἀρχόμενος μέλπειν δίζημαι, ἀγλαόμορφα
　　　Τέκνα Μνημοσύνης, πᾶν κράτος ὑμέτερον,
　　　Δίζημαι πρὸς Ἀπόλλωνος δνοφερὴν ὀλέκοντος,
30　Ὑμοῦ ἡγεμόνος, νύκτ' ἀδαημονίης,
　　　Οἴμης ἱμερτῆς δίζημαι πᾶσαν ἀρωγὴν
　　　Τοῦ Φοίβου ἤδη ἁπτομένου κιθάρης.

Textus: Tzechanes, Konstantinos (1776), *Carmen heroico-elegiacum ad sacratissimam et augustissimam totius Russiae Imperatricem Catharinam Secundam.* / Ἔπος ἡρωελεγεῖον πρὸς τὴν ἀείμνηστον πάσης Ῥωσσίας αὐτοκράτορα Αἰκατερίναν τὴν Δευτέραν, Leiden.

Sim.: 15 ὑψιπέτης ἀετός] cf. Hom. *Il.* 12.201, 219; 13.882; *Od.* 20.243 || 17 θεράποντες Ἄρηος] cf. Hom. *Il.* 2.110 et saepius || 19 αἰγιόχοιο Διός] cf. Hom. *Il.* 1.202 et saepius || 26 εὖχος ἀπειρέσιον] cf. *Anth. Gr. App., ep. ded.* 326.6

Poem in elegiac couplets to the philosopher and Empress of the undefeated Russians, Catherine the Second

(excerpt, ll. 9–32)

　　　So who is now going to blame me for my bold intention
　　　[10] to celebrate the Empress the way my spirit prompts me,
　　　Catherine, who received so much grace from God,
　　　　　which mind cannot apprehend, nor tongue could easily utter?
　　　The grace which most of the emperors long for,
　　　　　but even the most famous failed to obtain, the first among them
　　　[15] Peter, the high-flying eagle of the great-hearted Russians,
　　　　　the emperor who ruled alone, whose glory spreads far and wide.
　　　Therefore rejoice now, Russians, the faithful attendants of Ares,
　　　　　as Fate gave you Pallas as your empress,
　　　the third-born daugther of Aigis-bearing Zeus,

[20] immovable and fearless under her skin shield,
for which reason Zeus, yea, granted her unspeakably great fame and yet will give
   immense glory forever to her, the Wise One,
showing her stronger than the hateful enemies,
   she, who is devoted to the truth and the good.
[25] Thus, such a goddess – to Russians, who are mighty
   and war-loving, an immense object of boast –
I start to celebrate with my song, and I seek, you beauteous
   children of Mnemosyne, all of your power;
I seek it from Apollo, your master,
[30] who destroys the darkness of ignorance,
I seek for all the help in making a lovely song,
   now that Phoebus has already taken the lyre in his hands.

Metre: Elegiac couplets.

Notes: The poem about Belisarius, published together with three shorter epigrams in a booklet printed at Cambridge in 1776, is an allegoresis, apparently autobiographical in character, recounting Tzechanes' troubles in trying to obtain patronage for the continuation of his studies in Britain. Tzechanes used the apocryphal story first mentioned by Ioannes Tzetzes (*Chiliad*. III, 334–348) about Justinian's best general Belisarius, whom the emperor, consumed with envy, blinded so that he had to carry the note 'Give Belisarius an obol' and beg for alms on the streets of Constantinople. In the second half of the 18th century the motif of Belisarius' beggary became widely known because of a few popular literary and artistic works on the topic. Likening himself to Belisarius, Tzechanes tells the reader about the poverty he suffered for years, and the inexperience which made him metaphorically blind to human malice and envy. However, owing to our insufficient knowledge of Tzechanes' life, it is difficult to interpret all the content of the poem. Contemporary biographies mention only one stay by Tzechanes in Britain in 1773, whereas the poem mentions as many as three, only the last of which could be dated with certainty to the year 1776. By the same token, it is difficult to establish whom Tzechanes followed on his first visit to Oxford; one of the possible interpretations, if we assume that the poet's choice of words suggests the name of that man, is that the *famous Helladian* (Ἑλλάδος ἀνὴρ κλεινός, ll. 1–2) was Alexander Helladius, a Greek scholar and humanist who studied at the Greek College in Oxford during the first decade of the 18th century. Who invited Tzechanes to Paris remains a mystery. The epigram dedicated to Isaac Newton was printed in the same booklet as the previous poem, for obvious reasons, because Newton was an alumnus and professor at the University of Cambridge (1661–1696). Along with Newton's scientific excellence Tzechanes praises his enlightened attitude towards religion, which has often been identified as deism.

Similar in terms of philosophical and religious attitude, but more elaborate in poetic ornatus, Tzechanes' encomium on Empress Catherine the Great (1776, 45 elegiac couplets) showcases her enlightened government and the benefits that another Pallas or Sophia, as he calls her, is bestowing upon Russian society by promoting knowledge (see also Boulgaris, Palladoklis and Baldani in → **Russia**; Baffi in → **Italy**). At the same time, Tzechanes' surprisingly harsh criticism of both Eastern and Western Church establishments (ll. 57–86) makes this laudatory poem somewhat unconventional.

Biography: Konstantinos Tzechanes (Κωνσταντῖνος Τζεχάνης, Albanian Kostë Xhehani; Moschopole, c. 1741 – c. 1800) was a philosopher, mathematician, and poet of Aromanian descent. In his hometown he was taught grammar and poetry by Theodore Kavaliotis, the head of the famous *Nea Academia*. His family went to Hungary to pursue trading, but Tzechanes continued to attend school in Modra (Slovakia) for few years. They next moved to Vienna, but in 1766 Tzechanes departed for higher studies in Halle, Saxony, on foot and without money, and against his father's will. In Halle he studied philosophy and mathematics for about three years; while still a student he managed to publish his first treatise in mathematics (Halle 1769) and contributed to the philological research by one of his professors, the pioneering Albanologist Johann Thunmann. The reports on his wanderings after leaving Halle vary. Zaviras and other literary sources mention his attempt to enter the Academy of Göttingen, but the roster of students of the Leiden Academy and two booklets with Greek laudatory epigrams Tzechanes published there in 1769 and 1770 demonstrate that he was a student of Latin and Greek at the local high school from November 1769. Tzechanes was obviously still short of money, as he was enrolled there without paying any tuition. His poverty must have persisted in subsequent years – we find him in Cambridge in 1776, publishing a booklet of ancient Greek verse in which he presents himself as a student of philosophy and mathematics (*philosophiae et matheseos studiosus*) and desperately asks for financial support. According to Tzechanes' autobiographical poem in the booklet, he had made two earlier attempts to study in Britain, at the University of Oxford in particular, but both times he failed to receive support and did not feel welcome there. Equally unsuccessful, by his own account, was a period of time he spent in Paris, where he was invited by an unnamed fellow countryman. Literary sources also mention his visits to Amsterdam, Venice, Rome, Constantinople and Poland, but no firm data exist about these peregrinations, or about his later years and death, which allegedly took place in Leiden in 1786. In addition to several translations from and into ancient and modern Greek, Latin, and German, and two treatises on arithmetics (Halle 1769) and geometry (1774), written in modern Greek, Tzechanes composed and published several hundred encomiastic verses in ancient Greek, mostly in elegiac couplets and Sapphic stanzas, dedicated to his patrons and rulers, the last of which was printed in 1777.

Bibliography: Zaviras 1872, 394–397; Kourilas, Eulogios (1935), *Γρηγόριος ὁ Ἀργυροκαστρίτης: ὁ μεταφραστής τῆς Καινῆς Διαθήκης εἰς τὸ Ἀλβανικόν: ἤτοι αἱ βάσεις τῆς Ἀλβανικῆς φιλολογίας καὶ γλώσσης ἢ Ἀκαδημία τῆς Μοσχοπόλεως*, Athens, 126–131; Papahagi, Valeriu (1937), "Constantin Hagi Gheorghiu Gehani din Moscopole", in: *Revista Istorica* 23/7–9, 266–279.

Demetrios Darvaris (1757–1823)

ΣΑΠΦΙΚΟΝ εἰς τὴν τῆς Ῥωσσίας μεταβολὴν ἐπὶ ΑΛΕΞΑΝΔΡΟΥ [1819]

(excerptum, vv. 29–64)

    Φῶς σοφίης θ' ἱμερόεν πέφανται,
30 Δυσμαθίης τε σκότος ἐσκέδασται,
    Ὅττ' ΑΛΕΞΑΝΔΡΟΣ γε ἄναξε Δῖος·
        Χαίρετε λαοί.
    Φοῖβος ἀντέλλων ἀπ' ἄκρου πόλοιο
    Μέχρις ἄκρου λαμπετόει γε πᾶσι·
35 Τὼς ΑΛΕΞΑΝΔΡΟΣ κατέλαμψε πάτραν·
        Χαίρετε λαοί.
    Πρίν γε μὲν Μοῦσαι ἔχον Ἑλλάδ' αἶαν,
    Νῦν δὲ χώρην Ἑσπερίην· ὅθεν περ
    Αἶψα γῆν Ῥώσσων ἀπίκοντο πᾶσαι·
40   Χαίρετε λαοί.
    Τῇσι δ' ἱμερταὶ Χάριτές τ' ἔποντο,
    Ἥ τ' Ἀθηναίη κλυτὸς Ἑρμέας τε,
    Νῷ γ' ΑΛΕΞΑΝΔΡΟΥ καλιὴν ἔπηξαν·
        Χαίρετε λαοί.
45 Ἔνθ' ἀείδει θεῖος Ὅμηρος ἥρως,
    Πίνδαρος δ' ἀνδρῶν γαρύει ἄεθλα·
    Τήϊος μέλπει βιότοιο τερπνὰ
        Βαρβίτῳ ἡδύ.
    Σωκράτης νοῦν δαιμόνιος διδάσκει,
50 Ἦθος ἰθύνει δὲ Πλάτων ὁ θεῖος·
    Καὶ Σταγειρίτης ὁ σοφὸς χαράσσει
        Ὄργανον ἄλλο.
    Ὢ πόποι! Παρνασσὸν ὁρῶ, Ἑλικῶνα,
    Οὗ Διὸς Κοῦραι Χάριτές τε δῖαι
55 Ῥυθμῷ ὀρχεῦνται, λιγέως δ' ἀείδει

             Φοῖβος Ἀπόλλων.
        Δεῦτε δὴ κλειναὶ Χάριτες μάλ' ὦκα,
        Σὺν δὲ καὶ Μοῦσαι ἐρατειναί, ἁβρὸν
        Στέμμα Ἥρῳ, οὔτι ἐγὼ νόημι,
60   Πλέξατε δάφνης.
        Φοῖβ' Ἄπολλον, λάβ' ἀπὸ πατταλοῖο
        Γλυκερὴν φόρμιγγα τεήν· Ἄπολλον,
        Ἦκε Πίνδου ἐξ ὄρεος τάχιστα,
             Ἔννεπέ τ' ἄνδρα.

Textus: Darvaris, Demetrios (1819), *Τέτταρα μικρὰ ποιημάτια, ὧν τὰ μὲν δύο πρῶτα ἡρωελεγεῖα ἐγκωμιαστικὰ εἰς τοὺς Τρισεβαστοὺς Αὐτοκράτορας Αὐστρίας καὶ Ῥωσσίας Φραγκίσκον καὶ Ἀλέξανδρον τοὺς Εἰρηνοφίλους τε καὶ Εἰρηνοποιούς, τῶν δὲ λοιπῶν δύο τὸ μὲν σαπφικὸν εἰς τὴν τῆς Ῥωσσίας μεταβολὴν ἐπὶ Ἀλεξάνδρου, τὸ δὲ ἐπικήδειον εἰς τὸν ἄωρον θάνατον τῆς Σεβαστῆς Βιρτεμβέργης Ἀνάσσης Αἰκατερίνης...*, Vienna, 17–20.

Crit.: 34 λαμπετόει] more epico (cf. Hes. *Sc.* 390: ἄστρα λαμπετόωντα) || 41 τ' ἔποντο] θ' ἔποντο debuit || 53 ὁρῶ, 'λικῶνα] ita || 61 πατταλοῖο] παττάλοιο debuit

Sim.: 46 γαρύει ἄεθλα] cf. Pind. *Ol.* 1.3 || 57 μάλ' ὦκα] Hom. *Il.* 2.52 et saepius || 59 νόημι] hapax (more Aeolico) || 64 Ἔννεπέ τ' ἄνδρα] cf. Hom. *Od.* 1.1

A poem in Sapphic stanzas about the transformation of Russia during the reign of Alexander

(ll. 29–64)

    The desirable light of wisdom has shown up,
    [30] and the darkness of ignorance has been scattered,
    since the divine Alexander took the throne:
         Peoples, rejoice!
    Phoebus rising up from the heaven's top
    sheds light on everyone to the farthest end.
    [35] In the same way Alexander has given light to the fatherland:
         Peoples, rejoice!
    The Muses formerly possessed the land of Greece,
    now they own the West: from there
    they have, all of a sudden, come to the land of Russians:
    [40] Peoples, rejoice!
    The Muses are followed by the lovely Graces,
    and both Athena and the glorious Hermes.
    By Alexander's will they built a nest:
         Peoples, rejoice!
    [45] There sings the divine hero Homer,
    Pindar celebrates the contests of men,

the poet of Teos [Anacreon] praises the pleasures of life
   sweetly, with his lyre.
The heaven-sent Socrates teaches the mind,
[50] while the divine Plato guides morality:
The wise Stagirite [Aristotle] sharpens
   another *Organon*.
Alas, I look at Parnassus and Helicon,
where the daughters of Zeus and the divine Graces
[55] dance to the rhythm, and with a clear voice sings
   Phoebus Apollo.
So come here quickly, you famous Graces,
along with the lovely Muses: weave a graceful
garland of laurel for the hero – since I
[60]   can't do it myself!
Phoebus Apollo, grasp from the peg
your sweet-sounding lyre: Apollo,
come from the mountain of Pindus as fast as you can
   and sing of the man!

Metre: Sapphic stanzas.

Notes: A booklet published in Vienna in 1819 is the only evidence that Darvaris successfully composed poems in ancient Greek, a fact which dictionaries of literature have not mentioned thus far. This work was published by the Darvaris family, who intended to use the money from the sales of the booklet to support poor students of the Vienna-based Greek School. It contains an encomiastic poem (elegiac couplets, written in 1818) dedicated to the Emperor of Austria Francis II (1768–1835); two commendatory poems (elegiac couplets and sapphic stanzas, written in 1818) dedicated to the Emperor of Russia, Alexander I (1777–1825); and an elegy on the death of the Princess Catharina of Württemberg (1788–1819), Queen of Westphalia. In terms of form and content, the most interesting poem is an elegy to Emperor Alexander, consisting of 20 metrically almost impeccable Sapphic stanzas. Employing a plethora of reminiscences of ancient Greek culture, Darvaris commends the emperor's efforts to bring about enlightened changes in Russian society; he also credits him with a genuine dedication to peace and economic recovery in Russia. Darvaris, who was an enlightened scholar and educationist himself, was of course aware of the thorough reform of Russia's educational system. As a result of Alexander's efforts, the study of classical culture, especially Greek antiquity, became an integral part of the secondary school curriculum. The poet therefore rejoices that the Muses, who had once departed from Greece, no longer reside only in the West, but have finally found a new home in Russia, together with the best advocates of Greek poetry and philosophical thought.

Biography: Demetrios Darvaris (Δημήτριος Δάρβαρης/Δάρβαρις, Serbian Darvar; Kleisoura, Greece, 1757 – Vienna, Austria, 1823) was a pedagogical writer and poet of Wallachian descent and an exponent of the Greek Enlightenment. In 1769 he left Greece and settled in the part of Serbia controlled by Austria. After receiving elementary education in Zemun, Ruma and Novi Sad, where he started to learn ancient Greek, he attended the Academy of Bucharest until 1780. He completed his studies in Halle and Leipzig (1780–1783), where he studied philology and philosophy. After his studies in Saxony, Darvaris returned to Zemun and began to teach as a private tutor in 1785. His teaching there proved fruitful, as his pupils later distinguished themselves in a variety of social sectors. In 1795 he moved to Vienna, where he ran his family business while simultaneously serving as director of the Greek Orthodox community's school for many years. In his will he asked that the numerous books he had written (26 original titles and 11 translations, four of them from ancient Greek) be distributed amongst the schools operating in various provinces of the Habsburg Empire.

Bibliography: Papadrianos, Ioannis A. (1983), "The Greeks and the Serbs as an Integrated Society in Zemun during the Eighteenth Century", in: *Balkan Studies* 2, 565–582; Camariano-Cioran 1974, 274–276; Staikos/Slavenitis 2001, 120–145.

Nicolaus Androvich (1798–1857)

I. Τῷ αὐτῷ Λαμπρήδῳ χαλεπῶς νοσοῦντι [1826]

Ὄρσεο, Φοῖβε, φίλῳ καὶ Λαμπρήδῳ ἐπάμυνον
Θᾶσσον, ἐπεί ῥα νόσῳ ἀργαλέῃ ἔχεται·
Οὐδὲ γὰρ Ἄδμητον Μοῖραι Ἄϊδι προΐαψαν
Ἀζόμεναι μεγάλην Τοξοφόρου δύναμιν.
5 Ἀλλά, ἄναξ, ψυχὴ Λαμπρήδου σοι μέγ' ἀμείνων,
Ἀνδρὸς ἀεὶ δαίμων χεῖρ' ὑπερέσχε σοφοῦ.

II. Γαγιχίῳ γυναῖκα ἀγομένῳ [1826]

Οὐ δέμας οὐδὲ φυὴν Ἀφροδίτης ἐστὶ χερείων
Παρθένος, ἥν γαμέει ἱππότα Γαγίχιος,
Καὶ μία μὴν ἥγ' ἐστὶ θεάων· ὡς Θέτις εὐνῇ
Μυρμιδόνων βασιλεῖ καὶ φιλότητι μίγη.

III. Ὁδοιπόρος καὶ τύμβος [1826]

>   *ΟΔΟ.* Εἰπὲ τίν' ἀνθρώπων κεύθεις, τίνος εὔχεαι εἶναι
>   Τύμβος; *TYM.* Σοὶ μὲν ἐγὼν ἀτρεκέως ἐρέω·
>   Ἀνέρος, ὦ ξεῖν', ὧδε περικλυτοῦ ὀστέα κεῖται,
>   Τοῦ νῦν δὴ ψυχὴ ἐκ ῥεθέων πταμένη
> 5 Τείρεα καὶ νέφεα σκιόεντα ἔχουσ' ὑπὸ ποσσὶν
>   Τέρπεται Οὐλύμπου εἰσορόωσα σέλας.
>   *ΟΔΟ.* Εἴπ' ὄνομ' ὅ, ττί κεν ἄνδρα κάλεον; *TYM.* Τῷδ' οὔνομα ΘΩΜΑΣ,
>   Ἀλλ' ὅγ' ἔην ἀγαθῆς ΧΕΡΣΙΑΔΑΝ γενεᾶς.
>   Τίς μὲν ἄρ' ἦν ἔγνως, οἷος δέ τοι ἴσθι· τοκῆα,
> 10 Τοὺς δὲ φίλους ἑτάρους, πατρίδα καὶ μεγάλην,
>   Ἠδ' ἐσθλὸν πάσης εὖ εἰδόθ' ἀδελφὸν ἀοιδῆς,
>   Ἐννέα καὶ κούρας, ἃς τέκε Μνημοσύνη·
>   Ἶσον ἄχος πάντας θυμοφθόρον ἔλλαβε, πάντες
>   Ἴσως δ' ᾤμωξαν τἀνδρὸς ἀποφθιμένου.

Textus: Dubrovnik, Dominican monastery library, ms. 34-IX-1 (autographum), ff. 1v-5v; **I.** Androvich, Niccolò (1826), "[Epigramma greco]", in: Ignjat Đurđević, *L'ombra di Ovidio, ovvero Lodi della lingua illirica*, Ragusa, 14; **II.** Androvich, Nicolaus (1826), "ΕΠΙΓΡΑΜΜΑ", in: *Per le faustissime nozze del sig. cavaliere Geremia Gaguitsch consigliere onorario di S. M. I. R. di tutte le Russie colla signora Eustachia Lucich versi*, Ragusa, 8; **III.** Androvich, Nicolaus (1826), "ΕΠΙΓΡΑΜΜΑ", in: *In morte di Tommaso Chersa versi*, Ragusa, 6.

Crit.: plurimos accentus, in autographo et editionibus passim male positos, secundum normam hodiernam vocibus apposui

Sim.: I, 1 cf. Hom. *Il.* 17.171 ‖ **2** νόσῳ ἀργαλέῃ] cf. Hom. *Il.* 13.667 ‖ **3** Ἄϊδι προΐαψαν] cf. Hom. *Il.* 1.3 ‖ **4** cf. Quint. Smyrn. 12.386 ‖ **5** μέγ' ἀμείνων] cf. Hom. *Il.* 22.158, 333 ‖ **6** χεῖρ' ὑπερέσχε] cf. Hom. *Il.* 9.420
II, 1 cf. Hom. *Od.* 5.211-212 ‖ **3-4** εὐνῇ...μίγη] cf. Hom. *Il.* 6.25; *Od.* 5.126
III, 4 ψυχὴ...πταμένη] cf. Hom. *Il.* 16.856; 22.362 ‖ **5** νέφεα σκιόεντα] cf. Hom. *Il.* 5.525; 11.63 ‖ **13** ἄχος θυμοφθόρον] cf. Hom. *Od.* 5.716 ‖ **14** τἀνδρὸς ἀποφθιμένου] cf. Hom. *Il.* 18.499

To the same Urbano Lampredi, severely ill

>   Do not tarry, Phoebus, but fly to Lampredi's succour,
>   quickly, for he is struck with a terrible illness:
>   Even the Moirai did not dare to send Admetus to Hades,
>   for they feared the Archer and his great power.
>   [5] Be advised, Lord, that Lampredi's soul is much more valuable,
>   and that the god has always taken care of a wise man.

To Gagich, who is getting married

As fair as Aphrodite in stature and in face
  is the virgin the knight Gagich takes as his wife:
And indeed she is one of the goddesses: in the same manner did Thetis
  lie with the king of the Myrmidons [Peleus] in bed and love.

The traveller and the grave

T: Say whom of all men you hide. Of whom do you say you are the grave?
  G: I'll tell you, in truth:
Here, stranger, lie the bones of too famous a man,
  whose soul now, having flown off his limbs,
[5] with celestial bodies and dark clouds beneath its feet,
  rejoices to see the light of Olympus.
T: Tell me the name, whatever it would be. G: His name was THOMAS,
  and he belonged to the honourable family of Chersa.
Now that you know who he was, learn what kind of a man he was: his father,
[10] his dear friends, his great homeland,
and his most excellent brother, versed in all poetry,
  and the nine maids Mnemosyne gave birth to:
All of them had their hearts broken by the same sorrow,
  and all of them mourned his death in equal measure.

Metre: Elegiac couplets, mostly flawless.

Notes: In addition to Latin epigrams and Italian sonnets, Androvich wrote 10 Greek epigrams in Homeric style, composed during the 1820s, the heyday of Ragusan *Gelegenheitsdichtung*. The poems featured here were dedicated to prominent personalities from the Ragusan cultural milieu (Urbano Lampredi was a notable Italian scholar temporarily settled in Ragusa, Jeremija Gagich was the Russian consul in Ragusa, and Thomas Chersa was a Ragusan poet and diplomat) and published in collections of poems by various authors along with translations into Italian, Latin, German, French, and Croatian. Following the generation of internationally recognised Ragusan Greek scholars and translators of Homer, which included Raimondo Cunich and Bernardo Zamagna, Androvich represents the last surge of Greek scholarship in the city.

Biography: Nicolaus Androvich (Nikola Andrović; Republic of Ragusa/Dubrovnik, 1798–1857) was a polyglot and occasional poet. He was well regarded even outside the Ragusan community, especially because he was an autodidact in ancient Greek, which he managed to learn in an exceptionally short period of time. Although he was praised by contemporary Italian Hellenists Urbano Lampredi and Girolamo Amati as 'un giovane di alte speranze' because of his elegant poetic expression in ancient Greek, in his later life he completely gave up on poetry.

Bibliography: Bratičević, Irena (2019), "Grčki epigrami Nikole Androvića", in: *Musarum cultus. Zbornik u čast Marini Bricko*, Zagreb, 187–207; Demo, Šime (2019), "Stubborn Persistence at the Outskirts of the West: Latin in Nineteenth-Century Croatia", in: Christophe Bertiau/Dirk Sacré (eds.), *Le latin et la littérature néo-latine au XIXe siècle: Pratique et représentations*, Brussel, 115–132.

Farkas Gábor Kiss and András Németh
Hungary

Greek studies were brought to Hungary around the middle of the 15th century. Janus Pannonius (1434–1472) had already studied Greek under the guidance of Guarino Veronese in the 1440s in Ferrara (→ **Italy**), where translating Greek poems into Latin, and Latin poems into Greek was part of the curriculum (as witnessed by Battista Guarini's *De ordine docendi et studendi*). Janus celebrated Guarino as the guiding light of Greek studies in the West ('who gave back the land of Inachus to Latium', *Latio reddidit Inachiam*) and stressed the importance of studying Greek above all in his panegyric on his master (*Panegyricus in Guarinum*, ll. 725–732), because Greek is the language of intellectual life and poetry, blessed by the Muse (*Graiis ingenium, Graiis dedit ore rotundo / Musa loqui*, ll. 108–109). Still, none of Janus' Greek school exercises is known today. In Guarino's school in Ferrara, he became an excellent interpreter of Greek texts, and he also paraphrased many of the epigrams of the *Anthologia Graeca* in Latin verses. But it was then in Hungary that he translated a part of the sixth book of the *Iliad* into Latin verses and some works of Plutarch into Latin prose, in order to refresh his knowledge of Greek. No Greek poem by Pannonius is extant, nor by any other of the 15th century Hungarians who are known to have studied Greek in Italy (e.g., Péter Garázda in the 1460s, or Paulus Bánffy, who studied under Zaccaria Calliergi in Padua in 1502, or Johannes Vyrthesi/Vértesi, a pupil of Markos Mousouros in 1514) (→ **Italy, Greece**).

The Hellenizing Muse made its first appearance in Hungary in the 16th century under Erasmian influence (→ **Low Countries**). Jacobus Piso, the most significant Latin poet in Hungary in the first decades of the 16th century, praised his Dutch friend for his Greek knowledge in 1509 (*Graecae et Latinae literae, quibus ad invidiam usque excellis*).[1] And it was **Nicolaus Olahus/Oláh** (1493–1568), an admirer and later also friend of Erasmus, who composed the first two poems in Greek, while serving as a secretary of Mary of Hungary in the Netherlands in the 1530s. His two Greek funerary poems (one on Erasmus, the other on Klára Újlaki, an aristocratic noble lady, and mother of Oláh's friend, Ferenc Újlaki) reflect the occasional character of most Greek poems of this time. Oláh's secretary **Nicolaus Istvánffy** (1539–1615) continued this Erasmian tradition with a Greek translation inserted in his juvenile collection of poems. **Johannes Sambucus** (1531–1584),

---

1 Erasmus Roterodamus (1906), *Opus epistolarum*, I, ed. P.S. Allen, Oxford, 452–454.

an internationally well-known humanist, composed some 15 – mostly dedicatory – Greek poems throughout his life from a 1550 edition of Homer (for which he acted as a junior editor) to collections of emblem poems (*Emblemata* 1564 & 1566), which show a novel application of Greek poetry to the Renaissance emblematic genre. He started to study Greek in Vienna under Georg Rithaymer (whom he duly celebrated in a poem), and composed some Greek poems during his stay in Paris in 1551, where he became a student of Jean Dorat, and befriended the Hellenizing French circles (→ **France**).

Lutheranism and its educational agenda made the most significant impact on Hellenism in Hungary in the later 16th century (→ **Germany**). Valentin Wagner (c. 1515–1557), a German Protestant preacher in the Transylvanian city of Braşov, printed the first original Greek poem in the country at the end of his own Lutheran catechism, written in Greek in 1550 so that the students could practise Greek language and Lutheran doctrine at the same time. Philipp Melanchthon knew about Wagner's efforts already in 1545, and mentioned in a letter that his main aim was to spread Lutheranism among the neighbouring Greek-speaking communities of the Balkans (→ **Balkans**).[2] Wagner studied in Wittenberg, and the Saxon university town became the centre of all the Greek publishing activities of Hungarian Protestant scholars from the 1560s to the 1580s. Sophocles' *Electra* was translated into Hungarian by Péter Bornemissza under the influence of Melanchthon (Vienna, 1555), and Greek poems appeared in a collection of *propemptica* when Basilius Hellopoeus Szikszai left Wittenberg's Hungarian community of students in 1562 (authors included Basilius himself, his brother Valentinus, and Demetrius Fabricius Szikszai).[3]

Epithalamia, *propemptica*, dedicatory verses, and funerary poems remained the main genres of Greek poetry in later years. In 1567, **János Beregszászi** (Johannes Beregzazius) praised his teacher, Péter Károlyi, in a longer poem on the occasion of his wedding in Debrecen, just like Johannes Bonifacius (János Debreceni Joó) did in the same year. In 1571, the departure of Johannes Jantschius from Wittenberg was commemorated by Georg Henisch of Bardejov (who later became a well-known philologist in Augsburg), and his book was celebrated by Matthias Thoraconymus (Kabát) in Doric verses. In the same year, Mihály Varsányi, another student of Péter Károlyi, honoured his master's confutation of anti-Trinitarian doctrines with two Greek poems. The death of Basilius Fabricius was mourned

---

2 'ut puram Evangelii doctrinam in vicinas gentes, quae Graeca lingua utuntur, propagare possint.' *Corpus Reformatorum*, vol. 5, Halis Saxonum 1838, 771.
3 *Propemptica in discessum eruditione, virtute ac pietate ornatissimi viri D. Basilii Zykzaij Pannonii scripta a fratre et amicis*, Wittenberg, Schwenck, 1562. (VD16 ZV 21990)

by Vincentius L. Tonensis (Vince Tolnai?) in 1577; Péter Laskai Csókás (Petrus Lascovius de Barovia) dedicated his explanation of the Decalogue to the city of Debrecen with Greek poems in 1578 and encouraged the youth to study Greek in his *Speculum exilii*, published in Braşov (1581).

It seems that this Hellenizing trend was a direct influence of the Wittenberg Reform. As soon as ethnic Hungarian Protestants turned towards Calvinism in the late 1560s, and started to favour the University of Heidelberg instead of Wittenberg, their interest in composing Greek poetry seems to have faltered. When anti-Trinitarianism, the most revolutionary direction of Protestantism in Hungary, triumphed among Transylvanian Hungarians in the 1580s, their interest in Hellenic studies remained strong, especially under the influence of the radical thinker Jacobus Palaeologus (Giacomo da Chio).[4] Johann Sommer wrote a Greek funerary speech, György Enyedi translated the *Aethiopica* of Heliodorus into Latin (in manuscript), and he regularly cited the New Testament, Plato, or Homer in the Greek original in his Hungarian sermons held in the city of Cluj (Kolozsvár).[5] Nevertheless, it seems that no poetry was produced that could be connected to these branches of Protestantism in Hungary.

The Hellenizing Muse remained present in those parts of the country where the Lutheran Reform and the influence of Wittenberg were still strong, namely in the cities of Northern Hungary, where many Germans and Slovaks lived. Bartholomaeus Chryseus celebrated the wedding of Elias Schall in his native town of Banská Štiavnica (Schemnitz) in 1575, and Michael Marthius of Banská Bystrica (Neusohl) wrote a *propempticon* to his friend in 1589. This tendency continued well into the 17th century: Jeremias Spiegel composed a Greek paraphrase of Psalm 133 in Bardejov (1616) and *epithalamia*, propemptic poems, or epitaphs often appear in occasional publications in German towns (e.g., that of **Matthias Lochmann** in Levoča in 1658; the verses dedicated to Christian Seelman in Sopron in 1661, or the praise of the deceased Johann Lang by Georg Krieschke, the head of the local gymnasium in Levoča in 1647). In the 17th century, the teaching of Greek remained strong in the Lutheran schools of the mostly German-speaking towns of Bardejov, Kežmarok, Levoča, or Prešov in Upper Hungary (now Slovakia), as witnessed in the school play titled 'Dramatic School of Prešov' (*Lyceum*

---

[4] Most recently, see Rothkegel, Martin (2012) "Werdegang des Antitrinitariers Jacobus Palaeologus bis 1561. 1: Frate Jacobo da Scio und seine Anhänger in der Levante", in: *Acta Comeniana* 26, 7–69 and Rothkegel, Martin (2014), "Paleologo, Giacomo", in: *Dizionario Biografico degli Italiani* 80, 423–427.

[5] Poelchau, Lore (1997), "Johannes Sommer (1542–1574)", in: *Humanistica Lovaniensia* 44, 182–239; Balázs, Mihály/Keserű, Gizella (eds.) (2000), *György Enyedi and the Central European Unitarianism in the 16–17th Centuries*, Budapest.

Eperiense Dramaticum), in which the Greek language appears as an actor (1661). It seems significant that Hungarian Lutherans still turned to Greek, such as György Dömötöri, who celebrated the famous military hero Nicholas Zrínyi in a Greek poem in 1665; two years earlier, the death of the Lutheran nobleman István Vitnyédy (Wyttnyedy) had been commemorated by Greek poems in Tübingen. Even the author of the Greek poem celebrating the strongly anti-Protestant Emperor Leopold I, Joseph Guttovieni, was the director of a Lutheran school in Bratislava.

In the lack of thorough bibliographic studies, we know relatively little about Hellenic poetry in 18th-century Hungary. It seems that Greek epideictic poetry still remained fashionable among Protestant students (e.g., Andreas Parvi in Wittenberg in 1716, or Georgius Huszti in Franeker in 1735). Only a few mentions survive about the excellent Greek poetry of Samuel Szilágyi (1719–1785), a professor at the Calvinist academy of Debrecen.

Polyzoes Kondos (1760–1821) and **László Ungvárnémethi Tóth** (1788–1820) are already the representatives of a new age of Hellenism. The ancient and modern Greek poems of Polyzoes Kondos are part of the literature produced by the Greek diaspora of the Ottoman Empire,[6] of which Buda and Pest became significant centres around 1800. Fénelon's *Télémaque* was published in modern Greek translation there in 1801 by Dimitrios Govdelas,[7] and in the same year Konstantinos Koutzikos translated the life of Napoleon Bonaparte and the French *Amours de Carité et de Polydore* of Abbé Barthélémy (who in turn had claimed that his love novel was a translation from the Greek).[8] On the other hand, László Ungvárnémethi Tóth was a unique representative of sentimental bucolic poetry: while the emotions described by him are characteristic of the pre-Romantic (primarily German) bucolic poetry of the late 18th century, his tone and his elected

---

[6] See Sfoini, Alexandra (2015), "Transfert des idées par la voie de la traduction pendant l'ère révolutionnaire grecque (1797–1832)", in: *The Historical Review/La Revue Historique* 12, 47–74.

[7] See Stessi, Athina (2018), "Fénelon dans la culture néo-hellénique (XVIIIe-XIXe siècles)", in: *Dix-septième siècle* 278, 285–308.

[8] For other examples, see Horváth, András (1935), *Magyar-görög bibliográfia*, Budapest, 16–18. See in particular: Régi Magyar Könyvtár (RMK) III 591 (Johannes Bonifacius), RMK III 5340 (Johannes Jantschius), RMK III 612 (Mihály Varsányi), RMK III 7407 (Bartholomaeus Chriseus), RMK III 665 (Vincentius L. Tonensis), RMK III 674, Régi Magyarországi Nyomtatványok (RMNy) 483 (Péter Laskai Csókás), RMK III 716 (Tamás Fabricius Tolnai), RMK III 796 (Michael Marthius), RMK II 364 (Jeremias Spiegel), RMNy 2176 (Georg Krieschke), RMNy 2181 (Daniel Fabri), RMNy 2529 (Tobias Stephani), RMNy 2986 (to Christian Seelman), RMNy 3136 (for István Vitnyédy), RMNy 3259 (György Dömötöri), RMK III-18 33(Andreas Parvi), RMK III-18 157 (Georgius Huszti).

exquisite ancient Greek language harks back to Neoclassicism. The tradition of writing poetry in Greek is preserved up to this day by the classical scholar **Bence Fehér** (1968–), who both writes original poems and translates Hungarian poetry into ancient Greek.

[FGK]

General Bibliography

RMK = Régi Magyar Könyvtár I–IV (Budapest, 1879–1898).
RMNy = Régi Magyar Nyomtatványok I–IV (Budapest, 1971–2012).

228   I. SAMBVCI

EPITAPHIVM GENEROSI
adolescentis Georgij Bonæ Transyluani,
& tanquam fratris, qui obijt M. D. LIX.
ætatis suæ XX. VI. Septemb.

Ὦ ληθ' ἅπαση ἀρετῇ πάσας λιπόκοσμος ὁ Βῶνα,
Θαῦμα χρισογενῶν τῶν φίλος ἔσκε Θεῶν.
Ἥρπασε τεῦτον πανδαμάτωρ μοῖρ' οὐκ ἀέκοντος
Αὐτοῦ ἐπ' ἀΐδιον, κὶ βιοπόθητον ὄναρ.
Ὂν φίλοι, ὀρφανικὸς σὺν πᾶσιν ὀδύρεται οἶκος,
Ἥ ' μητῆς κήπου φεῦξεν ὁδ' αἰθερίου.

T⁖

Fig. 9: *Emblemata cum aliquot nummis antiqui operis, Ioannis Sambuci Tirnaviensis Pannonii*, Antverpiae: ex officina Christophori Plantini, 1564, 228: Greek epigram by Sambucus (see below, p. 458–460).

Nicolaus Olahus (Miklós Oláh, 1493–1548)

Epitaphium Erasmi [1537]

Σήματι τῷ κεῖται τὸ νεκρὸν φρονέοντος Ἐράσμου,
Αὐτὰρ ἔχει ψυχὴν οὐρανὸς ἀστερόεις.
Κλαίουσιν πάντες τούτου μόρον οἱ ἐνὶ κόσμῳ,
Ἀλλ᾽, ἄγε, χαίρουσιν πνεύματ᾽ ἐπουράνια.

Textus: *D. Erasmi Roterodami Epitaphia per clarissimos aliquot viros conscripta*, Lovanii, R. Rescius 1537, c. 5v; hinc Olahus, Nicolaus (1934), *Carmina*, ed. István Fógel/László Juhász, Lipsiae, 37 (no. 71).

Crit.: 1 τὸ ut vid. add. Craneveldius (vide ed. Fógel-Juhász, 48) | Ἐρασμοῦ Fógel-Juhász ‖ 4 πνεύματα οὐράνια ut vid. Olahus, corr. Craneveldius (vide ed. Fógel-Juhász, 48)

Sim.: 2 οὐρανὸς ἀστερόεις] cf. Hom. *Il.* 4.44 al.

Epitaph of Erasmus

The corpse of the wise Erasmus lies in this grave,
  but the starry sky possesses his soul.
Everyone in this world laments his fate,
  but, lo, the heavenly spirits rejoice.

Metre: Elegiac couplets (note the hiatus in l. 3).

Notes: This epigram testifies to Olahus' acquaintance with Erasmus of Rotterdam (→ **Low Countries**), as well as his admiration for his work.

Biography: Born in Nagyszeben (present-day Sibiu), Nicolaus Olahus started an early ecclesiastical career; in 1526 he became a secretary and counsellor of King Louis II and Queen Mary of Hungary. In 1531 he went to the Low Countries with Queen Mary of Hungary, who had become governor of the land in Brussels: there he kept in close contact with local humanists. In 1542, he returned to Hungary, and finally became the archbishop of Esztergom in 1553. He founded a college in Trnava (1558) and invited the Jesuits to Hungary (1561).

Bibliography: Szilágyi, Emőke R. (2015), "Nicolaus Olahus", in: David Thomas et al. (eds.), *Christian-Muslim Relations. A Bibliographical History, VII, Central and Eastern Europe, Asia, Africa and South America (1500–1600)*, Leiden, 201–206.

[FGK]

Johannes Sambucus (János Zsámboky, 1531–1584)

I. *Epitaphium generosi adolescentis Georgii Bonae Transylvani et tamquam fratris, qui obiit MDLIX, aetatis suae XX, VI. Septemb.* [1559]

Ὤλλεθ' ἅπασ' ἀρετὴ πάτρας, λιπόκοσμος ὁ Βῶνα·
  Θαῦμα χριστογενῶν τῶν φίλος ἔσκε Θεῶν.
Ἥρπασε τοῦτον πανδαμάτωρ μοῖρ' οὐκ ἀέκοντος
  Αὐτοῦ ἐπ' ἀΐδιον καὶ τριπόθητον ὄναρ.
5 Ὅν, φίλοι, ὀρφανικὸς σὺν πᾶσιν ὀδύρεται οἶκος,
  Ἡγητὴς κήπου φεῦξεν ὅδ' αἰθερίου.
Τὴν σοφίαν μεγάλου, πραπίδας, καὶ τὰς μελεδῶνας
  Ἡμῖν λυσιπόνῳ θυμὸς ἐν ἡσυχίᾳ.
Εὐσεβέων ἦν παῖς ἀγαθός, τῷ κρείσσον' ὀπηδεῖ,
10 Ἀενάῳ σύνεδρος νέκταρι κἀμβροσίᾳ.
Νείοθι τῆς πέτρης τὸν ἀδωροδόκητον ἀκεστὴν
  Προσδέκεται κριτήν, τοῦ πλέον' ὅσσ' ἂν ἔφυ.

Textus: *Emblemata cum aliquot nummis antiqui operis,* Ioannis Sambuci Tirnaviensis Pannonii, Antverpiae: Chr. Plantin, 1564[1], 228; 1566[2], 197; 1569[3], 211.

Crit.: 1 ἅπασ' 1566, 1569: ἅπαση 1564 || **6** ὅδ' edd., correxi | αἰθερίου: ἀθερίου 1566, 1569 || **9** ὀπηδεῖ edd., correxi (an ὀπήδει?) || **10** Αενάω 1566, 1569 | κἄμβροσία 1564 || **12** ὅσσ': ὁσσ' 1564, 1566, 1569 | ἂν ἔφυ: ἀνέφυ 1566, 1569.

Sim.: 1 λιπόκοσμος] hapax leg. || **2** χριστογενῶν] hapax leg. || **3** πανδαμάτωρ μοῖρ'] cf. Arist. epigr. 43.2 Rose in Peplo (*App. Anth. Gr., epigr. sepulchr.* 97.2) || **8** θυμὸς ἐν ἡσυχίᾳ] cf. *Anth. Pal.* 7.408.4

Epitaph of the noble young man Georgius Bona from Transylvania, almost a brother, who died at 20 on 6. Sept. 1559

All the virtue of the fatherland has gone, as Bona left the universe: he was a miracle for the Christians, and dear to the Gods. All-conquering fate has ravished him, though not against his own will, into an unseen, and thrice-longed for dream. His orphaned house mourns him, my friends, with all men; [5] this leader of the heavenly garden has fled. Now finally the heart of this man, who was great in his wisdom, spirit, and sufferings, rests in peace, which releases us from our toils. He was a good child of pious parents, he followed the Almighty, [10] and sits now among ever-flowing nectar and ambrosia. Under the stone, he awaits the incorruptible judge, the healer, from whom all greater things were born.

Metre: Elegiac couplets.

Notes: Nicolaus Olahus (see above) entrusted the education of his nephew Georgius (György) Bona (1539–1559) to the young humanist Johannes Sambucus, who became his tutor on his study trip to Padua in 1553. Bona started to study Greek in 1555, and he composed several dedicatory poems to the publications of his master. After returning to Vienna in 1557, he fell sick and died in his uncle's castle in 1559. His death was commemorated by Sambucus in this emblem.

II. *De obitu Oporini* [1568]

Αἴ, θάνε χαλκογράφων βασιλεύς, μέγα θαῦμα πόνοισι,
 Θησαυρούς τε λιπών, τοῦ κλέος οὐράνιον.
Πῶς τιν' Ὀπωρινοῦ θυμὸς πραπίδες τε λάθοιεν,
 Δώρων οὖ τυπικῶν πάντες ἄπαντα γέμει;

Textus: Andreas Iociscus, *Oratio De Ortu, Vita Et Obitu Ioannis Oporini Basiliensis, Typographicorum Germaniae Principis, recitata in Argentinensi Academia ab Ioanne Henrico Hainzelio Augustano*, Argentorati: Th. Rihelius 1569, c. F7v.

Crit.: 1 θανε ed., correxi || 4 πάντες dubium

Sim.: 2 τοῦ κλέος οὐράνιον] cf. *Anth. Pal.* 9.485.7

On Oporinus' death

Oh, the king of the typographers has died, a great miracle for his labours:
 he left behind treasures, his fame is heavenly.
How could Oporinus' mind and spirit escape anyone's attention,
 as everybody and everything is full of his printed gifts?

Metre: Elegiac couplets.

Notes: Johannes Oporinus (1507–1568), the Basel printer and dissident thinker, was a close collaborator of Johannes Sambucus, with whom he published the historical work of Antonio Bonfini in 1568, and to whom he also promised the *editio princeps* of Nonnus' *Dionysiaca*. Sambucus arranged imperial privileges in Vienna for the publications of his friend, but these plans were hampered by Oporinus' death, and Nonnus' poem was then published by Plantin in Antwerp (1569).

Biography: Johannes Sambucus (János Zsámboky, 1531–1584), born to a wealthy family in Trnava, studied Greek in Vienna under Georg Rithaymer, and later moved on to the universities of Ingolstadt, Tübingen, Strasbourg, Paris, and Padua. After returning to Vienna, he became the imperial historian of Emperor Maximilian II, and gathered an exceptional manuscript collection, from which he published several Greek and Latin texts throughout his life. Although some of his plans were thwarted (e.g., the publication of Dioscorides' *Materia medica*), he prepared 32 critical editions in his life, many of which were *principes*. Besides these, he published a popular book of emblems, which was translated into Dutch, English, and French in the 16th century. His library was bought by the Emperor, and incorporated into the earliest stock of the Imperial Library in Vienna.

Bibliography: Almási, Gábor (2009), *The Uses of Humanism. Andreas Dudith (1533–1589), Johannes Sambucus (1531–1584), and the East Central European Republic of Letters*, Leiden; Almási, Gábor Kiss, Farkas Gábor (eds.) (2014), *Humanistes du bassin des Carpates II. Johannes Sambucus*, Turnhout.

[FGK]

Nicolaus Istvanffius (Miklós Istvánffy, 1538–1615)

Iacobi Sannazari, Graece (Patavii, 1555)

Μέμψατο τυτθὸν Ἔρωτά ποτ' Ἄρτεμις ἀστεροπητῇ,
Ὡς κεῖνος μεμαὼς ἐστιν ἐς ὅπλα λίαν.
Τόφρα πατὴρ κληθέντι βαρὺν ἐπέδειξε κεραυνόν
Χ', "Οὗτος οἰστόν", ἔφη, "παῖ, σὸν ἀποσκεδάσει."
5 Τῷ καὶ μείλιχος εἶπεν Ἔρως πτερὰ γοργὰ συνάρας·
"Θές σ' ἄπο τὴν βροντὴν καὶ πάλι κύκνος ἔσῃ."

Textus: Budapest, Bibl. Academiae Scientiarum Hungaricae, ms. M.Irod.Irók. 4-r.241/II, f. 39r (manu ipsius auctoris), unde ed. Iosephus Holub/Ladislaus Juhász, in: Nicolaus Istvanffy, *Carmina*, Lipsiae, 1835, 43 (no. 57).

Sim.: 1 cf. Nonn. *Dion.* 15.395 (μέμψατο δ' αὐτὸν Ἔρωτα) | ἀστεροπητῇ] e.g. *Il.* 7.442 al. || 6 καὶ πάλι κύκνος ἔσῃ] cf. *Anth. Pal.* 9.108 (Ὁ Ζεὺς πρὸς τὸν Ἔρωτα· Βέλη τὰ σὰ πάντ' ἀφελοῦμαι / χὠ πτανός· Βρόντα, καὶ πάλι κύκνος ἔσῃ)

By Jacopo Sannazaro, in Greek (Padua, 1555)

Once Artemis denounced little Eros to the lightning-maker [Zeus],
    saying that he was too keen on weapons.
Then the father summoned him and showed him his heavy thunderbolt,
    and said: 'Child, this will destroy your arrow.'
[5] And Eros replied to him sweetly, gathering his frightening wings:
    'Put down the thunder, and you will be a swan again.'

Metre: Elegiac couplets; with a lengthening of the final syllable of βαρύν in l. 3; l. 1 may be considered a *versus bipartitus*, but the author certainly intended a κατὰ τρίτον τροχαῖον caesura.

Notes: This poem survived in the manuscript collection of Istvánffy's poems, which were mostly composed in his youth. The Greek translation of Sannazaro's Latin epigram (*Epigr.* 2.22: *De Veneris nato questa est*),[9] which was in turn inspired by an epigram of the *Greek Anthology* (*Anth. Pal.* 9.108), demonstrates the humanist practice of translating texts from Latin into Greek and vice versa.

Biography: Miklós Istvánffy (1538–1615) was the son of Pál Istvánffy, an important courtier in the court of King John Szapolyai. Between 1553–1557, he spent five years in Padua accompanying the nephew of Nicolaus Olahus, archbishop of Esztergom (see above), on his study trip to Italy. Returning to Hungary, he became the secretary of the archbishop, and a member of the royal chancery of Emperor Maximilian II, a royal councillor, and finally vice-palatine of Hungary in 1581, holding various political and diplomatic charges until his death in 1615. During his lifetime, he wrote a monumental history of 16th-century Hungary in 34 books, which was published posthumously in 1622.

---

9 *De Veneris nato questa est Dictynna Tonanti, / Quod nimis ille puer promptus ad arma foret. / Tunc pater accito ostendens grave fulmen Amori, / 'Hoc tibi, saeve puer, spicula franget', ait. / Cui lascivus Amor motis haec reddidit alis: / Quid, si iterum posito fulmine cygnus eris?* (see Sannazaro, Jacopo (2009), *Latin Poetry*, transl. Michael C.J. Putnam, Cambridge Mass., 318).

Bibliography: Ács, Pál/Tóth, Gergely (eds.) (2018), "*A magyar történet folytatója*", Budapest; Berlász, Jenö (1961), "Istvánffy Miklós könyvtáráról", in: *Az Országos Széchényi Könyvtár Évkönyve 1959*, Budapest, 202–240.

[FGK]

Valentinus Hellopoeus Zykzai (Bálint Hellopoeus Szikszai)

Ad eundem D. Basilium Zykzai virum pietate et eruditione praestantem Carmen aliud προπεμπτικόν, scriptum a Valentino Hellopoeo Zykzai, εἰς μνημόσυνον sui erga illum studii et amoris [1562]

(excerptum, vv. 1–10, 26–47)

    Πάντ' ἀπέδωκε κακοῖς ζωὴ ἄνδρεσσιν ἀμείνω
    Πράγματα, τῶν δὲ τύχη ἐν τῷ βίῳ ἔπλετο μείζων
    ἢ ἀγαθῶν· χρὴ πασχέμεναι κακὰ πολλὰ δικαίους.
    Σκῆπτρα ἔχουσι κακοί, πλούτους, ἀγλαὰς βασιλείας,
5   Ἀκροπόλεις μεγάλας, δύναμιν, σύμμεικτον ἀρούρης
    Καρπόν, ἀεὶ δ' οἴνοιο πίθους ἅμα ἡδυπότοιο.
    Ἀλλ' οὐκ ἀθανάτην σοφίην ἴσασιν ἑλέσθαι·
    Ἥδε μόνη σφᾶς τῆλε ἀλεύεται, οὐδέ τ' ὀφέλλει,
    Καὶ μᾶλλον κραδίαις ἐσθλῶν βούλοιτο ἐπέσθαι,
10 Τοῖσι καὶ αὐτομάτη πέφυκε δείξασθαι ἑαυτήν.
    [...]
26 Καί σοι, ὦ ἡμετέρῳ ἄνερ κεχαρισμένε θυμῷ,
    Ταῦτα μέμηλε ἀεὶ νύκτας τε καὶ ἤματα πάντα
    Τοὔνομα ὥστε θεοῦ κλείειν τοῦ αἰὲν ἐόντος,
    Καὶ θ' ἅμα τῶν λαῶν πιστῶν μέγ' ὄνειαρ ἔσεσθαι,
30 Εἴνεκα τοῦ σοφίης πολλῶν μάλ' ἐέλδεαι ὄλβων,
    Κτήματα τοῦ κόσμου ἄλλοις καλὰ μὴ καλὰ λείπων,
    Ἀλλ' ὅτε Παννονικὴν θούρῳ πέρθοιεν Ἄρηϊ
    Αἱμάδομοι γαῖαν Τοῦρκοι θεοχριστόμαχοί τε,
    Ἐξέφυγον Μοῦσαι πάντες τάχα ἀρτιέπειαι,
35 Λείψασαι ὕδωρ Ἴστρου ἅλαδε προρέοντος.
    Ταῖς ἀπὸ μὲν πατρίδος θυμός σ' ἑσπέσθαι ἀνώγει,
    Ῥηϊδίως πάσας ἀλέγοντα ὁδοῖο μερίμνας.
    Πολλὰ γὰρ ἀνθρώποισιν ὁδοιπορίη κακὰ τίκτει,
    Τὰ κραδίῃ ἐλθών σου ἀγήνορι ἶφι φέρεσκες,
40 Εἰσόκε Λευκορίδος κατὰ σφᾶς κλυτὸν ἄστυ γε τέτμῃς.

Ἐνθάδε καὶ μετέπειτ', ἠθεῖε, μένων, Βασίλειε
Ἤκουσας θείης μεγάλοιο Μελάγχθονος αὐδῆς,
Τοῦ ῥα διδάσκοντος κειμήλι' ἐπὶ φρεσὶ θῆκας.
Ἀλλ' ὅτε μοῖρα κακὴ ὁσιωτάτου ἀνδρὸς ἀφεῖλε
45 Θυμὸν ἀπὸ μελέων, ὃς πρὸς θεὸν εἰλήλουθε,
Ἄλλων ἤκουσας ἀνδρῶν μελιηδέα μῦθον
Λευκορίδ' ἐν σοφίῃ πεπνυμένα πολλὰ λεγόντων.

Textus: *Propemptica in discessum eruditione, virtute ac pietate ornatissimi viri D. Basilii Zykzaij Pannonii scripta a fratre et amicis*, Witebergae: Schwenck, 1562, cc. B2v–B4r.

Crit.: 9 ἐσπέσθαι correxi: ἔσπεσθαι ed. || **31** Κτήματα correxi: Κτῆμα, τὰ ed. || **34** πάντες: πᾶσαι debuit || **39** ἶφι: ἴφι ed.

Sim.: 5 σύμμεικτον...καρπόν: cf. Hes. *op.* 563 || **6** οἴνοιο πίθους ἅμα ἡδυπότοιο] cf. Hom. *Od.* 2.340 (ἐν δὲ πίθοι οἴνοιο παλαιοῦ ἡδυπότοιο) || **7** ἀθανάτην σοφίην] cf. *Anth. Pal.* 11.28.5 || **26** κεχαρισμένε θυμῷ] cf. Hom. *Il.* 5.243 al. || **29** μέγ' ὄνειαρ] cf. Hes. *op.* 41, 346 al. || **32** θούρῳ...Ἄρηι] saep. apud Hom., cf. *Il.* 5.30 al. || **33** αἱμάδομοι et θεοχριστόμαχοι] hapax leg., ut vid. || **34** ἀρτιέπειαι] de Musis cf. Hes. *Theog.* 29 || **35** ἅλαδε προρέοντος] cf. Hes. *op.* 757 || **38** ἀνθρώποισιν...κακὰ τίκτει] cf. *Orac. Sib.* 3.235–236 || **39** κραδίη ἀγήνορι] ex Hom. *Il.* 9.635 al. (κραδίη καὶ θυμὸς ἀγήνωρ) || **44** μοῖρα κακή] cf. Hom. *Il.* 13.602

For the same Mr Basilius Zykzai, a man excellent in piety and learning, another poem written by Valentin Hellopoeus Zykzai, in memory of his love and friendship towards him [1562]

(excerpt, ll. 1–10, 26–479)

Life has conceded all the better things to the evil men, whose luck is always greater in life than that of the good people: the just ones have to suffer many bad things. Always the evil have the royal rule, the riches, the glittering kingdoms, [5] the great castles, the power, the various fruits of the earth, together with the large jars of sweet wine. But they do not know how to grasp the immortal wisdom, which alone keeps them far away, and does not strengthen them, as it would rather follow the hearts of the virtuous, [10] to whom by nature it spontaneously reveals itself.
[…]
But you, o man, beloved to our heart, you always took care about these things all the days and nights, so as to celebrate the name of the eternal God, and at the same time to be a great aid to the people of the faithful, [30] therefore you long very much for the manifold blessings of wisdom, leaving to others all the beautiful things of the world – which are not beautiful at all. But whenever the blood-thirsty Turks, enemies of God and Christ, destroyed the land of Pannonia with furious war, all the eloquent Muses fled swiftly, [35] leaving behind the water of the Danube, which flows into the sea.

Your heart ordered you to follow their path away from your fatherland, taking easily all the anxious thoughts about the road. Because travel brings a lot of trouble to men, which you robustly withstood with a heroic heart on the road, [40] until you reached them in the famous city of Wittenberg at last. And thereafter you remained there, virtuous Basilius, and listened to the divine voice of the great Melanchthon, whose treasure of learning you stored in your mind. But when evil fate took away [45] the soul of this holiest man from his limbs, and he went to God, you listened to the honey-sweet talk of other men, who taught many prudent things with wisdom in Wittenberg.

Metre: Hexameters. The poem contains many problematic hiatuses (ll. 2, 3, 4, etc.) and irregularities, such as short α before σφ- (l. 40), or the lengthening of ἀπό in line 45.

Notes: The addressee of the poem, Basilius (Balázs) Fabricius Zykzai (c. 1530–1576) was a compatriot of the author, who studied in Wittenberg from 1557 to 1562, and composed two Latin poems and a Greek prayer there. This long epigram belongs to a small collection of *propemptica* for Zykzai's departure from Wittenberg, written by several of his friends and colleagues.

Biography: Valentinus (Bálint) Hellopoeus Zykzai was born in Szikszó around 1540–45, and studied in Wittenberg from 1562 to 1566, where he became the senior of the Hungarian *coetus*. Soon after, he continued his studies in Geneva with Theodore Beza and in Zurich with Heinrich Bullinger. In Hungary, he became the pastor of the Reformed congregation in Eger (1567–1572) and Debrecen (1573–1575), where he died in 1575.

Bibliography: Szabó, András (2004), *A későhumanizmus irodalma Sárospatakon (1555-1593)* [The late humanist literature in Sárosp., 1562-1598], Debrecen, 39–50; Bernhard, Jan-Andrea (2015), *Konsolidierung des reformierten Bekenntnisses im Reich der Stephanskrone. Ein Beitrag zur Kommunikationsgeschichte zwischen Ungarn und der Schweiz in der frühen Neuzeit (1500-1700)*, Göttingen, 277–278.

[FGK]

Johannes Beregzazius (János Beregszászi, c. 1550–post 1583)

Epithalamion in honorem nuptiarum clarissimi et doctissimi viri D. Petri Carolii praeceptoris sui [1569]

(excerptum, vv. 75–86, 140–147)

75 Ὄλβιός ἐστιν ἀνὴρ ἑτάρην ἐκ παντὸς ὁμοίην
    ἤθεσιν εὑρίσκων. τῷ γὰρ μάλα ἔκλυον αὐτοί,
    ἄλγεα παῦρα πάνυ καὶ χάρματα πολλὰ φέροντε,
    ἀνὴρ ἡδὲ γυνή, ἐρέω· ὁ τρὶς ὄλβιός ἐστι.
    Δύσμορος ἀλλ᾽ ἔστιν καὶ ἀποτμότατος κατὰ γαίας,
80 ὅς γαμέει ψυχῆς τε βίου παντὸς τρόπου ἐχθρήν.
    σύμβασις οὐκ ἔστιν τούτων φιλότητος, ἄριστον
    οὐ κλέος, ὁ στυγερὸς πλὴν ἔστιν ἑαυτῷ ἐκεῖνος
    ἱέμενος θανάτου, ζώην καὶ ἀήδεα πράττει.
    Τρισμάκαρ οὖν, πολλῶν δὲ μακάρτατος ἔσσεται ἄλλων,
85 ΚΑΡΌΛΙΟΣ ποιμὴν λαοῦ θεράπων καὶ Ἰησοῦ
    ὀτρηρός, φιλέει θεὸς ὃν καὶ κήδεται αἰεί.
    [...]
140 Ἡδὲ πολυστάφυλον καὶ ἐϋκτίμενον πτολίεθρον
    ἔστι τὸ ΒΑΡΆΔΙΝΟΝ τ᾽ ὅθι καλλίροον ῥέει ὕδωρ
    Χρύσιος ἐκ πηγῆς, χρυσοῦ ὅθεν ἔστι γενέθλη,
    καὶ ποταμὸς χρυσοῦν νικᾷ δόξα τε πόσει τε.
    ἀμφὶ δὲ Παννονίης κλυτὰ δώματ᾽ ἔναιον ἄνακτες
145 ἐν χερσὶν σκῆπτρον, χρύσεον καὶ στέμμα ἔχοντες·
    ἐνθάδε ὃς ποιμὴν λαοὺς ποιμαίνει Ἰησοῦ.
    Τοὔνεκα χαῖρε, τέκος, καὶ δάκρυα βάλλε, ἄριστον.

Textus: Beregzazius, Iohannes (1569), *Ἐπιθαλάμιον in honorem nuptiarum clarissimi et doctissimi viri D. Petri Carolii praeceptoris sui*..., Vitebergae: I. Crato, cc. A2v–A3r (RMK III 591).

Crit.: 76 ἤθεσι ed., correxi || 77 φέρονται possis || 78 ὁ τρὶς: an ὅτις? || 83 ζώην: ζωὴν debuit || 141 τ᾽ ὅθι: θ᾽ ὅθι debuit || 142 γενέθλη: γενεθλή ed. || 143 χρυσοῦν: an χρυσόν? || 145 σκῆπτρον ed., correxi

Sim.: 76 τῷ γὰρ μάλα ἔκλυον αὐτοί] cf. Hom. *Il*. 1.618 et *Od*. 6.185 || **77–78** cf. Hom. *Od*. 6.183–185 || 79 ἀποτμότατος] cf. Hom. *Od*. 1.219 || 84 cf. Hom. *Od*. 6.158 (μακάρτατος ἔξοχον ἄλλων) || 85 θεράπων...ὀτρηρός] cf. Hom. *Od*. 4.23, 217 || 140 ἐϋκτίμενον πτολίεθρον] cf. Hom. *Il*. 2.501 et saep. || 144 κλυτὰ δώματ᾽ ἔναιον] cf. Hom. *Il*. 2.854 || 145 σκῆπτρον...καὶ στέμμα] cf. Hom. *Il*. 1.28

Epithalamium in honour of the wedding of the illustrious and most learned Mr Petrus Carolius, the author's preceptor

(excerpt, ll. 75–86, 140–147)

> [75] Happy is the man who finds a companion who is totally similar to him in her manners. In this case both man and woman get positive fame, bringing hardly any suffering and a lot of happiness, I say: he is thrice blessed.
> But ill-fated and the unhappiest on Earth is he [80] who marries a girl completely hostile in her soul and lifestyle. The conjunction of such people is not marked by love, their fame is not the noblest, he becomes hateful even to himself and wishing to die, and makes even life unpleasant.
> Therefore Károlyi will be thrice happy, [85] and happiest of many others, who busily serves as a pastor the people and Jesus, and who is beloved and cared for by God.
> [...]
> [140] And the city of Várad is well-built and rich in grapes, where the water flows by beautifully: it is called Körös [Chrysius] from the source which gives rise of gold, but the river overwhelms gold with its fame and water. Lords lived in its houses which are famous all around Pannonia, who have [145] power in their hands and a golden crown. He who is a pastor there, herds the flock of God. Therefore, be happy, my noble daughter, and cast away the tears.

Metre: Hexameters, with some irregularities (hiatuses in ll. 76, 78, 142, 145, 146, 147; irregular lengthening in l. 77 πάνυ).

Notes: This is the only known Greek poem of Beregszászi, which he published a year after his arrival to Wittenberg on the occasion of the wedding of his former master, Péter Károlyi, to Anna Beregdy in Várad. Péter Károlyi, his master (and later bishop of the Calvinist church), was a significant teacher of Greek in his own right, having published a Greek grammar in Cluj in 1567.

Biography: Born in Beregszász (now Berehovo, Ukraine), probably around 1550, János studied under Péter Károlyi in Cluj until 1567, and then in Várad in 1568. He began his university studies in Wittenberg as 'Iohannes Bergzasy Pannonius' on 30 August 1568. Beregszászi's departure from Várad to Wittenberg was celebrated by Lőrinc Beregszászi in a longer *propempticon* in 1568. After his return to Hungary, he became a Calvinist pastor in the county of Bereg, and later on somewhere at the estate of the Mágocsy family, where he is still mentioned alive in 1583.

Bibliography: Móré, Tünde (2015), *Ars peregrinandi. A 16. századi wittenbergi magyar peregrinusok neolatinbúcsúztatóverseinek vizsgálata hazai és nemzetközi kontextusban* [Ars peregrinandi. The Neo-Latin *propemptica* of the Hungarians in Wittenberg in the 16th century in the Hungarian and international context], diss. Debrecen.

[FGK]

Matthias Lochmann (17th c.)

<Epithalamium> [1658]

    Οἱ μουσῶν ἱερεῖς ἐν γηραλέοισι μύθοισιν
    (Ἐξ ὧν ἐστὶ παρών) γλαφυρῶς κατὰ πάντα λέγουσιν·
    Ὥστε πρὸς Ἥφαιστον φιλότας ποτὲ δύο μολίσκειν
    Καὶ ἀνυπερβλήτως αἰτίζειν ἔργμα τι αὐτόν·
5   Δῆθεν, ὁμοῦ μεταπλασθῆναι ἔχρηζον ἀπ' αὐτοῦ
    Εἰς μίαν ἀνθρώπου μορφὴν ἐκ τοῖς δυσὶ πρόσθε.
    Τοσσάτιος βρασμὸς τούτων ἦν στέρξιος ἄμφω!
    Νῦν ἐν γαμούντων ξυνωρίδι ταὐτὸ λεύσσειν
    Πᾶσιν ἐπιτρέπεται, οὓς φιλαλληλία πλάττει
10 Καὶ ὑποφαίνει σάρκα μίαν θεϊκὸν κατὰ ῥῆμα.
    Ἀρχηγὸς συνοικεσίου φιλίαν ταύτην ἐπικυροῖ,
    Ἵνα διὰ παντὸς λιγυρῶς θάλλῃ ἑκάτερθεν!

Textus: *GLÜKWÜNSCHENDES Ehren-gedicht auff...hochzeitlichen Freud- und Ehren-tag dess...Jacobi Günthers bey der Rechten beflissenen, dess...Andreas Günthers, jetziger Zeit wolverordneten Seelensorgers in Wallendorff und der königl. 24. Fraternität oratoris perpetui...ältesten...Sohnes, mit der...Anna gebohrnen Handlerin, dess...Georgii Keysmarkers,...Graffens der königl. 13. Städte hinterlassenen Frauen Wittib, welcher den 26. Maji 1658. Jahrs...vollzogen ward...verfertiget von denen...Bräutigam...Freunden*, Leutschau: bey Lorentz Brewern, 1658, A4 B4 = [8] fol – 4o: c. A4b.

Crit.: 1 γηραλεοῖσι μυθοῖσιν ed., correxi || **3** φιλότας] an pro φιλητάς? || **8** ταυτὸ λεύσσειν ed., correxi || **12** πάντος ed., correxi | ἑκάτερθεν correxi: ἑ- ed.

Sim.: 10 θεϊκὸν κατὰ ῥῆμα] cf. NT, *Matth.* 19.6, *Marc.* 10.8

<Epithalamium>

    In the old myths, the priests of the Muses
    (among whom there is one present) retell everything delicately,
    how once two lovers came to Hephaestus
    and persistently begged him to do a service for them,

[5] namely they asked to be transformed thenceforth
into one human shape from what were two before.
The fervour of their love burned them both so hotly!
Now it is possible for everyone to see the same
in the marrying couple: mutual love shapes them
[10] and shows them to be one single flesh, according to God's word.
May the Lord confirm this binding love of marriage
so that it may flourish harmoniously on both sides forever.

Metre: Hexameters, with many anomalies: ll. 3 (δύο with long ῠ), 5, 8, 9 (φῐλαλληλῐᾰ), 12 (ἵνα with long iota, διά with long alpha); l. 11 is hypermetric, etc. Note the tmesis in l. 2 κατὰ...λέγουσιν.

Notes: Matthias Lochmann's Greek *epithalamion* was published in 1658 together with other poems in German and Latin on the occasion of the wedding of Jakob Günther, son of Andreas Günther, Lutheran pastor at Szepesolaszi (Spišské Vlachy) and the perpetual orator of the confraternity of the twenty-four Royal towns of Szepes. The wedding took place on 26 May 1658. The bride was Anna Handler, the widow of Georg Keysmarker, former count of Szepes. The text shows many uncertainties both in metre and grammar: e.g. l. 6 ἐκ + dative!

Biography: Matthias Lochmann Jr was born in 1634 in a family of Lutheran pastors. He became a school rector in Szepesolaszi in 1658 and the Lutheran pastor of Szepessümeg in 1661.

Bibliography: *RMNy* IV 2275; *RMK* II 900; Szabó, András Péter (2019), "Mesterség és életstratégia. Evangélikus lelkészdinasztiák a 16–17. századi Felföldön" [Profession and life strategy: Dynasties of Lutheran pastors in Upper Hungary in the 16th-17th c.], in: *Credo* 25, 63–64.

[AN]

József Guttovieni (1602–post 1667)

Τὸ ἔπος ἀκρόστιχον Ἑλληνικόν· ΛΕΟΠΟΛΔΟΣ [1659]

Λεῖπε λύπην ταχέως ἡ Οὑννία Γῆ! ὅτι λῷστον
κοίρανον ὀρθῶς νῦν τὸν ΛΕΟΠΟΛΔΟΝ ἔχεις.
Ἐσθλός, φιλόπονος, καὶ ὁμῶς ἐπινίκιός ἐστι
ΡΩΜΑΙΟΣ ΚΑΙΣΑΡ Παιόνιός τε ἄναξ.
5 Ὄλβιος ἡ πέλεται βασιλεία ἐκείνη, ἄνακτα
ἥτις ἔχει ἀγαθόν, σώφρονα καὶ φρόνιμον.

Πάμφιλός ἐστιν ἄναξ τοιοῦτος, †ὁθῶστὲ† φιλεῖτε
οὗτος ἀπ' ἀνθρώποις ἐν χθονὶ πᾶσι μάλα.
Ὄμματα σοῦ ἐστὶ λίαν ἄγλαα καὶ ἀέτεια,
10   οὖν καλῶς ἀετοῦ νῦν παράσημα ἔχεις.
Λάμπε ἀεί, ΛΕΟΠΟΛΔΕ ἄναξ, καὶ ἐν χθονὶ πάσῃ
χρηστῶς τοῖς θνητοῖς μοῦνος ἄνασσε μάκραν·
Δωρέαν Οὐννιακὴν ἀπὸ ἔχθροις αἶψα φύλαττε
τὴν γεάν, εἰρήνην ποίεε καὶ στάθεραν.
15   Ὀρθόφρων †ἔσωτ†, ΛΕΟΠΟΛΔΕ, κάκους τὲ κόλαζε,
ἀλλὰ φιλεῖ κάλους, καὶ μέγα δῶρα φέρε.
Σωτὴρ Χριστέ, ἐμὴν τὴν εὐχὴν λάμβανε ταύτην,
σώζε ἄνακτα νέον καὶ ΛΕΟΠΟΛΔΟΝ, ἀμήν.

Textus: Guttovieni, József (1659), *Carmen Acrostichvm, Aug. Sacr. Et Invictissimi Principi...Leopoldo...Romanorum Imperatori...,* <Tyrnaviae>.

Crit.: 1. λείπε] debuit λεῖπε || **4** ῥωμαίος] debuit ῥωμαῖος | Παίονιός] debuit Παιόνιός || **5** ἤ] an ἦ? || **7** ὀθῶστὲ] utrum ὅδ' ὥστε an ὅ θ' ὥστε? | φιλεῖτε] pro φιλεῖται || **9** Ὄμματα σοῦ] debuit ὄμματά σου | ἐστὶ] an ἐστὶν? | ἄγλαα] debuit ἀγλαὰ || **12** debuit μακράν || **13** debuit Δωρεὰν || **14** debuit σταθεράν || **15** ἔσω] ἔσο νῦν tentaveris | κάκους τὲ] debuit κακούς τε || **16** φιλεῖ κάλους] debuit φίλει καλούς || **17** σωτὴρ] debuit σῶτερ || **18** σώζε] σῷζε debuit

Greek acrostic poem: LEOPOLDOS

Leave behind indeed, oh Hunnia, immediately the grief!
   Because you now finally have Leopold, the best ruler.
Excellent, industrious, as well as victorious, he is
   Roman Emperor, and King of Pannonia.
[5] **O**h, that kingdom is prosperous, which has
   a good, moderate, and prudent ruler.
People all over the world very much love him,
   he is such a unanimously beloved ruler.
Oh, you have overshining and eagle eyes,
[10] so you now rightly have the eagle's insignia.
LEOPOLD, our ruler, shine forever, and rule alone
   for long on the whole Earth for the benefit of the mortals.
Do keep guard the new gift-land of the Huns from the enemies,
   and do make the peace stay for long.
[15] **O**h Leopold, be of rightful mind, and punish the evils,
   but love the noble ones, and bring greatly gifts.
Save, oh Christ Saviour, the new King,
   LEOPOLD, receiving this prayer, amen.

Metre: Elegiac couplets, but with many prosodical problems: l. 3 φιλόπονον, 9 ἐστί (with long iota), 14 νέαν (with short α); many hiatuses; Hermann's bridge is violated several times: l. 5, 7, 15.

Notes: Guttovieni's Greek acrostic poem is part of a series of poems in various languages including Latin, Greek, Hungarian, and Slovakian, written in honour of the enthronement of Leopold I (1640–1705) as Holy Roman emperor in 1658 and as king of Hungary (and Bohemia) in 1657. He used the occasion of Leopold's visit in the Diet of Pozsony to gain the king's favour with his anthology of polyglot panegyric poems. He was rewarded through an office at the municipal council. – The printing shop in Tencsény did not have Greek types until 1670. Therefore, the Greek text, suffering from several spelling mistakes and unclarities, is inserted on a handwritten sheet in both surviving copies of the book (Budapest, National Széchényi Library, *RMK* I 951a and Prešov, State Scientific Library) between quires A and B, which included the other poems all published in print. Besides accentuation and orthography, perhaps partially due to the copyist, the text also displays some serious grammatical problems (e.g., ll. 8 and 13: ἀπό with dative!).

Biography: József Guttovieni was the rector of the Evangelical Lutheran Lyceum in Pozsony (Bratislava) between 1649 and 1659. He published various poems in Trencsény (Trenčín) in 1656 and 1659.

Bibliography: *RMNy* IV 2861; *RMK* I 951a.

[AN]

Isaac Zabanius (1632–1707)

Lyceum Eperiense Dramaticum, *Actus III. Scaena II. Lingua Ebraea, Graeca & Latina Graeca, Jambici* [1661]

†Ἑλληνίζων φωνηεν† εἰμί, πᾶσιν ἔθνεσι
Πρόδηλος καὶ διὰ τοῦ κόσμου πάντων μερῶν
Διαχυθεῖσα. Διά μου Ἀπόστολοι,
Μυστηρίων θεϊκῶν οἰκονόμοι καὶ Ἰησοῦ
5 Τοῦ Χριστοῦ Διάκονοι ἐκκλησίαν νέης
Τῆς Διαθήκης ἐφύτευσαν, διά μου λαμπρότατα
Τῆς Ἀχαΐας πρόσωπα καὶ αὐτὸς φιλοσόφων
Κορυφαῖος ταὐτοῦ δόγματα γέγραφεν.

Ἔνθεν γινώσκουσιν ἄπαντες ἐμέ
10   Φοίνικα πασῶν φωνῶν ἐπιφέρεσθαι.

Textus: *Lycevm Eperiense Dramaticvm, In quo, tragicus nonnullorum interitus ad cautionem, & flagrans quorundam in literas ardor ad Imitationem, Jvventvti Fragariæ, cumprimis verò Poetis proponitur*, Cassoviae: Apud Marcum Severinum, 1661, c. C6r [unicum exemplar adservatur Halis Saxonum, apud Universitäts- und Landesbibliothek Sachsen-Anhalt, III.A.214: vide http://digital.bibliothek.uni-halle.de/hd/content/structure/1762472].

Crit.: (numeri versuum ad scaenam spectant) **1** Ἑλληνίζων φωνηεν] fort. Ἑλλήνων seu Ἑλληνική φωνή voluit || **2** Προδηλέ ed., correxi | μεηρων ed., correxi || **4** θέικῶν ed. | οἰκόνομοι ms || **6** ἐφύθευσαν ed. || **7** φιλοσοφουτων ed., correxi || **9** Ενθεν ed. | εμε ed. || **10** φωνων ed.

Sim.: **4** μυστηρίων...οἰκονόμοι] cf. NT, *Cor. I*, 4.1 || **7–8** φιλ. κορυφαῖος] scil. Plato

The Dramatic School of Prešov, Act III, sc. II. The Hebrew, the Greek and the Latin language Greek, in iambics

I am the Greek language, familiar
to all nations and dispersed in all parts of the world.
It is through me that the Apostles,
the administrators of the divine mysteries,
[5] and the deacons of Jesus Christ planted the Church
of the New Testament, it is through me that the most brilliant
heroes of Achaia [Greece] gained glory and the Coryphaeus
of the philosophers himself has written his doctrines.
Hence everyone knows that I get
[10] the palm (of victory) over all languages.

Metre: Iambic trimeters, but with many flaws, e.g. l. 3 διᾳχυθεῖσα and διά (with long iota), a number of hiatuses, and several lines (e.g., ll. 8–10) not to be redeemed by conjecture.

Notes: The chief characters of this play, written at the Eperjes (Prešov) College in Latin and in three Acts, are speaking names, to be understood in Greek, such as Theuphobus ('fearing God'), Aretophilus ('friend of virtue'), Misocacus ('hating the evil'), Hypnophilus ('friend of sleep'), Merobibus ('drinking pure wine'), Ponophygus ('avoiding work'). They deplore their wasted years and find *Virtus* and *Luxuria* and their fellows as guides. School subjects such as Hebrew, Greek, Latin, grammar, poetry, natural sciences, mathematics, geometry, etc. are all personified. Act III, scene II includes the presentation of the three languages: Hebrew, Greek, and Latin. The place for the Hebrew text has been left blank to be supplied later by hand (which did not eventually happen in the only known copy). The Greek is printed with Greek types, but it is of very low quality. All the rest of the play is written in Latin with an attempt to realise a great variety of classical poetic metres (iambic trimeter, hexameter, Anacreontics, Sapphic, Alcaic, Asclepiads, and hendecasyllables). The text is one of the very few examples of Greek used in dramatic performances (see Herrichen → **Germany** and Christopherson → **Great Britain**).

Biography: The author was Isaac Zabanius (Czabán Izsák) (1632–1707), Lutheran pastor and professor of theology at Prešov College, where the actual play was performed and its text was published in 1661.

Bibliography: *RMNy* IV 2976; Mikles, Ján (1948), *Izák Caban - Slovenský atomista v XVII. storočí*, Bratislava.

[AN]

Polyzoes Kondos (Πολυζώης Κοντός, 1760–1821)

Κλίνη Ἀοιδὸν ἔχειν δοκέει ἀλγοῦντ' ἀλεγεινή [1797]

(excerptum, vv. 1–8)

    Ταρβαλέοι Θεοί! οὗ μ' ἐπέκλωσε τόσ' ἄλγεα Κλωθώ;
    Καί μοι νουσαλέῳ γένεθ' ἄψε' ἀναλκέα δεσμῷ,
    Γυιοβόρῳ μάστιγι τετηκότα, γείτονα πότμου·
    Σῶμα δ' ἐμὸν κεῖται, φεῦ, ἀργαλέῃ ἐνὶ κλίνῃ...
5   Αἲ αἲ Μοῖρ' ὀλοή· τὴν οὔτις ἀλεύεται ἀνδρῶν...
    Οἴχομαι· ἄνθρωποι δὲ μινυνθάδιοι τελέθουσι·
    Στυγέω ὄχλον ἀτερπῆ ἐριπλάγκτου βιότοιο·
    Ζῶ γὰρ ἐνὶ στήθεσσιν ἔχων ἀλίαστον ἀνίην.

Textus: Kondos, Polyzoes (1797), *Carmen heroicum compositum...dum...valetudinem recuperasset cura...Caroli Ferdinandi Stipsics*, Viennae: typis Markidum Pulio, 4.

Crit.: 2 γένετ' ἄψε' ed., correxi

Sim.: 1 ταρβαλέοι] adi. Nonnianum || **2** νουσαλέῳ γένετ' ἄψε' ἀναλκέα δεσμῷ] cf. Nonn. *Par. Jo.* 11.23 (νουσαλέῳ πεπεδημένος ἄψεα δεσμῷ) || **3** γυιοβόρῳ...πότμου] idem Nonn. *Par. Jo.* 11.11 || **5** Μοῖρ' ὀλοή, τὴν οὔτις ἀλεύεται ἀνδρῶν] cf. Hom. *Od.* 24.29 (μοῖρ' ὀλοή, τὴν οὔτις ἀλεύεται, ὅς κε γένηται); L. Rhodoman, *Arion* 553 (τὰν οὔτις ἀλεύεται ἀνδρῶν) || **6** ἄνθρωποι δὲ μινυνθάδιοι τελέθουσι] cf. Hom. *Od.* 19.328 || **7** ἐριπλάγκτου] hapax leg. ut vid. || **8** ἐνὶ...ἀνίην] cf. Hes. *Theog.* 611

An uncomfortable bed seems to keep the poet in pains

(excerpt, ll. 1–8)

> Terrifying Gods, why did Clotho assign to me such pains,
> and why did my limbs become frail through the chain of my sickness,
> weakened by the body-consuming whip, near to death?
> My body is laying, alas, in the torturing bed...
> Oh, oh death-fate Moira: whom no man can escape...
> I am gone: men live a short life and die:
> I hate the ugly trouble of the over-torturous life,
> Since I live with recurrent grief in my heart.[10]

Metre: Hexameters.

Notes: This *Carmen Heroicum* is dedicated to Ferdinand Stipsics (1754–1820), a physician and University Professor of Medicine in Pest (1783–1819), who healed the heavily sick poet. Kondos describes his heroic struggle of recovery from the heavy sickness in a very long and exhaustive poem (236 lines in Greek with facing Latin translation).

Biography: Born in Ioannina, Polyzoes Kondos was an author, priest, and professor. He began his studies in Ioannina and then continued them in Venice. He was then active as a teacher in Vienna, and ended up teaching at the school of Greek of Pest (1793), later in Tokaj and from 1805 in Bucharest. He was a prolific author of prose and poetry, mostly encomiastic works (in 1802 he addressed a small epos to Napoleon Bonaparte), and a translator as well. One of his most interesting works is the Greek *Dialogues of the Dead* on the model of Voltaire.

Bibliography: Κοντός, Πολυζώης (1783), *Νεκρικοὶ διάλογοι Γʹ*, συντεθέντες καὶ στιχουργηθέντες παρὰ τοῦ Αἰακοῦ εἰς τὸν Ἅδην προτροπῇ τοῦ Πλούτονος, ἔνθα καὶ ἐτυπώθησαν, ἐπιμελείᾳ καὶ διορθώσει τοῦ ʻΡαδαμάνθυος [sic], πρὸς ἡμᾶς δὲ μετεκομίσθησαν παρὰ τοῦ Ἑρμοῦ, Ἐν Ἅδου ἐπὶ τοῦ ἔτους 5793 [1783]. Zaviras, Georgios I. (1872), *Νέα Ἑλλάς*, Athens, 519–521.

[AN]

---

10 Author's own Latin translation: *Terribiles Dii! cur destinavit mihi tantos dolores Clotho? / Et morbi vinculis constricto membra sine viribus sunt, / Membra depascenti flagello consumpta, vicina morti: / Corpus vero meum jacet, heu!, molesto in lecto... / Heu! Heu! fatum perniciosum, quod nemo mortalium evitat... / Perii! Homines vero non diu durantes moriuntur. / Odi molestiam inamoenam vitae nimium errabundae; / Vivo enim in pectore habens perpetuam tristitiam.*

László Ungvárnémeti Tóth (1788–1820)

I. Παρθένος ἄχαρις [1818]

    Κύπριδος μὲν οὐκ ἔχουσα
    τὸν κεστόν, οὐκ ἔτ' οἶσθα
    φιλότητος, ἱμέροιο
    καὶ παρφάσεως τὸ χρῆμα·
5   ἄχαρις γάρ ἐσσι κώρα.
    Καὶ ἀγνοεῖς τὸν ἄνδρα,
    φρόνημά τ' ἀνδρὸς ἐσθλοῦ,
    μένος τε τοῦ νέοιο,
    ἔρωτα τοῦ ἀοιδοῦ,
10 φίλημα τοῦ ἐρῶντος,
    πειθώ τε τοῦ φιλοῦντος·
    ἄχαρις γάρ ἐσσι κώρα.
    Ἔσεται δὲ τοῦτο ἆμαρ,
    ὅκα κεστὸν Ἀφροδίτης
15 λαχοῦσα πολλὰ γνώσεις,
    καὶ ἔσται οὗτος ἀνήρ,
    ὃς τἄλλα σ' αὖ διδάξει·
    εἰ σάμερον τόδ' εἴη·
    καὶ ἐγὼν ἀνὴρ πέφυκα.

Textus: Ungvárnémeti Tóth, László (1818), *Görög versei magyar tolmácsolattal*, Pest, 44 (no. X).

Sim.: 2–4 cf. Hom. *Il.* 14.214–217 (κεστὸν ἱμάντα / … / ἔνθ' ἔνι μὲν φιλότης, ἐν δ' ἵμερος, ἐν δ' ὀαριστὺς / πάρφασις) || **13–14** ἔσεται δὲ τοῦτο ἆμαρ / ὅκα] cf. Hom. *Il.* 4.164; 6.448 (ἔσσεται ἦμαρ, ὅτ')

Graceless virgin

    Since you lack the charms
    of Cypris, you do not know
    the matter of love,
    desire and flirt,
    [5] because you are a graceless girl.
    You are inexpert on man,
    the thoughts of a gentleman,
    the passion of a youth,
    the desire of a poet,
    [10] the kiss of a lover,
    the persuasion of a kiss,
    because you are a graceless girl.
    The day will arrive when

you learn many such things,
[15] having discovered the charms of Aphrodite,
and the man will arrive,
who will teach you even the other things:
may it be this day today:
I am a man myself.

Metre: Anacreontics (iambic dimeters and anaclastic ionics *a minore*). The prosody is almost flawless, but one may note some hiatuses: ll. 9, 10, 13.

Notes: The elegant poem is Anacreontic in metre and theme. The line ἄχαρις γάρ ἐσσι κώρα is repeated twice like a refrain preparing the nice *pointe* at the closure of the poem. Of course the girl has *charis*, but she is still too young to know the power of love, or she does not acknowledge the love of the speaker. But the speaker is sure that this will happen one day and if it is today, he is ready to love her. As for the key word ἄχαρις, Ungvárnémeti makes a reference to Sappho fr. 49 Voigt (ἠράμαν μὲν ἔγω σέθεν, Ἄτθι, πάλαι ποτά.../ σμίκρα μοι πάις ἔμμεν' ἐφαίνεο κἄχαρις). One may also note some Doric forms (κώρα, ἆμαρ, ὄκα, σάμερον), a feature also common in the *carmina Anacreontea*.

II. Ἑταῖροι καὶ ἑταῖραι [1818]

Εἷς ἐμοί ἐστι φίλος, χίλιαι δὲ φιλοῦνται ἑταῖραι·
ἓν γὰρ ἔχω ἦτορ, τῶν δὲ πόθων χιλίους.

Textus: Ungvárnémeti Tóth, László (1818), *Görög versei magyar tolmácsolattal*, Pest, 66 (no. XIII).

Friends and girlfriends

I just have one friend, but I do love a thousand girlfriends,
  because I have one heart, but a thousand desires.

Metre: Elegiac couplet.

Notes: The epigram plays with the different meanings of ἑταῖρος ('comrade, friend') and ἑταίρα ('girl friend' or even 'prostitute').

III. Ἔρως, Ἄρης, Ζεύς [1818]

Πικρὸν Ἔρωτι βέλεμνον, Ἄρηϊ δὲ μακρὰ τέτυκτο
Ἔγχεα ἐκ χαλκοῦ, Ζεὺς δὲ κεραυνὸν ἔχει·
Εἰπέ μοι, ἢν τολμᾷς, ὦ Δύσπαρι· τίς σοι ἐκείνων
φέρτιστος δοκέει; ὡς τόδ' ἔοικε μαθεῖν.
5   Ἰσοκρατεῖς αὐτοὺς εἶναι φής, ὅττι ἅπαντες
τῶν παρὰ Κυκλώπων ὀξέα ὅπλα λάχον,
καλὸν ἐρωτηθεὶς λέλεχας, καὶ ταῖσι θεαῖσι
ταῦτ' ἀποκρίνεσθαι ὤφελες εἰν ὄρεσι.

Textus: Ungvárnémeti Tóth, László (1818), *Görög versei magyar tolmácsolattal*, Pest, 84 (no. XXXVI).

Crit.: 6 ὄξεα ed., correxi

Sim.: 1 πικρὸν...βέλεμνον] cf. e.g. Hom. *Il*. 22.206 (πικρὰ βέλεμνα) || 3 Δύσπαρι] cf. Hom. *Il*. 3.39; 13.769

Eros, Ares, and Zeus

Eros has a bitter arrow, Ares has got long spears
   made of bronze, Zeus has his thunderbolt:
tell me, if you dare, oh unhappy Paris: who of them
   is the mightiest to your mind, for it is important to know this.
You say that they are of equal strength because they all
   got their sharp weapons from the Cyclopes.
You gave a good answer to the question, you should
   have answered the same to the goddesses on the mountains.

Metre: Elegiac couplets. Elegant, one may only note some hiatuses: ll. 2, 4, 5, 6, 8.

Notes: This witty piece is a nice comment on Paris' judgement beginning with Eros, Ares, and Zeus: each of them has a weapon, and Paris judges them equal in power. At the end, the poet gives the poem a witty turn: if Paris had given such a Salomonic judgement also to the three goddesses, he might have been happier. This tempered, moderate wit can only be called classical and seems to reflect the time of its composition.

Biography: Being the son of a Lutheran pastor, a student of the Lutheran Colleges, first in Sárospatak, then in Eperjes (today Prešov in Slovakia), László Ungvárnémeti

Tóth later converted to Catholicism and studied medicine in Pest and Vienna. During his studies, he turned out to be gifted in languages, especially in poetry, and delved into Latin, Greek, and German. Encouraged by Ferenc Kazinczy (1759–1831), the leader of the Hungarian language reform movement, Ungvárnémeti tried to improve his mother tongue – among other means – by writing bilingual poems, in classical Greek and Hungarian, in one and the same poetic metre. His anthology of bilingual poems in a wide range of poetic metres and genres (hexameter, elegiac couplets, Alcaic and Sapphic stanzas, epigrams, Pindaric odes mostly on national subjects, Idylls in the style of Theocritus, and poetic letters in the style of Horace's *Epistulae*), equipped with a commentary in Hungarian, was published in 1818 in Pest. However, as can be expected, it did not enjoy wide circulation and remains a unique example of Hellenizing poetry in this scale and variety in Hungary. Sometimes the Greek version inspired the Hungarian one or vice versa. The selected pieces seem to have been conceived in Greek.

Bibliography: Ungvárnémeti Tóth, László (1818), *Görög versei magyar tolmácsolattal*, Pest 1818, 44, 60; Bolonyai Gábor (ed.) (2008), *Ungvárnémeti Tóth László művei*, Budapest, 376–378, 390, 406.

[AN]

Bence Fehér (1968–)

I. Κατὰ ψυχολόγου τινός [2010]

Ὡς μὲν ὁ ψυχόλογος κοπροδάκτυλος ἦλθεν ἐς ἄστυ,
    Κόπρος ἐγεννήθη Παιονίας ἀρετή.
Οἱ δ' ἔδδεισαν ἀνιστάμενοι, φαλλόν τε ἑαυτοῦ
    Χείρ' ἐπιμασσάμενος ὣς φάθ' ὁ ψυχόλογος·
5   Ὦ ξεῖν', ἀγγέλλειν τοῖς Παννονίοις, ὅτι τῇδε
    Κεῖμαι, τοὺς κείνων φαλλοὺς δεξόμενος.
Ὦ ἔχθιστ', ἐπέεσσιν ἐμὲ πρόσφης τοιούτοις;
    Παῖδας ἀποκτείνειν Παίονίους ἐθέληις;
Οὔτ' οὖν ἐσθῆτος δευήσεαι, ἀλλὰ τεῦ φαλλοῦ,
10 Ὧι δ' ἐπέοιχ' ἱκέτην ῥήτορα παιδοφιλεῖν.

Textus: Fehér, Bence (2000), *Főnixmadár*, Budapest: Orpheusz, 75.

Crit.: 1, 4 ψυχόλογος] debuit ψυχολόγος || 8 ἐθέληις] an ἐθέλεις?

Sim.: 1 ψυχόλογος] verbum apud veteres non legitur, in lingua neograeca inde a medio saeculo XIXº invenitur | κοπροδάκτυλος] neologismus, cf. ῥοδοδάκτυλος apud Homerum || 3 ἔδδεισαν forma Homerica || **4** χείρ᾽ἐπιμασσάμενος: cf. Hom. *Od.* 9.302, 19.480 | ὣς φάθ᾽] formula Homerica, cf. Hom. *Il.* 2.182 etc. || **5–6** cf. Hdt. 7.228.2 = *Anth. Pal.* 7.249 (Ὦ ξεῖν᾽, ἀγγέλλειν Λακεδαιμονίοις, ὅτι τῇδε / κείμεθα τοῖς κείνων ῥήμασι πειθόμενοι) || **7** ἐπέεσσιν...πρόσφης] cf. Hom. *Il.* 13.768 (προσέφη αἰσχροῖς ἐπέεσσιν) et sim. || **9** est parodia versus Hom. *Od.* 6.192 = 14.510, cuius clausula οὔτε τευ ἄλλου

Against a psychologist

Once a fecal fingered psychologist arrived to the city,
    Pannonia's virtue turned into dirt.
Some woke up from the shock, when the psychologist,
    while touching his membrum with his hand, said as follows:
[5] 'O stranger, please announce to the Pannonians that
    I lie here, expecting to receive their membra.'
O most hateful man, do you address me with such words?
    Do you wish to kill the Pannonian children?
Well, you will not need a cloak but your *membrum*,
[10] with which it is normal that a rhetor should corrupt his young client.

Metre: Elegiac couplets. There are some prosodical shortcomings: ll. 4 (short syllable at the middle caesura, or lengthening by final sigma), 6 (spondaic foot in the second *hemiepes*!), 9 (irregular clausula: ἀλλὰ τεῦ φαλλοῦ). l. 7 has a spondaic ending. Doubling of consonants in l. 3 (Homeric licence).

Notes: The epigram with iambic tone seems to denounce a pederast. Féher uses Homeric formulae (ἔδδεισαν, ὣς φάθ᾽) in order to contrast them with more explicit expressions (φαλλός, παιδοφιλεῖν). The intended effect is obviously to underscore the difference between appearance and being. This culminates in a parodistic version of the famous epigram on the Spartans killed in the Battle of Thermopylae: 'Oh stranger, tell the Lacedaemonians…'. The transformation of the Homeric ῥοδοδάκτυλος ('rosy-fingered'), an epithet of Eos (Dawn), into κοπροδάκτυλος is significant as well.

II. Sonnet V [2010]

Καλὴ μία τ᾽ εἶ καὶ μόνη, γύναι,
Σ᾽ ἔδωκε γὰρ ἡ ἐλεήσασα Μοῖρα.
Ἔγω δὲ τίς σοί εἰμι, οὐ μὲν οἶδα,
Τὸ δ᾽ οἶδα, πάντα σοί με δόμεναι.
5   Φιλεῖν σ᾽ ὑφ᾽ ἱμέρου διώκομαι
Φεύγειν σε μέλλων, οὔ πω σοι πέποιθα,

Ἀλλ' εἰ σὺ φεύγεις, πᾶν ἄλγος πέπονθα.
Σκληρὸν πρὸς κέντρα μοι λακτίζεναι.

Καὶ γὰρ φεύγεις μ' ὦκεις ὡς οὐχ ὁρῶσιν
10 Κύνες πρόκας ἐν ὕλαις, ἃς ἄγουσιν,
Φεύγει μ' οὕτως τὸ σὸν μέλαν κάρη.

Κάθηρόν νύν με τῶν ἐμῶν μεριμνῶν,
Ἀπόπροθέν σοῦ, ὡς ὑπ' ὀστρακισμῶν,
Μὴ βάλλε, ῥῦσαί μ', ὦ Καθαρίνη.

Textus: Fehér, Bence (2000), *Főnixmadár*, Budapest: Orpheusz, 13.

Crit.: 3 Ἔγω] debuit ἐγώ, sed fortasse colorem quendam Sapphicum petit noster || 8 an λακτιζέμεν? || 9 debuit ὠκεῖς, sed de barytonesi cf. etiam v. 3 || 11 οὕτως exspectaveris, sed ft. psilosis Aeolica ab auctore petita

Sim.: 5–7 cf. Sapph. fr. 1.21 || 8 πρὸς κέντρα μοι λακτίζεναι] proverbium Graecum, cf. Pind. *Pyth.* 2.95; Aesch. *Ag.* 1624; NT, *Act.Ap.* 26.14 etc.

Sonnet V

You are beautiful and unique, woman.
The Moira has given you to me in an act of mercy.
But who I am to you, I have no idea,
the one thing I know is to give to you the whole of me.

[5] I am urged by the desire to love you,
wishing to run away from you, not yet obedient to you,
but if you run away, all pain is mine.
It is hard to kick against the pricks.

And you run away from me: just like the dogs
[10] cannot see the quick roe deers which they are chasing in the forest,
likewise your black head is running away from me.

Please free me now from all my sorrow,
and do not throw me away from you as if with ostracism,
but rescue me instead, O Katharine.

Metre: Iambic pentameter [in Latin, not Greek terminology], catalectic and acatalectic; the French variant of the Petrarchan sonnet with the rhyme scheme: abba, abba, ccd, eed.

Notes: A love sonnet with rhyming endings. This form was also used by the Czech poet Jan Křesadlo (→ **Bohemian Lands**) in his sonnet cycle *Rozličnosti aneb xenoglossie* (no. 1: ΠΑΝΤΑ ΕΥΔΕΙ, no. 2: ΕΙΣ ΑΦΡΟΔΙΤΗΝ). Like Křesadlo, Fehér seems to allude in some places to Sappho.

III. Πτελέα πρὸς ἄμπελον [2010]

    Ἄμπελος μέν, παῖ, σύ μοι εἶ μέλαινα,
    Ἡ δὲ σή μοι γίγνεται οἶνος ὀργή,
    Μαίνομαι θυμῷ σὰ ἔπη πεπωκὼς
        Ἱέμενός σε.

5   Μαινόλις ῥῦσθαι πτελέα θέλουσα
    Ῥάβδον οἴνου σώφρονα, παῖδα δῖαν,
    Ἵσταμαι μείνασά σε καρπὸν ὀρθὴ
        Ἄχρι κεραυνοῦ.

    Τὰς δ' ἀλώπεκάς σ' ἐθέλω προφεύγειν,
10 Οἶσθα γάρ σ' εὖ μή τιν' ἐμοῦ γε χωρὶς
    Που φιλήσειν, ὡς ἐθέλεις πρέπει τε,
        Κύπριδος οἶνε.

Textus: Fehér, Bence (2000), *Főnixmadár*, Budapest: Orpheusz, 13.

Crit.: 4 σε] σου debuit

Sim.: 3 μαίνομαι θυμῷ] cf. Sapph. fr. 1.18 V. (μαινόλαι θύμωι) || 4 ἱέμενός σε] cf. clausulam in Hom. *Od.* 1.6 (ἱέμενός περ) || 9 Τὰς δ' ἀλώπεκάς σ' ἐθέλω προφεύγειν] cf. Phaedri de vulpe et uva fabulam (Phaedr. *fab.* 4,3)

The elm to the grapevine

    Oh girl, to me you are the dark bunched grapevine,
    to me your anger becomes wine,
    your words make me drunk, mad from desire,
        craving for you.

    [5] While seeking for safety I, the stupefied elm,
    stand straight awaiting your fruit, oh divine girl,
    the wine's sober wand,
        until the thunder.

I want to keep the foxes away from you,
[10] since you know well know that you will never love anyone
without me as you wish and your nature urges,
　O wine of Cypris.

Metre: Sapphic stanzas.

Biography: Bence Fehér (b. 1968) is a historian, philologist, and archaeologist. He got his degrees in Latin language and literature, archaeology, and Arabic language and literature. He was a professor at Pázmány Péter Catholic University (1998–2002) and Károli Gáspár University of the Reformed Church (2002–2018). His broad fields of interests include the history and Latin literature of ancient Pannonia, and the religions of classical Antiquity. He is the author of poems in various languages including Latin, classical Greek, classical Arabic, and even Etruscan. He has translated *The Tragedy of Man* by Imre Madách into Latin, and the first scene of the same play into classical Greek. He prefers lyric and erotic poetry.

Bibliography: https://hu.wikipedia.org/wiki/Fehér_Bence [accessed: August 2020]; Fehér, Bence (2000), *Főnixmadár*, Budapest.

[AN]

Fig. 10: Oxford, The Queen's College (on the wall of the Senior Common Room): War memorial with a Greek inscription by Edgar Lobel at its bottom (see below, p. 553f.).

Stefan Weise
Great Britain

The selection of Greek poetry from Great Britain which is presented here is by no means exhaustive or representative.[1] It attempts, however, to give some examples of the rich tradition of ancient Greek literary composition in Great Britain. As in other sections, the question of what region to examine arises here too, although it is on the whole much simpler.[2] This selection will focus especially on England, with Oxford and Cambridge taken as the main centres, despite the fact that Greek composition was also active in other centres of learning, such as Dublin[3] or Aberdeen (see **Geddes**, below). As such, this selection is only a modest starting point for more thorough future research.

In order to highlight the importance of Greek composition in Great Britain as part of higher culture and education,[4] our survey will start from the present and then work backward to the 16th century. It will be shown that Britain manifested significant differences from the development of Greek composition on the continent. Two phenomena stand out in particular: First, while the continent saw a decline in several countries during the 18th century, the practice of writing Greek poetry continued in Britain without notable interruption – this may be due to the rise of English classicism and the Enlightenment, which preceded corresponding developments on the continent, especially in Germany. Second, at the end of the 18th century and during the 19th century, several competitions were established, most of which continue to the present day, embedding this tradition more firmly than elsewhere. This is made immediately clear by a prominent example: In 2012, the former Mayor of London and present-day prime minister, Boris Johnson, recited a Greek ode composed by the British classicist **Armand D'Angour** (born in 1958) at the Opening Gala of the London Olympics. This certainly was one of very few occasions in our era that a modern poem in ancient Greek gained such public attention. The composition itself, however, had a long history, since D'Angour had already written a Greek ode for the Olympic games in Athens in 2004. This

---
1 I owe special thanks to Thomas Gärtner (Cologne) for valuable advice and inspiration.
2 The terms 'British' and 'English' are not used with a sharp distinction here. The choice of the caption 'Great Britain' instead of 'United Kingdom' or 'British Isles' is due to the fact that neither Ireland nor Northern Ireland are treated except for a short hint to Dublin in the following footnote.
3 Cf., e.g., Tyrrell 1890.
4 Rutherford 2017, 93, notes with regard to the late-Victorian period: 'For many highly educated men, immersion in the classics was a way of life rather than a body of knowledge'.

https://doi.org/10.1515/9783110652758-012

earlier ode, which was commissioned by Dame Mary Glen-Haig, hearkened back to the first Olympics of the modern age, which took place in Athens in 1896, for which an Englishman had similarly composed an ode in ancient Greek. This poet, who also took part in the games himself and recited his ode at the final ceremony, was **George Stuart Robertson** (1872–1967), a classical scholar from Oxford, where he had already twice won the Gaisford Prize.[5] D'Angour's recent composition shows to what degree Greek (and also Latin) verse composition has played an important role in British classical education since the 18th century, at which time it was losing its appeal in other countries, only to be re-established subsequently through the neo-humanistic movement: Two key examples of British self-conception through classicism are Lord Chesterfield and Dr Johnson, both of whom valued Greek highly.[6] In short, one might say that whereas Italy was the place where humanistic poetry written in Greek began and from which it spread across Europe during the 16th century, Britain is the country which has inspired and challenged other nations in this domain since the end of the 18th century.[7] This becomes evident when we consider the remarks of German scholars, who have regarded the British enthusiasm for Greek verses with either suspicion or admiration. Theodor Kock (1820–1901), for example, wrote in the Latin preface to his much-admired Greek translation of Goethe's *Iphigenie*, published in 1855:

> *Est quidem aliquid in tanta temporum iniquitate spei et solatii relictum. Sunt tamen, carissime magister, sunt qui veterum poetarum non solum lectione sed etiam imitatione hodie quoque delectentur: viget adhuc in Britannia, fidelissima horum studiorum nutrice, viget Oxonii et Cantabrigiae, locis omnium saeculorum fama celebratis, viget ad quietas argenteae Sabrinae ripas, viget in summo commerciorum strepitu ac tumultu antiquae poesis consuetudo et veneratio.*

> There is some hope and comfort left in these troubled times. In the present day, my dear teacher, there are some who still delight not only in reading the ancient poets but also in imitating them: Familiarity with and veneration of ancient poetry still flourishes in Britain, the most devoted nurse of these studies, flourishes at Oxford and Cambridge, places celebrated through the fame of every generation, flourishes on the quiet banks of the silver Severn, flourishes in the greatest noise and agitation of commerce.

---

5 For his prose composition *Herodotus in Britain*, see esp. Harrison 2020.
6 For the prominence of Greek and Latin verse composition as part of higher education in Britain, cf. Baldwin 1995, 1; Rebenich 2011, 54.
7 For a renewal of classical and notably Greek enthusiasm in England at the end of the 18th century, see Adams 2015, 115–130.

Matthew Adams explains the renewed enthusiasm for verse composition in 19th-century Britain as a reaction against the French revolution and the rise of Napoleon: 'The English aristocracy championed the call to freedom in the face of French totalitarianism, and they found support in the Athenian democracy' (Adams 2015, 116). He further explains: 'The status of Latin necessarily dwindled as English grew, and it was not until the nineteenth century that the status of Greek overtook that of Latin. Greek became fashionable where Latin was not, admired and respected where Latin was not; it was older, had no associations with the tyranny of Catholicism and its flame was delivered to a relatively small number of learners and kept alight in the classroom by men of genius' (Adams 2015, 120). Such 'men of genius' and representatives of this Hellenizing culture – 'Romantic heroes', as Christopher Stray calls them,[8] include the classicists **Richard Claverhouse Jebb** (1841–1905), **Walter Headlam** (1866–1908), and **Ronald A. Knox** (1888–1957). All three composed original pieces, and Knox especially for fun.

On the whole, 19th-century Greek composition in Britain consisted of two main types: translations of English or Latin poetry and prose into Greek, which became especially popular during the Victorian age,[9] and competition pieces. Anthologies representing each category continued to be published in significant numbers until the first half of the 20th century. Examples include *Musae Etonenses* (t. III, 1795), *Musae Cantabrigienses* (1810), *A Selection from the Greek Verses of Shrewsbury School* (1841), *Anthologia Oxoniensis* (1846), *Sabrinae corolla* (1850), *Some Oxford Compositions* (1949). The titles alone clearly indicate where verse compositions tended to be created: Cambridge, Oxford, Eton, and Shrewsbury.[10] These are, of course, the well-known elite universities and colleges in Britain, to which we can add Westminster and Winchester. Evidence for the widespread practice of Greek verse composition is also found in workbooks, such as those written by George Preston or Arthur Sidgwick and Francis David Morice.[11] Arthur Sidgwick is also an interesting example of the deep personal engagement

---

8 See Stray 1998, 68–74. Stray describes the composition of verses 'as a practice which sustains a sense of aesthetic and moral worth'.
9 Cf. Brink 1995, 126–129; Stray 1998, 124–126; Adams 2015, 129–130.
10 For verse composition at Eton, see Clarke 1945, 18–19, 23–24; Stray 1998, 69. For Shrewsbury, see Clarke 1945, 23–24; Stray 1998, 69; Adams 2015, 123–127 (on the headmasters, Samuel Butler and Benjamin Hall Kennedy).
11 Preston, George (1869), *Greek Verse Composition, For the use of Public Schools and Private Students*, Cambridge; Sidgwick, Arthur/Morice, Francis David (1885), *An Introduction to Greek Verse Composition With Exercises*, London.

with and love for Greek among 19th-century British men, since he used the language even in his personal diaries for delicate entries concerning his sexual life.[12] Alongside these, we also find a Greek conversational guide, titled *Greek and English Dialogues* (1871), by John Stuart Blackie.[13] These publications and the general flourishing of Greek studies must be understood in the context of the significant progression of British classical scholarship and the reputation it gained from the end of the 17th century onward, through the work of scholars such as **Joshua Barnes** (1654–1712), Richard Bentley (1662–1742), and **Richard Porson** (1759–1808), among others.

The most important competitions were and remain the Sir William Browne's Medal (also known as the Browne Medal) at the University of Cambridge and the Gaisford Prize (established in 1855) at the University of Oxford.[14] These two prizes, together with the Porson Prize, are illuminating with regard to the shift in practice from free composition to translation.[15] Whereas the Browne Medal, founded in the late 18th century, stuck to the concept of free composition on a given theme, the Gaisford Prize changed its requirements from free composition to translation, and the Porson Prize (established in 1817) solicited translations from the very beginning.[16]

The Browne Medal has been awarded since 1775.[17] The medals, originally three in number, required the composition of a Greek ode in imitation of Sappho, a Latin ode in the style of Horace, or the composition of two epigrams – one in Greek in the style of the *Greek Anthology*, and one in Latin in the style of Martial, each piece to be composed on a given theme.[18] Thus the form and content of the undergraduates' compositions depended on the competition's rules. The subjects, however, show a remarkable diversity and were often connected to contemporary events. With regard to the Sapphic odes, for example, themes included

---

12 See the very intriguing analysis by Rutherford 2017. Cf. also Ribeyrol 2013 on Swinburne.
13 See Sandys 1908, III.428. For Greek *Gesprächsbüchlein* in general, cf. also Weise 2016, 129–131.
14 For an incomplete list of winners of the Browne Medal, see https://en.wikipedia.org/wiki/Browne_Medal [accessed: August 2020]. A complete list of winners from 1775 to 1910 is published in Tanner 1917, 302–312. For a list of winners of the Gaisford Prize, see https://en.wikipedia.org/wiki/Gaisford_Prize [accessed: August 2020].
15 Cf. Brink 1995, 126–129; Adams 2015, 88–96.
16 Cf. Tanner 1917, 316–317. Prize-winning translations are collected in *Translations which have obtained the Porson Prize in the University of Cambridge* (Cambridge 1850; London ²1857; ³1871).
17 For the regulations and history of the Browne Medals, with special focus on its numismatic aspect, see Freemann 1946.
18 In 1858 the medal for the epigrams was split in order to honour both the Greek and the Latin compositions with a medal of their own. See Tanner 1917, 302; Freemann 1946, 437.

Bellum Americanum in 1776, *Bastilia expugnata* in 1790, and *Napoleon in insulam Sanctae Helenae ablegatus* in 1816. Some of these odes were published in the collection *Musae Cantabrigienses* in 1810. Not included in this collection was the ode *Georgium Sydus*, written by **Abraham Moore** (1766–1822) and awarded with the Browne Medal in 1787. This ode about the planet Uranus, which had been discovered in 1781 by William Herschel and named *Georgium sidus* in honour of King George III, is of special interest not only because of its subject but also because of the place of its publication. The ode, as far as I know, was never printed in Britain, but appeared in a collection of Neo-Latin poetry by the German scholar Christian Wilhelm Mitscherlich in 1793, together with only three other Greek pieces. Therefore this collection allows us to gauge British influence on Greek composition in Germany during this period. Moore's ode is also interesting on its own account, as it reflects an emerging interest in natural science, which was already being cultivated in 18th-century didactic poetry.

Didactic poetry is also represented in the supplements to the geographical poem by Dionysius Periegetes made by **Edward Wells** (1667–1727). As Dionysius' poem was used for contemporary geographical education, Wells wanted to add up-to-date information about the American continent and modern cities. Further back, we can find examples of 17th-century Greek verse production in the works of **John Milton** (1608–1674) and **James Duport** (1606–1679). Their poems, due to English Baroque taste, show a special tendency to employ with which remained typical of the British production in later periods too (e.g., Knox). Longer Greek compositions of the time often celebrate events of the royal family. The official congratulatory collections published by the universities of Oxford and Cambridge (1603–1763) regularly contained Greek contributions.[19] It seems that the wide spread of Greek poetry originated in the classicism of the Restoration era, when knowledge of Greek and Latin became the hallmark of the English 'gentleman'. A clear sign of this development is that, in addition to the examples cited above, we find Greek poems by many famous English writers down to the 19th century, such as Andrew Marvell (1621–1678),[20] the metaphysical poet **George Herbert** (1593–1633), Richard Crashaw (1612–1649),[21] John Milton, the famous Dr Johnson or **Samuel Johnson** (1709–1784), the romantic poet **Samuel Taylor Coleridge**

---

19 See Forster 1982, esp. 147.
20 Cf. Forster 1982, 150.
21 His Greek poems are printed in Martin, Leonard Cyrill (ed.) (1927), *The Poems English Latin and Greek of Richard Crashaw*, Oxford, 67–71, 377–378.

(1772–1834), and the Victorian poet **Algernon Charles Swinburne** (1837–1909).²² This is a notable contrast to other European countries, where Greek verse composition was mostly practised by professional classicists. The closest comparisons, perhaps, are Klopstock and Engels in Germany, Paulinus and Runeberg in Finland, Pascoli in Italy, and de Baïf and Chénier in France. It is further worthy of note that some of these Greek compositions by English poets also show strong features of their own personal writing style. This is especially true of Herbert and Swinburne.

In the 16th century, however, the interest in Greek verse composition in England had been considerably less prominent than in other European countries, despite the work of important English Hellenists, such as William Grocyn (c. 1446–1519), Thomas Linacre (1460–1524), or Richard Croke (c. 1489–1558; see also → **Germany**) at the beginning of the century.²³ One may also recall that Erasmus came to England at that time in order to learn Greek. The initial enthusiasm spread by Englishmen who were trained in Italy quickly became attenuated, and the introduction of Greek types in printing was considerably delayed. The first book to contain Greek script was printed in 1521,²⁴ and the first major book in Greek was printed in 1543 (two homilies by Chrysostom, edited by John Cheke).²⁵ Micha Lazarus therefore distinguishes three periods of development in 16th-century Britain: 1) 1490s to 1530s: Greek studies by individual enthusiasts and Erasmian humanists, 2) 1530s to 1560s: Reformation Greek at the universities, 3) 1560s to 1600: further establishment of Greek in Elizabethan universities and schools.²⁶ A major influence on the establishment of Greek in English universities was Erasmus' stay in England.²⁷ After the beginning of the Reformation on the continent, however, Greek seems to have been considered dangerous and heretical.²⁸ This phase of reduction and absence of Greek, which lasted between 1520 and 1560, was finally brought to an end with the accession of Queen Elizabeth I

---

22 Cf. Haynes 2003, 10. I do not share, however, his general judgement 'that they [sc. the Greek poems by English poets] are like a dog walking on his hind legs; though not done well, we are surprised to see them done at all.' Cf. Baldwin 1995, 2, with regard to Latin.
23 For a more detailed analysis, see Lazarus 2014. With regard to Latin translations from Greek, see also Binns 1990, 215–240.
24 See Adams 2015, 57.
25 See Milne 2007, 678.
26 See Lazarus in http://hellenic-institute.uk/research/etheridge/Lazarus/Tudor-Greek.html [accessed: September 2020].
27 See Goldhill 2002, 14–59.
28 Cf. Adams 2015, 61.

in 1558 and the firm establishment of Protestantism.[29] Elizabeth I was herself taught Greek by Roger Ascham, who mentions in his *Scholemaster* that 'she readeth here now at Windsore more Greeke every daye, then some Prebendaris of this Church doth read Latin in a whole weeke.'[30] It may be because of this well-known fame that **George Etheridge** (1519–1588?) composed a lengthy Greek encomium on Henry VIII to mark the occasion of the Queen's visit to Oxford in 1566. It was King Henry VIII himself who established the Regius Professorship of Greek at the Universities of Cambridge in 1540 and Oxford in 1546, a moment which Lazarus considers of highest significance for the permanent establishment of Greek studies in Britain.[31] Indeed, we find that many of the *regii professores* – including **John Cheke** (1514–1557), the first Regius Professor of Greek at Cambridge – composed Greek poems (from this selection see also George Etheridge, **Andrew Downes**, and **James Duport**).

Although 16th-century England is generally lacking in Greek compositions, there is one text of special interest for the history of Greek writing as a whole: the Greek tragedy *Jephthah*, written by the Catholic scholar **John Christopherson** (†1558) and probably performed at Cambridge. This is a rare example of a dramatic text and therefore earns a special place of honour. Also noteworthy is the fact that – due to the rapid changes in the political and religious landscape under Edward VI, 'Bloody' Mary, and Elizabeth I – we find major Greek compositions not only by Protestant authors like Cheke but also by Catholic scholars, such as Etheridge and Christopherson.[32] However, the schism between these two groups becomes evident in the debate about the correct pronunciation of Greek which was provoked by Cheke and Thomas Smith. Cheke and Smith advocated for the 'new', restored (Erasmian) pronunciation, whereas conservative circles adhered to the 'traditional' (Reuchlinian) pronunciation. The conflict culminated in the prohibition of the new pronunciation by Cambridge Chancellor Stephen Gardiner in 1542.[33] In the end, however, the new pronunciation prevailed.

---

29 See especially Adams in https://www.bl.uk/greek-manuscripts/articles/greek-in-elizabethan-england [accessed: September 2020], with manuscript examples of complimentary Greek verses addressed to Edward VI, Henry VIII and Elizabeth I from the British Library (notably Royal MS 12 A XXXIII from Winchester College, Royal MS 12 A XXX from Eton College and Royal MS 12 A LXVII from St Paul's School).
30 Ascham, Roger (1571), *The Scholemaster* [...], London, 21.
31 See Lazarus 2014, 453.
32 Prominent later authors who converted to Catholicism were Richard Crashaw and Ronald A. Knox.
33 Cf. Tilley 1938, 440–441.

On the whole, the British verse composition provides a great variety of forms and metres. As in other regions, hexameters and elegiac couplets make up a huge proportion of the total. There are, however, also a large number of compositions in iambic trimeters and Sapphic stanzas, mostly because of the competitions described above. We even find a number of Pindaric odes, dating from at least 1695 to the present.[34] Although a general overview of Greek verse composition in Great Britain is lacking,[35] it is notable that in his famous *History of Classical Scholarship*, **John Edwin Sandys**, who himself won several prizes for composition (Browne Medal in 1865, Porson Prize in 1865 and 1866), was eager to mention Greek compositions by English scholars and even provided some quotations. Since then, many studies on the reception and influence of classics and classical education have appeared, in form of articles, monographs, or editions.[36] In future research, it would without doubt be worthwhile to explore the compositions made for competitions such as the Browne Medal at Cambridge, whose manuscript volumes are still extant,[37] or the Gaisford Prize at Oxford, in greater detail. Stephen Harrison made an interesting start in this direction with his analysis of the 'Herodotean' pieces from the Gaisford Prize. Although Harrison states that the 'elite culture' which put forth all these products is 'now dead and gone',[38] this is, as we have seen above, only partly true. Certainly, Greek – including Greek verse composition – is no longer part of general education as it was in the 19th century: Compulsory Greek was abolished at Cambridge in 1919, and compulsory Latin in the 1960s.[39] Yet, the 'Oxbridge' competitions still exist, and Britain was the site of composition not only for the modern Olympic odes by Armand D'Angour, but also for the Greek *Ode to Stalin* and the *Astronautilia* written by the Czech poet **Jan Křesadlo** (Václav Pinkava, 1926–1995) in Colchester, where he lived following his escape from Czechoslovakia in 1968 (see → **Bohemian Lands** and the Oxford inscription, below).

---

34 See Päll (forthcoming).
35 A good introduction to the topic, especially regarding the social dimension of Greek, is to be found in Haynes 2003, 10–17. Some very short hints are to be found in Bulwer 2019, 282–287.
36 See especially Fobes 1928 for Christopherson, Morrison 1983 for Coleridge, Blair 1985 for Herbert.
37 See Cambridge University Library, ms. UA. Char.I.3–6 (covering the prizewinning odes from 1775 until 1867).
38 Harrison 2020, 245. See also Päll (forthcoming) on Pindaric odes in the United Kingdom.
39 Cf. Stray 1998, 265–270, 293–295; Rutherford 2017, 110 and 112.

General Bibliography

Adams, Matthew (2015), *Teaching Classics in English Schools, 1500–1840*, Newcastle upon Tyne.
Baldwin, Barry (1995), *The Latin & Greek Poems of Samuel Johnson. Text, Translation and Commentary*, London.
Binns, James Wallace (1990), *Intellectual Culture in Elizabethan and Jacobean England. The Latin Writings of the Age*, Leeds.
Blair, Rhonda L. (1985), "George Herbert's Greek Poetry", in: *Philological Quarterly* 64.4, 573–584.
Brink, Charles O. (1985), *English Classical Scholarship: Historical Reflections on Bentley, Porson, and Housman*, Cambridge.
Bulwer, John (2019), "United Kingdom (Royaume Uni)", in: Francisco Oliveira/Ramón Martínez (eds.), *Europatrida*, Coimbra, 277–287.
Clarke, Martin L. (1945), *Greek Studies in England 1700–1830*, Cambridge.
Clarke, Martin L. (1959), *Classical Education in Britain 1500–1900*, Cambridge.
Forster, Harold (1982), "The Rise and Fall of the Cambridge Muses (1603–1763)", in: *Transactions of the Cambridge Bibliographical Society* 8.2, 141–172.
Freeman, Sarah Elizabeth (1946), "The Browne Prize Medals", in: *Bulletin of the History of Medicine* 19.4, 433–449.
Gelfert, Hans-Dieter (²2005), *Kleine Geschichte der englischen Literatur*, München.
Goldhill, Simon (2002), *Who needs Greek? Contests in the Cultural History of Hellenism*, Cambridge.
Harrison, Thomas (2020), "Herodotus's Travels in Britain and Beyond. Prose Composition and Pseudo-Ethnography", in: Thomas Harrison/Joseph Skinner (eds.), *Herodotus in the Long Nineteenth Century*, Cambridge et al., 244–273.
Haynes, Kenneth (2003), *English Literature and Ancient Languages*, Oxford.
Lazarus, Micha (2014), "Greek literacy in sixteenth-century England", in: *Renaissance Studies* 29.3, 433–458.
Lazarus, Micha (2016), "Greek in Tudor England", in: *The Etheridge Project* (http://hellenic-institute.uk/research/Etheridge/Lazarus/Tudor-Greek.html [accessed: September 2020]).
Milne, Kirsty (2007), "The Forgotten Greek Books of Elizabethan England", in: *Literature Compass* 4.3, 677–687.
Morrison, Anthea (1983), "Samuel Taylor Coleridge's Greek Prize Ode on the Slave Trade", in: John Richard Watson (ed.), *An Infinite Complexity: Essays in Romanticism*, Edinburgh, 145–160.
Musae Cantabrigienses; seu carmina quaedam numismate aureo Cantabrigiae ornata et Procancellarii permissu edita, Londini 1810.
Päll, Janika (forthcoming), "Greek Pindaric ode in the United Kingdom", in: Ivo Volt (ed.), *Hortus Floridus*, Tartu.
Rebenich, Stefan (2011), "Klassische Bildung", in: Michael Maaser/Gerrit Walther (eds.), *Bildung. Ziele und Formen, Traditionen und Systeme, Medien und Akteure*, Stuttgart/Weimar, 51–55.
Rutherford, Emily (2017), "Arthur Sidgwick's Greek Prose Composition: Gender, Affect, and Sociability in the Late-Victorian University", in: *Journal of British Studies* 56, 91–116.
Sandys, John Edwin (1908), *A History of Classical Scholarship*, vol. ii–iii, Cambridge.

Stray, Christopher (1998), *Classics Transformed. Schools, Universities, and Society in England, 1830–1960*, Oxford.
Tanner, Joseph Robson (ed.) (1917), *The Historical Register of the University of Cambridge being a supplement to the Calendar with a record of university offices honours and distinctions to the year 1910*, Cambridge.
Tilley, Arthur (1938), "Greek Studies in England in the Early Sixteenth Century", in: *English Historical Review* 53, 221–239, 438–456.
Tyrrell, Robert Yelverton (1890), *Dublin Translations into Greek and Latin*, Dublin/London.
Weise, Stefan (2016), "'Ἑλληνίδ' αἶαν εἰσιδεῖν ἱμείρομαι – Neualtgriechische Literatur in Deutschland (Versuch eines Überblicks)", in: *Antike und Abendland* 62, 114–181.

Abbreviated Titles

AC = Venn, John/Venn, John A. (eds.) (Part I 1922–27, Part II 1940–54), *Alumni Cantabrigienses. A Biographical List of All Known Students, Graduates and Holders of Office at the University of Cambridge, from the Earliest Times to 1900*, Cambridge.
DNB = Stephen, Leslie/Lee, Sidney (1885–1900), *Dictionary of National Biography*, London (online: https://en.wikisource.org/wiki/Dictionary_of_National_Biography,_1885–1900).
EB = Hoiberg, Dale H. (ed.) (2002), *The New Encyclopaedia Britannica. Micropaedia*, vol. 1–12, Chicago et al.
ODNB = Matthew, Colin/Harrison, Brian (ed.) (2004), *Oxford Dictionary of National Biography*, vol. 1–60, Oxford (online: https://www.oxforddnb.com).

John Cheke (1514–1557)

Mariae Cicellae Epitaphium. I. C. [1544?]

Ὀστέα τῆς Μαρίας Σισέλλης ἐνθάδε κεῖται,
πνεῦμα τελευτώσης κύριος αὐτὸς ἔχει.
Ἡ πατρὸς μητρός τ' ἀγαθοῖν ἀνδρός τ' ἀγαθοῖο
οὖσα, καλῷ θάνατον καλὸν ἔθηκε βίῳ.

Textus: [Cheke, John] (1551), *De obitu doctissimi et sanctissimi theologi doctoris Martini Buceri...Item, Epigrammata varia cum Graecae* [sic] *tum Latinè conscripta...*, Londini, n IIr. (unde Strype 1821, 166).

Crit.: 1 ἔνθαδε ed., correxi || 2 αὐτός ed., correxi || 3 πάτρος ed., correxi || 4 καλῶ ed., correxi | θανατόν καλόν ed., correxi

Sim.: 2 ἐνθάδε κεῖται] de clausula cf. e.g. Greg. Naz. *Anth. Pal.* 8.71.1; 8.81.1 etc.

Epitaph of Mary Cecil by J(ohn) C(heke)

Here lie the bones of Mary Cecil;
   the Lord himself has the spirit of the dead woman.
As she had a good father and mother, as well as a good husband,
   she made her death noble through her noble life.

Metre: Elegiac couplet (flawless).

Notes: This funerary epigram was written for Cheke's sister Mary, who married William Cecil in 1541 and died in 1544. The poem is skilfully structured and masterfully composed (although the accents, if indeed they are due to Cheke himself, reveal some tentativeness). The first two lines contrast body (ὀστέα) and soul (πνεῦμα) with their places of rest, earth (ἐνθάδε) and heaven (κύριος). The poet locates the name of the deceased in between. The last two lines celebrate her parents and her husband, culminating in the juxtaposition of beautiful death (θάνατον καλόν) and beautiful life (καλῷ...βίῳ). Arthur Tilley criticised the epigram for being poor in quality and having two grammatical errors (Tilley 1938, 443). This harsh evaluation appears to be unjustified, however. The epigram was published in a collection of consolatory verses on the death of Martin Bucer

(1491–1551).⁴⁰ In addition to Cheke's Greek verses about the deaths of his daughter and Bucer, the collection contains a considerable quantity of Greek poems by Nicholas Carr (1524–1549) (anacreontics and elegiac couplets),⁴¹ Christopher Carlile (see *AC* I.1,293; iambics and hexameters), Henry Ayland (see *AC* I.1,59; iambics), John Frere/Fryer (see *AC* I.2,183; iambics and elegiac couplets), Ἵμερος Βοϊτῶνος (William Boyton[?], see *AC* I.1,197; iambics), and John Culpeper (see *AC* I.1,431; elegiac couplets). Perhaps it is no coincidence that this considerable quantity of Greek poems first (?) appears in a collection for a 'German' Protestant reformer (Bucer was appointed Regius Professor of Divinity at the University of Cambridge in 1549 and died in 1551; subsequently, during the reign of Mary, his corpse was exhumed and publicly burnt for heresy), since Greek writing was better established in Germany at this period (→ **Germany**).

Biography: John Cheke (1514–1557) was the first Regius Professor of Greek at the University of Cambridge (1540–1551) and 'one of the principal restorers of Greek learning in England' (*DNB*). He was also tutor to Prince Edward who knighted him, once he became king, in 1552. Cheke studied at St John's College, Cambridge (fellow from 1529, BA in 1529/30, commenced MA in 1533). Being a Protestant, he left England after Mary's accession, but he was arrested in Belgium and jailed in the Tower of London, where he was forced to publicly renounce his Protestantism. He was said to have died of shame in 1557, although modern researchers suspect that the cause of his death rather was an influenza epidemic. William Cecil (1520/21–1598), who married Cheke's sister Mary in 1541, was among his students at Cambridge. In addition to the epigram about the death of his sister, we also possess a Greek letter written to Cecil,⁴² the quality of which Tilley regards as 'no better than his verse' (Tilley 1938, 443 fn. 2). As a Greek scholar, Cheke published influential letters on Greek pronunciation and printed the first major book in Greek in England, containing two homilies of John Chrysostom with Latin translation (Binns 1995, 222–223).

Bibliography: Strype, John (1821), *The Life of the Learned Sir John Cheke, Kᵗ.* […], Oxford; Nichols, John Gough (ed.) (1857), *Literary Remains of King Edward the Sixth*, London; Sandys 1980, II.231–233; *DNB* 10, 178–183; Tilley 1938, 439–440, 443, 454; Johnson, S.R. (1982), "Cheke, John (1514–57)", in: S.T. Bindoff, *The History of Parliament: the House of Commons 1509–1558* (online: https://www.historyofparliamentonline.org/volume/1509-1558/member/cheke-john-1514-57;

---

40 For a detailed description, see Nichols 1857, 305–307 fn. 3.
41 For Carr, see Tilley 1938, 444. Carr succeeded Cheke as Regius Professor of Greek from 1547 to 1549.
42 See Strype 1821, 176.

accessed: September 2020); Binns 1995, 222–223; Bryson, Alan (2004/2018), "Cheke, Sir John", in: *ODNB* online (https://doi.org/10.1093/ref:odnb/5211).

George Etheridge (1519–1588?)

Ἐγκώμιον τῶν πράξεων καὶ τῶν στρατηγημάτων τοῦ Ἐνρίκου ὀγδόου ἐμφανεστάτου βασιλέως [1566]

(excerptum, vv. 221–246)

    Οὐδένα μὴν ἔλαθέν γ' Ἐνρῖκος ἄναξ πολύκλειτος
    Πάντα περὶ πλείστου γράμματ' ἄριστα ποιῶν·
    Ἔστι δὲ τῆς ἀρετῆς ῥίζη τὰ γράμματα πάσης,
    Τοὺς δὲ θεοῦ δούλους χρὴ ἀρετήν γε φιλεῖν.
225 Τόσσον γὰρ χωρὶς ἀρετῆς τὰ γράμματα χραισμεῖ,
    Ὅσσον ἄνευ ψυχῆς σώματα τεθνεότα,
    Καρπὸν δ' ὡς ἀπολυμαίνεσθαι γαῖα πέφυκε
    Αὐχμώδης, ὑετός γ' ἤν ποτε οὐχὶ βρέχει·
    Οὕτως ἡ παιδεία τρόπων μετέχουσα κακίστων
230 Φθίνει (τῆς ἀρετῆς νοσφὶν ἐοῦσα) νόον.
    Γράμματα γοῦν ταύτην ἔπορεν βασιλῆος ἕκητι,
    Ὅς γ' ἔτι νῦν ἀνθεῖν γράμματα πάντα ποιεῖ·
    Τῶν Μουσῶν μὲν ἐρᾶτο, ἐπεὶ τὰ γράμματα αὐτὸς
    Οἶδεν, καὶ πολλῶν ἦν μάλ' ἐπιστάμενος,
235 Καὶ τοῖς σπουδαίοις τὰ χρήματ' ἔδωκεν ἀφειδῶς,
    Ὡς ἄψωσι λόγων, ὧν κλέος ἐστὶ μέγα·
    Τὰς γὰρ ἐπιστήμας ἐπὶ μισθοῖς οὐκ ἀρ' ὀλίγοις
    Ἀνθεῖν ἀμφοτέραις ταῖς ἐκέλευε σχολαῖς.
    Μάρτυρες οἱ Κανταβρίγιοί τε καὶ Ὀξονιαῖοι,
240 Ὅσσοι ταῖς βίβλοις νοῦν προσέχουσι καλαῖς,
    Οὕνεκα δὲ γλώσσας διδασκέμεναί γε μαθητὰς
    Τοὺς ἑρμηνευτὰς πρῶτος ἔδωκεν ἔχειν·
    Οἱ νομοδίδακταί γε, θεολόγοι οἵ τε ἰατροὶ
    γλῶσσά τε Ἑλλήνων Ἑβραϊκοί τε λόγοι
245 Τὴν εὐεργεσίαν προϋπαρξαμένην βασιλῆος
    Δηλώσουσιν ἀεί γ' ἀνδράσιν ἐσσομένοις.

Textus: ms. London, British Library, Royal MS 16 C X, fol. 18r–19r (unde editio digitalis: http://hellenic-institute.uk/research/Etheridge/ [accessed: July 2020]).

Crit.: 230 νοσφὶν] post correcturam ms., νόσφιν debuit || 237 ἀρ'] ms., ἄρ' debuit || 243 νομοδιδάκταί γε] νομοδιδάκται γε debuit || 245 προϋπαρξαμένην scripsi suadente Pontani: πρόυπ- ms.

Sim.: 223 τῆς ἀρετῆς ῥίζη τὰ γράμματα πάσης] cf. Joh. Chrys. PG 47.373.44 (ῥίζα τῆς πολλῆς ἀρετῆς); PG 55.341.56–57 (τοῦτο ἀρετῆς ἁπάσης ῥίζα); 55.631.55–56 (ῥίζα πάσης ἀρετῆς) || **234** ἐπιστάμενος] cf. eadem sede Archil. fr. 1.2 West; Solon fr. 13.52 West || **236** κλέος ἐστὶ μέγα] cf. Greg. Naz. *Anth. Gr. App., epigr. demonstr.* 161.1 (sed iunctura κλέος μέγα iam apud Homerum legitur) || **242** ἑρμηνευτάς] verbum pedestre || **243** νομοδίδακται] verbum pedestre, cf. Plut. *Cat. Mai.* 20; Artem. 2.29 || **246** ἀνδράσιν ἐσσομένοις] cf. Hes. *Op.* 56

Encomium on the deeds and stratagems of the most notable King Henry VIII

(excerpt, ll. 221–246)

> Everybody noticed that our very famous Lord Henry valued all the best disciplines greatly. Learning is the root of all virtue, and the servants of God must embrace virtue. [225] For learning without virtue helps as much as dead bodies without a soul and just as the dry earth which rain never wets naturally destroys the fruit,[43] learning which fosters the worst manners likewise [230] harms the mind, being devoid of virtue. But learning gave virtue according to the will of the King, who now makes all learning flourish. He loved the Muses, since he knew the sciences and was well versed in many of them. [235] He has also given money to scholars, without regard to costs, so that they might embrace the disciplines whose glory is great. He ordered that the sciences should be fostered at both schools through high salaries. The inhabitants of Cambridge and Oxford [240] who are interested in the best books are witness to this, since he was the first to give them translators to teach the languages to pupils. The teachers of law, the theologians, and the physicians, the language of the Greeks, and Hebrew literature [245] will forever show the benefits once received from the King to future men.

Metre: Elegiac couplets (note internal correption in l. 232 ποιῶν and 242 ποιεῖ, *thesis in arsi* in l. 235, hiatuses in ll. 234, 243, 254, παιδείᾰ in l. 239, irregular lengthening in l. 251 δῐδασκέμεναι, l. 253 νομοδίδακται [ῐ] and θεολόγοι [first o long!], σχ as single consonant in l. 248)

Notes: Deprived of his Regius Professorship at Oxford University, Etheridge composed a lengthy Greek encomium on the occasion of Queen Elizabeth I's visit to Oxford in 1566 in the hope of regaining his former position. One may assume that the encomium was not delivered, as Etheridge no longer held an official position at the university; in all likelihood, it was simply handed over to the Queen by its

---

[43] The translation published on the website of *The Etheridge Project* offers the following: 'or as fruit that has been produced by the earth only to be destroyed by drought, which rain never moistened'.

author. It appears that Etheridge knew that Elizabeth had enjoyed some training in Greek and therefore hoped to gain her favour through his Greek poem; however, no reaction is recorded. In order to avoid direct criticism and also to highlight his career under Henry VIII, Etheridge – a staunch Catholic – chose Elizabeth's father as the main subject of his encomium. In the excerpt provided here, he praises the king's patronage of learning, an obvious invitation to the Queen to follow in Henry's footsteps and to reinstate Etheridge as Regius Professor. Etheridge uses no specific poetic language. The main models which he references are Homer, Plutarch's *Life of Artaxerxes*, Justin Martyr, and some Church Fathers.[44]

Biography: George Etheridge (Etherege/Ethrygg) was a Catholic scholar, physician, and Regius Professor of Greek at the University of Oxford (1547–1550, 1554–1559). He was educated at Corpus Christi College, Oxford (BA in 1539, MA in 1543, BM in 1545). In 1547, after gaining King Henry VIII's favour, he was appointed to the Regius Professorship of Greek; he was dismissed from this position under Edward VI. During Mary I's reign he briefly regained his former position and was active in the repression of Protestants, taking part in the trial of the prelates Cranmer, Ridley, and Latimer. After the accession of Elizabeth I, he was permanently deprived of his professorship, although he continued to reside in Oxford till his death, working as a physician. His Catholic faith was the cause of imprisonments during his later life. Several of his works and musical compositions are preserved in manuscript form. In addition to the handwritten encomium for Queen Elizabeth I (see above) and a Greek hexameter poem on Thomas Wyatt's conspiracy against Queen Mary I, Etheridge also published a Greek translation of the second book of Virgil's *Aeneid* in 1553,[45] and towards the end of his life (1588) he published a medical book titled *In libros aliquot Pauli Aeginetae hypomnemata quaedam seu observationes medicamentorum* (accompanied by a Greek dedicatory letter).[46] In 2016, researchers affiliated with the British Library and the Hellenic Institute at Royal Holloway, University of London, published a digital edition of Etheridge's encomium, which they dedicated to Queen Elizabeth II to mark the 60th anniversary of her accession to the throne.

---

44 Cf. Wright, Christopher (2016), "The Text", in: *The Etheridge Project* http://hellenic-institute.uk/research/Etheridge/Author-and-Text/Text.html [accessed: September 2020].
45 Etheridge, George (1553), *Publii Vergilii Maronis Aeneidos liber secundus: Graecis versibus redditus*, Londini.
46 Cf. Wright, Christopher (2016), "The Author", in: *The Etheridge Project* http://hellenic-institute.uk/research/Etheridge/Author-and-Text/Author.html [accessed: September 2020].

John Christopherson (†1558)

Τραγῳδία Ἰεφθάε [1544–1547]

(excerptum, vv. 1110–1124, 1135–1148: Χο(ρός) = chorus, Οἰκέ(της) = famulus)[47]

1110 Χο. ὦ οἶκος ἐξωλὴς πάνυ.
 θεοῦ θέλημα παντελῶς
 γένοιτο· κάλλιστον τόδε.
 κραίνει δ' ἀέλπτως πολλάκις
 τὰ πολλὰ πανσθενὴς θεός.
1115 ἐκ τῶν μελάθρων ἐξιὼν
 δοῦλος τὰ πάντα φθέγξεται.
 Οἰκέ. πάρεστέ μοι γέροντες, ἔρχομαι λέγειν
 θαυμαστὰ περὶ καλῆς κόρης Ἰεφθάε·
 ἐπεὶ γὰρ ἱκόμεσθα πρὸς βωμὸν θεοῦ,
1120 ἐπὶ σφαγὰς στείχει πατὴρ ἄκων τέκνου.
 κείνη πατέρα κηλεῖν κατήρξατο πρόφρων.
 ἔλεξε τοιάδ'· 'ὦ πάτερ, τί δακρύεις;
 γήθει τελευτᾶν παῖδα σοῦ πάτρης πέρι.
 περὶ παντὸς Ἰσραὴλ καλόν μοι φῶς λιπεῖν.'
 [...]
1135 τέλος δὲ σῶμ' ἔκυψε πρὸς βωμὸν θεοῦ.
 πατὴρ ἐλάζετο ξίφος τλήμων μόλις.
 ἤρετο σμικρόν· πίπτει χάμαζε εὐθέως.
 ἀνιστὰς αὖθις ἤρξατο πλήττειν γοῶν.
 ἀλλ' οὐκ ἐᾷ νόος. βοᾷ κλαυθμοῦ μέτα·
1140 'ὦ παῖ, σὺ λάβε ξίφος. πατρὸς κόψον κάρα.
 ἐγὼ γὰρ ἔσσομαι τὸ θῦμα σοῦ πέρι.
 ὄλωλα δύσποτμος. Τί φῶς δέρκω τάλας;'
 πενθοῦσι πάντες. ἀλλὰ 'σπεύδειν (φασί) χρή·
 τριβὴ στόνον μείζω φέρει.' κεῖνος πότε
1145 τῷ φασγάνῳ κόπτεν τερὲν κόρης κάρα.
 ἔρευσεν αἷμα. βωμὸς εὐγενεῖ φόνῳ

---

[47] I am very grateful to Richard Hunter and Nicolas Bell (Cambridge) for providing copies of both the manuscripts and the print edition.

ἐστέψατ'. ἀσπαίρει τὸ σῶμα πρὸς βραχύ.
ἤρξαντο πάντες δακρύειν πικρῶς κόρην.

Textus: mss. T = Trinity College, Cambridge, MS. 0.1.37, ff. 56v–58r; J = St John's College, Cambridge, MS.287.H.19 (folia non numerata); ed. = Fobes 1928, 152–156.

Crit.: 1110 ἐξωλῆς] ἐξώλης debuit || 1115 ἐξίων] ἐξιὼν debuit || 1117 πάρεστε μοι T || 1124 παντὸς J: πάντος T || 1135 τέλος δὲ J: τέλοσδε T || 1137 χάμαζε] χαμᾶζε debuit || 1139 ἐᾶ ... βοᾶ] ἐᾷ ... βοᾷ debuit || 1140 λάβε] λαβὲ debuit || 1142 δέρκω τάλας J: ἔτι βλέπω T || 1143 φασί J: φασι T || 1144 κεῖνος πότε J: κεῖνος ποτε T: κεῖνός ποτε debuit || 1145 κόπτεν J: κόπτειν T | τέρεν debuit || 1146 βωμός] an βωμόν?

Sim.: 1111–1112 θεοῦ θέλημα παντελῶς / γένοιτο] cf. NT *Mt.* 6.10 (γενηθήτω τὸ θέλημά σου) || 1113–1114 cf. *Christus patiens* 1131 (πολλά τ' ἀέλπτως πολλάκις κραίνει Θεός) || 1119 ἐπεὶ γὰρ ἱκόμεσθα] cf. Eur. *IA* 1543 | πρὸς βωμὸν θεοῦ (vid. etiam 1135)] clausula Euripidea, cf. *IA* 1555 (πρὸς βωμὸν θεᾶς) || 1120 ἐπὶ σφαγὰς στείχει] cf. Eur. *IA* 1548 (ἐπὶ σφαγὰς στείχουσαν εἰς ἄλσος κόρην) || 1122 ἔλεξε τοιάδ'. ὦ πάτερ] cf. Eur. *IA* 1552 (ἔλεξε τοιάδ'· Ὦ πάτερ, πάρειμί σοι) | ὦ πάτερ, τί δακρύεις;] cf. Soph. *El.* 827 (ὦ παῖ, τί δακρύεις;) || 1136 πατὴρ...τλήμων] cf. Eur. *Med.* 1204 || 1139 βοᾶ κλαυθμοῦ μέτα] cf. LXX *Jud.* 14.16 (καὶ ἐβόησε φωνῇ μεγάλῃ μετὰ κλαυθμοῦ) || 1146 βωμὸς εὐγενεῖ φόνῳ] cf. Eur. *IA* 1595 (βωμὸν εὐ. φ.) || 1147 cf. Eur. *IA* 1587 (ἔλαφος γὰρ ἀσπαίρουσ' ἔκειτ' ἐπὶ χθονί)

Tragedy Jephthah

(excerpt, ll. 1110–1124, 1135–1148)

CHO.: O wholly cursed house! May God's will happen absolutely: This is entirely right! Almighty God often accomplishes most things beyond all hope. – [1115] A servant is coming from the house and will tell us everything.
SERVANT: Come to me, elders. I will tell you incredible things about the beautiful daughter of Jephthah. For as we came to the altar of God, [1120] the father went to the sacrifice of his child against his will. The girl, however, kindly began to charm her father. She spoke as follows: 'O father, why are you crying? Rejoice that your child is going to die for your homeland. It is good for me to leave the light for all of Israel! [...]'
[1135] Finally she stooped her body to the altar of God. The miserable father took the sword with toil and pain. He raised it a little but then dropped immediately on the ground. He stood up again and began to strike while weeping, but his mind did not let it happen. He shouted with tears, saying: [1140] 'O my child! Take the sword and cut off your father's head. For I will be the sacrifice for you. I am ruined by an unlucky fate! Why should I see the light anymore?' Everyone was mourning, but they said: 'We have to hurry. Delay brings bigger sorrow.' Then, at some time [1145] he cut off the soft head of the girl with his sword. The

blood ran down and the altar was crowned with her noble blood. The body still gasped for a short time. Then everybody began to bewail the girl bitterly.[48]

Metre: Iambic dimeters (ll. 1110–1116), iambic trimeters (ll. 1117ff.). Several violations of Porson's Law.[49]

Notes: Christopherson's *Jephthah* is one of very few examples of modern drama written in ancient Greek (cf. Herrichen and Richter → **Germany**; Rissa → **Italy**), and it is beyond question a highlight in 16th-century Greek verse composition. Two autographs of the Greek text are preserved, one at Trinity College and the other at St John's College, Cambridge. Each copy has its own dedicatee, the one at Trinity William Parr (T), the other at St John's Cuthbert Tunstall (J). A modern edition was published by Francis Howard Fobes in 1928. There is also a Latin version, preserved in a manuscript of the Bodleian Library (MS. Tanner 466) and dedicated to King Henry VIII (facsimile edition in Upton 1988). According to Christopherson's preface, the Greek version was composed prior to the Latin, which was written for easier comprehension: *atque vt totam Tragoediam primo graece scriptam facilius quisque intelligere possit, eam latine ijsdem metri generibus expressi* (MS. Tanner 466, p. 3). The text can be dated between 1544 and 1547 (most scholars consider 1544 the year of completion). Christopherson obviously hoped to succeed John Cheke (see above) as Regius Professor of Greek when the latter became tutor to Prince Edward (Upton 1988, 4–5). Whether Christopherson's Greek text was actually performed is not entirely certain (Fobes 1928, 9; Upton 1988, 4). The plot is taken from chapter 11 of the *Book of Judges*. Christopherson uses classical features of Attic tragedy: monologue, dialogue, chorus, messenger's report, and *stichomythia*. The prologue and the *epeisodia* are written

---

48 Author's own Latin translation (Bodleian Library, MS. Tanner 466, p. 52–53): **Cho:** [...] *O admodum infoelix domus. / Fiat voluntas Numinis· Namque istud in primis decet· / Deus repente praepotens / Permulta saepe perficit. / Ex aedibus nunc exiens / Seruus docebit omnia. /* **Fam:** *Adeste mihi senes relatum ad uos eo / miranda, de formosa Iephte filia. / Postquam venimus sacram ad aram numinis, / Lento gradu caedem occupat prolis pater. / Lenire coepit illa genitorem lubens, / Faturque talia· O pater quid ingemis? / Lętare quod proles cadat pro patria. / Decus est enim mihi ob Israel luce eximi. / [...] / Tandem ad dei aram corpus inflexit volens. / Aegre pater sumit manu ensem ferreum / Leuatque paululum, atque humum mox cecidit. / Iterumque surgens coedere incipit anxius. / Non sinit animus. Lugubrem vocem edidit. / O gnata cape tu ensem· Patris caput amputa. / Pro te lubenter victima ero nunc filia. / Perij miser· quid cerno lucem perditus? / Luxere cuncti· Sed propere obire incitant. / Gemitum mora auget· ille tandem ense ęreo / Tenerum abscidit ceruicibus prolis caput· / Cruor effluit· respersa sunt altaria / Cęde generosa· corpus ad tempus micat· / Deflere cuncti filiam luctu graui.*

49 For a detailed analysis of Christopherson's treatment of the metre, see Fobes 1928, 17–18.

in iambic trimeters, the choral parts in anapaests (*parodos*, second and fourth *stasimon*), trochaic dimeters (first *stasimon*), στίχοι χορικοὶ μικτοί (third *stasimon*), and iambics (fifth *stasimon*, *exodos*). The various metres are also noted in the manuscript. In addition to the Greek text of the play itself, Christopherson included a dedicatory letter, written in Latin, explanatory Latin verses, a Greek hypothesis, and the obligatory list of τὰ τοῦ δράματος πρόσωπα. The lines excerpted here come from the final part of the play, including the end of the fifth *stasimon* and the messenger's report on the death of Jephthah's daughter. The dramatic account of the sacrifice is mainly inspired by Euripides' *Iphigenia at Aulis* (see Fobes 1928, 152). The excerpt also shows Christopherson's talent in developing the characters' emotions (cf. Fobes 1928, 12–13). One may note, finally, that Christopherson made use of the late antique/Byzantine *Christus patiens* (see ll. 1113–1114), which may have been his model for the combination of Euripidean drama and biblical narrative.

Biography: John Christopherson was an English Catholic scholar at the University of Cambridge. He was educated at Pembroke Hall and St John's College. After his graduation in 1541, he first became a fellow at Pembroke, then at St John's (1542), and afterward at Trinity College (1546). After the accession of Edward VI, he left Cambridge and moved to Louvain. During Mary I's reign, he returned and was appointed master of Trinity College (1553). He subsequently became chaplain and confessor to Queen Mary I, dean of Norwich (1554–1557), and finally bishop of Chichester in 1557, a position he held until his death in 1558. He was imprisoned after the accession of Elizabeth I for a sermon criticising the Protestant faith. Among his scholarly achievements are Latin translations of Philo Judaeus (1553), and of Eusebius and other church historians (printed posthumously in Louvain in 1569) (cf. Binns 1995, 218–222). However, their quality is not held in high regard.

Bibliography: *DNB* 10, 293–295; Wright, Jonathan (2004/2005), "Christopherson, John", in: *ODNB* online (https://doi.org/10.1093/ref:odnb/5373); Boas, Frederick (1914), *University Drama in the Tudor Age*, Oxford, 43–62; Fobes, Francis Howard (ed.)/Sypherd, Wilbur Owen (1928), *Jephthah by John Christopherson. The Greek text edited and translated into English*, Newark, Delaware; Upton, Christopher (ed.) (1988), *John Christoperson, IEPHTE. William Goldingam, HERODES*, Hildesheim/Zürich/New York; Streufert, Paul D. (2008/2016), "Christopherson at Cambridge: Greco-Catholic Ethics in the Protestant University", in: Jonathan Walker/Paul D. Streufert (eds.), *Early Modern Academic Plays*, Farnham/Burlington, 45–64; Norland, Howard B. (1995), "Christopherson's Jephthah", in: Id., *Drama in Early Tudor Britain, 1485–1558*, Lincoln/London, 306–318; Binns 1995, 218–222.

Andrew Downes (1549?–1628)

Εἰς τὴν τελευτὴν τῆς μακαριωτάτης Ἠλισάβετ βασιλείας [1603]

Ἤνυσεν Ἠλισάβετ βίον, ἤνυσεν ἡ μακαρῖτις,
Ὄλβια πάντα λαχοῦσα, τὰ ἂν θνητοῖσι γένοιτο.
Εὐφημεῖν θέμις ἐστὶ καὶ οὐ θρηνεῖν ἀπιοῦσαν.
Οὐκ ἔτι γὰρ δήπου χαμαὶ ἐρχομένοις ὁ ὕπερθεν
5 Οὐρανὸς ἀμβατὸς ἦν κατὰ Πίνδαρον. ἄλλα δ' ὑπῆρξεν
Ἀθρόα πάντ' ἐπὶ γῆς οἱ, ἄγε ζηλωτὰ τέτυκται·
Νῖκαι παμμεγέθεις καὶ δυσμενέων κράτος ἀνδρῶν,
Καὶ τὸ ὑπεκπροφυγεῖν πολλὰς μικρῶν ἐπιβουλάς,
Τῆς θείας ὅγε δεῖγμα σαφέστατόν ἐστιν ἀρωγῆς,
10 Ἀρχομένων εὔνοια φίλων, δέος ἀντιπάλων δέ,
Εὐσεβίης ἀρετῆς τε καὶ εὐτυχίης μέγα κῦδος,
Δόξα καλή, βαθὺ γῆρας, ἐπὶ φρένες ἔμπεδοι αἰεί,
Ὃ σπάνιον τελέθει βασιλεῦσι μέγα κρατέουσι.
Μυρία δ' ἄλλ' ἐπὶ τοῖσιν ἐν ἀνθρώποις περίπυστα.
15 Οὐδὲ γάρ οἱ τάγε πάντ' ἂν ἀριθμήσειε προσόντα,
Οὐδ' εἴ τῳ δέκα μὲν γλῶσσαι, δέκα δὲ στόματ' εἴη.
Τοὔνεκα χρὴ βασιλίδα περικλείτην μακαρίζειν
Αὐτήν, ὑμνεῖν δὲ κλέος ἄφθιτον οὐρανόμηκες.
Σῶμα μὲν ἐν κόλποις ἔπεσεν χθονός, αὐτὰρ ἀπῆλθε
20 Ψυχὴ ἐς αἰθέρα δῖον ἀεὶ μακάρεσσι συνεῖναι.

ἐποίησεν Ἀ. Δουνῆς.

Textus: Downes, Andrew (1603), "Εἰς τὴν τελευτὴν τῆς μακαριωτάτης Ἠλισάβετ βασιλείας", in: *Threno-thriambeuticon. Academiae Cantabrigiensis ob damnum lucrosum, & infoelicitatem foelicissimam, luctuosus triumphus*, Cantabrigiae, 58.

Crit.: 11 ἀρητῆς ed. || 12 γήρας ed. || 19 ἔπεσε ed. (sed vix legi potest), ἔπεσεν Pontani: an ἔχεται (coll. *Anth. Gr.* 16.31.1)?

Sim.: 4 χαμαὶ ἐρχομένοις] circumlocutio Homerica, vid. *Il.* 5.442 (χαμαὶ ἐρχομένων τ' ἀνθρώπων). Cf. etiam *Hymn. Hom. Vest.* 2; Hes. *Theog.* 272 || 4–5 noster alludit ad Pind. *Pyth.* 10.27 (ὁ χάλκεος οὐρανὸς οὔ ποτ' ἀμβατὸς αὐτῷ) || 11 μέγα κῦδος] iunctura Hom., cf. e.g. *Il.* 9.673 || 12 βαθὺ γῆρας] cf. Greg. Naz. *Anth. Pal.* 8.16.3 et al. | φρένες ἔμπεδοι] iunctura Hom., vid. eadem sede *Od.* 10.493 || 13 μέγα κρατέουσι] de iunctura cf. e.g. Hom. *Il.* 16.172 (μέγα κρατέων ἤνασσε) || 16 cf. Hom. *Il.* 2.489 (οὐδ' εἴ μοι δέκα μὲν γλῶσσαι, δέκα δὲ στόματ' εἶεν) || 18 κλέος...οὐρανόμηκες] cf. Ar. *Nub.* 459; *Anth. Pal.* 7.84.1 et al.; κλέος ἄφθιτον iam Homericum, vid. *Il.* 9.413 || 19–20 cf. Speusipp. *Anth. Gr.* 16.31.1–2 (σῶμα μὲν ἐν κόλποις κατέχει τόδε γαῖα Πλάτωνος / ψυχὴ δ' ἰσόθεος τάξιν ἔχει μακάρων). Vide etiam *Anth. Pal.* 7.61.1–2 (γαῖα μὲν ἐν κόλποις κρύπτει τόδε σῶμα Πλάτωνος / ψυχὴ δ' ἀθάνατον τάξιν ἔχει μακάρων).

On the death of the most blessed Queen Elizabeth

Elizabeth has finished her life, the blessed Elizabeth has finished it after gaining all the good available to mortals. It is meet and right to honour the deceased and not to bewail her. For heaven above [5] was no longer accessible for the people wandering on earth, according to Pindar, but she had all other things on earth which are enviable: great victories and power over hostile men, the ability to escape the numerous attacks of mean men (a clear sign of divine assistance), [10] the favour of friendly subjects and the fear of her enemies, the great glory of piety, virtue and good luck, good fame, old age, and a consistently stable mind (which is rare with powerful kings), and, in addition to these, innumerable other things well known among men. [15] Therefore, nobody could count all the things which belong to her, not even if he had ten tongues and ten mouths. This is the reason why we must bless the Queen herself and sing her imperishable glory high as heaven. Her body has fallen into the bosom of earth, but her soul has flown [20] to divine heaven to be forever with the blessed ones.

Written by A(ndrew) Downes.

Metre: Hexameters. Note βασιλῖδα instead of βασιλίδα with artificial lengthening (l. 17).

Notes: Downes' poem on the death of Queen Elizabeth I is printed in a collection of memorial verses, published by the University of Cambridge. It is the only poem in Greek. Although Downes integrates phrases from various ancient models (notably Homer, Pindar, and the *Greek Anthology*), his diction is rather prosaic, and the compositional idea is simple: There is no reason to mourn for the Queen's death, as she had all goods and advantages on earth, and her soul is now in heaven.

Biography: Andrew Downes (Δουνῆς) was Regius Professor of Greek at the University of Cambridge (from 1586 until his retirement in 1625) and an important promoter of Greek. Born in or about 1545, Downes received his classical education at Shrewsbury and later at St John's, Cambridge (BA in 1570–71, fellow from 1571, commenced MA in 1574, senior fellow from 1580, BD in 1582). He was also a member of the committee for the revision of the authorised version of the Bible. As a scholar, he published especially on ancient orators. We owe to him an edition of Lysias' first speech for Eratosthenes (Cambridge 1593) and *praelectiones* on Demosthenes' *De pace* (London 1621).[50] In addition to his poem on the death of Elizabeth, Downes composed Greek pieces on various occasions (e.g., on the deaths of

---

50 Cf. Binns 1995, 235.

James I, Dr Whitaker, and Prince Henry) and also wrote Greek letters to Isaac Casaubon (→ **Switzerland**).

Bibliography: *DNB* 15, 392–393; Leedham-Green, Elisabeth/Wilson, Nigel G. (2004), "Downes, Andrew", in: *ODNB* online (https://doi.org/10.1093/ref: odnb/ 7972); Sandys 1908, II.336–337; Forster 1982, 147; Binns 1995, 235.

George Herbert (1593–1633)

Memoriae matris sacrum [1627]

(nr. XVI)

    Χαλεπὸν δοκεῖ δακρῦσαι,
    Χαλεπὸν μὲν οὐ δακρῦσαι·
    Χαλεπώτερον δὲ πάντων
    Δακρύοντας ἀμπαύεσθαι.
5   Γενέτειραν οὔ τις ἀνδρῶν
    Διδύμαις κόραις τοιαύτην
    Ἐποδύρεται πρεπόντως.
    Τάλας, εἴθε γ' Ἄργος εἴην
    Πολυόμματος, πολύτλας,
10 Ἵνα μητρὸς εὐθενούσης
    Ἀρετὰς διακριθείσας
    Ἰδίαις κόραισι κλαύσω.

Textus: Herbert, George (1627), "Memoriae Matris Sacrum", in: John Donne, *A sermon of commemoration of the Lady Danuers...*, London, [I 3v] (14) (unde Hutchinson 1941, 430).

Crit.: 5 Γενετείραν ed. || 8 εἴθεγ' ed. || 12 κλαύσῳ ed.

Sim.: 1–4 cf. *Anacreont.* 29 (χαλεπὸν τὸ μὴ φιλῆσαι, / χαλεπὸν δὲ καὶ φιλῆσαι· / χαλεπώτερον δὲ πάντων / ἀποτυγχάνειν φιλοῦντα) || 9 πολυόμματος] cf. Luc. *Dial. D.* 7 (de Argo)

To the memory of my mother

(nr. 16)

    It seems difficult to start crying,
    and it seems difficult not to start crying:
    but it seems more difficult than anything else
    to stop crying.

[5] No man can bewail
such a mother with his two eyes
in a worthy manner.
Alas, I wish I were many-eyed Argus,
I, who endure much,
[10] so that I might bewail
the distinguished virtues of my flourishing mother
with my own eyes.

Metre: Anaclastic ionic dimeter.

Notes: The poem presented here is part of a Latin-Greek cycle of poems which was composed by Herbert on the occasion of his mother's death in 1627. The cycle, titled *Memoriae matris sacrum*, consists of nineteen poems: fourteen in Latin (nos. I–XIII, XIX) and five in Greek (nos. XIV–XVIII). The five Greek epigrams, which are interwoven thematically with the Latin ones, represent a wide array of forms and metres: The framing poems, nos. XIV and XVIII, are written in elegiac couplets, no. XV in iambic trimeters, no. XVI in anaclastic ionic dimeters, and no. XVII in hexameters. No. XVI imitates the Anacreontic style. Blair calls it 'the most touching of all of Herbert's Greek poems' (Blair 1985, 576). The short poem is arranged in three parts. The beginning (ll. 1–4) is a general statement: It is difficult to stop crying. These lines are inspired by *Anacreont*. 29, a four-line poem on kissing. Herbert replaces the original φιλῆσαι ('to kiss') with δακρῦσαι ('to cry'). The second part (ll. 5–7) gives the reason for crying: No man can appropriately bewail the death of his mother with his two eyes (διδύμαις κόραις). The final part (ll. 8–12) is a prayer: Herbert, in his grief, would like to be 'many-eyed' Argos, in order to be able to weep for his mother with his own eyes (ἰδίαις κόραις). The poem thus starts from a general statement and comes, finally, to Herbert himself. The multiplication of eyes is, of course, a rhetorical *auxesis*, mirroring the overwhelming sorrow (ll. 8–9: τάλας...πολύτλας).

Biography: George Herbert (1593–1633) was an English clergymen and poet, one of the so-called metaphysical poets. He was educated at Westminster School (from 1604) and at Trinity College, Cambridge (from 1609). Among his teachers at Cambridge University was the Regius Professor of Greek, Andrew Downes, himself a poet of Greek verses (see above). In 1618, Herbert was appointed as praelector in Rhetoric, and he was elected orator of the university in 1620, a position from which he resigned in 1627, upon being ordained deacon. Later, he was ordained as a priest and became the rector of Bemerton. His collected poems were published posthumously by his friend Nicholas Ferrar under the title *The Temple: Sacred Poems and Private Ejaculations* in 1633. Herbert himself published several

Greek and Latin poems during his academic career at Cambridge, contributing *inter alia* to the official poetry collections which the University issued on special occasions (cf. Forster 1982, 155).

Bibliography: *EB* s.v. Herbert, George; Wilcox, Helen (2004), "Herbert, George", in: *ODNB* online (https://doi.org/10.1093/ref:odnb/13025); Hutchinson, Francis Earnest (ed.), *The Works of George Herbert*, Oxford 1941; Forster 1982, 150; Blair, Rhonda L. (1985), "George Herbert's Greek Poetry", in: *Philological Quarterly* 64.4, 573–584; Freis, Catherine/Freis, Richard/Miller, Greg (eds.) (2012), *George Herbert: Memoriae matris sacrum = To the Memory of my Mother: A Consecrated Gift. A Critical Text, Translation, and Commentary*, Fairfield, CT [non vidi].

John Milton (1608–1674)

In Effigiei Ejus Sculptorem [1645]

Ἀμαθεῖ γεγράφθαι χειρὶ τήνδε μὲν εἰκόνα
Φαίης τάχ' ἄν, πρὸς εἶδος αὐτοφυὲς βλέπων·
Τὸν δ' ἐκτυπωτὸν οὐκ ἐπιγνόντες, φίλοι,
Γελᾶτε φαύλου δυσμίμημα ζωγράφου.

Textus: Milton, John (1645), *Poems of Mr. John Milton, both English and Latin, Compos'd at several times*, London, frontispiece; Hawkings 1824, 353.

Sim.: 4 δυσμίμημα] neologismus

On the engraver of his portrait

This image is drawn by an incompetent hand,
you might say, if you look at the natural shape.
Thus, if you do not recognise the depicted person, my friends,
then laugh at the poor imitation by the careless artist.

Metre: Iambic trimeters. Violation of (the later discovered) Porson's Law in l. 4 (cf. Burney 1824, 361).

Notes: This witty epigram is printed below a picture of Milton on the frontispiece of his *Collected Poems* from 1645. Milton was not satisfied with the picture and took revenge by inserting this insulting Greek poem which, apparently, the artist could not understand: an early example of the British use of Greek as a means of hidden mockery and entertainment. The critic Charles Burney severely criticised

Milton's handling of the language: 'This Epigram is far inferior to those, which are preserved in the Greek Anthologia, on Bad Painters. It has no point: it has no αφελεια. It is destitute of poetical merit, and appears far more remarkable for its errors than for its excellencies. To confess the truth, the Poet does not appear to have suspected, that while he was censuring the *Effigiei Sculptor*, he was exposing himself to the severity of criticism, by admitting, into his verses, disputable Greek and false metre' (Burney 1824, 360). Burney then criticised especially the position of μέν in l. 1, the meaning of αὐτοφυές and ἐκτυπωτόν in l. 2–3 and the construction of γελᾶν with the accusative, as well as the neologism δυσμίμημα, in l. 4. Burney's hypercriticism, however, does not do justice to Milton's joke, which in fact bears witness to Milton's great skill in adapting the language to his intentions. What would be more appropriate than δυσμίμημα, unheard of and at the same time violating Porson's Bridge, to express the ineptitude of the *sculptor*?

Biography: John Milton, 'one of the greatest poets of the English language' (*EB*) and author of the famous epic *Paradise Lost*, was born in 1608. He was educated at St Paul's School in London and at Christ's College, Cambridge (BA in 1629, MA in 1632), before making a journey to Italy (1638–1639). During the Commonwealth, he was secretary of foreign languages, but he retired after the Restoration. Important works include his elegy *Lycidas* (1638), the plays *Comus* (1637) and *Samson Agonistes* (1671), the epics *Paradise Lost* (1667) and *Paradise Regain'd* (1671), and the treatises *Of Education* (1644) and *Areopagitica* (1644), the latter a plea for freedom of speech. The titles alone indicate the symbiosis of classical and Christian elements.[51] In addition to his English works, he also authored Latin, Italian, and a very few Greek poems (see Hawking 1824, 351–353). In the 18th and 19th centuries, Milton's poems – whole or in excerpts – were often translated into Greek. Richard Dawes (see below) tried his hand at a translation of book one of *Paradise Lost*, for example, and Edward Greswell (1797–1869) published a complete Greek translation of Milton's plays *Samson Agonistes* and *Comus* (Oxford 1832).

Bibliography: Sandys 1908, II.344–348; *EB* s.v. Milton, John; Campbell, Gordon (2004/2009), "Milton, John", in: *ODNB* online (https://doi.org/10.1093/ref: odnb/18800); Gelfert ²2005, 109–113. On his use of Greek and his Greek poems: Burney, Charles (1824), "Notes on the Greek Verses", in: Edward Hawkins (ed.), *The Poetical Works of John Milton*, vol. IV, Oxford, 357–361; Dillon, John B. (1984), "Milton's Latin and Greek Verse: An Annotated Bibliography", in: *Milton Studies* 19, 227–307; Hale, John K. (1995), *Milton's Languages: The Impact of Multilingualism on*

---

51 For Milton's knowledge and use of Greek literature in his own works, see Hale 2016.

Style, Cambridge, 43–46; Hale, John K. (2016), "A Study on Milton's Greek", in: *Milton Studies* 57, 187–210; Bulwer 2019, 282f.

James Duport (1606–1679)

Homeri *Culex, Sive,* Ὁμηρόκεντρα εἰς τὸν Κώνωπα στηλιτευτικά. ***Cùm ob aquarum restagnationem insolitâ Culicum copiâ infestaremur, mense* Julio 1661**

Ad Virum Ὁμηρικώτατον D. Joannem Cottonum, *Equitem Baronettum*

```
     Κώνωψ ὦ λιγύφωνε, μελικτὰ καὶ ἠχέτα κώνωψ,
     Κώνωψ ὦ κυνόμυια κακή, αἱμηπότα κώνωψ,
     Κώνωψ, ὦ σαλπιγκτά, βριήπυε, αἵματος ἆτε,
     Ἄρεος ἀνδροφόνοιο κασίγνητ', ἀλλοπρόσαλλε,
5    Εἴθε σ' ἀράχνια λεπτὰ περιπροχυθέντα δαμάζοι
     Δεσμός τ' ἀργαλέος, πάλαι ὡς ἀΐδηλον Ἄρηα
     Κύπριδι μισγόμενον, σέ τε κωνωπεῖον ἐρύκοι.
     Σχέτλιε, τίπτ' ἐθέλεις δάκνων ἐρεθιζέμεν ἄνδρας,
     Ὡς γίγας ἢ γέρανος πυγμαίοις τ' ἄμμι μάχεσθαι;
10   Τίπτε τόσον νύσσεις τέρενα χρόα νυκτὸς ἀμολγῷ;
     Νὺξ ἄρα νύγματός ἐστι φερώνυμος ὑμετέροιο;
     Νύξ, ὅτι νύξαι ἔθος τότε κωνώπεσσι μάλιστα;
     Πῆ φέρεαι διὰ νύκτα βαρύβρομος ἔνθα καὶ ἔνθα,
     Νύκτα δι' ὀρφναίην, ὅτε θ' εὑδέμεναι θέμις ἐστί;
15   Τίφθ' ὥς, ὦ Πολύφημ', ἀρήμενος ὧδ' ἐβόησας
     Νύκτα δι' ἀμβροσίην καὶ ἀΰπνους ἄμμε τίθησθα;
     Ἡμεῖς οὔ τί σε πω κακὸν ἔρδομεν, οὐδ' ἠβαιόν,
     Κείμεθα δ' εὔκηλοι, σὺ δὲ μαίνεαι οὐκέτ' ἀνεκτῶς,
     Ἄμμιν ἐφαλλόμενος βροτολοιγῷ ἶσος Ἄρηι
20   Ῥινοτόρῳ, στυγερῷ· ὥς σε γλυκὺς ἵμερος αἱρεῖ
     Αἵματος ἡμετέρου, σοὶ δ' οὐ κόρος, οὐδέ τι φειδώ.
     Ὡς ἄμοτον θύεις, εἴ που μέγα κύρμα κιχείης,
     Ἀνδρόμεα κρέ' ἔδων, Κώνωψ, αὐτὸς δέ τε Κύκλωψ,
     Αἷμα μέλαν πίνων, ἐπεὶ ἐν χροῒ ῥάμφος ἔπηξας.
25   Ὡς σευ ἀπὸ στόματος τέταται δολιχόσκιος αἰχμή,
     Σμερδαλέη προὔχουσα, λιλαιομένη χροὸς ἆσαι,
     Ὡς βδέλλη σύ γ' ὅμαιμος ὁμοῖός τ' ἔπλεο πάμπαν,
     Αἵματος ἀνδρομέου σίφων, ὀλοώτατε Κώνωψ.
     Εἴθ' οὖν λευγαλέῳ θανάτῳ πανάποτμος ὄλοιο,
30   Κύρῳ ὁμῶς, λιαροῖο βεβαμμένος αἵματος ἀσκῷ,
     Οὗπέρ σ' ἔλλαβε δίψα, βρότου κεκορημένος ἄδδην.
```

Textus: Duport, James (1676), *Musae subsecivae seu Poetica Stromata*, Cantabrigiae, 221–222.

Crit.: 15 ἀρήμενος] ἀρημένος debuit || **17** οὔτι σέ πω debuit || **22** Ὥς corr.: Ὡς ed.

Sim.: de tota re cf. Mel. *Anth. Pal.* 5.151–152 || **1** ἠχέτα κώνωψ] cf. Hes. *Op.* 582 || **2** ὦ κυνόμυια] cf. *Anth. Graec.* 16.9.1 (ὦ γαστὴρ κυνάμυια) | αἱμηπότα] cf. A.D. *Adv.* 189,10 || **3** βριήπυε] cf. Hom. *Il.* 13.521 (de Marte) || **4** cf. Hom. *Il.* 4.441 (de Eride): Ἄρεος ἀνδροφόνοιο κασιγνήτη ἑτάρη τε || **5** ἀράχνια λεπτά] iunctura Homerica, vid. *Od.* 8.280 || **6** ἀΐδηλον Ἄρηα] clausula Homerica, vid. *Od.* 8.309 || **8** cf. Hom. *Od.* 9.494 (σχέτλιε, τίπτ' ἐθέλεις ἐρεθιζέμεν ἄγριον ἄνδρα) || **10** νυκτὸς ἀμολγῷ] clausula Homerica, vid. *Il.* 11.173; 15.324 etc. || **14** cf. Hom. *Il.* 10.83, 386 (νύκτα δι' ὀρφναίην, ὅτε θ' εὕδουσι βροτοὶ ἄλλοι) || **15–16** = Hom. *Od.* 9.403–404 || **17** οὐδ' ἠβαιόν] clausula Homerica, vid. *Il.* 2.380 et al. || **18** σὺ δὲ μαίνεαι οὐκέτ' ἀνεκτῶς] cf. Hom. *Il.* 8.355 (de Hectore): ὃ δὲ μαίνεται οὐκέτ' ἀνεκτῶς || **19** βροτολοιγῷ ἶσος Ἄρηι] = Hom. *Il.* 11.295; 13.802 (de Hectore) || **19–20** Ἄρηι / ῥινοτόρῳ] cf. Hom. *Il.* 21.391–392 (Ἄρης / ῥινοτόρος) || **20** γλυκὺς ἵμερος αἱρεῖ] = Hom. *Il.* 3.446; 14.328 || **21** οὐδέ τι φειδώ] cf. Hom. *Od.* 14.92; 16.315 (οὐδ' ἔπι φειδώ) || **23** ἀνδρόμεα κρέ' ἔδων] = Hom. *Od.* 9.297 || **26** λιλαιομένη χροὸς ἆσαι] = Hom. *Il.* 21.168 (cf. etiam *Il.* 11.574; 15.317) || **28** αἵματος ἀνδρομέου σίφων] cf. Mel. *Anth. Pal.* 5.150.1–2 (αἵματος ἀνδρῶν / σίφωνες) || **29** λευγαλέῳ θανάτῳ] iunctura Homerica, vid. *Il.* 21.281; *Od.* 5.312 (bis eadem sede) | πανάποτμος] cf. Hom. *Il.* 24.255, 493 || **30–31** de re cf. Hdt. 1.214.

Homer's *Culex*, or an invective Homeric cento against the mosquito, (written) when we were attacked by an unusual mass of mosquitoes because of the stagnation of waters in July 1661

To the most Homeric man, Sir John Cotton, baronet knight

Mosquito, you clear-voiced singer and chirping mosquito, mosquito, you bad dog-fly, blood-drinking mosquito, mosquito, you loud-shouting trumpeter, insatiate of blood, fickle brother of man-slaying Ares! [5] May thin spider-webs be poured all around you and a strong bond subdue you as once happened to destructive Ares when he had intercourse with Cypris [Aphrodite]. And may a couch with mosquito curtains keep you away. You merciless mosquito, why do you want to provoke men by biting them and to fight against us like a giant or a crane against the Pygmies? [10] Why do you prick the soft skin like this at the dead of night? Is this why *nyx* [night] is named after your *nygma* [jab]? Is it called *nyx* since it is then that mosquitoes jab [*nyxai*] the most? To what end do you hurry loud-roaring hither and thither during night, during black night, when it is meet and right to sleep? [15] Why, Polyphemus, do you shout like this, as if you were distressed, during ambrosian night, and make us sleepless? We are not yet doing you any harm, not at all: We are lying silently, but you rage in a manner no longer tolerable by attacking us like [20] hide-piercing, hateful Ares, the plague of men. In this way, a sweet desire for our blood takes possession of you, and you have no satiety nor any mercy. In this way, you rage whenever you find a big prey anywhere, and you eat human flesh, you mosquito and at the same time Cyclops, and you drink dark blood when you have put your beak into the skin. [25] In this way, a shadow-casting spear is stretched out from your mouth, a terrible spear projecting and wishing to hurt the skin. In this way, you are of the same blood and similar in all ways to a leech, you sucker of human blood, most wretched mosquito. May you all-haplessly die a wretched death [30] like King Cyrus, dipped in a wineskin full of the warm blood you thirst for, satiated to your fill with gore.

Metre: Hexameters (hiatuses in ll. 2, 3, 19, 20; *spondiacus* in l. 17).

Notes: This Homeric cento continues the long tradition of Greek and Latin mosquito-poetry, seen also in other Humanist Greek authors and collections (e.g., Poliziano → **Italy** and Heinsius → **Low Countries**). The theme is already present in the *Greek Anthology* (*Anth. Pal.* 5.151; cited above in the apparatus *ad* l. 28). Duport gives the form a comic spin by introducing scenes and formulae from the *Odyssey*, and especially by comparing the mosquito with the Cyclops Polyphemus (ll. 15, 23) and Ares (ll. 6, 19). In ll. 10–12, clever wordplay connects the word for night (Greek νύξ) with the mosquito's jab (Greek νύγμα/νύσσω). This predilection for puns seems to be distinctive to Duport.[52] As a whole, the poem exhibits Duport's humour and his skill in using Homeric language. The poem was written shortly after the Restoration of King Charles II in 1660. Sir John Cotton (1621–1702; educated at Magdalene, Cambridge), to whom it is dedicated, was elected Member of Parliament for Huntingdon in the Cavalier Parliament in 1661. His 'recorded speeches were plentifully adorned with classical tags'.[53] One may therefore assume that the poem has some political relevance in displaying Duport's royalist attitude.

Biography: James Duport (1606–1679) was Regius Professor of Greek at the University of Cambridge and a prolific composer of Greek and Latin verse. He got his education at Westminster School and at Trinity College, Cambridge (BA in 1627, MA in 1630), where he was elected fellow in 1627. From 1639 until 1654 he held the Regius Professorship of Greek. During the interregnum of Cromwell (1654–1658), he continued lecturing as senior fellow at Trinity College. After the Restoration, his professorship was restored, but he resigned from the position and instead became dean at Peterborough (1664) and later master of Magdalene College, Cambridge (1668–1679). He published several poetic works in Greek and Latin. Besides the collection *Musae subsecivae* (1676), he wrote Greek paraphrases of books from the Old Testament: *Job* (1637: Θρηνοθρίαμβος), *Proverbs*,

---

[52] The *DNB* notices that 'he was extremely fond of puns and verbal quibbles, and when he was deputed regius professor and styled "pater" he could not forbear saying "Sum paterculus, sed non Velleius".'

[53] On Cotton's political activity, see http://www.historyofparliamentonline.org/volume/1660-1690/member/cotton-john-i-1621-1702 [accessed: August 2020].

Ecclesiastes, Song of Songs (1646: Σολομῶν ἔμμετρος), and *Psalms* (1666: Δαβίδης ἔμμετρος). He even translated the *Book of Common Prayer* into Greek (1665). In his *Homeri Gnomologia* (1660), he collected important sayings from the Homeric poems. He also devoted scholarly works to Theophrastus' *Characters* and to Demosthenes.

Bibliography: Sandys 1908, II.349–350; *DNB* 16, 239–241; O'Day, Rosemary (2004/2008), "Duport, James", in: *ODNB* online (https://doi.org/10.1093/ref: odnb/8301).

Edward Wells (1667–1727)

Τῆς πάλαι καὶ τῆς νῦν οἰκουμένης περιήγησις [1704]

(excerptum, vv. 1004–1029)

Κεφ. λ' Περὶ τῆς Ἀμερικῆς ἢ τῆς ἐπὶ δύσιν Ἰνδικῆς γῆς.

Ἀμερικὴν ἰσθμὸς διατέμνεται ἄνδιχα γαίην
1005 στεινὸς καὶ νοτίου πόντου μέσος ἠδὲ βορείου,
ὅν ῥά τε καὶ Δαριηνὸν ἐπωνυμίην ἐνέπουσι.
τοῦ δ' ὕπερ Ἀμερικὴ τετανυσμένη ἐστὶ βορείη,
νέρθε δὲ τοῦ νοτίη· ἐρέω ταπρῶτα βορείην.
 Ἀμφ' ἀκτὰς βορεήτιδας Ὑδσονίῳ ἐπὶ κόλπῳ
1010 ἔνθα νέη τέταται Καμβρίς, νέη ἔνθα Βρετανίς.
 Ἑξείης Φραγκῶν πεδίον νέον ἐκτετάνυσται
ἀμφὶς ἐΰρρείταο Κανάδου αἰπὺ ῥέεθρον·
οὕνεκά μίν θ' ἑτέρως γαίην καλέουσι Κανάδην·
ἐνθάδ' ὑπὲρ ποταμὸν Κηβεκκίδος ἐστὶ πτόλεθρον.
1015 Κεῖθεν ὑπὲρ ῥηγμῖνα βορειάδος ἀμφιτρίτης
Ἄγγλων μακρὰ νότονδε νέμονται ἔκγονοι ἀνδρῶν.
οἱ μὲν ναιετάουσι νέης λιπαρὸν πέδον Ἄγγλης,
ἐνθάδ' ὑπειράλιον Βοστωνίδος ἐστὶ πτόλεθρον·
οἱ δέ τε χῶρον ἰδὲ πόλιν Ἠβοράκοιο νέοιο·
1020 οἱ δὲ νέης πέδον ἀμφότερον ναίουσιν Ἰέρσης·
οἱ δέ τε καὶ Πέννου γαίην πάρος ὑλήεσσαν,
ἐνθάδ' εὔκτίμενον Φιλαδελφίας πτολίεθρον.
οἱ δ' αὖθις πεδίον καὶ ἐπώνυμον ἄστυ Μαρίας.
οἱ δέ τε παρθενικῆς τόδ' ἐπώνυμον οὖδας ἀνάσσης,
1025 ἐνθάδ' ἐπωνυμίην Ἰακώβου ἐστὶ πτόλεθρον·
οἱ δέ τ' ἐπίκλησιν Καρόλου πέδον ἠδὲ πτόλεθρον,
Ἀγγλιακῶν ὑπὲρ ἠπείροιο πανύστατοι ἀνδρῶν.
 Ἑξείης γαίη παραπέπταται ἀνθεμόεσσα
ἐς νότον, ἧχί περ ἀγχίαλος δόμος Αὐγουστίνου.

Textus: Wells, Edward (1704), *Τῆς πάλαι καὶ τῆς νῦν οἰκουμένης περιήγησις sive Dionysii Geographia Emendata & Locupletata Additione scil. Geographiae Hodiernae Graeco Carmine pariter donatae* [...], Oxford, 38–40.

Sim.: 1006 ἐπωνυμίην ἐνέπουσι] cf. Dionys. Per. 543 (ἑ. καλέουσιν) || **1007** τετανυσμένη] cf. eadem sede Dionys. Per. 174 || **1009** ἀμφ' ἀκτὰς βορεήτιδας] = Dionys. Per. 243 (sed βορεώτιδας) || **1011** ἐκτετάνυσται] = (eadem sede) Dionys. Per. 772 || **1012** αἰπὺ ῥέεθρον] cf. Dionys. Per. 49 || **1014** πτόλεθρον] apud veteres non legitur; pro πτολίεθρον || **1015** βορειάδος ἀμφιτρίτης] = Dionys. Per. 297 || **1017** λιπαρὸν πέδον] cf. Dion. Per. 227, 357, 858 || **1018** ὑπειράλιον...πτόλεθρον] cf. Dionys. Per. 851 (ὑπειράλιον πτολίεθρον) || **1022** ἐϋκτίμενον...πτόλεθρον] coniunctura Homerica, cf. *Il.* 2.501,505 etc. || **1023** ἐπώνυμον ἄστυ] cf. Ap. Rhod. *Argon.* 1.1346 || **1024** ἐπώνυμον οὖδας] cf. Nonn. *Dion.* 13.125 (οὖδας ἐπώνυμον) || **1027** ἠπείροιο πανύστατοι] = Dionys. Per. 218 (ἡ. π. Αἰθιοπῆες) || **1028** γαίη ... ἀνθεμόεσσα] cf. Hes. *Theog.* 878 | γαίη παραπέπταται] cf. Dionys. Per. 1107 (παραπέπταται αἶα)

Description of the ancient and the new world

(excerpt, ll. 1004–1029)

Chapter 30: About America or West India

A narrow isthmus divides the American continent: [1005] It lies between the southern and the northern sea, and they call it 'Isthmus of Darien' by name. Beneath lies South America. I will talk first about North America. Around the northern shores at the Hudson Bay [1010] lies New Cambria on one side, New England on the other. Next to this lies the new land of the French around the strong stream of the fair-flowing Canada River. Therefore, they also call the land Canada. Above the river, there is the city of Quebec. [1015] From that region above the edge of the northern sea, the offspring of English men reign far to the south. They inhabit the fruitful plain of New England. Here lies the city of Boston at the sea. Some inhabit the place and city of New York, [1020] others the two plains of New Jersey. Yet others inhabit the formerly wooded land of Penn [Pennsylvania]. There lies the well-built city of Philadelphia. Others inhabit the land and city named after Mary [Maryland], others the soil named after the Virgin Queen [Virginia]: [1025] There lies the city of James [Jamestown]. Others inhabit the land and city named after Charles [Carolina]. These are the Englishmen furthest south on the continent. Next to this, the flourishing land [Florida] extends to the south, where the house of Augustine [St Augustine/San Agustín] lies next to the sea.[54]

---

54 Author's Latin translation: *Americanam* Isthmus bifariam dissecat terram / [1005] Angustus, mediusque maris australis & Borealis, / Quem etiam *Darienum* cognomento dicunt. / Supra hunc *America* extenta est *Borealis*, / Infra vero hunc *australis*: dicam imprimis Borealem. / Circa littora Borealia, *Hudsonium* ad *Sinum*, / [1010] Heic *nova* porrigitur *Cambria*, illic *nova Britania*. / Deinceps *Francia nova* extenditur, / Utrinque ad pulchriflui *Canadae* altum fluentum: /

Metre: Hexameters (*spondiaci* in ll. 1015, 1021). Hiatuses in ll. 1008, 1009, 1012, 1016, 1025, missing main caesura in l. 1019 and 1027, lengthening of -ία in l. 1022 (Φιλαδελφίας).

Notes: This excerpt is taken from Wells' augmented version of Dionysius' geographical poem Οἰκουμένης περιήγησις from the Roman imperial period. Wells published this text for the first time in 1704. He added continents, modern states, and cities not mentioned by Dionysius, e.g. Amsterdam, New York, Mexico, and Taiwan. The excerpt presented here treats North America. Although written in hexameters, the language is very simple and concentrates on providing information for pupils. Nevertheless, Wells makes use of many Dionysian words and phrases.

Biography: The mathematician, geographer, and divine Edward Wells (born in 1667) was educated at Westminster School (from 1680) and Christ Church, Oxford (from 1686). After graduation (BA in 1690 and MA in 1693), he became rector of Cotesbach, Leicestershire, in 1701/02, and later of Bletchley, Buckinghamshire, in 1716. In 1704, he published for the first time his edition of Dionysius' geographical poem with modern additions and maps. This book saw several reprints within his lifetime (1709, 1718) and throughout the 18th century (1726, 1738, 1761). Among Wells' many works, we also find an edition of Xenophon's *Memorabilia* and *Apology* (1690), as well as several other theological, mathematical, and geographical writings (esp. biblical geography).

Bibliography: *DNB* 60, 227–228; Mayhew, Robert J. (2004/2009), "Wells, Edward", in: *ODNB* online (https://doi.org/10.1093/ref:odnb/29012); Brodersen, Kai (1996), "Principia Geographiae: Antike Texte im frühen Erdkundeunterricht", in: *Anregung* 42, 29–43; Jacob, Ch. (1990), *La Description de la terre habitée de Denys d'Alexandrie ou la leçon de géographie*, Paris (239–252, 253–265: French translation).

Quapropter ipsam etiam terram aliter vocant *Canadam*, / Ubi super fluvium *Quebecciae* est oppidum. / [1015] Illinc super littus maris septentrionalis, / Longe ad austrum incolunt Anglis prognati: / Hi quidem inhabitant pingue solum *Angliae novae*, / Ubi maritimum *Bostoniae* est oppidum; / Illi autem regionem & oppidum *Eboraci novi*: / [1020] Alii vero geminum solum incolunt *novae Iersae*; / Alii etiam *Penni* terram olim *Sylvosam*, / Ubi bene structum *Philadelphiae* oppidum; / Alii rursus solum & oppidum cognomine *Mariae*; / Alii etiam à *Virginia* denominatam terram Regina, / [1025] Ubi cognomento *Jacobi* est *oppidum*; / Alii etiam cognomine *Caroli terram & oppidum*, / Anglicorum hominum super continentem extremi. / Deinceps terra expanditur *Florida* / Ad Austrum, ubi maritima domus *Augustini*.

Joshua Barnes (1654–1712)

ΕΠΙΝΙΚΙΟΝ,
ὑπὲρ τοῦ ἀνικήτου ἡγεμόνος **ΜΑΡΛΒΟΡΙΟΥ,**
Τοῦ τὰς Βαβαρῶν τε καὶ Γαλατῶν στρατιὰς
Ἐν ἀγροῖς Βλεναμείοις πέρυσι νενικηκότος,
Ἀνακρεόντειον, ὑπὸ Ἰησοῦ τοῦ Βαρνεσίου. [1705]

Ὅτ' Ἀνακρέων λυρῳδὸς	Lyricus Poeta *Teîus*
Μάλα καλὰ Μαρλβόροιο	Ut ad alta Tecta venit
Ἀφίκανεν ἐς μέλαθρα,	Ducis ille *Marlboraei*,
Ἀνέβωσεν εὐθὺ χαίρων·	Resonabat ore laetus:
5 "Δότε μοὶ λύρην Ὁμήρου,	"Date mî chelyn *Homeri*,
Ἅμα φοινίαισι χορδαῖς·	Licet huic cruenta chorda;
Παφίης δὲ θῆλυς ὀμφὴ	*Veneris*que mollis Echo
Ἑκὰς ἱστάτω μάλιστα·	Procul hinc facessat almae:
Βρόμιός τε πουλυγηθὴς	*Bromius*que perjocosus,
10 Φιλοπαίγμονές τε Βάκχαι.	Jocularíaeque *Bacchae*.
Ἀπὸ τοῦδε γὰρ χρόνοιο,	Quiâ namque tempore ex hoc
Πολεμοκλόνους κυδοιμοὺς	Rapidos ego tumultus,
Ἐναρίμβροτόν τε φλοῖσβον	Truculentiámque *Martis*,
Προβέβουλα καὶ προήρευν	Animo magis petisso,
15 Διονυσίων τὲ κώμων,	*Dionysiis*que Thyrsis,
Ἀφροδισίων τὲ φίλτρων.	*Amathusiis*que Curis.
Ἀπὸ τοῦδ' ἐφανδάνει μοὶ	Et abhinc mihi placebit
Ἀλαλητὸς ἀνδροφόντης	Homocîda clamor ille,
Γαλατῶν τε τῶν ἐς Ἴστρον	Gemitusque *Gallicorum*
20 Στόνος αἰνὸς ἐμπεσόντων	Gravis incidentium *Istro*;
Βαβαρῶν τ' ἀποστατούντων	*Bavarûm* rebelliúmque
Σκέδασις φυγή τ' ἀεικής.	Fuga, dissipante Marte.
Βλεναμηΐου φορεῦμαι	*Blenameias* feror nunc
Πεδίοιο πὰρ γεφύρας,	Acies per & Phalangas;
25 Ἵνα Φλανδρίων φέριστοι,	Ubi *Flandrici* Dynastae,
Ἵνα τὲ πρόμοι Βρεταννῶν·	Ubi Principes *Britanni*.
Ὁ μὲν Εὐγένης δαΐφρων,	Viden', *Eugenes* ut Heros,
Λοδοβῖκος ἐκ Βαδῆνος	*Ludovicus* ut *Badenus*,
Ὅ τε Μαρλβόρειος Ἄγγλων	Ut & ille *Marlboraeus*,
30 Μεγαλητόρων Στράταρχος	Acie decorus *Anglâ*,
Πολέμου τριπλῆν ἔθηκαν	Triplicem necis dederunt
Ζαμενεστάτην θύελλαν·	Gravidam malis procellam!
Ἀετοὶ δὲ καὶ Λέοντες	*Aquilae* sed & *Leones*,
Βρετανῶν τε Φλανδρίων τὲ	*Alemannici*que & *Angli*,
35 Κατὰ Λειρίων βοῶσι	Mala *Liliis* minantur
Μάλα καλλίνικον αὐδήν·	Fremitu potentiori.

	Ἀνὰ δ' ἐξέβωσεν Ἀὴρ	Sed & ipse clamat Aër,
	Ὑπὸ πυρπνόων βελέμνων	*Reboante* Machinarum
	Στεροπήν τε καὶ κεραυνὸν	Strepitu, fragore magno,
40	Στομάτοσφιν ἐξεμεύντων·	Nebulam ignis evomentûm:
	Μετὰ μίγνυται δὲ κλαγγὴ	Quibus adde Tympanorum
	Τυπάνων τὲ βυρσονώτων	*Cybeleïum* tumultum,
	Μελέων τὲ χαλκοφώνων	Querulam Tubaeque vocem,
	Χρεμετισμάτων δέ θ' ἵππων	Fremitum simúlque Equorum,
45	Ἀνέρων τ' ἀποφθαρέντων	Hominúmque decidentûm,
	Ἐπινίκιόν τε δρώντων.	Superantiúmque bello.
	Ὁ δὲ Μαρλβόρειος ΑΝΝΗΣ	Ibi *Marlboraeus*, altae
	Βασιληΐδος στρατηγὸς	Celerum Tribunus ANNAE,
	Ἀνεμοστρόφῳ θυέλλῃ	*Aquiloniae* procellae
50	Ἴσος ὢν ἐμαίνετ' ἔγχει·	Similis, furebat Ense;
	Παρὰ δ' αἰνετῶς ἔθυνον	Laterique perfurebant
	Κρατερόφρονες Βρεταννοί.	Animo bono *Britanni*:
	Παρ' ὅτοισι δῖα Νίκη	Propè quos decora *Nice*
	Πολύχρυσα πῆλεν ὅπλα·	Quatiebat Arma pulchra,
55	Στέφανον δ' ἄρηρε λαμπρὸν	Capitíque *Marlboraeo*
	Κεφαλῇφι Μαρλβορείῃ·	Dabat inclytam coronam.
	Πρὸ δὲ τοῖο δείν' ἔθυνον	Faciem sed ante *Terror*,
	Βλοσυρωψ ὅμιλος Ἄρευς,	Metuendus & furebat,
	Φόβος αἰνὸς ἠδὲ Δεῖμος	Genus acre *Martis*, *Horror*,
60	Ἔριδός τε βλέμμα λυγρόν·	Rabiémque *Rixa* Spargens.
	Στυγερὸς γὰρ οἷος Ἀστὴρ	Rutilúmque quale sydus,
	Ἐν ὀπωριναῖσιν ὥραις	Ubi sicca torret Aestas,
	Κακόν ἐστι σῆμα θνητοῖς·	Mala fert necémque Terris:
	Γαλάταισι τοῖος ἥρως	Ità *Gallicis* micabat
65	Πυρόεντ' ἔλαμψε χαλκῷ,	Metuendus *Anglus* heros,
	Φοβερώτερος Δράκοντος.	Magis horridus Dracone.
	Ὁ μέγας δ' ὁ κλεινὸς αὐτὸς	Sed atrox, cruentus ille
	Γαλατῶν πρόμος Τάλαρδος	Comes atque Dux, *Talardus*,
	Στεφανηφόροιο πίπτων	Redimita procidebat
70	Παρὰ ποσσὶ Μαρλβόροιο,	Statim ad ora *Marlboraea*,
	Ὄνομ' ΑΝΝΙΚΟΝ προτείνας,	Per & alma nomina ANNAE,
	Βίον εἷλεν ἀντὶ Νίκης·	Sibi repperit salutem.
	Λεόπολδος αὐτοκράτωρ	*Leopoldus* Imperator,
	Ὑπὸ Μαρλβόρου σαωθεὶς	Ducis arte liberatus,
75	Κράτος ἀμφέπει Βρεταννῶν·	Populum fovet *Britannum*.
	Σκυθικὸς δ' ἄφαρ τύραννος	*Scythicus* sed ille *Turca*
	Ἄγαταί τε καὶ τέθηπε	Metuit stupétque frendens,
	Τὸν ὅλον παρόντα Κόσμον	Spatiosus omnis Orbis
	Ὑπὸ χερσὶ τῆς ἀνάσσης	Manibus sub *Anglicanae*
80	Κατακοιρανεῖσθαι ΑΝΝΗΣ."	Quòd abhinc regatur ANNAE."

Textus: Barnes, Joshua (ed.) (1705), *Anacreon Teius, Poeta Lyricus, Summâ Curâ & Diligentiâ, ad fidem etiam Vet. MS. Vatican. Emendatus* [...], Cantabrigiae, s.p. (post Epistolam dedicatoriam).

Crit.: 10 Φιλοπαίγμονες] Φιλονπαίγμονες ed. || **13** φλοῖσβον] φλοῖοβον ed.

Sim.: 5–6 ~ Anacreont. 2,1–2 (Δότε μοι λύρην Ὁμήρου / φονίης ἄνευθε χορδῆς) || **9** Βρόμιός τε πουλυγηθής] cf. Hes. Theog. 941 (Διώνυσον πολυγηθέα); Op. 614 || **10** φιλοπαίγμονές τε Βάκχαι] cf. Anacreont. 3.3 (φιλοπαίγμονες δὲ Βάκχαι) || **12** πολεμοκλόνους κυδοιμούς] cf. Batr. 4 (πολεμόκλονον ἔργον Ἄρηος), vid. etiam 275 et Hymn. Orph. 32.2 (de Minerva) || **13** ἐναρίμβροτον] cf. Pind. Isthm. 8.53 || **18** ἀλαλητὸς ἀνδροφόντης] cf. Hom. Il. 18.149 (ἀλαλητῷ ὑφ' Ἕκτορος ἀνδροφόνοιο), de forma ἀνδροφόντης cf. Aesch. Sept. 572 || **20** στόνος αἰνός] cf. Quint. Smyrn. 3.512 || **22** σκέδασις] cf. Hom. Od. 1.116; 20.225 || **32** ζαμενεστάτην θύελλαν] cf. Opp. Hal. 2.226 (ζαμενεῖς τε θυέλλας) || **38** πυρπνόων βελέμνων] cf. Aesch. Pr. 917 (πύρπνουν βέλος) || **42** βυρσονώτων] neologismus || **43** χαλκοφώνων] cf. Hom. Il. 5.785 (de Stentore: μεγαλήτορι χαλκεοφώνῳ); Hes. Theog. 311 (de Cerbero); de forma cf. Plin. NH 37.154 || **49** ἀνεμοστρόφῳ θυέλλῃ] = Anacreont. 38.14 || **50** ἐμαίνετ'] cf. Anacreont. 9.4, 10, 13 || **58–60** cf. Hom. Il. 4.440; 11.36–37, vid. etiam Il. 15.119; Hes. Theog. 933–934 || **69** στεφανηφόροιο] cf. Anacreont. 55.1 (στ. μετ' ἦρος)

Anacreontean victory song by Joshua Barnes for the undefeated General Marlborough, who defeated the troops of the Bavarians and the Gauls on the fields of Blenheim a year ago

When Anacreon, the lyre-playing singer, came to the very beautiful house of Marlborough, he immediately shouted with joy: [5] 'Give me the lyre of Homer together with its bloodstained strings. The female voice of the Paphian goddess [Aphrodite] shall stand very far away, as will delightful Bromius [Dionysus] [10] and the playful Bacchae, because from this time on, I prefer the sounds and the men-killing noise of war over Dionysiac festivals [15] and Aphrodisian lovecharms.

From now on, the men-killing war-cry, the grim groaning of the Gauls [Frenchmen] invading the Danube [20] and the scattering and shameful escape of the departing Bavarians appeal to me. I hurry through the battle lines of the plain of Blenheim, [25] where the best of the Flandrians, where the leaders of the Britons, the warlike Eugene, Ludwig from Baden and Marlborough, [30] the general of the heroic Anglians, have started a triple-raging storm of war.

The eagles and lions of the Britons and Flandrians [35] shout against the Lilies with very victorious voice: The air screamed with fire-breathing weapons disgorging flashes and thunderbolts [40] from their mouths. Between them, the scream of kettledrums with leather skin mingles with the noise of metallic-sounding melodies, the whinnying of horses, [45] killed men and those who sing a song of victory.

But Marlborough, the general of Queen Anne, [50] rages with his spear like a storm fed by the wind. Next to him, the stout-hearted Britons rush in praiseworthy fashion. Next to them, the divine Nike [Victory] brandished her golden weapons: [55] She placed a radiant crown on Marlborough's head. Before him, the grim-looking company of Ares, terrible Phobos [Fear] and Deimos [Terror], [60] as well as the mournful sight of Eris, rush terribly. Just as the hated star is a bad sign for mortals at the time of late summer, this hero sent light [65] against the Gauls with his fiery metal, much more terrible than a dragon. The great and famous general of the Gauls himself, Tallard, fell down [70] at the feet of victorious Marlborough, and, by calling upon the name of Queen Anne, chose life instead of victory. Emperor Leopold, saved by Marlborough, [75] honours the British army, and the Scythian tyrant wonders and is astonished that the whole world [80] is ruled by the hands of Queen Anne.

Metre: Anacreontics (anaclastic Ionic dimeter: ⏑⏑ – ⏑ – ⏑ – x).

Notes: Barnes' Anacreontic song, printed as part of an edition of Anacreon's and other Anacreontic poems, celebrates the victory of the British army under the command of John Churchill, the first Duke of Marlborough, in the battle of Blenheim (1704). In this battle, which was the first major episode of the War of the Spanish Succession, the allied troops of Emperor Leopold (l. 73), guided by Prince Eugen of Savoy (l. 27), and the English army under the Duke of Marlborough defeated the French army under Marshal Tallard (l. 68), together with their Bavarian allies (l. 21). Barnes consciously reverses the Anacreontic tradition, which rejects epic subjects such as battles (e.g., *Anacreont.* 2, 9, 23) by letting Anacreon himself declaim at Marlborough's house a lengthy renouncement of his former attitude while celebrating Marlborough's (and Queen Anne's) victory. The inversion becomes obvious through the quotation of *Anacreont.* 2.1–2 (9–10) Δότε μοι λύρην Ὁμήρου / φονίης ἄνευθε χορδῆς ('Give me the lyre of Homer without the bloody string') in ll. 5–6. Barnes replaces φονίης ἄνευθε χορδῆς with ἅμα φοινίαισι χορδαῖς (l. 6): 'together with his bloodstained strings'. Further linguistic signals of this new 'epic' Anacreontism are the many compound adjectives, not attested in the Anacreontic songs (e.g., πολεμόκλονος, ἐναρίμβροτος, χαλκόφωνος). This encomiastic reuse of ancient forms and the mixture of genres (Anacreontic, epic, and Pindaric *epinikion*) is a typical element of Baroque literature trying to surpass the Ancients. One may compare the anti-Anacreontic ode by Herrichen (→ **Germany**), which celebrates (tea-)water instead of (Anacreontic) wine. Johnson (see below) subsequently also translated a Latin epigram on Marlborough into Greek, combining martial and erotic elements (cf. Baldwin 1995, 113–115). In the context of Barnes' edition, the ode serves, of course, as a suitable praise of its dedicatee, although Johnson ridiculed it as an 'instance of servile absurdity' (ibid.).

Biography: Joshua Barnes was a classical scholar and professor of Greek at the University of Cambridge. Born in 1654, he was educated at Christ's Hospital and Emmanuel College, Cambridge (BA in 1675, MA in 1679, BD in 1686). He became a professor in 1695. Among his philological works are editions of Euripides (1694), Anacreon (1705), and Homer (1710–11). Although his qualities as a critic have had a mixed reception (Bentley describes him as 'one of a singular industry and a most diffuse reading'), his talent in speaking and writing Greek is often mentioned. Already in one of his early works, titled *Gerania, or the discovery of a little sort of people anciently discoursed of, called Pygmies* (1675), he inserted some Greek verses. The work is noteworthy insofar as it might have inspired Swift's *Voyage to Lilliput*. It is said that Barnes died shortly after a quarrel with a rival editor of Anacreon, William Baxter, in 1712. In the appendix to his *Anacreon*, he lists titles of poems he planned, but never published, like Ἀλεκτρυομαχία, Σπειδηριάς ('a poem in Greek macaronic verse upon a battle between a spider and a toad'), and Φληιάς ('a supplement to the old ludicrous poem under that title at Trinity House in Cambridge, upon the battle between the fleas and a Welshman').

Bibliography: *DNB* 3, 250–252; Sandys 1908, II.357–358; Haugen, Kristine L. (2004), "Barnes, Joshua", in: *ODNB* online (https://doi.org/10.1093/ref:odnb/ 1470).

Richard Dawes (1708–1766)

ΕΙΔΥΛΛΙΟΝ ΘΡΗΝΟΘΡΙΑΜΒΙΚΟΝ [1727]

ΠΑΛΑΙΜΩΝ, ΔΑΜΟΙΤΑΣ, ΘΥΡΣΙΣ

  Τὸν ποτὲ Δαμοίταν καὶ Θύρσιν ὀπάονας εὑρὼν
  Ἄμφω ἀμείβεσθαι δεδαημένω, ἄμφω ἀείδειν,
  Πρὸς χώρην δρυμοῖσιν ἐπίσκιον ἦλθε Παλαίμων·
  Αὐτίκα δὲ πταμένοις κούρους ἐπέεσσι προσηύδα—
5 ΠΑΛ. Ὧδε, Νέοι, θερμῶν ἀπάνευθ' Ὑπερίονος αὐγῶν
  Πυκναὶ ξὺν μελίῃς τείνουσι σκεπάσματα φηγοί·
  Ἡδὺ δὲ γόγγυζον πράως παραλείβεται ὕδωρ·
  Ὧδε κατὰ χλωρὴν ποίην, ἴτε, σῶμα κεκμηκὸς
  Ἡδυλόγην κελαδεῖτε κατακλίνοντες ἀοιδήν·
10 Ἡδυλόγην κελαδεῖτε μέλος περὶ τεθνειῶτος
  Ἀλβιόνων ΒΑΣΙΛΕΩΣ τε καὶ ΥΙΟΥ λειπομένοιο.
  Ἄρχετε δὴ μολπῇσιν ἀμοιβαίῃσιν ἐρίζειν,
  Ἄρχετ', ἀμοιβαίην Μοῦσαι φιλέουσιν ἀοιδήν.
  Τοίοισι προσέειπε Νέους ἐπέεσσι Παλαίμων·
15 Οἱ δ' ἐπιπειθόμενοι φίλου μύθοισιν ἑταίρου
  Παυσόμενον σκιεροῖς ὑπὸ δένδρεσι σῶμα τίθησαν.
  Δαμοίτας δ' ἐξαῦτις ἐπήρξατο πρῶτος ἀείδειν—
   ΔΑΜ. Οὐκέτι χαιρούσης ἀπ' ἐμεῦ ἐσακούσετε φωνῆς,
  Οὔρεα καὶ δρυμοί, λυσιπαίγμονος οὐκέτι πλήκτρου·
20 Οὐκέτ' ὀπηδεύει λιγύφωνος ἔμοιγε Θάλεια·
  Τέρψις ἑκὰς ἀπέφευγεν· ἀναιδὴς ἔκλυσε δίνη
  Τὸν Μούσης φίλον Ἄνδρα, τὸν οὐ Χαρίτεσσιν ἀπεχθῆ.

Θρηνῴδεων ἔξαρχε μέλων, ἄγε, Μοῦσα· θανόντος
Αἰάζω ΒΑΣΙΛΗΟΣ, ἐπαιάζοιτε Βρέταννοι.
25 Οἷα δ' ἐν ὑψηλῆς Μελίη ὑπεραίρεται ὕλης·
Τόσσον ὑπερλάμπεσκε ΓΕΩΡΓΙΟΣ ἐν Βριτόνεσσι
Παντοίης ἀρέτῃσιν ὑπὲρ προτέρων Βασιλήων·
Τοιοῦτος μὲν ἔην, (ὡς νῦν ὄφελές γε καὶ εἶναι)
Τοιοῦτον δ' ἄρ' ἐόντα δυσήνιος ἔλλαβε μοῖρα.
30 Ἀμφηχοῖ ἔγκοιλα 'ΓΕΩΡΓΙΟΣ ὄλλυται' οὔρη·
Φύλλα, λύπης σημεῖον, ὀρεινοὶ ἀπέκδυτε δρυμοί·
Ἄνθεα σαθρωθέντα προσουδίζοιτε κάρηνα·
Ἄλγος δ' οἱ ποταμοὶ παρέχοιτ' ὀκνηρὰ ῥέοντες
Θρηνῴδεων ἔξαρχε μέλων, ἄγε, Μοῦσα· θανόντος
35 Αἰάζω ΒΑΣΙΛΗΟΣ, ἐπαιάζοιτε Βρέταννοι.
Φοῖβε, κατάκρυψον ἀχέων νεφέλῃσι πρόσωπον·
Ἄστροις σὺν πενθοῦσιν ὑπὸ χθόνα δῦθι Σελήνη·
Νὺξ ἐπιγιγνέσθω πολυώδυνος· ἀμφὶ δὲ γαίῃ
Ἀενάοις ἀχλῦσι περιβληθεῖσα στενάζοι.
40 Κλαυθμώδη θαμιναὶ χείτωσαν ἀηδόνες ὀμφήν·
Κλαυθμώδη δὲ λυπεῖσα βοὴν ἀναπεμπέτω Ἠχώ.
Εὐγνώστους ποταμοὺς βαρύφωνοι λείπετε κύκνοι,
Κάδδ' ἐπικηδείην ποιεῖτε θανούμενοι αὐδήν.
Θρηνῴδεων ἔξαρχε μέλων, ἄγε, Μοῦσα· θανόντος
45 Αἰάζω ΒΑΣΙΛΗΟΣ, ἐπαιάζοιτε Βρέταννοι.
Δαμοίτας μὲν τοῖον ἀεισάμενος ἀπέληγεν.
Εἶτα δ' ἀμοιβαίην ὑπελάμβανε Θύρσις ἀοιδήν—
ΘΥΡ. Χαίροις, ὦ κύδιστε ΓΕΩΡΓΙΟΥ ΥΙΕ Ἄνακτος,
ΥΙΕ Ἄναξ, Μεγάλοιο ἀρειότερος Γενετῆρος·
50 Οὔποτε ΣΕΙΟ κλέους ἐπιλήσομαι, ἀλλὰ προθύμως
Ἀείσω πρῶτόν τε καὶ ὕστατον ἕν τε μέσοισι.
Λήγετε θρηνῴδεων Μοῦσαι, ἴτε, λήγετ' ἀοιδῶν.
Μηκέτ' ΕΔΟΥΑΡΔΟΥΣ κλαίοι ΚΑΡΟΛΟΥΣ τε θανόντας,
Μηκέτι δ' ΕΝΡΙΚΟΥΣ καὶ ἀγακλειτὸν ΓΥΛΙΕΛΜΟΝ,
55 Μήκετ' ἀγαυότερον δὲ ΓΕΩΡΓΙΟΝ αἶα Βρετάννη·
Καὶ γὰρ ΕΔΟΥΑΡΔΩΝ ἀρέται ΚΑΡΟΛΩΝ τ' ἐρικύδεων,
ΕΝΡΙΚΩΝ, ΓΥΛΙΕΛΜΟΥ ἰδ' ἐνδόξου Γενετῆρος
Φαίνονται ἐν ΣΟΙγε, ΓΕΩΡΓΙΟΥ ἀγλαὸς ΥΙΟΣ.
Ἄρχετε χαρμόφρονος, Μοῦσαι φίλαι, ἄρχετ' ἀοιδῆς.
60 Ἀλβιόνων, ἄγε, κοῦροι ἐριστικὸν εἴπατ' ἔπαινον,
Εἴπατε τῷ ΒΑΣΙΛΗΙ πολυφθόγγοισιν ἐν ᾠδῆς·
Νικᾶτ' Οὐργίλιον, νικᾶτ' ᾄδοντες Ὅμηρον,
Οὐδ' ἅλις ᾀσόμενοι· ἀναρίθμητός γε μὲν ἄμμος.
Ἄρχετε χαρμόφρονος, Μοῦσαι φίλαι, ἄρχετ' ἀοιδῆς.
65 Πᾶσα πολυχρονίῳ πληροίη καρδία τέρψει·
Κτήνη ἐν ἡδυγέλωσιν ἀγαλλιάσασθε νομῆσιν·
Αὐτόματοι σκιρτᾶτε δρύες, σκιρτᾶτε δὲ βουνοὶ
Μείζονι γηθοσύνῃ, ἢ ὅταν θαμινῆς ἅμα πέτρης
Θρηικίην ἅπτοντι λύρην ἐφέπεσθε μελῳδῷ.

70   Ἄρχετε χαρμόφρονος, Μοῦσαι φίλαι, ἄρχετ' ἀοιδῆς.
    Μηκέτι τερπνοτάτην αἴη θαύμαζε Βρετάννη
    Ἀρχαίου βασιλείαν ἐπιφθονέουσα Κρόνοιο·
    Νῦν ὄντως ἄρα σοὶ χρύσειος ἐπήλυθεν αἰών.
    Ἄρχετε χαρμόφρονος, Μοῦσαι φίλαι, ἄρχετ' ἀοιδῆς.
75   Ἄμμι νεοκτήτῳ στιλβηδόνι πάντα γελῶσιν·
    Οὐδὲ μὲν ἦν πᾶσιν φάος ἔθνεσι Φοῖβος ἀφαιρῇ,
    Ἣν δὲ Σεληναίη τε καὶ ἄστερες· οὐδὲ μὲν οὕτως
    Ἡμέτερον παύσειε φόως· ἴδιός γε Βρετάννη
    Ἀσπασίως τρίλλιστος ἐπήλυθε Φωσφόρος αἴη.
80   Χαίροις, ὦ κύδιστε ΓΕΩΡΓΙΟΥ ΥΙΕ Ἄνακτος,
    ΥΙΕ Ἄναξ, Μεγάλοιο ἀρειότερος Γενετῆρος·
    Οὔποτε ΣΕΙΟ κλέους ἐπιλήσομαι, ἀλλὰ προθύμως
    Ἀείσω πρῶτόν τε καὶ ὕστατον ἔν τε μέσοισιν.
    Ὣς μετὰ Δαμοίταν Θύρσις μὲν ἔληγε μελῳδῶν.
85   Τῶν δ' ἄρ' ἀεισαμένων οὕτως διέκρινε Παλαίμων—
    ΠΑΛ. Κοῦροι, ἐπιστήμη μεγάλη, ἡδεῖα δὲ μοῦσα
    Ἀμφοτέρων· σὺ δέ, Θύρσι, πολὺ νίκησας ἀείδων,
    Οὐδὲ τόσον νίκησας, ὅσῳ θέμα φέρτερον εὗρες.

Textus: Dawes, Richard (1727), "ΕΙΔΥΛΛΙΟΝ ΘΡΗΝΟΘΡΙΑΜΒΙΚΟΝ", in: *Academiae Cantabrigiensis Luctus in obitum serenissimi Georgii I. εὐεργέτου Magnae Britanniae, &c. Regis: et Gaudia ob potentissimi Georgii II. Patriarum virtutum ac solii haeredis successionem pacificam simul et auspicatissimam*, Cantabrigiae, Iv–I 2v.

Crit.: **1** Τὸν ποτὲ] Τόν ποτε exspectaveris || **7** γογγύζον debuit || **9–10** Ἡδυλόγην] ἡδύλογον exspectaveris || **22** Μούσης: -σης ed. || **23 (34, 44)** Θρηνωδέων ... μέλων] θρηνωδέων ... μελῶν debuit || **27** ἀρέτῃσι] ἀρετῇσι debuit || **28** ἂν ὄφελεν? || **41** λυπεῖσα] ἂν pro λυπηθεῖσα?, λυποῦσα deliberat Pontani || **52** θρηνώδεων] θρηνωδέων debuit || **56** ἀρέται] ἀρεταί debuit | ἐρικύδεων] ἐρικυδέων debuit || **62** Οὐργίλιον ed.: an Οὐιργίλιον? || **77** ἄστερες] ἀστέρες debuit

Sim.: **2** cf. [Theoc.] *Id.* 8.4 (ἄμφω συρίσδειν δεδαημένω, ἄμφω ἀείδεν) || **7** παραλείπεται ὕδωρ] cf. Theoc. *Id.* 1.8 (καταλείβεται ὑψόθεν ὕδωρ) || **9–10** ἡδυλόγην ... / ἡδυλόγην] cf. Pind. *Ol.* 6.96; *Anth. Pal.* 5.137.2; 7.159.2 || **13** ἀμοιβαίην Μοῦσαι φιλέουσιν ἀοιδήν] cf. Verg. *ecl.* 3.59 (*amant alterna Camenae*) | ἀμοιβαίην...ἀοιδήν] cf. Theoc. *Id.* 8.31 || **19** λυσιπαίγμονος] cf. *Anacreont.* 49.10 (λυσιπήμων West, sed λυσιπαίγμων P) || **21–22** ἔκλυσε δίνη / Τὸν Μούσης φίλον Ἄνδρα, τὸν οὐ Χαρίτεσσιν ἀπεχθῆ] cf. Theoc. *Id.* 1.140–141 (ἔκλυσε δίνη / τὸν Μοίσαις φίλον ἄνδρα, τὸν οὐ Νύμφαισιν ἀπεχθῆ) || **24 (35, 45)** Αἰάζω ΒΑΣΙΛΗΟΣ, ἐπαιάζοιτε Βρέταννοι] cf. Bion *Ep. Ad.* 6, 15 (αἰάζω τὸν Ἄδωνιν· ἐπαιάζουσιν Ἔρωτες) || **29** ἔλλαβε μοῖρα] cf. Hom. *Il.* 5.83 et al. (ἔλλαβε...μοῖρα κραταιή) || **38** πολυώδυνος] cf. Theoc. *Id.* 25.238 (πολυώδυνος ἰός) || **50–51 (82–83)** cf. Thgn. 1–4 (...οὔποτε σεῖο / λήσομαι ... / ἀλλ' αἰεὶ πρῶτόν τε καὶ ὕστατον ἔν τε μέσοισιν / ἀείσω || **52** Λήγετε θρηνώδεων Μοῦσαι, ἴτε, λήγετ' ἀοιδῶν] cf. Theoc. *Id.* 1.127,131 et al. (λήγετε βουκολικᾶς, Μοῖσαι, ἴτε λήγετ' ἀοιδᾶς) || **59 (64, 70, 74)** ἄρχετε..., Μοῦσαι φίλαι, ἄρχετ' ἀοιδῆς] cf. Theoc. *Id.* 1.104,108 et. | χαρμόφρονος] cf. *Hymn. Hom. Merc.* 127 || **63** ἀναρίθμητός γε μὲν ἄμμος] cf. Pind. *Ol.* 2.98 (ψάμμος ἀριθμὸν περιπέφευγεν) || **66** ἡδυγέλωσιν] cf. *Hom. Hymn.* 19.37; *Anth. Pal.* 5.135.4 || **67** de re cf. Nonn. *Dion.* 47.113 (καὶ δρύες ὠρχήσαντο καὶ ἐσκίρτησαν ἐρίπναι) || **79** τρίλλιστος ἐπήλυθε Φωσφόρος] cf. Hom. *Il.* 8.488 (τρ. ἐ. νὺξ ἐρεβεννή, oppositio in imitando)

Lamentful and triumphant idyll

Characters: Palaemon, Damoetas, Thyrsis

When Palaemon once found his fellows Damoetas and Thyrsis both able to respond, both able to sing, he came to a place, shadowy with thickets. Immediately he spoke to the boys with flying words:

[5] PAL.: 'Here, youngsters, far away from the warm beams of Hyperion [sun], close-laid oaks and ashes make a shelter, and sweet water flows, softly roaring. Here in the green grass, come ye, lay down your exhausted bodies and sing loudly a sweet-worded song, [10] sing a sweet-worded melody upon the deceased KING of the Albions [Britons] and the SON he left behind. Start to compete with alternating songs, start! The Muses love the alternate song!'

With these words Palaemon spoke to the youngsters [15] and they obeyed the words of their dear companion and laid their bodies to pause under the shadowy trees. Then Damoetas started to sing first:

DAM. 'You will no longer hear from me a rejoicing voice, you mountains and thickets, no longer the playful lyre. [20] Clear-voiced Thalia does not follow me anymore. Joy has gone apart. A greedy eddy has washed away the man, who was beloved by the Muses and not hated by the Graces.
Come, Muse, begin the mournful songs: I bewail the dead KING, may you Britons bewail him with me.
[25] Just as the ash excels in high forests, so did GEORGE with all his virtues surpass in splendour the previous kings among the Britons. Such he was (oh, would you be now too!), and the ungovernable Moira took him away although he was such a man.
[30] The hollow mountains echo: 'GEORGE is dead!' You thickets in the mountains, take off your leaves as a sign of sorrow. You flowers, dash your withered heads to the ground. You rivers, flow reluctantly and show your pain.
Come, Muse, begin the mournful songs: [35] I bewail the dead KING, may you Britons bewail him with me.
Phoebus, cover your face with clouds in sadness. Selene [moon], sink under the earth together with the mourning stars. A very painful night shall come and the earth shall groan, surrounded by ever-lasting mist.
[40] Nightingales shall shed a sobbing voice together. Distressed Echo shall send back the sobbing sound. You swans with your deep voices, leave your well-known rivers and make a funeral ode, as if you were about to die.
Come, Muse, begin the mournful songs: [45] I bewail the dead KING, may you Britons bewail him with me.'

When Damoetas had sung this, he stopped. Then Thyrsis took over the alternate song:

THYR.: 'May you rejoice, most glorious SON of King GEORGE, Lord SON, more valiant than your great genitor. [50] I will never forget YOUR glory, but I will sing it first and last and in between.

Come, Muses, stop the mournful songs! Britain may no longer bewail its dead EDWARDs and CHARLES's, no longer its HENRYs and the most famous WILLIAM, [55] no longer its very brilliant GEORGE, for the virtues of its EDWARDs and famous CHARLES's, its HENRYs, WILLIAM and the glorious Father can be seen in You, brilliant SON of GEORGE.

Dear Muses, begin the joyful song! [60] Come, you sons of the Albions, speak a rival praise, say it to the KING in multilingual songs. Defeat Virgil with your songs, defeat Homer and you will still not sing enough: The sand is uncountable.

Dear Muses, begin the joyful song! [65] Every heart shall be filled with long-lasting joy. You cattle, rejoice in your sweet-laughing pastures. You oaks, spring spontaneously, spring, you hills, with greater joy than whenever you follow the singer [Orpheus] touching his Thracian lyre together with the crowded rocks.

[70] Dear Muses, begin the joyful song! Britain, no longer admire with envy the most pleasant reign of ancient Kronos: For now the Golden Age has really come to you.

Dear Muses, begin the joyful song! [75] Everything is laughing for us with a newly gained brightness. Even if Phoebus or Selene and the stars will take the light away for all people, not even thus our light would stop. Its very morning star, often prayed for, has gladly come to Britain.

[80] May you rejoice, most glorious SON of King GEORGE, Lord SON, better than your great genitor. I will never forget YOUR glory, but I will sing it first and last and in between.'

In this manner, Thyrsis stopped singing after Damoetas. [85] As they had sung, Palaemon made his decision as follows:

PAL.: 'Youngsters, your knowledge is great and the muse of both of you is sweet, but you, Thyrsis, have won by far with your song, but you have not won as much as you have found a better subject.'

Metre: Hexameters. Several instances of hiatus: ll. 18, 25, 30, 48, 49, 52, 58, 68, 73, 80, 81, 86. In l. 6 σκ do not cause position. *Spondiacus*: l. 10. Artificial lengthening: l. 15 (φίλου), 46 (ἀεισάμενος), 87 (πολύ), but in l. 72 βασιλείαν with short second alpha.

Notes: This idyll is a contribution by Richard Dawes to a university volume composed in 1727 on the occasion of the death of George I and the accession of his son George II. The undergraduate Dawes chose the form of a bucolic contest between Damoetas and Thrysis, well-known figures from the bucolic world of Theocritus (Thyrsis is the singer of a bucolic song in Theocritus' first idyll, and Damoetas features as a singer in the sixth idyll), with the Virgilian Palaemon as a judge (cf. Verg. *ecl.* 3.50). Unlike most Theocritean bucolics, Dawes' idyll is not purely dramatic but has a narrator, who introduces characters and the setting (ll. 1–4) and marks the change of speakers (ll. 14–17, 46–47, 84–85). The structure is very simple. After the narrator's introduction Palaemon invites Damoetas and Thyrsis to sing about the king's death and the accession of his son. Damoetas starts with a dirge on the king's death, marked by the refrain θρηνῴδεων ἔξαρχε μέλων, ἄγε, Μοῦσα· θανόντος / αἰάζω ΒΑΣΙΛΗΟΣ, ἐπαιάζοιτε Βρέταννοι. The second line of this refrain is a clear reference to the *Epitaphios Adonidos*. Thyrsis answers Damoetas with a song of joy, celebrating the accession of George II. His song is characterised by the refrain ἄρχετε χαρμόφρονος, Μοῦσαι φίλαι, ἄρχετ' ἀοιδῆς, which is inspired by the refrain of Thyrsis' song in Theocritus' first idyll. Dawes' poem closes with a final statement by the judge, Palaemon, declaring Thyrsis the winner of the contest. One may compare this political idyll with the one composed by Kollár for Empress Maria Theresa (→ **Austria**). Like Kollár and other modern bucolic poets, Dawes combines elements of the Theocritean and Virgilian traditions: The juxtaposition of grief and joy is certainly inspired by Virgil's fifth eclogue on the death and *apotheosis* of Daphnis.[55]

Biography: Richard Dawes (1709–1766) was a classical scholar and schoolmaster. He studied at Emmanuel College, Cambridge (BA in 1730, MA in 1733), where, still an undergraduate, he contributed to the university's official volume the here selected Greek idyll on the death of George I and the accession of George II. He also published a partial translation in Greek hexameters of book I of Milton's English epic *Paradise Lost* (1736). In 1738, he became schoolmaster in Newcastle-upon-Tyne. His most important scholarly work is the *Miscellanea Critica*, published in 1745, which makes contributions to textual criticism and Greek grammar (well known is 'Dawes' Canon', which declares 'that the first subjunctive aorist, active and middle, was a solecism after ὅπως μή and οὐ μή').[56] In this book, he also attacks Bentley, despite being deeply inspired by the latter's work. Cobet notes this about his writings: *non tantum locis corruptis clara lux affulget sed paulatim addiscitur ars quaedam, qua verum cernere et eruere et ipse possis*[57] – 'not only does clear light shine on corrupted passages, but one also gradually learns a sort of art which enables you to see and find the truth for yourself'.

---

55 For the typical convergence of Theocritean and Virgilian features in early modern bucolic poetry, cf. also Barton (177–195), Van Sickle (77–97) and Weise (157–175) in Anne-Elisabeth Beron/Stefan Weise (eds.) (2020), *Hyblaea avena. Theokrit in römischer Kaiserzeit und Früher Neuzeit*, Stuttgart.
56 See Sandys 1908, II.415.
57 Cited from Sandys 1908, II.416.

Bibliography: Sandys 1908, II.415–416; Luard, H.R./Skedd, S.J. (2004), "Dawes, Richard", in: *ODNB* online (https://doi.org/10.1093/ref:odnb/7333); Clarke 1945, 52–54.

Samuel Johnson (1709–1784)

<Epitaphium in Olivarium Goldsmith> [1774]

Τὸν τάφον εἰσοράας τὸν Ὀλιβαρίοιο, κονίην
  Ἄφροσι μὴ σεμνήν, Ξεῖνε, πόδεσσι πάτει·
Οἷσι μέμηλε φύσις, μέτρων χάρις, ἔργα παλαιῶν,
  Κλαίετε ποιητήν, ἱστορικόν, φυσικόν.

Textus: Smith, David Nichol/McAdam, Edward L. (eds.), *The Poems of Samuel Johnson*, Oxford 1941, 171.

Crit.: 1 εἰσοράας ed.: εἰσοράᾳς debuit

Sim.: 1 Τὸν τάφον εἰσοράας] cf. *Anth. Pal.* 7.330.1 (τὴν σορόν, ἣν ἐσορᾷς)

<Epitaph on Oliver Goldsmith>

You see the tomb of Oliver. Please,
  stranger, don't trample on the holy ashes with senseless feet.
You who care for nature, gracious metres, and the works of the Ancients,
  bewail the poet, historian, and physician.

Metre: Elegiac couplets (flawless; the long ι in l. 1 κονίην is also common in Homer).

Notes: The selected text by Johnson is a cleverly composed funerary epigram on the Irish writer and physician Oliver Goldsmith (1728–1774). Johnson inserted this composition into a letter to Bennet Langton. The structure follows ancient epigrams by talking to an unknown stranger passing by (l. 2 Ξεῖνε) (cf. also Baldwin 1995, 112–113). Johnson combines this form with skilful praise of the deceased. One may note the elegant corresponding *tricola* and *asyndeta* in the second couplet (φύσις, μέτρων χάρις, ἔργα παλαιῶν – ποιητήν, ἱστορικόν, φυσικόν), the first also complying with Behaghel's 'Law of Increasing Terms'. Gennadius, for this reason, rightly states that 'it is an epitaph full of classic grace and solemnity' (Gennadius 1899, 38). Johnson later also supplied a Latin prose epitaph for Goldsmith's monument in Westminster Abbey (Baldwin 1995, 112).

Biography: Samuel Johnson *alias* Dr Johnson (1709–1784) was an important English critic, poet, and essayist of the Classical (Georgian) era. He was educated at Oxford, and from 1737 onward he lived in London. His renown as a critic is founded on his *Dictionary of the English Language* (1755) and *The Lives of the Most Eminent English Poets* (1777). His lasting fame as 'the most distinguished man of letters in English history' (Rogers 2004/2009), however, is mostly due to James Boswell's biography, titled *The Life of Samuel Johnson* (1791). His prose style, known as 'Johnsonese', was regarded as exemplary for English classical prose (see Gelfert ²2005, 170).

Bibliography: Rogers, Pat (2004/2009), "Johnson, Samuel", in: *ODNB* online (https://doi.org/10.1093/ref:odnb/14918); Gennadius, Ioannes (1899), "Dr. Johnson as a Grecian. A paper read before the Johnson Club on June 8, 1889", in: *Johnson Club Papers by Various Hands*, London, 17–48; Baldwin, Barry (ed.) (1995), *The Latin & Greek Poems of Samuel Johnson. Text, Translation & Commentary*, London; Gelfert ²2005, 168–170.

Richard Porson (1759–1808)

‹In Godofredum Hermannum› [1803]

Ὁ μετρικὸς ὁ σοφὸς ἄτοπα γέγραφε περὶ μέτρων.
Ὁ μετρικὸς ἄμετρος, ὁ σοφὸς ἄσοφος ἐγένετο.

Textus: Luard 1867, 87.

‹Against Gottfried Hermann›

The metrician, the wise man, has written strange things about metrics.
The metrician has become unmetrical, the wise man unwise.

Metre: Iambic trimeters (with all long syllables resolved).

Notes: Porson inserted this distich into a letter to Andrew Dalzel, dated 3 September 1803.[58] He is making fun of the German philologist Gottfried Hermann (1772–1848), who had authored a special treatise on Greek metre, titled *De Metris Poëtarum*, in 1796, shortly before Porson's edition of Euripides' *Hecuba*. Porson

---

58 See Luard 1867, 85–92.

integrated criticism of Hermann into the preface of his 1797 *Hecuba* edition. Hermann reacted by editing a rival edition in 1800. Porson responded again at greater length in a supplement to his re-edition of *Hecuba* in 1802.[59] This supplement contained the famous *lex Porsoniana* (see Clarke 1937, 70). In his letter to Dalzel, Porson first cites an epigram by an 'Etonian' friend about Hermann: 'Νήϊδες ἐστὲ μέτρων, ὦ Τεύτονες· οὐχ ὃ μὲν, ὃς δ' οὔ· / Πάντες, πλὴν ἙΡΜΑΝΝΟΣ· ὃ δ' ἙΡΜΑΝΝΟΣ σφόδρα Τεύτων', and then renders it into English: 'The Germans in Greek / Are sadly to seek; / Not five in five score, / But ninety-five more: / All; save only HERMAN, / And HERMAN's a German.' Finally, before citing the selected verses, he explains: 'It is a known principle in iambic verse, that the iambic may be resolved into a tribrach, in any place but the last. As Mr. Herman has not given any striking instances of this resolution in his incomparable treatise, I shall try to supply the defect.' The whole affair is a fine example of philologic rivalry seasoned with English humour.

Biography: Next to Bentley, Richard Porson (1759–1808) was one of the most important English Hellenists. He received his classical education at Eton and Trinity College, Cambridge. At Cambridge University, he gained the Craven Scholarship in 1781, the Chancellor's Medal in 1782 and became fellow of Trinity College in 1782. In 1792, he was elected Regius Professor of Greek but lived mainly in London, where he died in 1808. His major achievements are in the field of textual criticism and metrics, notably the discovery of Porson's Bridge. After his death, the Porson Prize (from 1817) and the Porson Scholarship were established in his honour.[60] Unlike the Browne Medal (see above), the Porson Prize requires not original composition but the translation of a set text into Greek. Collections of the prize-winning translations appeared under the title *Translations which have obtained the Porson Prize* in 1850, 1857, and 1871. Porson himself ridiculed original compositions and criticised, for example, Coleridge's prize-winning ode (see Coleridge, below), but he also wrote several Greek verses, especially for the purpose of mockery.[61] His clear Greek handwriting inspired a Greek typeface which is named after him and which has been used by Cambridge University Press since 1809 (cf. Morson 2004/2018).

Bibliography: Sandys 1908, II.424–430; Morson, Geoffrey V. (2004/2018), "Porson, Richard", in: *ODNB* online (https://doi.org/10.1093/ref:odnb/22550); Luard, Henry Richards (ed.) (1867),

---

59 Cf. Sandys 1908, II.427–428; Clarke 1937, 68–70.
60 For a list of winners prior to 1910, see Tanner 1917, 317.
61 Cf. also Clarke 1945, 84 and Brink 1985, 128.

The Correspondence of Richard Porson, Cambridge; Clarke, M.L. (1937), *Richard Porson. A Biographical Essay,* Cambridge; Brink 1985, 99–113.

Abraham Moore (1766–1822)

Georgium Sydus [1787]

(excerptum, vv. 1–24, 89–100)

In maximis Comitiis July 1.ˢᵗ 1788

    Ταλόθεν τὸ φέγγος ἀγαστὸν ὄρφνας
    Ἐκ μυχῶν ἔφλεξε· Σοφῶν δ' ἀθρῶν τις
    Εὐσκόποις φρουρῇσι φύλαξεν ὄσσων·
        Ἀστέρα δ' ἔγνω
5   Τόνδ' ἰδών, νεώτατον Οὐρανοῦ παῖδ'·
    Ὡς ἴδ', ὡς τέθαπεν! ἐμοὶ δ' ἂρ ὕμνων
    Νὶν χλιδῆς στέψοντι δι' αἰθέρος κού-
        φα πέταται φράν.
    Ποῖ δ' ἑλῶν κίχοιμ' ἄν; ἐπ' ἄντυγός τευ
10 Θοῦ μ' ἀγώνων οὐρανίων θεωρόν,
    Εὐφρόνα γλαυκῶπι, τεᾶς τ' ἀφ' ἕδρας
        Κλεῖθρα χάλαξον·
    Ὡς ἴδοιμ' ἄν, χωρὶς ἃ γᾶς πέπρακται,
    Τῶν δ' ἄνω τὰ κρυπτά· Σὺ δ', Ἐρσχελεῦ, 'μᾶς
15 Ποῦ γέγραψαι τᾶς κραδίας; ἐπεί τιν
        Ἄμβατος αἰθήρ·
    Σοί γαρ ὀππάτεσσι δέδωχ' ὁ Λυγκεὺς
    Οἷς δεδορκέναι· τάδ' ἔχων, τὰ θνατοῖς
    Ἀστιβῆ πόδεσσι, φραδὰν συθεὶς πτε-
20   ροῖσιν ἐπόπτῃ.
    Τάς θ' ὁδοὺς Νεύτωνος, ὁ θεοῖς ἴσος φώς,
    Προὐστάλη· τειρῶν τ' ἴδε δυσκρίτους εὖ
    Ἀντολὰς πάντων τε δύσεις, πόλος τά τ'
        Ἐστεφανῶται.
    [...]
    Χαῖρ', ἄωτον Οὐρανιδᾶν, ἐμᾶς γᾶς
90 Φαιδρὸν ἀγλάϊσμα· βλέπου σόν, ὦναξ,
    Ἐγγραφὲν δέλτοισι τὸ κῦδος ἄστρων·
        Σοὶ δὲ τὰ μάσσω
    Πὰρ σκοπεῖν· οἴακα νέμων φυλάττεις
    Πρᾶγος ἐν πρύμνῃ πόλεως· σάλῳ τὰν
95 Σὴ κακῷ τυπεῖσαν ἔσωσε βουλή.
        Νῦν δέ νιν εὔπλους
    Λίσσομαι, πέμψαι τις ἐφ' ὅρμον οὖρος·

Σοί τ' ἀεὶ πλέοντι τὸ κύριον φῶς
Αἰσίως ὕπερθεν ἐπιφλέγοιτ' ἐπ-
100   ώνυμος ἀστήρ.

Textus: ms. = Cambridge University Library, ms. UA Char.I.4., pp. 181–187; ed. = Mitscherlich, Christoph Wilhelm (ed.) (1793), *Eclogae recentiorum carminum Latinorum*, Hannover 1793, 261–266 (sine accentibus).

Crit.: 5 Τονδ' ms. || **9** ἐλῶν] ἐλῶν ms. post correcturam || **11** ἕδρα ms. || **16** ἀμβατὸς debuit || **17** Σοὶ γὰρ debuit || **24** ἐστεφάνωται debuit || **90** ὦναξ debuit || **92** δε ms.

Sim.: 3 φρουρῇσι...ὄσσων] cf. Soph. *Trach.* 225–226 (ὄμματος φρουράν) || **6** ὡς ἴδ', ὡς τέθαπεν] cf. Theoc. *Id.* 3.42 (ὡς ἴδεν, ὣς ἐμάνη) et al. || **7** χλιδῆς στέψοντι] cf. Soph. *El.* 52–53 (χλιδαῖς / στέψαντες) || **12** κλεῖθρα χάλαξον] cf. Eur. *Hipp.* 808 (χαλᾶτε κλῇθρα) || **16** Ἄμβατος αἰθήρ] oppositio in imitando, cf. Pind. *Pyth.* 10.27 (ὁ χάλκεος οὐρανὸς οὔ ποτ' ἀμβατὸς αὐτῷ) || **17** ὀππάτεσσι] de forma cf. Sapph. fr. 31.11 Voigt || **22–23** τειρῶν τ'...δυσκρίτους / ἀντολὰς...τε δύσεις] cf. Aesch. *Pr.* 457–458 (ἀντολὰς ἐγὼ / ἄστρων ἔδειξα τάς τε δυσκρίτους δύσεις) || **22–24** τειρῶν... /...πάντων..., πόλος τά τ' / ἐστεφάνωται] cf. Hom. *Il.* 18.485 (τὰ τείρεα πάντα, τά τ' οὐρανὸς ἐστεφάνωται) || **91** ἐγγραφὲν δέλτοισι] cf. [Aesch.] *PV* 789 (ἐγγράφου...δέλτοις φρενῶν) || **93–94** οἴακα νέμων φυλάττεις / πρᾶγος ἐν πρύμνῃ πόλεως] cf. Aesch. *Sept.* 2–3 (φυλάσσει πρᾶγος ἐν πρύμνῃ πόλεως / οἴακα νωμῶν)

George's star

(excerpt, ll. 1–24, 89–100)

[Delivered] on Commencement Day, July 1st, 1788

An admirable light has shone forth from the distant corners of darkness: One of the wise men kept watching it with his attentive eyes and recognised

[5] this star, when he saw it, as the youngest child of Uranus [Heaven]. When he saw it, how he did wonder! Thus, as I will crown him with the ornaments of hymns, my spirit easily flies through heaven.

Where could I drive to reach him? [10] O Night with your gleaming eyes, make me an observer of the struggles in heaven on your chariot, and open the lock bars of your seat

so that I might see what has happened far away from earth and see the secrets of heaven. But you, Herschel, [15] in which part of my heart are you engraved, as the heaven is easy to ascend for you?

Hence, Lynceus has given you the gift to see with his eyes. With their help, you departed with the wings of mind and [20] see now what is not to be trodden by mortal feet.

And Newton, the god-like man, was sent to these paths before. He observed well the risings and settings of all the stars which heaven has all round it. [...]

Hail, you best of Uranus' children, [90] beaming ornament of my country. Behold, ruler, your glory written on the tablets of the stars. You are allowed

to consider greater things: Managing the helm of government, you guard the affairs of the state on the stern. [95] Your counsel saved the state beaten by evil swell of the sea. Now I beg that a fair wind may

send it to the harbour. And when you are sailing, may the lawful light, [100] the star named after you, always shine above for you auspiciously.

Metre: Sapphic stanzas. According to Greek metrics the fourth syllable of the first three lines of the stanza is treated as an *anceps* (short: ll. 1, 5, 6, 9, 17, 18, 19, 89, 90, 95, 98, 99). Interlinear elision (*synapheia*): ll. 5/6, 23/24.[62] Hyphenation between third and fourth lines of the stanza: ll. 7/8, 19/20, 99/100.[63]

Notes: This prize-winning ode (Browne Medal, 1787) celebrates the discovery of the planet Uranus in 1781 by the astronomer William Herschel (1738–1822), who called the planet *Georgium sidus* ('George's star') in King George's honour. The poem is in many ways remarkable, first of course because of its fascination with astronomy. This interest in science can also be observed in other contemporary compositions such as the Latin didactic poem *Navis aëria* (1768) by the Ragusian poet Bernardo Zamagna.[64] In case of Cambridge it may also be motivated by the influence of Newton, who has been professor of Mathematics at Cambridge (cf. also Tzechanes → **Balkans**). *Laus Astronomiae* is the theme of another prize-winning ode from 1793 by John Keate (see Coleridge, below). Further, the ode was printed not in Britain but in the German collection *Eclogae recentiorum carminum* by Christoph Wilhelm Mitscherlich in 1793. This may be due to the fact that King George III was not only King of the United Kingdom but also Duke and Prince-

---

62 Cf. Musae Cantabrigienses 1810, IV–V: *Vocalis eliditur à Sappho et Catullo in fine tertii versûs, ab Horatio in fine primi, secondi, et tertii. Nobis autem regula in Graecis ita se habere videtur. Monosyllaba in ε desinentia elidi licet in fine cujusvis versûs, praeter Adonicum: hypermonosyllaba verò non nisi in fine tertii; duo enim priores versus integri sunt et absolute, tertius verò atque Adonicus in unum decurrunt.*
63 Cf. Musae Cantabrigienses 1810, IV: *Divisionem vocis in fine tertii tantùm versus fieri licet.*
64 Cf. Schindler, Claudia (2020), "Lehrdichtung als Science-Fiction. Fakten und Fiktionen in Bernardo Zamagnas *Navis aeria* (1768)", in: Stefan Weise (ed.), *Litterae recentissimae*. Formen und Funktionen neulateinischer Literatur vom 19. Jahrhundert bis zur Gegenwart, Innsbruck, 17–30.

Elector of Brunswick-Lüneburg, while Mitscherlich was a professor at Göttingen University, that is a university in the Duchy of Brunswick-Lüneburg, founded in 1732/34 by King George II. Mitscherlich's version of Moore's ode has no accents.[65] An autograph is preserved in the first of the three folio volumes kept in the Cambridge Universities Archives, where the odes which had won the Browne Medal were collected (cf. Morrison 1983, 145). The notice 'In maximis Comitiis July 1.st 1788' indicates that Moore recited the ode on Commencement Day, viz. a congregation in the Senate House, 'when prize exercises were recited…and all MAs and Doctors in all faculties were created.'[66] Moore's language draws especially on Attic tragedy (Sophocles, Euripides, and Aeschylus). It has a Doric flavour (notable through several instances of Doric ᾱ, e.g., l. 1 ταλόθεν, 6 τέθαπεν, etc.); Aeolic features, however, are not discernible.[67] One may compare in this regard the Sapphic odes by Coleridge and especially by Headlam to gauge the development in the philological treatment of Sappho.

Biography: Abraham Moore was a British barrister and Member of Parliament. Born in 1766, Moore went to Eton, where he became a King's Scholar in 1778. He later studied at King's College, Cambridge and won the Browne Medal in 1786 (Latin ode) and 1787 (Greek ode). Afterwards, he entered the service of the 1st Earl Grosvenor and died of yellow fever in New York in 1822. After his death, his friends published his translation of Pindar. He himself only published one English poem, titled *Niagara*, in 1822.

Bibliography: Fisher, D.R. (ed.) (2009), *The History of Parliament: The House of Commons 1820–1832*, Cambridge (online: https://www.historyofparliamentonline.org/volume/1820-1832/member/moore-abraham-1766-1822 [accessed: September 2020]).

---

[65] It is interesting that the same phenomenon can be observed in one of the autographs of Coleridge's ode. Cf. Morrison 1983, 149.

[66] See https://www.lib.cam.ac.uk/university-archives/glossary/commencement [August 2020]. Cf. also Morrison 1983, 148.

[67] On the choice of dialect, cf. *Musae Cantabrigienses* 1810, VI: *Sunt qui hujusmodi carminum dialectum ad Sapphûs et Pindari normam exigi debere affirmant, quibus non omninò obsequimur: quid enim vetat ea in quâvis dialecto conscribere, si in Pindaricâ licet, quae à Sapphicâ plurimùm distat? Hoc verò cavendum esse statuimus, ne cum Aeolicâ et Doricâ confundantur Ionica vel Attica dialectus, quod persaepe factum esse vidimus.*

Samuel Taylor Coleridge (1772–1834)

Sors misera Servorum in insulis Indiae occidentalis [1792]

(excerptum, vv. 1–28, 57–64, 93–100)

In maximis Comitiis Jul. 3. 1792.

    Ὦ σκότω πύλας, Θάνατε, προλείπων
    Ἐς γένος σπεύδων ἴθι ζεύχθεν ἄτᾳ·
    Οὐ ξενισθήσῃ γενύων σπαράγμοις,
        Οὐδ' ὀλολύγμῳ,
5   Ἀλλὰ δ' αὖ κύκλοισι χοροιτύποισιν,
    Κ' ἀσμάτων χαρᾷ· Φοβερὸς μὲν ἐσσί,
    Ἀλλ' ὁμῶς Ἐλευθερίᾳ συνοικεῖς,
        Στυγνὲ Τύραννε.
    Δασκίοις τεῦ αἰρόμενοι πτεροῖσι
10 Τραχὺ μακρῷ Ὠκεανῷ δι' οἶδμα
    Ἀδονᾶν φίλας ἐς ἕδρας πέτωνται,
        Γᾶν τε πατρῴαν
    Ἔνθα μὰν ἔρασται ἐρωμένῃσιν,
    Ἄμπι κρουνοῖσιν κιτρίων ὑπ' ἀλσῶν,
15 Οἷα πρὸς βροτῶν ἔπαθον βροτοί, τὰ
        Δεινὰ λέγοντι.
    Φεῦ· κόρῳ Νᾶσοι φονίῳ γέμουσαι
    Δυσθεατοῖς ἀμφιθαλεῖς κακοῖσι,
    Πᾶ νοσεῖ Λιμός, βρέμεταί τε πλάγα
20   Αἱματόεσσα,
    Ἀμμέων ἴω· ποσάκις προσῆξεν
    Ὀππάτεσσι δακρυόεσσ' ὀμίχλη,
    Ποσσάκις κ' ἅμα κραδία στέναξεν!
        Αἰνοπαθεῖ γὰρ
25 Δουλίᾳ γέννᾳ βαρέως συναλγῶ,
    Ὡς ἀφωνήτῳ στεναχεῦντι πένθει,
    Ὡς πόνων δίναις στυγερῶν κυκλοῦνται,
        Τέκνα Ἀνάγκας.
    […]
    Ἀλλὰ τίς μ' ἄχω μελίγαρυς, οἷαι
    Δωριᾶν ῥιπαὶ κιθαρᾶν, προσέπτα;
    Τίς ποτιστάζει ψιθύρισμον ἅδυν
60   Μάλθακα φώνα;
    Οἴ! ὁρῶ Κήρυκ' Ἐλέῳ, κλάδοισιν
    Ὡς κατάσκιον κεφαλὰν ἐλαίας!
    Οἴ! λόγων τέων γάνος, Ἰλβρεφωρσεῦ,
        Χρύσεον αἴω!

[...]
Χαῖρ', ὃς εὖ νωμᾷς Ἐλέω τὸν οἴακ'!
Ἐργμάτων καλῶν Ἀγάπη πτεροῖσι
95 Δακρύων ἔντοσθε γέλωτα θεῖσα
  Σὲ στεφανώσει.
Ἤδε Μοῖσα, τᾶν Ἀρετᾶν ὀπαδός,
Σεῖο μεμνᾶσθαι συνεχῶς φιλήσει·
Τλαμόνων ἤδ' εὐλογίαις πρὸς αἴθερ'
100   Οὔνομ' ἀίξει.

Samuel Taylor Coleridge, Coll. Jes. Scholaris

Textus: a) mss.: A = University Archives Cambridge, Char.I.4, pp. 230-233; B = 'Salston' collection of Coleridge's early letters (formerly in the possession of Lady Cave) [non vidi], b) edd.: Campbell, James Dykes (ed.), *The Poetical Works of Samuel Taylor Coleridge*, London 1893, 476–477 (edition princeps); Morrison 1983, 150–156.[68]

Crit.: 5 χορotυποῖσιν A || 6 κάσμάτων scripseris || 11 πέτονται Pontani || 18 δυσθεάτοις debuit || 21 πρόσηξεν A || 26 πενθεῖ A || 27 κύκλουνται A || 93 ὅς A | νωμᾷς A

Sim.: 1 σκότῳ πύλας...προλείπων] cf. Eur. *Hec.* 1–2 (Polydorus mortuus loquitur) (ἥκω...σκότου πύλας / λιπών) || 5 κύκλοισι χοροιτύποισιν] cf. Opp. *H.* 3.250 (χοροιτύπον...κύκλον) || 18 ἀμφιθαλεῖς κακοῖσι] cf. Aesch. *Ag.* 1144 (ἀμφιθαλῆ κακοῖς) || 19–20 πλάγα / Αἱματόεσσα] cf. Aesch. *Cho.* 468 (αἱματόεσσα πλαγά) || 21–22 προσῆξεν / Ὀππάτεσσι δακρύεσσ' ὀμίχλη] cf. [Aesch.] *PV* 144–146 (φοβερὰ δ' ἐμοῖσιν ὄσσοις ὀμίχλα προσῇξε πλήρης δακρύων) || 57–58 τίς μ' ἄχω...προσέπτα] cf. Aesch. *Pr.* 115 (τίς ἀχώ, τίς ὀδμὰ προσέπτα μ' ἀφεγγής) || 59 ψιθύρισμον ἄδυν] cf. Theoc. *Id.* 1.1 (ἁδύ τι τὸ ψιθύρισμα) || 59–60 ποτιστάζει.../ μάλθακα φωνά] cf. Pind. *Pyth.* 4.137 (μαλθακᾷ φωνᾷ ποτιστάζων ὄαρον) || 61–62 ὁρῶ Κήρυκ' Ἐλέω, κλάδοισιν / Ὡς κατάσκιον κεφαλὰν ἐλαίας] cf. Aesch. *Ag.* 493–494 (κῆρυκ' ἀπ' ἀκτῆς τόνδ' ὁρῶ κατάσκιον / κλάδοις ἐλαίας) || 93 νωμᾷς...τὸν οἴακ'] cf. Aesch. *Sept.* 2 (οἴακα νωμῶν) || 97 Ἀρετᾶν ὀπαδός] cf. Pind. *Nem.* 3.8 (ἀρετᾶν τε δεξιωτάταν ὀπαδόν)

The miserable fate of the slaves on the islands of western India [America]

(excerpt, ll. 1–28, 57–64, 93–100)

> O Death, leave the gates of darkness and go quickly to the people oppressed by misery: You will not be received with chattering of teeth nor loud crying,

---

[68] I follow A.

[5] but on the contrary with circular dances and the joy of songs. Although you are terrible, you live together with Freedom, hateful tyrant.

Lifted up by your thick-shaded wings, they fly [10] through the rough water of the bright Ocean to the lovely seats of joys and to their homeland,

where the lovers tell their beloved ones around the fountains under groves of citron-trees the terrible things [15] which mortals have suffered from mortals.

Alas, you islands full of murderous insolence, all-abounding with evils terrible to see, where Hunger is sick and [20] the bloody stroke [of the whip] is roaring.

Alas for us! How often came a tearful darkness to our eyes, and how often did our heart sigh at the same time! For I deeply

[25] sympathise with the suffering generation of slaves as they sigh with voiceless sorrow and as they are surrounded by the eddies of hateful labours, these children of Violence. [...]

Which sweet-voiced echo has come to me like the quivering notes of Doric lyres? Which [60] gentle voice let fall her sweet whisper?

Ah, I see the Herald of Compassion like a head covered with branches of the olive-tree! Ah, I can hear the golden brightness of your words, Wilberforce! [...]

Hail to you who handle well the helm of Compassion! The Love of your good works will crown you with her wings [95] after she has given laughter among the tears.

And the Muse, fellow of the Virtues, will ever love to commemorate you, and [100] your name will hasten towards heaven through the praises of the miserable.

Metre: Sapphic stanzas. According to Greek metrics the fourth syllable of the first three lines of the stanza is treated as an *anceps* (short: ll. 1, 6, 11, 13, 15, 21, 22, 23, 62, 63, 94, 97). Interlinear elision (*synapheia*): ll. 93/94, 99/100. Hyphenation between third and fourth lines of the stanza: ll. 7/8, 19/20, 99/100. Hiatus: ll. 9, 10, 28.[69]

Notes: As a student at Cambridge, Coleridge was eager to win the Browne Medal. In a letter to his brother George from 1791, he writes: 'I am reading Pindar, and composing Greek verse, like a mad dog. I am very fond of Greek verse, and shall

---

[69] Cf. *Musae Cantabrigienses* 1810, V: *Vocalium hiatus nimis licenter quidam admiserunt; quod in constrictis hujusmodi metris minùs rectè fieri judicamus. Semel in Sapphûs fragmento inter simplices vocales occurrit γλῶσσα ἔαγε; ubi corruptelam dudum corrigere tentârunt viri doctissimi.*

try hard for the Brown's Prize ode' (Griggs ²1966, 17). He submitted his compositions three times for the competitions of 1792, 1793, and 1794 but he only won with his ode against slavery in 1792. In 1793, he was defeated by John Keate (*Laus Astronomiae*),[70] and in 1794, by Samuel Butler. Although the themes were provided,[71] the abolition of slavery was a theme Coleridge cherished dearly and treated repeatedly in subsequent compositions (see Morrison 1983, 148). In a contemporary letter to his brother, Coleridge himself identified this Greek ode as 'my chef d'oeuvre in poetical composition' (Griggs ²1966, 34). In contrast to Moore's ode (see above), which precedes that of Coleridge by only four years, Coleridge tries to give his Greek a more Aeolic flavour by using recessive accentuation and psilosis, both, however, irregularly and inconsistently (see Morrison 1983, 147). On the whole, the poem is more Doric than Aeolic, which is certainly due to its main linguistic models, Pindar and Aeschylus. The famous philologist Richard Porson (see above) ridiculed the Greek expression of the ode by asserting that 'he could have shown "134 examples of bad Greek" in it' (see Morrison 1983, 147). The composition itself culminates in a praise of William Wilberforce (1759–1833), a member of the British parliament since 1780 and passionate advocate of the abolition of slave trade.

Biography: Samuel Taylor Coleridge was an important poet of English Romanticism. Born in 1772, he was educated at Christ's Hospital, London and at Jesus College, Cambridge. In 1796, he published his first poetry collection, titled *Poems on Various Subjects*. In 1798, he co-published with the poet William Wordsworth, his close friend, the *Lyrical Ballads*, which contain his most famous poem, *The Rime of the Ancient Mariner*. The *Lyrical Ballads* are regarded as the beginning of English Romanticism. Other famous works are the two poems *Christabel* and *Kubla Khan*, and the *Biographia Literaria*. Together with Wordsworth, he twice visited Germany (1798 and 1828). Since his youth, he consumed laudanum and later became addicted to it. He died in 1834.

Bibliography: Beer, John (2004/2008), "Coleridge, Samuel Taylor", in: *ODNB* online (https://doi.org/10.1093/ref:odnb/5888); Griggs, Earl Leslie (²1966), *Collected Letters of Samuel*

---

[70] Keate's prize-winning ode is published in the collection *Musae Cantabrigienses* (Cambridge 1810, 114–120). Although the Greek text of Coleridge's second ode was not preserved, an English translation by Southey survived. See Morrison 1983,146.

[71] The tradition has continued until the present day. In 2019/20, the competitors 'for a Greek Ode, not exceeding fifty lines in length, or Greek Elegy, not exceeding one hundred and fifty lines in length', had to write on 'The Sirens'. See https://www.student-funding.cam.ac.uk/sir-william-brownes-medals-201920 [August 2020].

Taylor Coleridge, vol. I, Oxford; Morrison, Anthea (1983), "Samuel Taylor Coleridge's Greek Prize Ode on the Slave Trade", in: J.R. Watson (ed.), *An Infinite Complexity: Essays in Romanticism*, Edinburgh, 145–160; Karagiorgos, Panos (2015), "Samuel Taylor Colerigde's Greek Ode", in: Id., *Anglo-Hellenic Cultural Relations*, Cambridge, 61–66.

William Duguid Geddes (1828–1900)

ΣΚΟΛΙΟΝ
(*Adversus nimium librorum studium.*) [1882?]

Ὦ γλύκιστε, τί δὴ βίβλους βιβρώσκων
παντοίους, ἔαρ ἄνθος ἡδὺ πνεῖον
ὀλέσεις βίου; λῆγε νόον
μισόγελων τρέφων, ἄρχεο παιγνίας.

Textus: Geddes, William D. (1882), *Flosculi Graeci Boreales*, Londini, 230.

Crit.: 4 μισόγελων] more Attico acuitur

Sim.: 4 μισόγελων] cf. Alex. Aet. fr. 7.2 Powell

Skolion
(Against the excessive study of books)

O my dear, why are you going to destroy
the sweet bloom of your life, which smells of spring,
by consuming all kinds of books? Stop nurturing
a laughter-hating mind and start to play.

Metre: ll. 1–2 Phalaecians, l. 3 syncopated dodrans and 1 choriamb, l. 4 double dodrans (this stanza is used in several ancient *skolia*).[72]

Notes: This is a rare example of a modern Greek *skolion* (drinking song).[73] *Skolia* were short poems to be performed at symposia. A collection of such works was

---

[72] For metric analysis see Budelmann, Felix (ed.) (2018), *Greek Lyric. A Selection*, Cambridge, 267–268.
[73] There are also two Greek *skolia* (1850) by the famous German philologist Karl Lachmann. See Hertz, Martin (1851), *Karl Lachmann. Eine Biographie*, Berlin, XVII.

transmitted by Athenaeus. Here, Geddes uses a metrical pattern typical of the form to express a witty paraenesis (especially funny in a learned collection of poems like Geddes' own): Don't waste your life time reading books; start to have fun instead.

Biography: William Duguid Geddes (1828–1900) appears here as a representative of Greek composition in Scotland. He was a professor of Greek at the University of Aberdeen (1855–1885). As a scholar, he published an edition of Plato's *Phaedo* (1863) and contributed to the Homeric question (*The Problem of the Homeric Poems*, 1878). As a defender of Greek writing, he collected Greek translations and original compositions by himself and other members of his university in the volume *Flosculi Graeci Boreales* (1882). The collection has a patriotic intention. In the Latin preface, Geddes states that he had taken the risk of collecting the pieces, *ut quid in hac re Scotia posset experirer, et patriae meae titulos doctrinae illius politissimae, qua Anglorum Academiae, inde a Porsoni viri illustrissimi temporibus, unicae pollere existimantur, Graecae scilicet poeseos, aliqua ex parte meo ipsius meorumque commilitonum Marte vindicarem* (Geddes 1882, V–VI) – 'in order to experience what Scotland is able to do in this area and to claim for my homeland, partly through my own work and partly through that of my fellows, the honours of an exquisite art like Greek poetry, in which the English academies are supposed to excel alone from the time of the famous Porson onward.'

Bibliography: Sandys 1908, III.428; Pollard, A.F./Smail, Richard (2004), "Geddes, Sir William Duguid", in: *ODNB* online (https://doi.org/10.1093/ref:odnb/10492).

Algernon Charles Swinburne (1837–1909)

ΕΠΙΓΡΑΜΜΑΤΑ ΕΠΙΤΥΜΒΙΑ ΕΙΣ ΘΕΟΦΙΛΟΝ [1872], V

Ὦ θεῷ φίλ' Ἀπόλλωνι, θεῶν φίλτατε φιλτάτῳ,
Πειθοῦς ἱμεροέσσας τέκνον, ἤ σ' Εὐφροσύνης φράσω;
καρδίας γε πεδήσας ἐπέων χρυσοδέτων πέδαις
ἄλλων, σὴν δὲ κόμην Πιερίδων δησάμενος πλόκοις,
5 νῦν δὴ παυόμενος τερπνοτάτης ἐν βιότῳ λύρας
εὔδιος, ἀμβροσίαν ἡμῖν ἀεὶ μνημοσύνην λιπών.

Textus: Swinburne, Algernon Charles (1873), "ΕΠΙΓΡΑΜΜΑΤΑ ΕΠΙΤΥΜΒΙΑ ΕΙΣ ΘΕΟΦΙΛΟΝ.", in: Lemerre, Alphonse (ed.), *Le tombeau de Théophile Gautier*, Paris, 172.

Crit.: 1 φίλ': φιλ' ed.

Funerary epigrams on Théophile, No. 5

O, beloved by the god Apollo, O most beloved by the most beloved of the gods,
should I call you child of charming *Peitho* [Persuasion] or of *Euphrosyne* [Merriment]?
Since you have bound the hearts of others with the fetters of your golden words
and bound your hair with wreaths of the Pierides [Muses];
now you peacefully cease from the lyre, which was most delightful in life,
leaving us an immortal memory forever.

Metre: *Asclepiadeus maior* (gl^{2c}).

Notes: These lines, written in the Asclepiadean metre, conclude a cycle of five Greek epigrams celebrating the death of the French author Théophile Gautier (1811–1872). They were inserted into a memorial book for Gautier which was edited by Alphonse Lemerre in 1873. Swinburne's polyglot contribution consisted of two poems in English, two in French, one in Latin, and five in Greek. Gautier was a key figure of the Paris *Bohème* and a member of the *Club des Hachichins* (1844–1849), a group of intellectuals testing the effects of various drugs, especially hashish. He authored several novels, short stories, and an important poetic collection, called *Émaux et camées* (1852). In choosing the Asclepiadean metre, Swinburne had in mind perhaps Horace *carm.* 1.11, the famous *carpe diem* poem. Swinburne's elegant poem is well structured into three parts: ll. 1–2 address the deceased Gautier in form of a question ('Should I call you son of Peitho or of Euphrosyne?'), ll. 3–4 seem to give an answer – Gautier bound the hearts of others with his words and adorned his hair with wreaths of the Muses: Thus, he is a son of both; ll. 5–6 remember his death and praise the eternity of his poetry. In his poem, Swinburne, though not using any special classical phrasing, carefully arranges the words within the line (note the enjambement in ll. 4 and 6), plays with repetition and abundant expression (l. 1 θεῷ φίλ'...θεῶν φίλτατε φιλτάτῳ, 3 πεδήσας...πέδαις), and uses well-chosen epithets (l. 2 Πειθοῦς ἱμεροέσσας, 3 ἐπέων χρυσοδέτων, 5 τερπνοτάτης...λύρας, 6 ἀμβροσίαν...μνημοσύνην). This artistic character may reflect the artifice of Gautier's own poetry, for Gautier prominently offers a theory of the concept of *l'art pour l'art* in the preface to his novel *Mademoiselle de Maupin* (1835).

Biography: Algernon Charles Swinburne (1837–1909) was a famous English poet of the Victorian era. He received his classical training at Eton (1849–1853/54) and Balliol College, Oxford (1856–1860), but left Oxford without taking his final exams. His early works provoked scandal because of his predilection for sadomasochism and homoeroticism. Notable were his connections to French writers and poets, such as Victor Hugo, Charles Baudelaire, and Guy de Maupassant. He was very proud of his knowledge of classical languages and asked his former professor, Benjamin Jowett, for advice and correction of his Greek verses (cf. Ribeyrol 2013, 5). His abilities, however, were judged variously (see Haynes 200, 383). In addition to the cycle of epigrams for the dead Gautier, a lengthy Greek dedication in elegiac couplets to Walter Savage Landor precedes his drama *Atalanta in Calydon* (1856).[74] He also used Greek in his correspondence. Ribeyrol summarises Swinburne's erudite polyglossia as follows: 'Whereas the winged words of Homer or Aeschylus were officially made to function metonymically as signifiers of classical authority in both his poetry and essays, discreet parodic sub-versions of canonic authors in those published texts suggest that the poet also considered Greek as a convenient cultural veil for more questionable desires to which he openly gave vent in his private correspondence' (Ribeyrol 2013, 28). In another poem of the Gautier cycle, indeed, Swinburne characterises Gautier as Hermaphroditus.

Bibliography: Rooksby, Rikky (2004/2009), "Swinburne, Algernon Charles", in: *ODNB* online (https://doi.org/10.1093/ref:odnb/36389); Haynes, Kenneth (ed.) (2000), *Algernon Charles Swinburne. Poems and Ballads & Atalanta in Calydon*, London; Ribeyrol, Charlotte (2013), "'It's bawdier in Greek': A.C. Swinburne's Subversions of the Hellenic Code", in: *Cahiers victoriens et édouardiens* [En ligne] 78 Automne, 2013, mise en ligne le 01 septembre 2013, consulté le 06 septembre 2020 URL: http://journals.openedition.org/cve/897; DOI: https://doi.org/10.4000/cve.897

---

[74] See Haynes 2000, 242–244 and 383–385.

Richard Claverhouse Jebb (1841–1905)

ΤΩι ΕΝ ΒΟΝΩΝΙΑι ΠΑΝΕΠΙΣΤΗΜΙΩι ΕΚΑΤΟΝΤΑΕΤΗΡΟΣ ΟΓΔΟΗΣ ΕΟΡΤΗΝ ΑΓΟΝΤΙ. [1888]

(excerptum, vv. 1–22, 147–154)

  Μᾶτερ ἀρχαία σοφίας, ὅθεν Εὐρώπᾳ πάλαι   στρ. α'.
  τᾶς ὀρθοβούλου φῶς Θέμιτος νέον ὦρτο,
  ἐργμάτων ἴαμα βιαιοτάτων, στυγνᾶν ἐλατήριον ἀτᾶν,
  Εὐνομίας ἀγανὸς κάρυξ βροτοῖς,
5 χείματος ὡς δνοφεροῦ
  ὅτε φοινικάνθεμον
  ἦρ πεδάμειψαν γύαι,

  φαιδίμας χαῖρ' Ἰταλίας θύγατερ, τᾶν ἀστέων   ἀντ. α'.
  πρέσβιστον ἐξ ἄλλων ἐφίλασεν Ἀθάνα,
10 παῖς θ' ὁ Λατοίδας, ὅ τ' ἐλευθερίᾳ χαίρων πολιάοχος Ἑρμᾶς·
  νῦν σε μάλ' ἀδυπνόοις δαιδαλλέμεν
  καίριον εὐλογίαις,
  ὅθ' ἑορτᾶς γεύεαι
  παντοσέμνου χάρματος·

15 Ὧραι γὰρ ἐπερχόμεναι θνατοῖς Διὸς   ἐπ. α'.
  εἰς ἑκατοντάδας ὀκτὼ δὴ τελέας ἐτέων
  δόξαν ἐϋστέφανον Βονωνίας
  μαρτυρέοντι γεγάκειν·
  τᾷ καὶ ἀγαλλόμεναι ξείνων πολυγαθέες ἶλαι
20 παντοδαπᾶν ἀπὸ πεμφθεῖσαι πολίων ποτινίσονθ' ἑστίαν
  φιλτάταν Πιερίεσσι, τεὰν
  κοινᾷ κλεΐξοισαι χάριν.

[...]

  τοιόνδε τὶν εὐσεβὲς ἄγκειται γέρας   ἐπ. ζ'.
  ματροπόλει παρ' ἀποίκων· οἷα Καληδόνιον
  καὶ τόδ' ὑπεὶρ ἅλα πέμπεται μέλος,
150 οἴκοθεν οἴκαδ' ἔπουρον[23],
  τηλεπόροι' ἀπὸ Κλώτας[24] Ἰταλὸν ἐς πρυτανεῖον·
  φαντὶ δὲ καὶ Βορέαν ἰοστεφάνων ἀπ' Ἀθανᾶν ἁρπάσαι
  τὰν Ἐρεχθηΐδα, καλλιρόου
  παίζοισαν Ἰλισσοῦ πέλας.

²³ Ad exemplar Universitatis Bononiensis a Nicolao V., Pontifice Summo, A.D. 1450 constituta est Universitas Glasguensis, quam instituta ann. 1482 condita vigere praedicant 'per accepta privilegia matris nostre Studii Bononiensis, omnium universitatum liberrime'.
²⁴ Clyde flumen.

Textus: [Jebb, Richard C.] (1888), *Universitati litterarum et artium Bononiensi ferias saeculares octavas pridie Idus Iunias anno p. n. C. MDCCCLXXXVIII celebranti*, Cantabrigiae; Id. (1907), *Translations into Greek and Latin Verse*, Cambridge, 264–273.

Sim.: 2 ὀρθοβούλου...Θέμιτος] cf. [Aesch.] *PV* 18 || **3** στυγνᾶν ἐλατήριον ἀτᾶν] cf. Aesch. *Cho.* 968 (ἀτᾶν ἐλατηρίοις) || **4** κάρυξ] de accentu cf. e.g. Pind. *Nem.* 8.1 || **6–7** φοινικάνθεμον / ἦρ] cf. Pind. *Pyth.* 4.64 || **8–9** ἀστέων / πρέσβιστον] cf. Aesch. *Sept.* 390 (πρέσβιστον ἄστρων) || **14** παντοσέμνου] cf. Aesch. *Eu.* 637 || **18** γεγάκειν] cf. Pind. *Ol.* 6.49 || **20** cf. Pind. *Ol.* 6.99 (ἀπὸ...τειχέων ποτινισόμενον) || **147** τοιόνδε τὶν...ἄγκειται γέρας] cf. Pind. *Ol.* 11.7–8 (αἶνος Ὀλυμπιονίκαις / οὗτος ἄγκειται) || **152** ἰοστεφάνων ἀπ' Ἀθανᾶν] cf. Pind. *Fr.* 76 || **150** οἴκοθεν οἴκαδ'] = Pind. *Ol.* 6.99.

To the University of Bologna celebrating its eighth centenary

(excerpt, ll. 1–22, 147–154)

> Old mother of wisdom, from where the new light of the right-counselling Themis once came to Europe, remedy for all violent acts, catharsis of hateful sins, you gentle herald of Good order [*Eunomia*] for mortals, [5] just like when the lands exchange purple-flowered spring for dark winter,
>
> hail, daughter of famous Italy, whom Athena, [10] the son of Leto [Apollo], and Hermes, the protector of the city, who loves freedom, all loved as the most honoured of all cities: Now it is time to embellish you with the most sweet-breathing praises, as you taste the joy of the all-majestic feast.
>
> [15] For the Horai, coming from Zeus to the mortals, testify that the well-crowned fame of Bologna has subsisted for eight complete centuries of years. Therefore, gladsome troops rejoice, [20] sent from manifold cities, and come to your house, which is very dear to the Pierides [Muses], in order to praise publicly your grace. [...]
>
> Such a pious present is laid up for you, mother city, by your colonists: Therefore this Caledonian song is sent over the sea [150] from home to home, from the far-distant Clyde to the Italian Senate House. They also say that Boreas stole the daughter of Erechtheus from violet-crowned Athens, while she was playing near the beautiful-flowing Ilissus.

Metre: Dactylo-epitrites (following Pind. *Ol.* 8):[75] **str./ant.** e – D – e ‖ – e – D x ‖ e x D x D – ‖ D – e ‖ D ‖ d² – e ‖ E, **ep.** – D – e ‖ D – D ‖ D ⌣ e ‖ D – ‖ D – D – ‖ D – D – e ‖ e D ‖ – E

Notes: This gratulatory ode in the Pindaric style is one of four major odes composed by Jebb (see below). Jebb's friend, the poet Alfred Tennyson (1809–1892), refers to it in verses dedicated to him: 'Fair things are slow to fade away, / Bear witness you, that yesterday / From out the Ghost of Pindar in you / Roll'd an Olympian; [...]'[76] Jebb, as a professor at Glasgow University (cf. l. 151: Clyde river), wrote this ode in 1888, on the occasion of the celebrations of the eighth centenary of the University of Bologna. His metric model is Pindar's 8th *Olympian* (as also in his Pindaric rendering of Leopardi's *Sopra il monumento di Dante*; cf. Päll [forthcoming]). Jebb's ode consists of seven triads (strophe, antistrophe, epode). As he has, unlike Pindar, no victory to celebrate, the greater part of the poem (ἀντ. β'– ἐπ. ς') consists of a list of important learned men from Bologna, starting with the jurists Irnerius and Bulgarus and ending with philologists and poets (Jebb also included a reference to Clotilde Tambroni, herself a Greek poetess → **Italy**). A long mythological account in the manner of Pindar is therefore missing, but Jebb adds a reference to the rape of Oreithyia by Boreas at the end of his poem as a comparandum to the foundation of Glasgow University through the acceptance of privileges from its 'mother', Bologna. The reference to the ματρόπολις Bologna in the last stanza also serves as a sort of *Ringkomposition* that connects the end to the beginning, where Bologna is called 'old mother of wisdom' (l. 1 μᾶτερ ἀρχαία σοφίας).

Biography: Richard Claverhouse Jebb (1841–1905) was a classical scholar and professor of Greek at Glasgow University (1875–1889) and the University of Cambridge (1889–1905: Regius Professor of Greek). He studied at Trinity College, Cambridge and won the Porson Prize in 1859. In 1869, he was elected Public Orator of the University of Cambridge. He received many other honours, among them the knighthood in 1900. Important scholarly works include especially his edition of Sophocles (1883–96) and that of the newly discovered Bacchylides (1905). Other works in his scholarly oeuvre concern the Attic orators and the history of classical scholarship (e.g., a book on Bentley). He excelled not only as a scholar but also

---

75 The analysis uses the following abbreviations, established by Paul Maas: e = – ⌣ –, E = – ⌣ – – – ⌣ – (= e – e), D = – ⌣⌣ – ⌣⌣ –, d¹ = – ⌣⌣ –, d² = ⌣⌣ –.
76 Tennyson, Alfred (1889), *Demeter and other poems*, London, 12. Cf. also Lloyd-Jones 2004/2016.

as a poet. His translations into Greek and Latin are assembled in volumes published between 1873 and 1907 (second edition). Sandys counts three Pindaric odes among the most notable of his Greek works: a rendering of Browning's *Abt Vogler* (Jebb ²1907, 2–15), a rendering of Rann Kennedy's *The Reign of Youth* (Jebb ²1907, 274–311) and the gratulatory ode on the eighth centenary of the University of Bologna which is presented here (cf. Sandys 1908, III.414). A fourth Pindaric ode is Jebb's translation of Leopardi's *Sopra il monumento di Dante che si preparava in Firenze* (Jebb ²1907, 240–263; cf. also Päll [forthcoming]). Jebb's talent as a Greek versifier was also admired by Wilamowitz (→ **Germany**; cf. Brink 1995, 146).

Bibliography: Jebb, Richard C. (1873/²1907), *Translations into Greek and Latin Verse*, Cambridge; Sandys 1908, III.413–415; Brink 1985, 143–148; Lloyd-Jones, Hugh (2004/2016), "Jebb, Sir Richard Claverhouse", in: *ODNB* online (https://doi.org/10.1093/ref:odnb/34166); Päll (forthcoming).

George Stuart Robertson (1872–1967)

ΑΘΗΝΑΙΣ [1896]

ἀνδρῶν τηλεδαπῶν ἑσμὸν ἀείσομαι βαρβάρων,   [στρ. α´][77]
αὐτὸς συμπεδέχων κρατεροῦ πόνου, οὐ
βάρβαρον στράτευμα·
ἀκαμαντόποδος γὰρ ὁρμᾷ μάχας
5 ἦλθον, ἦλθον, ἰώ,

ματρός τ' ἐσσυμένοι καλλιχόρων τεχνᾶν ἱμέρῳ,   [ἀντ. α´]
κάλλους ματρός, ἰοστεφάνου πόλιος,
καὶ κλέους, Ἀθανᾶν.
ἴτ', ἀδελφεοί, ὕμνῳ ὀρθώσατ' ἐγ-
10 κωμίων ἄωτον·

ἔστω δ' ἄμμι θεὸς γλυκὺ λαῖτμα πλέουσι   [ἐπ. α´]
ναυσίπομπος αὐδᾶς,
πληχθέντες γὰρ ἔρωτ' ἐρατεινοτάτας παρθένου
νῦν διαστείβομεν θάλασσαν.

---

77 The indentation and paragraphs of the original print are rather confusing: they are, therefore, not followed here. The notation of strophe (στρ.), antistrophe (ἀντ.) and epode (ἐπ.) are mine.

15 μᾶτερ, δόξαν ἔχεις ξεινοσύνας ἀεὶ πανδόκου,　　　　　　[στρ. β′]
    καί σοι μαρτυρέει μένος ἱρὸν Ὀρέσ-
    του θεᾶς φυγόντος,
    λύτρον ᾧ γ᾽ ἀβλαβοῦς ἔδωκας βλάβας·
    ἄμμε δ᾽, ὦ κλεεννά,

20 εὔφρων δεξαμένα γ᾽ ἀγλαΐαισι νικαφόροις　　　　　　　　[ἀντ. β′]
    ἄθλων σῶν πέλασον μεθέποντας ἑκὰς
    σὴν χάριν κλέος τε.
    ἄποθεν γὰρ ἐπερχόμεσθ᾽ ἀθρόοι,
    τοὺς γὰρ Ἀγγλίαθεν

25 ἔσσευεν φιλότιμος ἔρως ἐφορᾶν χώ-　　　　　　　　　　[ἐπ. β′]
    ραν, ὅθ᾽ ἀμφὶ καλᾷ
    αὐτοὶ μαρνάμενοί ποτ᾽ ἐλευθερίᾳ, σὺν δὲ Μοι-
    σᾶν τέκνον, τὸν βίον προῆκαν·

    τοὺς δ᾽ ἄθλων μοι ἄνακτας πόρεν ὀλβία Γαλλία,　　　　[στρ. γ′]
30 τοὺς δ᾽ ἀθρέω βαθὺ λήϊον Οὑγγαρίας
    Τευτόνων τ᾽ ἔχοντας,
    στρατὸν οὐδ᾽ Ἀμέριστος αἶ᾽ ἐξέπεμ-
    ψεν δρόμοις ἀφαυρόν.

    Πηλέος δὴ λέγεται καὶ Θέτιος γάμοισιν θεῶν　　　　　[ἀντ. γ′]
35 ἡρώων τε χορὸν μέγα δῶμα γερᾶ-
    ραι· σοί, ὦ πάνολβε,
    πατρίδος πάρα νῦν Πατήρ, τῆς ἐμῆς
    προσφιλὴς ὅμαιμος·

    Μοσκώων τε γάνος πάρα, χἄτερος αἶαν　　　　　　　　　[ἐπ. γ′]
40 πατρίαν Ἀλέξαν-
    δρος τῆς σῆς πεδαμείβει. ἀγάλλεο δ᾽, ὦ φιλτάτα,
    καὶ δέκευ δωρεὰν ἀοιδᾶς.

Textus: Cook, Theodore A. (1908), *The Cruise of the Branwen being a short history of the modern revival of the Olympic Games, together with an account of the adventures of the English fencing team in Athens in MCMVI*, Privately published, 55–56; D'Angour 2011, 192–193.

Crit.: 6 ἐσσύμενοι debuit || 32 στράτον ed., correxit Pontani || 35 χόρον ed., correxi || 37 Πατηρ, ed., correxi

Sim.: 1 ἀνδρῶν τηλεδαπῶν] = Hom. *Od.* 6.279 || 2 κρατεροῦ πόνου] cf. Quint. Smyrn. 7.526 (κρατεροῖο πόνοιο) || 4 ἀκαμαντόποδος] verbum Pindaricum, cf. *Ol.* 3.3; 4.1; 5.3 || 7 ἰοστεφάνου] epitheton Athenarum etiam apud Pind. fr. 76; Ar. *Ach.* 637; *Eq.* 1323 || 9–10 ὕμνῳ...ἐγκωμίων ἄωτον] cf. Pind. *Pyth.* 10.53 (ἐγκωμίων...ἄωτος ὕμνων) || 12 ναυσίπομπος αὐδᾶς] cf. Eur. *Ph.* 1712 (ναυσίπομπον αὔραν) || 19 κλεεννά] de forma cf. Pind. *Pyth.* 5.20 || 20 ἀγλαΐαισι νικαφόροις] de iunctura cf. Pind. *Ol.* 13.14 || 30 βαθὺ λήϊον] iunctura epica, cf. *Il.* 2.147; 11.560; *Od.* 9.134; Hes. *Sc.*

288 || **36** πάνολβε] cf. Aesch. *Supp.* 582 || **41** πεδαμείβει] de forma cf. Pind. *Ol.* 12.12 || **42** δέκευ δωρεάν] cf. Pind. *Ol.* 5.3 (δέκευ Ψαύμιός τε δῶρα)

For Athens

Taking part myself in the hard labour, I will sing the swarm of barbarian men – no barbarian army – coming from far countries. [5] For they came, they came – io! –, driven by the desire to fight, untiring in foot, and by longing for the mother of the arts of beautiful dancing, the mother of beauty and of glory, the violet-crowned city: Athens. Come, brothers, raise up with song [10] the finest praises: The god of voice shall be a ship-wafting companion for us swimming on the sweet waves, for we cross now the sea, smitten by the love for the loveliest maiden.

[15] Mother, you carry ever since the fame of all-receiving hospitality. And the holy force of Orestes, who took flight from the goddesses [= Furies], bears witness for you: You gave him release from unharming damage. Thus, O you famous (city), [20] receive us graciously and give us victorious triumph in your Games, as we are pursuing from far off your grace and glory. We come together from far away, as the love for glory has driven Englishmen [25] to visit the place where they themselves and the child of the Muses [= Byron] once gave their lives, while fighting for beautiful freedom,

and blessed France has given me the lords of the Games, [30] and I see also others who dwell in the deep cornfield of Hungary and of the Teutons, nor did the *Undivided* [Gr. *A-meristos*] land [= United States of *America*] send an army powerless in running. It is said that [35] a troop of gods and heroes honoured the house at the wedding of Peleus and Thetis. Here the Father of the Country [King George I of Greece], beloved brother of my own country,[78] comes to you, O you truly happy (city)! The joy of the Muscovites is present[79] and [40] a second Alexander[80] exchanges his homeland for yours. Exult, O dearest one, and receive the gift of song.

Metre: Pindaric (after the model of Pind. *Ol.* 5): *strophe/antistrophe*: gl^c cr || pher^ 2d || ith || ^gl cr || ith; *epode*: pher^{2d} || ith || gl^d cr || 2 cr ba

Notes: This Pindaric ode by Robertson was delivered on 3 April 1896 before King George I of Greece at the final ceremony of the first Olympic Games of modern times in the rebuilt Panathenaic Stadium in Athens. The official report describes the reaction as follows: 'The King lent a most attentive ear to the recital of those

---

[78] Princess Alexandra, George I's sister, was married with the late King Edward VII.
[79] This may be King George I's wife Queen Olga Constantinovna.
[80] Who is meant here is not totally clear. It cannot be Emperor Alexander III, who died in 1894. Perhaps Robertson addresses Oleksiy Butovsky, a general of the Russian army and member of the first International Olympic Committee. But to mention the general and not another member of the royal family at the end of the ode seems rather unusual. Morshead's English translation also seems to contradict this interpretation: 'An Alexander comes, of royal line— / Quitting his land for thine!'

beautiful verses, and the audience cheered heartily when the poet had finished speaking. After having warmly congratulated Mʳ Robertson the King stepped on a sort of platform, erected before the Royal seats [...]' (Lambros/Polites 1896, 111). Robertson chose Pindar's fifth *Olympian* ode as a model for the metre and also inserted some verbal echoes into his ode, notably at the end (l. 42 ~ Pind. *Ol.* 5.3). Just like the Pindaric model, Robertson's ode consists of three repeated triadic systems. The first system (ll. 1–14) treats the arrival of the foreigners in Athens, the second Athens' hospitality (ll. 15–28), and the third the present feast (ll. 16–42). Thus, the poem follows Robertson's own journey from England to Greece. He also cleverly integrates mythological references, first to Orestes' reception in Athens as an example of Athenian hospitality, and then to the marriage of Peleus and Thetis as a comparison to the present feast. With regard to his audience (although one might doubt that they were able to understand him), Robertson enumerates some of the participating nations, specifically, the English, the French, Germans, Hungarians, and Americans (ll. 23–33), and addresses King George I (and his wife?) at the end (ll. 36–41). The English, of course, get special attention, as Robertson recalls their participation in the Greek War of Independence and the death of the 'child of the Muses', Lord Byron (ll. 24–28). The Greek text of the ode was published together with an English translation by the classicist Edmund Doidge Anderson Morshead in a volume by Theodore Andrea Cook, who was a member of the International Olympic Committee, in 1908.

Biography: Sir George Stuart Robertson was participant in the first Olympic Games of modern times in Athens in 1896, where he gained a third place in the tennis doubles. Born in 1872, he studied at New College, Oxford. He later became a lawyer and was knighted in 1928. In addition to his Olympic Ode, he composed another remarkable Greek prose piece of special wit, titled *Herodotus in Britain*, a description of Britain in Herodotean style, which was awarded with the Gaisford Prize for Greek Prose in 1895 (see Harrison 2020); a year before this, he won the Gaisford Prize for Greek Verse for a translation of Shakespeare's *Henry IV*, Part II, Act 2, Scene 2.

Bibliography: Lambros, Sp.P./Polites, N.G. (1896), *The Olympic Games B.C. 776. – A.D. 1896.* [...], Athens/London; D'Angour, Armand (2011), "Pindar at the Olympics: the Limits of Revivalism", in: Barbara Goff/Michael Simpson (edd.), *Thinking the Olympics. The Classical Tradition and the Modern Games*, Bristol, 190–203; https://en.wikipedia.org/wiki/George_S._Robertson [accessed: August 2020]; Päll (forthcoming); Harrison 2020.

Walter Headlam (1866–1908)

I. Hunting-crop [ante 1908]

    Μάστιξ ἱππελάτειρα, πυλῶν ἐπανοίκτρι' ἀγροίκων
      λάτρι, σὲ μὲν τρισσαὶ παρθένοι ἱππόδαμοι
    ἀντ' ὀλίγων μέγα δῶρον ἐμοὶ χαρίσαντο Φιλιππίς,
      Νικώ, Ψιχάριον, ζεῦγος ἀδεισίπονον.
5 ὦ κραδίης μοχλευτί, σὺ δ' εἰπέ μοι· οὐ γὰρ ἔμοιγε
      εὑρετά· πῶς ταύτης ἀντὶ φιλοφροσύνης
    ταῖς κούραις τίσαιμ' ἂν ἴσην χάριν; εἴθε γένοιο
      Κίρκειος τέχνης ῥάβδος ἀπειρεσίης,
    μὴ μὴν ἀλλάξων φύσεως τύπον, ἀλλ' ἵνα θείης
10   ἀθανάτους ἅσπερ νῦν ἔλαχον χάριτας.

Textus: Headlam 1910, 27.

Crit.: 9 θέιης ed.
Sim.: 1 ἱππελάτειρα] cf. Orph. *Hymn.* 32.12 (de Minerva) || **3** ἀντ' ὀλίγων μέγα δῶρον] cf. Call. *ep.* 48.3 || **4** ἀδεισίπονον] neologismus || **8–9** de re cf. Hom. *Od.* 10.238–240

Hunting-crop

    Crop, you driver of horses, serving as opener of rustic gates,
      three maids, tamers of horses,
    have given you as a great gift for small merits to me – the three are Philippis,
      Nico, Psicharion, a trio not afraid of work:
[5] O you who heave up my heart, tell me, for I cannot
      find a solution: How could I return equal thanks
to the girls for their kindness? May you become
      Circe's magic wand of immense craft
not in order to change natural shapes, but in order to make
[10] immortal the gratitude they have now obtained.

Metre: Elegiac couplets (flawless).

II. To Mary [1905?]

Μᾶτρος ὦ φίλας ἔρατον γένεθλον,
χαῖρέ μοι, χρυσοπλόκαμ', ἔν τε βούλαις
εὐλόγοις σόφα πάϊ καὶ χόροισιν
   ἐν νεογυίαις.
5 ὄλβιον λέγω πάτερ' ὀλβίαν τε
μάτερ' ἅ σ' ἐγείνατο κἀνέθρεψεν
ἁλίκεσσι χάρμα παλαιτέροισί τ'
   εὔφιλες ἔρνος.
ἔσσεται καὶ κῆνο τάχ' αὖθις ἆμαρ
10 ἄνικ' ὀμμιμνασκομένα σὺ φάσεις,
"εἶδε χοὖτος ἄρ' ἔμε χἄδιόν μ' ἔθ-
   νασκε φιλήσαις."

Textus: Headlam 1910, *Poems* 101 (nr. LII).

Crit.: 2 ἔν corr.: ἐν ed. || **6** ἅ ed.: ἅ debuit Aeolice | σ' corr.: σ, ed. || **9** ἆμαρ corr.: ἀμαρ ed. || **10** ἄνικ' ed.: ἄνικ' debuit Aeolice (cf. Theoc. *Id.* 29.33) || **11** χἄδιόν] χἀδιόν ed.

Sim.: 2 χρυσοπλόκαμ'] cf. *Hymn. Hom. Ap.* 205 (de Latona) || **4** νεογυίαις] verbum Pindaricum, cf. *Nem.* 9.24; fr. 123.9 M. || **6** μάτερ' ἅ σ' ἐγείνατο κἀνέθρεψεν] cf. Hom. *Od.* 2.132 (ἥ μ' ἔτεχ', ἥ μ' ἔθρεψε) || **8** εὔφιλες] verbum Aeschyleum, cf. *Ag.* 34 (εὐφιλῆ χέρα) || **9** ἔσσεται καὶ κῆνο τάχ' αὖθις ἆμαρ] cf. Hom. *Il.* 4.164; 6.448 (ἔσσεται ἦμαρ ὅτ' ἄν ποτ' ὀλώλῃ Ἴλιος ἱρή) || **10** ὀμμιμνασκομένα] de forma cf. Theoc. *Id.* 30.22

To Mary

O lovely offspring of a kind mother, hail, goldenhaired girl, skilled in rational counsels and in dances with your young limbs.
[5] I call happy your father and happy your mother, who gave you birth and brought you up as a joy for those of your age and a well-loved youngster for the elders.
Soon, however, there will be the day, [10] when you will remember and say: 'So, this one saw me too and died more pleasantly, after having kissed me.'

Metre: Sapphic stanzas (according to Greek practice the fourth syllable of the hendecasyllabic lines is sometimes short, see ll. 1, 3, 5, 6, 7, 11; interlinear elision: l. 7/8; interlinear hyphenation: l. 11/12).

Notes: Two very elegant poems of Hellenistic grace and spirit. The first, skilfully structured in three parts, is an epigrammatic response to a gift: a hunting-crop given to the speaker by three young, horse-riding ladies (their Greek names are obviously invented: Φιλιππίς, the female 'who loves horses', Νικώ, the 'victorious', Ψιχάριον, 'little crumb', but they remind us of many similar names in Hellenistic epigrams too; for Νικώ see, e.g., *Anth. Pal.* 5.150.2). In pure Hellenistic fashion, Headlam does not address those who made the gift directly but asks the hunting-crop how he should return the favour. The second poem, written in Sapphic stanzas and Aeolic dialect, celebrates a young girl, obviously too young for the speaker, who is wholly enchanted by her skills and charm. At the end, therefore, the poet sketches a vision in which the girl will receive the news of the speaker's death at some future time and remember, how he kissed her. The poem, however, was apparently written rather for the mother (and the father), not the girl, in order to pay them an honest compliment. The 1910 edition provides an explaining note: 'Addressed to the Hon. Mary Gardner, aged nine, daughter of Lord and Lady Burghclere' (Headlam 1910, 101). The Hellenistic manner of these poems is best compared to the poetry of Wilamowitz (→ **Germany**), who was himself enchanted by Headlam's verses (see below).

Biography: Walter Headlam was a classical scholar at the University of Cambridge. Born in 1866, he was educated at Harrow and King's College, Cambridge, where he remained as fellow and lecturer until his sudden death in 1908. As a student he won several awards, including the Browne Medal for both Greek and Latin odes (both in 1885 and 1886, and again in 1887, together with the medal for the Latin epigram),[81] as well as the Porson Prize. He unsuccessfully applied for the Regius Professorship of Greek, despite delivering a highly admired lecture. His research concentrated on Hellenistic poetry (Meleager, Herodas), Greek drama (Aeschylus), and textual criticism. He published some of his translations from Greek into English and English or German into Greek in a volume titled *A Book of Greek Verse* (1907). Sandys, who closes his *History of Classical Scholarship* with Headlam, reports that 'only nine days before his death, he had the pleasure of meeting Wilamowitz, who, in the course of his brief visit to Cambridge, said of some of Walter Headlam's Greek verses that, if they had been discovered in an Egyptian papyrus, they would immediately have been recognized by all scholars as true Greek poetry' (Sandys 1908, III.485). Wilamowitz even composed a Greek epigram on his dead colleague, ending with the lines: καὶ νῦν Μοῖρα σ' ἄωρον ἀφήρπασεν, οἷς δὲ μέμηλεν / Ἑλλὰς τὰς πολλὰς ἐλπίδας ἠφάνισεν. / κἠμοὶ πικρότερον μὲν ἴσως ἄχος αὐτὸν ἰδόντι / ἄρτι σε· πλὴν ὁπόταν σῇσιν ἀηδονίσιν / ἐντύχω, αὐδῆς αὖθις ἐν οὔασι σῆς ἐπορούσει / φθόγγος, ζῶντα δ' ἀεὶ τὸν φίλον

---

[81] Cf. Tanner 1917, 310.

ἀσπάσομαι.⁸² – 'And now the Moira has taken you prematurely away, but for those who care for Greece, she has destroyed the greatest hopes. And for me too in like manner, who just saw you yourself, it is a quite bitter sorrow. Only whenever I encounter your nightingales, the sound of your voice will come back to my ears and I will greet the friend who is always alive.'

Bibliography: N.N. (1908), "Dr. Walter Headlam, 1866–1908", in: *The Classical Review* 22/5, 163–164; Sandys 1908, III.484–485; Wilson, Nigel G. (2004), "Headlam, Walter George", in: *ODNB* online (https://doi.org/10.1093/ref:odnb/33784); Headlam, Walter (1910), *His Letters and Poems with a Memoir by Cecil Headlam and a Bibliography by L. Haward*, London.

Ronald A. Knox (1888–1957)

A Fragment of a Telephoniazusae [1918]

Σνώξ. Τηλεφωνία

1   Σν.   ὦ οὗτος, οὗτος, οὔτ' –
      Τη.   ἀριθμός, εἰ δοκεῖ;
      Σν.   ὀκτὼ διπλοῦς, ὦ, πέντε, Παδίγγου πόλις.
      Τη.   ὀκτώ, διπλοῦς ὦ, πέντε, Παδίγγου πόλις;
      Σν.   οὐκ ἐς κόρακας; μὰ τὸν Δί', ἀλλ' ὀκτὼ διπλοῦς.
5   Τη.   βρεκεκεκὲξ κοὰξ κοάξ, βρεκεκεκὲξ κοάξ,
           ὦ οὗτος οὗτος· βρεκεκεκὲξ κοάξ·
      Σν.   ὦ φίλτατον πρόσφθεγμα σὺν χρόνῳ φανὲν
           ξένου πατρῴου Βιγγός, ἀσμένως σ' ἔχω.
      Τη.   ποίου σὺ Βιγγός; ἐν βραχεῖ γὰρ εἰκάσαι
10   οὔπω τιν' οἶδα τοῦτ' ἐπωνομασμένον.
      Σν.   σὺ δ' εἶ τίς;
      Τη.   ὅστις εἰμί; Φωθερίγγιος.
      Σν.   ὀκτὼ διπλοῦς, ὦ, πέντε καταλεχθεὶς σύ γε;
      Τη.   οὐκ, ἀλλὰ πέντε, τέσσαρες, τρεῖς, ἐννέα.
      Σν.   ἥμαρτον, ὡς ἔοικεν· ἐκκωδώνισον.
15   Τη.   Βρεκεκεκὲξ κοὰξ κοάξ· ὤόπ, ὤόπ, ὤόπ, ὤόπ·
           βρεκεκεκὲξ κοάξ,
           ὦ οὗτος οὗτος·
      Σν.   πρὸς θεῶν, ὅστις περ εἶ,

---

82 Reported in: *The Classical Review* 22/5, 1908, 163. See also Headlam 1910, 7–8. The 'nightingales' mentioned in Wilamowitz's verse may be an allusion to Callimachus' touching epigram for his fellow poet Heraclitus (*Anth. Pal.* 7.80.5). πολλὰς ἐλπίδας certainly alludes to *Anth. Pal.* 7.453, another funerary epigram by Callimachus.

	ἄνω μολὼν τὸν Βίγγα κατακάλει δόμων.
Τη.	(μυγμός).
20 Σν.	ἀλλ' ἡδέως κλύοιμ' ἄν, εἰ λάκοις μέγα.
Τη.	ὡς οὐ παρόντος ταῦτ' ἐρωτήσας μάθε.
Σν.	πότερον θανόντος ἢ 'ποδημοῦντος λέγεις;
Τη.	θάρρει, κάτεισι· κᾆτ' ἀπαγγεῖλαι τί χρή;
Σν.	ὁ Σνὼξ λέγων·
Τη.	Βλώξ;
Σν.	Σνὼξ μὲν οὖν.
Τη.	ὁ Σνωγμένων;
25 Σν.	ΣΝΩΞ, Σνῶκα, Σνωκός, Σνωκί· σῖγμα νῦ – κλύεις;
Τη.	καὶ μὴν ὅδ' αὐτὸς ἐξ ἀγρῶν κατέρχεται.
	(μυγμός).
	ὦ οὗτος οὗτος· Βὶγξ λέγει· κοὰξ κοάξ,
	βρεκεκεκὲξ κοὰξ κοάξ, βρεκεκε –
	(Silence)

Textus: primum in periodico scholae Shrewsburianae *The Salopian* 1918,[83] tum Eyres, Laurence E. (ed.) (1959), Ronald Knox, *In Three Tongues*, London, 34–35.

Sim.: 1 (6, 17, 28) ὦ οὗτος, οὗτος] = Ar. *Vesp.* 1364 || **2** εἰ δοκεῖ] cf. in fine versus etiam Ar. *Av.* 1597 || **5–6 (15–16, 28–29)** cf. Ar. *Ran.* 209–210, 220, 223 etc. (βρεκεκεκὲξ κοὰξ κοάξ) || **7** ὦ...χρόνῳ φανέν] cf. Eur. *El.* 578 (ὦ χρόνῳ φανείς) | φίλτατον πρόσφθεγμα] cf. Eur. *Tro.* 1184 (φίλα διδοὺς προσφθέγματα); Nic. Eug. *De Dros. et Char.* 8.101 (ὦ φίλον πρόσφθεγμα) || **11** σὺ δ' εἶ τίς; ὅστις...;] Ar. *Av.* 630 (σὺ δ' εἶ τίς; ὅστις; χρησμολόγος), 997 (σὺ δ' εἶ τίς ἀνδρῶν; ὅστις εἴμ' ἐγώ; Μέτων) || **15** ὠόπ, ὠόπ, ὠόπ, ὠόπ] cf. Ar. *Ran.* 180, 208 || **19 (27)** μυγμός] Aesch. *Eu.* 117, 120 (sonus Furiarum) || **22** πότερον θανόντος ἢ 'ποδημοῦντος λέγεις] cf. Eur. *Alc.* 520 (πότερον θανούσης εἶπας ἢ ζώσης ἔτι;)

A Fragment of a Telephoniazusae

Snox, Telephonia

Sn.: Hello, hello, hell-
Tel.: Number, please.
Sn.: Double eight, O dear, five, Paddington.
Tel.: Eight, double o, five, Paddington?
Sn.: No, for god's sake! Double eight!
[5] Tel.: Brekekekex koax koax, brekekekex koax,
Hello, hello, brekekekex koax …

---

83 The first publication place as noted in Eyres could not be confirmed yet, but Dr Robin Brooke-Smith, Taylor Librarian and Archivist at Shrewsbury School, to whom I owe special thanks, pointed to a reprint under the heading '25 years ago' in *The Salopian* March 1943, 248–249.

Sn.: O lovely voice of my father's
friend Binx, finally appeared. I am happy to hear you.
Tel.: Which Binx? Upon quick reflection,
[10] I don't know anyone with this name.
Sn.: Who are you?
Tel.: Who I am? Fotherings.
Sn.: Double eight, O, five, is that your number?
Tel.: No! Five, four, three, nine!
Sn.: I was obviously mistaken. Please let it ring.
[15] Tel.: Brekekekex koax koax: oop, oop, oop, oop,
brekekekex koax.
Hello, hello?
Sn.: By the gods, whoever you may be,
go up and call Binx from the house.
Tel.: (muttering)
[20] Sn.:I would be happy to listen to you, if you could speak loudly.
Tel.: You must know that he whom you are asking for is not here.
Sn.: Do you say this because he is dead or because he is abroad?
Tel.: Don't be afraid: He is coming down. And what should I announce?
Sn.: This is Snox speaking.
Tel.: Blox?
Sn.: Snox, that is.
Tel.: Snotheris?
[25] Sn.: *SNOX, Snóka, Snokós, Snokí*: Sigma nu – do you understand?
Tel.: Yes, he is coming from outside.
(muttering)
Hello, hello? Binx is speaking: koax koax,
brekekekex koax koax, brekeke –
(Silence)

Metre: Iambic trimeters; ll. 19 and 27 *extra metrum*.

Notes: Knox has written an entertaining parody of Greek Comedy, using phrases from and allusions to Greek drama. The title, *Telephoniazusae* ('*Telephoning women*' or rather '*Telephonists*'), evokes similar titles from Aristophanes (*Thesmophoriazusae*) and Theocritus (*Adoniazusae*) but uses the neologism τηλεφωνιάζω. From the outset, this establishes a witty frame for the scene, as does the personification of Τηλεφωνία (similar to Aristophanic personifications, such as Δημοκρατία in *Knights*). A further strategy which makes the scene especially funny is the combination of sound problems in modern telephoning with the onomatopoetic creations of Old Comedy and Greek tragedy. To imitate interference and background noise, Knox uses the croaking sound from Aristophanes' *Frogs* (βρεκεκεκὲξ κοὰξ κοάξ, ll. 5–6, 15–16, 28–29) three times. Another representation of interference (given as a note *extra metrum*, represented here as 'muttering') is the word μυγμός (l. 19), which is borrowed from Aeschylus' *Eumenides*. An educational background might be alluded to through the recitation of case forms of the name Σνώξ in l. 25. The whole scene is remarkable in two ways: first, because of its fine English wit, second, as an example of original 'dramatic' poetry. Although it was quite usual to translate scenes from English (especially Shakespearean) dramas into Greek, original pieces were rare (cf. Christopherson, above). Certainly, Knox' scene was only intended to be read, as becomes clear from the frequent quotations from Greek literature, but it could also be imagined as a short sketch. The naming Σνώξ, clearly playing on 'Knox', gives the piece a touch of self-mockery.

Biography: Ronald Arbuthnott Knox was an author of crime fiction and a Roman Catholic priest. He was educated at Eton College and studied at Oxford University, where he won the Gaisford Prize for Greek Verse Composition in 1908, with a translation of Robert Browning's *Pippa Passes*, Part III into Theocritean hexameters,[84] and the Chancellor's Prize for Latin Verse Composition in 1910. He subsequently became an influential theologian. Although he started out as an Anglican priest (1912), he converted to Catholicism in 1917, under the influence of Gilbert Keith Chesterton. From 1915 to 1916, Knox served as a schoolmaster at Shrewsbury School, from 1919 to 1926 at St Edmund's College, Ware. Many of his Greek translations and jokes, such as the text presented here or his *Jabberwocky* in iambics (Ἴαμβρωξ ἰαμβικῶς), were printed in *The Salopian*, a magazine at Shrewsbury School.

Bibliography: Eyres, Laurence E. (ed.) (1959), Ronald A. Knox, *In Three Tongues*, London; Gilley, Sheridan (2004/2016), "Knox, Ronald Arbuthnott", in: *ODNB* online (https://doi.org/10.1093/ref:odnb/34358); https://en.wikipedia.org/wiki/Ronald_Knox#Roman_Catholic_Church [accessed: August 2020]

---

[84] Printed in Eyres 1959, 2–13.

Greek Inscription at The Queen's College, Oxford [1951]

ΤΟΥΤΩΝ ΤΟΙΟΥΤΩΝ ΤΕ ΚΑΤ ΑΙΘΕΡΑ ΚΑΙ ΚΑΤΑ ΠΟΝΤΟΝ
ΚΑΙ ΚΑΤΑ ΓΗΝ ΑΡΕΤΗ ΣΩΣΕ ΦΑΝΕΙΣΑ ΠΑΤΡΑΝ
ΠΑΡ Δ ΗΒΗΝ ΕΒΑΛΟΝΤΟ ΚΑΙ ΕΣ ΤΕΛΟΣ ΩΠΑΣΕ ΔΑΙΜΩΝ
ΤΟΙΣ ΜΕΝ ΝΟΣΤΟΝ ΕΧΕΙΝ ΤΟΙΣΙ ΔΕ ΤΗΝΔΕ ΛΙΘΟΝ[85]

Textus: Monumentum Oxoniense collegis aulae Reginae bello altero mundano occisis dedicatum (The Queen's College, Oxford, on a wall of the College's Senior Common Room; see fig. 10, above)[86]

Sim.: 1–2 κατ' αἰθέρα καὶ κατὰ πόντον / καὶ κατὰ γῆν] cf. *Anth. Pal.* 14.64.2–3 (aenigma Sphingis): ὅσσ' ἐπὶ γαῖαν / ἑρπετὰ κινεῖται ἀνά τ' αἰθέρα καὶ κατὰ πόντον ‖ **3** ὤπασε δαίμων] clausula saepius apud poetas epicos aetatis posterioris legitur, cf. Opp. *H.* 1,661; Quint. Smyrn. 7,67; Nonn. *Dion.* 47,66

‹Greek inscription›

> The virtue of these men and others of the same kind, displayed in the skies, at sea
>   and on earth, saved their homeland.
> They risked their youth, and God fulfilled
>   for some of them the fate of returning home and for the others of having this stone.

Metre: Elegiac couplets (flawless).

Notes: This is one of several Greek – and many Latin – inscriptions in Oxford.[87] The inscription honours 'the men of this College [*sc.* The Queen's College, Oxford] who fell in the war of 1939–1945'. The monument which records the names of the fallen was officially unveiled on 25 April 1951 and sits on the wall of the College's Senior Common Room, opposite First World War memorials which are on the walls of the Library. The Greek verses are at the bottom of the inscription, beneath the names (see fig. 10). It is said that the last two words (τήνδε λίθον) hint at the author of these lines, as the last letter of τήνδε and the first of λίθον are the initials

---

85 With accents: Τούτων τοιούτων τε κατ' αἰθέρα καὶ κατὰ πόντον / καὶ κατὰ γῆν ἀρετὴ σῶσε φανεῖσα πάτραν, / πὰρ δ' ἥβην ἐβάλοντο καὶ ἐς τέλος ὤπασε δαίμων / τοῖς μὲν νόστον ἔχειν, τοῖσι δὲ τήνδε λίθον.
86 I owe my knowledge of this inscription to two different sources: Václav Z.J. Pinkava, the son of Jan Křesadlo (→ **Bohemian Lands**), and Filippomaria Pontani, via Prof. Michael D. Reeve (Cambridge). I am very grateful to each of them. For further information on the memorial, I am much obliged to Michael Riordan, Archivist of The Queen's College, Oxford.
87 For other Greek inscriptions, see Adams 2015, 9, 18, 22.

of Edgar Lobel (1888–1982), the famous editor of the Oxyrhynchus Papyri and Fellow at The Queen's College from 1927.[88] The Czech author Jan Křesadlo (Václav Pinkava), who wrote the Greek science-fiction epic *Astronautilia* (→ **Bohemian Lands**), mentions this inscription in an interview given at the Viola Theatre in Prague in 1992 and recites the verses by heart.[89] He knew them because his son Václav Z.J. Pinkava had studied at The Queen's College.

Bibliography: Adams, Reginald H. (2015), *Latin Inscriptions in Oxford. Inscriptiones aliquot Oxonienses*, Oxford (cites some Greek inscriptions but does not mention the one presented here); Queen's College Archives, FB621 (small file of correspondence relating to the memorial).

Armand D'Angour (1958–)

Alcaic Greek Ode for the London Olympics [2012]

a) Attice

ἴδεσθε καινὸν πῦρ τόδ' Ὀλυμπικόν,
ὅ γ' ἐξέλαμψε πρόσθε καθ' Ἑλλάδα.
ἀλλ' ἡδέως δέχεσθε τἆθλα
Λονδινίου ποταμοῦ παρ' ὄχθας.

5 ὑμνεῖτε δ' αἴγλην ἀντιπάλων σοφῶν,
στρατὸς γὰρ ἦλθεν ἐκ περάτων χθονός·
καὶ χρὴ μεγίσταις ᾧδ' ἀοιδὸν
ἀμφ' ἀρεταῖσι καθ' ἅρμ' ἐλαύνειν.

πλῆθος θεατῶν μυρίον ὄψεται
10 ὁρμὴν τρεχόντων καὶ λιπαρὰν χάριν,
σπουδήν τ' ἐρεσσόντων ἑταίρων
ἀκροβατῶν τε δοκοὺς πατούντων.

θεάσεται δὲ χάρματι τοξότην
τείνοντα νευράν, καὶ ποδὶ σωφρόνως
15 τὸν ἱππότην στρέφοντα πῶλον
ἀστεροπῆς τε σέλας θεούσης.

b) Aeolice

ἴδεσθε· καῖνον πῦρ τόδ' Ὀλύμπικον,
τό γ' ἐξέλαμψε πρόσθε κὰτ Ἕλλαδα.
ἀλλ' ἀδέως δέκεσθ' ἄεθλα
Λονδινίω ποτάμω πὰρ ὄχθαις.

ὔμνητε δ' αἴγλαν ἀντιπάλων σόφων,
στρότος γὰρ ἦλθεν ἐκ περάτων χθόνος·
καὶ χρὴ μεγίσταισ' ᾧδ' ἄοιδον
ἀμφ' ἀρέταισι κὰτ ἄρμ' ἐλαύνην.

πλῆθος θεάταν μύριον ὄψεται
ὄρμαν δρομήων καὶ σταδίω χάριν,
σπούδαν τ' ἐρεσσόντων ἐταίρων
ἀκροβάταν τε δόκοις ματέντων.

θεάσεται δὲ χάρματι τοξόταν
τείνοντα νεύραν, καὶ σοφίας πέδα
τὸν ἴππόταν στρέφοντα πῶλον
ἀστερόπας τε σέλας θεοίσας.

---

[88] Lobel's authorship is confirmed by archival material at The Queen's College (Queen's College Archives, FB621).
[89] Source: Václav Pinkava, personal communication. The interview, with English subtitles, has been uploaded to Youtube by Křesadlo's son. See https://www.youtube.com/watch?v=bWm9Bfc9ZGA [September 2020].

πρέψουσι δ' αὐλοὶ καὶ τύπανον βρόμῳ τιμῆς φλεγούσης πολλὰ καθ' ἡμέραν· ὄχλος δ' ἀΰσει καλλίνικε 20 χρύσε' ἄεθλ' ἐσιδὼν φέροντας.	πρέψουσι δ' αὔλοι καὶ τύπανον βρόμωι, τίμας φλεγοίσας πολλὰ κὰτ ἀμέραν· ὄχλος δ' ἀΰσει καλλίνικε χρύσι' ἄεθλ' ἐσίδων φέροντας.
δεῦτ' αὖτε γῆν ἐς τήνδε περίρρυτον· ἄρχων γὰρ ἄγχι καὶ πρύτανις βαρύς. νίκη δ' ἀρίστοις αἰὲν ἔστω· νῦν κρότος, αἶψα δὲ τἆθλ' ἀγέσθω.	δεῦτ' αὖτε γᾶν ἐς τάνδε περίρρυτον, ἄρχων γὰρ ἄγχι καὶ πρότανις βάρυς. νίκα δ' ἀρίστοιο' αἰὲν ἔστω· νῦν κρότος, αἶψα δ' ἄεθλ' ἀγέσθω.

Textus: a) versio Attica: https://www.armand-dangour.com/wp-content/uploads/2012/09/Olympic-Ode-for-Press.pdf [accessed: September 2020]; b) versio Aeolica: textus mihi ab auctore ipso electronice missus est

Alcaic Greek Ode for the London Olympics

Behold this new Olympic fire, which has formerly shone in Greece. Receive with pleasure the Games at the shores of London's river.
[5] Sing the glory of skilled rivals, for their team came from the ends of the world. And the singer must drive his chariot around the greatest virtues.
A countless mass of spectators will see [10] the onrush and brilliant grace of the runners as well as the effort of the rowers and the acrobats balancing on beams.
They will observe with joy the archer drawing his bowstring and [15] the rider prudently guiding his horse with his foot and the brightness of the running bolt.
The pipes and the drum will sound loud and clear through the noise of glory burning often every day: The mass will yell hurrah [20] when they see the ones who have earned golden prizes.
Come to this country surrounded by water, for an important ruler and a magistrate is near. Victory shall be always for the best. Now, applause and let the games begin immediately.[90]

---

90 The author's own poetic translation into English: 'This new Olympic flame behold / that once burned bright in Greece of old; / with happy hearts receive once more / these Games revived on London's shore. / [5] Praise rival teams, in sport allied, / as athletes stream from far and wide; / the poet too must take the road / conveying praise to victory owed. / Millions of watchers will embrace / [10] the passion of each close-run race, / the efforts of the rowing teams / and gymnasts balancing on beams. / They will observe with rapt delight / the archer draw his bowstring tight, / [15] the skillful rider guide her horse, / and lightning bolt around the course. / The pipes will play, the drum resound, / as medallists are daily crowned; / the crowd's hurrah will reach the skies / [20] when victors hoist the golden prize. / Now welcome to this sea-girt land, / with London's Mayor and co. at hand. / Good luck to all who strive to win: / applaud, and let the Games begin!'

Metre: Alcaic stanzas.

Notes: This is the second of two Olympic Odes composed by D'Angour for the Olympic Games: the first for the Games held in Athens in 2004, and the second for those held in London in 2012. These odes continue a tradition which goes back to Robertson's Greek ode for the first Olympic Games in Athens in 1896 (see above). The ode written by D'Angour was performed for the first time by Boris Johnson, then Mayor of London, at the Opening Gala of London's Olympic Games at the Royal Opera House on 23 July 2012. D'Angour wrote two versions, the first in Aeolic[91] and the second – at the request of Johnson – in Attic dialect, for the performance at the Gala. D'Angour is said to have included in his text and translation some puns on the names of well-known athletes (e.g., l. 16 ἀστεροπῆς 'bolt' ~ Usain Bolt, l. 17 αὐλοί 'pipes' ~ Ben Pipes) and Johnson himself (l. 22 πρύτανις **βαρύς** ~ **Boris** Johnson).[92] Accompanied by the English translation, the Attic version was also engraved on a privately-sponsored plaque, which was installed near a bridge in London's Olympic Park.

Biography: Armand D'Angour, born in 1958, is a classical scholar and musician who works at the University of Oxford. He was educated at Eton College and at the University of Oxford, where he won both the Gaisford Prize for Greek Prose in 1981 and the Chancellor's Latin Verse Prize. In addition to his classical education, he studied cello in the Netherlands. Since 2000, he has been a Fellow in Classics at Jesus College, Oxford. His research covers various areas of Greek philology, but especially ancient Greek music, lyric, and philosophy. Next to his two Olympic Odes, D'Angour has also written a Greek continuation of Sappho's famous fr. 31 Voigt (Φαίνεταί μοι κῆνος) and composed music in the ancient Greek style for performances of Euripides' *Alcestis*. Other Greek, Latin, and English occasional poems are assembled on his personal homepage.

Bibliography: D'Angour, Armand, "Pindar at the Olympics: the Limits of Revivalism", in: Barbara Goff/Michael Simpson (eds.), *Thinking the Olympics. The Classical Tradition and the Modern Games*, Bristol 2011, 190–203; https://en.wikipedia.org/wiki/Armand_D%27Angour [accessed:

---

[91] I owe special thanks to the author for providing me the Aeolic version and answering further questions.
[92] Cf. Bulwer 2019, 285 and https://www.ox.ac.uk/news/2021-07-23-mayor-read-out-oxford-university-classicists-olympic-ode [accessed: December 2020].

August 2020]; https://www.armand-dangour.com (personal homepage) [accessed: August 2020]; Bulwer 2019, 285–287; Päll (forthcoming).

Ὕμνος πρὸς τὴν παρθένον Μαρίαν διὰ τὸ
τὸ ἔργον τετελῆσθαι.

Ἀθανάτων βασίλισσαν ἀείδομαι, ἠδὲ καὶ ἀνδρῶν,
Καὶ αὐτὴν σε θύγατρα θεῦ, καὶ μητέρ' ἐοῦσαν,
Κέρην τῆς ἄγνης, καὶ Ἰωακίμοιο μέγον τος,
ἁγνὴν δὲ ἄκοιτιν Ἰωσήφε ζαθέοιο,
Θαῦμα βροτοῖς, καὶ τοῖς θείοις μακάρεσσιν ὀλύμπε·
σεμνοτάτην πάντων, ἃς ἔβλεπε γαῖα, γυναικῶν
αἰδοίην, χρυσοστέφανον, καὶ ἱμερόεσαν·
χρυσόθρονον βασίλισσαν ἐν θεανῷ ἀστερόεντι,
εἶδεν τὴν ζωήν, καὶ μείλιχα δῶρα διδοῦσαν·
πότνιαν ἔντε βροτοῖσι, καὶ ἀθανάτοισι θεοῖσιν,
ἣν πάντες μάκαρες τίουσιν ὄλυμπον ἔχοντες,
ἥντε καλῶς μὲν ἀοιδοὶ ψάλλουσιν δὲ ἄνδρες
λαῷ ἐνὶ μάκαρι· φωνῇ δὲ πρὸς θεὸν ἄλλον
εὐχομένων θνητῶν, καὶ παρθένε ἔαν' ἐπέσχεν
ἠδ' ἣν χρίσῳ τὰς κείνων ἐφραδεν εὐχάς,
αἶψα συναιρομένη, καὶ μείλιχα δῶρα ἰοῦσα.

Τοὔνεκα μελπομένην μὲν ἀείσω παρθένον ἁγνὴν,
ἣν τόκε πελοιοτος (ἀγνὸς πρὶν) πεσσῶν αἶψα
ἐν χθονὶ Ἰδυμαίης κατὰ Ἰορδάνοιο ῥέεθρον·
ἠδὲ μὲν αἰδοίη παρὰ μητρὶ τιθεύετο Κόρη
τερπῇ, ἀγλαομόρφος, ἐρασμίη, ἀγλαόθυμος·
ἀλλ' ὅτε δὴ χρόνος εἶκε, περιπλομένων ἐνιαυτῶν,
μητρὸς ὑπὸ θερίσκης τριετὴς παιδίσκη ἐδόθη
τροφῇ ἱερεῖ θεοκωσομένη ἐπὶ ναὸν.
ἔνθα παρασκευαζομένη τ' εὐσχήμονα ἔργα,
τὴν σοφίαν τ' ἐδιδάχθη ἁπλῶς, ὥστε εὐσεβῆ ἤθη,

Filippomaria Pontani
Iberia

A commonplace in the study of Iberian humanism is that neither Spain nor Portugal ever witnessed a true Hellenic Renaissance, as compared with that of Italy, Germany or France: the reasons for this state of affairs have been detected in the geographical marginality of the Iberian peninsula, in the instability due to prolonged warfare, and above all in the 'integralism' of the Spanish intellectual elite, for whom classical culture represented less an object of study *per se* than a tool that was propaedeutic to an accomplished theological and philosophical instruction. The student of Greek and Latin was faced with a lower social prestige, a higher degree of exposure to the ecclesiastical Inquisition, and above all to a limited circulation and production of printed books in Greek.[1] Classical instruction continued to play a relatively limited role in Spanish academic and artistic culture through the 19th century: when in 1891 the University of Salamanca appointed the young Miguel de Unamuno to the chair of Greek, the writer Juan Valera famously joked: 'ninguno sabe griego' ('nobody knows Greek'), but 'hemos dado la cátedra al único que podrá saberlo' ('we have given the chair to the only person who could know it').[2]

Despite this discouraging panorama, since the early 16th century a number of Iberian scholars and *literati* did acquire a good knowledge of Greek, first through their studies in other European countries, then thanks to the establishment of various chairs of Greek language and literature in the Iberian peninsula. The first professor of Greek at Salamanca (1495–1523) was Aires Barbosa (†1540),[3] one of the Portuguese pupils of Angelo Poliziano in Florence (→ **Italy**)[4] and later

---

[1] See Fernández Galiano, Manuel (ed.) (1977), *Humanismo español en el siglo XIX*, Madrid, esp. 5–29 (José Antonio Pérez Rioja, "Ranz Romanillos, traductor de Isócrates y Plutarco") and 31–65 (Manuel Fernández Galiano, "Humanismo y literatura en el siglo XIX español").
[2] See Fernández Galiano, Manuel (1965–1966), "Unamuno helenista", in: *Estudios Clásicos* 9, 289–298 and 10, 219–221.
[3] de Pina Martins, José Vitorino (1986), "Sur la spécificité de l'humanisme portugais au XVIe siècle", in: *Romanistik in Geschichte und Gegenwart* 20, 316–337. Tavares de Pinho, Sebastião (1999), "Aires Barbosa, pedagogo e poeta", in: *Actas do I Congresso Internacional "Humanismo Novilatino e Pedagogia (Gramáticas, Criações Maiores e Teatro)"*, Braga, 131–148. Tavares de Pinho 1984, 88–91.
[4] Others were Caiado, Figueiredo, Teixeira: see Sánchez Tarrio, Ana Maria (ed.) (2015) (ed.), *Leitores dos Clásicos*, Lisboa.

https://doi.org/10.1515/9783110652758-013

a distinguished poet;[5] amongst his pupils was 'el Comendador Griego', namely Hernán Núñez de Guzmán, the owner of a remarkable library, and Barbosa's successor in the chair of Greek at Salamanca.[6]

Still, of the first generations of Iberian Hellenists very few scholars attained such a degree of familiarity with Greek as to be able to compose prose or verse: in the fifth volume of the Polyglot Bible printed at Alcalá de Henares in 1514, the three Spanish curators (Juan de Vergara, Bartolomeo de Castro, and Hernán Núñez de Guzmán) added one Latin epigram each, whereas only the Greek and the Italian editor (Demetrios Doukas and Vettor Fausto) were bold enough to write a short poem in Greek: Doukas, incidentally, had been appointed in 1513 as the first teacher of Greek at the Complutensian University.[7] Perhaps the earliest Greek epigram by an Iberian author to appear in print was the short tetrastichon by which the Portuguese Diogo Pires/Didacus Pyrrhus (1517–1599) mourned over Erasmus' death in 1536,[8] but Pires later moved to Dubrovnik, where he played a decisive role in Greek studies of the Balkan region (→ **Balkans**). Emigration also played an important role in the 16th century: one need just think of Juan de Verzosa (1523–1574), who probably learned Greek in Leuven and wrote a number of unpublished Greek epigrams,[9] or of such a good Hellenist as the Avilan **Pedro Núñez Vela** (†1580), who in the 1540s converted to Protestantism and moved to Switzerland, where he used Greek for his encomiastic epigrams and odes, including a long thanksgiving to the Senate of the city of Berne.

Portugal boasted a priority over Spain in the advancement of humanism.[10] In fact, Portuguese humanism, although it remained an overwhelmingly Latin phenomenon, had started early in the shadow of Poliziano and Erasmus, and the creation of the University of **Coimbra** had contributed an important international dimension to it.[11] However, the triumph of the Counter-Reformation and the

---

5 See Barbosa, Aires (2013), *Obra poética*, ed. Sebastião Tavares de Pinho/Walter de Medeiros, Lisboa: no Greek epigrams are recorded.

6 See de Andrés 1988, 59–73. Signes Codoñer, Juan/Codoñer Merino, Carmen/Domingo Malvadi, Arantxa (eds.) (2001), *Biblioteca y epistolario de Hernán Núñez de Guzmán (el Pinciano)*, Madrid.

7 He will remain there until 1518: see de Andrés 1988, 17–22, and → **Greece**.

8 First published in 1537, then in Erasmi Roterodami *Opera omnia* I, Lugduni Batavorum 1703, c. *********3v.

9 Leiden, Universiteitsbiblioteek, ms. VUL 103: Raf van Rooy is currently editing this material.

10 Gil 1981, 52–53.

11 de Pina Martins, José Vitorino (1973), *Humanismo e Erasmismo na cultura portuguesa do século XVI*, Lisboa; da Costa Ramalho, Américo (1998–2000), *Para a historia do humanismo em Portugal*, I–IV, Coimbra/Lisboa. See most recently Berbara, Maria/Enenkel, Karl A. (eds.) (2012),

establishment of the Jesuits, both in the Colégio das Artes at Coimbra (1555),[12] and then in the Colégio do Espíritu Santo at **Évora** (1557),[13] marked the turning-point of Portuguese humanism towards a looser engagement with classical antiquity. While until 1580 Greek epigrams, of religious, funerary, or encomiastic content, appeared frequently in the poetic collections stemming from the colleges of Coimbra and Évora (some of them penned by important intellectuals such as **Cipriano Soares**), after that date the very knowledge of Greek became more and more suspect to the Inquisition, and quickly faded away, only to be partially recovered in the late 18th century.

In Renaissance Spain, while Greek was taught in several universities (Alcalá, Salamanca, Valencia, Barcelona; the chairs at Valladolid and Zaragoza were short-lived experiments), the practice of Greek composition was not especially widespread: some university curricula did prescribe the exercice of translation from Latin into Greek, and the 1565 reform at Alcalá invited students that they 'compongan versos, diálogos o discursos por escrito o de viva voz'; but apparently the same students complained that Greek was not adequately taught as a living language, and neither their professors nor the Jesuit colleges that flourished in Spain over the decades (indeed, much less interested in Greek than their Portuguese counterparts) ever favoured this exercise.[14]

However, Greek versification proved particularly popular in Valencia, a city whose enthusiasm for Hellenic studies was precocious and remarkable:[15] the practice of writing in Greek (not only *pièces d'occasion*, but also religious poems) was initiated by two doctors in the 1540s, **Miguel de Ledesma** (†1547) and Pedro Jaime Esteve; it later influenced Ledesma's pupil Pedro Juan Núñez (perhaps Spain's most important philologist together with Francisco de Vergara),[16] as well as their successor Juan Lorenzo Palmireno (1514–1579), the author of an entire Greek dialogue and a Greek preface to his edition of Horapollo's *Hieroglyphica*.[17] It was no doubt this heritage, together with a great intellectual ambition and an

---

Portuguese Humanism and the Republic of Letters, Leiden/Boston. On Coimbra, see Tavares de Pinho 1984, 91–102.
12 Tavares de Pinho 1984, 102–109.
13 da Silva, Augusto (ed.) (2009), *A universidade jesuítica de Évora*, Evora; Soares da Cunha 1999 (see esp. José Lavajo, "As humánidades em Évora", pp. 43–75, and 483f.).
14 López Rueda 1973, 258–263, and 269–286 on the teaching of Greek in the Jesuit colleges.
15 García Martínez 1980; Pérez i Durà, Jordi/Estellés, José Maria (eds.) (1998), *Los humanistas valencianos y sus relaciones con Europa: de Vives a Mayans*, Valencia; Gil 1981, 56–57.
16 See Barbeito Díez, Pilar (2000), *Pedro Juan Núñez, humanista valenciano*, Valencia; Fernandez Galiano, Manuel (1980), *Dos discursos en griego de la Barcelona del siglo XVI*, Madrid.
17 López Rueda 1973, 128–130.

immense devotion to learning, that induced, some decades later, the Valencian scholar **Vicente Mariner** (†1642) to produce, together with a large amount of translations and Latin poems, hundreds of Greek epigrams dedicated to friends, patrons, saints, etc.: yet none of this ever made it to the press, and Mariner's achievements, admirable as they are even in their imperfection, were thus doomed to almost total oblivion.

The three splendid monographs that describe Greek studies in Spain from 1500 until 1800 show *ad abundantiam* the decadence of linguistic competence over the centuries:[18] after the frequent attacks of the Inquisition on professors of Greek in the late 16th century,[19] most Jesuit colleges did not offer a decent curriculum of Greek, and at public universities some of the recruited professors were of Greek descent rather than Spaniards (e.g., Constantino Sofía at Toledo, Diogenes Aramonero and Neophytos Rhodinos at Salamanca: they all wrote very modest Greek epigrams), and most could not boast any real knowledge of ancient Greek literary language: their teaching was thus confined to an elementary grammatical parsing with the help of Francisco de Vergara's handbook.[20] Exceptions such as Martín Miguel Navarro, an obscure deacon of the cathedral at Tarragona who wrote a Sapphic ode to the philhellene pope Urbanus VIII (→ **Italy**),[21] or such as **Gonzalo Correas** (1571–1631), whose own Greek verse is far from perfect and who lived in a city (Salamanca) where the printing of Greek characters had become an almost unsurmountable problem, only go to confirm the rule. Correas' Anacreontic for the birth of a royal *infante*, however, tells us that Greek poetry did find its place in public ceremonies and feasts promoted by the University of Salamanca.

Nor did Greek studies fare better in Spain during the course of the 18th century: Gregorio Mayans famously observed in 1767 that nobody knew Greek in Spain except **Manuel Martí** (1663–1737), another Valencian who spent a long time abroad, and who tried his hand at light Greek versification for private communication.[22] The outcome of the Greek studies carried out at Madrid's royal colleges and libraries was largely unsatisfactory, as can be gathered by simply

---

[18] López Rueda 1973 (403–406 on Greek composition); de Andrés 1988 (302–308 on Greek composition); Hernando 1975 (283–294 on Greek composition). A shorter synthesis in Gil Fernández, Luis (2008–2009), "La enseñanza universitaria del griego y su valorización social", in: *Res Publica Litterarum*, Suppl. Tradición clásica y universidad, Madrid, 1–22.
[19] The implicit idea was that *qui graecizabant, lutheranizabant*: see Gil 1981, 205–212.
[20] See López Rueda 1973, 233–265; de Andrés 1988, 21–180; Gil 1981, 213–215.
[21] It is preserved in Madrid, Biblioteca Nacional, ms. 6685, f. 252v–253r.
[22] See Gil, Luis (1995), "El griego en la educación de las élites españolas del siglo XVIII", in: *Bulletin Hispanique* 97, 279–298.

glancing at the poor quality of **José Rodríguez de Castro**'s (ca. 1739–1789) celebrated *Congratulatio* to King Charles III (1759); not to mention the sometimes embarrassing imitations, translations from Latin, and letters in Greek that blossomed throughout the country (Ignacio López de Ayala attempted an idyll in Theocritean style; Pedro Mercado translated into Greek the *Officium Beatae Virginis*; Juan de Cuenca translated in Greek Augustine's *Sermo de expositione fidei*; Francisco Antonio González de Torres translated excerpts from Luis de Granada's *Guia de pecadores*; several scholars wrote Greek epistles to Antonio Campomanes). The case of **Antonio Martínez de Quesada**'s (1718–1751) original hymn to the Virgin (penned at the end of a complex exegetical work on Hesiod's *Theogony*) remains isolated.

In fact, after decades of neglect it was only in the 1770s that chairs of Greek started to be re-established in Spanish universities: this new interest was made possible in part thanks to the ban on the Jesuits in 1767 (the only Jesuit college with a certain interest in Greek studies, that of **Villagarcía de Campos**, had been shaped by the wise reform of Francisco Javier Idiáquez in 1755–1762), and in part through the general re-organisation of the *Plan de Estudios* (1771) promoted by Antonio Campomanes – one of the fondest supporters of Greek in modern Spain – on behalf of King Charles III.[23] However, perhaps the most interesting results in the field of Greek versification were achieved by those Jesuits (e.g., **Manuel Lassala**, **Manuel Aponte**) who moved to Italy after the ban, and thus could interact with the local cultural and academic *milieu*.

Despite the slow recovery of academic teaching of Greek, the 19th century did not witness a new wave of the Hellenizing Muse. A Greek encomium for Queen María Cristina de Borbón written by Antonio Vera in 1832 (produced in the frame of such an important institution as Madrid's Real Academia Grecolatina) seems to follow the rules of modern rather than ancient metre, although the language – far from being poetically convincing – still largely adheres to ancient models.[24] And very little can be found in later decades (the 20th-century Portuguese professor **Francisco Rebelo Gonçalves** (1907–1982) is again the exception that confirms the rule): it is noteworthy that even in contemporary academia, now that the teaching of Greek occupies a firm place in Spanish universities,[25] the practice

---

[23] Hernando 1975, 17–32 and 85–100; Gil, Luis (1978), *Campomanes, un humanista en el poder*, Madrid. Gil 1981, 176–178 and 546–551.

[24] Hualde Pascual, Pilar (2005), "Un poema griego inédito en honor de la Reina María Cristina de Borbón, encontrado en la Real Academia de la Historia", in: *Boletín de la Real Academia de la historia* 202, 281–306.

[25] Lasso de la Vega y Sánchez, José (ed.) (1992), *La enseñanza de las lenguas clásicas*, Madrid.

of writing Greek epigrams appears to be exceedingly rare – as opposed to what happened and happens in other countries, and as opposed to what happened in Spain with Latin versification. Throughout the central decades of the 20th century Latin verse of all kinds (but not a single Greek piece) found its natural venue on the pages of the famous periodical *Palaestra Latina* – a publication not devoid of influences from the Catholic Church, and partly resonating with the conservative ideological overtones that accompanied the dark years of Franco's regime.

General Bibliography

DBE = *Diccionario Biográfico Español*, Madrid 2009–2013.
de Andrés, Enriqueta (1988), *Helenistas españoles del siglo XVII*, Madrid.
García Martínez, Sebastián (1980), "Sobre la introducción del helenismo en la Universidad de Valencia durante la primera mitad del Quinientos", in: *Actes du premier Colloque sur le pays valencien à l'époque moderne*, Pau, 383–397.
Gil, Luis (1981), *Panorama social del humanismo español*, Madrid.
Hernando, Concepción (1975), *Helenismo e Ilustración (el griego en el siglo XVIII español)*, Madrid.
López Rueda, José (1973), *Helenistas españoles del siglo XVI*, Madrid.
Soares da Cunha, Mafalda (ed.) (1999), *Do mundo antigo aos novos mundos: humanismo, classicismo e notícias dos descobrimentos em Évora*, Lisboa.
Tavares de Pinho, Sebastião (1984), "Les études de grec à l'Université de Coimbra", in: *L'Humanisme Portugais et l'Europe. Actes du XXIe Colloque International d'Études Humanistes*, Paris, 87–109 (transl. and revised in Id. (2006), *Humanismo em Portugal* II, Lisboa, 297–322).

Miguel de Ledesma (†1547)

Cento Homericus de Christi passione [1545]

(excerptum, vv. 36–60)

36 Αἶψα κακῷ τούτων πάντων ταῦτ᾽ ἥνδανε θυμῷ,
 Χριστὸν ἀποκτείνειν, δοῦναι καὶ δῶρα Ἰούδᾳ
 ἄγλαα· κ᾽εὐθὺς Ἰουδαίους ζώννυσθαι ἄνωγαν
 παμπόλλους ἐπὶ νυκτί, ἐδύσσατο νώροπα χαλκὸν
40 ὅστις ἰὼν λόγχην τε φέρων καὶ φάσγανον ὀξύ.
 λαμπάδες ἐν τούτοις πολλαί, πολλοί τε κεν ἴπνοι
 φαῖνον, καὶ αἰχμαὶ λάμπον, κράτων τρυφαλεῖαι
 πόρρωθεν, κέλαδός τε ποδῶν ἠκούετο πουλύς.
 Αὐτὰρ ἐπεὶ κόσμηθεν σύν θ᾽ ἱερεῦσι ἕκαστοι,
45 ἐξέσσυντο πυλῶν, τῶν ἡγεμόνευε Ἰούδας,
 καὶ δαίμων τούτων πυμάτας ὤτρυνε φάλαγγας.
 Τοῖσι τρὶς Σωτὴρ μέγα εὔχετο χεῖρας ἀνασχών·
 νόσφιν ἀγωνίζων φάσκεν πατρὶ ἶφι μέδοντι·
 "Ὦ πάτερ οὐρανόθεν μεδέων κύδιστε μέγιστε,
50 τοῦτον τὸν θάνατον λυγρὸν δέπας ἆρ᾽ ἀπ᾽ ἐμεῖο,
 εἰ δρᾶσθαι δύναται. Ἀλλ᾽ οὐκ ἐμὰ ῥήματ᾽ ἀκούσῃς,
 ἀλλ᾽ ἄγε ὅττ᾽ ἐθέλησθα, καὶ ὡς τετελεσμένον ἔστω.
 Βούλομ᾽ ἀποθνήσκειν, λυτρεύσω πταῖσμα γονῆος
 οὐλόμενον, τὸ θνητοῖς ἄλγεα μυρί᾽ ἔθηκεν,
55 πολλάς τ᾽ ἰφθίμους ψυχὰς ποτὶ τάρταρα πέμψεν."
 Ὣς ἔφατ᾽ εὐχόμενος Χριστὸς τρίς, τρὶς δ᾽ ἐκίχανεν
 εὕδοντας γ᾽ ἑτάρους, περὶ δ᾽ ἀμβρόσιος κέχυθ᾽ ὕπνος.
 Στὰς δὲ ὑπὲρ κεφαλῆς Πέτρον πρὸς μῦθον ἔειπε·
 "Καρτερόθυμε Σίμων, εὕδεις; ἐνταῦθά μοι εἰπὲ
60 πῶς μὴ ἀγρυπνεῖν μετ᾽ ἐμοῦ ὥραν μίαν ἔσχες;"

Textus: *Graecarum Institutionum compendium* a Michaële Hieronymo Ledesma Valentino medico conscriptum, Valentiae, excudebat Ioannes Mey, 1545, cc. 94r–100r (95r).

Crit.: 36 ταῦθ᾽ ἥνδανε debuit || **38** ἀγλαὰ debuit || **40** an φέροι? || **41** ἱπνοί debuit || **42** τρυφάλειαι debuit || **43** κελαδός: correxi || **50** θάναθον et mox ἆρ᾽: correxi || **52** ὣς debuit | ἔστω: correxi || **53** λιτρεύσω: correxi (sed potius λυτρώσω debuit) || **55** ἰφθύμους: correxi || **57** εὐδοντάς debuit | ὕμνος: correxi

Sim.: de historia cf. NT, *Matth.* 26.2-4, 39-40, 47-48 || **36** ἥνδανε θυμῷ] *Il.* 1.24 etc. || **37** Χριστὸν ἀποκτείνειν] idem Nonn. *Par. Jo.* 5.66 || **38** ἄγλαα] cf. *Il.* 1.213 etc. | ζώννυσθαι ἄνωγαν] *Il.* 11.15 || **39** ἐδύσσατο νώροπα χαλκόν] *Il.* 2.578, 11.16 || **40** φάσγανον ὀξύ] cf. *Il.* 22.306 al., praes. *Od.* 10.145 || **41** ἴπνοι] cf. Arist. *Pax* 841 || **42** αἰχμαὶ λάμπον] cf. *Il.* 6.319, 8.494 | κράτων] de forma cf. *Od.* 22.309 | τρυφαλεῖαι] cf. *Il.* 10.76 etc. || **44** cf. *Il.* 3.1 || **45** ἐξέσσυντο πυλῶν] cf. *Il.* 7.1 || **46** πυμάτας ὤτρυνε φάλαγγας] *Il.* 4.254 || **47** μέγα εὔχετο χεῖρας ἀνασχών] cf. *Il.* 1.450 et 3.275 || **48** ἶφι μέδοντι] sim. *Il.* 1.38 al. (ἶφι ἀνάσσεις) || **49** cf. *Il.* 3.276, 320, 7.202, 24.308 || **52** sim. *Od.* 14.54 (ὅττι μάλιστ' ἐθέλεις, de Iove); ἐθέλησθα saepius apud Hom. (*Il.* 1.554 etc.) | καὶ — ἔστω] cf. *Il.* 9.310 || **54–55** *Il.* 1.2–3 || **56** cf. *Il.* 1.43 et saepius || **56–58** ἐκίχανεν — κεφαλῆς] cf. *Il.* 2.18–20 || **58–59** cf. *Il.* 2.59–60 (et 23.68–69, 24.682–683) | καρτερόθυμε] *Il.* 5.277

Homeric cento on the Passion of Christ

(excerpt, ll. 36–60)

[36] Immediately the evil spirit of them all took this decision:
to kill Christ and to offer splendid presents
to Judas. And straight away they ordered masses of Jews
to gird up their loins in the night: all those walking
[40] with a spear and a sharp sword wore flashing bronze.
Amid them many lanterns and many torches were shining,
and the spearheads glittered from afar, and so did helmets
on the heads, and a great noise of walking feet was heard.
Then after everyone got ready, they came out of the doors
[45] together with the priests, under the guide of Judas,
while the devil was stirring up their rearguard.
Thrice did the Saviour pray loudly for them raising his hands:
moving to another place he argued and said to the Father, the powerful ruler:
  'O greatest and noblest Father, ruler of the sky,
[50] push away from me this sad cup of death,
if that can be done. But no, do not listen to my words,
and do whatever you wish, and thus may it be done.
I want to die, I shall redeem the accursed fault of the forefather,
which brought about many evils for the mortals,
[55] and sent many valiant souls to the Underworld.'
So spoke Christ in his three prayers, and thrice did he find
his disciples asleep: divine sleep was poured upon them.
He approached Peter's head and said to him:
'O strong-hearted Simon, are you sleeping? Tell me now,
[60] why didn't you find one hour to stay awake with me?'

Metre: Hexameters. Greek prosody earned a place in Ledesma's *Compendium*, hence in his Greek poetry mistakes are not frequent (see however the app. crit.), aside from some ugly hiatuses (ll. 37, 39, 44, 48, 58, 60); metre often follows the Homeric prototype, and bipartite hexameters are rare (ll. 44, 54).

Notes: Introduced by a polemical epigram against a certain Zoilus (Honorato Juan, a former pupil of Juan Luis Vives), in which Ledesma appeals to Galen in order to defend his activity as both a doctor and a Hellenist, the *Compendium* is rounded off by two original Greek pieces, called *exercitamenta*. One is a prose oration in which the letter *tau* responds to the letter *sigma* (modelled on Lucian's dialogue *Lis consonantium*); the other is our *Cento Homericus de Christi Passione* (*inc.* Ζωοτόκον θάνατον Χριστοῦ πολυτλήμονος, *expl.* ἐπὶ δὲ στενάχοντο γυναῖκες), not exactly a cento in the narrow sense of the term, but a poem in 323 hexameters that freely reworks and combines lines and hemistichs from archaic Greek epic. This poem enjoyed wide popularity in learned Spain: it was even translated into Latin, together with other classical texts, by Vicente Mariner. In our excerpt (an amplification of the episode described in NT, *Matth.* 26), at least one passage displays not only the adoption of Homeric language and style, but also a skilful attention for the context of the prototype: ll. 56–60 are an overt allusion to Agamemnon's dream in *Iliad* 2. While there is no clear trace that Ledesma had read the *Christus patiens* (a Byzantine cento on the passion of Christ from Euripides and other tragedians), l. 37 is one of the few but relevant clues pointing to Ledesma's knowledge of Nonnus' hexametrical version of the Passion of Christ in book 19 of the *Paraphrase of the Gospel according to St John*. It can also be argued that in other parts of his *Cento* Ledesma imitated Politian's epigram IX on the *Pater Noster* (→ **Italy**).

Biography: Miguel Jerónimo de Ledesma († Valencia 1547) studied medicine and ancient Greek at the University of Alcalà, and in his capacity as a physician was a renowned supporter of the Galenic method: together with the other doctor Pedro Jaime Esteve, he also became the most accomplished teacher of Greek in Valencia, one of the most important centres of Spanish Hellenism from the 16th through the 19th century (from Oliver to Palmireno, from Mariner to Manuel Martí and Lassala). In Valencia, Ledesma taught Greek language and medicine from 1531 until his death in 1547, training pupils such as the important humanist Pedro Juan Núñez, and composing a *Compendium* of Greek grammar that declaredly aimed to improve on the *De Graecae linguae grammatica* of his former teacher Francisco de Vergara (1537), and even on Guillaume Budé's *Commentarii linguae Graecae*.

Bibliography: López Rueda 1973, 123–125, 147–153 and 339; García Martínez 1980; Báguena Cervellera, Maria José (2012), in: *DBE* 29, 316f.

Anonymous from Évora

In Olyss(iponam) [1554]

Ὅπλοις καὶ πλούτῳ ταύτῃ ἐστὶ περίβωτος
   ἡ πόλις, ἀνθρώποις κληζομένη μαχίμοις,
οἴκων ἀγλαΐῃ καὶ πύργοις καὶ πολυόλβῳ
   κλεινὴ ὠκεανῷ καὶ ποταμῷ πλατέϊ.
5 νῆας ἔχει μεγέθει θαυμαστὰς καὶ τῷ ἀριθμῷ,
   ἃς καλὸς τηρεῖ κυδάλιμός τε λιμήν.
ταῦτα χρόνος τήκει· ἀρετὴ οὖν σοῦ βασιλῆος
   πλείω καὶ μείζω σοι γέρα δῆτα πόρεν.

Textus: ms. Évora, Biblioteca Pública CXIII/1-10, f. 15v.

Crit.: Tit. *Olyss.*, supplevi || 4 ὠκεάνῳ, correxi || 7 σου, correxi || 8 πόρεν: δίδοι a.c.

Sim.: 1–2 περίβωτος...κληζομένη] cf. *Anth. Pal.* 9.62.1–2 (de Ilio) || **4** ποταμῷ πλατέϊ] cf. *Anth. Pal.* 9.147.4 || **6** καλὸς...λιμήν] cf. *Od.* 6.263 (de Ithaca) || **7** χρόνος τήκει...γέρα πόρεν] cf. *Anth. Pal.* 9.704.1–4

On Lisbon

This city is well-known for its weapons and its wealth,
   celebrated for its warlike men,
it is famous for its splendid houses and towers,
   for the wealthy ocean and the large river.
[5] It has ships remarkable in size and number,
   which are kept in a good and renowned harbour.
But all this is consumed by time: hence no doubt the virtue of your king
   brings you more numerous and more considerable gifts.

Metre: Elegiac couplets. Prosody and metre are generally sound, with the exception of l. 1 where ἐστὶν should be read instead of ἐστί; there are minor vagaries in the handling of hiatus (l. 4) and of *correptio attica* (see ll. 1, 3, 5 vs. l. 7).

Notes: After Coimbra, Évora was one of the most important centres of learning in 16th-century Portugal: Diogo Pires was born there in 1517; the humanist Nicolas Clénard (†1542) once reported that he had found in the city many people fluent in both Latin and Greek; the College of the Jesuits, founded in 1559, was particularly active; some Greek epigrams honouring the visit of Cardinal Michele Bonelli ('Alexandrinus') at Évora in 1571 are preserved in the poetic miscellany ms. Évora,

Bibl. Publ. CVIII/2-7, ff. 9–15. Ms. CXIII/1-10 also preserves a collection of miscellaneous poems by members of the College, mostly in Latin. The date 1554 occurs on f. 13v, and it must refer at least to the epigrams of this section, some of which celebrate King John III (the βασιλεύς mentioned here in l. 7) and his brother Luís de Portugal as still being alive – the latter died in 1555 (see below). The quality of the Greek pieces in this manuscript is uneven, and mainly modest: in our epigram, which might well be an autograph (no indication of authorship is preserved in the whole section), the poetic style is marred by incorrect forms (l. 1 ταύτη for αὕτη), superfluous adverbs (l. 8 δῆτα) and a general tone of prose (esp. l. 5). Still, the author displays some familiarity with the epigrams of the *Greek Anthology* on cities; the praise of Lisbon is based on its most obvious natural and anthropic features.

Bibliography: da Silva, Augusto (2009) (ed.), *A universidade jesuítica de Évora (1559–1759)*, Évora (esp. the article by Maria do Céu Fonseca, pp. 137–156); Soares da Cunha 1999, 483f.

Cipriano Soares (1524–1593)

I. *Ep. Principis Lodoici* [1555]

Πῶς μέγας ἐν μικρῷ τούτῳ τύμβῳ κατάκειται,
εὐνομίης σοφίας εὐσεβίης τε φάος;
σῶμα μὲν ἐν τύμβῳ μικρῷ μικρὸν κατάκειται·
οὐδὲν θαυμαστόν, ὦ παροδῖτα, βλέπεις.
5 ἡ ψυχὴ πλούτου μέτοχος καὶ φωτὸς ἀληθοῦς,
ἣν ποθέεσκε πάλαι, τάξιν ἔχει μακάρων.

II. *Epita. Prin. Lodoici* [1555]

Λυσιάδης τὸ γένος, Λοδόϊκος δ' οὔνομα, θείαις
φεῦ ἀρεταῖς ἥρως ἄξιος αἶ πατέρων,
ἐν βαιῷ κεῖται σηκῷ, μέγα χάρμα δικαίως
τῆς γαίης πάσης, ἀλλὰ μάλιστα πάτρας.
5 ὁ ψυχῆς πλοῦτον ζητῶν μόνον, ἔξοχ' ἄριστος,
ὁ σκοτινοῦ κόσμου δεύτερος ἀέλιος,
αἶ αἶ σκηπτούχου βασιλῆος παῖς καὶ ἀδελφὸς
κεῖται, τῆς σοφίας εὐσεβίας τε φάος.
μὴ σύγκρινε μέγαν βαιῷ σηκῷ, φίλε ξεῖνε·
10 ἐν γαίῃ πλοῦτον μηδὲ θανὼν ἀγαπᾷ.

Textus: Lisboa, Biblioteca Nacional, ms. 3308, pp. 31–32.

Crit.: II.10 θανῶν ms., correxi

Sim.: I.1 μικρῷ...κατάκειται] cf. e.g. *Anth. Pal.* 16.21.3 || **2** εὐσεβίης φάος] cf. Nonn. *Par. Jo.* 4.246, sed prob. hic formulas Latinas ("lux sapientiae et pietatis" vel sim.) resp. || **4** οὐδὲν θαυμαστόν] praeter multa loca scriptorum cf. e.g. Thgn. 1.25 | ὦ παροδῖτα] cf. *Anth. Pal.* 7.198.1 (item de tumulo parvo) || **5** φωτὸς ἀληθοῦς] scil. Dei, cf. NT, *Jo.* 1.9; de πλοῦτος ἀληθής item saepius apud Patres Christianos (vide tamen etiam *Anth. Pal.* 10.41.1) || **6** τάξιν ἔχει μακάρων] cf. epitaphium Platonis, *Anth. Pal.* 7.61.2 et 16.31.2
II.1 cf. *Anth. Pal.* 9.63.1 (Λύδη καὶ γένος εἰμὶ καὶ οὔνομα) || **3** βαιῷ] cf. *Anth. Pal.* 7.2b.1 | μέγα χάρμα] cf. *Il.* 24.706 || **5** ψυχῆς πλοῦτον] cf. supra I.5, praes. *Anth. Pal.* 10.41.1 | ἔξοχ᾽ ἄριστος] cf. *Il.* 9.638 || **6** δεύτερος ἀέλιος] cf. *Anth. Pal.* 7.6.2 et 9.422.6 || **7** σκηπτούχου βασιλῆος] cf. *Il.* 1.279, 2.86 etc.

Epitaph of Prince Luís

Why does a great man rest in such a small grave,
   the light of good government, wisdom, and piety?
His small body rests in a small grave:
   you are not seeing anything strange, o passer-by.
[5] But his soul, which partakes of true wealth and light,
   has its long-desired place among the blessed.

Epitaph of Prince Luís

A Lusiad by birth, Lodovicus by name, lo!, a hero
   worthy of his forefathers thanks to his divine virtues,
this man now lies in a small tumulus, despite having been a great joy
   for the entire earth, but above all for his fatherland.
[5] He who only sought the soul's riches, by far the greatest,
   the second sun of the gloomy universe,
lo! lo! the child and brother of a sceptre-bearing king,
   lies here, the light of wisdom and piety.
Do not compare, dear stranger, the great man with his small grave:
[10]   even after his death he still does not love earthly riches.

Metre: Elegiac couplets. Soares' familiarity with Greek prosody and metre is shown by the fact that both epigrams are virtually flawless, if we overlook the incorrect itacistic form σκοτινός for σκοτεινός in II.6, and the prosodical consideration (also sporadically attested in Greek and Latin versification) of ξ as a simple rather than a double consonant (II.9 ξεῖνε).

Notes: This poem belongs to a collection produced in the Colégio das Artes of Coimbra (founded in 1547, since 1555 run by the Jesuits), arguably the most important centre of Jesuit humanistic learning after the College in Rome. While initially placed under the shadow of Erasmian doctrine, the Colégio awarded a small but not insignificant place to the study of Greek (other institutions in Coimbra might have done the same, even if one should not trust the legend that in the Monastery of Santa Cruz, Latin and Greek were spoken fluently by all students). The two bulky mss. Lisboa, Biblioteca Nacional 3308 and Coimbra, Bibl. Univ. 993 represent tomes I (1555–1572) and II (1572–1579) of a collection *Rerum scholasticarum quae a patribus ac fratribus huius Conimbricensis Collegii scriptae sunt*: within this vast poetical output (chiefly in Latin, more rarely in Portuguese), the encomiastic and religious elements are of course dominant.

Our two pieces belong to a section of nine epitaphs marked as *a P. Cypriano*, which clearly points to Soares' authorship (autography cannot be ruled out). The epigrams mourn the death of the duke of Beja Luís de Portugal (1506–1555), the son of King Manuel I and the brother of King John III: renowned for his intellectual qualities and military skills, this prince took part in the conquest of Tunis (1535). The epitaphs revolve around the rather trivial *topos* of the contrast between the importance of the dead person and the modesty of his burial: they are inspired by an attentive reading of the *Greek Anthology*, and this might also explain a certain irregularity in their dialectal features (e.g., εὐνομίης σοφίας in I.2 and elsewhere).

Biography: Cipriano Soares (Ocaña 1524 – Plasencia 1593), a Spaniard by birth, was active in Portugal as a professor of rhetoric at the Colégio das Artes of Coimbra, where he achieved great fame and popularity: his three books *De arte rhetorica* (1562), which mainly elaborate on the doctrines of Aristotle, Cicero, and Quintilian, became the standard syllabus for students of Jesuit colleges in Europe until the end of the 18th century (it was openly recommended in the 1599 *Ratio studiorum*).

Bibliography: Flynn, Lawrence J. (1956), "The De arte rhetorica of Cyprian Soarez S.J.", in: *Quarterly Journal of Speech* 42, 367–374; Lavajo, José (1999), "As humanidades em Évora", in: Soares da Cunha 1999, 43–75 (esp. 63–65); Fernandes Pereira, Belmiro (2005), *Retórica e eloquencia em Portugal na época do Rinascimento*, Coimbra, 550–584; Tavares de Pinho, Sebastião (2006), "Literatura humanística inédita do Colégio das Artes da Universidade de Coimbra no século XVI", in: Id., *Humanismo en Portugal. Estudos II*, Lisboa, 323–344.

Pedro Núñez Vela (†1580)

Περὶ τῆς συγκλήτου τῆς Βερναίης [1570]

(excerptum, vv. 113–139)

    Αὕτη ἐλευθέριος δύναται βουλὴ καλέεσθαι·
    καὶ γὰρ καδδύναμιν ἀνθρώποις αἰὲν ἀρήγει
115 τερπομένη μοῦνον μελλούσης ἐλπίδι τέχνης,
    οὐδέ τινος καρποῦ παρεόντος τυγχάνει ἄλλου.
    Πάντα τὰ σὰ Χριστῷ γε μέλοι, σύγκλητε μεγίστη,
    τὸν δὲ τεὸν πλοῦτον Θεὸς ἄβροτος αἰὲν ἀέξοι.
    οὐ γὰρ ὑπαὶ γαίης, ὡς πολλοί, κτήματα κεύθεις
120 ἀλλά νυ δευομένοις χαίρεις διὰ δῶρα νέμουσα,
    καὶ δ' ἐξωτερικοῖς ἀνθρώποις, θαῦμα πυθέσθαι.
    Παῦρα πρὸς ἀλλοτρίους ἐστ' εὖ διακείμενα ἔθνη·
    ἔθνεα πάντα φιλεῖς κραδίῃ, σύγκλητε μεγίστη,
    ἀσπάζῃ τε φίλως, δύνασαί γ' ὅτε ἐλπίδι χαίρειν
125 τοῦ κεν τὸν κρατερὸν ποτὲ δοξασθῆναι ἄνακτα.
    Ἀλλοτρίους ἀγαπᾷς, ὧν εἷς ἐγὼ ἐνθάδε ναίω,
    τὸν σύ γε πολλὰ φιλεῖς καὶ φέρβεις κηρόφιν αἰεὶ
    ἶσον γιγνομένοις ἐν τῇ σέο πατρίδι γαίῃ.
    Τῆς ἕνεκα χάριτος πειρήσομαι ἠδὲ πονήσω
130 καδδύναμιν χάριτας ἀγαθὰς γλυκεράς τ' ἀποδοῦναι
    καί τοι πείθεσθαι νύκτας τε καὶ ἤματα πάντα.
    Καὶ γὰρ ὅταν σὺ θέλῃς με διδάσκειν Ἑλλάδα φωνὴν
    τούσδε νέους, περὶ τοῦτο τρόπον κατὰ πάντα πονήσω,
    πάντα τε κινήσω λίθον ἱέμενός τοι ἀρέσσαι,
135 καὶ Θεοῦ ἡμετέρου ζωῆς μοι δῶρα διδόντος
    γλώττῃ Ῥωμαίῃ τε καὶ Ἑλλάδι κάλλος ἀείδειν
    σῆς ἀρετῆς, ἰδὲ σῶν προγόνων πάνυ τίμια ἔργα
    εἰρήνης κατὰ καιρὸν ἰδὲ πτολέμοιο κακοῖο
    τείνων νεῦρα πάνυ πειρήσομαι, αἴ κε τύχοιμι.

Textus: Petri Nunii Velii Abulensis *Dialecticae Libri tres*...Eiusdem *Poematiorum Graecorum Liber unus*, cum Latina eorum ad verbum interpretatione e regione posita, Basileae: apud Petrum Pernam 1570, 198

Crit.: 115 μαλλούσης, correxi || **118** τεὸν scripsi (cf. "tuas divitias" in transl. Latina): θεόν | ἄμβροτος possis || **122** ἔθνην, correxi || **124** ὅτε: ὅτι possis

Sim.: 114 (et 130) καδδύναμιν] ex Hes. *Op*. 336, ubi codd. plerique et edd. κὰδ δύναμιν || **121** sim. *Il*. 5.725 et saepius (θαῦμα ἰδέσθαι) || **126** ἐνθάδε ναίω] cf. fort. Nonn. *Dion*. 26.22, vel potius formulam Homeri ἐνθάδε ναιετάειν (cf. *Od*. 6.245 al.) || **127** κηρόφιν] ex Hsch. κ 2558 (ubi explicatur ἐκ τῆς ψυχῆς) || **131** sim. νύκτας τε καὶ ἤματα (*Il*. 18.340 etc.) et ἤματα πάντα in clausula (*Il*. 8.539

et saepius) || **132** Ἑλλάδα φωνήν] cf. *Anth. Pal.* 9.451.4 || **134** πάντα...λίθον] proverbium, e.g. Zenob. 5.63 L.-S., *Anth. Pal.* 5.40.5 al. || **138** cf. *Il.* 1.284 al. (πολέμοιο κακοῖο) || **139** cf. *Il.* 5.279 (πειρήσομαι αἴ κε τύχωμι)

On the Senate of Berne

(excerpt, ll. 113–139)

> This Parliament can be called liberal,
> for it always helps the people as much as it can
> [115] and it rejoices only in the hope of future progress,
> without looking for any other gain at present.
> May all your decisions be dear to Christ, o highest Senate,
> and may the immortal God always increase your wealth.
> For you do not conceal riches under the earth, like many others,
> [120] but you rejoice in distributing gifts to the people in need
> and (wonderful to know) even to foreign people.
> Few nations are well disposed towards foreigners:
> you love in your heart all nations, o highest Senate,
> and you welcome them willingly, since you can rejoice in the hope
> [125] that the mighty Lord will be thus glorified.
> You love foreigners, and I am one of them, I who live here
> cherished by your love and always nourished from your heart
> in the same way as those who were born in your homeland.
> Because of this favour I shall try and seek
> [130] to reciprocate with good and sweet gratitude as best I can
> and to obey you for all days and all nights.
> And if you ask me to teach the Greek language
> to these youths, I shall do everything I can in this respect,
> and I shall go to any length to comply with your request,
> [135] and if our God gives me the gift of life,
> I shall strain every nerve and attempt, in case I may succeed,
> to sing in Latin and Greek the beauty of your virtue,
> and the much honoured deeds of your ancestors
> both in times of peace and of evil war.

Metre: Hexameters. Núñez Vela's versification is virtually flawless, with only one bipartite hexameter (l. 134) and slightly problematic metrical lengthenings of ἕνεκα in l. 129 (ἕνεκεν would solve the matter) and πάνυ in l. 139.

Notes: The prefatory letter to the three books of Vela's *Dialectica* (to which the Latin and Greek *poëmatia* serve as an appendix in the first edition of 1570, though not in the second one of 1578), expresses the author's thanks for the hospitality and the favour he has enjoyed in Switzerland. The long hexametrical poem on

Berne's Senate thus becomes a praise of this institution, which is presented as a model of effectiveness, democracy, and political intelligence. Vela's Greek versification – which he otherwise uses for encomiastic pieces – is generally adequate, though absolutely unpoetic (with some imperfections, see e.g. the misplaced δέ in l. 121 and σέο in l. 128) and with few unequivocal reminiscences of ancient poetic diction; in this frame, the erudite recovery of a term attested only in Hesychius' lexicon stands out (l. 127).

Biography: Not much is known about Pedro Núñez Vela (ca. 1500 – Lausanne 1580): a member of an illustrious family from Ávila, he fled from Iberia after his conversion to Protestantism, and his travels took him to Padua (where he came into contact with the local Aristotelian tradition), Rome, Geneva, and other European cities. A Ramist philosopher and a learned Hellenist, he finally settled down in Lausanne, where the Senate of Berne (since 1536 one of the largest city-states in Europe) granted him a pension and then a professorship of Greek, which he held from 1567 until his death.

Bibliography: Boehmer, Edward (1883), *Spanish Reformers of two Centuries from 1520*, II, Strassburg/London, 145–162; Bécares Botas, Vicente (2006), "Pedro Núnez Vela, helenista y heterodoxo", in: *Silva* 5, 7–19; Ceccarelli, Andrea (2015), "Un inedito commento rinascimentale a Lucrezio", in: *Giornale critico della filosofia italiana* 2, 233–263.

Anonymous from Coimbra (Nicolau Pimenta?)

Σεβαστιανῷ βασιλεῖ τρίκωλος τετράστροφος [1577–78]

```
       Ὕδωρ ἄριστον μὲν πέλεται· ὁ δὲ
       πῦρ ἠΰτε χρυσὸς νυκτὶ διαπρέπει
             καὶ χρυσοκολλήτοισι λάμπει
4                ἥλιος ἐμβεβαὼς δίφροισιν.
       Εἰ δ' ἄνδρα θεῖον νῦν φίλον ἔλδεαι,
       ὦ ἦτορ, ὑμνεῖν, εἰ μέγα γαρύεν
             ἐσθλὸν μελιφθόγγοισι Μούσαις
8                καὶ μεγάλου βασιλῆα κόσμου,
       κλεινὴν Σεβαστοῦ αὐδάσομεν βίαν
       πύλας τε ὕμνων τῷδε ἀνοίξομεν
             ὃς χειρὶ πόλλ' ἔσχ' ἀμφέπει τε
12               σκᾶπτα μενεπτολέμων ἀνάκτων,
       ὃς σὺν τυράννοις ἔθνεα βαρβάροις
       δεινοῖσιν ὅπλοις ἐκπολεμήσατο
             αἴας τε χώρας, ἐσχάτου τε
```

16	εὐρέας ὠκεανοῖο κόλπους.
	Αὐτὰρ τίς ὕμνων δαιδαλόεν κλέος
	κλυταῖσι θυμοῦ ἡδύνατο πτυχαῖς,
	ἴσον τίς αὐδᾶν ἀστέρεσσι
20	πῦρ σθένε τᾶν ἀρετᾶν φαεινόν;
	Μήτηρ ἐπειδή μιν τέκε νήπιον,
	μήτηρ τὸ κλεινὸν τοῦ μεγαλήτορος
	Κάρλοιο τέκνον, κ' ἐστάλαξεν
24	εἰς χέλεα βρέφεος τὸ νέκταρ,
	ἐξ οὐρανοῖο ἐς χθόνα αὐτίκα
	αὐτὰς θεοῦ πέμψαντος ἀπήλυθον,
	δέξαντο χερσὶν ἀμβροτοισιν
28	ἀσπασίως Ἀρεταὶ φύοντα,
	καὶ κρατὶ εὔτυκτον στεφάνην τότε
	καλὴν ἔθηκαν, στήθεσιν ἀμφὶ δὲ
	δειρῇ τε ὅρμοις χρυσέοισι
32	κόσμεον. Αὐτὰρ ἐπειδὴ αὐταὶ
	κόσμον τεθήκασιν περὶ τῷ χροΐ,
	δῖον λαβοῦσαι αἱ Χάριτες βρέφος
	ξανθοῖσι καὶ παμπορφύροισιν
36	ἄνθεσιν ἐνδυκέως ἔθρεψαν.
	Καὶ μὴν ἀγάλλει καὶ μεγαλοπρεπῶς
	θείοισι δώροις αὐτὸν ἀμείβετο
	καὶ πάντ' ἀκούει θ' ἕσπερος †τάη
40	ἡ ῥοδοδάκτυλος ὄπτετ' ἠώς.

Textus: Coimbra, Biblioteca Geral da Universidade, ms. 993, f. 145r/v.

Crit.: 13 τυραννοῖς ms. ‖ 16 ὠκεανοῖο ms. ‖ 17, 19 τις ms. ‖ 21–22 μητὴρ (bis) ms. ‖ 23 Καρλοῖο ms. ‖ 25 οὐρανοῦ ms. ‖ 29 εὔτικτον ms. ‖ 34 δίου ms. ‖ 39 πάντα ἀκούει ms.

Sim.: 1–6 cf. Pind. *Ol.* 1.1–4 ‖ **3–4** χρυσοκ. — δίφροισιν] cf. Eur. *Phoen.* 2 ‖ **7** μελιφθόγγοισι Μούσαις] cf. Pind. *Ol.* 6.21 ‖ **9** κλεινὴν βίαν] cf. Eur. *Phoen.* 56 | αὐδάσομεν] cf. Pind. *Ol.* 1.7 ‖ **10** πύλας ὕμνων] cf. Pind. *Ol.* 6.27 ‖ **11–12** ἀμφέπει σκᾶπτα] cf. Pind. *Ol.* 1.12 ‖ **14** δεινοῖσιν ὅπλοις] cf. *Il.* 10.254 al. ‖ **17** ὕμνων — πτυχαῖς] cf. Pind. *Ol.* 1.105 ‖ **23–24** κ' ἐστάλ. — νέκταρ] cf. Pind. *Pyth.* 9.62–63 ‖ **29–33** cf. *Hymn. Hom. Ven.* 7–14 ‖ **35** cf. Pind. *Ol.* 6.55

Ode to King Sebastian in quatrains of three different verses

    Water is the best thing; gold
glares like fire at night
        and the sun shines, stepping
[4]   on gold-rimmed carts.
O my heart, if you now wish to celebrate
a divine man, to praise highly

                with honey-tongued Muses a valiant
[8]   king of the wide world,
we shall sing the renowned power of Sebastian
and we shall open to him the doors of hymns
                to him whose hand has conquered so much and holds
[12]   the sceptres of brave war-like rulers,
to him who has overcome in battle with terrible weapons
populations ruled by barbarian tyrants,
                and regions of the earth, and vast gulfs
[16]   of the outer ocean.
But who could voice the artistic renown of his hymns
through the illustrious folds of his mind,
                who managed to extol like the stars
[20]   the gleaming fire of his virtues?
Just after his mother gave birth to her baby,
his mother, the glorious offspring of mighty Charles,
                and spilt from her breast
[24]   the nectar to the baby's lips,
immediately the Virtues, sent by God,
descended from sky to earth,
                and held gladly in their immortal hands
[28]   the new-born child:
they put on his head a well-wrought, beautiful
crown, and they adorned his chest
                and his neck with golden
[32]   necklaces. Then once they
had put these adornments on his body,
the Graces took the divine baby
                and they fed him tenderly
[36]   with blond and purple flowers.
And both the western star... and the rosy-fingered
dawn listen to him and watch him,
                and glorify him and reward him
[40]   magnificently with divine gifts.

Metre: Ten Alcaic stanzas, probably modelled on the Latin pattern (chiefly attested in Horace). The title τρίκωλος τετράστροφος is often applied by Latin humanist poets to stanzas consisting of three different verse types (*kola*) in four lines (τετράστιχος would be more correct). Aside from some disturbing hiatuses (e.g., ll. 10, 29) and a couple of morphological oddities (e.g., l. 19 ἀστέρεσσι for ἀστράσι, l. 24 χέλεα for χείλεα, l. 40 ὅπτετ', the mysterious τάη in l. 39), there are few metrical problems: both the οὐρανοῦ (for οὐρανοῖο) in l. 25, and other minor orthographical or prosodical flaws should probably be corrected – there is no indication that we are dealing here with an autograph.

Notes: This poem belongs to the same collection mentioned above (Cipriano Soares): it might well be by the same author of the Greek ode *De Diva Elisabet* that immediately precedes it in the Coimbra manuscript, namely the Jesuit father Nicolau Pimenta (Santarem 1546 – Goa 1614), a student and later a professor of theology at Évora and Coimbra, and since 1592 the Jesuit General Visitor for India (his *De felici statu et progressu rei Christianae in India Orientali* was published in Konstanz in 1603). The dedicatee of our ode is King Sebastian of Portugal (1554–1578), the son of Prince John Manuel and Joanna of Austria (the daughter of Charles V: see ll. 22–23). No hint is made of Sebastian's premature death, whereas his expeditions against barbarian tribes are openly mentioned and praised (ll. 11–16, which may well refer to the colonial expansion in Angola, Mozambique, and Malacca during the early years of Sebastian's reign): it is therefore possible that the poem was written in the months preceding the Crusade against the infidels in Morocco, during which he died. The praise of Sebastian's early royal status (ll. 25–36) alludes to the fact that he inherited the throne at the age of three, soon after the death of his grandfather King John III. The ode displays clear Pindaric allusions, both in terms of structure (the opening is clearly reminiscent of the *Olympian* odes, particularly *Ol.* 1 and 6) and in terms of imagery (the 'doors of songs', the Charites, the Aretai, etc.): however, it also displays a certain familiarity with epic and tragic vocabulary.

Bibliography: Tavares de Pinho 1984; da Costa Ramalho, Américo (1988, 2000), *Para a história do Humanismo en Portugal* I, Lisboa, 49–74 and IV, Lisboa, 135–139 (originally published in 1982 and 1979); Tavares de Pinho, Sebastião (2006), "Literatura humanística inédita do Colégio das Artes da Universidade de Coimbra no século XVI", in: Id., *Humanismo en Portugal. Estudos II*, Lisboa, 323–344

Vicente Mariner (†1642)

I. *Ad D. Franc. de Quevedo* ἐπίγραμμα [ca. 1611–1618]

    Τῷ στίλβοντι νόῳ πάντων μέγα φέρτατος ἐσσί,
    μουσάων φωνὰς σοῦ στόμασιν δὲ χέεις.
    ὥσπερ χρυσοκόμης Φοίβου ἐρικυδέος υἱὸς
    σεμνῶν μουσοπόλων ἕδραν ἔχεις προτέραν.
5   σοῦ μελιφθόγγου ἔπη κρατέουσι μάλιστα θεαινῶν·
    λαμπρότατος πᾶσιν θαυμάσιός τε πέλεις.
    Μοῦσαι κοσμήσαντο σέθεν καλὰ ἔργα ἐπαίνοις
    δώρῳ θεσπεσίῳ καὶ πόρον οὐρανίοις.

Textus: Madrid, Biblioteca Nacional, ms. 9813, f. 578r (manu ipsius auctoris).

Crit.: 1 φέρτατός ἐσσι debuit ‖ 2 στόμασίν δε, correxi

Sim.: 1 μέγα φέρτατος] cf. *Il.* 16.21 al., vide etiam *Il.* 1.581 (πολὺ (alii μέγα) φέρτατός ἐστιν) et Quint. Smyrn. 1.649 (μέγα φέρτατοι εἰμέν) ‖ 3 χρυσοκόμης] de Apolline cf. Eur. *Tro.* 253–254, Ar. *av.* 216–217 | cf. *Od.* 11.576 (Γαίης ἐρικυδέος υἱόν) ‖ 5 μελιφθόγγου] adi. Pindaricum, cf. *Ol.* 6.21, *Isthm.* 2.7 et 6.9 ‖ 7–8 cf. Opp. *H.* 4.8–9 (Μοῦσαι κοσμήσαντο…δώρῳ θεσπεσίῳ καί μοι πόρον ὑμετέροισι)

Epigram for Don Francisco de Quevedo

You are by far superior to everyone for your gleaming mind,
    and you pour out from your mouth the voice of the Muses.
Like the gold-haired son of illustrious Phoebus
    you sit in the first rank among the revered poets.
[5] Your verses, o honey-voiced, win over those of the goddesses:
    you are the most brilliant and admired by everyone.
By a divine gift, the Muses adorned your beautiful works
    with praise, and offered them to the celestial gods.

II. *In Sanctum Xavierium pauperibus medentem epigramma* [ca. 1620]

Θέλγων ἀνθρώπων πολυαλγέα πήματα νούσων
    Φραγκίσκος βιότου δοὺς φάος ἦλθε μάκαρ.
Εἶδεν ἀκεστορίης μάλα φάρμακα πολλὰ Θεοῖο,
    ψυχὰς ἀνθρώπων δόγμασιν ἠκέσατο.
5 χεῖρας ὀρεγνύμενος κακὰ πένθεα πᾶσιν ἀλέξει,
    οὐρανὸν εἰς μακάρων αἰὲν ἄειρε βροτούς.
Μείλιχος εἷλε νόσους, σωτήριος ἄστρα ὀπάζει,
    λαὸν ὅλον Χριστοῦ ἦγε νόμοις ἁγίοις.
Χήρευεν δὲ μέλαθρα πολυκλαύτου Ἀχέροντος·
10 οὐράνιον πᾶσιν δῶκε βίοιο τέλος.

Textus: Madrid, Biblioteca Nacional, ms. 9807, p. 389 (manu ipsius auctoris).

Sim.: 1 ex *Hymn. Orph.* 67.2 (ad Asclepium) ‖ 3 cf. *Anth. Pal.* 7.559.1 (εἶδεν Ἀκεστορίη); de φάρμακα πολλά cf. fort. *Od.* 4.230 ‖ 4 cf. *Anth. Pal.* 7.108.2 (ψυχὰς ἀνθρώπων γράμμασιν ἠκέσατο, de Apolline et Platone) ‖ 5 cf. Mosch. *Europa* 112 (χεῖρας ὀρεγνυμένη; vide etiam *Anth. Pal.* 7.506.6) ‖ 9 ex *Anth. Pal.* 16.270.3 (de Galeno)

Epigram on St Xavier healing the poor

Beguiling the painful sufferings of human diseases
 blessed Francis gave the light of life and arrived here.
He saw a great many medicines of God's healing art,
 and treated with doctrines the human souls.
[5] Reaching out his hands he protects everyone from bad sorrows,
 and he has always extolled mortals to the sky of the Blest.
A sweet man, he has defeated diseases; a saviour, he leads to the stars
 steering a whole population according to Christ's holy laws.
The halls of mournful Acheron have become empty:
[10] he has given to everyone a heavenly life-end.

III. *Ad invictissimum et potentissimum Hisp(aniae) et Ind(iae) regem Philippum quartum M(agistri) Vincentii Marinerii Valentini epigramma* [ca. 1630–1632]

Σμήνεα Μουσάων μέλι μὲν σοῦ χείλεσι θῆκαν,
 τέκνον καὶ σὲ ἔδον πληθόμενον σοφίης.
Καὶ σοφίη σε φίλησε χάριν στάζουσα προσώποις
 ὑψόθι καὶ πάντων σοῦ νόον ἦγε μέγαν.
5 μειλιχίης οἴηκα φέρεις ἐν χερσὶ γαλήνης
 ἤνοιξας δὲ θύρας εὐεπίης γλυκερῆς.
βήματα μοῦνος ἔβης καλῶν θεοτευχέα Μουσῶν,
 ὅττι νόου φέγγος δ' ἀστυφέλικτον ἔχεις.
Σοὶ Χαρίτων δὲ τριὰς καὶ σοὶ πάλι Φοῖβος Ἀπόλλων
10 ἐγγὺς ἔην σεόθεν χερσὶν ἐφαψάμενος.
ἤδη καὶ προφέρεις πάντων πεπνυμένα εἰδώς
 καὶ ὑπὸ Μουσάων πρῶτος ἔκεισο θρόνον.
Σὺ χθονὸς Ἰσπανίας φάος ἐξαίρεις ἐς Ὄλυμπον·
 ἡμῶν ἐσσὶ χάρις καὶ Χαρίτων κραδίη.

Textus: Madrid, Biblioteca Nacional, ms. 9805, p. 11 (manu ipsius auctoris).

Crit.: 6 ἤνοιξας scripsi: ἔνιξας ms.

Sim.: 1 μέλι...χείλεσι θῆκαν] de imagine cf. *Anth. Pal.* 16.210.6 (et 5.32.3) et *vitam Pindari* 8.12–13 Dr. || 2 ἔδον] cf. Hes. *Theog.* 30 (et Hsch. ε 490) | πληθόμενον σοφίης] cf. *Anth. Pal.* 6.293.4 || 3 cf. Io. Gaz. *Descr. Mundi* 2.71 (χάριν στάζουσα ῥεέθροις) || 5 cf. Io. Gaz. *Descr. Mundi* 2.75 (μειλιχίης οἴηκα κυβερνητῆρα γαλήνης) || 7 θεοτευχέα] ex Io. Gaz. *Descr. Mundi* 2.51 || 8 cf. Greg. Naz. *Carm.*, *PG* 37. 1553.7 (κάλλος νόος...ἀστυφέλικτον) || 9 Χαρίτων τριάς] cf. *Anth. Pal.* 5.260.7 || 10 σεόθεν] cf. *EtGud* 404, 3 Stef. | χερσὶν ἐφαψάμενος] cf. Thgn. 1.6 (de Apollinis matre) || 11 πεπνυμένα εἰδώς] cf. *Od.* 4.696 al.

To the most powerful and invincible Philip IV, king of Spain and India, epigram of Vicente Mariner from Valencia

Swarms of Muses put honey on your lips,
   and they made you their son, full of wisdom.
And wisdom kissed you, dropping elegance on your face,
   and enhanced your mind above all others.
[5] You hold in your hands the helm of sweet peace
   and you have opened the doors of pleasant eloquence.
You have walked alone on the divine tribunes of the beautiful Muses
   because your mind displays an unshaken splendour.
The three Graces and then again Phoebus Apollo
[10] have stood by you, touching you by hand.
Hence you are superior to all by your knowledge
   and you have occupied the first rank below the throne of the Muses.
You raise to the Olymp the light of the land of Spain:
   you are our grace and at the same time the heart of the Graces.

Metre: Elegiac couplets. Mariner's hexameters are generally good (Hermann's Bridge is violated in I.5), and prosodical mistakes are limited to the earliest text (I.4 ἕδραν should have long α; the second syllable of I.5 μελιφθόγγου is impossibly shortened as if by *correptio*; in III.6 ἔνιξας is just an oversight for the correct ἤνοιξας; an ugly hiatus in III.2 σὲ ἕδον).

Notes: The three epigrams can be dated on the basis of the manuscripts that carry them. The first one (equipped with a Latin translation on the *verso* of the same page)[26] is dedicated to the great Spanish poet Francisco de Quévedo (1580–1645); the second one is a tribute to the Jesuit saint Francis Xavier (1506–1552), and it can safely be dated to 1620, the year of a letter to André Schott preserved on pp. 395f. of the same manuscript; the third one (also followed by a Latin version) is an encomium of the learned king of Spain Philip IV (1605–1665, in power from 1621). All three texts develop an encomiastic tone, adapting it to the object of praise. Mariner is conversant with Greek poetic diction, as is shown by the manifold references to epic and epigrammatic vocabulary: at times, he adopts ancient lines wholesale in his epigrams (I.7–8 are a refined tribute to Oppian; II.1, 4, and 9 are taken from ancient poems dealing with doctors, and cleverly interwoven

---

26 *Fulgenti ingenio cunctorum es maximus ipse: / Musarum vocem nam vomis ore tuo / auricomique velut Phoebi quoque filius idem / prima inter cunctos carmine sede micas. / quaeque tuo iam melle fluunt stillantia verba / et Musas vincunt, te rutilumque vehunt. / Laudibus et Musae tua gesta tulere supernis, / divino in caelos munere teque locant.*

into the fabric of the praise of Francis Xavier; III.3–7 are partly indebted to John of Gaza's hexametrical *Descriptio mundi*). Mariner's style is on the whole not very elegant, though one cannot reproach him except for the incorrect use of particles (δέ in I.2 and III.8), and some semantic *abusiones* (in I.4 ἕδραν ἔχεις προτέραν is explained in the Latin version as *prima…sede micas*; in III.2 ἕδον means *peperere*, as in the Latin version, rather than 'gave', as it should).

Biography: Vicente Mariner (†Valencia 1642) was born in Valencia in the last third of the 16th century; he studied rhetoric and theology in his hometown, then moved to Madrid, where he worked as a private teacher for the Duke of Lerma and for the Duke of Uceda, and he got acquainted with many intellectuals such as Lope de Vega and Quévedo; he finally became a librarian at the Escorial in 1633. According to his lengthy self-presentation, during his life Mariner translated into Latin – beside a number of patristic or religious works – various Greek poets with the respective ancient exegesis: Homer (with D-scholia and Eustathius' commentaries), Hesiod, Theocritus, Lycophron, Apollonius Rhodius, then the scholia to Sophocles, Euripides, and Pindar, etc. He counted his own original output in Greek and Latin at 350,000 lines, with over 8,000 epigrams; he must be considered by far the most prolific poet in ancient Greek in modern Iberia. This unceasing activity, quite unparalleled in his day, did not always result in perfection. Above all, only a part of Mariner's achievements eventually arrived to the press: despite the 9 books of *Opera omnia* printed at Tornay in 1633, most of his works lie unpublished in the manuscripts of Madrid's Biblioteca Nacional and of Valencia's Biblioteca Universitaria; only in recent years have some of them become the object of fresh scholarly investigation.

Bibliography: de Andrés 1988, 272–299 (esp. 274–281), 307–310 and 375–387 (list of his works); de Andrés, Gregorio (1979), "Cronología de las obras del polígrafo Vicente Mariner", in: *Cuadernos Bibliográficos* 38, 139–152; García de Paso Carrasco, Maria Dolores/Rodríguez Herrera, Gregorio (1996), *Vicente Mariner y sus traducciones de la* Ilias *y de la* Odyssea, Cordoba; Iid. (eds.) (2012), *Vicente Mariner. Breve Antología*, Vigo-Pontevedra (esp. 11–33).

Gonzalo Correas (1571–1631)

Anacreonteiadonike
Ode dicolos distrofos in genesin Principis [1630]

    Τὸν παῖδα νῦν Φιλίππου
      τοῦ βασιλῆος
    μέλει πάρεστιν ᾄδειν
4   ἄμμι λιγέως.
    Ἰβηρίῃ φὺς ἔσται
      φῶς ἐπιλάμπον,
    φόβος δὲ τοῖς ἀπίστοις
8   πᾶσί τε θάμβος.
    Χάριν γονεῦσιν ἴδμεν
      τοῦ γεγαῶτος
    ὑπεύθυνοι μεγίστην
12   δαίμοσι πρώτως.
    Σχολὴ σοφῶν ἀμείνων
      ἐν Σαλαμάνκᾳ
    δείκνυσι τῶν ἀνάκτων
16   σφῶν τε τὸ χάρμα.
    Καὶ σὺν κόραις χορεῦσαι
      ταῖς Ἑλικῶνος
    αἱ Τορμίδες παρέσταν,
20   ὡς καλοφώνως.
    Ἐσέρχετ' ὔμμες ἆσσον
      ᾆσμ' ἀποδόντες
    ὦ μύσται Ἱπποκρήνης
24   τἆθλα λαβόντες.

Textus: *Fiestas de la Universidad de Salamanca* al nacimiento del Príncipe D. Baltasar Carlos Domingo Felipe V.N.S. siendo retor D. Lope de Moscoso, hijo de los Marqueses de Tavana...dirigidas al excelentissimo Señor D. Gaspar de Guzman, Conde de Olivares..., Inpresas en Salamanca por Iacinto Tabernier, 1630, p. 302.

Crit.: 21 ἐσέρχεσθ' (quod metro repugnat) debuit || 22 ἆσμ', correxi

Anacreontic-adonic ode in distichs of two different lines, in honour of the birth of the Prince

Now we want to sing
  in high-pitched verse
the son of Philip,
[4] our king.
Once born, he will be a light
  shining over Spain:
the terror of the infidels,
[8] admired by everyone.
We express our greatest
  gratitude to the parents
of the newborn, being subject
[12] ever since to their divinity.
The wise men at Salamanca's
  best school
show the joy of the masters
[16] and their own.
And the nymphs of the Tormes
  have come to dance
with the maidens of Helicon –
[20] what a sweet voice!
Come closer, come
  and give your song,
you prize-winning initiated
[24] of the Hippocrene.

Metre: Anacreontic ode. The title (followed in the page by a metrical scheme of the *anacreontica* and of the *adonika*) describes this ode as consisting of couplets combining a catalectic iambic dimeter (very common in Anacreontic odes) with an adonian (with the adonians rhyming two by two): this is a very common pattern in Latin odes of the same genre (cf. also Herrichen → **Germany**). Prosody and metre are not always flawless (e.g., l. 4 λιγέως does not scan in the adonean; l. 11 ὑπεύθυνοι should have a long υ). A note following the ode in the original print reads: *Cum antiqua mensura servat rhythmum Hispanicum de Seghidillas*, i.e. this ode follows not only the anacreontic rhythm, but also the tempo of the Castilian folk songs (and dances) known as *seguidillas*.

Notes: This ode belongs to the texts in various languages (Latin, Spanish, Greek, and Hebrew) read at the University of Salamanca in honour of the birth of Prince Baltasar Carlos (1629–1646), the first male son of King Philip IV and the obvious heir to the throne until his premature death at 17: the *Fiestas* gather all these poetic contributions, but the Greek pieces (this one and an epigram by Lorenzo Blasco) are added only *après coup* in the last pages of the book (pp. 302–304), for it had previously proved impossible to find Greek characters for the press, and 'a este genero de Poesias faltándoles sus propios carácteres les falta el alma, y pierden mucho de la magestad y estimación, que se les deve' (p. 275). As in epigrammatic literature, and in Anacreontic poetry in general, there is a certain inconsistency in terms of dialectal patina (see l. 4 ἄμμι, l. 21 ὔμμες); due to the virtuoso *tour de force* imposed by metre and rhyme, the syntax is sometimes compressed and prosastic (with incorrect active ἐσέρχετ(ε) in l. 21 being the only major grammatical flaw, aside from the rather cryptic meaning of ll. 11–12), and real poetic reminiscences are rare; l. 20 καλοφώνως seems to be an *hapax*, and so is no doubt the name of the nymphs of Salamanca's river, Τορμίδες (l. 19).

Biography: Gonzalo Correas (Jaraiz de la Vera, Cáceres 1571 – Salamanca 1631) studied theology and ancient Greek at Salamanca's Collegium Trilingue, and was then active as a teacher of Greek and Hebrew at Salamanca University from 1598. A translator of Epictetus' *Handbook* and the author of important handbooks of Greek grammar – first the *Prototypi grammatici canones* (Salamanca 1600), then the *Arte griega* (Valladolid 1627) –, Correas was also very active in the field of Spanish grammar, particularly with the unsuccessful proposal of a brand-new orthographical system for Castilian. He wrote Anacreontic odes and sonnets in Greek, most notably those dedicated to the death of King Philip III in 1621, which were collected as models of Greek versification at the end of the *Arte griega* (pp. 136–139).

Bibliography: de Andrés 1988, 35–46 and 305–306; de Bustos Tovar, José Jesús (1998), "Las propuestas ortográficas de Gonzalo Correas", in: *Dicenda* 16, 41–62; Infantes, Victor (2010), in: *DBE* 14, 712–715.

Manuel Martí (1663–1737)

Συμποτικὸν ἀστέισμα *sive Lusus Convivalis, Imitatio Odae I. Anacreonticae* [1725]

Ποίεέ μοι τὸ σκύφος μέγα πάντων ἠδὲ βάθιστον,
ὡς Ἡρακλεέους, Νέστορος ὥς τε δέπας.
Οὐ Σάτυρον γλυφθέντ' ἐθέλω, οὐ Πᾶνα τὸν αἰσχρόν
βούλομαι, ἡμίθεον μήθ' ὑπεραλλόμενον,

5   Οὐ γὰρ μαρνάμενον πρὸς δῖαν Ἀχιλλέα Τροῖαν,
       οὔτε φλόγ' ἐννυχίᾳ αἰθομένην γε πόλιν,
    Οὐκὶ μάχας δίφρους τε, στρατοὺς ἢ τεύχεα φρικτά·
    Παλλὰς ἐμοῦ ἔκαθεν καὶ βροτολοιγὸς Ἄρης.
    Κύπριν ἐγὼ γλυφθεῖσαν ἐρῶ, τῷ σώματι γυμνήν,
10   ἡδυγέλαιον ἅμα χ' ἁπαλόχρωτα θεόν.
    Ὦσι πέριξ ταύτης Χάριτες τρεῖς, ὦσιν Ἔρωτες
       μύριοι· αἱ κύλικες τὸν φιλέουσιν ἔρων.
    Ἄρτεμιν ἔγγλαψον μετὰ πάρθνοις, οὐ τὸ βέλεμνον
       χερσὶ φέρουσαν ὅμως καὶ πτοέουσαν ὄρη,
15 Ἀλλ' ὡς Ἀκταίων θηρῶν ἀνὰ πίδακα ταύτην
       βέβλεφεν, ἐν μέσσοις ὕδασι νιπτομένην.
    Ἀμφ' ἑλικοῖς ὁ νέος Βρόμιος κεράεσσι γεγράφθω,
       ἐκ πύξου φυσῶν πνεύματι φυσαλίδα.
    Πρόσθε καλοὶ βότρυες, πρὸς τοῖς ποσὶ κάνθαρος εἴη,
20   καὶ στέφος οἰνάρεον τοὺς τρίχας ἀμφιδέῃ.
    Αἱ Μοῦσαι Φοῖβός τε γεγραμμένα ἡμῖν ἔσωνται,
       αἱ μὲν ἀείδουσαι, ὁ δὲ κρέκων κίθαριν.
    Πάντα πλέω κισσῶν βοτρύων τε τὰ πάντα κορύμβων·
    Αὕτη μοι ἔσεται παγχαρίεσσα κύλιξ.

Textus: Emmanuelis Martini ecclesiae Alonensis decani *Epistolarum libri duodecim*, Mantuae Carpetanorum: apud Joannem Stunicam, 1735 (Amstelodami: Smith et Wetstein, 1738), p. 259 = c. Kk2 (epist. VI.15).

Crit.: 1 πάντως ἥδε βάθυστον, correxi || 5 Τροίαν debuit || 17 ἑλίκεσ(σ)ι debuit || 21 ἥμιν debuit || 23 πλέα debuit

Sim.: 2 de Heraclis poculo cf. Athen. 11.469d, de Nestoris poculo cf. *Il.* 11.632–637 || 7 cf. e contrario *Il.* 3.328 al. (τεύχεα καλά) || 8 βροτολοιγὸς Ἄρης] cf. *Il.* 5.518, 846 etc. || 10 ἡδυγέλαιον] sim. *Anth. Pal.* 5.135.4 (ἡδύγελως) || 12 ἔρων] de forma cf. *Anth. Pal.* 9.39.2 || 18 φυσαλίδα] de subst. cf. Ar. *Lys.* 1245, Hsch. φ 1042 || 20 οἰνάρεον] de adi. cf. Theoc. *Id.* 7.134 || 23 sim. e.g. Aesch. *Pers.* 603 (πάντα μὲν φόβου πλέα); hederae vineaeque sunt Bacchi insignia

Sympotic wit
or
Convivial Game
(Imitation of the first Anacreontic Ode)

Make my cup very big and deepest of all,
   like Heracles' cup, and Nestor's.
In the carving I do not want a Satyr, nor ugly Pan
   nor a leaping demigod,
[5] no Achilles fighting against divine Troy,

no city burning in night flames,
no battles or carts and armies, nor terrible weapons:
may both Pallas and man-slaying Ares be far from me.
I fancy carved Cypris, with her naked body,
[10] the sweetly smiling, soft-skinned goddess.
Around her may fly the three Graces, and thousands
of Erotes: cups fancy eros.
Carve Artemis amid her virgins: not, however, when she carries
the dart in her hands and frightens the mountains,
[15] but such as hunting Actaeon saw her in that fountain,
taking a bath in those waters.
Let young Bromios be carved on the curved handles,
blowing with his breath a pipe of boxwood.
Let nice grapes be in the foreground, a drinking-cup at his feet,
[20] and let a crown of vine-leaves bind his hair.
May the Muses and Phoebus be carved for us,
the former singing, the latter playing the kithara.
All is full of ivy, all is full of grapes and ivy fruits:
This will be for me the most beautiful cup.

Metre: Elegiac couplets. There is one clear mistake (ὁ in the *longum* of the second hemistich of the pentameter l. 22; but see also the app. crit.), and several surprising peculiarities: the prosodical consideration of the double consonants as simple (l. 1 σκύφος, l. 7 στρατούς) and morphological monsters created *metri causa* (l. 2 Ἡρακλεέους, l. 13 πάρθνοις for παρθένοις).

Notes: The elegy features as an appendix to a letter of 10 Dec. 1725, to Juan Interián de Ayala, a member of the Real Academia de la Lengua. While written in a relatively fluid style, the poem does not lean on specific literary models, nor does it show a distinctive imitation of ancient Greek prototypes; on the other hand, it carries several grammatical and syntactical peculiarities (hesitation between οὐ and μή in ll. 2–8; the elided dative φλόγ' in l. 6; the verb ἐρῶ with accusative in l. 9; the placing of the article τὸν in l. 12; the adj. ἑλικός for ἕλιξ in l. 17; the rare subj. ἔσωνται in l. 21), and a couple of interesting *hapax legomena* (l. 10 ἡδυγέλαιος, l. 13 ἐγγλάπτειν, l. 24 παγχαρίεσσα).

Biography: Manuel Martí Zaragoza (Oropesa del Mar 1663 – Alicante 1737) was one of the most important Spanish humanists of his time. He studied philosophy and theology in Valencia and then moved to Rome in 1686, where he served various cardinals, he learned to read and write Greek and, as a prolific Latin writer and poet, he entered the Academy of Arcadia with the name of Eumelus Olenius.

He later came back to Spain as a dean of Alicante; he travelled to Valencia, Madrid, Sevilla, Madrid again, and finally settled down in Alicante; he showed a scholarly interest in the ruins of Saguntum and Itálica; during his most prolific years in the capital (1704–1711) he completed a translation of Eustathios of Thessalonike's commentary to *Iliad* I–VIII (never published) and a penetrating study on the origins of the *Greek Anthology*, which he knew intimately. His *Epistolarum libri XII*, published with the help of his friend Gregorio Mayans, attest to his remarkable network of scholars and learned friends, and contain some of his Greek pieces, including his translations of some epigrams of Martial (*epist.* 6.13).

Bibliography: Hernando 1975, 17, 164–177, 245–251, 284f., 454f. Gil, Luis (1997), "El deán Martí y la Antología Griega", in: Mestre, Antonio (ed.), *Humanismo y pervivencia*, Cadiz, 33–65; Mestre Sanchis, Antonio (2002), *Manuel Martí, el Deán de Alicante*, Alicante; Id. (2012), in: *DBE* 32, 766–770.

Antonio Martínez de Quesada (1718–1751)

Ὕμνος πρὸς τὴν παρθένον Μαρίαν διὰ τὸ ἔργον τετελῆσθαι [1743–1747]

Ἀθανάτων βασίλισσαν ἀείδομαι ἠδὲ καὶ ἀνδρῶν,
καὶ αὐτήν γε θύγατρα Θεοῦ καὶ μητέρ' ἐοῦσαν,
κούρην τῆς Ἄννης καὶ Ἰωχίμοιο γέροντος,
ἁγναίην δὲ ἄκοιτιν Ἰωσήφου ζαθέοιο,
5   θαῦμα βροτοῖς καὶ τοῖς θείοις μακάρεσσιν Ὀλύμπου
σεμνοτάτην πάντων, ἃς ἔβλεπε γαῖα, γυναικῶν,
αἰδοίην, χρυσοστέφανον καὶ ἱμερόεσσαν,
χρυσόθρονον βασίλισσαν ἐν οὐρανῷ ἀστερόεντι,
ἔνθεν τὴν ζωὴν καὶ μείλιχα δῶρα διδοῦσαν,
10 πότνιαν ἔν τε βροτοῖσι καὶ ἀθανάτοισι θεοῖσιν,
ἣν πάντες μάκαρες τίουσιν Ὄλυμπον ἔχοντες,
ἥν τε καλαῖς μὲν ἀοιδῇσι ψάλλουσιν οἱ ἄνδρες
γαίῃ ἐνὶ μακρῇ, φωνὴ δὲ πρὸς οὐρανὸν ἦλθεν
εὐχομένων θνητῶν καὶ παρθένου οὔατ' ἐπέσχεν,
15 ἠδ' υἱῷ Χριστῷ τὰς κείνων ἔφραδεν εὐχάς,
αἶψα συναιρομένη, καὶ μείλιχα δῶρα ἰεῖσα.
    Τοὔνεκα μελπόμενος μὲν ἀείδω παρθένον ἁγνήν,
ἣν τέκε πουλυέτουσ' (ἄγονος πρίν) πισύνη Ἄννα
ἐν χθονὶ Ἰδουμαίης κατὰ Ἰορδάνοιο ῥέεθρον.
20 Ἥδε μὲν αἰδοίη παρὰ μητρὶ τιτθεύετο κούρη
ἱερή, ἀγλαόμορφος, ἐρασμίη, ἀγλαόθυμος.
Ἀλλ' ὅτε δὴ χρόνος ἔσκε, περιπλομένων ἐνιαυτῶν,
μητρὸς ὑπὸ θρήσκης τρίενος παιδίσκη ἐδόσθη

τῷ εἰῷ ἱερέι θρησκευσομένη ἐπὶ ναοῦ.
25 Ἔνθα παρασκευαζομένη τ' εὐσχήμονα ἔργα,
τὴν σοφίαν τ' ἐδιδάχθη ὁμῶς τά τε εὐσεβῆ ἤθη,
οὖσα πάις καλή τ' ἀγάμητός τ'. Αὐτὰρ ἔπειτα
ἀνδρὶ ἐνυμφεύθη θεόθεν κόρη· ἀλλὰ τότ' αὐτὴ
καὶ μένε παρθενίας τηροῦσα τὸ ἀγλαὸν ἄνθος.
30 Οὔ κε γὰρ ἤ ποτ' Ἰωσήφῳ χαρίεντι μέμικται,
τὴν συνιοῦσα κλίνην, ἀλλ' ἦν ἀμίαντος ἔπειτα,
ὡς ἀγάμητος ἐοῦσα, καὶ οὔ ποτε ἀνέρα ἔγνω.
Τὴν γὰρ ὁ τῶν ἀνδρῶν γενέτωρ Θεός, αἰθέρα ναίων,
ἐξέλεγ' ἐσσομένην θείων τ' οἴκημα ἐάων.
35 Ἤτοι μὲν μετέπειτ' Ἁγίου δ' ἐκ Πνεύματος αὐτὴ
γαστρὶ ἐνὶ κλειτῷ πατέρος λόγον ἀντιλέληγεν,
ὃς γεγονὼς ἄνθρωπος ἁμαρτίας θεραπεύοι.

Textus: Madrid, Biblioteca de la Univ. Complutense, ms. 191: *Hesiodus Mythicus-Mysticus* (vide fig. 11), ed. Lamata Meana, Silvia (1998), "Un texto en griego inédito del humanismo español del siglo XVIII", in: *Epos* 14, 563–580 (unde textum sumo).

Crit.: Tit. τετελέσθαι debuit ‖ **6** πασῶν debuit ‖ **13** φωνή δε ms., correxi ‖ **15** εὔχας ms., correxi ‖ **23** ἐδόθη debuit ‖ **35** μετέπειθ' debuit

Sim.: 1 cf. *Hymn. Hom.* 12.1 (ἀθανάτην βασίλειαν), necnon e.g. Hes. *Op.* 668 (Ζεὺς ἀθανάτων βασιλεύς) ‖ **4** ἀγναίην] adi. apud Hsch. α 646 tantum occurrit ‖ **5** θαῦμα βροτοῖς] cf. *Od.* 11.287 ‖ **7** αἰδοίην χρυσοστέφανον] ex *Hymn. Hom. Ven.* 1 ‖ **8** χρυσόθρονον] cf. *Hymn. Hom.* 12.1 | ἐν οὐρανῷ ἀστερόεντι] cf. *Il.* 4.44 et saep. ‖ **9** μείλιχα δῶρα διδοῦσαν (cf. etiam v. 16)] cf. *Hymn. Hom. Ven.* 2 ‖ **10** ἀθανάτοισι θεοῖσιν] clausula Homerica, cf. *Il.* 1.520 et saep. ‖ **11** cf. *Hymn. Hom.* 12.4-5 (ἥν πάντες μάκαρες κατὰ μακρὸν Ὄλυμπον ἀζόμενοι τίουσιν) ‖ **13** sim. Hes. *Theog.* 685 (φωνὴ…ἵκετ' οὐρανόν) ‖ **15** ἔφραδεν] de forma aoristi cf. *schol. Dion. Thr.* 493.12 al. ‖ **17** παρθένον ἁγνήν] in clausula cf. Greg. Naz. *Carm.*, PG 37.586.4; *Orac. Sib.* 2.312 et saep. ‖ **18** πουλυέτους'] cf. *Orac. Sib.* 3.369 al. (πουλυετής) ‖ **19** cf. *Il.* 21.25 (ποταμοῖο κατὰ δεινοῖο ῥέεθρα), 23.205 et Hes. *Theog.* 695 (Ὠκεανοῖο ῥέεθρα) etc., sed vide praes. Nonn. *Par. Jo.* 10.141 (Ἰορδάνοιο ῥεέθροις) ‖ **20** cf. *Od.* 8.420 (μητρὶ παρ'αἰδοίῃ) ‖ **21** ἀγλαόμορφος] saep. in hymnis, cf. *Anth. Pal.* 9.525.2, *Hymn. Orph.* 14.5 etc. | ἀγλαόθυμος] cf. *Anth. Pal.* 15.40.25 et 31 ‖ **22** ex *Od.* 1.16 (ubi ἔτος ἦλθε) ‖ **23** θρήσκης] de adi. cf. Hsch. θ 737 | τρίενος nescio unde (fort. e Theophr. *Hist. Pl.* 4.11.5; cf. lat. *triennis*) ‖ **27** ἀγάμητος] cf. Hsch. α 300 ‖ **29** ἀγλαὸν ἄνθος] cf. Tyrt. fr. 10.28 et Thgn. 1.1008 (de ἥβη); de flore virginitatis cf. Orph. *Arg.* 1339, sed saep. apud patres Christianos ‖ **33** cf. *Il.* 2.412 (αἰθέρι ναίων) ‖ **34** ἐάων] cf. *Il.* 24.528 al.

Hymn to the Virgin Mary for the completion of the work

I sing the queen of the immortals and of men,
She who is both daughter and mother of God,
daughter of Anna and old Ioachim,
chaste spouse of holy Joseph,

[5] a wonder for mortals and for the divine blest of the Olymp,
holiest of all the women that the earth has ever seen,
venerable, gold-crowned, charming,
queen on a throne of gold in the starry sky,
whence she gives life and sweet gifts;
[10] powerful among mortals and immortal gods,
honoured by all the inhabitants of the Olymp,
celebrated in beautiful songs by men
on the vast earth; the voice of praying mortals
arrived to the sky and captured the ears of the virgin,
[15] and she drew to their prayers the attention of Christ her son,
and immediately helped them and sent sweet gifts.
   Therefore I sing and celebrate the chaste virgin
begotten by elderly and obstinate Anna (hitherto sterile)
in the land of Idumaia next to river Jordan.
[20] This girl was brought up close to her venerable mother,
a holy, beautiful, desirable, noble-hearted child.
But when the years went by and the time came,
as a three-year-old child she was given by her pious mother
to the good priest so that she might be presented to the temple.
[25] There she accomplished splendid deeds,
she learned both wisdom and the pious manners,
being a nice and unmarried child. Then the girl
by divine will was married to a man; but even then
she kept the gleaming flower of virginity.
[30] For she never had intercourse with handsome Joseph
entering their bed, but she remained undefiled even afterwards,
as if she were unmarried, and she never knew a man.
For God the father of men, living in the skies,
chose her to be the home of all divine goods.
[35] And then by virtue of the Holy Spirit she received
in her illustrious bosom the Word of the Father,
which became man and saved us from sins.[27]

---

27 **Author's own Latin translation:** *Reginam cano Divorum simul, atque virorum, / et natam, matremque Dei, cum sit simul Annę, / Ioachimique senis proles, et pura verendi / uxor Iosephi: mortalibus omnibus ingens / Prodigium, ac alto sidentibus ęthere Divis. / Non venerabilior fuit hâc, vel castior ulla / Foemina de cunctis, quas vidit terra creatas. / Hęc serto aurato rutilans, venerabilis, atque / Chara, thronoque sendens* [sic] *aurato in culmine cęli / Stellati regina micat, dans indè misellis / Vitamque, ac animos nobis, et dulcia dona, / Aeternis veneranda Deis, veneranda virisque. / Hanc, qui sidereas ędes, qui candidi Olympi / culmen habent, semper foelices, atque beati / Laudibus extollunt: huic non incondita fundunt / carmina, qui terras habitant; sed voce sonorâ / concelebrant homines, et pulchris cantibus ipsam. / Vox autem miserûm tristi é tellure precantûm / in cęlum scanditque, et virginis occupat aures. / Illa preces horum commendat, cunctaque nato /*

Metre: Hexameters. Quesada's verses are far from flawless; while some 'irrational' lengthenings can easily be explained *metri causa*, the hiatuses in ll. 4, 16, 26, 28, 29, 32 are very harsh, and in l. 19 only a couple of problematic elisions (χθόν' Ἰδουμαίης κατ' Ἰορδάνοιο) could save the metrical pattern of the verse. In l. 20 the first syllable of τιτθεύετο is considered as short despite the double consonant, in l. 24 probably the form ἱερεῖ – the only remotely possible one – is meant; in l. 37 the iota of ἁμαρτίας is wrongly taken as long.

Notes: The introductory section of this hymn (which rounds off the *Hesiodus mythicus-mysticus*, the ἔργον mentioned in the title) relates some biographical episodes of the Virgin, whereas the rest of the poem is made of a series of salutations (χαιρετισμοί) and words of praise. Lamata Meana has already insisted on the blend of dialectal features in the hymn, as well as on the use of 'pagan' epithets for God and other entities of the Christian religion. Quesada's diction is marred by a number of true mistakes (l. 6 πάντων for πασῶν; l. 18 πουλυέτουσ(α) for πουλυετής; l. 23 ἐδόσθη for ἐδόθη; l. 24 a mysterious εἰῷ, probably some form of ἑῷ; l. 31 transitive σύνειμι; l. 35 aspiration missing in the elision; l. 36 a nonexistent form ἀντιλέλην, which defies analysis), and by some less idiomatic expressions or syntactic oddities (e.g. l. 1 ἀείδομαι in the middle voice, probably mutuated from the future ᾄσομαι, frequent in hymns; l. 6 ἔβλεπε γαῖα; l. 25 θρησκευσομένη in the sense of 'to be introduced to the temple rites' rather than 'worshipped'; l. 33 ναίω with accusative rather than local dative; the use of the article is often very free). This said, the *apparatus fontium* shows Quesada's acquaintance with both lexicography (from which he takes some very peculiar items) and Greek poetry, especially with the hymnic genre that represents his main source of inspiration.

---

vota suo Christo paritèr, citóque advenit ipsa / *Auxilium pręstans miseris, et dulcia dona.* / *Iccirco* [sic] *celebrans intactam canto puellam,* / *quàm peperit longęva (prius non foeta) monenti* / *confidens Domino, campo in regionis Idumę* / *Ad Iordanis aquas, multùm venerabilis Anna.* / *Illa autèm crescebat ibi veneranda puella* / *Matre sub augustâ, sacra, et pulcherrima formâ,* / *splendentique animo: sed ubi, currentibus annis* / *tempus erat, postquam jam tres compleverat annos,* / *Sacra sacerdoti templo exercenda dabatur.* / *Illa ibi persanctis exercita moribus, omnem* / *Doctrinam, moresque pios, et legis honorem* / *Perdidicit, perstans pulchra, atque innupta puella.* / *Posteà sed, cęlo sic disponente, venusto* / *Nupsit sponsa viro ; sed tunc permansit, ut antè,* / *florem conservans, et virginitatis honorem.* / *Non etenim charo Iosepho mixta subivit* / *unquam communem lectum, sed perstitit indè* / *incorrupta, virumque suum non novit in ęvo.* / *Hanc hominum genitor, qui altum colit ęthera, legit* / *ut Divinorum domus esset plena bonorum.* / *Scilicet unde eadem (mirum!) de flamine sancto* / *Ventre suo patris Verbum concepit in almo,* / *Quod tunc factus homo sanaret crimina nostra.*

Biography: Antonio Martínez de Quesada (Cuenca? 1718 – Alcalá 1751) studied Greek at Alcalá, where he lived his short life as an employee of the Library of the Colegio Mayor de San Ildefonso, and died in poverty and distress. A Latin poet and a specialist in history and theology, Quesada displayed his philological skill in an autograph manuscript now kept in the library of the Universidad Complutense, containing a large commentary to Hesiod's *Theogony* (written between 1743 and 1747), with a special attention to all its possible allegorical readings, especially those pertaining to etymology and to its relationship with the Bible. The *Hesiodus Mythicus-Mysticus* has been described as one of the best philological achievements of the 18th century in Spain: it is followed by a hymn to the Virgin Mary in 147 Greek hexameters.

Bibliography: Lamata Meana 1998 (see above Textus); Gil, Luis (1974), "Un helenista español desconocido: Antonio Martínez de Quesada (1718-1751)", in: *Boletin de la Real Academia Española* 54, 379–437; Romero Recío, Mirella (2012), in: *DBE* 33, 493; Romero Recío, Mirella (2003), "Religión y politica en el siglo XVIII: el uso del mundo clásico", in: *'Ilu Revista de ciencias de las religiones* 8, 127–142.

José Rodríguez de Castro (ca. 1739–1789)

Ὑπὲρ βασιλέως ζωῆς [1759]

Ὦ Μοῖραι ἐρέβους δεινωποῦ ἔκφυλον ἔθνος,
Αἱ δὲ βίου 'νθρώπων νήθουσαι στήμονα λεπτόν,
Καὶ ἐνόσω ἀρέσκει εἴθαρ λύετε ῥάμμα,
Ἔργον νήλεον ὑμῶν ἀσπασίως καταθέσθε,
5   Ζωῆς κλωστῆρ' ἄνακτος διαγράφετε χρείας,
Ἧς τε ἔχουσιν εὔορκοι ὄντως ἀρχόμεν' αὐτοῦ·
Βάσκανον οὖν Θεῖον δ' ἐπιχειροῖ στήμονα κόπτειν,
Πλῆγμά γε καίριον ἄφαρ ἐφ' ἡμῶν στρέψατε κάρᾳ.
Ὑμῶν ἓν λίαν ἐξαιτοῦμεν, ἂν' ἤμματα ζωῆς
10 Τοῦ Κάρλου ῥυθμεῖσθαι ἀνά γε τὰ καλὰ ψυχῆς·
Τὰ εἰν τῷ νῷ χωρεῖτ' αὐτῷ ἐκδιανύσθαι.

Textus: Σύγχαρμα τῷ βασιλεῖ κρατίστῳ Καρόλῳ ἐπὶ τῷ εὐθύνειν αὐτὸν τοὺς οἴακας τῆς Ἱσπανίας / *Congratulatio Regi praestantissimo Carolo quod clavum Hispaniae teneat*, Matriti: ex typographia Antonii Perez de Soto 1759, p. Xii.

Crit.: 2 αἳ debuit || **3** potius ἐν ὅσῳ || **4** νηλεές debuit | κατάθεσθε debuit || **7** ἐπιχειρεῖ debuit || **8** γὲ (idem l. 10), correxi || **9** ἤμματα, correxi || **10** ριθμῖσθαι, correxi || **11** εἶν, correxi

Sim.: 1 δεινωποῦ] de adi. cf. Hes. [*Sc.*] 514 et Hsch. δ 514 || **11** ἐκδιανύσθαι] hapax ut vid.

For the King's life

O Moirai, you stranger nation of tremendous hell,
you who weave the thin thread of human life,
and, whenever it pleases you, suddenly undo the fabric,
give up willingly this cruel practice of yours,
[5] prolong the thread of our lord's life in view of the need
that his faithful subjects really have of him:
Some envious Divinity attempts to cut off his thread,
so please deviate immediately the fatal blow on our head.
We ask you one thing only, to measure the threads
[10] of Charles' life according to his moral virtues;
do allow him to realise the plans in his mind.

Metre: Hexameters. The author is plainly incapable of handling Greek prosody and metre properly; there are problems with hiatus, aphaeresis (ll. 2, 3), diaeresis (l. 3 εἴθαρ, but the whole line is problematic), elision (l. 6 ἀρχόμεν[οι]), quantities (ll. 5, 10, 11 etc.); there are bipartite hexameters (ll. 4, 6; see also l. 11 with a series of spondees); but above all ll. 5, 8, 10 are simply metrically untenable, and by no means easy to correct.

Notes: The *Congratulatio* expressed Spain's mourning for the loss of King Ferdinand, but also the relief at the prospect of the consecration of King Charles III, who had already demonstrated his ability as a ruler in Southern Italy. The lines presented here correspond to the last section of the poem, and in their expressive awkwardness and lack of plausible literary allusions, they show how episodic and confused the Greek literary culture of Castro was – as opposed to his Latin eloquence, which enabled him to produce a much more convincing Latin version of the same invocation 'pro vita regis' on the facing page.[28]

Biography: Born in Galicia around 1739, Joseph Rodríguez de Castro studied Classics and Oriental languages at the Jesuit Colegio Imperial in Madrid; he later worked for a long time at the Royal Library, helping *inter alia* J. Iriarte complete

---

[28] *O proles Erebi diri, et crudelis, acerba / Quae nes vitae hominum subtilia stamina fluxae, / Dum placet extemplo fatalia fila revolvis: / Officium crudele tuum depone libenter, / Et nostri CAROLI filum metire secundum / Vota peregregii populi flagrantis amore / Illius lucis, cuius tutamine dulci / Indiget, ut prorsus sibi commoda cuncta supersint. / Si quis Divorum tentet discindere livens / Principis excelsi filum, te poscimus omnes, / In nos convertas hunc ictum, sospite Rege. / Atque quod enixe plena te voce precamur, / Ut dulcis grataeque dies meteris amoenos / Vitae iuxta animi CAROLI pulcherrima Regis, / Vivere tuque sinas, donec quae mente recepit / Perficiat plane Princeps celeberrimus ipse.*

the Catalogue of Greek manuscripts, and composing an ambitious *Biblioteca Española* (only two volumes published, 1781–1786) that gathered critical profiles of Spanish authors of different ages. His *Congratulatio regi Carolo*, a trilingual poem (Greek, Latin, and Hebrew) written at 20 for the accession to the throne of King Charles III, earned him precocious literary glory, despite the modesty of its results.

Bibliography: Hernando 1975, 292; Fernandez Sanchez, José (1987), "José Rodríguez de Castro, criado de S.M. en la Biblioteca Real", in: *Homenaje a Justo García Morales*, Madrid, 155–171; Sanchez Mariana, Manuel (2013), in: *DBE* 43, 936f.

Poetry from the Jesuit college of Villagarcía de Campos

I. Roque Menchaca (1743–1810) Εἰς τὸν παῖδα Ἰησοῦν [ca. 1760–1767]

Αἰθέρι καὶ γῆσιν δυνατὸν δὴ μακρὸν ἄνακτα
ἐν φάτνῃ μικρᾷ ψύχεα δεινὰ κακοῖ.
Μικκύλος οὗτος ἁμῶν αἰτεῖ τοῖς δάκρυσιν ἦτορ,
καὶ δ' ἀπορεῖς αὐτῷ δοῦναι ἅπαντα σέο;

Textus: Madrid, Biblioteca Nacional, ms. 3771, f. 189r.

Crit.: accentus spiritusque prorsus omisit auctor, praeter 2 κακοῖ, 3 αἰτεῖ, 4 δοῦναι: cett. ipse restitui

Sim.: 3 μικκύλος] prob. e Moschi *Am. Fug.* (*Anth. Pal.* 9.440) 13

On the child Jesus

In a small manger a terrible cold distresses the great Lord,
    powerful in the sky and in the countries of the earth.
This small baby begs our heart with his tears:
    do you hesitate to give all you have to him?

II. Miguel Macías (ca. 1745–1817)
Epigramma Graecum in Patrem Rectorem [ca. 1760–1767]

Πηγὴ ξήρ' ἐνταῦθα λέγῃ Φονσήκ' ἀπὸ πάντων,
 παιδείᾳ δὲ βρέχεις ἤτορα τάρχόμενα.
Εὔκολος εἶ αὐτός, σύνφημι, πολλάκις ἀλλὰ
 χειρουργοῦ δίκην εἰδότος πικρὰ πρίεις.

Textus: Madrid, Biblioteca Nacional, ms. 3771, f. 175v.

Crit.: accentus spiritusque prorsus omisit auctor, praeter 1 πηγὴ, 2 δὲ, 3 σύνφημι: cett. ipse restitui ‖ 3 πολάκις

Greek epigram for the Father Rector

> O Fonseca, here you are called by everyone 'a dry source',
> but you inundate with doctrine the souls of your subjects.
> You have a mild character yourself, I agree, but often like an expert
> surgeon you saw away the bitter evils.

Metre: Both texts are in elegiac couplets, and both are marred by prosodical mistakes (I.3 ἁμῶν with short α; II.1 the elision of long α in ξηρά and in Φονσήκα); ll. 3 and 4 of Macías' text do not scan (σύνφημι and εἰδότος have untenable prosody).

Notes: Both texts are accompanied by a metrical Latin translation, Macías' also by a Spanish one.[29] Menchaca's poetic diction is very rudimentary, with several mistakes (l. 1 the plural of γῆ, and μακρός for μέγας, l. 3 the position of δέ, l. 4 the strange *iunctura* ἄπαντα σέο, probably translating *cuncta tui* or the like); Macías' Greek is no less problematic, but the topic is less conventional, and the idea of etymologising the name of the rector (*fons-seca*) is witty. It must be stressed that both authors were very young, and that these exercises stem from their formative years at Villagarcía de Campos.

---

[29] I. Menchaca: *Coelis et terra longe lateque potentem / Praesepe in parvo frigora taetra premunt. / Parvulus hic lacrimis deposcit pectora nostra, / Et dubitas illi cuncta referre tua?* II. Macías, Latin: *Fons sterilis quamvis cunctis Fonseca voceris, / Doctrinae cumulo subdita corda iugas. / Tutemet es facilis, fateor, sed saepe peritus / Chirurgus veluti, Rector, acerba secas.* Macías, Spanish: 'Fuente seca tu nombre significa, / Mas no obstante, Fonseca, tu nos riegas, / Y con tu ciencia a todos nos sosiegas. / Blando es tu natural, así lo creo, / Mas si nuestra sobervia lo mereze, / Por lo vivo nos sayas, aunque esquece.'

Biographies: The Jesuit college of Villagarcía de Campos, near Valladolid, was one of the few institutions of its kind where Greek was taught, actively practised, and even printed, in the frame of a relatively advanced *curriculum studiorum*. Greek was not compulsory for pupils, but since it could become an important tool for future theologians, it was taught in a special academy guided by Father José Petisco: amongst the texts studied we find Aesop, Homer, Demosthenes, St Basil, the *Batrachomyomachia*, and even poets such as Pindar, Anacreon and Theocritus, *modo sint expurgati*. This special curriculum was then refined in the second half of the 18th century by Father Francisco Javier de Idiáquez, and Villagarcía de Campos became a model of Jesuit instruction for the whole of Spain. Ms. 3771 of the Biblioteca Nacional in Madrid contains a number of Latin and Greek verse compositions by pupils of this College. Of the two authors considered here, Roque Menchaca (Llodio, Oviedo 1743 – Orvieto 1810) became a prominent Jesuit father, who fled to Italy after the ban on the Jesuits in Spain in 1767, and settled in Bologna, where he edited and translated the letters of St Ignatius of Loyola and of St Francis Xavier; he later moved to Naples and finally to Orvieto after Bonaparte's ban on the Jesuits in 1806. Miguel Macías (Paredes de Nava, Palencia ca. 1745 – Villagarcía 1817), on the other hand, entered the college of Villagarcía in 1760 and after the 1767 ban he also fled to Italy (Rimini); he came back to Spain in 1798 and settled in Palencia, but lived long enough to see the final re-instauration of the Company of Jesus in Spain in 1814.

Bibliography: Fernandez Martin, Luis (1953), *El Colegio de Humanidades de Villagarcía dos Campos de 1742 a 1757*, Madrid; Hernando 1975, 85–91, 420f.; Pérez Picón, Conrado (1983), *Un Colegio ejemplar de letras humanas en Villagarcía de Campos (1576–1767)*, Santander. On Menchaca: Verd Conradi, Gabriel Maria (2004), "El P. Roque Menchaca, San Ignacio y el Soneto 'No me mueve, mi Dios, para quererte'", in: *Archivo Teológico Granadino* 67, 109–145; Batllori, Miguel (1996), "Tres ex-jesuitas españoles en la formación de Angelo Mai: Pignatelli, Andrés, Menchaca", in: *La cultura hispano-italiana de los jesuitas expulsos*, Madrid, 97–104. On Macías: Pérez Picón, Conrado (1982), *Villagarcía de Campos. Estudio histórico-artístico*, Valladolid, 177f. and 251f.

Manuel Lassala y Sangermán (1738–1806)

‹Ad cardinalem Boncompagnium› [1785]

Ζεὺς μὲν ἔδωκε σοφοὺς τῆς δίας Παλλάδος υἱοὺς
νῦν δοκίμοις σώζειν πράγματα κοινὰ νόμοις·
Νεκκῆρ', Ἀνθοφαλόν, Πίττον, Καυνίτζιον ἄλλοις,
κοσμοκράτῃ Ῥώμῃ τὸν δ' Εὐεταιριάδην.

Textus: Valencia, Biblioteca de la Universidad, ms. 573/16, no. 5, unde Carbonell Boria, Maria José/Sanchis Llopis, Jordi (1989), "Poemas en griego de Manuel Lassala", in: *Actas del VII Congreso Español de Estudios Clásicos*, III, Madrid, 405–411: 409.

Crit.: (omnia corr. edd. principes praeter 3 Νεκῆρα) **1** δῖας ms. ‖ **2** δοκιμοῖς ms. ‖ **3** Νεκῆρα ms. ‖ ἄλλοῖς ms. ‖ **4** κοσμοκρατῇ ms. (κοσμοκράτορι debuit)

Sim.: 1 δίας Παλλάδος] cf. Eur. *Phoen.* 666–667 ‖ **2** δοκίμοις…νόμοις] cf. Arist. fr. 548.8 Rose (de Zaleuco) ‖ σώζειν πράγματα κοινά] cf. Eur. *Iph. Taur.* 1062

‹For Cardinal Boncompagni›

> Zeus has now allowed the wise children of divine Pallas
>   to save the common good by excellent laws:
> for other nations these are Necker, Floridablanca, Pitt, Kaunitz,
>   and for world-ruling Rome it is Boncompagni.

Metre: Elegiac couplets. Metre and prosody are correct: the only peculiarity is the (legitimate) internal *correptio* of the diphthongue in the newly created name Εὐεταιριάδης.

Notes: This short epigram belongs to a series of thirteen *poésies d'occasion* written by Lassala in Bologna, in the same milieu where Manuel Aponte (see below) and Clotilde Tambroni (→ **Italy**) practiced their poetic vein in Greek. The text was no doubt conceived as a short celebrative piece on the promotion of Cardinal Ignazio Gaetano Boncompagni Ludovisi (1743–1790), the former papal legate in Bologna, to the rank of Secretary of State of Pope Pius VI (1785; he remained in office until 1789). This specific political context also explains the juxtaposition of Boncompagni with other outstanding members of the European political scene, made explicit in the author's Latin version:[30] the powerful French minister Jacques Necker (1732–1804, in office until 1790), the Spanish prime minister José Moñino y Redondo, count of Floridablanca (1728–1808), the English prime minister William Pitt Jr. (1759–1806), the Austrian chancellor Wentzel Anton von Kaunitz-Rietberg (1711–1794, in office until 1792). Beside the poetic echoes of the first distich (which attest to a certain familiarity with Greek literary language), the main interest of this epigram lies in the Greek rendering of the proper names in ll. 3–4, chiefly in the etymological calques Ἀνθοφαλός (ἄνθος 'flower' = 'flor' +

---

[30] *Jupiter dedit sapientes divinae Palladis filios / Nunc dignis servare rem publicam legibus; / Necker, Floridablanca, Pitt, Kaunitz aliis, / Romae terrarum dominae Boncompagnium.*

the rare φαλός 'white' = 'blanco') for Floridablanca, and Εὐεταιριάδης (εὖ 'well' = 'bene, buono' + ἑταῖρος 'friend' = 'compagno') for Boncompagni.

Biography: The Jesuit Lassala (Valencia 1738 – Valencia 1806) was trained in his hometown, and fled after the ban on the Jesuits issued in Spain in 1767. He spent 32 years in Italy, chiefly between Ferrara and Bologna, where he authored several dramas, translations, philosophical works in Latin, Spanish or Italian: many of his works are still unpublished and preserved to this day in the mss. Valencia, Biblioteca de la Universidad 573 and 574; in 1798, he returned to Valencia, where he continued his literary activity. In Italy he entered the glorious Accademia dell'Arcadia in 1775, with the name of Eurylius Cleoneus: it should be recalled that several of the members of this institution tried their hand at Greek versification (→ **Italy**).

Bibliography: Carbonell Boria/Sanchis Llopis 1989 (see above Textus); Astorgano Abajo, Antonio (2012), in: *DBE* 29, 168–172.

Benito Pardo Figueroa y Valladares (1755–1812)

Εἰς τὴν Σεβαστὴν Βασίλισσαν Βορυσσῶν [1806]

"Αἰνῶς ἀθανάτῃσι θεῇς εἰς ὦπα ἔοικεν"
θεῖος Ὅμηρος ἔφη δ' ἀζόμενος δ' Ἑλένην·
Ἀλλὰ σὲ πότνιαν εἰδὼν νῦν κεν φῇ πὲρ ἰσοῦσαν
Παλλάδι σωφροσύνην, Κύπριδι δ' εἰς χάριτα.

Textus: *Memorial Literario o Biblioteca Periodica de Ciencias y Artes* VII (1806), 329

Crit.: Tit. Βασίλισαν ed., correxi || **1** θέης ed., correxi || **2** Ὁμήρος ed., correxi | δάζομενος δ' Ελενην ed., correxi || **3** ποτνιαν ειδων νύν κὲν ed., correxi (ἰδών debuit) | ἴσουσαν ed., correxi || **4** Παλλάδι debuit

Sim.: 1 cf. *Il.* 3.158 || **2** θεῖος Ὅμηρος] saep., e.g. *Anth. Pal.* 7.3.2, 7.4.1, 7.7.1 etc.

For the Venerable Queen of the Prussians

'She looks incredibly like the immortal goddesses in her aspect,'
  thus wrote divine Homer in veneration of Helen:
But seeing you now, most powerful lady, he would say that you equal
  Pallas by your wisdom, the Cyprian goddess by your grace.

Metre: Elegiac couplets; l. 3 is a bipartite hexameter.

Notes: The epigram was printed in the *Memorial literario*, arguably the most important literary journal of the Spanish Enlightenment (1784–1808, but 1801–1808 in its last series), together with its Spanish translation.[31] The lady here celebrated is the beautiful Queen Luise of Prussia (1776–1810), the wife of Friedrich Wilhelm III: it is interesting to remark that in October 1806, just three months after the publication of Pardo's epigram, the royal couple had to flee Berlin because of Napoleon's fulminating invasion (culminated in the battle of Jena). Pardo's Greek is very rudimentary (the wrong use of δέ and περ in ll. 2–3, the wrong participle εἰδών for ἰδών in l. 3), and one wonders if some orthographical mistakes should not be ascribed to the author rather than to the publisher.

Biography: Benito Pardo Figueroa y Valladares (Fefiñanes, Pontevedra 1755 – Riga 1812) made a brilliant career in the army and, after some years spent in Paris, served as an ambassador to Prussia (Berlin) since March 1806, and then to Russia (Moscow) from 1808 until Napoleon's invasion in 1812. During his political and military activity, Pardo also wrote some Latin poems and an essay on Raphael and Greek painting.

Bibliography: Ozanam, Didier (2010), in: *DBE* 40, 59f; Larriba, Elisabel (2010), "La última salida al ruedo del *Memorial literario*", in: *Cuadernos de Ilustración y Romanticismo* 16, 1–88.

---

[31] '"Retrato fiel de las celestes Diosas": / Homero llama á la gentil Helena; / Mas si viese las prendas generosas / Que adornan tu beldad de gracias llena, / Te igualára á Minerva en la cordura, / Y a la madre de Amor en la hermosura.'

Manuel Aponte (1737–1815)

Ἐν εὐτυχεῖ
νόστῳ πρὸς ἱερὰν αὐτοῦ ἕδραν τοῦ Ἁγιωτάτου
χ᾽Ὑπάτου Ἀρχιερέως Κυρίου ἡμῶν Πίου
τοῦ Ἑβδόμου

Σαπφικὸν εἶδος
Εἰς Ῥώμην [1815]

    Χαῖρέ μοι Ῥώμα λαβέουσα κῦδος,
    οἷον ἐξαίφνης γελανεῖ προσώπῳ
    δῶκεν Ὕψιστος, μέγα θαῦμα, Κόσμῳ,
4   Ποιμένα δέξον.
    Εὖτε δ᾽ ἡρπάσθη ἀπό σευ μελάθρων
    εἰς μέρη Βορρᾶ κρατερῶς ἀπαχθεὶς
    δὴ τότ᾽ αὐχμώσης τραφερῆς τε χ᾽ὑγρῆς
8   Πείρατα πενθεῖ.
    Νῦν σε δεῖ φαιδρὰν περὶ κηρὶ μᾶλλον
    εὔγμασιν, φωναῖς, λιγυροῖς τε σείστροις,
    τυμπάνοις κ᾽ αὐλοῖς Πόλον εἰς ἀεῖραι
12   Σὸν γάνος αἰπύ.
    Τόσσον οὐ Καῖσαρ ποτε προυλέλαμπεν,
    ἅρματ᾽ Ἐσσῆνας πολίων ὑφέλκων,
    ὅσσον ὥριστος παραφαίνεθ᾽ Οὗτος
16   Θεῖος ἀρητήρ.
    Κεῖνος ἄρ χρυσῆν ἐνέδυνε πόρπην·
    Ἀλλ᾽ ὅ γ᾽ εἰν ἑσμῷ ἀρετῶν κρατίστων
    ἀσφαλῶς βαίνει θρόνον αἰὲν ἄκρον
20   ἀμφ᾽ ἀσάλευτον.
    Ἄσμενοι Χριστοῦ μεγάλου λαχόντι
    κάρτος ἠδ᾽ εἶδος δύναμίν τε τιμῆς,
    ἀξίως αὐτῷ προφέρωμεν αἴνους
24   ὅττι τάχιστα.
    Μᾶλλον ὑμνῶμεν Θεὸν αἰναληθῆ,
    εὐσεβῆ δῆμον φιλέονθ᾽, ὃς αὖθις
    ἐν Πίου νόστῳ ἀνέφηνε Ῥώμην
28   αἰὲν ἄνασσαν.

Textus: Alla Santità di Pio VII P.O.M. felicemente regnante pel suo glorioso ritorno a Roma nel giorno xxiv maggio MDCCCXIV...*Applausi poetici*, Ferrara: per Gaetano Bresciani, 1815, pp. cxlvi–cxlviii.

Crit.: 4 δέξου debuit || 13 Καῖσάρ ποτε debuit || 20 ἀμφασάλευτον ed., correxi

Sim.: 1 χαῖρέ μοι 'Ρώμα] idem Melinno, *Suppl. Hell.* 541.1 (11 ἀσφαλῶς cf. hic v. 19) || **2** γελανεῖ] cf. Pind. *Ol.* 5.2 et *Pyth.* 4.181 || **7** cf. *Il.* 14.308 et *Od.* 20.98 (ἐπὶ τραφερήν τε καὶ ὑγρήν); de re cf. Melinn. *Suppl. Hell.* 541.10 (στέρνα γαίας καὶ πολιᾶς θαλάσσας) || **10** εὔγμασιν] cf. Call. *Hymn.* 5.139 || **14** ἐσσῆνας] de subst. cf. Hsch. ε 6335 || **18** ἐσμῷ ἀρετῶν] cf. e.g. Them. *de philanthr.* 5a

On the merry return of the Holiest and Sublime Pontiff, our Lord Pius VII, to His Holy See

Sapphic Ode – To Rome

>Hail, o Rome, who have retrieved the glory
>that suddenly with cheerful glance the Highest
>tributed to you – what a wonder for the World:
>[4] welcome the Shepherd!
>When he was driven away from your palaces,
>being violently abducted to the Northern lands,
>since then the territories of the thirsty, the dry
>[8] and the damp earth were mourning.
>Beaming of joy in your heart, you should now
>extol your sublime happiness to the sky
>with prayers, songs, high-pitched rattles,
>[12] drums and flutes.
>Not even Caesar did ever shine as bright,
>dragging on his cart the Kings of cities,
>as has appeared This excellent
>[16]   Divine priest.
>For Caesar wore a golden brooch,
>whereas the other one amid the greatest virtues
>keeps proceeding safely towards the unshaken,
>[20] highest throne.
>Let us voice in happiness, immediately,
>worthy praises of him, who obtained by lot the power,
>the beauty, and the strong honour
>[24] of the great Christ.
>Let us sing even more the true, powerful God,
>who loves the pious people, who once again
>with Pius' return has made Rome
>[28] forever the queen of cities.

Metre: Sapphic stanzas. Both metre and prosody are generally flawless: only in l. 16 ἀρητήρ has a long α, not a short one as Aponte believes.

Notes: This ode (accompanied by a facing Italian translation)[32] is clearly inspired by the Sapphic *Ode to Rome* of the Hellenistic poetess Melinno, and it belongs to a sylloge of miscellaneous, mostly anonymous Latin and Italian poems (sonnets, *canzoni*, longer compositions) in honour of Pope Pius VII (1742–1823), a native of Cesena (Emilia). The 'return' to Rome celebrated here is a major event in Italian history, namely the end of the long period of papal captivity that had started in July 1809, when Napoleon's soldiers had kidnapped the Pope and brought him to Savona and later to Fontainebleau, where he had to accept very harsh conditions in exchange for freedom. Napoleon's defeat at Leipzig in 1813, however, accelerated his return to Italy, and in 1814 he was able to reach the Holy See through an adventurous journey and after spending some happy weeks in Bologna, Imola, and Forlì. Aponte (who signed the Greek compositions of this book on p. cl) writes a plausible and learned hymn, although he does not lean on a single poetic model. There are some problems, e.g. irrational 'distractions' (l. 1 λαβέουσα for λαβοῦσα), incorrect diathesis (l. 4 δέξον rather than δέξου), implausible forms (the perfect προυλέλαμπεν in l. 13 has an irrational augment), some semantic peculiarities (l. 12 αἰπύ is probably used in the sense of ὑψηλόν). But note the interesting *hapax* αἰναληθής (l. 25).

Biography: Manuel Rodríguez Aponte (Oropesa, Toledo 1737 – Bologna 1815) entered the Jesuit order in 1753, and two years later he was sent to the Philippines, where he was active as a missionary and as a professor of philosophy at the Colegio de San Ignacio of Manila. In Manila, Aponte was struck by the 1767 ban on the Jesuits: he came back to Spain and immediately took refuge in Bologna, where, from 1794, he held the professorship of Greek, teaching *inter alios* the well-known intellectual and poet Clotilde Tambroni (→ **Italy**), who later became his successor in that chair. Aponte wrote grammars and handbooks of Greek, and he translated passages of Homer into Spanish verse; in Greek he wrote some letters, an idyllion

---

32 'Salve, o mia Roma, che alla gloria antica / Aggiungi della nuova il bel fulgore, / Or che ti rende Dio con fronte amica / Il tuo Pastore. // Quando rapito da' regali tetti / Al Franco Regno a forza fu condutto, / La Terra, il Mar, le Stelle in tetri aspetti / Piansero a lutto. // Or ti fa lieta che tu n'hai ben onde, / E suoni tua letizia in canti e gridi: / Rimbombi Eco del Tebro in sulle sponde, / E al Ciel la gridi. // Non con più gloria entrò l'alte tue mura / Cesar traendo i Re schivi di vita, / Di Lui che vien da guerra acerba e dura / Divo Levita. // S'ei le vie corse colle schiere intorno, / Che menava cattive al Campidoglio, / Delle chiare virtudi il Padre adorno / Ascende al soglio. // Or per noi non si taccia l'alto merto, / Perché di Roma il fren riprende in mano / e torna del gran Manto ricoverto / Signor Sovrano; // E a Dio si volga il canto che s'adopra, / Onde le genti e la Città latina / Alle cose mortal vada di sopra / Sempre Regina.'

(1813) and other shorter pieces (some of which are preserved in ms. Ferrajoli 514 of the Vatican Library).

Bibliography: Piñero, Félix (1978), "Los estudios helénicos de Manuel Aponte", in: *Actas del V Congreso Español de Estudios Clásicos*, Madrid, 703–708; Baldini, Ugo/Brizzi, Gian Paolo (2010), *La presenza in Italia dei gesuiti iberici espulsi*, Bologna, 243; Fernández Arillaga, Inmaculada (2010), in: *DBE* 4, 354f.

Francisco Rebelo Gonçalves (1907–1982)

I. Εἴς τινα γυναῖκα [1967]

Πρὸς τὸν ἐρῶνθ' ἃ λέγεις ὀμνῦσ' Ἔρον ὅρκον ἐφ' ὅρκῳ,
ταῦτα γράφειν δεῖ πάντ' εἰς ἄνεμον καὶ ὕδωρ.

Textus: Rebelo Gonçalves, Francisco (1967), "Ἐπιγράμματια", in: *Euphrosyne* n.s. 1, 335f = Id. (1995), *Obra completa*, I, Lisboa, Fundação Calouste Gulbenkian, p. 805

Sim.: 2 cf. e.g. Soph. fr. 811 R. (ὅρκους ἐγὼ γυναικὸς εἰς ὕδωρ γράφω)

To a woman

Whatever you say to your lover swearing one oath after the other by Eros,
all that should be written on sand or water.

II. Δένδρα καὶ βίβλοι [1973]

Τρισόλβιος πᾶς ὅστις ὢν φημῶν ἑκὰς
δεινοῦ τε τῆς πόλεως ψόφου
θάλλονθ' ἑαυτοῦ δένδρα σιγηλὸς βλέπει
χαίρει τ' ἀνειλίσσων βίβλους.

Textus: Rebelo Gonçalves, Francisco (1973), "Δένδρα καὶ βίβλοι", in: *Euphrosyne* n.s. 6, 379 = Id. (1995), *Obra completa*, I, Lisboa, Fundação Calouste Gulbenkian, p. 809

Sim.: 1 τρισόλβιος...ὅστις] cf. *Anth. Pal.* 5.94.3

Trees and books

> Thrice merry the man who far from the voices
>   and the terrible noise of the city
> looks in silence to his trees in blossom
>   and rejoices in browsing books.

Metre: The first text is in elegiac couplets, the second in iambic distichs (one trimeter + one dimeter).

Notes: Rebelo Gonçalves published frequently short epigrams in Greek and Latin on the Portuguese periodical of Classical Studies *Euphrosyne*: his Greek output embraces some light *pièces d'occasion*, an inscription in honour of the humanist André de Resende, and translations of sonnets by Luís de Camões. The first of our two epigrams is a declared imitation of Catullus 70.3–4 (*sed mulier cupido quod dicit amanti / in vento et rapida scribere oportet aqua*), although the mediation of Sophocles' *gnome* can also be discerned. The other epigram (dated Ἐν Μάφρᾳ, i.e. in Rebelo Gonçalves' summer house in Mafra, in the district of Lisbon) is equipped with a Latin and a Portuguese translation.[33]

Biography: One of the most important philologists of 20th-century Portugal, Francisco da Luz Rebelo Gonçalves (Santarém 1907–1982) was a professor of Portuguese Language and Philology at Coimbra, Lisbon, and São Paulo, and the author of an important dictionary of Portuguese and of a treatise on Portuguese orthography. A militant humanist, he also taught classical philology and favoured the comparative study of the ancient and the modern world.

Bibliography: Rebelo Gonçalves, Francisco (1995–2002), *Obra completa*, ed. Maria Inês Rebelo Gonçalves, I–III, Lisboa.

---

33 Latin: *Felix ter ille qui procul rumoribus / et urbis horrido sono / tacens virentes arbores videt suas / librosque gaudet volvere.* Portuguese: 'Feliz três vezes quem, fugindo às atoardas / E à da cidade barulheira atroz, / Vê, silencioso, vicejando suas árvores / E em ler seus livros se recreia e folga.'

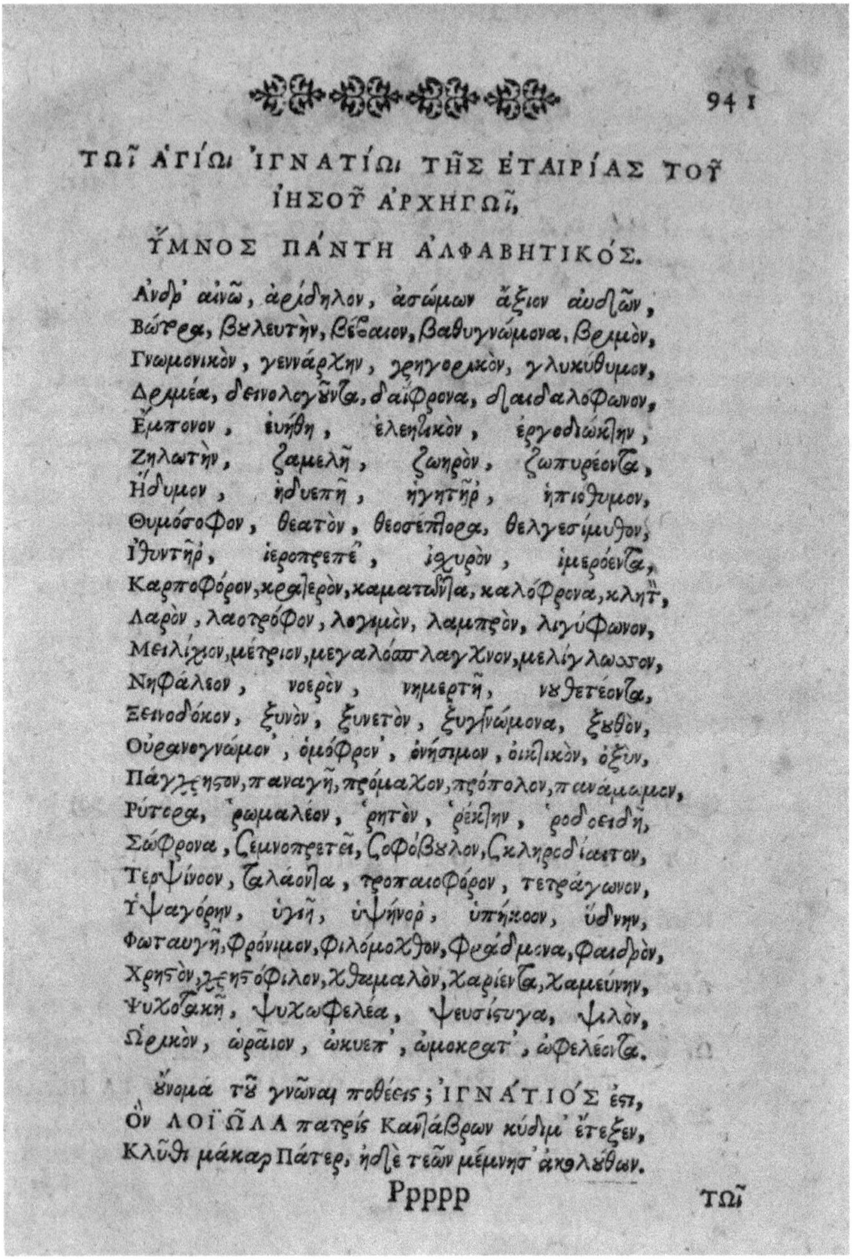

941

ΤΩι ΑΓΊΩι ΙΓΝΑΤΊΩι ΤΗΣ ΕΤΑΙΡΊΑΣ ΤΟΫ̓
ΙΗΣΟΫ̓ ΑΡΧΗΓΩι.

ΫΜΝΟΣ ΠΑΝΤΗ ΑΛΦΑΒΗΤΙΚΌΣ.

Ἄνδρ' αἰνῶ, ἀρίδηλον, ἀσώμων ἄξιον αὐδῶν,
Βώρεα, βυλευτὴν, βέβαιον, βαθυγνώμονα, βερμὸν,
Γνωμονικὸν, γεννάρχην, γρηγορικὸν, γλυκύθυμον,
Δερμέα, δεινολογῦντα, δαίφρονα, δαιδαλόφωνον,
Ἔμπονον, εὐήθη, ἐλεητικὸν, ἐργοδιώκτην,
Ζηλωτὴν, ζαμελῆ, ζωηρὸν, ζωπυρέοντα,
Ἥδυμον, ἡδυεπῆ, ἡγητῆρ', ἠπιόθυμον,
Θυμόσοφον, θεατὸν, θεοσέπτορα, θελγεσίμυθον,
Ἰθυντῆρ', ἱεροπρεπέ', ἰσχυρὸν, ἱμερόεντα,
Καρποφόρον, κεφαλερὸν, καματωδῆα, καλόφρονα, κλητ',
Λαρὸν, λαοτρόφον, λογιμὸν, λαμπρὸν, λιγύφωνον,
Μειλίχιον, μέτριον, μεγαλόσπλαγχνον, μελίγλωσσον,
Νηφάλεον, νοερὸν, νημερτῆ, νυθετέοντα,
Ξεινοδόκον, ξυνὸν, ξυνετὸν, ξυγγνώμονα, ξυθὸν,
Οὐρανογνώμον, ὁμόφρον', ὀνήσιμον, οἰκτιρικὸν, ὀξὺν,
Πάγχρηστον, πανάγη, πρόμαχον, πρόπολον, πανάλωμον,
Ῥυτερα, ῥωμαλέον, ῥητὸν, ῥέκτην, ῥοδοειδῆ,
Σώφρονα, σεμνοπρεπεῖ, σοφόβυλον, σκληροδίαιτον,
Τερψίνοον, ταλάσιφα, τροπαιοφόρον, τετράγωνον,
Ὑψαγόρην, ὑγιῆ, ὑψήνορ', ὑπήκοον, ὕδνην,
Φωταυγῆ, φρόνιμον, φιλόμοχθον, Φραζμενα, φαιδρὸν,
Χρηστὸν, ξρηστόφιλον, χθεμαλὸν, χαρίεντα, χαμεύνην,
Ψυχοδάκη, ψυχωφελέα, ψευσίσυγα, ψιλὸν,
Ὠρικὸν, ὥραιον, ὠκυεπ', ἀμοκρατ', ὠφελέοντα.

ὄνομα τῶ γνῶναι ποθέεις; ΙΓΝΑΤΙΟΣ ἐςὶ,
Ὃν ΛΟΪΌΛΑ πατρὶς Καντάβρων κύδιμ' ἔτεξεν,
Κλῦθι μάκαρ Πάτερ, ἠδ|ὲ τεῶν μέμνησ' ἀκολύθων.

Ppppp ΤΩι

Fig. 12: *Thesauri Polonolatinograeci Gregorii Cnapii e Societate Iesu tomus secundus* [...], Cracoviae: Sumptu & Typis Francisci Caesarii, 1626, 941: alphabetic hymn on Ignatius of Loyola by Gregorius Cnapius (see below, p. 636–639).

Tomas Veteikis (in collaboration with Gościwit Malinowski and Bartosz Awianowicz)
Poland and Lithuania

The present collection is a small part of the overall corpus of poems written and printed in ancient Greek in the area of the former Polish-Lithuanian Commonwealth and its two descendant countries, present-day Poland and Lithuania. Despite certain difficulties of territorial and national attribution,[1] the texts and authors in this section were chosen so as to meet one of the following criteria: 1) the texts are closely related (by their contents or through their target audience) either to the former Polish Crown and the Grand Duchy of Lithuania prior to the period of Great Partitions (1772–1795), or to the modern states of Lithuania and Poland; 2) the authors either have their origins in the aforementioned areas (which vary throughout the various historical periods) or they share close personal ties with Polish and Lithuanian contexts and personalities.[2]

The collection has been restricted due to lack of space, and it also suffers from the relatively poor state of research on this sort of texts, which mostly survive scattered in handwritten copies or obscure prints, both in the Polish and in the Lithuanian tradition. Since the longer poems and the manuscript texts are currently less well explored, we have only included short compositions (not exceeding 50 lines) that have appeared in print. The sheer quantity of poems, according to the data gathered by Polish and Lithuanian researchers, point to the Renaissance and Early Baroque (roughly the 16th and 17th centuries) as the period of greatest prosperity of Greek studies and literature in Lithuania and Poland, as reflected also in the overall revival of humanistic studies in Western Europe and the influence of this revival on local educational trends and culture. The traces of Greek literature in later centuries (from the 18th to the 21st) are considerably smaller, due to the general decline of Greek studies in favour of modern languages, as well as to some other local circumstances: despite our unsatisfactory understanding of the texts of this period in their entirety, two examples from this latter period have been included into the present collection, namely the only

---

1 Present-day Poland and Lithuania are just the remnants of that complex and shifting geopolitical formation that was the Polish-Lithuanian Commonwealth.
2 As a consequence, this section does not aim at covering the texts of modern Russia, Belarus, Ukraine, Latvia, Estonia, despite the fact that some of their territories (including some important cultural centres) were for some time constituent parts of the Polish Kingdom and the Grand Duchy of Lithuania.

https://doi.org/10.1515/9783110652758-014

known elegiac couplet of the 18th century[3] and one *poème d'occasion* that is based on the imitation of Pindaric metre and style by the *poeta doctus* **Jerzy Danielewicz**, illustrious representative of contemporaneous Polish and Lithuanian professors of Greek. Other (mostly unpublished) texts of contemporary academic poets remain yet to be discovered.[4]

Our selection of texts from the 16th and 17th centuries followed a number of criteria, including general relevance, political and intellectual authority, religious and academic affiliation of the authors and of their addressees, contents and style of each text, number and quality of its copies and academic success (both contemporaneous and posthumous). Only the (currently) best known and best revised pieces have found their place in this anthology:[5] among the main sources for the selection was the anthology of Greek poetry in Poland edited by Janina Czerniatowicz (Czerniatowicz 1991, abridged Cz in the critical comments of the present section), which contains 119 different poems by 81 authors, along with the references to a few unpublished texts and 8 texts of other Polish-Lithuanian Hellenists that were either no longer to be found or excluded due to technical reasons. Other sources for the selection of the texts included the PhD thesis by Tomas Veteikis (here cited as Vet 2004), containing 24 new texts from the 16th and 17th centuries that are not covered by Czerniatowicz, as well as recent finds and discussions by classical scholars from Poland and Lithuania (Bartosz Awianowicz, Katarzyna Gara, Gościwit Malinowski, Mindaugas Strockis, Tomas Veteikis, Sławomir Wyszomirski, and Henrikas Zabulis).[6]

Only a handful of the selected authors may be considered professional Greek-writing poets (i.e. scholars who have published books or left numerous handwrit-

---

[3] The elegiac couplet was printed in the 1729 polyglot edition, briefly described in Veteikis 2004 and reproduced as a facsimile in Ulčinaitė 2010, 262.
[4] Another interesting instance of a *poesis docta* can be found in a post by Gosciwit Malinowski in the electronic database *Hellenopolonica*: https://hellenopolonica.blogspot.com/2015/04/carmen-epinicium.html?view=flipcard
[5] This is why a couple of poems composed by students of the Academy of Vilnius (Franciscus Lacki and Nicolaus Zaleski) were chosen over less studied works by more renowned poets of the same period; moreover, these examples of occasional gratification and consolation to famous noblemen were preferred to similar poems of a lesser scholarly status (i.e. composed basically by students), drawn from collections of other schools (mostly Jesuit colleges).
[6] Only a few of these materials have been published so far. Cf. Wyszomirski 1993; Zabulis 2000; Gara 2014; Juchnevičienė/Strockis 2015. Some further discoveries (by Malinowski, Awianowicz, and Veteikis) remain unpublished. Taking into account the handwritten material (esp. Cod. Oss. 1137 and other manuscripts), Veteikis has calculated an approximate total number of 300 poems, representing roughly 12,000 lines.

ten poems). These were chiefly university professors, talented students at remarkable schools or individuals with educational, philological, or publishing experience.[7] Although some are not to be associated with any one particular educational centre, we cannot strictly detach any from the sphere of education and publishing: a common humanistic education ties all these authors together, and the majority can be connected with the most famous centres of education in Lithuania and Poland, such as the Academy of Cracow (the oldest in the region) or the Jesuit College and Academy of Vilnius (active since the 1570s), together with the respective printing houses. Greek poetry from other major educational centres (the Academy of Zamość, various Jesuit colleges, the gymnasia of Protestant and Orthodox communities, Königsberg University) is not included in this collection, with only the exception of a poem by a prominent Hellenist of German origin, **Michael Retell** (c. 1530–1576), active in Toruń and Gdańsk. His fellow-countryman, Johannes Mylius, was similarly included in this collection due to his close relations with the Polish and Lithuanian ruling elite.

The majority of the addressees of the Greek texts were either noblemen of political and religious standing, including rulers (esp. Sigismund II August, Stephen Báthory, Sigismund III Vasa), or members of the academic community. Sometimes the addressees were of collective nature: the inhabitants of a city, the members of an academic society, famous schools, or the universal recipient of prayers and devotion (the God of the Psalms and Gospels or the Christian saints, dear to the poet's country or surrounding community). All this shows the predominantly high-brow character and moral standards of such poetry, features that are evident in the poems of the present selection.

With respect to genres, the present selection reflects the general features of the currently inventoried Greek poetic material of our region, which largely consists of small-scale poems in the form of elegies, hymns, or epigrams with encomiastic or didactic content. Some texts have explicit indications of their genre or can be indirectly associated with one, such as epinician (by **Niegoszewski**), epitaph (by **Zaleski**), *epithalamion* (by Retell), or abecedarion/alphabetic hymn (by **Cnapius**). Almost all the poems show a blend of Greco-Roman and Christian motifs and a mixture of linguistic features that include ingredients from the epic dialect (with sporadic Dorisms and Aeolisms), from classical Attic and post-classical (esp. Biblical-Patristic) Greek and some neologisms. The predominant metres are dactylic hexameter and elegiac couplet, but in order to give a flavour of the variety of metrical experiments, we also include examples of other classical metres, such as the

---

7 Cf. Czerniatowicz 2013, 408.

Sapphic stanza and the Phalaecian hendecasyllable. Moreover, two poetic compositions even allow a double metrical analysis: the Sapphic stanzas of the ***Odarion* to St Casimir** can also be interpreted as rhymed accentual-syllabic verse, while the Greek part of the multilingual *Epinicion* by Niegoszewski consists of two quasi-Pindaric strophes, one of them being simply twenty hexameters, the other implying the almost unchanging repetition of a strophe from one of Pindar's epinician odes.

The selected poems also feature a remarkable variety of themes and moods: exhortations to the young and to men of letters to study law, live a pious life and observe Christian values and a 'Sarmatian' mentality[8] (see the poem by **Przyłuski**); congratulations on the occasion of marriages or the solemn receptions of visiting bishops (poems by Retell and **Lacki**); expressions of grief and respect through *topoi* of consolation for the family members of deceased noblemen (poem by Zaleski); the glorification of saints and prayers to God (Lord's prayer by **Mylius**; anonymous *Odarion* to St Casimir; Cnapius' *abecedarion* to St Ignace of Loyola); praise of outstanding military and cultural leaders (Jan Zamojski in the *Epinicion* by Niegoszewski; Meletius Smotrytsky in the *epos encomiasticon* by **Żórawski**).

Regrettably, several outstanding Hellenists could not be included in the present edition, and they deserve at least a brief mention here. Among them are several professors of the Academies of Cracow, Vilnius, and Zamość, and of the gymnasium at Toruń: Stanisław Marennius (c. 1532–1580), Andreas Schoenaeus (1552–1615), Adam Draski (c. 1587–1648), representing Cracow; Urban Brillius (?–1630) and Szymon Birkowski (1574–1626), representing Zamość; Kasper Pętkowski (1554–1612) and Thomas Klage (c. 1598–1664), representing Vilnius; Adam Freitag Maior (?–1621), representing Toruń.

General Bibliography (including special and conventional abbreviations)

Special abbreviations appearing only in the *apparatus criticus* of this section
- ed. 1548 (etc.) = edition of that year described in the subsection 'Textus'
- edd. = all the editions described in the subsection 'Textus' and/or all the editions seen by the editor of the present section of the anthology

---

8 'Sarmatian' refers to the popular cultural ideology of the Polish-Lithuanian nobility (*szlachta*) based on the belief that the Poles originated from the Sarmatians (in the Greco-Latin terminology), Iranian tribes that lived north of the Black Sea.

- edd. post 1626 (etc.) = all the editions after the edition of the year 1626 (or other which is indicated by number) which were inspected by the editor of the present collection

Abbreviations of bibliographical collections

Estr. = Estreicher, Karol et al. (1891–2014), *Bibliografia polska. 140,000 druków.* Cz. 3 (wieki XV–XVIII), vols. XII–XXXVI, Krakow.
NK = *Nowy Korbut* (1963–1965), ed. Roman Pollak et al., *Piśmiennictwo staropolskie*, 3 vols., Warszawa.
PSB = *Polski słownik biograficzny*, 52 vols. (1935–), ed. Władysław Konopczyński et multi alii, Kraków, Wrocław et al.
VASL = *Vilniaus akademijos spaustuvės leidiniai 1576–1805*, (1979), eds. Konstancija Čepienė/ Irena Petrauskienė, Vilnius.
VD = *Verzeichnis der im deutschen Sprachbereich erschienenen Drucke des 16. Jahrhunderts*, ed. Irmgard Bezzel, Claudia Fabian, Stuttgart, 1983–2000, 25 vols.

Selection of editions of Humanist Greek poetry and secondary literature

Awianowicz, Bartosz (2009), "Humanizm renesansowy w miastach Prus Królewskich", in: *Humanizm. Idee, nurty i paradygmaty humanistyczne w kulturze polskiej. Syntezy*, t. 2: *Humanizm. Historie pojęcia*, Warszawa, 149–197.
Backus, Irena (2006), "Early Christianity in Michael Neander's Greek-Latin edition of Luther's Catechism", in: Christopher R. Ligota/Jean-Louis Quantin (eds.), *History of Scholarship. A Selection of Papers from the Seminar on the History of Scholarship Held Annually at the Warburg Institute*, Oxford, 197–230.
Baldzuhn, Michael (2015), "Mylius, Johannes", in: Wilhelm Kühlmann/Jan-Dirk Müller/Michael Schilling u. a. (eds.), *Frühe Neuzeit in Deutschland 1520–1620. Literaturwissenschaftliches Verfasserlexikon* (VL 16), Bd. 4, Berlin/Boston, 546–554.
Barycz, Henryk (1969), *Z dziejów polskich wędrówek naukowych za granicę*, Wrocław.
Czerniatowicz, Janina (ed.) (1991), *Corpusculum poesis Polono-Graecae saeculorum XVI–XVII (1531–1648)*, Wrocław (= Cz in *app. crit.*)
Czerniatowicz, Janina (2013), "Greek Poetry Composed by Polish Authors in the 16th and 17th Centuries", in: *Eos* C 2013 / fasciculus extra ordinem editus electronicus (ISSN 0012-7825), 403–423 [orig. publ. in: *Eos* 72 (1984), 189–206].
Gara, Katarzyna (2014), "The Greek Hymns of Gregorius Cnapius", in: *Terminus* 16/4 (33), 411–430.
Goedeke, Karl (2011), *Grundriss zur Geschichte der Deutschen Dichtung aus den Quellen*. Zweite...Auflage. Bd. II. Viertes Buch: *Von der Reformation bis zum dreissigjährigen Kriege*, Berlin.
Günther, Johannes (1858), *Lebensskizzen der Professoren der Universität Jena seit 1558 bis 1858: Eine Festgabe zur dreihundertjährigen Säcularfeier der Universität am 15., 16. und 17. August 1858*, Jena.

Juchnevičienė, Nijolė/Strockis, Mindaugas (eds.) (2015), "Addenda Lituanica", in: *Senosios graikų kalbos chrestomatija* [*Reading book on ancient Greek*], Vilnius, 119–135 (= JuStr2015 in *app. crit.*)

Ławińska-Tyszkowska, Janina/Szastyńska-Siemion, Alicja (1985), "Z greckiej twórczości Stanisława Niegoszewskiego", in: *Eos* 73, 69–80.

Łempicki, Stanisław (1925/26), "Manucjusze weneccy a Polska : (karta z dziejów humanizmu w Polsce)", in: *Pamiętnik Literacki: czasopismo kwartalne poświęcone historii i krytyce literatury polskiej*, 22/23/1/4, 124–188.

Nadolski, Bronisław (1969), "Humanizm w murach Gimnazjum Toruńskiego", in: *Rocznik Toruński* 3, 29–54.

Narbutienė, Daiva/Narbutas, Sigitas (eds.) (1998), *Index librorum Latinorum Lituaniae saeculi septimi decimi*, Vilnius.

Narbutienė, Daiva/Narbutas, Sigitas (eds.) (2002), *Index librorum Latinorum Lituaniae saeculi quinti decimi et sexti decimi*, Vilnius.

Nekraševič-Karotkaja, Žanna (2019), "Widmungsgedichte von Johannes Mylius aus Liebenrode: zum Programm der humanistischen Katechese und religiösen Versöhnung in der Reformationszeit", in: *Neulateinisches Jahrbuch* 21, 273–307.

Niekraszewicz-Karotkaja, Żanna (2018), "Рэнесансная сядзіба Муз у Заблудаве: педагагічная і творчая дзейнасць Іагана Мюліуса пад патранатам Грыгорыя Хадкевіча", in: *Беларутэністыка Беластоцка* 10, 323–338.

Nowak-Dłużewski, Juliusz (1966), *Okolicznościowa poezja polityczna w Polsce: czasy Zygmuntowskie*, Warszawa.

Peressin, Roberto (2016), "The Lord's Prayer in Six Greek Dialects. A Curious Variation on a Renaissance Linguistic Topic", in: *Language and Literary Studies of Warsaw. Rocznik Naukowy Lingwistycznej Szkoły Wyższej w Warszawie*, Nr 6, Warszawa, 187–210.

Squire, Michael (2011), *The* Iliad *in a Nutshell: Visualizing Epic on the* Tabulae Iliacae, Oxford.

Strockis, Mindaugas (2001), "Graikų kalbos kirčiavimas ir eilėdara XVII a. Vilniaus universitete. Grigaliaus Sventickio *Odarion*", in: *Literatūra* 43/3, 106–116 (includes first modern edition of the *Odarion* from the *Theatrum S. Casimiri* (1604) in Lithuania) (= Stro2001 in *app. crit.*).

Strockis, Mindaugas (2002), "Graikų kalbos kirčiavimo teorijos ir Grigaliaus Sventickio *Odarion* (1604) eilėdara", in: *Literatūra* 44/3, 87–96.

Strockis, Mindaugas (2007), *Klasikinių kalbų kirčio žymėjimo įtaka lietuvių kirčio žymėjimui*. Daktaro disertacija. Humanitariniai mokslai, filologija, 04H. [*The Influence of Greek and Latin Accentuation on Lithuanian Accent Notation*. Doctoral dissertation. Humanities, Philology, 04H.] Vilnius (pp. 58–60 contain an edition of the *Odarion*, repeated from Stro2001).

Ulčinaitė, Eugenija (ed.) (2010), *Kalbų varžybos: Lietuvos Didžiosios Kunigaikštystės valdovų ir didikų sveikinimai* [Studies of the Palace of the Grand Dukes of Lithuania, vol. 5], Vilnius.

Veteikis, Tomas (2004), "Priedai" [Additions], in: *Graikų kalbos studijos ir graikiškoji kūryba Lietuvoje XVI–XVII amžiuje*, Daktaro disertacija. Humanitariniai mokslai, filologija, 04H. Vilnius [*Greek studies and Greek literature in 16–17th century Lithuania*. Doctoral dissertation. Humanities, Philology, 04H. Vilnius, 2004], 234–261 (first compendium of the printed Greek poems from 16th–17th centuries Lithuania) (= Vet2004 in *app. crit.*).

Veteikis, Tomas (2006), "Graikiško *Odarion*'o (1604) Šv. Kazimiero garbei autorystės problema", in: *Literatūra* 48/3, 89–103.

Veteikis, Tomas (2017), "The Cato Graeco-Latinus by Johannes Mylius: a Monument from the Early Stage of the Humanist Education in Lithuania", in: Arne Jönsson/Gregor Vogt-Spira (eds.), *The Classical Tradition in the Baltic Region: Perceptions and Adaptations of Greece and Rome*, Hildesheim/Zürich/New York, 391–406.

Veteikis, Tomas (2018), "Imitation of the *Carmina Moralia* of St. Gregory of Nazianzus in the 16th-century Greek Poetry of Lithuania", in: Janika Päll/Ivo Volt (eds.), *Hellenostephanos. Humanist Greek in Early Modern Europe. Learned Communities between Antiquity and Contemporary Culture*, Tartu, 336–378 (esp. 347–348).

Weise, Stefan (2016), "'Ἑλληνίδ' αἶαν εἰσιδεῖν ἱμείρομαι – Neualtgriechische Literatur in Deutschland (Versuch eines Überblicks)", in: *Antike & Abendland* 62, 114–181.

Wierzbowski, Teodor (1889–1894), *Bibliographia polonica XV ac XVI saeculorum* [...], vol. 1–3, Warszawa.

Wolf-Dahm, Barbara (1996), "Szembek, Christoph Andreas Johannes", in: *Biographisch-Bibliographisches Kirchenlexikon* (BBKL). Bd 11, Herzberg, 375–377.

Wyszomirski, Sławomir (ed.) (1993), *Ieremiae Voinovii Carmina Latina et Graeca nunc primum in unum volumen collecta*, Thorunii.

Zabulis, Henrikas (2000), "Epitalamos Jono Bretkūno dukrai Barborai", in: *Knygotyra* 36, 275–289.

Jacobus Prilussius (c. 1512–1554)

AD IUVENES POLONOS, ut pacis bellique iura hic a legumlatoribus praescripta seruent, literisque ac militiae studeant, contentione forensi posthabita. Iac. Pril. [1548; 1553]

Σαρματίης ἐφορᾶν τὸ συνέδριον ὅστις ἁπάντων
Σκηπτροφόρων ἐθέλης καλάς τε θέμιστας ἀκούειν,
Ἃ σοὶ προσφέρομεν, πρόφρων λάβε βίβλια ταῦτα,
Ἔνθ' οἱ νῦν ζῶντες θὲν ἔτι μὴν ψηφοφοροῦσι,
5 Πῶς δεῖ ἐν εἰρήνης ἀγορᾷ πολέμου θορύβῳ τε
Σαυτὸν ἔχειν, τί δ' ἀεὶ μελετᾷν τὸν ποιμένα λαῶν
Καὶ σκοπέειν τά τ' ἐόντα τά τ' ἐσσόμενα πρό τ' ἐόντα.
Χαῖρε, Λάχου τέκνον, θεσμοὺς τηροῦ τε δικαίους,
Πλήν γε καλῶς ζηλοῦ μιμούμενος ἔργα κάλιστα
10 Μουσάων, κ' εἰρήνης τέκτονος ἔργον Ἄρηος.
Πιερίδων θεράπων λίαν ὄλβιός ἐσσι καὶ ἐσθλός,
Πάντα φρονῶν, πολιτῶν λαμπρός τε ῥυμός τε κραταιός.
Τὴν κακότητα νικεῖ διὰ θάρσος χ' ὅπλα πονήρων
Αἵματι φοινικόεις Θεός, αὐτῷ χριστὸς ἀγῶνι.
15 Εἰ δὲ μή, ἀλλὰ θέλης μᾶλλόν τι φιλαίτιος εἶναι,
Σοῦ καὶ ἔρις κακόχαρτος ἔχει καὶ θυμὸν ἐγείρει
Εἶναι ὀπιπτεύοντ' ἀγορᾶς δοῦλόν τε κριτάων,
Δωροφάγον δικαιοδόταν σὺ τάχιστα πανώλης
Τρέψεις, ὡς Τιτυὸς κραδίᾳ τὸν γύππον ἐν Ἄιδου
20 Οὐκ εἰδὼς παῦσιν νύκτωρ καὶ ὀϊζυρὸς ἦμαρ.

Textus: ed. 1548 = [1] *Statuta Regni Poloniae methodica dispositione, propter faciliorem omnium causarum ex iure antiquo et novo definitionem, conscripta, ac Divi Sigismundi Augusti [...] nec non eius [...] Senatus simulque equestris ordinis legatorum iudicio ac censurae in Conventione Regni Generali Petricovien(si) anno 1548 exhibita...* Crac.(oviae) apud Viduam Hierony.(mi) Viet(oris), [s. a.; = 1548?], f. [A_iv verso][9]; ed. 1553 = [2] *Leges seu Statuta ac Privilegia Regni Poloniae omnia, hactenus magna ex parte uaga, confusa et sibi pugnantia: iam aute(m) in gratiam D. Sigismundi Augusti Regis Poloniae et in usum Reipublicae ab Iacobo Prilusio [...] collecta, digesta, et conciliata...*[ex coloph.: "[...] partim in Sczuczin, partim [Cracoviae] sub Arce Cracovien(si) [...]", 1553, f. [e_4] verso (adiectum Praefationi auctoris); Czerniatowicz 1991, 154–156 (ed. 1548); Czerniatowicz 1991, 156 (ed. 1553).

Crit.: tit. [1]AD IVVENES POLONOS, VT PACIS BELLIQVE / Iura, hic a Legumlatoribus praescripta seruent: lite- / risque ac Militiae studeant, contentione / forensi posthabita. / Iac. Pril. ed. 1548:

---

[9] Edition available online: https://www.dbc.wroc.pl/dlibbra/publication/10884/edition/9726 [accessed: February 2021].

⁽¹⁾SERVENTUR Cz : ⁽²⁾sine titulo ed. 1553 || **1** Σαρματιῆς edd. | ἐφορᾶν debuit || **2** καλάς τε θέμιστας ἀκούειν ed. 1553: μεγάλους ἀκούειν τε θέμιστας ed. 1548 || **3** Ἅς σοι possis, sed prob. ad βιβλία spectat rel. | πρόφρων λάβε βίβλια ταῦτα ed. 1553: λάβε βίβλια ταῦτα συνόψεις ed. 1548 | λαβὲ debuit | βιβλία debuit || **4** Ἔνθ' οἱ scripsi: Ἔνθ'οἷς edd.: ἔν θ' οἷς Cz | ζῶντες θεν ἔτι edd.: ζῶντές θεν ἔτι Cz: fort. debuit ζῶντες δὲν ἔτι sive ζῶντες θέμ' ἔτι? | ψηφοφόρουσὶ ed. 1548: ψηφόφορουσί ed. 1553, corr. Cz || **5** πολεμοῦ edd. | θορίβωτε edd., corr. Cz | **6** σ'αυτὸν edd.: σαυτὸν Cz | ἔχειν edd., corr. Cz || **7** σκοπεειν ed. 1548: σκόπεειν ed. 1553, corr. Cz | ἐσσόμενα ed. 1553 | ἔοντα (alterum) edd., corr. Cz || **8** Λαχουτέκνον ed. 1548: Λάχουτέκνον ed. 1553, corr. Cz | τηροῦτε δικαίους ed. 1548: τηροῦτεδικαίους ed. 1553: τηροῦ τε δικαίους Cz | **9** Πλήνγε edd.: πλήν γε Cz | ζήλου debuit || **10** εἰρηνητέκτονος edd., Cz: correxi || **11** ὄλβιός ἐστι ed. 1548: ὄλβιος ἔσσι ed. 1553, Cz || **12** Παντ'αφρόνων, πολιτῶν λαμπρόστε, ρυμόστε κράταιος ed. 1548: πανταφρόνων πολιτῶν λαμπρός τε, ρυμός τε κραταιός Cz: Ἔσσεαι αἰχμητής κρατερὸς λαμπρός τε πολίτης ed. 1553 || **13** κακοτητα ed. 1548: κακοτήτα ed. 1553, corr. Cz | θάρσου edd., correxi | πονηρῶν debuit || **14** χρηστὸς ed. 1548: χριστὸς ed. 1553: Χριστὸς Cz || **16** ἔρις ed. 1548 || **18** σὺ ταχύστα edd., corr. Cz || **19** Θρέψεις debuit | ὁς ed. 1548: ὅς ed. 1553 | τύτιος edd. | τοὺς γῦπας debuit | ἄδου edd. | **20** παύσιν edd. | ὀΐζυρος edd.: οἰζυρὸς Cz | ἦμαρ edd., corr. Cz

Sim.: **3** λαβὲ βιβλία ταῦτα] cf. LXX Jer 39.14 (Λαβὲ τὸ βιβλίον τῆς κτήσεως τοῦτο) || **6** Σαυτὸν ἔχειν] cf. Ps.-Pythag. *Carm. aur.* 14 (= Stob. *Flor.* 3.1.11.7) | ποιμένα λαῶν] cf. Hom. *Il.* 1.263; 2.243 etc. || **7** τά τ' ἐόντα...πρό τ' ἐόντα] cf. Hom. *Il.* 1.69–70 (de Calchante); Hes. *Theog.* 38 (de Musis); et alii || **10** ἔργον Ἄρηος] cf. Hom. *Il.* 11.734; *Hom. Hymn. Ven.* 10; *Batr.* 4 et 130; et alii || **11** Πιερίδων θεράπων] cf. Hes. *Theog.* 100 (Μουσάων θεράπων); Ar. *Av.* 909; et alii || **14** Αἵματι φοινικόεις] cf. Hes. [*Sc.*] 194; Hom. *Il.* 23.717 (αἵματι φοινικόεσσαι) || **16** Σοῦ καὶ ἔρις κακόχαρτος ...θυμὸν ἐγείρει] cf. Hes. *Op.* 28 || **17** Εἶναι ὀπιπτεύοντ' ἀγορᾶς] cf. Hes. *Op.* 29 (ὀπιπτεύοντ' ἀγορῆς...ἐόντα) || **18** Δωροφάγον] cf. Hes. *Op.* 39, 221, 264 || **19** ὡς Τιτυὸς...ἐν Ἄιδου] cf. Hom. *Od.* 11.576–581

To the Polish youth, so that they may observe here the rights of peace and war prescribed by the law-givers, and that they may study liberal arts and warfare while postponing the forensic contest. Jac(obus) Pril(ussius)

Whoever wishes to look upon the council board of all the sceptre-bearers of Sarmatia and to hear of their good laws, please take these books, which we are offering to you, in which those who are still alive deliberate [5] how you should behave in public places during peacetime and in the uproar of war, and why the shepherd of the people should always ponder on and consider the present, the future and the former state of affairs. Hail, child of Lech, and respect righteous laws, only emulating and imitating the best works [10] of the Muses and the actions of Ares, the carpenter of peace. You are an exceedingly fortunate and faithful servant of the Pierian Muses, understanding everything, an illustrious and mighty helm for the citizens. God, crimson with blood, anointed with battle itself, overcomes through courage and armour the wickedness of the malicious. [15] But if, rather, you prefer to be more liable to censure, and if strife, rejoicing in evil, holds and stirs up your heart to be a spy of public affairs and a slave to judges, then, utterly abandoned, you will very quickly feed the gift-devouring judge, just as Tityus feeds the vulture in Hades with his heart [20] without knowing any pause throughout the night and remains lamentable during the day.

Metre: Hexameters. Note misprint or unmetrical first syllable: Ἄ σοὶ (l. 3), metrical lengthening: ἔτῑ (l. 4, with following μ), artificial correction (violating morphology): ἔργα κάλιστα [! = κάλλιστα] (l. 9); l. 13 νικεῖ instead of νικᾷ with short ι.

Notes: This poem was published in two different editions of Polish law (1548 and 1553), arranged by the same author and handed over to the King of Poland and Lithuanian Grand Duke Sigismund II August (1520–1548–1572) and intended for use by citizens of the Polish-Lithuanian state. In both publications the poem is the same in the majority of lines, but there is one significant difference in the middle of the poem, where lines 11 and esp. 12 have different wordings that altogether provide the poem with different meaning.

Biography: Jacobus Prilussius (Jakub Przyłuski, Iacobus Prilusius Iessovius, c. 1512–c. 1554 Szczucin), a Polish lawyer, political writer, poet, and translator of supposedly noble origin, was educated in philological and juridical subjects, as well as in Latin, Greek, and Hebrew, in the Benedictine circles of Jeżów (hence his cognomen Iessovius), perhaps in Cracow. During roughly 1535–1540 he worked as a secretary in the court of the Voivode of Cracow, Piotr Kmita, where he was influenced by current trends of juridical, philosophical, and religious thought. From 1540 to 1548, he worked as the town scribe of Przemyśl, before entering the service of the Provost of Mościska (Ukr. Мостиська), and finally becoming a Calvinist. From 1551 onward, he worked as a scribe for the land court of Cracow and belonged to a circle of intellectuals that included Stanisław Orzechowski, Marcin Krowicki, and Andrzej Frycz Modrzewski. In the last years of his life, he established his own printing house in Szczucin nad Wisłą (Lesser Poland), a village he owned, but soon he transferred it to Cracow and there published the most important work of his life, *Leges seu statuta ac privilegia Regni Poloniae* (1553), a six-book compendium of laws, statutes, and privileges of the Polish Crown dedicated to Sigismund II August. His other major works include *Statuta Regni Poloniae methodica dispositione propter faciliorem omnium causarum ex iure antiquo et novo definitionem conscripta* (Cracoviae 1548), a non-extant Latin translation of Homer's *Iliad*, and a number of occasional poems in Latin and Greek that were published in Cracow between 1545 and 1548.

Bibliography: Estr. XXV, 375–376; Czerniatowicz 1991, 153–156; *PSB* XXIX, 206; *NK* (=*Nowy Korbut*) III, 138–139.

Johannes Mylius (†1575)

ΠΡΟΣΕΥΧΗ ΚΥΡΙΑΚΗ. ΜΑΤΘΑΙΟΥ Ϛ' [1561; 1568]

    Θεῖοι δεῦτε χοροὶ ποιεῖν δεήσεις,
    Ὡς ἄναξ ἐδίδασκε Χριστὸς αἰτεῖν.
    Ὦ πάτερ βασιλεῦ πόλου καὶ αἴης,
    Ὅστις ἡμετέρας κλύεις ἀοιδῆς,
5 Ναίων οὐρανίης ἕδρας ἐν ἄκρῳ,
    Σεῦ τὸ οὔνομα ἐν βροτοῖσιν ἱρὸν
    Εἴη καὶ βασιλὴ τεὴ προσέλθοι.
    Πάντα, ὡς σὺ θέλεις, καλῶς γένοιτο,
    Ἐν γαίῃ καθ' ὅσον καὶ ἐν τ' Ὀλύμπῳ.
10 Ἡμῖν δὸς τὸ ἐπάρκιον τοῦ ἄρτου,
    Καὶ ποίμαινε τροφῇ τὸ σῶμα ἡμῶν.
    Ἡμᾶς δὸς πάρεσιν λαβεῖν ὀφειλῆς,
    Ὡς καὶ τὴν ἄφεσιν λάβεν τις ἄλλος,
    Ἡμῖν ὃς γέγονεν βαρὺς καὶ ἐχθρός.
15 Μὴ πείραζε τεοὺς κακοῖσι δμῶας,
    Οὓς δαίμων ποθέει τάχιστ' ἀμαυροῦν,
    Ῥῦσον ἔκ τε κακῶν καὶ ἐκ πονηροῦ.
    Ταῦτα ῥηϊδίως τελεῖν γε οἶδας·
    Πάντων γὰρ βασιλεὺς κράτει ἀνάσσεις,
20 Καὶ ἔχεις δύναμιν μένουσαν αἰεί,
    Πέλεις ἔξοχος ἔν τε δόξῃ ἄλλων.

Textus: ed. 1561 = Τὰ τῆς Χριστιανῶν κατηχήσεως μέρη κεφαλαιωδῶς μέτροις Ἑλληνικοῖς συγγεγραμμένα παρὰ τοῦ Ἰωάννου Μυλίου Λιβενρόδεως, Cracoviae, Lazarus Andreae impressit, 1561, f. A₃ verso–[A₄] recto; ed. 1568a = Iohannis Mylii Libenrodensis, Poetae Laureati, *Cato Graeco-Latinus. Praecipua Christianae pietatis Capita.* Μελέται D. Andreae et D. Alexandri Chodcievitiorum, illustrium magni Lithuaniae Ducatus Equitum. Omnia in gratiam studiosae iuventutis publicata. [...] (ex coloph.: Lipsiae, Iohannes Rhamba excudebat) M. D. LXVIII., f. C₅ recto-verso; ed. 1568b = Ioannis Mylii Libenrodensis, Poetae Laureati, *Sacrorum Carminum liber primus*, in: Poëmata Ioannis Mylii Libenrodensis, Poetae Laureati, ex dioecesi generosorum Comitum de Hoenstein..., [s. l. = Lipsiae?] M. D. LXVIII., f. [M₆] recto-verso.

Crit.: 5 ἄκρῳ edd. 1568 (= ed. 1568a et ed. 1568b) || 7 βασιλεία sive βασιληίη fort. debuit, metro tamen resultat | τέη edd. 1568 || 9 Εν γαίῃ edd. 1568 | ἐντ' ὀλύμπῳ edd. 1568 || 10 ὑπάρκιον edd. 1568 || 11 τροφῇ ed. 1568a || 15 τέους edd. 1568 || 17 Ῥῦσαι debuit

Sim.: 3–17 Ὦ πάτερ...καὶ ἐκ πονηροῦ] cf. NT *Mt.* 6.9–13 || 3 πόλου καὶ αἴης] cf. Max. Conf. *Hymn.* 1.9 || 5 οὐρανίης ἕδρας] cf. Soph. *Phil.* 1413–1414; Eur. *Tro.* 1078 (οὐράνιον ἕδρανον) || 21 Πέλεις ἔξοχος...ἄλλων] cf. Hom. *Il.* 6.194 (ἔξοχον ἄλλων); 9.631, 641; *Od.* 5.118; 6.158 et al.

LORD'S PRAYER. Gospel of Matthew <Chapter> 6

Come here, divine choirs, in order to say prayers, asking as Lord Christ taught you: Oh, Father, King of the vault of heaven and earth, who gives ear to our song, [5] who lives on the summit of the throne of heaven, let Your name be hallowed among mortals and let Your kingdom come. Let everything happen properly according to Your wish, on earth as much as in Olympus (Heaven). [10] Give us sufficient bread, and nourish our bodies with food. Grant us to receive remission of debt just as forgiveness was granted to him who became burdensome and hateful to us. [15] Don't test Your servants, whom the devil desires to annihilate, with evils. Save us both from evils and from wickedness, for You are able to fulfil all this easily. For You, the King, reign over everything with power, [20] and You have the power that remains forever, and You are eminent even in the judgement of others.

Metre: Phalaecians. Instances of hiatus: τὸ οὔνομα ἐν (l. 6); τὸ ἐπάρκιον (l. 10). Note the new form βασιλή (l. 7), probably invented to fit the metre.

Notes: The poem is printed in several 16th-century editions with no significant differences. In all of them, this poem is an integral part of the collection but is not the first poem. The poem contains Latin paraphrases. The content of the Greek poem follows the text of the Gospel of Matthew, but its language imitates phrases from Homer as well as from classical and post-classical authors, and it has obvious features of the epic dialect, although it also contains a number of forms typical of Attic Greek. As it was first published in Cracow with a dedication to Nicholas Radvila the Black (1515–1565), it can be assumed that this and other religious poems were dedicated to the Lithuanian and Polish Evangelical communities, especially to the noble families of this denomination who consistently recruited private teachers for their children and developed plans to set up training centres for their children in their own countries.

Biography: Johannes Mylius Libenrodensis (Johann Mylius aus Liebenrode, ?–1575 Jena), well versed in Latin and Greek, was educated in the monastic school of Ilfeld (the cradle of the 'Ilfelder Dichterschule', see → **Germany**) and at the University of Cracow (1560–62), where he published his first books of religious poetry and entered into close contact with various Polish and Lithuanian intellectuals (Nicholas Radvila the Black, Wojciech Wędrogowski, Feliks z Sierpca, and others); he lived in the courts of Stanislaw Maciejowski, Castellan of Sandomierz, and Gregory Chodkiewicz, Elder of Vilnius, training their sons in Latin and Greek literature. In 1564, he escorted the boys Andreas and Alexander Chodkiewicz to Vienna and continued his own unfinished studies there. In 1565, while in Vienna, he was ordained *Poeta laureatus* by Emperor Maximilian II and was promoted to the nobility. That same year, Mylius published in Vienna two editions of his collection of poems about the triumphs of Christian saints, Ἱερονῖκαι, one of which he dedicated to Emperor Maximilian II, and the other to the Polish and Lithuanian ruler Sigismund August, as well as a poem of certain importance to Lithuanian history, *Victoria de Moschis reportata*, which expressed praise to Sigismund August and the poet's patron Gregory Chodkiewicz, hero of the battle of the Ula river (January 26, 1564). From about 1567 onward, Mylius focused on his own studies and the perfection of his teaching skills in the German Protestant universities of Wittenberg, Leipzig, and Jena. In 1568, he took on a professorship of Greek at Jena University, subsequently defending theses on secular and divine law and teaching Hebrew there. Meanwhile, he continued to train children of Polish and Lithuanian noblemen and published his own and his Polish-Lithuanian students' poetic works, composed during his stay at the court of Gregory Chodkiewicz. In the last years of his life, Mylius worked on a Latin translation of Luther's *Kleiner Katechismus*, which in his early years he had translated into Greek and had given to his teacher Michael Neander for revision (first ed. in Basel 1558). He died on 3 July 1575. His rich poetic legacy, containing numerous Greek compositions, is attested in several publications, such as Τὰ τῆς Χριστιανῶν κατηχήσεως μέρη (Cracow 1561), *Poëmata* (Leipzig 1568), and *Cato Graecolatinus* (Augsburg 1566; Leipzig 1568).

Bibliography: Günther 1858, 168; Wierzbowski II, 122f. (no. 1444); Estr. XXII 655–657; Nowak-Dłużewski 1966, 202, 205–207, 381; Barycz 1969, 86–87; Banach, Andrzej K. (1977), "Mylius, Jan", in: *PSB* XXII/2, fasc. 93, 354; VD16 M 7391–7392, VD16 ZV 3168; Backus 2006, 200; Baldzuhn 2015, 546–554; Veteikis 2017; Niekraszewicz-Karotkaja 2018; Nekraševič-Karotkaja 2019.

Michael Retellius Sittaviensis (c. 1530–1576)

ΣΥΓΧΑΡΙΣΤΙΚΌΣ ΛΌΓΟΣ ΕἸΣ ΓΆΜΟΝ ΛΟΥΚᾶ ΣΧΑΧΜΆΝΝΟΥ τοῦ τῆς πολιτείας τῶν Τορυνιέων ὑπάτου. [1571?]

(A) ΠΡῸΣ ΝΥΜΦΊΟΝ

(Αα) Χάριτες.
  Ὡς ἀλλήλας ἀγκαλίσι προσπτυξάμεθ' ἡμᾶς,
    ὣς ἐν ἔρωτ' ὤμων ἀντεχόμεσθα φίλω,
  ἄμπελος ἀμφιβαλεῖν πτελέαν καθὰ δένδρον ἔωθε,
    οὕτω γαμβρὲ φίλην ἀμφιβαλοῦ γαμέτιν.

(Αβ) Θάλεια.
5   ἔμπλεον εὔχομαι ὔμμι τύχην μάλα χαρμοσυνάων,
    δῶμα γέλω πλῆρες παίγμασιν εὐθαλέειν.
    ἀμφοῖν εὐρώστοιν ὑγίεια ἑκάστοτε μίμνοι.
    σφῶΐ κε ποιώῃ μακροβίους ὁ θεός.

(Αγ) Ἀθήνη.
    σεμνὸν ἔφυν καθάπερ θεῖον, καὶ τὸν τρόπον ἁγνά,
10 ἤθεα πάγχυ τρόπων ἤρεσέ μοι θαλερῶν
    τῆς σοφίας, φρενὸς ἢ πινυτῆς τις ἐπίτροπος οὖσα,
    εὔχομαι ἠγαθέην σφωΐ θεοῖο φρόνιν.

(Β) ΠΡ᾽ΟΣ Ν᾽ΥΜΦΗΝ.

(Βα) Ἐρατώ.
    οὐράνιος θεόφιν Κύπρις ἤϊα, οὐκ Ἀφροδίτη
    χερσαίη, ὅτ᾽ ἄφρων ἡ ῥυπαρὰ γέγαε.
15 ὔμμι θάλοι στοργὴ περὶ κῆρι μὲν ὄφρα δύναισθε
    ὑμμέων ἀμφαγαπᾶν κάλλιμα τέκνα δόμου.

(Ββ) Εὐσέβεια.
    γνῶσιν ἀληθέα ὔμμι θεὸς τοῦ ῥήματος οἷο
    δώῃ, πνεῦμ᾽ ἱερόν, δῶρα θεοφροσύνης.
    μῖσος ἀπῇ, φυγέτω ἔρις, ἢ δασπλῆτις Ἐριννύς.
20 ἁγνὸς ἐπευχάων νωλεμὲς ἔστε νεώς.

(Βγ) Ὑμέναιος.
    ἁβρὸς ἀπειρολεχὴς περὶ παρθενίας μάλα πολλά
    εὔχετ᾽, ἄρ᾽ ἡγεῖται μοῦνον ἒ πότνον ἔμεν.
    συζυγίης ἀτὰρ ἱρὸς ἔρως τις ἐτήτυμός ἐστι
    παρθενίῃ, καὶ ἀδεῖν τὴν μόνον ἴσθι θεῷ.

Textus: Μιχαήλου Ῥετελλίου *Ποιημάτων Ἑλληνικῶν βίβλοι δύο*. Michaelis Retellii *Poematum Graecorum libri duo. Τοῦ αὐτοῦ ἐκείνου λόγων βίβλος μία. Eiusdem autoris orationum liber unus.* Dantisci: Excudebat Iacobus Rhodus, M. D. LXXI., Lib. II, f. E4v–E5r.

Crit.: 1 ὣς debuit ǁ **2** ὣς debuit | φίλῳ ed.: φίλων vel φίλῳ possis ǁ **8** σφωΐ κε ποιώῃ ed., ποιοίη possis | μακριβίους ed. ǁ (Αγ) ἀθήνη ed. ǁ **11** πινυτῆς τὶς ed. ǁ **12** σφῶΐ debuit ǁ **15** ὕμμι debuit ǁ **19** δασπλῖτις ed. ǁ **23** ἔρως τις debuit ǁ ἁδεῖν ed.

Sim.: 2 ὣς...ἀντεχόμεσθα] cf. Basil. *Is.* (*Enarratio in prophetam Isaiam*) 4.133 (τῷ νυμφίῳ Λόγῳ...οἰονεὶ ἐρωτικῶς ἀντεχομένη) ǁ **3** ἄμπελος ἀμφιβαλεῖν πτελέαν] cf. Clem. Al. *Strom.* 6.15.117.3 (τὴν ἄμπελον ἡ πτελέα εἰς ὕψος ἀνάγουσα); cf. Herm. *Pastor* 51 (Parabola 2) ǁ **11–12** φρενὸς ἢ πινυτῆς...φρόνιν] cf. [!] *Anth. Gr. Appendix* (Epigrammatis addenda), Epigr. 2.198b.12 = IG (Kolbe) V 1.960 (καὶ πινυτῆς ἐρατῆς καὶ φρενὸς ἠγαθ[έης]) ǁ **13–14** οὐράνιος...Κύπρις...οὐκ Ἀφροδίτη / χερσαίη] cf. Xen. *Symp.* 8.9 (μία ἐστὶν Ἀφροδίτη ἢ διτταί, Οὐρανία τε καὶ Πάνδημος); cf. Paus. 8.32.2; cf. Plotin. *Enn.* 6.9.9; *Anth. Pal.* (Theoc.) 6.340.1–2; et al. ǁ **15** περὶ κῆρι] cf. Hom.

Il. 4.46; 4.53; 13.119 etc. || **16** κάλλιμα τέκνα] cf. *Hom. Hymn.* 31.5 || **18** θεοφροσύνης] verbum perrarum, cf. Hsch. θ 325 || **19** δασπλῆτις Ἐρινννύς] cf. Hom. *Od.* 15.234 || **21** ἀπειρολεχής] cf. Ar. *Thesm.* 119; Euseb. *Praep. evang.* 4.23.7 (*Anth. Gr. Appendix* (Oracula) 193.3) || **22** πότνον] forma masc. generis nusquam ante usitata || **23** ἐτήτυμός ἐστι] cf. Nonn. *Par. Jo.* 6.56; 7.156

Congratulatory song on the occasion of the wedding of Lucas Schachmann, Mayor of the City of Toruń

To the Bridegroom

Charites [Graces]
Just as we have embraced one another in our arms,
    likewise in love we cling to the shoulders of our beloved,
just as the grapevine is accustomed to embrace the elm tree,
    so too, bridegroom, embrace your beloved wife.

Thalia
[5] I wish that you might have a destiny filled with joys,
    and that your home might bloom with laughter and leisure.
May health and strength remain in both of you without end,
    and may God thus make you both long living.

Athena
As I was born as a sacred deity and pure in character,
[10]   I liked above all the habits of the blooming manners
of wisdom: being a protector of the wise mind,
    I pray that you might receive holy prudence from God.

To the Bride

Erato
I came from the gods as heavenly Cypris, not as terrestrial
    Aphrodite, when this sullied and foolish goddess was born.
[15] May love bloom in your hearts so that you might
    embrace with love the beautiful children of your house.

Eusebeia [Piety]
May God give to you the true knowledge of His own
    word, the Holy Spirit, the gifts of divine thought.
Let hatred cease, let Strife or the frightful Erinys run away.
[20] You will be forever the chaste temple of prayers.

Hymenaeus [Hymen]
The graceful, unwedded man prays frequently about
    virginity, and he therefore thinks that he himself alone is the master.

> And yet, virginity is a certain, genuine, and holy desire
> of union: remember that this alone pleases God.

Metre: Elegiac couplets. Instances of epic correption: εὔχομαι ὔμμι (l. 5); καὶ ἀδεῖν (l. 24); Attic correption: Κύπρις ἤϊα (l. 13); hiatus: ἀληθέα ὔμμι (l. 17); synizesis: ὑμμέων (l. 16).

Notes: This poem is printed in Book 2 of one of Retellius' collections of Greek poems (it is the 12th poem in the general list), published in Gdańsk in 1571; the two volumes of poems were also bound together with a short collection of his Greek speeches (5 in total). This is one (but not the only) poem related to a wedding, namely an *epithalamion* created for Lucas Schachmann (1521–1578), Mayor of Toruń. According to its content, it is a pious wish for the bride and contains references to the pious Christian marriage. With respect to its language and symbolism, however, the poem also incorporates ancient Greek elements, including phrases from Homer and other classical and postclassical authors: it displays features of the epic-Ionic dialect, with sporadic inclusion of Attic forms, rarities and morphological experiments (e.g., πότνον).

Biography: Michael Retellius Sittaviensis (Michael Retell, Michał Retell, c. 1530 Zittau/Żytawa – 1576 Gdańsk), a German-Polish poet and pedagogue, was educated in Frankfurt/Oder and Gdańsk (from 1558); a professor of rhetoric and poetics in the Academic Gymnasium of Gdańsk, he was the assistant of the rector Heinrich Möller in organising theatrical performances, as well as the author of poems in Greek and Latin. His collection of Greek poems was published in Gdańsk in 1571 (*Poematum Graecorum libri duo*) and contained paraphrases of St Paul's letters, *epithalamia*, *epicedia*, and other poems on religious, mythological and sometimes practical matters (e.g., ancient ships and navigation). Most of his Latin works were published together in Gdańsk in 1574 under the title *Epimythia in historias et fabulas*; despite its title, this book contained not only mythological verses filled with *gnomae*, but also a substantial collection of epigrams (*Liber epigrammatum*) and elegies (*Libri elegiarum duo*) filled with various details of daily life in Gdańsk, as well as short exercises in Latin and Greek. In the last year of his life, he was pastor of St Bartholomew's "Church" in Gdańsk.

Bibliography: Estr. XXVI, 271–272; Wierzbowski, III, no. 2560; Nadolski 1969; Nowak, Zbigniew (1988–1989), "Retell Michał", in: *PSB* XXXI, 146–147; Awianowicz 2009, 163–166; Goedeke 2011, 105 (no. 105).

Franciscus Lacki

ΤΟΥ ΑΥΤΟΥ ΒΑΛΕΡΙΑΝΟΥ
ΠΡΟΣ ΤΗΝ ΛΙΤΟΥΑΝΙΑΝ [1581]

Πῦρ θέτε ἀκάματον, παιήονα πρόφρονι θυμῷ,
Πάντες Βιλναῖοι, ᾄδετ', ἀρηΐφιλοι.
Ἄνθεσι πορφυρέοισι καλὰς κοσμεῖτε πλατείας,
Τοίχους ἀργυρέοις στρώμασιν ἀσκέετε,
5 Χαίρετ', ἐπειδὴ ὁρᾶν ἐάᾳ πόκα πότνια μοῖρα,
Ἔστιν ἐπεὶ φιλέειν ἀνέρα θεσπέσιον,
Ἀνέρα, ὃς περὶ καὶ ἀγορὰς καὶ ἔργα τέτυκτο
Ἄλλα βροτῶν· δίων τὸ κράτος οὐρανόθεν.
Χαῖρέ μοι, ὦ φίλε ξεῖνε, ἀεί τοι εὖ τε γένοιτο,
10 Αὐτὰρ ἔπειτ' ἄμμιν φαῖνέ σε μουσόφιλον,
Μοῦσαι γὰρ Σοφίης ταμίαι, Σοφίη δὲ ἄριστον
Φύλοις τῶν θνητῶν ἀθανάτων τε ὁμοῦ.
Σοὶ τριτάτην γενεὴν στεροπηγερέτα τελέσειε
Νέστορος ἠὲ θέλεις αὖτε Πλάτωνος ἔτος.

Textus: *Gratulationes Illustriss(i)mo ac Reverendiss(i)mo D(omi)no D. Georgio Radivilo, D. G. Episcopo Vilnen(si) Duci Olycen(si) etc., in primo felici atque exoptato eiusdem in suam Sedem adventu oblatae, a bonarum artium studiosa iuventute in Academia Vilnensi Collegii Societatis Iesu conscriptae*, Vilnae: Typis [...] D. Nic(olai) Christ(ophori) Radivili [...], Anno M. D. LXXXI. Mense Augusto. Martinus Kazymirien(sis), p. [48]. Editiones recentiores: Juchnevičienė/Strockis 126–127; Veteikis 2004, 236–237.

Crit.: 1 Παιήονα ed., corr. Cz || 3 Ανθεσι ed., corr. Cz || 4 ἀσκέετε ed., corr. Cz || 5 ἔαα ed., corr. Cz | ποκὰ debuit || 7 ὅς ed. || 8 Αλλα ed. (cf. ἄλλα JuStr2015): ἀλλὰ Cz || 9 Χᾶιρέ μοὶ ed., corr. Cz || 10 μουσόφιλον ed., Cz : μουσοφιλῆ JuStr2015 || 12 θανάτων ed., corr. JuStr2015 : θανάτων Cz || 14 ἠὲ θέλεις ed., sed fort. debuit ἦ ἐθέλεις aut ἢ ἐθέλεις : κὲ Cz (infeliciter tamen)

Sim.: 1 πῦρ...ἀκάματον] cf. Hom. *Il.* 5.4; 15.597–598, 731; 16.122, etc. *Od.* 20.123; 21.181 et mult. al. | πρόφρονι θυμῷ] Hom. *Il.* 24.140; *Od.* 16.257 et al. || 3 ἄνθεσι πορφυρέοισι] cf. Opp. *C.* 1.339; Clem. Al. *Strom.* 5.14.125.3.3 || 5 πότνια μοῖρα] cf. Eur. *IA* 1136 (hapax?) || 6 ἀνέρα θεσπέσιον] cf. Pl. *Tht.* 151b6; Synes. *Epist.* 105.32 || 7 Ἀνέρα, ὃς...τέτυκτο] cf. Hom. *Il.* 17.279 (de Aiace); *Od.* 11.550 (de eodem) || 9 Χαῖρέ μοι, ὦ...ξεῖνε] cf. Hom. *Il.* 23.19 et 179 (χαῖρέ μοι, ὦ Πάτροκλε); *Od.* 13.59 (χαῖρέ μοι, ὦ βασίλεια); *Od.* 1.123 (χαῖρε, ξεῖνε); *Od.* 8.408 = 18.122 = 20.199 (χαῖρε, πάτερ ὦ ξεῖνε) | ἀεί τοι εὖ τε γένοιτο] cf. Hom. *Od.* 8.408–409 = 18.122–123 = 20.199–200 (γένοιτό τοι ἔς περ ὀπίσσω / ὄλβος); cf. Eur. *Alc.* 626–627 (χαῖρε, κἂν Ἅιδου δόμοις / εὖ σοι γένοιτο) || 10 Αὐτὰρ ἔπειτ'] cf. Hom. *Il.* 1.51; 2.406 etc. || 11 Σοφίη δὲ ἄριστον] cf. Phil. *De migr. Abrah.* 28 (σοφία...ἄριστον ἐνδιαίτημα) || 12 Φύλοις τῶν θνητῶν] cf. Hom. *Hymn. Merc.* 578; *Hom. Hymn. Ven.* 3; *Or. Sib.* 11.95 | τῶν θνητῶν ἀθανάτων τε] cf. Hom. *Il.* 5.441–442; Bion. fr. 10, 11 (Gow) (θνατῶν ἀθανάτων τε πόθως); Greg. Naz. 3.1.1 (*Carm. Dogm.*), PG 37.452.1 = 3.1.2 (*Carm. Moral.*), PG 37.528.13 || **13–14** τριτάτην γενεὴν...Νέστορος] cf. *Or. Sib.* 3.135 (ἀλλ' ὅτε τὴν τριτάτην γενεὴν τέκε...); cf. schol. D

Hom. Il. 1.250 | στεροπηγερέτα] cf. Hom. *Il.* 16.298; Nonn. *Dion.* 8.370; Quint. Smyrn. 2.164 || **14** ἠὲ θέλεις] cf. Hom. *Il.* 1.133 et 15.132 (ἢ ἐθέλεις) | Πλάτωνος ἔτος] cf. etiam Lat. *magnus annus Platonis, magnus Platonis annus, annus Platonicus, annus mundanus* et sim.: cf. *Paradoxa regum et summi magistratus privilegia, dignitates et axiomata*...Iuliano Taboëtio autore..., Lugduni: Apud Theobaldum Paganum, 1560, 91–92: "Annus autem magnus vocatur annus Platonis continens annos 49000. quo temporis spatio nonum caelum suum complere debet revolutionem: post eius exitum omnia, quae prius fuerint, in eundem statum, syntaxin et formam redibunt. Quam Platonis sententiam repudiavit ut absurdam divus Aurelius."

(POEM) BY THE SAME VALERIANUS TO LITHUANIA

>Light the indefatigable fire and sing a paean with earnest heart,
>   all you citizen of Vilna [i.e. Vilnius], who are dear to Ares.
>Decorate the beautiful streets with purple blossoms,
>   dress the walls with silver carpets,
>[5] rejoice, because the mistress Moira now allows you to see,
>   because it is possible to love the divine man,
>the man who was well-versed both in speeches and in the other
>   deeds of mortals: the power of the saints is from heaven.
>Hail, my dear guest, let it be always well with you,
>[10] but then show yourself to us as an adept of the Muses,
>since the Muses are housekeepers of Wisdom, and Wisdom is the best thing
>   for the races of both mortals and immortals.
>May the lightning-rouser complete for you the third generation
>   of Nestor or, if you wish, even the year of Plato.

Metre: Elegiac couplets. Instances of hiatus: θέτε ἀκάματον (l. 1) (with metrical lengthening), καὶ ἀγορὰς (l. 7), δὲ ἄριστον (l. 11); diectasis: ἐάᾳ (l. 5).

Notes: This is the only Greek poem from the commemorative publication that honours the ingress of the Bishop of Vilnius, George Radvila (1556–1600), who replaced the recently deceased Bishop Waleryan Protasiewicz (Lith. Valerijonas Protasevičius, 1504–1579) in his see. The poem has a Latin paraphrase of the same length.[10] It is embedded in a cycle of poems written in the voice of the mentioned

---

10 The Latin version reads as follows: *Instaurate focis ignem, Paeana canentes, / Qui colitis Litavum Martia turba solum. / Purpureis nitidas violis ornate plateas, / Auleis paries cultus ubiq(ue) micet. / Gaudia quisq(ue) animo volvat, quia fata dedere, / Tam magni vobis ora videre viri. / Ora videre viri, magno quem munere summi / Hic rebus Divi praeposuere sacris. / Salve optate hospes, felicibus utere fatis; / Salve, et Musarum fac tueare decus. / Nam sophiae hae praesunt*

Waleryan, thereby not only expressing high appreciation for the new bishop, but also showing (indirectly) the outstanding merits of his predecessor: the latter sings exhortatory songs in Greek and Latin to the people of the Lithuanian capital and carries the message that this city is the centre of high intellectual culture. The fact that Vilnius had recently become the location of a university (in 1579) due to the efforts of Bishop Waleryan lies behind the lines of the poem. With respect to formal features, the poem reiterates a number of Homeric formulae with sporadic inclusions of phrases and allusions common to later poets and writers, especially philosophers and Christian theologians dear to Christian humanists and to Jesuits in particular.

Biography: Franciscus Lacki, student at the Vilnius Jesuit Academy in 1581, was the author of this short Greek poem and of its *versio Latina*, published in the collection titled *Gratulationes...D. Georgio Radivilo, D. G. Episcopo Vilnen(si)* (Vilnae 1581). Otherwise unknown, he might perhaps be identified with Franciscus Łącki (Franciszek Łącki 1562–1617), Suffragan Bishop of Włocławek from 1597 onward and also Titular Bishop of Margarita (Maktar).

Bibliography: Estr. XXVI, 72; VASL 16 (no. 38); Czerniatowicz 1991, 136f.; Narbutienė/Narbutas 2002, 96–98 (no. 90); Veteikis 2004, 236–237; Juchnevičienė/Strockis 2015, 126–127.

Stanislaus Niegossevius (c. 1565–1600)

‹In Joannem Zamoiscium› [1588]

ΕΠΑΜΙΝΩΝΔΑ‹Ι›

Ἄισατ' Ἰωάννην κύκνοι νῦν, ᾄσατε τῆνον
Ἄισμασι καὶ γλυκεροῖς ὑψίστῳ αἴρετ' Ὀλύμπῳ
Αὐγὴν ἀνθρώπων ἐπιείκελον ἀθανάτοισιν,
Αἴρετ' Ἰωάννην Μουσάων ἄξιον ἄνδρα,
5 Ἀμβρόσιον πίνοντα, Διὸς κοῦρον μεγάλοιο,
Καλὸν πὰρ θνητοῖς Ἐριούνιον, ἔξοχον ἄλλων·
Δυσμενέας πολεμεῖ, καὶ δή τ' ἐρρύσατο λαόν,
Καρτερόφρων αὐτός, σκηπτοῦχος, πολλὰ θεμίστωρ.
Χαῖρε πόλις δέσποινα, πόλις χαῖρ' ἤματα πάντα.
10 Σοὶ γὰρ δουλεύει, μέγα χάρμα Ζαμόσκιος ἀλφεῖ.

---

opibus, qua pulchrius est nil, / Quiq(ue) colunt pacem, quiq(ue) fera arma, viris. / Te Deus astripotens sanum per Nestoris annos, / Cecropii servet tempora sive Sophi.

Ἄνθρωπος μὲν ἐλεύθερος αἴην πατρίδα σώζει.
Βωμὸν Ἰωάννῃ, Νύμφαι, τῇδ' αἴρετε αἰεί.
Καὶ δότε νῦν στεφάνους, δότε νῦν καὶ στέμματα πολλά.
Ἄξιός ἐστι δρυὸς φύλλων τε καὶ ἄξιος ἀνθῶν
15 Χλωρίδος, ἔστιν ἀγάλματος ἄξιος, εἰ θεοειδής,
Ζεῦ, ᾗ πολλῆς μὲν δόξης βιοθάλμιος ἀνήρ.
Προσφιλὲς ἐσσόμενον δέρκω πάντεσσι Πολώνοις
Αὐτὸς γινώσκω κεφαλὴν καὶ ποιμένα λαῶν
Ὀξύτατον, χαλεπὸν πολέμου μεγάλοιο κεραυνόν,
20 Εἰρήνης τε φίλον, Μουσάων καὶ μέγ' ὄνειαρ.

ἈΝΤΙΣΤΡΟΦΉ.

Ἄριστος εὐφροσύνα
Πόνων κεκριμένων
Ἰατρός, αἱ δὲ σοφαί
Μοισᾶν θυγατέρες ἀοιδαί
25 Θέλξαν νῖν ἁπτόμεναι
Οὐ θερμὸν ὕδωρ τόσον
Γὲ μαλθακὰ τεύχει
Γυῖα, τόσσον εὐλογία
Φόρμιγγι συνάορος
30 Ῥῆμα δ' ἐρυμάτων χρονιώ-
τερον βιοτεύει
Ὅ τι κε σὺν χαρίτων τύχᾳ
Γλῶσσα φρενὸς ἐξέλοι βαθείας.

Textus: *Ad Illustriss(imum) Principem Ioannem Zamoiscium Regni Poloniae Magnum Cancellarium et Exercituum imper(atorem) P(atrem) P(atriae) Stanislai Niegossevvii Poloni Reipub(licae) Ven(etorum) Eq(uitis) Aurati Ἐπινίκιον* [s.l., s.a. = Venetiis 1588?], cc. D 2v–3r; Editio recentior: Czerniatowicz 1991, 143–146.

Crit.: I. Tit. ΕΠΑΜΙΝΩΝΔΑ ed. || **1** Ἀ᾽σατ᾽ ed., corr. Cz | ἄσατε ed., corr. Cz || **2** Ἀ᾽σμασι ed. || **5** Ἀμβροσίην fort. debuit (sic Cz) || **10** δουλεύεις ed., correxi: an δουλεύων? || **11** ἐλευθέρος ed., corr. Cz | σῴζει Cz || **12** Βόμον ed., corr. Cz || **15** ἔστι ed. | θεοειδής ed., corr. Cz || **17** Πολωνοῖς debuit || **18** γινόσκω ed., corr. Cz || **II. Tit.** ΑΝΤΙΣΤΡΩΦΗ ed., corr. Cz || **21** Ἀ᾽ρίστος ed., corr. Cz || **24** Μουσᾶν ed., corr. Cz || **25** νιν debuit || **26** Οὐδερμὸν ed., corr. Cz : cf. Οὐδὲ θερμὸν (*Pindari Olympia, Pythia, Nemea, Isthmia...*, [Venetijs in aedib. Aldi...], M. D. XIII] p. 156 = *Pindari Olympia, Pythia, Nemea, Isthmia. Caeterorum Octo Lyricorum carmina...*, Anno M. D. LX. Excudebat Henricus Stephanus..., p. 376) || **27** Γὲμαλδακὰ τένχει ed., corr. Cz || **30** ἐργμάτων fort. debuit | χρονίω ed., corr. Cz || **32** τύχα ed., corr. Cz

Sim.: 1 Ἄισατ᾽...κύκνοι] cf. Mosch. *Ep. Bion.* 14–15 (de cycnorum carmine tristi); Opp. *C.* 2.548 (de carmine tristi); cf. Greg. Paroem. 2, 78; 3, 84 (carmen cycnorum ante mortem) et mult. var.; Pl. *Phd.* 85b (de carmine laeto) | τῆνον] cf. Theoc. *Id.* 1.36; 1.71 et 72; 2.17 etc. | **3** ἐπιείκελον ἀθανάτοισιν] cf. Hom. *Il.* 1.265; 4.394; 11.60; *Od.* 15.414; 21.14; 21.37, et al. | **5** Διὸς κοῦρον μεγάλοιο] cf. Hom. *Il.* 6.304, 312; 9.536; 10.296; *Od.* 6.151, 323; 24.521 (Δ. κούρῃ μεγάλοιο); cf. Hom. *Il.* 9.502;

Hes. *Theog.* 81 (Δ. κοῦραι μεγάλοιο); cf. *Hom. Hymn. Diosc.* 9 (Δ. κούρους μεγάλοιο) || **6** Ἐριούνιον, ἔξοχον ἄλλων] cf. *Hom. Hymn. Pan.* 28 (Ἑρμείην); Hom. *Il.* 20.72 (ἐρ. Ἑρμῆς); 24.360, 440, 457 etc.; cf. etiam Hom. *Il.* 6.194 (ἔξοχον ἄλλων) et al. || **7** καὶ δή τ' ἐρρύσατο λαόν] cf. *Hom. Hymn. Minerv.* 4 || **8** θεμίστωρ] cf. Hsch. θ 252 (hapax) || **9** Χαῖρε πόλις] cf. Eur. *El.* 1134; Greg. Naz. *carm.* 3.2.1 (*De seipso*), *PG* 37.1261.6 | χαῖρ' ἤματα πάντα] cf. Hom. *Il.* 24.491 (χαίρει...ἤματα πάντα); cf. Hom. *Il.* 8.539; 12.133 etc. || **10** μέγα χάρμα] cf. Hom. *Il.* 24.706; *Or. Sib.* 1.287; et al. | ἀλφεῖ] cf. Hsch. α 3330 (<ἀλφεῖν>· εὑρίσκειν); Ps.-Zonar. *Lexicon* 138.25; et al. || **11** αἴην πατρίδα] cf. Hom. *Il.* 2.157, 174; *Od.* 1.290 etc. (π. γαῖαν); cf. Hom. *Il.* 2.162; 2.178; 4.172; *Od.* 2.161 (π. αἴης) || **16** βιοθάλμιος ἀνήρ] cf. *Hom. Hymn. Ven.* 189 || **18** ποιμένα λαῶν] cf. Hom. *Il.* 1.263; 2.243 etc. || **19** πολέμου ... κεραυνόν] cf. Lucr. 3.1034 (*Scipiadas, belli fulmen*); Verg. *Aen.* 6.842–843 (*duo fulmina belli, / Scipiadas*) || **20** Εἰρήνης τε φίλον] cf. Greg. Naz. 3.1.2 (*Carm. Moral.*), *PG* 37.783.14 | Μουσάων καὶ μέγ' ὄνειαρ] cf. *Hymn. Orph. Prooem.* 14 Q. (Δικαιοσύνης τε καὶ Εὐσεβίης μέγ' ὄνειαρ) || **21–32** Ἄριστος εὐφροσύνα...ἐξέλοι βαθείας] cf. Pind. *Nem.* 4.1–8

‹For Jan Zamojski›

To Epaminondas

Sing of Ioannes now, swans, sing of him,
and raise him up with sweet songs to the highest Olympus,
raise up Ioannes, the gleam of men similar
to the immortals, a man worthy of the Muses,
[5] a man who drinks ambrosia, the son of mighty Zeus,
the beautiful luck bringer of mortals, eminent among others.
He fights the enemies, and he has rescued the people,
being stout-hearted, a sceptre-bearer, expert in many things.
Hail, o City, my mistress, hail forever, o City,
[10] since Zamojski finds great delight in serving you.
It is a free man who saves his fatherland.
You Nymphs, raise here an eternal altar to Ioannes
and give him now crowns, give him now many wreaths as well.
He is worthy of oak leaves and worthy of the blossoms
[15] of Chloris, of a statue, if he is godlike,
o Zeus, since he is a flourishing man of great renown.
I see the future well-disposed to all Poles,
I myself recognise the head and shepherd of the people,
the swiftest one, the heavy thunderbolt of great war,
[20] the friend of Peace, and the great support of the Muses.

Antistrophe.

The best healer
for toils judged successful
is joyous revelry, but songs too,
those wise daughters of the Muses,

[25] soothe them with their touch.
Not even warm water
relaxes the limbs
as much as praise,
the companion of the lyre.
For words live longer
[30] than deeds,[11]
words that, with the Graces' blessing,
the tongue is able to draw from the depths of the mind.[12]

Metre: ll. 1–20 hexameters with a small number of hiatuses (e.g., αἴρετε αἰεί in l. 12a and, easily resolvable, ἔστι ἀγάλματος in l. 15a); note that l. 11 is bipartite. *Antistrophe*: The metre corresponds to Pind. *Nem.* 4.1–13 (Aldus and Stephanus), a logoaedic sequence that implies a mixture of disyllabic and trisyllabic feet.

Notes: This poetic composition consists of two distinct poems: 20 hexameters and a 13-line Pindaric strophe. The latter, apart from one or two minor differences, corresponds perfectly to the opening strophe of Pindar's 4th *Nemean Ode*. Both Greek texts form part of a sophisticated, polyglot composition designed to glorify Jan Zamojski (1542–1605), one of the greatest Polish politicians, diplomats, and statesmen of the time and a key figure in the War of the Polish Succession (1587–1588): this event is possibly the inspiration for the inclusion of this work in the form of an epinician. Zamojski, who was also to become the object of an encomium by Laurentius Rhodoman (→ **Germany**), is praised here through comparison with other famous historical leaders of different nations. As can be inferred from the title of this two-strophe composition, the hero of the Greek people is represented here by the symbolic figure of Epaminondas, the famous Theban general of the 4th century BC, who surprisingly does not, however, play any significant role in the poem. As a result, the motivation for the poet's choice of this figure remains unexplained, but one may think of the combination of military virtue and musical/poetic skill traditionally connected with Epaminondas. The work makes use of Greek poetic vocabulary, Homeric phrases and, obviously, Pindaric quotations: it represents one of many contemporary 'experiments' of poetic form based on free interpretation of the epinician structure.

---

11 Niegoszewski's text has ἐρυμάτων ('safeguards'), not ἐργμάτων ('deeds'), as is found in most editions of Pindar.
12 The translation of the *Antistrophe* is based on the translation of Pind. *Nem.* 4.1–8 by William H. Race (1997) in: Pindar, *Nemean Odes; Isthmian Odes; Fragments*, Cambridge, MA.

Biography: Stanislaus Niegossevius (Stanisław Niegoszewski, Niegossewius, Niegosevius, c. 1565 Niegoszowice – c. 1600), Polish poet and improvisator, *homo multilinguis* (versed in Latin, Greek, Hebrew, Italian, and Spanish), Knight of the Golden Spur of the Republic of Venice (*eques auratus Reipublicae Venetae*), educated at Cracow Academy and at Padua University, friend and client to the foreman ('starosta') of Szydłów, Jakub Secygniowski (c. 1518–c. 1594), to the Paduan physician Albertino Bottoni (?–1596), and to the Venetian printer Aldo Manuzio il Giovane (Aldus Manutius the Younger, 1547–1597). During his stay in Venice in 1584, Aldo Manuzio organised a great show in the Church of St John and Paul (Basilica dei Santi Giovanni e Paolo), where Stanisław Niegoszewski gave improvised answers in versified form to questions concerning philosophical and theological subjects. As a testimony to that event, Manuzio published a short advertisement and an open letter to Jan Zamojski with an interesting engraving on the title page, containing a few examples of Niegoszewski's Latin *poesis artificiosa*.[13] Niegoszewski's major works include a handful of occasional poetry in Latin, such as *Xenium in expeditionem contra Moschos...Domino Iacobo Seczigniewski* (Cracoviae 1581), *Epigrammata Joanni Kochanovio, qui...nimis cito periit et immaturus* (Cracoviae 1584), *Ad Franciscum Gioiosium S.R.E. card. amplissimum ἀδελφὸς τεθνεώς* (Neapoli 1588), *Ad Sixtum V. Pontificem Opt.(imum) Max.(imum)...Λέων Νικητής* (Romae 1588), *Epithalamion...Janussi ducis Ostrogiae et Catharinae Lubomierska...* (Cracoviae 1598), Πρὸς Θεῖον Σιγισμόνδον Τρίτον Τῶν Πολωνῶν Βασιλέα...Στεφανηφορία (Romae 1588) – a long poem in Greek praising the Polish King and Lithuanian Grand Duke Sigismund III Vasa (1533–1586) –, as well as a short collection of multilingual versified eulogies in honour of the illustrious political leader Jan Zamojski, *Ad Illustriss.(imum) Principem Ioannem Zamoiscium Regni Poloniae Magnum Cancellarium...Ἐπινίκιον* [s.a., s.l. = Venetiis 1588?].

Bibliography: Estr. XXIII, 109–110; Wierzbowski, II, 171 (no. 1683); Łempicki (1925/26), 176–179; Ławińska-Tyszkowska 1985; Czerniatowicz 1991, 143–146; http://hellenopolonica.blogspot.com/2014/03/stanislaus-niegossevius.html [accessed: January 2021].

---

[13] For the digital edition of this letter (preserved in the Polish National Ossoliński Institute (Ossolineum), with the shelfmark XVI.F.4234), see this link: https://dbc.wroc.pl/dlibra/publication/6020/edition/5614/content [accessed: January 2021].

Nicolaus Zaleski (*fl.* 1595)

ΓΡΗΓΟΡΕΙΤΕ ΟΤΙ ΟΥΚ ΟΙΔΑΤΕ ΤΗΝ ΗΜΕΡΑΝ [1595]

Σήμερον ἠγερθείς, ἄνθρωπε, τό σ' ἔσχατον ἦμαρ
   Τῆς ζωῆς οἴου ἔμμεναι ἀργαλέας.
Μηδὲ ἀπημοσύναισιν ἀπερχομένῃσι πεπειθὼς
   Τόλμα ἐπισχέσθαι αὔριον ἀμφίβολον.
5 Πόλλ' ἄκρων πίπτει χειλῶν κύλικός τε μεταξύ.
   Ὥρα τε πολλὰ μόνη κἂν ἀέκοντι φέρει.
Κεῖνος μὲν παίζων ἔπεσεν, κεῖνος παρὰ δαιτὸς
   Ἐπνίγη, αὐτὰρ ὁ χθὲς ἐν κλισίῃσι σάος.
Ἄστατός ἐστι τροχός, μικρός τε πεπηγμένος οὗτος
10   Τυφλός, ἀείστρεπτος, πουλύτροπός τε βίος.

Textus: *Parentalia in obitum illustris et magnifici domini D. Georgii Chodkievicii, Generalis Capitanei Samogitiae etc. etc., a sodalibus congregationis Parthenicae, Academiae Vilnensis, Societatis Iesu, mortem sodalis sui et moderatoris quondam vigilantissimi deflentibus, conscripta.* Vilnae: In Typographia Academiae Societatis Iesu, Anno Domini 1595, f. E 1r. Editiones recentiores: Czerniatowicz 1991, 183; Veteikis 2004, 242; Veteikis 2018, 372 (Appendix 4c).

Crit.: tit. NICOLAI ZALESKI. ed. || **1** ἐγερθείς debuit (seu potius ἠγέρθης metri gratia) | τόσ' ed. || **2** ζώης ed., corr. Cz | ἀργαλεᾶς ed., corr. Cz || **3** Μήδε ed., corr. Cz | πεποιθὼς fort. debuit || **4** Τολμᾷ ed. || **5** Πόλλ' ed. | μετάξυ ed. || **6** κἄν ed.

Sim.: tit. cf. NT *Mt* 25.13; *Mc* 24.42 || **1** ἔσχατον ἦμαρ] cf. *Or. Sib.* 8.91; 8.310–311 || **2** Τῆς ζωῆς ... ἀργαλέας] cf. Greg. Naz. 3.1.2 (*Carm. Moral.*), PG 37.672.13 (Μεσσηγὺ ζωῆς τε καὶ ἀργαλέου θανάτοιο) || **3** Μηδὲ ἀπημοσύναισιν...πεπειθὼς] cf. Greg. Naz. 3.1.2 (*Carm. Moral.*), PG 37.914.12 (Ἄλγος ἀπημοσύνης πολλάκι κουφότερον) || **5** Πόλλ' ἄκρων...μεταξύ] cf. Arist. *Pseudepigrapha* 8.184 (523); Dion. Thrax fr. 36; Zenob. 5.71; *Anth. Pal.* 10.32 (Palladas); et al. (Πολλὰ μεταξὺ πέλει κύλικος καὶ χείλεος ἄκρου); cf. (aliis verbis) Hom. *Od.* 22.8–18; Lycoph. *Alex.* 488–490 || **7** Κεῖνος μὲν παίζων ἔπεσεν] cf. Machon (comic.) fr. 16 Gow, 290–292 || **7–8** παρὰ δαιτὸς / Ἐπνίγη] cf. Luc. *Macr.* 24 (de Sophocle); cf. *Appendix proverbiorum* 1.77 L. (de Terpandro) | παρὰ δαιτὸς /...αὐτὰρ...ἐν κλισίῃσι σάος] cf. Hom. *Il.* 19.179 || **9–10** Ἄστατός ἐστι...τε βίος] cf. Greg. Naz. 3.1.2 (*Carm. Moral.*), PG 37.787.14–788.1.

WATCH, FOR YOU DO NOT KNOW THE DAY

   Today, when you wake, o man, believe that this is the last day
     of your troublesome life.
   Nor dare, having believed in the transience of moments of serenity,
     to wait for the ambiguities of tomorrow.
   [5] Many things slip between the cup and the lips.
     One hour, even if you do not want it to, brings many things.

One has fallen down while playing, another has choked at the banquet,
   while the one who yesterday was confined to in his bed is fine.
This life is an unresting wheel, short and fixed,
[10]   blind, ever turning and fickle.

Metre: Elegiac couplets. Anomalous lengthening of the first syllable (morphological mistake) for the sake of metre: ἠγερθείς (l. 1); instances of correption: ἔμμεναι ἀργαλέας (l. 2); Τολμᾷ [sic] ἐπισχέσθαι (l. 4); less regular (before the diphthong): Ἐπνίγη, αὐτὰρ (note the short ι); less successful hiatus: Μηδὲ ἀπημοσύναισιν (l. 3).

Notes: This is one of nine short funeral consolation poems written by the students at the recently established Vilnius Jesuit Academy and printed in a commemorative publication dedicated to honouring the untimely death of Jurgis Chodkevičius (Jerzy Chodkiewicz, 1570–1595), a member of an illustrious family of Polish and Lithuanian magnates. This poem testifies to the study and imitation of Greek Christian poetry (with special attention to didactic poetry of Gregory of Nazianzus) at Vilnius Academy. The poem develops its main idea from the quotation from the Gospel, chosen as its title, about constant vigilance and readiness for death and for the coming of the Lord: it entwines the biblical motif with the classical and Christian *topoi* of the unpredictability of the moment of death, the brevity of life, the weakness of man, etc.

Biography: Nicolaus Zaleski, otherwise unknown, was a student at the Vilnius Jesuit Academy in the years 1595–1596. His only known work, apart from this poem, is *Aeternos erige muros*, which is a short Latin poem in *Threni in obitum...Nicolai Szymanowski, studiosi philosophiae in Aademia Vilnensi Societatis Iesu. A iuventute eiusdem Academiae conscripti* (Vilnae 1596).

Bibliography: Estr. XIV 178–179; VASL 21 (no. 72); Czerniatowicz 1991, 183; Narbutienė/Narbutas 2002, 148–152 (no. 213); Veteikis 2004, 242; Veteikis 2018, 336–378 (esp. 347–348).

Anomymous (probably Gregorius Święcicius)

ODARION [1604]

SCIENTIA LINGVARUM.
Κάζετ' ἀνθηρὸν Κασιμεῖρον ἱρόν,
Ζηνὸς ὦ φρουραὶ μεγάλοιο κοῦραι,
Ἀνέρας, Μοῦσαι, ζαθέους ὑδοῦσαι,
    Ἆισμα φιλοῦσαι.

CALLIOPE.
5 Ὃν κέλεις βάζειν πρόφρονές τε κάζειν
Ἄρχομεν, Μουσῶν Χαρίτων τε σοῦσον.
Ἦν ὁ εὔκλειος νέος, ἦν ὁ δῖος
    Ὄζος Ἄρηος.

CLIO.
Γηθέτω λαῶν γέα Σαρματάων,
10 Δῆμος ἆρ μᾶλλον Λιτάλων ἀγάλλων.
Νῦν ἑκὰς φόρτοι, παρέσοιντο χόρτοι,
    Ἦλθεν ἑορτή.

ERATO.
Οὗτος ἦν δῖος βασιλῆος υἱός,
Μήποτε στέργων φλυάρων παρέργων,
15 Οὓς μάλα ζητεῖ ποθέοντι στήθει
    Πάντοτε πλήθη.

THALIA.
Μίσεεν τιμὴν κενεάν τε φήμην,
Μίσεεν σαρκὸς σπατάλην ὁ ἀρχός,
Πᾶν ὁ τιμήσας μίσεος τὸ μῖσος
20   Ἁγνέσιν ἶσος.

MELPOMENE.
Ὕβριος γρυφὰς ἔρικ' ἠδὲ τρυφάς,
Πᾶν ἔρεικ' ἄξαι, ἔρικ' ἠδὲ τάξαι.
Τέρψεν ἀχθεινὰς ἀγέλας τε ξείνας,
    Τέρψεν ἀχῆνας.

TERPSICHORE.
25 Εὐλαβής, σώφρων, θεότητι πρόφρων,
Πολλάκ' εὐχωλῶν ὁ παρεῖχε μῶλον,
Πολλάκ' ἀνῆκον νύχιός τε σηκὸν
    Πολλάκ' ἐφήκων.

EVTERPE.
Ζῆσεν ἁγνεύων, σθενίους φονεύων
30 Νερτέρους, ῥητὴν φύγεν Ἀφροδίτην.
Κύπριδος μίσγειν προβέβουλε θνήσκειν,
Πότμον ἐπισπεῖν.

POLYHYMNIA.
Κάρτερον, φοῖβον, καθαρόν τ' ἔφηβον
Οὐρανῶν σῶκοί σε στέγουσι θῶκοι.
35 Ἔλλαβες θείων μενέχαρμος ἴων
Ἔνθα βραβεῖον.

VRANIA.
Πατρίδος γαίης κακὰ μῶν σὺ κλαίεις;
Σοί τ' ἄναξ παὸς τάλας ἠδὲ λαὸς
Λίσσεται, δῆμον πολεμοῦντα, λοιμὸν
40 Κἄπτρεπε λιμόν.

LINGVARVM SCIENTIA.
Δὸς Σιγισμούνδῳ Θεοῦ ἀργυροῦν δῶ,
Οὐλαδισλάῳ πάϊδ' ἠδὲ λαῷ
Δὸς κρατεῖν ἐχθρῶν, μακάρων τε λέκτρον
Βῆμεν ἄλεκτρον.

Textus: *Pompa Casimiriana, sive De Labaro D. Casimiri, Casimiri Regis Poloniae &c. F(ilii) Iagellonis N(epotis) M. D. Lith(uaniae) Principis etc. A Leone X. Pontif(ice) Max(imo) in Divos relati, ex urbe transmisso, et Vilnam Lithuaniae Metropolim solemni pompa, ad 6. Idus Maii, Anno M. DC. IV. illato, Quirini Cnogleri Austrii Sermo Panegyricus*, p. 104–106, in libro convoluto sub titulo: *Theatrum S. Casimiri, in quo ipsius prosapia, vita, miracula, et illustris pompa in solemni eiusdem apotheoseos instauratione*, Vilnae Lithuaniae Metropoli V. Id(us) Maii Anno D(omi)ni M. DC. IV. instituta graphice proponuntur. [...] Editum ibidem, eodem anno, operis Typographicis Academiae Societatis Iesu [= Vilnae 1604]. Editiones recentiores: Czerniatowicz, 1991, 167–169; Strockis 2001, 110–114; Juchnevičienė/Strockis, 129–133; Veteikis 2004, 244–246; Strockis 2007, 58–60.

Crit.: tit. ODARION (tantum) ed. : GREGORIUS SWIĘCICIUS / GRZEGORZ ŚWIĘCICKI (nomen hypothetici auctoris) Cz : <in D. Casimirum> Vet2004 || **2** Ζῆνοσ ὦ ed., corr. Cz || **4** Ασμα ed.: ᾄσμα Cz: ᾆσμα Stro2001 || **5** Ὄν ed.: Ὄν Cz: Ὄν Stro2001 | κέλειο, ed.: κέλεις Cz, Stro2001 (sine nota commatis): κέλη JuStr2015 | πρόφρονεστε ed., corr. Cz || **6** χαρίτωντε ed., corr. Cz || **7** Hv ed. || **9** Σαρματἄων ed., corr. Cz || **11** ἕκασ ed., corr. Cz || **15** Οὕς ed., corr. Stro2001 (οὕς) || **17** κενεάντε ed., corr. Cz || **18** σάρκοσ ed., corr. Cz | ἄρχοσ, ed.: Ἄρχος. Cz (notam commatis signo puncti mutavit): Ἀρχός, Stro2001 JuStr2015 || **20** Ἅγνεσιν ed., corr. Cz et al. (forma verbi insolita, fort. pro ἁγνοῖς metri gratia creata) | ἴσοσ ed., corr. Stro2001 || **21** Υβρισο ed., corr. Cz | γρυφᾶσ (verbum perobscurum, quod in dictionariis non reperitur)...τρύφασ ed., sed fort. debuit γρυπὰς...τρύπας (cum -ῡ-)?: γρύτας...τρυφάς Vet2004: γρυπὰς...τρυφάς Cz cum nota «rectius» in margine: γρίφας...τρυφάς Stro2001, JuStr2015 (sic et sensus, et Leoninitas vocum [sc. Grifas...trifas] servatur) || ἔρικ' ed., Cz: ἔριπ' Stro2001, JuStr2015 || **22** ἔρεικ'] ex rec. Vet2004: ἔρικ' (primum) ed.,

Cz: ἔρυκ' Stro2001 propter longam syllabam | ἔρικ' (alterum) ed., Cz: ἔριπ' Stro2001 JuStr2015 ||
23 ἀχθείνασ ed., corr. Cz | ἀγέλάστε ed., corr. Cz || **24** ἀχήνασ· ed., corr. Cz || **25** θέοτητι ed., corr.
Cz || **27** ἀνῆκον ed. et al., Cz tamen proposuit ανῆκεν [sic!] | νύχιόστε ed., corr. Cz || **28** ἐφήκων
ed. et al., Cz autem proposuit ἐφῆκεν || **31** Κυπρίδοσ ed. | μίσγειν] ex rec. Stro2001: μίσκειν ed. |
θνήσκειν debuit || **33** Καρτερόν, debuit | φοῖβον fort. debuit | κάθαρόν τ' ed., corr. Cz || **35** Ελλαβεσ
ed., corr. Cz | ἴων ed.: ἰὼν Cz et al. || **38** παὸς] ex rec. Stro2001: ταὸσ ed. || **41** Σιγισμούνδῳ] ex rec.
Cz: ΣΙΓΙΣΜΟΥΝΔΩ ed. || **42** Οὐλαδισλάῳ] ex rec. Cz: ΟΥΛΑΔΙΣΛΑΩ ed. | παῖδ', ed., corr. Stro2001
|| **43** μακάρωντε ed., corr. Cz | λέχτρον ed., corr. Cz || **44** Βήμεν ed., corr. Stro2001 (βῆμεν) et
Vet2004 | ἄλεκτρον] ex rec. Stro2001: ἄλεκτον ed.

Sim.: 2–3 Ζηνός...μεγάλοιο κοῦραι...Μοῦσαι] cf. Hom. *Il.* 2.598; Hes. *Theog.* 25; 81; Eumelus fr.
16.1 = Clem. Al. *Strom.* 6.2.11.1 et al. || **3** ὑδοῦσαι] verbum perrarum, cf. Nic. *Alex.* 47 (ὑδεῦσι), 525
(ὑδέουσι); cf. Callim. *Hymn* 1.76 (ὑδείομεν) || **7** Ἦν ὁ εὔκλειος νέος] cf. Eutr. (Paeanii translatio)
8.11 (ἦν εὐκλεὴς ἔτι νέος) || **8** Ὄζος Ἄρηος] cf. Hom. *Il.* 2.540, 704, 745, 842; 12.188 etc. || **9** λαῶν
γέα] cf. Hom. *Il.* 2.96 (γαῖα / λαῶν ἰζόντων); LXX *3 Reg.* 8.53 (τῶν λαῶν τῆς γῆς); LXX *Esd* 10.2 et
11; 20.29 (ἀπὸ λαῶν τῆς γῆς) || **11** Νῦν ἑκάς] cf. Hom. *Il.* 5.791 = 13.107; 20.354 || **12** Ἦλθεν ἑορτή]
cf. Thuc. 6.57; Mus. *Her. et Leand.* 42 || **15** Οὓς μάλα] cf. Hom. *Il.* 4.233 et 4.241 (τοὺς μάλα) || **17**
τιμὴν κενεὰν τε φήμην] cf. Clem. Al. *Quis div. salv.* 11.4 (φήμης κενῆς καὶ κενοδοξίας) || **18** σαρκὸς
σπατάλῃ] cf. Chrys. *In ep. ad Eph. hom. IV, PG* 62.41 (Φρόνημα τῆς σαρκός, τρυφή, σπατάλη);
Cyril. *De adoratione et cultu in spiritu et veritate, PG* 68.457 (γήϊνον δὴ τουτὶ σπαταλᾷ σαρκίον);
Ephr. Syr. *Serm. paraen. mon., Or.* 36 (σπατάλην καὶ φιλοκαλίαν σώματος) || **20** Ἀγνέσιν]
abnormis terminatio casus Dativi, nusquam ante usitata || **25** Εὐλαβής, σώφρων, θεότητι
πρόφρων] cf. Cedr. *Comp. hist.* 1.603 (Μαρκιανὸς...σώφρων καὶ περὶ τὸ θεῖον εὐλαβὴς καὶ
ὀρθόδοξος); cf. Ephr. Syr. *Chron.* 8470–8472 (δεσπότης Ἰωάννης, / ἀνὴρ ἀγαθός, εὐλαβής, νόμων
φύλαξ, / σώφρων) || **27–28** ἀνῆκον...ἐφήκων] cf. NT *Phlm.* 8 (ἐπιτάσσειν σοι τὸ ἀνῆκον); cf. Suid.
α 2405 (<Ἀνῆκον> δὲ τὸ πρέπον) || **29–30** σθενίους φονεύων / Νερτέρους] cf. Jo. Chrys. *In
resurrectionem Domini* (Spur.) 3 (ἡμέρα...ἐν ᾗ οἱ διὰ παντὸς ἰσχυροὶ καὶ βέβαιοι τῶν καταχθονίων
νόμοι ἥττηνται) || **31** προβέβουλε θνήσκειν] cf. Ion. fr. 53.4 (Snell) = fr. 7.3 (Page) = Phil. *Quod
omn. prob. lib. sit* 134 (θάνατον δ' ὅ γε δουλοσύνας προβέβουλε) || **32** Πότμον ἐπισπεῖν] cf. Hom.
Il. 7.52; *Od.* 4.562; 5.308; 12.342 etc.; Greg. Naz. 3.2.2 (*carm. quae spectant ad alios*), *PG* 37.1458.13
|| **34** Οὐρανῶν...θώκοι] cf. Greg. Naz. 3.2.2, *PG* 37.1464.3; Nonn. *Dion.* 2.572; 8.267 || **35–36** Ἔλλα-
βες...βραβεῖον] cf. NT *1 Cor* 9.24 (εἷς δὲ λαμβάνει τὸ βραβεῖον); cf. Ephr. Syr. *Sermo de paenitentia
et iudicio et separatione animae et corporis*, p. 238 (τὸ βραβεῖον τῆς νίκης ἀπολαβεῖν) et al. || **35**
μενέχαρμος] cf. Hom. *Il.* 14.376 (ἀνὴρ μ.); Nonn. *Dion.* 20.363 (μ. Ἄρης); 39.33 (μ. Ὑδάσπης) etc. ||
37 Πατρίδος γαίης] cf. Hom. *Il.* 2.162 (πατρίδος αἴης); 2.178; *Od.* 4.521; 13.696 etc.; *Od.* 10.49 (γαίης
ἄπο πατρίδος) | κακὰ...κλαίεις] cf. Soph. *El.* 1117 || **38** ἄναξ...τάλας] cf. Soph. *Aj.* 901–902 (ὤμοι,
κατέπεφνες, ἄναξ, / τόνδε συνναύταν, τάλας·) || **39** Λίσσεται] cf. Hom. *Od.* 8.30; Eur. *Alc.* 202 (καὶ
μή προδοῦναι λίσσεται) et al. || **39–40** λοιμὸν / Κἄπτρεπε λιμόν] cf. Philo *De ebr.* 78–79 (λιμὸν ἢ
λοιμὸν...εὐχαῖς καὶ θυσίαις ἀποτρέπεσθαι) || **41** Θεοῦ ἀργυροῦν δῶ] cf. Hes. *Theog.* 933 (χρύσεα
δῶ); Hom. *Il.* 7.363 (ἡμέτερον δῶ); 18.385; 18.424; *Od.* 1.176; 2.262 etc. || **43** κρατεῖν ἐχθρῶν] cf.
[Dem.] *Περὶ συντάξεως* 16; Cyrill. *Commentarius in Isaiam prophetam, PG* 70.65 (κατακρατεῖν
ἐχθρῶν) et al.

ODARION [Little song]

Scientia linguarum ['Knowledge of Languages']
Adorn the blooming, saintly Casimir,
You maiden-guards, daughters of great Zeus,
You Muses who tell of divine men,
[4] You who love song.

Calliope
We start to sing Him whom you order us to speak of
and adorn willingly, the lily of the Muses and the Graces:
He was a glorious youth, he was a godlike
[8] Offshoot of Ares.

Clio
Let the land of the Sarmatian people rejoice,
and even more so the folk of the Lithuanians at their prayers.
Now let all anxiety be gone, let the banquet appear:
[12] The feast has come!

Erato
This one was the godlike son of the king,
he has never been fond of the nonsense gossip
that the crowds always long for
[14] with craving hearts.

Thalia
The Prince hated honours and vain fame,
he hated the depravity of the flesh,
he who honoured the hatred of hatred
[18] was equal to the saints.

Melpomene
He has shattered the frippery (nests?)[14] and the wantonness of insolence,

---

14 The uncertain word γρυφάς may be interpreted in the following several ways: '(vultures') nests', 'lurking places', if interpreted as γρυπάς or γρύπας (cf. Hsch. γ 953 s.v. γρύπαι), 'frippery', if interpreted as γρύτας (as it is represented here) or 'obscure, enigmatic', if interpreted as γρίφας (perhaps in combination with τρυφάς), a very rare adjective used instead of γρῖφώδης, cf. the example of γρίφας in the neuter provided by Nicephorus Gregoras in *Historia Romana* 1.309: τά... βιβλίων αἰνιγματώδη καὶ γρῖφα διαλευκαίνων. I would even consider the more radical suggestion to take γρυφάς as a misprint instead of δρυφάς 'tearings, scrappings, fragments', and to change the accusative τρυφάς to the Doric genitive τρυφᾶς, which is attested in close connection to ὕβριος in an interesting fragment by Hippodamus the Pythagorean (Ἱπποδάμου Πυθαγορείου ἐκ τοῦ Περὶ πολιτείας): βασιλεία μὲν γὰρ θεομίματον πρᾶγμα καὶ δυσφύλακτον ὑπὸ ἀνθρωπίνας

he has completely abstained from leadership, even from command.
He has delighted the flocks of burdensome people and pilgrims,
[24] he has delighted the poor.

Terpsichore
Discreet, temperate, earnestly devoted to Divinity,
oftentimes did he offer [to God] his toil of prayers,
oftentimes even at night he was presenting [to God] what is proper,
[28] he, who was oftentimes approaching the Temple.

Euterpe
He lived keeping purity; slaying the powerful
subterraneans, he escaped the common Aphrodite.
Rather than coupling with Cypris, he preferred to die,
[32] to face his fate.

Polyhymnia
You, the powerful, bright and chaste youngster,
You are protected by the solid seats of Heavens.
For steadfastness in battle you have gained
[36] the prize of violets.

Urania
Don't you lament the misfortunes of your fatherland?
Both the king, your kinsman and the miserable folk of yours
now beg you: avert the hostile people, the plague,
[40] and avert famine.

Linguarum scientia
Grant the silver house of God to Sigismund,
and grant to his son Vladislaus and to the people
to surpass the foes and step into the innocent
    couch of the blessed.

Metre: Sapphic stanzas (with rhyme inside each line and, in addition, between the third line and the adonian: the rhyme is perfect when the Byzantine pronunciation and Latin accentuation are applied). The Sapphic stanzas have only a few inaccuracies, specifically when a long syllable is used where a short one is required by metre (φλυάρων (ᾱ) l. 14, μίσεος l.19), or vice versa (τρυφᾶς, l. 21; ἀνῆκον, l. 27).

ψυχᾶς· ταχέως γὰρ ὑπὸ τρυφᾶς καὶ ὕβριος ἀλλάσσεται (Stob. *Flor.* 4.1.95.51–54). If so, then the hypothetical line that results (ὕβριος δρυφᾶς ἔρικ' ἠδὲ τρυφᾶς) could be translated as follows: 'He has shattered the fragments of insolence and wantonness'.

Notes: This is a poem printed in the complex edition bearing the title of the first section of texts *Theatrum S. Casimiri...* (Vilnius 1604). This ensemble of texts contains a large prose overview or report-like panegyric (*sermo panegyricus*) which carries the separate title *Pompa Casimiriana* and was authored by Quirinus Cnogler (c. 1580 – post 1622), and which gives an account of the solemn celebration of the canonisation of St Casimirus (Lith. Kazimieras, Pol. Kazimierz), a member of the royal family of the Lithuanian Grand Dukes and Polish Kings, on 10–12 May 1604. As far as can be understood from this report, the *Odarion* was publicly recited or sung by a group of students from Vilnius Academy, and was probably later given to the author of the panegyric (Cnogler), along with other texts (poems, languages, dialogues) that were performed during the festival. Researchers have noticed that the poem imitates the Sapphic stanza (the same metre which was used in the first Latin hymns glorifying this saint, which were composed in the 16th century by Zacharias Ferreri), but it is not only longer than its predecessors but also shows dual versification, both quantitative and accentual (Sapphic lines can be broken into rhymed halves with Latin dynamic accent). The language of this ode has ingredients from archaic, classical, and postclassical authors; moreover, it displays an impressive number of very rare or elsewhere unattested lexical and morphological units. Some words, however, seem to be the result of misprint, so that some lines have acquired quite interesting semantic aspects and sound like a riddle. Of course, the general frame of facts and the message inherent in the poem do not deviate from those of the official *Vita S. Casimiri* (published in the same book, *Theatrum S. Casimiri...*).

Biography: Gregorius Swięcicius (Grigalius Sventickis, Sviencickis, Grzegorz Święcicki, 1577–1617), popularly credited with the authorship of the poem, was a famous canonic of the Vilnius chapter who participated actively in the concluding stage of the long process of the canonisation of St Casimirus, the patron saint of Lithuania and Poland. As a delegate of the Vilnius bishop Benediktas Vaina (Benedykt Wojna) and the Vilnius chapter, in the spring of 1602 he went to Rome, where eventually, on 7 November of the same year, Pope Clement VIII signed the *breve* (*Quae ad sanctorum*) carrying the approval of Casimirus' canonisation. In May 1603, Swięcicius brought to Vilnius the *breve* and the flag (*labarum*), which were solemnly carried in the procession of 10–12 May 1604. On this occasion, he organised the printed edition of the documents concerning St Casimirus' life, his canonisation and the contemporary festivities. Swięcicius is generally held to be the author of the large book *Theatrum S. Casimiri* (Vilnae 1604), although not all parts of it come from his pen. One of the most important of his literary works is included in this book: this is the life of St Casimirus, written in Latin. He is also believed by some scholars to be the author of the Greek *Odarion*, which is composed in rhyming Sapphic stanzas. Other candidates to the authorship of the poem are Lars Bojer, professor of rhetoric at Vilnius Academy during that period and Joannes Krajkowski, the author of another Greek *Odarion* to St Casimirus (on his poem, cf. Veteikis 2004, 248-249).

Bibliography: Estr. XXX, 88; Bieliński, Józef (1899-1900), *Uniwersytet Wileński (1579 – 1831)*, Kraków, II, 620-621; III, 478; VASL 146 (no. 936); Czerniatowicz 1991, 167-169; Narbutienė/Narbutas 1998, 249-250 (no. 1124); Strockis 2001; Strockis 2002; Veteikis 2004, 244-246; Juchnevičienė/Strockis 2015, 129-133; Veteikis 2006; Strockis 2007, 57-70.

Gregorius Cnapius (c. 1564–1638)

ΤΩ͂Ι ΆΓΊΩΙ ΊΓΝΑΤΊΩΙ ΤΗ͂Σ ΈΤΑΙΡΊΑΣ ΤΟΥ͂ ΊΗΣΟΥ͂ ΆΡΧΗΓΩ͂Ι, Ὕ́ΜΝΟΣ ΠΆΝΤΗΙ ΆΛΦΑΒΗΤΙΚΌΣ [1626]

Ἄνδρ' αἰνῶ ἀρίδηλον, ἀσώμων ἄξιον αὐδῶν,
Βώτορα, βουλευτήν, βέβαιον, βαθυγνώμονα, βριμόν,
Γνωμονικόν, γεννάρχην, γρηγορικόν, γλυκύθυμον,
Δριμέα, δεινολογοῦντα, δαΐφρονα, δαιδαλόφωνον,
5 Ἔμπονον, εὐήθη, ἐλεητικόν, ἐργοδιώκτην,
Ζηλωτήν, ζαμελῆ, ζωηρόν, ζωπυρέοντα,
Ἥδυμον, ἡδυεπῆ, ἡγητῆρ', ἠπιόθυμον,
Θυμόσοφον, θεατόν, θεοσέπτορα, θελγεσίμυθον,
Ἰθυντῆρ', ἱεροπρεπέ', ἰσχυρόν, ἱμερόεντα,
10 Καρποφόρον, κρατερόν, καματῶντα, καλόφρονα, κλητόν,
Λαρόν, λαοτρόφον, λόγιμον, λαμπρόν, λιγύφωνον,
Μειλίχιον, μέτριον, μεγαλόσπλαγχνον, μελίγλωσσον,
Νηφάλεον, νοερόν, νημερτῆ, νουθετέοντα,
Ξεινοδόκον, ξυνόν, ξυνετόν, ξυγγνώμονα, ξουθόν,
15 Οὐρανογνώμον', ὁμόφρον', ὀνήσιμον, οἰκτικόν, ὀξύν,
Πάγχρηστον, παναγῆ, πρόμαχον, πρόπολον, πανάμωμον,
Ῥύτορα, ῥωμαλέον, ῥητόν, ῥέκτην, ῥοδοειδῆ,
Σώφρονα, σεμνοπρεπῆ, σοφόβουλον, σκληροδίαιτον,
Τερψίνοον, ταλάοντα, τροπαιοφόρον, τετράγωνον,
20 Ὑψαγόρην, ὑγιῆ, ὑψήνορ', ὑπήκοον, ὕδνην,
Φωταυγῆ, φρόνιμον, φιλόμοχθον, φράδμονα, φαιδρόν,
Χρηστόν, χρηστόφιλον, χθαμαλόν, χαρίεντα, χαμεύνην,
Ψυχοτακῆ, ψυχωφελέα, ψευσίστυγα, ψιλόν,
Ὡρικόν, ὡραῖον, ὠκυέπ', ὠμοκράτ', ὠφελέοντα.
25 Οὔνομα τοῦ γνῶναι ποθέεις; ἸΓΝΆΤΙΟΣ ἐστι,
Ὅν ΛΟΙΩΛΑ πατρὶς Καντάβρων κυδίμ' ἔτεξεν.
Κλῦθι, μάκαρ Πάτερ, ἠδὲ τεῶν μέμνησ' ἀκολούθων.

Textus: *Index rerum insigniorum et adnotationum ad criticen et variam eruditionem pertinentium, in primo tomo positarum vel ei hîc adnexarum. Ab auctore confectus vel potius affectus.*[...], in: *Thesauri Polono-Latino-Graeci* Gregorii Cnapii e Societate Iesu *tomus secundus Latino-Polonicus...,* Cracoviae: Sumptu, et Typis Francisci Cezarii, Anno Domini. M. DC. XXVI, p. 39 (= p. 941 totius operis): cf. supra fig. 12. Editiones recentiores: Czerniatowicz 1991, 109–110; Veteikis 2004, 257–258; Gara 2014, 415–416.

Crit.: tit. ΤΩΪ ΑΓΙΩι edd. | ἸΓΝΑΤΙΩι ed. 1626 (= editio princeps, anni 1626): ἸΓΝΤΙΩι cett. edd. (= ceterae editiones) || ΠΑΝΤΗ edd. | ΑΛΨΑΒΗΤΙΚΟΣ edd. post 1644 (= edd. 1652, 1668, 1693) || **1** Ἀ'νδρ' edd., corr. Cz || **2** βεβαιον edd. post 1626 (= edd. 1644, 1652, 1668, 1693) || **3** γρηγορικον, edd. 1668, 1693 | γλυκύθωμον edd. || **4** δαιδαλοφωνον edd. post 1626 || **6** Ζηλωτόν Cz || **7** ἠπιόθυμον edd. 1626, 1644, corr. Cz: ἠπιοθυμον cett. edd. || **9** ἱεροπρεπέ' ed. 1626: ἱεροπρεπέ cett. edd.: ἱεροπρεπῆ Cz | ἰσχυρὸν, edd., corr. Cz || **11** λογιμὸν, edd. || **13** Νηφαλέον seu Νηφάλιον debuit: Νηφάλιον Cz | νουθετέιοντα ed. 1644: νουθετέοντα cett. edd. || **14** ξυνον edd. post 1626 || **15** Οὐρανογνώμον edd. post 1644 || **16** παναμομον edd. post 1626 || **17** ῥέκτήν edd. 1668, 1693 | ῥοδειδῆ edd. 1668, 1693 || **18** σεμνοπρετεῖ ed. 1626: σεμνοπρεπεῖ cett. edd. | σκηροδήαιτον ed. 1644, Cz: σκληροδίτον edd. 1668, 1693 || **21** φόνιμον edd. 1668, 1693 | φιλόμοχθο edd. 1668, 1693 || **25** οὔνομα edd., corr. Cz | γνν(αι) ed. 1693 || **26** Ὅν edd. post 1626: ὅν Cz | πατρίς edd.

Sim.: 1–24 cf. *Anth. Pal.* 9.524; 9.525 (cf. imprimis 4 γλυκύθυμον, 9 θελγεσίμυθον, 24 ψευσίστυγα, 25 ὠκυεπῆ); cf. Greg. Naz. 3.1.2 (*Carm. Moral.*), *PG* 37.908–909; de testimoniis papyraceis carminum similium cf. Squire 2011, 96, n. 39 || **26** κυδίμ' ἔτεξεν] cf. Hes. *Theog.* 938 (τέκε κύδιμον Ἑρμῆν); Clem. Al. *Strom.* 1.21.105.5.3 || **27** Κλῦθι, μάκαρ Πάτερ] cf. Aesch. *Cho.* 139 et 332; cf. Greg. Naz. 3.1.1 (*Carm. Dogm.*), *PG* 37.517.4 et al.

ENTIRELY ALPHABETIC HYMN TO SAINT IGNATIUS, INITIATOR OF THE SOCIETY OF JESUS

I praise the man who is very conspicuous, worthy of incorporeal songs,
pastor, counsellor, steadfast, deeply wise, solid,
fit to judge, founder of the family, wakeful, gentle-minded,
discerning, marvellous in speech, prudent, clever-voiced,
[5] industrious, good-hearted, merciful, taskmaster,
zealous admirer, very strong, lively, inspiring,
pleasant, sweet-speaking, leader, gentle of mood,
wise from his heart, worthy of sight, God-worshipper, soft-speaking,
guide, beseeming a holy man, strong, charming,
[10] fruitful, mighty, toiling, cheerful-minded, the invoked one,
lovely, tending the people, notable, illustrious, clearvoiced,
mild, moderate, high-spirited, honey-tongued,
sober, reasonable, infallible, admonishing,
hospitable, approachable, intelligent, indulgent, agile,
[15] expert in the heavens, smooth-minded, profitable, compassionate, swift,
all-useful, all-hallowed, fighter on the frontlines, temple-servant, all-blameless,
defender, robust, famous, active worker, rose-like,

sound-minded, solemn-looking, wise adviser, living austere life,
heart-gladdening, patient, bringing victory (trophies), perfect,
[20] sublime speaker, healthy, exalting men, giving ear, experienced,
illuminating, sensible, lover of hardship, clever, beaming,
honest, trusty friend, reverent, graceful, finding his bed on the ground,
soul-melter, soul-benefactor, hating falsehood, unarmed,
youthful, mature, quick-speaking, strong-shouldered, helping. –
[25] You desire to know the name of this man? – He is IGNATIUS,
whom LOYOLA, the glorious fatherland of the Cantabri[15], has brought forth.
Give ear, blessed Father, and remember your followers.

Metre: Hexameters. Instance of correption: ὡραῖον (l. 24); Attic correption: βαθυγνώμονα (l. 2), οὐρανογνώμον' (l. 15); a case of metrical lengthening: ΙΓΝΑΤΙΟΣ (l. 25). The compound consonants ξ and ψ do not cause lengthening in the penult dactyls in line 14 (ξυγγνώμονα, ξουθόν) and line 23 (ψευσίστυγα, ψιλόν), respectively.

Notes: This poem (cf. fig. 12, above) by Gregorius Cnapius (Grzegorz Knapski), written in honour of St Ignatius of Loyola (1491–1556), perhaps in the spring of 1622, was printed at the end of vol. 2 (the Polish-Latin section) of his dictionary, *Thesaurus Polono-Latino-Graecus* (ed. princeps 1626), along with two more poems written for the co-founder of the Society of Jesus, Francis Xavier (1506–1552). As stated by the author himself in a brief note to the first of these Latin works, Cnapius publicly presented his texts during the canonisation ceremony held in Cracow for the two Spanish Jesuit saints (shortly after receiving the announcement of the proclamation of these men as saints in Rome on 12 March 1622). In terms of genre, this work imitates both the alphabetic poems (called *abecedaria*) of the *Greek Anthology* and by Gregory of Nazianzus and some fully epithetical hymns of the Orphic tradition. Cnapius calls it an *elogium*, perhaps partly because the poem has the aspect of a reverential commemoration of a deceased person, characteristic of tombstone inscriptions, and partly because of the inclusion of praise of deeds and virtues, characteristic of Greek εὐλογίαι (one of the etymological roots for the late-Roman concept of *elogium*).

Biography: Gregorius Cnapius (Grzegorz Knapski, Knapiusz, c. 1564 Grójec – 1638 Cracow), was a Polish philologist, lexicographer, and paremiographer, well versed in Latin and Greek; a poet, a Jesuit pedagogue, and a priest, he was educated in Warsaw and in Jesuit colleges at Kalisz (he entered the society here

---

15 The *Cantabri* were an ancient people of Northern Spain.

in 1585), Pułtusk, Vilnius, Braniewo (Braunsberg), and Poznań. In the period between 1594 and 1598, he accomplished a full course of theology at Vilnius Academy. In 1598, he became prefect of schools in Poznań and was ordained a priest. From 1603 to 1613 he stayed in Lublin, Cracow and Poznań, then lived four years (1614–1617) in Lwów and Jarosław, and finally (from 1619 until his death) again in Cracow. His major works include *Philopater* and *Felicitas*, school dramas (tragedies) created during his stay at Vilnius Academy (1594–1598); *Eutropius*, a school tragedy written in 1604 and performed in the presence of the Bishop of Cracow, Bernard Maciejowski; *Thesaurus Polonolatinograecus seu Promptuarium linguae Latinae et Graecae* (ed. princeps: Cracoviae 1621, vol.1; 1626, vol. 2; 1632, vol. 3), the largest lexicographical work of the Polish language until the 19th century, which went through many posthumous reprints (e.g., vol. 1 alone had 35 editions until 1793). Three poems in Greek, dedicated to Ignatius of Loyola and Francis Xavier, are inserted in the second volume of the *Thesaurus Polonolatinograecus*. In the third volume of his *Thesaurus*, Cnapius provided an invaluable collection of thousands of proverbs in three languages (Polish, Latin, and Greek), for which he not only used the usual classical sources, but also created a number of Greek proverbs of his own, some of which he rendered in metre (for the collection of these Greek *adagia*, see Czerniatowicz 1991, 50–80).

Bibliography: Estr. XIX, 335; Czerniatowicz 1991, 109–110; Veteikis 2004, 257–260; Gara 2014.

Nicolaus Żórawski (1595–c. 1655)

Μαΐστορος Νικολάου Ζοραβίου τῆς φιλοσοφίας διδασκάλου εἰς τὴν τοῦ ἐν Θεῷ αἰδεσίμου Μελετίου Σμοτρισκίου, εἰρημένου Ἀρχιεπισκόπου Πολοζκίου, Ἐπισκόπου Βιτευσκίου καὶ Μσκισλαβίου, Ἀρχιμανδρίτου Βιλνωουίαθι, *Παραίνεσιν*, ἔπος ἐγκωμιαστικόν [1629]

    Οἱ μὲν δράξαντες πολέμους ἐπὶ πατρίδος αἴας
      Χαίρουσιν διὰ τοῦ αἵμα φόνοιο χέειν.
    Ἄλλος μαρμαρέῳ βριαρὰν χθόνα σχίζει ἀρότρῳ,
      Καρποὺς εὐτροφέους ὅστις ἰδεῖν γλίχεται.
5   Ἄλλος προσβάλλει κενεῷ τῷ πνεύματι λαῖφος,
      Ὕδατος ἐνδέχεται καὶ κακὰ πολλὰ τάλας.
    Εἰσὶν ὁμηγερέες τινὲς ὑψηλοῖς ἐν ὄρεσσι,
      Λίστροις ἀργαλέως χρυσὸν ὀρυττόμενοι.
    Εἰσὶν τοῖς δὲ μέλει κίθαρις μαλακὴ καὶ ἀοιδή,

10 Τοῖς τέρπειν κῆρ καὶ δαῖτας ὀλέσσαι ἀεί.
    Ἀλλ' οὐ Σμοτρικίου λίαν ταῦθ' ἥνδανε θυμῷ,
    Μηδὲ λιλαιόμενος γηΐνα δὴ πέλεται.
    Ἔργον κεῖνος ἔχει, τὸ ἄξιόν ἐστι ἀμοιβῆς
    Ἀϊδίου, καὐτὸν πάντοτε δόξα μένει,
15 Ἔργον, ὅπερ μὴ μοῦνον ἐπευφήμησαν ἅπαντες
    Ἄνθρωπ' ὠκύμορ', ἀλλ' ἀθανάτοισι δοκεῖ.
    Ὅς μὲν γὰρ ὀρόων ἔχθιστον δαίμονα ψυχὰς
    Ἑλλήνων πολλὰς ἑλκέμεναι Ἄϊδι,
    Οὓς ἔρυσεν περὶ τὴν πίστιν τὰ σφάλματα πολλά,
20 Σχίσμα τε πρὸς Πάππαν καὶ ἔρις ἀσκελέως,
    Καὶ ἀμαθία παχύς, δύσρηκτον δὴ μάλα φλαῦρον,
    Καὶ βάσις ἐν κόσμῳ ἔπλετο ὅττι κακοῦ,
    Πρῶτον ἐρυσσάμενος κινδύνου ἔλκεθ' ἑαυτόν,
    Ζεύγνυται καὶ Ῥώμῃ, δόγμ' ἐχεπευκὲς ἀφείς.
25 Ἥ τε παραίνεσσιν ποτὶ Ῥώσσους γράψε τοιαύτην
    Ἧι θέλγητρον δρᾷ ὄφρα σέβεσθαι Θεόν
    Αὐτὸς ἔων κεφαλὴ πρότερον τοῦ σχίσματος οὔλου
    Εἰρήνης καὶ νῦν αὐτός ἐστιν κεφαλή.
    Ὥστε, πάτερ βέλτιστε, περίσχεο πώεος αὐτοῦ
30 Ἐκ τούτ' ἐλπίζων οὐ μικρὸν ἆθλον ἔχειν.

Textus: *Paraenesis, abo Napomnienie, od w Bogy Wielebnego Meletiusza Smotryskiego, Rzeczonego Archiepiskopá Połockiego, Episkopá Witepskiego y Mścisławskiego, Archimándrytę Wileńskiego y Dermańskiego, do Prżezacnego Bráctwa Wileńskiego*, Cerkwie S. Duchá; A w osobie iego, do wszystkiego tey strony Narodu Ruskiego uczynione; Anno 1628. Decembr(is) 12...., W Krakowie, W Druk(arni) Andrz(eja) Piotrk(owczyka)...Roku 1629, in fine operis, [N₃] recto-verso. Editiones recentiores: Czerniatowicz 1991, 184–186; Veteikis 2004, 250–252.

Crit.: tit. Μ Α Ι Σ Τ Ο Ρ Ο S ed. (separatim ab aliis vocabulis tituli scriptum), corr. Cz | Σμοτρισκιου ed., corr. Cz | Μσκισλαβίου ed., Μστισλαβίου Cz || **4** εὐτροφέας debuit? || **5** προσβαλλεῖ ed., corr. Cz | κενέῳ τῷ πνευματι ed., corr. Cz || **6** ἐνδεχέται ed., corr. Cz || **7** Ε'ισίν ed., corr. Cz | ὁμιγέρεές τινες ed.: ὁμογερέες τινες Cz | ὄρεασσι ed., corr. Cz || **8** ὀρυττομενοι ed. || **9** Ε'ισίν ed., corr. Cz || **10** ὀλέσσαι ed., Cz: ἀλέσσαι Vet2004 || **11** ταυτ' ed., corr. Cz | ἥνδανε ed. || **12** γηΐινα ed., corr. Cz || **13** κεινος ed., corr. Cz | ἄξιον ἔστε ed. || **14** κάυτὸν ed. || **15** ἐπεὐφήμησαν ed., corr. Cz | ἄπαντες ed., corr. Cz || **17** Ὁ ed. || **19** ἔρῠσεν ed., corr. Cz | πίσιν ed., corr. Cz || **20** Σχίσμάτε ed. | ἀσκελεῶς ed. || **21** ἀμάθεια fort. debuit (propter metrum) | παχέως (cum synizesi) fort. debuit (rectae consecutionis verborum causa) || δυσρρηκτον ed., corr. Vet2004 || **22** ἔπλετο] ἔπλεται ed., Cz: πέπληται Vet2004 || **23** ἑαυτον ed., corr. Cz || **24** ἀφεις ed., corr. Cz || **25** Ἥτε] sic Vet2004: Ἥτα ed., Cz | παραίνεσσιν] sic Vet2004: παραίνεισιν ed. | ποτὶ] sic Vet2004: ποδί ed.: ποδι' Cz || **26** ἧ ed.: ἥ Cz | σέβεαθαι ed.: σεβέασθαι Cz || **27** ἐὼν debuit | ὄυλου ed., corr. Cz || **29** περισχεο ed., corr. Cz | πωεος ed., corr. Cz || **30** τουτ' ed., corr. Cz

Sim.: 1–10 Cf. Himer. *Or.* 68.50–54 || **1** πατρίδος αἴας] cf. Hom. *Il.* 2.162 (π. αἴης); 2.178; 4.172 etc. || **5** κενεῷ τῷ πνεύματι] cf. Herm. *Pastor* 43.17 (πνεύματι τῷ ἐπιγείῳ καὶ κενῷ) || **7** ὑψηλοῖς ἐν ὄρεσσι] cf. Ap. Rhod. *Argon.* 4.287; Dion. Per. 315 (Ῥιπαίοις ἐν ὄ.); Callim. *Hymn.* 1.51; Quint. Smyrn. 1.799 (Ἰδαίοις ἐν ὄ.); Orph. *Arg.* 515 (ἀρκτῴοις ἐν ὄ.) || **9** μέλει κίθαρις μαλακὴ καὶ ἀοιδή] cf. Hom. *Od.* 1.159; *Hom. Hymn. Ap.* 188 || **10** τέρπειν κῆρ] cf. Hom. *Il.* 1.474 (φρένα τέρπετ'); cf. *Hom. Hymn. Merc.* 565 (φρένα τέρπε) et al. || **11** Ἀλλ' οὐκ…ταῦθ' ἤνδανε θυμῷ] cf. Hom. *Il.* 1.24; 1.378; 15.674; *Od.* 10.373 || **13** ἄξιόν ἐστι ἀμοιβῆς] cf. Hom. *Od.* 1.318; cf. Luc. *Tyrannicida* 11 || **14** πάντοτε δόξα μένει] cf. Evagr. *Sent. ad virg.* 18 || **16** ἀλλ' ἀθανάτοισι δοκεῖ] cf. Hom. *Il.* 10.440–441 || **21** δὴ μάλα] cf. Hom. *Il.* 9.348; *Od.* 15.401 et al. || **22** βάσις ἐν κόσμῳ] cf. Phil. *De Somniis* 1.134 (κλῖμαξ τοίνυν ἐν μὲν τῷ κόσμῳ συμβολικῶς λέγεται ὁ ἀήρ, οὗ βάσις μέν ἐστι γῆ, κορυφὴ δ' οὐρανός) || **24** δόγμ' ἐχεπευκὲς ἀφείς] cf. Hom. *Il.* 1.51 || **29** περίσχεο πώεος αὐτοῦ] cf. Hom. *Il.* 1.393 || **30** οὐ μικρὸν ἄθλον] cf. Pl. *Phdr.* 256 d5–6

Poem of praise by Master Nicolaus Żórawski, teacher of philosophy, for the *Παραίνεσις* (*Exhortation*) (written) by the venerable in God Meletius Smotrytsky, the nominated Archbishop of Polotsk, Bishop of Vitebsk and Mstislavl, Archimandrite in Vilnovia

Those who win wars for the fatherland
  rejoice when shedding blood of murder.
Another man cleaves solid earth with the gleaming plough:
  He strives to see well-nourished fruits.
[5] Another one throws the sail against the idle wind,
  and he, poor him, receives many evils from the water.
There are some groups of comrades in the mountain heights
  who dig up gold with shovels among great toils.
There are some who prefer to play the tender lyre and sing,
[10] who always care for the delight of the heart and the consumption of meals.
But these (occupations) were never very dear to Smotrytsky's heart,
  nor does he desire earthly things.
He has a job that is worthy of eternal
  recompense, and eternal glory awaits him;
[15] a job, that has not only been praised by all
  the early-dying humans; but that is also favoured by the immortals.
For he, seeing that the most hateful demon dragged
  many souls of Greeks to Hades –
that their many mistakes in terms of faith dragged them relentlessly away,
[20] as did the schism and strife against the Pope
and the mass stupidity, that most unbreakable silliness –
  and (seeing) that the footstep of evil was gaining on the world,
first he escaped the danger and dragged himself away,
  binding himself fast to Rome and abjuring the piercing dogma.
[25] He then wrote to the Ruthenians an exhortation of such a kind
  as to put a spell (on them) to (compel them to) revere God.
Although previously he himself was a leader of that baneful schism,
  now he himself, the same person, is the leader of peace.

Thus, our most excellent Father, embrace your flock,
[30]   with the hope of gaining from it not a small reward.

Metre: Elegiac couplets. Instances of correption: σχίζει ἀρότρῳ (l. 3); καὶ ἀοιδή (l. 9); anomalous correption and prosodical mistakes (note that in few cases consonant clusters with σ [στ, σχ] are treated as one consonant): χθόνα σχίζει (l. 3); γράψε τοιαύτην (l. 25), αὐτός ἐστιν (l. 28); hiatus: καὶ ἔρις (l. 20), καὶ ἀμαθία (l. 21; note the anomalous scansion of -θῑ-ᾰ); ἔπλετο ὅττι (l. 22); diectasis: ὁρόων (l. 17); artificial lengthening: παραίνεσσιν (l. 25); unusual morphology and syntax for the sake of metre: εὐτροφέους instead of εὐτροφέας (l. 4); ἀμαθία παχύς instead of ἀμαθ(ε?)ία παχεῖα (l. 21)

Notes: This is a poem printed on the final two pages of a book by the Uniate Bishop Meletius Smotrytsky (1577–1633), a convert from Orthodoxy: containing an open letter and popularly known by its shortened title, *Paraenesis abo Napomnienie* (Cracow 1629); the book is addressed to the Church of the Orthodox Brotherhood of the Holy Spirit in Vilnius and to the entire Ruthenian nation of that region, regarding the contemporary problems of the Orthodox Christian community and the necessity of its reunion. The author of the poem (Żórawski) praises the author of the letter (Smotrytsky) for his wise choice of confessional conversion and for his boldness in addressing the entire Ruthenian nation with an appeal to unity with the Roman Church. The poem is a mixture of Homeric forms and phrases and the vocabulary of texts of later times: some forms are created artificially on the basis of models in the epic dialect. The poem is noteworthy for its long priamel construction, which broadly echoes famous examples by ancient poets such as Sappho, Pindar, and Horace, and, more closely imitates several sections from Himerius' *Oration 68* (see the *app. sim.* above).

Biography: Nicolaus Żórawski (Nicolaus Zorawsky, Zorauski, Mikołaj Żórawski, 1595 Lublin – c. 1665 Kraków), son of Nicolaus (*notarius juratus* of Lublin), was educated at the Academy of Cracow and the University of Padua, and acted as a private doctor to the Polish kings Sigismund III Vasa (1566–*1632*), Władysław IV Vasa (1595–*1648*) and John II Casimir Vasa (1609–*1672*); he became a royal mathematician, astronomer and astrologist to the kings Władysław IV (from 1633) and Jan Kazimierz. He was also the author of calendar predictions in Polish (*Hemerologeion abo kalendarz świąt rocznych i biegów niebieskich*, from 1638 onward?) and German (from 1642 onward), as well as a professor of mathematics, astrology, and Greek at Cracow Academy. According to some bibliographical sources, Żórawski made translations into Greek of several works by Cicero (such as *Pro Archia poeta, Pro* *lege Manilia, Laelius sive de amicitia*, and *De officiis*) for students' use, but only a small portion of them survived.¹⁶ He also left us an interesting translation of the Lord's Prayer into several dialects of Greek (Attic, Aeolic, Ionic, Doric, Koine and 'the dialect used by the masses in Constantinople').¹⁷ Through his series of German calendars, he is also famous as the founder of the tradition of the German 'Crackauer Schreib Calender', printed in Vienna.

Bibliography: Orgelbrand, Samuel (1868), *Encyklopedia Powszechna* (*Universal Encyclopedia*), 28, Warszawa, 1074; Estr. XXVIII, 330 (on this poem); XIV, 255; XXXVI, 123–129 (about other works); Czerniatowicz 1991, 184–186; Veteikis 2004, 250–252; Peressin 2016.

Anomymous (18th century)

Graece [1729]

Τίς δ' οὐ νῦν χαίρῃ, Σὺ ὅταν, Θεοείκελε Ξεῖνε,
 Ἡμῖν ἐρχόμενος χάρματα πυκνὰ φέρεις;

Textus: *Universitas linguarum Magno Palaemonii Orbis et Urbis Hospiti Celsissimo...Domino Christophoro Joanni Comiti in Słupow Szembek Sacri Romani Imperii Principi, Episcopo Varmiensi et Sambiensi, Terrarum Prussiae Praesidi, Cum demississimo Cultu proposita ab Academica Universitate Vilnensi Soc(ietatis) Jesu*, Anno qVo PraesVL atqVe PrInCeps IngreDItVr VILnaM. [= 1729], f. [3]r. Editiones recentiores: Veteikis 2004, 261; Ulčinaitė 2010, 262.

Crit.: 1 οὐκ ed. | Χαιρη ed., corr. Vet2004, sed fort. debuit χαίρει (post οὐ) | ὀτὰν Θεοεικελε Ξεῖνε ed., corr. Vet2004 || **2** Ἡμῖν ed., corr. Vet2004 | ἐρχομένος ed. | πύκνα φερείς ed., corr. Vet2004

Sim.: 1 Τίς δ' οὐ νῦν χαίρει] cf. Eur. fr. 272.2 Kn. = Stob. *Flor*. 4.24d.49.2 (τίς δ' οὐχὶ χαίρει νηπίοις ἀθύρμασιν;); Epict. *diss*. 4.4.24 (τίς ἡμῶν οὐ χαίρει τῇ πανηγύρει ταύτῃ) | Θεοείκελε Ξεῖνε] cf. Hom. *Il*. 1.131 = 19.155 (de Achille); *Od*. 3.416 (de Telemacho) et al.

---

16 All these translations were considered lost (cf. Czerniatowicz 1991, 186), but in the past few years, fresh information concerning the newly discovered printed edition of the translation of the speech in defence of poet Archias (*Μάρκου Τυλλίου Κικέρωνος, ὁ ὑπὲρ τοῦ Ἀρχίου Ποιητοῦ λόγος*) has appeared (Peressin 2016, 188 n. 1.).
17 For detailed discussion, see Peressin 2016 (https://www.researchgate.net/publication/316608604_Language_and_Literary_Studies_of_Warsaw_vol_6_2016).

In Greek

> Who does not rejoice now whenever you, godlike Guest,
>   come to us, bringing much joy?

Metre: Elegiac couplet, with a single instance of artificial correption in l. 1, where ξ does not cause the lengthening of the preceding syllable.

Notes: This anonymous Greek distich is so far the only example to represent Greek literary compositions by Polish and Lithuanian authors in the 18th century. Together with its Latin *Paraphrasis*,[18] it expresses the simple idea of the cheerful greeting of a noble guest, who has been long awaited by the local Catholic community in its entirety. This poem is part of a multilingual collection of the Vilnius Jesuit Academy, dedicated to Christophorus Joannes Szembek (1680–1740), Count of Słupów, Bishop of Chełm (from 1711), Przemyśl (from 1719), Warmia and Semba (from 1724), on the occasion of his visit to Vilnius in 1729. The Greek poem and the Hebrew one preceding it, which together open the collection, are the shortest in the whole collection and contain fewer details and allusions concerning both the identity of the person praised and Polish-Lithuanian realities in comparison with those written in Latin, Slavonic, Polish, French, German, Lithuanian, and Latvian.

Bibliography: Wolf-Dahm 1996; Veteikis 2004, 93–95, 261; Ulčinaitė 2010, 262.

Jerzy Kazimierz Danielewicz (1942–)

PROFESSORI GEORGIO ŁANOWSKI SEPTUAGENARIO [1990]

>   Ὕμνον ὀρθῶσαι μελιαδέα με χρή
>   σάμερον, Μοισᾶν δόσιν ἠυκόμων
>   ἄνδρα τ' ἔνδοξον κελαδεῖν,
>   ὅσπερ ἄρτι γ' ἑβδομήκοντ' ἐκτελέων ἐνιαυτοὺς
> 5 ἐμπρέπει περικλυτός
>   ἀνέρων κύκλῳ σοφωτάτων ἀρετᾶς ἕνεκεν.
>
>   σὺν δίκᾳ γλαυκόχροα κόσμον ἐλαίας
>   σαῖς ἐθείραις ἀμφιβαλεῖν θέλομεν·

---

18 *Quis non gauderet, dum Tu, Celsissime Princeps, / Nobis adveniens, Gaudia multa vehis?*

```
      τῷ βίῳ νίκας ἔτυχες.
10   μουσικᾶς ἄωτον Ἑλλάνων δυνατός γ' ἐπιδεῖξαι
      σοῖς φίλοις, Γεώργιε,
      ἐσσὶ χάρμ' εὐήρατόν τε καὶ πολύβουλος ἀγός.

      ὡς ὅτε συμποσίου θάλλοντος αἱρεῖ
      οἰνοδόκον φιάλαν τις
15   ποτιφόρων ἄρξαις δ' ἐπέων ἑτάροις
      φερτάτοισιν ἀνδιδοῖ παρ' ἑστίᾳ,
      βούλομαι κἀγὼ προπίνειν σοὶ μέλος.
      ἵλαος δ' εἴη θεός
      ἠδὲ νόσους ἀπαλάλκοι τὶν βαρείας ἔργα τε καλὰ πόροι· πίτνει βροτοῖσιν
20   ἐν μιᾷ μοίρᾳ χρόνου τερπνὰ πάντα Ζηνὸς αἴσᾳ.
```

Textus: carmen primum editum est in: *Eos. Commentarii Societatis Philologae Polonorum* 88 (1990), 7.

Sim.: 1 Ὕμνον ὀρθῶσαι] cf. Pind. *Ol.* 3.3 || **1–2** χρή / σάμερον] cf. Pind. *Pyth.* 4.1 || **2** Μοισᾶν δόσιν ἠυκόμων] cf. Pind. *Ol.* 6.91; 7.7 || **3** ἄνδρα τ' ἔνδοξον κελαδεῖν] cf. Pind. *Ol.* 2.2 || **4** ἐκτελέων ἐνιαυτούς] cf. Pind. *Pyth.* 4.104 || **7** σὺν δίκᾳ] cf. Bacchyl. 13.165 | γλαυκόχροα κόσμον ἐλαίας] cf. Pind. *Ol.* 3.13 || **10** μουσικᾶς ἄωτον] cf. Pind. *Ol.* 1.15 || **13** ὡς ὅτε συμποσίου θάλλοντος] cf. Pind. *Isthm.* 6.1 || **14** οἰνοδόκον φιάλαν] cf. Pind. *Isthm.* 6.40 || **15** ἄρξαις δ' ἐπέων] cf. Pind. *Pyth.* 4.30–31 (φιλῶν δ' ἐπέων / ἄρχετο) || **16** φερτάτοισιν ἀνδιδοῖ] cf. Pind. *Isthm.* 6.39 | παρ' ἑστίᾳ] cf. Pind. *Ol.* 12.14 || **17** βούλομαι κἀγώ] cf. Eur. *El.* 299 (βούλομαι κἀγὼ μαθεῖν); cf. *Anth. Pal.* 11.359.3 (βούλομαι κἀγὼ λέγειν) || **18** ἵλαος δ' εἴη θεός] cf. Theoc. *Id.* 27.16 (ἵλαος Ἄρτεμις εἴη); cf. Greg. Naz. 3.2.2 (*Quae spectant ad alios*), *PG* 37 1536, 8 (ἐπὴν Θεὸς ἵλαος εἴη); et al. || **19** νόσους ἀπαλάλκοι τὶν βαρείας] cf. Pind. *Ol.* 8.85 (ὀξείας δὲ νόσους ἀπαλάλκοι) | **20** ἐν μιᾷ μοίρᾳ χρόνου] cf. Pind. *Ol.* 7.94 | τερπνὰ πάντα] cf. Pind. *Ol.* 14.5–6 (σὺν γὰρ ὑμῖν τά <τε> τερπνὰ καί / τὰ γλυκέ' ἄνεται πάντα βροτοῖς) | Ζηνὸς αἴσᾳ] cf. Pind. *Ol.* 9.42

TO PROFESSOR JERZY ŁANOWSKI THE SEPTUAGENARIAN

It behoves me to raise a hymn
today, a gift of the fair-haired Muses,
and to sing loudly of the man of high repute,
who, having just now completed seventy years,
[5] shines with his renown
in the circle of the wisest men, on account of his virtue.

We rightly wish to put around your hair
the grey-coloured ornament of olive:
you gained a victory with your entire life.
[10] You, who are able to show the flower of Greek music
to your friends, you, George,
are both a lovely source of delight and a versatile master.

As when at the peak of a banquet, someone
takes a goblet that holds wine
[15] and, having started with suitable words, delivers it to the most excellent
friends who are sitting near the fireplace,
so I desire to offer to you this song as a drinking gift.
May God be propitious
and let Him keep from you heavy diseases and bring good deeds: in one portion of time,
[20] all the delights fall to the mortals through Zeus' decree.

Metre (indicated by the author himself): Dactyloepitr. A[1]
ΣTP e–D–|²e–D|³e–d||⁴E–D–||⁵E||⁶E⌣D|||
EΠ D–e–||²D–|³⌣⌣e–D|⁴E⌣e||⁵E–e||⁶E||⁷D–e–D–e–||⁸EE–|||

Notes: This poem is printed on the opening pages of volume 78 of *Eos*, the Polish journal of classical philology, and serves as a supplement to the dedication to the famous Polish philologist Jerzy Łanowski (Georgius Arvalis, 1919–2000), professor at Wrocław University and author of numerous scholarly works in the field of Greek literature.

Biography: Jerzy Kazimierz Danielewicz (b. 1942) is a Polish classical philologist, a specialist of Latin and Greek literature and culture, a translator, an editor and a *poeta doctus*, educated at the Adam Mickiewicz University of Poznań (MA in 1964, PhD in 1969, Dr. Hab. in 1976). Since 1964, he has been an active member of the *Societas Philologa Polonorum* and, since 2010, of the Polish Academy of Sciences, and he is a permanent participant in the educational and research projects of Adam Mickiewicz University, as well as of other institutions and associations. Among his numerous articles and books on Classics, one can find the following: *Morfologia hymnu antycznego. Na materiale greckich zbiorów hymnicznych*, Poznań 1976; *Liryka starożytnej Grecji*, Wrocław 1984, 1987, 2006 (with Włodzimierz Appel and Alicja Szastyńska-Siemion; new edition: Warszawa-Poznań 1996 and 2001); *Anakreont i anakreontyki*, Warszawa 1987 (with Alicja Szastyńska-Siemion); *Alkajos i Safona*, Warszawa 1989; *Miary wierszowe greckiej liryki. Problemy opisu i interpretacji*, Poznań 1994 (English version: *The Metres of Greek Lyric Poetry. Problems of Notation and Interpretation*, Bochum 1996); *Liryka grecka*, vol. 2: *Melika*, Warszawa-Poznań 1999; *Posejdippos. Epigramy*, Warszawa 2004; *Atenajos. Uczta mędrców*, Poznań 2010 (with Krystyna Bartol); *Komedia grecka od Epicharma do Menandra. Wybór fragmentów*, Warszawa 2011 (with Krystyna Bartol). As a poet, he has published five occasional poems (two in classical Greek and three in classical Latin) in honour of famous professors, such as Wiktor Steffen (*Symbolae Philologorum Posnaniensium* 1,

1973, 5), Mieczysław Brożek (*Eos* 74, 1986, 5f.), Jerzy Łanowski (*Eos* 78, 1990, 7) and Andrzej Wójcik (*Symbolae Philologorum Posnaniensium* 19, 2009, 15).

Bibliography: http://www.koinonema.umk.pl/pl/koinotai.html [accessed: January 2021] (author's personal data and selected works); http://ifk.amu.edu.pl/__data/assets/pdf_file/0010/126946/Jerzy-Danielewicz-bibliografia.pdf (bibliographical list of Danielewicz's works).

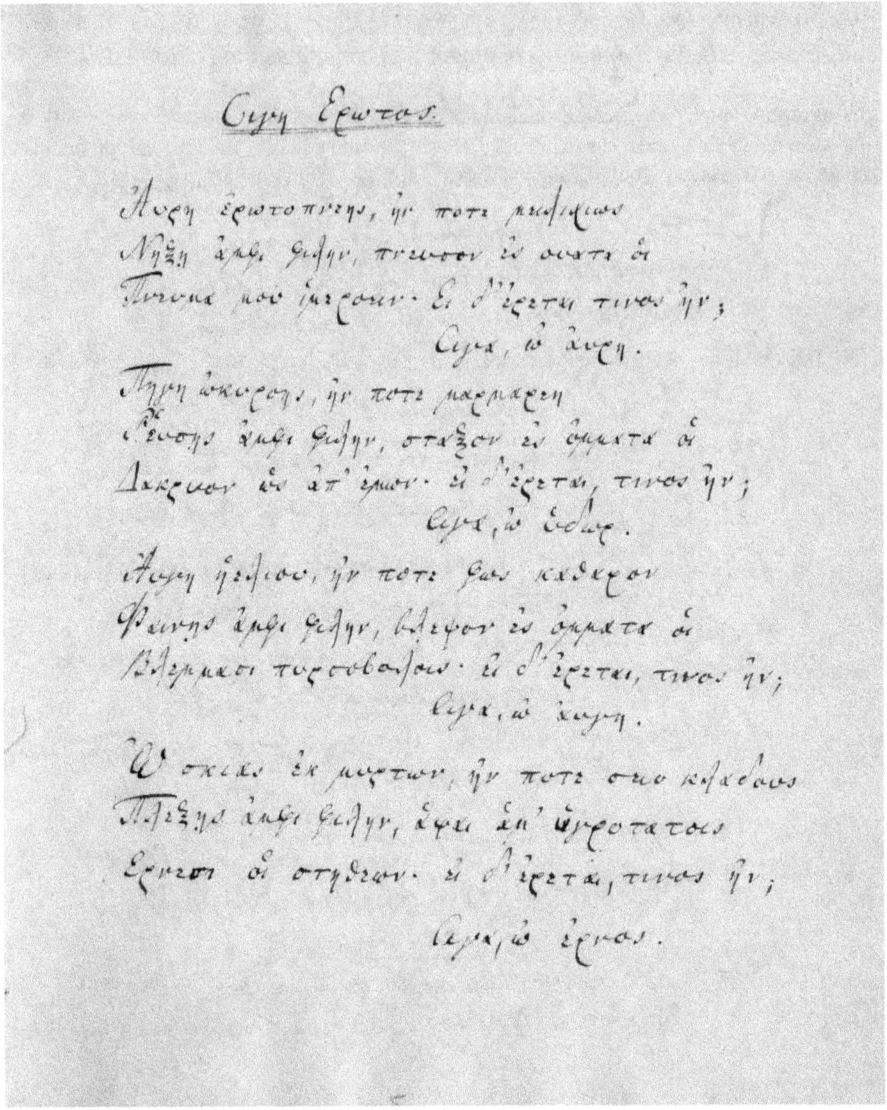

Fig. 13: St Petersburg, Russian National Library, ms. F. 608, I, 4802, f. 5v: autograph of Σιγη Ερωτος by Graefe (see below, p. 674–677; one may note that Graefe does not use accents in his autograph).

Elena Ermolaeva
Russia

Kievan Rus' came into contact with Greek culture in the 10th century, when it inherited the Orthodox Christian faith from the Byzantine Empire. Byzantine Greek served as a basis for the Cyrillic script in South and East Slavic languages, to which Russian belongs. Russian monks made regular pilgrimages to Constantinople and Mt. Athos where they acquired a good knowledge of Greek.[1] In 1518, **Maxim the Greek** (Michael Trivolis, or Maksim Grek in Russian) (1470–1556), an erudite Greek monk, humanist scholar, and theologian, came to Muscovy (Moscow) from Mt. Athos in order to correct and translate Greek canonical, theological, and liturgical texts at the request of Grand Prince Vasily III (1479–1533). Maxim, who had studied ancient languages and philosophy in Italy, where he had rubbed shoulders with Ianos Laskaris, Aldo Manuzio, Angelo Poliziano, Pico della Mirandola, and other humanists (→ **Italy**), not only brought Byzantine theology to Moscow but also Renaissance ideas.[2]

In 1685–1687 the first institution of higher education, called the Slavo-Greco-Latin Academy, was set up in Moscow: Greek and Latin writing and the *septem artes liberales* were taught there under the guidance of the **Leichoudes brothers**, Ioannikios (1633–1717) and Sophronios (1653–1730), both Greek monks educated at Padua University: they came to Moscow on the recommendation of Dositheos II, the Patriarch of Jerusalem.[3]

At the beginning of the 18th century, after the reforms of Peter the Great (1672–1725), the role of Latin became more important, since the entry of Russia into the family of European countries, which he initiated, required an acquaintance with the basic values of West-European culture, for which Latin was the perfect tool.[4] In the 18th century, the Academy of Sciences and the European-style Gymnasium, where both ancient languages were taught, were established in St Petersburg. Gottlieb Siegfried Bayer (1694–1738), a German classical scholar and Orientalist, was a professor of Greek and Roman antiquities at the Academy from 1726 until 1737. At the same time, Greek language remained obligatory in religious schools, where future Orthodox priests were educated; later, in 1797, the Alexander Nevsky Theological Academy was founded. Empress Catherine II (1729–1796) had an ambitious plan, the so-called Greek Project, to divide the Ottoman Empire

---
1 Gavrilov 2002, 1014–1030; id. 2010, 12–32.
2 Bulanin 1991.
3 Chrissidis 2016; Fonkich 2003.
4 Wes 1992.

between the Russian and Habsburg Empires and to restore the Byzantine Empire with its capital in Constantinople.[5] After the Russian victories in the Turkish wars, the land of New Russia (Novorossia) was founded in the Southern regions around the Black Sea.

Eugenios Boulgaris (1716–1806), a significant figure of the Greek Enlightenment (→ **Greece**), was invited by the Empress to the Russian court after he had translated into Greek (from a French translation) her famous *Nakaz* ('Instruction') of 1767, a document recommending a new code of laws for the Russian Empire.[6] In 1775, Boulgaris became the first Archbishop of the newly created Eparchy of Novorossia. Boulgaris dedicated his translation of Virgil's *Aeneid* into ancient Greek to Catherine II, who in his view was to restore Hellenism at the expense of the Ottoman Empire. During this time, the number of odes in honour of Catherine II and her favorites reached almost epidemic proportions, with ancient Greek odes and their Russian translations being particularly popular.[7] The Greek Project ended with the death of the Austrian Emperor Joseph II in 1790. Nevertheless, along with other factors, it stimulated Russian neo-classicism, and particularly a growing interest in the artistic theories of Johann Joachim Winckelmann (1717–1768); the first translations of Homer and other works of ancient Greek literature, including philosophy, into Russian; and the compilation of art and book collections, etc. In particular, Catherine II ordered the compilation of a catalogue of the Greek manuscripts belonging to the library of the Holy Synod of the Russian Orthodox Church. This catalogue was created by Christian Friedrich Matthaei (1744–1811), a German classicist and palaeographer, who was a professor of ancient languages at Moscow University. In 1805, he edited the full catalogue in Latin, titled *Accurata codicum Graecorum manuscriptorum Bibliothecarum Mosquensium Sanctissimae Synodi notitia et recensio*.

The famous family of Alexander Ypsilanti (1792–1828), a national hero in the Greek war of independence, and Count Ioannis Antonios Kapodistrias (1776–1831), the Foreign Minister of the Russian Empire and later the President of the First Hellenic Republic, promoted Greek education and culture in Russia, especially in Southern Russia, where many native Greeks lived. The first systematic archaeological excavations were started in the former ancient Greek colonies of Chersonesus and Panticapaeum in 1830–1840, and later enriched the Hermitage Museum with a collection of ancient art which, starting in 1852, was maintained

---

5 Gavrilov 2010, 50–64.
6 Batalden 1982; Gavrilov 2010, 65–70.
7 Cf. e.g. Pontani 2017, 334 about an ode to Catherine by Pasquale Baffi (→ **Italy**); Ermolaeva 2019, 375–386.

and studied by Ludolf Stephani (1816–1887), who mainly published on the Bosporus antiquities in the Hermitage.

The Department of Classics at St Petersburg University opened in 1819, when the university was re-founded; **Christian Friedrich Graefe** (1780–1851), a pupil of the famous classicist Gottfried Hermann (1772–1848), became its first professor.[8] In the 19th century, the Russian gymnasium was remodeled on the German classical *Gymnasium* and, as a result, the extensive net of classical education reached almost every large Russian city, since access to universities was open only to the graduates of classical gymnasia.

Classical philology, which flourished in Russia primarily from the time of Peter I and Catherine II onward, was intensively developed in 19th century, thanks to the efforts of such scholars as August Nauck, Lucian Müller, Karl Lugebil, Pjotr Nikitin, **Fyodor Korsch** (1843–1915), Fyodor Sokolov, and many others, and reached its full efflorescence at the beginning of the 20th century.[9] Byzantine studies successfully progressed under Vasily Vasilevsky (1838–1899); epigraphical studies of the Black Sea region developed under Vasily Latyshev (1855–1921); and Viktor Jernstedt (1854–1902), Nauck's pupil, became the first Russian papyrologist. Tadeusz Zieliński (1859–1944), a classical philologist and a professor at St Petersburg University (1890–1922), translated and published the complete tragedies of Sophocles as a *pendant* to the Euripides translation by Innokenty Annensky (1855–1909), a classicist and a poet; subsequently, **Vyacheslav Ivanov** (1866–1949), a symbolist poet, translated almost all of the tragedies of Aeschylus.

After 1917, however, classical education and scholarship came to a halt for many years. During the Soviet era, classical scholarship had to reckon with the closing of university chairs and gymnasia, the repression of scholars and students, and an official ideology bred on aggressive ignorance: it was nonetheless preserved, hanging by a thread, by those firm of mind and spirit, such as Sergey Zhebelev, Georgy Zereteli, Nikolay Novosadsky, Salomo Luria, **Jakob Borovsky**, Sergei Sobolevsky, Andrey Jegunov, Aristid Dovatur, and, subsequently Alexander Zaitsev. In 1932, the Department of Classical Philology was revived in Leningrad, and in 1934 in Moscow.

The rebirth of classical education in Russia began only with the *perestroika* in the late 1980s. In 1989, the *Gymnasium Classicum Petropolitanum* was founded by classicists who enthusiastically longed to revive the humanistic tradition of teaching Latin and ancient Greek together with mathematics.[10] Orthodox schools

---

8 Verlinsky 2013, 162–204.
9 Smyshlyayeva 2015; Gavrilov/Shaburina 2021 (forthcoming).
10 Zelchenko 2013, 289–296.

appeared with the support of the Russian Orthodox Church and the Patriarchate: pupils could study the language of the New Testament and the Church Fathers, orthodox liturgy and Byzantine Greek. Active contacts were reforged between Russian classical departments and scholars and their colleagues from Europe and America. In 1994, the *Bibliotheca Classica Petropolitana* was established, an independent research centre and reference library, along with *Hyperboreus*, a journal for classical philology.

The tradition of versification in ancient Greek started with Maxim the Greek in the 16th century, when Humanist Greek began to replace the vernacular Greek of Byzantine scholars. In the 18th century, erudite Greeks in the entourage of Catherine II, such as Boulgaris, Palladoklis, and Baldani, composed secular poetry in and made translations into ancient Greek. At the beginning of the 19th century, academics like Graefe brought in their erudite Greek versification, influenced by the trends current in European classical philology during its Golden Age; their versification and translations reflect a peculiar development of Russian classical scholarship.

From the 18th century on, the majority of poems were occasional ones, such as laudatory odes, jubilee poems, *carmina gratulatoria*, dedications to emperors and members of the imperial family, to patrons, friends, colleagues, and graduate students, book epigrams, along with erudite exercises, macaronic epistles, and translations from modern or classical poets. The prevailing metres were hexameters, elegiac couplets, iambic lines of different length as well as Sapphic and Alcaic stanzas; trochaic lines, anapaests, phalaecians, and anacreontic metres also occur.

General Bibliography

Batalden, Stephen K. (1982), *Catherine II's Greek Prelate Eugenios Voulgaris in Russia, 1771–1806*, New York.

Budaragina, Olga/Keyer, Denis/Verlinsky, Alexander (eds.) (2010), Alexander Gavrilov, *O filologakh i filologii* [On Philologists and Philology], St Petersburg.

Bulanin, Dmitry (1991), *Antichnyye traditsii v russkoj literature XI–XVI vv.* [Antiquity in Russian Literature of the 11th and 16th centuries], München.

Chrissidis, Nikolaos (2016), *An Academy at the Court of the Tsars: Greek Scholars and Jesuit Education in Early Modern Russia*, DeKalb, IL.

Ermolaeva, Elena (2019), "Neo-Hellenic poetry in Russia: Antonios Palladoklis (1747–1801) and Georgios Baldani (about 1760–1789)", in: *Hyperboreus* 25/2, 375–386.

Fonkich, Boris (2003), *Grecheskie rukopisi i dokumenty v Rossii v XIV – nachale XVIII v.* [Greek Manuscripts and Documents in Russia through the 14th – Beginning of the 18th Centuries], Moscow.

Gavrilov, Alexander (1995), "Russian Classical Scholarship in the 20th Century", in: Gregory Nagy/Victor Bers (eds.), *The Classics in East Europe: Essays on the Survival of a Humanistic Tradition*, Worcester, MA, 61–81.

Gavrilov, Alexander (2002), "Russland", in: Hubert Cancik/Helmut Schneider (eds.), *Der Neue Pauly*, Stuttgart and Weimar, 1014–1030 (English translation in: Hubert Cancik/Helmut Schneider/Manfred Landfester (eds.), *Brill's* New *Pauly: Encyclopedia of the Ancient World. Classical Tradition*, vol. 5, Leiden 2010, 1–18, s.v. "Russia").

Gavrilov, Aleksandr (2010), "Antichnoe nasledie v Rossii (IX–XX vv.)" [Ancient Heritage in Russia (Ninth–Twentieth Centuries)], in: Budaragina/Keyer/Verlinsky 2010, 12–32.

Gavrilov, Aleksandr/Shaburina, Tatiana (eds.) (2021), *Slovar, Peterburgskogo Antikovedenija 19 – nachala 20 vv.* [A Dictionary of Classical Studies in St Petersburg of the 19th and Early 20th Centuries], St Petersburg (in print).

Pontani, Filippomaria (2017), "*Graeca per Italiae fines*. Greek poetry in Italy from Poliziano to the present", in: Stefan Weise (ed.), *HELLENISTI! – Altgriechisch als Literatursprache im neuzeitlichen Europa*, Stuttgart, 311–347.

Smyshlyayeva, Vera (2015), *Rossiiskie filologi–klassiki XIX veka."Germanovskoe napravlenie"* [Russian Classical Philologists of 19th c. influenced by G. Hermann], St Petersburg.

Verlinsky, Alexander (2013), "Philologia inter Disciplinas: The Department of Classics at St Petersburg University 1819–1884", in: *Hyperboreus* 19/1–2, 162–204.

Wes, Marinus A. (1992), *Classics in Russia 1700–1855: Between Two Bronze Horsemen*, Leiden/New York/Köln.

Zelchenko, Vsevolod (2013), "Gymnasium Classicum Petropolitanum", in: *Hyperboreus* 19/1–2, 289–296.

Maxim the Greek (1470–1556)

<In fraudem Hellenicam> [c. 1552]

(excerptum, vv. 357–380)

      τοῦτο τέλος ἀτρεκῶς σοφίης ἱερᾶς τῷ ἐραστῇ
        αὐτῷ ἑνωθῆναι τῶν ἐφετῶν τῷ ἄκρῳ·
      οὐχὶ γραωδῶν καὶ σαπρῶν διὰ γνώσιος ὕθλων
360 καὶ Ἀκαδημαϊκῆς στωμύλου εὐφραδίης,
      ἀλλ' ἀκριβεῖ φυλακῇ τῶν τοῦ ὑψίστου ἐφετμῶν
      ψυχῆς τ' ἀκακίῃ καὶ χθαμαλοφροσύνῃ,
      σωφροσύνῃ θ' ἱερᾷ καὶ μακροθύμῳ πραότητι
      καὶ ἀδόλῳ πάντας πρὸς μέροπας ἀγάπῃ.
365 οἷς ὁ κατ' εἰκόνα χειρὶ θεοῦ πλασθεὶς ἐπάνεισι
      δόξαν ἐπὶ πρώτην αἶψα πάλιν σφετέρην·
      οἷσπερ ἀμοιβὴ οὗτοι ὁ ἐκ μερόπων βραχυτερπής,
      ἀλλ' ὁ ὑφ' ὑψίστου μὴ πέρας αἶνος ἔχων
      καὶ τέλος, αὐτοῦ τοῦ θείου κάλλους κατατρυφᾶν
370 αὐτοῖς ἐν δαπέδοις τοῖς ὑπερουρανίοις·
      μὴ τῷ τῆς κενῆς καλλιφραδίης Κεκροπΐδος
      κηληθμῷ λοιπὸν θελγόμενοι κενεῶς
      τῇ τῆς δυσσεβίης ἀπολειφθῶμεν ἐν ὀμίχλῃ,
      τὴν δ' ἐν τῇδ' ἄθεον κευθομένην ἀπάτην
375 ἐκ ψυχῆς μισήσαντες, ἐπιμαστεύσωμεν
      τὴν εὐαγγελικὴν ἀπλανέ' ἀτρεκίην.
      ἧς δι' ἐπιγνόντες ἕν' ἄναρχον ἀεί τε ἐόντα
      πανάγαθον κύριον παμμεδέοντα θεόν,
      πρηνεῖς δεῦτε πεσόντες ἐνώπιον αὐτοῦ ἐς αἶαν,
380 κράξωμεν· "δούλων φεῖσαι, ἄναξ, σφετέρων."

Textus: Wien, Österreichische Nationalbibliothek, ms. Phil. gr. 202, 8r–15v; Ševčenko 1997b, 181–276.

Crit.: 358 αὐτῶ ms., correxit Ševčenko | ἑνωθῆναι ms., correxit Ševčenko | τὸ ms., correxit Ševčenko || **359** διαγνώσιως ms., correxit Ševčenko || **360** ἀφρασίης vel ἀφραδίης ms., correxit Ševčenko, cf. slav. высокоумиемъ || **361** ὑψιστου ms., correxit Ševčenko || **362** χθαμολοφροσύνη ms., correxit Ševčenko || **366** ἐπιπρώτην ms., correxit Ševčenko | σφετέρων ms.: σφετέραν Ševčenko, fortasse σφετέρην || **367** οἷς σφετέρων περ (σφετέρ del.) ms., correxit Ševčenko || **371** τῆς κενῆς ms.: fortasse τῆσδε κενῆς vel τῆς κενεῆς | Κεκροπΐδος ms.: Κεκροπίδος Ševčenko || **372** κηληθμῶ ms., correxit Ševčenko || **373** ὀμίχλη ms., correxit Ševčenko || **377** ἕνν ἄρχον ms., correxit Ševčenko || **378** παναγαθον sine accentu ms., correxit Ševčenko

Sim.: 357 τέλος...σοφίης] cf. *Anth. Pal.* 7.93.1 | σοφίης ἱερᾶς...ἐραστῇ] cf. M. Psell. *poem.* 23.61 West. || **358** τῶν ἐφετῶν τῷ ἄκρῳ] cf. Greg. Naz. *in laud. Heronis*, PG 35.1200.5 || **359**

γραωδῶν καὶ σαπρῶν] cf. Ar. *Pax* 698 (γέρων ὢν καὶ σαπρός) | ὕθλων] cf. Pl. *Tht.* 176b (ὕθλος γραῶν): ad mythum alludit, cf. Lampe s.v. γραωδῶς ‖ **362** χθαμαλοφροσύνῃ] cf. Greg. Naz. *carm.*, PG 37.784.10 ‖ **363** cf. NT *epist. Coloss.* 3.12 ‖ **364, 367** μέροπας, μερόπων] vox epica ‖ **365** κατ' εἰκόνα...πλασθείς] cf. LXX, *Gen* 1.26; *Ps* 118.73; e.g. Basil. *orat.*, PG 31.1681.41 ‖ **367** βραχυτερπής] cf. Nicetae Byzantini *refut. Mohamedis* 804c ‖ **375** ἐπιμαστεύσωμεν] cf. Ap. Soph. 73.30, Etym. Magn. 361.52 ‖ **380** δούλων φεῖσαι] cf. LXX, *Ps* 18.14.

⟨Against Hellenic deceit⟩

(excerpt, ll. 357–380)

> The very goal for the admirer of holy wisdom is precisely to be united with the acme of desirable things, not through the knowledge of small, rotten old wives' talk, [360] nor of verbose academic high-mindedness, but through meticulous respect of the Highest One's orders and by keeping an innocent soul, a humble frame of mind, holy prudence, generous gentleness, and true love towards all human beings. [365] With these virtues, he who was created by the hand of God after His image will quickly come back to his previous glory. For these virtues, the reward is not human praise, which brings a brief pleasure, but the praise of the Highest One, which has no limit; the ultimate goal is to enjoy Divine beauty [370] in the spaces beyond Heaven. Let us therefore not get lost in the mist of impiety, attracted by the charms of the idle beauty of Cecropian [*sc*. Attic] eloquence, but, hating with all our heart [375] the godless error abiding in it, let us search for the unerring Evangelical truth, with the help of which we shall recognise the one Lord God, who is without beginning, eternal, absolutely good, sovereign and all-ruling, and let us fall prone before Him and cry: 'Have mercy on your slaves, O Lord.'

Metre: Elegiac couplets. Note the Homeric lengthenings with final -ς (ll. 357, 375, 377) and -ν (l. 373). Peculiar scansions are μακροθύμῳ (l. 363) with short -υ- and κενῆς (l. 371), whose first syllable is taken as long. Note also πανάγαθον (l. 378) with long first alpha.

Notes: The Viennese manuscript with two longer poems in ancient Greek elegiac couplets by Maxim the Greek was published with many mistakes by P. Bushkovich (Bushkovich 1984) and then revised, translated, and compared with the Church Slavonic prose version by I. Ševčenko (Ševčenko 1997b). The poems are Ἔπη ἡρωελεγιακὰ προτρεπτικὰ εἰς μετάνοιαν ('Verses in elegiac couplets exhorting to repentance', 122 lines) and an invective against Hellenic deceit, 380 lines (without a Greek title). They appear to be poetical versions of two Church Slavonic prose theological treatises: *O pokajanii* ('*On repentance*') and *Slovo oblichitelno na ellinskuju prelest'* ('*Invective against Hellenic deceit*'). The approximate date of the manuscript, which belonged to the collection of the Hungarian humanist and collector of manuscripts Iohannes Sambucus (1531–1584; → **Hungary**), is 1552–1579. The colophon is dated to the year 7060 (1551/1552), and is particularly interesting:

> Μακροβίῳ τῷ πολυθρυλλήτῳ ἐραστῇ πάσης σοφίης ἱερᾶς ὁ Μίνιμος μᾶλλον ἢ Μάξιμος, ὁ ποτ' ἑλλάδιος νῦν καὶ ὑπερβόρειος χαίρειν ἐν κυρίῳ. Τὸ βραχὺ φιλοπόνημα τοῦτο δεξάμενος ἐπιδιώρθωσον [sic] αὐτὸ ἐν οἷσπερ δόξει ἐσφάλθαι, καὶ ἐπιδιωρθωθέν σοι μὴ βυθοῖς λήθης ἀξιῶ σε παραδοθήτω, ἀλλὰ καὶ ἄλλοις φιλαρέτοις ἐπιγνωσθήτω· καὶ εἰ μὴ πάντας ἀλλ' ἴσως τινὰς ἐκσπάσει τῆς ὑπερβαλούσης ἐρωμανίης αὐτῶν, ἧς νοσοῦσιν ἀκρατῶς, περὶ τὰ ἑλληνικὰ στωμύλματα· ἔρρωσο, ἀγαπητὲ ἑταῖρε καὶ ἀδελφὲ ἐν κυρίῳ· ζξ'· ἐκ πόλεος Μοσχοβίου τῆς βασιλευούσης πάσης τῆς ἀνωτάτου Ῥωσίας.[11]

Maxim's addressee is an unknown person with the Greek name or pseudonym Makrobios, 'possibly a punning nickname understandable only to those who were initiates' (Ševčenko 1997b, 231). ὁ Μίνιμος μᾶλλον ἢ Μάξιμος is a conventional disparaging self-presentation. This seems to confirm that, while in Russia, Maxim might have maintained his contacts with Italian and/or Greek correspondents, and that, in all probability, he wrote elegiac couplets in ancient Greek for his erudite European readers, while Church Slavonic prose was reserved for his Russian audience. The paradox is striking that Maxim wrote formally good ancient Greek poetry in order to avert his readers from displaying any interest in Greek poetry by the Ancients, especially considering that his poetical skill and rhetorical *eloquentia* could be appreciated only by highly literate readers.

Biography: Maxim the Greek (Michael Trivolis), a Greek monk, humanist scholar, and theological writer, was born in 1470 in Arta, Greece. Around 1480, he went to Corfu, where he studied philosophy and rhetoric; then, together with Ianos Laskaris, who was a friend of Michael's uncle, Demetrius, he went to Florence as a pupil at the *Studio*, where Laskaris taught. Laskaris introduced him to Marsilio Ficino, Giovanni Pico della Mirandola, and Angelo Poliziano (→ **Italy**).

---

11 Translation: 'To Macrobius, the well-known admirer of every holy wisdom, the *minimus*, rather than *Maximus*, who was formerly a Greek, and now, in addition, is an Hyperborean, <sends> greetings in the Lord. Having received this brief work, correct it in what seems to be wrong, and, thus corrected, do not, please, abandon it to the depths of forgetfulness, but let it be known also to other lovers of virtue: it will draw out of the exceeding frenzy for the fineries of Hellenic style, if not all, at least some of those who suffer terribly from that disease. Farewell, beloved friend and brother in the Lord. Year 7060 [= 1552], from the city of Moscow which rules over all the northernmost Russia.' The reading ἀνωτάτου is proposed by Ševčenko 1997b (αἰωτάτου 'eternal' Bushkovitch 1993; or ἁγιωτάτου 'most holy'?). On ἐρωμανίης see *AP* 5. 220, 2; 255, 12; 293, 2; Ianos Laskaris *Epigr.* 15, 12 Meschini.

In Florence, Michael became a follower of Girolamo Savonarola and entered the monastery of San Marco as a Dominican friar. Later, he moved to Venice, where he took part in the Aldine circle, together with Markos Mousouros and other scholars. In 1504, he returned to Greece and to Orthodoxy and became a monk of the Vatopedi Monastery on Mt. Athos, where his teacher was the famous Manuel, the Great Rhetor. At Vatopedi he took a new name, Maximos. In 1516–1518 he acted as a missionary from the Vatopedi Monastery to Moscow at the request of Grand Prince Vasily III in order to correct the religious texts that were used in Russia at that time. First, he dictated a Latin translation of the Psalter with commentaries to Moscow scribes, who in turn translated it into Church Slavonic. He then entered the religious disputes between the so-called Non-possessors and Possessors and took part in the editing of the corrected critical Slavonic version of the Byzantine ecclesiastical laws supporting the ideas of the Non-possessors. As a result, in 1525 and 1531, he was punished as a heretic and exiled to the Iosifo-Volokolamsk Monastery and then to the Tver' Otroč Monastery. In about 1548, Tsar Ivan the Terrible released Maxim showing for him proper public respect. Maxim spent his last years in the Trinity Sergijev Monastery near Moscow, where he was buried. Afterwards, he was recognised as a saint by the Eastern Orthodox Church. His oeuvre consists of theological treatises and essays of exegetical, ethical, dogmatic, and polemical character, as well as epistles, *consolationes*, and translations into Church Slavonic from the Church Fathers, the *Acts*, *Epistles*, commentaries, and other works. In Moscow, he composed several ancient Greek poems and probably translated them into Church Slavonic prose.

Bibliography: Denissoff, Élie (1943), *Maxime le Grec et l'Occident*, Paris; Haney, Jack V. (1973), *From Italy to Muskovy: The Life and Works of Maxim the Greek*, München; Sinicyna, Nina (1977), *Maksim Grek v Rossii* [Maxim Grek in Russia], Moscow; Bulanin, Dmitry (1984), *Perevody i poslanija Maksima Greka* [Translations and Epistles by Maxim the Greek], Leningrad; Bushkovitch, Paul (1984), "Two Unknown Greek Texts of Maxim the Greek", in: *Jahrbücher für Geschichte Osteuropas* 32/4, 559–561; Bushkovitch, Paul (1993), "Maksim Grek—poet-giperboreyets [Maxim Grek as a 'Hyperborean' poet]", in: *Trudy Otdela Drevherusskoj Literatury* 47, 215–228; Ševčenko, Ihor (1997a), "On the Greek Poetic Output of Maksim Grek", in: *Byzantinoslavica* 58/1, 1–70; Ševčenko, Ihor (1997b), "On the Greek Poetic Output of Maksim Grek", in: *Palaeoslavica* 5, 181–276; Ševčenko, Ihor (1998), "Gleaning 1: On the Term ‚αἰωτάτου 'Ρωσίας' in Maksim Grek Once More and on Prince Vasiliy III's Purported «Admonitiones» to the Future Ivan IV", in: *Palaeoslavica* 6, 291–294; Speranzi, David (2010), "Michele Trivoli e Giano Lascari. Appunti su copisti e manoscritti greci tra Corfù e Firenze", in: *Studi Slavistici* 7, 263–297; Bulanin, Dmitry (2017), "Maksim Grek: grechesky pisatel' ili moskovsky knizhnik?" [Maxim the Greek: Was he a Greek Litterateur or an Expert in Muscovite Writings?], in: *Studia Slavica et Balcanica Petropolitana* 2, 85–98.

Eugenios Boulgaris (1716–1806)

I. Εἰς τὸν Ἑλληνιστὶ μεταφρασθέντα ΟΥΙΡΓΙΛΙΟΝ ἐπίγραμμα [1791]

Ἄσθμα Ὁμηρικὸν ἐν χείλεσσι Μάρωνος ἄυσε,
 Παλλάδος ἐντολίῃ, γῆρυν ἑλὸν προτέρην.
Οὐχ ὧδε φθονέει κοτέει τε Ἀοιδὸς Ἀοιδῷ,
 Οὕνεκα Μοῦσα μία πνεῦσεν ἐν ἀμφοτέροις.

Textus: Boulgaris, Eugenios (1791), *Aeneidis P. Virgilii Maronis libri XII Graeco carmine heroico expressi notisque perpetuis illustrati*, I, Petropoli, in Academia Scientiarum, p. ****v.

Crit.: 2 ἐντολίῃ] metri gratia fortasse pro ἐντολῇ ‖ 4 Οὕνεκα correxi: Οὔνεκα ed.

Sim.: 1 ἄυσε [ῡ] saepe in Homero, cf. *Il.* 3.81; 8.160 etc. ‖ 3 cf. Hes. *Op.* 25–26

Epigram on the translation of Virgil into ancient Greek

The breath of Homer cried out through the lips of Maro,
 by order of Pallas, taking an ancient voice.
In this way, neither Poet is envious of or angry with the other,
 since one and the same Muse breathed through both.

Metre: Elegiac couplets; note the hiatus in l. 1 (Ἄσθμα Ὁμηρικόν).

Notes: This epigram concludes a long prefatory letter in Greek to Empress Catherine, to whom the Greek translation of the *Aeneid* is dedicated ('by order of Pallas' means here 'by order of Catherine'). It makes clear Boulgaris' ambition to make Virgil speak with Homer's voice and style.

II. ‹*Vergilii Aeneis Graece*› [1791]

(excerptum, *Aen.* 1.1–7)

Τεύχε' ἀείδω Ἄνδρα τε, ὃς πρῶτος δὴ Τροίης
Ἔξορος Ἰταλίηνδ' ὑπὸ Μοιρῶν ἦλθεν ἰδ' ἀκτάς
Λαβινίους, ἀνὰ γῆν τ' ἀνὰ πόντον πόλλ' ἐπαληθείς,
Δαιμονίῃ τε βίῃ διά θ' Ἥρης μνήμονα μῆνιν
5 Νηλεέος· πολέμῳ πολλὰ τλὰς κτίζεν ὅτ' ἄστυ,

Ἐν δ' εἰσῆγε θεοὺς Λατίῳ, γένος ἔνθα Λατίνων
Ἀλβάνιοί τε πάτρες καί γ' αἰπῆς Τείχεα Ῥώμης.¹²

Textus: Boulgaris 1791 (vide supra), 3–5.

Sim.: 1 ἀείδω Ἄνδρα τε, ὅς...] cf. *Il.* 1.1 et *Od.* 1.1 || 3 πόλλ' ἐπαληθείς] cf. *Od.* 4.81

‹Virgil's *Aeneid* in Greek›

(excerpt, *Aen.* 1.1–7)

The arms, I sing, and the man who, exiled by the Moirai, first came from Troy to Italy and to the Lavinian shores, having wandered much over land and sea because of heaven-sent violence which was due to pitiless Hera's [5] unforgetting wrath; he had suffered much in war when he built a city and brought his gods to Latium, whence came the Latin race, the lords of Alba, and the high walls of Rome.

Metre: Hexameters. The first line is a *spondiacus*, and there are many hiatuses. A peculiar form is πάτρες (l. 7).

Notes: The translation seems to be mostly *ad verbum*; l. 3. ἀνὰ γῆν τ' ἀνὰ πόντον is a calque of *terra marique*.

III. Ὑψηλότατε καὶ λαμπρότατε ΠΡΙΓΚΙΨ φιλελληνέστατε! [1786]

(excerptum, vv. 59–64)

```
     Ἡμὲν οἳ ἀκτῇσιν Μαιώτιδος οἰκία πῆξαν,
60   Ἠδέ θ' οἳ ἔνθα ῥέει χεῦμα Βορυσθένιον,
     Ἔνθα καὶ ἄλλοτ' ἔην ποτ' ἀποίκισις ἐκ ῥὰ Μιλήτου
     Καὶ πόλις εὐδαίμων, Ὄλβιος ἦ ὄνομα,
     Ἐνθαδὶ Ἑλλάδα τὴν πάρος αὖθις δοῦναι ἰδέσθαι,
     Φαίδιμε ΠΟΤΤΕΜΚΙΝ, Σός κεν ἄεθλος ἔοι!
```

---

12 Latin original: *Arma virumque cano, Troiae qui primus ab oris / Italiam, fato profugus, Laviniaque venit / litora, multum ille et terris iactatus et alto / vi superum saevae memorem Iunonis ob iram; / multa quoque et bello passus, dum conderet urbem / inferretque Deos Latio: genus unde Latinum / Albanique patres atque altae moenia Romae.*

Textus: Boulgaris, Eugenios (1786), *Opera Georgica et Aeneis Graeco carmine heroico expressa notisque perpetuis illustrata*, I, Petropoli, in Academia Scientiarum, 2–4 (3).

Sim.: 60 χεῦμα] cf. Pind. *Nem.* 9.39 (χεῦμα Σκαμάνδρου) || **64** φαίδιμε] cf. Hom. *Il.* 4.505 (de Hectore); *Od.* 2.386, etc.

To the most great and excellent philhellene Prince

(excerpt, ll. 59–64)

> Those who built houses on the shore of lake Maeotis [*scil.* Sea of Azov],
> [60] and those who did so where the stream Borysthenes [*scil.* Dnepr] flows,
> where formerly there was the colony from Miletos
>   and the prosperous city by the name of Olbia,
> here may your labour be – o famous Potemkin –
>   to let us see again the Greece of old.
>
> [transl. Batalden 1982, 72, adapted]

Metre: Elegiac couplets.

Notes: The ode consists of 66 lines and is dedicated to Prince Grigory Potemkin, the Governor General of Novorossia, a key figure behind Empress Catherine II's strategy in the Black Sea and in the eastern region. As Archbishop of Slaviansk and Kherson, Boulgaris was in close cooperation with Grigory, and, in 1786, when publishing his translation of Virgil's *Georgics* in ancient Greek, he equipped it with a dedicatory ode, in which he pinned his hopes on Potemkin as the new force of a revived Hellenism. Olbia was an ancient Greek city founded by colonists from Miletus in the 7th c. BC. In addition to the list of toponyms in this ode, Boulgaris and Potemkin created Greek names for many cities including Sevastopol', Melitopol', Mariupol', Theodosia, Eupatoria, and Odessa.

Biography: Eugenios Boulgaris was born on the island of Corfu. He was an important scholar of the Greek Enlightenment and a prominent Orthodox educator. In 1753–1759, he was rector of the Athonite Academy, where he taught philosophy and mathematics. Subsequently, he became the head of the Patriarchal Academy in Constantinople. In 1771, he arrived in St Petersburg, at the invitation of Empress Catherine II. Before Catherine, he presented himself as 'Slavo-Bulgarian by origin, Greek by birth, Russian by inclination...'. In 1775, he became the first Archbishop of the newly created Eparchy (Diocese) of Slaviansk and Kherson. Catherine II invited Orthodox Greeks to settle along with Russians in the Novorossia and Azov areas to the north of the Black Sea, the region recently conquered by Russia from the Ottoman Crimean Khanate. In 1776, Boulgaris was made an honorary member of the Imperial Academy of Sciences in St Petersburg. Boulgaris's massive four-volume translation of Virgil's *Georgics* and *Aeneid* into ancient Greek, which incorporated his copious commentary and notes, written in ancient Greek in the style of Eustathius of Thessalonica, was published between 1786 and 1792 by the Academy of Sciences in St Petersburg, together with his dedications to Catherine II and Prince Grigory Potemkin. With his translations of Vergil, he intended to enlighten those Greeks who lived in Novorossia and Azov. Boulgaris died on 27 May 1806 in St Petersburg and was buried in the Saint Alexander-Nevsky Monastery.

Bibliography: Batalden, Stephen K. (1982), *Catherine II's Greek Prelate Eugenios Voulgaris in Russia, 1771–1806*, New York; Gavrilov, Aleksandr (2010), "Arhiepiskop Evgeniy Bulgaris" [Archbishop Eugeny Bulgaris], in: Budaragina/Keyer/Verlinsky 2010, 65–70.

Antonios Palladoklis (1747–1801)

I. Στίχοι εἰς τὴν στολὴν τὴν Ἑλληνικὴν ἣν οὐκ ἀπηνήνατο ἀμφιέσασθαι ἡ Μεγίστη Αὐτοκράτωρ [1771]

(excerptum, vv. 25–34)

25 Μέγας δ' Ἀλέξανρός τε Περσέων θρόνῳ
   Πάλαι καθεσθείς, ΤΗΝ δ' ἰδών, τὰ φωνέει·
   ΑΙΚΑΤΕΡΙΝΑΝ ΤΗΝ ΜΕΓΑΛΗΝ νῦν βλέπω
   Φοροῦσαν εἷμα καὶ στολὴν Μητρὸς μέθεν...
   Ὦ 'ναξ Πόλου, δός, κἀξίωσον δαρκέειν
30 ΑΙΚΑΤΕΡΙΝΑΝ κἄν Ἀλεξάνδρου στέφει,
   Ὥσπερ φιλοῦσαν ἔκ τε κήρος ἡμέας,
   Οὕτω τροποῦσαν Μουσταφᾶν ἀλαζόνα,
   Ὡς 'γὼ τρόπαιον κὰδ Δαρείου στησάμην,
   Ἐμοί τε αἰχμῇ καὶ ψυχῆς κάλλει ἸΣΗΝ.

Textus: Palladoklis, Antonios (1771), *Στίχοι εἰς τὴν στολὴν τὴν Ἑλληνικὴν ἣν οὐκ ἀπηνήνατο ἀμφιέσασθαι ἡ Μεγίστη Αὐτοκράτωρ*, St Petersburg, 3.

Crit.: 29 κἀξίωσον debuit, sed more temporis crasis cum iota subscripto | δαρκέειν] metri gratia pro δρακεῖν

Verses on the Hellenic garment in which the Great Empress did not disdain to dress Herself

(excerpt, ll. 25–34)

> [25] When Alexander the Great was once sitting on the throne of the Persians,
> seeing HER, he said:
> 'Now, I look at EKATERINE the GREAT
> in the garment and dress of my Mother...
> O Lord of heaven, give me the honour to look
> [30] at EKATERINE also in the wreath of Alexander.
> Exactly as she loves us from her heart
> and therefore puts to flight boastful Mustapha,
> likewise I have erected the trophy of Darius' defeat
> because she is my equal in the spear and the beauty of her soul.'

Metre: Iambic trimeters.

Notes: This poem, consisting of 34 lines with its Russian translation *en regard* (Стихи на платье греческое, в кое Ея Величество соизволило одеваться в маскараде) was dedicated to Empress Catherine II on the occasion when, during a bal masqué, she put on a Greek dress, that she pretended was the garment of Olympias, the mother of Alexander the Great. In keeping with a long-standing Byzantine equivalence, the Turks are called 'Persians' and are *de facto* equated with them; accordingly, Catherine II is shown as a spirit descending from Alexander the Great himself.

II. Ὠιδὴ τῷ Ἐκλαμπροτάτῳ Κόμητι Ἀλεξίῳ Γρηγοριάδῃ τῷ Ὀρλώβ [1771]

(excerptum, vv. 15–30)

> 15 Μῆτερ ποθητή, λῆγε δάκρυ' ἐκχέειν,
> Κ' ἐφ' ἁρπαγείσῃ 'λευθερίῃ ἀλγέειν·
> Ἰδοὺ ἀπ' Ἄρκτου Ἀγαμέμνων ἵπταται
> Δυσμάς τε ἐλθὼν ἁρπαγῇ τιμωρέει,
> Ὧι δὴ ἕπονται ἄλκιμοι Μυρμιδόνες,
> 20 Αἴας τ' Ἀχιλλεύς, τοῖς Ἀγαρηνοῖς στόνοι·
> Ἰδού γε Ἥρως ἵπτατ' ΟΡΛΩΒ Ῥωσίης,
> ΟΡΛΩΒ ποθητὸς καὶ λίην ἡμῖν φίλος,
> Ὧιπερ Ποσειδῶν δάφνινον πλέκει στέφος·
> Πτηνῶν δ' ἐφ' ἅλμης μηχανῶν τοῦ Δαιδάλου

25 Ἡφαιστοτεύκτων πτὰς ὅδε φλογοπνόων,
Τῇ μὲν Κεραυνὸν, τῇ δὲ δὴ Ἴριν φέρει
ΑΙΚΑΤΕΡΙΝΗΣ, προῖκ', ἈΝΑΣΣΗΣ, ΔΕΥΤΕΡΑΣ,
Ὅπως πατάξῃ τὸν στερήσανθ' ἡμέας
Ἐλευθερίης, οἶκτον ἐμφάνῃ ἔτι
30 Σοὶ τῇ παθούσῃ δεινὰ μακρῷ ἐν χρόνῳ.

Textus: Palladoklis, Antonios (1771), *Ὠιδὴ τῷ Ἐκλαμπροτάτῳ Κόμητι Ἀλεξίῳ Γρηγοριάδῃ τῷ Ὀρλώβ*, St Petersburg, 4.

Crit.: 18 ἁρπαγῇ correxi: ἅρπαγ' ἥ ed. || 24 ἅλμης correxi: ἄ- ed. || 25 Ἡφαιστοτεύκτων correxi: Ἡφεστοτεύκτων ed.

Sim.: 25 Ἡφαιστοτεύκτων] cf. Soph. *Phil.* 987 | φλογοπνόων] hapax leg. ut vid.

Ode to His Excellency, Count Alexei Grigoryevich Orlov

(excerpt, ll. 15–30)

> [15] Dear Mother, stop shedding tears
> and suffering because Thy freedom was stolen.
> Here, Agamemnon flies from the North
> and, having come to the West, seeks revenge for this loss:
> Brave Myrmidons accompany him,
> [20] together with Ajax and Achilles, sources of woe for the Agarenes.
> Here flies Orlov, the hero of Russia,
> Orlov who is desired and exceedingly beloved by us,
> for whom Poseidon weaves a laurel wreath.
> Flying above the sea on Daedalus' winged machines
> [25] made by Hephaestus and breathing flames,
> he brings the thunderbolt in one hand and Iris in another,
> the gift of EMPRESS EKATERINE THE SECOND,
> So as to strike down the one who deprived us of freedom,
> to show compassion for You,
> [30] who have suffered awful pains for a long time.

Metre: Iambic trimeters (iambic trimeter, with masculine and feminine rhyme *aabb*, in the Russian translation, also). Note the peculiar lengthening of the first alpha in l. 17 Ἀγαμέμνων.

Notes: This poem of 350 verses in ancient Greek was dedicated – together with its poetic translation into Russian (Ода Его Сиятельству графу Алексею Григорьевичу Орлову) and notes in ancient Greek and Russian – to the victorious Count Alexei Orlov (1737–1807) upon the defeat of the Turks at Chesme in

1770. Palladoklis addresses Greece as Μῆτερ ποθητή (l. 15) and describes to her in vivid language how the Russian fleet destroyed the Ottoman navy. Orlov is compared to Agamemnon, who came from the North to seek revenge from the Agarenes (Muslims) for having deprived the Greeks of their freedom; the Turkish fleet is called the Hundred Headed Hydra; Typhon eventually burns Troy. The edition was decorated with miniatures, in particular with the image of Pallas Athena on p. 20.

III. Ὠιδὴ τῷ Ἐκλαμπροτάτῳ Κόμητι Γρηγορίῳ Γρηγοριάδῃ τῷ ὈΡΛΩΒ [1771]

(excerptum, vv. 109–120)

  Ῥωσσίη γὰρ κλῦσεν ἐμῶν ὀδυρμῶν,
110 Ὀρφανοῖσ' ἀσπὶς τελέθουσα αἰέν,
  Οἳ δι' ἅλμης ἠδ' ὀρέων πύλας νῦν
    Ἧκον ἄρ οἴκτων.

  Χεῖρ' ὀρεγνὺς εὐμενέως ἔμοιγε,
  Ὥπ' ἐς οἰκτρόν μευ ἐπιδὼν φιλόφρων
115 Νῦν ὁ Κλεινὸς καὶ Μεγάδοξος ὈΡΛΩΒ
    Συμπαθέων μοι.

  Οὓς κλίνει δ' οὗτος στοναχῇσ' ἐμοῖο,
  Τοῦ φρενῶν ὀφθαλμὸς ἄρ' ἔστ' ἀϋπνῶν,
  Ὄφρ' ἀταρτηρὰν μέο μοῖραν ἄρδην
120   Ἐξολοθρεύσῃ.

Textus: Palladoklis, Antonios (1771), *Ὠιδὴ τῷ Ἐκλαμπροτάτῳ Κόμητι Γρηγορίῳ Γρηγοριάδῃ τῷ Ὀρλώβ*, St Petersburg, [6].

Crit.: 112 Ἧκον correxi: Ἡ- ed.

Sim.: 113 Χεῖρ' ὀρεγνύς] cf. Hom. *Il.* 1.351; 22.37 (χεῖρας ὀρεγνύς) ‖ 115 μεγάδοξος] hapax leg. ut vid.

Ode to His Excellency Count Grigory Grigoryevich Orlov

(excerpt, ll. 109–120)

> Russia, ever being the shield of orphans,
> [110] listened to my wailings
> which, flying over sea and mountains, have now
>   reached the gates of compassion.
> <Orlov> stretches a hand to me in friendly fashion,
> looking favourably at my pitiable face,
> [115] Orlov, who is famous and widely known,
>   and now sympathises with me.
> He inclines his ear to my groaning,
> and the eye of his mind is tireless
> so as to overturn utterly
> [120]   my baneful doom. [...]

Metre: Sapphic stanzas. Note in l. 117 κλίνει with short iota.

Notes: This Greek poem of 192 lines in Sapphic stanzas was edited together with a Russian poetic translation (Ода Его Сиятельству графу Григорию Григорьевичу Орлову) in iambic dimeters. The dedicatee, Grigory Orlov (1734–1783), was a favorite of Catherine II: together with his brothers, he organised a palace coup in 1762 to overthrow Emperor Peter III in favour of Ekaterina Alexeyevna (born Princess Sophie of Anhalt-Zerbst). Following this, the Orlovs were elevated to Counts, and then, in 1772, Grigory rose to Prince. He was famous as a philhellene and patron of Greek culture. In this ode, Hellas, 'famous Mother of heroes', is shown as a poor and disconsolate woman who complains about her miserable present, remembers her glorious past, and asks Orlov to be her patron and to defend her from the 'evil Agarene dogs'.

IV. Ὠιδὴ τῷ Ἐξοχωτάτῳ Συμεῶνι Κυριλλιάδῃ τῷ Ναρίσκην Τῷ κορυφαίῳ Στρατηγῷ, τῷ τῆς Μεγίστης Αὐτοκράτορος Ἀρχικυνηγῷ...τῷ Φιλέλληνι καὶ Φιλοξένῳ [1771]

(excerptum, vv. 1–8, 41–44)

> Χαρίεσσα Μοῦσα ᾆσον,
> Τίς ἔγνω βίον περαιοῦν
> Ὄφελος φέροντα πᾶσι;
> Τίς ἀδεῖ τε Δημιουργῷ;

5   Τίς Νέκταρος μεθέξει;
    Τίνα θρυλλέει ὁ αἰών;
    Τίς ἀνώτερός γε λήθης;
    Τίς ἄναξ πέλει ἑαυτοῦ;
    [...]
41 Τοίου βίου Ναρίσκην
    Δείκνυσιν εἰκόν' ἡμῖν,
    Ποδὶ ἀτρεκεῖ τε βαίνων,
    Φύσεως νόμον τε πληρῶν.

Textus: Palladoklis, Antonios (1771), *Ὠιδὴ τῷ Ἐξοχωτάτῳ Συμεῶνι Κυριλλιάδῃ τῷ Ναρίσκην*..., St Petersburg.

Crit.: 4 ἀδεῖ prob. tamquam forma a verbo ἀνδάνω derivata servandum || 44 τε scripsi: γε ed.

Ode to his Excellency, the Commander-in-Chief Semen Kyrillovich Naryshkin, the hospitable and philhellenic First Hunter of the Highest Empress

(excerpt, ll. 1–8, 41–44)

Sing, graceful Muse:
Who knows how to lead a life
that brings advantage to all?
Who will please the Creator?

[5] Who will take his share of the Nectar?
Who is the object of secular talk?
Who is above oblivion?
Who is the master of himself?
[...]
[41] Naryshkin shows us
an example of such a life,
stepping with sure foot,
and fulfilling the law of nature.

Metre: Anacreontic metre.

Notes: The poem consists of 29 stanzas (116 lines). It was dedicated to the nobleman Semen Naryshkin (1710–1775), a famous *bon vivant* who for a long time lived in Paris, was active in the circle of Diderot and Falconet, and later served as a Russian ambassador to Great Britain.

Biography: Antonios Palladoklis (Antonij/Anton Pavlovich Palladoklis in Russian), a native Greek born in Mytilene, became a Russian subject and had a distinguished career in Russia as a translator and diplomat. He studied first in Athens, then, from 1762, in the *Collegium Kijevoense Mohileanum* in Kiev, and from 1766, in the *Collegium Charcoviense*, the Slavo-Greco-Latin school at Kharkov (1721–1840). In 1768–1770, he was a teacher of ancient Greek and Latin at the Holy Trinity Orthodox Seminary near Moscow. In 1770, he was appointed as a translator of Greek, Latin, Turkish, Italian, and Romanian at the *Collegium* in Foreign Affairs in St Petersburg. In 1775–1779, he worked at the Russian embassy in Constantinople; from 1783 until 1797, he served as a Russian consul in Dalmatia; in 1800, he was appointed General Consul of Russia in Ragusa. Between 1771 and 1780, at the time of the Russian victories during the Russo-Turkish War, he published in St Petersburg six bilingual laudatory odes in ancient Greek and Russian, in various types of metre: hexameters, elegiac couplets, Sapphic stanzas, iambic dimeters, and trimeters. These odes were written in honour of Catherine II (1771), Counts Alexei (1771) and Grigory Orlov (1771), Count Nikita Panin (1771), and General Semen Naryshkin (1771); then came the poem *To Kherson* (Εἰς Χερσῶνα, 1780). The editions of the bilingual odes were decorated with miniatures and published at the expense of the author at a print run of 100 copies for each booklet. Palladoklis also completed two long historical epic poems in Russian on the Russo-Turkish war: *Calliope* (1775, 73 pages) and *Clio* (1781), the latter in the form of a dialogue between Ottoman [Osman] and the Muse of History, Clio; these poems bore dedications in ancient Greek to, respectively, Catherine II and Prince Grigory Potemkin, philhellenic patrons of the Greeks. Catherine, in whom Greeks put their hopes of freeing Greece from the Turks, was compared with Alexander the Great and portrayed as both Themis and Pallas. The name of Palladoklis was either a felicitous real name or a pseudonym chosen to glorify the Russian Pallas, Catherine II.

Bibliography: Sazonova, Lidiya (1999), "Palladoklis Anton Pavlovich", in: Aleksandr Panchenko (ed.), *Slovar' russkikh pisatelej XVIII veka* [A biographical dictionary of Russian writers of 18th c.], St Petersburg 1999, vol. 2 (K–P), 405–406; Pryakhin, Jurij (2008), *Greki v istorii Rossii XVIII–XIX vekov* [Greeks in Russian History of 18–19th centuries], St Petersburg; Davies, Brian L. (2015), *The Russo-Turkish War, 1768–1774. Catherine II and the Ottoman Empire*, London; Arsh, Grigory (2018), "Greko-russkij pisatel' I diplomat" [Greek and Russian writer and diplomat], in: Olga Sokolovskaya (ed.), *1000 let vmeste: klyuchevyje momenty istorii Rossii i Gretsii* [1000 Years Together: Key Milestones of Russian and Greek History], Moscow, 100–109. On his Greek poems: Ermolaeva 2019.

Georgios Baldani (c. 1760–1789)

Ὠιδὴ ἐπὶ τοῖς Πανηγυρικοῖς, Πανευδαιμονεστάτοις, Πανευθύμοις Γενεθλίοις Κωνσταντίνου Παυλείδου Μεγάλου Ἡγεμόνος Ῥωσσίης [1779]

(excerptum, vv. 21–30, 41–50)

  Ῥώς, ἴσχεο καὶ μεῖο κλῦθι,
  Ἆμαρ τόδε γηθόσυνόν σοι,
  Αὐδάν τε ἐμὰν χαρίεσσαν
  Αἴῃ ἁπάσῃ φέρε πρόφρων.
25 Νῦν Ῥωσσιίη βρέφος ἄλλο
  Φαιδρὸν Μαρίης τε καὶ Παύλου
  Λεύσσει, μεδέοντ' ἐρατεινόν·
  Ὕμμιν γέρας αὖθι παρεῖχε
  Θεῖον, κλέος ᾧτινι φάνδην
30 Ἧς Ῥωσσιίης ὄφρ' ὀφέλλῃ.
  [...]
  Ἦμος ῥὰ Θεὰ καταθνητοῖς
  Μυθήσατο ἀγγελιείην,
  Πνεῦσάν θ' ἅμα αὖραι λιγεῖαι,
  Αἴθρης τε σέλας πόλος εἷλε,
45 Ἠδ' ἀθάνατοι λίπον ἁγνὰ
  Οὐλύμπια δώματα, δῦσαν
  Γαῖάν τε, γέρας τε ἔχοντες
  Χειροῖν περικλυτὸν ἅπαντες,
  Ἷξον μετὰ Φοῖβον φανέντα
50 Νέβης βορέαο [...]

Textus: Baldani, Georgios (1779), Ὠιδὴ ἐπὶ τοῖς Πανηγυρικοῖς, Πανευδαιμονεστάτοις, Πανευθύμοις γενεθλίοις Κωνσταντίνου Παυλείδου Μεγάλου Ἡγεμόνος Ῥωσσίης, St Petersburg.

Crit.: 23 Αὐδάν correxi: Ἄυδὰν ed. || 27 Λεύσσει: Λούσσει ed. || 41 Ἦμός ῥα debuit || 43 Πνεῦσάν θ' correxi: Πνεῦσαν τ' ed.

Sim.: 29 φάνδην] cf. Hsch. ε 1791 (ἐκφάνδην· φανερῶς) || 44 Πνεῦσάν θ' ἅμα αὖραι λιγεῖαι] cf. Hom. Od. 4.567 (λιγὺ πνείοντος ἀήτας)

Ode for the festive, all-blessed, all-delightful birth of Constantine Pavlovich Great Leader of Russia

(excerpt, ll. 21–30, 41– 50)

>Ros, hold your breath and listen to me,
>this day is joyful for Thee.
>Willingly bring my pleasant voice
>to all the Earth.
>[25] Russia now sees another cheerful
>child of Mary and Paul,
>a lovely king:
>The Divinity has offered him to you as a gift,
>so as to increase through him the glory
>[30] of his Russia manifestly for whomever.
>[...]
>As soon as the goddess gave
>the message to the mortals,
>at the same time the sweet sounding winds blew,
>daylight lit up the sky,
>[45] all the immortals left their holy
>houses on Olympus, went down
>to Earth, with an outstanding gift in
>their hands. They came
>to Phoebus, who had appeared
>[50] on the northern Neva banks.

Metre: Paroemiac (an an⌣), with a number of prosodical mistakes (in addition, l. 49 does not scan correctly, as περικλυτός should have a short υ).

Notes: In Baldani's poem of 80 lines, the goddess Iris informs the entire world that the second child of Mary and Paul has been born in Russia. Paul is the future Emperor Paul I (1754–1801), and Mary is the future Empress Maria Fyodorovna, born Duchess Sophia Dorothea of Württemberg (1759–1828). Empress Catherine II gave her grandson, who was expected to become the future Emperor of Constantinople, once it had been liberated by the Russians, the name of Constantine.

Biography: Georgios (Georgij in Russian) Baldani, a native Greek, studied at the Greek Gymnasium of St Petersburg (the Corps of Foreign Co-Religionists), which was established by Catherine II in 1775. His extraordinary career as a poet seems to have started with his *Ode to Catherine II Great Empress of all Russia, the real Patroness of Greeks* (1779), written when he was still a gymnasium pupil, 'in Helleno-Greek', as he himself proclaimed in the title of a separate edition, in which his ode was presented with a Russian translation. In 1779 and 1781, he completed Greek odes with Russian translations to celebrate the birth and the name-day of Grand Duke Constantine Pavlovich; in 1782, he wrote an ode in ancient Greek with a Russian translation *en regard* for the birthday of Catherine II. His Russian version of the ode for the birth of Constantine Pavlovich (1779) is very similar (even down to the number of lines, i.e. 80) to the ode dedicated to the same event by the famous Russian poet Vassily Petrov (1736–1799). In 1780, Baldani translated into ancient Greek Petrov's ode to Prince Grigory Potemkin (1778), following the triadic structure of ancient choral lyric: strophe – antistrophe – epode. In 1781, he translated another laudatory ode by Petrov to Potemkin (1777), using various metres in an imitation of ancient choral lyric.

Bibliography: Kibalnik, Sergej (1999), "Georgij Baldani", in: Alexandr Panchenko (ed.), *Slovar' russkikh pisatelej XVIII veka* [A biographical dictionary of Russian writers of 18th c.], St Petersburg, vol. 1 (A–I), 55. On his Greek poems: Ermolaeva 2019.

Christian Friedrich Graefe (1780–1851)

I. "Ἀδελφοὶ ἐχθροί" Τραγῳδία ἐκ τῶν τοῦ Σχιλλέρου Δρᾶμα πρῶτον. Σκηνὴ α΄ [post 1799]

Μήτηρ ἄνασσα, Γέροντες

<u>Μήτηρ</u>. Πεισθεῖσ' ἀνάγκῃ οὐκ ἐμῷ βουλήματι
Ἐξῆλθον, ὦ γέροντες οἱ τὰ πρῶτ' ἐκεῖ,
Ἔμπροσθεν ὑμῶν, ἥσυχον λιποῦσ' ἐμὸν
Στέγος, γυναικείην τε παστάδ', ὄμματα
5 Φέρουσα πέπλων γύμν' ἐς ὄψιν ἀρσένων.
Χήρην γὰρ ἐχρῆν, ἥτις ἄνδρα φίλτατον,
Σὺν δ' ἀνδρὶ φῶς βίου τε δόξαν ὤλεσεν,
Μορφῆς ἑῆς μέλαιναν ὄψιν ὄμμασι
Πλήθους καλύπτειν ἐντὸς ἐν σιγῇ δόμων.
10 Ἄγει δὲ δαίμων σὺν βίᾳ μ' ἀμείλιχος
Καιρός τε δεινός, παγκράτωρ βίου θεός,
Ἐς τοῦτ' ἐμοί γ' ἄηθες ἤδη φῶς πόλου.
Οὔπω σελήνη δισσὸν ἐξέπλησε φῶς,
Ἐξ οὗ μὲν ἄνδρα καὶ τύραννον ἐν πόλει
15 Ἐβάστασ' εἰς μνημεῖον ἥσυχον τάφου,
Ὃ ἦν πτόλεως ἀρχηγὸς εὐκρατὴς ἀεί,
Ὑμῖν δ' ἀμύνων ἐν σθένει βραχίονος,
Φόβος δ' ἐν ἐχθροῖς, οἷς πτόλις κυκλουμένη.

Φροῦδος μὲν αὐτός ἐστι, πνεῦμα δ' εὐγενὲς
20 Ζώει πατρὸς παιδοῖν ἔτ' ἔμφυτον δυοῖν,
Οἳ τῆσδε γῆς μετ' αὐτόν εἰσιν ἕρματα.
Ὑμεῖς δ' ἐκείνους εἴδετ', ἐν νέῳ σθένει
Ὡς ηὐξάνο<ν>το, πῶς δ' ἐτῶν ἅμ' ηὔξετο,
Οὐκ οἶδ', ἀλάστορός τινος σπαρὲν χερί,
25 Μῖσος δύσοιστον, αὐτάδελφον, ἔμπεδον·
Ῥῆξαν δὲ παίδων τοῦτο νοῦν ὁμόφρονα·
Δεινὴν τέθηλεν εἰς ἀκμὴν ἀκμῇ βίου.
Οὔπω γέγηθα σφᾶς ἰδοῦσ' ὁμόφρονας
Ἣ πρίν ποθ' ἓν στάξασα τοῖς δισσοῖς γάλα,
30 Ἴσον φιλοῦσα γαστρὸς ὡς μιῆς βάρος.
Εὖ δ' οἶδα, πῶς φιλοῦσιν ἄμφω μητέρα,
Καθ' ἕν γε τοῦτο παῖδες ὄνθ' ὁμόφρονες·
Τὰ δ' ἄλλα πάντα νοῦν ἔρις φέρει δίχα.
Ἕως γὰρ οὖν πατὴρ μὲν αὐτὸς ηὐτύχει,
35 Οὗτος καθεῖργεν ἄμφω σὺν δίκῃ μιᾷ·
Ζυγὸν δὲ δισσοῖς ἐμβαλὼν δυσέξιτον
Ἕνωσεν αὐτοὺς ὑφ' ἑνὸς βαρήματος.
Ἐχρῆν ἀνόπλους ἄλλον ἄλλῳ προσπελᾶν,
Μηδ' αὖ καθεύδειν ἐν δόμων ἑνὶ στέγει.
40 Οὕτω μὲν εἶρξε δυσφόροις προστάγμασιν
Ὀργῆς βίαιον αἷμα δυσσεβεστάτης·
Ἀλλ' ἔμφυτον τῇ καρδίᾳ μῖσος μέσῃ
Ἔμεινεν ἔμπεδον. Βίᾳ γὰρ ὃς κρατεῖ,
Φράξαι τι πηγῆς βαιὸν οἶμ' α<ἰ>σχύνεται,
45 Ὡς καὶ θαλάσσης κύματ' εἴργειν οἷος ὤν.

Textus: St Petersburg, Russian National Library, ms. F.608, I, 4802.

Crit.: accentus in ms. omissos addidi || **18** κυκλουμένη correxi: κεκλουμενη ms. || **23** ηὐξάνο<ν>το supplevi || **36** ἐμβαλὼν correxi: ἐμβαλον ms. || **37** ἕνωσεν correxi: Ἐνωσεν ms. | ὑφ' correxi: ὑφ ms. || **44** α<ἰ>σχύνεται correxi: ἀσχυνεται ms. || **45** θαλασσης ante correcturam ms.

Sim.: **10** Ἄγει δὲ δαίμων σὺν βίᾳ μ' ἀμείλιχος] cf. Godofredi Hermanni translationem e Schilleri dramate *Piccolomini* (act. III sc. 9: ἕλκει δὲ βίᾳ δαίμων ἀφανεῖ) || **11** παγκράτωρ] cf. Isidor. *Hymn.* 4.23; *Chr. Pat.* 1339 || **18** Φόβος δ' ἐν ἐχθροῖς, οἷς πτόλις κυκλουμένη] cf. Godofredi Hermanni translationem e Schilleri dramate *Wallensteinii Mors* (act. IV, sc. 10: φόβοισι πάντοθεν κεκλησμένοι) || **25** δύσοιστον] cf. Soph. *OC* 1688; *Phil.* 508; Aesch. *PV* 690; *Cho.* 745 | αὐτάδελφον] Aesch. *Sept.* 718; Soph. *Ant.* 1, 503, 696 etc. || **35** δίκῃ μιᾷ] cf. Eur. *Or.* 1244 || **36** δυσέξιτον] hapax in Diod. Sic. 3.44.1 || **40** δυσφόροις] cf. Soph. *Aj.* 51; 642; *OT* 87; *El.* 143 || **41** δυσσεβεστάτης] cf. Aesch. *Sept.* 598; Soph. *Ant.* 514.

The Hostile Brothers. A Tragedy by Schiller

First Act, First Scene

DONNA ISABELLA in mourning; the ELDERS OF MESSINA.

ISABELLA.
Forth from my silent chamber's deep recesses,
Gray Fathers of the State, unwillingly
I come; and, shrinking from your gaze, uplift
The veil that shades my widowed brows: the light
And glory of my days is fled forever!
And best in solitude and kindred gloom
To hide these sable weeds, this grief-worn frame,
Beseems the mourner's heart. A mighty voice
Inexorable – duty's stern command,
Calls me to light again.
Not twice the moon
Has filled her orb since to the tomb ye bore
My princely spouse, your city's lord, whose arm
Against a world of envious foes around
Hurled fierce defiance! Still his spirit lives
In his heroic sons, their country's pride:
Ye marked how sweetly from their childhood's bloom
They grew in joyous promise to the years
Of manhood's strength; yet in their secret hearts,
From some mysterious root accursed, upsprung
Unmitigable, deadly hate, that spurned
All kindred ties, all youthful, fond affections,
Still ripening with their thoughtful age; not mine
The sweet accord of family bliss; though each
Awoke a mother's rapture; each alike
Smiled at my nourishing breast! for me alone
Yet lives one mutual thought, of children's love;
In these tempestuous souls discovered else
By mortal strife and thirst of fierce revenge.
While yet their father reigned, his stern control
Tamed their hot spirits, and with iron yoke
To awful justice bowed their stubborn will:
Obedient to his voice, to outward seeming
They calmed their wrathful mood, nor in array
Ere met, of hostile arms; yet unappeased
Sat brooding malice in their bosoms' depths;
They little reek of hidden springs whose power
Can quell the torrent's fury: scarce their sire
In death had closed his eyes, when, as the spark

That long in smoldering embers sullen lay,
Shoots forth a towering flame; so unconfined
Burst the wild storm of brothers' hate triumphant
O'er nature's holiest bands.[13]

[transl. from the German D. Lodge, 1841]

Metre: Iambic trimeters. Resolutions do not occur in Graefe's iambic trimeter. Porson's Law is broken four times in ll. 2, 12, 31, 38, 45.

Notes: Graefe had the opportunity to translate Schiller while he was in the presence of the great German philologist Gottfried Hermann, who himself translated four parts from Schiller's *Wallenstein* trilogy (1799). Hermann certainly must have encouraged his students to try the same exercise – if not directly, then at least by the example of his own translations. Graefe only translated the subtitle of Schiller's play 'die feindlichen Brüder', perhaps in order to avoid the specific allusion to Messina in favour of the more ancient-sounding 'enemy brothers'. His μήτηρ (unlike Schiller's non-Greek 'Isabella') is reminiscent, rather, of the mother of Eteocles and Polynices.

---

13 German original text: Fr. Schiller. *Die Braut von Messina oder die feindlichen Brüder*. Ein Trauerspiel mit Chören, 1803. Erster Auftritt. Donna Isabella in tiefer Trauer, die Ältesten von Messina stehen um sie her. Isabella: Der Noth gehorchend, nicht dem eignen Trieb, / Tret' ich, ihr greisen Häupter dieser Stadt, / Heraus zu euch aus den verschwiegenen / Gemächern meines Frauensaals, das Antlitz / [5] Vor euren Männerblicken zu entschleiern. / Denn es geziemt der Wittwe, die den Gatten / Verloren, ihres Lebens Licht und Ruhm, / Die schwarz umflorte Nachtgestalt dem Aug / Der Welt in stillen Mauern zu verbergen; / [10] Doch unerbittlich allgewaltig treibt / Des Augenblicks Gebieterstimme mich / An das entwohnte Licht der Welt hervor. / Nicht zweimal hat der Mond die Lichtgestalt / Erneut, seit ich den fürstlichen Gemahl / [15] Zu seiner letzten Ruhestätte trug, / Der mächtigwaltend dieser Stadt gebot, / Mit starkem Arme gegen eine Welt / Euch schützend, die euch feindlich rings umlagert. / Er selber ist dahin, doch lebt sein Geist / [20] In einem tapfern Heldenpaare fort / Glorreicher Söhne, dieses Landes Stolz. / Ihr habt sie unter euch in freud'ger Kraft / Aufwachsen sehen, doch mit ihnen wuchs / Aus unbekannt verhängnisvollem Samen / [25] Auch ein unsel'ger Bruderhaß empor, / Der Kindheit frohe Einigkeit zerreißend, / Und reifte furchtbar mit dem Ernst der Jahre. / Nie hab' ich ihrer Eintracht mich erfreut; / An diesen Brüsten nährt' ich beide gleich, / [30] Gleich unter sie vertheil' ich Lieb' und Sorge, / Und beide weiß ich kindlich mir geneigt. / In diesem einz'gen Triebe sind sie Eins, / In allem Andern trennt sie blut'ger Streit. / Zwar, weil der Vater noch gefürchtet herrschte, / [35] Hielt er durch gleiche Strenge / Gerechtigkeit die Heftigbrausenden im Zügel, / Und unter eines Joches Eisenschwere / Bog er vereinend ihren starren Sinn. / Nicht waffentragend durften sie sich nahn, / [40] Nicht in denselben Mauern übernachten. / So hemmt' er zwar mit strengem Machtgebot / Den rohen Ausbruch ihres wilden Triebs; / Doch ungebessert in der tiefen Brust / Ließ er den Haß – der Starke achtet es / [45] Gering, die leise Quelle zu verstopfen, / Weil er dem Strome mächtig wehren kann.

II. Εἰς Ὅμηρον [post 1797]

Οὐκέτ' ἔρις πόλεων περὶ θείκελόν ἐστιν Ὅμηρον,
  Ἐξ οὗ αἰνοβίης τλήμονα ῥῆξε λύκος.

Textus: St Petersburg, Russian National Library, MS department, F. 608, I, 4802.

Sim.: 1 de re cf. *Anth. Gr.* 16.297–298 et al. | θείκελον] dub. l. in Ar. *Lys.* 1252 || **2** αἰνοβίης] *Anth. Pal.* 7.226.1 (Anac.)

On Homer

No longer do the cities quarrel over godlike Homer,
  since a mighty strong wolf rent the poor man.

Metre: Elegiac couplet.

Notes: Graefe's epigram is a free translation of Friedrich Schiller's distich *Der Wolfische Homer* ('Sieben Städte zankten sich drum, ihn geboren zu haben, / Nun, da der Wolf ihn zerriß, nehme sich jede ihr Stück'), which was published among the satirical *Xenien* by Goethe and Schiller in *Musen-Almanach* (Tübingen 1797) as an answer to Friedrich August Wolf's *Prolegomena ad Homerum* (1795).

III. Σιγὴ Ἔρωτος [post 1810]

Αὔρη ἐρωτοπνεής, ἥν ποτε μειλιχίως
Νήξῃ ἀμφὶ φίλην, πνεῦσον ἐς οὔατά οἱ
Πνεῦμά μου ἱμερόειν· εἰ δ' ἔρεται "τίνος ἦν;"
  Σίγα, ὦ αὔρη.

5   Πηγὴ ὠκυρόης, ἥν ποτε μαρμαρέη
Ῥεύσῃς ἀμφὶ φίλην, στάξον ἐς ὄμματά οἱ
Δάκρυον ὡς ἀπ' ἐμῶν· εἰ δ' ἔρεται "τίνος ἦν;"
  Σίγα, ὦ ὕδωρ.

Αὐγὴ ἠελίου, ἥν ποτε φῶς καθαρὸν
10 Φαίνῃς ἀμφὶ φίλην, βλέψον ἐς ὄμματά οἱ
Βλέμμασι πυρσοβόλοις· εἰ δ' ἔρεται "τίνος ἦν;"
  Σίγα, ὦ αὐγή.

Ὦ σκιὰς ἐκ μύρτων, ἥν ποτε σεῖο κλάδους
Πλέξῃς ἀμφὶ φίλην, ἅψαι ἅμ' ὑγροτάτοις

15 Ἔρνεσί οἱ στηθέων· εἰ δ' ἔρεται "τίνος ἦν;"
    Σίγα, ὦ ἔρνος.

Textus: St Petersburg, Russian National Library, ms. F. 608, I, 4802, f. 5v.

Crit.: accentus in ms. omissos addidi

Sim.: 1 ἐρωτοπνεής] hapax leg. || 2 ἐς οὔατα] cf. Nonn. *Dion.* 3.54 et *passim*; cf. *Anth. Pal.* 5.303.1 || 11 πυρσοβόλοις] cf. *Anth. Pal.* 12.196.2

Silence of Eros

Wind sweet-blowing and gentle,
If thou blow upon my darling,
Breathe a whisper in her ear.
    Soft thou be if asked, 'who's here?'

[5] Rivulet swift-flowing and clear,
If thou come upon my darling,
Spray her face as if with tear.
    Soft thou be if asked, 'who's here?'

Morning bright and bathed in sunlight,
[10] When thou shine upon my darling,
Eye her sending shafts of fire.
    Soft thou be if asked, 'who's here?'

Woodland dark and myrtle-grown,
When thy shade falls on my darling,
[15] Touch her bosom swishing near.
    Soft thou be if asked, 'who's here?'.[14]

[Transl. from the Russian Tatiana Kostyleva, 2018]

---

14 Dershavin's original text: Тихий, милый ветерочик, / Коль порхнешь ты на любезну, / Как вздыханье ей в ушко шепчи. / Естьли спросит: чье? – молчи. / [5] Чистый, быстрый ручеёчик, / Естьли встретишь ты любезну, / Как слезинка ей в лицо плещи. / Естьли спросит: чье? – молчи. / Ясный, ведренный денёчик, / [10] Как освятишь ты любезну, / Взглядов пламенных ей брось лучи. / Естьли спросит: чьи? – молчи. / Темный, миртовый лесочик, / Как сокроешь ты любезну, / [15] Тихо веткой грудь ей щекочи. / Естьли спросит: кто? – молчи.

Metre: Graefe's stanza comprises three pentameters (2 hem x 3) and an adonean (as in the last line of a Sapphic stanza), a structure that seems to be his own invention, not paralleled in Greek poetry. The striking feature of its prosody is the large number of hiatuses, *certo certius* deliberate, no less than thirteen over the span of only four stanzas. Especially significant in this respect is the conclusive adonean: Σίγα, ὦ αὔρη / Σίγα, ὦ ὕδωρ / Σίγα, ὦ αὐγή / Σίγα, ὦ ἔρνος.

Notes: Graefe's poem translates Gavriil Derzhavin's *Modesty*, itself a free translation of the Italian poem *Amor timido* by Metastasio (1698–1782), for which Derzhavin used a *verbum pro verbo* translation by Nicolay Lvov (1753–1803). Derzhavin also translated into Russian from the *Anacreontica*, the *Greek Anthology*, and Sappho. It seems, then, that his imitations from the Greek sounded quite authentic to Graefe and inspired him to render into ancient Greek this very poem, also stylised by Derzhavin as an epigram from the *Greek Anthology*. Graefe's Greek version of Derzhavin is elegant and is far from being a slavishly literal translation. One may note the occurrence of lexical items from the *Anthology* and particularly from Nonnus's *Dionysiaca*, which Graefe himself edited between 1819 and 1826: the very title might have been influenced by Nonnus, *Dionysiaca* 33.107–108: καὶ Ἔρωτος ἐς οὔατα μάρτυρι σιγῇ / ψευδομένης ἀγόρευε δολόφρονα μῦθον ἀνάσσης. Graefe's manuscript, now preserved in St Petersburg, must have been put together during his stay in Russia, although several of its parts may have been composed at different times.

Biography: Christian Friedrich (Fyodor Bogdanovich in Russian) Graefe was born in Chemnitz (Saxony) on 1 July (N. S.) 1780. At the age of seven, Graefe became a pupil at the Lyceum in Chemnitz. From 1799, he studied theology and philology at the University of Leipzig. Graefe belonged to the first generation of pupils studying in Leipzig under the great Gottfried Hermann (1772–1848; →**Germany**). After graduating from the university, Graefe became a private tutor ('Erzieher') and was later, in 1806, enlisted by Hermann to teach in Livonia in the family of *Landrath* Karl Gustav Samson von Himmelstjerna, whose third daughter, Hedwig, would later become Graefe's wife. In 1810, on the advice of Mikhail Speransky, Graefe arrived in St Petersburg as a Professor of Greek at the Alexander Nevsky Theological Academy, founded in 1797. The following year, after engaging Graefe as a private tutor of ancient Greek, Sergey S. Uvarov, superintendent of St Petersburg Educational District, secured for him a position as Professor of Latin – and, in 1815, of Greek – at the Pedagogical Institute, a teacher training college that had been founded in 1804. After the Pedagogical Institute was reorganised by Uvarov into the University of St Petersburg (1819), Graefe became the first Professor of Greek and then Latin, and, in 1829, of ancient Greek literature. In 1818, he became a corresponding member and, in 1820, a full member of the Imperial Academy of Sciences. From 1817 onward, he worked as Custodian of the Collection of Antiquities and Coins in the Imperial Hermitage, a title later changed, in 1840, to Honorary Director of the Collection. Graefe's own strong points were in the field of textual criticism and linguistics; following the advice of Hermann, Graefe edited the *Dionysiaca* by Nonnus of Panopolis in 1819–1826. Just like Hermann, furthermore, Graefe habitually expressed himself in Latin and Greek, occasionally writing poetry *captandae benevolentiae causa*.[15] On 12 December 1851, Graefe passed away in St Petersburg and was buried at the Smolensky Lutheran Cemetery ('Der Deutsche Evangelisch–Lutherische Smolenski–Friedhof').

Bibliography: Eckstein, Friedrich August (1871/2005²), *Nomenclator philologorum*, Leipzig, 173; Bursian, Conrad (1879), "Gräfe, Christian Friedrich", in: *Allgemeine Deutsche Biographie* 9, 555–556; Schmid, Georg (1886), "Zur russischen Gelehrten Geschichte. S.S. Uwarov und Christian Friedrich Graefe", in: *Russische Revue* 26, 77–108, 156–167; Verlinsky, Alexander (2013), "Philologia inter Disciplinas: The Department of Classics at St Petersburg University 1819–1884", in: *Hyperboreus* 19, 162–204; Smyshlyayeva, Vera (2015), *Rossiiskie filologi-klassiki XIX veka. "Germanovskoe napravlenie"* [Russian Classical Philologists of 19th c. influenced by G. Hermann], St Petersburg, 124–127. On his Greek poems: Ermolaeva, Elena (2018), "Friedrich Schiller and Gavriil Derzhavin in Greek: Translations by Christian Friedrich Graefe (1780–1851)", in: *Philologia Classica* 13/1, 165–180.

---

15 The list of Graefe's published Latin and Greek poetry (*Gelegenheits-Schriften*), in: *Bulletin de la classe des sciences historiques, philologiques et politiques de l'Académie Impériale des Sciences de St.-Pétersbourg* 9/22–24, 1852, 367f.: 1. *Gallorum sub Brenno in Graecia clades et infamia nostris temporibus in memoriam revocata*. MDCCCXII; 2. ΥΜΝΟΣ ΕΙΣ ΝΕΜΕΣΙΝ ΕΝ ΤΗΙ ΝΙΚΗΙ ΚΑΙ ΤΩΙ ΝΟΣΤΩΙ ΑΛΕΞΑΝΔΡΟΥ ΤΟΥ ΣΕΒΑΣΤΟΥ. *Hymne à Nemesis à l'occasion du triumphe et du retour de Sa Majesté l'Empereur*. Par le Dr. F. Graefe. St. Petersbourg. 1814; 3. ΣΕΡΓΙΩΙ ΣΙΜΩΝΟΣ ΟΥΒΑΡΟΦ ΓΥΜΝΑΣΙΑΡΧΟΝΤΙ. Ἐν τῇ τοῦ Γυμνασίου χορηγίᾳ. MDCCCXVI; 4. *Ad imaginem Alexandri I. imperatoris et auctoris omnium Rossorum in museo numismatico Imp. Academiae Scient. Petropoli positam* Cal. Mart. MDCCCXXIV; 5. ΤΗΙ ΚΑΙΣΑΡΕΙΑΙ ΠΕΡΙ ΕΠΙΣΤΗΜΩΝ ΑΚΑΔΗΜΙΑΙ ΤΗΙ ΕΝ ΠΕΤΡΟΥ ΠΟΛΕΙ ΤΗΝ ΕΚΑΤΟΝΤΟΥΤΙΝ ΕΑΥΤΗΣ ΠΑΝΗΓΥΡΙΝ ΤΟ ΠΡΩΤΟΝ ΑΓΟΥΣΗΙ ΤΗΙ ΚΘ ΤΟΥ ΔΕΚΕΜΒΡΙΟΥ ΤΟΥ ΑΩΚΦ (ΑΩΚΣ? — ΕΕ) ΕΤΟΥΣ; 6. *Der Kaiserlichen Akademie der Wissenschaften zu St Petersburg bey ihrer ersten Saecular-Feier den XXIX. December MDCCCXXVI. Für wenige aus dem Griechischen übersetzt vom Verfasser*; 7. Η ΚΙΩΝ ΤΟΥ ΑΓΓΕΛΟΥ. ΤΗΙ Α ΜΗΝΟΣ ΑΥΓΟΥΣΤΟΥ ΕΤΟΥΣ ΑΩΛΔ; 8. *Imperatori Augustissimo Domino suo Clementissimo quid pro tot ac tantis beneficiis Universitas Literaria debeat*? Oratio in solemni Universitatis inauguratione habita a Fr. Graefo. Petropoli MDCCCXXXVIII.

Fyodor Yevgenievich Korsch (1843–1915)

I. Εἰς τὴν Ὁμήρου Ἰλιάδα τὴν ὑπὸ Νικολάου Γνέδιτς μεταπεφρασμένην [1886]

    Ληξάσης ἀίω θείης Ἑλληνίδος αὐδῆς,
        Θαμβέω δ', ὡς μεγάλου πρέσβεος ἐγγὺς ἐών.

II. Πρὸς Οὐεστφάλιον [1886]

    Αἱ μὲν Λύκηον τᾷ δυναμίτιδι
    'Ὑπ' οὐδενίσταν οἴχετ' ἐς ἀέρα,
        Οὐκ ἔστιν ὅττι μὴ δεδόρκων
            Σκεῦος ἔχησθα περ' ὀππάτεσσιν.

5   Αἱ δ', ὡς ἔολπα, σῶος ἐπὶ χθόνι
    Ἴμερτον ἀλίω προτόρης φάος,
        Δίκαιος ἔσσι τοῦτο δέχθαι,
            Ὃ χθὲς ἔμα παράκοιτις εὗρεν.

Textus: ΣΤΕΦΑΝΟΣ. *Carmina partim sua Graeca et Latina partim aliena in alterutram linguam ab se conversa elegit recensuit in ordinem redegit Theodorus Korsch Mosquanus,* Hauniae: sumptibus librariae Gyldendalianae (Hegeliorum patris et filii). Typis Schultzianis, 1886, 24 et 47; Korsch, Fyodor E. (2012), in: *Aristeas* 6, 2012, 42 et 64.

Sim.: I.1 αὐδῆς] in fine versus cf. Hom. *Il.* 1.249; *Od.* 2.268; 21.411 || **2** θαμβέω] in princ. versus cf. Hom. *Il.* 1.199; *Od.* 1.323.
II.4 ἔχησθα] cf. Hom. *Il.* 19.180 | ὀππάτεσσιν] cf. Sapph. fr. 31.11 V || **5** ἔολπα] vox epica || **6** ἵμερτον] cf. Alc. fr. 117b.5 | ἀλίω φάος] cf. Sapph. fr. 56.1 V (φάος ἀλίω) || **8** παράκοιτις] epicum, cf. Hom. *Il.* 1.557; 4.60 etc.

On Homer's *Iliad* translated by Nikolay Gnedich

    I hear the divine Hellenic voice, long silenced,
        and I am astonished, as if being in presence of the great old man.

To Westphal

If the Lyceum is blown up
by nihilists using dynamite,
   it will be impossible for you who cannot see
     with your eyes to get things.

[5] But, if, as I hope, you, safe and sound on the ground,
see the desired light of the sun,
   it is right for you to receive
     what my wife found yesterday.

Metre: I. Elegiac couplet. II. Alcaic stanzas (in Aeolic dialect).

Notes: I. The first complete hexameter translation of the *Iliad* into Russian, by the poet Nikolay Gnedich (1784–1833), appeared in print in 1829 and was received by the reading public with enthusiasm and acclaim. In 1830, the famous Russian poet Alexander Pushkin wrote an epigram in praise of Gnedich, which Korsch translated into ancient Greek in the dialect of Homer.[16]

II. The poem to Westphal is an occasional letter equipped with notes in ancient Greek; it tells the story of Westphal's spectacles getting lost in the wood, being found by the wife of the author, and being restored to their rightful owner, together with a small Greek poem:

> Ῥοδόλφος Οὐεστφάλιος, ὁ εὐδοκιμήσας ἐπὶ μετρικῇ, παραγενόμενός ποτε τῷ ποιητῇ εἶπεν ὅτι οἱ λεγόμενοι οὐδενισταὶ ἀπειλήσειαν τὸ Λυκεῖον τὸ Νικολάου τοῦ Καισαρίδου, οὗ τότε κατῴκει, ταύτῃ τῇ νυκτὶ καταλύσειν τῇ νῦν πολυθρυλήτῳ δυναμίτιδι. Ἀπελθὼν δ' ἐπ' οἴκου δῆλος ἐγένετο τὴν αὑτοῦ διόπτραν καταλιπών. Τῇ δ' ὑστεραίᾳ ὁ ποιητὴς αὐτὴν ἀνευρὼν ἀπέπεμψε μετὰ τοῦδε τοῦ ποιηματίου.

> Rudolf Westphal, the famous metrician, once visited the poet and told him that the so-called nihilists had threatened to blow up the Lyceum of Prince Nikolai, where he lived at that time, with the now famous dynamite on that very night. When he returned home, it became clear that he had left his glasses behind. On the next day, the poet found them and sent them back together with the following little poem.

Rudolf Westphal (1826–1892) was a German classical philologist and the editor of *Scriptores metrici graeci* (Leipzig 1866). From 1875 to 1879, he taught at Moscow Imperial Lyceum in Memory of Prince Nicolay, a privileged boarding school for

---

[16] The Russian original: Слышу умолкнувший звук божественной эллинской речи; / Старца великого тень чую смущенной душой.

the aristocracy with an in-depth programme in ancient languages (1868–1917). The *poemetto*, presented here, written in the Aeolic dialect, testifies to Korsch's friendship with Westphal. It wittily integrates into the archaic dialect Greek versions of modern terms: δυναμῖτις for 'dynamite' (a term, coined from the Greek word δύναμις by Korsch himself, after its invention by Alfred Nobel in 1867), and οὐδενίστας (Aeolic form for Attic οὐδενιστής) for the French word 'nihiliste' (first attested in 1877).

Biography: Fyodor Korsch was an honoured professor of classics and Oriental languages at Moscow University and a member of the Imperial Academy of Sciences. His scope was broad enough to include Slavistics, Indo-European linguistics, and the theory of versification, metre and translation. He published translations into Russian from the Latin of Catullus and Propertius, from the Slovene of the Romantic poet France Prešeren, and from German. In 1886, he edited a poetry anthology titled *Stephanos*, which consisted of 17 Greek and 88 Latin poems, including both original works and translations into ancient Greek and Latin from Russian, German (e.g., Goethe and Schiller), Arabic, Persian, Sanskrit, Armenian, and Slovene (Prešeren). The anthology also included translations Korsch had made from ancient Greek into Latin (Soph. *Ant.* 781sqq.; Sappho fr. 1 etc.).

Bibliography: Grushka, Apollon (1916), *Fyodor Jevgenyevich Korsch (Necrologue)*, Moscow.

Vyacheslav I. Ivanov (1866–1949)

I. G.A. Rachinsky [1910?]

Πρόμαντις οἰκτιρμῶν τε τοῦ Πατρὸς φίλοις
πέφυκας εἰρήνης τε συντεθλιμμένοις,
αὐτὸς συνοικτείρας μέν, ἐν καιρῷ δέ πως
θεοπροπήσας εὐστόμως νέαν χάριν·
5   σὺν τοιγαροῦν χαῖρ', ὠγάθ' ἐν Χριστῷ φίλε.

II. M.I. Rostovtsev [1910?]

Φθορᾶς μὲν ἐκσώσαντι τὸν πάλαι σπόρον,
πόνου δ' ἄελπτον καρπὸν ἀντείλαντί σοι
σπείρας ἀπαρχῶν αὐξίμῳ φέρω χάριν.

III. F.F. Zieliński [1910–1912]

Δελφίδος ἑρμηνεῦ καὶ βακχευτῶν ὑποφῆτα,
ἐξ Ἀίδαο δόμων ἀγκαλέσας Ἑλένην,
ἧς φάτιν ἡδυμελῶς ἑλληνίδα φωνησάσης
ἔκλυες ἀνταυδᾶν καλὰ διδασκόμενος,
5   ὄλβιε, χαῖρε φίλει τε συνένθεον, Ἑλλάδος εἴπερ
μουσοπόλω συνερᾶν εὐχόμεθ' ἀμφοτέρω.

Textus: Ivanov, Vyacheslav (1912), *Nezhnaja tajna* [Soft Secret], *Humanorum studiorum cultoribus*, St Petersburg, 112–113; Id. (1979), *The Complete Works in four Volumes*, 3, Brussels, 59.

Sim.: I.1 Πρόμαντις οἰκτιρμῶν τε τοῦ Πατρός] cf. NT *Cor.* ii.1.3.2 (ὁ Πατὴρ τῶν οἰκτιρμῶν καὶ Θεὸς πάσης παρακλήσεως); NT *Rom.* 12.1.1 (Παρακαλῶ οὖν ὑμᾶς, ἀδελφοί, διὰ τῶν οἰκτιρμῶν τοῦ Θεοῦ) || 4 θεοπροπήσας] cf. Hom. *Il.* 1.109; 2.322; *Od.* 2.184; Pind. *Pyth.* 4.190.
III.4 cf. Sol. fr. 18 W. (πολλὰ διδασκόμενος) || 5 συνένθεον] hapax leg. ut vid. || 6 μουσοπόλω] cf. Eur. *Alc.* 445

To G.A. Rachinsky

You are a preacher of the Father of mercy
and of peace for friends distressed,
for you yourself have pity upon them, but over time
you somehow become a prophet of a new delight with propitious words:
[5] hence, my dear friend, rejoice together in Christ.

To Michael Rostovtsev

To you, who saved the seed of old from death,
who raised the unhoped-for fruit of work,
who promoted the growth of the first offerings, I, the sower, bring [my] thanks.

To F.F. Zieliński

You, interpreter of the Pythia and exegete of the Bacchae,
  you who invoked the ghost of Helen from Hades,
to whom you listened when she was speaking sweetly in Greek,
  and to whom you learned to reply with beautiful words,
[5] you, blessed, rejoice and love [me] full of the god together [with you], if we,
  both servants of the Muses, boast to love Hellas together.

Metre: I–II: Iambic trimeters, III: Elegiac couplets.

Notes: I. Grigory Alekseyevich Rachinsky (1859–1939) was a religious philosopher and translator. In Ivanov's epigram, there is evidently a deliberate mixture of pagan and Christian vocabulary. It starts with the pagan πρόμαντις ('prophet') and continues with the 'Father of mercies and peace', which recalls the wording of the New Testament formula and the Prayer for Christmas: Θεὸς ὢν εἰρήνης, Πατὴρ οἰκτιρμῶν, / τῆς μεγάλης Βουλῆς σου τὸν Ἄγγελον, / εἰρήνην παρεχόμενον, ἀπέστειλας ἡμῖν ('As Thou art God of peace and Father of mercies, / Thou hast sent unto us Thine Angel of great counsel, / granting us peace'). This choral ode, the *Irmos* of the morning service for Christmas, was sent by Rachinsky, in Moscow, to Ivanov, in St Petersburg on a card dated 25 December 1910. Ivanov's Greek poem seems to have been his answer to this greeting. Note the expressive repetition of σύν (συντεθλιμμένοις, συνοικτείρας and σύγχαιρε *in tmesi*) and the deliberate repetitions of *clausulae* (τοῦ Πατρὸς φίλοις – ἐν Χριστῷ φίλε).
II. Mikhail Ivanovich Rostovtsev (1870–1952) was a historian of the ancient world and professor first at St Petersburg University (1901–1918) and later at Yale University (1925–1944). His friendship with Ivanov began in 1893 in Rome, where Ivanov was writing his Latin dissertation about tax farming in the Roman Republic (*De societatibus vectigalium publicorum populi Romani*), and Rostovtsev his own, about the wall paintings of Pompeii. Rostovtsev changed his scientific focus under the influence of Ivanov, among others, and began to work on the *History of Tax Farming in the Roman Empire: From Augustus to Diocletian*. After returning to Russia, Rostovtsev completed his dissertation and published it in 1899, becoming a professor at St Petersburg University and later an academician. Ivanov seemed to be more of a poet, a leader of the symbolist movement and a philosopher of mysticism. He wrote his epigram in gratitude for Rostovtsev's efforts to encourage him to complete and publish his dissertation in 1910, i.e. to save his *opus magnum* (which he called τὸν πάλαι σπόρον) from oblivion, and to receive πόνου δ' ἄελπτον καρπόν, the unhoped-for new grain. In these lines Ivanov gives a *sui generis* poetical paraphrase of two famous parables in the New Testament, the *Parable of the sower* (Mark 4.3–8) and *Parable of the growing seed* (Mark 4.26–29).
III. Tadeusz Stefan (in Russian Faddey Frantsevich) Zieliński (1859–1944) was a classical philologist and professor at St Petersburg University (1890–1922) and then, at Warsaw University (1922–1939). Zieliński enriched Russian culture with his translations of ancient poetry, including the complete tragedies of Sophocles in 1914–1915, which are still considered classics. In his Greek epigram, Ivanov compares Zieliński to an ancient prophet, an interpreter of Apollo and Dionysus –

Zieliński, an extremely popular and charismatic lecturer on ancient religion and literature, and a brilliant translator and scholar, could be seen as a kind of mediator between antiquity and his contemporaries – and at the same time, he compares him to a mediaeval philosopher, Goethe's Faust who summoned Helen of Troy from Hades to partake of eternal beauties. The last lines seem to hint that Zieliński and Ivanov shared the idea of a new Renaissance of classical antiquity, this time in the Slavic world.

Biography: Vyacheslav Ivanovich Ivanov was a symbolist poet, a literary critic, a classical scholar, and a translator. He studied history, philology, and philosophy at the University of Moscow, and later, in 1886–1891, he was a student at the University of Berlin, where he attended lectures by Theodor Mommsen, Eduard Zeller, Ernst Curtius, and others, preparing his dissertation under Otto Hirschfeld. During his stay in Germany, he was influenced by the philosophy of Friedrich Nietzsche and the German Romantics. In his treatises on Dionysus *The Hellenic Religion of the Suffering God* (1904) and *Religion of Dionysus* (1905), he followed the ideas of Nietzsche's *The Birth of Tragedy*. In 1924, Ivanov emigrated from the Soviet Union to Rome, where he found a job *inter alia* as a professor of Old Church Slavonic at the *Collegium Russicum*. He died in 1949 and was buried at the Cimitero Acattolico. His translations of, e.g., Sappho, Alcaeus, Pindar, the almost complete tragedies of Aeschylus, and the sonnets of Petrarch, are still considered classics.

Bibliography: Ivanov, Vyacheslav (tr.) (1989) *Eskhil. Tragedii* [Aeschylus. Tragedies], ed. by Nikolay Balashov/Dmitry Ivanov/Mikhail Gasparov/Gasan Guseinov/Nikolai Kotrelev/Victor Jarcho, Moscow; Bongard-Levin, Grigory (1997), "M.I. Rostovtsev i Vyach. I. Ivanov" [M.I. Rostovtsev and Vyach. I. Ivanov], in: *Skifskii Roman* [Scythian Novel], Moscow, 248–258; Takho-Godi, Elena (2002), "Dve sudby nedarom svyazuet vidimaya nit" [A visible thread connects two destinies not by chance], in: Daniela Rizzi/Andrej Shishkin (eds.), *Archivio russo-italiano II. Collana di Europa Orientalis*, Salerno, 181–276 (Publication of the letters by F. Zieliński to V. Ivanov and the articles by F. Zieliński about V. Ivanov); Zieliński, Thadeusz (1933), "Poeta Odrodzenia Słowiańskiego: Więcysław Iwanow", in: *Pion*, Warszawa, 12; Zieliński, Thadeusz (2012), *Mein Lebenslauf*, ed. by Michael von Albrecht, Berlin; Lapo-Danilevsky, Konstantin (ed.) (2019), *Alkey i Sapfo v perevode Vyach. Ivanova* [Alcaeus and Sappho in translation by Vyach. Ivanov], St Petersburg. On his Greek poems: Ermolaeva, Elena (2019), "Grecheskoye poslaniye Vyach. Ivanova G.A. Rachinskomu" [The Greek poem by Vyach. Ivanov to G.A. Rachinsky], in: *Philologia Classica* 14/1, 121–130; Ermolaeva, Elena (2020), "Three Greek Poems by the Neohumanist Vyacheslav Ivanov (1866–1949)", in: Mika Kajava/Tua Korhonen/Jamie Vesterinen (eds.), *MEILICHA DÔRA. Poems and Prose in Greek from Renaissance and Early Modern Europe*, Helsinki, 333–348.

Iakob M. Borovsky (1896–1994)

I. ‹*De S. A. Zhebelevii studiis ante annos abhinc XLV inchoatis*› [1937]

Ἐτῶν τεσσαράκοντα πέντε κλεινῶν
δι' ὧν γράμμασιν ὧν φάος μέγιστον
πᾶσι τοῖς ἀγαθοῖς φέρεις μάθησιν,
πολλὴν ἀντίδοσιν δίκαιος ἦσθα,
5 ὦ διδάσκαλε, νῦν λαβεῖν παρ' ἡμῶν.
Ἀλλ' οὐκ ἄξια σοῦ πορεῖν ἔνεστιν.
Ἧττον δ' εἰ σθένομεν, τοσοῦτον ἴσθι
συγχαίροντας ὁμοῦ καὶ εὐσεβοῦντας
εὔχεσθαι περὶ σοῦ τὰ πάντ' ἄριστα.

Textus: Gavrilov, A.K. (2004), "Я.М. Боровский как редактор и поэт", in: *Philologia Classica* 6, 99–112: 110; Borovsky, Iakob M. (2009), *Opera Philologica*, St Petersburg, 425.

Sim.: 2 φάος μέγιστον] cf. Eur. *Bacch*. 608 ‖ 6 Ἀλλ' οὐκ ἄξια σοῦ] cf. Ael. Arist. *Πρεσβευτικὸς πρὸς Ἀχιλλέα* 23 (p. 807.11 Behr)

‹On the forty-fifth anniversary of S. A. Zhebelev's scholarly activities›

Since you have been bringing education to all who are noble for forty-five illustrious years, being the greatest light of learning, o master, it is fair that now [5] you should receive a big repayment from us. But it is impossible to deliver gifts worthy of you. Be sure, however, that even if we have inadequate strength, we wish you all the best, piously rejoicing together with you.

Metre: Phalaecians.

Notes: Sergei Aleksandrovich Zhebelev (1867–1941), a full member of the Russian/Soviet Academy of Sciences, was an eminent classical philologist and a historian of the ancient world, as well as a specialist in epigraphy and archaeology. He began his scholarly work in 1890 at the Museum of Antiquities of St Petersburg University, where he later became a professor. Borovsky was among his pupils.

II. Ἐπιτύμβιον *Salomoni Luriae* [1970]

Μὴ κλαύσητε, φίλοι, τὸν ἐμὸν τάφον· οὐκ ἐτεῇ γὰρ
ἐνθάδε νῦν κεῖμαι ὀστέα καὶ κονίη,
ἀλλά μευ ἀίδιον μετὰ πᾶσι νοήματα μίμνει
Ἑλλήνων σοφίην εὖ παραδεξαμένοις.

Textus: Luria, Salomon (ed.) (1970), *Democritea*, Leninopoli, 5, 618; Borovsky, Iakob M. (2009), *Opera Philologica*, St Petersburg, 448.

Sim.: 1 μὴ κλαύσητε] cf. LXX, *Ezechiel* 24. 23. 3 | ἐτεῇ] cf. Democr. fr. 49.7 DK || **2** ὀστέα καὶ κονίη] cf. *Anth. Pal.* 5.85.4; 7.284.4 (ὀστέα καὶ σποδιή(ν)); 8.229.1-2 (ὀστέα μοῦνα κεύθω καὶ σποδιὴν τοῖσιν ἐπερχομένοις) || **3–4** νοήματα...σοφίην εὖ παραδεξαμένοις] cf. Pind. *Ol.* 7.72 (σοφώτατα νοήματα...παραδεξαμένους)

Epitaph for Salomo Luria

Don't weep, friends, on my tomb, as, verily,
it is not me, the bones and ashes, that lie here now,
but my thoughts remain forever with all those
who received well the wisdom of the Greeks.

Metre: Elegiac couplets.

Notes: The epitaph for Professor Salomo Luria (1891–1964) was set in stone on Luria's grave at the cemetery of Lviv (Ukraine). Luria graduated from the Faculty of History and Philology of St Petersburg University in 1913, where he was a pupil of Sergey Zhebelev, Mikhail Rostovtsev, and Tadeusz Zieliński. He corresponded with Ulrich von Wilamowitz-Moellendorff (→ **Germany**), Michael Ventris and others. His broad scholarly interests, including the history of science and mathematics – from Babylonian times up to Bonaventura Cavalieri and Leonhard Euler, whom he translated into Russian – were reflected in his numerous books (*Anti-Semitism in the Ancient World*, Petrograd 1922; Berlin 1923; *The Infinitesimal Theory of the Ancient Atomists*, Moscow/Leningrad 1935, etc.) and in over two hundred articles. In 1949, Luria was accused of cosmopolitanism and expelled from the Academy of Sciences and the Department of Classical Philology of Leningrad University, where he had been working as a professor of ancient Greek. In 1953, Luria became professor at Lviv University in Ukraine. The main work of his life – the annotated fragments of Democritus (*Democritea*, Leninopoli 1970) – was published by his colleagues after his death together with Borovsky's epigram and its translation into Russian.

III. A.K. Gavrilov [1991]

Βιβλίον, Ὠλέξανδρε, τόδ' ἔστω σοι παρ' ἐμεῖο
σύμβολον ἀψευδὲς καλλιφυεῦς φιλίας
ἠδὲ προπεμπτικὸν εὖ μὲν ἐπ' ἠέρος ὔμμε πέτεσθαι,
εὖ δ' ἀπονοστῆσαι πολλὸν ἀεξομένους.

Textus: Borovsky, Iakob M. (2009), *Opera Philologica*, St Petersburg, 453.

Sim.: 2 καλλιφυεῦς] cf. Nonn. *Dion.* 5.198, 15.171, 16.76

For A.K. Gavrilov

This book, o Alexander, let it be for you from me
a sure proof of beautiful friendship,
and let it escort you in flying well through the air
and in coming back safely with much profit.

Metre: Elegiac couplets.

Notes: This is a dedication written in the book by Ulrich von Wilamowitz-Moellendorff, *Euripides Herakles* I–III, Darmstadt 1959 (repr. of the 1907 and 1895 editions), presented to Alexander Konstantinovich Gavrilov, Borovsky's student and colleague, on 3 May 1991, upon his departure for the USA with his wife and daughter for a year of study at the Institute for Advanced Study in Princeton. In 1993, Gavrilov went on to receive the New Europe Prize in Berlin and in the same year he founded the *Bibliotheca Classica Petropolitana*, an independent research centre and reference library, along with *Hyperboreus*, a journal for classical philology, and a Russian almanac *The Ancient World and Us* ('*Drevnii mir i my*'), which publishes studies in the history of classics and its heritage in Russia and Western Europe.

Biography: Iakob Markovich Borovsky was a professor at the Classics Department of St Petersburg University, a researcher, translator, and a Neo-Latin poet. 47 of his Latin poems and 12 Greek poems (written between 1935 and 1991, many after he turned 90) were published in: Eberle 1961, 23–25; *Carmina Latina recentiora*, Leichlingiae 1974, 225–226; journals such as *Vox Latina*, *Atene e Roma*, and *Greece & Rome*. The majority of these were occasional poems: jubilees (*In diem natalem Horati, In diem natalem Ovidi, Carmen natalicium Lomonosovianum*, ΕΙΣ ΠΕΝΤΗΚΟΝΤΑΕΤΙΑΝ ΦΙΛΟΛΟΓΙΚΗΣ ΕΡΓΑΣΙΑΣ ΣΕΡΓΙΟΥ ΖΕΒΕΛΕΦ, etc.), book inscriptions, dedications to his friends and colleagues (*Illustrissimo Hugoni Henrico Paoli*, 1962; *To M. von Albrecht*, 1992; ΑΛΕΞΙΑΙ ΘΕΟΔΩΡΙΔΟΥ ΔΙΔΑΣΚΑΛΩΙ ΣΟΦΩΤΑΤΩΙ ΕΥ ΠΡΑΤΤΕΙΝ, 1983, etc.).

Bibliography: Eberle, Iosephus (ed.) (1961), *Viva Camena. Latina huius aetatis carmina*. Cum commentariolo Iosephi et Linae IJsewijn-Jacobs ‚De litteris Latinis recentioribus', Turici et Stuttgardiae (pp. 23–26: selection of Borovsky's Latin poems, with a short biography on p. 201); Pacitti, Guerino (1962), "La predica di un filologo russo", in: *Studi romani* 10, 54–56; Borovskij, Iacob M. (1985), "Iacobus Borovskij, professor Leninopolitanus", in: *Vox Latina* 21, 80, 295; Borovsky, Iacob M. (1993), "URSS: De philologia Classica", in: *La filologia greca e latina nel secolo XX*, Vol. 2, Pisa, 789–796; Gavrilov, Aleksandr/Zelchenko Vsevolod/Shaburina Tatiana (eds.) (2009), I.M. Borovsky. *Opera Philologica*, St Petersburg; Gavrilov, Aleksandr (2010), "Trudy i dni J. M. Borovskogo" [Works and Days of I.M. Borovsky], in: Budaragina/Keyer/Verlinsky 2010, 158–192; Gavrilov, Aleksander (2013), "Jakov M. Borovski, pesnik latinščine v Sovjetski zvezi" [Jakov M. Borovskij: Poet of Latin in the Soviet Union"] (transl. by Sonja Zupančič), in: *Keria: Studia Latina et Graeca* XV/2, 23–34.

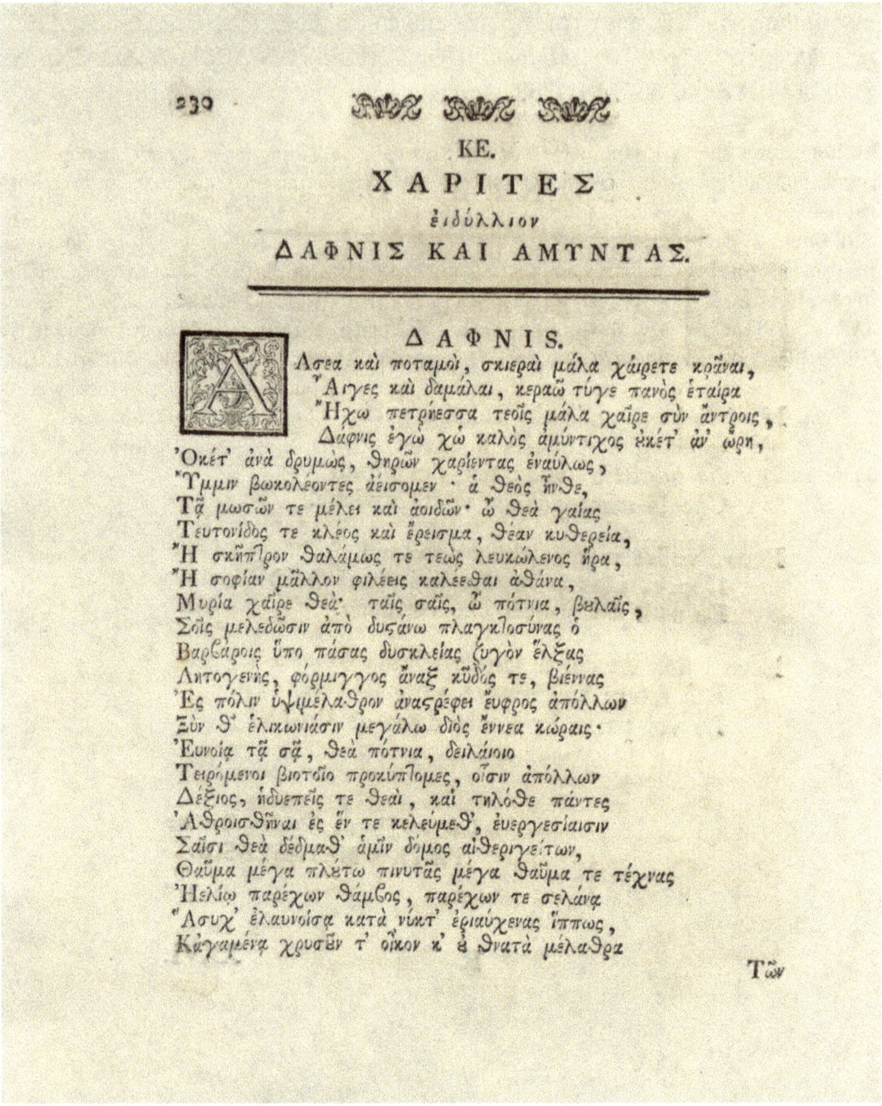

ΚΕ.
ΧΑΡΙΤΕΣ
ειδύλλιον
ΔΑΦΝΙΣ ΚΑΙ ΑΜΥΝΤΑΣ.

ΔΑΦΝΙΣ.

Άσεα καὶ ποταμοὶ, σκιεραὶ μάλα χαίρετε κρᾶναι,
Ἄιγες καὶ δαμάλαι, κεραῷ τύγε πανὸς ἑταίρα
Ἠχὼ πετρήεσσα τεοῖς μάλα χαῖρε σὺν ἄντροις,
Δαφνὶς ἐγὼ χὠ καλὸς ἀμύντιχος ἐκετ' ἀϋ ὤρη,
Οκέτ' ἀνὰ δρυμὼς, θηρῶν χαρίεντας ἐναύλως,
Ὕμμιν βωκολέοντες ἀείσομεν· ἁ θεὸς ἴν θε,
Τᾷ μωσῶν τε μέλει καὶ ἀοιδῶν· ὦ θεὰ γαίας
Τευτονίδος τε κλέος καὶ ἔρεισμα, θεὰν κυθερεία,
Ἡ σκῆπρον θαλάμως τε τεὼς λευκώλενος ἦρα,
Ἡ σοφίαν μᾶλλον φιλέεις καλέεσθαι ἀθάνα,
Μυρία χαῖρε θεά· ταῖς σαῖς, ὦ πότνια, βελαῖς,
Σοῖς μελεδῶσιν ἀπὸ δυσάνω πλαγκλοσύνας ὁ
Βαρβάροις ὑπὸ πάσας δυσκλείας ζυγὸν ἔλξας
Λητογενής, φόρμιγγος ἄναξ κυδὺς τε, βιέννας
Ἐς πόλιν ὑψιμέλαθρον ἀναςρέφει εὐφρος ἀπόλλων
Σὺν θ' ἑλικωνιάσιν μεγάλω διὸς ἐννεα κώραις·
Εὐνοίᾳ τᾷ σᾷ, θεὰ πότνια, δειλάιοιο
Τειρόμενοι βιοτοῖο προκύπτομες, οἷσιν ἀπόλλων
Δέξιος, ἠδυεπείς τε θεαὶ, καὶ τηλόθε πάντες
Ἀθροισθῆναι ἐς ἕν τε κελεύμεσθ', εὐεργεσίαισιν
Σαῖσι θεὰ δέδμαθ' ἁμὶν ὅμως αἰθερηγείτων,
Θαῦμα μέγα πλέτω πινυτᾶς μέγα θαῦμα τε τέχνας
Ἠελίω παρέχων θάμβος, παρέχων τε σελάνα
Ἀσυχ' ἐλαυνοίσᾳ κατὰ νύκτ' ἐριαύχενας ἵππως,
Κἀγαμένα χρυσέῶν τ' οἶκον κ' ἁ θνατὰ μέλαθρα

Τῶν

Fig. 14: First page of Kollár's poem *Charites* (see below, p. 698–707) from Franz Christoph Scheyb (ed.) (1756), *Musae Francisco et Mariae Theresiae augustis congratulantur ob scientias, bonasque artes eorum iussu et munificentia Vindobonae restitutas*, Vindobonae, p. 130. Photo: Österreichische Nationalbibliothek, Vienna.

William M. Barton, Martin M. Bauer, and Martin Korenjak
Austria

Austria within its present borders has existed only since 1919. Before that, its respective regions belonged to the much larger Habsburg Monarchy. Its history and development were intertwined with that of the other parts of this political entity, notably Hungary and Bohemia.

The preconditions for the development of a 'neo-ancient' Greek literature were less promising in Austria than in other European countries in two respects: First, while the Reformation gained some ground in many parts of the Habsburg Monarchy during the 16th century, it was resolutely suppressed and ultimately marginalised by the rulers. By and large, the Habsburg lands either remained Catholic or soon reverted to Catholicism. For this reason, the reformatory enthusiasm for Greek as the language of the New Testament was scarcely seen in Austria. After the Council of Trent had decided that the Latin *Vulgata* should remain the fundamental text of Catholicism, deeper study of the Greek New Testament and of Greek in general became less of a priority. Second, Austria had virtually no tradition of learned Greek philology of the kind that flourished in Italy, the Netherlands, Germany, France, and England, where many learned men acquired an intimate knowledge of the language of the ancient Greeks.[1] All in all, then, ancient Greek received but little attention in early modern Austria. The onset of German new humanism ('Neuhumanismus') in the later 18th century[2] eventually brought a change, but this trend, too, originated in the Protestant world and caught on in Austria only with some delay and in attenuated form.

None of the above is to say that there were no possibilities at all to learn ancient Greek in the centuries before. Regular instruction in that language had been provided at the University of Vienna by a *Graecarum literarum professor* since 1523.[3] From the second half of the 16th century, the Jesuits opened a number of schools in Austria (Vienna 1553, Innsbruck 1562, Graz 1573, Klagenfurt 1604 etc.). Their syllabus, the generally mandatory *Ratio Studiorum*, which was issued in a preliminary form in 1582 and in its definitive form in 1599,[4] prescribed five to seven years of Greek for every student of a Jesuit school. However, such Greek

---

1 Cf. Pfeiffer 1982.
2 Cf. Blankertz/Matthiessen 2001.
3 See Gastgeber 2012, 109.
4 See Lukács 1986 and → **General Introduction**.

school exercises as have been preserved[5] demonstrate that the pupils' actual command of Greek remained far below their command of Latin. Over the centuries, the *Ratio* served as a model for the syllabuses of other orders such as the Benedictines or Piarists, and therefore provided some Greek education in their schools, too. A higher level was reached when the state gradually took over the educational system and initiated a series of reforms, which were in part inspired by the ideas of German new humanism and therefore tended to promote Greek, in the later 18th and early 19th centuries.[6] In humanist gymnasia, Greek was among the most important disciplines. Over the following decades and centuries, however, its role in the curriculum was gradually eroded, especially after the Second World War. Today, Greek is an optional school subject at best, while it is still an established discipline at university.

As the composition of poetry requires accomplished levels of control and understanding of the respective language, it comes as no surprise that the development of Austro-Greek poetry reflects to some degree the aforementioned trends in religious and educational history. In the earlier periods, publications of Greek verse appear to be even scarcer than the rather unhelpful preconditions would lead one to expect. (What may exist in manuscript is unknown at present except for some chance finds.) Moreover, Greek prints seem to have been restricted to Vienna until the 19th century. In fact, we have been able to discover only one slim volume of Greek poetry for the whole of the 16th century. This publication, Georg Fabricius' and **Andreas Charopus'** Ἐπιθαλάμια (1563), clearly was an offshoot of the vogue for Greek studies in Germany initiated by Melanchthon (→ **Germany**), as it was dedicated to the latter's pupil Georg Tanner, who himself taught Greek at the University of Vienna. After that, scarcely any pertinent material is to be detected until the middle of the 18th century, when **Adam František Kollár** (1718–1783) published a Greek idyll in a collected volume in honour of Maria Theresia and her husband Emperor Francis I (1756). Again, this remained quite an isolated phenomenon. At least Kollár's Greek (as also that of his later followers from the 19th century onwards) contrasts favourably with Charopus' often hopelessly erroneous language.

At the end of the 18th century and the beginning of the 19th, some volumes of Greek poetry were published in Vienna quite independently of native Austrian developments. At that time, a community of several hundred Greek immigrants,

---

[5] For prose and poetry respectively, see Korenjak/Schaffenrath/Šubarić/Töchterle 2012, 302–303 and 401.
[6] See the index of Engelbrecht 1984, 538 s.v. 'Griechisch'.

mostly merchants, had settled in the capital and developed some noteworthy literary activity. For several decades, Vienna became the most important printing place of what is known today as the Greek Enlightenment. Publishers of Greek descent, such as Georgios Vendotis and the brothers Poulios, alongside local publishing houses printed Greek newspapers, calendars, and political pamphlets as well as translations of German, French, Italian and English works.[7] For their authors, ancient Greek was not a newly-discovered language learned from grammars and the perusal of the ancient classics, but an older variety of their everyday speech. What they wrote was not always neo-ancient Greek in the sense in which this term is used in the present volume, but rather occupied various points on a scale between classical Greek and an early version of the 'katharevousa'. For poetry, however, classical Greek was apparently preferred. Dimitrios Karakassis, a Greek doctor from Bucharest, published five books of medical didactic poetry in iambic trimeters and dactylic hexameters along with various other poems, all with facing Latin translation (Ποιημάτια ἰατρικά, Vienna 1795). The Ὀρθόδοξος ὑμνῳδὸς ἤτοι ἱερὰ φιλοσοφία ἐν μέτροις Πινδαρικοῖς (Vienna 1802) by Sergios Makraios was a collection of religious hymns in Pindaric metres.

The majority of genuinely Austrian poems in ancient Greek, in contrast, were inspired by the arrival of German new humanism in the 19th century. From the middle of that century to the beginning of the 20th, a number of schoolmen successfully tried their pen at various genres of Greek poetry. The Tyrolian Franciscan friar **Bernhard Niedermühlbichler** (1798–1850) not only appended a number of Greek epigrams – the first Greek poems known to us that were printed outside Vienna – to a collection of Latin ones (1844), but also issued an extensive volume of mostly sacred Greek poetry in an astonishing variety of metres (1847). **Ludwig Mayr**'s (1851–1944) charming crossover of *laudes urbium* and didactic epic on the city of Graz was one of the few Greek poems from Austria to make it through more than one edition (1897, ²1902). The well-known lexicographer **Josef M. Stowasser** (1854–1910) translated the anthem of the Danube Monarchy into Greek elegiacs (1902). He did the same with many so-called 'Schnadahüpfeln', a traditional form of improvised verse from the Austro-Bavarian region, in order to demonstrate the latter's functional equivalence with the elegiac couplet (*Griechische Schnadahüpfeln*, Vienna/Leipzig 1903).

With the decline of Greek in the 20th and 21st centuries, the number of scholars willing and able to perform such feats of linguistic prowess also diminished. Nonetheless, the scholarly and academic tradition of writing neo-ancient Greek verse has continued until recently in the work of such gifted individuals as Paul

---

7 Cf. Polioudakis 2008, 120–134.

Raimund Lorenz from the University of Vienna. If poems such as his birthday congratulation to his colleague Kurt Smolak[8] or his partial translation from the neo-Latin *Fasti Austriae* in celebration of the 16th congress of the *International Association for Neo-Latin Studies* in Vienna[9] have been the swansong of the Austro-Greek muse, only time will tell.

General Bibliography

Blankertz, Herwig/Matthiessen, Kjeld (2001), "Neuhumanismus", in: Dieter Lenzen (ed.), *Pädagogische Grundbegriffe*, 6th ed., Reinbek, vol. 2, 1092–1103.

Engelbrecht, Helmut (1984), *Geschichte des österreichischen Bildungswesens: Erziehung und Unterricht auf dem Boden Österreichs*, vol. 3: Von der frühen Aufklärung bis zum Vormärz, Vienna.

Gastgeber, Christian (2012), "Der Beginn der Griechischstudien im Wiener Humanismus an der Wende vom 15. zum 16. Jahrhundert", in: *Sborník Národního Muzea v Praze / Acta Musei Nationalis Pragae, series C: Historia Litterarum* 57, 103–109.

Korenjak, Martin/Schaffenrath, Florian/Šubarić, Lav/Töchterle, Karlheinz (eds.) (2012), *Tyrolis Latina. Geschichte der lateinischen Literatur in Tirol*, Vienna et al.

Lukács, Ladislaus (ed.) (1986), *Ratio atque institutio studiorum (1586, 1591, 1599)*, Rome.

Pfeiffer, Rudolf (1982), *Die Klassische Philologie von Petrarca bis Mommsen*, Munich.

Polioudakis, Georgios (2008), *Die Übersetzung deutscher Literatur ins Neugriechische vor der Griechischen Revolution von 1821*, Frankfurt a. M. et al.

Römer, Franz/Bannert, Herbert/Klecker, Elisabeth/Gastgeber, Christian (eds.) (2015), *Fasti Austriae 1736: Ein neulateinisches Gedicht in fünfzehn europäischen Sprachen*, Vienna.

---

8 See *Wiener Studien* 122, 2009, 4–5.
9 Römer et al. 2015, 40–43.

Andreas Charopus (fl. 1561–1569)

I. Ἐγκώμιον τῆς συζυγίας [1563]

Ἔστιν ἀρειότερον ζώειν εὐσχήμονα ἤπερ
ἀγλευκῆ κρυερὸν καὶ θεῷ εἶναι ἀεί.
Συγγαμίης καθαρῆς μοῦνος βίος ἔμπεδός ἐστι
καὶ πολὺς οὐ νικῶν πρὸς κακότητα βροτούς.
5 Ὄλβια πολλὰ πατὴρ ἀνδρῶν τε θεῶν τε δίδωσι
τοίοις, οἵ τ' ἀγανοὶ ὄντες ἄγουσι βίον.
Τοῖς πόρνοισι δ' ἀραῖα καὶ ἄλγεα μυρία βάλλει,
τοῦ Ἄϊδος φρικτοὺς καρχαλίους τε λύκους.

II. *Aliud* [sc. *epithalamium*] *Andreae Charopi Longeleusini Austrii*

Ἔννεπε Μοῦσα ἐμοί, τῷ νῦν τέρπονται ἅπαντες
ἐν τοῖς ἄστρασιν οἵ γε θεοὶ καὶ ἔπαρσιν ἔχοντες
(αἱ Χάριτες δὴ συγγαμίας σημεῖα διδοῦσι).
Αὐτὸς ὁ γὰρ Κρονίδης ὑψίζυγος αἰθέρι ναίων
5 καὶ σκηπτοῦχος ἐν εὐδένδρῳ παραδείσῳ Ὀλύμπου
τοῦ λαμπροῦ, πάντων ὁ πατὴρ ἀνδρῶν τε θεῶν τε,
τοὺς συνυπάρχοντάς τε χοροϊτυπός ἐστι φιληδῶν.
Ἡ Κύπρις δὲ χορεύει ὁμοῦ καὶ Παλλὰς Ἀθήνη,
ἀλλὰ θεὰ πρώτην Εὐρώπια τάξιν ἄγει τε
10 σκαίρουσ', ἄστρα κυβερνῶντες λοιποὶ δὲ ἕπονται.
Ταῦτα τί μὲν θέλει, ἔννεπέ μοι, δεδαῶσα Θάλεια·
ἆρα παρ' ἅμμιν ὅτ' ἐστί τις, ᾧ νεφεληγερέτα Ζεύς
εὔχεται, οὐρανόθεν ῥὰ γυναῖκά τε καλλιπάρειον
ἐγκατάζευγε, φιλῶν σπουδαίους ἄνδρας ἀληθῶς;
15 – Ναί. – Τίνι; – Ταννήρῳ ἀγαθῷ τε καλῷ τε Γεοργῷ,
ὃν σοφίας στέφανον καὶ δῶρα σεβαστὰ φέροντα
θαυμάζει καὶ ἔτιε Βιενναῖόν γε μὲν ἄστυ,
καῖσαρ ὅπου σὺν τῷ βασιλεῖ παῖδές τε καὶ αὐτῶν
καὶ πολλοὶ βίον ὑψηλόφρονες αἰὲν ἄγουσι
20 ἄρχοντες πᾶσαν γαῖαν δῆμόν τε ταγαῖον.
– Ἔνθα καὶ εἰπέ μοι, οἷαν ἔδωκε τῷ ἀνέρι νύμφην
παντοκράτωρ ὁ θεός· μῶν ὡρική ἐστι καὶ ἁβρά;
– Ἔστι. – Ὅπως αὐτὴν δὲ καλεῖτε; – Ἐναισίμη Ἄννα.
– Ἆρά γε παρθένος; – Οὐχ, ὅτι καὶ πρόσθεν τινὰ εἶχε
25 ἰητρόν, πολλῶν τῶν ἀνδρ' ἀντάξιον ἄλλων,
μουσικτὴν ἔξαλλον, ὃν ἀγλαόμορφος Ἀπόλλων
κοσμήσας χαρίεν μεγάλου Κρονίδεω διὰ βουλάς

νῦν βλέπει ἐν κοίλῳ, πρός τ' ἀλλήλους γε ἀδελφοί
κοινολογοῦνται, ἐν ὑψίστοις ἀγαπῶντες ἐόντα
30 καὶ δοξάζοντες Χριστὸν κλείουσιν ἀοιδαῖς.
– Εὖγε, σοὶ εὐχόμενος, Τάννηρε, διδάσκαλε λῷστε,
συγχαίρω τε καταντιβολῶ εὐήμερα πολλά.
οὐκ ἐν συζυγίᾳ, σύ γε νυμφίε καὶ σύ γε νύμφη,
συμβαίνῃ θ' ὑμῖν κακὰ ἤ τ' ἀποτεύγματα ὦσι.
35 Ἄξιος εἶ τε τεῆς ταύτης ὁμοδεμνίου αἰεί,
ἣν ἀρεταὶ μεγάλαι ποτέ σοί γε ἔτικτον ἐν αὐτῷ
οὐνόματ' εὐσεβέος Χριστοῦ πανακοῦς τε Θεοῦ τε,
ὅς ῥα τεὴν νύμφην, τεὰ σώματα καί σε ἀνέξει,
ῥυσκόμενος σώσει, ὑπερασπίζων τε φυλάξει
40 καὶ παισὶν σέ γε οὐκ ὀλίγοις πόρρωθεν ἀμείψει.
Ἄξιος εἶ ταύτης νύμφης, Τάννηρε, καὶ αὕτη
ἀξία ἐστὶ τεῶν ἀρετῶν ἤθους τε σεβαστοῦ·
ὡς ἢ ἐερσήεσσα ἔῃ, μὴ γλῶττα ἐμεῖο
ῥητρεύειν δύναται· σύ γε σπουδαῖός τε καὶ ἐσθλός·
45 οὐ μὴ δικολόγος Κικέρων ἢ φέρτερος Ὀρφεύς
Ὑβλητῶν ἢ Κεκροπίδαι οἱ ἀνέρες ἠέ
ἔννοος ὧδε Μάρων τε καὶ οὔποτε ὧδε Περικλῆς
καὶ πάντες βάζειν Ἕλληνές τ' ἀρκετοί εἰσι.
Αὐτὸς ὁ γὰρ Φοῖβος σὺν ταῖς σέ γε ἐννέα Μούσαις
50 καὶ Χάριτες χρησταὶ κόσμησαν ἀναρρίπτοντες,
πότνιά τοι Πειθὼ θεὰ καὶ γλαυκῶπις Ἀθήνη
τῶν ἀρετῶν ἀγανὸν σοφίας καὶ ἐφήρμοσε κόσμον.
Ἐντεῦθεν γίνεταί σοι, τοὔνεκα ταῦτα δίδωσι
τέκμορα γομφοπαγοῦς ναὶ μὴν αἴνοιο Φίλιππος,
55 οὔνομα ὃς περὶ τῆς δαερᾶς γῆς εἶχε Μελάγχθων
καὶ πολλοί θ' ἕτεροι ἄνδρες πανάριστοι, ἔγωγε
ὧν ἀθέλω καταριθμεῖσθαί ῥα συνώνυμα ἤδη.
Οὐδεὶς γὰρ δύναται τὸ ποιεῖν κατὰ χεῖρα καὶ ἆσσον,
κύριος ἀλλὰ θεός τε καὶ ἄγγελοι αὐτοῦ ἅπαντες,
60 οἳ μέτροις κρείττουσι ποτὲ ψήλωσιν ἐν ἄστροις,
ποῖά σοι ἀθανάτου σοφίας καρπώματα, νυμφῶν,
καί τ' ἀρετῆς θείως φανερᾶς ἐγκώμια δῶκαν.
Ταῦτά σοι ἔγραφον εὐχόμενος τοῖς πράγμασι σεῖο
πάντ' ἀπὸ οὐρανίοιο πατρός τε καὶ υἱοῦ αὐτοῦ,
65 ὃν διὰ σωσάμενοι ζῶμεν μακαρώτατα. Χαῖρε
καὶ σὺν τῇ νύμφῃ βιοθάλμιος οὖλε φιλητῇ.

Textus: Fabricius, Georg/Charopus, Andreas (1563), *Ἐπιθαλάμια εἰς τοὺς τοῦ Γεωργίου Ταννήρου...καὶ τῆς...Ἄννας...γάμους, ἀπὸ τοῖν αὐτοῦ ἀκροάταιν καὶ μαθηταῖν τοῦ Γεωργίου Φαβρικίου Παλατεινοῦ καὶ Ἀνδρείου Χαροποῦ Αὐστρίου...Epithalamia in nuptias...Georgii Tanneri...ac...Annae...a Georgio Fabricio Palatino et Andrea Charopo Longeleusino Austrio...conscripta*, Viennae Austriae: excudebat Michael Zimmermann, cc. A1v, A3v–4r.

Crit.: Orthographiam, spiritus, accentus, interpunctionem plerumque tacite nostrae aetatis normis accommodavi, soloecismos et errores morphologicos metricosque autem non correxi, graviores in apparatu commemoravi.
I. 5 Τοίοις et ἀγανοί scripsi: Τοιατί et ἀγ- ed.
II. 7 χοροιτύπος debuit || **9 τε**] sensu caret, metri causa tantum insertum videtur || **10** λοιποί scripsi: λοιπαί ed. || **11** τί μὲν θέλει scripsi: τι ἐνθέλει ed. | δεδαυῖα debuit || **12** ὅτ' scripsi: ὅ ed. || **15** Γεωργῷ debuit || **17** ἔτιε scripsi: ἐταῖε ed. || **18** ὅπου scripsi: ὁποῦ ed. | αὐτῶν scripsi: ἀντῶν ed. || **19** ὑψηλόφρονες scripsi: ἠψθλόφρονες ed. || **21** οἷαν ἔδωκε] οἷαν δῶκε debuit || **24** εἶχε scripsi: οὖχε ed., poeta fortasse per composita in -οὖχος exeuntia decepto || **31 (et 41)** Ταννηρέ ed., correxi || **32** καὶ ἀντιβολῶ possis || **50** ἀναρρίπτοντες scripsi: -ρύπτ- ed. || **51** γλαυκῶπις scripsi: γρ- ed. || **55** εἶχε scripsi: ἦχε ed. || **60** κρείττουσι] inauditum, perperam ex κρείττοσι creatum || **63** σοι scripsi: σοῖο ed.

Sim.: I. 2 ἀγλευκῆ] vox pedestris || **3** συγγαμίης] cf. Hsch. σ 2685 | βίος ἔμπεδός ἐστι] cf. Greg. Naz. *Carm.*, PG 37.1427.13 (μούνης δὲ ζωῆς καθαρῆς βίος ἔμπεδος αἰεί) || **5** πατὴρ ἀνδρῶν τε θεῶν τε] formula epica (e.g. Hom. *Il.* 1.544) || **7** ἄλγεα μύρια] cf. Hom. *Il.* 1.2 (μυρί' Ἀχαιοῖς ἄλγε' ἔθηκε) || **8** καρχαλίους τε λύκους] cf. Triph. 615
II. 1 Ἔννεπε Μοῦσα ἐμοί] cf. Hom. *Od.* 1.1 (ἄνδρα μοι ἔννεπε, Μοῦσα) || **4** Κρονίδης ὑψίζυγος, αἰθέρι ναίων] formula epica (e.g. Hom. *Il.* 4.166, Hes. *Op.* 18), cuius partes et separatim occurrunt || **5** ἐν εὐδένδρῳ παραδείσῳ] cf. Nonn. *Par. Jo.* 3.86 || **6** πατὴρ ἀνδρῶν τε θεῶν τε] v. supra I.5 || **7** φιληδῶν] poeta cum accusativo coniungit || **9** Εὐρώπια] ex Hesychio ε 7163, qui aliud nomen Iunonis esse affirmat || **11** ἔννεπέ μοι] v. supra 1 || **12** νεφεληγερέτα Ζεύς] formula epica (e.g. Hom. *Il.* 1.511) || **13** γυναῖκα τε καλλιπάρειον] epithetum (quod hic perperam scribitur) in sermone epico saepe pulchritudinem femineam designat (e.g. Hom. *Il.* 1.143 Χρυσηΐδα καλλιπάρηον) || **14** ἐγκατάζευγε] verbum ex Soph. *Aj.* 736 sumptum || **15** ἀγαθῷ τε καλῷ τε] iuncturam καλὸς κἀγαθός variat || **16** σοφίας στέφανον] cf. Ar. *Av.* 1274 || **20** cf. fort. Hom. *Od.* 8.555 | ταγαῖον ex Hesychio τ 12 (sed primum α longum esse oportebat) || **21** Ἔνθα καὶ εἰπέ μοι] initium carminis respicit, v. ad 1 || **22** παντοκράτωρ] vox sermone Christiano usitatissima || **25** ἰητρόν, πολλῶν τῶν ἄνδρ' ἀντάξιον ἄλλων] ex Hom. *Il.* 9.401 (ἰητρὸς γὰρ ἀνὴρ πολλῶν ἀντάξιος ἄλλων) || **26** μουσικήν] ex Hsch. μ 1750 | ἀγλαόμορφος Ἀπόλλων] cf. *Anth. Pal.* 9.525.2 || **27** μεγάλου Κρονίδεω διὰ βουλάς] contaminatio formularum epicarum Διὸς μεγάλου διὰ βουλάς (e.g. Hes. *Theog.* 465) et Κρονίδεω διὰ βουλάς (e.g. Hes. *Op.* 71) || **28** κοίλῳ] i.e. coelo || **30** κλείουσιν ἀοιδαῖς] cf. Hes. *Theog.* 44 || **32** καταντιβολῶ] ex Ar. fr. 603 K.-A., cf. Poll. 1.26; sensum verbi distorquet poeta || **35** ὁμοδεμνίου] cf. Aesch. *Ag.* 1108 et Musae. 70 || **39** ῥυσκόμενος] de verbo cf. *Il.* 24.730 || **43** ἐερσήεσσα] adi. ex Hom. *Il.* 24.419 || **44** ῥητρεύειν] verbum ex Lycoph. *Alex.* 1400 || **46** ὑβλητῶν] ex Hesychio υ 30 || **51** γλαυκῶπις Ἀθήνη] iunctura epica (e.g. Hom. *Il.* 1.204) || **54** γομφοπαγοῦς] ex Ar. *Ra.* 824 (ῥήματα γομφοπαγῆ), ubi Aeschyli sermo irridetur || ναὶ μήν] cf. *Anth. Pal.* 7.541.5, sicut hic ad laudem augendam || **55** δαερᾶς] ex Hesychio δ 30 || **57** ἀθέλω] (i.e. nolo) a poeta perperam inventum || **59** κύριος ἀλλὰ θεός τε καὶ ἄγγελοι] sermo Christianus || **66** βιοθάλμιος] ex *Hymn. Hom. Ven.* 189

Praise of the marriage

It is better to live in good order than to live savagely and always be odious to God. Only life in pure marriage is steady and as a rule does not win people over to wickedness. [5] Many riches the father of men and gods gives to those who lead their life gently. But to the whoremongers, he flings down numberless curses and sufferings, as well as the terrible, fierce wolves of the Netherworld.

Another [marriage song], by Andreas Charopus from Langenlois, an Austrian

Tell me, Muse: What are all the gods in the stars now so joyful and full of elation (as the Charites give signs of a marriage)? For the son of Kronos [scil. Zeus] himself, who sits on a high throne, lives in the ether and [5] holds the sceptre in the paradise-garden of luminous Olympus with its beautiful trees, the father of all men and gods, he is beating a dancing rhythm and delighting those who are with him. Cypris [scil. Aphrodite] and Pallas Athene are likewise dancing. But the skipping goddess Europia [scil. Hera] is leading the first row, [10] and the other gods who govern the stars are following her. What does this mean? Tell me, Thalia, because you know it. Is this because there is someone among us to whom Zeus, the gatherer of clouds, wishes all the best and with whom, from his seat in the sky, he has coupled a woman of fair cheeks, because he truly loves good men? [15] – Yes! – With whom? – With the good and handsome Georg Tanner, whom, with his garland of wisdom and his venerable gifts, the city of Vienna admires and honours – Vienna, where the Emperor with the king, their children and many high-minded men always lead their life, [20] reigning over the whole land and its obedient people. – At this point, tell me also, what sort of a girl God, the almighty, has given to the man? Is she in her prime and pretty? – Yes! – What is her name? – Righteous Anna. – And is she a virgin? – No, since previously she had a [25] physician, a man worth many others, a special friend of the Muses: Apollo, the god with shining body, has honoured him delightfully according to the plans of Kronos' great son [scil. Zeus] and now looks at him in the sky, and the brothers converse with each other; they love [30] and celebrate with songs Christ who is in the uppermost place. – Bravo, I pray for you, Tanner, best teacher, I share your joy and wish you many happy tidings. May you not, while you, groom, and you, bride, are married, experience bad things, and may there be no failures. [35] You are always worthy of your bedmate here, who was once generated for you by the great virtues in the very name of pious Christ and of the all-healing God, who will sustain your bride, your body and yourself, who will give you shelter and keep you safe, will keep his shield over you and protect you [40] and will reward you with not just a few children in the future. You are worthy of this girl, Tanner, and she is worthy of your virtues and your venerable character. How dew-fresh she is, my tongue cannot tell. You in turn are good and noble. [45] Certainly, not even Cicero, the advocate, or Orpheus, who is better than all seers, or the men who descend from Cecrops [Athenians], or wise Maro [Vergil] and Pericles and all the Greeks – they would never be able to express this fittingly. Phoebus himself with the nine Muses [50] and the skillful Graces have honoured and exalted you and lady Peitho [goddess of persuasion] and the owl-eyed goddess Athena have equipped you with the illustrious adornment of the virtues and wisdom. For this reason it happens to you, that Philipp, [55] who has got his name 'Melanchthon' from the black earth, verily gives you these firm testimonies of praise, as do also many other very excellent men, whose names I do not want to enumerate any longer. For nobody can do this [i.e. praise you] easily and quickly, only God the Lord and all His angels, [60] who once will sing to the accompaniment of the lyre in better metres, what profit of deathless wisdom, o groom, and what eulogies of your evident virtue they have divinely given to you. That's what I have written, praying for your affairs all the best from the Father in Heaven and his Son, [65] saved by whom we live most happily. Goodbye, live hale and hearty with your beloved bride!

Metre: Elegiac couplets (I), hexameters (II). In a free extension of Homeric usage, hiatus is admitted after a final short vowel (e.g. ll. 1, 10, 23, 24, 28 of the *epithalamium*), and a final long vowel is not shortened in this position (e.g. ll. 15, 32). In l. 21, the second syllable of οἶαν (debuit οἴαν) is shortened *metri causa*. In l. 53, there is a diaeresis after the third foot. Also note the *spondiacus* in l. 50.

Notes: Together with the introductory epigram, Andreas Charopus' *epithalamium* for his teacher of Greek Georg Tanner is the first specimen of Greek poetry on record to have been published by an Austrian author in Austria (the other *epithalamium* in the slim volume is by the Palatinate Georg Fabricius, 1516–1571). While the epigram praises marriage in general, the *epithalamium* focuses on the wedding at hand. In doing so, it neatly falls into two parts. In the first (ll. 1–30), the poet asks the Muse Thalia why all gods of the Greek pantheon are happy and excited, and having learned that it is because of Tanner's marriage, he inquires further about the circumstances of the event. In part two (ll. 31–66), Charopus turns toward the groom and apostrophises him directly, heaping praise on him and his bride, an otherwise unknown widow named Anna. This praise culminates – confessional differences notwithstanding – in Philipp Melanchthon's enthusiasm for Tanner (who had been his disciple in Wittenberg). The poem ends with good wishes for the couple's future matrimony. The poem's structure is thus fairly standard, combining elements ultimately derived from Statius and Claudian in a way that is redolent of a multitude of early modern *epithalamia*. The Greek is not standard, however. It is so full of lexical, syntactical (esp. aleatory use of particles, irrational use of subjunctive), and metrical errors that the editor has a hard time deciding what he should let stand and what he should correct. In spite of Charopus' best efforts to please his teacher of Greek by writing a Greek poem, he only succeeded in showing how far 16th-century Austria lagged behind countries like Italy and Germany in this respect.

Biography: Andreas Charopus called himself 'Langoleusensis' and, with a fanciful allusion to ancient Eleusis, 'Longeleusinus', in his publications. On 11 July 1567, he was crowned as *poeta laureatus* on behalf of Emperor Maximilian II. His published œuvre comprises over a dozen panegyrical poems. Most of these are short contributions to collections, but in two cases, he was sole and main author respectively, and in two others one of two authors. With two exceptions (Frankfurt 1575, Leipzig 1599), all publications in which he participated appeared between 1561 and 1569 in Vienna. One can thus reasonably surmise that he lived in that city during the 1560s and was well connected there. The full title of our publication attests that he was a disciple of its addressee Georg Tanner who taught Greek at the University of Vienna. Moreover, he was likely to have been friends with Paulus Melissus Schede (1539–1602), with whom he not only shared pages in many volumes, but also published three volumes in tandem. Perhaps Charopus was roughly the same age as his more famous colleague. Apart from the diploma attesting to his coronation and his publication record, his life seems to have left no further traces.

Bibliography: Flood, John L. (2006), *Poets Laureate in the Holy Roman Empire. A Bio-bibliographical Handbook* (4 vols.), Berlin, vol. 1, 313–314.

[MK]

Adam František Kollár (1718–1783)

Χάριτες, εἰδύλλιον [1756]

ΔΑΦΝΙΣ ΚΑΙ ΑΜΥΝΤΑΣ

ΔΑ. Ἄλσεα καὶ ποταμοί, σκιεραὶ μάλα χαίρετε κρᾶναι,
αἶγες καὶ δαμάλαι, κεραῶ τύγε Πανὸς ἑταίρα,
Ἠχὼ πετρήεσσα, τεοῖς μάλα χαῖρε σὺν ἄντροις·
Δάφνις ἐγὼ χὠ καλὸς Ἀμύντιχος οὐκέτ᾽ ἂν᾽ ὤρη,
5 οὐκέτ᾽ ἀνὰ δρυμώς, θηρῶν χαρίεντας ἐναύλως,
ὔμμιν βωκολέοντες ἀείσομεν· ἁ θεὸς ἦνθε,
τᾷ Μωσῶν τε μέλει καὶ ἀοιδῶν· ὦ θεὰ γαίας
Τευτονίδος τε κλέος καὶ ἔρεισμα, θέαν Κυθερεία,
ἢ σκῆπτρον θαλάμως τε τεὼς λευκώλενος Ἥρα,
10 ἢ σοφίαν μᾶλλον φιλέεις καλέεσθαι Ἀθάνα,
μυρία χαῖρε, θεά· ταῖς σαῖς, ὦ πότνια, βουλαῖς,
σαῖς μελεδῶσιν ἀπὸ δυστάνω πλαγκτοσύνας ὁ
βαρβάροις ὑπὸ πάσας δυσκλείας ζυγὸν ἕλξας
Λητογενής, φόρμιγγος ἄναξ κῦδός τε, Βιέννας
15 ἐς πόλιν ὑψιμέλαθρον ἀναστρέφει εὔφρος Ἀπόλλων
ξύν θ᾽ Ἑλικωνιάσιν μεγάλω Διὸς ἐννέα κώραις·
εὐνοίᾳ τᾷ σᾷ, θεὰ πότνια, δειλαίοιο
τειρόμενοι βιότοιο προκύπτομες, οἷσιν Ἀπόλλων
δεξιὸς ἡδυεπεῖς τε θεαί, καὶ τηλόθε πάντες

20 ἀθροισθῆναι ἐς ἓν κεκελεύμεθ'· εὐεργεσίαισιν
σαῖσι, θεά, δέδμαθ' ἁμὶν δόμος αἰθεριγείτων
θαῦμα μέγα πλούτῳ πινυτᾶς μέγα θαῦμά τε τέχνας
ἡελίῳ παρέχων θάμβος, παρέχων τε σελάνᾳ
ἄσυχ' ἐλαυνοίσᾳ κατὰ νύκτ' ἐριαύχενας ἵππως,
25 κἀγαμένᾳ χρυσοῦν τ' οἶκον κ' οὐ θνατὰ μέλαθρα
τῶν κώραισιν ἑαῖς κοτέει Ζεύς, ἀθάνατοί τε
ἁμῖν βασκαίνοντι καὶ οὐρανόθεν ποθέοντι.
Ἀλλ' ἄγε, βωκόλ' Ἀμύντα, ἐπὴν καὶ ὥρα ἀφέρπεν
ἐς πόλιν, ἃν ποταμῶν Ἴστρος βασιλεύτατος ἄλλων,
30 πηλώδης τε Βιέννα ῥέει πάρα· σύλλεγ', Ἀμύντα,
ποιμενικᾶς κόσμον πενίας καλάμως δόνακάς τε·
ἦ γὰρ ἅμ' ἀοῖ φαινομένᾳ καλύβαν τε λιπόντες
μισθωτόν τε βίον Ἴστρῳ ποτὶ μακρὰ ῥέεθρα
ἔρψομες.
ΑΜ.   Ὦ φίλε Δάφνι Διὸς πεφιλαμένε κώραις,
35 σπεύδεν χρὴ βραδέως ἀνετοίμως εἰς ὁδὸν ἄνδρας·
ἐς πόλιν ἔς τε θεᾶς ἱερὸν λῇς ναὸν ἱκέσθαι,
αὐτὰρ πᾷ θυσίαι, Δάφνι φίλε, πᾷ ἑκατόμβαι;
ΔΑ. Τῆνα μὲν οὐχ ἁμῶν, τὸ δ' ἐφ' ἁμῖν· τᾷ ποτὶ κράνᾳ
τᾷδε καθίξαντες Σικελὰν συνθῶμεν ἀοιδάν,
40 ἢ «Χάριτες» ἢ «Νόστος Ἀθάνας» τὰν ἐπίκλησιν.
Ἀθανάτοις θνατοῖς τε φίλοι γ' ὕμνοι καὶ ἀοιδαί.
ΑΜ. Καλὸν (ἐμὶν δοκέει) καὶ σύμφρονα μῦθον ἔειπας.
Καὐγούστῳ πόκα καὶ Πτολεμαίῳ καὶ Βερενίκᾳ
ἄνδανε ποιμενικὸν μέλος, ἄνδανε Δωρὶς ἀοιδά·
45 ἅπτεο σύριγγος, φίλε Δάφνι, καὶ ἄρχεο πρᾶτος.
ΔΑ. Κύνθιε, Παρνασσῶ μεδέων, εἴ τοί γε Βιέννα
ὑψιμεδεῦσα φίλη, νεοκτίστοισι μελάθροις,
καὶ μεγάροισι τεοῖς εἰ τέρπεαι, εἰς ἐμὸν ἦτορ
ἔρχεο, πότνε πάτερ, καί μοι συνάεισον ἄνασσαν
50 τὰν σάν, Αὐσονίου Ζανὸς κυδρὰν παράκοιτιν.
ΑΜ. Μῶσαι Πιερίδες, θεῖον γένος, εἴ τι Βιέννα
ἠνεμόεσσ' ὔμμιν μέλει, εἰ, δόμον οὐρανομήκη
δερκόμεναι, γηθεῖτε κατὰ θυμὸν κραδίαν τε,
πέμπετ' ἐπὶ πραπίδεσσιν ἐμαῖς Παρνάσσιον ὀμφάν
55 εἰς ἔπος ὑμετέρας εὐεργέτιδος βασιλείας.
ΔΑ. Κᾶπον ἐς εὐανθῆ κῶρος στεφανοπλόκος ἐνθὼν
παπταίνει πολυανθὲς ἔαρ πρασιᾶς τε βρυοίσας
ἄνθεσι παντοδαποῖς ἀπορῶν, πόθεν ἄρξεται ἔργω.
Δηλομένῳ κἠμὶν κατερεῖν ἀρετάς τε κλέη τε,
60 τοῖσι θεὸς χαρίεσσαν ἐκόσμησεν βασίλειαν,
οὐκ ἔντι κατὰ χεῖρ' ἐξευρέμεν ἔμπρεπον ἀρχάν.
ΑΜ. Πρὰν Κορύδων κἠγὼν ἐς τὰν πόλιν ἄγομες ἄρνας
κἤνθομες ἐς ναόν (Κορύδων ὁδὸν ἡγεμόνευεν),
ναὸν δαιδάλεον χρυσῷ χ' ἑτερόχροϊ κόσμῳ,
65 ἀχράντῳ μέγα δῶμα κόρας θεόπαιδα τεκοίσας.

Ὡς ἴδον, ἐξεπλάγην, τὰν δ' ἀμφασία λάβε γλῶσσαν·
ταὐτὸ πάθω καὶ νῦν παντοῖον ἀπείρονα κόσμον
Ῥωμαίας οὐχ οἷός τ' ὢν καταλέξαι Ἀθάνας.
ΔΑ. Τὰν κράναν τάνδ' ἀργύρεον φέρε πρᾶτον, Ἀμύντα,
70 ἢ δάφνας ὄσδῳ ἤπερ τανυφύλλω ἐλαίας
ἠὲ ῥόδοις στέψωμεν, ἐπὴν ἐναλίγκιός ἐντι
Μωσάων εὐεργέτιδι πότνα βασιλείᾳ.
ΑΜ. Τὰν πλάτανον τάνδ' ὑψίκομον φέρε, Δάφνι, σελίνοις
εὐόδμοις ἢ λευκοΐοις στεφάνοισι καὶ αὐτοὶ
75 ἄνθεσι τὰς κεφαλὰς πεπυκασμένοι ἱμερόεσσι
κοσμήσωμεν, ἐπὴν ταύταν παρόμοιος ἂν' ὕλαν
ἐννέα ματρὶ θεᾶν πάσας ἀρετᾶς τε τιθήνᾳ.
ΔΑ. Ὡς ἀνὰ λειμῶνας παγαῖον σκίδναται ὕδωρ
μυρία φῦλα τρέφον βοτανῶν καὶ μυρία δένδρων
80 ἄνθεσι μὲν κάλλος παρέχον, δένδροισι δὲ καρπόν·
ὣς καὶ παντοίαισιν εὐεργεσίαισι σεβαστὰ
καὶ κόσμῳ κόσμον παρέχει καὶ πάντα τιθεύει.
ΑΜ. Δέρκεο τὰν πλατάνιστον ἀν' ὕλαν σεμνὸν ἄνασσαν,
ὄρνιχας ὡς φιλέει, λαλαγεῦντας δ' ὡς ἐσακούει,
85 ὥς σφισι φυλλάττοισα μόρον δολόεντ' ἀπαμύνει·
οὕτω Μωσάων φιλεῖ ὄρνιχας Αὐστριὰς Ἥρα
καὶ μολπαῖς αὐτῶν προσέχει, σκέπει, ἀμφαγαπάσδει.
ΔΑ. Ὡς φίλα μοχθεύσαις κατ' ἔαρ ἴα ξουθὰ μελίσσαις,
ἄνθεσι τοὶ ζέφυροι, φιλοτέκνοις ματράσιν ἄρνες·
90 Παιονίδος γαίας οὕτω μενέχαρμον ἄνασσαν
ἀτρεκέως στέργοντι τοὶ ἀρχόμενοί τε φίλοι τε.
ΑΜ. Ὅσσον δειλαίνοντι Διὸς μεγάλοιο κεραυνῶς
πεῦκαι καὶ πίτυες κενεαυχέες ὀφρυόεσσαι,
ἀνίχ' ὑπὸ βρονταῖσι μέγας πελεμίζετ' Ὄλυμπος·
95 δυσμενέες τόσον Αὐστριακὰς τρομέοντι φάλαγγας
καὶ κράτος ὀμβριμόθυμον ἀνασσάτω βασιλείας.
ΔΑ. Ἐν δένδροις κέδρος, ῥόδον ἐν φυτοῖσιν, ἐν ἄστροις
φωσφόρος, ἀνθεμόεν πολυόλβοις εἶαρ ἐν ὥραις·
ἐν βασιλεῦσιν ἐρισθενέσιν τε καὶ ἡγεμόνεσσι
100 Παιονίδος γαίας βασιλὶς μάλα φέρτατός ἐντι.
ΑΜ. Αἰετὸς ἐν πτανοῖς, πολυτίμοις ἔν τε μετάλλοις
χρυσός, μάργαρον ἐν λάεσσιν, ἐν ἰκμάσιν οἶνος,
σκηπτούχοις μετὰ δεσποίναις, κρατεραῖσιν ἀνάσσαις,
θεσπέσιον χαρίεσσα μετέπρεπεν Αὐστριὰς Ἥρα.
105 ΔΑ. Πρόφρων, μείλιχος, ἡδυεπής, χαρίεντι προσώπῳ,
εὐμενέως αἰεὶ φαίνοισά τε κηδομένη τε
λαοῦ νηρίθμου τε σιδηροφόρων στρατοῦ ἀνδρῶν,
Εὐρώπᾳ παρέχοισ' εἰρήναν ὀλβιοδῶτιν,
ἀσυχίας πολέμω τε θεὰ κλειδοῦχος ἐοῖσα.
110 ΑΜ. Ἔνδοξον Καρόλου πόκα Καίσαρος αἷμα λαχοῖσα,
Ἀρτέμιδος μέγεθος, κάλλος χρυσᾶς Κυθερείας,
Ἥρας σκῆπτρα, φυὰν τεχνάων ματρὸς Ἀθάνας.

Καίσαρι εὐναθεῖσα καὶ εὐτυχέεσσι γενέθλαις
Καίσαρας ὠδίνασα, πόθον καὶ χάρμα βροτοῖσιν.
115 ΔΑ. Πᾷ φερόμεσθ', ἦ πᾷ φρένας ἐκπεποτάμεθ' Ἀμύντα;
Αἴνων μνασθείσας ταχέως λήγωμες ἀοιδᾶς·
αἰσχρὸν Μῶσα κόλαξ, θνατοῖς κοὐ τέρπετ' ἐπαίνοις
σκηπτροφόρος βασιλίς, αἱ κἀξιέπαινος ἐοῖσα·
μᾶλλον ὀφειλομένας ἁμῖν ἐκτιέμεν εὐχὰς
120 ἐμπρέπει οὕνεκ' εὐεργεσιάων· αἰθέρι ναίων
ὦ πάτερ, ὁ κτίσας λόγῳ οὐρανὸν ἠδὲ θάλασσαν,
κόσμου παμβασιλεῦ, πανυπέρτατε, κοίρανε πάντων,
εὐχωλᾶς ἐπάκοισον ἐμᾶς· μέγα ἄστυ Βιέννας
καὶ τὼς σὼς βασιλῆας, ἄναξ, σὺν θάλλεσι θείω
125 ἀρωγοῖσι δόμῳ παντὸς δεινοῖο φυλάσσοις.
ΑΜ. Αὐτόπατορ, πάντεσσιν ὅμως καὶ ῥίζα καὶ ἀρχά,
παμμεδέων, τῷ γαῖα ποδῶν στήριγμα τέτυκται,
ἱκεσίας ἐπάκοισον ἐμᾶς· σέλας ἠελίοιο
εἰσόκα δειλοῖσιν λάμπεν μερόπεσσιν ἐπείκεις,
130 παμφαίνειν τε δίδως λαμπρὰν διὰ νύκτα σελάναν
Αὐστριακοῖς νίκας σκήπτροις καὶ κῦδος ὀπάσδοις.

Textus: T = Kollár, Adam F. (1756), "Χάριτες, εἰδύλλιον", in: Franz Christoph Scheyb (ed.), *Musae Francisco et Mariae Theresiae augustis congratulantur ob scientias, bonasque artes eorum iussu et munificentia Vindobonae restitutas*, Vindobonae: J.T. Trattner, 130–141 (cap. 26): vid. fig. 14; K = Kollár, Adam F. (1762?), *Χάριτες, εἰδύλλιον seu Gratiae Francisco et Mariae Theresiae augustis in solennibus Minervae augg. munificentia et iussu Vindobonam reducis habitae*, Vindobonae: L.J. Kaliwoda.

Crit.: accentus plerosque tacite correxi et ad normam reduxi (auctoris tamen videntur e.g. εὐεργετίς vv. 55 et 72, ἔοισα v. 118, ἐκτίεμεν v. 119 etc.) || **7** Τευτονίθος K || **9** σκᾶπτρον K || **12** δυστήνω K || **20** κεκελεύμεθ' scripsi: τε κελεύμεθ' TK || **30** πηλώδης K: πηλώθης T || **31** καλάμως δόνακάς T: αὔλως καλάμως K || **35** Σπεύδειν K || **40** Σικελὰν scripsi: Σικιλὰν TK || **42** ἐμοὶ K || **44** Πτολεμαίῳ correxi: Πτολομαίῳ TK || **50** Αὐσονίῳ K || κἠμοὶ K || **61** ἔμπρεπον TK: ἐμπρεπῆ possis || **85** φυλλάττοισα T: φυλάττοισα K || **86** Οὕτω T: Ὥς καὶ K || **98** πολυόλβοις correxi: πολυόλβαις TK || **100** φερτάτα possis || **107** στρατῷ K || **117** μνασθείσας correxi ex errato typographi μνᾶς θείστας: μεμναμένας K || **124** θάλλεσι scripsi: θάλεσι K: θάλεσσι T | θείου K || **125** δόμου K | φυλάττοις K

Sim.: 1 Ἄλσεα καὶ ποταμοί] Hom. *Il.* 20.8–9; cf. *Anth. Pal.* 8.129 (κρῆναι καὶ ποταμοὶ καὶ ἄλσεα); Thgn. 2.1252 || **2–3** Ἠχὼ πετρήεσσα] *Anth. Pal.* 16.154.1 (Ἠχὼ πετρήεσσαν ὁρᾷς, φίλε, Πανὸς ἑταίρην); cf. Nonn. *Dion.* 6.313 || **4** χὠ καλὸς Ἀμύντιχος] ex Theoc. *Id.* 7.132 || **5** θηρῶν...ἐναύλως] Hom. *Hymn. Ven.* 123–124 || **9** λευκώλενος Ἥρα] cf. e.g. Hom. *Il.* 1.195; 1.208; 1.595 et saepius || **12** πλαγκτοσύνας] cf. Hom. *Od.* 15.343; Nonn. *Dion.* 2.692. || **14** Λητογενής] *Anth. Pal.* 9.525.12 || **15** ὑψιμέλαθρον] cf. *Hymn. Hom. Merc.* 103al. | εὔφρος] ex Suid. ε 3814 || **16** μεγάλω Διὸς ἐννέα κώραις] cf. Hes. *Th.* 76 (ἐννέα θυγατέρες μεγάλου Διός); Hes. *Th.* 60 (ἐννέα κώραις) || **19** ἡδυπεῖς] cf. Hes. *Theog.* 965 || **21** δόμος αἰθεριγείτων] ex Nonn. *Par. Jo.* 5.1 || **22** θαῦμα τέχνας] *Anth. Pal.* 16.105.1 || **23** ἠελίῳ παρέχων θάμβος] *Anth. Pal.* 9.811.2 || **24** ἐριαύχενας ἵππως] e.g. Hom. *Il.* 10.295 || **25** χρυσοῦν τ' οἶκον] Pind. *Isthm.* 4.101 || **28–29** ἀφέρπεν / ἐς πόλιν] cf. Theoc. *Id.* 4.29 (ἐπεὶ ποτὶ Πίσαν ἀφέρπων ποταμῶν βασιλεύτατος ἄλλων); cf. Dion. Per. 353 (de Thybri) || **31** καλάμως δόνακάς τε] cf. *Hymn. Hom. Merc.* 47 || **32** ἅμ' ἀοῖ φαινομένᾳ] cf. Hom. *Il.* 9.618 al. || **33** ποτὶ μακρὰ ῥέεθρα] cf. Quint. Smyrn. 9.44 || **36** Σπεύδεν χρὴ βραδέως] Suet. *Aug.* 25.5 etc., locutio notissima (cf. Erasm. *Adag.* 2.1.1) || **37** Ἀυτὰρ πᾷ θυσίαι…πᾷ ἑκατόμβαι] cf. Luc. *JTr* 13 || **39** τᾷδε καθίξαντες] Theoc. *Id.* 1.12 | Σικελὰν…ἀοιδάν] cf. Mosch. 3.8 et iterationes || **44** ποιμενικὸν μέλος] cf. *Anth. Pal.* 9.584.12 (ποιμενικὸν φθέγμα) | Δωρὶς ἀοιδά] Mosch. *Ep. Bion.* 12 || **45** ἄρχεο πρᾶτος] e.g. Theoc. *Id.* 9.1 (Βουκολιάζεο Δάφνι, τὺ δ' ᾠδᾶς ἄρχεο πρᾶτος); cf. Theoc. *Id.* 6.5; 8.32 || **48** μεγάροισι τεοῖς] Hom. *Od.* 1.295; *Anth. Pal.* 11.295.1 etc. || **49** πότνε] inauditum, sed e voce πότνια excogitatum || **50** κυδρὰν παράκοιτιν] cf. Hom. *Od.* 11.580 al. || **52** δόμον οὐρανομήκη] cf. Musae. 187 || **54** πέμπετ' ἐπὶ πραπίδεσσιν ἐμαῖς] cf. Orph. *A.* 4 || **57** Κᾶπον…ἐνθών] cf. Theoc. *Id.* 1.47–53 (puerulus ad hortum texens): κῶρος…αὐτὰρ ὅγ' ἀνθερίκοισι καλὰν πλέκει ἀκριδοθήραν || **56** πολυανθὲς ἔαρ] *Hymn. Hom.* 19.17 || **58** ἀπορῶν πόθεν ἄρξεται ἔργω] Theoc. *Id.* 17.9–10 || **63** ὁδὸν ἡγεμόνευεν] cf. Theoc. *Id.* 11.27 || **64** ἑτερόχροϊ κόσμῳ] cf. Nonn. *Par. Jo.* 2.97; *Dion.* 5.131 || **66** τὰν δ' ἀμφασία λάβε γλῶσσαν] sim. Ap. Rhod. *Argon.* 3.284 (τὴν δ' ἀμφασίη λάβε θυμόν) || **67** πάθω] praesens e verbo πάσχω creatum || **70** τανυφύλλῳ ἐλαίας] cf. e.g. Hom. *Od.* 13.102; 23.195 etc. || **73–74** σελίνοις / εὐόδμοις] Theoc. *Id.* 3.23 || **74–76** ἢ λευκοῖσι στεφάνοισι…ἱμερόεσσι / κοσμήσωμεν] cf. *Anth. Pal.* 11.19.3 || **84** Ὄρνιχας…λαλαγεῦντας] Theoc. *Id.* 5.48 || **85** μόρον δολόεντ'] cf. Opp. *H.* 2.156; 4.120 || **92** Διὸς μεγάλοιο κεραυνώς] cf. Hom. *Il.* 14.417; 21.198 || **94** βρονταῖσι…πελεμίζετ'] cf. Hes. *Theog.* 458 || **96** ἀνασσάτω] de adi. cf. Theoc. *Id.* 6.46 || **100** μάλα φέρτατός ἐντι] cf. Quint. Smyrn. 8.459 || **105** μείλιχος, ἡδυεπής] *Anth. Pal.* 8.12.3; 8.124.3 | χαρίεντι προσώπῳ] Hom. *Il.* 18.24 (de Achille) || **107** σιδηροφόρων στρατοῦ ἀνδρῶν] cf. Nonn. *Par. Jo.* 18.29 || **108** εἰρήναν ὀλβιοδῶτιν] cf. *Hymn. Orph.* 65.9 || **110** αἷμα λαχοῖσα] cf. Musae. 30 || **111** χρυσᾶς Κυθερείας] cf. e.g. Hom. *Il.* 3.64; *Od.* 8.337 || **115** πᾷ φρένας ἐκπεποτάμεθ'] Theoc. *Id.* 2.19; 11.72 || **116** λήγωμες ἀοιδᾶς] Eur. *Med.* 421; *Anth. Pal.* 7.612.3 || **122** κοίρανε πάντων] cf. *Anth. Pal.* 1.23.1 || **123** εὐχωλᾶς ἐπάκοισον] cf. Anacr. fr. 357.8 Page || **126** ῥίζα καὶ ἀρχά] cf. Greg. Naz. *carm.*, PG 37.551.7 || **127** γαῖα ποδῶν στήριγμα] cf. *Orac. Sib.* 1.139 || **128** σέλας ἡελίοιο] cf. e.g. *Anth. Pal.* 15.29.2; Eur. *Tro.* 860; *El.* 866 || **129** δειλοῖσιν … μερόπεσσιν] cf. Greg. Naz. *carm.*, PG 37.972.7 || **131** κῦδος ὀπάσδοις] cf. Hom. *Il.* 7.205 al.

Graces. An idyll

DAPHNIS and AMYNTAS

DAPHNIS: Farewell you woods and rivers, and you shady fountains a fond farewell,
my goats and calves, and you stony Echo, the partner
of horned Pan, a fond farewell to you along with your caves!
I, Daphnis, and handsome young Amyntas here will no longer sing to you
[5] on our way to the mountains or the glades – the cosy homes of wild animals
among the pastures. For that Goddess has now come
who pays attention to the Muses and poets. Oh Goddess!
glory and sustenance of the German lands, Cytherian for your aspect,
or, on account of your sceptre and your palaces, white-armed Hera,
[10] or, because of your wisdom, Athena, if you prefer rather so to be called,
myriad greetings Goddess! With your council, oh Queen,
with your care, from his terrible wanderings
the son of Leto, who drew the yoke of every indecency

at the hands of the barbarians, the master and glory of the lyre,
[15] returns to the high-walled city of Vienna, that happy Apollo,
along with the nine Heliconian daughters of great Zeus.
Through your good will we, who have been worn out, resurge, Goddess and Queen, from
a cruel life that wears us out, we to whom Apollo
and the sweet-singing Goddesses are kind. We all from far away
[20] are commanded to come together now. With your favourable deeds
Goddess, a home for us has been built which touches the sky,
a great wonder of wealth and a great wonder of the wise arts
which stirs amazement in both Helios [the sun] and Selene [the moon]
while she quietly drives her high-necked horses by night
[25] in wonder at the golden house, not a mortal hall,
for which Zeus bears a grudge against his own daughters, and for which the immortals
envy us and feel desire from high in the skies.
But come now, shepherd Amyntas, now it is time to creep away
to the city, along which run the Danube, most kingly of rivers,
[30] and the muddy Vienna. Take with you, Amyntas,
your shepherd's pipes and reeds, the symbol of poverty;
for truly daybreak will begin to shine at any moment, and after leaving our cottages
behind and our salaried working-life, we will start our journey towards the
wide streams of the Danube.

AMYNTAS: O dear Daphnis, beloved by Zeus' daughters,
[35] men not ready for the road should make haste slowly.
You want to arrive to the city and the sacred temple of the goddess,
but where are the victims, dear Daphnis, where are the offerings of a hundred oxen?

DA.: Those things are not our care, but this is up to us: sitting down
here at this spring, let us compose a Sicilian song,
[40] 'Graces' or 'Athena's Return' as a name for it,
by both the Gods and men, indeed, songs and hymns are beloved.

AM.: Good and propitious advice (it seems to me) you speak,
for Augustus once, for Ptolemy and Berenice too
was the shepherd's tune pleasing, and they liked Dorian song.
[45] Take up your shepherd's pipe, dear Daphnis, and begin first.

DA.: Cynthius [= Apollo], ruler of Parnassus, if high-ruling Vienna is endeared to you,
if you are delighted by the new-built rooves
and your large halls, come to my heart,
Lord father, and sing along with me for your
[50] Lady, the lovely wife of Ausonian Zeus.

AM.: Muses from Pieria, godly stock, if you care for windy Vienna
if, looking at the sky-scraping house,
you delight in both heart and mind, send to
my heart the Parnassian voice for

[55] a hymn for your benefactor, the Queen.

DA.: A boy weaving a crown having entered into a flowering garden
takes a good look at the blooming spring and the flower beds
full with various blossoms, is helpless as to where he will start the job.
So it is for me, while wanting to tell of the goodness and fame
[60] with which Zeus has honoured the beautiful queen:
I am not able to find at hand a fitting start.

AM.: Earlier on, Corydon and I brought our lambs to the city
and we went to the temple (Corydon led the way),
a temple curiously decorated with varied gold ornament,
[65] a great house of the undefiled girl who gave birth to the godly child.
And when I saw it, I was struck and speechlessness took my tongue.
I suffer the same now and I'm not able to describe the Roman Athena's
boundless decoration on all sides.

DA.: First of all, Amyntas, let us adorn the silver-coloured fountain here,
[70] either with a branch of laurel, or of long-leaved olive,
or with roses, since it is like
our benefactor, the ruling Queen of the Muses.

AM.: The towering sycamore, come on, Daphnis, with sweet-smelling
parsley, or with white wreaths let us dress it,
[75] being crowned ourselves with precious flowers on our heads,
since this wood is thus similar
to the nursing mother of the nine Goddesses and of everything good.

DA.: Just as the fountain's water scatters through the pastures
supporting countless races of plants and countless trees,
[80] and bringing beauty to the plants and fruit to the trees;
thus the reverend one with every type of good deed
offers order to the world and provides everything.

AM.: Look at the sycamore, as an adored princess of the woods,
how it loves the birds, how it listens to those singing,
[85] how it keeps crafty fate away from them through its protection;
thus Austrian Hera loves the Muses' birds,
and she hears their rhythms, shields them and holds them dear.

DA.: Just as in spring the yellow violets are beloved to the working bees,
the zephyrs to the flowers, the lambs to the child-loving mothers;
[90] thus truly do all her subjects and friends love
the battle-steady queen of the Paeonian land.

AM.: As much as the high raised pines and conifers fear
the bolts of mighty Zeus

when great Olympus is shaken by his thunders,
[95] so much do enemies fear the Austrian phalanxes
and the mighty strength of the invincible Queen.

DA.: Just as the cedar among trees, the rose among flowers, among stars
the morning-star and the flowery spring among the rich seasons,
among the powerful kings and rulers,
[100] thus the queen of the Pannonian land is indeed the bravest.

AM.: Just as the eagle amongst the birds, and among the valuable metals
gold, the pearl among stones, wine among liquids,
thus between sceptre-bearing ladies, the powerful mistresses,
the lovely Austrian Hera stands out wonderfully.

[105] DA.: Earnest, kind, eloquent, and with a lovely face,
graciously offering herself always and caring for
her people, and for an immeasurable army of iron-bearing men
providing happy peace to Europe,
this is the Goddess in charge of peace and war.

[110] AM.: Having once been allotted the glorious blood of Emperor Charles,
she has the height of Artemis, the beauty of the golden Cytherian,
the sceptre of Hera, the genius of Athena, mother of arts,
a bride for the Emperor and happily giving birth
to other Emperors, who are a joy and pleasure for mankind.

[115] DA.: Where are we off to?! Or where are our minds taking us, Amyntas?
Let us stop quickly with these commemorative songs of praise
the muse of flattery is shameful and neither does the sceptre-bearing queen
enjoy mortal eulogy, even though she is praiseworthy anyway;
rather we should bring out the required prayers
[120] because of her good deeds, O Father,
you who live in heaven, you who made heaven and the sea with a word,
king of the whole cosmos, the highest of all, ruler of everything,
listen to my prayers: The great city of Vienna,
and your kings, Lord, may you protect them
[125] together with the offshoots of the divine house that keep it away from every evil.

AM.: Your own father, the root and origin equally of everything,
the guardian of everything, for whom the earth is made as a support for the feet,
hear my prayer; you send the light of the sun
to shine on wretched mankind,
[130] and you make the bright light of the moon shine all round through the night:
may you also grant victories and honour to the Austrian sceptres.

Metre: Hexameters. Note in l. 7 (and 17) θεά (with ᾰ), 12 ἀπὸ δυστάνω (-o is lengthened), 13 βαρβάροις (with second ᾱ), 125 ἀρωγοῖσι (with long ᾱ), and some lengthenings *in arsi* or through consonants (33 βίον, 61 ἔντī, 72 εὐεργέτιδῖ, 88 ἔᾱρ, ἴα). There is a *spondiacus* in l. 17 and a rhyme in l. 27 (βασκαίνοντι...ποθέοντι). Note also the monosyllable ὸ at the end of l. 12.

Notes: Kollár's *Χάριτες* was published as part of the *Musae Francisco et Mariae Theresiae augustis congratulantur* [...], a panegyrical volume, which celebrated the opening of the new Aula of Vienna University, symbolic for contemporary reforms in the Austrian study system under Empress Maria Theresia, as well as for the university's efforts to move away from the influence of the Jesuit order. Ostensibly, the poem takes its inspiration in form, language, scenery, characters, literary *topoi*, and overall structure from Theocritus and the bucolic tradition that followed him. The opening lines (esp. 1–6 and 29–34) display, however, a violent rejection of traditional symbols of the pastoral world and the rustic life. Following an allegorical/autobiographical reading of the piece – standard for bucolic literature in the Renaissance and Early Modern period – we hear here a literary echo of Kollár's decision to leave his life in the noviciate in northern Slovakia, to join the court library in the Habsburg capital and support his family. Kollár was to become best known in his later years for his strong support of Maria Theresia's reforms, both political and educational. His eloquent passages on the miserable state of the lives of peasants and workers in the Kingdom of Hungary, and in support of a fairer social system in later works (cf. his *De originibus et usu perpetuo potestatis legislatoriae circa sacra apostolicorum Regum Ungariae*, Vienna 1764), are also perhaps prefigured in Daphnis' rejection of ποιμενικᾶς κόσμον πενίας καλάμως δόνακάς τε (l. 31) and the μισθωτόν [...] βίον (l. 33). Following the bucolic tradition, Kollár uses the Doric dialect. One may note e.g. δήλομαι (δηλομένῳ) as a dialectal equivalent for βούλομαι in l. 59.

Biography: Adam F. Kollár (1718–1783) was born in Terchová, Slovakia (then the Kingdom of Hungary) to modest parents. After his birth, his parents moved repeatedly, first to Banská Bystrica (Besztercebánya), where their son attended a Jesuit middle school. He would later use the town's Latin name (*Neosolium*) as an epithet to his own name in some of his Latin publications. He continued his education in Banská Štiavnica (Selmecbánya), and graduated in the university town of Trnava (Nagyszombat) before joining the Jesuit order. He attended the Jesuit college at Vienna, and taught briefly in Liptovský Mikuláš (Liptószentmiklós) before returning to Vienna to continue his studies. Kollár demonstrated a wonderful potential for languages early on. He began his studies of theology at the University of Vienna with two years of Hebrew along with Persian and Turkish. He left the Jesuits upon graduation. He then began his career at the Imperial Royal Library in 1748 as a scribe, and lectured on classical Greek at the University of Vienna between 1748 and 1751. He eventually became chief librarian and councillor at the court of the Habsburgs. Most of his appointments were readily approved by Empress Maria Theresia, with whom he curried favour, and whose policies he underpinned with his scholarship. With his training in Turkish, Persian, the classical languages, and numerous other languages (cf. Schulze → **Germany**), Kollár was able to edit and publish numerous manuscripts and earlier volumes from the collections of the Imperial Library. His annotated editions of texts in Turkish, Persian, and Arabic, with which he began his list of publications in the years just before his *Χάριτες*, were particularly successful. This editorial work, in addition to his familiarity with the linguistic and cultural diversity of his native Kingdom of Hungary, made him an early student of ethnology. He would famously become the first scholar to use and define this term in his *Historiae jurisque publici regni Ungariae amoenitates* of 1783. Kollár influenced many of Empress Maria Theresia's reforms, including her ordinance of the *Ratio educationis* in 1777, which aimed to standardise teaching methods, curricula, and textbooks.

Bibliography: Tibenský, Ján (1983), *Slovenský Sokrates. Život a dielo Adama Františka Kollára*, Bratislava; von Wurzbach, Constantin (1864), "Kollár von Keresztén, Adam Franz", in: *Biographisches Lexikon des Kaiserthums Österreich* XII, Vienna, 324–325. Historical Context: Csizmadia, Andor (1982), *Adam Franz Kollár und die ungarische rechtshistorische Forschung*, Vienna; Karner, Herbert/Rosenauer, Artur/Telesko, Werner (2007), *Die Österreichische Akademie der Wissenschaften: das Haus und seine Geschichte*, Vienna; Klingenstein, Grete (1979), "Bildungskrise. Gymnasien und Universitäten im Spannungsfeld theresianischer Aufklärung", in: Walter Koschatzky (ed.), *Maria Theresia und ihre Zeit: eine Darstellung der Epoche von 1740 – 1780 aus Anlaß des 200. Todestages der Kaiserin*, Vienna, 213–223. On the poetic collection: Gottsched, Johann Christoph (1757), *Das Neueste aus der anmutigen Gelehrsamkeit*, Leipzig, 7 st. 9 (Herbstmond), 692–699; st. 10 (Weinmond), 773–781; Lesigang-Bruckmüller, Annamaria (2008), "Musae Francisco et Mariae Theresiae Augustis congratulantur. Eine Festschrift zur Eröffnung der Neuen Aula der Wiener Universität", in: Christian Gastgeber/Elisabeth Klecker (eds.), *Neulatein an der Universität Wien. Ein literarischer Streifzug*, Vienna, 383–414; Barton, William M. (2020), "Adam Franz Kollár's Χάριτες (1756). Theocritean Praise of Maria Theresa in Mid-Eighteenth-Century Vienna", in: Anne-Elisabeth Beron/Stefan Weise (eds.), *Hyblaea avena. Theokrit in römischer Kaiserzeit und Früher Neuzeit*, Stuttgart, 177–195.

[WB]

Bernhard Niedermühlbichler (1798–1850)

I. <*Epigramma* 227> [1844]

> Μὴ ὡς ἀχρεῖόν τινα ἡγοῦ τὸν πλεονέκτην·
> ὠφέλιμόν τι πέλει χρῆμα τοιοῦτος ἀνήρ.
> Ζῶν μὲν ἔτ' οὔ τι δίδωσ', ὑΐ εἴκελος· ἀλλὰ τεθνηκὼς
> σφαττομένοιο πολὺ πλεῦνα δίδωσιν ὑός.

II. <*Epigramma* 229> [1844]

> Οὐκ ἂν ἐγὼ τὰ φίλων πάντ' εἶναι κοινὰ γενοίμην
> ἔξαρνος· κοινόν γ' ἀργύριον τὸ ἐμὸν
> σοὶ κἀμοὶ νομίσας ἔλες. εἴθε μὲν οὖν κοινῷ γ' ὥς, –
> νῦν δὲ μόνος τούτῳ χρῇ, φίλε, ὡς ἰδίῳ.

Textus: Niedermühlbichler, Bernhard (1844), *Epigrammata novi ex parte generis*, Innsbruck, 33–34 (nr. 227 et 229).

Sim.: I.1 πλεονέκτην] verbum pedestre || 2 ὠφέλιμον] verbum pedestre (praeter Eur. *Ion* 138) || 4 πλεῦνα] forma Ionica, rara in carminibus (sed cf. *Anth. Pal.* 6.296.5; 12.205.3; 16.256.4)
II.1 τὰ φίλων πάντ' εἶναι κοινά] proverbium commune, e.g. Eur. *Or.* 735; Plat. *Leg.* 5.739b–c; Arist. *EN* 8.9.1 (1159b31); in Latinum verterunt inter alios Mart. 2.43.1; Erasmus, *Adagia* 1.1.1.

<Epigram 227>

> Don't think that a greedy man is of no avail!
> In fact, such a man is truly a useful creature.
> Though while still alive he doesn't yield anything, like the pig,
> after his death, however, he gives far more than a slaughtered pig.[10]

<Epigram 229>

> I would not deny that between friends, all is common.
> Indeed, you have taken my money, assuming that it was common

---

[10] **Author's Latin translation:** *Ne quasi nulli rei esse avarum existimes: nam utilis quaedam res est ejusmodi homo. Vivus quidem adhuc nil praebet, porco assimilis: at mortuus mactato longe plura dat porco.*

between you and me. If only you used it like a common good –
but now, my friend, you use it yourself, as if it were yours alone.[11]

Metre: Elegiac couplets.

Notes: In a slim volume, Niedermühlbichler published a collection of 225 Latin and twelve Greek epigrams. The Latin pieces are mostly based on puns and wordplay, exploiting the language's tendency towards homographs and polysemy to the fullest. Wittier in content, yet more traditional in style, are his Greek epigrams. Epigram 227 (here no. I) is a good example of Niedermühlbichler's epigrammatic technique, with the antithesis ζῆν–θανεῖν featuring also in other epigrams and the unexpected comparison to a pig. Epigram 229 (here no. II) is Niedermühlbichler's take on the well-known Greek proverb κοινὰ τὰ τῶν φίλων, which features in several philosophical discussions as well as tragedy and comedy. It also found its way into several ancient and early modern collections of proverbs and emphatically opens the *Adagia* of Erasmus. An epigrammatic predecessor is Martial 2.43, where a rich acquaintance of the epigrammatic 'I' is mocked for quoting the proverb often, but not actually sharing his wealth.

III. Ἡ κυριακὴ προσευχή, ἀμειβομένοις ἐξαμέτροις καὶ πενταμέτροις ἐκφραζομένη [1847]

Ἡμετέρειε Τοκεῦ, ὁ ἐνουράνιός, Σε ἕκαστος
   δοξάζοιμεν ἀεί, κηρόθι ἀζόμενοι·
Σοὶ δ' ἀπὸ τοῦδ' ὕποχοι πειθοίμεθα πάντες ἄνακτι,
   καὶ Σὺ ἕοις βασιλεὺς ἦμιν ἀειχρόνιος·
5 πᾶν τε, τόπερ Σὺ θέλεις, καὶ οἱ ἐνταῦθα θέλοιμεν,
   ὡς ἐθέλουσ' ἔμπης χ' οἱ ἐν ἐπουρανίοις.
Δὸς δέ, ὅσων χρεία ἡμῖν, καὶ τήμερον αὖθις,
   μηδὲ Τεῶν τέκνων λῆγε προκηδόμενος.
Συγγνώμης δὲ τύχοι παρὰ Σοῦ τὸ πλημμελὲς ἡμῶν,
10   καὐτοὶ δ' ἀλλήλοις εἶμεν ἀμνησίκακοι.
Πειρασμῶν πάντων δὸς κρείσσονας ἄμμε γενέσθαι,
   καὶ κατανικῆσαι πᾶν τὸ πονηρὸν ἐόν. –
Δέξαι δὴ ἀμάς, ἐπακούσας, ὦ Πάτερ, εὐχάς,
   ἀχρείοις περ ἐοῦσ' ἄμμι Σὺ χρηστὰ μέδου.

---

11 **Author's Latin translation:** *Non ego, amicorum omnia esse communia, infitias iero: meum quippe argentum, tibi ac mihi commune ratus, tulisti! quo utinam saltem ut communi (utaris), – ast nunc solus, amice, illo uteris ut proprio!*

15 Σοὶ κλέος εἰν Υἱῷ καὶ Πνεύματι ἔμπεδον αἰεί,
    Σοὶ κλέος ἐν Σαυτῷ, ἡμετέρειε Γονεῦ!

Textus: Niedermühlbichler, Bernhard (1847), *ΕΥΧΟΛΟΓΙΟΝ, ἐμμέτρως ξυγγεγραμμένον καὶ ὕμνους τὸ πολὺ περιέχον*, Innsbruck, 17.

Sim.: 1 Ἡμετέρειε] verbum rarissimum (Anacr. fr. 392 Page; Anaxandr. fr. 9 K.-A.) | ἐνουράνιος] sermo mysticus ac Christianus (sed vide *Anth. Pal.* 9.223.2) || **4** ἀειχρόνιος] *Anth. Pal.* 12.229.4 (hapax legomenon) || **9** Συγγνώμης δὲ τύχοι παρὰ Σοῦ τὸ πλημμελές] cf. Diog. Laert. 4.54 || **10** ἀμνησίκακοι] sermo Christianus || **11** Πειρασμῶν] sermo Christianus || **15** ἔμπεδον αἰεί] e.g. Solon fr. 15.3 W.; Thgn. 1.317; 1.319; Ap. Rhod. *Argon.* 1.1076; Orph. *A.* 347; Nonn. *Par. Jo.* 14.63; frequenter in carminibus Christianis; cf. etiam Hom. *Il.* 15.683; *Od.* 7.259

The Lord's Prayer, fashioned in alternating hexameter and pentameter verses

    Our heavenly Father, may each one of us
        praise You always deeply in awe.
    May we all, your subjects, obey You our Lord from now on,
        and may You be our everlasting king.
5   Everything that You wish, may we down here also want,
        as they wish among the folks in heavens.
    Give us, then, as much as we need, also today again,
        and do not cease protecting Your children.
    May our inadequacy be pardoned by You,
10 and may we ourselves be forgiving towards one another.
    Allow that we be stronger than all temptations,
        and that we may completely defeat all wickedness.
    O Father, having listened to our prayers, please receive them
        and provide useful things for us who are useless ourselves.
15 May there be glory for You, in your Son and in the Holy Spirit on and on always,
        and glory for You in Yourself, our Father!

Metre: Elegiac couplets (with loose handling of hiatus).

Notes: Niedermühlbichler's *Εὐχολόγιον* represents the result of an ambitious project to render numerous forms of Christian prayer in ancient Greek verse (a practice frequently found elsewhere in humanistic Greek poetry: e.g. Poliziano → **Italy**). The author's primary motivation for this undertaking, as he underlines in the introduction to his 350-page work, is to experience sweet and pleasant effect of prayer in a foreign tongue. After an opening poem in praise of prayer generally, the volume is arranged with the prose texts of numerous biblical prayers followed by Niedermühlbichler's various poetic renderings of these pieces, frequently rather free and ornate in character – as here – when compared to the base text. His rendering of the *Pater noster* in elegiac couplets, presented here, is the first of two adaptations of this key prayer. The Greek prose version of the Lord's Prayer provided by Niedermühlbichler follows that of the *Divine Liturgy of Saint John Chrysostom*: cf. ἐπὶ τῆς γῆς (line 5) and the aorist ἀφίεμεν (line 8). While in the prose he omits the priest's closing doxology (ὅτι σοῦ ἐστιν ἡ βασιλεία καὶ ἡ δύναμις καὶ ἡ δόξα εἰς τοὺς αἰῶνας· ἀμήν) common in the Byzantine Rite and attested in John Chrysostom's *Divine Liturgy*, it is nonetheless echoed in the final four lines of his poetic rendering. The fifth and sixth foot of Niedermühlbichler's line 15 (ἔμπεδον αἰεί), for example, mirror the adverbial εἰς τοὺς αἰῶνας of the liturgical text. Interesting evidence of the contemporary reception of the *Εὐχολόγιον* is preserved in Innsbruck's literary magazine *Der Phönix*, where an article on the life of the famous polyglot Cardinal Giuseppe Gasparo Mezzosanti records his being presented with Niedermühlbichler's verse collection as a gift. Mezzosanti apparently responded by citing Horace's tag from *Ars poetica* 351–352: *Verum ubi plura nitent in carmine, non ego paucis / offendar maculis ...*

Biography: Bernhard Niedermühlbichler was a pupil at the Franciscan Gymnasium in Hall i.T. where he finished his studies in the *humaniora* in 1816. After leaving school, he joined the Franciscan order and later returned to his *alma mater* in 1826, first as a teacher of grammar and then from 1828 onwards as professor of humanities. In 1838 he went on to become the Gymnasium's Prefect. Having retired from his career at the school, Niedermühlbichler took up a role as lecturer in canon law in his order's monastery in Hall. He died here on 7 April 1850.

Bibliography: Holaus, Pascal Maximilian (1876), *Programm des K.K. Obergymnasiums zu Hall. Am Schlusse des Schuljahres 1875–76*, Innsbruck, 26, 29. On the *Εὐχολόγιον*: a parallel Latin translation of the work was published by the author himself in the same year as the Greek original: Niedermühlbichler, Bernhard (1847), *Liber precationum metrice graeco sermone conscriptus*, Innsbruck; Mitterrutzner, Johann Chysostomus (1850), "Cardinal Josef Mezzosanti (1774–1849). Biographische Skizze", in: *Der Phönix: Zeitschrift für Literatur, Kunst, Geschichte, Vaterlandskunde und Wissenschaft* VI, 27f. On the *Epigrammata*: Schaffenrath, Florian (2012), "Dichtung: Von der Vertreibung der Jesuiten bis zur Revolution 1848", in: Martin Korenjak/Florian Schaffenrath/Lav Šubarić/Karlheinz Töchterle (eds.), *Tyrolis Latina: Geschichte der lateinischen Literatur in Tirol. Band II. Von der Gründung der Universität Innsbruck bis heute*, Vienna/Cologne, Weimar, 919–940: 935.

[MB/WB]

Ludwig Mayr (1851–1944)

Χαρίτων πόλις [1897/²1902]

(excerptum, vv. 395–490)

395 Ἀνθρώπων δ' ἀγοραὶ πλήθουσι κατὰ πτολίεθρον.
    Μεστοὶ μὲν τάλαροι καρπῶν τε καὶ ὄψου ἔασιν,
    ἐν δὲ τραπέζαισιν κρέα πολλὰ βοῶν τε συῶν τε
    κεῖται, πρὸς δ' αὐλιζομένου βοὸς ἔντερα πολλὰ
    ἔμπλεια κνίσης τε καὶ ἥπατος ἠδὲ γάλακτος
400 ἠὲ καὶ αἵματος ὀπτῆσαι ποτιδόρπιον ἀστοῖς.
    Ἀμφὶ δὲ κοινοβίῳ μοναχῶν θαλερὰς μάλα πολλὰς
    πωλεῦσ' ὄρνιθας, τάς τε Στυρίη τρέφει αἶα,
    χῆνας καὶ νήττας ἁπαλοτρεφέας τε κάπωνας.
    Μόσχων δ' αὖ ἀγορὴ ποταμοῦ προπάροιθε τέτυκται,
405 καὶ δ' ἰχθῦς περνᾶσι πέρην ποταμοῖο ῥεέθρων,
    οἵους περ Μοῦρός τε τρέφει Ἴστρος τ' ἰοειδής. –
    Ἀνθρώπων δ' ἄρα παντοίων πλήθουσιν ἀγυιαί.
    Οἱ μὲν ἴασι κατὰ πρῆξιν κραιπνοῖσι πόδεσσιν
    ἂμ πόλιν, οἱ δ' ἐφορῶσι μάλ' ἐνδυκέως, ἃ πρόθεντο
410 πρηκτῆρες, νυκτός γ' ἠλέκτορι παμφανόωντα.
    Ἄλλοι δ' αὖτις μαψιδίως ἀλάονται ἐπ' ἦμαρ
    παρθενικὰς μάλ' ὀπιπτεύοντες καλλιπαρήους.
    Ἄλλοι δ' αὖ παρελαύνουσιν τλητούς περ ὁδίτας
    ἅρματ' ἀεὶ κραιπνῶς ὡς εἰ ἀνέμοιο θύελλα.
415 Ἅρμα δὲ θαυμάσιον στίλβει αἴθωνι σιδήρῳ·
    ἦ ῥα σιδήρειος δίφρος δύο τ' ἀγκύλα κύκλα,
    ἀλλήλων μετόπισθεν ἐερμέν' ὕπερθέ τε οἴηξ,
    ᾧ τ' ἰθύνεται ἅρμ', ἵνα μὴ βλάπτησιν ὁδίτην·
    ἄξοσι δ' αὖ παρὰ λαμπροτάτοις τέταται ἑκάτερθε
420 πηδάλιον· τὸ δ' ἀμοιβηδὶς πατέει γε ποδοῖιν
    ῥηϊδίως ἐλατὴρ πρήσσων μάλα ῥίμφα κέλευθον.
    Ἅρμα γὰρ ἀσφαλέως θέει ἔμπεδον, οὐδέ κεν ἴρηξ
    κίρκος ὁμαρτήσειεν, ἐλαφρότατος πετεηνῶν.
    Ἀλλὰ καὶ ὣς τρέχει ἡσυχίῃ πολυδαίδαλον ἅρμα·
425 κύκλων γὰρ καθύπερθεν ἐπίσσωτρα προσάρηρεν
    μαλθακά· κεῖνο δ' ἄρ' ἄκληρός κέ τις οὐ κτεατίζοι.
    Ἦ τοι καὶ θρασέαι θαμὰ παρθένοι ἠδὲ γυναῖκες
    πάντοσ' ἐπισταμένως γε σιδήρεον ἵππον ἐλαύνειν
    εὔχονται, πολλαὶ δ' ἀλέονται ἀδευκέα φῆμιν,
430 μή ποτέ τις εἴπησιν ἰδὼν ἐς πλησίον ἄλλον·
    "ὢ πόποι, οὐχ ὁράᾳς σύ γ' Ἀμαζόνας ἀντιανείρας,
    πληξίππους, αἳ νῦν τροχαλίστριαι ἔνθα καὶ ἔνθα
    φοιτῶσ', ἀνθρώποις πολλοῖς μέγα θαῦμα ἐοῦσαι;

Μή ποτ' ἐμοὶ τοιήδ' ἄλοχος κεκλημένη εἴη·
435 ἦ γὰρ ἐμοὶ πολὺ κείνη ἀρείων φαίνεται εἶναι,
ἥ κεν ἔπη τὰ ἃ ἔργα περιφραδέως κατὰ οἶκον,
οἷά τ' ἔοικεν, ἐπίστηταί τ' ἐὺ δαῖτα πένεσθαι."
Ὣς ποτέ τίς κ' εἴποι - - - - -
Ἦ τοι ὅθεν περ ὀρίνονται εὖρός τε νότος τε
440 καὶ βορέης αἰθρηγενέτης ζέφυρός τε δυσαής,
πάντοθεν ἀνθρώπους φορέουσ' ὑπὸ θερμῷ ἀϋτμῇ
ἅρματα καρπαλίμως ποτὶ ἄστυ ὁδοὺς ἀνὰ λείας,
αἵ τε κατέστρωνται πυκνῶς αἴθωνι σιδήρῳ,
εἴτε διὲξ ὀρέων τυκταὶ εἴτ' αὖ πεδίοιο.
445 Ὣς δ' αὔτως ἁρματροχιαί γε σιδήρεαί εἰσιν
ἂμ πόλιν· αὐτὰρ ὕπερθεν ἔτειναν πείσματα χαλκοῦ,
ὥς τ' ἄρα τείνουσιν πετεηνοῖς ἕρκε' ὀλοιά·
τὰς δὲ καθ' ἅρματα σεύονται ἠλέκτορος ὁρμῇ,
ἀλλ' ἦ πόλλ' ἐπίβαθρα ὀπηδός γ' αἰτεῖ ἕκαστον. –
450 Αὐτὰρ ὑπὲρ πτολιέθρου ἄνευθ' ἄλλων ἔχει οὖρος,
ᾧ ἔνι δένδρεα μακρὰ πεφύκασι τηλεθόωντα,
ἔνθα περ ὄρνιθες τανυσίπτεροι εὐνάζονται.
Αὖθι μὲν ὑψηλοὺς πύργους καὶ τεῖχος ἔδειμαν
οἱ πρότεροι, ἵν' ἀμύναιεν σφετέροισι τέκεσσιν
455 ἄνδρας δυσμενέας τε καὶ αἰνὴν δηϊότητα.
Νῦν δ' αἰπήν γε κέλευθον ἐλαύνετ' ἄνω τε κάτω τε
ἀντιόωντα δύ' ἅρμαθ', ἅ τ' οὔτε ποδώκεες ἵπποι
οὔτε τοι ἡμίονοι κρατερώνυχες ἐντεσιεργοί
ῥίμφα φέρουσ', ἀλλ' ἲς ἠλέκτορος ὀβριμοεργοῦ.
460 Πολλοὶ μὲν ξεῖνοί τε καὶ ἀστοὶ ἄνω τε κάτω τε
ἀσπάσιοι οἰχνεῦνται ἰδὲ πτολίεθρον ὕπερθεν
ὀφθαλμοῖς ὁρόωσιν ἀκούοντες μελπήθρων,
οἷς κραδίην θέλγουσι χελιδόνες Ἰστρογένειαι
εἴαρι φαινόμεναι· ἐπεὶ ἂν δέ τ' ἐπὶ κνέφας ἔλθῃ,
465 δὴ τότ' ἀπ' ἀκροτάτης κορυφῆς αἰεὶ ἐπιλάμπει
νύκτα δι' ὀρφναίην ἠλέκτωρ ἥλιος ὥς,
ἐντὸς γὰρ μεγάρων δαίνυντ' ἐρικυδέα δαῖτα,
τερπόμενοι μολπῇ τε καὶ ὀρχηθμῷ καὶ ἀοιδῇ.
Ἄγχι δὲ κυκλοτερὴς ἕστηκεν πύργος ἀτειρής,
470 ἐξ οὗ ἀκούσειάς κεν ἀεὶ τρὶς ἐπ' ἤματι χαλκέου
τῆλε φθεγγομένης ὀπὸς ἠελίου ἀνιόντος,
καὶ ὅτ' ἂν ἠέλιος μέσον οὐρανὸν ἀμφιβεβήκῃ,
καὶ ὁπότ' ἂν δύῃ λαμπρὸν φάος ἠελίοιο.
Εἰσὶ δ' ὑπ' αἰθούσῃ δολίχαυλα δύ' ὅπλ' ἐρίδουπα
475 πῦρ ἐρέοντα πόληϊ ὀλοιόν, ἐάν τι γένηται·
εἰσὶ δὲ καὶ φύλακες πυρὸς αὐγὴν σημανέοντες.
Ἐγγύθι δ' αὖ κεν ἴδοις κισσῷ πεπυκασμένα τείχεα
καὶ φρέαρ εὐποίητον, ὃ βάρβαροι ἄνδρες ὄρυξαν·
τοῖα γὰρ ἐν δεσμοῖς ζωάγρια τοί γ' ἐτέλεσσαν
480 πολλὰ μάλ' ἄκοντες· κρατερὴ δ' ἐπέκειτο ἀνάγκη.

Ἄγχι δὲ λαΐνέη ἕδρη, λυγροῖς ἀραρυῖα
σήμασιν, ᾗ φασιν σεμνόν ποτ' ἐπίσκοπον ἦσθαι·
τὸν μὲν δήθ' ἐνὶ πύργῳ ἐρύκακον· οὐδ' ἄρ' ἔμελλε
δηρὸν ἔτ' ὄψεσθαι λαμπρὸν φάος ἠελίοιο·
485 αὐτόθι γὰρ θάνατος τῷ γ' ἀβληχρὸς μάλα ἦλθεν.
 Αὐτὰρ τόσσον ἔνερθεν, ὅσον τε γέγωνε βοήσας,
τετράπλευρον πύργον ἔδειμαν, σῆμα πόληος,
τηλεφανέα, τὸν δὴ ἱερόν φασ' ἔμμεναι Ὡρέων,
Ζηνὸς καὶ Θέμιδός γε θυγατρῶν, αἵ τε κελεύθους
490 σημαίνουσιν ἀεὶ νυκτός τε καὶ ἤματος ἀστοῖς.

Textus: Mayr, Ludwig (²1902), *ΧΑΡΙΤΩΝ ΠΟΛΙΣ. Die Stadt der Grazien. Beschreibung der Stadt Graz nebst den wichtigsten Sagen aus Stadt und Umgebung*. Griechisch und Deutsch, Graz (editio princeps: *ΧΑΡΙΤΩΝ ΠΟΛΙΣ. Die Stadt der Grazien. Griechisch und Deutsch*, Graz 1897).[12]

Crit.: 450 οὖρος correxi: οὑρὸς Mayr || 461 οἰχνεῦνται suadente Weise correxi: ὀχνεῦνται Mayr || 474 ἐρίδουπα correxi: ἐρίδυυπα Mayr

Sim.: 397 τραπέζαισιν] Pind. *Ol.* 50 | κρέα πολλὰ βοῶν] Hom. *Il.* 8.231 || 398 αὐλιζομένου βοός] cf. Hom. *Od.* 12.265 || 399–400 ἔμπλεια κνίσης τε καὶ — αἵματος] cf. Hom. *Od.* 18.119 et 20.26 || 402 τρέφει αἶα] Nic. *Ther.* 388, 759 || 403 χῆνας καὶ νήττας] cf. Ar. *Pax* 1004 | ἀπαλοτρεφέας] Hom. *Il.* 21.363 || 404–405 ποταμοῦ – ποταμοῖο] cf. Hom. *Il.* 21.185–186 || 405 πέρην ποταμοῖο ῥεέθρων] Theoc. 25.19 || 408–411 κατὰ πρῆξιν — μαψιδίως ἀλάονται] cf. Hom. *Od.* 3.372-373 || 408 κραιπνοῖσι πόδεσσιν] Opp. *C.* 2.268 || 409 ἂμ πόλιν] Ap. Rhod. *Argon.* 1.165; 2.996 || 410 πρηκτῆρες] Hom. *Od.* 8.162 pro mercatoribus | ἠλέκτορι παμφανόωντα] cf. Hom. *Il.* 6.513; 19.398 || 412 παρθενικὰς — ὀπιπτέυοντες] cf. Hom. *Od.* 19.67 || 414 ὡς εἰ ἀνέμοιο θύελλα] apud Homerum passim; *Il.* 23.366 etiam de curribus || 415–420 ἅρμα δέ — πηδάλιον] cf. e.g. Hom. *Il.* 5.720-732 || 417 οἴηξ] cf. Hom. *Il.* 24.269 || 418 ἰθύνεται ἅρμ'] cf. Hom. *Il.* 11.528; Hes. [*Sc.*] 324; Nonn. *Dion.* 14.40; 37.165; 38.199 || 421 πρήσσων μάλα ῥίμφα κέλευθον] cf. Hom. *Il.* 14.282; 23.501; *Od.* 13.83 || 422–423 ἀσφαλέως — ἐλαφρότατος πετεηνῶν] Hom. *Od.* 13.86-87 || 425 ἐπίσσωτρα προσάρηρεν] cf. Hom. *Il.* 5.725 || 426 ἄκληρος] cf. Hom. *Od.* 11.490 (hapax legomenon) || 428 ἵππον ἐλαύνειν] cf. Hom. *Od.* 5.371 || 429 ἀλέονται ἀδευκέα φῆμιν] cf. Hom. *Od.* 6.273 || 430 τις εἴπῃσιν ἰδὼν ἐς πλησίον ἄλλον] cf. e.g. Hom. *Il.* 2.71 vel *Od.* 10.37 et saepius || 431 Ἀμαζόνας ἀντιανείρας] Hom. *Il.* 6.186 || 432 τροχαλίστριαι] apud veteres non legitur || 434 μή ποτ' ἐμοὶ τοιήδ' ἄλοχος κεκλημένη εἴη] cf. *Hymn. Hom. Ven.* 148 | 436 περιφραδέως] Hom. *Il.* 1.466; 2.429; 7.318; 24.624; *Od.* 14.431; 19.423 || 437 δαῖτα πένεσθαι] cf. e.g. Hom. *Od.* 3.428 vel 22.199 || 438 ὥς ποτέ τίς κ' εἴποι] cf. Hom. *Il.* 6.479 || 439–440 εὖρος τε νότος τε / καὶ βορέης αἰθρηγενέτης ζέφυρός τε δυσαής] Hom. *Od.* 5.295 || 442 καρπαλίμως ποτὶ ἄστυ] cf. Hom. *Il.* 3.116–117 | ὁδοὺς ἀνὰ λείας] cf. Hom. *Od.* 10.103 || 443 αἴθωνι σιδήρῳ] cf. e.g. Hom. *Il.* 4.485; 7.473; 20.372; Hes. *Op.* 743 || 445 ἁρματροχιαί] cf. Hom. *Il.* 23.505 (hapax legomenon) || 446 ἂμ πόλιν] cf. v. 409 || 446–447 ἔτειναν πείσματα — ὁλοιά] cf. Hom. *Od.* 22.465-472 || 448 ἠλέκτορος] cf. Hom. *Il.* 6.513; 19.398; *Hymn. Hom. Ap.* 369 (de Sole) || 450 ἄνευθ' ἄλλων] Hom. *Il.* 22.39; *Od.* 16.239 || 451 δένδρεα

---

[12] I would like to thank Irina Tautschnig and Rupert Rainer for their valuable help with the transcription and the *similia*. – MB

μακρὰ πεφύκασι τηλεθόωντα] Hom. *Od.* 7.114; cf. *Od.* 5.238; 5.241 || **452** ἔνθα – εὐνάζονται] Hom. *Od.* 5.65 || **453** ὑψηλοὺς πύργους καὶ τεῖχος ἔδειμαν] Hom. *Il.* 7.436–437 || **454** σφετέροισι τέκεσσιν] Hes. [*Sc.*] 247 || **455** ἄνδρας δυσμενέας] Hom. *Il.* 10.40; aliis in casibus saepius | αἰνὴν δηϊότητα] aliis in casibus apud Homerum passim || **456** αἰπήν γε κέλευθον] cf. Quint. Smyrn. 5.55 || **457** ποδώκεες ἵπποι] Hom. *Il.* 23.376; Hes. [*Sc.*] 191; cf. etiam *Il.* 17.614; ὠκέες ἵπποι *Il.* 16.866; 23.373 || **458** ἡμίονοι κρατερώνυχες ἐντεσιεργοί] cf. Hom. *Il.* 24.277 || **459** ῥίμφα φέρουσ'] cf. Hom. *Il.* 17.458 | ἠλέκτορος] vide supra v. 448 || **460** πολλοὶ μὲν ξεῖνοι] cf. Hom. *Od.* 19.379 || **462** μελπήθρων] cf. Hom. *Il.* 13.233; 17.255; 18.179; Nonn. *Dion.* 5.521 semper de cibo canum || **463** κραδίην θέλγουσι] cf. Triph. 464 | Ἰστρογένειαι] apud veteres non legitur || **464** εἴαρι] cf. Opp. *C.* 1.376–392 | ἐπὶ κνέφας ἔλθῃ] cf. Hom. *Il.* 2.413; 11.194; 11.209; 17.455; *Od.* 5.225 || **465** ἀπ' ἀκροτάτης κορυφῆς] Hes. *Th.* 62; cf. etiam *Il.* passim || **466** νύκτα δι' ὀρφναίην] Hom. *Il.* 10.83; 10.276; 10.386; *Od.* 9.143; *Hymn. Hom. Merc.* 578 | ἠλέκτωρ] vide supra v. 448 || **467** ἐντὸς γὰρ μεγάρων] cf. Hom. *Od.* 22.172 | δαίνυντ' ἐρικυδέα δαῖτα] Hom. *Il.* 24.802; *Od.* 3,66; 13.26; 20.280; cf. *Od.* 10.182 || **468** τερπόμενοι – ἀοιδῇ] cf. Thgn. 1.791 | μολπῇ τε καὶ ὀρχηθμῷ] cf. Hom. *Il.* 13.637; *Od.* 23.145; Triph. 342; Quint. Smyrn. 13.3 | ὀρχηθμῷ καὶ ἀοιδῇ] *Hymn. Hom. Ap.* 149; Hes. [*Sc.*] 282 || **469** κυκλοτερής] Hom. *Od.* 17.209 (hapax legomenon) || **470** τρὶς ἐπ' ἤματι] cf. Hom. *Od.* 12.105 || **470–471** χαλκέου – ὀπός] cf. Hom. *Il.* 18.222 || **471** ἠελίου ἀνιόντος] Hom. *Il.* 8.538; 22.135; Ap. Rhod. *Argon.* 4.125–126 || **472** ἠέλιος μέσον οὐρανὸν ἀμφιβεβήκῃ] Hom. *Il.* 8.68; 16.777; *Od.* 4.400 || **473** λαμπρὸν φάος ἠελίοιο] Hom. *Il.* 1.605; 5.120; 8.485; Hes. *Op.* 155 || **474** ὑπ' αἰθούσῃ] Hom. *Il.* et *Od.* passim; ὑπ' αἰθούσῃ ἐριδούπῳ *Od.* 3.399; 3.493; 7.345; 20.176; 20.189 | δολίχαυλα] cf. Hom. *Od.* 9.156 (hapax legomenon) || **475** πῦρ – ὀλοιόν] cf. Hom. *Od.* 12.68 || **476** πυρὸς αὐγήν] cf. Hom. *Il.* 9.206; 18.610; *Od.* 6.305; 23.89; *Hymn. Hom. Ven.* 86 || **480** κρατερή δ' ἐπέκειτο ἀνάγκη] cf. Hom. *Il.* 6.458 || **481–482** λυγροῖς – σήμασιν] cf. Hom. *Il.* 6.168; Quint. Smyrn. 12.529 || **484** δηρὸν – ἠελίοιο] Hom. *Il.* 5.120 || **485** θάνατος τῷ γ' ἀβληχρὸς μάλα] cf. Hom. *Od.* 11.134–135; 23.281–282 || **486** τόσσον ἔνερθεν, ὅσον] Hom. *Il.* 8.16 || **487** τετράπλευρον] verbum pedestre | πύργον ἔδειμαν] Ap. Rhod. *Argon.* 4.517; cf. Hom. *Il.* 7.437–438 || **488** τηλεφανέα] Hom. *Od.* 24.83 (hapax legomenon) || **489** Ζηνὸς καὶ Θέμιδός γε θυγατρῶν] cf. *Hymn. Orph.* 43.1 || **489–490** κελεύθους – νυκτός τε καὶ ἤματος] cf. Hom. *Od.* 10.86; Pind. *Pyth.* 4.195; Parm. DK 28 B 1.11

The City of the Graces

(excerpt, ll. 395–490)

> [395] Throughout the city the marketplaces are brimming with people.
> Baskets are filled with fruits and produce,
> beef and pork is placed on the counters,
> and besides that, also many entrails of the displayed bull
> filled with lard and liver and milk
> [400] or with blood to be roasted, a supper for the townsmen.
> Around the monastery lots of luscious poultry
> are sold, reared by the Styrian soil:
> geese and ducks and well-fattened capons.
> Near to the river the veal market is set up,
> [405] and beyond the streams of the river fish are sold,

which the river Mur and violet-faced Danube have bred.
The streets are crammed with people of all sorts.
Some go after their business on swift feet
throughout the city; others are inspecting very carefully,
[410] what the merchants have on display, at night illuminated by electric light.
Still others are randomly roaming the streets by day,
looking around after fair-cheeked maidens.
Others again drive their vehicles past the steadfast wanderers,
ever-swiftly like the swirl of the wind.
[415] This wondrous vehicle blazes from glittering iron:
iron is the seat, iron are the two curved wheels,
fastened together in a row, one in the back of the other, and above all the handle,
with which the vehicle is steered, lest it damage the wanderer.
On each side of the gleaming axes a peddle is fastened:
[420] the driver treads them in turn with his feet
and covers his path without effort.
For the vehicle runs forever easily; even the circling hawk
would miss it, the swiftest of all birds.
Nevertheless the artfully wrought vehicle runs in silence:
[425] For soft tires are fixed around the wheels;
therefore a poor man would not be able to acquire it.
But also bold maidens as well as bold women
boast to be versed in steering the iron horse in any direction,
whilst many others shun the bitter gossip,
[430] lest upon seeing them someone say to his neighbour:
'Oh shame, do you not see those men-matching Amazons,
driving the iron horse, who are now going hither and thither
by cycling, being a great wonder to many people?
Be it so that such a woman may never be called my wife!
[435] For to me a better woman seems to be her,
who wisely pursues her domestic chores,
as it is fit, and knows to prepare a meal.'
Like that someone could say – – – – – –
From all directions, where the East and the South wind,
[440] the aether-born North and the ill-blowing West wind are roused,
steam-driven coaches quickly bring the people
to the city, driving on smooth pathways,
which are firmly laid out, made of glittering iron,
whether built through mountains or in the lowland.
[445] In the same way there are also iron railways
everywhere in the city. But above them metal wires are stretched out,
like deathly nets are laid out for birds:
along them the coaches are moved by the power of electricity,
but the conductor demands a high fare from everyone.
[450] Above the city, there is a mountain, apart from the others,
where large and blooming trees grow,
on which the long-winged birds build their nests.

There the ancients built high towers and walls
to fend off from their children
[455] evil-minded foes and dreadful battle.
But now two coaches are going up and down on a rocky pathway,
meeting in the middle. Neither swift-footed horses
nor mules with mighty hooves working in harnesses
draw them so quickly, but the power of electricity, a worker of great deeds.
[460] Many strangers and townsmen appreciate being carried up and down
and seeing the city from above
with their eyes and listening to the dance-songs,
with which the 'Swallows' enchant the hearts, coming from the Danube
and appearing in spring. For when dusk falls,
[465] then electric light is always shining from the highest summit
through the dark night like the sun.
Inside the hall they eat a glorious meal
rejoicing in dance, music, and song.
Nearby a circular, never-yielding tower stands,
[470] out of which you could hear an iron voice thrice a day,
a far-sounding one: at sunrise,
and when the sun has just reached the middle of the sky,
and when the bright light of the sun sets.
In a portico, there are two resounding weapons with long tubes,
[475] which tell the city of deadly fire, if it happens:
there are also guardians, which indicate the gleam of fire.
Next to them you could see the walls, overgrown with ivy,
and a well-made well, dug out by barbarians:
Laid in chains, such a ransom they paid for having their life spared,
[480] and though they were very unwilling, mighty necessity forced them.
Nearby there is a stone seat, furnished with baneful signs,
on which, they say, a noble bishop once sat down.
They had kept him in the tower for a long time, and so
he would not see the bright light of the sun any longer:
[485] on this very spot, Death came upon him very gently.
Only so far below, as one reaches with his calls,
they had built a four-sided tower, the town's landmark,
being seen from afar. They call it the sanctuary of the Hours,
the daughters of Zeus and Themis, which always show
[490] the paths of the night and the day to the townsmen.

Metre: Hexameters. Note short α in πεφύκασι l. 451.

Notes: This panegyric epyllion on Graz belongs to the sub-genre of *laudes urbium*. Its title features a Latin pun on the (originally Slavic) name of the city; the Graces also act as the eponymous goddesses and guardians of the city throughout the work. Χαρίτων πόλις was first published in 1897, with the revenue going to the pilgrimage church of Maria Grün in the outskirts of Graz. This first edition consisted of 326 dactylic hexameters with facing German verse translation, without any further paratexts. Due to the remarkably positive reception from both the press and the public, Mayr decided to publish an extended version five years later. The second edition (1902) consists of 927 hexameters, almost three times the length of the first edition, and features a preface and a short commentary. In the additional verses Mayr presents places and sights not covered in the earlier version; he also supplements several legends and short historical narratives. The most interesting modifications are updates which offer a glimpse into the changes in everyday life in a mid-size Austrian city circa 1900. For example, in 1897 the trams in Graz are still horse-drawn; however, Mayr hints already at future electrification (Mayr 1897, ll. 218–223). In the second edition, the verses in question are replaced with a praise of the new electric tramway, although the public transport still seems to be overpriced in Mayr's opinion (ll. 445–449 above). Typical for the time was also the formation of all-female dance bands, such as the 'Wiener Schwalben' ('Viennese Swallows'), who regularly performed at the terrace restaurant on the 'Grazer Schloßberg' during the summer months (alluded to in l. 463). Overall, *Χαρίτων πόλις* is a well-written epyllion featuring Homeric epic language and style as well as numerous intertextual allusions to the *Iliad* and the *Odyssey*. A striking example is the description of bicycles in the manner of Iliadic chariots (ll. 413–426). Some accounts are clearly meant satirically, such as the jocular depiction of female cyclists (ll. 427–438), while the Homeric Greek sometimes serves as an amusing *Verfremdungseffekt*. In other passages, however, Mayr adopts a more serious tone, as in the earnest praise of the city and its surroundings at the beginning of the piece (not included in this selection). A particularly felicitous use of a Homeric simile occurs in l. 447, where the overhead cables of the newly built tramway are compared to bird nets. Also notable is the deliberately unfinished l. 438 (already present in the first edition and imitated in the German translation), surely a gesture of reverence towards the 'Latin Homer' Vergil and his *tibicines* ('half-finished hexameter lines').

Biography: Ludwig Mayr was professor of classical languages at the 'k. k. I. Staatsgymnasium' in Graz (the successor of the old Jesuit gymnasium, today's 'Akademisches Gymnasium'). He was born on 3 July 1851 in Bozen in South Tyrol. His family then moved to Innsbruck before 1854, where Mayr attended the gymnasium and studied German and classical philology at the university. He worked as a teacher in Bozen and Marburg an der Drau (Maribor), before he came to Graz in 1891. After retiring in 1905, he moved back to South Tyrol, where he died on 6 July 1944 in Lana. *Χαρίτων πόλις* is Mayr's only known literary work.

Bibliography: Pietsch, Wolfgang Josef (2004/5), "Chariton Polis – Die Stadt der Grazien. Ludwig Mayr und sein Lobgedicht auf die Stadt Graz", in: *Jahresbericht des Akademischen Gymnasiums Graz*, 5–16.

[MB]

Josef Maria Stowasser (1854–1910)

Das Gott erhalte [1902]

(excerptum, vv. 1–8)

    Ὦ θεὸς οὐρανόθεν μεδέων, σῶσόν τε φύλαξόν θ'
    ἡμετέρην γαίην καίσαρά θ' ἡμέτερον,
    τῆς ὀρθῆς δόξης ὑπερείσμασιν ἰσχυρωθεὶς
    ἡμᾶς οὗτος ἀεὶ χερσὶ σοφαῖς ἀγάγοι.
5   Γενναίως τε καὶ ἀνδρείως διαδήματι πατρῶν
    αὐτοῦ ἀμύνωμεν, ὅστις ἂν ἐχθρὸς ἔῃ,
    αἰεὶ δ' Ἀψβούργων μεγάλων τὸ στέμμα κλεεννὸν
    εὐθύνοι πότμον τῆς χθονὸς Αὐστριακῆς.

Textus: Stowasser, Josef M. (1902), "Das Gott erhalte – griechisch und lateinisch", in: *Achtundzwanzigster Jahresbericht über das k.k. Franz Joseph-Gymnasium in Wien. Schuljahr 1901/1902*, Wien, III.

Sim.: 1 οὐρανόθεν μεδέων] e formula Homerica -θεν μεδέων (e.g. Hom. *Il.* 3.276 Ἴδηθεν μεδέων) et voce Homerica οὐρανόθεν contaminatum || **3** ὀρθῆς δόξης] circumlocutio vocis ὀρθοδοξίας || **4** χερσὶ σοφαῖς] cf. Marc. Mus. *In Platonem* 66 (vide huius voluminis **capitulum Graecum**); χειρόσοφος Luc. *Rh.Pr.* 17, *Lex.* 14 || **7** κλεεννόν] forma Aeolica (e.g. Pind. *Pyth.* 4.280)

May God preserve

(excerpt, ll. 1–8)

    O God who reigns from the heavens, keep safe and sound and guard our country and our emperor! Strong through the strut of the correct faith, may this man always guide us with his wise hands! [5] Gallantly and bravely let us defend the crown of his fathers against any enemy! May the glorious crown of the great Habsburgs always direct Austria's fate![13]

Metre: Elegiac couplets. Note *longum in arsi* in l. 6.

Notes: In the 19th and early 20th centuries, school teachers were exhorted to publish specimens of their scholarly expertise in their schools' annual reports. While these were usually articles on specific research questions, Stowasser here shows his unusual prowess in Greek and Latin as well as his patriotism in the form of a translation of the Austrian anthem into both of these languages. The anthem, written in this version for Emperor Franz Joseph I by Johann Gabriel Seidl on a tune by Joseph Haydn and officially adopted in 1854, celebrates the harmony between the Austrian population and its ruler. It officially comprised six stanzas, of which only the first four were sung in the early 20th century (stanzas 5 and 6 being dedicated to the emperor's wife and first born son, both of whom were already deceased at the time). Stowasser consequently translated only the first four stanzas, of which the very first of the Greek version is displayed here. The four-footed trochees of the original were turned into elegiac couplets by the translator: this amounted to extending the single lines from 7–8 to 12–17 syllables. The additional space was taken up partly by the numerous Greek particles, partly by bigger (e.g., οὐρανόθεν μεδέων, l. 1; γενναίως τε καὶ ἀνδρείως, l. 5) and smaller additions (ὀρθῆς, l. 2), as well as by more complex syntax ('jeden Feind' becomes ὅστις ἂν ἐχθρὸς ἔῃ, l. 6). Stowasser not only writes impeccable Greek, his translation also shows the ambition to stylistically improve upon the original. This can be seen in the opening direct address to God, which transforms the poem into a kind of prayer, and in the beautiful chiasm that makes l. 2 into a *versus serpentinus*, but particulary in the repeated addition of the adverb ἀεί/αἰεί (ll. 4, 7). Stowasser thus anticipates the eternity motif which provides a crowning finish to the anthem (str. 4, l. 8: 'Österreich wird ewig stehn', Αὐστριακῶν ἀρχὴ ἔσται ἐς ἀΐδιον); this then results in a harmonious ring composition.

---

13 The German original translated by Stowasser reads: 'Gott erhalte, Gott beschütze / unsern Kaiser, unser Land! / Mächtig durch des Glaubens Stütze / führ' er uns mit weiser Hand! / Laßt uns seiner Väter Krone / schirmen wider jeden Feind: / Innig bleibt mit Habsburgs Throne / Österreichs Geschick vereint.' The English translation is based not on the original, but on Stowasser's version. The Latin version reads: *O deus in caelis, salva servaque, precamur, / vitam Caesaris ac dulce solum patriae! / Pollens atque potens fidei munimine sacrae / nos ducat sapiens ille regatque manu; / nos vero semper clarum diadema parentum / hostes contra omnes protueamur ei, / firmiter ut coniuncta throno sceptroque potenti / Habsburgi maneant, Austria, fata tua.*

Biography: Josef Maria Stowasser was born in 1854 in Troppau in Austrian Silesia (today Opava, Czech Republic). He studied classics and German at the University of Vienna from 1872 to 1876. Since 1878, he taught at various gymnasia, most of the time (from 1885 to 1908) at Vienna's Franz-Joseph-Gymnasium. His activity as a teacher, interrupted only by a study tour to Italy in 1881, came to an end when he had to retire due to health reasons two years before his death in Vienna in 1910. Today, Stowasser is still famous as the author of the eponymous Latin-German school dictionary ('Der Stowasser'), which has been revised several times and uninterruptedly remained in print since its first edition in 1894. He was also a charismatic teacher, a fanciful etymologist and, last but not least, a playful poet, who translated, besides the specimen on record here, Greek verse into Austrian dialect and vice versa.

Bibliography: "Stowasser Josef Maria", in: *Österreichisches Biographisches Lexikon 1815–1950*, vol. 13, Vienna 2007–2010, 334.

[MK]

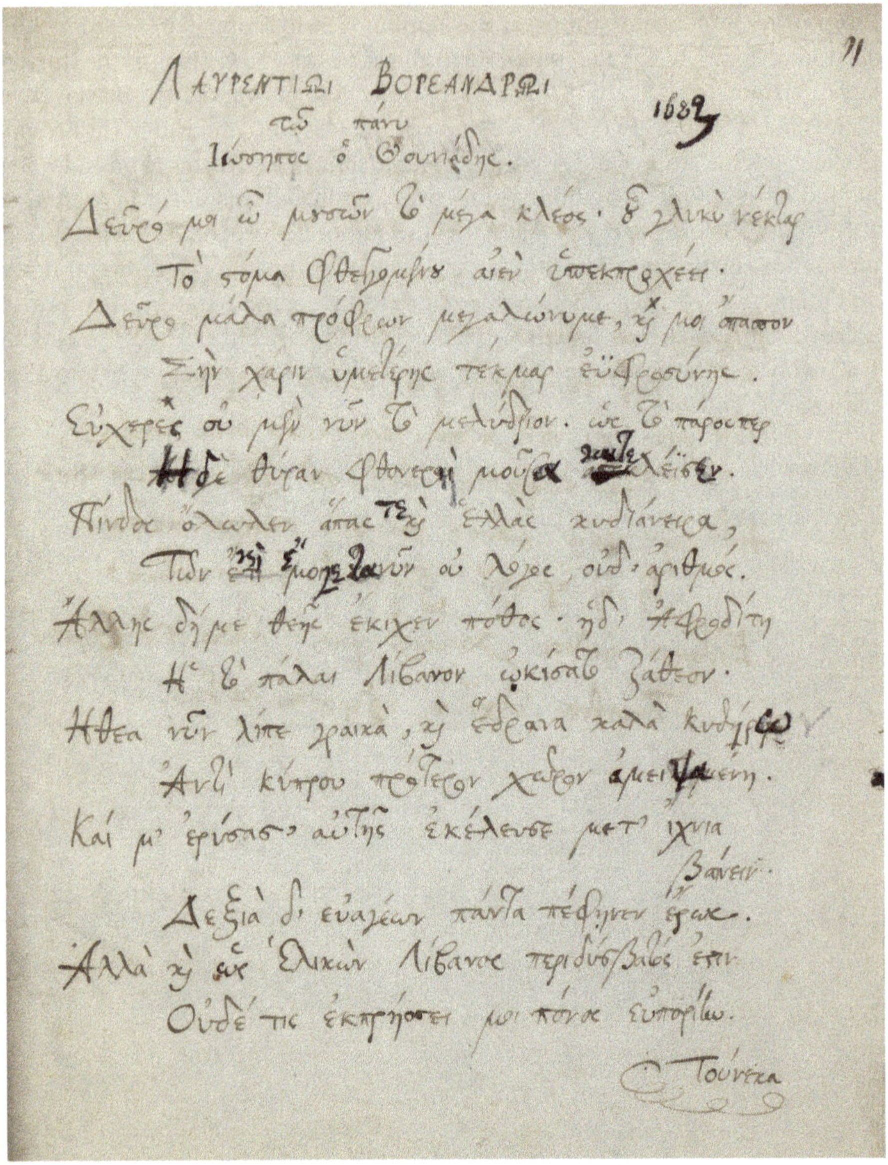

ΛΑΥΡΕΝΤΙΩΙ ΒΟΡΕΑΝΔΡΩΙ
τῶ πάνυ 1689
Ἰώσηπος ὁ Θουνιάδης.

Δεῦρό μοι ὦ μουσῶν τὸ μέγα κλέος, ὁ ἡλικὺ νεκτὰρ
  Τὸ στόμα φθεγομένης αἰεὶ ὑπεκπροχέει·
Δεῦρο μάλα ποθέων μεγαλώνυμε, καὶ μοι ὄπασσον
  Σὴν χάριν ὑπηδερης τέκμαρ εὐφροσύνης.
Εὔχερες οὐ μὲν νῦν τὸ μελιστάγιον, ὡς τὸ πάρος περ
  Ἡδὲ θυγατρὶ φθονερὴ μοῦσα καυτὰ ἔλιπεν.
Πίνδος ὁλωλεν ἅπας τε ἡ Ἑλλὰς κυδιάνειρα,
  Τῶν ἐμοὶ ἐτέων οὐ λόγος, οὐδ᾽ ἀριθμός.
Ἄλλης δή με θεῆς ἔκιχεν πόθος, ἡδ᾽ Ἀφροδίτη
  Ἥ τε πάλαι Λίβανον ᾤκισε ζάθεον.
Ἥ θεα νῦν λίπε γραικά, καὶ ἕδρανα καλὰ κυδρὰ ἐω
  Ἀντὶ κύπρου πετραῖον χῶρον ἀμειψαμένη.
Καί μ᾽ ἐρύσασ᾽ αὐτῆς ἐκέλευσε μετ᾽ ἴχνια
                                      βαίνειν·
  Δεξιὰ δ᾽ εὐαγέων πάντα πέφηνεν ἐμοί.
Ἀλλὰ καὶ ἐκ ἡλικῶν Λίβανος περιδύσσηβες ἐστί
  Οὐδέ τις ἐκπήσει μοι πόνος εὐπορίην.

                                    Θουνέα

Fig. 15: *Carmina Graeca JOSEPHI THUNII Autographa* (Linköping Diocesan Library, W 40), p. S5: manuscript page providing a Greek poem by Josef Thun (see below, p. 749–752) to his fellow poet Laurentius Norrmannus.

Johanna Akujärvi, Tua Korhonen, Janika Päll, and Erkki Sironen
Nordic Countries

1 The principles of choice

As stressed by J. IJsewijn in the context of Neo-Latin studies, humanist *Res Publica Litterarum* does not follow regional borders.[1] The 'Nordic countries' are here understood as a cross-section of countries belonging to the modern Nordic Council and the Baltic Assembly, including poems from authors whose birth places lie within the borders of modern Sweden (14), Finland (7), Estonia (3), Latvia (1), Denmark (5), and Iceland (1). These poems are a small sample of the whole corpus of known Nordic Humanist Greek poetry, which exceeds 2100 texts for the countries of the former Swedish Empire; the size of the Danish corpus remains unknown.

The Nordic Greek poetry tradition was at its strongest in the Early Modern period. Excepting Denmark, this means that the greater part of this poetry was created during the Swedish Empire, when Sweden ruled over Finland (including Carelia), Estonia and Latvia (including Livonia and Curonia). The nature of Greek poetry from these countries does not reflect the wide-ranging origins of its authors, many of whom were active in different parts of the kingdom.[2] The Danish tradition, though rich and likely the oldest in the region, is underrepresented here as a result of the slight attention it has received from Danish scholarship.[3] For historical reasons, the traditions of Norway and Iceland are treated here together with Denmark.[4]

The study of Humanist Greek in the Swedish Empire began in the 18th century with E. M. Fant's and M. Floderus' disputations, which present the history and provide text samples of Humanist Greek. After a period of neglect, it has

---

[1] IJsewijn 1990, 39. Although IJsewijn used regional-ethnic criteria in his account of Neo-Latin literature, he was not rigid and discussed travelling humanists in several sections, corresponding to the times and places of their activity. The same broad approach has been used by Fant 1775–1786; Floderus 1785–1789; Collijn 1927–1938; Collijn 1942–1946.
[2] These countries are considered together also in IJsewijn 1990, 274–283. Regional differences appear mainly in the periods of activity (depending on political history) and in the language choice of polyglot poetry.
[3] See only now Gottschalck 2019.
[4] As already IJsewijn 1990, 263–273. For a similar combination of Nordic and Baltic, see Merisalo/ Sarasti-Wilenius (1994) (including also Lithuania, which in this anthology is together with Poland).

https://doi.org/10.1515/9783110652758-017

been resumed by the editors of this section, now united in the *Helleno-Nordica* project (led by Johanna Akujärvi).[5]

2 Humanist Greek Literature in Nordic countries: history

Nordic Humanist Greek literature began much later than Neo-Latin literature[6] and is limited primarily to learned circles, with some minor engagement from members of the courts (although kings, queens, and noblemen often figure as adressees of the longest and most eloquent Greek poems).[7] The role of the Reformation (particularly the Lutheran church) for its beginning and development was crucial; in Scandinavia, the systematic study of and education in Greek began primarily as a means for reading and translating the Bible. Greek was not taught by Byzantines or Greek émigrés or by Italian humanists, but learned from books and by travelling to (Protestant) universities, mostly in Germany, before a new educational system had been established after the reformation in the former Swedish Empire. The initial stages in the 1550s are characterised by wandering poets (see Jespersen under Denmark, Krüger under Estonia) and students at German universities; hence their earliest poems were printed abroad, in places such as Wittenberg, Rostock, Jena, Lübeck, Leiden, and Amsterdam. The availability of printing types in Greek was decisive for the flourishing of Humanist Greek poetry. In some Nordic countries Greek types started to be used in the last three decades of the 16th century: occasional Greek poems were published in Copenhagen in 1568 and in Sweden the first Greek prints were school texts: *Catechesis Christianorum Graeca* and an edition of Isocrates' *Oratio ad Demonicum* (now lost). Both were printed in 1584 in Stockholm by Andreas Gutterwitz and edited by Jacobus Erici, professor of Greek at the Royal College, where the study of languages – not only of Latin, but also of Greek and Hebrew – was encouraged.

---

5 *Helleno-Nordica. The Humanist Greek Heritage of the Swedish Empire*, funded by the Swedish Research Council (project no. 2016-01881) under the auspices of which this section was written.
6 The information in this subchapter is mainly based on Fant 1775–1786 and Floderus 1785–1789, more recent overviews are Korhonen 2007 and Päll 2020a. Data collected during earlier projects and now under the leadership of Johanna Akujärvi will be published in the Helleno-Nordica project database at Tartu University Library, http://humgraeca.utlib.ut.ee.
7 See Korhonen 2009.

In Sweden, Johannes Rudbeck played a key role as stimulus to the establishment of Greek studies. As a professor at Uppsala University he held a private collegium where Latin and Greek were the only spoken languages (1610–1613), and, as bishop in Västerås, he founded the first Swedish gymnasium in that city. The writing of Greek poetry became far more common after the reform of the Swedish school system in the first decades of the 17th century. It was not until the 1620s that Uppsala University became financially secure and began to function effectively again after a series of reforms. Moreover, several new universities and gymnasia were founded and endowed with well-educated professors and well-equipped printing houses. The most important of these institutions were the gymnasia in Västerås (1623), Tartu/Dorpat and Turku/Åbo (1630), Riga and Tallinn/Reval (1631), as well as the universities in Tartu (1632), Turku (1640), and Lund (1666). Additionally, Greek was studied at several other schools. A first flourishing of Humanist Greek in the Nordic countries occurred from the middle of the 1630s until the 1650s, after which interest in it weakened due to the outbreak of the plague and the Second Northern War (1655–1661). A second peak began towards the end of the 17th century, but this time with several marked differences between the countries. The tradition was strong in Sweden, Finland, and Denmark, but not in Estonia and Latvia, especially after the beginning of the Great Northern War (1700–1721) and the ensuing Russian rule. After the closing of the Tartu-Pärnu University (1710), the Humanist Greek poetry tradition continued in Riga and Tallinn Gymnasia and in connection to the court in Jelgava/Mitau until the 1730s. Approximately midway through the 18th century the tradition started to weaken in Sweden, Finland, and Denmark as well – now for poetic rather than political reasons – although poems continued to be written until the end of the century.

The 19th century marked a fresh start for Greek studies, strongly anchored in the altered framework of classical scholarship: Tartu University was reopened in 1802, Turku University relocated to Helsinki in 1828, and Uppsala, Lund, and Copenhagen Universities continued to develop the teaching of classical languages and philology. Now the practice of writing in Greek was confined to a very small circle of academics, schoolteachers even. In the 20th and 21st centuries there are still some professors of Greek or Latin who continue to write and publish Greek dedicatory epigrams in the universities of Sweden, Finland, and Estonia.

3 The Character of Humanist Greek Literature in the Nordic Countries

Nordic Humanist Greek starts with occasional poetry and epigrams in the middle of the 16th century (Peder Aagesen and Jacob Jespersen from Denmark, Laurentius Petri Gothus from Sweden). These included poems for weddings, funerals, and paratexts in various types of prints. During the same period, the first local example of a most sublime genre, namely verse oration (written for public recitation, but often also printed)[8], appeared with a religious hexameter oration published in Wittenberg in approximately 1555 by Gregor Krüger (see Introduction to Estonia), followed by a hexameter paraphrasis on the episode of Heracles' choice in Xenophon's *Memorabilia* by **Ivar Borrichius** (Leiden 1595, see Denmark). The production of Greek hexameter orations flourished in Uppsala between 1640 and 1680 and also includes panegyrical orations; the most notable specimen from the Nordic countries is **Johan Paulinus'** *Finlandia*, published in Uppsala in 1678 (see Finland). Another highly esteemed genre, the Pindaric ode, is represented by German-born Heinrich Vogelmann in Tartu (see Introduction to Estonia) and an anonymous Swedish author in Uppsala (Ζαχαρίᾳ Πλαντίνῳ εἰς τὴν αὐτοῦ δάφνην, 1711). Both are congratulations for major academic achievements.

The printed books, academic dissertations, and orations from Sweden, Finland, and Estonia are characterised by a great number of dedications and congratulations – most often written by fellow students, but sometimes by professors too. Some of these texts are in Greek.[9] Additionally, Greek occurs in occasional poetry commemorating notable events in the life and death of the addressees, whether educated people, nobility, or royalty. After Swedish, Latin, and German, Greek is the fourth most common language in Swedish collections

---

[8] Public presentation of (verse) orations on different festive occasions was established as an institutionalised practice at least in German and Swedish universities (but also outside the academic context) from the mid-16th century onwards. Due to overlaps between 'genre' and 'form', verse oration has sometimes not been classified as a genre in its own right, e.g. religious orations and Bible paraphrases in hexameters can be regarded together as Biblical epic. See Czapla, Ralf Georg (2013), *Das Bibelepos in der Frühen Neuzeit*, Berlin/Boston. More on this: Weise 2020, 39; Päll 2018, 73–83.

[9] On Greek paratextual material in dissertations from the Universities of Uppsala and Lund, see Akujärvi (forthcoming); Turku, see Korhonen 2004, 284–346, 355–372; Tartu, see Päll 2018, 84–90.

of occasional poetry.¹⁰ It seems that Greek was an option for the author whenever the adressee had an academic background in Greek.¹¹

In the Nordic Greek corpus, the ancient and modern poetic genres are represented primarily by innumerable congratulatory epigrams, but epyllia, hymns, elegies, satires, eidyllia, lyric poems, centos, and paraphrases were written as well, alongside some instances of drama (see Sweden). Almost all possible types of metrical forms are present, but hexameters and elegiac couplets prevail and only some types of lyric verses (anacreontics, sapphics, iambic verse) are used more than sporadically. As elsewhere in Europe, Humanist Greek metrics are often influenced by the (Neo-)Latin tradition, which can be seen in a preference for certain types of caesurae and epodic verses.¹² In addition to verse, two other text types occur among the occasional texts: Greek lapidaries (likely influenced by the widely popular Latin and vernacular lapidary texts)¹³ and short congratulatory prose texts, which were especially popular at the end of the 17th and in the 18th century and result partly from the Greco-Latin *progymnasmata* tradition.¹⁴ Among the figures and formal devices we find numerous different types of acrostics (from verse-initial to full verse acrostics), tautogrammatic poems, anagrams, figurative poetry, palindromes, chronostichs, dialogues, ekphraseis, and echo-poems in Greek.

Multilingualism is a common context for Humanist Greek. Out of three types of polyglot poetry clusters, two can be found in the Nordic countries. One of these, which includes different biblical and oriental languages (Hebrew, Greek, Latin, Syriac, Aramaic, Arabic, etc.), appears almost exclusively in Uppsala where the required printing types were available earlier. The other is universally popular, extending from simple Greek-Latin and Greek-Latin-vernacular poem clusters to poems with many different vernaculars; here the language choice varies from region to region and can reach up to 10 different languages as in the sumptuous *Europa in luctu* on the death of King Charles XI in 1697 (see also Latvia).¹⁵ Occasionally, ancient or modern literature is translated into Greek; this is most frequent in the 19th century when the practice of writing Greek became even more exclusively academic and translation was often used in dissertations

---

10 Hedin 2020. For Tartu, see Kriisa 2018.
11 See Kaju 2016 and Päll 2010.
12 See Andrist/Lukinovich 2005, 691–692. For an overview of metres, see Päll 2020a, 435–437.
13 See Ridderstad 1975; Kajanto 1994 and Weise 2016, 137 and 164 (for Germany).
14 See Korhonen 2004, 62f, 161f., 375 and Päll 2012.
15 The third type, aspiring to include as many different languages as possible, has not been found in Nordic countries: for its background, see Päll/Valper 2014, 25f., 34. For language variation, see Kriisa 2018.

as an academic exercise (see Sweden); the same trend can be seen in other countries.[16] From the 19th century onwards, epigram is the dominant genre, though with a few notable exceptions, such as attempts at drama and a satiric epos (see Sweden and Finland).

The practice of Humanist Greek entails more than just the writing of poetry. Teaching manuals and text editions from the Nordic countries occasionally included Greek prose prefaces and dedications, and a number of letters and stipendium applications were written in Greek.[17] What seems to be peculiar to Sweden (who imported the tradition from Germany), is a strong tradition of disputing in Greek, as is testified by more than 40 printed and manuscript disputations in Greek from 1620 to the 1820s.[18] In addition to verse orations, mentioned above, students composed and delivered Greek prose orations on different subjects as well: both the disputations and the orations can be seen as a side-practice to the more usual Latin examples.[19]

The language of Nordic Humanist Greek is a mixture of different dialects with a Homeric and Attic flavour, although the Atticizing tendency becomes stronger towards the 18th century.[20] The syntax, particularly the use of particles, can occasionally be described as unusual. In versification, the rules of ancient prosody (avoidance of hiatus, attention to the positions of the caesurae) tend to be ignored in the 16th and 17th century, but are mostly observed from the 19th century onwards, corresponding to the growing impact of modern classical scholarship.

[JP/JA/TK, with ES]

---

16 For translation in an academic context in Sweden and Finland, see Akujärvi 2017; Akujärvi (2020a); for Great Britain, see Päll (forthcoming); for Germany, see Weise 2016, 161–164; see also Pontani 2017, 335–338 for the exclusively academic context in Italy.
17 Korhonen 2004, 135–148.
18 See Korhonen 2010; Korhonen 2018 and the list of unpublished Greek dissertations in Korhonen 2020. For Swedish and German tradition from 1604 till the 19th century, see Päll (2020b) with a catalogue of all known Greek disputations in the Appendix.
19 See Sironen 2018; Korhonen 2004, 392–420; an edition of unpublished orations found in manuscripts is being prepared by Erkki Sironen, to appear in 2021.
20 For language usage in orations, see Sironen 2018; for language usage of Johan Paulinus, Sironen 2000; for language usage in disputations, Korhonen 2004 (passim); for the orthography, Päll 2005.

General Bibliography for the Nordic Countries

Akujärvi, Johanna (2017), "*Suethice*. On 19th century Swedish university translations of ancient literature", in: Arne Jönsson/Gregor Vogt-Spira (eds.), *The Classical tradition in the Baltic Region. Perceptions and Adaptations of Greece and Rome*, Zürich/New York, 253–274.

Akujärvi, Johanna (2020a), "Translation in university dissertations. A study of Swedish (and Finnish) dissertations of the 19th century and earlier", in: Meelis Friedenthal/Hanspeter Marti/Robert Seidel (eds.), *Early Modern Disputations and Dissertations in an Interdisciplinary and European Context*, Intersections, Leiden/Boston, 779–813.

Akujärvi, Johanna (forthcoming), "*Versificandi mania*. University teaching of Greek and Greek verses in dissertations", in: Federica Ciccolella (ed.), *When Greece flew across the Alps: The Study of Greek in Early Modern Europe*, Leiden.

Andrist, Patrick/Lukinovich, Alessandra (2005), "POESIS ET MORES: Florent Chrestien, Joseph-Juste Scaliger, et les *Psaumes* en vers du *Bernensis* A 69", in: Antje Kolde/Alessandra Lukinovich/André-Louis Rey (eds.), κορυφαίῳ ἀνδρί. *Mélanges offerts à André Hurst*, Genève, 673–715.

Collijn, Isak (1927–1938), *Sveriges bibliografi intill år 1600*, I-III, Uppsala.

Collijn, Isak (1942–1946), *Sveriges bibliografi. 1600-talet*, I-II, Uppsala.

Fant, Erik Michael (1775–1786), *Historiola litteraturae Graecae in Svecia. Specimen* I-XII, Uppsala (Diss.).

Floderus, Matthias (1785–1789), *De poëtis in svio-Gothia Graecis. Specimen* I-IV. Uppsala (Diss.).

Gottschalck, Rasmus (2019), "Denmark", in: Francisco Oliveira/Ramón Martínez (eds.), *Europatrida*, Coimbra, 59–70.

Hedin, Östen (2020), "Tillfällesdikten på Kungliga biblioteket. Ett okänt kapitel i bibliotekets historia", in: Arne Jönsson et al. (eds.), *Att dikta för livet, döden och evigheten. Tillfällesdiktning under tidigmodern tid/Poems for Life, Death and Eternity. Occasional poetry in the Early Modern period*, Göteborg/Stockholm, 683–725.

IJsewijn, Jozef (1990), *Companion to Neo-Latin Studies,* Vol.1, Leiden.

Kajanto, Iiro (1994), "On Lapidary Style in Epigraphy and Literature in Sixteenth and Seventeenth Century", in: *Humanistica Lovaniensia* 43, 137–172.

Kaju, Katre (2016), "Keelevalik Tartu *Academia Gustaviana* aegses pulmaluules (1632–1656)" [The Choice of the Language in the Wedding Poetry from the Period of *Academia Gustaviana* (1632–1656) in Tartu], in: *Eesti Ajalooarhiivi toimetised* 12 (19), 50–82.

Korhonen, Tua/Oksala, Teivas/Sironen, Erkki (eds.) (2000), *Johan Paulinus (Lillienstedt): Finlandia*, Helsinki.

Korhonen, Tua (2004), *Ateena Auran rannoilla: Humanistikreikkaa Kuninkaallisesta Turun akatemiasta*, http://urn.fi/URN:ISBN:952-10-1812-7, Diss. Helsinki.

Korhonen, Tua (2007), "Der frühe Philhellenismus und die Griechisch-Tradition in Finnland des 17. und 18. Jahrhunderts", in: Evangelos Konstantinou (ed.), *Ausdrucksformen des europäischen und internationalen Philhellenismus vom 17.–19. Jahrhundert*, Frankfurt am Main, 61–67.

Korhonen, Tua (2009), "Christina of Sweden and her knowledge of Greek", in: *Arctos* 43, 41–56.

Korhonen, Tua (2010), "The dissertations in Greek supervised by Henrik Ausius in Uppsala in the middle of the seventeenth century", in: Janika Päll/Ivo Volt/Martin Steinrück (eds.), *Classical tradition from the 16th century to Nietzsche*, Tartu, 89–113.

Korhonen, Tua (2018), "Classical authors and pneumatological questions. Greek dissertations supervised by Johannes Gezelius the Elder at the University of Tartu", in: Päll/Volt 2018, 158–184.

Korhonen, Tua (2020), "Disputing and writing dissertations in Greek: Petrus Aurivillius' Περὶ τῆς ἀρετῆς (Uppsala, 1658)", in: Meelis Friedenthal/Hanspeter Marti/Robert Seidel (eds.), *Early Modern Disputations and Dissertations in an Interdisciplinary and European Context. Intersections*, Leiden/Boston, 703–727.

Kriisa, Kaidi (2018), *Multilingual Practices in the Early Modern Academia Dorpatensis (1632–1710)*, Tartu.

Merisalo, Outi/Sarasti-Wilenius, Raija (eds.) (1994), *Mare Balticum - Mare Nostrum. Latin in the countries of the Baltic Sea (1500-1800)*, Helsinki.

Päll, Janika (2005), "Far Away from Byzantium: Pronunciation and Orthography of Greek in the 17th Century Estonia", in: Ivo Volt/Janika Päll (eds.), *Byzantino-Nordica. Acta Societatis Morgensternianae* 2, Tartu, 86–119.

Päll, Janika (2012), "The Practice of Chreia at the Academia Gustavo-Carolina (1690–1710) in Dorpat (Tartu)", in: Astrid Steiner-Weber *et al.* (eds.), *Acta Conventus Neo-Latini Upsaliensis: Proceedings of the Fourteenth International Congress of Neo-Latin Studies*, Leiden/Boston, 789–800.

Päll, Janika (2018), "Humanist Greek in Early Modern Estonia and Livonia", in: Päll/Volt 2018, 57–112.

Päll, Janika (2020a), "Hyperborean flowers: Humanist Greek around the Baltic Sea", in: Natasha Constantinidou/Han Lamers (eds.), *Receptions of Hellenism in Early Modern Europe*, Leiden/Boston, 410–438.

Päll, Janika (2020b, in print), "Greek Disputations in German and Swedish Universities and Academic Gymnasia in the 17th and Early 18th Century", in: Meelis Friedenthal/Hanspeter Marti/Robert Seidel (eds.), *Early Modern Disputations and Dissertations in an Interdisciplinary and European Context. Intersections*, Leiden/Boston, 728–778.

Päll, Janika (forthcoming), "Greek Pindaric ode in the United Kingdom", in: Ivo Volt/Janika Päll/Neeme Näripä (eds.), *Hortus Floridus*, Tartu.

Päll, Janika/Valper, Eve (2014), *Βάρβαρος οὐ πέλομαι… "I'm not a barbarian…." The humanists in and about the Greek language*, Tartu.

Päll, Janika/Volt, Ivo (eds.) (2018), *Hellenostephanos*, Tartu.

Pontani, Filippomaria (2017), "*Graeca per Italiae fines*. Greek poetry in Italy from Poliziano to the present", in: Stefan Weise (ed.), *HELLENISTI! Altgriechisch als Literatursprache im neuzeitlichen Europa*, Stuttgart, 311–347.

Ridderstad, Per S. (1975), *Konsten att sätta punkt. Anteckningar om stenstilens historia 1400–1765*, Stockholm.

Sironen, Erkki (2000), "Notes on the Language of Johan Paulinus' *Finlandia*. A Baroque Eulogy in Greek Verse", in: *Arctos* 24, 129–147.

Sironen, Erkki (2018), "'Dialectal' Variation in Humanist Greek Prose Orations in the Great Empire of Sweden (1631–1721)", in: Päll/Volt 2018, 130–143.

Weise, Stefan (2016) "'Ἑλληνίδ' αἶαν εἰσιδεῖν ἱμείρομαι – Neualtgriechische Literatur in Deutschland (Versuch eines Überblicks)", in: *Antike und Abendland* 62, 114–181.

Sweden

The Swedish corpus of Humanist Greek poetry (and prose) is perhaps one of the largest in Europe after the German and British ones, estimated to be between 1600 and 2000 texts, of which more than 1500 have been described already.[21] Consequently, it is also rich in forms and metres, comprising examples of virtually every genre of ancient and Humanist Greek poetry excepting, perhaps, a lengthy epic.

Swedish Humanist Greek begins with the adopted poet Heinrich Moller from Hessen and the Swede Laurentius Petri Gothus (1529/1530–1579, professor of Greek, later archbishop of Sweden), both of whom presented Crown Prince Erik XIV with Latin elegiac paraphrases of historiographical works such as Johannes Magnus' *Gothorum Sveonumque historia* (including episodes from Herodotus' *Histories* that are appropriated into the ancient/Gothic history of Sweden) that present favourable interpretations of the Gothic/Swedish past and are used as cautionary paradigms; both prints include substantial Greek paratexts before or after the main texts of the prints (printed in Wittenberg in 1557 and 1559, respectively).[22] Other Swedes followed soon after, at first writing and publishing abroad: Olaus Martini (1557–1609, also archbishop of Sweden) published a Greek gratulation for the *laurea magistralis* of Christian Ruuth (Rostock 1584), who was a student from Viborg (Carelia, Finland, now Russian Federation).[23] In 1597, Jonas Nicolai Kylander published a Σύγχαρμα in Wittenberg.[24]

Towards the end of the 16th century, when Greek studies had been established in universities and schools, and printing houses furnished with Greek types, professors and students soon produced Greek poems in great quantities. Several of the early professors of Greek at Uppsala University were prolific Greek poets, particularly Johannes Stalenus (1624–1640) and **Henrik Ausius** (1640–

Most of the overview of this part is based on Fant 1775–86 and Floderus 1785–89, with earlier discussion in Korhonen 2004, and the ongoing research of Johanna Akujärvi which will be published in articles to appear, if not stated otherwise. For the authors edited here, we also refer to the notes to the poems.

---

21 The release of the database of Humanist Greek texts. Vol. 1. Nordic countries in preparation, under http://humgraeca.utlib.ut.ee.
22 On these prints, see Akujärvi 2020b and Nordgren 2019, 265, 267f.
23 Text reprinted in Nordgren 2019, 265, 268f.
24 See Floderus 1785, 3f. and Fant 1775, I, 22.

1659). A testament to the successful development of Greek studies in Sweden under their leadership is the great number of Greek poems written by their students.[25] During their professorships many Greek student orations were presented and printed;[26] Ausius presided over at least five Greek disputations and wrote numerous poems (see below).

Greek studies were often carried on in families and across borders. Under Ausius' guidance, the brothers Nicolaus and Jonas Jonae Salanus wrote hexameter orations, and the Paulinus brothers from Finland wrote poetry in Turku and Uppsala (see Finland). The Holstenius and Gezelius families had Hellenists in many generations, active in different parts of the kingdom. Many poets practised a range of genres. For instance, as a student, **Petrus Aurivillius** (1637–1677) defended a Greek disputation under Ausius, wrote a panegyrical epitaph on the death of two members of the De La Gardie family, and composed a prose oration; and as a professor of Greek at Uppsala, he still produced numerous epigrams. Shortly after, **Johan(nes) Columbus** (1640–1684), called a Swedish Flaccus, wrote highly accomplished Greek poetry.

Laurentius Norrmannus was professor of Greek at Uppsala (1651–1703). His verse oration Λόγος ἔμμετρος ἐς Χριστὸν Θεάνθρωπον from his years at Strängnäs Gymnasium remains unpublished,[27] whereas his occasional poetry and long-form prose panegyric have been printed. Other important Greek poets were **Martin Brunnerus** (1627–1679), who started as a professor of Greek advancing to professor of theology and pastor, and **Johan(nes) Bilberg** (1646–1717), a professor of sciences who both wrote Greek poetry and translated two poems by Propertius into Greek (see below). Uppsala University was the largest centre of Humanist Greek in Sweden and accordingly the greatest amount of Greek poetry was printed there, but the gymnasium and printing houses in Stockholm were not unimportant: several lengthier Greek works, like orations, were sometimes delivered at Uppsala or Turku, but printed in Stockholm. The Strängnäs and Västerås gymnasia, where many famous Nordic Hellenists started their studies, and the University of Lund were important centres as well. Active in these centres were, among others, Andreas Erici Thermaenius, lector of Greek in Västerås, who has left behind many fine poems, **Caspar Weiser** (c. 1627–1686), who studied in Denmark and was a professor at Lund University before he was exiled, and **Josef Thun** (1661–1721), lector in

---

[25] As noted by Annerstedt 1877–1931, I, 248.
[26] See Korhonen 2010, 89–113, for the orations, Korhonen 2004, 392–420, 460-462 and Sironen 2018, 133–136.
[27] An edition of Norrmannus' oration and other unpublished Greek orations is being prepared by Erkki Sironen.

Strängnäs for more than 20 years, who is perhaps the most notable Humanist Greek poet from the Nordic countries; his legacy of both published and unpublished Greek poetry is considerable (see below and cf. fig. 15, above).[28]

The peaks of Humanist Greek poetry in Sweden took place midway through the 17th century and during the transition from the 17th to the 18th century. Although the most substantial mass of poetry comprises academic congratulations – in particular paratextual congratulatory texts printed in dissertations[29] – important Greek panegyrics for royalty and high court members were also written; in these the role of Queen Christina is often emphasised, but the De La Gardie and Oxenstierna families should not be forgotten as supporters of Greek studies. From the 1730s onwards, writing Greek poetry becomes rarer, but there is still experimentation with genres, e.g. a Cubus poem from 1754.[30] Overall, during the latter half of the 18th century, the practice of Greek (occasional) poetry was changing. This is in line with other changes in the field of literature as not only the use of learned languages continued to decrease but also the total amount of occasional poetry within the traditional publication channels plummeted between the 1770s and 1790s.[31]

In the late 18th century the Humanist Greek tradition all but died, but even in the 19th century isolated occasional poems in Greek occur, though by then their character had changed according to the new (romantic and classicistic) poetic ideal; one is printed below (**Erik Engelbert Östling**, 1807–1870). During the course of the 19th century, several dissertations either written in Greek or containing Greek translations of Latin or modern literature were published. Classical examples were imitated in a Greek tragedy by Albert Johansson, *Nupta Fluvii* (Vänersborg 1891). However, these are academic exercises for an academic public. From the late 19th century onwards, Humanist Greek poetry from Sweden has been mostly written by and for classical scholars such as **Johan Bergman** (1864–1951), who worked in Tartu and Stockholm, or by professors of Greek in Lund, such as the prominent Hellenists **Albert Wifstrand** (1901–1964) and **Jerker Blomqvist** (1938–).[32]

[JA]

---

28 On Thun, see also Akujärvi 2018; Ead. 2020c.
29 On Humanist Greek texts in dissertations, see Akujärvi (forthcoming).
30 See Akujärvi (forthcoming).
31 Statistics in Hansson 2011, 37–71.
32 For some further poets and poems (Petrus Rezandrus, E. Runnerberg, Carl Brunius) see also Nordgren 2019.

Special Bibliography

Akujärvi, Johanna (2018), "*Efter som iag intet monument efter mig hafwer*. Josef Thun som humanistgrekisk diktare", in: Elin Andersson/Emil Stenback (eds.), *Böckerna i borgen. Ett halvsekel i Roggebiblioteket*, Stockholm, 163–182.

Akujärvi, Johanna (2020b), "Neo-Latin texts and Humanist Greek paratexts. On two Wittenberg prints dedicated to crown prince Erik of Sweden", in: Mika Kajava/Tua Korhonen/Jamie Vesterinen (eds.), *Meilicha dôra. Poems and Prose in Greek from Renaissance and Early Modern Europe*, Helsinki, 75–104.

Akujärvi, Johanna (2020c), "Greek occasional poetry from the Swedish Empire. The case of Josephus Thun", in: Arne Jönsson *et al.* (eds.), *Att dikta för livet, döden och evigheten. Tillfällesdiktning under tidigmodern tid/Poems for Life, Death and Eternity. Occasional poetry in the Early Modern period*, Göteborg/Stockholm, 61–68.

Annerstedt, Claes (1877–1931), *Upsala universitets historia*. 1–3 & 1–5 suppl. Uppsala.

Hansson, Stina (2011), *Svensk bröllopsdiktning under 1600- och 1700-talen. Renässansrepertoarernas framväxt, blomstring och tillbakagång*, Göteborg, 37–71.

Nordgren, Lars (2019), "Sweden (Suède)", in: Francisco Oliveira/Ramón Martínez (eds.), *Europatrida*, Coimbra, 265–276.

Sironen, Erkki (forthcoming 2021), *Zehn Reden auf griechisch aus Schweden (1658–1797). Erstausgabe mit Übersetzung und Wortregister*, Lund.

Henrik (Henricus) Ausius (1603–1659)

Ad...M. Nicolaum Salanum [1656]

Ὥσπερ ἐνὶ καθαρῷ φέρεται λειμῶνι μέλισσα
ἐμματέουσα ἐπεὶ λέγεται πολυποίκιλα ἄνθη,
ὣς σπουδὴν χ' ὁρμὴν μελετᾷς, τιμιώταθ' ἑταῖρε,
ἔργον ἀοίδιμον· ἠδ' χερσὶν ὑποθήκας ἑλίσσεις,
5 δείγματα ποιητῶν, οὓς ἠγαθέης πέδον εἶχεν
Ἑλλάδος· εἶτα δὲ μὴ παῦσαι νεότητι ἀρήγων.

Textus: *Gnomologia: In qua Memorabilia Dicta & Illustres Sententiae ... Ad certos titulos, secundum ordinem Alphabeticum...* A Nicolao Jonae Salano, Uppsala [1656], [ ]:(4v)

Crit.: 3 ὣς scripsi: ὡς ed. | τιμιώταθ' ἑταῖρε scripsi: τιμιώτατ' ἑταῖρε ed. || 4 ἠδ' sic ed.: fortasse pro ἢ || 5 πέδον correxi: πεδὸν ed.

Sim.: 1 ἐνὶ ... λειμῶνι] cf. Theoc. *Id.* 26.5 || **1–4** de comparatione anthologistae cum ape cf. Clem. Al. *Strom.* 1.1.11.2 || **1–2** μέλισσα / ἐμματέουσα] cf. Nic. *Ther.* 809 (κέντρον γὰρ πληγῇ περικάλλιπεν ἐμματέουσα [*sc.* μέλισσα]); de sensu cf. Hsch. ε 2363 || **4** ἔργον ἀοίδιμον] cf. Tryph. 126 || **4–5** χερσὶν ... δείγματα] cf. Hor. *Ars P.* 268–269 (*exemplaria...versate manu*) || **5–6** ἠγαθέης ... Ἑλλάδος] cf. *Carm. pop.* fr. 21 *PMG* ex Plut. *Lys.* 18.3 (Ἑλλάδος ἀγαθέας).

To...Master Nicolaus Salanus

Like a bee flies on a pure meadow,
when it searches and gathers manifold flowers,
so do you, most valued friend, exercise effort and zeal
with regard to this work celebrated in song. In your hands you turn over pieces of advice,
[5] samples from the poets, whom the soil of holy
Hellas bore. So, do not stop helping the youth!

Metre: Hexameters. The stress tends to occur in the longum of the two or three last metra; this is observed throughout in ll. 3 and 4, in l. 4 where the quantity of syllables appears to be ignored (otherwise, note irrational lengthening of χερσίν – if not to be read ἠδὲ χεροῖν *metri gratia* – and uncalled for shortening of ὑποθήκας (or: short alpha as a Doric touch?)); irrational lengthening in l. 1 of ἐνί, likely following the pattern of Hom. *Il.* 2.137 (εἴατ' ἐνὶ μεγάροις) and other occurrences of the same phrase in the same position of the verse; hiatus in l. 2 *bis*, 6.

Notes: In these congratulatory verses printed in a collection of Greek dicta, Ausius stresses the diligence of the collector Nicolaus Salanus (1620–1671), by employing a conventional bee simile. As students at Uppsala University, Nicolaus Salanus and his brother Jonas authored Greek hexameter orations and occasional poetry – though their treatment of the Greek language, prosody, and metre at times borders on maltreatment. He published the *Gnomologia* as *lector Graecae linguae* at Stockholm Gymnasium. Ausius' last verse stresses the usefulness of the collection for schoolboys; its usefulness was increased by each Greek excerpt being translated into Latin.

Biography: Born in 1603, Henrik Ausius enrolled at Uppsala University in 1627. He was appointed *collega* at Stockholm's *Collegium illustre* in 1629, but resumed his studies at Uppsala the following year thanks to a scholarship, and travelled to Oxford and Leiden as tutor to the sons of the nobleman Carl Bonde. From December 1640 he was professor of Greek at Uppsala University until his death in 1659. Under his guidance, Greek studies at Uppsala flourished: the production of Greek poetry increased and a number of Greek dissertations were written and defended. Ausius also held the position of professor *extra ordinarius* of Swedish and Roman law (1646–1651), most likely for economic reasons.

Bibliography: Kuylenstierna, Carl Wilhelm Ulf (1920), "Ausius, Henrik", in: *Svenskt biografiskt lexikon 2*, 499–500. Ausius as professor of Greek: Annerstedt 1877–1931, 1.409. Ausius' Greek dissertations: Korhonen 2010. On his Greek poems: Fant 1775–86, 1.78–81; Floderus 1785–89, 20–23. On the Salanus brothers: Fant 1775–86, 1.84–88; Floderus 1785–89, 23–31.

[JA]

Petrus Aurivillius (1637–1677)

Λόγος ἐπιτάφιος [1663]

(excerptum, vv. 20–37, 170–176)

20 οἵη περ φύλλων γενεή, τοίη δὲ καὶ ἀνδρῶν.
Ὥς ῥα χαμαιγενέων θνητῶν ἀριδείκετα τέκνα
ἀρτιφανῆ ἔβλαστ' ἐνὶ τῷ παλιναυξέι κόσμῳ.
Τοῖσιν ἔδωκε Θεὸς γενετὴρ νόον ἰθυκέλευθον
σώματ' ἐν ἀνδρομέῳ, καίπερ μινυώριον εἴη.
25 Οὐ σμικρὸν τέρπει ἁπαλόχροα τέκνα τοκῆας·
ἀβρῶς γλακτοφάγοις εὐτερπέ' ὄρινε γέλωτα,

γαργαρίσασ᾿ υἱοῖς μήτηρ ἀεὶ ἠπιόδωρος·
τῆδ᾿ ἐπιμειδιόωσι, πατρὸς κραδίη δὲ γέγηθε
παρστάντος· μετέπειτα δὲ ἀρτιθαλῆ υἱὸν ἥβης
30 πρῶτ᾿ ἔμεναι πιστὸν Μουσῶν λάτριν φιλομόλπων
πατρῴη κέλ᾿ ἐφημοσύνῃ, μύθους τε δαῆναι
θεσπεσίους, Ἄρεος μεθέπειν καὶ θέσκελα ἔργα
δουρικλύτου. τὸν μὲν κούφῃ λάβεν ἔνδοθεν ἐλπίς.
Αἶψα γὰρ ἦλθε κιὼν θάνατος, νέφος ἀμφικαλύπτων
35 πυκνὸν καὶ στυγερόν, παρὰ σῆμα νέεσθαι ἄνωγε
δεινὸς ἀμείλικτός τε. Κατεκλάσθη δὲ φίλον κῆρ
ἀγγελίῃ λυγρῇ τοκέων βίον ἄρτι ποθούντων.
[...]
170 Ἡρτύνονθ᾿ ἵπποι λασιαύχενες, ὀξὺ θέοντες,
στάντο καὶ εἰνοδίου πρήσσειν πεδίου μεμαῶτες·
Ἐμμαπέως δὲ τότ᾿ ἦλθε δραμὼν κλειτὸς ΙΑΚΩΒΟΣ
ΑΥΓΟΥΣΤΟΣ, κρατερός τ᾿ ἐρυσάρμονα ἵππον ἔσηρε
κούφαισιν παλάμαις, καὶ οὐ κείνοιο νόησε
175 ἄγριον ὀργήν· αἶψα φρύαξε δὲ ὄβριμος ἵππος,
λάκτισε καὶ κὰρ ἴφθιμον παιδὸς θαλεροῖο.

Textus: Aurivillius, Petrus [1663], Λόγος ἐπιτάφιος *nomini ac memoriae illustrissimorum olim juvenum...Dn. Jacobi Augusti de la Gardie...Dn. Johannis Caroli de la Gardie...*, Stockholm)(1v,)(4v–5r (4:o)

Crit.: 32 ἄρεος ed. || 26 γλακτοφάγοις] metri gratia pro γαλακτοφάγοις || 31 κέλ'] forma activi ex analogia || 173 ἔσηρε corr.: ἔσηρε ed.

Sim.: 20 = Hom. *Il.* 6.146 || 21 χαμαιγενέων ἀνθρώπων], cf. *Hymn. Hom. Ven.* 108; *Hymn. Hom. Cer.* 352; Hes. *Theog.* 879 | ἀριδείκετα τέκνα] Hes. *Theog.* 385, cf. Hereas *ap.* Plut. *Thes.* 20 (Hom. *Od.* 11.631 ἐρικυδέα τέκνα) || 22 ἀρτιφανῆ...κόσμῳ] cf. Nonn. *Par. Jo.* 16.77 (ἀρτιφανὴς βλάστησεν ἀνὴρ παλιναυξέι κόσμῳ), cf. Nonn. *Par. Jo.* 15.1; *Dion.* 25.542 || 23 νόον ἰθυκέλευθον] Nonn. *Par. Jo.* 12.158 (νόον ἰθυκέλευθον) || 25 ἀπαλόχροα τέκνα] cf. *Anth. Pal.* 12.133 (ἀπαλόχροα παῖδα) || 34 θάνατος, νέφος ἀμφικαλύπτων] Hom. *Il.* 16.350 (θανάτου δὲ μέλαν νέφος ἀμφεκάλυψεν), cf. *Od.* 4.180 || 36 κατεκλάσθη δὲ φίλον κῆρ] cf. Hom. *Od.* 10.198 (τοῖσιν δὲ κατεκλάσθη φίλον ἦτορ) || 170 ἵπποι λασιαύχενες] Soph. *Ant.* 350–351 (λασιαύχενά θ᾿ / ἵππον) || 176 κάρ] cf. Hom. *Il.* 16.392 (τὸ ἐξ ὀρέων ἐπικάρ), Hsch. ε 4828 (ἐπὶ κάρ· ἐπὶ κεφαλήν)

A Funeral Oration

(excerpt, ll. 20–37, 170–176)

[20] Just as is the generation of leaves, such is that also of men. So the glorious children of earth-born humans, recently come to light, flowered and were born in ever-regenerating cosmos. God the Creator gave them straight-going mind in a human body, although it may

be short-lived. [25] The soft-skinned babies did not give their parents little delight. Whenever the caring mother tickled her milk-eating sons gently, she excited delightful laughter; they smiled at her, and the father, standing by, rejoiced in his heart. Later he exhorted by paternal command his son just budding in his youth, [30] first, to be a faithful servant of song-loving Muses, to learn divine tales, to pursue the wondrous works of Ares, famed for his spear. Vain hope had him in its grip. For suddenly came death, covering him with a thick and abominable cloud, [35] horrible and cruel, and ordered him to come to the tomb. The hearts of the parents, who had recently hoped for life, were broken at the mournful message. [...]

[170] Shaggy-necked, quick-running horses were put in order; they stood, though they were eager to pass over the field beside the road. Then renowned, strong Jacob August came quickly, running; with his nimble hands he brushed the chariot-drawing horse and did not notice its [175] wild anger. Suddenly the mighty horse neighed and struck the strong head of the vigorous boy.

Metre: Hexameters (multiple hiatus).

Notes: Aurivillius wrote this funerary oration (264 verses) for the memory of two De La Gardie brothers. The funeral was held in Stockholm and the memorial in Uppsala where Aurivillius was a 'post-graduate' student of theology. Aurivillius' Latin dedication to the youngsters' father, an eminent figure in Swedish politics, Count Magnus De La Gardie, is dated 11 January 1663. The Greek text begins with a prose address (4 lines) to the 'directors and teachers of the Academy' as well as 'the servants of Muses'. The text concentrates on the elder brother, Jacob August, who studied at Uppsala and died there in a riding accident (see text, ll. 170–175). The younger brother, Johannes Carolus, died of an acute illness.

Biography: Petrus Aurivillius (1637–1677) was the son of a pastor in Knutby, near Uppsala, and enrolled at the University of Uppsala at the age of thirteen. He defended (and probably also wrote) a Greek dissertation in 1658, two Latin dissertations *pro gradu* in 1660 and 1661, and a dissertation *pro doctoratu* in 1664. He was appointed as an adjunct of the theological faculty in 1664, professor of logic and metaphysics in 1668 and professor of Greek as well as *professor extraordinarius* of theology in 1674. He presided for circa 50 dissertations and published a highly popular textbook on 'peripatetic' logic. Besides two Greek orations (the other so far unpublished) and a Greek dissertation (1658), Aurivillius wrote 24 Greek occasional poems – the first when he was only 16 years old.

Bibliography: Nelson, Axel Herman (1920), "Aurivillius, Petrus", in: *Svenskt biografiskt lexikon* 2, 465. Greek texts: Floderus 1785–1789, 38–43 (ll. 1–2, 16–9, 34–7, 170–5, 185–9, 258–264 reprinted); Fant 1775-86 II, 11–12; Korhonen 2020. Some of Aurivillius' prints and manuscripts (including this oration with corrections marked by a pen) are digitised in the database ALVIN, University of Uppsala, http://www.alvin-portal.org/alvin/home.jsf?dswid=-7645 [accessed: September 2019].

[TK]

Martin Brunnerus (1627–1679)

In tumulum...M. Jonae Columbi [1663]

ΑΝΔΡΑ ΙΘΑΓΕΝΗ ΕΥΦΥΑ ΕΛΛΟΓΙΜΟΝ ΓΛΥΚΥΘΥΜΟΝ
ΚΟΣΜΙΟΝ ΑΙΔΟΙΟΝ Τ ΗΝ ΟΔΕ ΤΥΜΒΟΣ ΕΧΕΙ.
ΘΡΕΜΜΑΤΑ ΟΥΨΑΛΙΑΣ ΒΙΟΘΑΛΜΙΟΣ ΕΙΤΑ ΔΙΔΑΞΑΣ
ΕΥΣΕΒΙΗΣ ΛΟΓΑΔΑΣ ΔΗΘΑ ΚΟΛΟΥΜΒΟΣ ΕΗΝ.[33]

Textus: *IN TUMULUM ... M. JONÆ COLUMBI olim in Academia Upsaliensi Poëseos Professoris, & totos postea annos Pastoris Ecclesiæ Dei in Husby Westmannorum*, s.a.; N. Rudbeckius, *Christeligh Lijk-Predikan Uthöfwer ... Her, M. JONA SVVENONIS COLUMBO ...*, Stockholm 1668, Eiii^v

Sim.: 2 ΤΥΜΒΟΣ ΕΧΕΙ] cf. *Anth. Pal.* 7.19.3 (Leon.) etc. || 3 ΒΙΟΘΑΛΜΙΟΣ (sc. ἀνήρ)] *hapax legomenon* in *Hymn. Hom.Ven.* 189 || 4 ΕΥΣΕΒΙΗΣ ΛΟΓΑΔΑΣ] hebraismus; cf. et *Caten. in Act. Apost.* 150.8

On the tomb...of Jonas Columbus

A man of native stock, good nature, high repute, charming mind,
   orderly and reverential, look!, is held by this mound.
Columbus, a long lived man, taught the nurslings of Uppsala
   and next the chosen pious ones for a long time; he was a dove.

Metre: Elegiac couplets (hiatus: l. 1 *ter*, 3).

---

[33] Minuscule version with accents: Ἄνδρα ἰθαγενῆ, εὐφυᾶ, ἐλλόγιμον, γλυκύθυμον, / κόσμιον αἰδοῖόν τ', ἤν', ὅδε τύμβος ἔχει· / θρέμματα Οὐψαλίας βιοθάλμιος εἶτα διδάξας / εὐσεβίης λογάδας δηθὰ Κολουμβος ἔην.

Notes: These verses, in the form of a literary epigram, were written in honour of Jonas Svenonis Columbus (1586–1663), who, after studies in Trondheim, Copenhagen and Uppsala (congratulatory verses addressed to his brother are preserved from his student years; magister in 1617), and after a *peregrinatio academica* to Germany in 1622, became lector of Greek at Västerås, later professor of poetry and music at Uppsala, and, finally, vicar and dean in (Dala-)Husby. In a manner familiar from the sepulchral epigrams of the *Anthologia Palatina*, the first couplet describes the character and manner of the deceased with a list of adjectives. Columbus' long period of activity and his advanced age are stressed – he lived to be nearly eighty years old in a period when living to sixty was considered an accomplishment – with the epithet βιοθάλμιος, a *hapax legomenon*, which is explained in early modern lexica as 'long lived' (e.g., Scapula 1628, s.v. ἅλις). The second couplet gives a succinct summary of Columbus' career as university professor at Uppsala (1625–1630) and vicar and dean of 'the chosen pious ones' in (Dala-)Husby (from 1631 until his death). The final words are a double play on Columbus' name, transcribed into Greek – both the Hebrew first name and the Latin surname mean 'dove'.

Biography: Martin Brunnerus, born 1627, enrolled at Uppsala University in 1645 and became *magister* in 1655. Between May 1657 and September 1658, he travelled to German, Dutch, and English universities. Soon after returning to Uppsala he succeeded Ausius as professor of Greek in 1659; in this role he lectured on and edited Palaephatus' *De incredibilibus* (1663) from a manuscript brought to Uppsala from Constantinople. He also worked on Moeris' and Thomas Magister's Atticistic lexical works, but never finished the planned editions. In 1666, Brunnerus took orders and advanced to professor of theology. He remained at Uppsala until his death in 1679. As a Greek poet Brunnerus was famed for writing little, and only terse epigrams.

Bibliography: Holm, Rurik (1926), "Brunnerus, Martin", in: *Svenskt biografiskt lexikon* 6, 530–536; Ekholm, R. (1929), "Columbus, Jonas Svenonis", in: *Svenskt biografiskt lexikon* 8, 755–761; Annerstedt 1877–1931, 2.2.285–288. Greek poems: Fant 1775–86, 2.16–22; Floderus 1785–89, 53f.

[JA]

Johan(nes) Jonae Columbus (1640–1684)

In nuptias Gustavi Elvii & Elisabeth [1664]

Ὤιχετο νὺξ γοερή, στυγερῶν γενέτειρα μεριμνῶν,
ᾤχετο, δῦ δὲ ῥόον βαθυδίνεος Ὠκεανοῖο.
Φωσφόρος ὦρσε γλυκὺ στίλβον σέλας. ᾧ παρομαρτεῖ
ἅρματ' ἐπὶ κροκοειδέϊ, δαιδαλέῳ, δροσόεντι,
5   ἠριγενεῖς ἐλάσασ' ἵππους ῥοδοδάκτυλος Ἠώς.
Νυμφίε, λῆγε γοῶν, σκέδασον δὲ τὰ πένθεα λυγρά,
ὅσσα τεὰς μάλα πολλὰ λάβε φρένας, ἠδέ σ' ἀνιᾷ.
Χαῖρε δὲ σὸν κατὰ θυμόν. ἐφέσπεται ἐσθλὰ κακοῖσι.
Ἠνίδε ἀντέλλει πολυήρατον αἴθριον ἦμαρ,
10 ὅττι γέ σοι ἄλοχον πινυτόφρονα, καλλιπάρῃον,
αἰδοίην τε φέρει, πασῶν ἄμπαυμα μεριμνῶν.
Σοὶ πλῆθος τούτοιο συνήδεται εἰλαπιναστῶν.
Φόρμιγγες δ' αὐλοῖσι μεμιγμέναι, ἦχον ἄρισται,
καλὰ λιγαίνουσιν, καὶ ἄγουσιν ἐφ' ἵμερον ἄνδρας
15 τῆς γλυκερῆς μολπῆς, καὶ ἀμύμονος ὀρχηθμοῖο.
Συγχαίρω καὶ ἔγωγ' ἀπεὼν περ μακρά, καὶ εὐχὰς
εὐμενέων ποιοῦμαι ἔπη ὑμενήϊα πέμπων.

Textus: *In nuptias reverendi & clarissimi viri D. Gustavi Elvii ... atque ... virginis Elisabeth ...*, Uppsala [1664], [2]

Crit.: 1, 2 ᾤχετο scripsi: ὤχετο ed.

Sim.: 1–6 ᾤχετο νὺξ ... γοῶν] de loco, sed per oppositionem cf. Ov. *Am.* 1.13.1–10 (*Iam super oceanum venit [Aurora] ... mane! ... nunc iuvat in teneris dominae iacuisse lacertis ... quo properas, ingrata viris, ingrata puellis? roscida purpurea supprime lora manu!*) || **1** νὺξ ... γενέτειρα] cf. *Hymn. Orph.* 3.1 || **2** βαθυδίνεος Ὠκεανοῖο] cf. Hom. *Od.* 10.511 (Ὠκεανῷ βαθυδίνῃ) || **3** παρομαρτεῖ] pedestre; verbum simplex poëticum || **4** ἅρματ' ἐπὶ κροκοειδέϊ] cf. Chrys. *pan. mart.* 1–3 PG 50.709 (ὑπὸ τὴν ἕω τὸν ἥλιον ... κροκοειδεῖς ἀφιέντα ἀκτῖνας) || **6** λῆγε γοῶν] cf. Bion 1.97 (λῆγε γόων) | πένθεα λυγρά] cf. Hom. *Il.* 22.242 (πένθεϊ λυγρῷ) et al. || **8** σὸν κατὰ θυμόν] cf. Hom. *Il.* 24.158 etc. | ἐφέσπεται ... κακοῖσι] cf. Hes. *Op.* 179 (μεμείξεται ἐσθλὰ κακοῖσιν) || **9** αἴθριον ἦμαρ] cf. J. *AJ* 18.285 (ἡμέραν αἴθριον) || **10–11** ἄλοχον ... αἰδοίην] cf. Hom. *Il.* 6.250 (παρ' αἰδοίης ἀλόχοισιν) et al. || **11** πασῶν ἄμπαυμα μεριμνῶν] cf. Hes. *Theog.* 55 (κακῶν ἄμπαυμά τε μερμηράων); Thgn. 1.343; Nonn. *Dion.* 17.74 || **12–15** πλῆθος ... ὀρχηθμοῖο] cf. Hom. *Il.* 18.491–495 (γάμοι τ' ἔσαν εἰλαπίναι τε ... ὀρχηστῆρες ἐδίνεον ... αὐλοὶ φόρμιγγές τε)] || **13** φόρμιγγες ... μεμιγμέναι] cf. Pind. *Ol.* 3.8–9 (φόρμιγγά τε ποικιλόγαρυν καὶ βοὰν αὐλῶν ἐπέων τε θέσιν ... συμμεῖξαι); Hor. *Ep.* 9.5–6 (*sonante mixtum tibiis carmen lyra, hac Dorium, illis barbarum*) || **14–15** ἵμερον ... ὀρχηθμοῖο] cf. Hom. *Od.* 23.144–145 (ἵμερον ... μολπῆς τε γλυκερῆς καὶ ἀμύμονος ὀρχηθμοῖο) || **16–17** εὐχὰς ... ποιοῦμαι] pedestre

On the wedding of Gustav Elvius and Elisabeth

Distressful night, mother of miserable worries, is gone, gone and plunged into the stream of deep-eddying Oceanus. The morning star stirred sweet glittering light; it is accompanied on her saffron-coloured, well wrought, misty carriage by rosy-fingered Eos (Dawn) driving early-born horses. [6] Bridegroom, stop groaning! Scatter the many mournful sorrows, that in great numbers have taken hold of your heart and plague you! Let your mind be cheerful! Good follows bad. See, a very lovely, bright day is dawning, [10] which brings you a wife – wise, with beautiful cheeks, revered: a rest from all worries. The crowd of guests rejoices with you at this. Lyres, with a most lovely ringing, mingled with pipes, create a beautiful clear sound and make men long for sweet song and irreproachable dance. [16] I, too, though I am far away, rejoice with you, and pray benevolently by sending wedding verses.

Metre: Hexameters (often allowing hiatus).

Notes: These Greek verses form part of a four-page wedding gratulation sent by Johan and his brother Samuel from Uppsala, where they studied at the university, to their home diocese, as Gustav Elvius, vicar in a parish not far from that of their father's, married the daughter of a vicar in Rättvik; a short Latin poem by a certain Ericus P. Schottenius is included on the last page of the print. Samuel's poem is a short Latin prayer for the newly-weds. Johan's contribution consists of two Latin pieces and one Swedish piece, in addition to the Greek poem, which appears first. Despite the occasional prosaic wording or turn of phrase, the Greek poem is characterised by a poetic style with adjectives that are used in both traditional combinations and more innovative ones, as in the description of Dawn, who is often described as ῥοδοδάκτυλος in the Homeric epics, but also with adjectives like κροκόπεπλος ('saffron-veiled') and ἠριγένεια ('early-born'). Here Columbus uses compounds with elements from these traditional adjectives (κροκοειδής and ἠριγενής) and ascribes them to Dawn's carriage and horses respectively. The Greek poem comprises four parts. (1) The dawn of the new day is described and the groom is exhorted to dismiss all sorrow and worries. Columbus thus reverses the *topos* of dawn separating rather than uniting two lovers, common in Latin love elegy and thematised in Ovid's *Amores* 1.13. (2) In line with the first part, the bride is designated as 'rest from all worries', and described with three adjectives from the Greek epic tradition, two of which are Homeric and often applied to wives (αἰδοῖος) and women (καλλιπάρῃος), while the other has much later origins and is applied to wily Odysseus (πινυτόφρων; likely inspired by Penelope being described as πινυτή in the *Odyssey*). (3) The four lines devoted to the wedding feast are replete with reminiscences from the Homeric epics – the wedding celebration described on the shield of Achilles (*Il.* 18.491–496) and the feigned wedding that Odysseus orchestrated to mask the massacre of the suitors (*Od.* 23.143–148). (4) The poet's congratulations and prayer to the happy couple, which he issues from a distance.

Biography: Johan(nes) Jonae Columbus, son of Jonas Columbus (celebrated by Brunnerus above), was *professor poëseos* and one of the most admired Swedish Latin poets of his times. His younger brother Samuel preferred Swedish over Latin, though neither of them was inept as a Greek poet. Born 1640, Johan enrolled at Uppsala University in 1659 after attending school in Kopparberget and Västerås. Master in December 1668, he was made *adjunctus* at the faculty of philosophy for the spring term of the next year. As *professor extraordinarius* of poetry (1671) he assumed the duties of the *professor ordinarius*, Lars Fornelius, too old and weak for teaching. After the passing of Fornelius, he was appointed *professor ordinarius* in 1673. Columbus lectured on a wide selection of Latin poetical texts, and as *locum tenens* for *professor Skytteanus* Elias Obrecht, he lectured on Latin historiography. He also edited *Incerti scriptoris Graeci Fabulae aliquot Homericae* (1678; attributed to Nicephorus Gregoras, in fact by Manuel Gabalas). Further, he planned to edit Valerius Flaccus' *Argonautica*, and took over Brunnerus' work on Moeris' *Atticista*, without finishing either project, most likely due to ill health. He died in 1684, only 44 years old. Though Columbus is best known for his Latin verses, his Greek poems demonstrate that he possessed a strong command of Greek too.

Bibliography: Ekholm, R. (1929), "Columbus, Johan(nes) Jonæ", in: *Svenskt biografiskt lexikon* 8, 761–767; Annerstedt 1877–1931, 2.2.281, 286–289; Berggren, Maria (2003), "Johannes Columbus (1640–1684) as an official poet", in: Outi Merisalo/Raija Sarasti-Wilenius (eds.), *Erudition and eloquence. The use of Latin in the countries of the Baltic Sea (1500–1800)*, Helsinki, 98–111; Hanselli, Per (1871), *Samlade vitterhetsarbeten. I. G. Stjernhjelm, G. Rosenhane och J. Columbus*, Uppsala, 309–388 (edition of select poems, including two Greek ones). Greek poetry: Fant 1775–86, 2.13–16 & 22f., Floderus 1785–89, 43–46.

[JA]

Laurentius Norrmannus/Lars Norrman (1651–1703)

Memoria M. Olavi Odhelii [1688]

Τὸν Χριστῷ φίλον ἄνδρα· τὸν οὐ Χαρίτεσσιν ἀπεχθῆ·
τὸν πατρὸς ἀθανάτου οὔ τι χερειότερον·
τὸν νέον ὨΔ'ΈΛΙΟΝ· φθονερὴ κατὰ γαῖα καλύπτει·
λείψαντ' οἰκτίστως ἠελίοιο φάος.
5 Ὅς ποτ' ὀπωρινῇ ὥρῃ, παρὰ θῖνα θαλάσσης,
νύκτα δι' ὀρφναίην, ὅν δε δόμον δε ἰών·
οἷος ἐών· δμωός τε ἄτερ· δαΐδων τε φαεινῶν·
ὕδασιν εἰν ὀλοοῖς ἐξαπόλωλε πεσών·
ὦκα δὲ ἐκ ῥεθέων πταμένη μέγαν οὐρανὸν ἷκεν
10 ψυχή· καὶ μακάρων ἐγκατάλεκτο χοροῖς.
Ὤλετο μὲν μένος ἠΰ· καὶ ἀγλαΐη· καὶ ὀπωπῆς
φέγγος· ἐπουρανίοις ἄστρασιν εἰδόμενον.
Ἀλλ' οὐκ εὐσεβίης κλέος ἀμφιβόητον ὀλεῖται·
οὐ πινυτοφροσύνης· οὐ πολυϊστορίης·
15 πολλὰ γὰρ ἀνθρώπων, πάτρηθεν ἀλώμενος, εἶδεν
ἄστεα· μαστεύων ἴχνεα τῆς σοφίης·
ἀνδρομέης δ' ἐλθὼν ἐπὶ πείρατα· αἰπὺν Ὄλυμπον
εἰσανέβη· θείην ἀμφαγαπαζόμενος.

Textus: *Breve epicedion memoriae ... M. Olavi Odhelii ... qui ... A. MDCLXXXVIII. Octob. d. V rebus humanis ereptus est*, Uppsala [1688], [3–4].

Crit.: 12 ἄστρασιν sic retinui collato Hdn. Περὶ Ἰλιακῆς προσῳδίας εἰς τὴν Χ 28, 3.2.119 Lentz

Sim.: 1 Τὸν ... ἀπεχθῆ] cf. Theoc. *Id.* 1.141 (τὸν Μοίσαις φίλον ἄνδρα, τὸν οὐ Νύμφαισιν ἀπεχθῆ) || **3** κατὰ ... καλύπτει] cf. Hom. *Il.* 14.114; 6.464 (καλύπτοι); *Anth. Pal.* 7.3 (Antip. Sid.) de Homero et frequens iunctura || **4** λείψαντ' ... φάος] cf. Hom. *Il.* 18.11 (λείψειν φάος ἠελίοιο); *Od.* 11.93 (λιπών) || **5** παρὰ ... θαλάσσης] cf. Hom. *Il.* 19.40; *Od.* 4.432 etc. || **6** νύκτα ... ὀρφναίην] cf. Hom. *Il.* 10.83 etc. | ὅν δε δόμον δε] cf. Hom. *Od.* 1.83 etc. || **7** οἷος ἐών] cf. Hom. *Il.* 18.115 (τοῖος ἐών) et al. saepe in init. versus || **9** μέγαν οὐρανόν] cf. Hom. *Il.* 1.497 | οὐρανὸν ἷκεν] cf. Hom. *Il.* 2.153 etc. || **9–10** ὦκα ... ψυχή] cf. Hom. *Il.* 16.856 et 22.362 (ψυχὴ δ' ἐκ ῥεθέων πταμένη Ἄϊδόσδε βεβήκει) || **10** μακάρων ... χοροῖς] cf. Nonn. *Dion.* 21.252 (οὐρανίων μακάρων χορόν) | ἐγκατάλεκτο] cf. Hom. *Od.* 4.451 (λέκτο) || **11** μένος ἠΰ] Hom. *Il.* 17.456 et al. || **11–12** ὤλετο ... φέγγος] cf. Nonn. *Dion.* 20.402 (ὤλεσε φέγγος ὀπωπῆς) || **12** ἄστρασιν εἰδόμενον] cf. *Hymn. Hom. Ap.* 441 (ἀστέρι εἰδόμενος) || **13** οὐκ ... κλέος ... ὀλεῖται] cf. Hom. *Il.* 2.325; 7.91 (κλέος οὔ ποτ' ὀλεῖται) et al. || **15** πάτρηθεν ἀλώμενος] cf. Ap. Rhod. *Argon.* 2.541 || **15–16** πολλὰ ... ἄστεα] cf. Hom. *Od.* 1.3 (πολλῶν δ' ἀνθρώπων ἴδεν ἄστεα) || **17** ἀνδρομέης ... πείρατα] cf. Hom. *Od.* 4.563 | πείρατα ... Ὄλυμπον] cf. Hom. *Il.* 5.367 et al. || **18** ἀμφαγαπαζόμενος] cf. Hom. *Il.* 16.192 et al.

Commemoration of Master Olaus Odhelius

The man beloved to Christ, not hated by the Graces, in no wise inferior to his immortal father, young Odhelius is covered by envious earth, after he most deplorably left the light of the sun. [5] Once in late summer, along the seashore, in murky nighttime, as he was walking towards his house, alone, with no servant or shining torch, he fell into deadly waters and perished. His soul fluttered quickly from his limbs, reached wide heaven, and was chosen into the choruses of the blessed. [11] Lost were a good spirit, splendour, and light of sight like the heavenly stars. But far-famed renown for piety shall not perish, nor that for ingeniousness, nor that for erudition. [15] For wandering from his native land, he saw many cities of men; in search for traces of wisdom, he reached the limits of the human one, climbed up steep Olympus and greeted with love divine wisdom.

Metre: Elegiac couplets (often allowing hiatus).

Notes: These verses commemorate Olaus Odhelius (1655–88), son of Ericus Odhelius (1620–66), professor at Uppsala, who met with premature death by drowning on an autumn evening. Odhelius was only a few years younger than Norrmannus, and had enrolled at Uppsala University two years after Norrmannus. On the title page, after listing Odhelius' titles (*magister* and *professor designatus* of theology in Tartu (Dorpat), death prevented him from taking up the post) and notable qualities (*pietas, virtus* etc.), Norrmannus adds two descriptives that hint at their relationship: *amicus* and *suus* συνοδοιπόρος – that is, 'friend' and 'fellow traveller'. Perhaps Norrmannus' first trip to the Continent coincided in part with Odhelius' long *peregrinatio academica* (1679–84). The poem is written in lapidary style where semicolon and comma are used to indicate both meaningful word and phrase units, as well as clause and caesura; the punctuation of the original is retained in the present edition qua conscious stylistic feature, both in spite of the fact that and because it constitutes an obstacle to a fluent reading of the text. This carefully composed poem is characterised by numerous echoes of Greek epic poetry – the Homeric epics in particular, but also Apollonius Rhodius' *Argonautica* and Nonnus' *Dionysiaca* – in the form both of unchanged direct loans and of adjusted formulae and phrases. In that context l. 14 is striking. This pentameter consists of two perfectly equal parts, separated by a semicolon, with two words each, two of which appear to be neologisms. Neither πινυτοφροσύνη nor πολυϊστορίη are attested according to the TLG, but both are transparent formations from the adjective πινυτόφρων ('wise-minded') and πολυΐστωρ ('very learned'), respectively.

Biography: After studies at the gymnasium in Strängnäs, Norrmannus came to Uppsala in 1668. Apart from three trips to Denmark and the Continent, Norrmannus remained at Uppsala throughout his career, despite offers of posts as professor and librarian at Lund University (in 1682 and 1683). At Uppsala he advanced from extraordinary professor of Greek and Hebrew (1682), to ordinary professor of logic and metaphysics (1684), Greek (1685), and theology (1693–1702), and was finally consecrated bishop of Göteborg, but without taking office because of his demise soon thereafter (1703). Following the example of his teachers Martin Brunnerus and Johannes Schefferus, Norrmannus edited several texts by Aelius Aristides and Thomas Magister as professor of Greek. After his promotion to the faculty of theology, he published very little. His Latin was as elegant as his Greek and so admired that one Greek and seventeen Latin orations were posthumously edited (1738).

Bibliography: Rudberg Stig Y. (1990-1991), "Norrmannus, Laurentius", in: *Svenskt biografiskt lexicon* 27, 599–601; Annerstedt 1877–1931, 2.2.283–289; Akujärvi 2020a. Edition of orations, including a Greek one: *Laurentii Norrmanni ... Orationes panegyricæ et nonnulla programmata, simul cum Caroli Lundii ... laudatione funebri et Andreae Norrelii ... praefatione*, Stockholm 1738. On his Greek poems: Fant 1775–86, 2.53–76, Floderus 1785–89, 46–52.

[JA]

Caspar Weiser (c. 1627–1686)

⟨*Ad regem Carolum undecimum*⟩ [1675]
יהוה

OLIVA *quae manu gestatur*.
ΓΑΒΡΙΗΛ. ΚΆΡΟΛΕ, Δῖε ἄναξ ἀνδρῶν, ὑψίθρονε, χαῖρε,
ἠνίδε τὸν στέφανον, δῶρον μεγάλοιο Θεοῖο
τοῦ ὑψιβρεμέτου, ὃς ὑπέρτατα δώματα ναίει,
διδόμενον τοί, τὸν σέο τῇ κεφαλῇ ἐπιβάλλω,
5   πρὸς μεγαλοβρεμέτου δόξαν, προβολήν θ' ὑπογείων.

PALMA, *cum aureo ense*.
ΡΑΦΑΗΛ. Σοί τε βοήθειαν βασιλευόντων Βασιλῆος
ἀγγέλλω πρὸς τοὺς ἐχθρούς, ἐὰν ἔννομα ῥέξῃς,
τιμήσῃς τε Θεόν, τὸν ὄλβια πλεῖστα διδόντα.
Ὀλβιοδαίμων ᾖς, βουλαὶ πολυφρόντιδες ἐχθρῶν,
10   τῶν τε πολυφλοίσβων, καὶ οὐλομένων ῥα πεσοῦνται.

Textus: *Arctoï solis tripudium, cùm ... Dn. Carolus undecimus ... Upsaliae, IV. Calendarum Octobris ... coronaretur,* Lund [1675], [2]

Crit.: 5 θ' ὑπογείων scripsi: τ' ὑπογείων ed.

Sim.: 1 δῖε ... ὑψίθρονε] cf. Quint. Smyrn. 2.86 (δῖον ἄνακτα); cf. Hom. *Il.* 2.434 etc. (ἄναξ ἀνδρῶν); Thdr. Prodromos *Epigr. in VT et NT* 1Reg.118b. (ἄναξ ὑψίθρονος) || **3** τοῦ ... ναίει] cf. Hes. *Op.* 8 (Ζεὺς ὑψιβρεμέτης, ὅς ὑπέρτατα δώματα ναίει) || **5** μεγαλοβρεμέτου] cf. Διὸς μεγαλοβρεμέταο hapax legomenon in Quint. Smyrn. 2.508 || **6** βασιλευόντων βασιλῆος] cf. *1Ep.Ti.* 6.15 (ὁ βασιλεὺς τῶν βασιλευόντων) || **7** ἔννομα ῥέξῃς] cf. *Carm. Aur.* 3 (ἔννομα ῥέζων) || **8** τιμήσῃς τε Θεόν] cf. *Carm. Aur.* 1–2 (ἀθανάτους ... θεούς ... τίμα) || **9** ὀλβιοδαίμων] cf. Hom. *Il.* 3.182 (Ἀτρεΐδη ... ὀλβιόδαιμον) | βουλαὶ πολυφρόντιδες] cf. *Anacreont.* 50.7 (πολυφρόντιδές τε βουλαί)

<To King Charles XI>

YAHWEH

Olive borne in hand.
Gabriel: Charles, noble lord of men, high-throned, hail. See, the wreath, a gift of great God, the high thundering, who dwells in the upmost palace, given to you. I put it on your head, for the glory of the great thunderer and for the protection against what is under ground.

Palm-branch with a golden sword.
Raphael: I bring news of help from the Lord of regents to you against your enemies, if you act according to the law and revere God, giver of the greatest gifts. You shall be blessed; the anxious designs of your enemies, loud-noised and accursed, will then be ruined.

Metre: Hexameters (often allowing hiatus and prosodic irregularities, such as the irregular lengthening of iota l. 4 διδόμενον and omicron l. 8 τόν).

Notes: Weiser had already courted Charles XI of Sweden with Greek verses in 1672 when the young monarch reached majority and acceded to the throne; the above Greek verses, followed by a long Latin poem in a four-page pamphlet, were delivered for the coronation in 1675. The grand occasion is reflected in the grand layout of the print, particularly of its second page, where the Greek poem is printed. On the top of the page, at its centre, is written the Hebrew tetragrammaton; below it are four stars and a sun. The two parts of the poem, lines addressed to the king by the archangels Gabriel and Raphael, respectively, are printed in parallel, separated by the king's crowned monogram. Above the names of Gabriel and Raphael, separated by the sun, the two Latin lines are printed, likely serving as descriptives of the two archangels. However, linguistically and stylistically the poem is simple; there are several epic reminiscences and a notable imitation of the *Golden verses* ascribed to Pythagoras, often used in school practice.

Biography: Born circa 1627, Caspar Weiser, or Casper Jacobsen Weiser, attended school and university in Copenhagen, Denmark, and obtained the master's degree in 1653. In 1655, he was appointed rector of the school in Kristianstad, in the province of Skåne, then still a part of Denmark. When Skåne (Scania) was surrendered to Sweden under the Treaty of Roskilde (1658), Weiser's career did not seem to suffer. In 1660, he advanced to rector of the school in Lund, canon of the cathedral, and prebend of Fjelie, a financially rewarding move. When Lund University was founded, Weiser was appointed professor, first of physics (1669), then poetry (1671), in addition to holding the above mentioned rectorate and prebend. Neither as teacher nor as poet did he stand high in his colleagues' estimation. Moreover, poetry proved to be Weiser's undoing. When hostilities between Sweden and Denmark were renewed and Skåne was invaded by Danish troops (1676), Weiser, unlike his colleagues, stayed in Lund and quickly composed and published a Latin poem with a Danish version, welcoming and honouring the king of Denmark. The fortunes of war soon turned, the Danes were driven out, and Weiser faced the consequences of high treason. His death sentence was turned into exile, but the poem was burned publicly by the executioner in Malmö (1677). After some difficult years in Copenhagen, Weiser continued to Christiania (Oslo), in Norway, where he lived out his life as lector of theology.

Bibliography: Carlquist, Gunnar (1952), *Lunds stifts herdaminne från reformationen till nyaste tid*, II.4, Lund, 492–495; Rørdam, Holger Frederik (1891), "Skaaninger fra Adskillelsetiden. V. Professor Caspar Weiser i Lund", in: Id. (ed.), *Historiske samlinger og studier vedrørende danske forhold och personligheder især i det 17. aarhundrede*, København, 160–170. On Weiser as a Latin poet: Gejrot, Claes (1999), "The Rise and Fall of a Latin Poet. The Case of Caspar Weiser", in: Claes Gejrot/Annika Ström (eds.), *Poems for the occasion. Three essays on Neo-Latin Poetry from Seventeenth-Century Sweden*, Stockholm, 13–76.

[JA]

Josef Thun/Josephus Thunius (1661–1721)

I. *Hymnus in filium Dei* [1682]

(excerptum, vv. 1–13)

Ἔρρετέ μοι Ἑλικωνιάδες, νόθον εὖχος ἀοιδῶν
ἔρρε μοι Ἀργυρότοξε, σέθεν δ' οὐ μάντις ὑπάρχω,
οὐδὲ τρίπους μέλεται, ἀεσίφρονα χρησμὸν ἰάλλων,
οὐ Κίρρη, οὐδ' ἠλίθιαι Πίνδοιο κολῶναι.
5   Ὑψόσε νῦν δὲ καλεῦμαι ἐς οὐρανόν· ἔγρεο θυμέ,
ἔγρεο, καὶ γαίης ἀνεμώλια πέμπε ταλαίνης·
ΧΡΙΣΤΕ μέλος σύ μοι ἱμερόεν, σέο γ' αἰὲν ἀοιδή
ἐν στομάτεσσι γλυκεῖα πέλοι, φίλε σῶτερ ΙΗΣΟΥ!
Ἀρχόμενος δ' ὡς πρῶτα μετήϊες ἄνδρας ἔραζε
10 δώματος ἐξ ὑπάτοιο λιπὼν ‹Θεὸν› οὐρανίωνα,
τοῖς δὲ χαριζόμενος μόρον ἡμερόφοιτον ἄμυνας,
κῆρά τε περσεφόνην, καὶ ἀτειρέα πήματα θνητῶν.
Ἵλαθι παμβασιλεῦ, καὶ ἐμῇ χάριν ἔμβαλ' ἀοιδῇ.

Textus: *Amores sacri, sive Canticum canticorum Salomonis Elegis expressum ... Accedunt & alia varii argumenti Poëmatia Græca, omnia studio* Iosephi J. Tuhn [!] Sudermanniâ-Sveci, Stockholm 1682, C^r.

Crit.: 10 Θεὸν supplevi metri gratia

Sim.: 1–2 ἔρρετέ μοι...ἔρρε μοι] cf. Greg. Naz. *Carm.*, PG 37.1495.7 (ἔρρετέ μοι, βίβλοι πολυηχέες· ἔρρετε, Μοῦσαι) || **1** ἔρρετέ μοι Ἑλικωνιάδες] cf. Hes. *Theog.* 1 (Μουσάων Ἑλικωνιάδων ἀρχώμεθ') sed contrarie | νόθον εὖχος] cf. Greg. Naz. *Carm.*, PG 37.1229.10 (τίμιον εὖχος ἄνακτος) sed contrarie || **2** ἔρρε μοι Ἀργυρότοξε] cf. Hom. *Il.* 1.37 (κλῦθί μευ ἀργυρότοξ') sed contrarie || **3** ἀεσίφρονα χρησμόν] cf. Hom. *Il.* 21.302 (ἀεσίφρονι θυμῷ); Hes. *Op.* 315, 335 (ἀεσίφρονα θυμόν) etc. || **4** Πίνδοιο κολῶναι] cf. Verg. *E.* 10.11 (*iuga...Pindi*) || **5–6** ἔγρεο...ταλαίνης] cf. Io. Geometres *Carm.* 57.7 van Opstall (ἔγρεο, θυμὲ τάλαν, βλεφάρων ὕπνον ἔκτοθι πέμπε) || **7–8** μέλος...γλυκεῖα] cf. Pind. *Nem.* 5.2 (γλυκεῖ' ἀοιδά); Bion 2.1–2 (μέλος ἀδὺ...ἱμερόεν) || **10** δώματος...ὑπάτοιο] cf. Pind. *Ol.* 1.42 (ὕπατον...δῶμα) | ‹Θεὸν› οὐρανίωνα] cf. Hom. *Il.* 1.570 (θεοὶ Οὐρανίωνες) etc. || **11** ἡμερόφοιτον] hapax legomenon in Bas. *hex.* 8.7 || **13** παμβασιλεῦ] cf. *Sap.* 50.15 | χάριν ἔμβαλ' ἀοιδῇ] cf. *Hymn. Hom. Vest.* 5 (χάριν...ὄπασσον ἀοιδῇ)

Hymn to the Son of God

(excerpt, ll. 1–13)

> Begone, Heliconian ones (Muses), the false vaunt of singers; begone, silver-bowed Apollo, I am not your prophet; nor is the tripod, sending forth witless oracle, of concern to me; nor is Cirrha, nor the vain peaks of Pindus. [5] I call now aloft to heaven. Wake up, soul, wake up and send off the emptiness of the wretched world. Christ, you are a lovely tune for me; may your song forever be sweet in my mouth, beloved saviour Jesus!
> [9] Starting when you first walked among men after you had left God in heaven and come to earth from the hall above, you have favoured men by warding off doom that wanders at day, Persephone – death –, and unyielding misery from mortals. Be gracious, ruler of all, and instill grace into my song.

Metre: Hexameters (often allowing hiatus).

Notes: When Thun completed his studies in Turku, he published a small collection of poetry, both Latin – an elegiac paraphrase of the Song of Songs – and Greek – epigrams on the Apostles and on the benefactors of the young author, in addition to the *Hymn to the Son of God* (123 verses in all), the beginning of which is edited here. A likely inspiration of Thun's was Daniel Heinsius' hymn to Hesiod's Pandora and his collection of epigrams to Greek philosophers (in *Poemata Latina et Graeca* → **Low Countries**). Thun, however, chose strictly Christian content for the whole volume, and decided to not simply ignore but to explicitly reject the ancient tradition, while using traditional epic vocabulary. A model may have been Johan Paulinus' *Magnus Principatus Finlandia* (ll. 39–52), but to repudiate the heathen apparatus was a common strategy of Christian authors. In the above sample, the very beginning of the hymn, Thun thus drives away the Heliconian Muses, who open Hesiod's *Theogony*, silver-bowed Apollo, who is the cause of the plague that ravages the Achaean camp in the first book of the *Iliad*, and repudiates everything that reminds him of pagan inspiration. After that, he invokes divine inspiration and embarks on the hymnic narrative of the birth of Jesus.

II. *Ad Eundem* [1711]

> Μέμφετο ταῖς Μοίραις νεκύων βασιλεὺς ἀγέρωχος
> ὁ Πλούτων γρύξας χίλια παῦρα θανεῖν.
> Αἱ δὲ μελάμπεπλοι τὸν ΒΛΟΚΚΙΟΝ ᾐτιόωντο,
> ὃς χειρωνείῃ δῆσε χέρας παλάμῃ.

Textus: Block, Magnus Gabriel (1711), *Åtskillige anmärkningar öfwer närwarande pestilentias beskaffenhet motande, botande och utrotande...*, Linköping, [15].

Crit.: 4 δῆσε conieci: δῆσι ed.

Sim.: 1–2 βασιλεὺς ἀγέρωχος] cf. *Orac. Sib.* 3.202–203 (ἀγέρωχοι / βασιλῆες) || 2 γρύξας] verbum comicum et serum || 4 χειρωνείη] adjectivum medicinale

To the same [*sc*. M.G. Blockius]

> Pluto, lordly king of the dead, censured the Moirai:
> He grumbled that only a few thousands died.
> The black-robed ones (the Moirai) accused Blockius,
> who has bound their hands with his Chironian art.[34]

Metre: Elegiac couplets.

Notes: The severe outbreak of the bubonic plague of 1710–11, which began in Stockholm with the arrival of refugees from the eastern parts of the crumbling Swedish Empire and spread quickly, raged particularly fiercely in Östergötland, where Magnus Gabriel von Block was district medical officer. Thanks to Block's successful treatment of the epidemic, mortality was low. Thun's epigram is one of several gratulatory paratexts printed in Block's monograph, in which he describes the effects of the recent outbreak and how Block responded to it. The tone of Thun's epigram is light and jocular, describing how Pluto complained to the Moirai about the shortage of new arrivals to the realm of the dead; the reason for this, they explain, is that their hands have been checked by someone who masters the handicraft of the centaur Chiron, who according to myth had healing powers. Μέμφομαι ('to blame') occurs frequently in funerary epigrams of the *Anthologia Palatina*, but the one blaming is never Pluto nor any of the Netherworld deities.

Biography: Josef Thun, or Josephus Thunius in Latin and Θουνιάδης in Greek, was born in Tunsäter, not far from Nyköping, in 1661. He attended school and gymnasium in Strängnäs. After a short stay at Uppsala University (1679), he studied at Turku from 1679 to 1682. Latin, Greek, and Hebrew were his main

---

34 The author's own Latin translation, printed after the Greek text: *Incusat Parcas Pluto, cui tristia parent / Tartara, conquestus millia pauca mori. / Ast in BLOCKiadem rejectant crimina tanta / Qui Chironéa vinxerat arte manus.*

subjects. He spent the greater part of the 1680s at the newly reopened Lund University as tutor of the nobility. From 1688 he served as lector in Strängnäs, first *poëseos*, then of Greek, and, finally, of theology and minister (ordained in 1694). He declined professorships in both Turku and Tartu-Pärnu. From 1712 he was dean of Nyköping's western parish; he remained in that position until his death in 1721. Thun was a prolific and much admired Greek poet; more than 70 pieces of varying length by him are preserved in print or manuscript. His plan to edit his own collected Greek poems, with the help of Petrus Hedelinus (see below) came to nothing due to the ravages of war, ill health, and death.

Bibliography: Hagström, Klas Alfred (1898), *Strengnäs stifts herdaminne*, II, Strängnäs, 312–315; Lundström, Ruth (1976), "Josef Thun och Bibliotheca Thuniana", in: Ead. (ed.), *Från biskop Rogge till Roggebiblioteket*, Stockholm, 102–112. On his Greek poems: Fant 1775–86, 2.76–80; Floderus 1785–89, 80–90; Korhonen 2004, 129–132; Akujärvi 2018 and 2020c.

[JA]

Johan Bilberg (1646–1717)

In eruditam disputationem...Iohannis Palmroots [1685]

Καλαὶ Ἀθῆναι, Παλλάδος κλεινὴ πτόλις,
σεβάσμιόν ποτ' ὄμμα γαίης Ἑλλάδος.
Ἡ τῆς αὑτῆς ἴδρις ἔκλυες πάλαι,
τὸ φασγάνων πνέουσα καὶ πυρὸς μένος.
5   Ἡ παντοίης μήτηρ ὁμοῦ παιδεύσεως
σοφὴ πέφυκας, πᾶσι τιμιωτάτη·
θρέπτειρα τῶν Μουσῶν πανάγρυπνός τ' ἔης,
γλώσσης τ' ἄγαλμα τῆς ἐλευθεροστόμου.
Τοίου κλέους δύστηνος ἐστερημένη,
10   πραθεῖσα νῦν τῶν βαρβάρων ὕπαι γοᾶς.
Στένω, δακρύσας δυστάλαινά σε στένω,
θεήλατόν τε τῆς τύχης καταστροφήν,
καὶ πότμον ἦ ῥ' ἄποτμον ἐν βραχεῖ χρόνῳ.
Σέλας τὸ σὸν γὰρ εἰς τόδ' ἦλθε συμφορᾶς,
15   πασῶν σε τεχνῶν ὥστ' ἄϊδριν ἔμμεναι,
ὠδῖνας εἰ μὴ τῶν ἐλαιῶν ἐκδρέπειν.
Ἔρρει σθένος, γλῶσσ' ἐστι μιξοβάρβαρος,
μάτην Ἀθήνας εἰν Ἀθήναις καὶ σέβω.

Textus: Lagerlööf, Petrus/Palmroot, Johannes (1685), *Historiola linguae Graecae*, Uppsala, [5] (dissertation).

Crit.: 7 Μουσῶν correxi: Μυσῶν ed. | ἕης scripsi: ἕες ed.

Sim.: 1 Παλλάδος ... πτόλις] cf. Ar. *Plut.* 772 (Παλλάδος κλεινὸν πέδον), sed Παλλάδος κλεινὴν πόλιν in St.Byz. α 34 Billerbeck (Ἀθῆναι) citante Ar. *Plut.* || **2** ὄμμα ... Ἑλλάδος] cf. Arist. *Rh.* 1411a5 (τὴν Ἑλλάδα ἑτερόφθαλμον); Aristid. *pac. Athen.* 405.27 Dind. (τῆς Ἑλλάδος τοῖν ὀφθαλμοῖν τὸν ἕτερον); Lib. *Or.* 18.27 (τῆς Ἑλλάδος ὀφθαλμοῦ, τῶν Ἀθηνῶν) || **4** πνέουσα ... μένος] cf. Hom. *Il.* 6.182 (ἀποπνείουσα πυρὸς μένος) || **5** παιδεύσεως] cf. Thuc. 2.41.1 τήν τε πᾶσαν πόλιν τῆς Ἑλλάδος παίδευσιν εἶναι || **7** πανάγρυπνος] hapax legomenon in *Anth. Pal.* 7.195.5 (Mel.) || **8** γλώσσης ... ἐλευθεροστόμου] cf. Aesch. *Supp.* 948–949 (ἐλευθεροστόμου / γλώσσης) || **11** στένω, δακρύσας] cf. Eur. *Ph.* 1311 | δυστάλαινα adjectivum tragicum || **13** πότμον ... ἄποτμον] cf. Eur. *Hipp.* 1144; *Ph.* 1306 | ἐν βραχεῖ χρόνῳ] cf. Aesch. *Pers.* 713 || **16** ὠδῖνας ... ἐλαιῶν] cf. Nonn. *Dion.* 29.189 (χυτὰς ὠδῖνας ἐλαίης) et *Dion.* 33.7 || **17** μιξοβάρβαρος] adjectivum tragicum initio | γλῶσσ' ... μιξοβάρβαρος] cf. Luc. *JTr.* 27 (τὴν φωνὴν ἰδιώτης καὶ μιξοβάρβαρος); Philostr. *VS* 2.1 p. 563 Olearius (ἡμιβαρβάρῳ γλώττῃ) || **18** cf. Mich. Choniates *Carm.* 10.17 (οἰκῶν Ἀθήνας οὐκ Ἀθήνας που βλέπω) | μάτην ... σέβω] cf. *Is.* 29.13 μάτην σέβονται (= *Mt.* 15.9, *Mc.* 7.7)

On the learned dissertation...of Jonas Palmroot

Beautiful Athens, the famed city of Pallas, once the august light of Hellenic soil, who was formerly spoken of as skilled in battle cry, breathing the might of swords and fire, [5] who at the same time was the wise mother of various schools, most valuable to all; you were an ever wakeful rearer of the Muses, and a delight to the free-spoken tongue. Wretched, deprived of such glory, [10] sold by barbarians, you now weep. I sigh, I cry and sigh over you, most miserable one, your godsent reversal of fortune, your destiny truly turned into nothing in a short time. For your light came to such a misfortune, [15] that you are ignorant of all arts, other than plucking the birthpangs of olives. Gone is your strength; your tongue is semi-barbarian; in vain I revere Athens in Athens.

Metre: Iambic trimeters (hiatus l. 1).

Notes: This eulogy of Athens and lament of its present state is printed in a dissertation on the history of the Greek language. It is intended as a gratulation to the respondent (Jonas Palmroot, future professor at Uppsala), but as such it is unusual. It does not praise the addressee, but dwells exclusively on the topic of the dissertation. Bilberg equates Athens with Greece and praises it for its military strength, its fostering of learning, poetry, and freedom of speech, all of which are now gone, 'sold by barbarians', which is likely a reference to the Ottoman conquest and the rule of the last remains of the Byzantine Empire. In addition, Athens has lost its strength and purity of language, the 'tongue' having become semi-barbarian. This is a complaint familiar from works such as Philostratus' *Lives of the Sophists* (2.1, p. 553 Olearius), and common in Byzantine times and in the Renaissance. In a poem on Athens, the choice of iambic metre, uncommon in

Greek poetry from the Swedish Empire, is particularly apt not only because of its association with Attic tragedy and comedy but also because it allows for numerous verbal echoes of Attic drama.

Biography: Johan Bilberg was born in 1646 in Mariestad. After studies at Uppsala and a long *peregrinatio* to courts and universities of Europe as tutor to the son of Tord Bonde, the king's councillor (1673–7), he was appointed professor of mathematics at Uppsala University in 1679. Bilberg's work in the field of mathematics, physics, and astronomy includes several important contributions to the field, but when he advanced to professor of theology in 1689, he was wholly devoted to that field. In 1692 he became dean and vicar in Örebro, and in 1701 bishop of Strängnäs, where he died in 1717. Bilberg was admired for his scholarship, and, though classical philology was not his primary study, he was similarly admired for his Latin as well as Greek poetry; in his old age he still translated some Propertius into Greek.

Bibliography: Nilsson, Alb. (with H.J. Heyman) (1924), "Bilberg, Johan", in: *Svenskt biografiskt lexikon* 4, 310–315; Annerstedt 1877–1931, 2.2.317–326. On his Greek poems: Fant 1775–86, 2.38–40; Floderus 1785–89, 64–69; Korhonen 2004, 295f.; Korhonen 2008, 61.

[JA]

Petrus Hedelinus (–1721)

<In laudem Josephi Thunii> [1721?]

Ἥρωας μὲν Σκαλιγέρους· Κασαυβονίους τε·
Σαλμασίους τε σέβω· Εἰνσιάδας τε σέβω·
ἀλλοδαπῶν Ἑλληνοδικέων· τῶν δ' ἔνδοθι πάτρης
τὸ πλέον ἠγασάμην τῆς Βορεηνορέης.
5   Ἐξ οὗ δ' αὖ τὸ φόως Βορεανδρικὸν ἔσβεσε μοῖρα
ἦν πάρος· εἰμὶ δ' ὅλος νῦν· ΦΙΛΟΘΟΥΝΙΑΔΗΣ.

Textus: *Acta literaria Sveciae*, edita Upsaliae, Trimestre primum anni MDCCXXI, 182.

Crit.: 6 εἰμὶ correxi: εἶμι ed.

Sim.: 3 Ἑλληνοδικέων] cf. Pind. *Ol.* 3.12, praeterea nomen prosaicum | ἔνδοθι πάτρης] cf. Quint. Smyrn. 1.70 || 6 ἦν πάρος ... νῦν] cf. Hom. *Od.* 19.549 (ἦα πάρος, νῦν αὖτε)

⟨Praise of Josef Thun⟩

Scaligers and Casaubons I revere as heroes, Salmasiuses and Heinsiuses, too, among foreign judges of Hellenes. Of those in our country I admired the Boreandrean [*sc.* Muse, lyre, *vel sim.*] more. [5] But, since the Boreandric light was put out by destiny, I used to be and am now a complete – Thuno-phile.

Metre: Elegiac couplets.

Notes: These verses honouring Josef Thun (see above) were published in the first quarter of *Acta literaria Sveciae* of 1721 as an appendix to a notice announcing Thun's intention to publish a collection of his Greek poems, and at the same time informing of the passing of their author. Letters by Thun show how important Hedelinus' work had been in the preparation of the edition. Here Hedelinus sets Thun side by side with prominent protestant continental Hellenists, scholars, and text editors who were also admired as Neo-Latin and Humanist Greek authors. Βορέανδρος, referred to with the circumlocutions τῆς Βορεηνορέης and τὸ φόως Βορεανδρικόν, is Laurentius Norrmannus (see above), who on occasion used the Greek translation of his name, viz. 'North-man', for signing his Greek poetry. Norrmannus may be considered to have been the closest Swedish equivalent to the Scaligers etc. of continental Europe. Thun, lector of Strängnäs Gymnasium and dean of Nyköping, stands comparison with them only as a Greek poet. ΦΙΛΟΘΟΥΝΙΑΔΗΣ is created to Θουνιάδης, the Greek name Thun used on occasion.

Biography: Little is known about Petrus Hedelinus. He entered Strängnäs Gymnasium in 1694 where Josef Thun was one of his teachers. After studies at Uppsala University he became *magister* in 1710. He was appointed lector at Karlstad Gymnasium in 1719. Hedelinus assisted Josef Thun in collecting and copying his Greek poems; his death in March 1721 was a serious setback for Thun's edition. Like most Swedes writing Greek, Hedelinus had a modest career and made minimal impact on the annals of Swedish education, history, etc., but, unlike most, he had a talent for Greek poetry which enabled him to write *Musis et Apolline dextro* in the words of Floderus.

Bibliography: Edestam, Anders (1975), *Karlstads stifts herdaminne från medeltiden till våra dagar*, I, Karlstad, 185. On his Greek poems: Fant 1775–86, 3.5f.; Floderus 1785–89, 97–102; Korhonen 2004, 36; Akujärvi 2018, 2020c.

[JA]

Erik Engelbert Östling (1807–1870)

Memoria beati Esaiae Tegnér [1847]

(excerptum, vv. 1–17)

    Θειότερον τί θέημα, τί μεῖζον δεινότερόν τε,
    ἢ ἐπὶ πέτρῃ στάντα ἰδεῖν εἰς κύματα πόντου
    ἠέλιον καταδύντα, λιπόντα δ' ἄρ' οὐρανὸν εὐρύν;
    Ἱμερόεν φθινύθει φέγγος, πάντῃ δὲ φέρονται
5   ἔνθα καὶ ἔνθα σκιαί, δροσερὸν σκέπας ἐκτανύουσαι
    καὶ ποταμοὺς ἄνα, καὶ λίμνας, καὶ ἀν' οὔρεα μακρὰ
    ἄνθεσιν ἕρσῃ δευομένοις νεύουσι κάρηνα·
    παύει δ' ἄλσει ἔνι σκιερῷ μέλος ὄρνεα ἡδύ,
    ἐν θάμνοις σκοπέλοις τε ἑὰς ὑποδύντα καλιάς.
10 Αὐτίκα κοιμηθέντος ἀνάσσει Νὺξ ἐρεβεννὴ
    κόσμου, σκῆπτρον ἔχουσα χερί· πάντ' εἶδος ἀτερπὲς
    ἐνδύεται, καὶ θυμὸς ἐνὶ στήθεσσι φίλοισιν
    ἀνδρός, ὅτις συνετός, κινεῖται πολλά τε πάσχει.
    Εἰκόνα οἱ δοκέει γὰρ ἰδεῖν, ὡς πάντ' ἐπὶ γαῖαν
15 φθαρτά θ' ὁμοῦ καὶ ἄπιστα, βραχεῖ εὔτρεπτά τ' ἐν ὥρῃ·
    εἰκόνα σεμνοτάτην τ' ἀνδρὸς προφερεστέρου ἄλλων,
    οὗ βίον ἐκλείποντος ἄφαρ νὺξ πάντα καλύπτει.

Textus: *Memoriam beati Esaiae Tegnér episcopi Vexionensis olim Graecae linguae professoris poëtae divini Graeco carmine pie celebravit* E.E. Östling Eloq. et poes. Lector, Örebro 1847, [3].

Crit.: 6 ἄνα correxi: ἀνὰ ed. || 6–7 μακρὰ ἄνθεσιν scripsi: μακρά. Ἄνθεσιν ed.

Sim.: 1 θειότερον τί θέημα] cf. Basil. *Is.* 7.199 Trevisan (Τί ... θειότερον ἄκουσμα, ἢ θέαμα) | τί μεῖζον δεινότερόν τε] cf. D. Chr. 11.29 (τί μεῖζον ἢ δεινότερον) || **2** κύματα πόντου] cf. Quint. Smyrn. 2.217; Nonn. *Dion.* 6.310 etc. || **3** ἠέλιον καταδύντα] cf. Hom. *Il.* 1.601 etc. | οὐρανὸν εὐρύν] cf. Hom. *Il.* 3.364 etc. || **6** οὔρεα μακρὰ] cf. Hom. *Il.* 13.18 etc. || **8** ἄλσει ... σκιερῷ] cf. Ap. Rhod. *Argon.* 4.1715 || **10** Νὺξ ἐρεβεννὴ] cf. Hes. *Theog.* 213; *Op.* 17 || **11** σκῆπτρον ... χερί] cf. *Orac. Sib.* 5.415 (σκῆπτρον ἔχων ἐν χερσίν); Alex. Aphr. *in Metaph.* 821 Hayduck (Νὺξ 'σκῆπτρον ἔχουσ' ἐν χερσὶν...'), Syrian. *in Metaph.* 182 Kroll | εἶδος ἀτερπές] cf. Eudoc. *mart. S. Cypr.* 2.122 || **12** θυμὸς ... φίλοισιν] cf. Hes. fr. 315 Merkelbach & West || **13** κινεῖται ... πάσχει] cf. Arist. *de An.* 416b31 (ἡ δ' αἴσθησις ἐν τῷ κινεῖσθαί τε καὶ πάσχειν) et saepe

Commemoration of Esaias Tegnér of blessed memory

(excerpt, ll. 1–17)

> What sight is more divine, what more powerful and awesome, than to stand on a cliff and to gaze towards the waves of the sea at the sun setting and leaving the vast sky? [4] The lovely light vanishes, the shadows are carried hither and thither on every side, spreading out a dewy covering along rivers and seas, and throughout high mountains flowerheads drop, moist with dew. In the shady grove birds cease their sweet song, and slip into their nests in bushes and on peaks. [10] Now dark Night rules the world lulled to sleep, with a scepter in her hand. All is clothed in joyless shape, and the spirit in a man's breast, if he is wise, is moved and deeply affected. [14] For it seems to him that he sees an image of how everything on earth is perishable, not to be trusted, short and easily overturned in a short time; and the most august image of a man, more excellent than others, after whose death all is suddenly enveloped by night.

Metre: Hexameters; note l. 11 χερί with ῑ; allowing hiatus: without elision or shortening of vowel in l. 2 (ἢ ἐπί); probably legitimised by former digamma in ll. 2 (στάντα ἰδεῖν), 8, 9, 14.

Notes: These lines open a 78 verses long hexametric tribute to Esaias Tegnér (1782–1846), printed one year after his death. After studies at Lund University and after holding lesser teaching and administrative positions at the university, Tegnér became professor of Greek at Lund in 1812, on which occasion the Greek chair in Lund was separated from that of Oriental languages for the first time since the early 18th century. Ordained in 1812, Tegnér advanced to bishop of Växjö in 1824, a position he held until his death. Tegnér was a notable poet, and from 1819 a member of the Swedish Academy. After Östling's romantic, lyrical introduction, which melancholically contemplates the stillness of dusk and the arrival of night, the better part of the celebration is devoted to the poet Tegnér. Given the prominence of sun and light in Tegnér's poetry, Östling's likening his death to the setting of the sun gains added significance.

Biography: Not much is known about Erik Engelbert Östling. Born in 1807, the son of a rural court judge, he studied at Uppsala where he wrote and defended the wholly Greek dissertation *ΠΕΡΙ ΤΩΝ ἘΛΕΥΣΙΝΙΩΝ ΔΙΗΓΗΣΙΣ* in November 1828. After a period as *docens* of Latin at Uppsala, Östling left the university as he was appointed *lector eloquentiae et poëseos* at Karlstad in 1842. He remained there until his death in 1870.

Bibliography: Edestam, Anders (1975), *Karlstads stifts herdaminne från medeltiden till våra dagar*, I, Karlstad, 170.

[JA]

Johan Bergman (1864–1951)

Carmen Graecum. Πάντα ῥεῖ. [1926]

Ἡδὺ μέν ἐστι βροτοῖσι φανὲν φάος Ἡελίοιο·
ἀλλ' ὑπ' ὄρεσσι ταχέως σβήσεται ἑσπερίοις·
Ἡδὺς μὲν Ζέφυρος, θαλερῷ λειμῶνι χορεύων,
κύματα θωπεύων, ἄλσεσι κάρτα φίλος·
5   ἀλλ' ἔσται ταχέως στυγερὴ ναύταισι θύελλα,
ἧς περιδινούσης δένδρα περιστενάχει.
Ἡδέα χρήματα πολλά τε καὶ χρυσὸς πολύτιμος·
ὄλβος ἐν ἀνθρώποις ταῦτα πολὺς λέγεται.
τερπνὸν δ' οὐδὲν ἔχει· τάχα δ' αἱρήσουσιν ἅπαντα
10   κληρονόμοι ῥυπαραῖς χείρεσιν ἁρπαλέως.
"Ἀλλὰ τὸ κάλλος ὅμως, δῶρον χρυσέης Ἀφροδίτης
καὶ φιλότης γε κορῶν· μή τά γ' ἀνάξια φῇς."
Ταῦτα μὲν οὖν· λείψει σε χάρις θ' ἥβη τ' ἐρατεινή,
σπευδόντων ὡρῶν θεῖναι ἔτεσσι τέλος·
15   ἀμφικαλύψει ἅπαξ χρόα καλὸν γαῖα μέλαινα,
καὶ τότε τίς τέρψις; τίς χαρίεσσα κόρη;
Ἔκλιπε μὲν χειμών, ἔαρος βλέψεν φίλον ὄμμα,
ἀλλ' ἐπὶ γήραϊ σῷ οὐκ ἔσεται νεότης.
Πάντα γὰρ ἀλλοιοῦται· ὑπάρχει δ' ἔμμονον οὐδέν
20   ἐν βίῳ ἀνθρώπων· πᾶν φύγεν ὡς νεφέλαι.

Textus: Bergman, Johannes (1926), *Carmina novissima. Carmina latina uno carmine graeco adiecto*, Stockholm, 38.

Crit.: 11 χρυσέης debuit || 14 σπευδόντων] σπευδουσῶν debuit

Sim.: 1 Ἡδὺ μέν ἐστι βροτοῖσι] cf. Eur. *Andr*. 781 (ἡδὺ μὲν γὰρ αὐτίκα τοῦτο βροτοῖσιν) | φάος Ἡελίοιο] formula Homerica || 3–4 cf. Anacreont. 41.1–4 (ἦ καλόν ἐστι βαδίζειν, / ὅπου λειμῶνες κομῶσιν, / ὅπου λεπτὸς ἡδυτάτην / ἀναπνεῖ Ζέφυρος αὔρην); Paul. Silent. *Descr. Ambonis* 226 (καὶ θαλερῷ λειμῶνι) || 7–10 cf. Thgn. 1.719–728 (Ἴσόν τοι πλουτοῦσιν, ὅτῳ πολὺς ἄργυρός ἐστιν / καὶ χρυσὸς καὶ γῆς πυροφόρου πεδία...ὅταν δέ κε τῶν ἀφίκηται / ὥρη, σὺν δ' ἥβη γίνεται ἁρμοδία, / ταῦτ' ἄφενος θνητοῖσι· τὰ γὰρ περιώσια πάντα / χρήματ' ἔχων οὐδεὶς ἔρχεται εἰς Ἀίδεω / οὐδ' ἂν ἄποινα διδοὺς θάνατον φύγοι οὐδὲ βαρείας / νούσους οὐδὲ κακὸν γῆρας ἐπερχόμενον) || **11–13** cf. Mimn. fr. 1.1 (τίς δὲ βίος, τί δὲ τερπνὸν ἄτερ χρυσῆς Ἀφροδίτης), 3 (κρυπταδίη φιλότης καὶ μείλιχα δῶρα καὶ εὐνή) || **13** cf. Anac. fr. 395.3–4 PMG (χαρίεσσα δ' οὐκέτ' ἥβη / πάρα) et formulam Homericam χαριεστάτη ἥβη || **15** ἀμφικαλύψει...καλόν] cf. Hes. *Op.* 198 (λευκοῖσιν φάρεσσι καλυψαμένω χρόα καλόν | γαῖα μέλαινα] cf. Hom. *Il.* 2.699 (ζωὸς ἐών· τότε δ' ἤδη ἔχεν κάτα γαῖα μέλαινα) || **16** cf. supra ad v. 11–13 || **17** φίλον ὄμμα] cf. *Anth. Gr. App.*, *epigr. sepulchr.* 670.2

Greek poem. Everything flows

Sweet is for mortals the shining light of the sun, but it will rapidly disappear below the western mountains. Sweet is the western wind when it dances on a blooming meadow, when it caresses the waves, it is very dear to the groves, [5] but a storm will rapidly come, loathsome for seamen, and when it whirls around, the trees groan. Sweet is great property and much-revered gold, among men this is called great fortune, [9] but it holds nothing delightful: soon greedy heirs will take everything with their dirty hands. 'Nevertheless, there is beauty, the gift of the golden Aphrodite, and the love of maidens! Do not say it is worthless!' That is indeed so: but grace and lovely youth will leave you as the seasons rush to put an end to the years. [15] One day the black earth will cover your beautiful body, and then, what is delight? what is a lovely girl? Winter has left, it has caught a glimpse of the lovely eye of spring, but your old age is not going to be followed by youth. All things change and nothing is stable in the life of men; everything takes flight like clouds.

Metre: Elegiac couplets.

Notes: The poem, which takes its title from Heraclitus, expresses ideas about the fragility of life and the passing nature of joy, found passim in archaic Greek poetry (Mimnermus, Theognis, Solon, Simonides or Archilochus, but also Homer) and Horace, but without many direct loans.

Biography: Johan (Johannes) Bergman was born in Sweden and held many different teaching posts in Göteborg, Uppsala, and Stockholm, working also for the *Thesaurus Linguae Latinae* and participating in archaeological excavations. From 1919 to 1923, he was professor of Latin philology and literature and archaeology at the University of Tartu, but returned later to Sweden. He was active in politics, a leading figure in the Swedish temperance movement and a member of the Riksdag.

Bibliography: Piirimäe, Helmut (ed.) (1994), *Eesti ülikooli algus*, Tartu, 61; Jacobson, G. (1922), "Bergman, Johan", in: *Svenskt biografiskt lexikon* 3, 620–627.

[JP]

Albert Wifstrand (1901–1964)

Till Frithiof Pontén [1961]

Ἐννάκι πέντ' ἔτη ἐστίν, ἀφ' οὗ σεο χεῖρέ μ' ὁδηγεῖν
ἤρξαντ' ἀρχόμενον βῆτα καὶ ἄλφα λέγειν·
εἴ τι δ' ἐν Ἑλλήνων συγγράμμασι προσμεμάθηκα,
τοῖς παρὰ σοῦ πρώτοις ἐστὶν ἐποικοδομή.

Textus: Wifstrand, Albert (1961), *Bakgrunder. Uppsatser om tider och tänkesätt*, Lund, [5].

Sim.: 1 σεο ... ὁδηγεῖν] cf. LXX, *Ps.* 138.10 (ἡ χείρ σου ὁδηγήσει με) || 2 βῆτα ... λέγειν] cf. *Anth. Pal.* 11.437.2 (Arat.) (βῆτα καὶ ἄλφα λέγων) || 4 ἐποικοδομή] cf. [Long.] *Subl.* 11.1–2 (αὔξησιν ... τοῦτο δὲ εἴτε διὰ τοπηγορίαν ... εἴτ' ἐποικοδομίαν ἔργων ἢ παθῶν (μυρίαι γὰρ ἰδέαι τῶν αὐξήσεων) γίνοιτο)

To Frithiof Pontén

It has been nine times five [= 45] years since your hands began to guide me as I was beginning to read *alpha* and *beta*. If I know now anything more in Greek literature, that is a superstructure to the first teachings that came from you.[35]

Metre: Elegiac couplets.

Notes: With this dedication to his former school-teacher of Greek, Frithiof Pontén (author of a Greek textbook for beginners, first published in the 1920s and still in use), Albert Wifstrand celebrates the important role played by school-teachers in the future studies and careers of their former pupils.

Biography: Born in 1901, Albert Wifstrand studied classical and Semitic languages at Lund University; he became doctor with a dissertation on the *Greek Anthology* in 1926. He was immediately promoted to associate professor (docent) of Greek language and literature. Moreover, he regularly acted as a professor in the absence of the holder of the Greek chair in Lund, Claes Lindskog, who was a member of the Swedish Riksdag and thus occupied in Stockholm. Wifstrand was then promoted to *professor ordinarius* in 1935 and held the chair until his death

---

35 The author's own Swedish translation, printed after to the Greek text: 'Fem och fyrtio år ha förrunnit, sen jag begynte / först under ledning av dig stava på grekiska ord. / Vad jag må därutöver ha lärt i hellenernas skrifter / bygger på vad du en gång fäste i ynglingens håg.'

in 1964. His scholarly interests were broad, but he had a particular interest in Greek poetry and metrics. He was not only the author of an important study on the Greek hexameter from Callimachus to Nonnus (1933), but also composed Greek poems himself. These are generally short epigrams addressed to friends and colleagues, and they were often presented as inscriptions in books he gifted, some of which have been collected in Lund University Library.

Bibliography: Hanell, Krister (1965), "Albert Wifstrand", in: *Kungl. humanistiska vetenskapssamfundet i Lund. Årsberättelse 1964–1965*, Lund, 19–26; Palm, Jonas (1965), "Albert Wifstrand", in: *Vetenskaps-societeten i Lund. Årsbok 1965*, Lund, 159–171.

[JA]

Jerker Blomqvist (1938–)

Tullia Linders [1990]

ΕΛΛΑΔ ΥΠΕΡΒΟΡΕΗΙ ΔΙΕΡΕΥΝΗΣΑΣΑ ΦΡΟΝΗΣΕΙ
ΤΥΛΛΙΑ ΗΔ ΕΤΕΡΟΙΣ ΣΟΥ ΜΕΤΑΔΟΥΣΑ ΝΟΟΥ
ΠΟΛΛΩΝ ΕΚ ΧΕΙΡΩΝ ΔΕΞΑΙ ΔΩΡΟΝ ΤΕ ΓΕΡΑΣ ΤΕ
ΠΟΛΛΗΣ ΑΝΤ ΑΡΕΤΗΣ ΣΟΙ ΠΡΟΣΟΦΕΙΛΟΜΕΝΟΝ[36]

Textus: *Opuscula Atheniensia* 18, 1990, [5]

Sim.: 4 ΠΟΛΛΗΣ ΑΝΤ ΑΡΕΤΗΣ] de iunctura cf. Isoc. *Antid.* 37; Pl. *Leg.* 678a9 etc.

Tullia Linders

Tullia, with Hyperborean prudence you have scrutinised Hellas
   and shared your thoughts with others.
From the hands of many accept this offering, a gift of honour,
   which is due to you for your great accomplishment.

Metre: Elegiac couplets (note l. 2 hiatus as prosodic pause after ΤΥΛΛΙΑ).

---

[36] Minuscule version: Ἑλλάδ' Ὑπερβορέῃ διερευνήσασα φρονήσει, / Τυλλία, ἡδ' ἑτέροις σοῦ μεταδοῦσα νόου, / πολλῶν ἐκ χειρῶν δέξαι δῶρόν τε γέρας τε / πολλῆς ἀντ' ἀρετῆς σοι προσοφειλόμενον.

Notes: Published at the head of a special issue of *Opuscula Atheniensia* dedicated to Tullia Linders (1925–2008), professor of classical archaeology and ancient history at Uppsala from 1979 to 1991, this is the first of five Greek epigrams that Blomqvist produced for *Opuscula Atheniensia* as a member of the journal's editorial committee (the last one appeared in 2001). It is published anonymously, as are all the Greek dedicatory texts published on similar occasions in that journal, both before and after Blomqvist's time. Unlike his later epigrams, Blomqvist has not yet broken with the tradition of printing the epigram in majuscles and without punctuation. This epigram adheres to the common structure of dedicatory epigrams: the dedicatee is identified, the reason why the gift is given is described only briefly, and the dedicatee is exhorted to accept the gift.

Biography: Jerker Blomqvist is professor emeritus, formerly professor of Greek language and literature at Lund University. Born in 1938, Blomqvist studied the ancient languages at Lund University, where he also took the doctorate in Greek with a dissertation on Greek particles in Hellenistic prose (1969). Having taught at Lund and Uppsala, Blomqvist was appointed professor of classical philology at the University of Copenhagen in 1980. He returned to Lund when he was appointed professor of Greek language and literature in 1987, and remained in that position until his retirement in 2003. Blomqvist's scholarly interests are wide, but he has published mainly on Greek language and linguistics (particles in particular), language history, and Greek sceptics; with Ole Jastrup, meanwhile, he has produced a Greek grammar that is used in first-cycle Greek courses in all Scandinavian countries.

Bibliography: *Jerker Blomqvist*, in: *Nationalencyklopedin*, http://www.ne.se/uppslagsverk/encyklopedi/lång/jerker-blomqvist [accessed: December 2018].

[JA]

Finland

The first Greek poems were printed in Finland no earlier than 1648, when the University of Turku (founded in 1640) had acquired Greek printing types. Until then, Finnish scholars published their poems elsewhere. According to present knowledge, the first poems were by Aeschillus Petraeus in Wittenberg in 1623 and in Rostock in 1628. However, several Finns are known to have made efforts to learn Greek long before that. Mikael Agricola (1510–1557), the bishop of Turku and a leading proponent of the Protestant Reformation in Finland, studied in Wittenberg under the supervision of Philipp Melanchthon, while a certain Matthias Marci taught elementary Greek (according to his own report) at the University of Rostock during the 1580s. At the same time, elementary Greek was included in the curriculum of Finnish schools.

There are approximately 400 Humanist Greek texts, both poems and prose, from Finland (including Carelia). The Finnish corpus as a whole includes various types of occasional poetry, particularly funerary poems, texts for academic occasions, but also hexameter orations. The corpus is reasonably rich in forms and metres and includes rare forms like a tautogrammatic and a macaronic Greek poem, a Theognis cento, and several cento-like imitations. A specific feature of Turku Greek texts is the great amount of short prose congratulations during the last decades of the 17th century.[37] Another peculiar feature is six applications for scholarships in Greek.

During the first several decades at Turku University (the Royal Academy of Turku), many congratulations were written by professors and students who came from Sweden, such as Professor Petrus Laurbecchius and Josef Thun (see **Sweden** above) who studied at Turku and wrote several Greek poems there before returning to Sweden. Some important Hellenists of Swedish origin, such as Nicolaus Nycopensis and **Johannes Gezelius Sr** (see Estonia), enjoyed the better part of their academic or clerical career in Turku, but produced most of their Greek poems as students and teachers in Tartu.

The richest period of Humanist Greek poetry in Turku took place between the 1670s and 1710s. Numerous poems were written by students, some of them rather long, like Georgius Ståhlberg's *epibaterion* (1689) and, in prose, Burgman's oration lamenting the death of Charles X (delivered in Turku, printed in Stockholm 1660). The most notable example from this period is the hexameter oration *Magnus*

---

[37] The influence can be seen also in Tartu during the 1690s, where more than half of the Greek texts were in prose; probably also thanks to Finnish students, such as Ericus Castelius. See Päll 2010, 135–138.

Principatus Finlandia, a *laus patriae* by **Johan Paulinus** (ennobled Lillienstedt). This oration was delivered and published in Uppsala (1678), but more than likely was at least partially composed in Turku. It played an important role in the development of the national political identity of the country, first under Swedish, then under Russian rule. Johan and his brothers Simon and Henrik wrote several Greek poems and Greek occasional texts in prose. Simon, later professor of Greek and Hebrew, and his colleagues, Professors Ericus Falander (ennobled Tigerstedt) and David Lund, both prolific authors of Greek occasional poetry, had an impact on the Greek compositions of their students. Some Greek poems were written by professors of eloquence, such as **Martin Miltopaeus** (1631–1679) and **Christiernus Alander** (1660–1704); others were written by the elite of Finnish cultural history, e.g. the first high-quality poets who ever published in Finnish, **Johannes Cajanus** (1655–1681) and Henrik Lilius, the Fennophile Daniel Juslenius, the Wolfian philosopher **Johan Welin** (1705–1744) and the economist Anders Chydenius.

When the university reopened in 1722 after its shutdown during the Great Northern War (1700–1721), a new subgenre emerged: Greek dedications in disputations. In spite of this, the writing of Humanist Greek occasional poetry never fully recovered in Turku after the war. The last Greek congratulation to a disputation was published in 1786. Just before the university relocated to the new capital, Helsinki, the future Finnish national poet **Johan Ludvig Runeberg** (1804–1877) composed a satiric Ἔπος γελοῖον (1826). In the 20th and 21st centuries the Finnish tradition has since been revived by Erkki Sironen.[38]

[TK]

The overview in this sub-chapter is based on Korhonen 2004 (with an English summary). The bibliographies by Melander 1951–1959 and Vallinkoski 1962 contain useful indices with references to Greek occasional texts. See also SKB.

---

38 Senior Lecturer of Ancient Greek Sironen has composed c. 25 Greek epigrams for various occasions. One of them was written for the conferment ceremony of the Faculty of Arts at the University of Helsinki in 2000 celebrating Maarit Kaimio, the then professor of Greek language and literature in Helsinki: Τᾶσδε παναγύριος ἀρχαγὸς τιμαθέτο / τοῖσδε ἄρκτοις μικκοῖς ἀντὶ ἀγαθῶν μεγάλων. / χθὲστεφανόθεμες, τὰ δὲ νῦν ἔστι ἐν Σϝεαβόργοι / ἐκτὸς τᾶς τελετᾶς, νάσοι ἐν ἀμφιρύται ('Let the leader of this celebration be honoured with these small bears for her great good deeds. Yesterday we got our wreaths, but this takes place at Sveaborg, outside the ceremony, on a sea-girt island'). The poem is published in Nikkarinen 2001, 4 (a facsimile drawing of the poem in archaising Corinthian lettering) and in Korhonen/Sironen 2018, 28. Small bears in the poem refer to the joint gift, a necklace with tiny bears, which the *promovendi* in classics gave to Professor Kaimio on the degree ceremony cruise day. [ES]

Special Bibliography

Korhonen, Tua (2002), "Γλῶττα eller γλῶσσα: att skriva grekiska dikter under barocktiden", in: Hans-Erik Johannesson (ed.), *Mimesis förvandlingar. Tradition och förnyelse i renässansens och barockens litteratur*, Göteborg, 179–192.

Korhonen, Tua (2004), *Ateena Auran rannoilla*, http://urn.fi/URN:ISBN:952-10-1812-7, diss. Helsinki.

Korhonen, Tua (forthcoming), "How to Versify in Greek in Turku (Finland). Greek Composition at the Universities of the Swedish Empire During the Seventeenth Century", in: Federica Ciccolella/Luigi Silvano (reds.), *Graecia transvolavit Alpes: The Study of Greek in Early Modern Europe*. Leiden.

Korhonen, Tua/Sironen, Erkki (2018), *The Exhibition "Humanist Greek from Finland" 22 August – 5 October 2018*, Helsinki.

Melander, Toini (1951–1959), *Personskrifter hänförande sig till Finland 1562-1713: bibliografisk förteckning*, Helsinki.

Nikkarinen, Jakke et al. (eds.) (2001), *Promotio ordinis philosophorum Universitatis Helsingiensis MM*, Helsinki.

Päll, Janika (2010), "Humanistengriechisch im alten Estland und Nord-Livland", in: Janika Päll/Ivo Volt/Martin Steinrück (eds.), *Classical Tradition from the 16th century to Nietzsche*, Tartu, 114–147.

SKB = Laine, Tuija/Nyqvist, Rita (1996) (eds.), *Suomen kansallisbibliografia/ Finlands nationalbibliografi / Finnische Nationalbibliographie 1488–1700*, Helsinki.

Vallinkoski, Jorma (1962), *Turun Akatemian väitöskirjat 1642–1828*, Helsinki.

Martin Miltopaeus (1631–1679)

Gamelia [1652]

    Μοῦσαι καὶ Χάριτες, κοῦραι Διὸς ὥριον ἀνδρός
        ἐς γάμον ἐλθοῦσαι ψάλλετε καλὸν ἔπος·
    Οὗτος ἀνὴρ χρυσοῦ τε καὶ ἀργύρου ἀντερύσασθαι
        ἄξιος, ἐν τιμίοις πράγμασι γιγνόμενος.
5   Βέλτερος ἢ πλουτοῦντος ἔφυ σεσοφισμένος ἀνήρ·
        νυμφίος ἐστὶ σοφός, ΒΗΡΓΙΟΣ ἐστὶ παχύς.
    Παρθενικὴν κάλλος (τί γὰρ ἡδύτερον καὶ ἄρειον;)
        κοσμεῖ τὴν νύμφην καὶ μάλ᾽ ἐπισταμένην.
    Οὐδέν, ΠΕΤΡ᾽, ἀγαθῆς γλυκερώτερόν ἐστι γυναικός·
10 ταύτης ναιχὶ Θεὸς μάρτυς ἀληθοσύνης.
    Φάρμακον οὖσ᾽ ἀνδρὸς δὴ πταίσματα πολλὰ συναιρεῖ·
        τερπωλὴ νικᾷ πάντα σὺν εὐφροσύνῃ.
    Νῦν δὲ μέσην παρὰ παῖδα λαβὼν ἀγκῶνα φίλησον·
        στέργε τεὴν ἄλοχον γήραος ἄχρι φίλην.
15 Εἰρήνη καὶ πλοῦτος ἔχοι θάλαμον στεφανοῦντες
        σφωΐτεροι δὲ κακὰς φεύγετε τὰς ἔριδας
    καί τε ἄνευ τέκνων ὅτι οὐ γλυκερὸς γάμος ἐστίν,
        παιδοτόκον θάλαμον κ᾽ εὔχομαι ὔμμιν ἐγών.
    Ὕστερον οὐρανόθι πιστοὶ συγχαίρετε Χριστῷ
20 τούτων οὐδέν τι ἄλλ᾽ ἐπιτερπνότερον.

Textus: *Gamelia, festivis thalami honoribus…Petri Andreae Bergii Sudermanni…Helenae Henrici f. Carsteniae*, Turku: Petrus Wald, 1652, A4v (4:o)

Crit.: 8 κοσμεῖ; τὴν ed. || 9 ἀγαθῆς γλυκερώτερόν ἐστι corr.: ἀγατῆς γλυκυρώτερον ἐστὶ ed. || 10 ταύτης correxi] ταυτῆς ed. || 11 ἄνδρος ed. || 13 νῦν δὲ correxi: νῦνδε ed. | ἀγκῶνα correxi: ἀγκῶντε ed. || 15 στεφανοῦντες correxi: στεφανόντες ed. || 17 ἐστίν, scripsi: ἐστὶν; ed.

Sim.: 1–2 cf. Thgn. 15–16 (Μοῦσαι καὶ Χάριτες, κοῦραι Διός, αἵ ποτε Κάδμου / ἐς γάμον ἐλθοῦσαι καλὸν ἀείσατ᾽ ἔπος) | ὥριον…γάμον] cf. Hes. *Op.* 697 || 3–4 cf. Thgn. 77–78 (πιστὸς ἀνὴρ χρυσοῦ τε καὶ ἀργύρου ἀντερύσασθαι / ἄξιος ἐν χαλεπῇ, Κύρνε, διχοστασίῃ) || 5 cf. Ps.-Phoc. 130 (βέλτερος ἀλκήεντος ἔφυ σεσοφισμένος ἀνήρ) || 7 cf. Ps.-Phoc. 195 (Στέργε τεὴν ἄλοχον· τί γὰρ ἡδύτερον καὶ ἄρειον) || 9–10 cf. Thgn. 1225–1226 (οὐδέν, Κύρν᾽, ἀγαθῆς γλυκερώτερόν ἐστι γυναικός· / μάρτυς ἐγώ, σὺ δ᾽ ἐμοὶ γίνου ἀληθοσύνης) || 11 cf. Joh. Chrysost. *In epistulam i ad Corinthios*, PG 61.223.15–16 (καὶ γὰρ λιμήν ἐστιν ἡ γυνή, καὶ φάρμακον εὐθυμίας μέγιστον) || 12 cf. Thgn. 1068 (τερπωλὴ νικᾷ πάντα σὺν εὐφροσύνῃ) || 13 cf. Thgn. 265 (ed. Gezelius 1646) ἔνθα μέσην παρὰ παῖδα λαβὼν ἀγκῶν᾽ ἐφίλησα (Thgn. 265 (*hodierni*) ἔνθα μέσην περὶ παῖδα) || 14 cf. Ps.-Phoc. 196 (ἢ ὅταν ἀνδρὶ γυνὴ φρονέῃ φίλα γήραος ἄχρις) || 20 cf. Thgn. 1066 (τούτων οὐδὲν †τιτ† ἄλλ᾽ ἐπιτερπνότερον)

Wedding song

Muses and Charites, daughters of Zeus, who have come to the wedding that celebrates the man at the right age, please sing a beautiful song. This man is worth his weight in gold and silver as he performs valuable tasks. [5] A man with wisdom is indeed better than a rich one. The bridegroom is wise, Bergius is a man of substance! Beauty (for what is sweeter and better than it?) graces the maidenly bride who is very capable too. Petrus, there is nothing sweeter than a good wife: [10] God bears verily witness to this truth. Being man's medicine she takes away many setbacks; joy together with delight conquers all. Now, take the girl by her waist and kiss her. Love your dear wife until old age. [15] May peace and wealth decorate your bedchamber with garlands. And the two of you: do avoid evil disputes. And since marriage without children is not sweet, I wish you a bedchamber that favours child-birth. In the hereafter, rejoice faithfully with Christ in Heaven; [20] nothing else is more delightful than that.

Metre: Elegiac couplets; note hiatus in ll. 3, 7, 17, 18, 20; *brevis pro longo* in l. 4 (τιμίοις); l. 19 (οὐρανόθι with long ι); l. 20 follows Theognidean tradition.

Notes: Miltopaeus – a 21-year-old student while writing this poem – imitates Theognis' verses at a basic level (*imitatio servilis*), sometimes, however, with *interpretatio Christiana* (l. 10: in Theognis' verse, the witness is the poetic 'I'). Some gnomic verses from the collection attributed to the archaic poet Phocylides are used too. Both Theognis and Ps-Phocylides were popular text-book material for studying Greek in early modern Europe. The addressee of this wedding poem is Petrus Bergius (1612–1691), who, as professor of Greek and Oriental languages, is likely to have inspected Miltopaeus' poem before its publication.

Biography: Martin Miltopaeus (1631–1679) was born in Turku, enrolled at the university in 1647 and graduated six years later. Miltopaeus did not study abroad and his family background was not academic (the name Miltopaeus is a curious half-Greek form of *Ruskeapää* ('Redhead')). As professor of *eloquentia* from 1660 until his early death, Miltopaeus published among other things a popular treatise on rhetoric (*Institutiones oratoriae*, 1669) and supervised dissertations not only in his discipline but on history, politics, and physics. He was an industrious writer of Latin occasional verses and composed two poems in Greek (in 1652 and 1657). He is remembered for his support of freedom of speech in the era of Orthodox Lutheranism.

Bibliography: Kotivuori, Yrjö, *s.v.* "Miltopaeus, Mårten", in: https://ylioppilasmatrikkeli.helsinki.fi [accessed: April 2019]; Kallinen, Maija (1995), *Change and Stability. Natural Philosophy at the Academy of Turku 1640–1713*, Helsinki, 82–85. On his Greek poems: Korhonen 2004, 225f., 300.

[TK]

Johan Cajanus Jr (1655–1681)

‹In disputationem philosophicam de somniis scriptam› [1675]

Ὕπνος ὅταν μέλιτος γλυκίων βλεφάροισιν ἐφίζει
ἡμῶν καὶ μαλακῷ δέει ἄμφω φάεα δεσμῷ
τῆμος ὑφερπύζει παμποίκιλον ἔθνος ὀνείρων,
πολλάκι μὲν λυγροῖς φαντάσμασι, πολλάκι δ' αὖτε
5 τερπνοῖς ἐμπαῖζον τοῖς εὕδουσιν μερόπεσσιν.
Νῦν ἄγε δή, φίλε ΜΥΡΙΧ, ἐπεὶ μελετήματι δηλοῖς
ἀκριβεῖ πᾶσαν γένεσιν καὶ φῦλον ὀνείρων,
μισθὸν τῶν μεγάλων καμάτων σοι ἐπεύχομαι ἡδύν.

Textus: Andreas Norcopensis/Nordenhielm (pr.) & Johannes Mürick (resp.), *Disputatio philosophica de Somniis*, Stockholm: Nils Wankijff, 1675,)(4v (8:o).

Crit.: 5 ἔμπαιζον ed.

Sim.: 1–2 cf. Mosch. *Eur.* 3–4 (ὕπνος ὅταν μέλιτος γλυκίων βλεφάροισιν ἐφίζων / λυσιμελὴς πεδάᾳ μαλακῷ κατὰ φάεα δεσμῷ); cf. Hom. *Il.* 1.249 || 3 ὑφερπύζει] vide Scapula 1637, 519 s.v. ἕρπω: ὑφερπύζω = ὑφέρπω *subrepo, subserpo, clam serpo* | ἔθνος ὀνείρων] cf. Mosch. *Eur.* 5 (εὖτε καὶ ἀτρεκέως ποιμαίνεται ἔθνος ὀνείρων) || 5 ἐμπαῖζον...μερόπεσσιν] cf. *Anth. Pal.* 10.70.1–2 (Εἰ βίον ἐν μερόπεσσι Τύχης παίζουσιν ἑταῖραι / Ἐλπίδες) || 6 Νῦν ἄγε δή] cf. Quint. Smyrn. 2.153 (νῦν δ' ἄγε δή κοίτοιο), sed ἄγε δή, νῦν e.g. Pl. *Soph.* 235a10 || 7 φῦλον ὀνείρων] cf. Hes. *Theog.* 212 (φῦλον Ὀνείρων)

‹On a philosophical dissertation on dreams›

When Sleep, sweeter than honey, alights on our eyelids and binds both eyes with a soft bond, then the manifold clan of dreams creeps secretly in, teasing sleeping mortals often with sad images, but often also [5] with pleasurable ones. Now, since you, dear Mürick, present the full origin and tribe of dreams in your exact dissertation, I pray for you a pleasurable reward for your great efforts.

Metre: Hexameters (hiatus in ll. 2, 8).

Notes: In this congratulation for a dissertation on dreams, Cajanus imitates verses taken from the poem *Europa* by Moschus and a phrase from Hesiod's *Theogony*. Besides a congratulatory text, Cajanus' poem attempts to render something of the enigmatic nature of dreams. The dissertation itself provides citations in Greek from Plutarch, Theocritus, *New Testament* and from the same passage of Hesiod's *Theogony* (211–3), which Cajanus used in the dissertation itself.

Biography: In the annals of Finnish literary history, Johan (Johannes/Juhana) Cajanus is mentioned as the composer of the most highly acclaimed (non-oral) poem in Finnish of his time, *Etcös ole ihmis parka, aiwan arca* ('Are you not a poor thing?', 23 stanzas), dealing with the transience of human life and combining classical with Kalevala metre. A son of a vicar and county dean in Paltamo of Kainuu (*Cajania*) in northern Finland, Cajanus enrolled at the University of Uppsala in 1671 and graduated eight years later. His dissertation (*De mundi anima* I–II, 1679) aroused strong polemics due to its ideas touching on Cartesianism. However, the next year, Cajanus was appointed an extra ordinary professor of philosophy at the Royal Academy of Turku. Cajanus wrote some occasional poems in Latin but this is his only known contribution in Greek.

Bibliography: Rapola, Martti et al. (1963), *Suomen kirjallisuus II*, Helsinki, 277–283; Laitinen, Kai (1985), *Literature of Finland: An Outline*, Helsinki 1985, 42; Kallinen 1995, 300–308. On the Greek poem: Korhonen 2002, 182f.

[TK]

Johan Paulinus (1655–1732)

Magnus Principatus Finlandia, Epico Carmine depicta [1678]

(excerptum, vv. 124–139)

  Τῇδ' ἐνὶ Ἡσυχίῃ βίον οἰκονομοῦσι Πολῖται
125 Ἁπλοϊκόν, Δόλος αἰνὸς ἄπεστ', ἀπόεστι δὲ ψεῦδος,
  Μήδεα λοξά, στρεβλαὶ Τέχναι, Στροφαὶ ἀλλοπρόσαλλαι.
  Ἐκδημεῖ δὲ δύσαυλος Ἔρις καὶ Φύλοπις αἴθοψ.
  Ἐκδημεῖ Φθόνος ἠδ' Ἔχθος στυγεραί τε Ἀπειλαί.
  Ἐκδημεῖ δ' Ὑπερηφανίη σὺν ἀγάνορι Κόμπῳ
130 Σὺν Κώμῳ τ' ὀλοῷ Σπατάλῃσί τ' ἐγερσιγύναιξι.
  Δαισὶ γὰρ ἀθρύπτησιν ἑὰς κοσμοῦσι τραπέζας,
  Εἷμα δὲ τηλεδαπὸν μαλακὰς ἁβράς τε χιτῶνας,
  Ἀλλοτρίους χαιτῶν πλοκάμους καὶ λοξὰ Κορύμβων
  Ἅμματα χλευάζουσι μόνον πινυτόφρονι θυμῷ.
135 Ἀλλὰ κακὴν Πενίην, ἣν Ἀνδράσιν Ὄκνος ὀφέλλει
  Σὺν Λύπαις στυγεραῖς, ἅμα σὺν κακοφράδμονι Λιμῷ
  Χώρης Φιννονίης καμάτων ἐξήλασε σπουδή.
  Τὴν δὲ Φιλαργυρίην, ῥίζαν κακότητος ἁπάσης,
  ΟὙ τιμῶσιν ὁμῶς ὀλιγαρκέα θυμὸν ἔχοντες.

Textus: Secundum editionem criticam anno 2000 factam, vide Korhonen/Oksala/Sironen (eds.) 2000, 204, 215, 219 (by E. Sironen).

Crit.: vide cap. "Apparatus criticus & de edendo textu" in: Korhonen/Oksala/Sironen 2000, 204–207) || **135** ἦν Sjöström, Hanselli || **137** Φιννοίνης Sjöström, Hanselli || **132** χιθῶνας ed., correxi

Sim.: 125 cf. Hom. *Il.* 22.94 (ἔδυ δέ τέ μιν χόλος αἰνός) || **125–129** cf. Hes. *Theog.* 226–32 || **127** δύσαυλος Ἔρις] cf. *Anth. Pal.* 9.266.6 | aliter ac Homerus φύλοπις αἰνή, lusit Paulinus || **130** cf. Angeli Politiani *Ep.* LVII 5 (ed. Pontani): τὸν κῶμόν τ' ᾄδοντας ἐγερσιγύναικα πλανήτην || **131** cf. Ps-Pyth. *Carm. aur.* 35 (εἰθίζου δὲ δίαιταν ἔχειν καθάρειον, ἄθρυπτον) || **133** cf. Ps-Phoc. 211 (μὴ κορυφὴν πλέξῃς μήθ' ἄμματα λοξὰ κορύμβων) || **134** πινυτόφρονι θυμῷ] Nonn. *Dion.* 16.185; 47.238 || **135** πενίη semel apud Hom. *Od.* 14.157 (ὃς πενίῃ εἴκων ἀπατήλια βάζει), pluries apud Hes., e.g. in *Op.* 495 et 638 || **136** κακοφράδμων vix in Graecitate antiquitatis || **138** cf. Ps-Phoc. 42 (Ἡ φιλοχρημοσύνη μήτηρ κακότητος ἁπάσης) || **139** ὀλιγαρκέα] cf. Luc. *Tim.* 57

Finlandia

(excerpt, ll. 124–139)

> Here the citizens live a simple life in peace; terrible fraud is absent, there is no lying, no treacherous counsels, no crooked deceptions, no fickle twists. [127] Inhospitable conflict and flashing battle are in exile as well as malice, hatred, and terrible threats, along with pride and arrogant haughtiness, together with ruinous revelry and dainty feasts that stir women. [131] In fact, they adorn their own tables with solid foods; they only make fun of exotic garments and delicate, soft clothing, as well as others' curly wigs and oblique knotted decorations — prudently they make fun of these. [135] However, as for wretched poverty, procured by hesitation to mankind, together with miserable sufferings as well as hunger which will make you foolish — eagerness for toil has ousted poverty from the territory of Finland. [138] But avarice, the origin of all wretchedness, they (the Finns) do not value, because they have a content mind.

Metre: Hexameters (hiatus in ll. 124, 126, 128; ll. 125, 126, 137 handling double consonants ψ, στρ, σπ as single); l. 129 note the Doric form ἀγάνορι.

Notes: The selected passage consists of a description of the Finnish simple way of life, a central part of the 379-verse epic *Finlandia*. The versified speech imitates and emulates numerous Greek authors. Its post-Homeric vocabulary forms more than 75% of the poem, and much of this language potentially consists of Paulinus' own coinages. Homeric formulae are consciously modified; most of the noun-epithets are innovated into rare combinations or are unparalleled in Homer. Paulinus seems to imitate 'contemporary' writers, namely Angelo Poliziano and Martin Crusius (see Korhonen 2000). Capital initial letters are a regular feature of poetry from the 17th century – they denote important nouns that the author wishes to highlight and emphasise. *Finlandia* features 311 cases of capital initials. At the level of ideas, the key sources of inspiration for *Finlandia* are Hesiod's *Works and Days* as well as Virgil's *Georgics*.

Biography: Johan Paulinus (in 1690 ennobled as Lillienstedt) was a gifted poet from Pori (on the western coast of Finland); he remained reasonably active as a poet into the 1690s. He started writing poems in Latin at the Royal Academy of Turku in 1672, after which he set to publishing in Greek in 1675. In 1677, Paulinus moved to Uppsala to study jurisprudence, but soon came out with his Greek poem *Finlandia*, which he had composed aged 22. During the 1680s, he enjoyed further fame with his Baroque poems in Swedish, served Sweden as an official, and eventually became a count. His much-admired *Finlandia* has been translated four times into Finnish, once into Swedish and English; one commentary in Finnish exists.

Bibliography: Korhonen/Oksala/Sironen (eds.) 2000, 8–32, 178–179 (by Korhonen). *Finlandia*: Sironen 2000, 129–147; Korhonen, Tua (2000), "Rhetorical Strategies in Johan Paulinus' (Lillienstedt) *Finlandia* (1678). A Versified Oration in Greek from the Baroque Period", in: *Arctos* 34, 63–87; Korhonen, Tua (2008), "Apostrophe and Subjectivity in Johan Paulinus Lillienstedt's *Magnus Principatus Finlandia* (1678)", in: Pernille Harsting/Jon Viklung (eds.), *Rhetoric and Literature in Finland and Sweden, 1600–1900*, Copenhagen, 27–65 (translation into English 52–61).

[ES]

Christiernus Alander (1660–1704)

Ad juvenem…in rhetore musico disputantem, dn. Samuelem Preutz [1703]

Τερπιάδης κῦδος φέρε καὶ μέγ' ὄνειαρ ἀοιδῆς
αὐτοδίδακτος ἐών, ᾧ μὲν Θεὸς ἐν φρεσὶν οἴμας
παντοίας ἐνέφυσεν, ἔοικε δὲ οἷ παραείδων,
τούτῳ γὰρ Ὀδυσεὺς δῷ ζωὴν κἄν γε χολωθείς
5 τοῖς μνηστῆρσιν, οἳ μὲν λυγρὸν πότμον ἐπέσπον,
ἀλλά γε Τερπιάδης τότ' ἀλύσκανε κῆρα μέλαιναν,
καὶ φόρμιγξ μὲν τοῦτον ἐρύσσατο καὶ ἐσάωσεν.
Ταῦτα Τερπιάδης· ἀλλ' Τερψιχόρη μάλ' ἀγλαία
καὶ ἕτεραι Μῶσαι καὶ Φοίβῳ πᾶς ἀτάλαντος
10 τὴν αὐδήν, ἔπεα ὡς πρὸς ἄρμιγγα μελίζων,
ὡς σύ, διογενὲς ΠΡΕΥΤΖ, δέλτῳ σῇ ἐνὶ φράζεις,
τοῦτον τέρψις ἀεὶ καὶ πότνιον ἕσπεται κῦδος.

Textus: Christiernus Alander (*pr.*) & Samuel Preutz (*resp.*), *Rhetor musicus: seu specimen academicum, de vi & usu musices in rhetorica...*, Turku: Johan Wall, 1703, [a5] (4:0).

Crit.: 3 ἔοικε correxi: ἔοικα ed. ‖ 4 δω ed. ‖ 6 ἀλύσκανε correxi: ἐλύσκαζε ed. ‖ 8 ἀλλ' Τερψιχόρη ed. *sic*! ǀ ἀγλαΐα ed. ‖ 10 ἅρμιγγα correxi: ἁρμίγγα ed. hapax ‖ 12 πότνιον] cf. πότνια ut adiectivum

Sim.: 2–3 cf. Hom. *Od.* 22.347–349 (αὐτοδίδακτος δ' εἰμί, θεὸς δέ μοι ἐν φρεσὶν οἴμας / παντοίας ἐνέφυσεν· ἔοικα δέ τοι παραείδειν / ὥς τε θεῷ) ‖ 5 λυγρὸν πότμον ἐπέσπον] cf. Hom. *Od.* 22.317 (ἀεικέα πότμον ἐπέσπον) ‖ 6 cf. Hom. *Od.* 22.330 (Τερπιάδης δ' ἔτ' ἀοιδὸς ἀλύσκανε κῆρα μέλαιναν) ‖ 7 ἐρύσσατο καὶ ἐσάωσεν] cf. Hom. *Od.* 22.372 (ἐρύσσατο καὶ ἐσάωσεν)

On the young man disputing in the *Rhetor musicus*..., Mr Samuel Preutz

Phemius, the son of Terpes obtained fame and great profit from his song, although he was autodidact. God planted all sorts of songs in his heart – and Phemius seemed to sing to Him [= God]. For Odysseus gave him his life, despite his being angry with the [5] suitors, who met a cruel doom. But the son of Terpes escaped black fate; the lyre saved him and gave him safety. This much on the son of Terpes, but glorious Terpsichore, the other Muses and everyone who is equal to Phoebus [10] in his voice as he sings to the accompaniment of the organ (*harminx*) – joy and revered renown will always follow him, as you, divine Preutz, tell in your 'writing-tablet'.

Metre: Hexameters (poor knowledge of metre, multiple hiatus, prosodical problems, see ll. 6, 8, 9, several bipartite hexameters), lengthening through final -ρ (l. 4), -ν (l. 5) and -ς (l. 10), short syllable before ζ (l. 6), long σύ in (l. 11).

Notes: Phemius, the son of Terpes was the bard in Odysseus' court. He was forced to sing to the suitors of Penelope during Odysseus' absence. In this congratulatory poem for a dissertation on music, Alander plays with the homophonic words *Terpiades* (Terpes' son), Terpsichore (the Muse of dancing and chorus song often depicted holding a lyre), and *terpsis* 'joy'. The respondent, Samuel Preutz (or Prytz), was the organist at the Great Cathedral of Turku. His instrument is referred to in l. 10: ἅρμιγξ (ἁρμίγγα in the print, cf. φόρμιγξ). This term is not to be found in modern or early modern lexica, so it may have been invented by Alander. Instead, Angelo Poliziano uses the word ὄργανον for an organ in his titles of two epigrams (Pontani 2002, 164 (no. 37), 207–8 (no. 51)). Alander's *interpretatio Christiana* changes the meaning of Homer's verse: in Alander's view, Phemius is, in fact, singing to 'him' (l. 3); that is, to the Christian God. The subject of ἔοικα in the *Odyssey* (22.347–9) is Phemius who promises to sing to Odysseus as to a god (ὥς τε θεῷ). In general, Alander's Greek poems contain exceptional allusions (in the context of *Regia Academia Aboensis*) to the Greco-Roman culture, which is why the poem deserves to be presented here despite its many shortcomings.

Biography: Alander was the son of the vicar of Finström in Åland, which is a large island between Finland and Sweden. He was formally enrolled at the Royal Academy of Turku at only the age of nine. After one year at the University of Uppsala, he graduated from Turku in 1682. He was nominated the professor of *eloquentia* in 1692. As a professor, he supervised a dissertation on Phocylides' poem on women, which included the text and a commentary (1698), and he also composed five Greek congratulations for dissertations.

Bibliography: Stiernman, Anders Anton (1712), *Aboa literata*, Stockholm, 112–114, Kotivuori, *s.v.* "Alander, Krister", https://ylioppilasmatrikkeli.helsinki.fi/ [accessed: April 2019]. On his Greek poems: Korhonen 2004, 285, 335–338. Dissertation and poem digitised: https://www.doria.fi/handle/10024/50699.

[TK]

Johan Welin (1705–1744)

Ad tumulum...Hermanni Witte [1728]

(excerptum, vv. 57–64)

 γυμνὸν καὶ φαλακρὸν λίαν τε μέγ' εἶχε κάρηνον·
 αἱ ῥῖνες μὴ σάρκ' εἶχον, παρὰ χόνδρον ἄνικμον·
 ὑστέρει ἠδ' ἐρυθρῶν χειλῶν παντός τε ἐνούλου·
60 ὡς ὁ κύων διόπερ λευκοὺς παρέδειξεν ὀδόντας.
 Ἐν μέσῳ ἰσχνὸς ἔην ὥσπερ μυρμήκιον ἦ τι.
 Οἱ πόδες ἀμφότεροι ὥσπερ δύο βάκτρα ἄσαρκοι.
 Ἐν σκαιῇ χειρὶ κλεψύδραν εἶχε σαφηνῶς·
 τὴν φρικτὴν δρεπάνην νώτῳ βάσταζεν ἀπηνής,
 [...]

Textus: *Ad tumulum...Hermani Witte cum...solemni pompâ terrae mandaretur gremio...nomine nationis suae Borea-Fennicae cecinit Johannes Welinus*, Turku: E. Flodström 1728, [p. 2, vv. 57–64] (2:o).

Crit.: 61 ἦ τι correxi: ἤτι ed. | μυρμήκιον] scripsit noster speciem quandam araneae intelligens (Philum. *Ven.* 15.1) pro μύρμηξ || **62** ἀμφότεροι correxi: ἀμφότεραι ed.

Sim.: 57 γυμνὸν καὶ φαλακρόν] cf. Theod. Prodrom. *Carmina historica* 59.87 (ἐπεὶ φαλακρὸν καὶ θεοῦ γυμνὸν σκέπης) || **58** ἄνικμον] cf. Plu. *Prim. frig.* 951b (ὁ δ' ἄνικμος καὶ ξηρὸς (*sc.* ἀήρ)) || **60** λευκοὺς...ὀδόντας] cf. Hom. *Il.* 5.291 (λευκοὺς δ' ἐπέρησεν ὀδόντας) || **63** ἐν σκαιῇ χειρί] cf. Hes. *Theog.* 178–179 (χειρὶ /σκαιῇ) | σαφηνῶς] cf. Thgn. 1.963

To the tomb...of Hermann Witte

(excerpt, ll. 57–64)

> He [= Death] had an unclad, bald, and too big skull; his nose was fleshless, so near to a dry gristle; he had no red-coloured lips, no gums. [60] Hence, like a dog he exhibited his white teeth. His waist was narrow as if it were a waist of some kind of ant indeed. Both his legs were without flesh like two sticks. In his left hand he clearly held an hourglass and on his back the ungentle one bore an awful reaping-hook [...]

Metre: Hexameters.

Notes: This Greek funerary poem in memory of Herman Witte, bishop of Turku, is exceptional for its length (127 lines, making it the longest occasional Greek poem published in Finland) and for its fictional framework. It is composed of three parts. (1) A description of the sun setting and various birds going to rest (ll. 1–28). (2) An account of a dream vision of the poetic 'I' (ll. 29–96). (3) *Lamentatio, laudatio, consolatio,* the expected *topoi* of a funerary poem (ll. 97–127). The above excerpt is from the dream vision, from the beginning of an encounter between the narrator and a personified incarnation of Death beside the shore of a silent stream where a beautiful palm tree (φοῖνιξ) grows. One may compare this baroque ecphrasis of Death with a similar passage in Laurentius Rhodoman's *Arion,* originally published circa 1567 (ll. 491–495, see Weise 2019), though there are no verbal reminiscences. After the description of Death (ll. 57–64), a short dialogue follows, before Death cuts the palm tree, which metamorphoses into the deceased Bishop Witte. The Greek word φοῖνιξ means 'palm tree', and the polysemous homonym refers to the mythological, regenerating bird, phoenix – an obvious association (cf. *Ps.* 92:13 and its interpretation) also here evoking the 'ornithological' beginning of the poem. Furthermore, the palm tree/phoenix may also allude to the Royal Academy of Turku, which was back in operation again after the Russian occupation of Finland and the evacuation of the university to Sweden during the Great Nordic War. The deceased Bishop Witte had compared the Academy with the phoenix in his speech at the reopening of the university in 1722.

Biography: Johan Welin was the first Finn who was accepted into the Royal Society (London) and is remembered for introducing Christian Wolff's ideas in Turku. He was a son of a vicar of Lappo, near Turku, and enrolled at the Royal Academy of Turku in 1724. After graduation, he was appointed adjunct at the faculty of philosophy in 1732. Soon after that, he met Wolff in Marburg and on Wolff's recommendation he was elected professor of logic and metaphysics in Turku *in absentia*. However, he remained on the Continent, travelling also to England, France, and Italy, but visited Turku only occasionally. His life ended spectacularly when his house in Paris burned down in a fire. Welin wrote occasional poetry in many languages. In addition to one in Hebrew and two in Greek, he wrote poems in Latin, Swedish, German, and French, and at least one letter in Italian.

Bibliography: Vallinkoski, Jorma (1947), "Juhana Welin, wolffilainen filosofi, runoilija ja seikkailija", in: *Historiallinen arkisto* 52, 213–276 [Summary in German; a list of Welin's work on pp. 271–274]. On his Greek poems: Korhonen, Tua (2002), "Döden med en myras midja. En grekisk gravdikt av Johan Welin (1728)", in: Janne Pölönen/Eero Jarva (eds.), *Antiquitas Borea*, Oulu, 56–70.

[TK]

Johan Ludvig Runeberg (1804–1877)

Ἡ Ἀνάκρισις ἀκαδημαϊκή. Ἔπος γελοῖον [1826]

(excerptum, vv. 1–11)

    Μῆνιν ἄειδε, Θεά, Οὐαλληνίου ὀκρυόεσσαν
    Θυμοβόρην στυγερήν θ', ἧς εἵνεκα πόλλ' ἐπάθοντο
    Ἄλγεα λυγρὰ νέοι, Ἀκαδημίας ἄνθεα καλά·
    Οἳ δ' ἄρ' ἐπειγόμενοι καὶ βιβλία συχνὰ φέροντες
5 Στεῖχον ἐς ἄγκρισιν λαιψηρά τε γούνατ' ἐνώμων,
    Γηθόσυνοι μὲν εἰδυίης πραπίδεσσι πιθόντες.
    Αὐτὰρ ὅτ' εὔτυκτον πρὸς δῶ Ἰωάννου ἵκοντο,
    Οὐκ ἔτ' ἐνὶ φρεσὶ ᾗσ' ἔχαρον· τὸν δ' ἔνδοθι τέτμον
    Μικρὴν ἀμφιέποντα καλὴν δέ τε βιβλιοθήκην.
10 Οὐδ' ἄρα τοὺς γήθησεν ἰδών, ἀτὰρ ὄψ' ὁ γεραιός
    Νεῦσεν ἀσπάζων αὐτούς θ' ἕζεσθαι ἄνωγεν.

Textus: ex apographis AB edidit Zilliacus (1969, vid. bibl.), additis signis diacriticis et apparatu critico necnon erroribus aliquot purgatis; collatis micropelliculis litteras in initio cuiusque versus magnas retinui erroresque Zilliaci reliquos correxi

Crit.: Tit. Ανακρισις Ακαδημικη B ‖ **1** θεα] B; Υαλληνιου AB, corr. Zilliacus ‖ **4** επειγομενοι A, ιδρωοντες B; ~~εχοντες~~ B ‖ **5** αν'κρισιν A ‖ **6** γητοσυνοι A; ιδυϊης B ‖ **9** Πικρην AB, Μικρὴν corr. Heikel ‖ versus additicii post v. **9:** Ητοι ὁ δη Κελσον στιβαρον, μεγα αχθος αρουρης / βαιν' εν χερσιν εχων, εν δ' ομμασι αινοθεν αινως / καμματος τε κακος σπουδη τε καλη πολεμιχθην B, om. A

Sim.: 1 cf. Hom. *Il.* 1.1–2 (μῆνιν ἄειδε, θεά, Πηληιάδεω Ἀχιλῆος / οὐλομένην); ὀκρυόεσσαν cf. Hom. *Il.* 6.344 (κακομηχάνου ὀκρυοέσσης) ‖ **5** cf. Hom. *Il.* 2.833 et 11.331 (στείχειν ἐς πόλεμον φθισήνορα); cf. Hom. *Il.* 22.144 (λαιψηρὰ δὲ γούνατ' ἐνώμα) ‖ **6** cf. e.g. Hom. *Il.* 1.608 (Ἥφαιστος ποίησεν ἰδυίῃσι πραπίδεσσι) ‖ **7** cf. Hom. *Il.* 10.566 ‖ **8** φρεσὶ ᾗσ'] cf. Hom. *Il.* 13.609 ‖ **10** cf. Hom. *Il.* 4.283 (καὶ τοὺς μὲν γήθησεν ἰδὼν κρείων Ἀγαμέμνων)

The Academic Examination. A Ludicrous Poem

(excerpt, ll. 1–11)

> Sing, o goddess, of the dreadful, soul-devouring and miserable wrath of Wallenius, for which youngsters — the virtuous youth of the Academy — suffered many tearful griefs. [4] With numerous books they were marching in a hurry to an examination, in rapid movement, happy and having faith in their wise thoughts. [7] But when they had arrived at the well-constructed abode of Johannes, they were no longer happy in their mind: they found Wallenius inside, attending to his small but fine library. [10] He was not glad to see them — much later the old man nodded for a greeting and commanded the students to sit down.

Metre: Hexameters (altogether seven hiatuses: ll. 1, 3, 7, 8, 11).

Notes: Generally speaking, Runeberg's poem conforms to the standards of a satiric tendency that emerged from the 19th century onwards (cf. Křesadlo → **Bohemian Lands**, Richter → **Germany**, Knox → **Great Britain**, Fehér → **Hungary**, Vitelli and Rissa → **Italy**). The opening scene of this 97-verse outburst depicts young students of the Royal Academy of Turku sitting in an examination to be held by the much maligned Professor J. F. Wallenius (1765–1836). The 22-year-old student Runeberg composed his burlesque epyllion after having read Homer, Sophocles, and Thucydides. Hence the Homeric vocabulary pervades the text with ca. 90 percent. In contrast to Johan Paulinus' *Finlandia* from 1678, Runeberg's text includes the trite Homeric connecting particle αὐτάρ and features small particles (such as δέ, δή, μήν, ῥα) much more often. Furthermore, typically for an unchecked student text, numerous metric mistakes remain: in our specimen e.g. in lines 3, 5, 6, 7, and 11 (to be read as Ἀκαδημίᾱς, ἄγκρῑσιν, μὲνν, Ἰωάννου, νεῦσενν). Perhaps the three extra verses between ll. 9–10 in copy B were too Homeric (cf. 9α ἄχθος ἀρούρης = *Il.* 18.104; 9β αἰνόθεν αἰνῶς = *Il.* 7.97) to deserve inclusion in the second copy A.

Biography: Johan Ludvig Runeberg (1804–1877) was a renowned poet, regarded even as the national poet of Finland. He wrote in Swedish, and thus also influenced the literature of Sweden. He was one of the founders of the Finnish nation as a cultural and political entity. He evolved as a poet during the 1830s thanks to his knowledge of classical literature (he disputed on the function of the chorus in Greek tragedy), which deepened through his teaching activities in Helsinki and Porvoo.

Bibliography: Laitinen 1985, 51–55. Greek poem: *editio princeps* by Henrik Zilliacus, in: Gunnar Tideström/Carl-Eric Thors (eds.) (1969), *Samlade skrifter av Johan Ludvig Runeberg VIII: 1 Uppsatser och avhandlingar på latin*, Helsingfors, 95–98 (https://litteraturbanken.se/forfattare/RunebergJL/titlar/); commentaries and translations into Swedish and Finnish: Heikel, Ivar A. (1904), "En grekisk dikt af J.L. Runeberg", in: *Joukahainen* 12, 75–83; Henrik Zilliacus, in: Gunnar Tideström/Carl-Eric Thors (eds.) (1972), *Samlade skrifter av Johan Ludvig Runeberg XVII. Översättning och kommentar till Uppsatser och avhandlingar på latin*, Helsingfors 120–124 (https://litteraturbanken.se/forfattare/RunebergJL/titlar/); Oksala, Teivas (1987), "Professorinpilkkaa à la J.L. Runeberg", in: *Kanava* 15, 508–509.

[ES]

Estonia and Latvia (Early Modern Estonia, Livonia, and Curonia)

Humanist Greek in the Swedish oversea provinces corresponding to the modern states of Estonia and Latvia is understood in different ways.[39] There is no certain evidence of ethnic Estonians or Latvians writing in Greek before the 21st century. However, several Baltic German students and professors wrote and published Greek poems either at home (in the Baltic countries) or during their studies abroad. As in other parts of Sweden, academics, clerics, and merchants were mobile: at the University of Tartu (and Pärnu) we find also Greek poetry by students and professors from Germany, Sweden, Finland, and Ingria. From Tallinn we have a Greek poem by a student from Curonia, and from Riga several poems by **Martin Francke** (*fl.* 1647–1653), born in Narva (Estonia). So, as the literary life of the region, also its Humanist Greek was flourishing.[40]

The corpora of Humanist Greek poetry from Estonia and Latvia are much smaller than in Sweden or Finland: 108 texts from the only early modern university of the region, the University of Tartu/Tartu-Pärnu (1632–1656 and 1690–1710), active for only fifty years, and 99 texts from the Gymnasia of Tallinn (53) and Riga (41) and the court of Jelgava/Mitau (5) despite their much longer period of activity. This reveals the importance of universities for the study and practice of Greek. Together with texts in manuscripts, from abroad and more recent poems, the 'Estonian' corpus extends to 179 and the 'Latvian' to 47 Humanist Greek texts (mostly poetry).

In Estonia (Early Modern Estonia and Northern Livonia), Humanist Greek starts with scholars of German origin.[41] Gregor Krüger Mesylanus, being a stipendiary of Tallinn City Council directed his poetry to readers in Tallinn and Riga and sent in 1554 a set of 6 poems, 5 of which are Greek, from Berlin to Tallinn. At approximately the same time he published a Greek hexameter oration *Carmen de dignitate et excellentia doctrinae coelestis* in Wittenberg. When Estonian gymnasia and universities were opened in the 1630s, the first professors were mostly invited from Germany.[42] One of them, Peter Götsch, professor of Greek and

---

[39] This account is mostly based on Päll 2010 and 2018, see recently also Bērziņa 2018. For bio-bibliographical information about local students, see Tering 1984 and 2018. The bibliographies are Jaanson 2000, Klöker 2005/2 and T. Reimo et al. (to appear in 2021); Garber et al. 2001–2009; Šiško 2013.
[40] See Klöker 2005, 47 (a.o.).
[41] The overview, if not stated otherwise, is based on Päll 2010, 2018, and 2020a.
[42] See Tering 1984, 19–37.

oriental languages, presented in 1632 an inaugural oration in Greek hexameters (*Christognosia,* Tartu 1633) for which he was congratulated with a Greek Pindaric ode by Heinrich Vogelmann, another German-born scholar.[43] Götsch also published several shorter Greek poems, which abound in loans from ancient authors.

David Cunitz, student in Tartu and from 1643 professor of poetics at Tallinn Gymnasium, published in 1642 two Greek verse orations: a paraphrasis of the Gospel of Matthew in Uppsala and a Christmas oration in Rostock. Several other professors of Tallinn Gymnasium published Greek poems, such as Rector Heinrich Vulpius Sr and professors of Greek Georg Schultz (born in Tallinn) and Reiner Brockmann (born in Mecklenburg), who in addition to a Theocritus-cento and other Greek occasional poems also wrote the first poems in Estonian.[44] At Tallinn Gymnasium local schoolboys also wrote Greek poems, such as Heinrich Vulpius Jr and Joachim Salemann. Several of them continued their studies abroad, congratulating each other with Greek poems on academic occasions, like Eberhard Müller and **Georg Dunte** (1631–1677) in Wittenberg. After 1710, the writing of Greek poetry continued for a while in Tallinn, but ceased after 1734.

After the reopening of the university in 1802, at least three Greek poems were published in the 19th century, but none in the 20th (except the poem by **Johan Bergman**, professor of classics from Sweden; see above). Attempts to revitalise the tradition are being made in the 21st century.

In Latvia (Early Modern Southern Livonia and Curonia) the humanist centres were the Riga Academic Gymnasium and the court of Mitau (Jelgava) in Curonia. Greek had been taught in Riga already in the 16th century, but Humanist Greek poems were not published until the printing house of Riga Gymnasium had been furnished with new types.[45] Of the 47 Latvian Greek poems (from 1632–1731) known today, most are from Riga Gymnasium, including *epithalamia* and *epicedia* for local dignitaries, but also an *epicedium* on the death of Gustav II Adolf of Sweden and a poem in Anacreontics for the opening of the University of Tartu (both by Aggaeus Friderici).[46] As in Tallinn, both professors and students came from Germany, but the impact of local youngsters and professors is greater in Riga, corresponding to its more prominent political and cultural position. Among the more prolific authors are Johannes Hörnick (*collega* at Riga

---

43 Published in Päll 2001.
44 See Priidel 2000. For his Theocritean cento, see Päll 2013.
45 Bērziņa 2018, 40–44. The subchapter (if not stated otherwise) is based on Bērziņa 2018, Päll 2020a, Šiško 2013, and Garber 2004.
46 The latter is edited and discussed in Viiding/Päll 2004.

Gymnasium) with six and Arnold Fuhrmann (pastor at Riga Cathedral) with four poems. Martin Francke from Narva published three Greek poems during his studies at Riga Gymnasium.

The variety of metres in Riga is broad, including different iambic metres, phalaecians, and epodic forms that are found in Horace. The Riga corpus also comprises many anagram poems, intricate use of acrostics, and several polyglot poems. Among the latter, a 9-language *epithalamium* by Henning Witte was recently found in Göttingen University Library by Jürgen Beyer. Students of Latvian German origin also published their poetry elsewhere, as Arnold Mahlstedt in Tartu[47] and Erich Nothmann in Kiel.[48]

In Curonia, only five poems between 1695 and 1731 were published; most of these, as characteristical in Mitau court, are polyglot poems by Christian Bornmann.

[JP]

Special Bibliography

Bērziņa, Gita (2018), "16th–17th-century Greek texts at the Academic Library of the University of Latvia", in: Janika Päll/Ivo Volt (eds.), *Hellenostephanos. Humanist Greek in Early Modern Europe. Learned Communities between Antiquity and Contemporary Culture*, Tartu, 40–56.

Garber, Klaus et al. (eds.) (2001–2009), *Handbuch des personalen Gelegenheitsschrifttums in europäischen Bibliotheken und Archiven*, Hildesheim.

Jaanson, Ene-Lille (2000), *Druckerei der Universität Dorpat 1632–1720*, Tartu.

Klöker, Martin (2005), *Literarisches Leben in Reval in der ersten Hälfte des 17ten Jahrhunderts (1600–1657)*, 1. *Darstellung*, Tübingen.

Klöker, Martin (2005): *Literarisches Leben in Reval in der ersten Hälfte des 17ten Jahrhunderts (1600–1657)*, 2. *Bibliographie der Revaler Literatur. Drucke von den Anfängen bis 1657*, Tübingen.

Päll, Janika (2001), "Pindarlektüre an der Academia Gustaviana: Henricus Vogelmannus' *Ode prosphonetike*", in: *Studia Humaniora Tartuensia* 2.A.2, 1–16 = https://doi.org/10.12697/sht.2001.2.A.2 [accessed: September 2020].

Päll, Janika (2013), "Eesti bukoolikast", in: *Keel ja Kirjandus* 6, 420–439.

Reimo, Tiiu e.a. (to appear in 2021), *Eesti võõrkeelne raamat ja Estonica 1508-1830*, Tallinn.

Priidel, Endel (ed.) (2000), Reiner Brockmann, *Teosed = Reineru Brokmannu poiemata*, Tartu.

Šiško, Silvija (2013), *Gesamtkatalog der fremdsprachlichen Altdrucke Lettlands. 1588-1830*. Reihe A, Riga.

---

47 Edited by Janika Päll with a commentary in Viiding/Orion/Päll 2007, 230–237 and 408f.
48 *Pie Defunctis manibus...Joh. Pauli Dassovii*, Kiel 1706.

Tering, Arvo (ed.) (1984), *Album Academicum der Universität Dorpat (Tartu) 1632–1710*, Tallinn.
Tering, Arvo (2018), *Lexikon der Studenten aus Estland, Livland und Kurland an europäischen Universitäten 1561–1800*, Köln.
Viiding, Kristi/Päll, Janika (2004), "Die Glückwunschgedichte der Rigaer Gelehrten zur Inauguration der Academia Gustaviana im Jahre 1632", in: *Humanistica Lovaniensia* 53, 299–321.
Viiding, Kristi/Orion, Jana/Päll, Janika (eds.) (2007), *O Dorpat, urbs addictissima musis*, Tallinn.

Estonia

Johannes Gezelius Sr (1615–1690)

<*Epithalamium*> [1642]

Κἂν γλυκερὸν χαλεπῶς πονέουσιν ἀεὶ ἀνάπαυμα
ἔστι, λίαν τοῖς διψῶσι γλυκὺ πηγίδιόν τε,
τοῖς τε πλάνοις ὁδός ἐστι γλυκεῖα, γλυκεῖα πυρή τε
τοῖς ψυχροῖς, τοῖς λυπηροῖς γλυκὺς ἡδυλόγος μέν,
5 τὸν δὲ γάμον γαμέειν γλυκερώτερόν ἐστιν ἤ εἰσι
πηγίδιόν θ' ὁδός, ἡδυλόγος τ' ἀνάπαυμα πυρή τε.

Textus: *Novis Nuptiarum honoribus Dn. Simonis Skragge...Sara PederssDotter*, Tartu 1642.

Sim.: 1 πονέουσιν ἀεὶ ἀνάπαυμα] cf. LXX, *Is.* 28.12.1 (Τοῦτο τὸ ἀνάπαυμα τῷ πεινῶντι καὶ τοῦτο τὸ σύντριμμα, καὶ οὐκ ἠθέλησαν ἀκούειν) || **2** πηγίδιον] cf. *Suda* π 1489 (Πηγίδιον· ἡ μικρὰ πηγή) || **5** γλυκερώτερόν ἐστιν] Thgn. 1225 (Οὐδέν, Κύρν', ἀγαθῆς γλυκερώτερόν ἐστι γυναικός)

<Wedding song>

As much as for those who work hard rest is always sweet, and for those who are very thirsty a small stream of water is sweet, and for wanderers a road is sweet, and a bonfire is sweet for the cold, and for mourners a mild-speaking man is sweet, [5] to be wed in matrimony is sweeter than the stream and the road, the mild-speaker, the rest and the bonfire.

Metre: Hexameters (note hiatus in l. 1).

Notes: This, the first poem of a three-language wedding poem cluster by Gezelius, appears in a collection of *epithalamia* by the 'Muses of Embecca' (viz. of Emajõgi, the river that flows through Tartu), initiated by the professor of poetics and rhetoric of Tartu University, Lorenz Luden (1592–1654). For his Greek poems, Gezelius often borrows a verse or a motif from classical or Christian literature. This *epithalamium* in the form of a priamel presents a list of sweet notions (ll. 1–4, 6), all of which pale in comparison to the sweetness of marriage (l. 5). The source of the list is Christian literature in general (e.g., Psalm 106 with references to the right way, the hungry and the thirsty); the structure of priamel, which repeats the list at the end of the poem, is rare, but a possible influence could be an anonymous Greek epigram (possibly by Reiner Brockmann), published in Tallinn under the title *De vitae humanae fugacitate*, and presenting a free translation of Henricus Ranzovius' Latin epigram).⁴⁹ In polyglot clusters by Gezelius the poems are often complementary to each other: here the Greek poem states the general truths, the Swedish poem adresses the bride and the groom personally in their native language, and the Latin poem includes more general well-wishes and the *votum*. The language of the poem receives an epic flavour from non-contracted forms and the particle τε (which can occur prepositively and function as a filler, when a short syllable is needed).

Biography: Johannes Gezelius Sr (Gävle, 1615 – Turku, 1690) studied at Västerås Gymnasium, and at Uppsala and Tartu Universities (mag. phil. Tartu 1641, doct. theol., Uppsala 1661). He worked at Tartu University as a professor of Greek and Hebrew (from July 1642 until Summer 1649, officially until July 1650) and possibly as an adjunct for theology too (in 1649). After different ecclesiastic positions in the Swedish Empire he became the bishop of Turku in 1664. There he made major contributions to a new Bible translation and reorganised the school system of Finland. In Tartu he published several manuals for teaching Greek, including an edition of wisdom literature, a Greek grammar (at least 30 reprints), a Greek translation of J. A. Comenius' *Ianua linguarum*, and a Greek-Latin lexicon; in Turku he edited a selection of Aesop's *Fables* and Greek pericopes of the New Testament, both with Latin translations. He presided over at least 40 Greek disputations (8 extant) and wrote more than 30 occasional poems in Greek (mostly in Tartu). The addressees, Simon Skragge (a quaestor of Finland) and his bride Sara Pedersdotter (a daughter of Captain Peter Nilsson), were married on 20 February 1642 in Ropka near Tartu.

Bibliography: Laasonen, Pentti (1997/2012), "Gezelius, Johannes vanhempi", in: *Kansallis-biografia-verkkojulkaisu*, Helsinki, http://www.kansallisbiografia.fi/kansallisbiografia/henkilo/2252 [accessed: May 2017]; Mustelin, Olof: "Johannes Gezelius", in: *Svenskt biografiskt lexikon* 17, 101–104, https://sok.riksarkivet.se/sbl/artikel/13047 [accessed: May 2017]; Friedenthal, Meelis/Päll, Janika (2017), "Pneumatoloogiast üldiselt ja Johannes Gezeliuse kreekakeelsetest pneumatoloogilisest disputatsioonidest spetsiifiliselt", in: *Acta et Commentationes Archivi Nationalis Estoniae* 1(32), Tartu, 183–237: 205–208; Kolk, Kaspar (2018), "Dissemination and survival of a book printed in 17th century Tartu: the case of Johannes Gezelius' *Lexicon Graeco-Latinum* (1649)", in: Päll/Volt 2018, 144–157: 145. Gezelius as a Hellenist: Korhonen 2004, 89–99; Korhonen 2018, 158–184; Päll 2020a, 421–427, 435.

[JP]

---

49 See *Ehren-gedächtnüs, Auff den trawrigen...* (Tallinn, 1636) and *Delitiae Poetarum Germanorum*, Vol. 5, Frankfurt 1612, 539.

Ericus Harckman (before 1637–1679)

‹Epithalamium› [1643]

"Ἔμμορε μὲν τιμῆς ὅς γ' ἔμμορε γείτονος ἐσθλοῦ" –
μείζονος ἀλλ' ἔτυχεν τιμῆς ἀγαθῆς ἀλόχοιο
κυρῶν, ἧς (ἣν χρηστή 'στι) γλυκερώτερον οὐδέν.
Γείτονα μὲν καλὸν τίς γ' ἀρνεῖται μέγ' ὄνειαρ
5 ἔμμεναι, ἐν χαλεποῖς τοῖς δυστυχέουσι μάλιστα;
Τούτου ὅμως δοκίμη παράκοιτις πολλὸν ἀμείνων
γίνεται, ἣ παρὰ-μὲν-μίμνει καλοκαγαθὴ αἰέν
ἐξ ἀρχῆς καὶ μεσσόθι καὶ μέχρι γήραος οὐδοῦ.
Γειτονέων δ' οὐχ' ὡδὶ χρόνον ξύμπαντα ὁπηδεῖ,
10 πολλάκις οὐκ ἐπὶ κινδύνοις μένει, ἀλλ' ἀποφεύγει.
Ὄντως ἐστὶ θεοῦ δῶρον γαμετὴ παναρίστη,
καὶ δίδοται αὐτῇ τῷ δ' ἀνδρὶ φοβουμένῳ αὐτόν.
Εὐδοκίμης τί ἀκοίτιος ἡδύτερον καὶ ἄρειον;
Ἠνὶ λάχες τυ ΚΑΘΗΓΗΤΉ ΓΕΖΗΛΙΕ Κεδνέ,
15 τοιούτου δώρου, γοῦν παμπήδην Νεόνυμφε
χαῖρέ γε τῷ δώρῳ καὶ τέρπεο σὸν κατὰ θυμόν:
ἀνδράσιν εἰσέμεναι μὴ πᾶσ' ἔξεστι Κόρινθον.

Textus: *Sacris nuptiarum honoribus...Dn. M. Johannis Georgii Gezelii...Gertrude...Guthemii*, Tartu, 1643.

Crit.: 1 ἐσθλοῦ corr.: ἐθλοῦ ed. ‖ 7 καλοκαγαθὴ] pro καλοκαγαθὸς ‖ 10 κινδύνοις corr.: Κύνδυνοις ed. ‖ 13 Εὐδοκίμης] pro εὐδοκίμου ‖ 14 ΚΑΘΗΓΗΤΉ] pro Καθηγητά ‖ 15 παμπήδην corr.: παμπήδη ed.‖ 17 εἰσέμεναι] pro εἰσίμεναι

Sim.: 1 Ἔμμορε μὲν...ἐσθλοῦ] cf. Hes. *Op.* 347 (Ἔμμορέ τοι τιμῆς...ἐσθλοῦ) ‖ 2–3 μείζονος...γλυκερώτερον οὐδέν] cf. Thgn. 1225 (Οὐδέν, Κύρν', ἀγαθῆς γλυκερώτερόν ἐστι γυναικός); Eur. fr. 463.4 (εἰ δέ τις κυρεῖ γυναικὸς ἐσθλῆς) ‖ 4 Γείτονα...ὄνειαρ] cf. Hes. *Op.* 346 (πῆμα κακὸς γείτων, ὅσσον τ' ἀγαθὸς μέγ' ὄνειαρ) ‖ 8 ἐξ ἀρχῆς...οὐδοῦ] cf. Hes. *Op.* 368–369 (Ἀρχομένου δὲ...μεσσόθι φείδεσθαι) et Ps-Phoc. 230 (ζωὴν ἐκτελέοιτ' ἀγαθὴν μέχρι γήραος οὐδοῦ) ‖ 11 θεοῦ...παναρίστη] Greg. Naz. *Anth. Pal.* 8.162.5 (τοῦτό σοι εὐσεβίης ἱερὸν γέρας, ὦ παναρίστη) ‖ 12 τῷ δ'... φοβουμένῳ αὐτόν] Did. Caec. in *Ps.*, fr. 1174 (τῷ δὲ φοβουμένῳ τὸν κύριον δῶρον θεοῦ δίδοται κοινωνός τις καὶ σύζυγος, οὐχ ἡ τυχοῦσα γυνή), *Prov.* 19.14.2 (παρὰ δὲ θεοῦ ἁρμόζεται γυνὴ ἀνδρί); *Ps.* 111.1 (Μακάριος ἀνὴρ ὁ φοβούμενος τὸν κύριον) ‖ 13 cf. Ps.-Phoc. 195 (ἡδύτερον καὶ ἄρειον) ‖ 15 παμπήδη] Thgn. 1.615 (Οὐδένα παμπήδην ἀγαθὸν καὶ μέτριον ἄνδρα) ‖ 16 χαῖρέ γε...θυμόν] cf. Hes. *Op.* 358 (χαίρει τῷ δώρῳ καὶ τέρπεται ὃν κατὰ θυμόν) et al. ‖ 17 ἀνδράσιν...Κόρινθον] cf. Zenob. *Cent.* 5.37 (Οὐ παντὸς ἀνδρὸς εἰς Κόρινθον ἔστ' ὁ πλοῦς); Strab. 8.6.20; 12.3.36; Hor. *Epist.* 1.17.36 (*non cuivis homini contingit adire Corinthum*), et M. Henschel in *Nuptiarum solemnitati...Erici zur Beecken...Elisabetham zur Telte...*, Tallinn, 1642, v. 11 (*Paucis duntaxat contingit adire Corinthum*).

‹Wedding song›

He who has received a good neighbour, has received a reward. But he has received a bigger reward who has a good wife: nothing is sweeter than her (if she is good). Who would deny that a nice neighbour [5] is a big advantage, especially for the unfortunate who are in trouble? Yet, an esteemed housewife is much better than a neighbour, as she stays by your side always beautiful and good, from the beginning, in the middle and until the threshold of old age. A neighbour does not accompany you like that all the time; [10] in dangers he often does not stay, but runs away. Actually, an excellent wife is a gift from God and she is given to the man who fears Him. What is better and sweeter than a well-reputed wife? – Behold! You, Illustrious Teacher Gezelius, have received [15] such a gift, thus, always, Groom, be grateful for your gift and be happy in your heart: not every man has the chance to arrive to Corinth.

Metre: Hexameters (several hiatuses, multiple lack of central caesura).

Notes: This poem appeared in another wedding collection by the 'Muses of Embecca' (see Gezelius above). It is based on popular motives from recommended school authors Hesiodus and Theognis. A comparison favouring a good wife over other things occurs often in Early Modern *epithalamia*, but Harckman reverses the motive of the luck of having a good wife with Hesiod's verse about the importance of having a good neighbour: instead of a good neighbour, who runs to help, he presents a good wife who remains while the neighbour runs away. He concludes with a commonplace that a good wife is a gift from God and a popular proverb which states that luck is a rare thing. Harckman's diction is typical of the period: he takes liberties in metre, uses a mixture of different dialects, and creates new forms based on analogy. He seems uneasy with the tmesis, indicating it in the orthography (παρὰ-μὲν-μίμνει in l. 7; cf. also Arnoldus Engel in → **Bohemian Lands**).

Biography: The author of the poem, Ericus Harckman, was from Västmanland in Sweden and had studied for several years in Uppsala before enrolling at Tartu (in 1642). He participated as a *respondens* in the first Greek disputation of Johannes Gezelius Sr on pneumatology (1644), published a Greek gratulation for a disputation of a co-student (1645) and received Greek gratulations from Gezelius and Ericus Holstenius for participation in a disputation series on the Gospel of John (1646).[50] After studying theology at Tartu, he worked between 1653–1675 as a pastor in Uusi Puura (Nowabura) in Ingria. The addressees are Gezelius and his bride

---

50 For the poems, see Jaanson 2000, Nos. 466 and 521.

Gertrud, the daugther of Petrus Guthemius, Pastor at Riga St Jacob's Church. The wedding took place on 26 June 1643 in Riga.

Bibliography: Väänänen, Kyösti (1987), *Herdaminne för Ingermanland*, Helsinki, 202. On his Greek works: Korhonen 2004, 222–223; the disputation: J. Gezelius (praes.), E. Harckman (resp.), *Τῆς πνευματικῆς συζήτησις πρώτη*, Tartu 1644 is re-edited by Janika Päll and Meelis Friedenthal, in: Friedenthal/Päll 2017, 208–235.

[JP]

Georg Dunte (1631–1677)

<In laudem M. Eberhardi Mulleri> [1654]

Τίπτε σὲ ὑμνήσω, Σοφίης πολυήρατον ὄμμα,
ὅς σεο θυμὸν ἀεὶ γλυκεραῖς βοσκαῖσι πιαίνεις
τῆς διδαχῆς τε γλίχῃ; Μελέτην σέθεν ἀστερόεντι
οὐρανῷ ἐγκολποῦν μεγάλου οὐκ ἔστι πόνοιο
5   πρᾶγμα· τεὴν ἀρετὴν βροτοὶ ἔνθα καὶ ἔνθα βριῶσιν,
ὥστε μοι οὐδετέραν καταλειπέμεν ἤδη ἄρουραν.
Οὐχ' ἧττον δὲ φιλεῖ, ὅτ' ἐπαινετός ἐσσι ἐπαινεῖν,
ὅττί σοι οὐκ ἄλλον μελέδημα νεώτερον ἦτο
ἀντ' ἐρατῆς σοφίης, οὐ μαλθακὸς ὕπνος ἢ οἶνος
10 λυσίκακος, λευκώλενοι οὐκ ἢ καλλιπάρῃοι
παρθένοι, οὔτε σχολὴ ὀλεσήνωρ. Ἀγλαὸς ἥβη
ἦμός σου φέρεται τὰ ἐς ἔργα δορυσσόα λάβρως·
ἠνίδε! νῦν, κακόχαρτε, καὶ ἠνίδε, δυσκέλαδ' αὐτόν,
ὃς δεκάτη μοίρᾳ καθέδραν, πεπνυμένα εἰδώς
15 βῆσεν, ἀμυνόμενος πρὸ ἐριγδούποιο ἀέθλου!
λειριοεσσάων γένος εὖγε ! καὶ εὖγε κοράων.
Γυιοκόροι δὲ ὀπηδοῖεν φθονεροῖσι μέριμναι,
μέχρις ἂν ἵκωνται δνοφεροῖς ὑπὸ κεύθμασι γαίης!
Πατρίδα κοσμήσων, λιπαρὴν πόλιν, ἀλλὰ Σὺ μᾶλλον,
20 ζωὴν ἐκτέλεσον θαλερὴν μέχρι γήραος οὐδοῦ!
Χ' οὕτω μὴ θανάτου σε μέλαν νέφος ἀμφικαλύψει.

Textus: *Exercitationum philologicarum in psalmum primum, septima...praeside Andrea Sennerto...respondente M. Eberhardo Mullero, Revaliensi Livono*, Wittenberg: Röhner 1654 (VD17 3:022202Y).

Crit.: 2 ὅς corr.: ὅστ (stigma) ed. || 3 Μελέτην corr.: Μελετὴν ed. || 5 βριῶσιν] fortasse pro βρύουσιν || 11 ὀλεσήνωρ corr.: ὀλόσηνωρ ed. || 18 κεύθμασι retinui pro κεύθεσι, cf. edd. vet. || 20 οὐδοῦ correxi: οὐδῷ ed.

Sim.: **1** Σοφίης...ὄμμα] cf. Steph. Alc. 2.232 (τὸ τῆς σοφίας ἀναβλέπουσιν ὄμμα), *Ep. Pauli ad Eph.* 1.18 (ὁ πατὴρ τῆς δόξης, δώῃ ὑμῖν πνεῦμα σοφίας...πεφωτισμένους τοὺς ὀφθαλμοὺς τῆς καρδίας) || **3–4** ἀστερόεντι οὐρανῷ] formula epica, e.g. Hom. *Il.* 4.44 (οὐρανῷ ἀστερόεντι) || **4** μεγάλου...πόνοιο] cf. Joh. Chrys. *in Acta ap.*, PG 60.285 (ὅτι ἄπονόν ἐστι πρᾶγμα, ἐὰν θέλωμεν) || **5** βριῶσιν] cf. Hes. *Op.* 5 (ῥέα μὲν γὰρ βριάει, ῥέα δὲ βριάοντα χαλέπτει) || **8** ἦτο] cf. Ps-Zon. ε 638 (τὸ τρίτον ἦτο) || **8–9** οὐκ ἄλλον...σοφίης] cf. Thgn. 1.789–90 (Μήποτέ μοι μελέδημα νεώτερον ἄλλο φανείη / ἀντ' ἀρετῆς σοφίης τ') | μαλθακὸς ὕπνος] cf. Thgn. 1.470 (θωρηχθέντ' οἴνωι μαλθακὸς ὕπνος ἔλῃ) || **9–10** ἢ οἶνος λυσίκακος] cf. Thgn. 1.475–476 (μέτρον γὰρ ἔχω μελιηδέος οἴνου / ὕπνου λυσικάκου μνήσομαι) | **10** λευκώλενοι...καλλιπάρῃοι] epice || **11** σχολὴ ὀλεσήνωρ] cf. Thgn. 1.399 (αἰδεῖσθαι δὲ φίλους φεύγειν τ' ὀλεσήνορας ὅρκους); LXX *Eccl.* 10.18 (ἐν ἀργίᾳ χειρῶν στάξει ἡ οἰκία) | Ἀγλαὸς ἥβη] cf. Thgn. 1.985 (παρέρχεται ἀγλαὸς ἥβη) || **12** φέρεται...λάβρως] cf. Thgn. 1.987–988 (αἵ τε ἄνακτα φέρουσι δορυσσόον ἐς πόνον ἀνδρῶν / λάβρως) || **13** κακόχαρτε...δυσκέλαδ'] cf. Hes. *Op.* 195–196 (ζῆλος δ'.../ δυσκέλαδος κακόχαρτος ὁμαρτήσει στυγερώπης) || **14** δεκάτῃ μοίρᾳ] cf. Hes. *Theog.* 789 (Ὠκεανοῖο κέρας, δεκάτη δ' ἐπὶ μοῖρα δέδασται) | πεπνυμένα εἰδώς] formula epica, e.g. Hom. *Od.* 4.696 || **15–16** πρὸ ἐριγδούποιο... λειριοεσσάων] cf. Hes. *Theog.* 41 (Ζηνὸς ἐριγδούποιο θεᾶν ὀπὶ λειριοέσσῃ) || **17** Γυιοκόροι...μέριμναι] Hes. *Op.* 66 (γυιοβόρους μελεδώνας), cf. mss Hes. *Op.* 66 et Ps.Zon. 459.22 (Ἡσίοδος· καὶ γυιοκόρους μελεδώνας) || **18** μέχρις ἂν ἵκωνται] cf. Ap. Rhod. *Argon.* 4.1234 (μέχρις ἵκοντο) | δνοφεροῖς ὑπὸ κεύθμασι γαίης] cf. Thgn. 1.243 (ὅταν δνοφερῆς ὑπὸ κεύθμασι γαίης), edd. veteres et Gezelius 1646 || **19** Πατρίδα...πόλιν] cf. Thgn. 1.947 (πατρίδα κοσμήσω, λιπαρὴν πόλιν) || **20** ζωὴν...οὐδοῦ] cf. Ps-Phoc. 230 (ζωὴν ἐκτελέοιτ' ἀγαθὴν μέχρι γήραος οὐδοῦ) || **21** Χ' οὕτω μὴ θανάτου... ἀμφικαλύψει] cf. Thgn. 1.707 (ὅντινα δὴ θανάτοιο μέλαν νέφος ἀμφικαλύψῃ)

⟨Praise of Eberhard Müller⟩

Why should I start to praise you, most beloved eye of Wisdom, you who always fatten your soul on sweet pasturages and strive after learning? To bring your practice into the embrace of the starry sky is not a matter of great toil; [5] mortal men augment your virtue here and there, so that they do not leave either field to me. But it is nonetheless pleasing to praise you, since you are praiseworthy, when you do not have any other newer care in place of beloved wisdom: not soft sleep nor wine, [10] the end of evil, not maidens with white arms or beautiful cheeks, nor idleness, the destroyer of men, so long as your brilliant youth mightily strives towards lance-brandishing works. See, you, who rejoice in evil and you who have a malicious tongue, look at him, [14] who, wisely knowing, in the tenth hour has stepped up onto the podium defending himself in the loud-roaring combat! Well said, delicate-voiced race! Well said, race of maidens! May the limb-gnawing sorrows follow those who are jealous, until they arrive down under the dark holes of earth! [19] But you, as a decoration for your fatherland, wealthy town, moreover, bring your life to its accomplishment, blooming until the threshold of the old age! And thus the dark cloud of death will not cover you.

Metre: Hexameters (multiple hiatus, absence of central caesura, in l. 11 double consonant (written with a ligature σχ) in σχολή not causing position).

Notes: This congratulation for a dissertation features countless words from ancient poetry, but direct cento-like loans are rare (which results in numerous hiatuses). The poem begins with a *topos* concerning the difficulty of praising in a novel way (with a metaphor of a field) an already praised young man who values wisdom over other virtues. In lines 12–18 the occasion of the poem (university disputation) is presented as a fight where the adressee will prevail over his opponents. The poem ends by wishing Müller a worthy and beneficial life in his homeland.

Biography: Georg Dunte was a son of Ludwig Dunte, the deacon in Tallinn St Olai Church. He was born in Tallinn, studied in Tartu, Giessen, Wittenberg (*magister* in 1653), and Rostock, and became professor of Greek at the Gymnasium of Tallinn in 1672. He published at least four Greek poems: in 1651 in Tallinn a wedding poem for Georg Salemann, the above poem in Wittenberg in 1654, and two *epicedia* (one in 1672 for Merchant Georg Ohm and the other in 1676 for Gebhard Himsel, Tallinn City physician and professor of mathematics at the gymnasium). The addressee, Eberhard Müller (†1660), was also from Tallinn. He had studied in Stettin, Tartu, Wittenberg (*magister* in 1653, adjunct of philosophy in 1654), Leipzig, and Rostock, was a pastor in Thorn, and died without returning to his homeland. He participated actively in disputations during his studies in Germany, and published fine Latin poetry, a speech in Hebrew, and at least one Greek poem (a gratulation to Hermann Kahl in Wittenberg, 1653). He received a collection of poetry for his master's degree, including a Latin poem by Dunte (*Bona Verba...Eberhardum Mollerum*, Wittenberg 1653), possibly referred to in l. 5.

Bibliography: Dunte in Klöker, 2005.1, 662–663; Tering 2018, 274 (no. 1527); Müller in Klöker 2005.1, 208–210, 216, 705; Tering 2018, 491 (no. 3420). Works: Klöker 2005.2. On his Greek poetry: Päll 2018, 90f.

[JP]

Latvia

Martin Francke (*fl.* 1647–1653)

ΦΆΡΜΑΚΟΝ ΘΑΝΑΤΆΓΩΓΟΝ [1652]

    Ἀντὶ κράτους θανάτου ἐν κήποις φάρμακον οὐδέν,
        οὕτως λέγει τὸ πλῆθος
    ἰητρῶν βίβλοισιν ἐαῖς ἐν ταῖς μεγάλαισιν.
        Τί Πνεῦμα Κοιράνοιο;
5   Ἰσραῆλος ὕδωρ πηγῆς, ἄνθος τε Σαρῶνος,
        καὶ ῥίζα τοῦ Ἰέσσε,
    τῆς ζωῆς δένδρον καὶ ἀεὶ θάλλουσα ἐλάτη,
        ἀπολλύειν ὄλεθρον
    (ἐκ τούτων ἄρα σοι ποιῆς ἔκλειγμα) δύνανται
10   αἰώνιόν τε ζήσεις.

Textus: *Christliche Sterbens-Gedancken, Welche über...Herrn GEORG HEKK*, Riga: Gerhard Schröder 1652, B3v–B4r (in Bibliotheca Universitatis Upsaliensis, Sv Personverser 4to).

Crit.: tit. θαναταγωγόν debuit || **3** βίβλοισιν corr.: βιβλυισιν ed. || **9** δύνανται corr.: δύναται ed.

Sim.: 1 Ἀντὶ...οὐδὲν] *Regimen Sanitatis Salernitanum* v. 178 (Cap. LX, *De Salvia*, 2) *Contra vim mortis non est medicamen in hortis* || **5** Ἰσραῆλος ὕδωρ πηγῆς] cf. LXX (Regnorum IV = Regum II Mas), 5.12 πάντα τὰ ὕδατα Ισραηλ | ἄνθος τε Σαρῶνος] *Carm. Sal.* 2.1 (Ἐγὼ ἄνθος τοῦ πεδίου), cf. Lutherbibel: *Ich bin eine Blume zu Saron* || **5–6** ἄνθος...ῥίζα τοῦ Ἰέσσε] *Is.*11.1–10 (Καὶ ἐξελεύσεται ῥάβδος ἐκ τῆς ῥίζης Ιεσσαι, καὶ ἄνθος ἐκ τῆς ῥίζης ἀναβήσεται) || **7** Τῆς ζωῆς δένδρον] cf. *Gen.* 2.9 (*lignum etiam vitae in medio paradisi*, sed LXX τὸ ξύλον τῆς ζωῆς) | ἀεὶ θάλλουσα ἐλάτη] pino semper viridi in loco symboli Nativitatis civitas Rigensis se primam uti credit || **10** αἰώνιόν τε ζήσεις] cf. NT *Joh.* 11.25 (Ἐγώ εἰμι ἡ ἀνάστασις καὶ ἡ ζωή· ὁ πιστεύων εἰς ἐμὲ κἂν ἀποθάνῃ ζήσεται, καὶ πᾶς ὁ ζῶν καὶ πιστεύων εἰς ἐμὲ οὐ μὴ ἀποθάνῃ εἰς τὸν αἰῶνα).

Death-banishing Medicine

    There is no medicine in the gardens against the strength of death,
        so tells the majority
    of doctors in their big books.
        What is the Spirit of the Lord?
    [5] The water of the fountain of Israel, the Flower of Sharon,
        the Root of Jesse,
    the Tree of Life and the Evergreen Fir-tree

can abolish the peril of death.
Thus you should make these a medicine for yourself,
[10] and you will live forever.

Notes: The poem is preceded by an anagram poem by Francke, based on the anagram *Dunst/Stund* ('haze'/'hour'), combining the German phraseologism 'to disappear into a blue haze' and motives from the Psalms.[51] The Greek poem begins with a popular quotation from *Regimen sanitatis* (but in Greek) and continues with *loci* of funeral sermons on Christ, Faith, and Resurrection. Francke's diction is epic in tone due to its mixture of Ionic and epic forms (Ἰητρῶν, βίβλοισιν, ἑαῖς) and analogy based forms (κοιράνοιο). His choice of metre is quite typical for Humanist Greek poetry from gymnasia, which seems to prefer Latin epodic forms.

Biography: Martin Franck(e) was born in Narva (he referred to himself as a Livo), possibly a son of Jacob Franck from Turku, pastor of a Finnish-Estonian parish in Narva. He studied briefly at Tartu University, Riga Gymnasium (where he published several poems in Greek and Latin), and Königsberg University. It is likely that he also published a Latin poem in Tallinn in 1647. According to the title-page of the collection, the deceased, Georg Hekk (Heck), a merchant and the elder of the Great Gild in Riga, died on 29 August and was buried on 5 September 1652 with a ceremony in Riga Cathedral.

Bibliography: Tering 2018, 309; Garber 2004 (Bd. 12–15). On his poetry: Berziņa 2018, 49, n.20; Kaju Katre (2010), "Die Heinrich Stahl gewidmeten Hochzeitssammlungen", in: Janika Päll/Martin Steinrück/Ivo Volt (eds.), *Classical Tradition from the 16th century to Nietzsche*, Tartu, 28f.

[JP]

---

[51] The poem: 'In Nebel-blauer Dunst muss Flügel schnell verstiben, Im Fall er durch die Lufft vom Winde wird getriben: So fleucht die Stunde hin, der Stunde gleich die Zeit, Und mit der Zeit der Mensch, wohin ? zur Ewigkeit' ('Into a foggy-blue haze the bird has to be striven fast, when it will be thrown down through the air by the winds. So flees the hour, the time equals to an hour, and with the time, where goes the man? To eternity.'). Cf. Ps. 89 by Luther: 'Ach wie flüchtig, ach wie nichtig ist der Menschen Leben. Wie ein Nebel bald entstehet und auch wieder bald vergehet, so ist unser Leben, sehet!'

Denmark, Norway, and Iceland

Copenhagen University (founded in 1479) remained the only university in Denmark until the 19th century. In no small part thanks to the support of King Christian II, a humanistic impulse and an interest in Greek studies is discernible in Copenhagen as early as the 1520s. The first Danish print containing Greek words was a eulogy of the king published by Mathias Gabler in 1521.[52] The first Danish poet to write in Greek was probably the Catholic, wandering humanist Jakob Jespersen (Jacobus Danus, Jacobus Jasperi, active 1529–1549) from Aarhus. Due to the Reformation, he did not return to Denmark after studying at the *Collegium trilingue*, but taught Greek in Leuven and also spent a long time in Antwerpen, where he published some Greek poems: Latin and Greek *epithalamia* for Christina of Denmark on her marriage with Francis, Duke of Lorraine, which included also a Homeric cento (*Epithalamium*, 1641) and four Greek poems with Latin translations (*Anactobiblion*, 1544).[53]

The Reformation in Denmark did not entail as severe a disruption in the educational system as in Sweden. After a short period of decline and inactivity in the 1530s, the university was refounded in 1539.[54] Humanist culture in Denmark was firmly established already by the 1550s, and the printing of Greek poetry in Denmark started in the second half of the 16th century. In 1568, Peder Aagesen (Petrus Haggaeus) had published a Greek *epithalamium* in Copenhagen. In 1572, Torben Nielsen from Ribe in southern Jutland (Thorbernus Nicolaus/Nicolai Ripensis) published a short hexameter wedding poem in Copenhagen.[55] Niels Lauridsen from Ribe (Nicolaus Laurentius Ripensis, c. 1547–1579) studied in Wittenberg and became a professor at Copenhagen University in 1574. He has published a Greek hexameter oration, which was based on synoptical Gospels, a set of Bible paraphrases in Greek and a Greek occasional poem for his master's degree.[56]

---

52 *In laudem illustrissimi invictissimique Christierni*, Copenhagen 1521. See Schwarz Lausten 1991a.
53 Cf. Schwarz Lausten 2003; Harstings 1994.
54 Schwarz Lausten 1991b.
55 *Epithalamia in nuptiis D. Thomae Gregorii Hemettensis...Ceciliae, D. Andreae Ljungii*, Copenhagen 1568; *In honorem nuptiarum Matthiae Lagonis...Mariae...Johannis Langii*, Copenhagen 1572. In 1575 he wrote a Greek *epicedium* in elegiacs, *Carmen funebre graecolatinum...Johannis Baldis*. S.l.s.a. (Wittenberg 1576 according to the catalogue of Danish Royal Library). Not much is known about his life.
56 *Historia resurrectionis Domini nostri* (Wittenberg 1574); *Cantica Mariae virginis, Zachariae et Simeonis* (Wittenberg 1575) and *Gratulatio in honorem Nic. Kragii & Christ. Michaelis Choagii* (Wittenberg 1575). For Lauridsen's biography, see Rørdam, Holger Frederik (1896), "Niels Lauridsen",

However, even when Greek printing types were available, it was not uncommon to publish abroad with a more accomplished printer, particularly longer books of prose or poetry. In 1578, the student Hans Olufsen Slangerup, later professor of theology in Copenhagen (1584–1596), demonstrated his prowess in the language by translating the second book of Cicero's *De officiis* into Greek and a speech of Demosthenes into Latin.[57] In 1595, **Petrus Ivarus Borrichius** (1563–1627) published in Leiden a hexameter paraphrase of the story of Hercules at the crossroads. In the 17th century, the Latinist, rector in Malmö, and vicar in Skåne (Scania) **Bertel Knudsen Aquilonius** (1588–1650) published a collection of Greek epigrams; **Peder Winstrup** (1605–1679; bishop of Lund both under Danish and Swedish rule, when the eastern provinces of Denmark became the southern provinces of Sweden 1658, with the Treaty of Roskilde) published his collected Greek and Latin poems twice. Another important Hellenist and Greek poet was Rasmus Polsen Vinding (Erasmus Paul Winding, 1615–1684), who was professor of Greek at Copenhagen University from 1648.[58] His Latin oration, *De regno hereditario* (1640), ends with a small collection of his Greek poems in elegiac verses (*Carmen ad dulcissimam Patriam*, six poems dedicated to Christian IV, and an epigram for Vinding by an unidentified poet).[59] As a classical scholar, he is famous for his study of the origins of the Greek language (*De literarum Graecarum origine*, 1661) and editions of Greek geographical authors.[60]

From 1380 to 1814, Norway was in union with Denmark while Iceland remained in union with Denmark until 1944. Norway is here half-represented by Borrichius, and, with regard to Iceland, at least two Greek poems are known, one an *epicedium* by **Torfi Pálsson**, printed in Copenhagen in 1695, and published by Sigurður Pétursson in 1998 (see below).[61] Whether Johannes Chrysorinus

---

in: *Dansk Biografisk Lexikon*, X, Copenhagen, 142. http://runeberg.org/dbl/10/ 0144.html [accessed: October 2020].
57 *Secundus liber M. T. Ciceronis de officiis, e latina lingua in Græcam, exercitii causa translatus*, Wittenberg 1578. Biographical details: Kornerup 1983³.
58 See Rørdam, Holger Frederik (1905), "Vinding, Rasmus", in: C.F. Bricka (ed.), *Dansk Biografisk Lexikon*, XIX, Copenhagen, 26–28.
59 Signed as: Γ. Νερρίεδος Ἀρμορικός.
60 For further Danish poets (notably Hans Jørgensen Sadolin and Peter Grib Fibiger) and poems see also Gottschalck 2019.
61 Another poem, a congratulation for a disputation, was written by Jón Þorkelsson Vídalín (1666–1720) to his brother Arngrímur, published in Copenhagen in 1688. We thank Gottskálk Jensson who first drew our attention to these poems and gave information pertaining to Vídalín's poem. See also Pétursson 2004, 297–300. Sigurður Pétursson, who originally found both of these poems and published the one presented here, died while we were finishing this part in 2020.

Thorcillius (1697–1759), also known as *quadrilinguis*, knew and wrote in Greek, remains unknown.[62]

JP/JA/TK

Special Bibliography

Gottschalck, Rasmus (2019), "Denmark (Danemark) ", in: Francisco Oliveira/Ramón Martínez (eds.), *Europatrida*, Coimbra, 59–70.

Harstings, Pernille (1994), "Jacob Jasparus (fl.1529-1549): 'Homerculus noster Danicus'", in: *Acta Conventus Neo-Latini Hafniensis*, Binghamton, 465–476.

Kornerup, Bjørn (1983³), "Slangerup, Hans Olufsen", in: *Dansk biografisk leksikon*, https://biografiskleksikon.lex.dk/Hans_Olufsen_Slangerup [accessed: September 2020].

Pétursson, Sigurður (2004), "Erlend tungumál á Íslandi á 16. og 17. öld" [Foreign languages in Iceland in the 16th and 17th centuries], in: *Skírnir* 178, 291–317.

Schwarz Lausten, Martin (1991a), "Københavns Universitet i Middelalderen 1479-ca. 1530", in: Svend Ellehøj/Leif Grane/Kai Hørby (eds.), *Københavns universitet 1497–1979*, I, København, 65–77.

Schwarz Lausten, Martin (1991b), "Københavns Universitet 1536-1588", in: Svend Ellehøj/Leif Grane/Kai Hørby (eds.), *Københavns universitet 1497–1979*, I, København, 85–92.

Schwarz Lausten, Martin (2003), "Jakob JESPERSEN", in: Peter G. Bietenholz (ed.), *Contemporaries of Erasmus*, Vol. 2, Toronto, 234–235.

---

62 In *Instrumentum Bibliographicum* to *Humanistica Lovaniensia*, Vol. XLI, 1992, 382–383 he is called 'quadrilinguis' with a reference to S. Pétursson, 'Jon Thorkelssons flersprogede Litteraere virke med udgangspunkt i hans hovedvaerk, Specimen Islandiae non-barbarae', *Lat. Nat. Nord.*, pp. 271–278.

Petrus Ivarus Borrichius (1563–1627)

Ξενοφῶντος Ἡρακλῆς [1595]

(excerptum, vv. 13–24)

13 Ἀλκείδης μένος Ἀμφιτρυωνιάδαο ἀτειρὲς
   καὶ κλέος, Αἰγιόχου Διὸς υἱὸς καρτερόθυμος
15 ἀκλειῶς ἐπειὴ βίον εἶλκεν ἐὸν δεκαοκτὼ
   τοὺς λυκάβαντας, ἐσῆλθεν μοῦνος ὑπόσκιον ὕλην
   εἴαρι ἀνθεμόενθ', ὅταν ἤματα μακρὰ πέλονται,
   ἠδὲ ἐφράζετο τὴν βιότοιο ἀταρπὸν ὁδεύοι,
   ἆρα ἀπραγμοσύνης ἀκολουθήσειεν ἀταρπῷ,
20 ᾗ νεμεσᾷ θεὸς αὖ πάντες τε καὶ ἄνδρες ἄριστοι,
   ἦ μᾶλλον βίον ἕλκοι, ὃς εἰς πόλον ὑψιμέλαθρον
   ἄνδρας ἄγει παναρίστους καὶ σοφὸν ἦτορ ἔχοντας.
   Ταῦτα δὲ τὠϋτέου νοέοντος ἐνὶ πραπίδεσσιν,
   ἠνὶ θεοὶ δύο καρπαλίμως αὐτόνδε προσῆλθον.

Textus: *Xenophontis Hercules, Carmine Graeco Heroico expositus*, a Pet. Ivaro Borrichio, Leiden 1595, 6–8.

Crit.: 18, 19 ἀταρπὸν, ἀταρπῷ correxi: ἄταρπον, ἀτάρπῳ ed. || **23** τὠϋτέου scripsi haesitans: τωϋτέου ed.

Sim.: 13–24 cf. Xen. *Mem.* 2.1.21 || **13** μένος ... ἀτειρές] cf. Hom. *Od.* 11.270 (Ἀμφιτρύωνος υἱὸς μένος αἰὲν ἀτειρής, cum var. lect. ἀτειρές) || **13–14** Ἀμφιτρυωνιάδαο ... Διὸς υἱός] cf. Hes. *Theog.* 316–317 (Διὸς υἱός ... Ἀμφιτρυωνιάδης) || **14** καρτερόθυμος] cf. Hom. *Il.* 5.277; 13.350 etc. || **16** ὑπόσκιον ὕλην] cf. Hom. *Il.* 15.273; *Od.* 5.470 (ἐς κλειτὺν ἀναβὰς καὶ δάσκιον ὕλην) || **17** εἴαρι ἀνθεμόενθ'] cf. Alcm. fr. 367; Quint. Smyrn. 2.601 | εἴαρι ... πέλονται] cf. Hom. *Od.* 18.367 (ὥρῃ ἐν εἰαρινῇ, ὅτε τ' ἤματα μακρὰ πέλονται) || **18** τὴν ... ὁδεύοι] cf. Nonn. *Par. Jo.* 14.21 (ζωὴ ἐγὼ βιότοιο καὶ ἀτραπός), Isocr. 1.5 (ὅσοι ... τοῦ βίου ταύτην τὴν ὁδὸν ἐπορεύθησαν) et plures || **18, 19** ἀταρπὸν, ἀταρπῷ] cf. Hom. *Il.* 17.743, *Od.* 14.1 || **19** ἀκολουθήσειεν ἀταρπῷ] cf. *Mc.* 10.52 (ἠκολούθει αὐτῷ ἐν τῇ ὁδῷ); *1 Ep.Clem.* 35.5 (ἀκολουθήσωμεν τῇ ὁδῷ) || **21** εἰς ... ὑψιμέλαθρον] cf. Nonn. *Par. Jo.* 14.110 || **22** σοφὸν ἦτορ] cf. *Ex.* 35.10 (σοφὸς τῇ καρδίᾳ); *Pr.* 10.8 (σοφὸς καρδίᾳ) etc.

Xenophon's Heracles

(excerpt, ll. 13–24)

When Alcides [= Heracles], the unyielding force and glory of the son of Amphitryo, the stronghearted son of aegis-bearing Zeus, had lived his life without distinction for eighteen years, he entered a shady forest alone [17] in flowery springtime, when the days become long, and pondered what way of life he should travel – should he follow the path of inaction, [20] which is resented by God and all the best men, or should he rather live a life that brings the very best men who are wise at heart to high-vaulted heaven. As he was contemplating these things in his mind, see!, two goddesses approached him swiftly.[63]

Metre: Hexameters (often allowing hiatus and occasionally ignoring central caesura; bipartite hexameters in ll. 16, 22).

Notes: After twelve verses of invocation of divine inspiration, these verses begin a more than 200 verses long hexameter paraphrasis of Prodicus' well-known tale of Hercules' choice between Virtue and Vice as recounted by Socrates in Xenophon's *Memorabilia* (2.1.21–34). This was a popular text in educational contexts in Protestant Europe, both in the original Greek and in translation into both Latin and various vernaculars (this episode was the first piece of ancient literature to be translated into Swedish) as well as in paraphrases. According to the preface, Borrichius made the paraphrasis for the benefit of the students of Herlufsholm to further encourage their Greek studies; he also stresses the fundamental importance of Greek for proper mastery of Latin. The print is dated 1595, the preface 1593; perhaps Borrichius used the text in manuscript form in the classroom prior to publication.

Biography: Petrus Ivarus Borrichius, or Peder Iversen/Iverssøn Borch, was born in 1563 in Denmark and died 3 April 1627 in Trondheim, Norway. Little is known of his career before 1584 when he is mentioned as a teacher in Denmark, first at Fredriksborg School in Hillerød and then in Sorø, where the school relocated to in 1586. In 1591, he was appointed rector of Herlufsholm School in Næstved, Denmark, a school renowned for its teaching in classics; Borrichius promoted Greek studies there. In 1594, he took the master's degree at the University of Copenhagen; in the same year he published two treatises in Rostock and a year later the *Xenophontis Hercules* in Leiden. He left Herlufsholm in 1595 possibly as a result of inadequate

---

[63] The author's own Latin translation, printed parallel to the Greek text and following it line by line without being hexametric: *Hercules indomitum robur Amphitryoniadae / Et gloria, Iovis Ægiochi filius magnanimus, / [15] Inglorius postquam vixisset decem & octo / Annos, solus ingressus est umbrosam sylvam / Vere florifero, quando dies longae sunt, / Et secum deliberavit quam vitae viam sequeretur, / Utrum Voluptatis viam sectaretur, / [20] Cui et Deus succenset et omnes homines boni, / Aut potius istam vitam viveret, quae in altum caelum / Viros ducit optimos et sapiens cor habentes. / Haec autem ipso cogitante in pectoribus, / Ecce binae Deae subitò ad ipsum accesserunt.*

salary; in 1599, he was appointed cantor and lector at the cathedral school in Trondheim. Due to the pestilence that was prevalent at the time, he did not take up his post until 1601. He remained in Trondheim until his death in 1627.

Bibliography: Thorkildsen, Dag (1999), "Borch (Borck), Peder Iverssøn (el. Iversen)", in: *Norsk biografisk leksikon*, 1, Oslo, 409; Rørdam, Holger Fredrik (1874), "Personalhistoriske bidrag fra det 17de Aarhundrede", in: *Kirkehistoriske samlinger*, 3.1, København, 318–326; Akujärvi, Johanna (2018), "Xenophon and Aisopos for the Swedish youth. On the earliest printed translations of ancient literature in Sweden", in: Päll/Volt 2018, 185–217.

[JA]

Bertel Knudsen Aquilonius (1588–1650)

I. *De Me* [1633]

Ἀλλάττουσιν ἔτη πολλούς· μέγας ἤρεσε πρόσθεν
αἶνος· πρὸς γαίας τῆλέ τε γνῶσιν ἵναι.
Νῦν λήθη μᾶλλον, νῦν κλῆρος ἄφημος ἀρέσκει,
ἐν μικρῷ τε ποθῷ πτὼξ ἄφαντός τε λαθεῖν.

Textus: Philomusi aphemi. *ΠΟΙΗΜΑΤΩΝ, quae quidem prodierunt liber XL. Ad Celsissimum Heroem Tagium Tottium, magn. Daniae Senatorem*, Rostock 1633, 15, 21 (copy used: Det Kgl. Bibliotek, Copenhagen, sign. 53,-21 8° 00130)

Crit.: 2 ἵναι ed. pro ἴμεν

Sim.: 3 ἄφημος] Hsch. α 8642 (ἄφημοι· ἀνώνυμοι, ἀκλεεῖς), *Suda* α 4604 (Ἄφημος· ἀπευθής) || 4 πτὼξ ἄφαντός τε λαθεῖν] cf. Hom. *Il.* 17.676 (οὐκ ἔλαθε πτώξ)

II. *Ad Deum* [1633]

Νῦν ἅλις εἰς μικρὰς σπουδὴν ἐπέθηκα μαθήσεις
ἐν βαιαῖς τε φίλως ἤν τε πέλον τε βίβλοις.
Ἂψ πόνον εἰς ὁσίας καὶ μῆτιν πᾶσαν ἀνοίσω
δουλεύει τε μόνῳ φρήν τε φύσις τε θεῷ.

Crit.: 2 ἤν τε πέλον τε scripsi: ἤντε πελόντε ed. || 3 ὁσίας scripsi: ὀσέας ed. || 4 φρήν τε] τε manu supra lineam additum ed. | φύσις scripsi: φύσίς ed.

About me

Years change many. Earlier, great reputation was pleasing: to have fame
   travel to countries and far away.
Now, rather oblivion, now a lot without fame is pleasing:
   in small circumstances, I long to escape notice, cowering and invisible.

To God

Now I have laid enough effort on slight learning,
   gladly I have been engaged in small books.
I shall bring labour and all my skill back again
   to the service of God, and my mind and body serve God only.

Metre: Elegiac couplets (note the wrong prosody of l. 4 ἄφαντος).

Notes: These poems come from a small collection of more than 80 Greek poems printed under the pseudonym Philomusus Aphemus; Aquilonius' authorship is marked as uncertain in bibliographical works, but seems to be confirmed by his reprinting of certain poems from this collection in later works. In addition to poems addressed to the nobleman Tage Tott (1580–1658), dedicatee of the volume, and other men of importance and rank, the collection includes a series of poems *De Me*, *Ad Deum*, and *Ad lectorem*, nearly all of which are meditations on the theme of change in the poetic 'I': the poet either renounces his frivolous and vainglorious aspirations in favour of a quiet life, or he rejects his vain and ephemeral literary pursuits in order to devote himself to the praise of God, as in the two poems above. These appear to reflect the change in the author's pursuits.

Biography: Bertel Knudsen Aquilonius (father's family name Nordrup Latinised; called himself also Toxotes; mother's family name Skytte Graecised) was born in 1588, the son of a vicar in Sjælland. Having finished school at the Gymnasium of Herlufsholm (1606), he travelled throughout Europe, reaching Turkey before returning to Denmark (1610). *Philosophiae magister* in 1612, he was appointed school rector in Malmø the same year, and a few years later he became preacher at the castle. In 1619, he was promoted to parish priest and rural dean. His literary output was considerable: he published hundreds of Latin poems across numerous collections, five *centuriae* of Latin letters, and perhaps another collection of Greek poems in addition to the one used here. After his move to the country, he seems to have devoted himself mainly to historical, linguistic, and poetic studies.

Bibliography: Carlquist 1963, 290–297; Ehrencron-Müller, H. (1924), *Forfatterlexikon omfattende Danmark, Norge og Island indtil 1814*, I, 133–136; Jensen, Minna Skafte (2017), "Nationalromantik og sprogteori. Bertil Knudsen Aqvilonius", in: Camilla Plesner Horster/Lærke Maria Andersen Funder (eds.), *Antikkens veje til renæssancens Danmark*, Aarhus, 181–199.

[JA]

Peder Winstrup (1605–1679)

I. *Studiosorum vitia nocturna* [1653]

a Νυκτοποτεῖν καὶ b νυκτοπονεῖν καὶ c νυκτοχαράσσειν,
d Νυκτομαχεῖν καὶ e νυκτομαθεῖν καὶ f νυκτοταράσσειν.
Haec vitanda tibi studiose, gens studiosa.
 a noctu potare. b noctu laborare. c noctu sculpere (lapides, ictu gladiorum). d noctu pugnare. e noctu studere. f noctu tumultuari.

II. *Votum autoris quotidianum* [1653]

Πρὸς πάντα ἔργα μεῖο
Πρὸς ἔργα πάντα μεῖο
Πρὸς πάντα μεῖο ἔργα
Πρὸς ἔργα μεῖο πάντα
5 Πρὸς μεῖο πάντα ἔργα
Πρὸς μεῖο ἔργα πάντα
Σοῦ πέμπε Χριστὲ πνεῦμα
Σοῦ πνεῦμα Χριστὲ πέμπε
Σοῦ Χριστὲ πέμπε πνεῦμα
10 Σοῦ Χριστὲ πνεῦμα πέμπε
Σοῦ πέπμε πνεῦμα Χριστέ
Σοῦ πνεῦμα πέμπε Χριστέ.
 i.e. Ad omnia opera mea tuum Christe mitte Spiritum.

Textus: *Petri P. Winstrupii Epigrammata. Liber II*, Copenhagen: Georg Holst 1653, 426, 428.

Night-time errors of students

Night-drinking and night-working and night-chiseling; night-fighting and night-studying and night-rumbling – this, my tribe of students, should be studiously avoided by you.

The author's daily prayer

Christ, send Thy Spirit to all my doings.

Metre: I. Hexameters, II: catalectic iambic dimeters (multiple hiatus).

Notes: Winstrup published his Latin and Greek epigrams in three books: the first includes poems on the articles of the Christian faith, the second and third include playful poems on different topics from theology to philology, as well as epigrams for different persons. His playful epigrams often use a macaronic mixture of Greek and Latin (occasionally even Hebrew and Latin) and neologisms. In the first poem Winstrup explains his Greek neologisms in Latin notes (as he often does). He loves to use repetition as a poetic device; in the second poem we see *transpositio* (*metathesis*).

Biography: Peder Winstrup (1605–1679) was born in Copenhagen, and studied in Rostock, Wittenberg, Leipzig, and Jena. After returning home he began to serve King Christian IV of Denmark. He was appointed bishop of Lund (in Scania) in 1638 and remained in this position until his death, both under Swedish and Danish rule. He also published his collected epigrams in Jena in 1632, an augmented and revised edition in Copenhagen in 1653; both editions include a Greek prose dedicatory letter addressed to the Danish Chancellor Christen Friis (1581–1639). Winstrup had a role in the opening of the University of Lund (1666). His literary legacy includes numerous Danish homilies, Latin academic dissertations, and historical and panegyric works (including *Cornicen Danicus* from 1639 (ed. 1644) in elegiac verses, dedicated to Christian IV) both in Latin and in vernacular. He also published a lengthy Greek paraphrase on the sufferings and death of Christ in 1808 hexameters (*Τοῦ Χριστοῦ Πάσχοντος Λύτρον Κοσμοσωτήριον. Paraphrasis sacrosanctissimae historiae passionis & Mortis Domini ... Iesu Christi*, Wittenberg 1576).

Bibliography: Hansson, Karl F. (1653), *Biskop Peder Winstrup*, 1605-1679, Lund; Kornerup, Bjørn (1979–1984), "Peder Winstrup", in: *Dansk Biografisk Lexikon*, Gyldendal (http://denstoredanske.dk/index.php?sideId=299424); Lagerås, Per (2016), "Från trädgård till grav: växterna i biskop Peder Winstrups kista", in: *Särtryk ur Ale* 4, 15–28; Sjöberg, Cajsa (2020), "Till Annas bröllop 1627. Några tillfällesdikter ur Peder Winstrups Epigrammata", in: Arne Jönsson/Valborg Lindgärde/Daniel Möller och Arsenii Vetuschko-Kalevich (eds.), *Att dikta för livet, döden och evigheten. Tillfällesdiktning under tidigmodern tid*, Göteborg/ Stockholm, 109–127.

[JP]

Iceland

Torfi Pálsson (1673–1712)

Ἐπιτάφιος καὶ θρῆνος [1695]

(excerptum, vv. 13–20)

> Τίπτε λόγοις χρήσει, αἴ αἴ νῦν φιλτάτου ἐμοῦ
>   χηρώθην φίλου, φεῦ τάλας; οἰχομένου.
> 15 Ὄντως ὃς πατρὸς θεοειδέος, οὐκ ὀλίγης τε
>   μητέρος, ἐς δὲ φάος ἤλυθεν εὐξαμένων.
>   Αἰέν, ζῶν, καλοῖς ἐπὶ γράμμασ' ἐδείξατο σπουδὴν
>   πλεῖον καὶ πάντων, πᾶσιν ἦν ἱμερόεις.
>   Καὶ σπλάγχνοισιν ἑοῖσι θεοῦ μέγαν οἶκτον ἐφείλξεν,
> 20   εἰρήνης φίλος, καὶ καθαρὸς κραδίην.

Textus: Ἐπιτάφιος καὶ θρῆνος διὰ θανάτου τοῦ...μείρακος ΒΙΓΦΟΥΣΟΥ [!] τοῦ ΙΩΝΑ [!] τοῦ ἐν τῇ γυμνασίᾳ τῇ Ἀφνικῇ περὶ τὴν θεολογίαν διατρίβοντος..., Copenhagen: Justinus Hög, 1695, 2:0.

Crit.: 1 λογοῖς ed. 13 ‖ Τίπτε conieci] Τὶ τὲ ed. | αἴ αἴ νῦν φιλτάτου ed. ‖ 15 ὀλίγης τὲ, ed. ‖ 17 Ἄιεν ed. ‖ 19 οἶκτον ed. | ἐφείλξεν debuit

Sim.: 14 χηρώθην] cf. Greg. Naz. *carm.*, PG 37.1447.11 ‖ 15–16 cf. Greg. Naz. *carm.*, PG 37.1447. 4–5 (Πατρὸς μὲν γενόμην θεοειδέος, οὐκ ὀλίγης δὲ Μητέρος· ἐς δὲ φάος ἤλυθον εὐξαμένης) ‖ 19–20 cf. Greg. Naz. *carm.*, PG 37.783.13–14 (Ὃς σπλάγχνοισιν ἑοῖσι Θεοῦ μέγαν οἶκτον ἐφέλκει, Εἰρήνης τε φίλος, καὶ καθαρὸς κραδίην)

Epitaph and lament

(excerpt, ll. 13–20)

> And why will one use words, ah ah, now when I, poor me, am bereaved of my dearest friend? He is gone. [15] Truly he went to the light as his divine father and not less worthy mother prayed for. Always he showed, as he lived, more diligence in his studies than all others, he was liked by all. And he will draw a great compassion of God with his own mercy, [20] a friend of peace, pure in heart.

Metre: Elegiac couplets, several metrical mistakes in ll. 13–14, 17–18, 20.

Notes: The poem is printed on a decorated sheet commemorating the early death of Vigfús Jónsson, who enrolled at the University of Copenhagen on 6 November

1694 to study theology and was buried in the Holy Trinity Chapel of Copenhagen on 16 December the same year. Pálsson's poem, 28 lines long with an elaborate heading, was published one year later. It is, however, almost a *cento* of Gregory of Nazianzus' poems;[64] only lines 4, 13–14, 17–18, and 23–24 are by Pálsson. The poem is thus an example of the method of learning to write Greek poems by combining one's own verses with those imitated or outright borrowed from verses by Greek authors.

Biography: Not much is known of Torfi Pálsson (1673–1712). He was born in Múlaþing (in the eastern part of Iceland) and went to Copenhagen together with his friend Vigfús Jónsson (1676–1694), the son of the bishop of the same diocese. After completing his studies, Pálsson became a vicar in southern Denmark. He never returned to his home country.

Bibliography: Pétursson, Sigurður (1998), "Vigfús Jónsson syrgður" ['Vigfús Jónsson mourned'], in: *Ritmennt* 3, 89–98 (Greek text and its translation and commentary in Icelandic language, summary in English; the picture of the poem on p. 96). Also available online: https://timarit.is/page/5427050#page/n91/mode/2up [accessed: November 2020].

[TK]

---

64 Lines 1–2, cf. *carm.*, PG 37.1287.3–4; l. 3 cf. PG 37.1353.12; ll. 5–12 cf. PG 37.779.1–8; ll. 15–16 see *supra*; ll. 19–20 see *supra*; ll. 21–22 cf. PG 37.784.1–2; ll. 25–26 cf. PG 37.1385.5–6; ll. 27–28 cf. PG 37.1428.7–8. Sigurður Pétursson, who published the poem in 1998, did not mention Pálsson's imitation of Gregory of Nazianzus.

List of Contributors

Johanna Akujärvi is Associate Professor of Greek and Research Fellow at the Centre of Languages and Literature at Lund University. Her research interests include Greek literature of the Roman Empire, narratology, and classical tradition. She has extensively worked on the classical tradition in Sweden: its educational contexts, Humanist Greek, and the history of Swedish translations of ancient literature. She is co-editor of the database *Oldtidens og middelalderens litteratur – i skandinaviske oversættelser* (http://skandinaviska-oversattningar.net), is finishing a monograph on the history of ancient literature in Swedish translation, and is project leader of two research projects in those fields: *Classics Refashioned. Swedish Translations of Ancient Literature* (VR 2016-01884) and *Helleno-Nordica. The Humanist Greek Heritage of the Swedish Empire* (VR 2016-01881).

Bartosz B. Awianowicz (PhD and habilitation in Humanities/Literary Studies at Nicolaus Copernicus University in Toruń, 2007 and 2013 respectively) is Professor at the Institute of Literary Studies at Nicolaus Copernicus University in Toruń. He has worked on the theory of ancient rhetoric and its reception in early modern Europe as well as on Latin and bilingual (Latin-Polish, Latin-Greek) panegyrics from the 16th and 17th centuries. He is editor and translator of Cicero's *De oratore* (2010), Latin panegyrics by Eliusz Pielgrzymowski (2012) and Andrzej Patrycy Nidecki (2016), as well as author of many articles on ancient and early modern rhetoric, Greek and Latin epigraphy and numismatic. Currently he participates in a project on Stefan Iavorskii and his intellectual milieu, and in the complete edition of the works by Jan Kochanowski.

William M. Barton is Key Researcher at the Ludwig Boltzmann Institute for Neo-Latin Studies, Innsbruck, and teaches several courses at the local University. His research has focussed principally on the representation of the natural world in the Latin and Greek literatures of the early modern period, including their reception of the long bucolic tradition and their use in contemporary natural philosophical debate. In the course of this work on literary landscapes, he recently produced a critical edition of the late antique *Pervigilium Veneris* (2018).

Martin M. Bauer is Postdoctoral Researcher at the Department of Classical Philology and Neo-Latin Studies at the University of Innsbruck. His broad research interests include Greek epic and lyric poetry, Greek epigraphy, and the reception of classical antiquity, on which he has published several articles. For his PhD, he worked on the image of Islam in Medieval Latin and Byzantine Greek literature, culminating in a new edition of Riccoldo da Monte di Croce's *Epistole ad Ecclesiam triumphantem* (2021). He is currently preparing a book-length study of audience(s) of and in Greek historiography.

Elena Ermolaeva is Associate Professor of Classical Philology at St Petersburg State University. Her main research interests include ancient Greek epic poetry and parody, lexicology, textual criticism, and history of classical scholarship. Her other research themes are the reception of the classics in Russian literature and Humanist Greek in Russia.

Jean-Marie Flamand (PhD at Paris-Sorbonne University in 1980), *Emeritus* Researcher at the Institut de Recherche et d'Histoire des Textes (CNRS, Paris), has worked for a long time on Greek Neoplatonism (Plotinus, Porphyry). His interests then turned towards the history of humanism and the transmission of texts (especially the tradition of Greek philosophy) in 15th/16th-century Europe.

Farkas Gábor Kiss (PhD Budapest, 2006) is a specialist on Latin and Hungarian literature of the later Middle Ages and the Renaissance in East and Central Europe. He has taught at the Ludwig Boltzmann Institute for Neo-Latin Studies at the University of Innsbruck, and is currently the head of the Department of Medieval and Renaissance Hungarian Literature at Eötvös Loránd University, Budapest. His interests include Central European humanism (Johannes Sambucus), the history of reading, the relationship between the vernaculars and Latin, and the late medieval art of memory. He is the leader of the research group 'Humanism in East Central Europe', and is preparing the *Companion to Humanism in Hungary*, an in-depth study of texts and transmissions of humanist authors from Hungary in the period 1420–1620.

Martin Korenjak is Professor of Classical Philology and Neo-Latin at the University of Innsbruck. He has worked on Greek and Latin poetry, literary theory and rhetoric, as well as on the reception of classical antiquity. In recent years, he is mainly concerned with Neo-Latin literature, in which field he has published an overview for a broader readership (*Geschichte der neulateinischen Literatur*, 2016) and an anthology (*Neulatein. Eine Textsammlung*, 2019).

Tua Korhonen, Associate Professor in Greek literature, is currently University Researcher at the Department of Languages (Greek and Latin) at the University of Helsinki, and a member of the project *Helleno-Nordica*. Besides 'Humanist Greek' in early modern Finland and Sweden (e-thesis 2004 on the subject), her other research interests include animals in antiquity.

Han Lamers is Professor of Classics at the University of Oslo. His research concentrates on scholarly, cultural, and ideological receptions of the classical heritage in (early) modern Europe. Recent publications concerning early modern Hellenism include *Receptions of Hellenism in Early Modern Europe, 15th-17th Centuries* (2019), co-edited by Natasha Constantinidou (University of Cyprus), and *Greece Reinvented: Transformations of Byzantine Hellenism in Renaissance Italy* (2015). He also edited a themed issue of the *International Journal of the Classical Tradition* on the history of Greek learning in early modern Europe (Volume 25, 2018, Issue 3) and translated Manuel Chrysoloras' *Comparison of New and Old Rome* (2019), with Nico de Glas, into Dutch.

Gościwit Malinowski (PhD and habilitation in Literary Studies/Ancient Greek Literature at the University of Wrocław, 1999 and 2007 respectively) is Professor at the Institute of Classical, Mediterranean and Oriental Studies at the University of Wrocław. He has worked on Hellenistic Greek historiography, the attitudes toward animals in the ancient world, the ancient and medieval image of East Asia in Greco-Latin literature, and the Greek sources on Polish history (hence his monograph *Hellenopolonica. Miniatures from the Polish-Greek history*). He currently participates in three projects: Roma Sinica Studies, the editions of the *Hodoeporicon* by Iakovos Miloitis and the *opera omnia* of Stanisław Niegoszewski, as well as biographies of Polish Philhellenes for the Society for Hellenism and Philhellenism.

Romain Menini (PhD at Paris-Sorbonne University, 2012) is Associate Professor at the Université Gustave Eiffel. His works focus on Renaissance literature and philology, and on Rabelais in particular (*Rabelais et l'intextexte platonicien*, 2009; *Rabelais altérateur. "Graeciser en François"*, 2014).

András Németh is Vice Director of the Editorial Service of the Vatican Apostolic Library as well as Curator of its Greek manuscripts. He coordinates various activities concerning palimpsests at the Vatican Library, and is preparing the catalogue of a select group of Greek codices. His publications include *The Excerpta Constantiniana and the Byzantine Appropriation of the Past* (CUP, 2018), which was shortlisted and highly commended by the judges of the Runciman Award 2019. Currently he is preparing a monograph on the Greek manuscripts of the Bibliotheca Corviniana.

Janika Päll, Professor and Head of the Department of Classical Philology at the College of World Languages and Cultures at the University of Tartu, also works as a researcher at Tartu University Library, leading the development of the Humanist Greek database (https://humgraeca.utlib.ut.ee/). Next to Humanist Greek, she has published on ancient Greek language and literature, ancient rhetoric and poetics, classical tradition and translation history. She is co-editor of *Acta Societatis Morgensternianae* and author of numerous translations of Greek and Roman literature into Estonian. Currently she is working on a monograph about Pindarising poetry in Greek.

Filippomaria Pontani is Professor of Classical Philology at the University of Venice Ca' Foscari. While primarily concerned with scholarship and manuscript transmission in the Byzantine and humanistic period (from Plutarch's *Natural Questions* to Planudes' edition of Ptolemy, down to Pletho's *De Homero*), he is currently editing the scholia to Homer's *Odyssey* (four volumes so far, 2007–2020; prolegomena: *Sguardi su Ulisse*, 2005). He has published extensively on Greek and Latin texts (from Sappho's *Nachleben* to Callimachus' *Aitia*, from Aeschylus' *Choephori* to Euripides' *Medea*, from the rise of ancient grammar to allegory and the literary *facies* of some ancient myths), as well as on Byzantine, Humanist (Poliziano's *Liber Epigrammatum Graecorum*, 2002; Kondoleon's *Scritti omerici*, 2018) and Modern Greek literature (*Poeti greci del Novecento*, 2010).

Vlado Rezar is Professor of Classical Philology at the University of Zagreb (Faculty of Humanities and Social Sciences). He is primarily concerned with text editing of works of Croatian Humanist writers (Ludovicus Cervarius Tubero's *Commentaria de temporibus suis*, 2001; Damianus Benessa's *De morte Christi*, 2006; Ludovicus Cervarius Tubero's *De origine et incremento urbis Ragusanae*, 2013; Damianus Benessa's *Poemata*, 2017; Nicolaus Petraeus' *Opuscula miscellanea*, forthcoming).

Luigi-Alberto Sanchi (PhD at Scuola Superiore di Studi Storici, San Marino, 2004) is Senior Researcher at the Institut Jean Gaudemet d'histoire du droit (CNRS, Paris), and focuses on the history of classical scholarship. Recently, he published a critical edition with French translation of Guillaume Budé's *De Asse et partibus eius*, books I–III (2018).

Erkki Sironen is since 2001 University Lecturer in Greek Language and Literature and Docent in Greek Philology at the University of Helsinki (where he has taught since 1982) as well as Docent of Ancient Languages and Culture at the University of Oulu since 1998. He is a member of the international research project *Helleno-Nordica*, presently editing ten orations in ancient Greek preserved in Swedish manuscripts. His other research interests include late antique and early Christian epigraphy (published *Inscriptiones Graecae* volumes include Attica [2008] and Corinthia [2018]), verse inscriptions of the imperial period (particularly from Greece and Cyprus), and Neo-Latin poetry of Sweden.

Marcela Slavíková is a classical philologist and an editor of Neo-Latin texts. She works as an editor of Comenius' *Opera omnia* at the Department of Comenius Studies and Early Modern Intellectual History, Institute of Philosophy, Czech Academy of Sciences in Prague. She specialises in the Latin correspondence of Johann Amos Comenius and in Neo-Latin and Humanist Greek poetry of Bohemian origin.

Martin Steinrück obtained his licentiate degree at Basel University, his degree of Docteur ès Lettres at Lausanne University, and his habilitation at Fribourg University (Switzerland), where he currently works as a Lecturer of Greek and Latin and also teaches literature. He has published about 20 monographs and books and numerous articles on Homer, iambography, versification, ancient literature and culture, but also on the classical tradition (including Humanist Greek). He is currently leading the Swiss National Science Foundation's project *Lectures de Jean Bollack* (http://p3.snf.ch/projects-185432).

Raf Van Rooy is Postdoctoral Researcher at KU Leuven and the University of Oslo, funded by the Research Foundation – Flanders, and the European Commission. His research focuses on the reception of ancient Greek language and literature in the early modern period. For his PhD, he investigated the development of the 'dialect' concept from ancient Greece to modern linguistics (*Language or Dialect? The History of a Conceptual Pair*, 2020) and early modern dialectology (*Greece's Labyrinth of Language*, 2020). As a postdoc, he has also studied the cross-linguistic application of Greek categories such as 'aorist' and 'article' and the association of Greek with vernacular tongues. Recently, he has broadened his interest to the teaching of ancient Greek language and literature in the Renaissance and the production of 'new ancient Greek' literature, both with a focus on the early modern Low Countries.

Tomas Veteikis (PhD in Classical Philology, Vilnius University, 2004), is Associate Professor at the Department of Classical Philology at Vilnius University. He has worked on ancient Greek prose, the Greco-Roman classical tradition and its reception, with a special focus on Neo-Latin and Renaissance Greek literature in early modern Lithuania. He has published a number of articles on ancient Greek rhetoric, co-edited and translated into Lithuanian various Neo-Latin texts (e.g., by Nicolaus Hussovianus, Matthaeus Praetorius, Nicolaus Christophorus Chalecki). His recent papers focus on the analysis of both Latin and Humanist Greek texts related to 16th- and 17th-century Lithuania. He currently participates in one local and two international projects related to the mentioned subjects.

Stefan Weise is Professor (*Juniorprofessor*) of Classical Philology/Ancient Greek at the University of Wuppertal. His main research interests include Greek epic and epigrams, late antique poetry, Humanist Greek, classical reception studies, and Neo-Latin. His PhD thesis was an edition and commentary of the Greek poems under the name of Claudian. Since then he has published several conference volumes (*HELLENISTI!*, 2017; *Litterae recentissimae*, 2020; *Hyblaea avena*, 2020, co-edited by Anne-Elisabeth Beron) and a book-length edition of the Greek Renaissance epyllion *Arion* by Laurentius Rhodoman (2019).

Kostas Yiavis is Assistant Professor of Comparative Literature at the University of Thessaloniki. He is interested in the ways in which literature confirms and unsettles other cultural discourses. Yiavis has edited *Imperios and Margarona* (2019), an intriguing Greek romance of the 16th century, straddling the medieval courtly and the Renaissance popular thought-worlds in East and West. A reader-friendly edition of this romance is in press, with a fresh study on the earliest printed literature for women in Greek.

Gerasimos Zoras is Professor of Italian and Comparative Literature at Athens University. He has edited poems in ancient Greek by Italian members of the Roman Accademia dell'Arcadia: *Ελληνόγλωσσα στιχουργήματα Ιταλών λογίων (ΙΖ'-ΙΘ' αιώνες). Η Ακαδημία Arcadia της Ρώμης και η ελληνική παράδοση* (1993), as well as texts in Italian by Heptanesian writers: *Risonanze italiane nel mare Ionio. Testi in italiano di poeti delle Isole Ionie* (2001). Recently he published a collection of eleven studies: *Sulle orme di Dante* (2021). He directs (since 2017) the annual journal *Rivista di letteratura comparata italiana, bizantina e neoellenica*. He is the President of the National Society of Greek Writers, an Honorary Member of the Società Dantesca Italiana in Florence and a Cavaliere of the Italian Republic.

Index Librorum Manuscriptorum

Page numbers with asterisk (*) indicate footnotes.

Antwerp, Plantin-Moretus Museum
– Arch. 1150 a.misc.: 264*

Berlin, Staatsbibliothek
– Lat. Fol. 239: 159

Bruxelles, Bibliothèque Royale de Belgique
– 8471–75: 231

Budapest, Library of the Academy of Sciences
– M.Irod.Irók. 4-r.241/II: 460

Budapest, National Széchényi Library
– Fol. Lat. 3606.II: VII, 410, 421

Cambridge, St. John's College Library
– 287.H.19: 499

Cambridge, Trinity College Library
– O.1.37: 499

Cambridge, University Library
– UA. Char.I.3–6: 490*
– UA. Char.I.4: 528, 532

Castelvecchio, Archivio Pascoli
– cart. LXII, busta 4: 135

Città del Vaticano, Biblioteca Apostolica Vaticana
– Barb. gr. 279: 118–119, 121–122
– Barb. gr. 463: 122
– Borg. gr. 22: 98
– Ferrajoli 514: 602
– Vat. gr. 12: 46
– Vat. gr. 1462: 55

Coimbra, Biblioteca Geral da Universidade
– 993: 571, 575

Dubrovnik, Archivum Monasterii Ragusini Fratrum Minorum (Franjevački samostan Male braće)
– 78: 411

Dubrovnik, Dominican monastery library (Dominikanski samostan)
– 34-IX-1: 448

Évora, Biblioteca Pública
– CVIII/2-7: 569
– CXIII/1-10: 568–569

Firenze, Biblioteca Medicea Laurenziana
– Plut. 31.21: 40
– Plut. 31.24: 40
– Plut. 55.18: 101
– Plut. 58.15: 91, 93
– San Marco 303: 102

Firenze, Biblioteca Marucelliana
– B.I.12: 126

Kassel, Universitätsbibliothek
– 2° Ms. poet. et roman. 7: 155

Leiden, Universiteitsbibliotheek
– SCAL 25: 244
– VUL 97: 241, 243
– VUL 103: 240–243, 560*

Linköping, Diocesan Library (Stiftsbiblioteket)
– W 40: 722

Lisboa, Biblioteca Nacional
– 3308: 570–571

London, British Library
– Add. 8236: 433
– Burney 371: 240

– Royal 12 A XXX: 489*
– Royal 12 A XXXIII: 489*
– Royal 12 A LXVII: 489*
– Royal 16 C X: 495
– Sloane 2764: 219*

Madrid, Biblioteca Nacional
– 3771: 593–595
– 6685: 562*
– 9805: 579
– 9807: 578
– 9813: 578

Madrid, Biblioteca de la Universidad Complutense
– 191: 558, 588

Milano, Biblioteca Ambrosiana
– D 450 inf.: 104
– R 110 sup.: 113–114

München, Bayerische Staatsbibliothek
– Nachlass Bruno Snell, Sign. Ana 490.B.II: 279*

Napoli, Biblioteca Nazionale "Vittorio Emanuele III"
– XIII.A.A.63: 108
– C.L. XXIV.11.b: 132

Nürnberg, Stadtbibliothek
– Cent. V App. 3: 155

Oxford, Bodleian Library
– Tanner 466: 500

Oxford, The Queen's College, Archives
– FB621: 554

Paris, Bibliothèque Nationale de France
– Dupuy 837: 252
– Dupuy 951: 230
– gr. 2879: 46
– gr. 3068: 54
– N.A.F. 6851: 395

Praha, Královská kanonie premonstrátů na Strahově
– DF V 20: 299

Praha/Litoměrice, The Museum of Czech Literature (Památník Národního Písemnictví), Literary Archive
– collection Jan Křesadlo, no. 2110: 303

Roma, Biblioteca Angelica
– C.4.13: 42

St Petersburg, Russian National Library (Rossijskaja nacional'naja biblioteka)
– F.608, I, 4802: 648, 671, 674, 675

Valencia, Biblioteca de la Universidad
– 573: 596–597
– 574: 597

Venezia, Biblioteca Nazionale Marciana
– Marc. gr. 198: 40–41
– Marc. gr. 333: 37–38

Wien, Österreichische Nationalbibliothek
– Phil. gr. 52: 423
– Phil. gr. 202: 654

Wolfenbüttel, Herzog August Bibliothek
– Guelf. 872 Novi: 323

Wrocław, Ossolineum Biblioteka
– 1137: 606*
– XVI.F.4234: 627*

Index Selectivus Personarum

Page numbers with asterisk (*) indicate footnotes; page numbers in bold indicate that the person is part of our selection.

Aagesen, Peder *vide* Haggaeus, Petrus
Achilles 278, 319*, 585, 663, 743
Actaeon 586
Adam 72
Admetus 448
Adonis 121
Adrastea 299, 300*
Aerichalcus, Sebastianus (Měděný, Šebestián) 8, 281*, **286–287**
Aeschylus 206, 219, 271–272, 278, 348, 369, 380, 400, 420, 530, 534, 538, 548, 552, 651, 683
Aesopus 595, 783
Agamemnon 319, 567, 663–664
Agricola, Rodolphus 217*
Ajax 663
Alander, Christiernus 764, **771–773**
Alcaeus 206, 303, 357, 683
Aleandro, Girolamo 50, 85, 114, 365
Alexander the Great 427, 544, 662, 667
Alexander I (emperor of Russia) 445–
Alexiou, Stylianos 36, **80–81**
Allacci, Leone 5, 10, 16–17, 27, 34–35, **66–70**, 87, 119, 122,
Amalteo, Giovan Battista 8, 13, 72, 86, **112–115**, 405,
Amalthea 227
Ammon (Zeus) 435–436
Ampelander (Rebmann), Valentin 312, 324–325
Amphitryo 56, 794
Amyntas 702–705
Anacreon 134, 193, 229, 234, 377, 392, 446, 516–518, 595
Androvich, Nicolaus 405, **447–450**
Antipater of Sidon 185
Apelles 45, 229
Aphrodite (Cypris; Cytherea; Paphia; Venus) 97, 99, 121, 180, 234, 254, 260, 364–365, 371, 375–376, 394, 396, 449, 474–475, 481, 509, 516, 586, 619, 634, 696, 702, 705, 759
Apollo (Phoebus) 51, 101, 104, 108–109, 193–194, 263, 266, 271–272, 288, 289*, 304, 325, 327, 344, 352, 359*, 371, 430, 442, 445–446, 448, 521–522, 537, 540, 578, 580, 586, 682, 669, 696, 703, 750, 772
Apollonius of Rhodes 41, 46, 114, 581, 745
Aponte, Manuel 9, 88, 131, 563, 596, **599–602**
Apostolis, Aristoboulos (Arsenios) 33, 41, 46, 50, **52–55**, 102, 226
Apostolis, Michael 41
Aquilonius, Bertel Knudsen 792, **796–798**
Aramonero, Diogenes 562
Aratus 114, 320, 354, 377
Archilochus 285, 325, 341, 356–357, 759
Arcudi, Francesco 34, 87, 119, **120–123**
Ares 104, 180, 200, 234, 364, 373, 422, 441, 476, 509–510, 516, 586, 613, 622, 633, 738
Argyropoulos, John 32, 83, 99
Arion 180–181
Aristophanes 50, 103, 109, 171, 206, 380, 388, 393, 404, 551
Aristotle 52, 102–103, 219, 226, 253, 331, 415, 427, 430, 446, 571
Artemis 197, 461, 586, 705
Ascham, Roger 489
Athena (Pallas) 244, 257, 263, 275, 296, 327, 379–380, 441, 443, 445, 540, 586, 596, 598, 619, 658, 664, 667, 696, 702–705, 753
Athenaeus 103, 331, 388, 536
Atlas 119
Aurivillius, Petrus 732, **736–739**

Ausius, Henrik (Henricus) 731–732, **735–736**, 740
Averani, Benedetto 88
Ayland, Henry 494
Aylmer, John 314

Bacchus *vide* Dionysus
Bade, Josse 360*, 382
Baffi, Pasquale 9, 13, 28, 88, **125–129**, 443, 650*
Baïf, Jean-Antoine de VII, 7, 358, 360, 369, **370–372**
Baïf, Lazare de 369, 371
Baldani, Grigory 443, 652, **668–670**
Barberini, Francesco 65, 122
Barberini, Maffeo (Pope Urbanus VIII) 6, 27, 87, 119, **123–125**
Barbosa, Aires 559–560
Barnes, Joshua 10, 486, **514–518**
Basil of Caesarea 93, 595
Belaras, Nikolaos 407
Belisarius 438–440, 442
Belleau, Rémy 360, **376–378**
Bembo, Pietro 43, 85, 103, 365
Benessa, Damianus 5, 13, 404, **411–414**
Bentley, Richard 10, 486, 517, 523, 526, 541
Bérauld, François 360, **372–374**
Beregzazius, Johannes (Beregszászi, János) 452, **465–467**
Berenice 703
Bergman, Johan(nes) 9, 733, **758–759**, 779
Beroe 260
Bessarion, Basilios 16, 32, **37–39**, 40–41
Beza, Theodorus (Théodore de Bèze) 8, 312, 330, 333, 364, 464
Bilberg, Johan 732, **752–754**
Binnart, Martin 261–264
Bion 243, 253, 260
Birkowski, Szymon 608
Bismarck, Otto von 210–211
Blackie, John Stuart 486
Blomqvist, Jerker 733, **761–762**
Blondetus, Franciscus 312, 333*
Bodoni, Giambattista 130–131
Boeckh, August 151–152, 178, 400

Boivin, Jean 9, 359, 391–393
Bojer, Lars 636
Bonamico, Lazaro 50, 85, **104–105**, 111
Bonifacius, Johannes 452, 454*
Boreas 79, 540–541
Bornmann, Christian 780
Borovsky, Iakob M. 10, 651, **684–687**
Borrichius, Petrus Ivarus 7, 27, 726, 792, **794–796**
Bouboulios, Nikolaos 35
Boulgaris, Eugenios 9, 28, 443, 650, 652, **658–661**
Bovillius, Petrus (Bouille, Pierre) 217*
Brâncoveanu, Constantine 406, 429
Brie, Germain de (Brixius, Germanus) 5, **364–365**
Brillius, Urban 608
Brockmann, Reiner 779
Brodeau, Jean 363
Bromios *vide* Dionysus
Brunius, Carl 733*
Brunnerus, Martin 732, **739–740**, 743, 746
Bucer, Martin 493–494
Budé, Guillaume 5, 7, 46, 360–361, 362–363, 365, 567, 805
Bullinger, Heinrich 310, 322, 464
Burghauser, Jarmil 283*
Burgman, Johannes 763
Butler, Samuel 485*, 534
Buxtorf, Johann Jakob 351
Byron, George Gordon VII, 4, 30, 36, 76, 77, 544–545

Caesar (Gaius Iulius) 142, 271–273, 307*, 600
Cajanus Jr, Johan 764, **768–769**
Callimachus 14, 186, 243, 260, 377, 549*, 761, 805
Calliope 73, 346, 633, 667
Camerarius, Joachim 6–7, 26, 57, 86, 112, 149, 163, **165–168**, 175, 308, 376, 420
Campanus, Johannes (Vodňanský, Jan) **295–296**
Campomanes, Antonio 28, 563
Carlile, Christopher 494
Carpzov, Friedrich Benedikt 193–194

Carr, Nicholas 494
Casaubon, Isaac 16, 64, 311, **328–331**, 382, 387, 504, 755
Caselius, Johannes 149, 164, **174–176**
Casimirus, St 635–636
Castellio (Châtillon), Sebastianus 26, 309, 313
Castrobello, Stephanus a (Beauchasteau, Étienne de) 312, 333
Catherine II (Empress of Russia) 9, 28, 88, 127–129, 441, 443, 649–651, 658, 660–662, 665, 667, 669–670
Catullus 7, 13, 76, 245–246, 249, 323, 389, 394, 603, 680
Cazzaniga, Ignazio 89
Cecrops 696
Cedrenus, Georgius 43
Celtis, Conrad 5, 148, **155–156**, 157, 345
Ceporinus, Jacobus (Wiesendanger, Jakob) 8, 310, **317–321**
Chalkondyles/Chalkokondyles, Demetrios 32, 41, 83, 98–99, 404
Champ-Renaud, Abraham 312, 314
Chapouthier, Fernand 359, **401–402**
Charites vide Graces
Charles III (King of Spain) 563, 592–593
Charles XI (King of Sweden) 727, 747
Charopus, Andreas 8, 690, **693–698**
Châtillon, Odet de 368–369
Cheke, John 26, 488–489, **493–495**, 500
Chénier, André 9, 359, **395–398**, 488
Chiron 751
Chloris 625
Chrestien, Florent 7, 196, 314, 361, **378–381**
Christ vide Jesus
Christian IV (King of Denmark) 792, 799
Christina (Queen of Sweden) 261, 733, 791
Christopherson, John 10, 26, 472, 489, 490*, **498–501**, 552
Chryseus, Bartholomaeus 453
Chrysogonos of Trebizond, Georgios 9, 407, **431–433**
Chrysoloras, Manuel 3, 25, 83, 804
Chrysostom vide John Chrysostom
Chydenius, Anders 764

Cicero, Marcus Tullius 142, 269, 354, 571, 642, 696, 792, 803
Ciriaco of Ancona 83
Claudian 697, 807
Clio 73, 344, 346, 630, 633, 667
Clotho 473
Cnapius, Gregorius VIII, 8, 604, 607–608, **636–639**
Coddaeus, Gulielmus (van der Codde, Willem) 242, 254, 257
Collinus, Matthaeus (Matouš) 26, 281–282, 285, **288–289**
Columbus, Johannes Jonae 732, **741–743**
Columbus, Jonas Svenonis 739–740, 743
Comnenos, Ioannes Molyvdos 9, 407, **426–429**
Corenzio, Belisario 34, **65–66**
Correas, Gonzalo 562, **582–584**
Cortona, Pietro 26, 86, **110–112**
Corybants 299
Corydon 222, 704
Crashaw, Richard 487, 489*
Crinesius, Christophorus 8, **297–298**
Croke, Richard 149, 164, 167, 488
Crusius, Martin 4, 7, 13, 27, 147, 150, **168–172**, 186, 196, 308, 388, 770
Cuenca, Juan de 563
Culpeper, John 494
Cunich, Raimondo 405, 449
Cunitz, David 779
Cupid vide Eros
Cybele 299
Cyclops 509–510
Cynthius vide Apollo
Cypris vide Aphrodite
Cytherea vide Aphrodite

Dacier, Anne 9, 206, 359, 390, 392
Daedalus 287, 663
Damoetas 521–523
Daneau, Lambert 311
Danès, Pierre 25, 365
D'Angour, Armand 29, 483–484, 490, **554–557**
Danielewicz, Jerzy Kazimierz 8, 10, 13, 29, 606, **644–647**
Daphnis 391, 523, 702–706

Darvaris, Demetrios 408, **444–447**
Dazzi, Andrea 85
Demeter 232, 247, 357
de Miro, Giovan Battista 88, 128
Demosthenes 164, 400, 404, 503, 511, 595, 792
dèr Mouw, Johan Andreas 4, 10, 29, 218–220, **270–276**
Derzhavin, Gavriil 676
Devaris, Matthaios 33
Dictys Cretensis 43
Dio Chrysostom 93, 331
Diogenes the Cynic 250
Diogenes Laertius 250, 329, 331, 359
Dionysus (Bacchus; Bromios) 185, 193, 247, 260–261, 379–380, 392, 516, 586, 682–683
Dolios 339
Dolscius, Paul 149, 164, 308, 313
Dömötöri, György 454
Dorat, Jean 7–8, 26, 235, 312, 360, **366–370**, 371, 377, 380, 452
Doukas, Demetrios 25, 32, **51–52**, 560
Downes, Andrew 489, **502–504**, 505
Draski, Adam 608
Du Bellay, Joachim 312, 360–361, 364, 369
Dunte, Georg 8, 779, **786–788**
Duport, James 196, 202, 252, 487, 489, **508–511**

Echo 702
Electra 96, 98–99, 452
Elizabeth I (Queen of England) 488–489, 496–497, 501, 503
Endymion 193
Engel (Angelus), Arnoldus 6, 283, **298–301**, 785
Engels, Friedrich 10, 29, 152, **207–209**, 488
Eos 435, 478, 742
Epaminondas 625–626
Eparchos, Antonios 33, **55–57**
Epicharmus 38, 273
Erasmus of Rotterdam, Desiderius 6, 16, 25, 103, 163, 174, 217, 219–220, **222–228**, 308, 365, 382, 388, 415, 451, 457, 488, 560, 709,
Erato 73, 346, 619, 633
Erinys 72, 170, 619
Eros/Erotes (Cupid) 97, 108–109, 160, 180, 205, 234–235, 260, 263, 356, 375, 392, 394, 461, 476, 586, 602, 675
Esteve, Pedro Jaime 6, 561, 567
Estienne, Henri II 5, 8, 196, 243, 307–308, 311, 314, 326, 329–330, 346, 361, 374, 376–377, 380, **381–382**
Estienne, Robert 8, 26, 307–308, 311, 346, 360, 369, 380, 382
Eteocles 29, 152, 208, 673
Etheridge, George 489, **495–498**
Euripides 41, 54, 164, 213, 275, 371, 380, 400, 402, 501, 517, 525, 530, 556, 567, 581, 651, 686, 805
Europia *vide* Hera
Euros 79
Eusebeia (personification) 619
Eustathius of Thessalonica 225*, 227, 581, 661
Euterpe 73, 346, 634
Eyth, Eduard 29, 147*, 152, **199–202**

Faberius, Martin 282*
Fabricius, Georg 690, 697
Fabricius, Johann Albert 194
Fabricius, Theodosius 188
Faesch, Sebastian 346, **347–349**, 352
Falander, Ericus 764
Fant, Erik Michael 17, 723, 724*, 731*
Fausto, Vettor 560
Favorino, Guarino 102
Faye, Antoine de la (Fayus, Antonius) 311
Fehér, Bence 11, 13, 455, **477–481**, 776
Fibiger, Peter Grib 792*
Filelfo, Francesco 1–2, 7, 13, 17, 32, 38, 84, **91–94**, 97, 112, 404
Filelfo, Senofonte 404
Finkelthaus, Wolfgang 169, 171
Flacius Illyricus, Matthias 405, 420
Floderus, Matthias 17, 723, 724*, 731*, 755
Foreestius, Johannes (von Foreest, Jan) 27, 44, 181, 219, **259–261**

Forteguerri (Carteromaco), Scipione 85, **100–103**, 254
Francis I (King of France) 6, 46, 57, 364–365, 369, 373, 380
Francius, Petrus (de Frans, Pieter) 9, 194, 219–220, 264–270, 391
Francis Xavier, St 579–581, 595, 638–639
Francke, August Hermann 196
Francke, Martin 778, 780, **789–790**
Freitag Maior, Adam 608
Frere/Fryer, John 494
Freyer, Hieronymus 17, 196
Friderici, Aggaeus 779
Friedländer, Paul 152, 213, **214–215**
Frischlin, Nicodemus 150, **184–186**, 308
Froben, Johann 243, 307, 376, 382
Führer, Rudolf 357
Fuhrmann, Arnold 780

Gabriel (archangel) 186–187, 747
Galen(us) 111, 566–567
Garbitius Illyricus, Matthias 8, 164, 405, **416–421**
Garibaldi, Giuseppe 89, 136
Gaurico, Pomponio 17, 86, **107–110**
Gautier, Théophile 4, 537–538
Gaza (Gazes), Theodore 41, 65, 83, 164
Geometres, John 31
George I (King of Greece) 544–545
George I (King of Great Britain and Ireland) 522–523
George II (King of Great Britain and Ireland) 522–523, 530
George III (King of the United Kingdom) 487, 529
Gessner, Konrad 7–8, 312, **321–326**, 339, 342
Gezelius Sr, Johannes 732, 763, **782–783**, 785
Goethe, Johann Wolfgang von 152, 206, 212–213, 484, 674, 680, 683
González de Torres, Francisco Antonio 563
Gothus, Laurentius Petri 726, 731
Gothus, Matthaeus 7–8, 12, 27, 147, 150, 164, **186–188**, 313
Götsch, Peter 778–779

Gozze, Ioannes 404
Graces (Charites) VIII, 56, 104, 109, 113, 445–446, 521, 576–577, 580, 586, 619, 626, 633, 688, 696, 702–703, 715, 717, 745, 767
Graefe, Christian Friedrich VIII, 9–10, 16, 28, 648, 651–652, **670–677**
Gregoras, Metrophanes 407
Gregory of Nazianzus 5, 18, 31, 59, 98, 111, 158, 264, 413, 629, 638, 801
Grocyn, William 488
Grotius, Hugo 8, 27, 220, **236–240**, 242–243, 245, 250, 252–253
Grynaeus, Simon 219, 226, 309
Guarino Veronese 451
Guttovieni, József 8, 454, **468–470**
Gwalther (Gualtherus), Rudolf 310

Haggaeus, Petrus (Aagesen, Peder) 726, 791
Haller, Johannes 312, 324, 325*
Harckman, Ericus **784–786**
Hasištejnský z Lobkovic, Bohuslav 281, **285–286**
Headlam, Walter 10, 13, 485, 530, **546–549**
Hedelinus, Petrus 752, **754–755**
Hegesander 171, 388*
Heinsius, Daniel 7, 27, 219–220, 239–240, 242–243, 245, **246–254**, 260–261, 510, 750, 755
Helen(a) 32, 43–44, 183, 589, 681, 683
Helios 180, 703
Hellopoeus *vide* Zykzai
Henisch, Georg 452
Henry VIII (King of England) 489, 496–497, 500
Hephaestus 180, 379, 467, 663
Hera 180, 696, 702, 704–705
Heracles/Hercules 7, 56, 104–105, 128, 192, 386–387, 585, 726, 792, 794–795
Heraclitus (philosopher) 759
Heraclitus (poet) 549*
Herbert, George 10, 487–488, 490*, **504–506**
Herder, Johann Heinrich VII, 306, **353–355**

Hermann, Gottfried 151, 204, 212–213, 525–526, 651, 673, 676–677
Hermes 76, 119, 327, 445, 540
Hero 51
Herodotus 74, 103, 181, 362, 382, 484*, 545, 731
Herrichen, Johann Gottfried 7, 9, 13, 28, 109, 151, **189–195**, 196, 267, 391, 472, 500, 517, 583
Herschel, William 487, 528–529
Hesiod 202, 253, 268, 285, 287, 294, 319
Hesychius of Alexandria 50, 103, 242, 255*, 258, 268, 574
Hippocrates 93, 111, 363
Hoděiovský, Jan (the Elder) 285, 289
Holstenius, Ericus 732, 785
Homer 5, 25, 33, 41, 50, 54, 83–84, 99, 101, 134, 163, 183, 213, 219, 227, 232, 239, 257–258, 260, 264, 278, 285, 303, 338, 348, 352, 369, 392–393, 397, 404, 418, 425, 445, 449, 452–453, 497, 503, 516–517, 522, 524, 538, 581, 595, 598, 601, 616, 620, 650, 658, 674, 678–679, 718, 759, 770, 776, 806
Horace 7, 13, 110, 196, 202, 205–206, 319, 325, 327, 341, 345, 376, 477, 486, 537, 576, 642, 711, 759, 780
Horai 540
Hörnick, Johannes 779
Huet, Pierre-Daniel 7, 267, **389–391**
Huszti, Georgius 454
Hydra 664
Hymen(aeus) 619
Hypischiotes, Michael Goras 408, **434–436**

Iamblichus 241
Icarus 75–76, 287
Idiáquez, Francisco Javier 563, 595
Ignatius of Loyola VII–VIII, 8, 107, 595, 604, 608, 637–639
Illuminati, Luigi 89, **141–142**
Ioannou, Philippos 11, 29, **74–76**
Iris 76, 663, 669
Istvanffius, Nicolaus (Istvánffy, Miklós) 5, 451, **460–462**
Ivanov, Vyacheslav I. 651, **680–683**

Jamot, Frédéric 217, 219, **232–235**, 314
Jason 113–114
Jebb, Richard Claverhouse 13, 485, **539–542**
Jeckelmann, Heinrich **334–336**
Jensius, Johannes 269
Jeremiah 169, 171, 335
Jespersen, Jakob 724, 726, 791
Jesus (Christ) 5, 58, 73, 87, 116, 124, 141, 170, 186–188, 190–191, 290, 299, 313, 323, 419–420, 422, 425, 433, 435, 463, 466, 469, 471, 566–567, 573, 579, 589, 593, 600, 616, 681, 696, 745, 750, 767, 790, 799
Johansson, Albert 10, 733
John Chrysostom 365, 374, 488, 494, 711
Johnson, Samuel 484, 487, 517, **524–525**
Junius (de Jon), Franciscus 311
Juslenius, Daniel 764

Kaibel, Georg 209–211, 213
Kalliergis, Zacharias 50, 102, 107
Kallistos, Andronikos 32–33, **39–42**, 57, 83
Karakassis, Dimitrios 691
Karyophylles, Ioannes Matthaios 34, **64–65**, 69
Kavalliotes, Theodoros 407
Keate, John 529, 534
Keramopoulos, Antonios 36, **78–79**
Kigalas, Ioannes 34
Klage, Thomas 608
Klopstock, Friedrich Gottlieb 13–14, 151, **197–198**, 488
Knauth, Samuel 196
Knox, Ronald A. 10, 29, 485, 487, 489*, **549–552**, 776
Köchly, Hermann VII, 146, **203–204**
Kock, Theodor 212, 213*, 484
Kokkos, Phrangiskos 34
Kolettis, Liberios 35
Kollár, Adam Franz VIII, 9, 13, 28, 523, 688, 690, **698–707**
Kondoleon, Christophoros 33
Kondos, Polyzoes 9, 28, 454, **472–473**
Koressios, Georgios 11, 34, **62–64**

Korsch, Theodorus (Fyodor Yevgenievich) 11, 13, 29, 651, **678–680**
Korydalleus, Theophilos 34
Kottounios, Ioannes 34–35
Krajkowski, Joannes 636
Křesadlo, Jan VII, 11, 13, 29, 280, 281*, 283, **301–305**, 480, 490, 553, 554*, 776
Krieschke, Georg 453, 454*
Kronos 119, 160, 380, 522, 696
Krüger Mesylanus, Gregor 8, 724, 726, 778
Kylander, Jonas Nicolai 8, 731
Kyminetes, Sebastos 407

Labé, Louise 7, 375–376
Lachmann, Karl 152, 535*
Lacki, Franciscus 606*, 608, **621–623**
Laertes 339
La Monnoye, Bernard de 7, 359, **393–395**
Lampsonius, Dominicus VII, 216, 227, **228–231**, 234, 266
Lamy, Pierre 362–363
Lapini, Walter *vide* Rissa, Alvaro
Laskai Csókás, Péter (Lascovius de Barovia, Petrus) 453, 454*
Laskaris, Ianos 5, 16–17, 25–26, 32–33, **44–47**, 50, 54, 57, 84–85, 98, 148, 161, 167, 254, 360*, 365, 404, 413, 649, 656
Laskaris, Konstantinos 32
Lassala y Sangermán, Manuel 9, 543, 567, **595–597**
Laurbecchius, Petrus 763
Lauridsen, Niels 791
Lavater, Johannes 310, **340–343**
Leander 51
Leda 43, 149, 179–181
Ledesma, Miguel de 5–6, 561, **565–567**
Leo X (Pope) 33, 46, 50, 54
Leo the Philosopher 61
Leonhartus, Albertus **293–294**
Leonidas 57
Leopardi, Giacomo 9, 89, **131–134**, 541–542
Leto 344, 430, 540, 702
Leuschner, Georg 196
Levakovich, Raphael 406, **424–426**
Lilius, Henrik 764

Linacre, Thomas 5, 103, 488
Linder, Emanuel 309*, 310
Linders, Tullia 761–762
Lizelius, Georg(ius) 17, 28, 148, 171, 196, 333
Lochmann, Matthias 453, **467–468**
López de Ayala, Ignacio 563
Lorenz, Paul Raimund 691–692
Louis XIV (King of France) 35, 69
Lucian of Samosata 46, 157, 223, 363, 567
Luís de Portugal 569, 571
Lund, David 764
Luria, Salomo 651, 685
Lycophron 366, 369, 371, 581
Lynceus 439–440, 528
Lysias 93, 503

Macías, Miguel 14, **594–595**
Mahlstedt, Arnold 780
Mai, Angelo 134
Maia 119
Makraios, Sergios 9, 72, 691
Malalas, John 43
Manuzio, Aldo 25, 33, 46, 50, 54, 85, **100–103**, 148, 156, 356, 404, 627, 649
Manuzio il Giovane, Aldo 627
Marennius, Stanisław 608
Margounios, Maximos 34, **60–61**
Maria Theresia (Holy Roman Empress) 690, 706–707
Mariner, Vicente 6, 562, 567, **577–581**
Maro *vide* Virgil
Marschalk, Nicolaus 148, 155, **158–159**
Marthius, Michael 453, 454*
Martí, Manuel 9, 562, 567, **584–587**
Martial 246, 486, 587, 709
Martinengo, Tito Prospero 8, 27, 87, **115–118**
Martínez de Quesada, Antonio VII, 558, 563, **587–591**
Martini, Olaus 8, 731
Marvell, Andrew 487
Mary I (Queen of England) 46, 229, 489, 494, 497, 501
Matthaei, Christian Friedrich 650
Mavrocordatos, Alexander 428

Maxim the Greek (Trivolis, Michael) 5, 9, 25, 649, 652, **654–657**
Maximilian I (Holy Roman Emperor) 69, 318–320
Maximilian II (Holy Roman Emperor) 423, 460–461, 617, 697
Mayr, Ludwig 10, 29, **712–719**
Meiler, Jacob **331–333**
Mekerchus, Adolphus 230
Melanchthon, Philipp 6, 25, 57, 112, 147, 149, 151, **162–165**, 167, 175, 183, 243, 287, 289, 308–309, 405, 420, 452, 464, 690, 696–697, 763
Melinno 601
Melissa 299, 300*
Melissus Schede, Paulus 698
Melpomene 73, 346, 633
Ménage, Gilles 7, 171, 359, **387–389**
Menchaca, Roque 14, **593–595**
Menelaos 43, 278
Mercado, Pedro 563
Metaxopoulos, Parthenios 407
Methodius of Olympus 121–123
Meursius, Johannes 242
Michelangelo Buonarroti 33, 45–46
Micyllus, Jacob(us) 26, 149, 166, 308, 420
Milo of Croton 63
Milton, John 3, 72, 487, **506–508**
Miltopaeus, Martin 764, **766–767**
Mimnermus 759
Mladenovich, Jovan 408, **437–438**
Mnemosyne 77, 182, 440, 442, 449
Moira/Moirai 166, 214, 380, 448, 473, 479, 521, 549, 592, 622, 659, 751
Molière (= Jean-Baptiste Poquelin) 359
Moller, Heinrich 731
Montaigne, Michel de 7, 383–384
Montmaur, Pierre de 388–389
Moore, Abraham 10, 487, **527–530**
More/Morus, Thomas 365
Morel, Fédéric II 373–374
Morgenstern, Christian 304
Moro, Antonio (Mor van Dashorst, Anthonis) VII, 216, 227, 229
Moschopolites, Gregorios Konstantinos 408

Moschos, Demetrios 16–17, 25, 32, **42–44**, 149*, 181
Moschus 134, 243, 253, 260, 768
Motte, Antoine Houdar de la 392
Mousouros, Markos 4, 16, 25, 33, 46, **47–51**, 52, 54, 57, 98, 103, 105, 109, 148–149, 164, 243, 254, 365, 451, 657
Müller, Eberhard 779, 787–788
Murray, Gilbert 2
Musculus, Wolfgang 312, 324
Muse(s) (Pierides) 53–54, 73, 135, 157, 165, 173, 182–184, 188, 201, 210, 214, 218, 238, 252, 263, 266, 268, 285, 296, 299, 304, 313, 335, 345–346, 352, 356–357, 368–369, 379–380, 392, 418, 422, 428, 430, 432, 439–440, 445–446, 451, 463, 496, 521–522, 533, 537, 540, 544–545, 576, 578, 580, 586, 613, 622, 625, 633, 645, 658, 666–667, 681, 696–697, 702–704, 738, 755, 772
Mylius, Johannes 7–8, 16, 147, 196, 607–608, **615–617**

Naiad(s) 49, 106
Navarro, Martín Miguel 7, 562
Neander, Michael 7, 26, 149–150, 164, 171, 175, 183, 188, 308, 617
Nestor 585, 622, 623*
Newton, Isaac 440, 442, 529
Nicander 377
Niedermühlbichler, Bernhard 11, 691, **708–711**
Niegossevius (Niegoszewski), Stanislaus 8, 176, **623–627**, 804
Nielsen, Torben 791
Nijhoff, Guillaume ('Pim') 274–275
Nonnus of Panopolis 5, 12, 18, 26, 84, 98–99, 164, 204, 253, 260–261, 264, 187, 423, 460, 567, 676–677, 745, 761
Norrmannus, Laurentius (Norrman, Lars) VIII, 722, 732, **744–746**, 755
Norsa, Medea 140
Notaras, Dimitrios 407, **429–431**
Nothmann, Erich 780
Notos 79
Núñez, Pedro Juan 561, 567
Núñez de Guzmán, Hernán 415, 560

Núñez Vela, Pedro 8, 312, 560, **572–574**
Nycopensis, Nicolaus 763
Nymphs 106–107, 583–584, 625

Occo III, Adolph 326
Ochsner, Konrad 311*, 339
Odysseus (Ulysses) 43, 319*, 338–339, 742–743, 772
Olahus, Nicolaus (Oláh, Miklós) 451, **457–458**, 459, 461
Oporinus, Johannes 8, 25, 172, 181, 188, 307, 309–310, 313, 366, 382, 459–460
Oppian 258, 380, 580
Oreithyia 541
Origen(es) 227, 352, 391
Orlov, Alexei 663, 665
Orlov, Grigory 667
Orpheus 368, 397, 425, 522, 696
Östling, Erik Engelbert 9, 733, **756–758**
Ovid 76, 269, 322–323, 371, 686, 742

Palaemon 521–523
Palaeologus, Jacobus (Giacomo da Chio) 453
Palladas 38
Palladoklis, Antonios 9, 443, 652, **661–667**
Pallas *vide* Athena
Palmireno, Juan Lorenzo 6, 561, 567
Pálsson, Torfi 792, **800–801**
Pan 95, 98, 585, 702
Pannonius, Janus 451
Paphia(n) *vide* Aphrodite
Pardo Figueroa y Valladares, Benito **597–598**
Paris (son of Priamus) 43, 476
Parvi, Andreas 454
Pascoli, Giovanni 17, 89, **134–137**, 488
Patousas, Georgios 35, **73–74**
Paul III (Pope) 33, 56
Paulinus, Henrik 764
Paulinus, Johan 5, 7, 15, 27, 488, 726, 728*, 732, 750, 764, **769–771**, 776
Paulinus, Simon 764
Peitho 537, 696
Peleus 449, 544–545
Penelope 339, 742, 772

Pericles 33, 57, 696
Persephone 232, 251, 750
Pétau, Denis 8, 27, 119, 361, **385–387**
Petit, Pierre 194, 267
Pętkowski, Kaspar 608
Petraeus, Aeschillus 8, 763
Petrarch (Petrarca, Francesco) 1, 5, 93, 115, 246, 479, 683
Peutinger, Conrad 160
Peutinger, Constantia 5, 148, 159–160
Phemius 772
Philaras, Leonardos 7, 34–35, **70–72**
Philip IV (King of Spain) 580, 583
Philodemus of Gadara 254
Phocylides 141, 767, 773
Phoebus *vide* Apollo
Pico della Mirandola, Giovanni 161, 649, 656
Pierides *vide* Muses
Pimenta, Nicolau **574–577**
Pindar 7, 10, 12–13, 25–26, 29, 31, 35, 41, 72, 76, 78, 86, 88, 114, 117–118, 128–129, 150, 164, 178, 186, 194, 208, 217*, 219–220, 234–235, 238–239, 245, 267, 278, 313–315, 320, 348, 369, 413, 418, 445, 477, 490, 503, 517, 530, 534–535, 541–542, 544–545, 577, 581, 595, 606, 608, 626, 642, 683, 691, 726, 779, 805
Pirckheimer, Willibald 5, 148, 155, **157–158**
Pires, Diogo *vide* Pyrrhus, Didacus
Planoudes/Planudes, Maximos 31, 363, 805
Plato 4, 25, 32–33, 38, 40–41, 46, 49–50, 57, 83, 98–99, 103, 201–202, 213, 215, 243, 254, 274–275, 311–312, 356–357, 362–363, 382, 433, 446, 453, 471, 536, 622
Pletho, Georgios Gemistos 32, 38, 41, 805
Plutarch 50, 52, 93, 157, 202, 278, 311, 363, 407, 451, 497, 768, 805
Pluto 751
Polanus, Henricus 8, **291–293**
Poliziano, Angelo 1, 4–6, 14, 17, 25, 32–33, 41, 46, 50, 84–86, **94–100**, 102, 112, 148–149, 159, 161, 167, 252, 254,

404, 413, 510, 559–560, 649, 656, 710, 770, 772, 805
Polydamas 63
Polyhymnia 345–346, 631, 634
Polynices 29, 152, 208, 673
Pontani, Filippo Maria 89*
Pontén, Frithiof 760
Porson, Richard 486, **525–527**
Portus, Aemilius (Porto, Emilio) 196, 311, 313, 329
Portus, Franciscus (Porto, Francesco) 34, 311, 314, 325–326, 329
Porzio, Gregorio 34, 87, **118–120**
Poseidon 133, 260, 663
Posselius, Johannes 8, 149, **172–174**, 196
Postelnikos, Ioannes 407
Potemkin, Grigory 660–661, 667, 670
Prilussius, Jacobus **612–614**
Prodicus 795
Prodromos, Theodore 31, 54
Prometheus 45, 420
Propertius 104, 246, 680, 732, 754
Prosdokonymus, Jan 282*
Protogenes 65–66
Psellos, Michael 53–54
Ptolemy (Claudius Ptolemy) 103, 158
Ptolemy III (King of Egypt) 703
Pylades 362
Pyrrhus, Didacus (Pires, Diogo) 26, 405, **414–416**, 560
Pythagoras 241, 748
Pythia 681

Quévedo, Francisco de 577–578, 580–581

Rabelais, François 4, 360, **362–363**, 805
Rebelo Gonçalves, Francisco 11, 563, **602–603**
Rebmann *vide* Ampelander
Reiske, Ernestine Christine 206
Retellius Sittaviensis, Michael 26, **617–620**
Reuchlin, Johannes 5, 148–149, **159–162**, 163–164, 217*, 319–320, 489
Reusner, Nicolaus 7, 13, 16, 147, 150, **176–179**, 196

Rezandrus, Petrus 733*
Rhea 119
Rhodinos, Neophytos 425, 562
Rhodoman, Laurentius 4, 7–8, 13, 27, 44, 117, 147, **179–184**, 187–188, 246, 308, 626, 774, 807
Richter, Julius 10, 29, 152, **204–207**, 500, 776
Rissa, Alvaro (Lapini, Walter) 10–11, 29, 90, **142–145**, 500, 776
Rithaymer, Georg 452, 460
Ritschl, Friedrich Wilhelm 152
Rittershausen, Konrad 61
Robertson, George Stuart 10, 13, 29, 484, **542–545**, 556
Robortello, Francesco 26, 72, 86, 175
Rodríguez de Castro, José 6, 563, **591–593**
Romanos the Melodist 31
Ronsard, Pierre de VII, 312, 358, 360, 366–369, 371, 377, 380, 388
Rostovtsev, Mikhail Ivanovich 680–682, 685
Runeberg, Johan Ludvig 11, 28, 688, 764, **775–777**
Runnerberg, E. 733*

Sadolin, Hans Jørgensen 792*
Saint-Martin, Jean de (Sammartinus, Johannes) **382–384**
Salanus, Jonas Jonae 732
Salanus, Nicolaus 735–736
Salemann, Georg 788
Salemann, Joachim 779
Sambucus, Johannes (Zsámboky, János) VII, 451, 456, **458–460**, 656, 804
Sannazaro, Jacopo 6, 109–110, 378, 461
Saphirides, Pavel (Paulus) 282*
Sappho 7, 88, 131, 157, 205, 212–213, 234, 285, 303, 345, 357, 375–376, 392, 475, 480, 486, 529*, 530, 556, 642, 676, 680, 683, 805
Satyrs 585
Scala, Alessandra 33, 97–99, 148, 161
Scaliger, Joseph Justus 7, 217, 219, 239, **243–246**, 248, 250, 253, 261, 308, 329–331, 387–388, 755

Schadewaldt, Wolfgang 213
Schiller, Friedrich (von) 10, 76, 212, 672–674, 680
Schmidius, Erasmus 196
Schoenaeus, Andreas 608
Schultz, Georg 779
Schulze, Johann Heinrich **195–197**, 707
Schweizer (Suicerus), Johann (Hans) Kaspar 311, 314, 352
Sebastian, St 6, 124
Sebastian (King of Portugal) 575–577
Selene 133–134, 193, 521–522, 703
Semitelos, Demetrios VII, 4, 30, 36, **77–78**
Serres, Jean de (Serranus, Johannes) 312, 314
Siciliano, Saverio 89
Sidgwick, Arthur 485
Silius Italicus 413
Simias of Rhodes 119
Simonides 53, 759
Skordylis, Zacharias 34, **58–59**
Slade, Matthew 268–269
Slangerup, Hans Olufsen 792
Snell, Bruno 219, 277–279
Soares, Cipriano 561, **569–571**, 577
Socrates 196, 446, 795
Sofía, Constantino 562
Solon 759
Sommer, Johann(es) 453
Sophianos, Michael 34
Sophocles 50, 96, 99, 202, 205, 371, 380, 393, 397, 452, 530, 541, 581, 603, 651, 682, 776
Sophronios of Jerusalem 61
Spanos, Alexios 35
Spiegel, Jeremias 8, 453, 454*
Ståhlberg, Georgius 763
Stalenus, Johannes 731
Stalin, Joseph 11, 302–305
Statius 697
Stier, Heinrich Christoph Gottlieb 208
Stowasser, Josef Maria 691, **719–721**
Strabo 331, 356–357
Strabo, Jakub 7, 282*, **290–291**
Strategos, Antonios 35
Stucki, Johann Rudolf 310, **337–340**
Stucki, Johann Wilhelm 311*, 339

Święcicius, Gregorius **630–636**
Swinburne, Algernon Charles 4, 10, 486*, 488, **537–538**
Synesius of Cyrene 61, 387
Szilágyi, Samuel 454

Tambroni, Clotilde 9, 88, **129–131**, 541, 596, 601
Tanner, Georg 690, 696–698
Tantalus 53, 206, 247
Tegnér, Esaias 756–757
Tennyson, Alfred 541
Terpander 366
Terpsichore 73, 344, 346, 630, 634, 772
Thalia 73, 344, 346, 521, 619, 630, 633, 696–697
Themis 327, 540, 667, 717
Themistocles 57
Theocritus 50, 84, 99, 101–102, 151, 192, 194, 222–223, 235, 239, 251, 253, 330, 371, 387, 404, 477, 522–523, 551–552, 563, 581, 595, 706, 768, 779
Theognis 164, 218, 232, 285, 351, 759, 763, 767, 785
Thermaenius, Andreas Erici 732
Theseus 128
Thetis 449, 544–545
Thiersch, Friedrich 151
Thoraconymus, Mathias 452
Thryllitsch, Georg Friedrich 196
Thucydides 103, 167, 776
Thun, Josef (Thunius, Josephus) VIII, 27, 722, 732, **749–752**, 755, 763
Thyrsis 521–523
Tiraqueau, André 4, 362–363
Tiresias 305
Tithonus 435–436
Tityus 614
Tolomei, Lattanzio VII, 82, 85, **105–107**
Tomann, Sadrach 310
Tommaseo, Niccolò 89
Tonensis, Vincentius L. 453, 454*
Tory, Geoffroy 361
Toussain, Jacques (Tusanus, Iacobus) 360, 365, 373–374
Triklinios, Demetrios 31
Turnèbe, Adrien 245, 378

Typhon 664
Tzechanes, Konstantinos 9, 407, **438–444**, 529
Tzetzes, Ioannes 31, 54, 442
Tzetzes, Isaac 31

Ueberweg, Friedrich 208
Ulysses *vide* Odysseus
Ungvárnémeti Toth, László 9, 28, 454, **474–477**
Urania 73, 346, 634
Uranus 528–529
Urbanus VIII (Pope) *vide* Barberini, Maffeo

Valla, Lorenzo 362
Van de Ven, Willem 218, **231–232**
Van Effenterre, Henri 80
Van Groningen, Bernard Abraham 218–219, 275, **277–279**
Van Schurman, Anna Maria 218
Van Wassenaer, Nicolaes Jansz. 7, 27, 219–220, **255–258**
Varsányi, Mihály 452, 454*
Včelín, Jakub 296
Vendotis, Georgios 691
Venus *vide* Aphrodite
Vera, Antonio 563
Vergara, Francisco de 561–562, 567
Vergil *vide* Virgil
Vernier, Léon 359, **398–400**
Verzosa, Juan de 560
Vídalín, Jón Þorkelsson 792*
Villa, Emilio 90*
Vinding, Rasmus Polsen (Winding, Erasmus Paul) 792
Virgil/Vergil 28, 66, 76, 109, 201, 269, 497, 522–523, 650, 658–661, 696, 718, 771
Vitelli, Girolamo 10, 90, **137–141**, 776
Vitrioli, Diego 89
Voetius, Gisbertus 218*
Vogelmann, Heinrich 726, 779
Vorstius, Adolphus 219*
Vulcanius, Bonaventura 8, 219, 235, **240–243**, 254, 261, 308
Vulpius Jr, Heinrich 779
Vulpius Sr, Heinrich 779

Wagner, Valentin 452
Weil, Henri/Heinrich 398–400
Weiser, Caspar 732, **746–748**
Welin, Johan 764, **773–775**
Wells, Edward 10, 487, **511–513**
Westphal, Rudolf 11, 679–680
Wettstein I, Johan Rudolf 310, **343–347**, 348,
Wettstein II, Johan Rudolf 310, 349, **350–353**
Wifstrand, Albert 733, **760–761**
Wilamowitz-Moellendorff, Ulrich von 2, 4, 10, 29, 152, **209–214**, 215, 542, 548–549, 685–686
Winckelmann, Johann Joachim 650
Winstrup, Peder 792, **798–799**
Witte, Henning 780
Wolf, Friedrich August 131, 674
Wolf, Hieronymus 178, 423
Wolff, Christian 775
Wyrffel, Georgius VII, 405, 410, **421–424**

Xenophon 93, 102, 145, 404, 513, 726, 794–795

Zabanius, Isaac (Czabán, Izsák) **470–472**
Zaleski, Nicolaus 606*, 607–608, **628–629**
Zamagna, Bernardo 405, 449, 529
Zamojski, Jan 175, 608, 625–627
Zephyrus 79
Zeus 45–46, 49–50, 56, 76, 104, 111, 119, 149, 160, 180–181, 183, 205, 227, 250, 252, 257, 272, 299, 327, 335, 350, 368–369, 380, 386, 394, 412, 422, 436, 440–442, 446, 461, 476, 540, 596, 625, 633, 646, 696, 703–704, 717, 767, 794
Zeuxis 45, 229
Zieliński, Tadeusz Stefan 651, 681–683, 685
Żórawski, Nicolaus 608, **639–643**
Zwinger, Jacob 310, 335–336, 339
Zwingli, Ulrich 310, 320, 325
Zykzai, Basilius Fabricius 462–464
Zykzai, Valentinus Hellopoeus (Szikszai, Bálint) **462–464**

Index Selectivus Rerum Memorabilium

Page numbers with asterisk (*) indicate footnotes.

academies
- Académie de Genève 26, 311–312, 329
- Académie française 390, 393, 395, 399–400
- Accademia degli Apatisti 88
- Accademia degli Infiammati 105
- Accademia degli Intronati 107
- Accademia degli Umoristi 120
- Accademia dell'Arcadia 6, 88, 128, 131, 586, 597, 807
- Accademia delle Notti Vaticane 114
- New Academy/Neakademia 85, 103
- New Academy of Moschopole 28, 407–408, 436
- Princely Academy of Bucharest 406–407, 429, 433, 447
- Royal Academy of Turku 27, 763, 769, 771, 773–776
- Vilnius Jesuit Academy 606*, 607–608, 623, 629, 635–636, 639, 644

acrostic VII, 60, 306, 313, 346, 348, 353–354, 359*, 433, 469–470, 727, 780
Aeolic *vide* dialect
Alcaic stanza *vide* metre
Anthologia Palatina/Planudea/Graeca
  (*Greek Anthology*) 5, 13, 25, 32, 46, 50, 84–85, 88, 99, 107, 109, 111, 157, 186, 225, 249, 251, 267, 269, 278, 287, 289, 345, 360*, 363, 405, 413, 451, 461, 486, 503, 507, 510, 569, 571, 587, 638, 676, 740, 751, 760
Arabic *vide* languages
Aramaic *vide* languages
Asclepiad *vide* metre
Attic *vide* dialect

Batrachomyomachia 201, 304, 393, 595
Bible, Biblical poetry 125, 294, 311, 313, 333, 360*, 501, 513, 607, 629, 710, 726*
Browne Medal *vide* prizes
bucolic *vide* pastoral

Calvinist, Calvinism 34, 87, 453–454, 466, 614
carmina figurata 119, 122
Catholic, Catholicism 4, 6, 8, 33–34, 38, 59, 61, 65–66, 72, 98, 107, 114, 147, 150, 171, 281, 286, 369–370, 403, 405, 407, 423, 425, 477, 485, 489, 497, 501, 552, 564, 644, 689, 791
cento 5, 88, 129, 136, 148, 161, 223–225, 264, 326*, 338, 509–510, 565–567, 727, 763, 779, 788, 791, 801
Church Slavonic *vide* languages
Classicism 151, 198, 455, 483–484, 487, 650
colleges
- Collège de Coqueret 26, 369, 371
- Collège royal 6, 25, 86, 235, 360, 378, 389, 393
- Collegio Greco 27, 34–35, 64, 65, 69, 72, 87, 119–120, 122
- Collegio Romano 5, 124
comedy *vide* genre
competition 10–11, 77, 160, 483, 485–486, 490, 534
correption (metric) *vide* prosody
Counter-Reformation 34, 87, 232, 560

dialect
- Aeolic 13, 93, 212–213, 276, 303, 445 (sim.), 479 (crit.), 530, 534, 547 (crit.), 548, 554, 556, 643, 679–680, 719 (sim.)
- Attic 13, 92, 96, 99, 136, 178, 220, 225, 239, 276, 322, 530, 535 (crit.), 554, 556, 607, 616, 620, 643, 680, 728, 740
- Doric 13, 76, 102, 130 (sim.), 136, 149, 178, 181, 194, 220, 239, 250, 267, 327 (sim.), 344 (crit.), 379 (sim.), 380, 452, 475, 530, 533–534, 633*, 643, 706, 735, 770
- Ionic 13, 136, 225, 264, 363, 530*, 620, 643, 708 (crit.), 790
dodecasyllable *vide* metre

Doric *vide* dialect
drama *vide* genre

elegiac couplet *vide* metre
Enlightenment 9, 28, 129, 194, 403, 447, 483, 598, 650, 660, 691
epic *vide* genre
epicedium *vide* genre
epigram *vide* genre
epitaph *vide* genre
epithalamium *vide* genre
epodic *vide* metre
epyllion *vide* genre

Gaisford Prize *vide* prizes
genre
– comedy 44, 54, 144, 206, 278, 287, 359, 551, 709, 754
– drama 10, 31, 69, 139–140, 144, 206, 212, 219, 278, 296, 453–454, 470–472, 489, 500–501, 522, 538, 548, 551–552, 597, 639, 727–728, 754
– epic 5, 11, 13, 43, 77, 89–90, 93, 98–99, 109, 114, 124, 134, 139–140, 149–150, 152, 183, 187, 198, 201–202, 204, 208, 213, 219–220, 224, 232, 250, 253, 257, 282–283, 287, 289, 291, 296, 300, 303–305, 313*, 319, 322, 339, 346, 357, 384, 397, 413, 423, 507, 517, 523, 554, 567, 577, 580, 607, 616, 620, 642, 667, 691, 718, 726*, 731, 742, 745, 747, 750, 769–770, 783, 790, 803–804
– epicedium 289, 342, 310, 319, 324, 326*, 336, 339, 342, 348, 620, 779, 788, 791*, 792
– epigram VII, 1, 3–7, 9–11, 13, 25–27, 31–36, 37–38, 40–41, 44, 46, 50, 52, 59, 61, 65–66, 69, 73–74, 76, 77, 79, 80, 83–86, 88–90, 97–100, 101–102, 104–105, 106–107, 109, 111–112, 115, 120, 122, 125, 131, 137, 140, 142, 145, 148–150, 152, 155–161, 163–167, 178, 185–186, 197, 202, 211–215, 216, 222, 242–243, 245, 250, 254, 267–268, 276, 278, 282, 285, 294, 312–313, 325, 329, 333*, 357, 358, 360, 363, 364–365, 366, 376–377, 382, 384, 389, 390, 394, 396, 404, 406–408, 413, 415, 420, 423, 425, 427–428, 431, 433, 434–436, 438, 440, 442–443, 449, 451, 456, 457, 461, 464, 475, 477, 478, 486, 493–494, 505, 506–507, 517, 524, 526, 537–538, 547–548, 549*, 560–562, 564, 566–567, 568–569, 570–571, 578–581, 584, 587, 594, 596, 598, 603, 607, 620, 627, 652, 658, 674, 676, 679, 682, 685, 691, 697, 708–709, 725–728, 732, 740, 750–751, 761–762, 764*, 772, 782–783, 792, 799, 805–806
– epitaph 4, 9, 38, 65–66, 105, 219–220, 223, 243, 288, 348, 381, 383–384, 457–458, 493, 524, 570, 607, 685, 732, 800
– epithalamium 8, 120, 264, 297, 338, 341–342, 420, 452–453, 465–466, 467–468, 607, 620, 627, 693, 697, 779–780, 782, 784–785, 791
– epyllion 10, 13, 32, 43, 149, 181, 260, 313, 335, 717–718, 776, 807
– hymn VII, 8–9, 14, 31, 41, 60–61, 89, 98, 108–109, 117, 127–128, 131, 133–134, 166, 181, 186, 260, 263, 303, 335, 338, 342*, 361, 368–369, 371, 378, 379–380, 425, 528, 558, 563, 576, 588, 590–591, 601, 604, 607, 635, 637–638, 645, 677*, 691, 703–704, 727, 749–750
– idyll 7, 9–10, 27, 31, 114, 134, 167, 189–192, 194, 222, 313, 330, 371, 477, 521–523, 563, 601, 690, 702, 727
– ode (except Pindaric) 4, 9, 11, 25, 29, 33, 41, 46, 49–50, 56–57, 76, 93, 130, 134, 145, 194, 197–198, 243, 254, 302–305, 369, 376, 380, 484–487, 490, 517, 521, 526, 529–530, 534, 554–556, 562, 575, 577, 582–583, 585, 600–601, 635, 660, 663, 665–666, 669–670, 682
– Pindaric ode 7, 26–29, 35, 72, 86, 88, 114, 117, 127–129, 150, 178, 186, 208, 236, 238–239, 313–314, 541–542, 544–545, 626, 650*, 726, 779
– skolion 535
– tragedy 10, 69, 90, 206, 213, 253, 272, 277–278, 397, 481, 489, 499–500, 530, 551, 639, 672, 683, 709, 733, 754, 777

Ginnasio greco 33, 50, 54
Greek War of Independence, Greek Revolution 28, 76, 545, 650

hapax legomena 4, 206, 220, 272, 319, 367, 584, 586, 601, 740
Hebrew *vide* languages
Hellenistic poetry 18, 87, 117, 119, 131, 152, 164, 181, 213, 366, 371, 377, 547–548, 601
hexameter *vide* metre
hiatus *vide* prosody
hymn *vide* genre

iambic trimeter *vide* metre
idyll *vide* genre
Iliad 99, 202, 208*, 242, 257, 281, 289, 319*, 405, 451, 567, 587, 614, 678–679, 718, 750
inscriptions VII, 4, 30, 38, 82, 106, 141, 146, 203, 223, 358, 371, 482, 490, 553–554, 603
Ionic *vide* Dialect

Jesuits, Jesuit order 6, 8, 26–28, 59, 64, 87–88, 124, 263, 281–283, 296, 300, 387, 405, 561–563, 571, 577, 580, 592, 593, 595, 597, 601, 606*, 607, 623, 629, 638, 644, 689, 706, 718

katharevousa 277*, 691

languages
– Arabic 298, 351, 390, 393, 481, 680, 707, 727
– Aramaic 298, 727
– Church Slavonic 425, 655–657, 683
– Hebrew 107, 148, 158–159, 160–161, 209, 291, 298, 310, 320, 324, 339, 349, 351, 374, 380, 387, 390, 471, 496, 583–584, 593, 614, 617, 627, 644, 707, 724, 727, 740, 746–747, 751, 764, 775, 783, 788, 799
– Syriac 107, 297–298, 390, 727
lengthening (metric) *vide* prosody

macaronic poetry/literature 11, 90, 518, 652, 763, 799
metre
– Alcaic stanza 7, 10, 12, 118, 477, 556, 576, 652, 679
– anapaest 144, 501, 652
– asclepiad 10, 12, 196, 345, 472, 537
– *bipartitus* 12, 40, 54, 56, 63, 74, 108, 130, 136, 166, 257, 335, 386, 431, 461, 566, 573, 592, 598, 626, 772, 795
– choriamb 119, 345, 354, 535
– dodecasyllable 31, 69
– elegiac couplet 31–32, 38, 46, 50–51, 54, 56, 59, 61, 63–65, 74, 76–77, 79–80, 83, 93, 97–98, 101, 104, 106, 111, 118, 122, 124, 130, 141, 155–158, 160, 163, 166, 170, 173, 185–186, 191–192, 202, 203, 212, 214, 219, 231, 235, 241–242, 245, 247, 249–252, 254, 257, 267*, 268, 275, 277, 285, 287, 289, 291, 294, 313, 327, 333, 336, 345–346, 348, 352, 355, 362, 364, 366, 371, 373, 377, 380, 381, 384, 388, 396, 399, 413, 415, 420, 423, 425, 428, 431–433, 436, 440–443, 446, 449, 457, 459, 461, 470, 475–478, 490, 493–494, 496, 505, 524, 538, 546, 553, 568, 570, 580, 586, 594, 596, 598, 603, 606–607, 620, 622, 629, 642, 644, 652, 655–656, 658, 660, 667, 674, 679, 682, 685–686, 691, 697, 709–711, 720, 727, 739, 745, 751, 755, 759–761, 767, 797, 800
– epodic 7, 12, 166, 324, 329, 727, 780, 790
– hexameter 7, 10, 12, 31, 40, 43, 54, 56, 63, 69, 74, 83, 97–98, 108–109, 114, 117–118, 119, 130, 136–137, 163–164, 180–181, 183–184, 185–186, 187, 191–192, 194, 201, 208, 213, 219, 224, 257, 260, 263–264, 292, 300, 302, 304–305, 313, 318–319, 324–325, 327, 329, 335–336, 338–339, 341, 350, 354–355, 357, 375–376, 382, 386, 390, 395, 402, 431, 464, 466, 468, 472–473, 477, 490, 494, 497, 503, 505, 510, 513, 522–523, 552, 566–567, 573, 580, 590–591, 592, 598, 607–608, 614, 626, 638, 652, 659,

667, 679, 691, 697, 706, 710, 717–718, 726–727, 732, 735–736, 738, 742, 747, 750, 757, 761, 763, 768, 770, 772, 774, 776, 778–779, 782, 785, 787, 791–792, 795, 799
– iambic dimeter 169, 186, 194, 222, 229, 266, 296–297, 324–325, 341, 375–376, 392, 475, 500, 583, 665, 667, 799
– iambic trimeter 10, 31, 69, 118, 139, 144, 175, 206, 211, 226–227, 272–273, 329, 345, 437, 471–472, 490, 500–501, 505–506, 525, 551, 662–663, 673, 682, 691, 753
– paroemiac 669
– Phalaecian 7, 12, 98, 186, 322, 345, 394, 535, 608, 616, 652, 684, 780
– Sapphic stanza 1, 4, 7, 10, 12–13, 33, 46, 76, 84, 92–93, 109, 118, 194, 235, 276, 291, 314, 345, 368–369, 444–446, 472, 477, 481, 486, 490, 529–530, 533, 547–548, 562, 600–601, 608, 634–636, 652, 665, 667, 676, 727
– *spondiacus* 201, 208, 275, 302, 362, 478, 510, 513, 522, 659, 697, 706
– trochaics 345–346, 501, 652
mosquitoes 97, 251–252, 509–510

names, Hellenized 156, 206, 324, 547–548, 656, 660, 755, 797
neologisms 4, 99, 105, 135, 144, 162, 165, 171, 180, 182, 187, 190, 210, 220, 239, 242, 245, 273, 275, 304, 384, 477, 506–507, 516, 546, 551, 607, 745, 799
Neuhumanismus/Neo-humanism 148, 659

occasional poetry 4, 85, 194, 219, 235, 279, 282, 294, 296, 313, 315, 324–325, 331, 335, 339, 342, 346, 349, 352, 405, 407–408, 425, 428, 433, 449, 451, 556, 606, 614, 627, 646, 652, 679, 686, 724, 726, 732–733, 736, 738, 763–764, 767, 769, 774–775, 779, 783, 791
ode *vide* genre
Odyssey 134, 202, 304–305, 325, 338–339, 370, 400, 405, 510, 718, 742, 772, 805

Olympic Games 29, 483, 544–545, 556
Orthodox, Orthodox Church 9, 35, 59, 66, 150, 403, 406, 425, 436, 438, 447, 607, 642, 649–652, 657, 660, 667

pagan, paganism 32, 50, 86, 98, 106, 117, 122, 124, 183, 220, 227, 335, 390, 590, 682, 750
paraphrase 5, 7–8, 31, 33, 50, 98, 124–125, 149, 171–172, 174, 311–314, 323, 333, 336, 451, 453, 510, 567, 616, 620, 682, 726*, 727, 731, 750, 791–792, 795, 799
parody 90, 144–145, 152, 389, 478, 538, 551, 803
paroemiac *vide* metre
pastoral, bucolic 5, 7, 9–10, 13, 53, 98, 125, 134, 191–192, 213, 260, 283*, 330, 384, 405, 454, 522–523, 706, 803
periodicals
– *Alindethra* 152
– *Eos* 646–647
– *Euphrosyne* 603
– *Memorial Literario* 598
– *Palaestra Latina* 564
– *The Salopian* 552
Phalaecian *vide* metre
Pléiade 6, 360, 377
poeta laureatus/poet laureate 156, 188, 424, 617, 697
Porson Prize *vide* prizes
prayer 95, 98, 141, 218, 231–232, 277–278, 290, 336, 338, 341, 346, 464, 469, 505, 511, 608, 616, 643, 682, 705, 710–711, 720, 742–743, 799
printer, printing 9, 14, 33–35, 47, 52, 59, 103, 107, 117, 130, 159, 172, 181, 218, 226*, 230, 263, 307, 309, 314*, 320, 329–330, 369, 374, 380, 382, 403, 407–408, 425, 428, 436, 460, 470, 488, 562, 607, 614, 627, 691, 724–725, 727, 731–732, 762–763, 779, 791–792, 797
prizes
– Browne Medal 13, 28, 486–487, 490, 526, 529–530, 533, 548

– Gaisford Prize 272*, 484, 486, 490, 545, 552, 556
– Porson Prize 486, 490, 526, 541, 548
prosody
– correption 156, 496, 614, 620, 629, 638, 642, 644
– hiatus 12, 38, 43, 51, 54, 57, 72, 74, 79, 92, 97, 122, 130, 160, 163, 170, 173, 180, 196, 201, 208, 302, 304, 319, 322, 327, 333, 350, 357, 380, 381, 386, 457, 464, 466, 470, 471, 475, 476, 496, 510, 513, 522, 533, 566, 568, 576, 580, 590, 592, 616, 620, 622, 626, 629, 642, 658, 659, 676, 697, 710, 728, 735, 738, 739, 742, 745, 747, 750, 753, 757, 761, 767–768, 770, 772, 776, 782, 785, 787–788, 795, 799
– lengthening 12, 40, 43, 54, 56, 122, 156, 160, 163, 180, 277, 380, 461, 464, 466, 478, 496, 503, 513, 522, 573, 590, 614, 622, 629, 638, 642, 644, 655, 663, 706, 735, 747, 772
Protestantism 6, 9, 26, 150, 184, 322, 324, 453, 489, 494, 560, 574

Ratio studiorum (Jesuit curriculum) 6, 27, 87, 405, 423, 571, 659
Reformation 25, 87, 161, 281, 308–309, 324, 359, 374, 380, 488, 689, 724, 763, 791

refrain 178, 475, 523
ring composition 339, 348, 541, 720
Russo-Turkish War 667

Sapphic Stanza *vide* metre
sesquipedalia verba, verba plaustralia 171, 388, 390
skolion *vide* genre
spondiacus *vide* metre
Syriac *vide* languages

tautogrammatic 727, 763
tea 9, 139–140, 193–194, 220, 266–267, 391, 517
tragedy *vide* genre
translations into Greek 7, 72, 141, 145, 151, 174, 178, 197–198, 212–213, 273, 311, 314, 394, 451, 461, 484, 486, 497, 507, 523, 526, 542, 545, 552, 561, 643, 650, 658–661, 672–676, 692, 720, 727–728, 783
Turks 10, 25, 33, 50, 57, 114, 129, 150, 163, 243, 268, 373, 422, 463, 662–663, 667

word-play 325, 329

Index Graecitatis (neologismi, hapax legomena, verba rara)

ἀγναῖος 585 (de Quesada, v. 4)
ἀδεισίπονος 546 (Headlam, I.4)
ἀειχρόνιος 709 (Niedermühlbichler, III.4)
ἀέτειος 469 (Guttovieni, v. 9)
ἀθέλω 694 (Charopus, II.57)
αἱμάδομος (?) 462 (Zykzai, v. 33)
αἱματοδιψαλέος 170 (Crusius, II.8)
αἱμηπότης 508 (Duport, v. 2)
αἰναληθής 599 (Aponte, v. 25)
ἄκληρος 712 (Mayr, v. 426)
ἀκμόνειος 118 (Porzio, v. 4)
ἀκρατοχανδοπότης 387 (Ménage, v. 2)
ἀλλοπροσαλλοκόλαξ 387 (Ménage, v. 1)
ἀλφοδότης 317 (Ceporinus, v. 8)
ἀμφιμάχητος 104 (Bonamico, v. 5)
ἀναγραμματοτεχνοποιητής 387 (Ménage, v. 3)
ἀραβημιγής 162 (Melanchthon, v. 3)
ἀργυρῶπις 131–132 (Leopardi, v. 3, 30)
ἁρματροχιή 713 (Mayr, v. 445)
ἄρμιγξ 771 (Alander, v. 10)
ἀρχιγονέτης 70 (Philaras, v. 19)
αὐτοβοῦς (= 'autobus') 142 (Rissa, v. 133)
ἄφημος 796 (Aquilonius, I.3)
ἀχόρηγος 244 (Scaliger, v. 6)
Βακχοφόνος 259 (Foreestius, v. 59)
βαρύνουσος 106 (Tolomei, v. 3)
βιβλοδότειρα 381 (Estienne, v. 1)
βιβλοθεουφυγάς 170 (Crusius, II.10)
βιοθάλμιος 739– 740 (Brunnerus, v. 3)
βλοσυρώψ 515 (Barnes, v. 58)
βομβαρδοξιφεσισχοινεγχεσιπυρδιαλέκτης 170 (Crusius, II.9)
βραχυτερπής 654 (Maxim the Greek, v. 367)
βυρσόνωτος 515 (Barnes, v. 42)
γενναιόφρων 138 (Vitelli, v. 63)
γεννάρχης 636 (Cnapius, v. 3)
γλυκίνας 138 (Vitelli, v. 58)
γομφοπαγής 694 (Charopus, I.54)
γραμματοληρολόγος 387 (Ménage, v. 4)
γραμμοτόκος 378 (Chrestien, v. 14)

γραοσόβης vel γραοσόβος 205 (Richter, v. 281)
γρυφάς 630, 633–634* (Święcicius?, v. 21)
γυιαρκής 67 (Allacci, v. 734)
δαιδαλόφωνος 636 (Cnapius, v. 4)
δεινολογέω 636 (Cnapius, v. 4)
δεισίθεος 439 (Tzechanes, II.10)
δευτερόποτμος 252 (Heinsius, V.5)
διαβολοσπερής 170 (Crusius, II.11)
διαλλήλως 109 (Gaurico)
δικορράπτης 376 (Belleau, v. 9)
διπυρίτης 138 (Vitelli, v. 58)
δολίχαυλος 713 (Mayr, v. 474)
δοξοπαλαιομαθής 387 (Ménage, v. 3)
δορίτολμος 421 (Wyrffel, v. 15)
δόρκα (= δέδορκα) 429 (Notaras, v. 3)
δυσέξιτος 671 (Graefe, I.36)
δυσμίμημα 506 (Milton, v. 4)
ἐγγλάπτω 585 (Martí, v. 13)
ἐγερσιγύναιξ 96 (Poliziano, III.5), 769 (Paulinus, v. 130)
εἰδωλοσεβαστής 169 (Crusius, II.3)
εἱματολευκοφόρος 169 (Crusius, II.1)
ἐκδιανύσθαι 591 (Rodríguez de Castro, v. 11)
ἔμπαγε (= ἔμπα γε) 123 (Barberini, v. 5)
ἐξαπατησιάδης 170 (Crusius, II.5)
ἐπανοίκτρια 546 (Headlam, I.1)
ἐπάψ 340 (Lavater, v. 14)
ἑπτάπεπλος 204 (Richter, v. 273, 275–277)
ἐρίπλαγκτος 472 (Kondos, v. 7)
ἐσθλοπόνος 181 (Rhodoman, II.16)
ἐσσήν 599 (Aponte, v. 14)
εὑρεσίτεχνος 75 (Ioannou, II.7)
Εὐρώπια 693 (Charopus, II.9)
εὔφρος 698 (Kollár, v. 15)
ἐχθροφόνος 255 (Wassenaer, v. 435)
ζαλοσύνα (= ζηλοσύνη) 179 (Rhodoman, I.949)
ζητοδιεργόβιος 169 (Crusius, II.2)
ἡδυγέλαιος 585 (Martí, v. 10)

ἡερόπλαγκτος 74 (Ioannou, I.6)
ἡμερόφοιτος 749 (Thun, I.11)
ἡρακλειόθυμος 209 (Wilamowitz, I.10)
θαμβοπαθέω 382 (Saint-Martin?, v. 2)
θειογραφικός 427 (Molyvdos Comnenos, v. 37)
θεμίπλεκτος 125 (Baffi, v. 17)
θεμίστωρ 623 (Niegossevius, v. 8)
θεοτευχής 579 (Mariner, III.7)
θεοφροσύνη 618 (Retellius, v. 18)
θεοχριστόμαχος 462 (Zykzai, v. 33)
θηρήτειρα 259 (Foreestius, v. 50)
θρασυμήχανος 74 (Ioannou, I.9)
ἱππογένης (debuit ἱππογενής) 165 (Camerarius, I.3), 182 (Rhodoman, crit. ad I.1–5)
ἱπποτρεχεδειπνοσοφιστής 387 (Ménage, v. 1)
Ἰταλίηθεν 100 (Forteguerri, v. 6)
κακοφράδμων 769 (Paulinus, v. 136)
καλλιτριχιπποβάτης 170 (Crusius, II.6)
καλοφώνως 582 (Correas, v. 20)
κάπων 712 (Mayr, v. 403)
καταλύτης 372 (Bérauld, v. 15)
καταντιβολέω 694 (Charopus, II.32)
Κελτοδουλεία 209, 211 (Wilamowitz, I.12)
κερδαλεοφρόνιμος 170 (Crusius, II.8)
κερματοθρασίδης 170 (Crusius, II.6)
κηληδών 367 (Dorat, II.27)
κηρόφιν 572 (Núñez Vela, v. 127)
κοπροδάκτυλος 477 (Fehér, I.1)
κοσμοθεωρέω 303 (Křesadlo, II.8)
κοσμοκράτης 595 (Lassala y Sangermán, v. 4)
κοσμοματαιόσοφος 170 (Crusius, II.10)
κοσμοτέχνης 47 (Mousouros, v. 9)
κοσμουπαντηπεροπευτής 170 (Crusius, II.5)
κραδίηθε 419 (Garbitius, III.3)
κραντορίη 426 (Molyvdos Comnenos, v. 30)
κρειοφαγαινοβόρος 387 (Ménage, v. 2)
κυκλοτερής 713 (Mayr, v. 469)
λάγηρ 301 (Křesadlo, I.16)
λαμπόπυγος 395 (Chénier, v. 2)
λεκτροδικαιόφυγος (debuit -δικαιοφύγος) 170 (Crusius, II.4)

λεξικοράπτης 241 (Vulcanius, II.3)
λεοντηδόν 62 (Koressios, v. 243)
λεοντοπάλης 104 (Bonamico, v. 2)
λιπαρόχροος 132 (Leopardi, v. 10)
λιπόκοσμος 458 (Sambucus, I.1)
λογέμπορος 225 (Erasmus, III.10)
λοξοδίκης 376 (Belleau, v. 4)
λυσιπαίγμων 518 (Dawes, v. 19)
μαστίκτωρ 270 (dèr Mouw, I.54)
μεγάδοξος 664 (Palladoklis, III.115)
μεγαλοβρεμέτης 746 (Weiser, v. 5)
μελάγχειρ 401 (Chapouthier, v. 8)
μηδοφόρος 317 (Ceporinus, v. 9)
μισόγελως 535 (Geddes, v. 4)
μισόνυμφος 262 (Binnart?, v. 15)
μονόπυλος 204 (Richter, v. 277)
μονοφεγγής 47 (Mousouros, v. 13)
μουσάναξ 367 (Dorat, II.51)
μουσικτής 693 (Charopus, II.26)
Μουσόδοτος 236 (Grotius, v. 153)
μωρεπιμωρότατος 387 (Ménage, v. 4)
ναυσίπομπος 542 (Robertson, v. 12)
νηπευθής 243 (Scaliger, v. 1)
νόημι 445 (Darvaris, v. 59)
νυκτιλαθραιοφάγος 389 (Huet, v. 3)
νυκτίσεμνος 270 (dèr Mouw, I.67)
νυκτομαθέω 798 (Winstrup, I.2)
νυκτοπονέω 798 (Winstrup, I.1)
νυκτοποτέω 798 (Winstrup, I.1)
νυκτοταράσσω 798 (Winstrup, I.2)
νυκτοχαράσσω 798 (Winstrup, I.1)
ὀλεσίπολις 334 (Jeckelmann, v. 3)
ὀλοοφρενιλαθραφυτευτής 170 (Crusius, II.7)
ὀρθοφρενιπλανής 170 (Crusius, II.12)
ὀρθοφρονέω 431 (Chrysogonos of Trebizond, v. 5)
οὐρανόδεικτος 350 (Wettstein II, v. 4)
παγχαρίεις 585 (Martí, v. 24)
παιηοσύνη 110 (Cortona, v. 15)
πάμφθαρτος 270 (dèr Mouw, I.73)
πανάγρυπνος 752 (Bilberg, v. 7)
πανδοτήρ 237 (Grotius, v. 174)
Πανιταλίδης 134 (Pascoli, v. 6)
πάνσκοπος 179 (Rhodoman, I.956)
παντάγαθος 654 (Maxim the Greek, v. 378; Wettstein II, 1)

παντοδάμας 419 (Garbitius, III.2)
παντόλεθρος 166 (Camerarius, II.4)
παντόσεμνος 539 (Jebb, v. 14)
παραλείβω 518 (Dawes, v. 7)
παχυοσκοτοεργοδιώκτης 170 (Crusius, II.11)
παυσανίας 211 (Wilamowitz, IIa.4)
πελαργόχρως 209 (Wilamowitz, I.9)
πενιχραλέος 190 (Herrichen, I.171)
πηγίδιον 782 (Gezelius Sr, v. 2, 6)
πινυτοφροσύνη 744 (Norrmannus, v. 14)
πιππίζω 393 (La Monnoye, v. 9)
πιστιδότειρα 419 (Garbitius, III.8)
πλοίαρχος 303 (Křesadlo, II.7)
ποικιλόγαρυς (= -γηρυς) 126 (Baffi, v. 44)
πολυκυδής 181 (Rhodoman, II.14)
πορνολαθραιοτρόφος 170 (Crusius, II.4)
πότνιος 343 (Wettstein I, v. 74)
πότνος 618 (Retellius, v. 22)
πρεμνόθεν 270 (dèr Mouw, I.64)
προφυλακτικόν 142 (Rissa, v. 140)
πτόλεθρον (= πτολίεθρον) 511 (Wells, v. 1014, 1026)
πυροδαίσιον 255 (Wassenaer, v. 428)
ῥάδιον (= 'radio') 142 (Rissa, v. 135)
ῥητρεύω 694 (Charopus, II.44)
ῥοδόμαζος 395 (Chénier, v. 1)
σαῦσε 189–190, 192 (Herrichen, I.165–167, 169, 171–171)
σαύσιον 189 (Herrichen, I.164)
σκοτοδερκής 96, 99 (Poliziano, III.11)
σμίγδην 105 (Tolomei, v. 2)
στερεός (= 'stereo') 142 (Rissa, v. 135)
συνένθεος 681 (Ivanov, III.5)
ταγαῖος 693 (Charopus, II.20)
ταρταρερινύμορος 170 (Crusius, II.12)
τεκνικός 328 (Casaubon, v. 2)
τέλθος 115 (Martinengo, v. 10)
τερπογυνής 366 (Dorat, I.2)
Τευτονικός 159 (Reuchlin, v. 10)
Τηλέγραφος 75 (Ioannou, II.tit.)
τηλέπομπος 270 (dèr Mouw, I.68)
τηλεφανής 714 (Mayr, v. 488)
Τηλεφωνία 549, 551 (Knox, *persona*)
τηλεφωνιάζω 551 (Knox, tit.)
τηξιμελής 110 (Cortona, v. 3)
τρισέραστος 414 (Pyrrhus, II.1)
τρισήλιος 60 (Margounios, v. 5)
τρισσοφαής 70 (Philaras, v. 16), 434 (Hypischiotes, II.6)
τροχαλίστρια 712 (Mayr, v. 432)
τυμπανοδέγμων 378 (Chrestien, v. 15)
ὑβλήτης 694 (Charopus, II.46)
ὑπεκπίνειν 270 (dèr Mouw, I.65)
ὑφεξείης 47 (Mousouros, v. 13)
ὑφερπύζω 768 (Cajanus Jr, v. 3)
ὑψικόλωνος 255 (Wassenaer, v. 445)
φαιναγιόφθαλμος 170 (Crusius, II.7)
φαινοσκυθρωποπρόσωπος 169 (Crusius, II.1)
φάνδην 668 (Baldani, v. 29)
φεψαλόω 271 (dèr Mouw, I.79)
φιλόκαντος 273 (dèr Mouw, II.21)
φιλόμολπος 737 (Aurivillius, v. 30)
φιλοποίμνιος 189 (Herrichen, I.149)
φιλόπυρος 244 (Scaliger, v. 8)
φίλυμνος 391 (Boivin, v. 6)
φλογιθαλπής 105 (Tolomei, v. 1)
φλογόπνοος 663 (Palladoklis, II.25)
φοιβομανής 370 (de Baïf, II.2,4)
φοινικάνθεμος 539 (Jebb, v. 6)
φραδμόνως 66 (Allacci, v. 723)
χαλκογράφος, Χαλκογραφίη 262 (Binnart?, v. 8), 379 (Chrestien, v. 27)
χαλκομέτωπος 379 (Chrestien, v. 26)
χαρμόφρων 519–520 (Dawes, v. 59, 64, 70, 74)
χαρτοπώλης 142 (Rissa, v. 137)
χιονόμορφος 179 (Rhodoman, I.953)
χρηματομισσοπράτης 169 (Crusius, II.2)
Χριστογενής 458 (Sambucus, I.2)
Χριστοκαθηματιοσταυρός 169 (Crusius, II.3)
Χριστοπόλος 419 (Garbitius, III.13)
Χριστοσεβής 323 (Gessner, II.3), 383 (de Saint-Martin?, v. 9)
Χριστοφιλέω 421 (Wyrffel, v. 20)
χρονόδειγμα 301 (Křesadlo, I.13)
ψυχόλογος (debuit ψυχολόγος) 477 (Fehér, I.1)
ψυχοφυής 47 (Mousouros, v. 6)
ὠκυγράφος 162 (Melanchthon, v. 13)
ὠμώδης 91 (Filelfo, v. 15)
ὠρολόγος 301 (Křesadlo, I.8,12)

www.ingramcontent.com/pod-product-compliance
Lightning Source LLC
Chambersburg PA
CBHW070208250426
43668CB00049B/1807